Essentials *of* Business Communication

9e

MARY ELLEN GUFFEY

DANA LOEWY

Professor Emerita of Business
Los Angeles Pierce College

Business Communication Program
California State University, Fullerton

SOUTH-WESTERN
CENGAGE Learning®

Australia • Brazil • Japan • Korea • Mexico • Singapore • Spain • United Kingdom • United States

Essentials of Business Communication
Ninth Edition

Mary Ellen Guffey, Dana Loewy

Vice President of Editorial, Business: Jack W. Calhoun

Publisher: Erin Joyner

Acquisitions Editor: Jason Fremder

Senior Developmental Editor: Mary H. Emmons

Editorial Assistant: Megan Fischer

Marketing Manager: Michelle Lockard

Content Project Manager: Jana Lewis

Media Editor: John Rich

Manufacturing Planner: Ron Montgomery

Marketing Communications Manager: Sarah Greber

Senior Art Director: Stacy Jenkins Shirley

Rights Acquisitions Specialist: Sam Marshall

Production Service: Cenveo Publisher Services

Internal Designer: KeDesign, Mason, OH

Cover Designer: KeDesign, Mason, OH

Cover Image: © Martin Barraud/Getty Images

For product information and technology assistance, contact us at
Cengage Learning Customer & Sales Support, 1-800-354-9706

For permission to use material from this text or product,
submit all requests online at **www.cengage.com/permissions**
Further permissions questions can be emailed to
permissionrequest@cengage.com

Library of Congress Control Number: 2011944636
ISBN-13: 978-1-111-82122-7
ISBN-10: 1-111-82122-4
Student Edition ISBN 13: 978-1-111-82123-4
Student Edition ISBN 10: 1-111-82123-2

South-Western
5191 Natorp Boulevard
Mason, OH 45040
USA

Cengage Learning products are represented in Canada by
Nelson Education, Ltd.

For your course and learning solutions, visit **www.cengage.com**
Purchase any of our products at your local college store or at our preferred online store **www.cengagebrain.com**

Printed in the United States of America
2 3 4 5 6 7 16 15 14

Dear Business Communication Student:

The **Ninth Edition** of ***Essentials of Business Communication*** offers you a four-in-one learning package including (a) an authoritative textbook, (b) a convenient workbook, (c) a self-teaching grammar/mechanics handbook, and (d) a comprehensive student Web site at **www.cengagebrain.com**.

Although much copied, ***Essentials*** maintains its leadership at the college level because of its effective grammar review, practical writing instruction, and exceptional support materials. In revising this Ninth Edition, we examined every topic and added new coverage with two themes in mind: technology and social media and their relevance to your future career success. Let us describe a few of the major improvements and features in the Ninth Edition:

- **Workplace relevance.** This edition continues to stress the practical and immediate importance of this course to your career success.
- **Integrated, cutting-edge coverage of digital tools and social media**. The Ninth Edition prepares you to become an effective communicator in today's challenging, wired, and mobile workplace. Every chapter has been thoroughly researched and updated to acquaint you with the latest trends in workplace communication technology.
- **More figures and model documents.** The Ninth Edition has been enhanced with numerous new figures and model documents that show the use of social media such as Facebook and Twitter, instant messages, podcasts, blogs, and wikis.
- **New *Technology in the Workplace* video**. Using humor to compare appropriate and inappropriate uses of social media, this new video helps you distinguish between professional and social uses of the Internet.
- **New application activities throughout.** Every chapter has 40 to 100 percent new activities including many recent and highly topical examples to prepare you for the high-stress modern workplace dominated by information technology.
- **Job search and interviewing coverage**. The Ninth Edition covers the latest trends and tips in preparing résumés and successful employment interviewing.
- **New grammar and writing improvement exercises**. One of the best ways to improve your writing skills is to revise poorly written messages. This edition provides many new grammar/mechanics exercises and new writing activities for you to hone your skills.
- **Premier Web site at www.cengagebrain.com**. All students with new books have access to chapter review quizzes, PowerPoint slides, and a wide assortment of learning resources.

The many examples and model documents in ***Essentials of Business Communication,* 9e,** including résumés and cover letters, have made this book a favorite to keep as an on-the-job reference.

We wish you well in your studies!

Cordially,

Mary Ellen Guffey & Dana Loewy

Guffey has updated tools and created new ways to keep you interested so you achieve success in this course and in real-life business communication. The following four pages describe features that will help make learning with Guffey... just that easy!

NEW AND KEY FEATURES

NEW Integrated Coverage of Digital Tools and Social Media

New Chapter 5, *Electronic Messages and Digital Media*, offers expansive coverage of digital tools in today's increasingly connected workplace. Plus, every chapter has been thoroughly researched and updated to acquaint you with the latest trends in workplace communication, including social media.

because they enable them to get answers quickly and allow multitasking.

Despite its popularity among workers, some organizations forbid employees to use instant messaging for a number of reasons. Employers consider instant messaging yet another distraction in addition to the interruptions caused by the telephone, e-mail, and the Web. Organizations also fear that privileged information and company records will be revealed through public instant messaging systems, which hackers can easily penetrate. Organizations worry about *phishing* (fraudulent) schemes, viruses, malware, and *spim* (IM spam).

Like e-mail, instant and text messages are subject to discovery (disclosure); that is, they can become evidence in lawsuits. Moreover, companies fear instant messaging and texting because businesses are required to track and store messaging conversations to comply with legal requirements. This task may be overwhelming. Finally, IM and texting have been implicated in traffic accidents and inappropriate uses such as the notorious *sexting*.

Organizations may ban instant messaging because of productivity, security, litigation, and compliance fears.

Best Practices for Instant Messaging and Texting

Instant messaging can definitely save time and simplify communications with coworkers and customers. Before using IM or text messaging on the job, however, be sure you have permission. Do not use public systems without checking with your supervisor. If your organization does allow IM and texting, you can use it efficiently and professionally by following these best practices:

- Learn about your organization's IM policies. Are you allowed to use instant messaging? With whom may you exchange messages?
- Don't text or IM while driving a car. Pull over if you must read or send a message.
- Make yourself unavailable when you need to complete a project or meet a deadline.

OFFICE INSIDER

"[B]ear in mind that messaging sessions can be stored, then copied and pasted elsewhere. . . . The term 'confidential' is somewhat rubbery these days, so . . . think before you hit that enter key."

—Michael Bloch, Taming the Beast, E-commerce development & Web marketing consultancy services

Chapter 5 Electronic Messages and Digital Media 117

NEW Social Media Figures and Model Documents

New figures and model documents show the professional use of social media such as Facebook and Twitter as well as highlight new communication tools such as instant messaging, podcasts, blogs, and wikis.

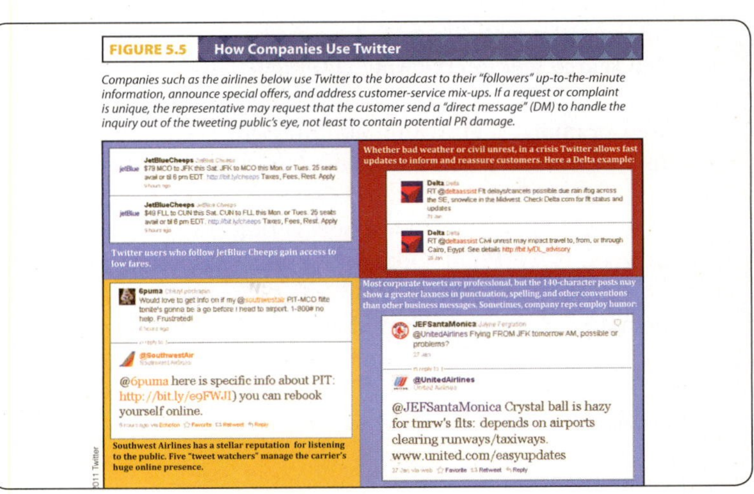

CengageNOW provides all of your learning resources in one intuitive program organized around the essential things you need to ace your course. It features personalized study, an integrated eBook, and much more!
www.cengage.com/coursemaster

TEAM WEB

5.15 Social Networking: Preparing a Professional LinkedIn Profile

Virtual networking on a professional networking site such as LinkedIn is an extension of seeking face-to-face contacts—the most effective way to find a job to date. Consider creating a credible, appealing presence on LinkedIn to make yourself attractive to potential business connections and hiring managers. Your LinkedIn site should serve purely to build your career and professional reputation.

Your Task. Go to **http://www.linkedin.com** and sign up for a free account. Follow the on-screen directions to create a profile, add a professional-looking photograph, and upload a polished résumé. You will be prompted to invite contacts from your e-mail address books. If your instructor directs, form teams and critique each other's profiles. Link to those profiles of your peers that have been prepared most diligently and strike you as having the best eye appeal.

NEW

Abundant Exercises and Activities
Extensively updated end-of-chapter exercises and activities provide a plethora of fresh, relevant activities for you to develop new skills. These exercises help you polish writing skills while creating an understanding of workplace communication challenges.

Expanded meguffey Premium Web Site for Students
A long-time leader in providing innovative, online resources, Guffey and Loewy have expanded the premium Web site to include robust resources that enhance learning.

Student Resources:

- **Abundant Grammar/Mechanics Resources**
- **Beat the Clock Game**
- **Chapter Review Quizzes**
- **Personal Language Trainer**
- **PowerPoint Chapter Reviews**
- **Workplace Simulations**
- **And More!**

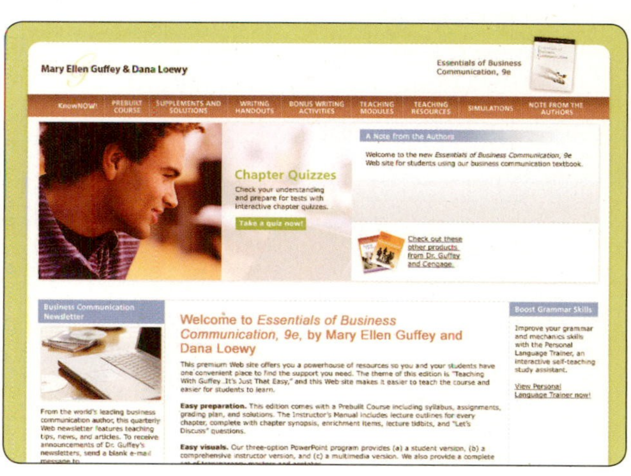

LEARNING WITH GUFFEY... IT'S JUST THAT EASY!

From headlines to hands-on, KnowNOW! brings you news that's making a difference in the world and in your course. Business communication-specific, digital online pages provide instant access to timely news with immediate applications for this course. News stories, organized by chapter and topic, include discussion questions and assignments.

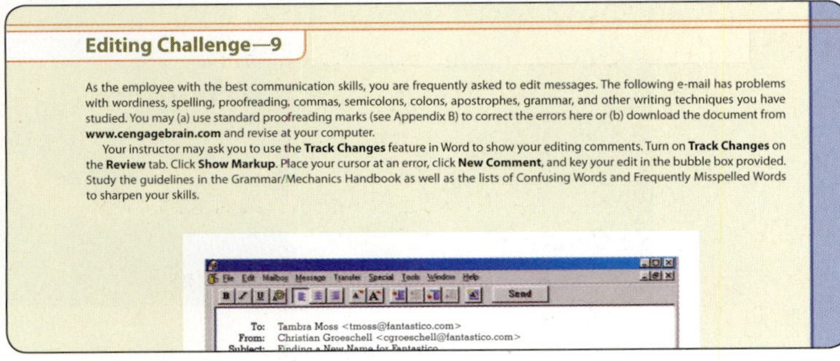

Editing Challenge—9

As the employee with the best communication skills, you are frequently asked to edit messages. The following e-mail has problems with wordiness, spelling, proofreading, commas, semicolons, colons, apostrophes, grammar, and other writing techniques you have studied. You may (a) use standard proofreading marks (see Appendix B) to correct the errors here or (b) download the document from **www.cengagebrain.com** and revise at your computer.

Your instructor may ask you to use the **Track Changes** feature in Word to show your editing comments. Turn on **Track Changes** on the **Review** tab. Click **Show Markup**. Place your cursor at an error, click **New Comment**, and key your edit in the bubble box provided. Study the guidelines in the Grammar/Mechanics Handbook as well as the lists of Confusing Words and Frequently Misspelled Words to sharpen your skills.

To: Tambra Moss <tmoss@fantastico.com>
From: Christian Groeschell <cgroeschell@fantastico.com>

NEW

Editing Challenge
(formerly Grammar/Mechanics Challenge)
These new exercises, at the end of each chapter, sharpen your skills in editing. You'll learn to apply writing techniques (such as conciseness, parallelism, and organization) as well as edit for grammar, spelling, punctuation, proofreading, and other potential writing challenges.

NEW

Workplace Simulations
Gain real-world training through these interactive case studies. Available at the premium student Web site, these simulations challenge you to use a variety of communication media to solve workplace problems.

WRITING PLAN FOR REFUSING TYPICAL REQUESTS AND CLAIMS

- **Buffer:** Start with a neutral statement on which both reader and writer can agree, such as a compliment, appreciation, a quick review of the facts, or an apology. Try to include a key idea or word that acts as a transition to the reasons.
- **Reasons:** Present valid reasons for the refusal, avoiding words that create a negative tone.
- **Bad news:** Soften the blow by de-emphasizing the bad news, using the passive voice, accentuating the positive, or implying a refusal. Suggest a compromise, alternative, or substitute, if possible. The alternative may be part of the bad-news section or part of the closing.
- **Closing:** Renew good feelings with a positive statement. Avoid referring to the bad news. Include resale or sales promotion material, if appropriate. Look forward to continued business.

Writing Plans
Clear, step-by-step writing plans structure the writing process so that you can get started quickly and stay focused on the writing experience.

Communication Skills: Your Ticket to Success

Workplace surveys and studies confirm that recruiters rank communication skills at the top of the list of qualities they most desire in job seekers. Such skills are crucial in a tight employment market when jobs are few and competition is fierce. In a recession, superior communication skills will give you an edge over other job applicants. A powerful career filter, your ability to communicate will make you marketable and continue to be your ticket to success regardless of the economic climate.

Perhaps you are already working or will soon apply for your first job. How do your skills measure up? The good news is that effective communication can be learned. This textbook and this course can immediately improve your communication skills. Because the skills you are learning will make a huge difference in your ability to find a job and to be promoted, this will be one of the most important courses you will ever take.

Small superscript numbers in the text announce information sources. Full citations appear at the end of the chapter. This edition uses a modified American Psychological Association (APA) reference format.

Why Writing Skills Matter More Than Ever

Today's workplace revolves around communication. Workers communicate more, not less, since information technology and the Internet have transformed the world of work in the last two decades. The modern office is mobile and fast paced. Technology enables us to transmit messages faster, farther, to potentially larger audiences, and more easily than in the past. Many people work together

2 Chapter 1 Communication Skills as Career Filters

Career Relevance
Because employers often rank communication skills among the most requested competencies, this text focuses on the link between excellent communication skills and career success—helping you see for yourself the critical role business communication plays in your life.

Bridging the Gap Videos
These video cases take you inside real companies, allowing you to apply your understanding of business communication concepts to actual business situations. Most videos conclude with a series of discussion questions and an application activity.

- **Understanding Teamwork: Cold Stone Creamery**
- **Writing Skills: The Little Guys**
- **Happy Cows in Harmony With Nature: Organic Valley**
- **Bad News: BuyCostumes**
- **Persuasive Request: Hard Rock Cafe**

Building Workplace Skills Videos
This video library includes high-quality videos to introduce and reinforce text-specific concepts such as building teamwork skills, applying writing techniques, delivering good and bad news, and making persuasive requests.

- **Career Success Begins With Communication Foundations**
- **Intercultural Communication at Work**
- **Guffey's 3-x-3 Writing Process Develops Fluent Workplace Skills**
- **Technology in the Workplace**
- **Smart E-Mail Messages and Memos Advance Your Career**
- **Effective On-the-Job Oral Presentations**
- **The Job Search**
- **Sharpening Your Interview Skills**

Office Insider
To accentuate how excellent communication skills translate into career success, the *Office Insider* demonstrates the importance of communication skills in real-world practice.

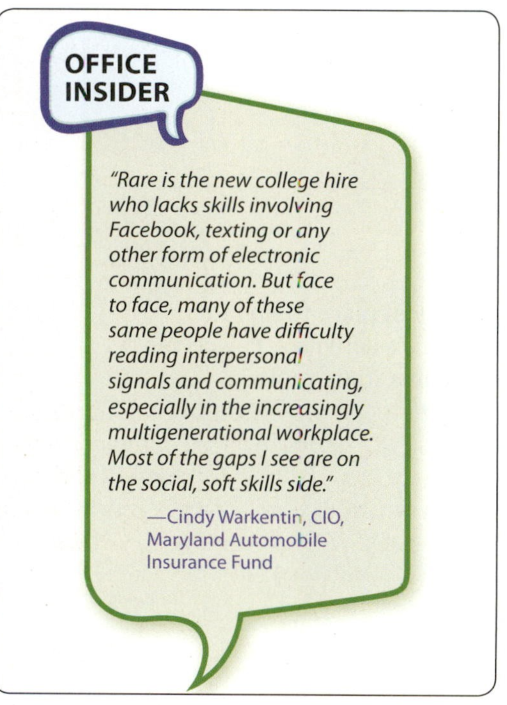

OFFICE INSIDER
"Rare is the new college hire who lacks skills involving Facebook, texting or any other form of electronic communication. But face to face, many of these same people have difficulty reading interpersonal signals and communicating, especially in the increasingly multigenerational workplace. Most of the gaps I see are on the social, soft skills side."
—Cindy Warkentin, CIO, Maryland Automobile Insurance Fund

Communication Workshops
Communication workshops develop critical thinking skills and provide insight into special business communication topics such as ethics, technology, career skills, and collaboration.

Ethics

Communication Workshop

Should Employers Restrict E-Mail, Instant Messaging, and Internet Use?

Most employees today work with computers and have Internet access. Should they be able to use their work computers for online shopping, personal messages, and personal work, as well as to listen to music and play games?

But It's Harmless
Office workers have discovered that it is far easier to shop online than to race to malls and wait in line. To justify her Web shopping at work, one employee, a recent graduate, said, "Instead of standing at the water cooler gossiping, I shop online." She went on to say, "I'm not sapping company resources by doing this."[31]

Those who use instant messaging say that what they are doing is similar to making personal phone calls. So long as they don't abuse the practice, they see no harm. One marketing director justified his occasional game playing and online shopping by explaining that his employer benefits because he is more productive when he takes minibreaks. "When I need a break, I pull up a Web page and just browse," he says. "Ten minutes later, I'm all refreshed, and I can go back to business-plan writing."[32]

Companies Cracking Down
Employers, however, see it differently. A recent survey reported that more than one fourth of employers have fired workers for misusing e-mail, and nearly one third have fired employees for misusing the Internet.[33] UPS discovered an employee running a personal business from his office computer. Lockheed Martin fired an employee who disabled its entire company network for six hours because of an e-mail heralding a holiday event that the worker sent to 60,000 employees. Companies not only worry about lost productivity, but they fear litigation, security breaches, and other electronic disasters from accidental or intentional misuse of computer systems.

What's Reasonable?
Some companies try to enforce a "zero tolerance" policy, prohibiting any personal use of company equipment. Ameritech Corporation specifically tells employees that computers and other company equipment are to be used only to provide service to customers and for other business purposes. Companies such as Boeing, however, allow employees to use faxes, e-mail, and the Internet for personal reasons. But Boeing sets guidelines. Use has to be of reasonable duration and frequency and can't cause embarrassment to the company. Strictly prohibited are chain let-

Guffey helps you learn to communicate effectively and professionally in today's workplace, no matter what career path you choose to follow. The exciting, new ***Essentials of Business Communication*, 9e,** is packed with resources to make learning business communication easier and more enjoyable. The premium student Web site houses powerful resources to help make learning with Guffey … just that easy.

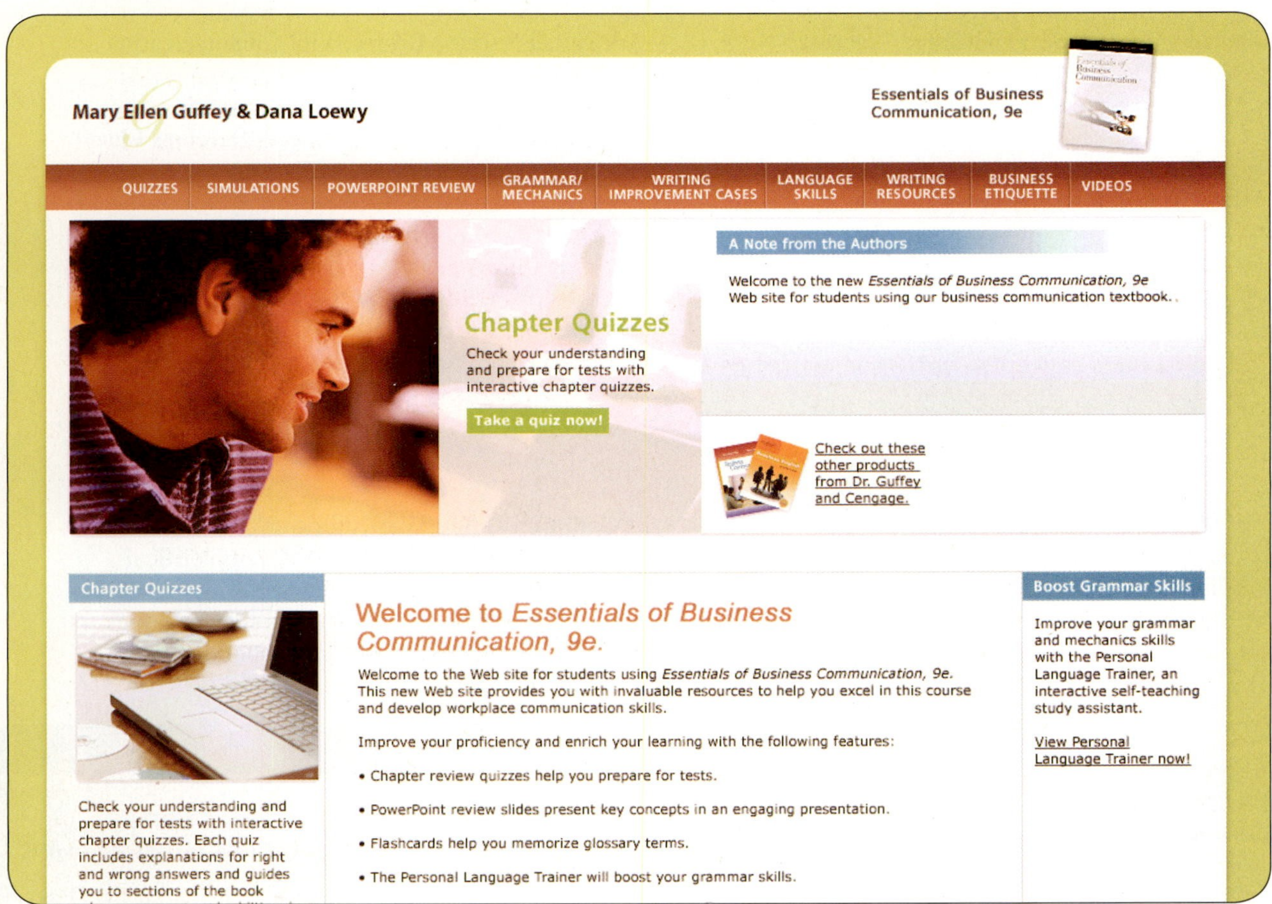

NEW

Student Support Web Site

Guffey and Loewy's premium student Web site gives you one convenient place to find the support you need. You can study with self-teaching grammar/mechanics activities, PowerPoint® slides, chapter review quizzes, Beat the Clock games, and other valuable study tools.

Access the meguffey Web site through www.cengagebrain.com.

DIGITAL TOOLS WITH GUFFEY... IT'S JUST THAT EASY!

The following features are all part of the Guffey and Loewy Premium Student Web site. Visit **www.cengagebrain.com** to use these tools today!

Beat the Clock Interactive Games
These fun but challenging interactive games give you an opportunity to review chapter concepts and make quick decisions in a game-like environment.

Chapter Review Quizzes
Chapter review quizzes help you prepare for tests and check your understanding of the most important concepts in each chapter. Plus, each question includes feedback to help you understand why your answers are right or wrong.

Grammar/Mechanics Checkups
Improve your grammar skills by completing these Grammar/Mechanics Checkups. Available in the textbook and at the student Web site, these Checkups review all sections of the Grammar/Mechanics Handbook.

Grammar/Mechanics Challenge Documents
Build your language skills by finding and correcting errors in the Grammar/Mechanics Challenge Documents. Save time re-keying these documents by downloading them from the Web site.

Personal Language Trainer
The Personal Language Trainer strengthens your language skills through a three-part program that reviews, strengthens, and measures your knowledge. You will begin with a diagnostic quiz to determine your personal fitness profile.

Online Writing Labs
This rich collection of Web sites provide relevant and publicly accessible online "handouts," style guides, and writing tips to help you in this course. You will find a variety of topics including citation formats, test-taking tips, grammar, and the writing process.

Dr. Guffey's Business Etiquette Guide
Do your table manners need to be polished before your next business dinner? Dr. Guffey explores 17 different business etiquette topics, including business dining, of interest to both workplace newcomers and veterans.

PowerPoint® Slides
You can review the most important topics of each chapter in these professionally designed PowerPoint slides. Study them before tests to check your understanding of key concepts.

How do you access the Guffey and Loewy Premium Web site?

1. To register a product using the access code found in your textbook, go to **http://login.cengagebrain.com**.

2. Register as a new user or log in as an existing user if you already have an account with Cengage Learning or **CengageBrain.com**.

3. Follow the online prompts.

Note: If you did not buy a new textbook, the access code may have been used. You can choose to either buy a new book or purchase access to the Guffey Premium Web site at **www.cengagebrain.com**.

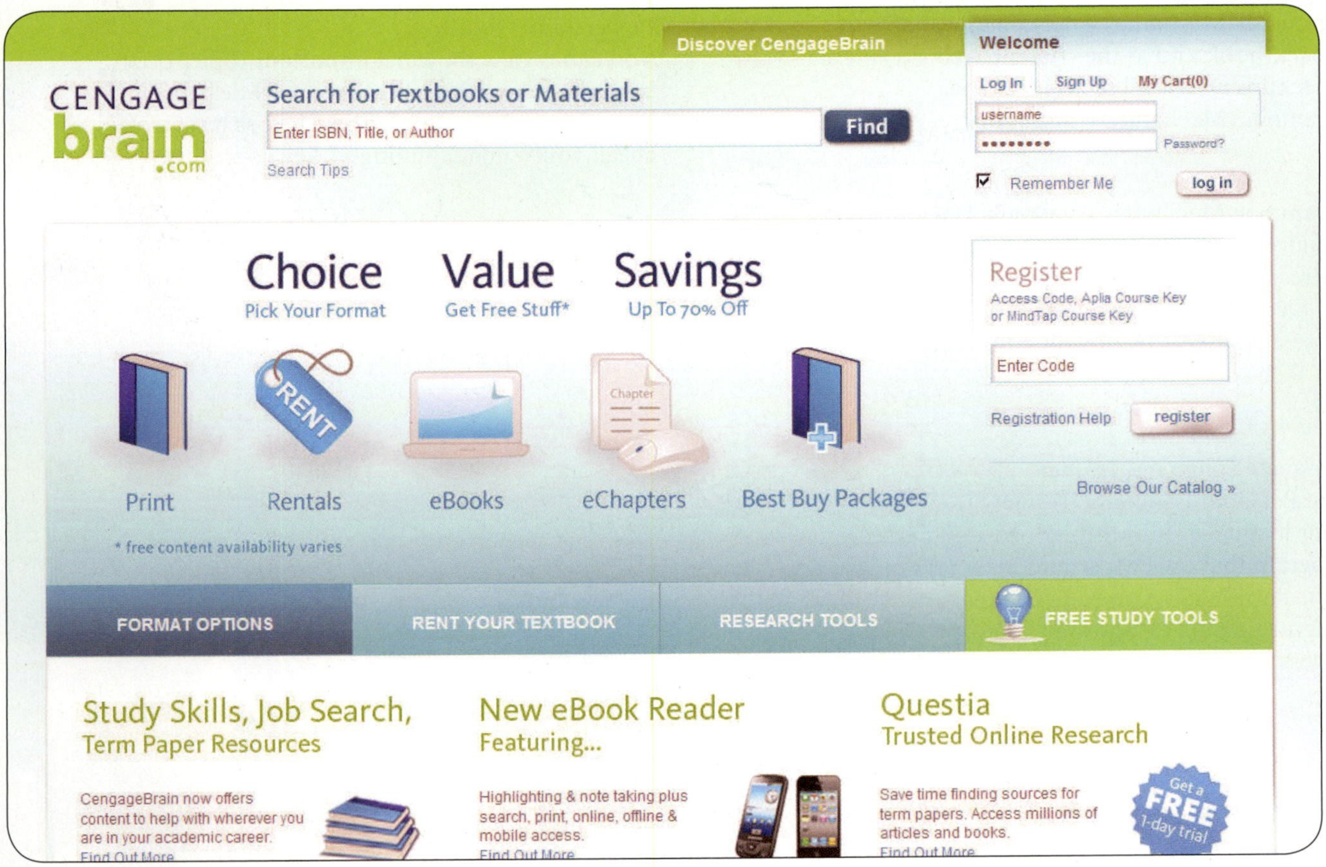

Discover CengageBrain
Welcome
Log In Sign Up My Cart(0)
username
Password?
Remember Me log in
CENGAGE brain .com
Search for Textbooks or Materials
Enter ISBN, Title, or Author
Find
Search Tips
Choice Pick Your Format
Value Get Free Stuff*
Savings Up To 70% Off
Print Rentals eBooks eChapters Best Buy Packages
* free content availability varies
Register
Access Code, Aplia Course Key or MindTap Course Key
Enter Code
Registration Help register
Browse Our Catalog »
FORMAT OPTIONS RENT YOUR TEXTBOOK RESEARCH TOOLS FREE STUDY TOOLS
Study Skills, Job Search, Term Paper Resources
CengageBrain now offers content to help with wherever you are in your academic career.
New eBook Reader Featuring...
Highlighting & note taking plus search, print, online, offline & mobile access.
Questia Trusted Online Research
Save time finding sources for term papers. Access millions of articles and books.
Get a FREE 1-day trial

BRIEF CONTENTS

CONTENTS

Unit 1 Workplace Communication Today 1

Unit 2 The Business Writing Process 35

Unit 3 Communicating at Work 105

Unit 4 Reports and Proposals 245

ABOUT THE AUTHORS

Dr. Mary Ellen Guffey

A dedicated professional, Mary Ellen Guffey has taught business communication and business English topics for over thirty years. She received a bachelor's degree, *summa cum laude,* from Bowling Green State University; a master's degree from the University of Illinois, and a doctorate in business and economic education from the University of California, Los Angeles (UCLA). She has taught at the University of Illinois, Santa Monica College, and Los Angeles Pierce College.

Now recognized as the world's leading business communication author, Dr. Guffey corresponds with instructors around the globe who are using her books. She is the founding author of the award-winning *Business Communication: Process and Product,* the leading business communication textbook in this country and abroad. She also wrote *Business English,* which serves more students than any other book in its field; *Essentials of College English*; and *Essentials of Business Communication,* the leading text/workbook in its market. Dr. Guffey is active professionally, serving on the review boards of the *Business Communication Quarterly* and the *Journal of Business Communication*, publications of the Association for Business Communication. She participates in national meetings, sponsors business communication awards, and is committed to promoting excellence in business communication pedagogy and the development of student writing skills.

Dr. Dana Loewy

Dana Loewy has been teaching business communication at California State University, Fullerton for the past fifteen years. She enjoys introducing undergraduates to business writing and honing the skills of graduate students in managerial communication. Most recently, she has also taught various German classes. Dr. Loewy is a regular guest lecturer at Fachhochschule Nürtingen, Germany. Having earned a PhD from the University of Southern California in English with a focus on translation, she is a well-published freelance translator, interpreter, brand-name consultant, and textbook author. Dr. Loewy has collaborated with Dr. Guffey on recent editions of *Business Communication: Process & Product* as well as on *Essentials of Business Communication.*

Fluent in several languages, among them German and Czech, her two native languages, Dr. Loewy has authored critical articles in many areas of interest—literary criticism, translation, business communication, and business ethics. Before teaming up with Dr. Guffey, Dr. Loewy published various poetry and prose translations, most notably *The Early Poetry* of Jaroslav Seifert and *On the Waves of TSF.* Active in the Association for Business Communication, Dr. Loewy focuses on creating effective teaching/learning materials for undergraduate and graduate business communication students.

ACKNOWLEDGMENTS

We gratefully acknowledge the following professionals whose excellent advice and constructive suggestions helped this and previous editions of *Essentials of Business Communication*:

Faridah Awang
Eastern Kentucky University

Joyce M. Barnes
Texas A & M University—Corpus Christi

Patricia Beagle
Bryant & Stratton Business Institute

Nancy C. Bell
Wayne Community College

Ray D. Bernardi
Morehead State University

Karen Bounds
Boise State University

Jean Bush-Bacelis
Eastern Michigan University

Cheryl S. Byrne
Washtenaw Community College

Mary Y. Bowers
Northern Arizona University

Steven V. Cates
Averett University

Lise H. Diez-Arguelles
Florida State University

Dee Anne Dill
Dekalb Technical Institute

Jeanette Dostourian
Cypress College

Nancy J. Dubino
Greenfield Community College

Cecile Earle
Heald College

Valerie Evans
Cuesta College

Bartlett J. Finney
Park University

Christine Foster
Grand Rapids Community College

Pat Fountain
Coastal Carolina Community College

Marlene Friederich
New Mexico State University—Carlsbad

JoAnn Foth
Milwaukee Area Technical College

Gail Garton
Ozarks Technical Community College

Nanette Clinch Gilson
San Jose State University

Robert Goldberg
Prince George's Community College

Margaret E. Gorman
Cayuga Community College

Judith Graham
Holyoke Community College

Bruce E. Guttman
Katharine Gibbs School, Melville, New York

Tracey M. Harrison
Mississippi College

Debra Hawhee
University of Illinois

L. P. Helstrom
Rochester Community College

Jack Hensen
Morehead State University

Rovena L. Hillsman
California State University, Sacramento

Karen A. Holtkamp
Xavier University

Michael Hricik
Westmoreland County Community College

Sandie Idziak
University of Texas, Arlington

Karin Jacobson
University of Montana

Bonnie Jeffers
Mt. San Antonio College

Edna Jellesed
Lane Community College

Pamela R. Johnson
California State University, Chico

Edwina Jordan
Illinois Central College

Sheryl E. C. Joshua
University of North Carolina, Greensboro

Diana K. Kanoy
Central Florida Community College

Ron Kapper
College of DuPage

Lydia Keuser
San Jose City College

Linda Kissler
Westmoreland County Community College

Deborah Kitchin
City College of San Francisco

Frances Kranz
Oakland University

Keith Kroll
Kalamazoo Valley Community College

Rose Marie Kuceyeski
Owens Community College

Richard B. Larsen
Francis Marion University

Mary E. Leslie
Grossmont College

Ruth E. Levy
Westchester Community College

Maryann Egan Longhi
Dutchess Community College

Nedra Lowe
Marshall University

Elaine Lux
Nyack College

Margarita Maestas-Flores
Evergreen Valley College

Jane Mangrum
Miami-Dade Community College

Maria Manninen
Delta College

Tim March
Kaskaskia College

Paula Marchese
State University of New York College at Brockport

Kenneth R. Mayer
Cleveland State University

Karen McFarland
Salt Lake Community College

Bonnie Miller
Los Medanos College

Mary C. Miller
Ashland University

Willie Minor
Phoenix College

Nancy Moody
Sinclair Community College

Nancy Mulder
Grand Rapids Junior College

Paul W. Murphey
Southwest Wisconsin Technical College

Jackie Ohlson
University of Alaska—Anchorage

Richard D. Parker
Western Kentucky University

Martha Payne
Grayson County College

Catherine Peck
Chippewa Valley Technical College

Carol Pemberton
Normandale Community College

Carl Perrin
Casco Bay College

Jan Peterson
Anoka-Hennepin Technical College

Kay D. Powell
Abraham Baldwin College

Jeanette Purdy
Mercer County College

Carolyn A. Quantrille
Spokane Falls Community College

Susan Randles
Vatterott College

Diana Reep
University of Akron

Ruth D. Richardson
University of North Alabama

Carlita Robertson
Northern Oklahoma College

Vilera Rood
Concordia College

Rich Rudolph
Drexel University

Joanne Salas
Olympic College

Rose Ann Scala
Data Institute School of Business

Joseph Schaffner
SUNY College of Technology, Alfred

Susan C. Schanne
Eastern Michigan University

James Calvert Scott
Utah State University

Laurie Shapero
Miami-Dade Community College

Lance Shaw
Blake Business School

Cinda Skelton
Central Texas College

Estelle Slootmaker
Aquinas College

Clara Smith
North Seattle Community College

Nicholas Spina
Central Connecticut State University

Marilyn St. Clair
Weatherford College

Judy Sunayama
Los Medanos College

Dana H. Swensen
Utah State University

James A. Swindling
Eastfield College

David A. Tajerstein
SYRIT College

Marilyn Theissman
Rochester Community College

Lois A. Wagner
Southwest Wisconsin Technical College

Linda Weavil
Elan College

William Wells
Lima Technical College

Gerard Weykamp
Grand Rapids Community College

Beverly Wickersham
Central Texas College

Leopold Wilkins
Anson Community College

Charlotte Williams
Jones County Junior College

Almeda Wilmarth
State University of New York—Delhi

Barbara Young
Skyline College

In addition to honoring these friends and colleagues, we extend our warmest thanks to the many skillful professionals at Cengage Learning/South-Western including president Jonathan Hulbert; vice president of editorial business, Jack Calhoun; editor in chief, Erin Joyner; acquisitions editor, Jason Fremder; marketing manager, Michelle Lockard; content project manager, Jana Lewis; senior art director, Stacy Shirley; and media editor, John Rich.

Preparing a comprehensive textbook plus all of its supplements for today's digital and evolving market requires an amazing amount of effort and skill. As we worked on the Ninth Edition of *Essentials of Business Communication,* your co-authors were involved in every aspect of the process—from creating the chapter files to selecting photos, writing PowerPoint content, checking all copyediting, proofreading all stages of page proofs (many times!), preparing the Instructor's Manual, and supervising all of the supplements.

However, we also recognize our many helpers. Special gratitude goes to our unsurpassed developmental editor and friend, Mary Emmons, for her remarkable insights, unflappable manner, professional support, steady guidance, and always sunny disposition. In addition to coordinating all of our efforts, Mary helped create an exceptionally helpful Instructor's Manual. For their outstanding work in developing testing and quiz materials, we thank Carolyn Seefer, Diablo Valley College; Catherine Peck and Jane Flesher, Chippewa Valley Technical College; and John Donnellan, University of Texas. For the exciting PowerPoint program, we are indebted to Carolyn Seefer, who worked closely with both authors in creating a warm, entertaining, and instructive set of slides for both students and instructors. In recognition of excellent editing, we commend Malvine Litten and her staff at LEAP Publishing Services Inc. for their effective shepherding of the Ninth Edition to its completion.

We are especially grateful for the support of our fellow professionals at the Association for Business Communication and to the many instructors and students who have made *Essentials of Business Communication* the leading text-workbook in the field.

Mary Ellen Guffey and Dana Loewy

UNIT 1

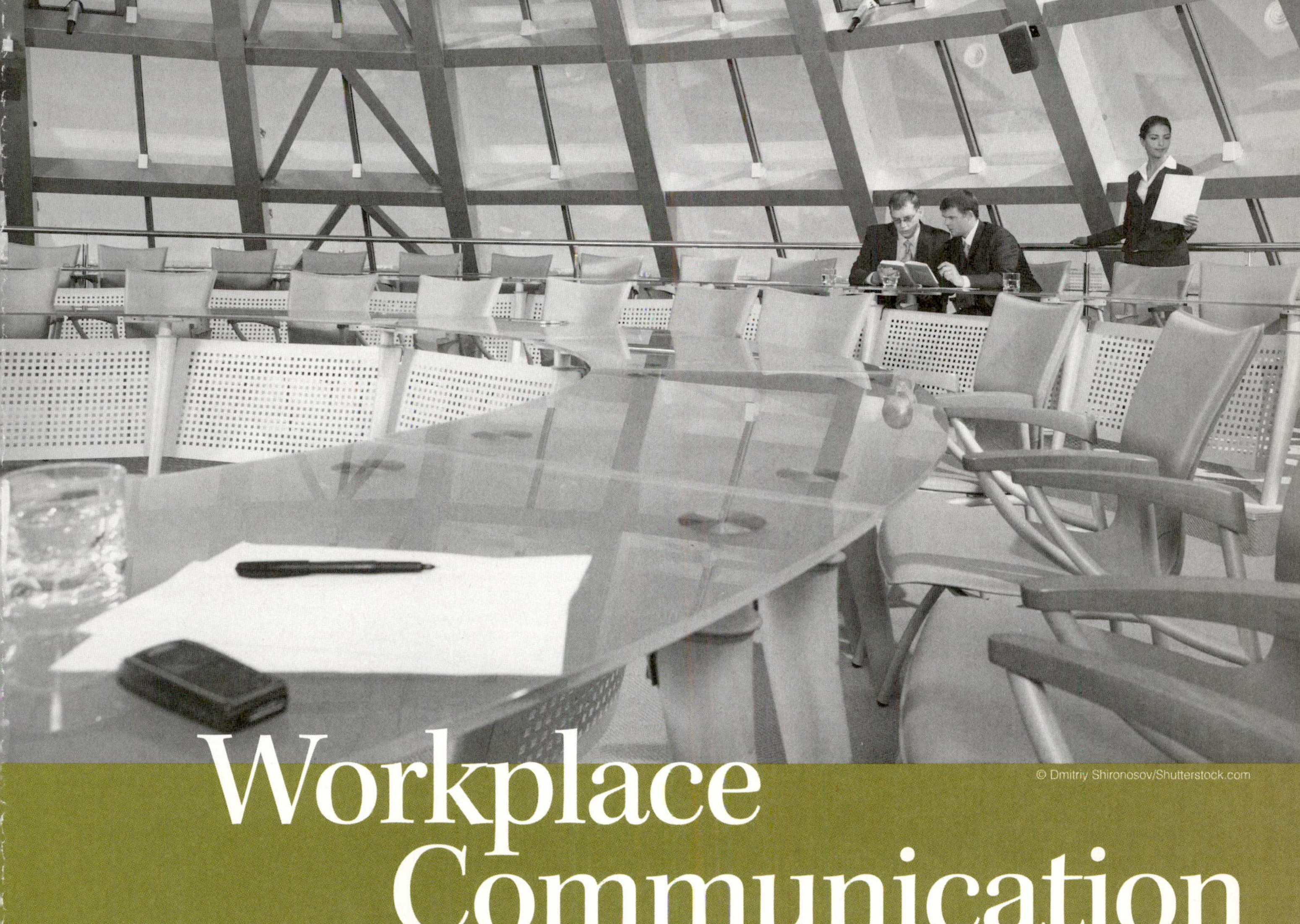

© Dmitriy Shironosov/Shutterstock.com

Workplace Communication Today

CHAPTER 1
Communication Skills as Career Filters

CHAPTER 1

Communication Skills as Career Filters

© Dmitriy Shironosov/Shutterstock.com

Go to **cengagebrain.com** and use your access code to unlock valuable student eResources.

OBJECTIVES

After studying this chapter, you should be able to

- Appreciate how solid communication skills will improve your career prospects and help you succeed in today's changing workplace.
- Understand the process of communication.
- Begin practicing your listening skills and confront barriers to effective listening.
- Explain the importance of nonverbal communication and of improving your nonverbal communication skills.
- Recognize how culture influences communication and explain five common dimensions of culture.
- Discuss strategies that help you overcome negative cultural attitudes and prevent miscommunication in today's diverse workplace.

Communication Skills: Your Ticket to Success

Workplace surveys and studies confirm that recruiters rank communication skills at the top of the list of qualities they most desire in job seekers. Such skills are crucial in a tight employment market when jobs are few and competition is fierce. In a recession, superior communication skills will give you an edge over other job applicants. A powerful career filter, your ability to communicate will make you marketable and continue to be your ticket to success regardless of the economic climate.

Perhaps you are already working or will soon apply for your first job. How do your skills measure up? The good news is that effective communication can be learned. This textbook and this course can immediately improve your communication skills. Because the skills you are learning will make a huge difference in your ability to find a job and to be promoted, this will be one of the most important courses you will ever take.

Small superscript numbers in the text announce information sources. Full citations appear at the end of the chapter. This edition uses a modified American Psychological Association (APA) reference format.

Why Writing Skills Matter More Than Ever

Today's workplace revolves around communication. Workers communicate more, not less, since information technology and the Internet have transformed the world of work in the last two decades. The modern office is mobile and fast paced. Technology enables us to transmit messages faster, farther, to potentially larger audiences, and more easily than in the past. Many people work together but are physically apart. They stay connected through spoken and written messages. Writing skills, which were always a career advantage, are now a necessity.[1] A survey of American corporations revealed that two thirds of salaried employees have some writing responsibility. About one third of them, however, do not meet the writing requirements for their positions.[2]

"Businesses are crying out—they need to have people who write better," said Gaston Caperton, business executive and College Board president.[3] The ability to write opens doors to professional employment. People who cannot write and communicate clearly will not be hired. If already working, they are unlikely to last long enough to be considered for promotion. Writing is a marker of high-skill, high-wage, professional work, according to Bob Kerrey, president of The New School university in New York and chair of the National Commission on Writing. If you can't express yourself clearly, he says, you limit your opportunities for many positions.[4]

OFFICE INSIDER

The founder of a New York public relations firm was shocked at how many college graduates failed the writing test he gives job applicants. He said, "We don't have the time to teach basic writing skills here."

Not surprisingly, many job listings explicitly ask for excellent oral and written communication skills. In a poll of recruiters, oral and written communication skills were by a large margin the top skill set sought.[5] Employers consistently state that communication skills are critical to effective job placement, performance, career advancement, and organizational success.[6] Among the top choices in two other polls were teamwork, critical thinking, analytical reasoning, and oral and written communication skills.[7]

If you believe that you will not need strong communication skills in a technical field such as accounting or information technology, think again. A recent poll of 1,400 chief financial officers sponsored by Accountemps revealed that 75 percent said that verbal, written, and interpersonal skills are more important today than they were in the past.[8] Even technical specialists must be able to communicate with others and explain their work clearly. A survey of Web professionals showed that those with writing and copyediting skills were far less likely to have their jobs sent offshore.[9] Another survey conducted by the Society for Information Management revealed that network professionals ranked written and oral communication skills among the top five most desired skills for new-hires.[10]

Looking and sounding professional gains you credibility on the job.

Businesses today generate a wide range of messages in a variety of media. In addition to traditional letters and memos, expect to communicate with the public and within the company by e-mail*, instant messaging and texting, company blogs, collaboration software such as wikis, and social media sites such as Facebook and Twitter. You will learn more about workplace communication technology in Chapter 5.

Regardless of career choice, writing is in your future. You will probably be sending many digital messages, such as the e-mail shown in Figure 1.1. In fact, e-mail is "today's version of the business letter or interoffice memo."[11] Because electronic mail and other digital media have become important channels of communication in today's workplace, all digital business messages must be clear, concise, and professional. Notice that the message in Figure 1.1 is more businesslike and more professional than the quick e-mail or text you might dash off to friends. Learning to write professional digital messages will be an important part of this course.

OFFICE INSIDER

"Rare is the new college hire who lacks skills involving Facebook, texting or any other form of electronic communication. But face to face, many of these same people have difficulty reading interpersonal signals and communicating, especially in the increasingly multigenerational workplace. Most of the gaps I see are on the social, soft skills side."

—Cindy Warkentin, CIO, Maryland Automobile Insurance Fund

What Employers Want: Professionalism

In addition to technical knowledge in business, your future employer will expect you to show professionalism and possess what are often referred to as "soft skills." Soft skills are essential career attributes that include the ability to communicate, work well with others, solve problems, make ethical decisions, and appreciate diversity.[12] Sometimes also called employability skills or key competencies, these soft skills are desirable in all business sectors and job positions.[13]

As much as businesses expect employees to act in a businesslike and professional manner, many entry-level workers are not ready or have the wrong attitudes. One employer was surprised that many of her new-hires had no idea that excessive absenteeism or tardiness was grounds for termination. The new employees also didn't seem to know that they were expected to devote their full energy to duties when on the job.

* The usage standard in this book is *Merriam-Webster's Collegiate Dictionary,* Eleventh Edition. Words such as *e-mail* and *Web* are in a state of flux, and a single standard has yet to establish itself. *Merriam-Webster's* continues to show conventional usage patterns.

FIGURE 1.1 **Businesslike, Professional E-Mail Message**

Because e-mail messages are rapidly replacing business letters and interoffice memos, they must be written carefully, provide complete information, and sound businesslike and professional. Notice that this message is more formal in tone than e-mail messages you might send to friends.

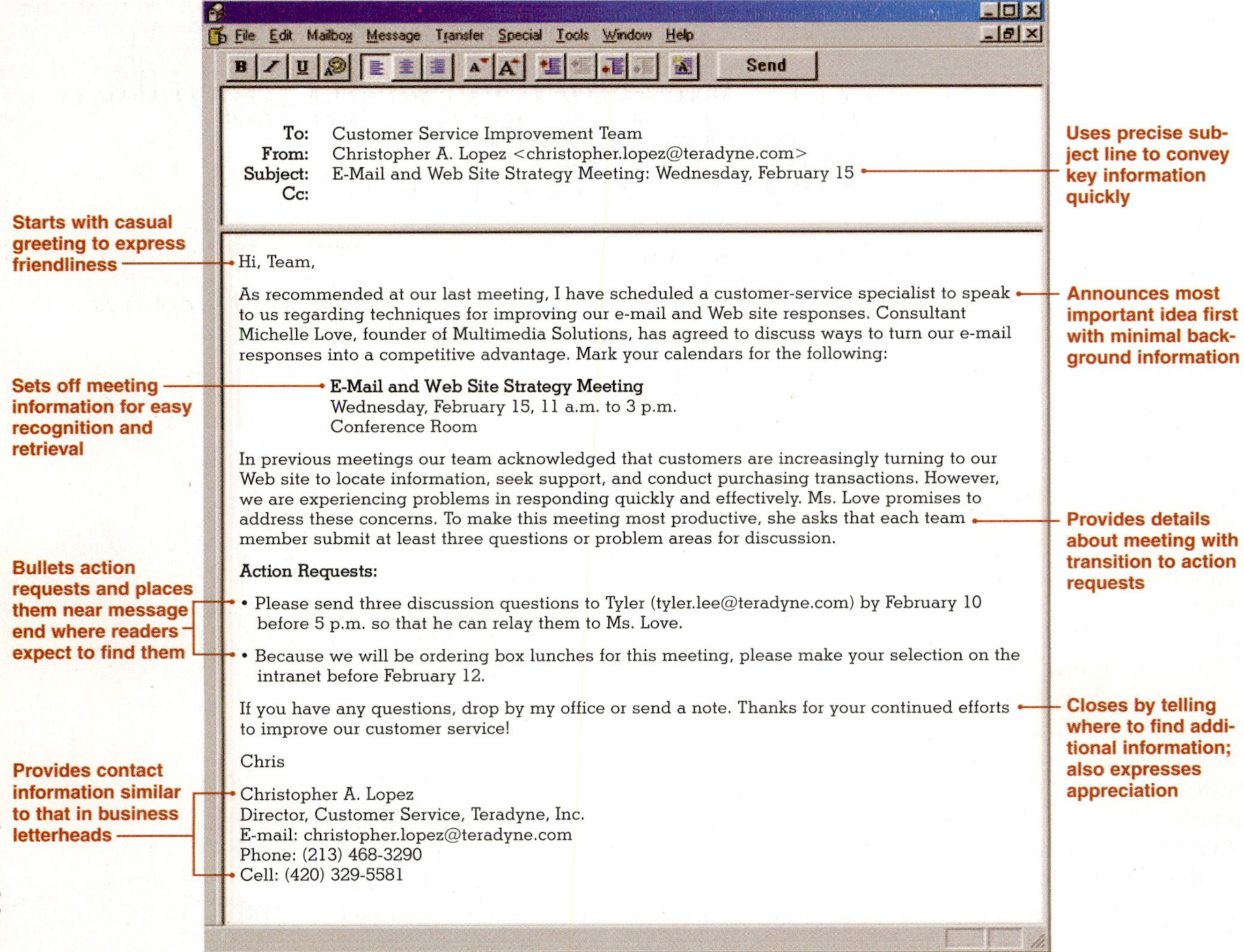

File Edit Mailbox Message Transfer Special Tools Window Help

Send

To: Customer Service Improvement Team
From: Christopher A. Lopez <christopher.lopez@teradyne.com>
Subject: E-Mail and Web Site Strategy Meeting: Wednesday, February 15
Cc:

Hi, Team,

As recommended at our last meeting, I have scheduled a customer-service specialist to speak to us regarding techniques for improving our e-mail and Web site responses. Consultant Michelle Love, founder of Multimedia Solutions, has agreed to discuss ways to turn our e-mail responses into a competitive advantage. Mark your calendars for the following:

E-Mail and Web Site Strategy Meeting
Wednesday, February 15, 11 a.m. to 3 p.m.
Conference Room

In previous meetings our team acknowledged that customers are increasingly turning to our Web site to locate information, seek support, and conduct purchasing transactions. However, we are experiencing problems in responding quickly and effectively. Ms. Love promises to address these concerns. To make this meeting most productive, she asks that each team member submit at least three questions or problem areas for discussion.

Action Requests:

- Please send three discussion questions to Tyler (tyler.lee@teradyne.com) by February 10 before 5 p.m. so that he can relay them to Ms. Love.
- Because we will be ordering box lunches for this meeting, please make your selection on the intranet before February 12.

If you have any questions, drop by my office or send a note. Thanks for your continued efforts to improve our customer service!

Chris

Christopher A. Lopez
Director, Customer Service, Teradyne, Inc.
E-mail: christopher.lopez@teradyne.com
Phone: (213) 468-3290
Cell: (420) 329-5581

One young man wanted to read Harry Potter novels when things got slow.[14] Other recent graduates had unrealistic expectations about their salaries and working hours.[15]

Projecting and maintaining a professional image can make a real difference in helping you obtain the job of your dreams. Once you get that job, you are more likely to be taken seriously and promoted if you look and sound professional. New-hires can sabotage their careers when they carry poor college habits into the business world. Banish the flip-flops, sloppy clothes, and IM abbreviations. Think twice about sprinkling your conversation with *like*, *you know*, and uptalk (making declarative sentences sound like questions). You don't want to send the wrong message with unwitting and unprofessional behavior. Figure 1.2 reviews areas you will want to check to be sure you are projecting professionalism. You will learn more about soft skills and professionalism in Chapter 11.

How Your Education Drives Your Income

College graduates with bachelor's degrees will earn nearly three times as much as high school dropouts.

The effort you invest in earning your college degree will most likely pay off. College graduates make more money, suffer less unemployment, and can choose from a wider variety of career options than workers without a college education.

FIGURE 1.2 Projecting Professionalism When You Communicate

	Unprofessional	Professional
Speech habits	Speaking in *uptalk*, a singsong speech pattern that has a rising inflection making sentences sound like questions; using *like* to fill in mindless chatter; substituting *go* for *said*; relying on slang; or letting profanity slip into your conversation.	Recognizing that your credibility can be seriously damaged by sounding uneducated, crude, or adolescent.
E-mail	Writing e-mails with incomplete sentences, misspelled words, exclamation points, IM slang, and senseless chatting. Sloppy, careless messages send a nonverbal message that you don't care, don't know, or aren't smart enough to know what is correct.	Employers like to see subjects, verbs, and punctuation marks. They don't recognize IM abbreviations. Call it crazy, but they value conciseness and correct spelling, even in brief e-mails.
Internet	Using an e-mail address such as *hotbabe@hotmail.com, supasnugglykitty@yahoo.com*, or *buffedguy@aol.com*.	An e-mail address should include your name or a relevant, positive, businesslike expression. It should not sound cute or like a chat room nickname.
Voice mail	An outgoing message with strident background music, weird sounds, or a joke message.	An outgoing message that states your name or phone number and provides instructions for leaving a message.
Telephone	Soap operas, thunderous music, or a TV football game playing noisily in the background when you answer the phone.	A quiet background when you answer the telephone, especially if you are expecting a prospective employer's call.
Cell phones and smartphones	Taking or placing calls during business meetings or during conversations with fellow employees; raising your voice (cell yell) or engaging in cell calls that others must reluctantly overhear; using a PDA during meetings.	Turning off phone and message notification, both audible and vibrate, during meetings; using your cell only when conversations can be private.

Moreover, college graduates have access to the highest-paying and fastest-growing careers, many of which require a degree.[16] As Figure 1.3 shows, graduates with bachelor's degrees earn nearly three times as much as high school dropouts and are almost three times less likely to be unemployed.

Writing is one aspect of education that is particularly well rewarded. A *Fortune* magazine article reported this finding: "Among people with a two- or four-year college degree, those in the highest 20 percent in writing ability earn, on average, more than three times what those with the worst writing skills make."[17] One corporate president explained that many people climbing the corporate ladder are good. When he faced a hard choice between candidates, he used writing ability as the deciding factor. He said that sometimes writing is the only skill that separates a candidate from the competition. A recent study confirms that soft skills such

FIGURE 1.3 Income and Unemployment in Relation to Education

Education	Median Weekly Earnings	Unemployment Rate
High school dropout	$ 440	14.6%
High school diploma	629	9.7%
Some college, no degree	699	8.6%
Associate's degree	761	6.8%
Bachelor's degree or higher	1,138	3.5%

Sources: U.S. Bureau of Labor Statistics. (2010). Current population survey: Education pays. Retrieved from http://www.bls.gov/emp/ep_chart_001.htm; and Crosby, O., & Moncarz, R. (2006, Fall). The 2004-14 job outlook for college graduates. *Occupational Outlook Quarterly, 50*(3), 43. Retrieved from http://www.bls.gov/opub/ooq/2006/fall/art03.htm

as communication ability can tip the scales in favor of one job applicant over another.[18] Your ticket to winning in a tight job market and launching a successful career is good communication skills.

Building Your Career Communication Skills With This Book

Developing career-boosting communication skills requires instruction, practice, and feedback from a specialist.

This book focuses on developing basic writing skills. You will also learn to improve your listening, nonverbal, and speaking skills. These basic communication skills include learning how to write an e-mail, letter, or report and how to make a presentation. Anyone can learn these skills with the help of instructional materials and good model documents, all of which you will find in this book. You also need practice—with meaningful feedback. You need someone such as your instructor to tell you how to modify your responses so that you can improve.

We have designed this book, its supplements, and a new companion Web site at **www.cengagebrain.com** to provide you and your instructor with everything necessary to make you a successful business communicator in today's dynamic but demanding workplace. Given the increasing emphasis on communication, many businesses are paying large amounts to communication coaches and trainers to teach employees the very skills that you are learning in this course. Your instructor is your coach. So, get your money's worth! Pick your instructor's brain.

To get started, this first chapter presents an overview. You will take a quick look at the changing workplace, the communication process, listening, nonverbal communication, the cultural dimensions of communication, and intercultural job skills. The remainder of the book is devoted to developing specific writing and speaking skills.

Advancing in a Challenging World of Work

Trends in the new world of work highlight the importance of communication skills.

The world of work is changing dramatically. The kind of work you will do, the tools you will use, the form of management you will work under, the environment in which you will be employed, the people with whom you will interact—all are undergoing a pronounced transformation. Some of the most significant changes include global competition, flattened management hierarchies, and team-based projects. Other trends reflect constantly evolving technology, the "anytime, anywhere" office, and an emphasis on ethics. The following overview of trends reveals how communication skills are closely tied to your success in a demanding, dynamic workplace.

- **Heightened global competition.** Because American companies are moving beyond domestic markets, you may be interacting with people from many cultures. As a successful business communicator, you will want to learn about other cultures. You will also need to develop intercultural skills including sensitivity, flexibility, patience, and tolerance.
- **Flattened management hierarchies.** To better compete and to reduce expenses, businesses have for years been trimming layers of management. This means that as a frontline employee, you will have fewer managers. You will be making decisions and communicating them to customers, to fellow employees, and to executives.
- **Increased emphasis on self-directed work groups and virtual teams.** Businesses today are often run by cross-functional teams of peers. You can expect to work with a team in gathering information, finding and sharing solutions, implementing decisions, and managing conflict. You may even become part of a virtual team whose members are in remote locations and who communicate almost exclusively electronically. Good communication skills are extremely important in working together successfully in all team environments, especially if members do not meet face-to-face.

Today's employees must be able to work on local as well as remote teams.

- **Innovative communication technologies.** New communication technology is dramatically affecting the way workers interact. In our always-connected world, businesses exchange information by using e-mail, instant messaging, text messaging, PDAs or smartphones, fax, voice mail, and powerful laptop computers and netbooks. Satellite communications, wireless networking, teleconferencing, and videoconferencing help workers to conduct meetings with associates around the world. Even social networking sites such as Facebook and Twitter as well as blogs, wikis (multiuser weblogs), and peer-to-peer tools help businesspeople collect information, serve customers, and sell products and services. Figure 1.4, on pages 8 and 9, illustrates many new technologies you will encounter in today's workplace.

- **"Anytime, anywhere" and nonterritorial offices.** Thanks largely to advances in high-speed and wireless Internet access, millions of workers no longer report to nine-to-five jobs that confine them to offices. They have flexible working arrangements so that they can work at home or on the road. The "anytime, anywhere" office requires only a mobile phone and a wireless computer.[19] Telecommuting employees now represent 11 percent of the workforce, and this number increases annually.[20] To save on office real estate, a growing number of industries provide "nonterritorial" workspaces. The first to arrive gets the best desk and the corner window.[21]
- **Renewed emphasis on ethics.** Ethics is once again a hot topic in business. Following the Enron and WorldCom scandals in the early 2000s, businesses responded with a flurry of programs emphasizing ethical awareness and training. Despite increased awareness, however, much training was haphazard[22] and characterized by lip service only. With the passage of the Sarbanes-Oxley Act, the government required greater accountability. Nevertheless, a calamitous recession followed, caused largely, some say, by greed and ethical lapses. As a result, businesses are now eager to regain public trust by building ethical environments. Many have written ethical mission statements, installed hotlines, and appointed compliance officers to ensure strict adherence to their high standards and the law.

After the corporate scandals in the early years of the new millennium and the steep recession that followed the banking crisis, ethics is again front and center in business.

These trends mean that your writing skills will constantly be on display. Those who can write clear and concise messages contribute to efficient operations and can expect to be rewarded.

Understanding the Communication Process

The most successful players in the new world of work will be those with highly developed communication skills. As you have seen, you will be communicating more rapidly, more often, and with greater numbers of people than ever before. Because good communication skills are essential to your success, we need to take a closer look at the communication process.

Just what is communication? For our purposes *communication* is "the transmission of information and meaning from one individual or group to another." The crucial element in this definition is *meaning*. Communication has as its central objective the transmission of meaning. The process of communication is successful only when the receiver understands an idea as the sender intended it. This process generally involves five steps, discussed here and shown in Figure 1.5, on page 10.

Communication is the transmission of information and meaning from one individual or group to another.

1. **Sender has an idea.** The form of the idea may be influenced by the sender's mood, frame of reference, background, culture, and physical makeup, as well as the context of the situation.
2. **Sender encodes the idea in a message.** *Encoding* means converting the idea into words or gestures that will convey meaning. A major problem in communicating any message verbally is that words have different meanings for different people. That's why skilled communicators try to choose familiar words with concrete meanings on which both senders and receivers agree.
3. **Message travels over a channel.** The medium over which the message is transmitted is the *channel*. Messages may be sent by computer, telephone, letter, or memorandum. They may also be sent by means of a report, announcement, picture, video, spoken word, fax, or other channel. Because messages carry verbal and nonverbal meanings, senders must choose channels carefully. Anything that disrupts the transmission of a message in the communication process is called *noise*. Channel noise ranges from static that disrupts

The communication process has five steps: idea formation, message encoding, message transmission, message decoding, and feedback.

FIGURE 1.4 Communication and Collaboration Technologies

Communication Technology Reshaping the World of Work

Today's workplace is changing dramatically as a result of innovative software, superfast wireless networks, and numerous technologies that allow workers to share information, work from remote locations, and be more productive in or away from the office. We are seeing a gradual progression from basic capabilities, such as e-mail and calendaring, to deeper functionality, such as remote database access, multifunctional devices, and Web-based collaborative applications.

Telephony: VoIP

Savvy businesses are switching from traditional phone service to voice over Internet protocol (VoIP). This technology allows callers to communicate using a broadband Internet connection, thus eliminating long-distance and local telephone charges. Higher-end VoIP systems now support unified voice mail, e-mail, click-to-call capabilities, and softphones (phones using computer networking). Free or low-cost Internet telephony sites, such as the popular Skype, are also increasingly used by businesses.

Open Offices

The widespread use of laptops, netbooks, wireless technology, and VoIP have led to more fluid, flexible, and open workspaces. Smaller computers and flat-screen monitors enable designers to save space with boomerang-shaped workstations and cockpit-style work surfaces rather than space-hogging corner work areas. Smaller breakout areas for impromptu meetings are taking over some cubicle space, and digital databases are replacing file cabinets.

Multifunctional Printers

Stand-alone copiers, fax machines, scanners, and printers have been replaced with multifunctional devices. Offices are transitioning from a "print and distribute" environment to a "distribute and print" environment. Security measures include pass codes and even biometric thumbprint scanning to make sure data streams are not captured, interrupted, or edited.

Handheld Wireless Devices

A new generation of lightweight, handheld smartphones provide phone, e-mail, Web browsing, and calendar options anywhere there is cell phone coverage or a Wi-Fi network. Devices such as the BlackBerry, the iPhone, and the Android phones now allow you to tap into corporate databases and intranets from remote locations. You can check customers' files, complete orders, and send out receipts without returning to the office.

Company Intranets

To share insider information, many companies provide their own protected Web sites called intranets. An intranet may handle company e-mail, announcements, an employee directory, a policy handbook, frequently asked questions, personnel forms and data, employee discussion forums, shared documents, and other employee information.

Voice Recognition

Computers equipped with voice recognition software enable users to dictate up to 160 words a minute with accurate transcription. Voice recognition is particularly helpful to disabled workers and to professionals with heavy dictation loads, such as physicians and attorneys. Users can create documents, enter data, compose and send e-mails, browse the Web, and control the desktop—all by voice.

Electronic Presentations

Business presentations in PowerPoint can be projected from a laptop or PDA or posted online. Sophisticated presentations may include animations, sound effects, digital photos, video clips, or hyperlinks to Internet sites. In some industries, PowerPoint slides ("decks") are replacing or supplementing traditional hard-copy reports.

Collaboration Technology: Rethinking the Way We Work Together ▸

New tools make it possible to work together without being together. Your colleagues may be down the hall, across the country, or across the world. With today's tools, you can exchange ideas, solve problems, develop products, forecast future performance, and complete team projects any time of the day or night and anywhere in the world. Blogs and wikis, also part of Web 2.0, are social tools that create multidirectional conversations among customers and employees. Web 2.0 moves Web applications from "read only" to "read-write," thus enabling greater participation and collaboration.

◂ Blogs, Podcasts, Wikis, and Tweets

A *blog* is a Web site with journal entries usually written by one person and comments by others. Businesses use blogs to keep customers and employees informed and to receive feedback. Company developments can be posted, updated, and categorized for easy cross-referencing. Blogs and other Web sites may feature audio and video files, *podcasts*, for listening and viewing or for downloading onto the computer and smartphone. A *wiki* is a Web site that allows multiple users to collaboratively create and edit pages. Information gets lost in e-mails, but blogs and wikis provide an easy way to communicate and keep track of what is said. Most companies are still trying to figure out how to harness Twitter for business. However, tech-savvy individuals already send *tweets*, short messages of up to 140 characters, to other users to issue up-to-date news about their products, to link to their blogs and Web sites, or to announce events and promotions.

▴ Voice Conferencing

Telephone "bridges" join two or more callers from any location to share the same call. ***Voice conferencing*** (also called ***audioconferencing***, ***teleconferencing***, or just plain ***conference calling***) enables people to collaborate by telephone. Communicators at both ends use enhanced speakerphones to talk and be heard simultaneously.

Web Conferencing ▸

With services such as GoToMeeting, WebEx, and Microsoft LiveMeeting, all you need are a PC and an Internet connection to hold a meeting (***webinar***) with customers or colleagues in real time. Although the functions are constantly evolving, Web conferencing currently incorporates screen sharing, chats, slide presentations, text messaging, and application sharing.

Videoconferencing ▸

Videoconferencing allows participants to meet in special conference rooms equipped with cameras and television screens. Groups see each other and interact in real time although they may be continents apart. Faster computers, rapid Internet connections, and better cameras now enable 2 to 200 participants to sit at their own PCs and share applications, spreadsheets, presentations, and photos.

▴ Video Phones

Using advanced video compression technology, video phones transmit real-time audio and video so that communicators can see each other as they collaborate. With a video phone, people can videoconference anywhere in the world over a broadband IP (Internet protocol) connection without a computer or a television screen.

◂ Presence Technology

Presence technology makes it possible to locate and identify a computing device as soon as users connect to the network. This technology is an integral part of communication devices including cell phones, laptop computers, PDAs, smartphones, and GPS devices. Collaboration is possible wherever and whenever users are online.

FIGURE 1.5 The Communication Process

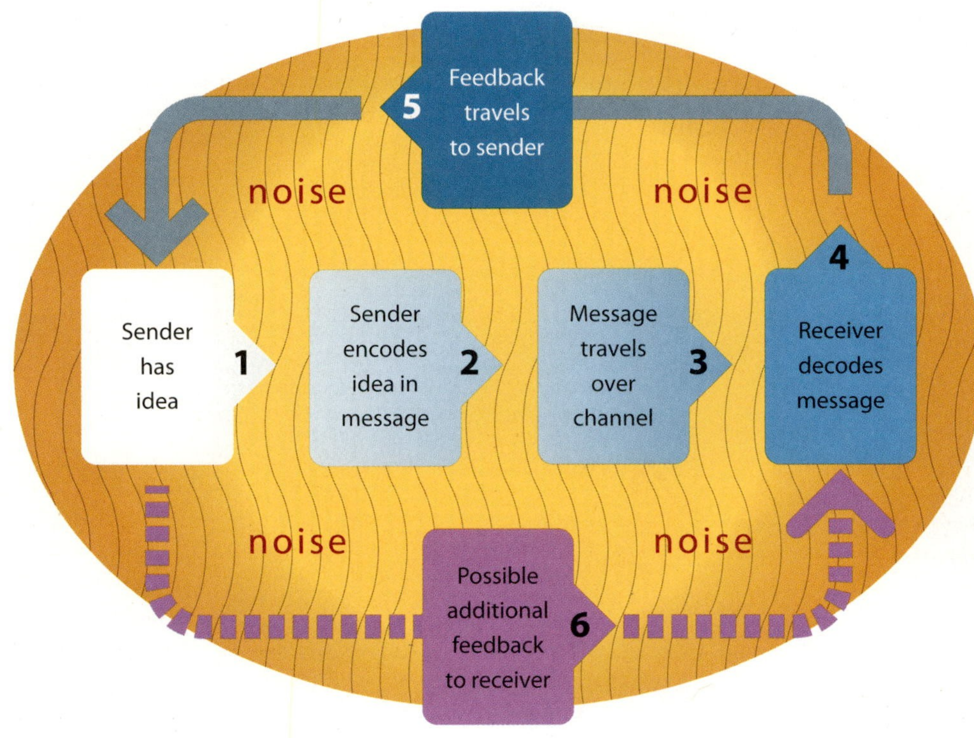

Note: A more comprehensive model of the communication process is available in the instructor's PowerPoint program.

OFFICE INSIDER

Did you know?
It is estimated that more than 50 percent of our work time is spent listening.
** Immediately following a 10-minute presentation, average people retain about half of what they hear and only one quarter after 48 hours.*
** Sixty percent of all management problems are related to listening.*
** We misinterpret, misunderstand, or change 70 to 90 percent of what we hear.*

—Valarie Washington, CEO, Think 6 Results

a telephone conversation to spelling errors in an e-mail or blog post. Such errors damage the credibility of the sender.

4. **Receiver decodes the message.** The person for whom a message is intended is the *receiver*. Translating the message from its symbol form into meaning involves *decoding*. Successful communication takes place only when a receiver understands the meaning intended by the sender. Such success is often hard to achieve because no two people share the same background. Success is further limited because barriers and noise may disrupt the process.
5. **Feedback travels to the sender.** The verbal and nonverbal responses of the receiver create *feedback*, a vital part of the entire communication process. Feedback helps the sender know that the message was received and understood. Senders can encourage feedback by asking questions such as, "Am I making myself clear?" and, "Is there anything you don't understand?" Senders can further improve feedback by delivering the message at a time when receivers can respond. Senders should provide only as much information as a receiver can handle. Receivers can improve the process by paraphrasing the sender's message. They might say, "Let me try to explain that in my own words," or, "My understanding of your comment is. . . ."

Improving Listening Skills

An important part of the communication process is listening. By all accounts, however, most of us are not very good listeners. Do you ever pretend to be listening when you are not? Do you know how to look attentive in class when your mind wanders far away? How about "tuning out" people when their ideas are boring or complex? Do you find it hard to focus on ideas when a speaker's clothing or mannerisms are unusual?

You probably answered *yes* to one or more of these questions because many of us have developed poor listening habits. In fact, some researchers suggest that we listen at only 25 to 50 percent efficiency. Such poor listening habits are costly in business and affect professional relationships. Messages must be rewritten, shipments reshipped, appointments rescheduled, contracts renegotiated, and directions restated.

To improve listening skills, we must first recognize barriers that prevent effective listening. Then we need to focus on specific techniques that are effective in improving listening skills.

Overcoming Barriers to Effective Listening

As you learned earlier, barriers and noise can interfere with the communication process. Have any of the following barriers and distractions prevented you from hearing what has been said?

Barriers to listening may be physical, psychological, verbal, or nonverbal.

- **Physical barriers.** You cannot listen if you cannot hear what is being said. Physical impediments include hearing disabilities, poor acoustics, and noisy surroundings. It is also difficult to listen if you are ill, tired, or uncomfortable.
- **Psychological barriers.** Everyone brings to the communication process a unique set of cultural, ethical, and personal values. Each of us has an idea of what is right and what is important. If other ideas run counter to our preconceived thoughts, we tend to "tune out" the speaker and thus fail to receive them.
- **Language problems.** Unfamiliar words can destroy the communication process because they lack meaning for the receiver. In addition, emotion-laden or "charged" words can adversely affect listening. If the mention of words such as *bankruptcy* or *real estate meltdown* has an intense emotional impact, a listener may be unable to think about the words that follow.
- **Nonverbal distractions.** Many of us find it hard to listen if a speaker is different from what we view as normal. Unusual clothing or speech mannerisms, body twitches, or a radical hairstyle can cause enough distraction to prevent us from hearing what the speaker has to say.
- **Thought speed.** Because we can process thoughts at least three times faster than speakers can say them, we can become bored and allow our minds to wander.
- **Faking attention.** Most of us have learned to look as if we are listening even when we are not. Such behavior was perhaps necessary as part of our socialization. Faked attention, however, seriously threatens effective listening because it encourages the mind to engage in flights of unchecked fancy. Those who fake attention often find it hard to concentrate even when they want to.
- **Grandstanding.** Would you rather talk or listen? Naturally, most of us would rather talk. Because our own experiences and thoughts are most important to us, we grab the limelight in conversations. We sometimes fail to listen carefully because we are just waiting politely for the next pause so that we can have our turn to speak.

Most North Americans speak at about 125 words per minute. The human brain can process information at least three times as fast.

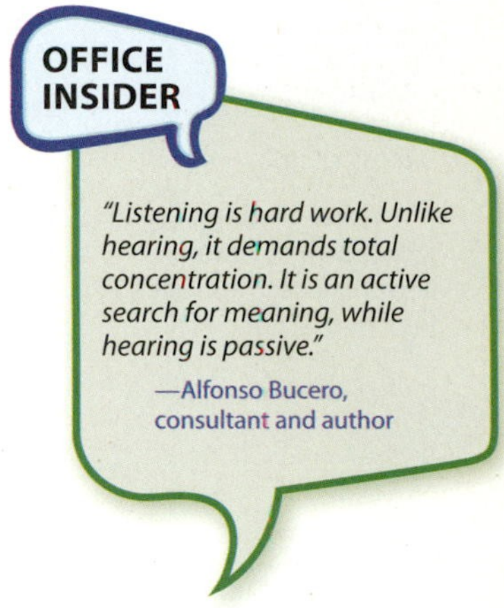

OFFICE INSIDER
"Listening is hard work. Unlike hearing, it demands total concentration. It is an active search for meaning, while hearing is passive."
—Alfonso Bucero, consultant and author

Building Powerful Listening Skills

You can reverse the harmful effects of poor habits by making a conscious effort to become an active listener. This means becoming involved. You can't sit back and hear whatever a lazy mind happens to receive. The following keys will help you become an active and effective listener:

- **Stop talking.** The first step to becoming a good listener is to stop talking. Let others explain their views. Learn to concentrate on what the speaker is saying, not on what your next comment will be.
- **Control your surroundings.** Whenever possible, remove competing sounds. Close windows or doors, turn off TVs and iPods, and move away from loud people, noisy appliances, or engines. Choose a quiet time and place for listening.

"How can I listen to you if you don't say the things I want to hear?"

- **Establish a receptive mind-set.** Expect to learn something by listening. Strive for a positive and receptive frame of mind. If the message is complex, think of it as mental gymnastics. It is hard work but good exercise to stretch and expand the limits of your mind.
- **Keep an open mind.** We all sift through and filter information based on our own biases and values. For improved listening, discipline yourself to listen objectively. Be fair to the speaker. Hear what is really being said, not what you want to hear.
- **Listen for main points.** Heighten your concentration and satisfaction by looking for the speaker's central themes. Congratulate yourself when you find them!
- **Capitalize on lag time.** Make use of the quickness of your mind by reviewing the speaker's points. Anticipate what is coming next. Evaluate evidence the speaker has presented. Don't allow yourself to daydream. Try to guess what the speaker's next point will be.
- **Listen between the lines.** Focus both on what is spoken and what is unspoken. Listen for feelings as well as for facts.
- **Judge ideas, not appearances.** Concentrate on the content of the message, not on its delivery. Avoid being distracted by the speaker's looks, voice, or mannerisms.
- **Hold your fire.** Force yourself to listen to the speaker's entire argument or message before reacting. Such restraint may enable you to understand the speaker's reasons and logic before you jump to false conclusions.
- **Take selective notes.** In some situations thoughtful notetaking may be necessary to record important facts that must be recalled later. Select only the most important points so that the notetaking process does not interfere with your concentration on the speaker's total message.
- **Provide feedback.** Let the speaker know that you are listening. Nod your head and maintain eye contact. Ask relevant questions at appropriate times. Getting involved improves the communication process for both the speaker and the listener.

Mastering Nonverbal Communication Skills

Understanding messages often involves more than merely listening to spoken words. Nonverbal cues, in fact, can speak louder than words. These cues include eye contact, facial expressions, body movements, space, time, territory, and appearance. All these nonverbal cues affect how a message is interpreted, or decoded, by the receiver.

Nonverbal communication includes all unwritten and unspoken messages, intended or not.

Just what is nonverbal communication? It includes all unwritten and unspoken messages, whether intended or not. These silent signals have a strong effect on receivers. But understanding them is not simple. Does a downward glance indicate modesty? Fatigue? Does a constant stare reflect coldness? Dullness? Aggression? Do crossed arms mean defensiveness? Withdrawal? Or just that the person is shivering?

Messages are even harder to decipher when the verbal and nonverbal cues do not agree. What will you think if Scott says he is not angry, but he slams the door when he leaves? What if Alicia assures the hostess that the meal is excellent, but she eats very little? The nonverbal messages in these situations speak more loudly than the words. In fact, researchers believe that over 90 percent of a message that we receive is nonverbal.

When verbal and nonverbal messages clash, listeners tend to believe the nonverbal message.

When verbal and nonverbal messages conflict, receivers put more faith in nonverbal cues. In one study speakers sent a positive message but averted their eyes as they spoke. Listeners perceived the total message to be negative. Moreover, they thought that averted eyes suggested lack of affection, superficiality, lack of trust, and nonreceptivity.[23]

Successful communicators recognize the power of nonverbal messages. Cues broadcast by body language might be helpful in understanding the feelings and attitudes of senders. It is unwise, however, to attach specific meanings to gestures or actions because behavior and its interpretations strongly depend on one's cultural background, as you will see.

Your Body Sends Silent Messages

Psychologist and philosopher Paul Watzlawick held that we cannot not communicate.[24] In other words, it's impossible to not communicate. This means that every behavior is sending a message even if we don't use words. The eyes, face, and body can convey a world of meaning without a single syllable being spoken.

Eye Contact. The eyes have been called the windows to the soul. Even if they don't reveal the soul, the eyes are often the best predictor of a speaker's true feelings. Most of us cannot look another person straight in the eyes and lie. As a result, in American culture we tend to believe people who look directly at us. Sustained eye contact suggests trust and admiration; brief eye contact signals fear or stress. Good eye contact enables the message sender to see whether a receiver is paying attention, showing respect, responding favorably, or feeling distress. From the receiver's viewpoint, good eye contact, in North American culture, reveals the speaker's sincerity, confidence, and truthfulness.

The eyes are thought to be the best predictor of a speaker's true feelings.

Facial Expression. The expression on a person's face can be almost as revealing of emotion as the eyes. Experts estimate that the human face can display over 250,000 expressions.[25] To hide their feelings, some people can control these expressions and maintain "poker faces." Most of us, however, display our emotions openly. Raising or lowering the eyebrows, squinting the eyes, swallowing nervously, clenching the jaw, smiling broadly—these voluntary and involuntary facial expressions can add to or entirely replace verbal messages.

Posture and Gestures. A person's posture can convey anything from high status and self-confidence to shyness and submissiveness. Leaning in toward a speaker suggests attraction and interest; pulling away or shrinking back denotes fear, distrust, anxiety, or disgust. Similarly, gestures can communicate entire thoughts via simple movements. However, the meanings of some of these movements differ in other cultures. Unless you know local customs, they can get you into trouble. In the United States and Canada, for example, forming the thumb and forefinger in a circle means everything is OK. But in parts of South America, the OK sign is obscene.

What does your own body language say about you? To take stock of the kinds of messages being sent by your body, ask a classmate to critique your use of eye contact, facial expression, and body movements. Another way to analyze your nonverbal style is to record yourself making a presentation. Then study your performance. This way you can make sure your nonverbal cues send the same message as your words.

Nonverbal messages often have different meanings in different cultures.

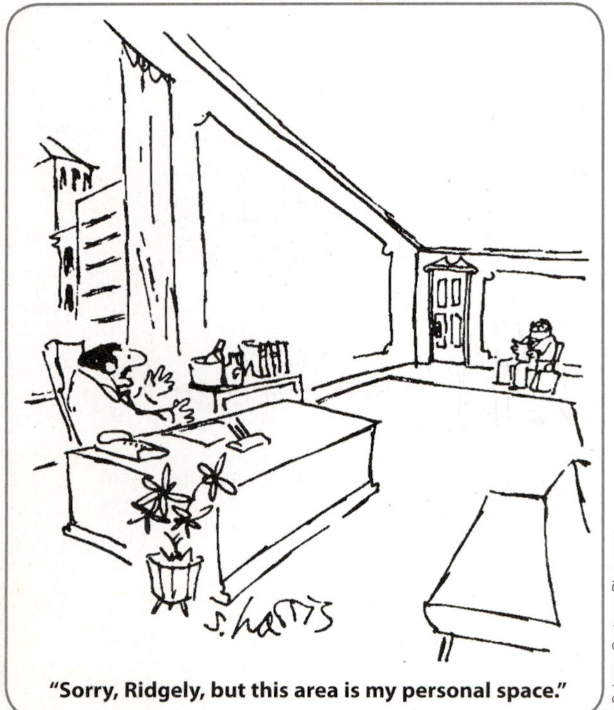
"Sorry, Ridgely, but this area is my personal space."

© ScienceCartoonsPlus.com

Time, Space, and Territory Send Silent Messages

In addition to nonverbal messages transmitted by your body, three external elements convey information in the communication process: time, space, and territory.

Time. How we structure and use time tells observers about our personalities and attitudes. For example, when Warren Buffett, industrialist, investor, and philanthropist, gives a visitor a prolonged interview, he signals his respect for, interest in, and approval of the visitor or the topic to be discussed.

Space. How we order the space around us tells something about ourselves and our objectives. Whether the space is a bedroom, a dorm room, an office, or a department, people reveal themselves in the design and grouping of their furniture. Generally, the more formal the arrangement, the more formal and closed the communication style. The way office furniture is arranged sends cues about how communication is to take place. Israeli diplomat Danny Ayalon caused an international incident after humiliating the Turkish ambassador by making him sit in a chair lower than his own. He also deliberately failed to put the Turkish flag on display.[26] Although Ayalon later apologized, his message was clear: He did not want his visitor to feel equal to him.

The distance required for comfortable social interaction is controlled by culture.

Territory. Each of us has a certain area that we feel is our own territory, whether it is a specific spot or just the space around us. Your father may have a favorite chair in which he is most comfortable, a cook might not tolerate intruders in the kitchen, and veteran employees may feel that certain work areas and tools belong to them. We all maintain zones of privacy in which we feel comfortable. Figure 1.6 illustrates the four zones of social interaction among Americans, as formulated by anthropologist Edward T. Hall.[27] Notice that Americans are a bit standoffish; only intimate friends and family may stand closer than about 1.5 feet. If someone violates that territory, Americans feel uncomfortable and may step back to reestablish their space.

FIGURE 1.6 Four Space Zones for Social Interaction

© iStockphoto.com/Morgan Lane Studios

Intimate Zone (1 to 1.5 feet)

© iStockphoto.com/Dean Mitchell

Personal Zone (1.5 to 4 feet)

© iStockphoto.com/Catherine Yeulet

Social Zone (4 to 12 feet)

© Kablonk Royalty-Free/Inmagine

Public Zone (12 or more feet)

Appearance Sends Silent Messages

Much like the personal appearance of an individual, the physical appearance of a business document transmits immediate and important nonverbal messages. Ideally, these messages should be pleasing to the eye.

"Now, Dan we're all equals here. Have a seat."

Eye Appeal of Business Documents. The way an e-mail, letter, memo, or report looks can have either a positive or a negative effect on the receiver. Sloppy e-mails send a nonverbal message that you are in a terrific hurry or that you do not care about the receiver. Envelopes—through their postage, stationery, and printing—can suggest routine, important, or junk mail. Letters and reports can look neat, professional, well organized, and attractive—or just the opposite. In succeeding chapters you will learn how to create business documents that send positive nonverbal messages through their appearance, format, organization, readability, and correctness.

The appearance of a message and of an individual can convey positive or negative nonverbal messages.

Personal Appearance. The way you look—your clothing, grooming, and posture—telegraphs an instant nonverbal message about you. Based on what they see, viewers make quick judgments about your status, credibility, personality, and potential. If you want to be considered professional, think about how you present yourself. One marketing manager said, "I'm young and pretty. It's hard enough to be taken seriously, and if I show up in jeans and a teeshirt, I don't stand a chance."[28] As a businessperson, you will want to think about what your appearance says about you. Although the rules of business attire have loosened up, some workers show poor judgment. You will learn more about professional attire and behavior in later chapters.

Building Strong Nonverbal Skills

Nonverbal communication can outweigh words in the way it influences how others perceive us. You can harness the power of silent messages by reviewing the following tips for improving nonverbal communication skills:

Because nonverbal cues can mean more than spoken words, learn to use nonverbal communication positively.

- **Establish and maintain eye contact.** Remember that in the United States and Canada appropriate eye contact signals interest, attentiveness, strength, and credibility.
- **Use posture to show interest.** Encourage interaction by leaning forward, sitting or standing erect, and looking alert.
- **Improve your decoding skills.** Watch facial expressions and body language to understand the complete verbal and nonverbal messages being communicated.
- **Probe for more information.** When you perceive nonverbal cues that contradict verbal meanings, politely seek additional cues ("I'm not sure I understand," "Please tell me more about . . .," or "Do you mean that . . .").
- **Avoid assigning nonverbal meanings out of context.** Don't interpret nonverbal behavior unless you understand a situation or a culture.
- **Associate with people from diverse cultures.** Learn about other cultures to widen your knowledge and tolerance of intercultural nonverbal messages.
- **Appreciate the power of appearance.** Keep in mind that the appearance of your business documents, your business space, and yourself sends immediate positive or negative messages to receivers.
- **Observe yourself on video.** Ensure that your verbal and nonverbal messages are in sync by recording and evaluating yourself making a presentation.
- **Enlist friends and family.** Ask friends and family to monitor your conscious and unconscious body movements and gestures to help you become an effective communicator.

Understanding How Culture Affects Communication

Verbal and nonverbal meanings are even more difficult to interpret when people come from different cultures.

Comprehending the verbal and nonverbal meanings of a message is difficult even when communicators are from the same culture. When they come from different cultures, special sensitivity and skills are necessary.

Negotiators for a North American company learned this lesson when they were in Japan looking for a trading partner. The North Americans were pleased after their first meeting with representatives of a major Japanese firm. The Japanese had nodded assent throughout the meeting and had not objected to a single proposal. The next day, however, the North Americans were stunned to learn that the Japanese had rejected the entire plan. In interpreting the nonverbal behavioral messages, the North Americans made a typical mistake. They assumed the Japanese were nodding in agreement as fellow North Americans would. In this case, however, the nods of assent indicated comprehension—not approval.

Every country has a unique culture or common heritage, joint experience, and shared learning that produce its culture. Their common experience gives members of that culture a complex system of shared values and customs. It teaches them how to behave; it conditions their reactions. Global business, new communication technologies, the Internet, and even Hollywood are spreading Western values throughout the world. However, cultural differences can still cause significant misunderstandings.

The more you know about culture in general and your own culture in particular, the better able you will be to adopt an intercultural perspective. In this book it is impossible to cover fully the infinite facets of culture. However, we can outline some key dimensions of culture and look at them from various points of view.

So that you will better understand your culture and how it contrasts with other cultures, we will describe five key dimensions of culture: context, individualism, formality, communication style, and time orientation.

Context

Low-context cultures (such as those in North America and Western Europe) depend less on the environment of a situation to convey meaning than do high-context cultures (such as those in China, Japan, and Arab countries).

Context is one of the most important cultural dimensions, yet it is among the most difficult to define. In a model developed by cultural anthropologist Edward T. Hall, context refers to the stimuli, environment, or ambience surrounding an event. Hall arranged cultures on a continuum, shown in Figure 1.7, from low to high in relation to context. Our figure also summarizes key comparisons for today's business communicators.

Communicators in low-context cultures (such as those in North America, Scandinavia, and Germany) depend little on the context of a situation to convey their meaning. They assume that listeners need to be briefed exactly and specifically to avoid misunderstandings. Low-context cultures tend to be logical, analytical, and action oriented. Business communicators stress clearly articulated messages that they consider to be objective, professional, and efficient. Words are taken literally.

Communicators in high-context cultures (such as those in China, Japan, and Arab countries) assume that the listener is already "contexted" and does not need much background information.[29] Communicators in high-context cultures are more likely to be intuitive and contemplative. They may not take words literally. Instead, the meaning of a message may be implied from the social or physical setting, the relationship of the communicators, or nonverbal cues. For example, a Japanese communicator might say *yes* when he really means *no*. From the context of the situation, the Japanese speaker would indicate whether *yes* really meant *yes* or whether it meant *no.* The context, tone, time taken to answer, facial expression, and body cues would convey the meaning of *yes.*[30] Communication cues are transmitted by posture, voice inflection, gestures, and facial expression.

FIGURE 1.7 **Comparing High- and Low-Context Communicators**

Culture has a powerful effect on business communicators. The following observations point out selected differences. Remember, however, that these are simplifications and that practices within a given culture vary considerably. Moreover, as globalization expands, low- and high-context cultures are experiencing change and differences may be less pronounced.

Business Communicators in Low-Context Cultures	Business Communicators in High-Context Cultures
Assume listeners know little and must be told everything directly.	Assume listeners are highly "contexted" and require little background.
Value independence, initiative, self-assertion.	Value consensus and group decisions.
Rely on facts, data, and logic.	Rely on relationships rather than objective data.
Value getting down to business and achieving results.	Value relationships, harmony, status, and saving face.
Keep business and social relationships separate.	Intermix business and social relationships.
Expect negotiated decisions to be final and ironclad.	Expect to reopen discussions of decisions previously negotiated.
Hold relaxed view toward wealth and power.	Defer to others based on wealth, position, seniority, and age.
Value competence regardless of position or status.	May value position and status over competence.
Have little problem confronting, showing anger, or making demands.	Avoid confrontation, anger, and emotion in business transactions.
Analyze meanings and attach face value to words.	May not take words literally; may infer meanings.

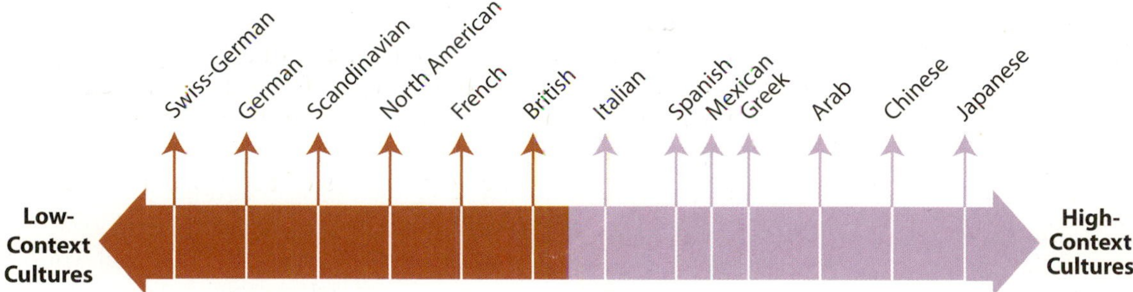

Individualism

An attitude of independence and freedom from control characterizes individualism. Members of low-context cultures, particularly Americans, tend to value individualism. They believe that initiative, self-assertion, and competence result in personal achievement. They believe in individual action and personal responsibility, and they desire a large degree of freedom in their personal lives.

Members of many low-context cultures value independence and freedom from control.

Members of high-context cultures are more collectivist. They emphasize membership in organizations, groups, and teams; they encourage acceptance of group values, duties, and decisions. They typically resist independence because it fosters competition and confrontation instead of consensus. In group-oriented cultures such as those in many Asian societies, for example, self-assertion and individual decision making are discouraged. "The nail that sticks up gets pounded down" is a common Japanese saying.[31] Business decisions are often made by all who have competence in the matter under discussion. Similarly, in China managers also focus on the group rather than on the individual, preferring a consultative management style over an autocratic style.[32]

Many cultures, of course, are quite complex and cannot be characterized as totally individualistic or group oriented. For example, European Americans are generally quite individualistic, whereas African Americans are less so, and Latin Americans are closer to the group-centered dimension.[33]

Formality

Tradition, ceremony, and social rules are more important in some cultures than in others.

People in some cultures place less emphasis on tradition, ceremony, and social rules than do members of other cultures. Americans, for example, dress casually and are soon on a first-name basis with others. Their lack of formality is often characterized by directness. In business dealings Americans come to the point immediately; indirectness, they feel, wastes time, a valuable commodity in American culture.

This informality and directness may be confusing abroad. In Mexico, for instance, a typical business meeting begins with handshakes, coffee, and an expansive conversation about the weather, sports, and other light topics. An invitation to "get down to business" might offend a Mexican executive.[34] In Japan signing documents and exchanging business cards are important rituals. In Europe first names are used only after long acquaintance and by invitation. In Arab, South American, and Asian cultures, a feeling of friendship and kinship must be established before business can proceed.

In Western cultures people are more relaxed about social status and the appearance of power.[35] Deference is not generally paid to individuals merely because of their wealth, position, seniority, or age. In many Asian cultures, however, these characteristics are important and must be respected. Deference and respect are paid to authority and power. Recognizing this cultural pattern, Marriott Hotel managers learned to avoid placing a lower-level Japanese employee on a floor above a higher-level executive from the same company.

Communication Style

Words are used differently by people in low- and high-context cultures.

People in low- and high-context cultures tend to communicate differently with words. To Americans and Germans, words are very important, especially in contracts and negotiations. People in high-context cultures, on the other hand, place more emphasis on the surrounding context than on the words describing a negotiation. A Greek may see a contract as a formal statement announcing the intention to build a business for the future. The Japanese may treat contracts as statements of intention, and they assume changes will be made as a project develops. Mexicans may treat contracts as artistic exercises of what might be accomplished in an ideal world. They do not necessarily expect contracts to apply consistently in the real world. An Arab may be insulted by merely mentioning a contract; a person's word is more binding.[36]

North Americans value a direct, straightforward communication style.

In communication style North Americans value straightforwardness, are suspicious of evasiveness, and distrust people who might have a "hidden agenda" or who "play their cards too close to the chest."[37] North Americans also tend to be uncomfortable with silence and impatient with delays. Some Asian businesspeople have learned that the longer they drag out negotiations, the more concessions impatient North Americans are likely to make.

Time Orientation

North Americans tend to correlate time with productivity, efficiency, and money.

North Americans consider time a precious commodity. They correlate time with productivity, efficiency, and money. Keeping people waiting for business appointments wastes time and is also rude.

In other cultures time may be perceived as an unlimited and never-ending resource to be enjoyed. A North American businessperson, for example, was kept waiting two hours past a scheduled appointment time in South America. She wasn't offended, though, because she was familiar with Hispanics' more relaxed concept of time.

The perception of time and how it is used are culturally learned. In some cultures time is perceived analytically. People account for every minute of the day. In other cultures, time is holistic and viewed in larger chunks. Western cultures tend to be more analytical, scheduling appointments at 15- to 30-minute intervals. Eastern cultures tend to be more holistic, planning fewer but longer meetings. People in one culture may look at time as formal and task oriented. In another culture, time is seen as an opportunity to develop an interpersonal relationship. In the announcements of some international meetings, a qualifier may be inserted after the meeting time. For example, "The meeting starts at 10 a.m. Malaysian time." This tells participants whether to expect fixed or fluid scheduling.

Learning Intercultural Workplace Skills

The global economy needs workers who not only master their technical skills but also can thrive on diverse teams and interact effectively with customers and clients at home and abroad. Even if you never seek an overseas work assignment, you will need to be able to collaborate with diverse coworkers right here at home. We will discuss how to overcome barriers to productive intercultural communication, develop strong intercultural skills, and capitalize on workplace diversity.

OFFICE INSIDER

"Not everyone can travel, but since we live and work in a global economy, we should expect undergraduate programs to prepare students with a fundamental understanding of the cultural differences, historical perspectives and common business practices employed by all the major countries within it."

—Craig Cuyar, CIO, Cushman & Wakefield Inc.

Conquering Ethnocentrism and Stereotyping

The process of understanding and interacting successfully with people from other cultures is often hampered by two barriers: ethnocentrism and stereotyping. These two barriers, however, can be overcome by developing tolerance, a powerful and effective aid to communication.

Ethnocentrism. The belief in the superiority of one's own culture is known as *ethnocentrism*. This natural attitude is found in all cultures. Ethnocentrism causes us to judge others by our own values. If you were raised in North America, the values described in the preceding sections probably seem "right" to you, and you may wonder why the rest of the world doesn't function in the same sensible fashion. A North American businessperson in an Arab or Asian country might be upset at time spent over coffee or other social rituals before any "real" business is transacted. In these cultures, however, personal relationships must be established and nurtured before earnest talks may proceed.

Ethnocentrism is the belief in the superiority of one's own culture and group.

Stereotypes. Our perceptions of other cultures sometimes cause us to form stereotypes about groups of people. A *stereotype* is an oversimplified perception of a behavioral pattern or characteristic applied to entire groups. For example, the Swiss are hardworking, efficient, and neat; Germans are formal, reserved, and blunt; Americans are loud, friendly, and impatient; Canadians are polite, trusting, and tolerant; Asians are gracious, humble, and inscrutable. These attitudes may or may not accurately describe cultural norms. But when applied to individual business communicators, such stereotypes may create misconceptions and misunderstandings. Look beneath surface stereotypes and labels to discover individual personal qualities.

A *stereotype* is an oversimplified behavioral pattern applied to entire groups.

Tolerance. Working with people from other cultures demands tolerance and flexible attitudes. As global markets expand and as our society becomes increasingly multiethnic, tolerance becomes critical. *Tolerance*, here, does not mean "putting up with" or "enduring," which is one part of its definition. Instead, we use *tolerance* in a broader sense. It means learning about beliefs and practices different from our own and appreciating them. One of the best ways to develop tolerance is to practice *empathy*. This means trying to see the world through another's eyes. It means being nonjudgmental, recognizing things as they are rather than as they "should be."

Developing intercultural tolerance means practicing empathy, being nonjudgmental, and being patient.

For example, in China, the American snack foods manufacturer Frito-Lay had to accommodate yin and yang, the Chinese philosophy that nature and life must balance opposing elements. Chinese consider fried foods to be hot and avoid them in summer because two "hots" don't balance. They prefer "cool" snacks in summer; therefore, Frito-Lay created "cool lemon" potato chips dotted with lime specks and mint. The yellow, lemon-scented chips are delivered in a package showing breezy blue skies and rolling green grass.[38] Instead of imposing the American view that potato chips are fine as a summer snack, Frito-Lay looked at its product through the eyes of its Chinese consumers and adjusted accordingly.

The following suggestions can help you prevent miscommunication in oral and written transactions across cultures.

Successful Oral Communication With Intercultural Audiences

To improve communication with nonnative speakers of English, speak slowly, enunciate clearly, observe eye messages, encourage feedback, check for comprehension, accept blame, don't interrupt, remember to smile, and follow up important conversations in writing.

When you have a conversation with someone from another culture, you can reduce misunderstandings by following these tips:

- **Use simple English.** Speak in short sentences (under 20 words) with familiar, short words. Eliminate puns, sport and military references, slang, and jargon (special business terms). Be especially alert to idiomatic expressions that can't be translated, such as *burn the midnight oil* and *under the weather*.
- **Speak slowly and enunciate clearly.** Avoid fast speech, but don't raise your voice. Overpunctuate with pauses and full stops. Always write numbers for all to see.
- **Encourage accurate feedback.** Ask probing questions, and encourage the listener to paraphrase what you say. Don't assume that a *yes*, a nod, or a smile indicates comprehension or assent.
- **Check frequently for comprehension.** Avoid waiting until you finish a long explanation to request feedback. Instead, make one point at a time, pausing to check for comprehension. Don't proceed to B until A has been grasped.
- **Observe eye messages.** Be alert to a glazed expression or wandering eyes. These tell you the listener is lost.
- **Accept blame.** If a misunderstanding results, graciously accept the responsibility for not making your meaning clear.
- **Listen without interrupting.** Curb your desire to finish sentences or to fill out ideas for the speaker. Keep in mind that North Americans abroad are often accused of listening too little and talking too much.
- **Smile when appropriate.** Roger Axtell, international behavior expert, calls the smile the single most understood and most useful form of communication in either personal or business transactions. In some cultures, however, excessive smiling may seem insincere.[39]
- **Follow up in writing.** After conversations or oral negotiations, confirm the results and agreements with follow-up letters. For proposals and contracts, engage a qualified translator to prepare copies in the local language.

You can improve intercultural written communication by adopting local styles, using short sentences and short paragraphs, avoiding ambiguous wording, and citing numbers carefully.

"He doesn't understand you. Try shouting a little louder."

Successful Written Communication With Intercultural Audiences

When you write to someone from a different culture, you can improve your chances of being understood by following these suggestions:

- **Consider local styles.** Learn how documents are formatted and how letters are addressed and developed in the intended reader's country. Decide whether to use your organization's preferred format or adjust to local styles.
- **Consider hiring a translator.** Engage a professional translator if (a) your document is important, (b) your document will be distributed to many readers, or (c) you must be persuasive.
- **Use short sentences and short paragraphs.** Sentences with fewer than 20 words and paragraphs with fewer than 8 lines are most readable.
- **Avoid ambiguous wording.** Include relative pronouns (*that, which, who*) for clarity in introducing clauses. Stay away from contractions (especially ones such as *Here's the problem*). Avoid idioms (*once in a blue moon*), slang (*my presentation really bombed*), acronyms (*ASAP* for *as soon as possible*), abbreviations (*DBA* for *doing business as*), and jargon (*input, output, clickstream*). Use action-specific verbs (*purchase a printer* rather than *get a printer*).

- **Cite numbers carefully.** For international trade it is a good idea to learn and use the metric system. In citing numbers, use figures (*15*) instead of spelling them out (*fifteen*). Always convert dollar figures into local currency. Avoid using figures to express the month of the year. In North America, for example, *March 5, 2012,* might be written as *3/5/12*, while in Europe the same date might appear as *5.3.12*. For clarity, always spell out the month.

You can expect to be interacting with customers and colleagues who may differ from you in race, ethnicity, age, gender, national origin, physical ability, and many other characteristics.

Globalization and Workplace Diversity

As global competition opens world markets, North American businesspeople will increasingly interact with customers and colleagues from around the world. At the same time, the North American workforce is also becoming more diverse—in race, ethnicity, age, gender, national origin, physical ability, and countless other characteristics.

No longer, say the experts, will the workplace be predominantly male or Anglo-oriented. The white non-Hispanic population of the United States is expected to drop from 79 percent in 1980 to 64 percent in 2020. The Hispanic population will climb from 6 percent to 17 percent, the African American population will increase from 12 percent to 13 percent, and the Asian population will rise from 2 percent to 6 percent.[40] In addition to increasing numbers of minorities, the workforce will see a big jump in older workers. By 2020, the number of workers aged fifty-five and older will grow to 20 percent.[41]

What do all these changes mean for you as a future business communicator? Simply put, your job may require you to interact with colleagues and customers from around the world. Your work environment will probably demand that you cooperate effectively with small groups of coworkers. What's more, these coworkers may differ from you in race, ethnicity, gender, age, and other ways.

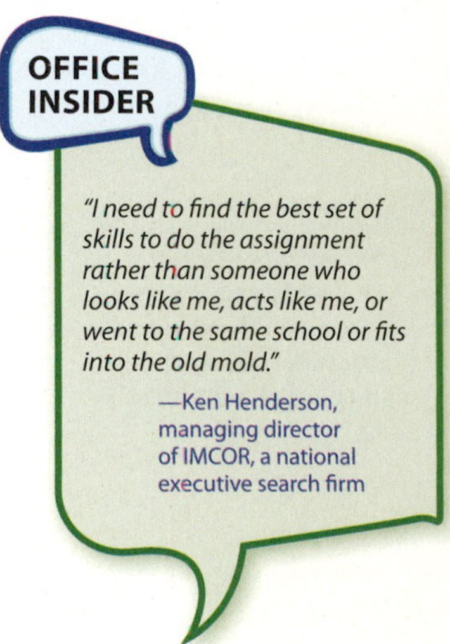

OFFICE INSIDER
"I need to find the best set of skills to do the assignment rather than someone who looks like me, acts like me, or went to the same school or fits into the old mold."
—Ken Henderson, managing director of IMCOR, a national executive search firm

Benefits of a Diverse Workforce

A diverse work environment offers many benefits and makes good business sense. Customers want to deal with companies that respect their values. They are more likely to say, "If you are a company whose ads do not include me, or whose workforce does not include me, I will not buy from you." A diverse staff is better able to read trends and respond to the increasingly diverse customer base in local and world markets.

At PepsiCo, work teams created new products inspired by diversity efforts. Those products included Gatorade Xtremo aimed at Hispanics as well as Mountain Dew Code Red, which appeals to African Americans. One Pepsi executive said that companies that "figure out the diversity challenge first will clearly have a competitive advantage."[42]

In addition, organizations that set aside time and resources to cultivate and capitalize on diversity will suffer fewer discrimination lawsuits, fewer union clashes, and less government regulatory action. Most important, though, is the growing realization among organizations that diversity is a critical bottom-line business strategy to improve employee relationships and to increase productivity. Developing a diverse staff that can work together cooperatively is one of the biggest challenges facing business organizations today.

"We need to focus on diversity. Your goal is to hire people who all look different, but think just like me."

Tips for Communicating With Diverse Audiences on the Job

Integrating all this diversity into one seamless workforce is a formidable but vital task. Harnessed effectively, diversity can enhance productivity and propel a company to success well into the twenty-first century. Mismanaged, it can become a tremendous drain on a company's time and resources. How companies deal

"As part of our commitment to cultural diversity, we've hired Ledyard, who has 8 earrings on various portions of his anatomy. . ."

with diversity will make all the difference in how they compete in an increasingly global environment. This means that organizations must do more than just pay lip service to these issues. Harmony and acceptance do not happen automatically when people who are dissimilar work together. The following suggestions can help you and your organization find ways to improve communication and interaction:

Successful communicators understand the value of differences, seek training, learn about their own cultures, make fewer assumptions, and build on similarities.

- **Understand the value of differences.** Diversity makes an organization innovative and creative. Sameness fosters an absence of critical thinking called *groupthink*. Case studies, for example, of the *Challenger* shuttle disaster suggest that groupthink prevented alternatives from being considered. Even smart people working collectively can make dumb decisions if they do not see different perspectives.[43] Diversity in problem-solving groups encourages independent and creative thinking.
- **Seek training.** Especially if an organization is experiencing diversity problems, awareness-raising sessions may be helpful. Spend time reading and learning about workforce diversity and how it can benefit organizations. Look upon diversity as an opportunity, not a threat. Intercultural communication, team building, and conflict resolution are skills that can be learned in diversity training programs.
- **Learn about your cultural self.** Begin to think of yourself as a product of your culture, and understand that your culture is just one among many. Try to stand outside and look at yourself. Do you see any reflex reactions and automatic thought patterns that are a result of your upbringing? These may be invisible to you until challenged by people who are different from you. Remember, your culture was designed to help you succeed and survive in a certain environment. Be sure to keep what works and yet be ready to adapt as your environment changes.
- **Make fewer assumptions.** Be careful of seemingly insignificant, innocent workplace assumptions. For example, don't assume that everyone wants to observe the holidays with a Christmas party and a decorated tree. Celebrating only Christian holidays in December and January excludes those who honor Hanukkah, Kwanzaa, and the Lunar New Year. Moreover, in workplace discussions don't assume that everyone is married or wants to be or is even heterosexual, for that matter. For invitations, avoid phrases such as *managers and their wives*. *Spouses* or *partners* is more inclusive. Valuing diversity means making fewer assumptions that everyone is like you or wants to be like you.

In times of conflict, look for areas of agreement and build on similarities.

- **Build on similarities.** Look for areas in which you and others not like you can agree or at least share opinions. Be prepared to consider issues from many perspectives, all of which may be valid. Accept that there is room for various points of view to coexist peacefully. Although you can always find differences, it is much harder to find similarities. Look for common ground in shared experiences, mutual goals, and similar values. Concentrate on your objective even when you may disagree on how to reach it.[44]

www.cengagebrain.com

Available with an access code, these eResources will help you prepare for exams:

- **Chapter Review Quizzes**
- **Personal Language Trainer**
- **PowerPoint Slides**
- **Flash Cards**

Summing Up and Looking Forward

This chapter described the importance of communication skills in today's fast-paced, mobile workplace and challenging economy. Writing skills are particularly important because businesspeople produce more written messages than ever before. Heightened global competition, flattened management hierarchies, team-based projects, constantly evolving technology, the "anytime, anywhere" office, and an emphasis on ethics are all trends that increase the need for good communication skills. To improve your skills, you should understand the communication process. Communication doesn't take place unless senders encode meaningful messages that can be decoded and understood by receivers.

One important part of the communication process is listening. You can become a more active listener by keeping an open mind, listening for main points, capitalizing on lag time, judging ideas and not appearances, taking selective notes, and providing feedback. The chapter also described ways to help you improve your nonverbal communication skills.

You learned about the powerful effect that culture has on communication, and you became more aware of the cultural dimensions of context, individualism, formality, communication style, and time orientation. Finally, the chapter discussed ways that individuals can learn intercultural skills and businesses can benefit from workforce diversity.

The following chapters present the writing process. You will learn specific techniques to help you improve your written and oral expression. Remember, communication skills are not inherited. They are learned, and anyone can learn to be a good communicator. Writing skills are critical because they function as a gatekeeper. Poor skills keep you in low-wage, dead-end work. Good skills open the door to high wages and career advancement.[45]

Critical Thinking

1. How is the writing that you and your peers are practicing every day by texting, e-mailing, or instant messaging different from the writing business professionals expect in the workplace? Will your employer benefit from your informal writing?
2. Name examples that illustrate the nonverbal cues we send by our use of time, space, or territory. How does our need for personal space or territory, for example, play out in the new, flexible "anytime, anywhere" workplace?
3. How are listening skills important to employees, supervisors, and executives? Who should have the best listening skills?
4. What arguments could you give for or against the idea that body language is a science with principles that can be interpreted accurately by specialists?
5. It is quite natural to favor one's own country over a foreign one. To what extent can ethnocentrism and stereotypes be considered normal reactions, and when do they become destructive and unproductive in the workplace?

Chapter Review

6. In what ways do communication skills act as a career filter?
7. Do business professionals think that college graduates today are well prepared for the communication and writing tasks in the workplace?
8. What are soft skills?
9. Will the time and money spent on your college education and writing training most likely pay off?

10. List seven trends in the workplace that affect business communicators. Be prepared to discuss how they might affect you in your future career.

11. List 11 techniques for improving your listening skills. Be prepared to discuss each.

12. Name at least five techniques that will help you build strong nonverbal skills.

13. Would your culture be classified as high- or low-context? Why?

14. What is ethnocentrism, and how can it be reduced?

15. List seven or more suggestions for enhancing comprehension when you are talking with nonnative speakers of English. Be prepared to discuss each.

Digital Study Tools [or] Premium Web Site

- **Chapter Review Quiz**
- **PowerPoint Slides**
- **Flash Cards**
- **Listening Quiz**
- **Personal Language Trainer**

Activities and Cases

1.1 Online Communication Skills Assessment: How Do You Rate?

This course can help you dramatically improve your business communication skills. How much do you need to improve? This assessment exercise enables you to evaluate your skills with specific standards in four critical communication skill areas: writing, reading, speaking, and listening. How well you communicate will be an important factor in your future career—particularly if you are promoted into management, as many college graduates are.

Your Task. Either here or at **www.cengagebrain.com**, select a number from 1 (indicating low ability) to 5 (indicating high ability) that best reflects your perception of yourself. Be honest in rating yourself. Think about how others would rate you. When you finish, see a rating of your skills. Complete this assessment online to see your results automatically!

Writing Skills	Low				High
1. Possess basic spelling, grammar, and punctuation skills	1	2	3	4	5
2. Am familiar with proper e-mail, memo, letter, and report formats for business documents	1	2	3	4	5
3. Can analyze a writing problem and quickly outline a plan for solving the problem	1	2	3	4	5
4. Am able to organize data coherently and logically	1	2	3	4	5
5. Can evaluate a document to determine its probable success	1	2	3	4	5
Reading Skills	Low				High
1. Am familiar with specialized vocabulary in my field as well as general vocabulary	1	2	3	4	5
2. Can concentrate despite distractions	1	2	3	4	5
3. Am willing to look up definitions whenever necessary	1	2	3	4	5
4. Am able to move from recreational to serious reading	1	2	3	4	5
5. Can read and comprehend college-level material	1	2	3	4	5
Speaking Skills	Low				High
1. Feel at ease in speaking with friends	1	2	3	4	5
2. Feel at ease in speaking before a group of people	1	2	3	4	5
3. Can adapt my presentation to the audience	1	2	3	4	5
4. Am confident in pronouncing and using words correctly	1	2	3	4	5
5. Sense that I have credibility when I make a presentation	1	2	3	4	5
Listening Skills	Low				High
1. Spend at least half the time listening during conversations	1	2	3	4	5
2. Am able to concentrate on a speaker's words despite distractions	1	2	3	4	5
3. Can summarize a speaker's ideas and anticipate what's coming during pauses	1	2	3	4	5
4. Provide proper feedback such as nodding, paraphrasing, and asking questions	1	2	3	4	5
5. Listen with the expectation of gaining new ideas and information	1	2	3	4	5

Total your score in each section. How do you rate?

22–24 Excellent! You have indicated that you have exceptional communication skills.
18–21 Your score is above average, but you could improve your skills.
14–17 Your score suggests that you have much room for improvement.
10–13 You need serious study, practice, and follow-up reinforcement.

Where are you strongest and weakest? Are you satisfied with your present skills? The first step to improvement is recognition of a need. The second step is making a commitment to improve. The third step is following through, and this course will help you do that.

WEB

1.2 Pumping Up Your Basic Language Muscles

You can enlist the aid of your author to help you pump up your basic language skills. As your personal trainer, Dr. Guffey provides a three-step workout plan and hundreds of interactive questions to help you brush up on your grammar and mechanics skills. You receive immediate feedback in the warm-up sessions, and when you finish a complete workout, you can take a short test to assess what you learned. These workouts are completely self-taught, which means you can review at your own pace and repeat as often as you need. *Your Personal Language Trainer* is available at your premium Web site, **www.cengagebrain.com**. In addition to pumping up your basic language muscles, you can also use *Spell Right!* and *Speak Right!* to improve your spelling and pronunciation skills.

Your Task. Begin using *Your Personal Language Trainer* to brush up on your basic grammar and mechanics skills by completing one to three workouts per week or as many as your instructor advises. Be prepared to submit a printout of your "fitness" (completion) certificate when you finish a workout module. If your instructor directs, complete the spelling exercises in *Spell Right!* and submit a certificate of completion for the spelling final exam.

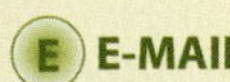

E-MAIL

1.3 Getting to Know You

Your instructor wants to know more about you, your motivation for taking this course, your career goals, and your writing skills.

Your Task. Send an e-mail or write a memo of introduction to your instructor. See Chapter 5 for formats and tips on preparing e-mails. In your message include the following:

a. Your reasons for taking this class
b. Your career goals (both temporary and long-term)
c. A brief description of your employment, if any, and your favorite activities
d. An assessment and discussion of your current communication skills, including your strengths and weaknesses

For online classes, write a letter of introduction about yourself with the preceding information. Post your letter to your discussion board. Read and comment on the letters of other students. Think about how people in virtual teams must learn about each other through online messages.
Alternatively, your instructors may assign this task as a concise individual voice mail message to establish your telephone etiquette and skills.

TEAM

1.4 Small-Group Presentation: Getting to Know Each Other

Many business organizations today use teams to accomplish their goals. To help you develop speaking, listening, and teamwork skills, your instructor may assign team projects. One of the first jobs in any team is selecting members and becoming acquainted.

Your Task. Your instructor will divide your class into small groups or teams. At your instructor's direction, either (a) interview another group member and introduce that person to the group or (b) introduce yourself to the group. Think of this as an informal interview for a team assignment or for a job. You will want to make notes from which to speak. Your introduction should include information such as the following:

a. Where did you grow up?
b. What work and extracurricular activities have you engaged in?
c. What are your interests and talents? What are you good at doing?
d. What have you achieved?
e. How familiar are you with various computer technologies?
f. What are your professional and personal goals? Where do you expect to be five years from now?

To develop listening skills, team members should practice the good listening techniques discussed in this chapter and take notes. They should be prepared to discuss three important facts as well as remember details about each speaker.

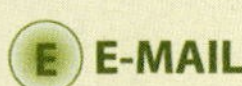

E-MAIL

1.5 Class Listening

Have you ever consciously observed the listening habits of others?

Your Task. In one of your classes, study student listening habits for a week. What barriers to effective listening did you observe? How many of the suggestions described in this chapter are being implemented by listeners in the class? Write a memo or an e-mail to your instructor briefly describing your observations. (See Chapter 5 to learn more about e-mails and memos.)

1.6 How Good Are Your Listening Skills? Self-Checked Rating Quiz

You can learn whether your listening skills are excellent or deficient by completing a brief quiz.

Your Task. Take Dr. Guffey's Listening Quiz at **www.cengagebrain.com**. What two listening behaviors do you think you need to work on the most?

1.7 Body Language

Can body language be accurately interpreted?

Your Task. What attitudes do the following body movements suggest to you? Do these movements always mean the same thing? What part does context play in your interpretations?

a. Wringing hands, tugging ears
b. Bowed posture, twiddling thumbs
c. Steepled hands, sprawling sitting position
d. Rubbing hand through hair
e. Open hands, unbuttoned coat

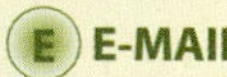

E-MAIL

1.8 Silent Messages

Becoming more aware of the silent messages you send helps you make them more accurate.

Your Task. Analyze the kinds of silent messages you send your instructor, your classmates, and your employer. How do you send these messages? Group them into categories, as suggested by what you learned in this chapter. What do these messages mean? Be prepared to discuss them in small groups or in an e-mail or memo to your instructor.

1.9 Universal Sign for "I Goofed"

In an effort to promote peace and tranquility on the highways, motorists submitted the following suggestions to a newspaper columnist.[46]

Your Task. In small groups consider the pros and cons of each of the following gestures intended as an apology when a driver makes a mistake. Why would some fail?

a. Lower your head slightly and bonk yourself on the forehead with the side of your closed fist. The message is clear: "I'm stupid. I shouldn't have done that."
b. Make a temple with your hands, as if you were praying.
c. Move the index finger of your right hand back and forth across your neck—as if you were cutting your throat.
d. Flash the well-known peace sign. Hold up the index and middle fingers of one hand, making a V, as in Victory.
e. Place the flat of your hands against your cheeks, as children do when they have made a mistake.
f. Clasp your hand over your mouth, raise your brows, and shrug your shoulders.
g. Use your knuckles to knock on the side of your head. Translation: "Oops! Engage brain."
h. Cover your eyes with one hand for a few seconds and then smile.
i. Place your right fist over the middle of your chest and move it in a circular motion. This is universal sign language for "I'm sorry."
j. Open your window and tap the top of your car roof with your hand.
k. Smile and raise both arms, palms outward, which is a universal gesture for surrender or forgiveness.
l. Use the military salute, which is simple and shows respect.
m. Flash your biggest smile, point at yourself with your right thumb and move your head from left to right, as if to say, "I can't believe I did that."

TEAM
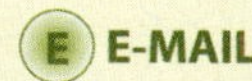

E-MAIL

1.10 The Silent Language of Tattoos: How Much Self-Expression on the Job?

Tattoos and piercings have gained in popularity among young Americans over the last two decades. Current findings by Pew Research Center suggest that nearly 40 percent of 18- to 29-year-olds and about one third of 30- to 45-year-olds sport a tattoo.[47] Employment services firm Challenger, Gray & Christmas reports that job candidates among the Millennials, also called Generation Y, do not particularly try to hide their body art. About 25 percent of this generation also show off piercings in places other than their earlobes.

CEO John Challenger suggests that a generational shift accounts for the changing mores: "Those making hiring decisions are younger and not as adherent to traditions about workplace appearance." Career expert Andrea Kay agrees, but she warns that acceptance among hiring managers varies by industry: Recruiters in the technology and retail fields may be more forgiving than those in banking and law. Tattoos and piercings send a strong message, and Kay cautions that if they make people at work uncomfortable, such decorations are detrimental. She has the following advice for job seekers: "People have adjusted their thinking in what is acceptable, but it still comes down to the impression you want to make on the people you're dealing with in your business." Many workplaces today have policies covering body adornment, some requiring employees with customer contact to conceal such decorations.

Your Task. In teams or in class, discuss tattoos as a form of self-expression in the workplace. Gauge the attitudes toward tattoos and piercings in your class. Consider the limits to self-expression on the job. Think about casual clothing or blogging and tweeting about your employer. What is different? What are some of the similarities between these various forms of self-expression? What types of nonverbal cues do body adornments send? Summarize your discussion orally or in an e-mail to your instructor. Alternatively, your instructor may ask you to post your responses to a Blackboard discussion board or some other forum that allows individual postings.

1.11 Workplace Writing: Separating Myths From Facts

Today's knowledge workers are doing more writing on the job than ever before. Flattened management hierarchies, heightened global competition, expanded team-based management, and heavy reliance on e-mail have all contributed to more written messages.

Your Task. In teams or in class, discuss the following statements. Are they myths or facts?

a. Because I'm in a technical field, I will work with numbers, not words.
b. Secretaries will clean up my writing problems.
c. Technical writers do most of the real writing on the job.
d. Computers can fix any of my writing mistakes.
e. I can use form letters for most messages.

1.12 Translating Idioms

Many languages have idiomatic expressions that do not always make sense to outsiders.

Your Task. Explain in simple English what the following idiomatic expressions mean. Assume that you are explaining them to nonnative speakers of English.

a. have an axe to grind
b. class act
c. ballpark figure
d. cold shoulder
e. loose cannon
f. get your act together
g. go overboard
h. keep on trucking
i. the bottom of the barrel

1.13 Analyzing Diversity at Pharma Giant Pfizer

Recently, pharmaceutical powerhouse Pfizer stepped up its diversity program. Its chief diversity officer, Karen Boykin-Towns, explained: "We asked ourselves, is it really all that it could be and are we capitalizing on diversity? We said, 'We can do more.' "

The company has created 53 Colleague Resource Groups (CRGs), whose focus is to foster an inclusive culture and contribute value to the business. These groups are open to everyone and are supported by senior executives who act as sponsors, including those who are ethnically or racially different from the groups they counsel. Some CRGs act as focus panels for corporate advertisements. Others serve on the Business Maximization Subcommittee, providing input on business issues that might affect diverse customers.

Moreover, Pfizer conducts an annual pay-equity analysis to ensure that women and people of color are not discriminated against in compensation—which is often a thorny issue in the battle for true inclusion. Recently, Pfizer India conducted focus groups of leading women in sales and high-profile female physicians to discuss career goals, challenges, and opportunities.[48]

Your Task. In what ways might Pfizer benefit by diversifying its staff? What competitive advantages might it gain? Outline your reasoning in an e-mail to your instructor. Alternatively, your instructor may want you to post your responses to a Blackboard discussion board or some other forum that allows individual postings by your class.

1.14 Capitalizing on Diversity: What to Do With Difference in Job Interviews?

Today's workforce benefits from diversity, and most businesses have embraced explicit nondiscrimination policies. The federal government and many state governments have passed legislation that makes it illegal to discriminate based on race, color, creed, ethnicity, national origin, disability, sex, age, and other factors such as sexual orientation and gender identity. Some public institutions have the most far-reaching nondiscrimination policies on their books—for example, the Massachusetts Institute of Technology (MIT): "The Institute does not discriminate against individuals on the basis of race, color, sex, sexual orientation, gender identity, religion, disability, age, genetic information, veteran status, ancestry, or national or ethnic origin."[49]

Your Task: Consider how such differences could affect the communication, for instance, between an interviewer and a job candidate. If negatively, how could the differences and barriers be overcome? Role-play or discuss a potential job interview conversation between the following individuals. After a while summarize your findings, either orally or in writing:

a. A female top executive is interviewing a prospective future assistant, who is male.
b. A candidate with a strong but not disruptive foreign accent is being interviewed by a native-born human resources manager.
c. A manager dressed in a conventional business suit is interviewing a person wearing a turban.
d. A person over fifty is being interviewed by a hiring manager in his early thirties.
e. A recruiter who can walk is interviewing a job seeker using a wheelchair.

Video Resources

Two video libraries accompany Guffey's *Essentials of Business Communication*, 9e. These videos take you beyond the classroom to build the communication skills you will need to succeed in today's rapidly changing workplace.

Video Library 1, *Building Workplace Skills*, includes seven videos that introduce and reinforce concepts in selected chapters. These excellent tools ease the learning load by demonstrating chapter-specific material to strengthen your comprehension and retention of key ideas.

Video Library 2, *Bridging the Gap*, presents six videos transporting you inside high-profile companies such as Cold Stone Creamery, The Little Guys, and Hard Rock Cafe. You will be able to apply your new skills in structured applications aimed at bridging the gap between the classroom and the real world of work.

We recommend three videos for this chapter:

Video Library 1: *Career Success Starts With Communication Foundations.* Made especially for Guffey books, this film illustrates the changing business world, flattened management hierarchies, the communication process, communication flow, ethics, listening, nonverbal communication, and other topics to prepare you for today's workplace. The film is unique in that many concepts are demonstrated through role-playing. Be prepared to discuss critical-thinking questions at the film's conclusion.

Video Library 1: *Intercultural Communication at Work.* This film illustrates intercultural misunderstandings when a Japanese businessman visits an American advertising agency that seeks his business. The agency owners, Rob and Ella, as well as the receptionist, Stephanie, make numerous cultural blunders because they are unaware of the differences between high- and low-context cultures. At the film's conclusion, you will have an opportunity to make suggestions for improving Rob and Ella's cultural competence.

Video Library 2: *Understanding Teamwork: Cold Stone Creamery.* This video highlights teamwork at Cold Stone Creamery, a fast-growing ice cream specialty chain. It shows team members behind the counter but also provides the inside scoop through the insights of Kevin Myers, vice president, marketing. You will see how teamwork permeates every facet of Cold Stone's corporate culture. Look for a definition of *team*, as well as six kinds of teams and the characteristics of successful teams.

Grammar/Mechanics Checkup

These checkups are designed to improve your control of grammar and mechanics, which includes punctuation, spelling, capitalization, and number use. The checkups systematically review all sections of the Grammar/Mechanics Handbook. Answers are provided near the end of the book. You will find a set of alternate Bonus Grammar/Mechanics Checkups with immediate feedback at your premium Web site, **www.cengagebrain.com**. These bonus checkups use different exercises but parallel the items that appear in the textbook. Use the bonus checkups to reinforce your learning.

Nouns

Review Sections 1.02–1.06 in the Grammar/Mechanics Handbook. Then study each of the following statements. Underscore any inappropriate form, and write a correction in the space provided. Also record the appropriate G/M section and letter to illustrate the principle involved. If a sentence is correct, write *C*. When you finish, compare your responses with those provided at the end of the book. If your answers differ, study carefully the principles shown in parentheses.

journeys (1.05d) **Example** Although one exciting trip ended, several new journies awaited the travelers.

__________ 1. Setting healthy workplace boundarys is an important task for new supervisors.

__________ 2. Be sure to read the FAQs before using that Web site.

__________ 3. Because world markets are expanding, many companys are going global.

__________ 4. Surprisingly, business is better on Sunday's than on weekdays.

__________ 5. She said that attornies are the primary benefactors of class action suits.

__________ 6. Only the Welches and the Sanchez's brought their entire families.

__________ 7. During the late 2000's, home values dropped precipitously.

__________ 8. Both editor in chiefs followed strict copyediting policies.

__________ 9. That financial organization employs two secretaries for four CPA's.

__________ 10. Voters in three countys refused to approve any new taxes.

__________ 11. Prizes were awarded to both runner ups in the essay contest.

__________ 12. Both cities are located in valleys that lie between mountains.

__________ 13. Our accountants insist that we list all income, expenses, and liabilitys.

__________ 14. Some typeface fonts make it difficult to distinguish between *t*'s and *i*'s.

__________ 15. Both of the homes of her brother-in-laws had many chimneys.

Editing Challenge — 1

As the employee with the best communication skills, you are frequently asked to edit messages. The following memo has faults in proofreading, grammar, spelling, punctuation, capitalization, word use, and number form. You may (a) use standard proofreading marks (see Appendix B) to correct the errors here or (b) download the document from **www.cengagebrain.com** and revise at your computer.

Your instructor may ask you to use the **Track Changes** feature in Microsoft Word to show your editing comments. In Word 2010, turn on **Track Changes** on the **Review** tab. Click **Show Markup**. Place your cursor at an error, click **New Comment**, and key your correction in the bubble box provided. **Hint:** In this memo you will have about 40 edits that you might combine in 30 **Track Changes** comments. Study the guidelines in the Grammar/Mechanics Handbook as well as the lists of Confusing Words and Frequently Misspelled Words at the end of the book to sharpen your skills.

MEMORANDUM

To: Jessica Wu-Santana

From: Martin Fitzgerald, Manager

Date: November 4, 201x

Subject: Suggestion for Telecommuting Successfully

To help you become an effective telecommuter Jessica, we have a few suggestion to share with you. I understand you will be working at home for the next nine months. The following guidelines should help you stay in touch with us and complete your work satisfactory.

- Be sure to check your message bored daily, and respond immediate to those who are trying to reach you.
- Check your e-mail at least 3 times a day, answer all messages promply. Make sure that you sent copys of relevant messages to the appropriate office staff.
- Transmit all spread sheet work to Scott Florio in our computer services department. He will analyze each week's activitys, and update all inventorys.
- Provide me with end of week reports' indicating the major accounts you serviced.

In preparing your work area you should make sure you have adequate space for your computer printer fax and storage. For security reasons you're working area should be off limits to your family and friends.

We will continue to hold once a week staff meetings on Friday's at 10 a.m. in the morning. Do you think it would be possible for you to attend 1 or 2 of these meeting. The next one is Friday November 17th.

I know you will enjoy working at home Jesica. Following these basic guidelines should help you accomplish your work, and provide the office with adequate contact with you.

Communication Workshop

Using Job Boards to Learn About Employment Possibilities in Your Field

Nearly everyone looking for a job today starts with the Web. This communication workshop will help you use the Web to study job openings in your field. Looking for jobs or internships on the Web has distinct advantages. For a few job seekers, the Web leads to bigger salaries, wider opportunities, and faster hiring. The Web, however, can devour huge chunks of time and produce slim results.

In terms of actually finding a job, the Web does not always result in success. Web searching seems to work best for professionals looking for similar work in their current fields and for those who are totally flexible about location. However, the Web is an excellent place for any job seeker to learn what is available, what qualifications are necessary, and what salaries are being offered. Thousands of job boards with many job listings from employers across the United States and abroad are available on the Web.

Career Application. Assume that you are about to finish your degree or certification program and you are now looking for a job. At the direction of your instructor, conduct a survey of electronic job advertisements in your field. What's available? How much is the salary? What are the requirements?

Your Task

- **Visit Monster.com (http://www.monster.com)**, one of the most popular job boards.
- **Study the opening page.** Ignore the clutter and banner ads or pop-ups. Close any pop-up boxes.
- **Select keyword, category, city, and state.** Decide whether you want to search by a job title (such as *nurse, accountant, project manager*) or a category (such as *Accounting/Finance, Administrative/Clerical, Advertising/Marketing*). Enter your keyword job title or select a category—or do both. Enter a city, state, or region. Click **Search**.
- **Study the job listings.** Click **Expand** to read more about a job opening. Click **More** to see a full description of the job.
- **Read job-search tips.** For many helpful hints on precise searching, click **Job search tips**. Browsing this information may take a few minutes, but it is well worth the effort to learn how to refine your search. Close the box by clicking the **X** in the upper right corner.
- **Select best ads.** In your career and geographical area, select the three best ads and print them. If you cannot print, make notes on what you find.
- **Visit another site.** Try **http://www.collegerecruiter.com**, which claims to be the highest-traffic entry-level job site for students and graduates, or **http://www.careerbuilder.com**, which says it is the nation's largest employment network. Become familiar with the site's searching tools, and look for jobs in your field. Select and print three ads.
- **Analyze the skills required.** How often do the ads you printed mention communication, teamwork, computer skills, or professionalism? What tasks do the ads mention? What is the salary range identified in these ads for the positions they feature? Your instructor may ask you to submit your findings and/or report to the class.

Communication Workshops (such as the one on this page) provide insight into special business communication topics and skills not discussed in the chapters. Topics include ethics, technology, career skills, and collaboration. Each workshop includes a career application to extend your learning and help you develop skills relevant to the workshop topic.

Endnotes

[1] Appleman, J. E. (2009, October). Don't let poor writing skills stifle company growth. *T + D, 63*(10), p. 10. Retrieved from http://search.ebscohost.com; Timm, J. A. (2005, December). Preparing students for the next employment revolution. *Business Education Forum, 60*(2), 55–59. Retrieved from http://search.ebscohost.com; Messmer, M. (2001, January). Enhancing your writing skills. *Strategic Finance*, p. 8. See also Staples, B. (2005, May 15). The fine art of getting it down on paper, fast. *The New York Times*, p. WK13(L).

[2] Do communication students have the "write stuff"?: Practitioners evaluate writing skills of entry-level workers. (2008). *Journal of Promotion Management, 14*(3/4), 294. Retrieved from http://search.ebscohost.com; The National Commission on Writing. (2005, July). Writing: A powerful message from state government. CollegeBoard. Retrieved from http://www.collegeboard.com/prod_downloads/writingcom/powerful-message-from-state.pdf; The National Commission on Writing. (2004, September 14). Writing skills necessary for employment, says big business. [Press release]. Retrieved from http://www.writingcommission.org/pr/writing_for_employ.html

[3] Survey shows workers should write better. (2004, September 14). Associated Press. Retrieved from MSNBC at http://www.msnbc.msn.com/id/6000685

[4] The National Commission on Writing. (2004, September 14). Writing skills necessary for employment, says big business. [Press release]. Retrieved from http://www.writingcommission.org/pr/writing_for_employ.html

[5] Employers rank top 5 candidate skills. (2010, January 20). [Weblog post]. Retrieved from http://blog.resumebear.com/2010/01/20/employers-rank-top-5-candidate-skills; Moody, J., Stewart, B., & Bolt-Lee, C. (2002, March). Showcasing the skilled business graduate: Expanding the tool kit. *Business Communication Quarterly, 65*(1), 23.

[6] Students don't write good. (2006, November). *Manufacturing Engineering, 137*(5), 27; Kinsman, M. (2004, February 1). Are poor writing skills holding back your career? *California Job Journal*. Retrieved from http://www.jobjournal.com/article_full_text.asp?artid=1039. See also Smerd, J. (2007, December 10). New workers sorely lacking literacy skills. *Workforce Management*, p. 6; Stevens, B. (2005, March). What communication skills do employers want? Silicon Valley recruiters respond. *Journal of Employment Counseling, 42*, 1; Gray, F., Emerson, L., & MacKay, B. (2005). Meeting the demands of the workplace: Science students and written skills. *Journal of Science Education and industry, 14*, 425–435.

[7] American Management Association. (2010). AMA 2010 critical skills survey: Executives say the 21st century requires more skilled workers. Retrieved from http://www.p21.org/documents/Critical%20Skills%20Survey%20Executive%20Summary.pdf; Vance, E. (2007, February 2). College graduates lack key skills, report says. *The Chronicle of Higher Education*, p. A30.

[8] Musbach, T. (2009, November 11). Secret weapon in the job hunt today: Personality. *FastCompany.com*. [Weblog post]. Retrieved from http://www.fastcompany.com/user/tom-musbach; Gallagher, K. P., Kaiser, K. M., Simon, J., Beath, C. M., & Goles, J. (2009, June). The requisite variety of skills for IT professionals. *Communications of the Association for Computing Machinery, 53*(6), 147. doi: 10.1145/1743546.1743584

[9] Willmer, D. (2009, April 21). Leveraging soft skills in a competitive IT job market. Computerworld.com. Retrieved from http://www.computerworld.com; Morisy, M. (2008, February 28). Networking pros can avoid outsourcing with soft skills. *Global Knowledge*. Retrieved from http://www.globalknowledge.com/training/generic.asp?pageid=2119&country=United+States; Stranger. J. (2007, July). How to make yourself offshore-proof. *Certification Magazine, 9*(7), 34–40. Retrieved from http://search.ebscohost.com

[10] Marsan, C. D. (2007, December 31). Job skills that matter: Where you can leave a mark. *Network World, 24*(50), 38–40. Retrieved from http://search.ebscohost.com/

[11] Robinson, T. M. (2008, January 26). Quoted in Same office, different planets. *The New York Times*, p. B5.

[12] Mitchell, G. A., Skinner, L. B., & White, B. J. (2010) Essential soft skills for success in the twenty-first-century workforce as perceived by business educators. *The Delta Pi Epsilon Journal, 52*(1). Retrieved from http://www.faqs.org/periodicals/201001/2036768821.html

[13] McEwen, B. C. (2010). Cross-cultural and international career exploration and employability skills. *National Business Education Association Yearbook 2010: Cross-Cultural and International Business Education*, 48, 142.

[14] King, J. (2009, September 21). Crossing the skills gap. *Computer world*, p. 30. Retrieved from http://search.ebscohost.com; Professional demeanor and personal management. (2004, January). *Keying In*, National Business Education Association Newsletter, p. 1.

[15] King, J. (2009, September 21). Crossing the skills gap. *Computerworld*, p. 30. Retrieved from http://search.ebscohost.com

[16] Crosby, O., & Moncarz, R. (2006, Fall). The 2004-14 job outlook for college graduates. *Occupational Outlook Quarterly, 50*(3), 43. Retrieved from http://www.bls.gov/opub/ooq/2006/fall/art03.htm

[17] Daniels, C. (2004, June 28). 50 best companies for minorities. *Fortune*, p. 136.

[18] Employers rank top 5 candidate skills. (2010, January 20). [Weblog post]. Retrieved from http://blog.resumebear.com/2010/01/20/employers-rank-top-5-candidate-skills

[19] Holland, K. (2008, September 28). The anywhere, anytime office. *The New York Times*, p. 14 BU Y.

[20] Telework trendlines. (2009, February). Retrieved from Worldatwork at http://www.workingfromanywhere.org/news/Trendlines_2009.pdf

[21] Holland, K. (2008, September 28). The anywhere, anytime office. *The New York Times*, p. 14 BU Y.

[22] DeMars, N. (2008, April). Office ethics: News from the front lines. *OfficePro*, p. 28.

[23] Burgoon, J., Coker, D., & Coker, R. (1986). Communicative explanations. *Human Communication Research, 12*, 463–494.

[24] Watzlawick, P., Beavin-Bavelas, J., & Jackson, D. (1967). Some tentative axioms of communication. In: *Pragmatics of human communication: A study of interactional patterns, pathologies and paradoxes.* New York: W. W. Norton.

[25] Birdwhistell, R. (1970). *Kinesics and context*. Philadelphia: University of Pennsylvania Press.

[26] Ravid, B. (2010, January 13). Peres: Humiliation of Turkey envoy does not reflect Israel's diplomacy. Haaretz.com. Retrieved from http://www.haaretz.com/news/peres-humiliation-of-turkey-envoy-does-not-reflect-israel-s-diplomacy-1.261381

[27] Hall, E. T. (1966). *The hidden dimension*. Garden City, NY: Doubleday, pp. 107–122.

[28] Wilkie, H. (2003, Fall). Professional presence. *The Canadian Manager, 28*(3), 14–19. Retrieved from http://search.ebscohost.com

[29] Davis, T., Ward, D. A., & Woodland, D. (2010). Cross-cultural and international business communication—verbal. *National Business Education Association Yearbook: Cross-Cultural and International Business Education*, p. 3; Hall, E. T., & Hall, M. R. (1990). *Understanding cultural differences.* Yarmouth, ME: Intercultural Press, pp. 183–184.

[30] Chaney, L. H. & Martin, J. S. (2000). *Intercultural business communication* (2nd ed.). Upper Saddle River, NJ: Prentice Hall, p. 83.

[31] Beamer, L., & Varner, I. (2008). *Intercultural communication in the global workplace*. Boston: McGraw-Hill Irwin, p. 129.

[32] Sheer, V. C., & Chen, L. (2003, January). Successful Sino-Western business negotiation: Participants' accounts of national and professional cultures. *The Journal of Business Communication, 40*(1), 62; see also Luk, L., Patel, M., & White, K. (1990, December). Personal attributes of American and Chinese business associates. *The Bulletin of the Association for Business Communication*, 67.

[33] Gallois, C., & Callan, V. (1997). *Communication and culture*. New York: Wiley, p. 24.

[34] Jarvis, S. S. (1990, June). Preparing employees to work south of the border. *Personnel*, p. 763.

[35] Gallois, C., & Callan, V. (1997). *Communication and culture*. New York: Wiley, p. 29.

[36] Copeland, L. & Griggs, L. (1985). *Going international.* New York: Penguin, p. 94. See also Beamer, L. & Varner, I. (2008). *Intercultural communication in the global workplace*. Boston: McGraw-Hill Irwin, p. 340.

[37] Copeland, L. & Griggs, L. (1985). *Going international.* New York: Penguin, p. 12.

[38] Flannery, R. (2005, May 10). China is a big prize. *Forbes, 173*(10), 163.

[39] Martin, J. S., & Chaney, L. H. (2006). *Global business etiquette*. Westport, CT: Praeger, p. 36.

[40] Karoly, L. A. & Panis, C. W. A. (2004). *The 21st century at work.* Santa Monica, CA: Rand Corporation, pp. 36–39.

[41] Ten Tips for the awkward age of computing. (n.d.). *Microsoft Accessibility, Technology for Everyone*. Retrieved from http://www.microsoft.com/enable/aging/tips.aspx

[42] Terhune, C. (2005, April 19). Pepsi, vowing diversity isn't just image polish, seeks inclusive culture. *The Wall Street Journal*, p. B4.

[43] Schoemaker, P. J. H., & Day, G. S. (2009, Winter). Why we miss the signs. *MIT Sloan Management Review, 50*(2), 43; Schwartz, J., & Wald, M. L. (2003, March 9). Smart people working collectively can be dumber than the sum of their brains. Appeared originally in *The New York Times*. Retrieved from http://www.mindfully.org/Reform/2003/Smart-People-Dumber9mar03.htm

[44] Simons, G., & Dunham, D. (1995, December). Making inclusion happen. *Managing Diversity*. Retrieved from http://www.jalmc.org/mk-incl.htm

[45] Kerrey, B. (2004). Quoted in National Commission on Writing: Writing skills necessary for employment, says big business. Retrieved from http://www.writingcommission.org/pr/writing_for_employ.html

[46] What's the universal hand sign for 'I goofed'? (1996, December 16). *Santa Barbara News-Press*, p. D2.

[47] Scenario based on Schepp, D. (2010, July 26). People@work: How to job hunt with tattoos. DailyFinance.com. Retrieved from http://www.dailyfinance.com/story/careers/tattoos-job-hunt-interviews-career/19566567/

[48] Love, A. (2010, May 14). Diversity as a strategic advantage. *BusinessWeek*. Retrieved from http://www.businessweek.com/print/managing/content/may2010/ca20100513_748402.htm

[49] MIT Reference Publications Office. (2009, December). Nondiscrimination policy. Retrieved from http://web.mit.edu/referencepubs/nondiscrimination/

Acknowledgments

p. 3 Office Insider based on Hendricks, M. (2007, July 2). Pen to paper. *Entrepreneur, 35*(7), 85–86.

p. 3 Office Insider based on King, J. (2009, September 21). Crossing the skills gap. *Computerworld*, p. 30. Retrieved from http://search.ebscohost.com

p. 10 Office Insider based on Washington, V. (n.d.). The high cost of poor listening. EzineArticles.com. [Weblog post]. Retrieved from http://ezinearticles.com/?The-High-Cost-of-Poor- Listening&id=163192

p. 11 Office Insider based on Bucero, A. (2006, July). Listen and learn. *PM Network*. Retrieved from http://search.ebscohost.com

p. 19 Office Insider based on King, J. (2009, September 21). Crossing the skills gap. *Computerworld*, p. 32. Retrieved from http://search.ebscohost.com

p. 21 Office Insider based on Papiernik, R. L. (1995, October 30). Diversity demands new understanding. *Nation's Restaurant News, 29*(43), 54. Retrieved from http://www.nrn.com

UNIT 2

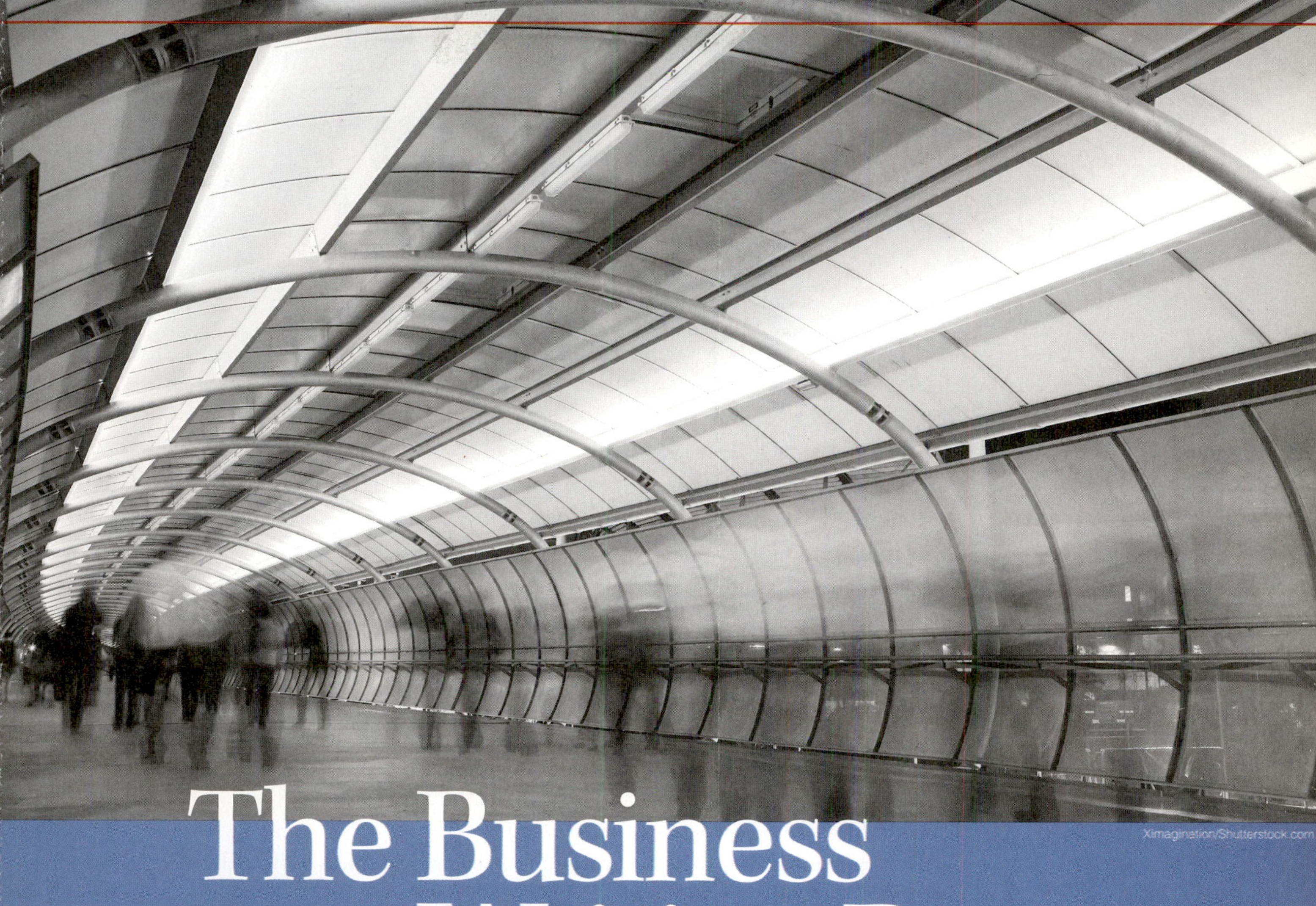

Ximagination/Shutterstock.com

The Business Writing Process

CHAPTER 2
Planning Business Messages

CHAPTER 3
Composing Business Messages

CHAPTER 4
Revising Business Messages

CHAPTER 2

Planning Business Messages

Go to **cengagebrain.com** and use your access code to unlock valuable student eResources.

Yuri Arcurs/Shutterstock.com

OBJECTIVES

After studying this chapter, you should be able to

- List goals for business messages and follow the three-phase writing process.
- Identify the purpose of a message and select the best communication channel.
- Anticipate and profile the audience for a message.
- Adapt your message to the task and to your audience by addressing audience benefits and cultivating a "you" view.
- Use skillful writing techniques including being conversational, professional, and courteous as well as using bias-free language, plain expression, and familiar words.

OFFICE INSIDER

When asked what communication skills employees needed, one recruiter said that new-hires "need the ability to take something that is awkwardly written and make it flow smoothly—to express business ideas in writing that is 180 degrees [different] from writing for English classes."

—Betsy Stevens, *Journal of Employment Counseling*

Understanding Business Writing Goals and the Writing Process

In the workplace you may be surprised to learn that business writing differs from other writing you may have done. When you prepared high school or college compositions and term papers, you probably focused on discussing your feelings or displaying your knowledge. Your instructors wanted to see your thought processes, and they needed assurance that you had internalized the subject matter. You may have had to meet a minimum word count. Business writers, however, have different goals. For business messages and oral presentations, your writing should be:

- **Purposeful.** You will be writing to solve problems and convey information. You will have a definite purpose to fulfill in each message.
- **Persuasive.** You want your audience to believe and accept your message.
- **Economical.** You will try to present ideas clearly but concisely. Length is not rewarded.
- **Audience oriented.** You will concentrate on looking at a problem from the perspective of the audience instead of seeing it from your own.

These distinctions actually ease the writer's task. You will not be searching your imagination for creative topic ideas. You won't be stretching your ideas to make them appear longer. Writing consultants and businesspeople complain that many college graduates entering industry have at least an unconscious perception that quantity enhances quality. Wrong! Get over the notion that longer is better. Conciseness and clarity are what count in business.

The ability to prepare concise, audience-centered, persuasive, and purposeful messages does not come naturally. Very few people, especially beginners, can sit down and compose a terrific e-mail, report, or presentation without training. However, following a systematic process, studying model messages, and practicing the craft can make nearly anyone a successful business writer or speaker.

Following a systematic process helps beginning writers create effective messages and presentations.

Following a Writing Process for Better Messages and Presentations

Whether you are preparing an e-mail, memo, letter, or oral presentation, the process will be easier if you follow a systematic plan. Our plan breaks the entire task into three phases: *prewriting, writing*, and *revising*.

The writing process has three parts: prewriting, writing, and revising.

To illustrate the writing process, let's say that you own a popular local McDonald's franchise. At rush times, you face a problem. Customers complain about the chaotic multiple waiting lines to approach the service counter. You once saw two customers nearly get into a fistfight over cutting into a line. What's more, customers often are so intent on looking for ways to improve their positions in line that they fail to examine the menu. Then they are undecided when their turn arrives. You want to convince other franchise owners that a single-line (serpentine) system would work better. You could telephone the other owners. But you want to present a serious argument with good points that they will remember and be willing to act on when they gather for their next district meeting. You decide to write an e-mail that you hope will win their support.

Prewriting. The first phase of the writing process prepares you to write. It involves *analyzing* the audience and your purpose for writing. The audience for your letter will be other franchise owners, some highly educated and others not. Your purpose in writing is to convince them that a change in policy would improve customer service. You are convinced that a single-line system, such as that used in banks, would reduce chaos and make customers happier because they would not have to worry about where they are in line.

The first phase of the writing process involves analyzing and anticipating the audience and then adapting to that audience.

Prewriting also involves *anticipating* how your audience will react to your message. You are sure that some of the other owners will agree with you, but others might fear that customers seeing a long single line might go elsewhere. In *adapting* your message to the audience, you try to think of the right words and the right tone that will win approval.

The second phase of the writing process includes researching, organizing the message, and actually writing it.

Writing. The second phase of the writing process involves researching, organizing, and then composing the message. In *researching* information for this letter, you would probably investigate other kinds of businesses that use single lines for customers. You might check out your competitors. What are Wendy's and Burger King doing? You might do some calling to see whether other franchise owners are concerned about chaotic lines. Before writing to the entire group, you might brainstorm with a few owners to see what ideas they have for solving the problem.

Once you have collected enough information, you would focus on *organizing* your letter. Should you start out by offering your solution? Or should you work up to it slowly, describing the problem, presenting your evidence, and then ending with the solution? The final step in the second phase of the writing process is actually *composing* the letter. Naturally, you will do it at your computer so that you can make revisions easily.

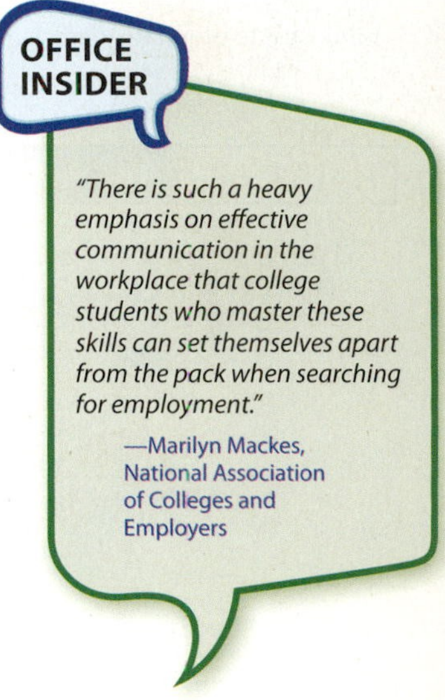

OFFICE INSIDER
"There is such a heavy emphasis on effective communication in the workplace that college students who master these skills can set themselves apart from the pack when searching for employment."
—Marilyn Mackes, National Association of Colleges and Employers

Revising. The third phase of the process involves revising, proofreading, and evaluating your letter. After writing the first draft, you will spend a lot of time *revising* the message for clarity, conciseness, tone, and readability. Could parts of it be rearranged to make your point more effectively? This is the time when you look for ways to improve the organization and sound of your message. Next, you will spend time *proofreading* carefully to ensure correct spelling, grammar, punctuation, and format. The final phase involves *evaluating* your message to decide whether it accomplishes your goal.

Scheduling the Writing Process. Although it seems as if you would proceed in a line through the three phrases, actually the process is not always linear. As shown in Figure 2.1, often the writer must circle back and repeat an earlier step. In addition, although Figure 2.1 shows the three phases of the writing process equally, the time you spend on each varies depending on the complexity of the problem, the purpose, the audience, and your schedule. One expert gives these rough estimates for scheduling a project:

Because revising is the most important part of the writing process, it takes the most time.

- Prewriting—25 percent (planning and worrying)
- Writing—25 percent (organizing and composing)
- Revising—50 percent (45 percent revising and 5 percent proofreading)

These are rough guides, yet you can see that good writers spend most of their time on the final phase of revising and proofreading. Much depends, of course, on your project, its importance, and your familiarity with it. What's critical to remember, though, is that revising is a major component of the writing process.

It may appear that you perform one step and progress to the next, always following the same order. Most business writing, however, is not that rigid. Although writers perform the tasks described, the steps may be rearranged, abbreviated, or repeated. Some writers revise every sentence and paragraph as they go. Many find that new ideas occur after they have begun to write, causing them to back up, alter the organization, and rethink their plan.

We have just taken a look at the total writing process. As you begin to develop your business writing skills, you should expect to follow this process closely. With experience, though, you will become like other good writers and presenters who alter, compress, and rearrange the steps as needed. At first, however, following a plan is very helpful.

Analyzing Your Purpose

The writing process begins with prewriting. The remainder of this chapter focuses on what you do in the important prewriting phase. You will learn to analyze the purpose for writing, anticipate how your audience will react, and adapt your message to the audience. Adaptation involves many good writing techniques that will give your messages a professional edge.

Identifying Your Purpose

The primary purpose of most business messages is to inform or to persuade; the secondary purpose is to promote goodwill.

As you begin to compose a message, ask yourself two important questions: (a) Why am I sending this message? and (b) What do I hope to achieve? Your responses will determine how you organize and present your information.

Your message may have primary and secondary purposes. For college work your primary purpose may be merely to complete the assignment; secondary

FIGURE 2.1 The Writing Process

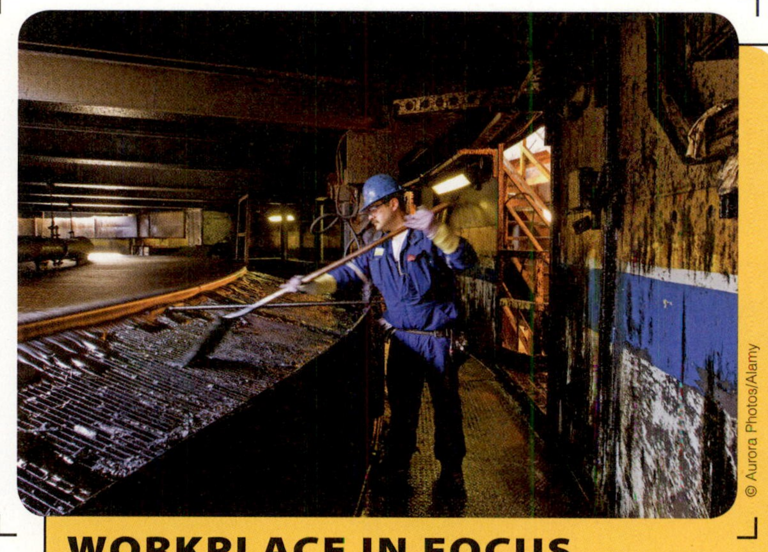

WORKPLACE IN FOCUS

With energy independence at the forefront of international concerns, many leaders have high expectations for Suncor Energy, a Canadian firm with a high-tech process for extracting oil from Alberta's bitumen-rich sands. The company recently rolled out "Oil Sands: The Next Generation," a communications blitz conveying Suncor's forwardlooking vision to more than 3,000 employees. The campaign included keynote speeches, newsletter inserts, offsite breakout meetings, and a Star Trek parody to motivate workers to double Suncor's oil sands production. Employee feedback surveys provided managers with a gauge of the campaign's effectiveness. ***Why might organizations use multiple communication channels to transmit messages?***

purposes might be to make yourself look good and to get a terrific grade. The primary purposes for sending business messages are typically to inform and to persuade. A secondary purpose is to promote goodwill. You and your organization want to look good in the eyes of your audience.

Selecting the Best Channel

After identifying the purpose of your message, you need to select the most appropriate communication channel. Some information is most efficiently and effectively delivered orally. Other messages should be written, and still others are best delivered electronically. Whether to set up a meeting, send an e-mail, or write a report depends on some of the following factors:

- Importance of the message
- Amount and speed of feedback and interactivity required
- Necessity of a permanent record
- Cost of the channel
- Degree of formality desired
- Confidentiality and sensitivity of the message

Choosing an appropriate channel depends on the importance of the message, the feedback required, the need for a permanent record, the cost, and the degree of formality, confidentiality, and sensitivity needed.

An interesting theory, called media richness, describes the extent to which a channel or medium recreates or represents all the information available in the original message. A richer medium, such as face-to-face conversation, permits more interactivity and feedback. A leaner medium, such as a report or proposal, presents a flat, one-dimensional message. Richer media enable the sender to provide more verbal and visual cues, as well as allow the sender to tailor the message to the audience.

Many factors help you decide which of the channels shown in Figure 2.2 is most appropriate for delivering a workplace message.

Switching to Faster Channels

Technology and competition continue to accelerate the pace of business today. As a result, communicators are switching to ever-faster means of exchanging information. In the past business messages within organizations were delivered largely by hard-copy memos. Responses would typically take a couple of days. However, that's too slow for today's communicators. They want answers and action now! Mobile phones, instant messaging, faxes, Web sites, and especially e-mail can deliver that information much faster than can traditional channels of communication.

FIGURE 2.2 Choosing Communication Channels

Channel	Best Use
Blog	When one person needs to present digital information easily so that it is available to others.
E-mail	When you need feedback but not immediately. Lack of security makes it problematic for personal, emotional, or private messages.
Face-to-face conversation	When you need a rich, interactive medium. Useful for persuasive, bad-news, and personal messages.
Face-to-face group meeting	When group decisions and consensus are important. Inefficient for merely distributing information.
Fax	When your message must cross time zones or international boundaries, when a written record is significant, or when speed is important.
Instant messaging	When you need a quick response from someone who is also online. Useful for fast answers in real time or for customer-service chats.
Letter	When a written record or formality is required, especially with customers, the government, suppliers, or others outside an organization.
Memo	When you want a written record to clearly explain policies, discuss procedures, or collect information within an organization.
Phone call	When you need to deliver or gather information quickly, when nonverbal cues are unimportant, and when you cannot meet in person.
Report or proposal	When you are delivering considerable data internally or externally.
Text messaging	When you need to connect with someone by smartphone but not necessarily in real time. Useful for leaving brief messages discreetly without having to call.
Voice mail message	When you wish to leave important or routine information that the receiver can respond to when convenient.
Video- or audioconference	When group consensus and interaction are important, but members are geographically dispersed.
Wiki	When digital information must be made available to others. Useful for collaboration because participants can easily add, remove, and edit content.

"I sent you an e-mail and forwarded a copy to your PDA, cell phone, and home computer. I also faxed a copy to your office, your assistant, and laptop. Then I snail-mailed hard copies to you on paper, floppy, and CD. But in case you don't receive it, I'll just tell you what it said..."

Within many organizations, hard-copy memos are still written, particularly for messages that require persuasion, permanence, or formality. They are also prepared as attachments to e-mails. However, the channel of choice for corporate communicators today is clearly e-mail. It's fast, inexpensive, and easy. Businesspeople are sending fewer hard-copy memos and letters. Web sites, e-mail, and even social media such as Twitter and Facebook now serve many customer-service functions.

Many businesses today communicate with customers through live chat, shown in Figure 2.3 Customers visit the company Web site and chat with representatives by keying their questions and answers back and forth. Customer-service representatives must have not only good keying skills but also an ability to write conversational and correct responses. One company found that it could not easily convert its telephone customer-service people to chat representatives because many lacked the language skills necessary to write clear and correct messages. They were good at talking but not at writing, emphasizing the point that the Internet has increased the need for good writing skills.

Whether your channel choice is live chat, e-mail, a hard-copy memo, a report, or a presentation, you will be a more effective communicator if you spend sufficient time in the prewriting phase.

FIGURE 2.3 Live Chat Connects Service Reps and Customers

Customer-service reps in chat sessions require solid writing skills to answer questions concisely, clearly, and conversationally. It takes special talent to be able to think and key immediate responses that are spelled correctly and are error-free.

Anticipating the Audience

A good writer anticipates the audience for a message: What is the reader or listener like? How will that person react to the message? Although you can't always know exactly who the receiver is, you can imagine some of that person's characteristics. For example, writers of direct-mail sales letters have a general idea of the audience they wish to target. Picturing a typical reader is important in guiding what you write. One copywriter at Lands' End, the catalog company, pictures his sister-in-law whenever he writes product descriptions for the catalog. By profiling your audience and shaping a message to respond to that profile, you are more likely to achieve your communication goals.

Profiling the Audience

Visualizing your audience is a pivotal step in the writing process. The questions in Figure 2.4 will help you profile your audience. How much time you devote to answering these questions depends greatly on your message and its context. An analytical report that you compose for management or an oral presentation before a big group would demand considerable audience anticipation. On the other hand, an e-mail to a coworker or a letter to a familiar supplier might require only a few moments of planning. No matter how short your message, though, spend some time thinking about the audience so that you can tailor your words to your readers or listeners. Remember that most readers or listeners will be thinking, "What's in it for me?" or, "What am I supposed to do with this information?"

By profiling your audience before you write, you can identify the appropriate tone, language, and channel for your message.

Responding to the Profile

Profiling your audience helps you make decisions about shaping the message. You will discover what kind of language is appropriate, whether you are free to use specialized technical terms, whether you should explain everything, and so on. You will decide whether your tone should be formal or informal, and you will select the most desirable channel. Imagining whether the receiver is likely to be neutral,

FIGURE 2.4 Asking the Right Questions to Profile Your Audience

Primary Audience	Secondary Audience
Who is my primary reader or listener?	Who might see or hear this message in addition to the primary audience?
What are my personal and professional relationships with that person?	How do these people differ from the primary audience?
What position does the person hold in the organization?	Do I need to include more background information?
How much does that person know about the subject?	How must I reshape my message to make it understandable and acceptable to others to whom it might be forwarded?
What do I know about that person's education, beliefs, culture, and attitudes?	
Should I expect a neutral, positive, or negative response to my message?	

"You haven't been listening. I keep telling you that I don't want a product fit for a king."

positive, or negative will help you determine how to organize your message.

Another advantage of profiling your audience is considering the possibility of a secondary audience. For example, let's say you start to write an e-mail to your supervisor, Sheila, describing a problem you are having. Halfway through the message you realize that Sheila will probably forward this message to her boss, the vice president. Sheila will not want to summarize what you said; instead she will take the easy route and merely forward your e-mail. When you realize that the vice president will probably see this message, you decide to back up and use a more formal tone. You remove your inquiry about Sheila's family, you reduce your complaints, and you tone down your language about why things went wrong. Instead, you provide more background information, and you are more specific in identifying items the vice president might not recognize. Analyzing the task and anticipating the audience will help you adapt your message so that you can create an efficient and effective message.

Adapting to the Task and Audience

Writers improve the tone of a message by emphasizing audience benefits, cultivating a "you" attitude, and using a conversational tone and inclusive language.

After analyzing your purpose and anticipating your audience, you must convey your purpose to that audience. Adaptation is the process of creating a message that suits your audience.

One important aspect of adaptation is *tone*. Conveyed largely by the words in a message, tone affects how a receiver feels upon reading or hearing a message. Skilled communicators create a positive tone in their messages by using a number of adaptive techniques, some of which are unconscious. Among the most important adaptive writing techniques are developing audience benefits and cultivating the "you" view.

Stressing Audience Benefits

Focusing on the audience sounds like a modern idea, but actually one of America's early statesmen and authors recognized this fundamental writing principle over 200 years ago. In describing effective writing, Ben Franklin observed, "To be good, it ought to have a tendency to benefit the reader."[1] These wise words have become a fundamental guideline for today's business communicators. Expanding on Franklin's counsel, a contemporary communication consultant gives this solid advice to his business clients: "Always stress the benefit to the audience of whatever it is you are trying to get them to do. If you can show them how you are going to save them frustration or help them meet their goals, you have the makings of a powerful message."[2]

Adapting your message to the receiver's needs means putting yourself in that person's shoes. It's called *empathy*. Empathic senders think about how a receiver will decode a message. They try to give something to the receiver, solve the receiver's problems, save the receiver's money, or just understand the feelings and position of that person. Which version of the following messages is more appealing to the audience?

Empathy involves shaping a message that appeals to the receiver.

Sender Focus	Audience Focus
All employees are instructed herewith to fill out the enclosed questionnaire completely and immediately so that we can allocate our training resource funds to employees.	By filling out the enclosed questionnaires, you can be one of the first employees to sign up for our training resource funds.
Our warranty becomes effective only when we receive an owner's registration.	Your warranty begins working for you as soon as you return your owner's registration.
We are proud to announce our new software virus checker that we think is the best on the market!	Now you can be sure that all your computers will be protected with our real-time virus scanning.

Cultivating the "You" View

Notice that many of the previous audience-focused messages include the word *you*. In concentrating on receiver benefits, skilled communicators naturally develop the "you" view. They emphasize second-person pronouns (*you, your*) instead of first-person pronouns (*I/we, us, our*). Whether your goal is to inform, persuade, or promote goodwill, the catchiest words you can use are *you* and *your*. Compare the following examples.

Because receivers are most interested in themselves, emphasize the word *you* whenever possible.

"I/We" View	"You" View
We are requiring all employees to respond to the attached survey about health benefits.	Because your ideas count, give us your thoughts on the attached survey about health benefits.
I need your account number before I can do anything.	Would you mind giving me your account number so that I can locate your records and help you solve this problem?
We have shipped your order by UPS, and we are sure it will arrive in time for your sales promotion December 1.	Your order will be delivered by UPS in time for your sales promotion December 1.

Although you want to focus on the reader or listener, don't overuse or misuse the second-person pronoun *you*. Readers and listeners appreciate genuine interest; on the other hand, they resent obvious attempts at manipulation. Some sales messages, for example, are guilty of overkill when they include *you* dozens of times in a direct-mail promotion. What's more, the word can sometimes create the wrong impression. Consider this statement: *You cannot return merchandise until you receive written approval.* The word *you* appears twice, but the reader may feel singled out for criticism. In the following version the message is less personal and more positive: *Customers may return merchandise with written approval.*

Another difficulty in emphasizing the "you" view and de-emphasizing *we/I* is that it may result in overuse of the passive voice. For example, to avoid *We will give you* (active voice), you might write *You will be given* (passive voice). The active voice in writing is generally preferred because it identifies who is doing the acting. You will learn more about active and passive voice in Chapter 3.

Emphasize *you* but don't eliminate all *I* and *we* statements.

In recognizing the value of the "you" attitude, writers do not have to sterilize their writing and totally avoid any first-person pronouns or words that show their feelings. Skilled communicators are able to convey sincerity, warmth, and

Employers are working hard to attract and retain Generation Y graduates for their organizations. Now reaching their mid-twenties, Gen Y-ers are generally optimistic, entrepreneurial, team oriented, and tech savvy. But they also have high workplace expectations and short attention spans—traits linked to the gotta-have-it-now digital culture. Accounting firms have begun using rap videos, online chat, and alternative work arrangements to recruit these young graduates before they lose interest and go elsewhere. ***When creating a message for a Generation Y audience, what benefits would you stress?***

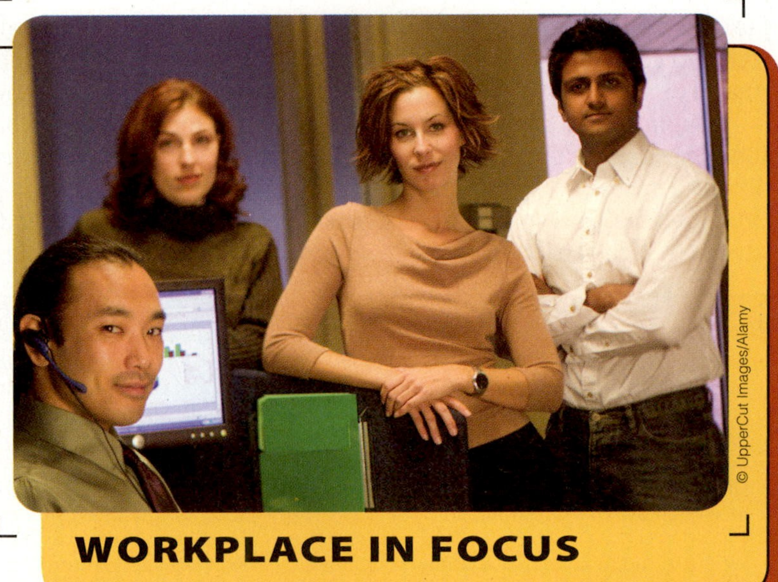

© UpperCut Images/Alamy

WORKPLACE IN FOCUS

enthusiasm by the words they choose. Don't be afraid to use phrases such as *I'm happy* or *We're delighted,* if you truly are. When speaking face-to-face, communicators show sincerity and warmth with nonverbal cues such as a smile and a pleasant voice tone. In letters, memos, and e-mail messages, however, only expressive words and phrases can show these feelings. These phrases suggest hidden messages that say *You are important, I hear you,* and *I'm honestly trying to please you.*

Developing Skillful Writing Techniques

Skillful writers employ a number of techniques that make their messages easy to read and effective. To help you make your messages stand out, this section teaches you to use conversational, professional, positive, and courteous expression. Other skillful writing techniques in this section include choosing bias-free language, plain language, familiar words, and precise expression.

Being Conversational but Professional

Strive for conversational expression, but also remember to be professional.

Most instant messages, e-mails, business letters, memos, and reports replace conversation. Therefore, they are most effective when they convey an informal, conversational tone instead of a formal, pretentious tone. Workplace messages should not, however, become so casual that they sound low-level and unprofessional.

Instant messaging (IM) enables coworkers to have informal, spontaneous conversations. Some companies have accepted IM as a serious workplace tool. With the increasing use of instant messaging and e-mail, however, a major problem has developed. Sloppy, unprofessional expression appears in many workplace messages. You will learn more about the dangers of e-mail in Chapter 5. At this point, though, we focus on the tone of the language.

To project a professional image, you must sound educated and mature. Overuse of expressions such as *totally awesome, you know,* and *like,* as well as reliance on needless abbreviations (such as *BTW* for "by the way" and *LOL* for "laughing out loud"), make a businessperson sound like a teenager. Professional messages do not include IM abbreviations, slang, sentence fragments, and chitchat. Strive for a warm, conversational tone that avoids low-level diction. Levels of diction, as shown in Figure 2.5, range from unprofessional to formal.

Your goal is a warm, friendly tone that sounds professional. Although some writers are too casual, others are overly formal. To impress readers and listeners, they use big words, long sentences, legal terminology, and third-person constructions. Stay

FIGURE 2.5 Levels of Diction		
Unprofessional (low-level diction)	**Conversational (midlevel diction)**	**Formal (high-level diction)**
badmouth	criticize	denigrate
guts	nerve	courage
pecking order	line of command	dominance hierarchy
ticked off	upset	provoked
rat on	inform	betray
rip off	steal	expropriate
Sentence example: If we just hang in there, we can snag the contract.	**Sentence example:** If we don't get discouraged, we can win the contract.	**Sentence example:** If the principals persevere, they can secure the contract.

away from expressions such as *the undersigned, the writer*, and *the affected party.* You will sound friendlier with familiar pronouns such as *I, we*, and *you.* Study the following examples to see how to achieve a professional, yet conversational tone:

Unprofessional	Professional
Hey, boss, Gr8 news! Firewall now installed!! BTW, check with me b4 popping the news.	Mr. Smith, our new firewall software is now installed. Please check with me before announcing it.
Look, dude, this report is totally bogus. And the figures don't look kosher. Show me some real stats. Got sources?	Because the figures in this report seem inaccurate, please submit the source statistics.

Overly Formal	Conversational
All employees are herewith instructed to return the appropriately designated contracts to the undersigned.	Please return your contracts to me.
Pertaining to your order, we must verify the sizes that your organization requires prior to consignment of your order to our shipper.	We will send your order as soon as we confirm the sizes you need.

Expressing Yourself Positively

You can improve the clarity and tone of a message if you use positive rather than negative language. Positive language generally conveys more information than negative language does. Moreover, positive messages are uplifting and pleasant to read. Positive wording tells what *is* and what *can be done* rather than what *isn't* and what *can't be done*. For example, *Your order cannot be shipped by January 10* is not nearly as informative as *Your order will be shipped January 20.* Notice in the following examples how you can revise the negative tone to reflect a more positive impression.

Positive language creates goodwill and gives more options to receivers.

Negative	Positive
This plan cannot succeed if we don't obtain management approval.	This plan can succeed if we obtain management approval.
Because you failed to include your credit card number, we can't mail your order.	We look forward to completing your order as soon as we receive your credit card number.
You cannot park in Lot H until April 1.	You may park in Lot H starting April 1.
You won't be sorry that	You will be happy that . . . .

OFFICE INSIDER

"Negative tone can hurt your company in many ways. It can lose customers, it can generate lawsuits and, if inflammatory rhetoric is found in a discoverable e-mail or log notes, a few words might cost your company a whopping settlement and punitive damages in a bad-faith lawsuit."

—Gary Blake, *National Underwriter Life & Health-Financial Services*

Being Courteous

Maintaining a courteous tone involves not just guarding against rudeness but also avoiding words that sound demanding or preachy. Expressions such as *you should, you must,* and *you have to* cause people to instinctively react with *Oh, yeah?* One remedy is to turn these demands into polite requests that begin with *Please*. Giving reasons for a request also softens the tone.

Even when you feel justified in displaying anger, remember that losing your temper or being sarcastic will seldom accomplish your goals as a business communicator: to inform, to persuade, and to create goodwill. When you are irritated, frustrated, or infuriated, keep cool and try to defuse the situation. In dealing with customers in telephone conversations, use polite phrases such as *It was a pleasure speaking with you, I would be happy to assist you with that,* and *Thank you for being so patient.*

Less Courteous	More Courteous and Helpful
This is the third time I have written! Can't you people get anything right?	Please credit my account for $40. My latest statement shows that the error noted in my letter of May 15 has not yet been corrected.
You should organize a car pool in this department.	Organizing a car pool will reduce your transportation costs and help preserve the environment.
Am I the only one who can read the operating manual?	Let's review the operating manual together so that you can get your documents to print correctly next time.

Choosing Bias-Free Language

In adapting a message to its audience, be sure your language is sensitive and bias-free. Few writers set out to be offensive. Sometimes, though, we all say things that we never thought might be hurtful. The real problem is that we don't think about the words that stereotype groups of people, such as *the boys in the mail room* or *the girls in the front office.* Be cautious about expressions that might be biased in terms of gender, race, ethnicity, age, and disability. Generally, you can avoid gender-biased language by leaving out the words *man* or *woman*, by using plural nouns and pronouns, or by changing to a gender-free word (*person* or *representative*). Avoid the *his or her* option whenever possible. It's wordy and conspicuous. With a little effort, you can usually find a construction that is graceful, grammatical, and unselfconscious.

Specify age only if it is relevant, and avoid expressions that are demeaning or subjective (such as *spry old codger*). To avoid disability bias, do not refer to an individual's disability unless it is relevant. When necessary, use terms that do not stigmatize disabled individuals. The following examples give you a quick look at a few problem expressions and possible replacements. The real key to bias-free communication, though, lies in your awareness and commitment. Be on the lookout to be sure that your messages do not exclude, stereotype, or offend people.

Gender Biased	Bias-Free
female doctor, woman attorney, cleaning woman	doctor, attorney, cleaner
waiter/waitress, authoress, stewardess	server, author, flight attendant
mankind, man-hour, man-made	humanity, working hours, artificial
office girls	office workers
the doctor . . . he	doctors . . . they

Gender Biased	Bias-Free
the teacher . . . she	teachers . . . they
executives and their wives	executives and their spouses
foreman, flagman, workman	lead worker, flagger, worker
businessman, salesman	businessperson, sales representative
Each employee had his picture taken.	Each employee had a picture taken. All employees had their pictures taken. Each employee had his or her picture taken.

Racially or Ethnically Biased	Bias-Free
An Indian accountant was hired.	An accountant was hired.
James Lee, an African American, applied.	James Lee applied.

Age Biased	Bias-Free
The law applied to old people.	The law applied to people over sixty-five.
Sally Kay, 55, was transferred.	Sally Kay was transferred.
a spry old gentleman	a man
a little old lady	a woman

Disability Biased	Bias-Free
afflicted with arthritis, suffering from . . ., crippled by . . .	has arthritis
confined to a wheelchair	uses a wheelchair

Using Plain Language and Familiar Words

In adapting your message to your audience, use plain language and familiar words that you think audience members will recognize. Don't, however, avoid a big word that conveys your idea efficiently and is appropriate for the audience. Your goal is to shun pompous and pretentious language. Instead, use "GO" words. If you mean *begin,* don't say *commence* or *initiate*. If you mean *pay*, don't write *compensate*. By substituting everyday, familiar words for unfamiliar ones, as shown here, you help your audience comprehend your ideas quickly.

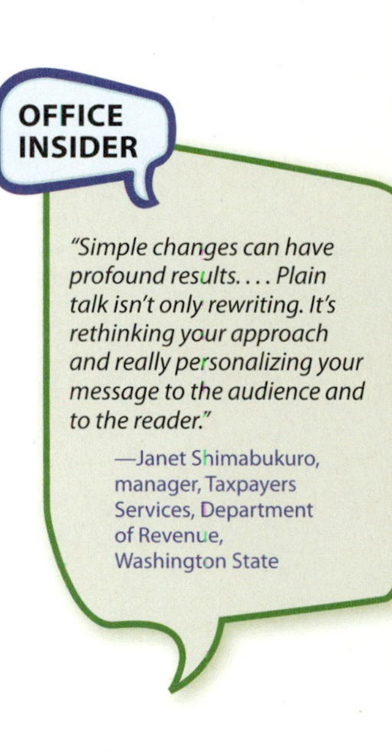
OFFICE INSIDER
"Simple changes can have profound results. . . . Plain talk isn't only rewriting. It's rethinking your approach and really personalizing your message to the audience and to the reader."
—Janet Shimabukuro, manager, Taxpayers Services, Department of Revenue, Washington State

Unfamiliar	Familiar
commensurate	equal
interrogate	question
materialize	appear
obfuscate	confuse
remuneration	pay, salary
terminate	end

At the same time, be selective in your use of jargon. *Jargon* describes technical or specialized terms within a field. These terms enable insiders to communicate complex ideas briefly, but to outsiders they mean nothing. Human resources professionals, for example, know precisely what's meant by *cafeteria plan* (a benefits option program), but most of us would be thinking about lunch. Geologists refer to *plate tectonics,* and physicians discuss *metastatic carcinomas.* These terms mean little to most of us. Use specialized language only when the audience will understand it.

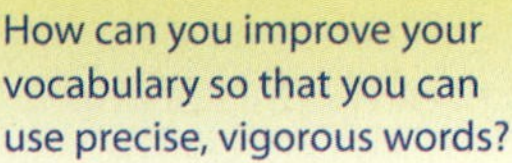

How can you improve your vocabulary so that you can use precise, vigorous words?

In addition, don't be impressed by high-sounding language and legalese, such as *herein, herewith, thereafter,* and *hereinafter.* Your writing will be better if you use plain language.

Employing Precise, Vigorous Words

Strong verbs and concrete nouns give receivers more information and keep them interested. Don't overlook the thesaurus (or the thesaurus program on your computer) for expanding your word choices and vocabulary. However, don't accept words whose meanings you don't fully understand. Whenever possible, use specific words as shown here.

Imprecise, Dull	More Precise
a change in profits	a 25 percent hike in profits
	a 10 percent plunge in profits
to say	to promise, confess, understand
	to allege, assert, assume, judge
to think about	to identify, diagnose, analyze
	to probe, examine, inspect

As you revise a message, you will have a chance to correct any writing problems. Notice in Figure 2.6 what a difference revision makes. Before revision, the message failed to use familiar language. Many negative ideas could have been expressed positively. After revision, the message is shorter, is more conversational, and emphasizes audience benefits.

www.cengagebrain.com

Available with an access code, these eResources will help you prepare for exams:

- **Chapter Review Quizzes**
- **Personal Language Trainer**
- **PowerPoint Slides**
- **Flash Cards**

FIGURE 2.6 Improving the Tone in an E-Mail Message

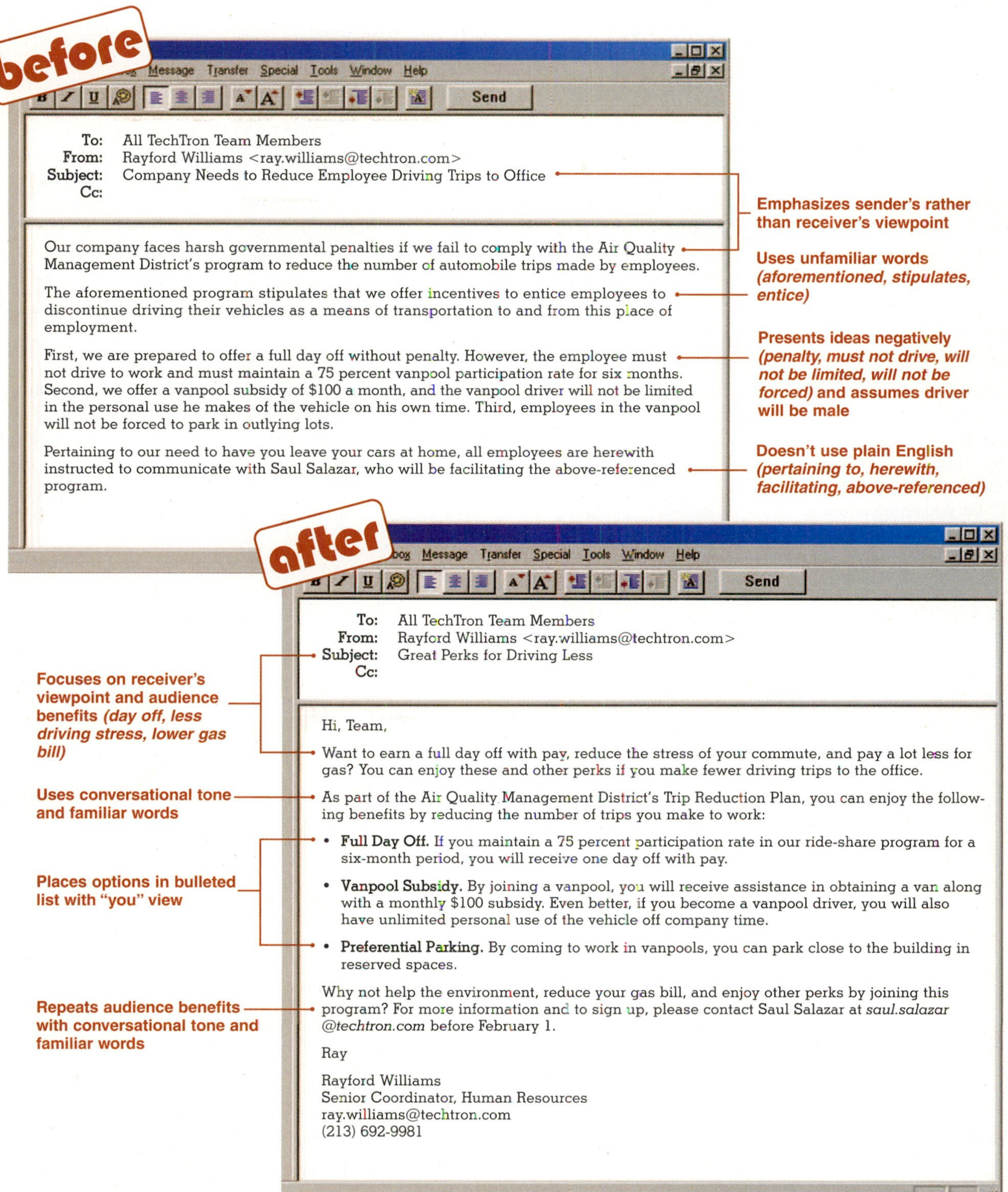

before

To: All TechTron Team Members
From: Rayford Williams <ray.williams@techtron.com>
Subject: Company Needs to Reduce Employee Driving Trips to Office
Cc:

Our company faces harsh governmental penalties if we fail to comply with the Air Quality Management District's program to reduce the number of automobile trips made by employees.

The aforementioned program stipulates that we offer incentives to entice employees to discontinue driving their vehicles as a means of transportation to and from this place of employment.

First, we are prepared to offer a full day off without penalty. However, the employee must not drive to work and must maintain a 75 percent vanpool participation rate for six months. Second, we offer a vanpool subsidy of $100 a month, and the vanpool driver will not be limited in the personal use he makes of the vehicle on his own time. Third, employees in the vanpool will not be forced to park in outlying lots.

Pertaining to our need to have you leave your cars at home, all employees are herewith instructed to communicate with Saul Salazar, who will be facilitating the above-referenced program.

Emphasizes sender's rather than receiver's viewpoint
Uses unfamiliar words *(aforementioned, stipulates, entice)*
Presents ideas negatively *(penalty, must not drive, will not be limited, will not be forced)* and assumes driver will be male
Doesn't use plain English *(pertaining to, herewith, facilitating, above-referenced)*

after

To: All TechTron Team Members
From: Rayford Williams <ray.williams@techtron.com>
Subject: Great Perks for Driving Less
Cc:

Hi, Team,

Want to earn a full day off with pay, reduce the stress of your commute, and pay a lot less for gas? You can enjoy these and other perks if you make fewer driving trips to the office.

As part of the Air Quality Management District's Trip Reduction Plan, you can enjoy the following benefits by reducing the number of trips you make to work:

- **Full Day Off.** If you maintain a 75 percent participation rate in our ride-share program for a six-month period, you will receive one day off with pay.
- **Vanpool Subsidy.** By joining a vanpool, you will receive assistance in obtaining a van along with a monthly $100 subsidy. Even better, if you become a vanpool driver, you will also have unlimited personal use of the vehicle off company time.
- **Preferential Parking.** By coming to work in vanpools, you can park close to the building in reserved spaces.

Why not help the environment, reduce your gas bill, and enjoy other perks by joining this program? For more information and to sign up, please contact Saul Salazar at *saul.salazar@techtron.com* before February 1.

Ray

Rayford Williams
Senior Coordinator, Human Resources
ray.williams@techtron.com
(213) 692-9981

Focuses on receiver's viewpoint and audience benefits *(day off, less driving stress, lower gas bill)*
Uses conversational tone and familiar words
Places options in bulleted list with "you" view
Repeats audience benefits with conversational tone and familiar words

Summing Up and Looking Forward

Good business writing is audience centered, purposeful, persuasive, and economical. To achieve these results, business communicators typically follow a systematic writing process. This process includes three phases: prewriting, writing, and revising. In the prewriting phase, communicators analyze the task and the audience. They select an appropriate channel to deliver the message, and they consider ways to adapt their message to the task and the audience. Effective techniques include spotlighting audience benefits, cultivating the "you" view, striving to use conversational language, and expressing ideas positively. Good communicators also use courteous and bias-free expressions, plain language, and familiar words.

Chapter 3 continues to examine the writing process. It presents additional techniques to help you become a better writer. You will learn how to collect and organize information into outlines and how to develop a variety of sentence types. In addition, you will study techniques for emphasizing ideas, using active and passive voice, developing parallelism, and avoiding misplaced modifiers. Finally, Chapter 3 teaches you how to draft powerful paragraphs.

Critical Thinking

1. When asked what business schools should teach more or less of, venture capitalist Guy Kawasaki said, "They should teach students how to communicate in five-sentence e-mails and with 10-slide PowerPoint presentations. If they just taught every student that, American business would be much better off."[3] Do you agree or disagree? Why?
2. Is it necessary to follow a writing process in preparing a short message? A long message? Why or why not?
3. In e-mails writers sometimes use abbreviations such as *FYI* ("for your information") and *ASAP* ("as soon as possible"). Other writers sometimes use *LOL* ("laughing out loud"), *4 u* ("for you"), and *gr8* ("great"). What's the difference between these abbreviations, and how do they contribute to one's professional image?
4. Which sentence sounds better? *You can't use the parking lot until July 1*, or *You may use the parking lot on July 1 and thereafter*?
5. To focus firmly on the "you" view, writers should scrub all uses of *I* and *we* from their writing. Do you agree or disagree? Why?

Chapter Review

6. Name four goals that business writers have when they prepare oral presentations and business messages.

7. Explain the three steps in the writing process.

8. Does the writing process always proceed from Step 1 through Step 3? Explain.

9. Which phase of the writing process should receive the most time? Why?

10. Why are businesspeople writing fewer interoffice memos and letters today?

11. Why is it important to profile the audience for a message?

12. List six factors that writers should consider when selecting an appropriate communication channel. Name one additional factor that you might consider in your business messages.

13. What special skills do customer-service representatives in chat sessions require?

14. In messages to customers, what's wrong with words such as *complaint, criticism, defective, failed, mistake,* and *neglected?*

15. What is bias-free language? Provide several examples of biased language and bias-free alternatives.

Writing Improvement Exercises

Audience Benefits and the "You" View

Your Task. Revise the following sentences to emphasize the perspective of the audience and the "you" view.

16. To help us process your order with our new database software, we need you to go to our Web site and fill out the customer information required.

17. Under a new policy, reimbursement of travel expenses will be restricted to those related to work only.

18. To avoid suffering the kinds of monetary losses experienced in the past, our credit union now prohibits the cashing of double-endorsed checks presented by our customers.

19. We are pleased to announce an arrangement with HP that allows us to offer discounted computers in the student bookstore.

20. We are pleased to announce that you have been approved to enroll in our management trainee program.

21. Our warranty goes into effect only when we have received the product's registration card from the purchaser.

22. Unfortunately, the computer and telephone systems will be down Thursday afternoon for upgrades to improve both systems.

23. As part of our company effort to be friendly to the environment, we are asking all employees to reduce paper consumption by communicating by e-mail and avoiding printing.

Conversational, Professional Tone

Your Task. Revise the following to make the tone conversational yet professional.

24. Pertaining to your request, the above-referenced items (printer toner and supplies) are being sent to your Oakdale office, as per your telephone conversation of April 1.

25. Kindly inform the undersigned whether or not your representative will be making a visitation in the near future.

26. It's totally awesome that we still got the contract, like, after the customer amped up his demands, but our manager pushed back.

27. BTW, dude, we've had some slippage in the schedule but don't have to dump everything and start from ground zero.

28. To facilitate ratification of this agreement, your negotiators urge that the membership respond in the affirmative.

29. R head honcho wz like totally raggety bkuz I wz sick n stuff n mist the team meet. Geez!

Positive and Courteous Expression

Your Task. Revise the following statements to make them more positive.

30. Customers are ineligible for the 10 percent discount unless they show their membership cards.

31. Titan Insurance Company will not process any claim not accompanied by documented proof from a physician showing that the injuries were treated.

32. If you fail to comply with each requirement, you will not receive your $50 rebate.

33. We must withhold remuneration until you complete the job satisfactorily.

34. Although you apparently failed to consult the mounting instructions for your Miracle Wheatgrass Extractor, we are enclosing a set of clamps to fasten the device to a table. A new set of instructions is enclosed.

35. Your application cannot be processed because you neglected to insert your telephone number.

Bias-Free Language

Your Task. Revise the following sentences to eliminate terms that are considered sexist or that suggest stereotypes.

36. Any applicant for the position of fireman must submit a medical report signed by his physician.

37. Every employee is entitled to see his personnel file.

38. All waiters and waitresses are covered under our new benefits package.

39. A salesman would have to use all his skills to sell those condos.

40. Executives and their wives are invited to the banquet.

Plain Language and Familiar Words

Your Task. Revise the following sentences to use plain language and familiar words.

41. We are offering a pay package that is commensurate with other managers' remuneration.

42. The seller tried to obfuscate the issue by mentioning closing and other costs.

43. Even after officers interrogated the suspect, solid evidence failed to materialize.

44. In dialoguing with the owner, I learned that you plan to terminate our contract.

Precise, Vigorous Words

Your Task. From the choices in parentheses, select the most precise, vigorous words.

45. Management is predicting a (change, difference, drop) in earnings after the first of the year.

46. Experts (predict, hypothesize, state) that the economy will (change, moderate, stabilize) by next year.

47. We plan to (acknowledge, announce, applaud) the work of outstanding employees.

48. After (reading, looking at, studying) the report, I realized that the data were (bad, inadequate, inaccurate).

Activities

Selecting Communication Channels

Your Task. Using Figure 2.2, suggest the best communication channels for the following messages. Assume that all channels shown are available. Be prepared to explain your choices.

49. As an event planner, you have been engaged to research the sites for a celebrity golf tournament. What is the best channel for conveying your findings?

50. You want to persuade your manager to change your work schedule.

51. As a sales manager, you want to know which of your sales reps in the field are available immediately for a quick teleconference meeting.

52. You need to know whether Amanda in Reprographics can produce a rush job for you in two days.

53. Your firm must respond to a notice from the Internal Revenue Service announcing that the company owes a penalty because it underreported its income in the previous fiscal year.

Video Resources

Video Library 1, *Building Workplace Skills.* Your instructor may show you a video titled ***Guffey's 3-x-3 Writing Process Develops Fluent Workplace Skills***. It shows three phases of the writing process including prewriting, writing, and revising. You will see how the writing process guides the development of a complete message. This video illustrates concepts in Chapters 2, 3, and 4.

Grammar/Mechanics Checkup—2

Pronouns

Review Sections 1.07–1.09 in the Grammar Review section of the Grammar/Mechanics Handbook. Then study each of the following statements. In the space provided, write the word that completes the statement correctly and the number of the G/M principle illustrated. When you finish, compare your responses with those provided near the end of the book. If your responses differ, study carefully the principles in parentheses.

its (1.09d) **Example** Our Safety Committee just submitted (its, their) report.

________ 1. We expected Mr. Thomas to call. Was it (he, him) who left the message?

________ 2. Every member of the men's bowling team must have (his, his or her, their) picture taken.

________ 3. Just between you and (me, I), a new salary schedule will soon be announced.

________ 4. (Who, Whom) did you say was having trouble with the virus protection software?

________ 5. Most applications arrived on time, but (yours, your's) was late.

________ 6. Because of outstanding sales, the company gave bonuses to Mark and (me, I).

________ 7. My friend and (I, me, myself) could not decide on an apartment to share.

________ 8. The offices are similar, but (ours, our's) is cheaper to rent.

________ 9. Please distribute the supplies to (whoever, whomever) ordered them.

________ 10. Everyone except the manager and (I, me, myself) was eligible for a bonus.

________ 11. No one is better able to lead the team than (he, him, himself).

________ 12. It became clear that (we, us) employees would have to speak up for ourselves.

________ 13. Someone on the women's team left (their, her) shoes in the van.

________ 14. Next year I hope to earn as much as (she, her, herself).

________ 15. Every homeowner should check (their, his or her, his) fire insurance.

Editing Challenge—2

As the employee with the best communication skills, you are frequently asked to edit messages. The following has errors in spelling, proofreading, verbs, plural nouns, pronouns, and other writing techniques studied in this chapter. You may (a) use standard proofreading marks (see Appendix B) to correct the errors here or (b) download the document from **www.cengagebrain.com** and revise at your computer.

Your instructor may ask you to use the **Track Changes** feature in Microsoft Word to show your editing comments. Turn on **Track Changes** on the **Review** tab. Click **Show Markup**. Place your cursor at an error, click **New Comment**, and key your edit in the bubble box provided. Study the guidelines in the Grammar/Mechanics Handbook as well as the lists of Confusing Words and Frequently Misspelled Words to sharpen your skills.

To: Marcella Richardson <marcella.richardson@beveragesinc.com>
From: Susan M. Wang <susan.wang@beveragesinc.com>
Subject: Your Request for Information on New Sweeteners
Cc:

Marcella,

Herewith is a summary of the investigation you assigned to Craig Brady and I pertaining to new sweeteners. As you know, Coca-Cola co. and PepsiCo inc. has introduced sweeteners that are new to the market. Totally awesome!

Coca-Cola brought out Sprite Green, a reduced calorie soft drink that contains Truvia, which it considers a natural sweetener because it is derived from an herb. The initial launch focused on locations and events oriented to teenagers and young adults. According to inside information obtained by Craig and I, this product was tested on the shelfs of grocerys, mass merchants, and conveience stores in 5 citys in Florida.

PepsiCo has it's own version of the herbal sweetener, however it was developed in collaboration with Green earth sweetener co. Its called Pure Via. The first products to contain the sweetner will be 3 flavors of zero-calorie SoBe Life-water. It may also be used in a orange-juice drink with half the calorys and sugar of orange juice.

BTW, approval by the Food and drug administration did not materialize automatically for these new sweeteners. FDA approval was an issue because studys conducted in the early 1990s suggested that their was possible adverse health effects from the use of stevia-based products. However the herb has been aproved for use in 12 countrys.

Both companys eventually received FDA approval and there products are all ready on the market. We cannot submit our full report until October 15.

Susan

Susan M. Wang
susan.wang@beveragesinc.com
Research and Development
Office: (927) 443-9920
Cell: (927) 442-2310

Communication Workshop:

Get Ready for Critical Thinking, Problem Solving, and Decision Making!

Gone are the days when management expected workers to check their brains at the door and do only as told. Today, you will be expected to use your brain and think critically. You will be solving problems and making decisions. Much of this book is devoted to helping you solve problems and communicate those decisions to management, fellow workers, clients, the government, and the public. Faced with a problem or an issue, most of us do a lot of worrying before separating the issues or making a decision. You can convert all that worrying to directed thinking by channeling it into the following procedure:

- **Identify and clarify the problem.** Your first task is to recognize that a problem exists. Some problems are big and unmistakable, such as failure of an air-freight delivery service to get packages to customers on time. Other problems may be continuing annoyances, such as regularly running out of toner for an office copy machine. The first step in reaching a solution is pinpointing the problem.
- **Gather information.** Learn more about the problem situation. Look for possible causes and solutions. This step may mean checking files, calling suppliers, or brainstorming with fellow workers. For example, the air-freight delivery service would investigate the tracking systems of the commercial airlines carrying its packages to determine what is going wrong.
- **Evaluate the evidence.** Where did the information come from? Does it represent various points of view? What biases could be expected from each source? How accurate is the information gathered? Is it fact or opinion? For example, it is a fact that packages are missing; it is an opinion that they are merely lost and will turn up eventually.
- **Consider alternatives and implications.** Draw conclusions from the gathered evidence and pose solutions. Then weigh the advantages and disadvantages of each alternative. What are the costs, benefits, and consequences? What are the obstacles, and how can they be handled? Most important, what solution best serves your goals and those of your organization? Here is where your creativity is especially important.
- **Choose the best alternative and test it.** Select an alternative, and try it out to see if it meets your expectations. If it does, implement your decision and put it into action. If it doesn't, rethink your alternatives. The freight company decided to give its unhappy customers free delivery service to make up for the lost packages and downtime. Be sure to continue monitoring and adjusting the solution to ensure its effectiveness over time.

Career Application. Let's return to the McDonald's problem (discussed on page 37) in which some franchise owners are unhappy with the multiple lines for service. Customers don't seem to know where to stand to be the next served. Tempers flare when aggressive customers cut in line, and other customers spend so much time protecting their places in line that they are not ready to order. As a franchise owner, you want to solve this problem. Any new procedures, however, must be approved by a majority of McDonald's owners in a district. You know that McDonald's management feels that the multiline system accommodates higher volumes of customers more quickly than a single-line system. In addition, customers are turned off when they see a long line.

Your Task

- Individually or with a team, use the critical-thinking steps outlined here. Begin by clarifying the problem.
- Where could you gather information? Would it be wise to see what your competitors are doing? How do banks handle customer lines? Airlines?
- Evaluate your findings and consider alternatives. What are the pros and cons of each alternative?
- Within your team choose the best alternative. Present your recommendation to your class and give your reasons for choosing it.

Communication Workshops, such as the one provided here, offer insight into special business communication topics and skills not discussed in the chapters. Topics include ethics, technology, career skills, collaboration, and other workplace issues. Each workshop includes a career application with a case study or problem to help you develop skills relevant to the workshop topic.

Endnotes

[1] Arnold, V. D. (1986, August). Benjamin Franklin on writing well. *Personnel Journal*, 17.

[2] Bacon, M. (1988, April). Quoted in Business writing: One-on-one speaks best to the masses. *Training*, 95. See also Danziger, E. (1998, February). Communicate up. *Journal of Accountancy*, 67.

[3] Bryant, A. (2010, March 21). Corner office: Guy Kawasaki. *The New York Times*, p. 7.

Acknowledgments

p. 36 Office Insider based on Stevens, B. (2005, March). What communication skills do employees want? Silicon Valley recruiters respond. *Journal of Employment Counseling*, *42*, 3.

p. 37 Office Insider based on Marilyn Mackes, National Association of Colleges and Employers, quoted in "Step up to the soft skills," (2004, January). *Keying In*, Newsletter of the National Business Education Association, p. 1.

p. 46 Office Insider based on Blake, G. (2002, November 4). Insurers need to upgrade their employees' writing skills. *National Underwriter Life & Health-Financial Services Edition, 106*(44), 35.

p. 47 Office Insider based on Shimabukuro, J. (2006, December 11). Quoted in Wash. state sees results from 'plain talk' initiative. *USA Today*, p. 18A.

Composing Business Messages

Go to
cengagebrain.com
and use your access code to unlock valuable student eResources.

Ilja Mašík/Shutterstock.com

OBJECTIVES

After studying this chapter, you should be able to

- Contrast formal and informal methods of researching data, and generate ideas for messages.
- Organize information into outlines.
- Compare the direct and indirect strategies for organizing ideas.
- Write effective sentences using four sentence types while avoiding three common sentence faults.
- Emphasize ideas, use active and passive voice effectively, achieve parallelism, and avoid dangling and misplaced modifiers.
- Draft powerful paragraphs that incorporate topic sentences, support sentences, and transitional expressions to build coherence.

Composing Messages on the Job

OFFICE INSIDER

Business executives and human resources staff rate writing skill as the most important skill that a new employee should possess.

—Workforce Readiness Project

Who me? Write on the job? Not a chance! Some people think they will never be required to write on the job. The truth is, however, that business, technical, and professional people are exchanging more messages than ever before. As a result, you can expect to be doing your share of writing on the job. The more quickly you can put your ideas down and the more clearly you can explain what needs to be said, the more successful and happy you will be in your career. Being able to write is also critical to promotions. That's why we devote three chapters to teaching you a writing process, summarized in Figure 3.1. This process guides you through the steps necessary to write rapidly but, more important, clearly. Instead of struggling with a writing assignment and not knowing where to begin or what to say, you are learning an effective process that you can use in school and on the job.

Chapter 2 focused on the prewriting stage of the writing process. You studied the importance of using a conversational tone, positive language, plain and courteous expression, and familiar words. This chapter addresses the second stage of the process: gathering information, organizing it into outlines, and composing messages.

FIGURE 3.1 The Writing Process

No smart businessperson would begin writing a message before collecting the needed information. We call this collection process *research*, a rather formal-sounding term. For simple documents, though, the process can be quite informal. Research is necessary before beginning to write because the information you collect helps shape the message. Discovering significant data after a message is completed often means starting over and reorganizing. To avoid frustration and inaccurate messages, collect information that answers these questions:

- What does the receiver need to know about this topic?
- What is the receiver to do?
- How is the receiver to do it and when?
- What will happen if the receiver doesn't do it?

Whenever your communication problem requires more information than you have in your head or at your fingertips, you must conduct research. This research may be formal or informal.

Formal Research Methods

Long reports and complex business problems generally require some use of formal research methods. Let's say you are a market specialist for Coca-Cola, and your boss asks you to evaluate the impact on Coke sales of New Age natural beverages. Or, assume you must write a term paper on the same subject for a college class. Both tasks require more data than you have in your head or at your fingertips. To conduct formal research, you could do the following:

Formal research may include searching libraries and electronic databases or investigating primary sources (interviews, surveys, and experiments).

- **Search manually.** You will find helpful background and supplementary information through manual searching of resources in public and college libraries. These traditional sources include books and newspaper, magazine, and journal articles. Other sources are encyclopedias, reference books, handbooks, dictionaries, directories, and almanacs.
- **Access electronically.** Much of the printed material just described is now available from the Internet, databases, CDs, or DVDs that can be accessed by computer. College and public libraries subscribe to retrieval services that permit you to access most periodic literature. You can also find extraordinary amounts of information by searching the Web. You will learn more about using electronic sources in Chapters 9 and 10.
- **Go to the source.** For firsthand information, go directly to the source. For the Coca-Cola vs. New Age beverages report, for example, you could find out

Good sources of primary information are interviews, surveys, questionnaires, and focus groups.

what consumers really think by conducting interviews or surveys, by putting together questionnaires, or by organizing focus groups. Formal research includes structured sampling and controls that enable investigators to make accurate judgments and valid predictions.

- **Conduct scientific experiments.** Instead of merely asking for the target audience's opinion, scientific researchers present choices with controlled variables. Let's say, for example, that Coca-Cola wants to determine what age group and under what circumstances consumers would switch from Coca-Cola to a New Age beverage. The results of experimentation would provide valuable data for managerial decision making.

Because formal research techniques are particularly necessary for reports, you will study resources and techniques more extensively in Chapters 9 and 10.

AP Photo/Paul Sakuma

WORKPLACE IN FOCUS

With tablet computers set to become top-selling gadgets over the next few years, marketers want to know how tight-lipped tablet leader Apple delivers iPad's remarkable quality and price advantages. Thanks to gadget teardown research from supply chain researcher IHS iSuppli, product managers for the Motorola Xoom, Samsung Galaxy Tab, and HP TouchPad can see what's inside iPad 2 and discover how much the unit costs to produce. *How might tablet developers use formal research to compete in the consumer electronics market?*

Informal Research and Idea Generation

Most routine tasks—such as composing e-mails, memos, letters, informational reports, and oral presentations—require data that you can collect informally. Here are some techniques for collecting informal data and for generating ideas:

- **Look in the files.** If you are responding to an inquiry, you often can find the answer to the inquiry by investigating the company files or by consulting colleagues.
- **Talk with your boss.** Get information from the individual making the assignment. What does that person know about the topic? What slant should be taken? What other sources would she or he suggest?
- **Interview the target audience.** Consider talking with individuals at whom the message is aimed. They can provide clarifying information that tells you what they want to know and how you should shape your remarks.
- **Conduct an informal survey.** Gather unscientific but helpful information by using questionnaires or telephone surveys. In preparing a memo report predicting the success of a proposed fitness center, for example, circulate a questionnaire asking for employee reactions.
- **Brainstorm for ideas.** Alone or with others, discuss ideas for the writing task at hand, and record at least a dozen ideas without judging them. Small groups are especially fruitful in brainstorming because people spin ideas off one another.

Informal research may include looking in the files, talking with your boss, interviewing the target audience, conducting an informal survey, and brainstorming.

Organizing to Show Relationships

Writers of well-organized messages group similar ideas together so that readers can see relationships and follow arguments.

Once you have collected data, you must find some way to organize it. Organizing includes two processes: grouping and strategizing. Well-organized messages group similar items together; ideas follow a sequence that helps the reader understand relationships and accept the writer's views. Unorganized messages proceed free-form, jumping from one thought to another. Such messages fail to emphasize important points. Puzzled readers can't see how the pieces fit together, and they become frustrated and irritated. Many communication experts regard poor organization as the greatest failing of business writers. Two simple techniques can help you organize data: the scratch list and the outline.

In developing simple messages, some writers make a quick scratch list of the topics they wish to cover. They then compose a message at their computers directly from the scratch list. Most writers, though, need to organize their ideas—especially if the project is complex—into a hierarchy, such as an outline. The beauty of preparing an outline is that it gives you a chance to organize your thinking before you get bogged down in word choice and sentence structure. Figure 3.2 shows a format for an outline.

OFFICE INSIDER

"Writing today is not a frill for the few, but an essential skill for the many."

—National Commission on Writing

The Direct Strategy

After developing an outline, you will need to decide where in the message to place the main idea. Placing the main idea at the beginning of the message represents the *direct strategy*. In the direct strategy the main idea comes first, followed by details, an explanation, or evidence. Placing the main idea later in the message (after the details, explanation, or evidence) reflects the *indirect strategy*. The strategy you select is determined by how you expect the audience to react to the message, as shown in Figure 3.3.

In preparing to write any message, you need to anticipate the audience's reaction to your ideas and frame your message accordingly. When you expect the reader to be pleased, mildly interested, or, at worst, neutral—use the direct strategy. That is, put your main point—the purpose of your message—in the first or second sentence. Compare the direct and indirect openings in an e-mail. Notice how long it takes to get to the main idea in the indirect opening.

Business messages typically follow either (a) the direct strategy, with the main idea first, or (b) the indirect strategy, with the main idea following an explanation and evidence.

FIGURE 3.2 Format for an Outline

Title: Major Idea or Purpose

I. First major component
    A. First subpoint
        1. Detail, illustration, evidence
        2. Detail, illustration, evidence
        3. Detail, illustration, evidence
    B. Second subpoint
        1.
        2.
II. Second major component
    A. First subpoint
        1.
        2.
    B. Second subpoint
        1.
        2.
        3

Tips for Making Outlines

- Define the main topic in the title.
- Divide the topic into main points, preferably three to five.
- Break the components into subpoints.
- Don't put a single item under a major component if you have only one subpoint; integrate it with the main item above it or reorganize.
- Strive to make each component exclusive (no overlapping).
- Use details, illustrations, and evidence to support subpoints.

FIGURE 3.3 Audience Response Determines Organizational Strategy

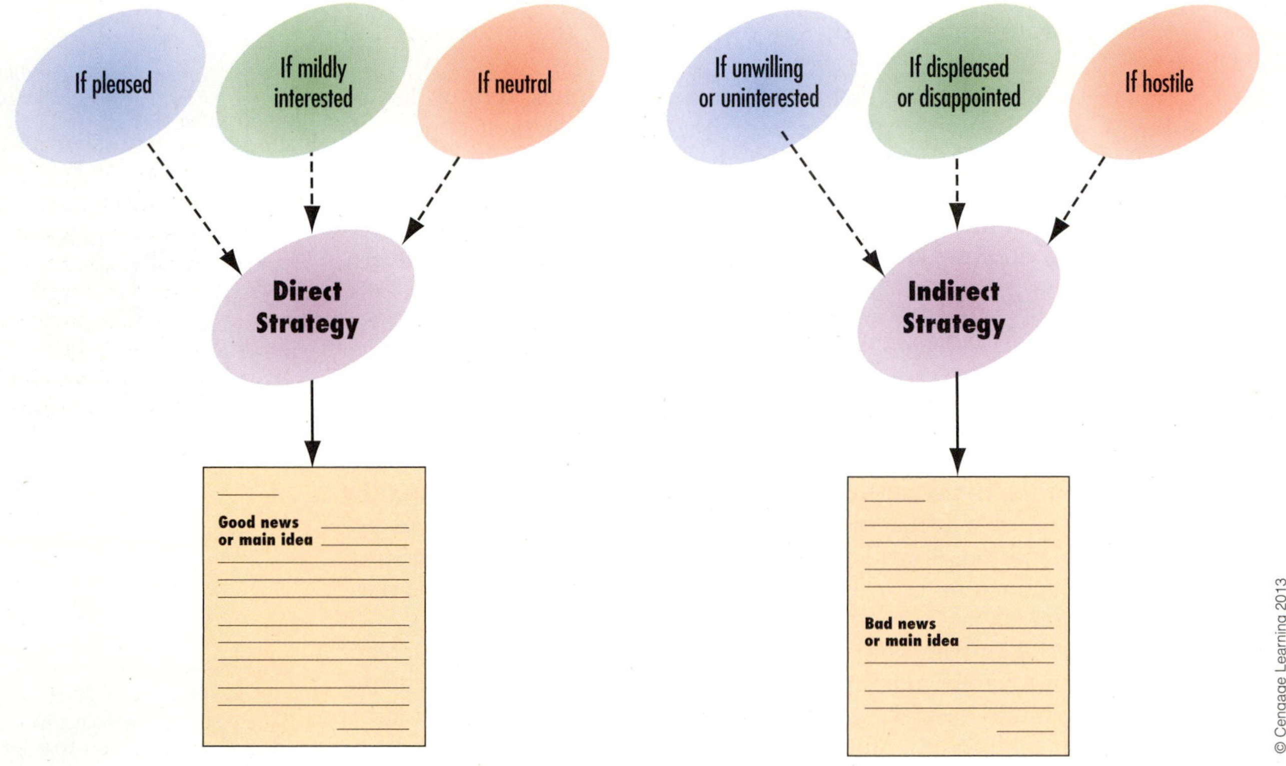

Indirect Opening	Direct Opening
For the past several years, we have had a continuing problem scheduling vacations, personal days, and sick time. Our Human Resources people struggle with unscheduled absences. After considerable investigation, the Management Council has decided to try a centralized paid time-off program starting January 1. We are pleased to send you this e-mail message, which will describe its benefits and procedures.	To improve the scheduling of absences, a new paid time-off program will begin January 1. Its benefits and procedures follow.

Explanations, background, and details should follow the direct opening. What's important is getting to the main idea quickly. This direct method, also called *frontloading*, has at least three advantages:

- **Saves the reader's time.** Many of today's businesspeople can devote only a few moments to each message. Messages that take too long to get to the point may lose their readers along the way.
- **Sets a proper frame of mind.** Learning the purpose up front helps the reader put the subsequent details and explanations in perspective. Without a clear opening, the reader may be thinking, *Why am I being told this?*
- **Prevents frustration.** Readers forced to struggle through excessive verbiage before reaching the main idea become frustrated. They resent the writer. Poorly organized messages create a negative impression of the writer.

Frontloading saves the reader's time, establishes the proper frame of mind, and prevents frustration.

This frontloading technique works best with audiences who are likely to be receptive to or at least not likely to disagree with what you have to say. Typical

U.S. Coast Guard photo

WORKPLACE IN FOCUS

When the Deepwater Horizon rig exploded in the Gulf of Mexico, millions of barrels of oil spread to coastlines, harming wildlife and displacing thousands of citizens. Although BP established a $20 billion emergency fund to compensate gulf coast businesses for their economic losses, victims became distressed when the independent agency in charge of financial disbursements sent form letters denying payment to more than 300,000 claimants, mostly for insufficient documentation on applications. *How should claims administrators organize messages when denying claims to disaster victims?*

business messages that follow the direct strategy include routine requests and responses, orders and acknowledgments, nonsensitive memos, e-mails, informational reports, and informational oral presentations. All these tasks have one element in common: none has a sensitive subject that will upset the reader.

The Indirect Strategy

When you expect the audience to be uninterested, unwilling, displeased, or perhaps even hostile, the indirect strategy is more appropriate. In this strategy don't reveal the main idea until after you have offered an explanation and evidence. The indirect strategy works well with three kinds of messages: (a) bad news, (b) ideas that require persuasion, and (c) sensitive news, especially when being transmitted to superiors. The indirect strategy has a number of benefits:

The indirect strategy works best when the audience may be uninterested, unwilling, displeased, or even hostile.

- **Respects the feelings of the audience.** Bad news is always painful, but the trauma can be lessened when the receiver is prepared for it.
- **Encourages a fair hearing.** Messages that may upset the reader are more likely to be read when the main idea is delayed. Beginning immediately with a piece of bad news or a persuasive request, for example, may cause the receiver to stop reading or listening.
- **Minimizes a negative reaction.** A reader's overall reaction to a negative message is generally improved if the news is delivered gently.

Typical business messages that could be developed indirectly include messages that refuse requests, reject claims, and deny credit. Persuasive requests, sales letters, sensitive messages, and some reports and oral presentations also benefit from the indirect strategy. You will learn more about how to use the indirect strategy in Chapters 7 and 8.

In summary, business messages may be organized directly, with the main idea first, or indirectly, with the main idea delayed. Although these two strategies cover many communication problems, they should be considered neither universal nor unquestionable. Every business transaction is distinct. Some messages are mixed: part good news, part bad, part goodwill, part persuasion. In upcoming chapters you will practice applying the direct and indirect strategies in typical situations. Eventually, you will have the skills and confidence to evaluate communication problems and develop a strategy based on your goals.

Constructing Effective Sentences

Using a variety of sentence types avoids boring, monotonous writing.

The most compelling and effective messages contain a variety of sentence patterns rather than repeating the same pattern. Effective messages also avoid common sentence faults, and they achieve emphasis and parallelism with special sentence-writing techniques.

Using Four Sentence Types to Achieve Variety

Messages that repeat the same sentence pattern soon become boring. The way you construct your sentences can make your messages interesting and readable. To avoid monotony and to add spark to your writing, use a variety of sentence types. You have four sentence types from which to choose: simple, compound, complex, and compound-complex.

A **simple sentence**, shown in the following example, contains one complete thought (an independent clause) with a subject (underlined once) and predicate verb (underlined twice):

Coca-Cola saw an opportunity.

A **compound sentence** contains two complete but related thoughts. The two thoughts (independent clauses) may be joined (a) by a conjunction such as *and, but*, or *or;* (b) by a semicolon; or (c) by a conjunctive adverb such as *however, consequently,* and *therefore.* Notice the punctuation in these examples:

Our team project was difficult.

Our team project was difficult; we were happy with the results.

Our team project was difficult; however, we were happy with the results.

A **complex sentence** contains an independent clause (a complete thought) and a dependent clause (a thought that cannot stand by itself). Dependent clauses are often introduced by words such as *although, since, because, when,* and *if.* When dependent clauses precede independent clauses, they always are followed by a comma.

When we finished our team project, we held a team party.

A **compound-complex sentence** contains at least two independent clauses and one dependent clause. Because these sentences are usually long, use them sparingly.

Although this team project is completed, soon we will begin work on another; however, it will be less challenging.

Controlling Sentence Length

Sentences of 20 or fewer words have the most impact.

Regardless of the type of sentence, remember that sentence length can influence readability. Because your goal is to communicate clearly, try to limit your sentences to 20 or fewer words. The American Press Institute reports that reader comprehension drops off markedly as sentences become longer:

Sentence Length	Comprehension Rate
8 words	100%
15 words	90%
19 words	80%
28 words	50%

Avoiding Three Common Sentence Faults

As you craft your sentences, beware of three common traps: fragments, run-on (fused) sentences, and comma-splice sentences. If any of these faults appears in a business message, the writer immediately loses credibility.

Fragments. One of the most serious errors a writer can make is punctuating a fragment as if it were a complete sentence. A fragment is usually a broken-off part of a complex sentence.

Fragments are broken-off parts of sentences and should not be punctuated as sentences.

Fragment	Revision
Because most transactions require a permanent record. Good writing skills are critical.	Because most transactions require a permanent record, good writing skills are critical.
The recruiter requested a writing sample. Even though the candidate seemed to communicate well.	The recruiter requested a writing sample even though the candidate seemed to communicate well.

Fragments often can be identified by the words that introduce them—words such as *although, as, because, even, except, for example, if, instead of, since, such as, that, which,* and *when*. These words introduce dependent clauses. Make sure such clauses always connect to independent clauses.

Run-On (Fused) Sentences. A sentence with two independent clauses must be joined by a coordinating conjunction (*and, or, nor, but*) or by a semicolon (;). Without a conjunction or a semicolon, a run-on sentence results.

When two independent clauses are run together without punctuation or a conjunction, a run-on (fused) sentence results.

Run-On	Revision
Most job seekers present a printed résumé some are also using Web sites as electronic portfolios.	Most job seekers present a printed résumé. Some are also using Web sites as electronic portfolios.
One candidate sent an e-mail résumé another sent a traditional résumé.	One candidate sent an e-mail résumé; another sent a traditional résumé.

Comma-Splice Sentences. A comma splice results when a writer joins (splices together) two independent clauses with a comma. Independent clauses may be joined with a coordinating conjunction (*and, or, nor, but*) or a conjunctive adverb (*however, consequently, therefore,* and others). Notice that clauses joined by coordinating conjunctions require only a comma. Clauses joined by a coordinating adverb require a semicolon. The three following examples illustrate three ways to revise comma splices. Notice that the first one uses a conjunction (*and*), the second uses a conjunctive adverb (*however*), and the third uses just a semicolon.

"Sentence fragments, comma splices, run-ons — who cares? I know what I meant!"

Comma Splice	Possible Revisions
Some employees responded by e-mail, others picked up the telephone.	Some employees responded by e-mail, and others picked up the telephone.
	Some employees responded by e-mail; however, others picked up the telephone.
	Some employees responded by e-mail; others picked up the telephone.

Improving Writing Techniques

Writers can significantly improve their messages by working on a few writing techniques. In this section we focus on emphasizing and de-emphasizing ideas, using active and passive voice strategically, developing parallelism, and avoiding dangling and misplaced modifiers.

Developing Emphasis

When you are talking with someone, you can emphasize your main ideas by saying them loudly or by repeating them slowly. You could even pound the table if you want to show real emphasis! Another way you could signal the relative importance of an idea is by raising your eyebrows or by shaking your head or whispering in a low voice. But when you write, you must rely on other means to tell your readers which ideas are more important than others. Emphasis in writing can be achieved primarily in two ways: mechanically or stylistically.

You can emphasize ideas mechanically by using underlining, italics, boldface, font changes, all caps, dashes, and tabulation.

Achieving Emphasis Through Mechanics. To emphasize an idea in print, a writer may use any of the following devices:

Underlining	Underlining draws the eye to a word.
Italics and boldface	Using *italics* or **boldface** conveys special meaning.
Font changes	Selecting a large, small, or *different* font draws interest.
All caps	Printing words in ALL CAPS is like shouting them.
Dashes	Dashes—used sparingly—can be effective.
Tabulation	Listing items vertically makes them stand out: 1. First item 2. Second item 3. Third item

Other means of achieving mechanical emphasis include the arrangement of space, color, lines, boxes, columns, titles, headings, and subheadings. Today's software and color printers provide a wonderful array of capabilities for setting off ideas. More tips on achieving emphasis are coming in Chapter 4, in which we cover document design.

You can emphasize ideas stylistically by using vivid words, labeling the main idea, and positioning the main idea strategically.

Achieving Emphasis Through Style. Although mechanical devices are occasionally appropriate, more often a writer achieves emphasis stylistically. That is, the writer chooses words carefully and constructs sentences skillfully to emphasize main ideas and de-emphasize minor or negative ideas. Here are four suggestions for emphasizing ideas stylistically:

- **Use vivid words.** Vivid words are emphatic because the reader can picture ideas clearly.

General	Vivid
One business uses *personal* selling techniques	*Avon* uses *face-to-face* selling techniques.
Someone will *contact* you *as soon as possible.*	*Ms. Stevens* will *telephone* you *before 5 p.m. tomorrow, May 3.*

- **Label the main idea.** If an idea is significant, tell the reader.

Unlabeled	Labeled
Consider looking for a job online, but also focus on networking.	Consider looking for a job online; but, *most important*, focus on networking.
We shop here because of the customer service and low prices.	We like the customer service, but the *primary reason* for shopping here is low prices.

- **Place the important idea first or last in the sentence.** Ideas have less competition from surrounding words when they appear first or last in a sentence. Observe how the concept of *productivity* can be emphasized by its position in the sentence:

Main Idea Lost	Main Idea Emphasized
Profit-sharing plans are more effective in increasing *productivity* when they are linked to individual performance rather than to group performance.	*Productivity* is more likely to be increased when profit-sharing plans are linked to individual performance rather than to group performance.

- **Place the important idea in a simple sentence or in an independent clause.** Don't dilute the effect of the idea by making it share the spotlight with other words and clauses.

Main Idea Lost	Main Idea Clear
Although you are the first trainee we have hired for this program, we had many candidates and expect to expand the program in the future. (Main idea is lost in a dependent clause.)	You are the first trainee we have hired for this program. (Simple sentence)

De-emphasizing When Necessary. To de-emphasize an idea, such as bad news, try one of the following stylistic devices:

You can de-emphasize ideas by using general words and placing the ideas in dependent clauses.

- **Use general words.**

Emphasizes Harsh Statement	De-emphasizes Harsh Statement
Our records indicate that *you were recently fired.*	Our records indicate that *your employment status has recently changed.*

- **Place the bad news in a dependent clause connected to an independent clause with something positive.** In sentences with dependent clauses, the main emphasis is always on the independent clause.

Emphasizes Bad News	De-emphasizes Bad News
We cannot issue you credit at this time, but we have a special plan that will allow you to fill your immediate needs on a cash basis.	Although credit cannot be issued at this time, you can fill your immediate needs on a cash basis with our special plan.

Using Active and Passive Voice

Writers prefer active-voice sentences because they are direct, clear, and concise; however, passive voice has distinct uses.

In composing messages, you may use active or passive voice to express your meaning. In active voice, the subject is the doer of the action (*The manager hired Jake*). In passive voice, the subject is acted upon (*Jake was hired [by the manager]*). Notice that in the passive voice, the attention shifts from the doer to the receiver of the action. You don't even have to reveal the doer if you choose not to. Writers generally prefer active voice because it is more direct, clear, and concise. Nevertheless, passive voice is useful in certain instances such as the following:

- **To emphasize an action or the recipient of the action.** *An investigation was launched.*
- **To de-emphasize negative news.** *Cash refunds cannot be made.*
- **To conceal the doer of an action.** *An error was made in our sales figures.*

How can you tell whether a verb is active or passive? Identify the subject of the sentence and decide whether the subject is doing the acting or is being acted upon. For example, in the sentence *An appointment was made for January 1*, the subject is *appointment*. The subject is being acted upon; therefore, the verb (*was made*) is passive. Another clue in identifying passive-voice verbs is that they generally include a *to be* helping verb, such as *is, are, was, were, be, being,* or *been*. Figure 3.4 summarizes effective uses for active and passive voice.

Achieving Parallelism

Balanced wording helps the reader anticipate and comprehend your meaning.

Parallelism is a skillful writing technique that involves balanced writing. Sentences written so that their parts are balanced or parallel are easy to read and understand. To achieve parallel construction, use similar structures to express similar ideas. For example, the words *computing, coding, recording,* and *storing* are parallel because the words all end in *-ing*. To express the list as *computing, coding, recording,* and *storage* is disturbing because the last item is not what the reader expects. Try to match nouns with nouns, verbs with verbs, and clauses with clauses. Avoid mixing active-voice verbs with passive-voice verbs. Your goal is to keep the wording balanced in expressing similar ideas.

FIGURE 3.4 Using Active and Passive Voice Effectively

Use active voice for directness, vigor, and clarity.

Direct and Clear in Active Voice	Indirect and Less Clear in Passive Voice
The manager completed performance reviews for all employees.	Performance reviews were completed for all employees by the manager.
Evelyn initiated a customer service blog last year.	A customer service blog was initiated last year.
IBM will accept applications after January 1.	Applications will be accepted after January 1 by IBM.
Coca-Cola created a Sprite page in Facebook to advertise its beverage.	A Sprite page was created in Facebook by Coca-Cola to advertise its beverage.

Use passive voice to be tactful or to emphasize the action rather than the doer.

Less Tactful or Effective in Active Voice	More Tactful or Effective in Passive Voice
We cannot grant you credit.	Credit cannot be granted.
The CEO made a huge error in projecting profits.	A huge error was made in projecting profits.
I launched a successful fitness program for our company last year.	A successful fitness program was launched for our company last year.
We are studying the effects of the Sarbanes-Oxley Act on our accounting procedures.	The effects of the Sarbanes-Oxley Act on our accounting procedures are being studied.

Lacks Parallelism	Illustrates Parallelism
The policy affected all vendors, suppliers, and *those involved with consulting.*	The policy affected all vendors, suppliers, and *consultants*. (Matches nouns)
Our primary goals are to increase productivity, reduce costs, and *the improvement of product quality*.	Our primary goals are to increase productivity, reduce costs, and *improve product quality*. (Matches verbs)
We are scheduled to meet in Atlanta on January 5, *we are meeting in Montreal on the 15th of March*, and in Chicago on June 3.	We are scheduled to meet in Atlanta on January 5, *in Montreal on March 15*, and in Chicago on June 3. (Matches phrases)
Shelby audits all accounts lettered A through L; accounts lettered M through Z are audited by Andrew.	Shelby audits all accounts lettered A through L; Andrew audits accounts lettered M through Z. (Matches clauses)
Our Super Bowl ads have three objectives: 1. We want to increase product use. 2. Introduce complementary products. 3. Our corporate image will be enhanced.	Our Super Bowl ads have three objectives: 1. Increase product use 2. Introduce complementary products 3. Enhance our corporate image (Matches verbs in listed items)

Avoiding Dangling and Misplaced Modifiers

For clarity, modifiers must be close to the words they describe or limit. A modifier dangles when the word or phrase it describes is missing from its sentence. For example, *After working overtime, the report was finally finished.* This sentence says the report was working overtime. Revised, the sentence contains a logical subject: *After working overtime, we finally finished the report.*

Modifiers must be close to the words they describe or limit.

A modifier is misplaced when the word or phrase it describes is not close enough to be clear. For example, *Firefighters rescued a dog from a burning car that had a broken leg.* Obviously, the car did not have a broken leg. The solution is to position the modifier closer to the word(s) it describes or limits: *Firefighters rescued a dog with a broken leg from a burning car.*

Introductory verbal phrases are particularly dangerous; be sure to follow them immediately with the words they logically describe or modify. Try this trick for detecting and remedying many dangling modifiers. Ask the question *Who*? or *What*? after any introductory phrase. The words immediately following should tell the reader who or what is performing the action. Try the *who?* test on the first three danglers here:

"To make this easy to read, I have divided it into three parts: A, B, and 3."

© Ted Goff www.tedgoff.com

Dangling or Misplaced Modifier	Clear Modification
Skilled at graphic design, the contract went to DesignOne.	Skilled at graphic design, DesignOne won the contract.
Working together as a team, the project was finally completed.	Working together as a team, we finally completed the project.
To meet the deadline, your Excel figures must be received by May 1.	To meet the deadline, you must send us your Excel figures by May 1.
The recruiter interviewed candidates who had excellent computer skills in the morning.	In the morning the recruiter interviewed candidates with excellent computer skills.
As an important customer to us, we invite you to our spring open house.	As you are an important customer to us, we invite you to our spring open house. *OR*: As an important customer to us, you are invited to our spring open house.

Drafting Powerful Paragraphs

A paragraph is a group of sentences about one idea. Paragraphs are most effective when they contain (a) a topic sentence, (b) support sentences that expand and explain only the main idea, and (c) techniques to build coherence.

Crafting Topic Sentences

Topic sentences explain the main idea of a paragraph and often appear first.

A topic sentence states the main idea of the paragraph. Business writers generally place the topic sentence first in the paragraph. It tells readers what to expect and helps them understand the paragraph's central thought immediately. In the revision stage, you will check to be sure each paragraph has a topic sentence. Notice in the following examples how the topic sentence summarizes the main idea, which will be followed by support sentences explaining the topic sentence:

> Flexible work scheduling could immediately increase productivity and enhance employee satisfaction in our entire organization. [Support sentences explaining flex scheduling would expand the paragraph.]
>
> The chat function at our main Web site is not functioning as well as we had expected. [Support sentences would describe existing problems in the Web chat function.]

Developing Support Sentences

Support sentences illustrate, explain, and strengthen the topic sentence.

Topic sentences summarize the main idea of a paragraph. Support sentences illustrate, explain, or strengthen the topic sentence. One of the hardest things for beginning writers to remember is that all support sentences in the paragraph must relate to the topic sentence. Any other topics should be treated separately. Support sentences provide specific details, explanations, and evidence:

> Flexible work scheduling could immediately increase productivity and enhance employee satisfaction in our entire organization. Managers would be required to maintain their regular hours. For many other employees, though, flexible scheduling permits extra time to manage family responsibilities. Feeling less stress, employees are able to focus their attention better at work; therefore, they become more relaxed and more productive.

Building Paragraph Coherence

Paragraphs are coherent when ideas are linked—that is, when one idea leads logically to the next. Well-written paragraphs take the reader through a number of steps. When the author skips from Step 1 to Step 3 and forgets Step 2, the reader is lost. Several techniques allow the reader to follow your ideas:

- **Repeat a key idea by using the same expression or a similar one:** *Employees treat guests as VIPs. These VIPs are never told what they can or cannot do.*
- **Use pronouns to refer to previous nouns:** *All new employees receive a two-week orientation. They learn that every staffer has a vital role.*
- **Show connections with transitional expressions:** *however, as a result, consequently*, and *meanwhile.* For a complete list, see Figure 3.5.

Controlling Paragraph Length

The most readable paragraphs contain eight or fewer printed lines.

Although no rule regulates the length of paragraphs, business writers recognize the value of short paragraphs. Paragraphs with eight or fewer printed lines look

FIGURE 3.5 Transitional Expressions to Build Coherence

To Add or Strengthen	To Show Time or Order	To Clarify	To Show Cause and Effect	To Contradict	To Contrast
additionally	after	for example	accordingly	actually	as opposed to
accordingly	before	for instance	as a result	but	at the same time
again	earlier	I mean	consequently	however	by contrast
also	finally	in other words	for this reason	in fact	conversely
beside	first	put another way	hence	instead	on the contrary
indeed	meanwhile	that is	so	rather	on the other hand
likewise	next	this means	therefore	still	previously
moreover	now	thus	thus	yet	similarly

inviting and readable. Long, solid chunks of print appear formidable. If a topic can't be covered in eight or fewer printed lines (not sentences), consider breaking it into smaller segments.

Composing the First Draft

Create a quiet place in which to write. Experts recommend freewriting for first drafts.

Once you have researched your topic, organized the data, and selected a pattern of organization, you are ready to begin composing. Communicators who haven't completed the preparatory work often suffer from "writer's block" and sit staring at a piece of paper or at the computer screen. Getting started is easier if you have organized your ideas and established a plan. Composition is also easier if you have a quiet environment in which to concentrate. Businesspeople with messages to compose set aside a given time and allow no calls, visitors, or other interruptions. This is a good technique for students as well.

As you begin composing, keep in mind that you are writing the first draft, not the final copy. Some experts suggest that you write quickly (*freewriting*). If you get your thoughts down quickly, you can refine them in later versions. Other writers, such as your authors, prefer to polish sentences as they go. Different writers have different styles. Whether you are a freewriter or a polisher, learn to compose your thoughts at your keyboard. You might be tempted to write a first draft by hand and then transfer it to the computer. This wastes time and develops poor habits. Businesspeople must be able to compose at their keyboards, and now is the time to develop that confidence and skill.

www.cengagebrain.com
Available with an access code, these eResources will help you prepare for exams:

- **Chapter Review Quizzes**
- **Personal Language Trainer**
- **PowerPoint Slides**
- **Flash Cards**

Summing Up and Looking Forward

This chapter explained the second phase of the writing process, which includes researching, organizing, and composing. Before beginning a message, every writer collects data, either formally or informally. For most simple messages, you would look in the files, talk with your boss, interview the target audience, or possibly conduct an informal survey. Information for a message is then organized into a list or an outline. Depending on the expected reaction of the receiver, the message can be organized directly (for positive reactions) or indirectly (for negative reactions or when persuasion is necessary).

In composing the first draft, writers should use a variety of sentence types and avoid fragments, run-on sentences, and comma splices. Emphasis can be achieved through mechanics (underlining, italics, font changes, all caps, and so forth) or through style (using vivid words, labeling the main idea, and positioning the important ideas strategically). Important writing techniques include skillfully using active- and passive-voice verbs, developing parallelism, and avoiding dangling or misplaced modifiers. Powerful paragraphs result from crafting a topic sentence, developing support sentences, and building coherence with the planned repetition of key ideas, the proper use of pronouns, and transitional expressions.

In Chapter 4 you will learn helpful techniques for the third phase of the writing process, which includes revising and proofreading.

Critical Thinking

1. What trends in business and what developments in technology are forcing workers to write more than ever before?
2. Molly, a 23-year-old college graduate with a 3.5 GPA, was hired as an administrative assistant. She was a fast learner on all the software, but her supervisor had to give her a little help with punctuation. On the ninth day of her job, she resigned saying: "I just don't think this job is a good fit. Commas, semicolons, spelling, typos. Those kinds of things just aren't all that important to me. They just don't matter."[1] For what kind of job is Molly qualified?
3. In a survey of teenagers, most admitted that they spend a considerable amount of their lives composing e-mails, instant messages, texts, and social network posts. Yet they did not consider these messages *real* writing.[2] What distinctions do you see between texting and workplace or academic writing?
4. When asked what to look for in hiring, Richard Anderson, CEO of Delta Air Lines, said, "You're looking for a really good work ethic [and] really good communication skills. More and more, the ability to speak well and write is important. You know, writing is not something that is taught as strongly as it should be in the educational curriculum."[3] Do you agree? In your education, was writing strongly taught?
5. **Ethical Issue:** Now that you have studied active and passive voice, what do you think when someone in government or business says that *mistakes were made*? Is it unethical to use the passive voice to avoid specifics?

Chapter Review

6. What are the three main activities involved in the second phase of the writing process?

7. Distinguish between formal and informal methods of researching data for a business message.

8. How do you make an outline?

9. What is *frontloading* and what are its advantages?

10. Distinguish between the direct and the indirect strategies. When is each appropriate?

11. How is a compound sentence different from a complex sentence? Give an example of each.

12. Distinguish between achieving emphasis mechanically and achieving it stylistically.

13. Ideally, sentences should be how long?

14. What is the difference between a topic sentence and support sentences?

15. What rule regulates the length of paragraphs?

Writing Improvement Exercises

Sentence Types

Your Task. For each of the numbered sentences, select the letter that identifies its type:

a Simple sentence
b Compound sentence
c Complex sentence
d Compound-complex sentence

16. Americans pride themselves on their informality. ________
17. When Americans travel abroad on business, their informality may be viewed negatively. ________
18. Informality in Asia often equals disrespect; it is not seen as a virtue. ________
19. The order of first and last names in Asia may be reversed, and this causes confusion to Americans and Europeans. ________
20. When you are addressing someone, ask which name a person would prefer to use; however, be sure you can pronounce it correctly. ________

Sentence Faults

Your Task. In the following, identify the sentence fault (fragment, run-on, comma splice). Then revise to remedy the fault.

21. Although they began as a side business for Disney. Destination weddings now represent a major income source.

22. About 2,000 weddings are held yearly. Which is twice the number just ten years ago.

23. Weddings may take place in less than one hour, however the cost may be as much as $5,000.

24. Limousines line up outside Disney's wedding pavilion, ceremonies are scheduled in two-hour intervals.

25. Many couples prefer a traditional wedding others request a fantasy experience.

Emphasis

Your Task. For each of the following sentences, circle (a) or (b). Be prepared to justify your choice.

26. Which is more emphatic?
    a. They offer a lot of products.
    b. CyberGuys offers computer, travel, and office accessories.
27. Which is more emphatic?
    a. Increased advertising would improve sales.
    b. Adding $50,000 in advertising would double our sales.
28. Which is more emphatic?
    a. We must consider several factors.
    b. We must consider cost, staff, and safety.
29. Which sentence places more emphasis on product loyalty?
    a. Product loyalty is the primary motivation for advertising.
    b. The primary motivation for advertising is loyalty to the product, although other purposes are also served.
30. Which sentence places more emphasis on the seminar?
    a. An executive training seminar that starts June 1 will include four candidates.
    b. Four candidates will be able to participate in an executive training seminar that we feel will provide a valuable learning experience.
31. Which sentence places more emphasis on the date?
    a. The deadline is April 1 for summer vacation reservations.
    b. April 1 is the deadline for summer vacation reservations.
32. Which is *less* emphatic?
    a. One division's profits decreased last quarter.
    b. Profits in consumer electronics dropped 15 percent last quarter.
33. Which sentence *de-emphasizes* the credit refusal?
    a. We cannot grant you credit at this time, but we welcome your cash business and encouage you to reapply in the future.
    b. Although credit cannot be granted at this time, we welcome your cash business and encourage you to reapply in the future.
34. Which sentence gives more emphasis to *leadership*?
    a. She has many admirable qualities, but most important is her leadership skill.
    b. She has many admirable qualities, including leadership skill, good judgment, and patience.
35. Which is more emphatic?
    a. We notified three departments: (1) Marketing, (2) Accounting, and (3) Distribution.
    b. We notified three departments:
        1. Marketing
        2. Accounting
        3. Distribution

Active-Voice Verbs

Your Task. Business writing is more forceful if it uses active-voice verbs. Revise the following sentences so that verbs are in the active voice. Put the emphasis on the doer of the action. Add subjects if necessary.

Example Antivirus software was installed on her computer.

Revision Madison installed antivirus software on her computer.

36. A company credit card was used by the manager to purchase office supplies.

37. To protect students, laws were passed in many states that prohibited the use of social security numbers as identification.

38. Checks are processed more quickly by banks because of new regulations.

39. Millions of packages are scanned by FedEx every night as packages stream through its Memphis hub.

Passive-Voice Verbs

Your Task. When indirectness or tact is required, use passive-voice verbs. Revise the following sentences so that they are in the passive voice.

Example Travis did not submit the proposal before the deadline.

Revision The proposal was not submitted before the deadline.

40. Accounting seems to have made a serious error in this report.

41. We cannot ship your order for smart surge protectors until May 5.

42. The government first issued a warning regarding the use of this pesticide more than 15 months ago.

43. Your insurance policy does not automatically cover damage to rental cars.

44. We cannot provide patient care unless patients show proof of insurance.

Parallelism

Your Task. Revise the following sentences so that their parts are balanced.

45. (**Hint:** Match verbs.) To improve your listening skills, you should stop talking, your surroundings should be controlled, be listening for main points, and an open mind must be kept.

46. (**Hint:** Match active voice of verbs.) Paula Day, director of the Okefenokee branch, will now supervise all Eastern Division operations; the Western Division will be supervised by our Oroville branch director, Reggie Kostiz.

47. (**Hint:** Match verb phrases.) Our newly hired employee has started using the computer and to learn her coworkers' names.

48. (**Hint:** Match adjectives.) Training seminars must be stimulating and a challenge.

49. Our new telecommunications software allows you to meet with customers over the Internet for training, Web-based meetings can be held, and other online collaboration within virtual teams is also facilitated.

50. We need more trained staff members, office space is limited, and the budget for overtime is much too small.

51. The application for a grant asks for this information: funds required for employee salaries, how much we expect to spend on equipment, and what is the length of the project.

52. Sending an e-mail establishes a more permanent record than to make a telephone call.

Dangling and Misplaced Modifiers

Your Task. Revise the following sentences to avoid dangling and misplaced modifiers.

53. When collecting information for new equipment, the Web proved to be my best resource.

54. To win the lottery, a ticket must be purchased.

55. The exciting Mandalay Bay is just one of the fabulous hotels you see strolling along the Las Vegas strip.

56. Angered by slow computer service, complaints were called in by hundreds of unhappy users.

Organizing Paragraph Sentences

Your Task. Study the following list of sentences from an interoffice memo to hospital staff.

1. *The old incident report form caused numerous problems and confusion.*
2. *One problem was that employees often omitted important information.*
3. *The Hospital Safety Committee has revised the form used for incident reports.*
4. *Another problem was that inappropriate information was often included that might expose the hospital to liability.*
5. *The Hospital Safety Committee has scheduled a lunchtime speaker to discuss prevention of medication mistakes.*
6. *Factual details about the time and place of the incident are important, but speculation on causes is inappropriate.*
7. *The new form will be available on April 1.*

57. Which sentence should be the topic sentence? ____________

58. Which sentence(s) should be developed in a separate paragraph? ____________

59. Which sentences should become support sentences? ____________

Building Coherent Paragraphs

Your Task. Revise the following paragraphs.

60. Improve the organization, coherence, and correctness of the following paragraph.

We feel that the "extreme" strategy has not been developed fully in the fast-food market. Pizza Hut is considering launching a new product called The Extreme. We plan to price this new pizza at $19.99. It will be the largest pizza on the market. It will have double the cheese. It will also have double the toppings. The plan is to target the X and Y Generations. The same target audience that would respond to an extreme product also reacts to low prices. The X and Y Generations are the fastest-growing segments in the fast-food market. These population segments have responded well to other marketing plans using the extreme strategy.

61. Use the following facts to construct a coherent paragraph with a topic sentence and appropriate transitional expressions in the supporting sentences.
    - *The federal government will penalize medical practices that don't adopt electronic medical records (EMRs).*
    - *Valley Medical Center is considering beginning converting soon.*
    - *Converting paper-based records to EMRs will be complex.*
    - *Converting will be technically challenging. It will probably be time-consuming and labor-intensive.*
    - *Converting should bring better patient care and maybe even lower costs in the long run.*
    - *The federal government provides funds to reimburse the cost of adopting the technology.*

62. Use the following facts to construct a coherent paragraph with a topic sentence and appropriate transitional expressions in the supporting sentences.
    - Nearly all teams experience conflict. They should recognize and expect it.
    - The most effective teams strive to eliminate destructive conflict and develop constructive conflict.
    - Destructive conflict arises when team members take criticism personally.
    - Destructive conflict poisons teamwork.
    - Conflict can become constructive.
    - Teams that encourage members to express their opinions may seem to be experiencing conflict when the opinions differ.
    - Better decisions often result when teams listen to and discuss many views.

Grammar/Mechanics Checkup—3

Verbs

Review Sections 1.10–1.15 in the Grammar Review section of the Grammar/Mechanics Handbook. Then study each of the following statements. Underline any verbs that are used incorrectly. In the space provided, write the correct form (or *C* if correct) and the number of the G/M principle illustrated. When you finish, compare your responses with those provided near the end of the book. If your responses differ, study carefully the principles in parentheses.

is ____ (1.10c) **Example** Are you certain that the database of our customers' names and addresses <u>are</u> secure?

______ 1. In the company's next annual report is a summary of our environmental audit and a list of charitable donations.

______ 2. Only one of the top-ranking executives have been insured.

______ 3. CityBank, along with 20 other large national banks, offer a variety of savings plans.

______ 4. Neither the plans that this bank offers nor the service just rendered by the teller are impressive.

______ 5. Finding a good bank and selecting a savings/checking plan often require considerable research and study.

______ 6. The budget analyst wants to know whether the Equipment Committee are ready to recommend a printer.

______ 7. Either of the printers that the committee selects is acceptable to the budget analyst.

______ 8. If Ms. Davis had chose the Maximizer Plus savings plan, her money would have earned maximum interest.

______ 9. Although the applications have laid there for two weeks, they may still be submitted.

______ 10. Jessica acts as if she was the manager.

_____________________ 11. One of the reasons that our Alaskan sales branches have been so costly are the high cost of living.

In the space provided, write the letter of the sentence that illustrates consistency in subject, voice, and mood.

_____________________ 12. a. If you read the instructions, the answer can be found.

b. If you read the instructions, you will find the answer.

_____________________ 13. a. All employees must fill out application forms; only then will you be insured.

b. All employees must fill out application forms; only then will they be insured.

_____________________ 14. a. First, take an inventory of equipment; then, order supplies.

b. First, take an inventory of equipment; then, supplies must be ordered.

_____________________ 15. a. Select a savings plan that suits your needs; deposits may be made immediately.

b. Select a savings plan that suits your needs; begin making deposits immediately.

Editing Challenge—3

As the employee with the best communication skills, you are frequently asked to edit messages. The following letter has faults in verbs, spelling, proofreading, sentence structure, parallelism, and other writing techniques studied in this chapter. You may (a) use standard proofreading marks (see Appendix B) to correct the errors here or (b) download the document from **www.cengagebrain.com** and revise at your computer.

Your instructor may ask you to use the **Track Changes** feature in Microsoft Word to show your editing comments. Turn on **Track Changes** on the **Review** tab. Click **Show Markup**. Place your cursor at an error, click **New Comment**, and key your edit in the bubble box provided. Study the guidelines in the Grammar/Mechanics Handbook as well as the lists of Confusing Words and Frequently Misspelled Words to sharpen your skills.

RAINTREE FINANCIAL SERVICES
CERTIFIED FINANCIAL PLANNERS
3392 Econlockhatchee Trail
Orlando, FL 32822-6588
407.891.2330
garth.peterson@raintree.com

Current date

Mrs. Julie Noriega
392 Blue Lagoon Way
Orlando, FL 32814

Dear Julie:

This is to inform you that, as your Financial Planner, I'm happy to respond to your request for clarification on the Tax status of eBay profits.

As you in all probability are all ready aware of, you can use eBay to clean out your closets or eBay can be used to run a small business. Your smart to enquire about your tax liability. Although there is no clear line that separates fun from profit or a hobby from a business. One thing is certin, the IRS taxs all income.

There are a number of factors that help determine whether or not your hobby should or should not be considered a business. To use eBay safely the following questions should be considered:

1. Do you run the operation in a businesslike manner? Do you keep records, is your profit and loss tracked, and how about keeping a seperate checking account?

2. Do you devote alot of time and effort to eBay? If you spend eighteen hours a day selling on eBay the IRS would tend to think your in a business.

3. Some people depend on the income from their eBay activities for their livelihood.

Are you selling items for more then they cost you? If you spend four dollars for a Garage Sale vase and sell it for fifty dollars the IRS would probably consider this a business transaction. All profits is taxable. Even for eBay sellers who are just playing around. If you wish to discuss this faarther please call me at 551-3791.

Sincerely,

Garth Peterson
Certified Financial Planner

Communication Workshop

Dos and Don'ts for Using Electronic Media Professionally

Dos: Know Workplace Policies and Avoid Private Use of Media at Work

- **Learn your company's rules.** One employee knew that her employer restricted personal use of work computers, but she believed it focused on Web surfing, not e-mail. She was stunned when her agency fired her after finding 418 personal e-mails on her PC.[4] Companies have been slow to adapt Internet policies to advances such as IM, texting, and tweeting. Being informed is your best protection.
- **Avoid or minimize sending personal e-mails, instant messages, and texts from work.** Even if your company allows personal use during lunch or after hours, keep it to a minimum. Better yet, wait to use your home computer to access your personal e-mail and social networking sites.
- **Separate work and personal data.** Keep information that could embarrass you or expose you to legal liability on your personal storage devices or hard drives, never on your office computer.

Dos: Treat All Online Speech as Public and Protect Your Computer

- **Be careful when blogging, tweeting, or posting on social networking sites.** A Canadian blogger lost his job for an entry that read, "Getting to blog for three hours while being paid: priceless."[5]
- **Keep your virus and malicious software protection current.** Always download the newest definitions and updates to your operating system, browser, antivirus program, and antispyware.
- **Pick strong passwords and vary them.** Use a combination of letters, numbers, and symbols. Select a different password for each Web service, and never use your Web passwords as PIN codes on credit or debit cards. Change your passwords every few months.
- **Keep sensitive information private.** Monitor the privacy settings on social networking sites, but don't trust the "private" areas on Facebook, Flickr, and other services that provide public access to most material they store.

Don'ts: Avoid Questionable Content, Personal Documents, and File Sharing

- **Don't send, download, print, or exhibit pornography, sexually explicit jokes, or inappropriate screen savers.** Anything that might "poison" the work environment is prohibited.
- **Don't download free software and utilities to company machines.** Employees can unwittingly introduce viruses, phishing schemes, and other cyber "bugs."

Career Application. One of the biggest problems of current organizations is developing appropriate electronic media policies. Many employees are unaware of the spoken and often unspoken rules of using electronic media on the job. What is allowed and what is prohibited?

Your Task. In teams discuss the preceding dos and don'ts. Do they seem reasonable? For example, should you store your music library and photos on company computers? How about sharing files and using file-sharing services? What harm could be done to the company? What could be wrong with downloading a movie during a slow period at work? How about using Google Docs?

Endnotes

[1] Booher, D. (2007). *The Voice of Authority.* New York: McGraw-Hill, p. 93.

[2] Lenhart, A., Arafeh, S., Smith, A., and Macgill, A. (2008, April 24). Writing, technology and teens. Pew Internet & American Life Project. Retrieved from http://www.pewinternet.org

[3] Anderson, R. as quoted in Bryant, A. (2009, April 26). He wants subjects, verbs and objects. *The New York Times,* p. 2 BU Y.

[4] Zetter, K. (2006, October). Employers crack down on personal net use: Misusing e-mail or browsing the wrong sites can cost you your job. *PC World,* p. 26. Retrieved from http://www.pcworld.com/article/126835/employers_crack_down_on_personal_net_use.html

[5] Breaton, S. (2007, January/February). Blogging: Priceless? *CA Magazine*, p. 13. Retrieved from http://search.ebscohost.com

Acknowledgments

p. 58 Office Insider based on Conference Board et al. (2006). Are they really ready to work? Retrieved from http://www.p21.org/documents/FINAL_REPORT_PDF9-29-06.pdf

p. 61 Office Insider cited in National Commission on Writing. (2003). The neglected "R": The need for a writing revolution. Retrieved from http://www.writingcommission.org/prod_downloads/writingcom/neglectedr.pdf

CHAPTER 4

Revising Business Messages

Go to

cengagebrain.com

and use your access code to unlock valuable student eResources.

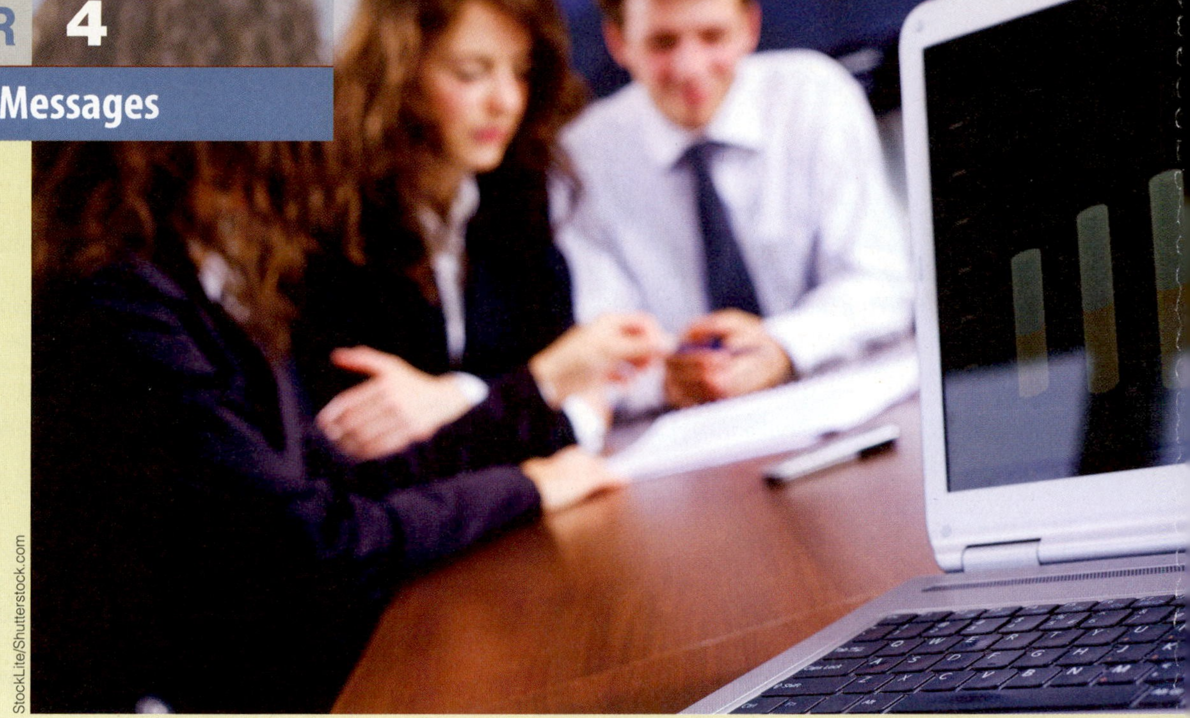

StockLite/Shutterstock.com

OBJECTIVES

After studying this chapter, you should be able to

- Enhance message conciseness by eliminating flabby expressions, limiting long lead-ins, dropping fillers, and rejecting redundancies.
- Revise messages to improve clarity by dumping trite business phrases, using jargon judiciously, avoiding slang, and dropping clichés.
- Revise messages to improve vigor and directness by unburying verbs, controlling exuberance, and choosing precise words.
- Understand document design and be able to use white space, margins, typefaces, fonts, numbered and bulleted lists, and headings to improve readability.
- Apply effective techniques for proofreading routine and complex documents both manually and digitally.

Managing the Process of Revision

Revision involves improving content, sentence structure, and design; proofreading involves improving grammar, spelling, punctuation, and mechanics.

One of the biggest problems with today's business messages is that they are written quickly and carelessly. Too many writers skip the last step in the writing process: revision. This chapter focuses on revising and proofreading. Revising involves improving the content and sentence structure of your message. It may include adding, cutting, recasting, reformatting, and redesigning what you have written. Proofreading involves improving the grammar, spelling, punctuation, and mechanics of your messages.

Rarely is the first or even the second version of a message satisfactory. Experts say that only amateurs expect writing perfection on the first try. The revision stage is your chance to make sure your message is clear, concise, and readable. This is the time when you will see how to draw out the major points and perhaps make a bulleted list so that the reader sees quickly what you mean.

Many professional writers compose the first draft quickly without worrying about language, precision, or correctness. Then they revise and polish extensively. Other writers, however, prefer to revise as they go—particularly for shorter business documents. Whether you revise as you go or do it when you finish a document, you will want to focus on concise wording.

Revising for Conciseness

In business, time is indeed money. Translated into writing, this means that concise messages save reading time and, thus, money. In addition, messages that are written directly and efficiently are easier to read and comprehend. In the revision process, look for shorter ways to say what you mean. Examine every sentence that you write. Could the thought be conveyed in fewer words? Your writing will be more concise if you eliminate flabby expressions, drop unnecessary introductory words, and get rid of redundancies.

OFFICE INSIDER

"Regardless of what you may have been taught in school, writing more doesn't necessarily equate to writing better—especially in a business environment, where time is precious. Don't bury your important points under unnecessary verbiage."

—Edwin Powell, *Office Solutions*

Eliminating Flabby Expressions

As you revise, focus on eliminating flabby expressions. This takes conscious effort. As one expert copyeditor observed, "Trim sentences, like trim bodies, usually require far more effort than flabby ones."[1] Turning out slim sentences and lean messages means that you will strive to "trim the fat." For example, notice the flabbiness in this sentence: *Due to the fact that sales are booming, profits are strong*. It could be said more concisely: *Because sales are booming, profits are strong.* Notice how the following flabby expressions could be said more concisely.

Main points are easier to understand in concise messages.

Flabby phrases can often be reduced to a single word.

Flabby	Concise
as a general rule	generally
at a later date	later
at this point in time	now, presently
despite the fact that	although
due to the fact that, inasmuch as, in view of the fact that	because
feel free to	please
for the period of, for the purpose of	for
in addition to the above	also
in all probability	probably
in the event that	if
in the near future	soon
in very few cases	seldom
until such time as	until
with regard to	about

Limiting Long Lead-Ins

Another way to create concise sentences is to delete unnecessary introductory words. Consider this sentence: *I am sending you this e-mail to announce that a new manager has been hired.* A more concise and more direct sentence deletes the long lead- in: *A new manager has been hired.* The meat of the sentence often follows the words *that* or *because,* as shown in the following:

Avoid long lead-ins that prevent the reader from reaching the meaning of the sentence.

Long Lead-Ins	Concise
We are sending this announcement to let everyone know that new parking permits will be available January 1.	New parking permits will be available January 1.
This is to inform you that you may find lower airfares at our Web site.	You may find lower airfares at our Web site.
I am writing this letter because Professor Brian Wilson suggested that your organization was hiring trainees.	Professor Brian Wilson suggested that your organization was hiring trainees.

Dropping Unnecessary *There is/are* and *It is/was* Fillers

In many sentences the expressions *there is/are* and *it is/was* function as unnecessary fillers. In addition to taking up space, these fillers delay getting to the point of the sentence. Eliminate them by recasting the sentence. Many—but not all—sentences can be revised so that fillers are unnecessary.

Wordy Fillers	Concise
There are only two administrative assistants to serve five managers.	Only two administrative assistants serve five managers.
There is a huge amount of work waiting for the temporary employee.	A huge amount of work is waiting for the temporary employee.
It was our auditor who discovered the theft.	Our auditor discovered the theft.

Rejecting Redundancies

Redundancies convey a meaning more than once.

Expressions that repeat meaning or include unnecessary words are redundant. Saying *unexpected surprise* is like saying *surprise surprise* because *unexpected* carries the same meaning as *surprise*. Excessive adjectives, adverbs, and phrases often create redundancies and wordiness. Redundancies do not add emphasis, as some people think. Instead, they identify a writer as inexperienced. As you revise, look for redundant expressions such as the following:

OFFICE INSIDER
"Employees, customers and investors increasingly want to be addressed in a clear and genuine way. Fuzzy and bombastic writing alienates these stakeholders."
—Ilja van Roon

Redundant	Concise
absolutely essential	essential
adequate enough	adequate
basic fundamentals	fundamentals *or* basics
big in size	big
combined together	combined
exactly identical	identical
each and every	each *or* every
necessary prerequisite	prerequisite
new beginning	beginning
refer back	refer
repeat again	repeat
true facts	facts

Revising for Clarity

Business writers appreciate clear messages that are immediately understandable. Techniques that improve clarity include dumping trite business phrases and avoiding slang, jargon, and clichés.

Dumping Trite Business Phrases

To sound "businesslike," many writers repeat the same stale expressions that other writers have used over the years. Your writing will sound fresher and more vigorous if you eliminate these phrases or find more original ways to convey the idea.

© AP Photo/Yomiuri Shimbun, Takuya Yoshino

WORKPLACE IN FOCUS

After a 9.0-magnitude Tokohu earthquake unleashed a devastating tsunami on northeastern Japan, attention turned to the Fukushima Daiichi power plant, where structural damage sparked worries that the facility's fuel rods would experience total meltdown. Scientists warned of the public's exposure to radioactive isotopes, and citizens flocked to drugstores to purchase doses of potassium iodide. Hazmat crews tested the Japanese people for contamination when radiation levels near the plant reached 400 millisieverts. ***How might writers report this historic event without using jargon?***

Trite	Improved
as per your request	as you request
pursuant to your request	at your request
enclosed please find	enclosed is/are
every effort will be made	we will try
in accordance with your wishes	as you wish
in receipt of	have received
please do not hesitate to	please
thank you in advance	thank you
under separate cover	separately
with reference to	about

Train yourself not to use these trite business expressions.

Avoiding Jargon and Slang

Except in certain specialized contexts, you should avoid jargon and unnecessary technical terms. Jargon is special terminology that is peculiar to particular activities or professions. For example, geologists speak knowingly of *exfoliation, calcareous ooze,* and *siliceous particles.* Engineers are familiar with phrases such as *infrared processing flags, output latches,* and *movable symbology.* Telecommunication experts use such words and phrases as *protocols, clickstream, neural networks,* and *asynchronous transmission.*

Jargon, which is terminology unique to certain professions, should be reserved for individuals who understand it.

Every field has its own special vocabulary. Using that vocabulary within the field is acceptable and even necessary for accurate, efficient communication. Don't use specialized terms, however, if you think your audience may misunderstand them.

Slang is composed of informal words with arbitrary and extravagantly changed meanings. Slang words quickly go out of fashion because they are no longer appealing when everyone begins to understand them. Consider the following statement of a government official who had been asked why his department was dropping a proposal to lease offshore oil lands: "The Administration has an awful lot of other things in the pipeline, and this has more wiggle room so they just moved it down the totem pole." He added, however, that

Slang sounds fashionable, but it lacks precise meaning and should be avoided in business writing.

the proposal might be offered again since "there is no pulling back because of hot-potato factors."

The meaning here, if the speaker really intended to impart any, is considerably obscured by the use of slang. If you want to sound professional, avoid expressions such as *snarky, lousy, blowing the budget, bombed,* and *getting burned.*

Dropping Clichés

Clichés are dull and often ambiguous.

Clichés are expressions that have become exhausted by overuse. Many cannot be explained, especially to those who are new to our culture. Clichés lack not only freshness but also clarity. Instead of repeating clichés such as the following, try to find another way to say what you mean.

below the belt	last but not least
better than new	make a bundle
beyond a shadow of a doubt	pass with flying colors
easier said than done	quick as a flash
exception to the rule	shoot from the hip
fill the bill	stand your ground
first and foremost	think outside the box
good to go	true to form

Revising for Vigor and Directness

Clear, effective business writing reads well and is immediately understood. You have already studied techniques for improving clarity and conciseness. You can also strengthen the vigor and directness of your writing by unburying verbs, controlling exuberance, and choosing precise words.

Unburying Verbs

Burying verbs in wordy noun expressions weakens business writing.

Buried verbs are those that are needlessly converted to wordy noun expressions. This happens when verbs such as *acquire, establish,* and *perform* are made into nouns such as *acquisition, establishment,* and *performance.* Such nouns often end in *-tion, -ment,* and *-ance.* Using these nouns increases sentence length, drains verb strength, slows the reader, and muddies the thought. Notice how you can make your writing cleaner and more forceful by avoiding wordy verb/noun conversions:

Buried Verbs	Unburied Verbs
conduct a discussion of	discuss
create a reduction in	reduce
engage in the preparation of	prepare
give consideration to	consider
make an assumption of	assume
make a discovery of	discover
perform an analysis of	analyze
reach a conclusion about	conclude
take action on	act

Controlling Exuberance

Occasionally we show our exuberance with words such as *very, definitely, quite, completely, extremely, really, actually,* and *totally*. These intensifiers can emphasize and strengthen your meaning. Overuse, however, sounds unbusinesslike. Control your enthusiasm and guard against excessive use.

Avoid excessive use of adverb intensifiers.

Excessive Exuberance	Businesslike
We *totally* agree that we *actually* did not *really* give his proposal a *very* fair trial.	We agree that we did not give his proposal a fair trial.
The manufacturer was *extremely* upset to learn that its printers were *definitely* being counterfeited.	The manufacturer was upset to learn that its printers were being counterfeited.

Choosing Clear, Precise Words

As you revise, make sure your words are precise so that the audience knows exactly what you mean. Clear writing creates meaningful images in the mind of the reader. Such writing is sparked by specific verbs, concrete nouns, and vivid adjectives. Foggy messages are marked by sloppy references that may require additional inquiries to clarify their meaning.

Less Precise	More Precise
She requested that everyone help out.	Our manager begged each team member to volunteer.
They will consider the problem soon.	Our steering committee will consider the recruitment problem on May 15.
We received many responses.	The Sales Division received 28 job applications.
Someone called about the meeting.	Russell Vitello called about the June 12 sales meeting

Plain Writing Movement

Many of the writing techniques you are learning are advocated in the Plain Writing Act recently passed by Congress. This act requires the federal government

to write documents—such as tax returns, federal college aid applications, and Veterans Administration forms—in simple, easy-to-understand language. Using plain language saves time and money for government agencies. For example, when the Veterans Benefits Administration revised a standard letter sent to veterans, inquiries dropped from an average of 1.5 calls for each letter sent to 0.27 calls.[2] Veterans could understand the plain version and didn't have to call for an explanation.

What does this new law mean for government workers? Just as you have been studying, they are being told to use the active voice, write short sentences and paragraphs, avoid redundancies and wordy expressions (*if* instead of *in the event that*), and use parallel phrasing. The new law also encourages writers to improve the readability of government documents by including white space, informative headings, and vertical lists. You will learn more about implementing these and other readability suggestions in the next section.

Designing Documents for Readability

Successful document design improves readability, strengthens comprehension, and enhances your image.

Well-designed documents improve your messages in two important ways. First, they enhance readability and comprehension. Second, they make readers think you are a well-organized and intelligent person. In the revision process, you have a chance to adjust formatting and make other changes so that readers grasp your main points quickly. Significant design techniques to improve readability include appropriate use of white space, margins, typefaces, numbered and bulleted lists, and headings for visual impact.

Employing White Space

Empty space on a page is called *white space*. A page crammed full of text or graphics appears busy, cluttered, and unreadable. To increase white space, use headings, bulleted or numbered lists, short paragraphs, and effective margins. As discussed earlier, short sentences (20 or fewer words) and short paragraphs (eight or fewer printed lines) improve readability and comprehension. As you revise, think about shortening long sentences. Also consider breaking up long paragraphs into shorter chunks. Be sure, however, that each part of the divided paragraph has a topic sentence.

Understanding Margins and Text Alignment

Business documents are most readable with left-aligned text and ragged-right margins.

Margins determine the white space on the left, right, top, and bottom of a block of type. They define the reading area and provide important visual relief. Business letters and memos usually have side margins of 1 to 1.5 inches.

Your word processing program probably offers four forms of margin alignment: (a) lines align only at the left, (b) lines align only at the right, (c) lines align at both left and right (*justified*), and (d) lines are centered. Nearly all text in Western cultures is aligned at the left and reads from left to right. The right margin may be *justified* or *ragged right.* The text in books, magazines, and other long works is often justified on the left and right for a formal appearance.

However, justified text may require more attention to word spacing and hyphenation to avoid awkward empty spaces or "rivers" of spaces running through a document. When right margins are "ragged"—that is, without alignment or justification—they provide more white space and improve readability. Therefore, you are best served by using left-justified text and ragged-right margins without justification. Centered text is appropriate for headings but not for complete messages.

Choosing Appropriate Typefaces

Times New Roman is a typeface with serifs; Arial is a typeface without serifs (*sans serif*).

Business writers today may choose from a number of typefaces on their word processors. A typeface defines the shape of text characters. As shown in Figure 4.1, a wide range of typefaces is available for various purposes. Some are decorative and useful for special purposes. For most business messages, however, you should choose from *serif* or *sans serif* categories.

Serif typefaces have small features at the ends of strokes. The most common serif typeface is Times New Roman. Other popular serif typefaces are Century, Georgia, and Palatino. Serif typefaces suggest tradition, maturity, and formality. They are frequently used for body text in business messages and longer documents. Because books, newspapers, and magazines favor serif typefaces, readers are familiar with them.

Sans serif typefaces include Arial, Calibri, Gothic, Tahoma, Helvetica, and Univers. These clean characters are widely used for headings, signs, and material that does not require continuous reading. Web designers often prefer sans serif typefaces for simple, pure pages. For longer documents, however, sans serif typefaces may seem colder and less accessible than familiar serif typefaces.

For less formal messages or special decorative effects, you might choose one of the happy fonts such as Comic Sans or a bold typeface such as Impact. You can simulate handwriting with a script typeface. Despite the wonderful possibilities available on your word processor, don't get carried away with fancy typefaces. All-purpose sans serif and traditional serif typefaces are most appropriate for your business messages. Generally, use no more than two typefaces within one document.

Capitalizing on Type Fonts and Sizes

Fonts include caps, boldface, italic, underline, outline, and shadow.

Font refers to a specific style (such as *italic*) within a typeface family (such as Times Roman). Most typeface families offer various fonts such as CAPITALIZATION,

FIGURE 4.1 Typefaces with Different Personalities for Different Purposes

All-Purpose Sans Serif	Traditional Serif	Happy, Creative Script/Funny	Assertive, Bold Modern Display	Plain Monospaced
Arial	Century	Brush Script	Britannic Bold	Courier New
Calibri	Garamond	Comic Sans	Broadway	Letter Gothic
Helvetica	Georgia	Gigi	Elephant	Monaco
Tahoma	Goudy	Jokerman	Impact	Prestige Elite
Univers	Palatino	Lucinda	Bauhaus 93	
Verdana	Times New Roman	Kristen	SHOWCARD	

Small Caps, **boldface**, *italic*, and underline, as well as fancier fonts such as outline and shadow.

As discussed in Chapter 5, font styles are a mechanical means of adding emphasis to your words. ALL CAPS, Small Caps, and **bold** are useful for headings, subheadings, and single words or short phrases in the text. ALL CAPS, HOWEVER, SHOULD NEVER BE USED FOR LONG STRETCHES OF TEXT BECAUSE ALL THE LETTERS ARE THE SAME HEIGHT, MAKING IT DIFFICULT FOR READERS TO DIFFERENTIATE WORDS. In addition, excessive use of all caps feels like shouting, and it irritates readers. **Boldface**, *italics*, and underlining are effective for calling attention to important points and terms. Be cautious, however, when using fancy or an excessive number of font styles. Don't use them if they will confuse, annoy, or delay readers.

During the revision process, think about type size. Readers are generally most comfortable with 10- to 12-point type for body text. Smaller type enables you to fit more words into a space. Tiny type, however, makes text look dense and unappealing. Slightly larger type makes material more readable. Overly large type (14 points or more), however, looks amateurish and out of place for body text in business messages. Larger type, however, is appropriate for headings.

Numbering and Bulleting Lists for Quick Comprehension

Improve the "skim value" of a message by adding high-visibility vertical lists.

One of the best ways to ensure rapid comprehension of ideas is with numbered or bulleted lists. Lists provide high "skim value." This means that readers can browse quickly and grasp main ideas. By breaking up complex information into smaller chunks, lists improve readability, understanding, and retention. They also force the writer to organize ideas and write efficiently.

In the revision process, look for ideas that could be converted to lists and follow these techniques to make your lists look professional:

- **Numbered lists:** Use for items that represent a sequence or reflect a numbering system.
- **Bulleted lists:** Use to highlight items that don't necessarily show a chronology.
- **Capitalization:** Capitalize the initial word of each line.
- **Punctuation:** Add end punctuation only if the listed items are complete sentences.
- **Parallelism:** Make all the lines consistent; for example, start each with a verb.

Numbered lists represent sequences; bulleted lists highlight items that may not show a sequence.

In the following examples, notice that the list on the left presents a sequence of steps with numbers. The bulleted list does not show a sequence of ideas; therefore, bullets are appropriate. Also notice the parallelism in each example. In the numbered list, each item begins with a verb. In the bulleted list, each item follows an adjective/noun sequence. Business readers appreciate lists because they focus attention. Be careful, however, not to use so many that your messages look like grocery lists.

Numbered List

Our recruiters follow these steps when hiring applicants:

1. Examine the application.
2. Interview the applicant.
3. Check the applicant's references.

Bulleted List

To attract upscale customers, we feature the following:

- Quality fashions
- Personalized service
- A generous return policy

Adding Headings for Visual Impact

Headings help writers to organize information and enable readers to absorb important ideas.

Headings are an effective tool for highlighting information and improving readability. They encourage the writer to group similar material together. Headings help the reader separate major ideas from details. They enable a busy reader to skim familiar or less important information. They also provide a quick preview or review. Headings appear most often in reports, which you will study more fully in Chapters 9 and 10. However, main headings, subheadings, and category headings can also improve readability in e-mails, memos, and letters. In the following example, they are used with bullets to summarize categories:

Category Headings

Our company focuses on the following areas in the employment process:

- **Attracting applicants.** We advertise for qualified applicants, and we also encourage current employees to recommend good people.
- **Interviewing applicants.** Our specialized interviews include simulated customer encounters as well as scrutiny by supervisors.
- **Checking references.** We investigate every applicant thoroughly. We contact former employers and all listed references.

In Figure 4.2, on page 94, the writer was able to convert a dense, unappealing e-mail into an easier-to-read version by applying document design. Notice that the all-caps font in the first paragraph makes its meaning difficult to decipher. Justified margins and lack of white space further reduce readability. In the revised version, the writer changed the all-caps font to upper- and lowercase and also used ragged-right margins to enhance visual appeal. One of the best document design techniques in this message is the use of headings and bullets to help the reader see chunks of information in similar groups. All of these improvements are made in the revision process. You can make any message more readable by applying the document design techniques presented here.

Recording Proofreading Edits Manually and Digitally

As you proofread, you will want to make changes or edits. You can do this immediately, or you can mark the document to show the edits. Marking edits is particularly important when you are collaborating or if you need a record of document changes. You can show edits manually or digitally. On printed documents you will manually use proofreading marks to show your edits. On digital documents you have a variety of electronic tools. However, before you study proofreading markup tools, you need to know what to watch for in proofreading both routine and complex documents.

What to Watch for in Proofreading

Once your message is in its final form, set aside time to proofread. Don't proofread earlier because you may waste time checking items that eventually are changed or omitted. Careful proofreaders check for problems in these areas:

Proofreading before a document is completed is generally a waste of time.

- **Spelling.** Now is the time to consult the dictionary. Is *recommend* spelled with one or two *c*'s? Do you mean *affect* or *effect*? Use your computer spell-checker, but don't rely on it totally.
- **Grammar.** Locate sentence subjects; do their verbs agree with them? Do pronouns agree with their antecedents? Review the principles in the Grammar/Mechanics Handbook if necessary. Use your computer's grammar checker, but don't let it replace careful manual proofreading.
- **Punctuation.** Make sure that introductory clauses are followed by commas. In compound sentences put commas before coordinating conjunctions (*and, or, but, nor*). Double-check your use of semicolons and colons.

FIGURE 4.2 Using Document Design to Improve Readability

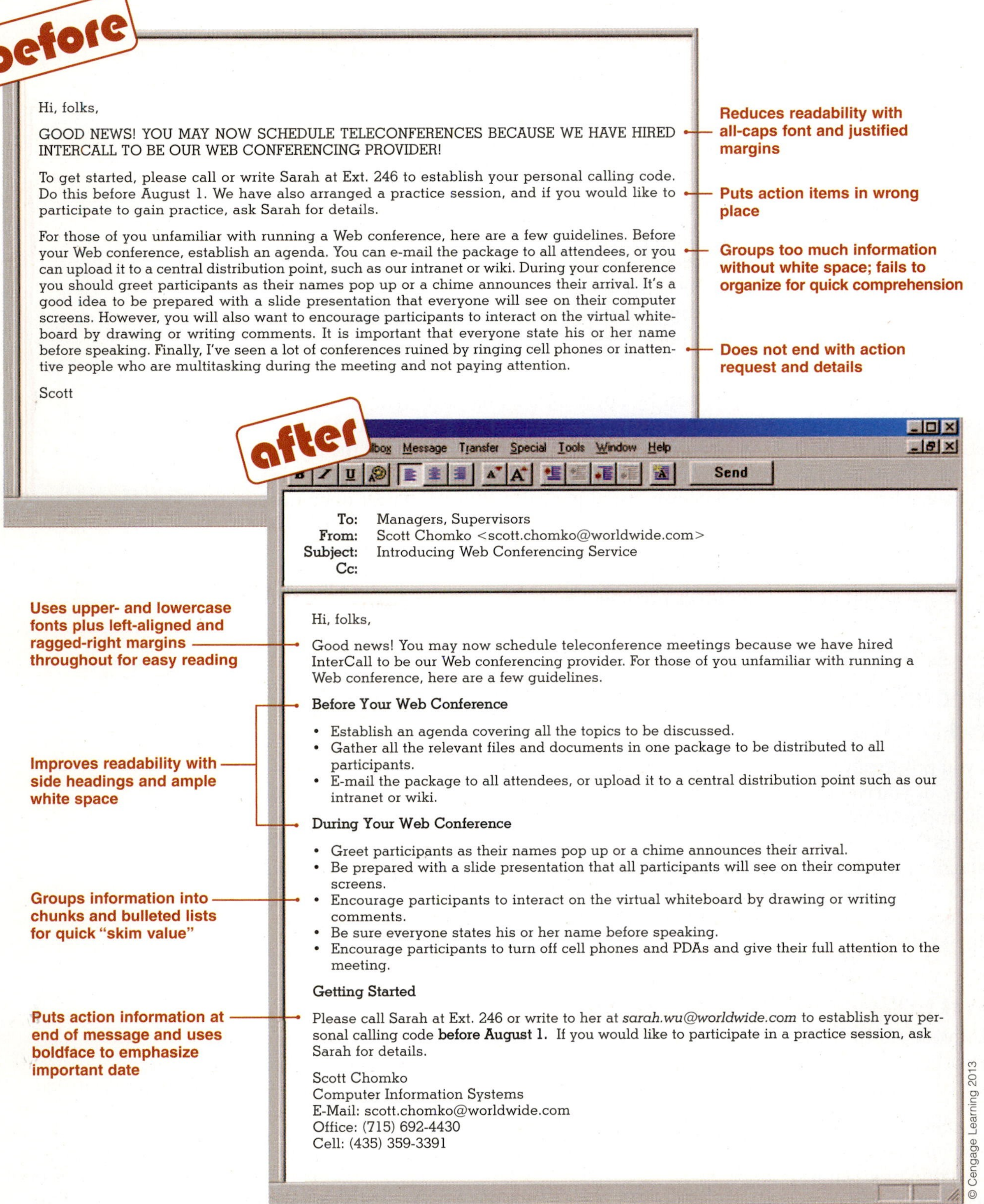

before

Hi, folks,

GOOD NEWS! YOU MAY NOW SCHEDULE TELECONFERENCES BECAUSE WE HAVE HIRED INTERCALL TO BE OUR WEB CONFERENCING PROVIDER!

To get started, please call or write Sarah at Ext. 246 to establish your personal calling code. Do this before August 1. We have also arranged a practice session, and if you would like to participate to gain practice, ask Sarah for details.

For those of you unfamiliar with running a Web conference, here are a few guidelines. Before your Web conference, establish an agenda. You can e-mail the package to all attendees, or you can upload it to a central distribution point, such as our intranet or wiki. During your conference you should greet participants as their names pop up or a chime announces their arrival. It's a good idea to be prepared with a slide presentation that everyone will see on their computer screens. However, you will also want to encourage participants to interact on the virtual whiteboard by drawing or writing comments. It is important that everyone state his or her name before speaking. Finally, I've seen a lot of conferences ruined by ringing cell phones or inattentive people who are multitasking during the meeting and not paying attention.

Scott

Reduces readability with all-caps font and justified margins
Puts action items in wrong place
Groups too much information without white space; fails to organize for quick comprehension
Does not end with action request and details

after

Message Transfer Special Tools Window Help
Send

To: Managers, Supervisors
From: Scott Chomko <scott.chomko@worldwide.com>
Subject: Introducing Web Conferencing Service
Cc:

Hi, folks,

Good news! You may now schedule teleconference meetings because we have hired InterCall to be our Web conferencing provider. For those of you unfamiliar with running a Web conference, here are a few guidelines.

Before Your Web Conference

- Establish an agenda covering all the topics to be discussed.
- Gather all the relevant files and documents in one package to be distributed to all participants.
- E-mail the package to all attendees, or upload it to a central distribution point such as our intranet or wiki.

During Your Web Conference

- Greet participants as their names pop up or a chime announces their arrival.
- Be prepared with a slide presentation that all participants will see on their computer screens.
- Encourage participants to interact on the virtual whiteboard by drawing or writing comments.
- Be sure everyone states his or her name before speaking.
- Encourage participants to turn off cell phones and PDAs and give their full attention to the meeting.

Getting Started

Please call Sarah at Ext. 246 or write to her at *sarah.wu@worldwide.com* to establish your personal calling code **before August 1.** If you would like to participate in a practice session, ask Sarah for details.

Scott Chomko
Computer Information Systems
E-Mail: scott.chomko@worldwide.com
Office: (715) 692-4430
Cell: (435) 359-3391

Uses upper- and lowercase fonts plus left-aligned and ragged-right margins throughout for easy reading
Improves readability with side headings and ample white space
Groups information into chunks and bulleted lists for quick "skim value"
Puts action information at end of message and uses boldface to emphasize important date

- **Names and numbers.** In proofreading, compare all names and numbers with their sources because inaccuracies are not immediately visible. Especially verify the spelling of the names of individuals receiving the message. Most of us are offended when someone misspells our name.

- **Format.** As you proofread, be sure that letters, printed memos, and reports are balanced on the page. Compare their parts and formats with those of standard documents shown in Appendix A. If you indent paragraphs, be certain that all are indented.

"But there can't be any errors. My grammar and spell checkers found nothing wrong!"

© Randy Glasbergen www.glasbergen.com

How to Proofread Routine Documents

Most routine messages, including e-mails, require a light proofreading.

- To proofread documents at your computer, use the down arrow to reveal one line at a time, thus focusing your attention at the bottom of the screen.
- Read carefully for faults such as omitted or doubled words. Be sure to use your spell-checker.
- To proofread printed letters or memos, read from a hard copy. You are more likely to find errors and to observe the tone when you do.

How to Proofread Complex Documents

Long, complex, or important documents demand more careful proofreading using the following techniques:

For complex documents, it is best to proofread from a printed copy, not on a computer screen.

- Print a copy, preferably double-spaced, and set it aside for at least a day. You will be more alert after a breather.
- Allow adequate time to proofread carefully. A common excuse for sloppy proofreading is lack of time.
- Be prepared to find errors. One student confessed, "I can find other people's errors, but I can't seem to locate my own." Psychologically, we don't expect to find errors, and we don't want to find them. You can overcome this obstacle by anticipating errors and congratulating, not criticizing, yourself each time you find one.
- Read the message at least twice—once for word meanings and once for grammar/mechanics. For very long documents (book chapters and long articles or reports), read a third time to verify consistency in formatting.
- Reduce your reading speed. Concentrate on individual words rather than ideas.

© AP Photo/News & Record, Joseph Rodriguez

WORKPLACE IN FOCUS

In situations like the one pictured here, typos are amusing. But in business situations, typos result in angry clients and lost profits. At Verizon a copy error on an employee benefit plan increased the balances of some 13,800 participants. The mistake nearly cost the phone company $1.67 billion, but the U.S. Seventh Circuit Court of Appeals ruled that Verizon could correct the error. One judge remarked, "People make mistakes, even administrators of ERISA plans." ***What can writers do to prevent costly typos?***

- For documents that must be perfect, have someone read the message aloud. The reader should spell names and difficult words, note capitalization, and read punctuation.
- Use standard proofreading marks, shown in Figure 4.3, to indicate changes.

Your computer word processing program may include a style- or grammar-checker. These programs generally analyze aspects of your writing style, including readability level and the use of passive voice, trite expressions, split infinitives, and wordy expressions. To do so, they use sophisticated algorithms (step-by-step procedures) to identify significant errors. In addition to finding spelling and typographical errors, grammar-checkers can find subject–verb problems, word misuse, spacing irregularities, punctuation problems, and other faults. However, they won't find everything. Although grammar- and spell-checkers can help you a great deal, you need to be the final proofreader.

Understanding Manual and Digital Proofreading

When revising printed documents, you will manually apply standard proofreading marks, such as those shown in Figure 4.3. Some people refer to this as "hard" proofing because you are marking hard copies. Today, however, you will often be proofreading and marking digital documents. This is especially true when you are collaborating with someone who is not nearby.

Revising digital documents with digital proofing tools is known as "soft" proofing. Soft proofing has many advantages. Corrections and edits can be transferred electronically among authors, editors, proofreaders, and typesetters—and then on to the printer without pen ever touching paper. Revising digitally can save mailing costs and days of production time by avoiding sending hard-copy proofs back and forth. The disadvantages of soft proofing include tired eyes, especially

FIGURE 4.3 Proofreading Marks

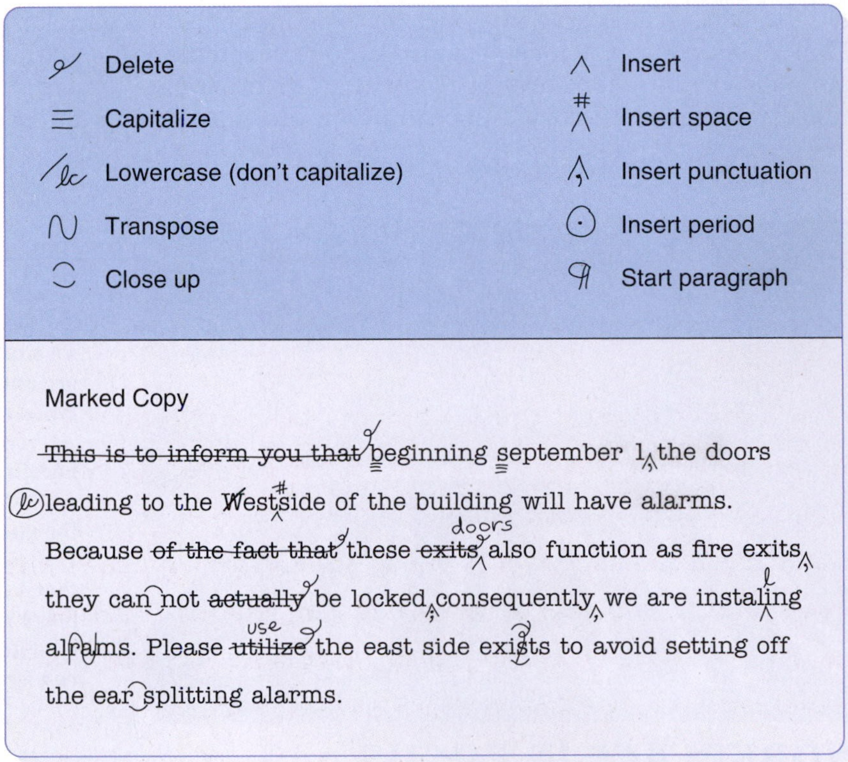

Mark	Meaning	Mark	Meaning
℘	Delete	∧	Insert
≡	Capitalize	# ∧	Insert space
/lc	Lowercase (don't capitalize)	∧ (with ,)	Insert punctuation
∩∪	Transpose	⊙	Insert period
⁀‿	Close up	¶	Start paragraph

Marked Copy

~~This is to inform you that~~ beginning september 1, the doors leading to the West side of the building will have alarms. Because ~~of the fact that~~ these ~~exits~~ doors also function as fire exits, they can not ~~actually~~ be locked, consequently, we are instaling alrams. Please ~~utilize~~ use the east side exists to avoid setting off the ear splitting alarms.

when you are working on long documents. An even greater disadvantage is the fear of losing your work because of a computer crash.

Regardless of its hazards, digital proofing is definitely a skill you should learn. You have a number of tool options. You might use simple word processing tools such as strikethrough and color. In the example shown in Figure 4.4, strikethroughs in red identify passages to be deleted. The strikethrough function is located on the **Font** tab in MS Word. We used blue to show inserted words, but you may choose any color you prefer. Another way to revise digitally is to use the MS Word **Comment** and **Track Changes** features, which are discussed and illustrated in the Communication Workshop feature starting on page 105.

How to Proofread and Revise PDF Files

As business writers depend more and more on PDF (portable document format) documents, you will want to learn how to edit them. A rich array of PDF tools from Adobe Acrobat can make markup and work flow fairly intuitive. That is, you can usually see how to perform a function without reading instructions. You can insert, replace, highlight, delete, or underline material as well as add notes, all with an insertion point that looks like that used in traditional proofreading, as shown in Figure 4.5. Adobe Acrobat enables you to add comments easily, but these markup tools require special software and practice to use effectively.

FIGURE 4.4 Showing Revisions Manually and Digitally

Revising Printed Documents Manually

~~This is a short note to let you know that,~~ as you requested, I ~~made an~~ investigat~~ion of~~ ed several of our competitors' Web sites. Attached ~~hereto~~ is a summary of my findings. ~~of my investigation.~~ I was ~~really~~ most interested in comparing ~~making a comparison of the employment of strategies for~~ marketing strategies as well as ~~the use of~~ navigational graphics ~~used~~ to guide visitors through the sites. ~~In view of the fact that~~ Because we will be revising our own Web site ~~in the near future,~~ soon I was ~~extremely~~ intrigued by the organization, ~~kind of~~ marketing tactics, and navigation at ~~each and~~ every site I visited.

Revising Printed Documents Digitally

~~This is a short note to let you know that, as~~ As you requested, I ~~made an investigation of~~ investigated several of our competitors' Web sites. Attached ~~hereto~~ is a summary of my findings. ~~of my investigation.~~ I was ~~really~~ most interested in ~~making a comparison of the employment of strategies for~~ comparing marketing strategies as well as ~~the use of~~ navigational graphics ~~used~~ to guide visitors through the sites. ~~In view of the fact that~~ Because we will be revising our own Web site ~~in the near future~~ soon, I was ~~extremely~~ intrigued by the organization, ~~kind of~~ marketing tactics, and navigation at ~~each and~~ every site I visited.

FIGURE 4.5 Proofreading and Marking PDF Files

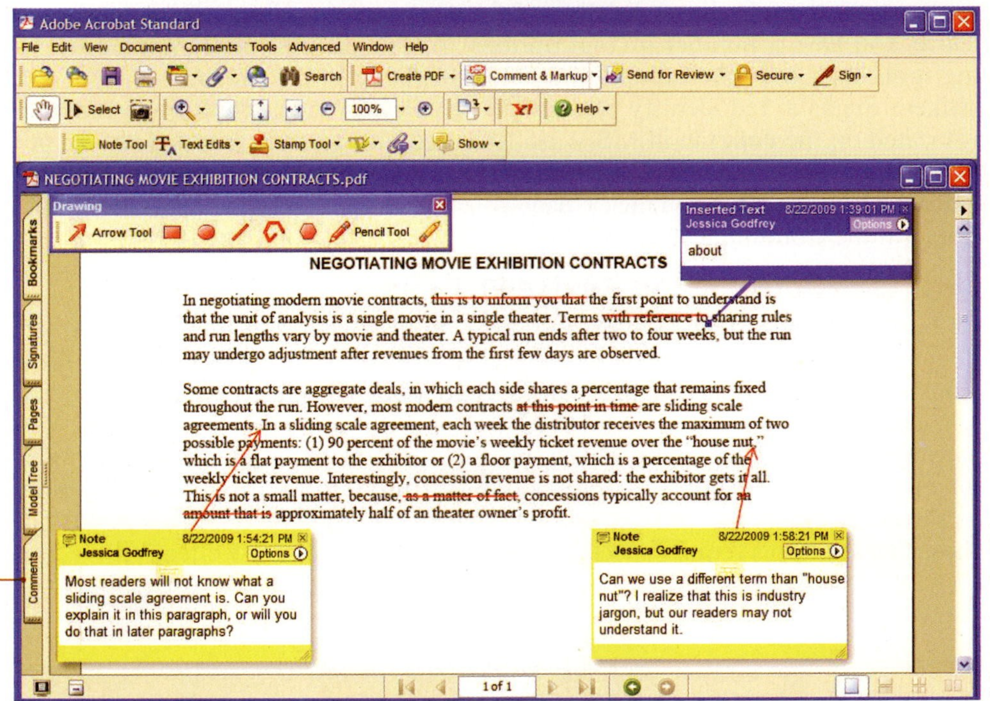

You may proofread and edit PDF files by using Adobe Acrobat software, which allows you to insert, replace, highlight, delete, and underline material as well as add notes.

www.cengagebrain.com

Available with an access code, these eResources will help you prepare for exams:

- **Chapter Review Quizzes**
- **Personal Language Trainer**
- **PowerPoint Slides**
- **Flash Cards**

Summing Up and Looking Forward

Revision is the most important part of the writing process. To revise for conciseness, look for flabby phrases that can be shortened (such as *at this point in time*). Eliminate long lead-ins (*This is to inform you that*), fillers (*There are*), and redundancies (*combined together*). To revise for clarity, dump trite business phrases (*pursuant to your request*), confusing jargon, slang, and clichés (*think outside the box*). To revise for vigor and directness, unbury verbs (use *examine* rather than *make an examination*), control exuberance, and choose precise words.

To improve readability, employ document design principles. Use ample white space, ragged-right margins, and appropriate typefaces and fonts. Include numbered lists and bulleted lists as well as headings to help readers comprehend messages quickly.

After revising a message, you are ready for the last step in the writing process: proofreading. Watch for irregularities in spelling, grammar, punctuation, names and numbers, and format. Although routine messages may be proofread on the screen, you will have better results if you proofread from a printed copy. Complex documents should be printed, put away for a day or so, and then proofread several times.

Manual proofreading requires the insertion of proofreading marks on hard copies. Digital proofing requires the use of electronic tools to show edits on digital documents. PDF (portable document format) documents call for special software to mark edits.

In these opening chapters, you have studied the writing process. You have also learned many practical techniques for becoming an effective business communicator. Now you can put these techniques to work. Chapter 5 introduces you to writing electronic messages and managing digital media. Later chapters present opportunities to apply the writing process and composition techniques to positive, negative, and persuasive messages as well as to reports and presentations.

Critical Thinking

1. You work in an insurance office where you are expected to use a book of boilerplate paragraphs to respond to customer inquiries. Many of these paragraphs use flabby expressions, trite business phrases, long lead-ins, and other writing faults you have studied. What should you do?
2. You have just submitted a beautifully researched report. But your supervisor focused on the two or three little errors that you missed and gave none of the praise you expected. Was this fair of your supervisor?
3. It's easy to use clichés because they just roll off the tongue. What's wrong with tried-and-true expressions such as *it is what it is* or *at the end of the day*?
4. Whether editing your own writing or someone else's, why is it important to use a set of standard proofreading marks?
5. How can you overcome defensiveness when your writing is criticized constructively?

Chapter Review

6. How is proofreading different from revising?

7. Why should business writers strive for conciseness?

8. What's wrong with expressions such as *due to the fact that* and *in view of the fact that*?

9. What's wrong with expressions such as *necessary prerequisite* and *small in size*?

10. Why should writers avoid the opening *I am sending this e-mail because . . .*?

11. Why should writers avoid opening a sentence or clause with *there is* or *there are*?

12. What is a buried verb? Give an original example. Why should writers avoid buried verbs?

13. What design techniques can you use to improve the readability of e-mails, memos, letters, and reports?

14. In proofreading, why is it difficult to find your own errors? How can you overcome this barrier?

15. What are the differences between editing manually and editing digitally? What tools are used for each?

Writing Improvement Exercises

Flabby Expressions

Your Task. Revise the following sentences to eliminate flabby phrases.

16. We cannot complete the construction at this point in time due to the fact that building costs have jumped at a considerable rate.

17. In the normal course of events, we would seek additional funding; however, in view of the fact that rates have increased, we cannot.

18. In very few cases has it been advisable for us to borrow money for a period of 90 or fewer days.

19. Inasmuch as our sales are increasing in a gradual manner, we might seek a loan in the amount of $50,000.

20. Despite the fact that we have had no response to our bid, we are still available in the event that you wish to proceed with your building project.

Long Lead-Ins

Your Task. Revise the following to eliminate long lead-ins.

21. This is an announcement to tell you that parking permits are available in the office.

22. We are sending this memo to notify everyone that anyone who wants to apply for telecommuting may submit an application immediately.

23. I am writing this letter to inform you that your new account executive is Edward Ho.

24. This is to warn you that cyber criminals use sophisticated tools to decipher passwords rapidly.

There is/are and *It is/was* Fillers

Your Task. Revise the following to avoid unnecessary *there is/are* and *it is/was* fillers.

25. There is a password-checker that can evaluate your password's strength automatically.

26. It is careless or uninformed individuals who are the most vulnerable to computer hackers.

27. There are computers in Internet cafes, at conferences, and in airport lounges that should be considered unsafe for any personal use.

28. A computer specialist told us that there are keystroke-logging devices that gather information typed on a computer, including passwords.

Redundancies

Your Task. Revise the following to avoid redundancies.

29. Because his laptop was small in size, he could carry it everywhere.

30. A basic fundamental of computer safety is to avoid storing your password on a file in your computer because criminals will look there first.

31. The manager repeated again his warning that we must use strong passwords.

32. Although the two files seem exactly identical, we should proofread each and every page.

Trite Business Phrases

Your Task. Revise the following sentences to eliminate trite business phrases.

33. Pursuant to your request, I will submit your repair request immediately.

34. Enclosed please find the list of customers that will be used in our promotion.

35. As per your request, we are sending the contract under separate cover.

36. Every effort will be made to proceed in accordance with your wishes.

Jargon, Slang, Clichés, Wordiness

Your Task. Revise the following sentences to avoid confusing jargon, slang, clichés, and wordiness.

37. Our manager insists that we must think outside the box in promoting our new kitchen tool.

38. Although we got burned in the last contract, you can be sure we will stand our ground this time.

39. Beyond the shadow of a doubt, our lousy competitor will make another snarky claim that is below the belt.

40. If you refer back to our five-year plan, you will see that there are provisions for preventing blowing the budget.

Buried Verbs

Your Task. Revise the following to unbury the verbs.

41. After investigating, the fire department reached the conclusion that the blaze was set intentionally.

42. Our committee promised to give consideration to your proposal at its next meeting.

43. When used properly, zero-based budgeting can bring about a reduction in overall costs.

44. Did our department make an application for increased budget support?

45. The budget committee has not taken action on any projects yet.

46. Homeowners must make a determination of the total value of their furnishings.

Precise, Direct Words

Your Task. Revise the following sentences to improve clarity and precision. Use your imagination to add appropriate words.

Example They said it was a long way off.

Revision Management officials announced that the merger would not take place for two years.

47. Someone told us that it would be available for rent soon.

48. Please contact us in the immediate future.

49. An employee from that organization notified us about the change in date for the event.

50. She said that the movie she saw was not very good.

Lists, Bullets, and Headings

Your Task. Revise the following sentences and paragraphs using techniques presented in this chapter. Improve parallel construction and reduce wordiness if necessary.

51. Revise the following by incorporating a numbered list.

    Computer passwords are a way of life at this point in time. In the creation of a strong password, you should remember a few things. First, you should come up with an eight-word phrase that is easy to remember, such as *my favorite uncle was a fireman in Cleveland.* Then take each of those words and the first letter should be selected, such as *mfuwafic.* The last step for creating a really strong password is to exchange—that is, swap out—some of those letters for characters and capital letters, such as *Mf@w&%iC.*

52. Revise the following by incorporating a bulleted list with category headings.

    Auto accidents account for a high number of accidental deaths. The most common causes of these accidents are due to the following causes. In all probability, the most common cause is distracted drivers. Makeup, cell phones, texting, food, and the morning newspaper are all common ways that drivers are being distracted. Another cause is most assuredly impaired driving. Alcohol and drugs impair judgment and reaction times. This obviously results in accidents. Another cause has got to be aggressive drivers. Being an aggressive driver instead of a defensive driver puts you at risk for getting involved in an accident. Finally, road rage is a significant cause. Drivers who get angry easily and then take it out on other drivers are one of the leading causes of accidents.

53. Revise the following by incorporating a bulleted list with category headings.

    There are many people today who want to improve their credit scores. Some simple tips for bumping up your score are obvious. For one thing, you should immediately fix mistakes. If you check your credit report (and you should at least once a year) and there are errors, you can dispute these and have them investigated. Another way to improve your credit score is to pay on time. At least 35 percent of your score is a direct result of your payment history. Next, you should make an effort to lower and reduce your balances. It may be difficult, but you should keep your personal credit balances as low as possible. The less you're using, the better for your score. Finally, making a habit of keeping older accounts will improve your score. This means that you should keep your older cards so that you have a longer history to share. It also shows stability.

Grammar/Mechanics Checkup—4

Adjectives and Adverbs

Review Sections 1.16 and 1.17 of the Grammar/Mechanics Handbook. Then study each of the following statements. Underscore any inappropriate forms. In the space provided, write the correct form (or *C* if correct) and the number of the G/M principle illustrated. You may need to consult your dictionary for current practice regarding some compound adjectives. When you finish, compare your responses with those provided at the end of the book. If your answers differ, carefully study the principles in parentheses.

point-by-point (1.17e) **Example: She made a point by point comparison of the items.**

______ 1. Web sites use state of the art technology to identify visitors.

______ 2. The newly developed software can combine thousands of lines of code very quick.

______ 3. Most Web visitors do not know that there online behavior is being studied.

______ 4. One company said that it only collected data, not identities.

______ 5. An investigative reporter analyzed the number of cookies placed on his computer over an 18 week period.

______ 6. The technology allows analysts to make site by site comparisons of data.

______ 7. When people land on a Web page, there data is scanned in a fifth of a second.

______ 8. Although some people make spur of the moment decisions, most make well-considered decisions.

______ 9. However, not all decisions that are made on the spur of the moment turn out bad.

______ 10. One new company has a well thought out plan for capitalizing on consumer behavior data.

______ 11. Rhonda felt badly when she learned that cookies and other tracking devices were installed on her computer.

______ 12. Of the two companies using behavior data at their Web sites, Capital One said that it was the most compliant with government regulations.

______ 13. A technician wondered whether he could make the scanner run more faster.

______ 14. Web sites now adjust their offers and appearance on a case by case basis.

______ 15. Every Web site hopes its technology will run smooth and fail to attract government intervention.

Editing Challenge—4

As the employee with the best communication skills, you are frequently asked to edit messages. The following e-mail has problems with flabby expressions, long lead-ins, *there is/are* fillers, redundancies, trite business phrases, and other writing techniques you have studied. You may (a) use standard proofreading marks (see Appendix B) to correct the errors here or (b) download the document from **www.cengagebrain.com** and revise at your computer.

Your instructor may ask you to use the **Track Changes** feature in Word to show your editing comments. Turn on **Track Changes** on the **Review** tab. Click **Show Markup**. Place your cursor at an error, click **New Comment**, and key your edit in the bubble box provided. Study the guidelines in the Grammar/Mechanics Handbook as well as the lists of Confusing Words and Frequently Misspelled Words to sharpen your skills.

To: Roger M. Karjala <r.m.karjala@firstbank.com>
From: Keiko Kurtz <k.kurtz@firstbank.com>
Subject: Suggestion for Improvement of Customer Relations
Cc:

Roger,

Because of the fact that you asked for suggestions on how to improve customer relations I am submitting my idea. I am writing you this message to let you know that I think we can improve customer satisfaction easy by making a change in our counters.

Last December glass barriers were installed at our branch. There are tellers on one side and customers on the other. The barriers have air vents to be able to allow we tellers to carry on communication with our customers. Management thought that these bullet proof barriers would prevent and stop thiefs from jumping over the counter.

However there were customers who were surprised by these large glass partitions. Communication through them is really extremely difficult and hard. Both the customer and the teller have to raise there voices to be heard. Its even more of a inconvenence when you are dealing with an elderly person or someone who happens to be from another country. Beyond a shadow of a doubt, these new barriers make customers feel that they are being treated impersonal.

I did research into the matter of these barriers and made the discovery that we are the only bank in town with them. There are many other banks that are trying casual kiosks and open counters to make customers feel more at home.

Although it may be easier said than done, I suggest that we actually give serious consideration to the removal of these barriers as a beginning and initial step toward improving customer relations.

Keiko Kurtz
E-mail: k.kurtz@firstbank.com
Support Services
(455) 549-2201

Communication Workshop

Revising and Editing Documents in MS Word

Collaborative writing and editing projects are challenging. Fortunately, Microsoft Word offers many useful tools to help team members edit and share documents electronically. Three simple but useful editing tools are **Text Highlight Color, Font Color**, and **Strikethrough,** which you learned about on page 97. These tools, included on the **Office Button Home** tab, enable reviewers to point out editing changes. For example, notice how you can use **Strikethrough** to delete a wordy lead-in or use yellow highlighting to call attention to a misspelled word:

> ~~This is just a note to let you know that~~ I would appreciate you're help in preparing the announcement about tornado safety tips.

Complex projects, however, may require more advanced editing tools such as **Track Changes** and **Insert Comments**.

Track Changes

To suggest specific editing changes to other team members, **Track Changes** is handy. When this command is in effect, all changes to a document are recorded in a different color, with one color for each reviewer. New text is underlined, and a vertical line appears in the margin to show where changes were made. Text that has been deleted is crossed out. Suggested revisions offered by different team members are identified and dated. The original writer may accept or reject these changes. In Word 2007, you will find **Track Changes** on the **Review** menu.

Insert Comments

By using **Insert Comments**, you can point out problematic passages or errors, ask or answer questions, and share ideas without changing or adding text. When more than one person adds comments, the comments appear in different colors and are identified by the individual writers' names and date/time stamps.

To use this tool in Word 2007, fill in the **User Information** section. To facilitate adding, reviewing, editing, or deleting comments, click the **New Comment** button on the **Review** tab. Then type your comment. In the **Draft** and **Outline** views, the reviewing pane opens on the left side or bottom of the screen so that you can enter a comment. In the **Print Layout** and **Web Layout** views, a new balloon appears on the right side of the screen. See the figure on page 104 illustrating the **Comment** feature.

Career Application. On the job, you will likely be working with others on projects that require written documents. During employment interviews, employers may ask whether you have participated in team projects using collaborative software. To be able to answer that question favorably, take advantage of this opportunity to work on a collaborative document using some of the features described here.

Your Task. Divide into two-person teams. Each partner edits the Editing Challenge exercise on the previous page. Download it from **www.cengagebrain.com** or keyboard it from the textbook. Edit the message, making all necessary corrections. Save the letter with a file name such as *YourName-Editing4*. Send an e-mail to your partner with the attached file. Ask your partner to make any further edits. The receiving partner uses font color, strikethrough, and the **Comment** feature to edit the partner's message. Print a copy of your partner's edited message before you edit it. Submit that copy along with a copy of your partner's message with your edits. Be sure to label each carefully.

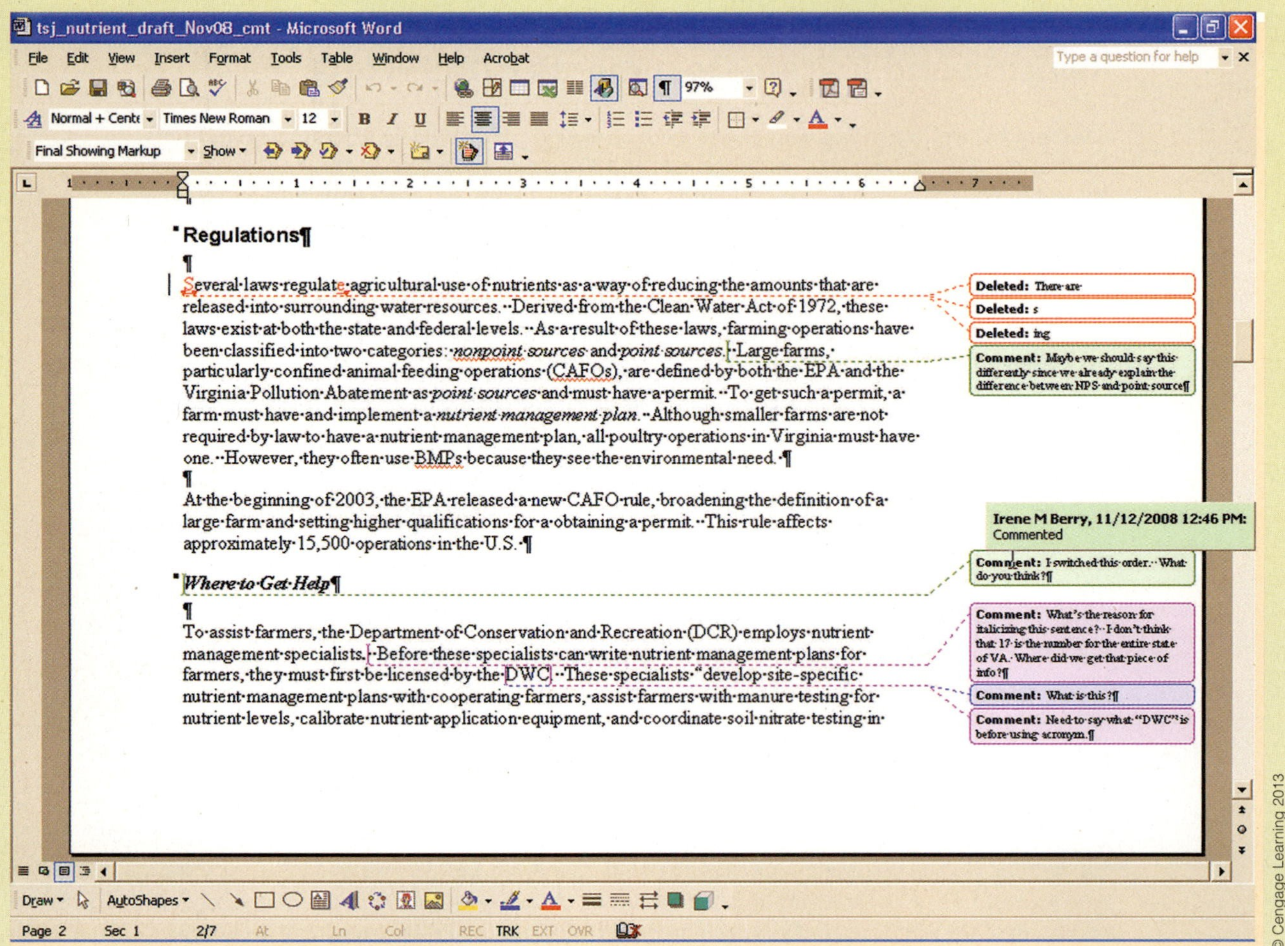
tsj_nutrient_draft_Nov08_cmt - Microsoft Word

Regulations

Several laws regulate agricultural use of nutrients as a way of reducing the amounts that are released into surrounding water resources. Derived from the Clean Water Act of 1972, these laws exist at both the state and federal levels. As a result of these laws, farming operations have been classified into two categories: *nonpoint sources* and *point sources*. Large farms, particularly confined animal feeding operations (CAFOs), are defined by both the EPA and the Virginia Pollution Abatement as *point sources* and must have a permit. To get such a permit, a farm must have and implement a *nutrient management plan*. Although smaller farms are not required by law to have a nutrient management plan, all poultry operations in Virginia must have one. However, they often use BMPs because they see the environmental need.

At the beginning of 2003, the EPA released a new CAFO rule, broadening the definition of a large farm and setting higher qualifications for a obtaining a permit. This rule affects approximately 15,500 operations in the U.S.

Where to Get Help

To assist farmers, the Department of Conservation and Recreation (DCR) employs nutrient management specialists. Before these specialists can write nutrient management plans for farmers, they must first be licensed by the DWC. These specialists "develop site-specific nutrient management plans with cooperating farmers, assist farmers with manure testing for nutrient levels, calibrate nutrient application equipment, and coordinate soil nitrate testing in

Deleted: There are

Deleted: s

Deleted: ing

Comment: Maybe we should say this differently since we already explain the difference between NPS and point source

Irene M Berry, 11/12/2008 12:46 PM: Commented

Comment: I switched this order. What do you think?

Comment: What's the reason for italicizing this sentence? I don't think that 17 is the number for the entire state of VA. Where did we get that piece of info?

Comment: What is this?

Comment: Need to say what "DWC" is before using acronym.

Endnotes

[1] Cook, C. K. (1985). *Line by line*. Boston: Houghton Mifflin, p. 17.

[2] Benefits of plain language. (n.d.). Retrieved from http://centerforplainlanguage.org

Acknowledgments

p. 83 Office Insider based on Powell, E. (2003, November/December). Ten tips for better business writing. *Office Solutions*, *20*(6), 36.

p. 84 Office Insider based on Ilja van Roon, quoted in Sorry, no more excuses for bad business writing. (2006, May 23). *PR Newswire*.

UNIT 3

© Dmitry Yashkin/Shutterstock.com

Communicating at Work

Electronic Messages and Digital Media

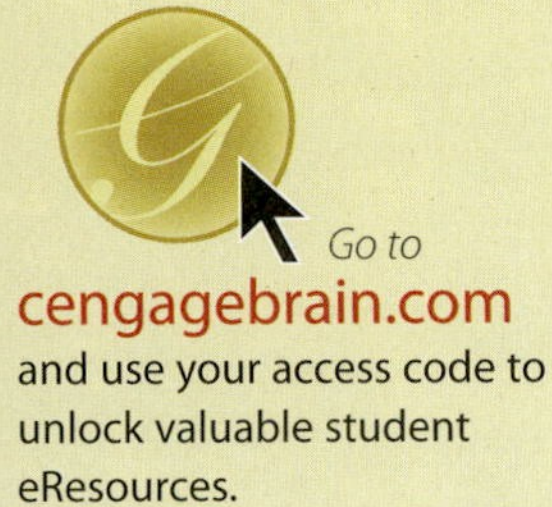

Go to
cengagebrain.com
and use your access code to unlock valuable student eResources.

Dmitriy Shironosov/Shutterstock.com

OBJECTIVES

After studying this chapter, you should be able to

- Understand how organizations exchange electronic and paper-based messages.
- Know when to send and how to organize e-mails and memos.
- Describe appropriate formats for e-mails and memos.
- Identify best practices for writing professional e-mails.
- Explain the business applications of instant messaging and texting.
- Discuss social networking sites, assess their advantages and their risks, and appreciate the potential of professional networking sites.
- Recognize the business uses of podcasts, blogs, and wikis; understand the distribution of Web content by real simple syndication (RSS) feeds; and describe the purpose of social bookmarking.

Communication Technology and the Information Flow in Organizations

Although today's workplaces are still far from paperless, increasingly, information is exchanged electronically and on the go. The Web has evolved from mere storage of passively consumed information to Web 2.0—a dynamic, interactive environment. Users are empowered, active participants who create content, review products, and edit and share information.

Ever more data are stored on and accessed from remote networks, not just individual computers. This storing and accessing of data along with software applications in remote network clusters, or "clouds," is called *cloud computing*. Mobile communication and cloud computing are the two prevailing technological trends today. In many businesses, desktop computers are fast becoming obsolete with the advent of ever-smaller laptops, netbooks, smartphones, tablets, and other compact mobile devices. Furthermore, virtual private networks (VPN) offer secure access to company information from any location in the world that provides an Internet connection.

Today's workforce must stay connected at all times. Knowledge and information workers are expected to remain tethered to their jobs wherever they are, even on the weekends or on vacation. The technological revolution of the last 25 years has resulted in amazing productivity gains. However, technological advances have also made 50-hour workweeks without overtime pay a reality for those "i-workers" lucky enough to snag or keep a promising position in a tough economy. Also, more employees than ever before are telecommuting.

You may already be sharing digitally with your friends and family, but chances are that you need to understand how businesses transmit information electronically and how they use new technology. This chapter explores professional electronic communication, specifically e-mail, instant messaging, text messaging, and corporate blogs. Moreover, you will learn about business uses of podcasts, wikis, and social networking sites. You will read about best practices in composing e-mails and interacting through other electronic media. Knowing how to prepare an effective message and understanding business technology can save you time, reduce stress, and build your image as a professional.

Organizing E-Mails and Memos

E-mail has replaced paper memos for many messages inside organizations and some letters to external audiences. However, paper-based documents still have their proper functions. Because they are committed to paper, hard-copy messages tend to carry more weight and are taken more seriously in certain situations. They are considered more formal than electronic communication. Moreover, even if e-mail writers have access to sophisticated HTML mail, the recipient may receive only plain-text messages. Poor layout and little eye appeal may result when elaborate formatting disappears on the receiver's end. The e-mail may also be difficult to print. This is why business communicators often deliver electronic copies of memos or letters as attachments accompanied by a brief e-mail cover message. PDF documents in particular guarantee that the reader receives a message that looks exactly as the writer intended it.

E-mails and memos inform employees, request data, give responses, confirm decisions, and provide directions.

Today it is estimated that on average more than 294 billion e-mails are sent each day worldwide.[1] E-mail growth has slowed recently, and rival services are booming. Twitter and Facebook, for example, offer faster, always-on connectedness. However, e-mail in the workplace is here to stay. Because e-mail is a standard form of communication within organizations, it will likely be your most common business communication channel. E-mails perform critical tasks such as informing employees, giving directions, outlining procedures, requesting data, supplying responses, and confirming decisions.

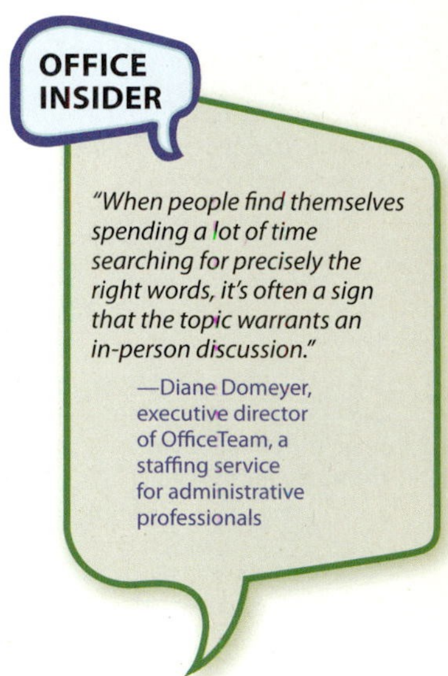

OFFICE INSIDER
"When people find themselves spending a lot of time searching for precisely the right words, it's often a sign that the topic warrants an in-person discussion."
—Diane Domeyer, executive director of OfficeTeam, a staffing service for administrative professionals

Knowing When to Send E-Mails and Memos

Before sending any message, you must choose a communication channel, as discussed in Chapter 2. E-mail is appropriate for short, informal messages that request information and respond to inquiries. It is especially effective for messages to multiple receivers and messages that must be archived (saved). An e-mail is also appropriate as a cover document when sending longer attachments.

E-mail, however, is not a substitute for face-to-face conversations, telephone calls, or business letters. Face-to-face conversations or telephone calls are better channel choices if your goal is to convey enthusiasm or warmth, explain a complex situation, present a persuasive argument, or smooth over disagreements. A recent research study revealed that managers and employees were adamant about using face-to-face contact, rather than e-mail, for critical work situations such as human resources annual reviews, discipline, and promotions.[2]

Although e-mail is more often used today, memos are still useful for important internal messages that require a permanent record or formality. For example, organizations use memos to deliver changes in procedures, official instructions, reports, and long internal documents. Whatever channel you choose, be sure it is comfortable to the receiver and appropriate for the organization.

Writing Informational E-Mails and Memos

In today's workplace you will probably write numerous informational e-mails and some hard-copy memos. Both kinds of messages usually carry nonsensitive information that is unlikely to upset readers. Therefore, these messages should be organized directly with the main idea first. The following writing plan will help you create information messages quickly:

Writing Plan for Informational E-Mails and Memos

- **Subject line:** Summarize the main idea in condensed form.
- **Opening:** Reveal the main idea immediately but in expanded form.
- **Body:** Explain and justify the main idea using headings, bulleted lists, and other high-skim techniques when appropriate.
- **Closing:** Include (a) action information, dates, or deadlines; (b) a summary of the message; or (c) a closing thought.

Subject Line. In e-mails and memos, an informative subject line is essential. It summarizes the central idea, thus providing quick identification for reading and for filing. Busy readers glance at a subject line and decide when and whether to read the message. E-mails without subject lines are often automatically deleted.

What does it take to get your message read? For one thing, stay away from meaningless or dangerous words. A sure way to have your message deleted or ignored is to use a one-word heading such as *Issue, Problem, Important,* or *Help.* Including a word such as *Free* is dangerous because it may trigger spam filters. Try to make your subject line "talk" by including a verb. Explain the purpose of the message and how it relates to the reader. Remember that a subject line is usually written in an abbreviated style, often without articles *(a, an, the)*. It need not be a complete sentence, and it does not end with a period. Subject lines should appear as a combination of uppercase and lowercase letters—never in all lowercase letters.

Poor Subject Lines	Improved Subject Lines
Trade Show	Need You to Showcase Two Items at Our Next Trade Show
Staff Meeting	Staff Meeting Rescheduled for May 12
Important!	Please Respond to Job Satisfaction Survey
Parking Permits	New Employee Parking Permits Available From HR

Direct e-mails and memos open by revealing the main idea immediately.

Opening. Because most e-mails and memos cover nonsensitive information, it can be handled in a straightforward manner. Begin by frontloading; that is, reveal the main idea immediately. Even though the purpose of the e-mail or memo is summarized in the subject line, that purpose should be restated—and amplified—in the first sentence. Busy readers want to know immediately why they are reading a message. Notice how the following indirect opening can be improved by frontloading.

Indirect Opening	Direct Opening
For the past six months the Human Resources Development Department has been considering changes in our employees' benefit plan.	Please review the following proposal regarding employees' benefits, and let me know by May 20 if you approve these changes.

Designed for easy comprehension, the body explains one topic.

Body. The body provides more information about the reason for writing. It explains and discusses the subject logically. Effective e-mails and memos generally discuss only one topic. Limiting the topic helps the receiver act on the subject and file it appropriately. A writer who, for example, describes a computer printer problem and also requests permission to attend a conference runs a 50 percent failure risk. The reader may respond to the printer problem but delay responding to or forget about the conference request.

The body of e-mails and memos should have high "skim value." This means that information should be easy to read and comprehend. As covered in the section on document design in Chapter 4, many techniques improve readability. You can use white space, bulleted lists, enumerated lists, appropriate typefaces and fonts, and headings. In the revision stage, you will see many ways to improve the readability of the body of your message.

Closing. Generally end an e-mail or a memo with (a) action information, dates, or deadlines; (b) a summary of the message; or (c) a closing thought. Here again, the value of thinking through the message before actually writing it becomes apparent. The closing is where readers look for deadlines and action language. An effective memo or e-mail closing might be, *Please submit your written report to me by June 15 so that we can have your data before our July planning session.*

Messages should close with (a) action information including dates and deadlines, (b) a summary, or (c) a closing thought.

In more detailed messages, a summary of main points may be an appropriate closing. If no action request is made and a closing summary is unnecessary, you might end with a simple concluding thought *(I'm glad to answer your questions* or *This sounds like a useful project)*. You need not close messages to coworkers with goodwill statements such as those found in letters to customers or clients. However, some closing thought is often necessary to prevent sounding abrupt. Closings can show gratitude or encourage feedback with remarks such as *I sincerely appreciate your help* or *What are your ideas on this proposal?* Other closings look forward to what's next, such as *How would you like to proceed?* Avoid closing with overused expressions such as *Please let me know if I may be of further assistance*. This ending sounds mechanical and insincere.

Applying E-Mail and Memo Formats

E-mails and hard-copy memos are similar in content and development, but their formats are slightly different. In this section you will learn how to format e-mails and memos, and you will learn how e-mails can serve as transmittal documents.

An e-mail contains guide words, an optional greeting, and a concise and easy-to-read message.

Formatting E-Mail Messages

Because e-mail is now a standard form of business communication, people are beginning to agree on specific formatting and usage conventions. The following suggestions identify current formatting standards. Always check with your organization, however, to observe its practices.

Guide Words. Following the guide word *To*, some writers insert just the recipient's electronic address, such as *michael.harding@schilling-voigt.com*. Other writers prefer to include the receiver's full name plus the electronic address, as shown in Figure 5.1. By including full names in the *To* and *From* slots, both receivers and senders are better able to identify the message. By the way, the order of *Date, To, From, Subject*, and other guide words varies depending on your e-mail program and whether you are sending or receiving the message.

Most e-mail programs automatically add the current date after *Date*. On the *Cc* line (which stands for *carbon copy* or *courtesy copy*), you can type the address of anyone who is to receive a copy of the message. Remember, though, to send copies only to those people directly involved with the message. Most e-mail programs also include a line for *Bcc (blind carbon copy)*. This sends a copy without the addressee's knowledge. Savvy writers today use *Bcc* for the names and

FIGURE 5.1 Formatting an E-Mail Message

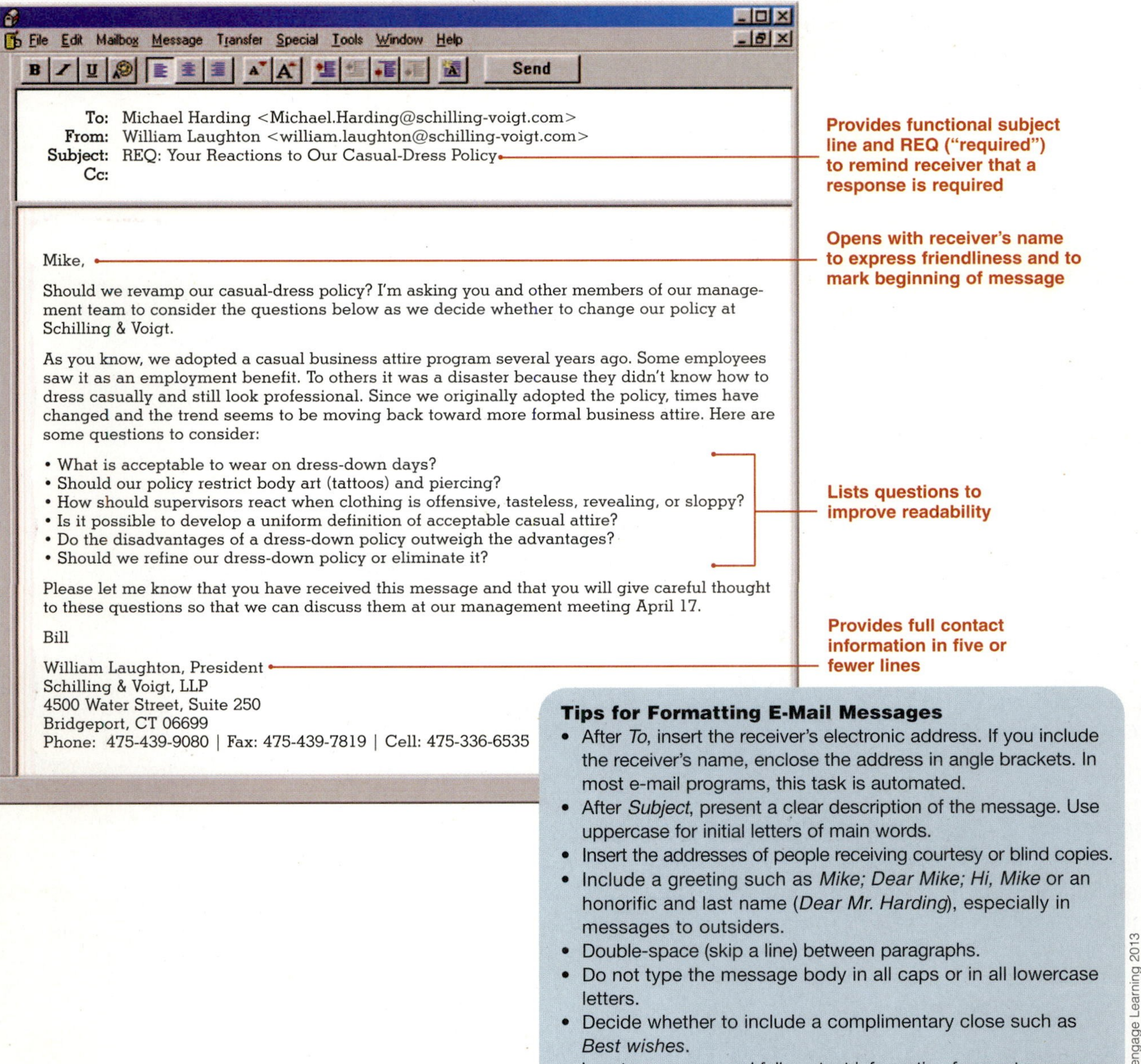

To: Michael Harding <Michael.Harding@schilling-voigt.com>
From: William Laughton <william.laughton@schilling-voigt.com>
Subject: REQ: Your Reactions to Our Casual-Dress Policy
Cc:

Mike,

Should we revamp our casual-dress policy? I'm asking you and other members of our management team to consider the questions below as we decide whether to change our policy at Schilling & Voigt.

As you know, we adopted a casual business attire program several years ago. Some employees saw it as an employment benefit. To others it was a disaster because they didn't know how to dress casually and still look professional. Since we originally adopted the policy, times have changed and the trend seems to be moving back toward more formal business attire. Here are some questions to consider:

- What is acceptable to wear on dress-down days?
- Should our policy restrict body art (tattoos) and piercing?
- How should supervisors react when clothing is offensive, tasteless, revealing, or sloppy?
- Is it possible to develop a uniform definition of acceptable casual attire?
- Do the disadvantages of a dress-down policy outweigh the advantages?
- Should we refine our dress-down policy or eliminate it?

Please let me know that you have received this message and that you will give careful thought to these questions so that we can discuss them at our management meeting April 17.

Bill

William Laughton, President
Schilling & Voigt, LLP
4500 Water Street, Suite 250
Bridgeport, CT 06699
Phone: 475-439-9080 | Fax: 475-439-7819 | Cell: 475-336-6535

Tips for Formatting E-Mail Messages

- After *To,* insert the receiver's electronic address. If you include the receiver's name, enclose the address in angle brackets. In most e-mail programs, this task is automated.
- After *Subject*, present a clear description of the message. Use uppercase for initial letters of main words.
- Insert the addresses of people receiving courtesy or blind copies.
- Include a greeting such as *Mike; Dear Mike; Hi, Mike* or an honorific and last name (*Dear Mr. Harding*), especially in messages to outsiders.
- Double-space (skip a line) between paragraphs.
- Do not type the message body in all caps or in all lowercase letters.
- Decide whether to include a complimentary close such as *Best wishes*.
- Insert your name and full contact information for most messages.

addresses of a list of receivers, a technique that avoids revealing the addresses to the entire group. On the subject line, identify the subject of the e-mail. Be sure to include enough information to be clear and compelling.

An e-mail greeting shows friendliness and indicates the beginning of the message.

Greeting. Begin your message with a greeting such as the following:

Hi, Kevin,	Thank you, Haley,
Greetings, Amy,	Dear Mr. Cotter,
Leslie,	Dear Leslie:

In addition to being friendly, a greeting provides a visual cue marking the beginning of the message. Many messages are transmitted or forwarded with such long headers that finding the beginning of the message can be difficult. A greeting helps, even if it is just the receiver's name, as shown in Figure 5.1.

Body. When preparing the body of an e-mail, use standard caps and lowercase characters—never all uppercase or all lowercase characters. Cover just one topic, and try to keep the total message under three screens in length. Remember to double-space between paragraphs. For longer messages prepare a separate file to be attached. Use the e-mail message only as a cover document.

Closing Lines and Signature Block. Some people sign off their e-mails with a cordial expression such as *Cheers*, *All the best*, or *Warm regards*. Regardless of the closing, be sure to sign your name. Messages without names become very confusing when forwarded or when they are part of a thread (string) of responses. It is also smart to include full contact information as part of your signature block. Some writers prepare a number of "signatures" in their e-mail programs, depending on what information they want to reveal. They can choose a complete signature with all their contact information, or they can use a brief version. See Figure 5.1 for an example of a complete signature.

E-mails are most helpful when they conclude with the writer's full contact information.

Formatting Office Memos

In the past interoffice memorandums were the primary communication channel for delivering information within organizations. They are still useful for internal messages that require a permanent record or formality.

Memo Forms and Margins. Memos include the basic elements of *Date, To, From*, and *Subject*. Large organizations may include other identifying headings, such as *File Number*, *Floor*, *Extension*, *Location*, and *Distribution*.

In preparing a memo on plain paper, set 1-inch top and bottom margins and left and right margins of 1.25 inches. Provide a heading that includes the name of the company plus "Memo" or "Memorandum." Begin the guide words a triple space (two blank lines) below the last line of the heading. Insert in bold the guide words: **Date:**, **To:**, **From:**, and **Subject:** at the left margin. The guide words may appear in all caps or with only the initial letter capitalized. Triple-space (set two blank lines) after the last line of the heading. Do not justify the right margins. As discussed in the document design section of Chapter 4, ragged-right margins make printed messages easier to read than right-justified margins do. Single-space the message, and double-space between paragraphs, as shown in Figure 5.2.

OFFICE INSIDER
E-mail is the digital equivalent of DNA evidence, the smoking gun: "E-mail has become the place where everybody loves to look."
—Irwin Schwartz, president of the National Association of Criminal Defense Lawyers

Preparing Memos as E-Mail Attachments. E-mail has become increasingly important for exchanging internal messages. However, it is inappropriate for long documents or for items that require formality or permanence. For such messages, writers may prepare the information in standard memo format and send it as an attachment to a cover e-mail.

In preparing e-mail attachments, be sure to include identifying information. Because the cover e-mail message may become separated from the attachment, the attachment must be fully identified. Preparing the e-mail attachment as a memo provides a handy format that identifies the date, sender, receiver, and subject.

To deliver a long or formal document, send a cover e-mail with an attachment.

Adopting Best Practices for Professional E-Mails

Wise e-mail business communicators are aware of the importance as well as the dangers of e-mail as a communication channel. They know that their messages can travel, intentionally or unintentionally, long distances. A hasty e-mail may end up in the boss's mailbox or be forwarded to an enemy. Making matters worse, computers—like elephants and spurned lovers—never forget. Even erased messages can remain on multiple servers that are backed up by companies or Internet

Despite its popularity, e-mail may be dangerous because messages travel long distances, are difficult to erase, and may become evidence in court.

FIGURE 5.2 Formatting a Memo That Responds to a Request

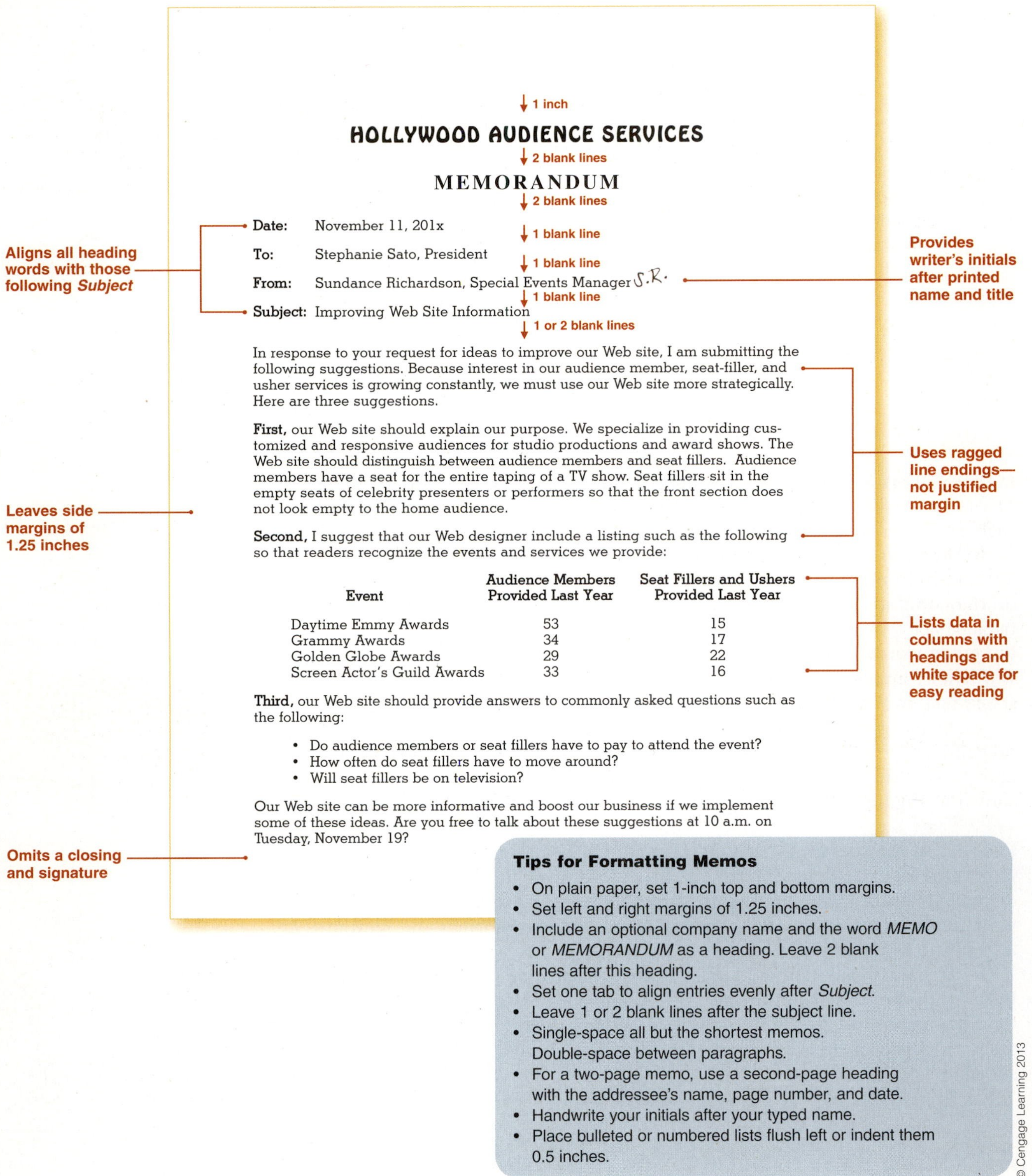

1 inch
2 blank lines
2 blank lines
1 blank line
1 blank line
1 blank line
1 or 2 blank lines
Aligns all heading words with those following *Subject*
Provides writer's initials after printed name and title
Uses ragged line endings—not justified margin
Leaves side margins of 1.25 inches
Lists data in columns with headings and white space for easy reading
Omits a closing and signature

HOLLYWOOD AUDIENCE SERVICES

MEMORANDUM

Date: November 11, 201x

To: Stephanie Sato, President

From: Sundance Richardson, Special Events Manager *S.R.*

Subject: Improving Web Site Information

In response to your request for ideas to improve our Web site, I am submitting the following suggestions. Because interest in our audience member, seat-filler, and usher services is growing constantly, we must use our Web site more strategically. Here are three suggestions.

First, our Web site should explain our purpose. We specialize in providing customized and responsive audiences for studio productions and award shows. The Web site should distinguish between audience members and seat fillers. Audience members have a seat for the entire taping of a TV show. Seat fillers sit in the empty seats of celebrity presenters or performers so that the front section does not look empty to the home audience.

Second, I suggest that our Web designer include a listing such as the following so that readers recognize the events and services we provide:

Event	Audience Members Provided Last Year	Seat Fillers and Ushers Provided Last Year
Daytime Emmy Awards	53	15
Grammy Awards	34	17
Golden Globe Awards	29	22
Screen Actor's Guild Awards	33	16

Third, our Web site should provide answers to commonly asked questions such as the following:

- Do audience members or seat fillers have to pay to attend the event?
- How often do seat fillers have to move around?
- Will seat fillers be on television?

Our Web site can be more informative and boost our business if we implement some of these ideas. Are you free to talk about these suggestions at 10 a.m. on Tuesday, November 19?

Tips for Formatting Memos

- On plain paper, set 1-inch top and bottom margins.
- Set left and right margins of 1.25 inches.
- Include an optional company name and the word *MEMO* or *MEMORANDUM* as a heading. Leave 2 blank lines after this heading.
- Set one tab to align entries evenly after *Subject*.
- Leave 1 or 2 blank lines after the subject line.
- Single-space all but the shortest memos. Double-space between paragraphs.
- For a two-page memo, use a second-page heading with the addressee's name, page number, and date.
- Handwrite your initials after your typed name.
- Place bulleted or numbered lists flush left or indent them 0.5 inches.

service providers. Increasingly, e-mail has turned into the "smoking gun" uncovered by prosecutors to prove indelicate or even illegal intentions.

In addition, many users complain of poorly written messages and "e-mail ping-pong." Inboxes overflow with unnecessary back-and-forth exchanges seeking to clarify previous messages.[3]

E-Mail Best Practices: Getting Started

"Be careful what you write. My wonderful, charming, brilliant boss reads everyone's e-mail."

© Randy Glasbergen www.glasbergen.com

Despite its dangers and limitations, e-mail is the No. 1 channel of communication. To make your messages effective and to avoid e-mail ping-pong, take the time to organize your thoughts, compose carefully, and consider the receiver. The following best practices will help you get off to a good start in using e-mail smartly, safely, and professionally.

- **Try composing offline.** Especially for important messages, use your word processing program to write offline. Then upload your message to your e-mail or copy and paste the text into the frame of your e-mail. This prevents "self-destructing" (losing all your writing through some glitch or pressing the wrong key) when working online.
- **Get the address right.** If you omit one character or misread the letter *l* for the number *1,* your message bounces. Solution: Use your electronic address book for people you write to frequently. Double-check every address that you key in manually. Don't accidentally reply to a group of receivers when you intend to answer only one.
- **Avoid misleading subject lines.** Make sure your subject line is relevant and helpful. Generic tags such as *Hi!* and *Important*! may cause your message to be deleted before it is opened.
- **Apply the top-of-screen test.** When readers open your message and look at the first screen, will they see what is most significant? Your subject line and first paragraph should convey your purpose.

Content, Tone, and Correctness

Although e-mail seems as casual as a telephone call, it definitely is not. Because it produces a permanent record, think carefully about what you say and how you say it.

Avoid sending sensitive, confidential, inflammatory, or potentially embarrassing messages because e-mail is not private.

- **Be concise.** Omit unnecessary information. Remember that monitors are small and typefaces are often difficult to read. Organize your ideas tightly. If you must send a long message, prepare an attachment and use the e-mail as a cover message.
- **Don't send anything you wouldn't want published.** E-mail creates a permanent record that does not go away even when deleted. Every message is a corporate communication that can be used against you or your employer. Don't write anything that you wouldn't want your boss, your family, or a judge to read.
- **Don't use e-mail to avoid contact.** E-mail is inappropriate for breaking bad news or for resolving arguments. For example, it is improper to fire a person by e-mail. It is also a poor channel for clashing with supervisors, subordinates, or others. Before risking hurt feelings, call or pay the person a visit.
- **Care about correctness.** People are still judged by their writing, whether electronic or paper based. Sloppy e-mail messages (with missing apostrophes, haphazard spelling, and jumbled writing) make readers work too hard. They resent not only the information but also the writer.
- **Care about tone.** Your words and writing style affect the reader. Avoid sounding curt, negative, or domineering.
- **Resist humor and sarcasm.** Without the nonverbal cues conveyed by your face and your voice, humor can easily be misunderstood.

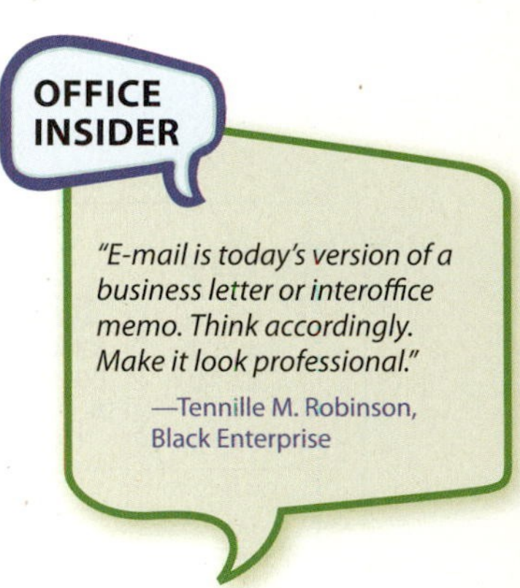

OFFICE INSIDER
"E-mail is today's version of a business letter or interoffice memo. Think accordingly. Make it look professional."
—Tennille M. Robinson, Black Enterprise

Netiquette

Although e-mail is a relatively new communication channel, a number of rules of polite online interaction are emerging.

- **Never send blanket copies and "spam."** Sending unsolicited advertisements ("spam") either by fax or e-mail is illegal in the United States. Address copies only to people who really need to see a message. It is unnecessary to document every business decision with an electronic paper trail.
- **Use capital letters only for emphasis or for titles.** Avoid writing entire messages in all caps, which is like SHOUTING.
- **Don't forward without permission, and beware of long threads.** Obtain approval before forwarding a message. Also beware of forwarding e-mail consisting of a long thread (string) of messages. Some content in bottom screens may be inappropriate for the third receiver. Aside from the issue of clutter, leaving sensitive information in the thread can lead to serious trouble.

Reading and Replying to E-Mail

Scan all messages before responding, paste in relevant sections, revise the subject if the topic changes, provide a clear first sentence, and never respond when angry.

The following tips can save you time and frustration when reading and answering messages:

- **Scan all messages in your inbox before replying to each individually.** Because subsequent messages often affect the way you respond, scan all messages first (especially all those from the same individual).
- **Print only when necessary.** Generally, read and answer most messages online without saving or printing. Use folders to archive messages on special topics. Print only those messages that are complex, controversial, or involve significant decisions and follow-up.
- **Acknowledge receipt.** If you can't reply immediately, tell when you can (*Will respond Friday*).
- **Don't automatically return the sender's message.** When replying, cut and paste the relevant parts. Avoid irritating your recipients by returning the entire thread (sequence of messages) on a topic.
- **Revise the subject line if the topic changes.** When replying or continuing an e-mail exchange, revise the subject line as the topic changes.
- **Provide a clear, complete first sentence.** Avoid fuzzy replies such as *That's fine with me* or *Sounds good!* Busy respondents forget what was said in earlier messages, so be sure to fill in the context and your perspective when responding.
- **Never respond when you are angry.** Calm down before shooting off a response to an upsetting message. You will come up with different and better options after thinking about what was said. If possible, iron out differences in person.

Personal Use

Remember that office computers are meant for work-related communication.

- **Don't use company computers for personal matters.** Unless your company specifically allows it, never use your employer's computers for personal messages, personal shopping, or entertainment.

- **Assume that all e-mail is monitored.** Employers legally have the right to monitor e-mail, and about 75 percent of them do.

Other Smart E-Mail Practices

Depending on your messages and audience, the following tips promote effective electronic communication.

Design your messages to enhance readability, and double-check before sending.

- **Design your messages effectively.** When a message requires several screens, help the reader with headings, bulleted lists, side headings, and perhaps an introductory summary that describes what will follow. Although these techniques lengthen a message, they shorten reading time.
- **Consider cultural differences.** Be clear and precise in your language. Remember that figurative clichés (*pull up stakes, play second fiddle,*) sports references (*hit a home run, play by the rules*), and slang (*cool, stoked*) may confuse nonnative speakers of English.
- **Double-check before hitting the** Send **button.** Avoid the necessity of sending a second message, which makes you look careless. Use your spell-checker, and reread for fluency before sending. Verify important facts and the spelling of names.

Using Instant Messaging and Texting Professionally and Safely

Making their way from teen bedrooms to office boardrooms, instant messaging (IM) and text messaging have become permanent and powerful communication tools. IM enables you to use the Internet to communicate in real time in private chat rooms with one or more individuals. It is like live e-mail or a text telephone call. More and more workers are using it as a speedy communication channel to exchange short messages.

Businesspeople use instant messaging to exchange ideas in real time in private chat rooms.

Text messaging, or texting, is another popular means for exchanging brief messages in real time. Usually delivered by smartphone, texting requires a short message service (SMS) supplied by a cell phone service provider.

How Instant Messaging and Texting Work

To send an instant message, you might use a client such as such as Microsoft's Windows Live Messenger, Yahoo! Messenger, and AOL's Instant Messenger, or newer services such as Google Talk, Digsby, and Trillian Astra that integrate social network updates.[4] Once the client is installed, you enter your name and password to log on. The software checks to see if any of the users in your contact list are currently logged in. If the server finds any of your contacts, it sends a message back to your computer. If the person you wish to contact is online, you can click that person's name and a window opens that you can enter text into. You enter a message, such as that shown in Figure 5.3, and click **Send**. Unlike e-mail, IM and texting provide no elaborate page layout options. The text box is small, and pressing the **Enter** key sends the message. Obviously, it is designed for brief but fast text interaction.

New applications allow people to use IM not only on their computers but also on their handheld devices such as the popular iPhone shown in Figure 5.4. Many smartphones work on a 3G or 4G cell phone network where they consume minutes, but they may also allow generally free Wi-Fi access where available.

Texting, on the other hand, usually requires a smartphone or PDA, and users are charged for the service, often by choosing a flat rate for a certain number of text or media messages per month. Lately, voice over Internet protocol (VoIP) providers such as Skype offer texting. For a small fee, Skype subscribers can send text messages to SMS-enabled cell phones in the United States and IM messages both domestically and internationally. Skype and other formerly computer-based applications are simultaneously available on mobile devices and are making communication on the go more convenient than ever before.

FIGURE 5.3 Instant Message for Brief, Fast Communication

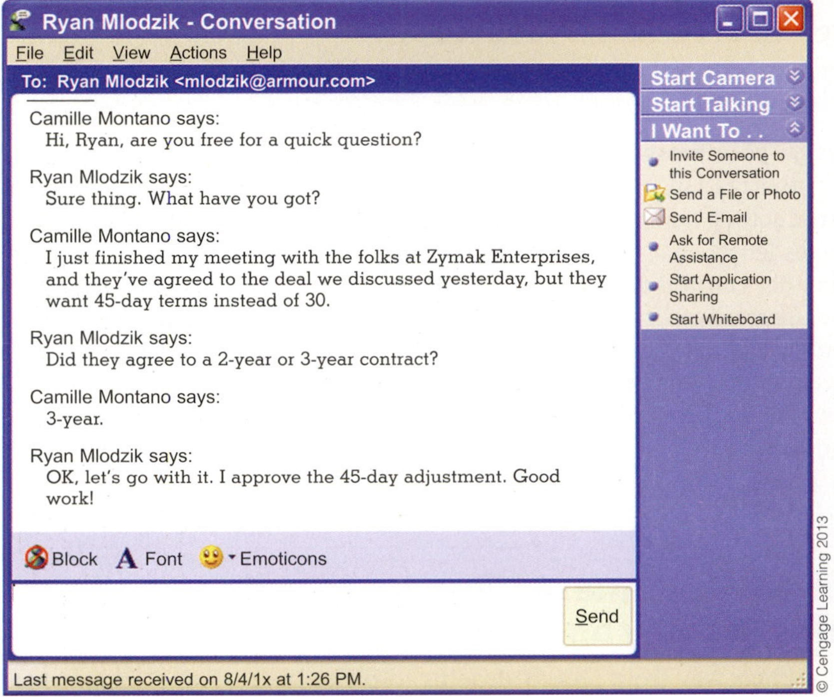

Pros and Cons of Instant Messaging and Texting

In today's fast-paced world, instant messaging (IM) offers numerous benefits. Its major attraction is real-time communication with colleagues anywhere in the world—so long as a cell phone signal or a Wi-Fi connection is available. IM is a convenient alternative to the telephone and may eventually even replace e-mail.

FIGURE 5.4 Texting and Instant Messaging with the iPhone

Apple's iPhone is one of the most popular handheld devices in the United States. Users like the touch-screen interface and access to countless smart applications ("apps"), many of which are free.

GRANTLAND®
ISN'T THIS NEW INSTANT MESSAGING SYSTEM GREAT? --
WE CAN COMMUNICATE INSTANTLY, IN REAL TIME, AND GET AN IMMEDIATE RESPONSE!
YES, BUT I LIKE THE OLD SYSTEM BETTER.
WHAT'S THAT?
WATCH.
HEY FRAN, I REALLY LIKED YOUR REPORT. LET'S TALK ABOUT IT.
SURE.
3320
www.grantland.net

Because IM allows people to share information immediately and make decisions quickly, its impact on business communication has been dramatic.

Like IM, texting can be a low-cost substitute for voice calls, delivering a message between private mobile phone users quietly and discreetly. SMS is particularly popular in Europe, New Zealand, Australia, and Asia.[5] In bulk text messages, companies around the world provide news alerts, financial information, and advertising to customers. Texts have been used in game shows for TV voting, in the United States most notably to select contestants on *American Idol*.

The immediacy of instant and text messaging has created many fans. A user knows right away whether a message was delivered. Messaging avoids phone tag and eliminates the downtime associated with personal telephone conversations. Another benefit includes "presence functionality." Coworkers can locate each other online, thus avoiding having to hunt down someone who is out of the office. Many people consider instant messaging and texting productivity boosters because they enable them to get answers quickly and allow multitasking.

Despite its popularity among workers, some organizations forbid employees to use instant messaging for a number of reasons. Employers consider instant messaging yet another distraction in addition to the interruptions caused by the telephone, e-mail, and the Web. Organizations also fear that privileged information and company records will be revealed through public instant messaging systems, which hackers can easily penetrate. Organizations worry about *phishing* (fraudulent) schemes, viruses, malware, and *spim* (IM spam).

Organizations may ban instant messaging because of productivity, security, litigation, and compliance fears.

Like e-mail, instant and text messages are subject to discovery (disclosure); that is, they can become evidence in lawsuits. Moreover, companies fear instant messaging and texting because businesses are required to track and store messaging conversations to comply with legal requirements. This task may be overwhelming. Finally, IM and texting have been implicated in traffic accidents and inappropriate uses such as the notorious *sexting*.

OFFICE INSIDER
"[B]ear in mind that messaging sessions can be stored, then copied and pasted elsewhere. . . . The term 'confidential' is somewhat rubbery these days, so . . . think before you hit that enter key."
—Michael Bloch,
Taming the Beast,
E-commerce
development &
Web marketing
consultancy services

Best Practices for Instant Messaging and Texting

Instant messaging can definitely save time and simplify communications with coworkers and customers. Before using IM or text messaging on the job, however, be sure you have permission. Do not use public systems without checking with your supervisor. If your organization does allow IM and texting, you can use it efficiently and professionally by following these best practices:

- Learn about your organization's IM policies. Are you allowed to use instant messaging? With whom may you exchange messages?
- Don't text or IM while driving a car. Pull over if you must read or send a message.
- Make yourself unavailable when you need to complete a project or meet a deadline.

- Organize your contact lists to separate business contacts from family and friends.
- Keep your messages simple and to the point. Avoid unnecessary chitchat, and know when to say goodbye.
- Don't use IM to send confidential or sensitive information.
- Be aware that instant messages can be saved. As with e-mail, don't say anything that would damage your reputation or that of your organization.
- If personal messaging is allowed, keep it to a minimum. Your organization may prefer that personal chats be done during breaks or the lunch hour.
- Show patience by not blasting multiple messages to coworkers if a response is not immediate.
- Keep your presence status up-to-date so that people trying to reach you don't waste their time.
- Beware of jargon, slang, and abbreviations, which, although they may reduce keystrokes, may be confusing and appear unprofessional.
- Respect your receivers by employing proper grammar, spelling, and proofreading.

Using Podcasts, Blogs, and Wikis for Business

Podcasts, blogs, and wikis are part of the new user-centered virtual environment called Web 2.0. Far from being passive consumers, today's Internet users have the power to create Web content; interact with businesses and each other; review products, self-publish, or blog; contribute to wikis; or tag and share images and other files. Individuals wield enormous power because they can potentially reach huge audiences. For this reason, businesses often rightly fear the wrath of disgruntled employees and customers. On the other hand, this connectedness also allows them to curry favor with influential plugged-in opinion leaders.

The democratization of the Web means that in the online world, Internet users can bypass gatekeepers who filter content in the traditional print and visual media. Hence, even extreme views often reach audiences of thousands or even millions. The dangers are obvious. Fact checking often falls by the wayside, buzz may become more important than truth, and a single keystroke can make or destroy a reputation. This section addresses prudent business uses of podcasts, blogs, and wikis because you are likely to encounter these and other electronic communication tools on the job.

Business Podcasts

Used by the news media, in education, and in corporate training, podcasts are digital audio or video files that can be downloaded to a computer or watched on a smartphone.

The words *broadcast* and *iPod* combined to create the word *podcast*; however, audio and video files can be played on any number of devices, not just Apple's iPod. Podcasts can extend from short clips of a few minutes to 30-minute or longer digital files. Naturally, large video files gobble up a lot of memory, so they tend to be streamed on a Web site rather than downloaded.

How Organizations Use Podcasts. Like blogging, podcasting has experienced large growth and has spread among various user groups online. Major news organizations and media outlets podcast radio shows (e.g., National Public Radio) and TV shows, from ABC to Fox. Podcasts are also used in education. Students can access instructors' lectures, listen to interviews, watch sporting events, and access other content. Apple's iTunes U is perhaps the best-known example of free educational podcasts from Berkeley, Stanford, and other universities. Unlike streaming video that users can view only with an active Internet connection, podcasts encoded as MP3 files can be downloaded to a computer, a smartphone, or an MP3 player to be enjoyed on the go, often without subsequent Web access.

Delivering and Accessing Podcasts. Businesses have embraced podcasting for sending audio and video messages that do not require a live presence yet offer a friendly human face. Because they can broadcast repetitive information that does not require interaction, podcasts can replace costlier live teleconferences. IBM is training its sales force with podcasts that are available anytime. Real estate agents create podcasts to enable buyers to take virtual walking tours of available properties at their leisure. HR policies can also be presented in the form of podcasts for unlimited viewing on demand or as convenient. Marketing pitches also lend themselves to podcasting.

Podcasts are featured on media Web sites and company portals or shared on social networking sites and blogs. They can usually be streamed or downloaded as media files. Really simple syndication (RSS) allows the distribution of current information published in podcasts, blogs, video files, and news items. Users can select RSS feeds from various sources and personalize the information they wish to receive.

Creating a Podcast. Producing a simple podcast does not require sophisticated equipment. With inexpensive recording, editing, and publishing software such as the popular Propaganda, ePodcast Creator, Audacity, or Gabcast, users can inform customers, mix their own music, or host interviews. In fact, any digital recorder can be used to create a high-quality simple podcast, especially if the material is scripted and well rehearsed. If you are considering creating your own podcast, here are a few tips:

Creating a simple, yet professional podcast is easy and relatively inexpensive.

- **Decide whether to record one podcast or a series.** You can create a one-time podcast for a specific purpose or a series of podcasts on a related subject. Make sure you have enough material to sustain a steady flow of information.
- **Download software.** The program Audacity is available for free; other popular recording and editing software programs are relatively inexpensive.
- **Obtain hardware.** Depending on the sound quality you desire, you may need a sophisticated microphone and other audio equipment. The recording room must be properly shielded against noise, echo, and other interference. Many universities and some libraries provide language labs that feature recording booths.
- **Organize the message.** Make sure your broadcast has a beginning, middle, and end. Build in some redundancy. Tell the listeners what you will tell them, then tell them, and finally, tell them what you have told them. This principle, known to effective PowerPoint users, also applies to podcasting. Previews, summaries, and transitions are important to help your audience follow the message.
- **Choose an extemporaneous or scripted delivery.** Think about how you will deliver the information, whether speaking freely or using a manuscript. Extemporaneous delivery means that you prepare, but you use only brief notes. It usually sounds more spontaneous and natural than reading from a script, but it can also lead to redundancy, repetition, and flubbed lines. Reading from a script, if done skillfully, can sound natural and warm. However, in the wrong hands, reading can come across as mechanical and amateurish.
- **Prepare and practice.** Before recording, do a few practice runs. Editing audio or video is difficult and time-consuming. Try to get your recording right, so that you won't have to edit much.
- **Publish and distribute your message.** If you post the podcast to a blog, you can introduce it and solicit your audience's feedback. Consider distributing your podcast by an RSS feed.

Professional Blogs and Twitter

A blog is a Web site with journal entries on any imaginable topic usually written by one person, although some blogs feature multiple commentators. Typically, readers leave feedback. Businesses use blogs to keep customers and employees informed and to interact with them. The biggest advantage of business blogs is that they potentially reach a far-flung, vast audience.

Blogs are online journals used by companies to communicate internally with employees and externally with customers.

Marketing firms and their clients are looking closely at blogs because blogs can produce unbiased consumer feedback faster and more cheaply than such staples of consumer research as focus groups and surveys. Employees and executives at companies such as Google, IBM, and Hewlett-Packard maintain blogs. They use blogs to communicate internally with employees and externally with clients. Currently, 78 (15.6 percent) of Fortune 500 companies are blogging.[6] As an online diary or journal, a blog allows visitors to leave public comments. At this time, writers have posted 163 million blogs, and this number is growing by about 76,000 blogs per day.[7]

Twitter falls between the blog and social media categories. It is often referred to as a microblogging service, but it also invites social networking. It allows users to share brief status updates called tweets about their lives and their whereabouts online. Twitter users can access the service by computer or with their smartphones.

In some industries, companies are using Twitter and other social media to monitor what is being said about them, to engage with customers, and to market to other businesses. In tweets of 140 characters or fewer, JetBlue and United offer special deals on flights. Social media veteran Southwest Airlines has a particularly impressive online presence, boasting 12 million monthly visits to its Web site, 1.3 million Facebook fans, and 1 million Twitter followers.[8] An early adopter of Facebook and Twitter, the quirky carrier appointed "tweet watchers" who troubleshoot air travelers' problems. JetBlue followed suit in responding to customer queries. Other airlines also tweet actively.[9] To view examples of typical customer-service tweets, see Figure 5.5.

How Companies Use Blogs

The potential applications of blogs in business are vast. Like other Web 2.0 phenomena, corporate blogs usually invite feedback and help build communities. Specifically, companies use blogs for public relations, customer relations, crisis communication, market research, viral marketing, internal communication, and recruiting.

Public Relations, Customer Relations, and Crisis Communication. One of the prominent uses of blogs is to provide up-to-date company information to the press and the public. Blogs can be written by executives or by rank-and-file

FIGURE 5.5 How Companies Use Twitter

Companies such as the airlines below use Twitter to the broadcast to their "followers" up-to-the-minute information, announce special offers, and address customer-service mix-ups. If a request or complaint is unique, the representative may request that the customer send a "direct message" (DM) to handle the inquiry out of the tweeting public's eye, not least to contain potential PR damage.

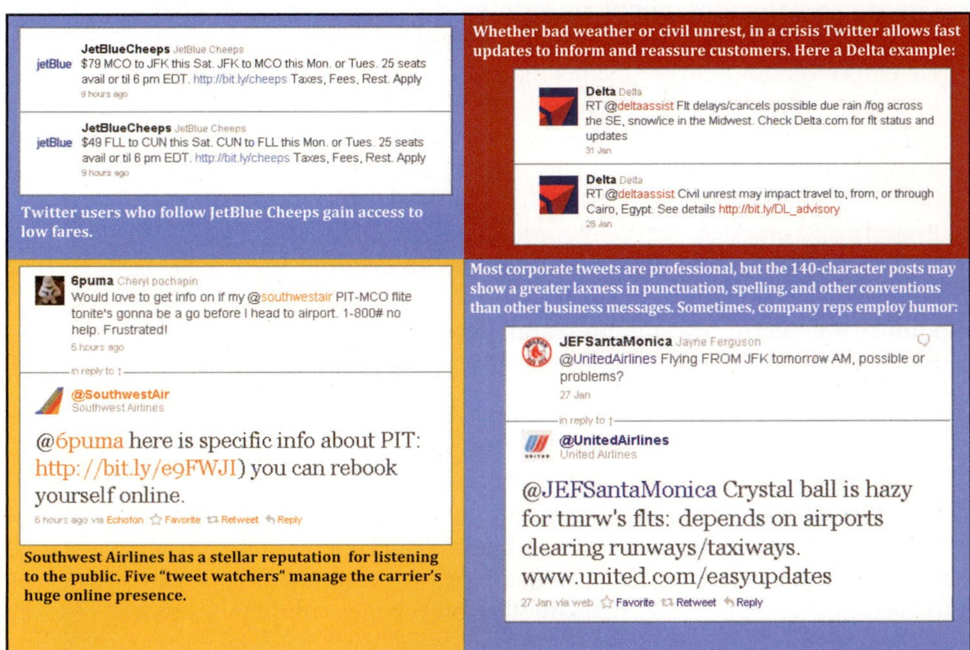

employees. General Electric's Global Research blog addresses industry insiders and the interested public. Similarly, after experimenting with in-house blogs and proprietary social networks, Best Buy introduced BBY, Best Buy Community, a blog and social networking site for employees and managers. The company's chief marketing officer, Barry Judge, runs a corporate blog on a Web site bearing his name.

A company blog is a natural forum for late-breaking news, especially when disaster strikes. Business bloggers can address rumors and combat misinformation. Although a blog cannot replace other communication channels in an emergency, it should be part of the overall effort to soothe the public's emotional reaction with a human voice of reason.

Market Research. Because most blogs invite feedback, they can be invaluable sources of opinion from customers and industry experts. In addition to monitoring visitor comments on their corporate blogs, many companies now have appointed employees who scrutinize the blogosphere for buzz and positive and negative postings about their organization and products.

Online Communities. Like Twitter, which has a loyal core following, company blogs can attract a devoted community of participants who want to keep informed about company events, product updates, and other news. In turn, those enthusiasts can contribute new ideas. Similar to Dell's IdeaStorm, Starbucks' blog Ideas In Action solicits product and service ideas from customers.

Internal Communication and Recruiting. Blogs can be used to keep virtual teams on track and share updates on the road. Members in remote locations can stay in touch by smartphone and other devices, exchanging text, images, sound, and video clips. In many companies, blogs have replaced hard-copy publications in offering late-breaking news or tidbits of interest to employees. They feature profiles of high-performing workers, information about benefits, and so forth.

Blogs mirror the company culture and present an invaluable opportunity for job candidates to size up a potential employer and the people working there.

Tips for Creating a Professional Blog

Blogging has grown up as a commercial activity and now offers sound business opportunities. Some bloggers make a living, although most remain unknowns in the boundless thickets of information on the Internet. To even have a shot at competing with established blog sites, consider the following guidelines for starting a successful business blog:

Like all business messages, blog entries must be well targeted, carefully crafted, and professional.

- **Identify your audience.** As with any type of communication, you must know your audience to decide what to write to get people to read your blog. Does your blog stand out? What makes you interesting and unique?
- **Find a home for your blog.** You can use software that will let you attach a blog function to your Web site. Alternatively, you can join a blog hosting site that will provide a link on your Web site to attract visitors. You can usually find templates and other options to help build traffic to your site, especially if you use trackers that identify recent posts and popular message threads. According to Blogtap, currently the top three blog hosting sites are WordPress, Google Blogger, and TypePad.[10]
- **Craft your message.** Blog about topics that showcase your expertise and insights. Offer a fresh, unique perspective on subjects your audience cares about. Your writing should be intriguing and sincere. Experts suggest that authors get to know the blogosphere in their industry and comment on what other bloggers are writing about. Stick with what you know.
- **Make "blogrolling" work for you.** Your goal is to attract repeat visitors to your blog. One way to achieve this objective is to increase traffic between blogs. "Blogrolling" means that you provide links to other sites or blogs on the Web

that you find valuable and that are related to your business or industry. Respond to other bloggers' postings and link to them.

- **Attract search engines by choosing the right keywords.** In headlines and text, emphasize potential search terms that may draw traffic to your site. Focus on one topic and use a variety of synonyms to propel your blog to the top of search engine listings. An import company doing business with China would want to stress the keywords *import* and *China* as well as *trade, Asia,* and so forth, in addition to more industry-specific terms, such as *toys.*
- **Blog often.** Provide fresh content regularly. Stay current. Stale information puts off visitors. Post short, concise messages, but do so often.
- **Monitor the traffic to your site.** If necessary, vary your subjects to attract interest. If traffic slows down, experiment with new themes while staying with your core business and expertise. Also, evaluate the effectiveness of your publishing platform. Some blog publishing sites are more valuable than others in increasing your blog's visibility to search engines.
- **Seek permission.** If you are employed, explore your company's blogging policy. Even if neither a policy nor a prohibition against blogging exists, avoid writing about your employer, coworkers, customers, and events at the office, however veiled your references may be. The Internet is abuzz with stories about bloggers who got fired for online indiscretions.
- **Stay away from inappropriate topics.** Whether you are a rank-and-file employee or a freelance blogger, remember not to write anything you wouldn't want your family, friends, and the public at large to read. Blogs are not private journal entries; therefore, don't entrust to them any risqué, politically extreme, or private information.

Wikis and Collaboration

Teams use wikis to create and edit documents whether across geographic distances and multiple time zones or in house.

At least as important to business as blogs are wikis. A wiki is a Web site that employs easy-to-use collaborative software to allow users to create documents that can be edited by tapping into the same technology that runs the well-known online encyclopedia Wikipedia. Large companies, such as BT Group (previously British Telecom), use wikis to connect company representatives with developers and create a community that will contribute to the knowledge base of a product or service.[11] With its Forum Nokia, the Finnish cell phone maker is one of many companies—for example, IBM, Microsoft, and Disney—that maintain wikis. Most corporate projects are facilitated with the help of wikis, a tool that is especially valuable across vast geographic distances and multiple time zones.

How Businesses Use Wikis. Far from being just a tool for geeks, wikis are used beyond information technology departments. The five main uses range from providing a shared internal knowledge base to storing templates for business documents.

- **The global wiki.** For companies with a global reach, a wiki is an ideal tool for information sharing between headquarters and satellite offices. Team members can easily edit their work and provide input to the home office and each other.
- **The wiki knowledge base.** Teams or departments use wikis to collect and disseminate information to large audiences creating a database for knowledge management. For example, an IT department may compile frequently asked questions that help users resolve the most common problems themselves. Human resources managers may update employee policies, make announcements, and convey information about benefits.
- **Wikis for meetings.** Wikis can facilitate feedback before and after meetings or serve as repositories of meeting minutes. In fact, wikis may replace some meetings, yet still keep a project on track. An often-cited example of a huge global wiki meeting is IBM's famous massive online discussion and brainstorming session that involved more than 100,000 participants from more than 160 countries.

- **Project management with wikis.** Wikis offer a highly interactive environment ideal for projects by enabling information to be centralized for easy access and user input. All participants have the same information available and can share ideas freely, more freely than in traditional face-to-face meetings. Instead of a top-down information flow, wikis empower employees and foster a team environment in which ideas can thrive.
- **Documentation and wikis.** Wikis can help to document projects large and small as well as technical and nontechnical. Wikis may also provide templates for reports.

How to Be a Valuable Wiki Contributor. Whether you wish to contribute to a wiki on the Web or at work, try to be an effective participant. As with most electronic communication, abide by the conventions of polite society, and follow commonsense rules. Show respect and watch out for improper or ambiguous language. Don't attack or otherwise severely criticize another contributor.

To be productive when working on a wiki project, be polite, follow the guidelines established by the editors, and respect other contributors.

Pay attention to correct grammar and spelling, and verify your facts. Every comment you contribute is essentially published on the Web and available to any reader. If the content appears on the company intranet, it is for the whole company to see. Wikipedia, a wiki that is trying to marry credibility with its desire for openness, recently tightened the rules for its editors after Internet vandals prematurely announced Senator Edward Kennedy's death and pronounced his colleague, Senator Robert Byrd, dead as well.

Follow the guidelines for contributors, and give credit where credit is due. Contributors to a wiki are part of a team, not individual authors who can reasonably expect recognition or maintain control over their writing. When borrowing, be sure to cite your sources to avoid plagiarism.

Negotiating Social and Professional Networking Sites

Far from being only entertaining leisure sites, social networking sites such as Facebook and Twitter are used by businesses for similar reasons and in much the same way as podcasts, blogs, and wikis. Social networking sites enable businesses to connect with customers and employees, share company news, and exchange ideas. Social online communities for professional audiences (e.g., LinkedIn) help recruiters find talent and encounter potential employees before hiring them.

Social networking sites allow businesses to connect with customers and employees, share company news, and exchange ideas.

How Businesses Use Social Networks

Some firms use social online communities for brainstorming and teamwork. They provide the collaboration tools and watch what happens. British Telecom (BT) has about 11,000 employees on Facebook in addition to offering its own internal social network. A British Telecom IT executive says that his company can observe online relationships to see how information travels and decision making occurs. The company is able to identify teams that form spontaneously and naturally and then assigns targeted projects to them. Idea generators are easy to spot. The BT executive considers these contributors invaluable, suggesting that "a new class of supercommunicators has emerged."[12] The key to all the new media is that they thrive in a highly mobile and interactive Web 2.0 environment.

Other companies harness the power of online communities to boost their brand image or to provide a forum for collaboration. McDonald's has a strong presence on Facebook boasting nearly 1.5 million "fans." The fast-food chain also maintains a private networking site, StationM, for its 650,000 hourly employees in 15,000 locations across the United States and Canada.[13]

McDonald's and BT Group (formerly British Telecom) are not the only companies running their own social networks. Insurer MetLife has launched connect. MetLife, an online social network collaboration tool. Resembling Facebook, this internal networking tool sits safely behind the corporate firewall.[14] Best Buy has created its own social network, Blue Shirt Nation, with currently more than 20,000 participants, most of them sales associates. IBM's in-house social network, Beehive, has 30,000 employees on it. Managers notice avid networkers who create buzz and promote the brand. The drawback is that quieter employees may be overlooked.[15]

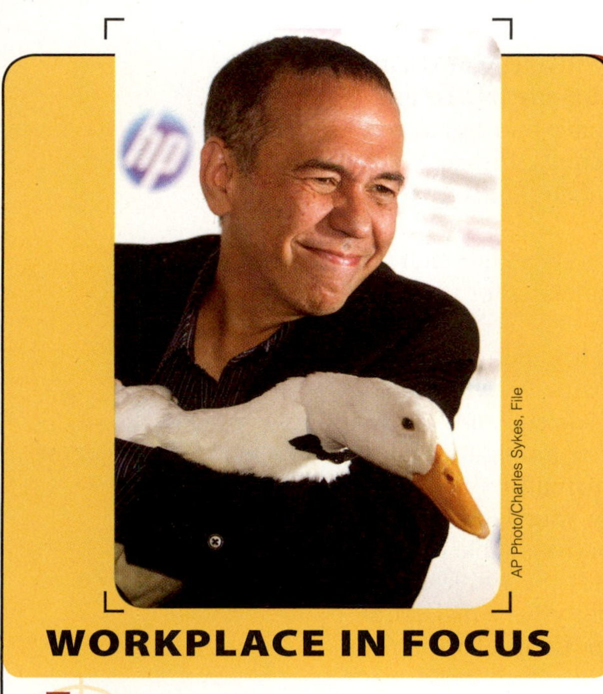

AP Photo/Charles Sykes, File

WORKPLACE IN FOCUS

The Aflac Duck lost his voice recently when long-time voice actor Gilbert Gottfried was fired for posting tasteless jokes on Twitter. With the commercial quacker quieted, Aflac advertised tryouts for a new spokesduck, including one ad that featured the iconic mascot in a black and white silent movie. During the spot, shouts of "Aflac!" appear on silent movie title cards as the flustered fowl rescues a damsel tied to a railroad track. How should professionals exercise caution when using digital media?

Potential Risks of Social Networks for Businesses

Online social networks hold great promise for businesses while also presenting some risk. Most managers want plugged-in employees with strong tech skills. They like to imagine their workers as brand ambassadors. They fantasize about their products becoming overnight sensations thanks to viral marketing. However, they also fret about incurring productivity losses, compromising trade secrets, attracting the wrath of huge Internet audiences, and facing embarrassment over inappropriate and damaging employee posts.[16]

Businesses take different approaches to the "dark side" of social networking. Some, such as Zappos.com, take a hands-off approach to employee online activity. Others, such as IBM, have drafted detailed policies to cover all forms of self-expression online. Some of IBM's guidelines include being honest about one's identity, accepting personal responsibility for published posts, and hitting **Send** only after careful thought. The technology giant asks its workers to avoid any controversies outside their professional role. The company wants workers to "add value" as they are building their social reputations, not dwell on trivia.[17] Finally, Enterprise Rent-A-Car and other organizations block some or all social sites.

Companies struggle with finding the right balance between permitting access to the Web and protecting security as well as ensuring productivity.

Younger workers in particular are often stunned when their employers block access to Facebook, Gmail, and other popular Web destinations. One 27-year-old Chicago resident complained about his former employer: "It was a constant battle between the people that saw technology as an advantage, and those that saw it as a hindrance."[18] The key is to strike a balance between allowing employees access to the Web and protecting security and ensuring productivity.

Tips for Using Social Networking Sites and Keeping Your Job

Experts agree that, as with any public online activity, users of social networking sites would do well to exercise caution. Privacy is a myth, and sensitive information should not be shared lightly, least of all risqué photographs. Furthermore, refusing "friend" requests or "unfriending" individuals could jeopardize professional relationships. Consider the following tip by career counselor Julie Powell[19] if you like to visit social networking sites and want to keep your job: Establish boundaries. Don't share information online that you would not be comfortable sharing openly in the office.

The advice to think twice before posting online applies to most communication channels used on the job. Facebook expert and blogger Nick O'Neill cautions account holders never to assume that the content they post on a social networking site is protected unless they have activated the privacy option. Many users leave their pages open and risk trouble with their employers by assuming that online

FIGURE 5.6 **Big Companies Rule on Facebook: Netflix**

Facebook recently reached 600 million users. The site allows registered users to create individual home pages and to choose from more than 200 groups based on their interests. Large corporations seem to thrive on Facebook. Slate magazine ranked Coca-Cola "first among companies with the best Facebook presences." Newer companies such as online film rental service Netflix may draw 100,000 fans, as opposed to Coca-Cola's whopping 5,300,000 fans.

AP Images/PRNewsFoto/Netflix, Inc.

> **OFFICE INSIDER**
>
> *Some see parallels between Web use on the job today and old-fashioned chatting around the water cooler or making personal phone calls, grudgingly accepted as they were by managers: "These two worlds will continue to collide until there's a mutual understanding that performance, not Internet usage, is what really matters."*
>
> —Gary Rudman, Consultant

comments are hidden from view.[20] Even privacy settings, however, do not guarantee complete protection from prying eyes.

Among the many risks in the cyber world are inappropriate photographs and making "friends" online. Tags make pictures searchable so that an embarrassing college incident may resurface years later. Another potential minefield, says consultant Rachel Weingarten, is rejecting friend requests from some colleagues while accepting such offers from others.[21] The snubbed coworker may harbor ill feelings as a result. Blocking a user for no apparent reason could also be interpreted as a rude rejection.

Harnessing the Potential of Professional Networking Sites

What are the potential rewards of using professional networking sites such as LinkedIn?

Experts agree that connecting online offers professional opportunities by expanding the traditional Rolodex. They see social networking online as a natural extension of work.[22] Small businesses may view such sites as forums for sharing slideshow presentations and other office documents. Artists may feature their work. Medical doctors can discuss surgical techniques with peers.

As we have seen, the lines between social and professional networking are increasingly blurry. However, among business-oriented Web sites where users can post job openings, résumés, and career profiles, LinkedIn is the most popular networking tool in the United States. A great value of such business networking sites is that they can serve as a source for referrals and recommendations. Job seekers can also browse jobs posted by a company with a LinkedIn presence.

While most social networking sites connect people in cyberspace, Foursquare's geosocial networking service connects people in real spaces. Launched in 2009, the location-sharing app encourages mobile device users to "check in" at local stores, restaurants, and offices. The GPS feature sends meet-up alerts whenever contacts from one's social network are in the vicinity. Professionals tout Foursquare's face-to-face networking potential; Starbucks uses the service to deliver mobile customer rewards programs. How is mobile computing changing the way we do business?

AP Photo/Russel A. Daniels

WORKPLACE IN FOCUS

Hiring experts agree that about three quarters of U.S. companies view social media—mostly LinkedIn—as indispensable outlets for recruiting.[23] They recommend that job seekers keep their profiles "clean"—that is, free of risqué photos, profanity, and negative comments. Instead, job candidates are encouraged to highlight awards, professional goals, and accomplishments. Although professional networking sites cannot replace face-to-face interviews, they allow hiring managers to form first impressions before inviting job hunters, or to vet interviewees being considered for an open position.

The advantages that social and professional networking sites offer recruiters and applicants are plain. In the right hands, the sites are inexpensive, simple, and fast ways to advertise current business opportunities and to connect. However, as innovative as this new type of job search seems to be, the basics remain the same. Candidates need to craft their profiles with the same care they use when putting together their traditional résumés and cover letters. The job hunter's public appearance online must always be professional, and the profile should be up-to-date. You will learn more about job searching online in Chapter 13.

Sharing Information Through RSS Feeds and Social Bookmarking

RSS feeds allow users to monitor many news sources at once.

You may wonder how businesspeople navigate the vast resources available on the Internet. Seeking information on the Web that is relevant to you and your business can be time-consuming. Really simple syndication (RSS for short) is a time-saver, allowing users to monitor many news sources in one convenient spot. Likewise, social bookmarking helps busy professionals stay informed about topics of interest and negotiate the vast information jungle of the Web.

Really Simple Syndication. RSS, a fast and easy way to search and manage information, is a data file format capable of transmitting changing Web content. News organizations, bloggers, and other online information providers syndicate (i.e., publish and distribute) their content to subscribers. RSS documents are called feeds or channels, and they can be read most efficiently with a Web-based feed reader (also known as an aggregator), an easy-to-use software application. Feeds help alert subscribers to up-to-the-minute blog entries, news items, videos, and podcasts from various sources.

How does RSS work? Each time a syndicated Web site is updated, a summary of the new information travels by RSS feed to the site's subscribers. Users can read RSS feeds within their Internet browsers and in e-mail programs such as MS Outlook, or use popular news aggregators such as Google Reader, Bloglines, SharpReader, NetNewsWire, and Straw. Web-based feed readers also work well with mobile devices, helping busy executives keep up with customized news feeds on the go.

Forward-looking companies such as retailer Target, online travel sites such as Travelocity, and many airlines have been using RSS feeds to alert customers to weekly sales and special offers.

Social Bookmarking. In the battle for "eyeballs" on the Internet, social bookmarking is another critical component. Business Web sites, blogs, and other online content gain an edge if readers link to them and, thus, share content with other online users. Digg, delicious, reddit, StumbleUpon, and squidoo are just a few of the many fast-growing social bookmarking and content aggregator (collector) Web sites. Social bookmarking helps users search, organize, manage, and store bookmarks on the Web with the help of metadata—that is, information tags or keywords.

In what ways is social bookmarking helpful to business users?

Many Web sites, blogs, and other content providers on the Internet offer various widgets or icons of social bookmarking sites to enable content sharing. Web publishers hope readers will link their information to social bookmarking sites and alert others to the information.

Perhaps you can see now how RSS feeds and social bookmarking sites could help you stay abreast of breaking news from many sources and save you valuable time. Whether you wish to grab a broadcast from CNN.com or check the most recent sports scores, look for the square orange RSS feed icon on your favorite Web sites or a rectangular button with the letters RSS or XML. On most high-traffic Web sites, you will also see Share links, or widgets, that will take you to social bookmarking sites.

www.cengagebrain.com

Available with an access code, these eResources will help you prepare for exams:

- **Chapter Review Quizzes**
- **Personal Language Trainer**
- **PowerPoint Slides**
- **Flash Cards**

Summing Up and Looking Forward

The information flow in business today is increasingly digital and mobile as the Web has evolved into an interactive medium inviting participation and interaction with large groups of people over large distances. Within organizations, internal messages in today's workplace usually take the form of e-mails, memos, and, to a lesser extent, instant messages and texts. E-mails and memos use a standardized format to request and deliver information.

Because most messages are exchanged electronically, this chapter presented many techniques for sending and receiving safe and effective e-mails, instant messages, and text messages. However, businesspeople are still using interoffice memos to convey confidential information, emphasize ideas, deliver lengthy documents, or lend importance to a message.

On the other hand, businesses are embracing modern communication technology such as podcasts, blogs, and wikis. You learned how to be safe and professional when recording a podcast, posting to a blog, and contributing to a wiki when collaborating with others. Companies also use social media sites to communicate with employees, customers, and job candidates, and you were introduced to tips that will keep you safe when using social and professional networking sites. The chapter also discussed how to select and organize information using RSS feeds and social bookmarking.

In Chapter 6 you will apply the direct strategy in composing e-mails, memos, and letters.

Critical Thinking

1. How does your use of e-mail, IM, texting, blogs, social media, and other current communication technologies with your friends and family compare with the business uses of these technologies that you learned about in this chapter?
2. Google CEO Eric Schmidt upset some by sketching his vision of a future in which targeted advertising will become so sophisticated that the search software will know exactly users' preferences and literally tell them what to do.

Google is already under fire for its Streetview software in Google Maps for breaching privacy, and this notion of artificial intelligence anticipating our needs makes many uncomfortable.[24] How do you view this expanded role of search software? What are the potential advantages and disadvantages?

3. A recent study suggests that American teenagers text away to the tune of about 80 messages a day, almost 2,300 a month. The dangers of texting while driving are well established, but what about texting while walking? A 15-year-old in New York state fell into an unsecured manhole while she was texting. Another texting teen was killed on a crosswalk. Who is at fault in these incidents, and do we need legal restrictions for distracted walkers who text?[25]

4. Media company ESPN recently created an official policy for social networking that affects all its prominent talent. The core message: "Assume at all times you are representing ESPN." Some sports bloggers have criticized the rules as too strict. Discuss the ramifications of the core statement.[26]

5. **Ethical Issue:** *Playboy* recently launched a new "office-safe" Web site, TheSmokingJacket.com, designed to entertain the magazine's core readership, males between the ages of twenty-five and thirty-four, as they goof off on the job. Hiding its true origin, the new Web site expressly wishes to reach bored men at work. Instead of nudity, it offers humor and related "cool" content. The lead producer of the stealth *Playboy* clone, Matt Gibbs, seems to have no qualms about tricking company firewalls: "The ideal is to be . . . the go-to site for those who are bored at work."[27] Analyze the ethics of (a) launching a Web site that deliberately targets office workers while they are on the job and (b) Web surfing while being paid to work. Could an argument be made for limited surfing that most would consider harmless? Under what circumstances and rules? What are the dangers of engaging in such behavior at work?

Chapter Review

6. List the typical components of direct e-mails and memos.

Subject line
opening
Body, Closing

7. Why do writers of most e-mails and memos frontload—that is, reveal the main idea immediately in the opening?

Because readers want to know what they are reading about immediatly.

8. Specify some of the key formatting and usage conventions for e-mails.

guide words body
Greeting closing lines

9. What are some of the dangers of e-mail?

You could send them to wrong person & unententionally.

10. Briefly describe the pros and cons of instant messaging and texting.

Pros: contacts immediatly
make decisions fast
low-cost

Cons: distractive
exposures

11. Suggest at least ten best practices for using IM and texting responsibly and professionally.

10

- Dont txt and Drive
- Learn policies
- organize contact lists
- respect recivers
- avoid jargon
- keep messages to a minimum
- keep them simple
- Do not use for sensetive messages.
- Be carefull what you say.

12. Describe the steps to creating a simple podcast.

Download software
obtain hardware
organize
prepare + practive
Publish.

13. What are blogs, and how do businesses use them?

web site with Journal entries.

They use them to keep employees + customers informed.

14. In what ways have businesses embraced social networking?

By contacting customers, share news + exchang Ideas.

15. What are RSS feeds and social bookmarking, and how do they help businesspeople navigate information on the Internet?

easy ways to search for information. By automatically traveling information.

Writing Improvement Exercises

Message Openers and Subject Lines

Your Task. Compare the following sets of message openers. Circle the letter of the opener that illustrates a direct opening. Write an appropriate subject line for each opening paragraph.

16. An e-mail requesting information about creating a Facebook presence:
    a. We want to start our business fan page on Facebook, but we are not sure how to ensure visibility and participation, and we worry about the privacy risks and data safety. We have many questions and would like information about Facebook and social media in general.
    b. Please answer the following questions about creating a business fan page on Facebook and protecting our network from intrusions and malicious attacks.

    Subject line:

17. An e-mail announcing a new day-care program:
    a. Employees interested in enrolling their children in our new low-cost day-care program are invited to an HR orientation on September 15.
    b. For several years we have studied the possibility of offering a day-care option for those employees who are parents. Until recently, our management team was unable to agree on the exact parameters of this benefit, but now some of you will be able to take advantage of this option.

    Subject line:

18. An e-mail message announcing an employee satisfaction survey:
    a. We have noticed recently an increased turnover among our sales staff. We are concerned about this troubling development and would like to study its causes. We have hired an outside consulting firm to gauge the attitudes of our salespeople in confidential qualitative interviews.
    b. The consulting firm Strelitz & Kaus Research Associates will soon conduct in-depth qualitative interviews to explore the satisfaction among our sales staff and recommend strategies to stem the tide of recent departures.

    Subject line:

19. A memo announcing a new procedure:
    a. It has come to our attention that some staff members write blogs, sometimes publicly addressing sensitive company information. We respect the desire of employees to express themselves and would like to continue allowing the practice, but we decided to provide binding rules to ensure the company's and the bloggers' safety.
    b. The following new policy for blog authors will help staff members to create posts that will maintain the integrity of the company's sensitive information and keep the writers safe.

    Subject line:

Opening Paragraphs and Subject Lines

Your Task. The following opening paragraphs to memos are wordy and indirect. After reading each paragraph, identify the main idea. Then, write an opening sentence that illustrates a more direct opening and include a subject line.

20. Several staff members came to me and announced their interest in learning more about telecommuting and government telework policies. As most of you know, these areas of concern are increasingly important for most government workers here in Washington, D.C. A seminar titled "Telecommuting and Telework Policies" is being conducted March 22. I am allowing the following employees to attend the seminar: Darrell Walters, Akil Jackson, and Amy Woods.

    Subject line:

21. Your MegaCorp Employees Association has secured for you discounts on auto repair, carpet purchases, travel arrangements, and many other services. These services are available to you if you have a Buying Power Card. All MegaCorp employees are eligible for their own private Buying Power Cards.

    Subject line:

Bulleted and Numbered Lists

22. E-mails and memos frequently contain bulleted or numbered lists, which you learned about in Chapter 4.

    Your Task. Revise the following wordy paragraph into an introductory statement and a short list with category headings (see p. 93 in Chapter 4). Should the list be numbered or bulleted?

Our office could implement better environmental practices such as improving energy efficiency and reducing our carbon footprint. Here are three simple things we can do to make our daily work practices greener. For one thing, we can power down. At night we should turn off monitors, not just log off our computers. In addition, we could "Light Right." This means installing energy-efficient lighting throughout the office. A final suggestion has to do with recycling. We could be recycling instantly if we placed small recycling bins at all workstations and common-use areas.

To improve environmental practices
• Power Down • recycle.
• Light right

23. **Your Task.** Revise the following wordy paragraph into an introductory statement with a concise list that has three bullet points. Could you use category headings for your bullet points?

If you are a job candidate interviewing for a job, you should follow a few guidelines that most people consider basic. You will be more successful if you do these things. One of the first things to do is get ready. Before the interview, successful candidates research the target company. That is, they find out about it. If you really want to be successful, you will prepare success stories. Wise candidates also clean up any digital dirt that may be floating around the Internet. Those are a few of the things to do before the interview. During the interview, the best candidates try to sound enthusiastic. They answer questions clearly but with short, concise responses. They also are prepared to ask their own questions. After the interview, when you can relax a bit, you should remember to send a thank-you note to the interviewer. Another thing to do after the interview is contact references. One last thing to do, if you don't hear from the interviewer within five days, is follow up with an inquiry.

For preparing for a job interveiw, some basic steps are.
• prepare for interveiw
• sound enthusiastic
• send a thank you.

Note: All Writing Improvement Cases are provided at **www.meguffey.com** for you to revise online.

Writing Improvement Cases

 **E-MAIL**

5.1 Information E-Mail: Confusion Over Fall Training Conference

Jim Morales' e-mail request is confusing to say the least. It would benefit from a better organization and visual presentation.

Your Task. Analyze the e-mail message. List its weaknesses. If your instructor directs, revise it.

To: Greta Targa <greta.targa@gamma.com>
From: Jim Morales <jim.morales@gamma.com>
Subject: HELP!
Cc:

As you already know, we have been working hard to plan the Gamma Fall Training Conference. It will be held in Miami. Here are the speakers I have lined up for training sessions. I'm thinking that on Tuesday, November 12, we will have Nicole Gold. Her scheduled topic is "Using E-Mail and IM Effectively." Anthony Mills said he could speak to our group on November 13 (Wednesday). "Leading Groups and Teams" is the topic for Mills. Here are their e-mail addresses: *tony.mills@sunbelt.net.* and *n.gold@etc.com.*

You can help us make this one of the best training sessions ever. I need you to send each of these people an e-mail and confirm the dates and topics. Due to the fact that we must print the program soon (by September 1), I will need this done as soon as possible. Don't hesitate to call if you have any questions.

Jim

1. List at least five weaknesses of this message.

2. Outline a writing plan (not the actual message) for this message.

Subject line:
Opening:
Body:

Closing:

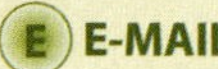

5.2 Information E-Mail: Disorganized Workshop Description

In her e-mail Eleanor Hutchinson is reporting about a recent workshop on workplace violence she attended. However, Eleanor presents the information in a rather haphazard fashion.

Your Task. Analyze the e-mail. List its weaknesses and then outline an appropriate writing plan. Can you think of a way to improve readability? If your instructor directs, revise it.

To: Mitchell Moraga <mitchell.moraga@media.com>
From: Eleanor Hutchinson <ehutchinson@media.com>
Subject: My Report
Cc:

Mitchell,

This is in response to your request that I attend the Workplace Issues and tell you about it. As you know, I attended the Workplace Issues conference on November 3, as you suggested. The topic was how to prevent workplace violence, and I found it very fascinating. Although we have been fortunate to avoid serious incidents at our company, it's better to be safe than sorry. Because I was the representative from our company and you asked for a report, here it is. Kit Adkins was the presenter, and she made suggestions in three categories, which I will summarize here.

Ms. Atkins cautioned organizations to prescreen job applicants. As a matter of fact, wise companies do not offer employment until after a candidate's background has been checked. Just the mention of a background check is enough to make some candidates withdraw. These candidates, of course, are the ones with something to hide.

A second suggestion was that companies should prepare a good employee handbook that outlines what employees should do when they suspect potential workplace violence. This handbook should include a way for informers to be anonymous.

A third recommendation had to do with recognizing red-flag behavior. This involves having companies train managers to recognize signs of potential workplace violence. What are some of the red flags? One sign is an increasing number of arguments (most of them petty) with coworkers. Another sign is extreme changes in behavior or statements indicating depression over family or financial problems. Another sign is bullying or harassing behavior. Bringing a firearm to work or displaying an extreme fascination with firearms is another sign.

I think that the best recommendation is prescreening job candidates. This is because it is most feasible. If you want me to do more research on prescreening techniques, do not hesitate to let me know. Let me know by November 18 if you want me to make a report at our management meeting, which is scheduled for December 3.

Ellie

1. List at least five weaknesses of this e-mail message.

2. Outline a writing plan (not the actual message) for this message.

Subject line:
Opening:
Body:

Closing:

5.3 Information Memo: Facts About Corporate Instant Messaging

The following memo reports information from a symposium, but it is poorly written.

Your Task. Analyze the message. List its weaknesses and then outline a writing plan. If your instructor directs, revise the message.

Date: March 4, 201x
To: Trevor Kurtz, CEO
From: Emily Lopez-Rush
Subject: Instant Messaging

Thanks for asking me to attend the Instant Messaging Symposium. It was sponsored by Pixel Link and took place March 2. Do you think you will want me to expand on what I learned at the next management council meeting? I believe that meeting is March 25.

Anyway, here's my report. Jason Howard, the symposium leader told us that over 80 million workers are already using instant messaging and that it was definitely here to stay. But do the risks outweigh the advantages? He talked about benefits, providers, costs involved, and risks. The top advantages of IM are speed, documentation, and it saves costs. The major problems are spam, security, control, and disruptive. He said that the principal IM providers for consumers were Windows Live Messenger, Yahoo Messenger, and AOL Instant Messenger. Misuse of IM can result in reductions in productivity. However, positive results can be achieved with appropriate use. Although some employees are using consumer IM services, for maximum security many organizations are investing in enterprise-level IM systems, and they are adopting guidelines for employees. These enterprise-level IM systems range in cost from $30 to $100 per user license. The cost depends on the amount of functionality.

This is just a summary of what I learned. If you want to hear more, please do not hesitate to call.

1. List at least five weaknesses of this e-mail message.

2. Outline a writing plan (not the actual message) for this message.

   Subject line:
   Opening:
   Body:

   Closing:

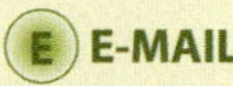
E-MAIL

5.4 Information E-Mail: Poorly Organized Message About Interns

The following message from the human resources director to project director Joshua Turck suffers from poor organization and murky focus.

Your Task. Determine what the main idea is and organize the message to develop that idea. Don't just rearrange the sentences.

To: Joshua Turck <joshua.turck@bayside.com>
From: Sable Johnson <sable.johnson@bayside.com>
Subject: Interns
Cc:

We do want a strong internship program that can provide us with superior, well-trained personnel; however, the program must meet government regulations.

Your inquiry about the status of our interns caused my staff and me to look into this matter more carefully. Our attorneys told us that all interns must be considered employees and paid at least the minimum wage. We learned that college students are legitimate only if they are receiving real training. Interns are not legitimate if they do any of the following: 1. If they displace a regular employee. 2. If they complete a client's work for which we bill. 3. If they are promised full-time jobs at the end of training.

I appreciate your bringing this to my attention. I would like to arrange for you to meet with the vice president and me to analyze this fall's internship program and consider changes.

Having every single intern sign a contract saying that they are willing to accept college credit in place of wages does not provide legal protection. An intern must do more than busy work.

After reviewing our complete program, changes must be made. We believe that future interns must have a structured training program. Let's meet to discuss!

Sable Johnson, Director
Human Resources

Activities and Cases

5.5 Instant Messaging at Local Auto Dealer

Read the following log of a live IM chat between a customer-service representative and a visitor to a Glendora car dealership's Web site.

Your Task. In class discuss how Alex could have made this interaction with a customer more effective. Is his IM chat with Mr. Rhee professional, polite, and respectful? If your instructor directs, rewrite Alex's responses to Mr. Rhee's queries.

Service rep:	Hey, I'm Alex. How's it goin? Welcome to Harkin BMW of Glendora!
Customer:	??
Service rep:	Im supposed to provid live assistance. What can I do you for?
Customer:	I want buy car.
Service rep:	May I have your name fist?
Customer:	Jin Bae Rhee
Service rep:	Whoa! Is that a dude's name? Okay. What kind? New inventory or preowned?
Customer:	BMW. 2011 model. for family, for business.
Service rep:	New, then, huh? Where are you from?
Customer:	What car you have?
Service rep:	We got some that will knock your socks off.
Customer:	I want green car, low mileage, less gasoline burn.
Service rep:	My man, if you can't afford the gas on these puppies, you shouldn't buy a Beemer, you know what I mean? Or ya want green color?
Customer:	?
Service rep:	Okeydoke, we got a full lineup. Which series, 3, 5, 6, or 7? Or an X3 or X5? A Z4 convertible?
Customer:	760 sedan?
Service rep:	Nope. We got just two 550i, one for $68,695 and one for 71,020
Customer:	Eureopean delivery?
Service rep:	Oh, I know zip about that. Let me find someone who does. Can I have your phone number and e-mail?
Customer:	i prefer not get a phone call yet... but 299-484-9807 is phone numer and jrhee@techtrade.com email
Service rep:	Awsome. Well give you a jingle back or shoot you an email pronto! Bye.

5.6 Information E-Mail: Choosing a Holiday Plan

In the past your company offered all employees 11 holidays, starting with New Year's Day in January and proceeding through Christmas Day the following December. Other companies offer similar holiday schedules. In addition, your company has given all employees one floating holiday. That day was determined by a company-wide vote. As a result, all employees had the same day off. Now, management is considering a new plan that involves a floating holiday that each employee may choose. Selections, however, would be subject to staffing needs within individual departments. If two people wanted the same day, the employee with the most seniority would have the day off.

Your Task. As a member of the human resources staff, write an e-mail to employees. This message should provide information as well as ask employees to choose between continuing the current company-wide uniform floating holiday and instituting a new plan for an individual floating holiday. Be sure to establish an end date.

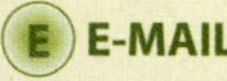 

5.7 Information E-Mail: Reaching Consensus About Business Attire

Casual dress in professional offices has been coming under attack. Your boss, Michael Harding, received the e-mail shown in Figure 5.1. He thinks it would be a good assignment for his group of management trainees to help him respond to that message. He asks your team to research answers to the first five questions in CEO William Laughton's message. He doesn't expect you to answer the final question, but any information you can supply to the first questions would help him shape a response.

Schilling & Voigt is a public CPA firm with a staff of 120 CPAs, bookkeepers, managers, and support personnel. Located in downtown Bridgeport, Connecticut, the plush offices on Water Street overlook Waterfront Park and the Long Island Sound. The firm performs general accounting and audit services as well as tax planning and preparation. Accountants visit clients in the field and also entertain them in the downtown office.

Your Task. Decide whether the entire team will research each question in Figure 5.1 or whether team members will be assigned certain questions. Collect information, discuss it, and reach consensus on what you will report to Mr. Harding. As a team write a concise one-page response. Your goal is to inform, not persuade. Remember that you represent management, not students or employees.

5.8 Instant Messaging: Practicing Your Professional IM Skills

Your instructor will direct this role-playing group activity. Using instant messaging, you will simulate one of several typical business scenarios—for example, responding to a product inquiry, training a new-hire, troubleshooting with a customer, or making an appointment. For each scenario, two or more students will chat professionally with only a minimal script to practice on-the-spot yet courteous professional interaction by IM. Your instructor will determine which software you will need and provide brief instructions to prepare you for your role in this exercise.

If you don't have instant messaging software on your computer or smart device yet, download the application first—for example, AOL's Instant Messenger, Yahoo Messenger, Microsoft's Windows Live Messenger, or Skype. Yahoo Messenger, for instance, allows you to IM your friends on Yahoo Messenger but also on Windows Live Messenger. You control who sees you online; if you don't wish to be interrupted, you can use stealth settings. All IM software enables users to share photos and large media files (up to 2 gigabytes on Yahoo). You can make voice calls and use webcam video as well. These advanced features turn IM software into a simple conferencing tool and video phone. You can connect with users who have the same software all around the world. Contrary to calling landlines or cell phones, peer-to-peer voice calls are free. Most IM clients also have mobile applications for your smartphone, so that you can IM or call other users while you are away from a computer.

Your Task. Log on to the IM program your instructor chooses. Follow your instructor's directions closely as you role-play the business situation you were assigned with your partner or team. The scenario will involve two or more people who will communicate by instant messaging in real time.

WEB

5.9 Podcast, Twitter, Texting: Analyzing a Podcast

Browsing the podcasts at iTunes, you stumble across the Quick and Dirty Tips series, specifically Money Girl, who dispenses financial advice. You sign up for the free podcasts that cover a variety of business topics. You also visit the Web site at **http://www.quickanddirtytips.com/**.

Your Task. Pick a QDNow.com podcast that interests you. Listen to it or obtain a transcript on the Web site and study it for its structure. Is it direct or indirect? Informative or persuasive? At your instructor's request, write an e-mail that discusses the podcast you analyzed. Alternatively, if your instructor allows, you could also send a very concise summary of the podcast by text message from your cell phone or an ultrashort tweet (140 characters or fewer) to your instructor.

WEB

5.10 Blog: Analyzing the Nuts About Southwest Blog

When you browse the Southwest Airlines blog, you will find the following terms of use:

> *We want to build a personal relationship between our Team and you, and we need your participation. Everyone is encouraged to join in, and you don't need to register to read, watch, or comment. However, if you would like to share photos or videos or rate a post, among other things, you will need to complete a profile. . . .*
>
> *This is the point where we insert the "fine print" and discuss the guidelines for posting. Nuts About Southwest is a moderated site because we want to ensure that everyone stays on topic—or at least pretty close to it. We would LUV for you to post your thoughts, comments, suggestions, and questions, but when you post, make sure that they are of general interest to most readers. Of course, profanity, racial and ethnic slurs, and rude behavior like disparaging personal remarks won't be tolerated nor published.*
>
> *Even though Nuts About Southwest is moderated, we pledge to present opposing viewpoints as we have done since our blog first went "live" several years ago, and we will strive to keep posts interesting, diverse, and multi-sided. Our Team wants to engage in a conversation with you, but not every post will receive a response from us. . . .*[28]

Your Task. Visit the Southwest.com blog at **http://www.blogsouthwest.com/about**. Click **About** and read the entire User Guide. In class, discuss the tone of the guidelines. How are they presented? Who is authoring the blog, and what is its purpose? What assumptions can you make about the company culture when you read the guidelines and the blog entries? If your instructor directs, write a clear, direct memo or an e-mail reporting your observations.

E-MAIL **WEB**

5.11 Blog and Wiki: Reviewing Fortune 500 Business Blogging Wiki

Here is your opportunity to view and evaluate a corporate blog. The site Socialtext.net is a wiki listing the 78 Fortune 500 companies that have a business blog at this time, defined as "active public blogs by company employees about the company and/or its products." You will find a range of large business organizations such as Amazon.com, Disney, Motorola, Safeway, and Toys"R"Us. Socialtext.net is hosting a wiki of reviews that critique Fortune 500 business blogs. The reviews are posted on a variety of blogs authored by various writers and hyperlinked to the Socialtext.net wiki.

Your Task. Browse the Fortune 500 Business Blogging Wiki at **http://www.socialtext.net/bizblogs/index.cgi**. Follow the links provided there to view some of the corporate blogs on the site. Select a company blog you find interesting, browse the pages, and read some of the contents. Pick a corporate blog that has already been reviewed by an independent blogger. Read the blogger's review. Consider the style and length of the review. If your instructor directs, write a brief informational memo or e-mail describing the business blog as well as its review, the style of the blogger's critique, the review's accuracy, and so forth.

Alternatively, your instructor may ask you to write an original review of a Fortune 500 company blog that has not yet been evaluated. You may be called on to write your own blog entry discussing an unreviewed company blog of your choice. You could compose the blog response in Microsoft Word or e-mail it to your instructor as appropriate.

 WEB

5.12 Twitter: Creating a Twitter Group

Twittgroups.com is designed to make microblogging useful for private individuals and businesses. The site is based on the premise that people like to talk with other like-minded people. Users come together in communities around specific topics (politics, sports, art, business, and so on). Twittgroups invites members to talk about the big news stories of the day, bounce ideas off other participants online, or just join the conversation—all in fewer than 140 characters. Your instructor may choose to create a public or private group for the class. Within this Twittgroup for your course, you may be asked to complete short assignments in the form of tweets. Posts in a private group are not shared with other general users, yet they should be relevant to the class content and professional.

Your Task. Use your Twitter username and password to log on at **http://twittgroups.com**. Sign into and follow the group designated by your instructor. Your instructor may ask you to comment on a topic he or she assigns or may encourage you to enter into a freewheeling discussion with other members of your class online. Your instructor may act as a group moderator evaluating the frequency and quality of your contributions.

5.13 Twitter: Learning to Write Superefficient Tweets

Twitter forces its users to practice extreme conciseness. Some music reviewers have risen to the challenge and reviewed whole albums in no more than 140 characters. National Public Radio put Stephen Thompson, one of its music editors, to the test. "I approach Twitter as a science," Thompson says.[29] He sees well-designed tweets as online equivalents of haiku, a highly structured type of Japanese poetry. Thompson believes that tweets should be properly punctuated, be written in complete sentences, and of course, not exceed the 140-character limit. His rules also exclude abbreviations.

Here are two samples of Thompson's mini reviews: "Mos Def is a hip-hop renaissance man on smart songs that look to the whole world and its conflicts. Slick Rick's guest spot is a nice touch." The second one reads: "The Phenomenal Handclap Band: Chugging, timeless, jammy throwback from eight shaggy Brooklyn hipsters. Starts slowly, gets hypnotically fun."[30]

Your Task. As an intern in Stephen Thompson's office, review your favorite album in 140 characters or fewer, following your boss's rules. After you have warmed up, your instructor may direct you to other concise writing tasks. Send a tweet to your instructor, if appropriate, or practice writing Twitter posts in Word. The best tweets could be shared with the class.

 WEB

5.14 Social Networking: Building an Online Community on Facebook

Chances are you already have a Facebook profile and communicate with friends and family. You may be a fan of a celebrity or a business. Now you can also become a fan of your business communication class if your instructor decides to create a course page on Facebook. The main purpose of such a social networking site for a class is to exchange links and interesting stories relevant to the material being learned. Intriguing tidbits and business news might also be posted on the "wall" to be shared by all signed-up fans. Everybody, even students who are quiet in class, could contribute. However, before you can become a fan of your business communication class, it needs to be created online.

Your Task. If you posted a profile on Facebook, all you need to do is search for the title of the newly created business communication Facebook page and become a fan. If you don't have an account yet, begin by signing up at **http://www.facebook.com**. On-screen prompts make it easy for you to build a profile.

 TEAM  WEB

5.15 Social Networking: Preparing a Professional LinkedIn Profile

Virtual networking on a professional networking site such as LinkedIn is an extension of seeking face-to-face contacts—the most effective way to find a job to date. Consider creating a credible, appealing presence on LinkedIn to make yourself attractive to potential business connections and hiring managers. Your LinkedIn site should serve purely to build your career and professional reputation.

Your Task. Go to **http://www.linkedin.com** and sign up for a free account. Follow the on-screen directions to create a profile, add a professional-looking photograph, and upload a polished résumé. You will be prompted to invite contacts from your e-mail address books. If your instructor directs, form teams and critique each other's profiles. Link to those profiles of your peers that have been prepared most diligently and strike you as having the best eye appeal.

Video Resources

This important chapter offers two learning videos.

Video Library 1: *Technology in the Workplace*.
Illustrating proper and improper use of today's technologies in the workplace, this video takes you to H. B. Jones, a small landscape design and supply firm. You will meet Elliott, the owner and founder; Helena, a competent office worker; James, East Coast manager; and Ian, an inept employee.

This fast-paced video gives you a glimpse of office workers using smartphones, computers, and other technologies on the job. Be watching for the attitudes of Ian, Elliott, James, and Helena toward their jobs and their use of company time. Who is using "Facespace" and why? Is James driving and accepting cell calls? Why does James complain about Elliott's e-mail and phone messages? This video moves so quickly that you may want to watch it twice to be able to answer the questions at the end of the video.

Video Library 2: ***Smart E-Mail Messages and Memos Advance Your Career***
Watch this chapter-specific video for a demonstration of how to use e-mail skillfully and safely. It will help you better understand the writing process in relation to composing messages. You will also see tips for writing messages that advance your career instead of sinking it.

Grammar/Mechanics Checkup—5

Prepositions and Conjunctions

Review Sections 1.18 and 1.19 in the Grammar Review section of the Grammar/Mechanics Handbook. Then study each of the following statements. Write *a* or *b* to indicate the sentence in which the idea is expressed more effectively. Also record the number of the G/M principle illustrated. When you finish, compare your responses with those provided at the back of the book. If your answers differ, study carefully the principles shown in parentheses. For more practice, you will find a set of Bonus Grammar/Mechanics Checkups with immediate feedback at your premium Web site, **www.cengagebrain.com**.

b (1.18a) **Example** a. Gentry graduated high school last year.
b. Gentry graduated from high school last year.

________ 1. a. What type of printer do you prefer?
b. What type printer do you prefer?

________ 2. a. I hate when my cell rings during meetings.
b. I hate it when my cell rings during meetings.

________ 3. a. Bullets make this message easier to read then that one.
b. Bullets make this message easier to read than that one.

________ 4. a. Blogrolling is when you provide links to other blogs.
b. Blogrolling involves the provision of links to other blogs.

________ 5. a. It seems as if we have been working on this project forever.
b. It seems like we have been working on this project forever.

________ 6. a. Does anyone know where the meeting is?
b. Does anyone know where the meeting is at?

________ 7. a. A wiki is better then a blog for workplace updates.
b. A wiki is better than a blog for workplace updates.

________ 8. a. Were you transferred to the home office in Seattle or to the office of the branch in Portland?
b. Were you transferred to the Seattle home office or the Portland branch office?

________ 9. a. Cloud computing is where your files and programs are stored in huge Internet data centers.
b. Cloud computing involves storing files and programs at huge Internet data centers.

________ 10. a. Where shall we move the computer to?
b. Where shall we move the computer?

________ 11. a. Job seekers should keep their online profiles free of risqué photos, profanity, and negative comments.
b. Job seekers should keep their online profiles free of risqué photos, profanity, and they should avoid negative comments.

________ 12. a. His blog comments were informative like we hoped they would be.
b. His blog comments were informative as we hoped they would be.

________ 13. a. Jeremy had an interest in and an aptitude for computer researching.
b. Jeremy had an interest and aptitude for computer researching.

________ 14. a. She joined both of the social networking sites.
b. She joined both social networking sites.

________ 15. a. As soon as she graduated college, she was eligible for the job.
b. As soon as she graduated from college, she was eligible for the job.

Editing Challenge—5

As the employee with the best communication skills, you are frequently asked to edit messages. The following e-mail has problems in proofreading, conversational tone, buried verbs, organization, list parallelism, and the subject line. You may (a) use standard proofreading marks (see Appendix B) to correct the errors here or (b) download the document from **www.cengagebrain.com** and revise at your computer.

Your instructor may ask you to use the **Track Changes** feature in Word to show your editing comments. Turn on **Track Changes** on the **Review** tab. Click **Show Markup**. Place your cursor at an error, click **New Comment**, and key your edit in the bubble box provided. Study the guidelines in the Grammar/Mechanics Handbook as well as the lists of Confusing Words and Frequently Misspelled Words to sharpen your skills.

To: Melody Menzes <melody@armorindustries.com>
From: Anthony Alvarado <anthony@armorindustries.com>
Subject: Need Your Help!
Cc:

Melody,

This is just a note to let you know that because of your excellent researching skills, the presidenet and the undersigned have selected you to work on a special project collecting information for next years annual report. You will in all probability need to visit each and every department head personal to collect department information individually from them.

The Corporate Communications division which oversee the production of the annual report is of the opinion that you should concentrate on the following items:

- specific accomplishments for the past year
- You should also find out about goals of each department for the coming year.
- in each department get names of interesting employees who have made a contribution to the department or ones who have contributed to the community.
- Be sure to ask about special events featuring outstanding employees and corporate officers.

Because of the fact that this is an assignment that is big in size, Darcy Coleman has been given the assignment of offering assistance to you. We made the decision that it was better to assign an assistant rather then have you be overwhelmed with the task.

Oh, one more thing. You should also be thinking about and collecting photos that illustrate employees and special events.

Inasmuch as the annual report must be completed by September first, you must submit this material to the undersigned by August 5th. We are grateful for your expertise and have confidence that you will do a terrific job.

Best,

Tony

Anthony Alvarado, Director
Human Resources Development
Armour Industries, Inc.
anthony@armourindustries.com
Cell: 761-662-8919

Communication Workshop

Should Employers Restrict E-Mail, Instant Messaging, and Internet Use?

Most employees today work with computers and have Internet access. Should they be able to use their work computers for online shopping, personal messages, and personal work, as well as to listen to music and play games?

But It's Harmless

Office workers have discovered that it is far easier to shop online than to race to malls and wait in line. To justify her Web shopping at work, one employee, a recent graduate, said, "Instead of standing at the water cooler gossiping, I shop online." She went on to say, "I'm not sapping company resources by doing this."[31]

Those who use instant messaging say that what they are doing is similar to making personal phone calls. So long as they don't abuse the practice, they see no harm. One marketing director justified his occasional game playing and online shopping by explaining that his employer benefits because he is more productive when he takes minibreaks. "When I need a break, I pull up a Web page and just browse," he says. "Ten minutes later, I'm all refreshed, and I can go back to business-plan writing."[32]

Companies Cracking Down

Employers, however, see it differently. A recent survey reported that more than one fourth of employers have fired workers for misusing e-mail, and nearly one third have fired employees for misusing the Internet.[33] UPS discovered an employee running a personal business from his office computer. Lockheed Martin fired an employee who disabled its entire company network for six hours because of an e-mail heralding a holiday event that the worker sent to 60,000 employees. Companies not only worry about lost productivity, but they fear litigation, security breaches, and other electronic disasters from accidental or intentional misuse of computer systems.

What's Reasonable?

Some companies try to enforce a "zero tolerance" policy, prohibiting any personal use of company equipment. Ameritech Corporation specifically tells employees that computers and other company equipment are to be used only to provide service to customers and for other business purposes. Companies such as Boeing, however, allow employees to use faxes, e-mail, and the Internet for personal reasons. But Boeing sets guidelines. Use has to be of reasonable duration and frequency and can't cause embarrassment to the company. Strictly prohibited are chain letters, obscenity, and political and religious solicitation.

Career Application. As an administrative assistant at Texas Technologies in Fort Worth, you have just received an e-mail from your boss asking for your opinion. It seems that many employees have been shopping online and more are using instant messaging. One person actually received four personal packages from UPS in one morning. Although reluctant to do so, management is considering installing monitoring software that not only tracks Internet use but also blocks messaging, porn, hate, and game sites.

Your Task

- In teams or as a class, discuss the problem of workplace abuse of e-mail, instant messaging, and the Internet. Should full personal use be allowed?
- Are computers and their links to the Internet similar to other equipment such as telephones?
- Should employees be allowed to access the Internet for personal use if they use their own private e-mail accounts?
- Should management be allowed to monitor all Internet use?
- Should employees be warned if e-mail is to be monitored?
- What reasons can you give to support an Internet crackdown by management?
- What reasons can you give to oppose a crackdown?

Decide whether you support or oppose the crackdown. Explain your views in an e-mail or a memo to your boss, Arthur W. Rose, *awrose@txtech.com*.

Endnotes

[1] Yarow, J. (2011, January 14). 107,000,000,000,000. Business Insider. Retrieved from http://www.businessinsider.com/internet-statistics-2011-1

[2] Kupritz, V. W., and Cowell, E. (2011, January). Productive management communication: Online and face-to-face. *Journal of Business Communication, 48*(1), 70–71.

[3] Hogan, R. C. (2006, February 16). Cure for an epidemic of bad e-mail—explicit business writing. eReleases. Retrieved from http://www.ereleases.com/pr/cure-for-an-epidemic-of-bad-emailexplicit-business-writing-6838

[4] Muchmore, M. (2010, August 11). The best IM clients. PC Mag. Retrieved from http://www.pcmag.com/article2/0,2817,2367620,00.asp

[5] Living the fast, young life in Asia. (2008, April). Change Agent. Retrieved from http://www.synovate.com/changeagent/index.php/site/full_story/living_the_fast_living_young_in_asia

[6] Fortune 500 business blogging wiki. (2009, October 1). Socialtext.net. Retrieved from http://www.socialtext.net/bizblogs/index.cgi

[7] BlogPulse Stats. (2011, June 1). Retrieved from http://www.blogpulse.com

[8] Brown, M. (2011, January 31). Southwest Airlines social media strategy—Lessons for all organizations. Social Media Today. Retrieved from http://socialmediatoday.com/mikebrown-brainzooming/266092/southwest-airlines-social-media-strategy-lessons-all-organizations

[9] Gardner, T. (2009, September 13). It may pay to Twitter. *Los Angeles Times*, p. L8.

[10] Scott, C. (2010, February 20). The best blogging sites and platforms. Blogtap. Retrieved from http://www.blogtap.net/the-best-blogging-sites-and-platforms-top-blog-sites

[11] FON Wiki. (2010, January 26). Retrieved from http://wiki.fon.com/wiki/Join_FON_Wiki_Team

[12] Baker, S., & Green, H. (2008, June 2). Beyond blogs: What business needs to know. *BusinessWeek Online*. Retrieved from http://www.businessweek.com/magazine/content/08_22/b4086044617865.htm?chan=technology_technology+index+page_top+stories

[13] Taking cues from Facebook. (n.d.). About McDonald's. Retrieved from http://www.aboutmcdonalds.com/mcd/students/did_you_know/taking_cues_from_facebook.html?DCSext.destination=http://www.aboutmcdonalds.com/mcd/students/did_you_know/taking_cues_from_facebook.html

[14] Conlin, M., & MacMillan, D. (2009, June 1). Managing the tweets. *BusinessWeek*, p. 21.

[15] Baker, S., & Green, H. (2008, June 2). Beyond blogs. *BusinessWeek*, pp. 46, 48.

[16] Conlin, M., & MacMillan, D. (2009, June 1). Managing the tweets. *BusinessWeek*, p. 20.

[17] Ibid., pp. 20-21.

[18] Irvine, M. (2009, July 12). Young workers push employers for wider Web access. *USA Today*. Retrieved from http://www.usatoday.com/tech/webguide/internetlife/2009-07-13-blocked-internet_N.htm

[19] Villano, M. (2009, April 26). The online divide between work and play. *The New York Times*. Retrieved from http://www.nytimes.com

[20] Ibid.

[21] Ibid.

[22] Ibid.

[23] Dougherty, C. cited in Hiring pros share insights about social networking. (2009). Network Pittsburgh. Retrieved from http://www.networkpittsburgh.com/articles/entry/Hiring-Pros-Share-Insights-About-Social-Networking-Sites

[24] Levine, B. (2010, August 18). Did you do bad? Google CEO says change your name. *Top Tech News*. Retrieved from http://www.toptechnews.com/story.xhtml?story_id=102009DI6CEO

[25] Based on McManus, K. (2009, October 20). Should walking while texting be illegal? [Weblog post]. Retrieved from http://www.responsibilityproject.com/blog/should-walking-while-texting-be-illegal-/?src=keyword_s=ggl_K=DangersOfTextMessaging_C=Law_G=WalkingTexting_Unsafe_M=broad#fbid=LbAqCqZ0KrL

[26] Wade, J. (2009, September 14). Managing the risks and rewards of social media, as illustrated by ESPN's new social networking policy. Risk Management Monitor. Retrieved from http://www.riskmanagementmonitor.com/managing-the-risks-and-rewards-of-social-media-as-illustrated-by-espns-new-social-networking-policy

[27] Babwin, D. (2010, July 20). Playboy's work-safe Website launches. Huffpost Media. Retrieved from http://www.huffingtonpost.com/2010/07/20/playboys-worksafe-website_n_652337.html

[28] Nuts about Southwest. (n.d.). Retrieved from http://www.blogsouthwest.com/about

[29] Greene, D. (Host). (2009, July 2). Twitter music reviews: Criticism as Haiku. *Morning Edition*. Washington, DC: National Public Radio. Retrieved from http://www.npr.org/templates/story/story.php?storyId=106178234

[30] Ibid.

[31] Irvine, M. (2009, July 12). Young workers push employers for wider Web access. *USA Today*. Retrieved from http://www.usatoday.com/tech/webguide/internetlife/2009-07-13-blocked-internet_N.htm; DeLisser, E. (1999, September 27). One-click commerce: What people do now to goof off at work. *The Wall Street Journal.* Retrieved from http://www.kenmaier.com/wsj19990927.htm

[32] Cheng, J. (2009, April 2). Study: Surfing the Internet at work boosts productivity. Ars Technica. Retrieved from http://arstechnica.com/web/news/2009/04/study-surfing-the-internet-at-work-boosts-productivity.ars; DeLisser, E. (1999, September 27). One-click commerce: What people do now to goof off at work. *The Wall Street Journal.* Retrieved from http://www.kenmaier.com/wsj19990927.htm

[33] Ford, J. (2009, November 9). Think twice about shopping online from work. Marketwatch.com. Retrieved from http://www.marketwatch.com/story/think-twice-about-shopping-online-from-work-2009-11-29; The 2007 electronic monitoring and surveillance survey. (2008, February 29). Retrieved from http://www.gpsdaily.com

Acknowledgments

p. 107 Office Insider cited in More clicks than conversations: Shift to e-mail in business makes crafting meaningful messages more important. (2007, December 12). *OfficeTeam*. [News release]. Retrieved from http://officeteam.rhi.mediaroom.com/index.php?year=2007&s=news_releases

p. 111 Office Insider cited in E-mail becoming crime's new smoking gun. (2002, August 15). *USA Today.com*. Retrieved from http://www.usatoday.com/tech/news/2002-08-15-email-evidence_x.htm

p. 113 Office Insider cited in Brown, P. B. (2008, January 26). Same office, different planets. *The New York Times*, p. B5. Retrieved from http://proquest.umi.com

p. 117 Office Insider cited in Bloch, M. (n.d.). Instant messaging and live chat etiquette tips. Taming the Beast. Retrieved from http://www.tamingthebeast.net/articles6/messaging-chat-etiquette.htm

p. 125 Office Insider based on Irvine, M. (2009, July 12). Young workers push employers for wider Web access. *USA Today*. Retrieved from http://www.usatoday.com/tech/webguide/internetlife/2009-07-13-blocked-internet_N.htm

CHAPTER 6

Positive Messages

Go to cengagebrain.com and use your access code to unlock valuable student eResources.

koh sze kiat/Shutterstock.com

OBJECTIVES

After studying this chapter, you should be able to

- Understand when business letters are more appropriate than e-mails and memos, and explain how business letters should be formatted.
- Write direct messages that make requests and respond to inquiries.
- Create effective and clear step-by-step instructions.
- Compose messages that make direct claims and voice complaints.
- Prepare adjustment messages that regain the confidence of customers and promote further business.
- Write goodwill messages that convey kindness and build a positive image of the writer and his or her company.

Positive Messages: Letters, E-Mails, and Memos

In the workplace, most messages are positive or neutral and, therefore, direct. Positive messages are routine and straightforward; they help workers in organizations conduct everyday business. Such routine messages include simple requests for information or action, replies to customers, and explanations to fellow employees. Other types of positive messages are instructions as well as direct claims and complaints. They may take the form of e-mails, memos, and letters. Memos are an important channel of communication within an organization while letters are a vital paper-based external channel. E-mail is increasingly used to communicate not only within an organization, but also with outside audiences.

Chapter 5 discussed electronic messages as well as memos and focused on their format and safe, professional use. This chapter will familiarize you with the direct writing plans for positive messages whether paper-based or electronic. First, though, you will learn when to respond by letter and how to format a business letter.

Understanding Business Letters

The principal channel for delivering messages outside an organization is business letters.

Despite the advent of e-mail and other electronic communication technologies, in certain situations letters are still the preferred channel of communication for delivering messages *outside* an organization. Positive, straightforward letters help organizations perform everyday business and convey goodwill to outsiders. Such letters go to suppliers, government agencies, other businesses, and, most important, customers. The letters to customers receive a high priority because these messages encourage product feedback, project a favorable image of the organization, and promote future business.

Even with the electronic media available today, a letter remains one of the most powerful and effective ways to get your message across. Although e-mail is incredibly successful for both internal and external communication, many important messages still call for letters. Business letters are necessary when (a) a permanent record is required; (b) confidentiality is paramount; (c) formality and sensitivity are essential; and (d) a persuasive, well-considered presentation is important.

Producing a Permanent Record. Many business transactions require a permanent record. For example, when a company enters into an agreement with another company, business letters introduce the agreement and record decisions and points of understanding. Although telephone conversations and e-mails may be exchanged, important details are generally recorded in business letters that are kept in company files. Business letters deliver contracts, explain terms, exchange ideas, negotiate agreements, answer vendor questions, and maintain customer relations.

Business letters are important for messages requiring a permanent record, confidentiality, formality, sensitivity, and a well-considered presentation.

Providing Confidentiality. Carefree use of e-mail was once a sign of sophistication. Today, however, communicators know how dangerous it is to entrust confidential and sensitive information to digital channels. A writer in *The New York Times* recognized the unique value of letters when he said, "Despite the sneering term *snail mail*, plain old letters are the form of long-distance communication least likely to be intercepted, misdirected, forwarded, retrieved, or otherwise inspected by someone you didn't have in mind."[1]

Conveying Formality and Sensitivity. Business letters presented on company stationery carry a sense of formality and importance not possible with e-mail. They look important. They carry a nonverbal message saying the writer considered the message to be so significant and the receiver so prestigious that the writer cared enough to write a real message. Business letters deliver more information than e-mail because they are written on stationery that usually is printed with company information such as logos, addresses, titles, and contact details.

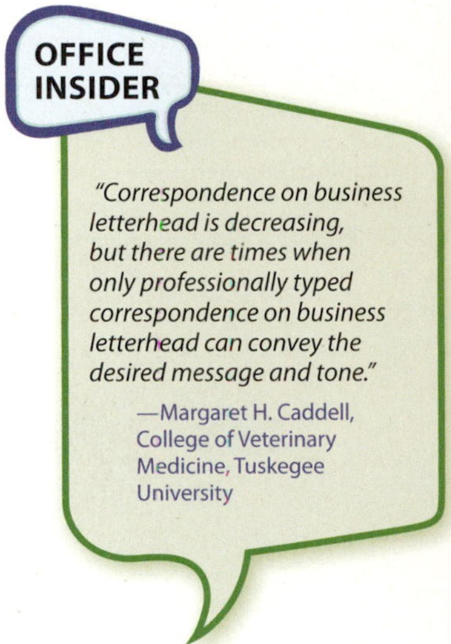

OFFICE INSIDER
"Correspondence on business letterhead is decreasing, but there are times when only professionally typed correspondence on business letterhead can convey the desired message and tone."
—Margaret H. Caddell, College of Veterinary Medicine, Tuskegee University

Delivering Persuasive, Well-Considered Messages. When a business communicator must be persuasive and can't do it in person, a business letter is more effective than other communication channels. Letters can persuade people to change their actions, adopt new beliefs, make donations, contribute their time, and try new products. Direct-mail letters remain a powerful tool to promote services and products, boost online and retail traffic, and solicit contributions. Business letters represent deliberate communication. They give you a chance to think through what you want to say, organize your thoughts, and write a well-considered argument. You will learn more about writing persuasive and marketing messages in Chapter 8.

Formatting Business Letters

A business letter conveys silent messages beyond that of its printed words. The letter's appearance and format reflect the writer's carefulness and experience. A short letter bunched at the top of a sheet of paper, for example, looks as though it were prepared in a hurry or by an amateur.

The block style is a popular business letter format.

For your letters to make a good impression, you need to select an appropriate format. The block style shown in Figure 6.1 is a popular format. In this style the parts of a letter—dateline, inside address, body, and so on—are set flush left on the page. The letter is arranged on the page so that it is centered and framed by white space. Most letters have margins of 1 to 1.5 inches.

In preparing business letters, be sure to use ragged-right margins; that is, don't allow your computer to justify the right margin and make all lines end evenly.

FIGURE 6.1 Formatting a Direct Request Business Letter in Block Style

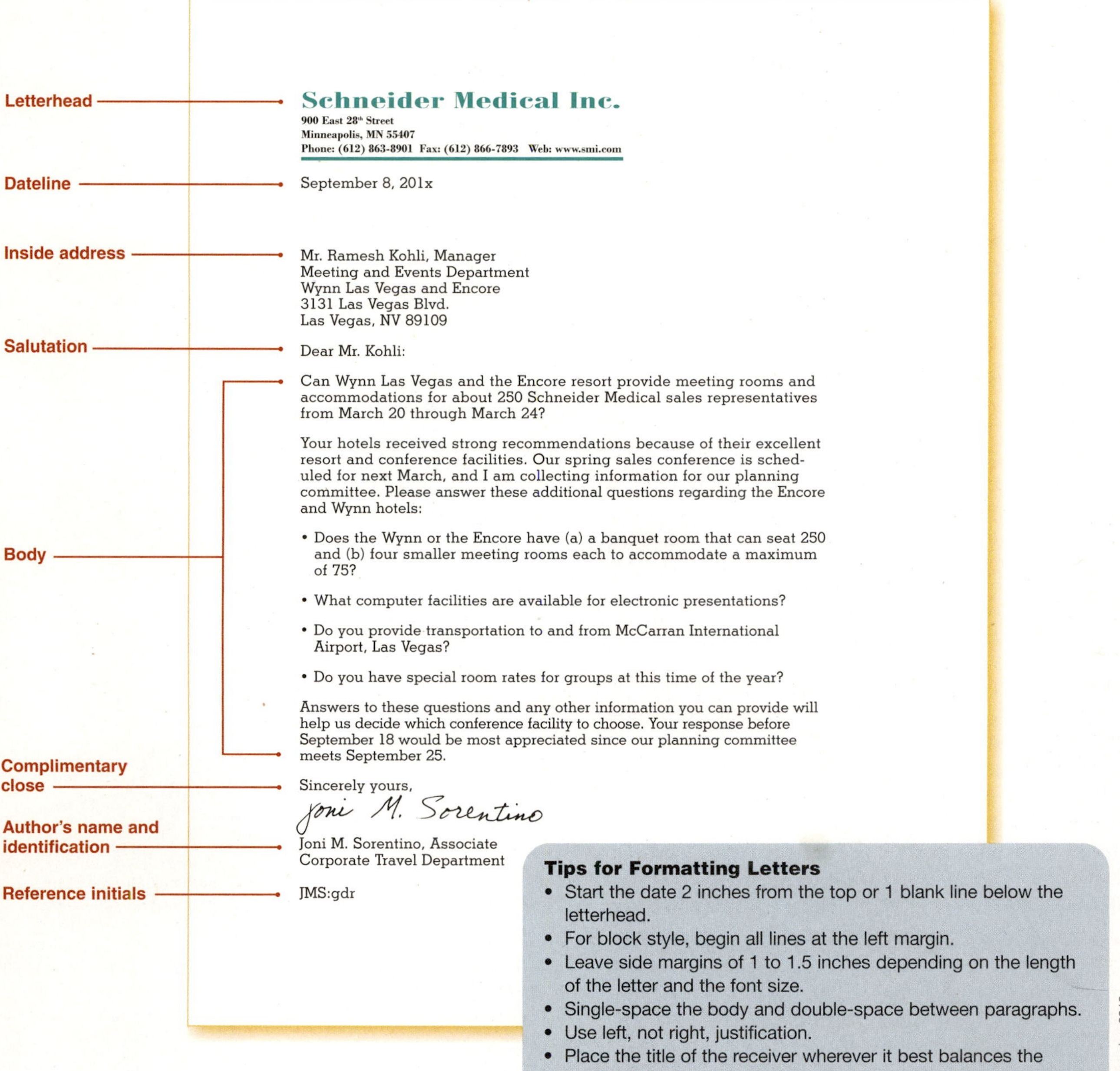

Letterhead
Dateline
Inside address
Salutation
Body
Complimentary close
Author's name and identification
Reference initials
Schneider Medical Inc.
900 East 28th Street
Minneapolis, MN 55407
Phone: (612) 863-8901 Fax: (612) 866-7893 Web: www.smi.com
September 8, 201x
Mr. Ramesh Kohli, Manager
Meeting and Events Department
Wynn Las Vegas and Encore
3131 Las Vegas Blvd.
Las Vegas, NV 89109
Dear Mr. Kohli:
Can Wynn Las Vegas and the Encore resort provide meeting rooms and accommodations for about 250 Schneider Medical sales representatives from March 20 through March 24?
Your hotels received strong recommendations because of their excellent resort and conference facilities. Our spring sales conference is scheduled for next March, and I am collecting information for our planning committee. Please answer these additional questions regarding the Encore and Wynn hotels:
• Does the Wynn or the Encore have (a) a banquet room that can seat 250 and (b) four smaller meeting rooms each to accommodate a maximum of 75?
• What computer facilities are available for electronic presentations?
• Do you provide transportation to and from McCarran International Airport, Las Vegas?
• Do you have special room rates for groups at this time of the year?
Answers to these questions and any other information you can provide will help us decide which conference facility to choose. Your response before September 18 would be most appreciated since our planning committee meets September 25.
Sincerely yours,
Joni M. Sorentino
Joni M. Sorentino, Associate
Corporate Travel Department
JMS:gdr
Tips for Formatting Letters
• Start the date 2 inches from the top or 1 blank line below the letterhead.
• For block style, begin all lines at the left margin.
• Leave side margins of 1 to 1.5 inches depending on the length of the letter and the font size.
• Single-space the body and double-space between paragraphs.
• Use left, not right, justification.
• Place the title of the receiver wherever it best balances the inside address.
• Place the title of the author wherever it best balances the closing lines.

Unjustified margins improve readability, say experts, by providing visual stops and by making it easier to tell where the next line begins. Although book publishers use justified right margins, as you see on this page, your letters should be ragged right. Study Figure 6.1 for more tips on making your letters look professional. If you have questions about letter formats, see Appendix A.

Direct Requests and Response Messages

Routine requests and replies follow a similar pattern, the direct strategy.

Most of your business messages will involve routine requests and responses to requests that are organized directly. Requests and replies may take the form of e-mails, memos, or letters. You might, for example, need to request information from a hotel as you plan a company conference. You might be answering an inquiry from a customer about your services or products. These kinds of routine requests and replies follow a similar pattern, as shown in the following writing plan:

WRITING PLAN FOR DIRECT REQUEST AND RESPONSE MESSAGES

- **Opening:** Ask the most important question first or express a polite command.
- **Body:** Explain the request logically and courteously. Ask other questions if necessary.
- **Closing:** Request a specific action with an end date, if appropriate, and show appreciation.

Creating Request Messages

Readers find the openings and closings of documents most interesting and often read them first.

When you are planning a message that requests information or action and you think your request will be received positively, start with the main idea first. The most emphatic positions in most documents are the opening and closing. Readers tend to look at them first. The writer, then, should capitalize on this tendency by putting the most significant statement first. The first sentence of a direct request is usually a question or a polite command. It should not be an explanation or justification, unless resistance to the request is expected. When the direct request is likely to be forthcoming, frontload your message, which means immediately tell the reader what you want.

A letter inquiring about hotel accommodations, shown in Figure 6.1, begins immediately with the most important idea: Can the hotel provide meeting rooms and accommodations for 250 people? Instead of opening with an explanation of who the writer is or how the writer happens to be writing this message, the letter begins directly.

Begin a direct request with the most important question or a summarizing statement.

If several questions must be asked, you have two choices. You can ask the most important question first, as shown in Figure 6.1. An alternate opening begins with a summary statement, such as *Please answer the following questions about providing meeting rooms and accommodations for 250 people from March 20 through March 24.* Avoid statements that begin with *Will you please* . . . . Although such a statement sounds like a question, it is actually a disguised command. Because you expect an action rather than a reply, you should punctuate this polite command with a period instead of a question mark. To avoid having to choose between a period and a question mark, just omit *Will you* and start with *Please answer.*

Providing Details in the Body

The body of a request message may contain an explanation or a list of questions.

The body of a message that requests information or action provides necessary details. Remember that the quality of the information obtained from a request depends on the clarity of the inquiry. If you analyze your needs, organize your ideas, and frame your request logically, you are likely to receive a meaningful answer that doesn't require a follow-up message. Whenever possible, focus on benefits to the reader (*To ensure that you receive the exact sweater you want, send us your color choice*). To improve readability, itemize the appropriate information in bullets or numbered lists. Notice that the questions in Figure 6.1 are bulleted, and they are parallel. That is, they use the same balanced construction.

Closing With Appreciation and an Action Request

In the closing tell the reader courteously what is to be done. If a date is important, set an end date to take action and explain why. Some careless writers end request messages simply with *Thank you,* forcing the reader to review the contents to

For a group project, middle schoolers at Portland's Mt. Scott Learning Center wrote letters to the Domtar Corporation urging the sustainable paper company to save forests. One letter referenced the class's green motto: "Don't be a Domtar." Eager to address students' concerns, CEO John Williams wrote a personal response and arranged for the vice president of sustainable development to visit the school. Students learned the amazing uses of recycled paper and got an inside look at how the paper industry promotes healthy forests. *What are tips for writing direct response letters?*

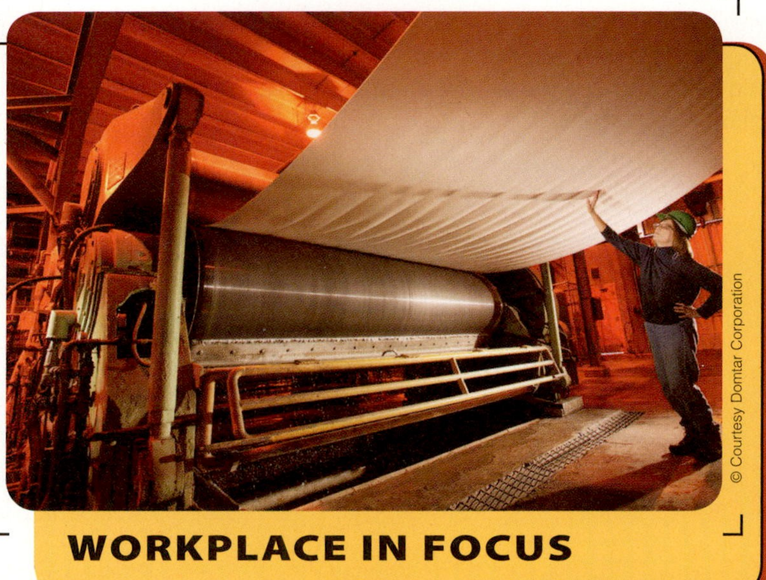
© Courtesy Domtar Corporation

WORKPLACE IN FOCUS

determine what is expected and when. You can save the reader time by spelling out the action to be taken. Avoid other overused endings such as *Thank you for your cooperation* (trite), *Thank you in advance for . . .* (trite and presumptuous), and *If you have any questions, do not hesitate to call me* (suggests that you didn't make yourself clear).

Showing appreciation is always appropriate, but try to do so in a fresh and efficient manner. For example, you could hook your thanks to the end date *(Thanks for returning the questionnaire before May 5, when we will begin tabulation).* You might connect your appreciation to a statement developing reader benefits *(We are grateful for the information you will provide because it will help us serve you better)*. You could briefly describe how the information will help you *(I appreciate this information that will enable me to . . .)*. When possible, make it easy for the reader to comply with your request *(Note your answers on this sheet and return it in the postage-paid envelope* or *Here is my e-mail address so that you can reach me quickly)*.

Responding to Requests

Often, your messages will respond directly and favorably to requests for information or action. A customer wants information about a product. A supplier asks to arrange a meeting. An employee inquires about a procedure, or a manager requests your input on a marketing campaign. In complying with such requests, you will want to apply the same direct pattern you used in making requests:

WRITING PLAN FOR LETTER, E-MAIL, AND MEMO REPLIES

- **Subject line:** Summarize the main information from your reply. (A subject line is optional in letters.)
- **Opening:** Start directly by responding to the request with a summary statement.
- **Body:** Provide additional information and details in a readable format.
- **Closing:** Add a concluding remark, summary, or offer of further assistance.

FIGURE 6.2 Customer Response E-Mail

File Edit Mailbox Message Transfer Special Tools Window Help

Send

To: Jeffrey White <Jeffrey.White@gmail.com>
From: Linda DeLorme<ldelorme@sonomasoft.com>
Subject: Your July 12 Inquiry About WorkZone Software
Cc:
Attached: WorkZone_Pamphlet.pdf (8099Kb)

Dear Mr. White:

Yes, we do offer personnel record-keeping software specially designed for small businesses like yours. Here are answers to your three questions about this software:

1. Our WorkZone software provides standard employee forms so that you are always in compliance with current government regulations.
2. You receive an interviewer's guide for structured employee interviews, as well as a scripted format for checking references by telephone.
3. Yes, you can update your employees' records easily without the need for additional software, hardware, or training.

Our WorkZone software was specially designed to provide you with expert forms for interviewing, verifying references, recording attendance, evaluating performance, and tracking the status of your employees. We even provide you with step-by-step instructions and suggested procedures. You can treat your employees as if you had a professional human resources specialist on your staff.

In the attached PDF copy of our pamphlet, you can find out more about WorkZone. To receive a preview copy or to ask questions about WorkZone and its use, just call 1-800-354-5500. Our specialists are eager to help you weekdays from 8 to 5 PST. If you prefer, visit our Web site to receive more information or to place an order.

Sincerely,

Linda DeLorme
Senior Marketing Representative
ldelorme@sonomasoft.com

Sonoma Software, Inc. | 520 Sonoma Parkway | Petaluma, CA 94539 | Phone (707) 784-2219 | Fax (707) 780-3838 | www.sonomasoft.com

Identifies previous correspondence and subject

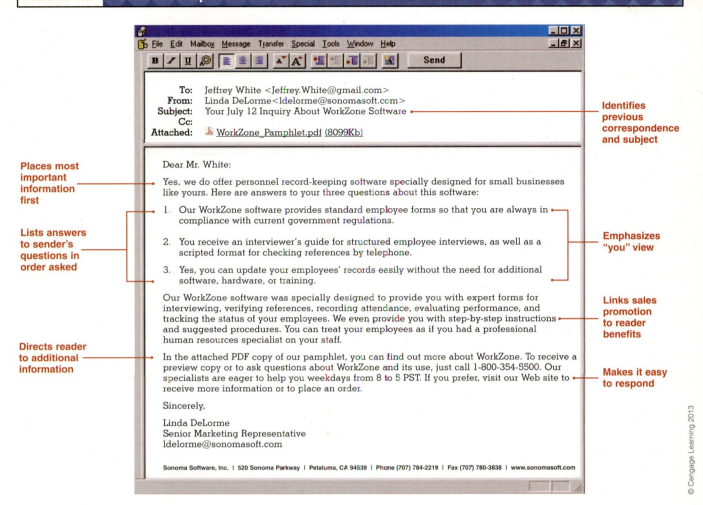

Places most important information first

Lists answers to sender's questions in order asked

Emphasizes "you" view

Links sales promotion to reader benefits

Directs reader to additional information

Makes it easy to respond

A customer reply e-mail that starts with an effective subject line, as shown in Figure 6.2, helps the reader recognize the topic immediately. The subject line refers in abbreviated form to previous correspondence and/or summarizes a message *(Subject: Your July 12 Inquiry About WorkZone Software)*. Knowledgeable business communicators use a subject line to refer to earlier correspondence so that in the first sentence, the most emphatic spot in a letter, they are free to emphasize the main idea.

In the first sentence of a direct reply e-mail, deliver the information the reader wants. Avoid wordy, drawn-out openings (*I am responding to your e-mail of December 1, in which you request information about . . .*). More forceful and more efficient is an opener that answers the inquiry (*Here is the information you wanted about . . .*). When agreeing to a request for action, announce the good news promptly *(Yes, I will be happy to speak to your business communication class on the topic of . . .)*.

In the body of your response, supply explanations and additional information. Because an e-mail, like any other document written for your company, is considered a legally binding contract, be sure to check facts and figures carefully. If a policy or procedure needs authorization, seek approval from a supervisor or executive before writing the letter.

When answering a group of questions or providing considerable data, arrange the information logically and make it readable by using lists, tables, headings, boldface, italics, or other graphic devices. When customers or

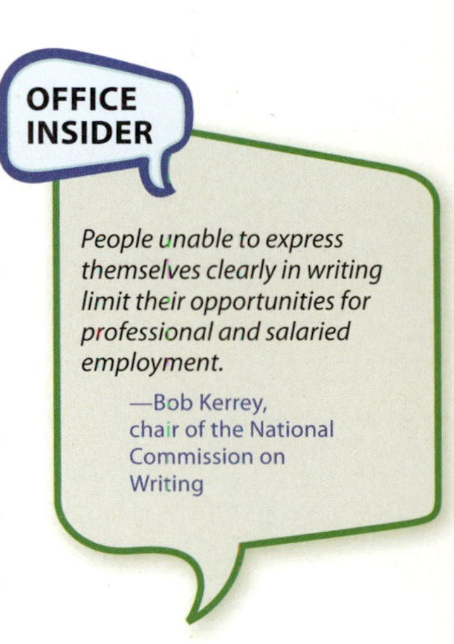

People unable to express themselves clearly in writing limit their opportunities for professional and salaried employment.

"You're right, it is difficult to assemble—we'll let the customers do it."

www.Cartoonstock.com

prospective customers inquire about products or services, your response should do more than merely supply answers. Try to promote your organization and its products. Provide helpful information that satisfies the inquiry, but consider using the opportunity to introduce another product as well. Be sure to present the promotional material with attention to the "you" view and to reader benefits *(You can use our standardized tests to free you from time-consuming employment screening)*.

In concluding a response message, make sure you are cordial and personal. Refer to the information provided or to its use *(The attached list summarizes our recommendations. We wish you all the best in redesigning your Web site.)*. If further action is required, help the reader with specifics *(The Small Business Administration publishes a number of helpful booklets. Its Web address is . . .)*. To prevent abruptness, include a pleasant closing remark that shows your willingness to help the reader. Tailor your remarks to fit this e-mail and this reader. Avoid signing off with clichés *(If I may be of further assistance, don't hesitate to . . .)*. In your e-mail provide an electronic signature block with your contact information to enable the reader to contact you for follow-up.

Instruction Messages

Instruction messages must clearly explain how to complete a task.

Instruction messages describe how to complete a task. You may be asked to write instructions about how to repair a paper jam in the photocopier, order supplies, file a grievance, or hire new employees. Like requests and responses, instruction messages follow a straightforward, direct approach. They must use plain English and be especially clear. Instructions are different from policies and official procedures, which establish rules of conduct to be followed within an organization. We are most concerned with creating messages that clearly explain how to complete a task.

Dividing Instructions Into Steps

Before writing instructions for a process, be sure you understand the process completely. Create logical steps in the correct order. Practice completing the procedure yourself first. Here is a writing plan that will help you get started:

WRITING PLAN FOR INSTRUCTION E-MAILS AND MEMOS

- **Subject line:** Summarize the content of the message.
- **Opening:** Expand the subject line by stating the main idea concisely in a full sentence.
- **Body:** Divide the instructions into steps. List the steps in the order in which they are to be carried out. Arrange the items vertically with bullets or numbers. Begin each step with an action verb using the imperative mood (command language such as *do this, don't do that*).
- **Closing:** Request a specific action, summarize the message, or present a closing thought. If appropriate, include a deadline and a reason.

The most effective way to list directions is to use command language called the imperative mood. Think recipes, owner manuals, and assembly instructions. The imperative mood differs from the indicative mood in that it requests an action, whereas the indicative mood describes a statement as shown here:

Indicative Mood	**Imperative (Command) Mood**
The contract should be sent immediately.	Send the contract immediately.
The first step involves loading the software.	Load the software first.
A survey of employees is necessary to learn what options they prefer.	Survey employees to learn the options they prefer.

If you are asked to prepare a list of instructions that is not part of a message, include a title such as "How to Clear Paper Jams." Include an opening paragraph explaining why the instructions are needed.

Revising a Message Delivering Instructions

Figure 6.3 shows the first draft of an interoffice memo written by Troy Bell. His memo was meant to announce a new method for employees to follow in advertising open positions. However, the tone was negative, the explanation of the problem rambled, and the new method was unclear. Notice, too, that Troy's first draft told readers what they *shouldn't* do (*Do not submit advertisements for new employees directly to an Internet job bank or a newspaper)*. It is more helpful to tell readers what they *should* do. Finally, Troy's first memo closed with a threat instead of showing readers how this new practice will help them.

In the revision Troy improved the tone considerably. The subject line contains a *please*, which is always pleasant to see even if one is giving an order. The subject line also includes a verb and specifies the purpose of the memo. Instead of expressing his ideas with negative words and threats, Troy revised his message to explain objectively and concisely what went wrong.

Troy realized that his original explanation of the new procedure was vague and unclear. To clarify the instructions, he itemized and numbered the steps. Each step begins with an action verb in the imperative (command) mode (*Write, Bring, Let,* and *Pick up*). It is sometimes difficult to force all the steps in a list into this kind of command language. Troy struggled, but by trying different wording, he finally found verbs that worked.

Numbered steps and action verbs improve the clarity of instructions.

Why should you go to so much trouble to make lists and achieve parallelism? Because readers can comprehend what you have said much more quickly. Parallel language also makes you look professional and efficient.

In writing messages that deliver instructions, be careful of tone. Today's managers and team leaders seek employee participation and cooperation. These goals can't be achieved, though, if the writer sounds like a dictator or an autocrat. Avoid making accusations and fixing blame. Rather, explain changes, give reasons, and suggest benefits to the reader. Assume that employees want to contribute to the success of the organization and to their own achievement. Notice in the Figure 6.3 revision that Troy tells readers that they will save time and have their open positions filled more quickly if they follow the new method.

Learning More About Writing Instructions

The writing of instructions is so important that we have developed a special bonus online supplement called *How to Write Instructions.* It provides more examples and information. This online supplement at **www.cengagebrain.com** extends your textbook with in-depth material including links to real businesses showing you examples of well-written instructions.

Learn more about how to write instructions in the special bonus online supplement called *How to Write Instructions* at **www.cengagebrain.com**.

FIGURE 6.3 Memo Delivering Instructions

before

Date: January 5, 201x
To: Ruth DiSilvestro, Manager
From: Troy Bell, Human Resources
Subject: Job Advertisement Misunderstanding

We had no idea last month when we implemented a new hiring process that major problems would result. Due to the fact that every department is now placing Internet advertisements for new-hires individually, the difficulties occurred. This cannot continue. Perhaps we did not make it clear at the time, but all newly hired employees who are hired for a position should be requested through this office.

Do not submit your advertisements for new employees directly to an Internet job bank or a newspaper. After you write them, they should be brought to Human Resources, where they will be centralized. You should discuss each ad with one of our counselors. Then we will place the ad at an appropriate Internet site or other publication. If you do not follow these guidelines, chaos will result. You may pick up applicant folders from us the day after the closing date in an ad.

Uses vague, negative subject line

Fails to pinpoint main idea in opening

Makes new process hard to follow

Uses threats instead of showing benefits to reader

after

MEMORANDUM

Date: January 5, 201x

To: Ruth DiSilvestro, Manager

From: Troy Bell, Human Resources TB

Subject: Please Follow New Job Advertisement Process

To find the right candidates for your open positions as fast as possible, we are implementing a new routine. Effective today, all advertisements for departmental job openings should be routed through the Human Resources Department.

A major problem resulted from the change in hiring procedures implemented last month. Each department is placing job advertisements for new-hires individually, when all such requests should be centralized in this office. To process applications more efficiently, please follow these steps:

1. Write an advertisement for a position in your department.
2. Bring the ad to Human Resources and discuss it with one of our counselors.
3. Let Human Resources place the ad at an appropriate Internet job bank or submit it to a newspaper.
4. Pick up applicant folders from Human Resources the day following the closing date provided in the ad.

Following these guidelines will save you work and will also enable Human Resources to help you fill your openings more quickly. Call Ann Edmonds at Ext. 2505 if you have questions about this process.

Employs informative, courteous, upbeat subject line

Combines "you" view with main idea in opening

Explains why change in procedures is necessary

Lists easy-to-follow steps and starts each step with a verb

Closes by reinforcing benefits to reader

Tips for Writing Instructions

- Arrange each step in the order it should be completed.
- Start each instruction with an action verb in the imperative (command) mood.
- Be careful of tone when writing messages that give orders.
- Show reader benefits if you are encouraging use of the process.

Direct Claims and Complaints

Claim messages register complaints and usually seek correction of a wrong.

In business, many things can and do go wrong—promised shipments are late, warrantied goods fail, or service is disappointing. When you as a customer must write to identify or correct a wrong, the letter is called a *claim*. Straightforward claims are those to which you expect the receiver to agree readily. Even these claims, however, often require a letter. Your first action may be a telephone call or an e-mail to submit your claim, but you may not be satisfied with the results. Claims written as letters are taken more seriously than telephone calls or e-mails, and they also establish a record of what happened. Straightforward claims use a direct approach. Claims that require persuasion are presented in Chapter 8.

WRITING PLAN FOR A DIRECT CLAIM

- **Opening:** Describe clearly the desired action.
- **Body:** Explain the nature of the claim, tell why the claim is justified, and provide details regarding the action requested.
- **Closing:** End pleasantly with a goodwill statement, and include an end date and action request, if appropriate.

Opening a Claim With a Clear Statement

When you, as a customer, have a legitimate claim or complaint, you can expect a positive response from a company. Smart businesses want to hear from their customers. They know that retaining a customer is far less costly than recruiting a new customer.

> The direct strategy is best for simple claims that require no persuasion.

Open a claim with a clear statement of the problem or with the action you want the receiver to take. You might expect a replacement, a refund, a new order, credit to your account, correction of a billing error, free repairs, free inspection, or cancellation of an order. When the remedy is obvious, state it immediately (*Please correct an erroneous double charge of $59 to my credit card for LapLink migration software. I accidentally clicked the Submit button twice*). When the remedy is less obvious, you might ask for a change in policy or procedure or simply for an explanation (*Because three of our employees with confirmed reservations were refused rooms September 16 in your hotel, would you please clarify your policy regarding reservations and late arrivals*).

Explaining and Justifying a Claim

In the body of a claim message, explain the problem and justify your request. Provide the necessary details so that the difficulty can be corrected without further correspondence. Avoid becoming angry or trying to fix blame. Bear in mind that the person reading your message is seldom responsible for the problem. Instead, state the facts logically, objectively, and unemotionally; let the reader decide on the causes. If sending a letter, enclose copies of all pertinent documents such as invoices, sales slips, catalog descriptions, and repair records. By the way, be sure to send copies and *not* your originals, which could be lost. When service is involved, cite the names of individuals you spoke to and the dates of calls. Assume that a company honestly wants to satisfy its customers—because most do. When an alternative remedy exists, spell it out (*If you are able to offer store credit only, please apply the second amount of $59 to your TurboSpeed software and a LapLink USB cable that I would like to buy too*).

> Providing details without getting angry improves the effectiveness of a claim message.

Concluding a Claim With a Specific Action Request

End a claim message with a courteous statement that promotes goodwill and summarizes your action request. If appropriate, include an end date (*I hope*

> Written claims submitted promptly are taken more seriously than delayed ones.

you understand that mistakes in ordering online sometimes occur. Because I have enjoyed your prompt service in the past, I hope that you will be able to issue a refund or store credit by May 2). Finally, in making claims, act promptly. Delaying claims makes them appear less important. Delayed claims are also more difficult to verify. By taking the time to put your claim in writing, you indicate your seriousness. A written claim starts a record of the problem, should later action be necessary. Be sure to keep a copy of your letter. When sending an e-mail, file an electronic copy of your customer claim in a folder for easy retrieval.

Putting It All Together and Revising

When Keith Krahnke received a statement showing a charge for a three-year service warranty that he did not purchase, he was furious. He called the store but failed to get satisfaction to his complaint. Then he decided to write. You can see the first draft of his direct claim letter in Figure 6.4. This draft gave him a chance to vent his anger, but it accomplished little else. The tone was belligerent, and the message assumed that the company intentionally mischarged him. Furthermore, it failed to tell the reader how to remedy the problem. The revision, also shown in Figure 6.4 tempered the tone, described the problem objectively, and provided facts and figures. Most important, it specified exactly what Keith wanted to be done.

Notice in Figure 6.4 that Keith used the personal business letter style, which is appropriate for you to use in writing personal messages. Your return address, but not your name, appears above the date.

Adjustments

Most companies make adjustments promptly because (a) customers can sue if they are harmed and (b) most businesses want to please customers and keep their business.

Even the best-run and best-loved businesses occasionally receive claims or complaints from consumers. When a company receives a claim and decides to respond favorably, the message is called an *adjustment*. Most businesses make adjustments promptly: they replace merchandise, refund money, extend discounts, send coupons, and repair goods. Businesses make favorable adjustments to legitimate claims for two reasons. First, consumers are protected by contractual and tort law for recovery of damages. If, for example, you find an insect in a package of frozen peas, the food processor of that package is bound by contractual law to replace it. If you suffer injury, the processor may be liable for damages. Second, and more obviously, most organizations genuinely want to satisfy their customers and retain their business.

© Ted Goff www.tedgoff.com

In responding to customer claims, you must first decide whether to grant the claim. Unless the claim is obviously fraudulent or excessive, you will probably grant it. When you say yes, your adjustment message will be good news to the reader. Deliver that good news by using the direct pattern. When your response is no, the indirect pattern might be more appropriate. Chapter 7 discusses the indirect pattern for conveying negative news.

You have three goals in adjustment messages:

- Rectifying the wrong, if one exists
- Regaining the confidence of the customer
- Promoting further business

FIGURE 6.4 Direct Claim Letter

before

Dear Good Vibes:

You call yourselves Good Vibes, but all I'm getting from your service is bad vibes! I'm furious that you have your salespeople slip in unwanted service warranties to boost your sales.

When I bought my Panatronic DVR from Good Vibes, Inc., in August, I specifically told the salesperson that I did NOT want a three-year service warranty. But there it is on my Visa statement this month! You people have obviously billed me for a service I did not authorize. I refuse to pay this charge.

How can you hope to stay in business with such fraudulent practices? I was expecting to return this month and look at HDTVs, but you can be sure I'll find an honest dealer this time.

Angrily,

- Sounds angry; jumps to conclusions
- Forgets that mistakes happen
- Fails to suggest solution

after

1201 Lantana Court
Lake Worth, FL 33461
September 3, 201x

Ms. Ernestine Sanborn
Manager, Customer Satisfaction
Good Vibes, Inc.
2003 53rd Street
West Palm Beach, FL 33407

Dear Ms. Sanborn:

Please credit my Visa account, No. 0000-0046-2198-9421, to correct an erroneous charge of $299.

On August 1, I purchased a Panatronic DVR from Good Vibes, Inc. Although the salesperson discussed a three-year extended warranty with me, I decided against purchasing that service for $299. However, when my credit card statement arrived this month, I noticed an extra $299 charge from Good Vibes, Inc. I suspect that this charge represents the warranty I declined. Enclosed is a copy of my sales invoice along with my Visa statement on which I circled the charge.

Please authorize a credit immediately and send a copy of the transaction to me at the above address. I'm enjoying all the features of my Panatronic DVR and would like to be shopping at Good Vibes for an HDTV shortly.

Sincerely,

Keith Krahnke

Keith Krahnke

Enclosure

- Uses personal business letter style
- States simply and clearly what to do
- Doesn't blame or accuse; uses friendly tone
- Explains objectively what went wrong
- Documents facts
- Summarizes request and courteously suggests continued business once problem is resolved

Tips for Submitting Claims

- Begin with a compliment, point of agreement, statement of the problem, brief review of action you have taken to resolve the problem, or clear statement of the action you want taken.
- Prove that your claim is valid; explain why the receiver is responsible.
- Enclose document copies supporting your claim.
- Appeal to the reader's fairness, ethics, legal responsibilities, or desire for return business.
- Avoid sounding angry, emotional, or irrational.
- Close by restating what you want done and looking forward to future business.

Airline troubles continue to mount as weary air travelers complain of lost luggage, long delays, canceled flights, and soaring ticket prices. In one customer-service debacle, major U.S. carriers shut down 3,700 flights in a single month after failing to meet safety inspections mandated by the Federal Aviation Administration. The grounded flights affected hundreds of thousands of passengers, underscoring the airline industry's last-place finish in a Consumer Satisfaction Index survey conducted by the University of Michigan. *What guidelines should airline companies follow when writing adjustment letters to disgruntled customers?*

© Image Source / Alamy

WORKPLACE IN FOCUS

A positive adjustment message follows the direct strategy described in the following writing plan:

WRITING PLAN FOR ADJUSTMENT MESSAGES

- **Subject line (optional):** Identify the previous correspondence and refer to the main topic.
- **Opening:** Grant the request or announce the adjustment immediately.
- **Body:** Provide details about how you are complying with the request. Try to regain the customer's confidence. Apologize, if appropriate, but don't admit negligence.
- **Closing:** End positively with a forward-looking thought; express confidence in future business relations. Include a sales promotion, if appropriate. Avoid referring to unpleasantness.

Revealing Good News Up Front in an Adjustment Message

Readers want to learn the good news immediately.

Instead of beginning with a review of what went wrong, present the good news immediately. When Kathy Nguyen responded to the claim of customer Ultima Electronics about a missing shipment, her first draft, shown at the top of Figure 6.5, was angry. No wonder. Ultima Electronics apparently had provided the wrong shipping address, and the goods were returned. Once Kathy and her company decided to send a second shipment and comply with the customer's claim, however, she had to give up the anger. Her goal was to regain the goodwill and the business of this customer. The improved version of her letter announces that a new shipment will arrive shortly.

If you decide to comply with a customer's claim, let the receiver know immediately. Don't begin your letter with a negative statement (*We are very sorry to hear that you are having trouble with your dishwasher*). This approach reminds the reader of the problem and may rekindle the heated emotions or unhappy feelings experienced when the claim was written. Instead, focus on the good news. The following openings for various letters illustrate how to begin a message with good news.

FIGURE 6.5 Customer Adjustment Letter

Dear Sir:

I have before me your recent complaint about a missing shipment. First, let me say that it's very difficult to deliver merchandise when we have been given the wrong address.

After receiving your complaint, our investigators looked into your problem shipment and determined that it was sent immediately after we received the order. According to the shipper's records, it was delivered to the warehouse address given on your stationery: 66B Industrial Lane, West Warwick, RI 02893. Unfortunately, no one at that address would accept delivery, so the shipment was returned to us. I see from your current stationery that your company has a new address. With the proper address, we probably could have delivered this shipment.

Although we feel that it is entirely appropriate to charge you shipping and restocking fees, as is our standard practice on returned goods, in this instance we will waive those fees. We hope this second shipment finally catches up with you at your current address.

Sincerely,

Fails to reveal good news immediately and blames customer

Creates ugly tone with negative words and sarcasm

Sounds grudging and reluctant in granting claim

DW **DIGITAL WAREHOUSE**
6 Business Park Drive
Branford, CT 06405

Phone: (203) 488-2202
Fax: (203) 489-3320
Web: www.dwarehouse.com

April 24, 201x

Mr. Robert Alarcon
Ultima Electronics
27 Wightman Street
West Warwick, RI 02893

Dear Mr. Alarcon:

Subject: Your April 19 Letter About Your Purchase Order

You should receive by April 26 a second shipment of the Blu-ray players, video game consoles, and other digital equipment that you ordered April 2.

The first shipment of this order was delivered April 10 to 66B Industrial Lane, West Warwick, RI. When no one at that address would accept the shipment, it was returned to us. Now that I have your letter, I see that the order should have been sent to 27 Wightman Street, West Warwick, RI 02893. When an order is undeliverable, we usually try to verify the shipping address by telephoning the customer. Somehow the return of this shipment was not caught by our normally painstaking shipping clerks. You can be sure that I will investigate shipping and return procedures with our clerks immediately to see if we can improve existing methods.

Your respect is important to us, Mr. Alarcon. Although our rock-bottom discount prices have enabled us to build a volume business, we don't want to be so large that we lose touch with valued customers like you. Over the years our customers' respect has made us successful, and we hope that the prompt delivery of this shipment will retain yours.

Sincerely,

Kathy Nguyen

Kathy Nguyen
Distribution Manager

c Joe Gonzalez
Shipping Department

Uses customer's name in salutation

Announces good news immediately

Regains confidence of customer by explaining what happened and by suggesting plans for improvement

Closes confidently with genuine appeal for customer's respect

When possible, begin with good news in adjustment messages.

You're right! We agree that the warranty on your American Standard Model UC600 dishwasher should be extended for six months.

You will be receiving shortly a new slim Nokia cell phone to replace the one that shattered when dropped recently.

Please take your portable Admiral microwave oven to A-1 Appliance Service, 200 Orange Street, Pasadena, where it will be repaired at no cost to you.

The enclosed check for $325 demonstrates our desire to satisfy our customers and earn their confidence.

In announcing that you will make an adjustment, try to do so without a grudging tone—even if you have reservations about whether the claim is legitimate. Once you decide to comply with the customer's request, do so happily. Avoid halfhearted or reluctant responses (*Although the American Standard dishwasher works well when used properly, we have decided to allow you to take yours to A-1 Appliance Service for repair at our expense*).

Explaining Compliance in the Body of an Adjustment Message

Most businesses comply with claims because they want to promote customer goodwill.

In responding to claims, most organizations sincerely want to correct a wrong. They want to do more than just make the customer happy. They want to stand behind their products and services; they want to do what's right.

In the body of the message, explain how you are complying with the claim. In all but the most routine claims, you should also seek to regain the confidence of the customer. You might reasonably expect that a customer who has experienced difficulty with a product, with delivery, with billing, or with service has lost faith in your organization. Rebuilding that faith is important for future business.

OFFICE INSIDER

"Even if the problem is not the company's fault, something like 'I'm sorry to hear that you're not satisfied with our service' is at least conciliatory, without involving the company [in] accepting any liability."

—Robert Ashton, business writing trainer and CEO of UK firm Emphasis

How to rebuild lost confidence depends on the situation and the claim. If procedures need to be revised, explain what changes will be made. If a product has defective parts, tell how the product is being improved. If service is faulty, describe genuine efforts to improve it. Notice in Figure 6.5 that the writer promises to investigate shipping procedures to see whether improvements might prevent future mishaps.

Sometimes the problem is not with the product but with the way it is being used. In other instances customers misunderstand warranties or inadvertently cause delivery and billing mix-ups by supplying incorrect information. Remember that rational and sincere explanations will do much to regain the confidence of unhappy customers.

In your explanation avoid emphasizing negative words such as *trouble, regret, misunderstanding, fault, defective, error, inconvenience,* and *unfortunately*. Keep your message positive and upbeat.

Deciding Whether to Apologize

Although apologies can be misconstrued and potentially trigger lawsuits, they are generally viewed favorably.

Whether to apologize is a debatable issue. Attorneys generally discourage apologies fearing that they admit responsibility and will trigger lawsuits. However, both judges and juries tend to look on apologies favorably. More than 20 U.S. states have passed some form of "apology laws" that would allow an expression of regret without fear that those statements would be used as a basis for liability in court.[2] Some business writing experts advise against apologies, contending that they are counterproductive and merely remind the customer of unpleasantness related to the claim. If, however, apologizing seems natural, do so.

People like to hear apologies. It raises their self-esteem, shows the humility of the writer, and acts as a form of "psychological compensation."[3] Don't, however, fall back on the familiar phrase, *I'm sorry for any inconvenience we may have caused.* It sounds mechanical and insincere. Instead, try something like this: *We understand the frustration our delay has caused you, We're sorry you didn't receive better service,* or *You're right to be disappointed.* If you feel that an apology is appropriate, do it early and briefly. You will learn more about delivering effective apologies in Chapter 7 in which we discuss negative messages.

The primary focus of an adjustment letter is on how you are complying with the request, how the problem occurred, and how you are working to prevent its recurrence.

Using Sensitive Language in Adjustment Messages

The language of adjustment letters must be particularly sensitive, because customers are already upset. Here are some don'ts:

Because customers are upset when making a claim, don't use negative words, don't blame the customer or individuals in your company, and don't make unrealistic promises.

- Don't use negative words *(trouble, regret, misunderstanding, fault, error, inconvenience, you claim)*.
- Don't blame customers—even when they may be at fault.
- Don't blame individuals or departments within your organization; it's unprofessional.
- Don't make unrealistic promises; you can't guarantee that the situation will never recur.

To regain the confidence of your reader, consider including resale information. Describe a product's features and any special applications that might appeal to the reader. Promote a new product if it seems appropriate.

Showing Confidence in the Closing

End positively by expressing confidence that the problem has been resolved and that continued business relations will result. You might mention the product in a favorable light, suggest a new product, express your appreciation for the customer's business, or anticipate future business. It is often appropriate to refer to the desire to be of service and to satisfy customers. Notice how the following closings illustrate a positive, confident tone.

> *You were most helpful in informing us of this situation and permitting us to correct it. We appreciate your thoughtfulness in writing to us.*
>
> *Thanks for writing. Your satisfaction is important to us. We hope that this refund check convinces you that service to our customers is our No. 1 priority. Our goals are to earn your confidence and continue to merit that confidence with quality products and excellent service.*
>
> *Your Asus Netbook will come in handy whether you are connecting with friends, surfing the net, listening to music, watching movies, or playing games. What's more, you can add an HD TV tuner and built-in GPS for a little more. Take a look at the enclosed booklet detailing the big savings for essential technology on a budget. We value your business and look forward to your future orders.*

Although the direct pattern works for many requests and replies, it obviously won't work for every situation. With more practice and experience, you will be able to alter the pattern and adapt your skills to other communication problems.

Goodwill Messages

Many communicators are intimidated when they must write goodwill messages expressing thanks, recognition, and sympathy. Finding the right words to express feelings is often more difficult than writing ordinary business documents. That is probably why writers tend to procrastinate when it comes to goodwill messages. Sending a ready-made card or picking up the telephone is easier than writing a message. Remember, though, that the personal sentiments of the sender are always more expressive and more meaningful to readers than are printed cards or oral messages. Taking the time to write gives more importance to our well-wishing. Personal notes also provide a record that can be reread, savored, and treasured.

Messages that express thanks, recognition, and sympathy should be written promptly.

In expressing thanks, recognition, or sympathy, you should always do so promptly. These messages are easier to write when the situation is fresh in your mind. They also mean more to the recipient. Don't forget that a prompt thank-you note carries the hidden message that you care and that you consider the event to be important. You will learn to write various goodwill messages that deliver thanks, congratulations, praise, and sympathy. Instead of learning writing plans for each of them, we recommend that you concentrate on the five Ss. Goodwill messages should be:

Goodwill messages are most effective when they are selfless, specific, sincere, spontaneous, and short.

- **Selfless.** Be sure to focus the message solely on the receiver not the sender. Don't talk about yourself; avoid such comments as *I remember when I . . . .*
- **Specific.** Personalize the message by mentioning specific incidents or characteristics of the receiver. Telling a colleague *Great speech* is much less effective than *Great story about McDonald's marketing in Moscow.* Take care to verify names and other facts.
- **Sincere.** Let your words show genuine feelings. Rehearse in your mind how you would express the message to the receiver orally. Then transform that conversational language to your written message. Avoid pretentious, formal, or flowery language *(It gives me great pleasure to extend felicitations on the occasion of your firm's twentieth anniversary).*
- **Spontaneous.** Keep the message fresh and enthusiastic. Avoid canned phrases *(Congratulations on your promotion, Good luck in the future).* Strive for directness and naturalness, not creative brilliance.
- **Short.** Although goodwill messages can be as long as needed, try to accomplish your purpose in only a few sentences. What is most important is remembering an individual. Such caring does not require documentation or wordiness. Individuals and business organizations often use special note cards or stationery for brief messages.

OFFICE INSIDER
"Saying 'Thank You' is an important concept in our business. When people are sincerely appreciated for their efforts, they tend to be more effective and do a better job."
—Nowell C. Wisch, editor of *Wearables Business* and veteran of the promotional products industry

Expressing Thanks

When someone has done you a favor or when an action merits praise, you need to extend thanks or show appreciation. Letters of appreciation may be written to customers for their orders, to hosts and hostesses for their hospitality, to individuals for kindnesses performed, and especially to customers who complain. After all, complainers are actually providing you with "free consulting reports from the field." Complainers who feel that their complaints were heard often become the greatest promoters of an organization.[4]

Because the receiver will be pleased to hear from you, you can open directly with the purpose of your message. The letter in Figure 6.6 thanks a speaker who addressed a group of marketing professionals. Although such thank-you notes

FIGURE 6.6 Thank-You Letter for a Favor

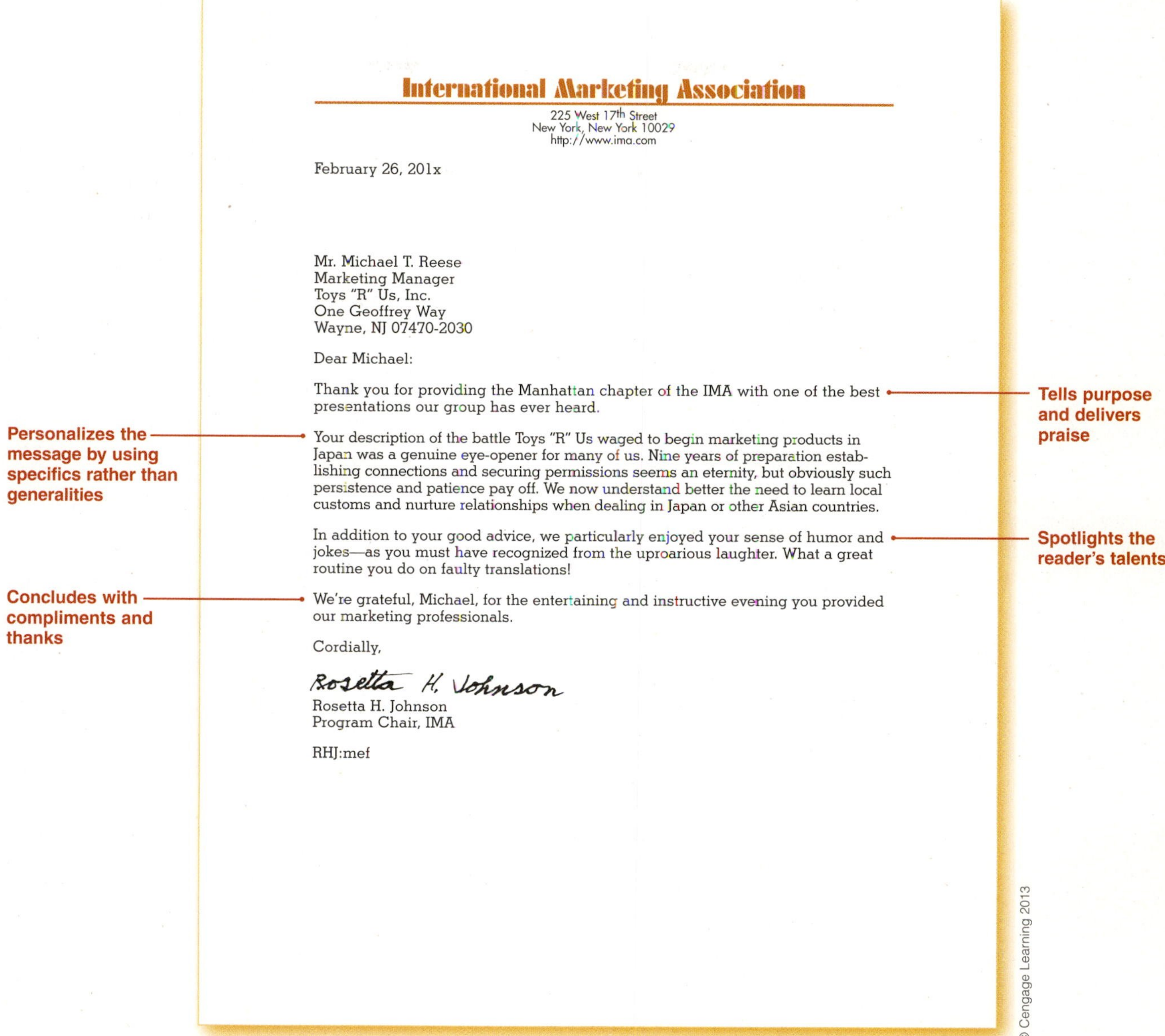
International Marketing Association

225 West 17th Street
New York, New York 10029
http://www.ima.com

February 26, 201x

Mr. Michael T. Reese
Marketing Manager
Toys "R" Us, Inc.
One Geoffrey Way
Wayne, NJ 07470-2030

Dear Michael:

Thank you for providing the Manhattan chapter of the IMA with one of the best presentations our group has ever heard.

Your description of the battle Toys "R" Us waged to begin marketing products in Japan was a genuine eye-opener for many of us. Nine years of preparation establishing connections and securing permissions seems an eternity, but obviously such persistence and patience pay off. We now understand better the need to learn local customs and nurture relationships when dealing in Japan or other Asian countries.

In addition to your good advice, we particularly enjoyed your sense of humor and jokes—as you must have recognized from the uproarious laughter. What a great routine you do on faulty translations!

We're grateful, Michael, for the entertaining and instructive evening you provided our marketing professionals.

Cordially,

Rosetta H. Johnson

Rosetta H. Johnson
Program Chair, IMA

RHJ:mef

Tells purpose and delivers praise
Personalizes the message by using specifics rather than generalities
Spotlights the reader's talents
Concludes with compliments and thanks

can be quite short, this one is a little longer because the writer wants to lend importance to the receiver's efforts. Notice that every sentence relates to the receiver and offers enthusiastic praise. By using the receiver's name along with contractions and positive words, the writer makes the letter sound warm and conversational.

Written notes that show appreciation and express thanks are significant to their receivers. In expressing thanks, you generally write a short note on special notepaper or heavy card stock. The following messages provide models for expressing thanks for a gift, for a favor, and for hospitality.

Expressing Thanks for a Gift. When expressing thanks, tell what the gift means to you. Use sincere, simple statements.

> *Thanks, Laura, to you and the other members of the department for honoring me with the elegant Waterford crystal vase at the party celebrating my twentieth anniversary with the company. The height and shape of the vase are perfect to hold roses and other bouquets from my garden. Each time I fill it, I will remember your thoughtfulness in choosing this lovely gift for me.*

Sending Thanks for a Favor. In showing appreciation for a favor, explain the importance of the gesture to you.

I sincerely appreciate your filling in for me last week when I was too ill to attend the planning committee meeting for the spring exhibition. Without your participation, much of my preparatory work would have been lost. Knowing that competent and generous individuals like you are part of our team, Mark, is a great comfort. Moreover, counting you as a friend is my very good fortune. I'm grateful to you.

Extending Thanks for Hospitality. When you have been a guest, send a note that compliments the fine food, charming surroundings, warm hospitality, excellent host and hostess, and good company.

Jeffrey and I want you to know how much we enjoyed the dinner party for our department that you hosted Saturday evening. Your charming home and warm hospitality, along with the lovely dinner and sinfully delicious chocolate dessert, combined to create a truly memorable evening. Most of all, though, we appreciate your kindness in cultivating togetherness in our department. Thanks, Jennifer, for being such a special person.

Responding to Goodwill Messages

Take the time to respond to any goodwill message you may receive.

Should you respond when you receive a congratulatory note or a written pat on the back? By all means! These messages are attempts to connect personally; they are efforts to reach out, to form professional and/or personal bonds. Failing to respond to notes of congratulations and most other goodwill messages is like failing to say "You're welcome" when someone says "Thank you." Responding to such messages is simply the right thing to do. Do avoid, though, minimizing your achievements with comments that suggest you don't really deserve the praise or that the sender is exaggerating your good qualities.

Answering a Congratulatory Note. In responding to congratulations, keep it short and simple.

Thanks for your kind words regarding my award, and thanks, too, for sending me the newspaper clipping. I truly appreciate your thoughtfulness and warm wishes.

Responding to a Pat on the Back. When acknowledging a pat-on-the-back note, use simple words in conveying your appreciation.

Your note about my work made me feel good. I'm grateful for your thoughtfulness.

Conveying Sympathy

Sympathy notes should refer to the misfortune sensitively and offer assistance.

Most of us can bear misfortune and grief more easily when we know that others care. Notes expressing sympathy, though, are probably more difficult to write than any other kind of message. Commercial "In sympathy" cards make the task easier—but they are far less meaningful than personal notes. Grieving friends want to know what you think—not what Hallmark's card writers think. To help you get started, you can always glance through cards expressing sympathy. They will supply ideas about the kinds of thoughts you might wish to convey in your own words. In writing a sympathy note, (a) refer to the death or misfortune sensitively, using words that show you understand what a crushing blow it is; (b) in the case of a death, praise the deceased in a personal way; (c) offer assistance without going into excessive detail; and (d) end on a reassuring, forward-looking note. Sympathy messages may be typed, although handwriting seems more personal. In either case, use notepaper or personal stationery.

Expressing Condolences. Mention the loss tactfully, recognize the good qualities of the deceased, assure the receiver of your concern, offer assistance, and conclude on a reassuring note.

We are deeply saddened, Gayle, to learn of the death of your husband. Warren's kind nature and friendly spirit endeared him to all who knew him. He will be missed. Although words seem empty in expressing our grief, we want you to know that your friends at QuadCom extend their profound sympathy to you. If we may help you or lighten your load in any way, you have but to call.

We know that the treasured memories of your many happy years together, along with the support of your family and many friends, will provide strength and comfort in the months ahead.

Conclude a condolence message on a positive, reassuring note.

Is E-Mail Appropriate for Goodwill Messages?

In expressing thanks or responding to goodwill messages, handwritten notes are most impressive. However, if you frequently communicate with the receiver by e-mail and if you are sure your note will not get lost, then sending an e-mail goodwill message is acceptable, according to the Emily Post Institute.[5] To express sympathy immediately after learning of a death or accident, you might precede a phone call or a written condolence message with an e-mail. E-mail is a fast and nonintrusive way to show your feelings. However, advises the Emily Post Institute, immediately follow with a handwritten note. Remember that e-mail messages are quickly gone and forgotten. Handwritten or printed messages remain and can be savored. Your thoughtfulness is more lasting if you take the time to prepare a handwritten or printed message on notepaper or personal stationery.

www.cengagebrain.com

Available with an access code, these eResources will help you prepare for exams:

- **Chapter Review Quizzes**
- **Personal Language Trainer**
- **PowerPoint Slides**
- **Flash Cards**

Summing Up and Looking Forward

Although e-mail is becoming an important communication channel for brief messages, both internal and external, business letters are still important. They are necessary for messages that must produce a permanent record, are confidential, convey formality and sensitivity, and deliver persuasive, well-considered ideas. In this chapter you learned to write direct messages that request information or action. You also learned to write instruction messages, direct claims, direct responses, adjustments, and a variety of goodwill messages. All of these routine messages, whether e-mails, memos, or letters, use the direct strategy. They open immediately with the main idea followed by details and explanations. But not all messages will carry good news. Occasionally, you must deny requests and deliver bad news. In Chapter 7 you will learn to use the indirect strategy in conveying negative news.

Critical Thinking

1. In an age when millions of e-mails are sent daily, does the writing of an "old-fashioned" business letter potentially provide a competitive advantage or reflect favorably on the writer? Under what circumstances and why?
2. The opening and the closing are the most emphatic parts of any message. How can writers avoid sounding demanding and abrupt in these two most important sections?
3. Is it true that the "squeaky wheel gets the most grease," meaning that the customer complaining the loudest and most aggressively will get noticed and receive the greatest concessions?
4. Why are apologies in business so complex and controversial?
5. **Ethical Issue:** Is it ethical to write a "hyped-up" letter of recommendation or one that is only lukewarm or vague? How would you feel if someone you trust wrote you either a letter of recommendation that stretches the truth or one that is less than glowing?

Chapter Review

6. How can you determine when it is appropriate to send an e-mail, a memo, or a letter?

7. Which silent messages does a business letter convey?

8. What does frontloading the message mean, and what are the advantages in direct requests?

9. Why are a plain *Thank you* or a standard phrase such as *Thank you in advance for your cooperation* undesirable in a closing of a business message?

10. How can you make messages delivering instructions most readable?

11. When should you write a claim letter instead of venting your frustration by e-mail?

12. Why should you state facts in a claim message logically, objectively, and unemotionally?

13. What are the two main reasons that motivate businesses to grant favorable adjustments to their customers if they have legitimate claims?

14. Why is positive language so important in adjustment messages, and what are some of the major don'ts?

15. Why are many communicators intimidated when they must write goodwill messages expressing thanks, recognition, and sympathy?

Writing Improvement Exercises

Improving Opening Paragraphs

Your Task. Revise the following openings so that they are more direct. Add information if necessary.

16. Despite the economy, Liberty Bank has been investigating the possibility of initiating an internship program within our Financial Services Department. I have been appointed as the point person to conduct research regarding our proposed program. We are fully aware of the benefits of a strong internship program, and our management team is eager to take advantage of some of these benefits. We would be deeply appreciative if you would be kind enough to help us out with answers to a number of specific questions.

17. My name is Kimberly Sanchez, and I am assistant to the manager of Information Services & Technology at Onyz, Inc. We are interested in your voice recognition software that we understand allows you to dictate and copy text without touching a keyboard. We are interested in answers to a number of questions, such as the cost for a single-user license and perhaps the availability of a free trial version. Will you please answer the following questions.

18. Your letter of March 4 has been referred to me. Pursuant to your inquiry, I have researched your question in regard to whether or not we offer our European-style patio umbrella in colors. This unique umbrella is one of our most popular items. Its 10-foot canopy protects you when the sun is directly overhead, but it also swivels and tilts to virtually any angle for continuous sun protection all day long. It comes in two colors: cream and forest green.

19. I am pleased to receive your inquiry regarding the possibility of my acting as a speaker at the final semester meeting of your business management club on May 2. The topic of online résumés interests me and is one on which I think I could impart helpful information to your members. Therefore, I am responding in the affirmative to your kind invitation.

20. So far I have been happy with my Timex Ironman watch, but lately it's been rather erratic. The display has been fading, and the numerals are hard to read. I suspected that a new battery was needed, but the problem remained even after a new one was inserted. I wore the watch while surfing and I suspect that water may have penetrated the watch. Can you recommend a convenient service location to have the watch looked at?

Writing Instructions

Your Task. Revise the following wordy, dense paragraphs into a set of concise instructions. Include an introductory statement.

21. Orders may be placed at our Web site by following certain steps. Here they are. As a visitor to our site, you should first look over everything and find the items you want from our catalog. Then your shopping cart is important. You will add items to your shopping cart. When you are finished adding things to your shopping cart, the next step is to proceed to checkout. But wait! Have you created a new account? After creating a new account, we next need to know what shipping address to ship your items to. We will also need to have you choose a shipping method. Then you will be expected to provide payment information. Finally, you are nearly done! Payment information must be provided, and then you are ready to review your order and submit it.

22. If you want to make a YouTube video, here are some important tips for those who have not done it before. First, you will need to obtain a video recording device such as a cell phone, webcam, or camcorder. Another thing you will have to do is make a decision on whether or not to make a video blog, comedy skit, how-to video, or a video that is about travel. Remember that your video must be no more than 15 minutes long for traditional YouTube membership accounts. You will want to create a video with good light quality, and that usually means daytime recording. Finally, be sure to use editing software to change or delete anything.

23. A number of employees have asked about how to make two-sided copies. Here's what to do. The copy for side 1 of the original goes face down on the Document Glass. Then the Document Cover should be closed. Next you should select the quantity that you require. To copy side 1, you should then press Start. Now you remove the first original and place the second original face down on the Document Glass. The Document Cover should be closed. Now you remove side 1 copy from the Output Tray. It should be inserted face down into the Paper Bypass Tray. Then select the Alternate Paper Tray and press Start.

Writing Improvement Cases

6.1 Direct Request: Workplace Security

The following letter requests information; however, the first draft suffers from many writing faults.

Your Task. Analyze the message. List its weaknesses and then outline an appropriate writing plan. If your instructor directs, revise the message. A copy of this message is provided at **www.meguffey.com** for revision online.

Current date

Mr. Gregory Howard, Sales Manager
HiTek Software and Computing
16544 Burt Street
Omaha, NE 68154-3749

Dear Sir:

Our insurance rates will be increased in the near future due to the fact that we don't have security devices on our computer equipment. Local suppliers were considered, but at this point in time none had exactly what we wanted. That's why I am writing to see whether or not you can provide information and recommendations regarding equipment to prevent the possible theft of office computers and printers. In view of the fact that our insurance carrier has set a deadline of April 1, we need fast action.

Our office now has 18 computer workstations along with twelve printers. We need a device that can be used to secure separate computer components to desks or counters. Would you please recommend a device that can secure a workstation consisting of a computer, monitor, and keyboard. We wonder if professionals are needed to install your security devices and to remove them. We are a small company, and we don't have a staff of maintenance people.

One problem is whether the devices can be easily removed when we need to move equipment around. We are, of course, very interested in the price of each device. What about quantity discounts, if you offer them.

Until such time as we hear from you, thank you in advance for your attention to this matter.

Sincerely,

1. List at least five weaknesses of this letter.

2. Outline a writing plan (not the actual message) for a direct request.

   Opening:
   Body:
   Closing:

6.2 Direct Response: Can Chatter Beat Facebook?

The following memo responds to a request for information about safer, more business-appropriate social networking services than Facebook and Twitter.[6]

Your Task. Analyze the following poorly written memo about Chatter, a new application created by enterprise software leader Salesforce.com with headquarters in San Francisco. List its weaknesses, and then outline an appropriate writing plan. If your instructor directs, revise the message. A copy of this message is provided at **www.meguffey.com** for revision online.

Date: March 4, 201x
To: Helen Lazar, CEO
From: Gilbert S. Luce
Subject: Chatter

Thanks for asking me to research and investigate potential alternatives to Facebook and Twitter. I stumbled upon Chatter, a new social networking service provided to its customers by San Francisco–based Salesforce.com, a fast-growing upstart whose stock has more than doubled over the last year, to $120 per share. I had fun doing research and would welcome another opportunity anytime. Let me know if you want me to present my findings to you and other executives in greater detail. Okay, back to Chatter and my report.

Imagine, a company that implements Chatter can expect its e-mail traffic to drop 40 percent as employees stay plugged in to the organization and remain connected. You can also track which workers add value to the company because you can keep an eye on deals being struck and monitor support staff members who excel at nipping problems in the butt.

The disadvantages of online social networks are obvious and clearly apparent. They sap and drain employees' time and productivity. Their openness creates a corporate security nightmare. Chatter, however, allows for virtual watercooler conversations but with limitations that are appropriate for business. Management can control and restrict access to sensitive information and records.

Salesforce.com is offering the Chatter service as part of its existing service to some 82,000 customers worldwide. Currently, about 20,000 companies have deployed Chatter, computer maker Dell and advertising agency Saatchi & Saatchi among them. At Dell, some 20,000 workers are on Chatter, allowing managers to track deals. As for the cost, Chatter is included at no extra charge in the monthly fees of $65–$125 for customer-relationship management and other Salesforce.com business software. As a stand-alone product, Chatter costs $15 a month per user.

Did I mention how Chatter works? It is a lot like Facebook and Twitter, but it asks what people are working on, not what is on their mind or what is happening. Salesforce.com calls Chatter a "real-time collaboration cloud," meaning that users need only a browser and an Internet connection to access it. Users create profiles, and their status updates center on questions, salient tidbits, and hyperlinks that are shared with coworkers in their personal networks. Together those comments and updates merge into a running feed. As on Twitter, employees can follow each other, their customers, and deals. Additional advantages are that (a) workers can connect with colleagues in the whole company, not just their workgroups, and (b) profiles are searchable for needed skills, say, if you need someone who speaks Mandarin and so forth. Chatter also makes suggestions to account users about people they should follow based on their past activities and job needs. Pretty nifty, isn't it?

This is just a summary of what I learned. If you want to hear more, please do not hesitate to call.

1. List the weaknesses of this memo.

2. Outline a writing plan for a direct response.

   Opening:
   Body:
   Closing:

6.3 Direct Claim: Rental Car Refund Complaint

The following letter conveys a complaint and makes a claim. However, its poor tone and expression may prevent the receiver from getting what she wants.

Your Task. Analyze the message. List its weaknesses and then outline an appropriate writing plan. If your instructor directs, revise the message. A copy of this message is provided at **www.meguffey.com** for revision online.

Current date

Mr. John Lear
Regional General Manager
Apex Car Rentals
4510 Cyprus Street
Denver, CO 80246

Dear Regional General Manager John Leer:

I have a horror story of gargantuan proportions to relate to you so that you know how incompetent the amateurish bozos are that work for you! You should fire the whole Colorado Springs airport branch. I'm tired of lousy service and of being charged an arm and a leg for extras that end up not functioning properly. Calling your company is useless because no one answers the phone or returns calls!

In view of the fact that my colleague and I were forced to wait for an hour for a car at Colorado Springs Airport on August 15, your local branch people gave us a free navigation device. That would have been really nice in the event that the thing had actually worked, which it didn't. We advised the counter person that the GPS was broken, but it took another half hour to receive a new one and to finally start our business trip.

Imagine our surprise when the "free" GPS showed up on our bill apparently costing a whopping $180, plus tax! What came next would qualify as some dark Kafkaesque nightmare. I spent hours over the next three weeks talking to various employees of your questionable organization who swore that only "the manager" could help me, but this mysterious person was never available to talk. At this point in time, I called your Denver Airport location again and refused to get off the phone until I spoke to "the manager," and, lo and behold, he promised to credit the cost of the GPS to our corporate account. Was my nightmare over? No!

When we checked the status of the refund on our credit card statement, we noticed that he had forgotten to add about $60 in taxes and surcharges that had also been assessed. So much for a full refund!

Inasmuch as my company is a new customer and inasmuch as we had hoped to use your agency for our future car rentals because of your competitive rates, I trust that you will give this matter your prompt attention.

Your very upset customer,

1. List at least five weaknesses of this letter.

2. Outline a writing plan for a claim request.

Opening:

Body:

Closing:

Activities and Cases

 **E-MAIL**

6.4 Direct Request: Pamper Palace Spa Worries About Duplicate Charges

As an assistant to Donna K. Lilly, the busy proprietor of Pamper Palace Spa in Weymouth, Massachusetts, you have been asked to draft an e-mail to Virtual Treasures asking about an apparent duplicate charge for a small trial order of massage oils. The Weymouth location of Pamper Palace Spa, a professional spa franchise operating nationwide, wanted to try Virtual Treasures' exquisite Tahitian Monoi Tiare coconut oils. After reading a French magazine, your boss had ordered a few bottles and a bar of soap for $58.88 to test the product, but when Ms. Lilly checked Pamper Palace Spa's business account online, she found what she believed to be a duplicate order. She wants you to write to Virtual Treasures and ask about the apparent error.

Donna Lilly is suspicious because a few weeks earlier, she had ordered a French press coffee pot for $19 to use in her office and received two pots. Her account was charged $38. She did not take any action, making good use of the two French press coffee pots in her business. For both orders, Ms. Lilly had used Virtual Treasures' EasyPay feature, a one-click convenience tool online. Now she worries that future orders may lead to costly duplicate shipments and double charges. The order was divided into two shipments, each with a different order number: #502-3385779-9590624 and #502-8112203-6442608. Donna Lilly may order large quantities of Monoi Tiare oil after trying the pending shipment.

Your Task. Write a direct request by e-mail to Virtual Treasures at *customer-care@virtualtreasures.com*. Inquire about the possible error stemming from the use of EasyPay. Format your e-mail correctly. Include the Pamper Palace Spa's location and your business e-mail, *info@pamperpalacespa.com*.

E-MAIL

6.5 Direct Request: Searching for a Social Media Maven

For most consumers, social media are just fun. Facebook, Twitter, blogs, and MySpace are amusing and a pleasant way to keep in touch with friends. Only recently have companies begun to recognize that social media can also make money, and suddenly, social media mavens are in great demand. Petco, supplier of pet supplies and services, recently hired Natalie Malaszenko as its director of social media and commerce. Her assignment at Petco was to envision and articulate the company's social media strategy for the future. To that end, she created fan pages on Facebook, opened several Twitter accounts, and wrote a company blog. In addition to Petco, other organizations have hired social media officers, including Sears Holdings, Panasonic, Citigroup, AT&T, Fiji Water, Go Daddy.com, and Harrah's Entertainment.

As the director of corporate communication for HomeCenter, a large home supply store, you are charged with looking into the possible hiring of a social media specialist. You know that other companies have both profited and been hurt by fast-moving viral news. Nobody wants to suffer the fate of United Airlines, which took a beating last year after ignoring a wronged passenger who was a musician. He posted a clever song about how the airline had broken his guitar, and the video skyrocketed into cyberspace with millions of viewers enjoying its YouTube ribbing. Social media mavens, companies hope, can monitor cyberspace and be ready to respond to both negative and positive messages. They can help build a company's brand and promote its online reputation. They can also develop company guidelines for employee use and encourage staffers to spread the good word about the organization.

To learn more about social media, you decide to go to Rick Trumka, who was recommended as a social media consultant by your CEO, David Seldenberg. You understand that Mr. Trumka has agreed to provide information and will be paid by HomeCenter.

This whole social media thing may be just another passing fad. You are not convinced that any real benefits would result from having a social media specialist on your staff. However, the CEO wants you to explore the possibilities. You decide that this is not a matter that can be handled quickly by a phone call. You want to get answers in writing.

Many issues concern you. For one thing, you are worried about the hiring process. You have no idea about a reasonable salary for a social media expert. You don't know where to place that person within your structure. Would the media maven operate out of corporate communications, marketing, customer service, or exactly where? Another thing that disturbs you is how to judge a candidate. What background would you require? Do colleges actually award degrees in social networking? How will you know the best candidate? And what about salary? Should you be promising a full-time salary for doing what most people consider to be fun?[7]

Your Task. Compose an e-mail inquiry to *rick.trumka@mediaresources.com*. Explain your situation and list specific questions. Mr. Trumka is not an employment source; he is a consultant who charges for his information and advice. Make your questions clear and concise. You realize that Mr. Trumka would probably like to talk on the phone or visit you, but make clear that you want a written response so that you can have a record of his information to share when you report to the CEO.

6.6 Direct Request: Raising Puppies to Become Guide Dogs

As an assistant in the Community Involvement Program of your corporation, you have been given an unusual task. Your boss wants to expand the company's philanthropic and community relations mission and especially employee volunteerism. She heard about The Seeing Eye, a program in which volunteers raise puppies for 14 to 18 months for guide dog training. She thinks this would be an excellent outreach program for the company's employees. They could give back to the community in their role as puppy raisers. To pursue the idea, she asks you to request information about the program and ask questions about whether a company could sponsor a program encouraging employees to act as volunteers. She hasn't thought it through very carefully and relies on you to raise logical questions, especially about costs for volunteers.

Your Task. Write a direct request letter to Susanna Odell, The Seeing Eye, 9002 East Chaparral Road, Scottsdale, AZ 85250. Include an end date and a reason.

WEB

6.7 Direct Request: Planning a Winter Retreat in Jackson Hole, Wyoming

Despite grim economic news, your employer, Stremer Media Group of Dallas, Texas, has had an excellent year and the CEO, Peter Stremer, would like to reward "the troops" for their hard work with a rustic yet plush winter retreat. The CEO wants his company to host a four-day combination conference/retreat/vacation for his 55 marketing and media professionals with their spouses or significant others at some spectacular winter resort. Ideally, the location would delight any taste, with activities ranging from dining and relaxing in style to downhill and cross-country skiing, snowboarding, snowmobile tours, and other winter sports.

One of the choices is Jackson Hole, Wyoming, a famous ski resort town with steep slopes and dramatic mountain views. The location is popular for its proximity to Grand Teton National Park, Yellowstone, and the National Elk Refuge. Mr. Stremer has asked you, as marketing manager, to write a letter so that you can have a permanent, formal record of all the resorts you investigate. You will also look into winter resorts in Utah and Colorado.

As you search the Web and investigate the options in Jackson Hole, you are captivated by the Four Seasons Resort, a five-star facility with outdoor pool, spa tub, ski in/ski out access, and an amply equipped gym and fitness room. Other amenities include an on-site spa with massage and treatment rooms, a sauna, and facial and body treatments. You can see that the guest rooms are well appointed with DVD players, MP3 docking stations, and coffee/tea makers. Bathrooms feature separate bathtubs and showers, double sinks, and bathrobes. For business travelers, the hotel offers complimentary wired high-speed Internet access, complimentary wireless Internet access, and multiline phones as well as fax availability.

The Web site of the Four Seasons Jackson Hole is not very explicit on the subject of business and event facilities, so you decide to jot down a few key questions. You estimate that your company will require about 50 rooms. You will also need two conference rooms (to accommodate 25 participants or more) for one and a half days. You want to know about room rates, conference facilities, A/V equipment in the conference rooms, and entertainment options for families. You have two periods that would be possible: December 15–19 or January 12–16. You realize that both are peak times, but you wonder whether you can get a discounted group rate. You are interested in entertainment on site, in Jackson Hole, and in tours to the nearby national parks. Jackson Hole airport is 4.5 miles away, and you would like to know whether the hotel operates a shuttle. Also, one evening the CEO will want to host a banquet for about 85 people. Mr. Stremer wants a report from you by September 15.

Your Task. Write a well-organized direct request letter to Denise O'Handley, Sales Manager, Four Seasons Resort, 7680 Granite Loop Road, Teton Village, WY 83025. You might like to take a look at the Four Seasons Resort Web site at **http://www.fourseasons.com/jacksonhole** and search for general information about Jackson, Wyoming.

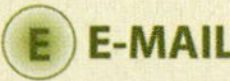

E-MAIL

6.8 Direct Response: Virtual Treasures Reassures Business Customer

Online retailer Virtual Treasures has received the direct request from Donna K. Lilly (see Activity 6.4), who is concerned that her company, Pamper Palace Spa, is being charged twice for the same order whenever she uses the convenience feature EasyPay. As customer care representative at Virtual Treasures, you investigate the request and find that Ms. Lilly ordered five items on September 16, which were divided into two orders. The first, #502-3385779-9590624, was for Monoi Tiare Tahiti (Gardenia) Bar Soap, 4.6 oz., and three 4-ounce bottles of coconut oil, Monoi Coco (Natural Coconut Oil), Monoi Pitate (Coconut Oil w/Jasmine) , and Monoi Santal (Coconut Oil w/ Sandalwood). Order #502-8112203-6442608 was for Monoi Tiare Tahiti (Coconut Oil w/Gardenia), also 4 ounces. The invoice total accurately read $58.88; there were no duplicate charges.

When you talk to your technical team, however, you learn that occasionally customer account statements have shown duplicate orders when EasyPay was activated. The IT people assure you that the technical malfunction has been fixed. You are glad that, in turn, you can now reassure the customer.

Each e-mail you send out for Virtual Treasures contains two standards links allowing customers to click answers to the options "Did we solve your problem?" or "If not, we are very sorry. Please click the link below." This second option also suggests to the customer to contact Virtual Treasures by telephone. Soliciting feedback from customers in every message serves the purpose to "build America's Friendliest Company."

Your Task. Write a direct reply e-mail to Donna K. Lilly. You may want to list the full order for reference. Ensure eye appeal and readability when writing and formatting your message.

 TEAM  WEB

6.9 Direct Response: Telling Job Applicants How to Make a Résumé Scannable

As part of a team of interns at the outdoor e-tailer Campmor.com, you have been asked to write a form letter to send to job applicants who inquire about your résumé-scanning techniques. The following poorly written response to an inquiry was pulled from the file.

Dear Ms. Fratelli:

Your letter of April 11 has been referred to me for a response. We are pleased to learn that you are considering employment here at Campmor, and we look forward to receiving your résumé, should you decide to send same to us.

You ask if we scan incoming résumés. Yes, we certainly do. Actually, we use SmartTrack, an automated résumé-tracking system. We sometimes receive as many as 300 résumés a day, and SmartTrack helps us sort, screen, filter, and separate the résumés. It also processes them, helps us organize them, and keeps a record of all of these résumés. Some of the résumés, however, cannot be scanned, so we have to return those—if we have time.

The reasons that résumés won't scan may surprise you. Some applicants send photocopies or faxed copies, and these can cause misreading, so don't do it. The best plan is to send an original copy. Some people use colored paper. Big mistake! White paper (8 1/2 × 11-inch) printed on one side is the best bet. Another big problem is unusual type fonts, such as script or fancy gothic or antique fonts. They don't seem to realize that scanners do best with plain, readable fonts such as Helvetica or Arial in a 10- to 14-point size.

Other problems occur when applicants use graphics, shading, italics, underlining, horizontal and vertical lines, parentheses, and brackets. Scanners like plain, unadorned résumés. Oh yes, staples can cause misreading. And folding of a résumé can also cause the scanners to foul up. To be safe, don't staple or fold, and be sure to use wide margins and a quality printer.

When a hiring manager within Campmor decides to look for an appropriate candidate, he is told to submit keywords to describe the candidate he has in mind for his opening. We tell him (or sometimes her) to zero in on nouns and phrases that best describe what they want. Thus, my advice to you is to try to include those words that highlight your technical and professional areas of expertise.

If you do decide to submit your résumé to us, be sure you don't make any of the mistakes described herein that would cause the scanner to misread it.

Sincerely,

Your Task. As a team, discuss how this letter could be improved. Decide what information is necessary to send to potential job applicants. Search the Web for additional information that might be helpful. Then, submit an improved version to your instructor. Although the form letter should be written so that it can be sent to anyone who inquires, address this one to Chiara Fratelli, 1019 University Drive, Boise, ID 83725.

 E-MAIL  WEB  TEAM

6.10 Direct Response: The Real-World Click Has Arrived

Online companies have enjoyed a distinct advantage over traditional brick-and-mortar retailers. On the Web, e-tailers can personalize deals to shoppers and allow instant price comparisons. They can establish a unique user profile based on the purchasing behavior of the customer and tailor special offers or recommendations to the shopper upon his or her next visit. Amazon.com and other e-commerce sites have mastered this technique.

Offline retailers, on the other hand, depend on foot traffic to make a sale and may never learn anything about a shopper who walks in, buys an item, and walks out again. However, as opposed to a Web site's visitors, a small proportion of whom actually make a purchase, traditional retailers experience a much higher "conversion rate," the percentage of patrons who walk into the store and actually buy an item. For example, about 20 percent of fashion shoppers buy a piece of clothing; in electronics, the percentage of store visitors who make purchases ranges from 40 to 60 percent.

New smartphone-centered services offered by cutting-edge tech entrepreneurs now promise to bridge the gap between e-commerce advantage and the traditional retail paradigm. Internet services such as Foursquare, Booyah, Shopkick, Gowalla, and, yes, Facebook, have begun to extend digital efficiencies to the physical retail world by enticing millions of consumers to digitally "check in" to real-world locations. With location-sensing technology, the visitor to a physical store is asked to open an app that sends this location information to selected friends. By checking in frequently, the user earns certain advantages such as gift certificates or a chance to win prizes. The services are designed to give brick-and-mortar businesses the opportunity to customize deals to patrons and to build enduring relationships with the otherwise anonymous walk-ins, potentially their best customers.

Big retailers are coming on board: Gap, Starbucks, Sephora, Best Buy, American Eagle, and Sports Authority all have forged partnerships with the upstart services. The digital check-in services try to make their interfaces interesting by using "game mechanics." In other words, they include gamelike features in their apps and help their retail partners—Sony and AT&T Wireless among them—to build game mechanics into their own Web sites as well. Traditional retailers are hoping that the services will catch on so that they will know—as an e-commerce Web site does—who their customers are, where they are, and even when they are nearby, potentially ready to spend.

Your boss, Jane McKinley, vice president of e-commerce and digital marketing at Verizon Wireless, heard that competitor AT&T Wireless is already using Scvngr. In groups or individually, research the following start-ups: Scvngr, Foursquare, Stickybits, Gowalla, Shopkick, and Booyah. Additionally, you could take a look at Barcode Hero and Facebook Places. Find out how they work, which retail partners they serve, how many users they have, and so forth.[8]

Your Task. Ms. McKinley asked you, a group of interns at Verizon Wireless, to conduct research that would help her decide whether any of the current Internet upstarts offering check-in services could benefit the company. She may request an e-mail or a memo about each individual service from the researcher or group assigned to it. If your instructor directs, later the contributions of each researcher or group might be combined in a direct response memo to Ms. McKinley.

6.11 Direct Response: Describing Your Major

A friend in a distant city is considering moving to your area for more education and training in your field. Your friend has asked you for information about your program of study.

Your Task. Write a letter describing a program in your field (or any field you wish to describe). What courses must be taken? Toward what degree, certificate, or employment position does this program lead? Why did you choose it? Would you recommend this program to your friend? How long does it take? Add any information you feel would be helpful.

E-MAIL

6.12 Instruction Message: What to Do in an Emergency

In talking with your boss, Sue Curry, one day, you learned that she was concerned about fires and safe evacuation in your office building. She thinks that you, as director of human resources, should prepare a set of procedures for employees to follow in case of fires. She also thinks that the two of you can work out the procedures in a conversation, and she begins talking with you.

She notes that if an employee sees a fire, that person should pull the alarm and call the fire department. The number of that department is 9-911. If the fire is small, the employee can attempt to extinguish it with a fire extinguisher. At this point, you ask your boss if the person who discovered the fire should also notify a supervisor, and your boss agrees. The supervisor is probably the one who should size up the situation and decide whether the building should be evacuated. You then begin to think about the evacuation process. What to do? Ms. Curry says that all doors should be closed and employees should secure their workstations. You ask what exactly that means, and she says employees should turn off their computers and put away important documents, but perhaps that information is unnecessary. Just stick to the main points, she says.

If employees are evacuating, they should go to the nearest exit in an orderly manner. In addition, it's very important that everyone remain calm. You ask about people with disabilities. "Sure," she says, "we should assist all visitors and persons with disabilities." Then Ms. Curry remembers that employees have been told about predetermined gathering places, and they should go there and wait for more instructions from floor monitors. It's also important that employees not reenter the building until given the all-clear. When they are outside, they should stay out of the way of fire department personnel and equipment.

"Do you have all the information?" she asks. "Great! Now prepare a draft memo to employees for my signature."

Your Task. Draft an e-mail or memo to employees from Sue Curry, CEO. Provide brief background data and explain the main idea. List clear fire instructions. Provide your name, title, and office phone number if receivers want more information.

6.13 Instruction Message: How to Copy Pictures and Text from PDF Documents

As a summer intern in the Marketing Department at Jovanovic Laboratory Supply, Inc., in Bozeman, Montana, you have been working on the company's annual catalog. You notice that staffers could save a lot of valuable time by copying and inserting images and text from the old edition into the new document. Your boss, Marketing Director Linda M. Trojner, has received numerous inquiries from staffers asking how to copy text and images from previous editions. You know that this can be done, and you show a fellow worker how to do it using a PDF feature called **Snapshot Tool**. Marketing Director Trojner decides that you are quite a tech-savvy student. Because she has so much confidence in you, she asks you to draft a memo detailing the steps for copying images and text passages from portable document format (PDF) files.

You start by viewing the **Tools** pull-down menu in an open PDF document. Depending on the Acrobat version, a feature called **Snapshot Tool** emerges either under **Basic** or under **Select & Zoom**. This feature is represented by a camera icon. To copy content, you need to select the part of the PDF document that you want to capture. The cursor will change its shape once the feature is activated. Check what shape it acquires. With the left mouse button, click the location where you want to insert the copied passage or image. At the same time, you need to drag the mouse over the page in the direction you want. A selected area appears that you can expand and reduce, but you can't let go of the left mouse button. Once you release the left mouse button, a copy of the selected area will be made. You can then paste the selected area into a blank Microsoft Office document, whether Word, Excel, or PowerPoint. You can also take a picture of an entire page.

Your Task. Prepare a memo addressed to Marketing Department staff members for the signature of Linda M. Trojner. Practice the steps described here in abbreviated form and arrange all necessary instructions in a logical sequence. You may need to add steps omitted here. Remember, too, that your audience may not be as computer literate as you are, so ensure that the steps are clear and easy to follow.

E-MAIL

6.14 Instruction Message: So Your Work Computer Won't Work?

As the manager of Computing Support Services for Primacy Group, a small financial services firm, you always tried to handle computer repairs on a personal level. In the past managers and employees called you when they had a problem, and you asked for details on the telephone and then sent one of your two tech assistants to clear up the problem. However, Primacy Group recently merged with Midstate Financial Providers, doubling the number of employees. You realize that to continue to provide timely and effective service, you must give up your personal approach and establish a set of instructions to be followed by anyone seeking help.

You must send an e-mail explaining the new instructions. Here's what you decided to do. First, you would tell staff members who are reporting a problem to close all software programs, reboot, and try again. It's surprising how many times this simple trick works. But if that doesn't work and a real problem persists, they should go to a Web page you have established. It's located at **http://www.primacysupport.com**. On this page, staff members should look for the tab that says **Service Request**. This is where you want them to give you information such as their name, room number, phone number, and e-mail address. But wait! If their computer is down, how can they fill out this Web form? You remember to insert an instruction telling them to go to another staff member's computer to access the Web page.

One of the most important pieces of information you will need is an explanation of what they were doing before and at the time of the problem. What happened? What did they see on the screen? Finally, you want to warn staff members not to try to repair computer equipment or printers themselves. No matter how much they know about computers, you don't want them to tamper with company equipment. It may result in more damage than necessary.

After a technician makes the repair, your department will send a Service Completion Report by e-mail. You would like staff members to tell whether the work was completed to their satisfaction. You are convinced that staff members will receive faster and better service if they follow this set of instructions.

Your Task. Write an e-mail to Primacy Midstate staff members explaining the new instructions for reporting computer problems. Be sure to list the steps to follow and end with a concluding paragraph.

6.15 Direct Claim: Botched Valentine's Day Surprise

Randy Pettit is very disappointed. He planned to surprise his girlfriend Sue at her workplace with beautiful roses and a vase for Valentine's Day. Sue works as an analyst for a major financial services company, and Randy knows that a generous bouquet sent there would impress not only Sue but also her colleagues and superiors. Randy had read favorable reviews on the Internet praising Bouquet International, a Swiss-based flower-delivery service operating worldwide. Because Valentine's Day was to fall on a Saturday, Randy requested that the flowers be sent a day before the big date.

Alas, upon the delivery of the bouquet in its flower-friendly packaging, Sue heard the sound of broken glass and refused the FedEx shipment. The delivery driver actually had advised Sue to return the package and took it back. Randy's surprise was ruined, and he was frustrated and angry with Bouquet International. On top of that, the same package with the identical tracking number was delivered to Sue's workplace again some three days after Valentine's Day. Sue was away, and a colleague signed for the package not knowing the history of the order. Sue later called FedEx to pick up the potentially less-than-fresh flowers.

However, about two weeks later, Randy's credit card statement showed the order number 106928959 and a charge of $73.25 from Bouquet International. Randy has friends and family on the East Coast and in Europe. He may potentially use Bouquet International's services to send flowers in the future. He decides to e-mail customer service to get his money back.

Your Task. Write a direct claim by e-mail to Bouquet International at *info@bouquetinternational.com* requesting a refund. Include the necessary information and organize it logically in a well-formatted, professional e-mail.

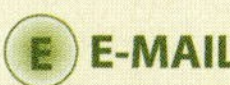

6.16 Direct Claim: Duplicate Delivery of Fourth of July Beads

Barbara DiDonato, owner of Great Stuff Gifts & Cards in Norfolk, Virginia, bought 3,000 multicolored (red, white, and blue) beads from Gift Shoppe in time for the huge Independence Day parade in town. The $600 shipment arrived by UPS two months before the holiday, and she had no problems selling all her beads in this patriotic town.

Much to her surprise, Barbara received another shipment of 3,000 beads from Gift Shoppe some 40 days after the Fourth of July holiday along with a new charge of $600 to her business credit account. She called Gift Shoppe and sent the package back by UPS, tracking number U3529803873838583833. She asked the customer-service representatives to issue a refund, but even after repeated phone calls, Gift Shoppe insisted that the returned package had not been received and a credit could not be issued. Unnerved, Barbara followed up with UPS and was stunned when the otherwise highly reliable shipper admitted that the package had apparently been lost in transit and was not to be found in the system. The last record was a pickup at Great Stuff. UPS suggested that Gift Shoppe make a claim for a refund because the shipment of beads was insured and it was clear that the package had left the Great Stuff premises.

Your Task. Write a courteous e-mail to Gift Shoppe at *info@giftshoppe.com* requesting $600 to be refunded to the company account. Clearly detail what happened to the return shipment by UPS.

6.17 Direct Claim: New Iron Gate Needs Work

You work for JPM, Johnson Property Management, in Portland, Oregon. Your employer specializes in commercial real estate. Just yesterday one of your business tenants in the trendy NW 23rd neighborhood complained about problems with an iron gate you had installed by Chung Iron Works just six months earlier, on August 20. Apparently, the two doors of the gate have settled and don't match in height. The gate gets stuck. It takes much force to open, close, and lock the gate. The iron gate was painted, and in some spots rust is bleeding onto the previously pristine white paint. The tenant at 921 NW 23rd Ave., Portland, OR 97210 is a petite shop owner, who complained to you about struggling with the gate at least twice a day when opening and closing her store.

You realize that you will have to contact the installer, Chung Iron Works, and request that the company inspect the gate and remedy the problem. Only six months have passed, and you recall that the warranty for the gate was for one year. To have a formal record of the claim and because Chung Iron Works does not use e-mail, you decide to write a claim letter.

Your Task. Address your letter to Jin Ree at Chung Iron Works, 2255 NW Yeon Avenue in Portland, OR 97210. To jog his memory, you will enclose a copy of the company's proposal/invoice. Your business address is 1960 NE Irving Street, Portland, OR 97209, phone (503) 335-5443 and fax (503) 335-5001.

6.18 Direct Claim: The Real Thing

Have you ever bought a product that didn't work as promised? Have you been disappointed in service at a bank, restaurant, department store, or discount house, or from an online merchant? Have you had ideas about how a company or organization could improve its image, service, or product? Remember that smart companies want to know what their customers think, especially if a product could be improved.

Your Task. Select a product or service that has disappointed you. Write a claim letter requesting a refund, replacement, explanation, or whatever seems reasonable. For claims about food products, be sure to include bar-code identification from the package, if possible. Your instructor may ask you to actually mail this letter. When you receive a response, share it with your class.

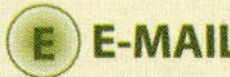

6.19 Adjustment: Responding to Valentine's Day Bouquet Crisis

Like your major competitor Fleurop Interflora, your employer, Swiss-based Bouquet International, offers same-day florist delivery of fresh flowers, plants, and gifts all over the world, aided by a global network of 20,000 associated florists. You like the company's cheerful motto: "Express yourself with a bouquet!"

You receive an e-mail from a frustrated Randy Pettit (See Activity 6.15), who requests a refund of $73.25 for a Valentine's Day bouquet that was delivered with a broken vase and subsequently refused only to be delivered again and sent back as before. You contact your shipping department about order number 106928959 to find out if more instances of broken vases have been reported or if this was an unfortunate but isolated incident. So far you haven't heard from your shipping department or from your contact at FedEx.

As an intern without your own e-mail account, you often write for your supervisor, Oksana Georgyevna Gotova, using her e-mail address, *oggotova@bouquetinternational.com*. You were tasked with delivering the good news to Randy Pettit at *rpettit@sbcglobal.net* that he will receive a credit of $73.25 and that his flower order was canceled. Tell him to check his next credit card statement for the refund. You know that all employees must always include the case ID number in every e-mail and encourage customers to do the same when contacting your company. Randy is a frequent customer.

Your Task. Draft the e-mail to Randy Pettit for your supervisor. Try to rebuild Randy's trust in your services. For your electronic signature, you may want to indicate that the company is headquartered in Switzerland at Stiegengasse 5, CH-8065 Zurich, phone + 41 (0) 45 763 36 77 and fax + 41 (0) 45 763 25 70.

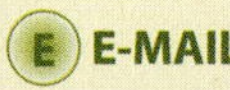

6.20 Adjustment: Refund for Duplicate Shipment and Charges Granted

Aubrey Gordy at Gift Shoppe Wholesale is terribly swamped, and in his despair he asks you to write an adjustment e-mail to Great Stuff owner Barbara DiDonato. Great Stuff of Norfolk, Virginia, had ordered 3,000 red, white, and blue beads for the Fourth of July parade for $600 (see Activity 6.16). Then, a month and a half after the patriotic holiday, Great Stuff received another 3,000-piece shipment of the same beads and was charged $600 again for this apparently unwanted batch of beads. A very good customer, Barbara DiDonato wants the $600 credited back to her business account. She swears she returned the second shipment of beads to you immediately by UPS, and as proof she lists the tracking number U3529803873838583833. Gift Shoppe Wholesale, however, has no record of a return shipment of beads from Barbara, nor can it find the tracking number.

After speaking to UPS, as Ms. DiDonato has suggested, you learn that the package has indeed vanished in transit and cannot be located. It disappeared without a trace after pickup at the Norfolk store. UPS promises to reimburse you for the lost shipment. You know that you need to inform Barbara DiDonato about the pending refund of $600 and process it as soon as possible.

Your Task. Write a polite adjustment e-mail to Barbara DiDonato announcing the refund and building goodwill.

6.21 Adjustment: Erroneous Charge for GPS Reversed

As assistant to John S. Lear, Regional General Manager at Apex Rent-a-Car, you read a shockingly irate complaint letter from a corporate customer (See Activity 6.3) addressed to your boss. Adriana Schuler-Reyes, Sales Manager for KDR Precision Components, Inc., in Phoenix, Arizona, has angrily detailed her tribulations with your company's Colorado Springs Airport branch.

Apparently, she and a colleague suffered long delays in obtaining their rental car. To compensate for the late car delivery, the customers received complimentary use of a navigation device, a $180 value plus taxes and surcharges that add up to another $60. However, at the end of their rental period, their bill reflected the full cost of the GPS. After multiple phone calls to the Colorado Springs Airport branch as well as to Apex Rent-a-Car corporate offices, Ms. Schuler-Reyes apparently was finally able to have the $180 credited to KDR's business account. However, soon she realized that the $60 levy had not been credited. She now wants the remainder of the refund. Ms. Schuler-Reyes has no confidence in the Colorado branch and is asking your boss to intervene on her behalf and reverse the remaining $60 charge.

Mr. Lear asks you to investigate what has gone so terribly wrong at the Colorado Springs Airport location. You learn that the branch is an independent franchisee, which may explain such a laxness in customer service that is unacceptable under corporate rules. In addition, you find out that the branch manager, Scott Brown, was traveling on company business during Ms. Schuler-Reyes' rental period and then left town to attend two management training seminars. Mr. Lear is concerned that Apex might lose this disappointed customer and decides to offer discount vouchers for KDR's next three rentals at 20 percent off each, valid at any U.S. branch. He wants to you to draft the letter and enclose the discount vouchers.

Your Task. Write a polite adjustment letter to Adriana Schuler-Reyes, KDR Precision Components, Inc., 2328 E Van Buren St., Phoenix, AZ 85006 to secure the customer's goodwill and future business.

 E-MAIL

6.22 Thanks for a Favor: Glowing Letter of Recommendation

One of your instructors has complied with your urgent request for a letter of recommendation and has given you an enthusiastic endorsement. Regardless of the outcome of your application, you owe thanks to all your supporters. Respond promptly after receiving this favor. Also, you can assume that your instructor is interested in your progress. Let him or her know whether your application was successful.

Your Task. Write an e-mail or, better yet, a letter thanking your instructor. Remember to make your thanks specific so that your words are meaningful. Once you know the outcome of your application, use the opportunity to build more goodwill by writing to your recommender again.

 TEAM  WEB

6.23 Thanks for a Favor: Business Etiquette Training Session

Your business communication class was fortunate to have the etiquette and protocol expert Pamela Eyring speak to you. A sought-after TV commentator and media personality, she runs the Protocol School of Washington, a training center for etiquette consultants and protocol officers. Ms. Eyring emphasized the importance of soft skills. She talked about outclassing the competition and dining like a diplomat. She addressed topics such as business entertaining, invitations, introductions, greetings, seating arrangements, toasting, eye contact, remembering names, and conversation skills. In the table manners segment, among other topics, she discussed dining dos and don'ts, host and guest duties, seating and napkin placement, place settings and silverware savvy, eating various foods gracefully, and tipping. With characteristic poise but also humor, Ms. Eyring brought utensils, plates, and napkins to demonstrate correct table manners.

The class was thrilled to receive hands-on training from a nationally known business etiquette expert who was able to lessen their fears of making fools of themselves during business meals or at business mixers.

Your Task. Individually or in groups, draft a thank-you letter to Pamela Eyring, director of The Protocol School of Washington, P.O. Box 676, Columbia, SC 29202. Check out the company's Web site **http://www.psow.edu**, or find The Protocol School of Washington on Facebook, where you can follow Ms. Eyring's frequent media appearances, interviews, and etiquette advice.

6.24 Thanks for the Hospitality: Boat Party and Harbor Cruise

You and other members of your staff or organization were entertained at an elegant dinner during the winter holiday season on board a large ship that was cruising the harbor of Marina Del Rey in California. The posh pleasure boat featured a live band, ballroom dancing, and a casino.

Your Task. Write a thank-you letter to your boss (supervisor, manager, vice president, president, or chief executive officer) or to the head of an organization to which you belong. Include specific details that will make your letter personal and sincere.

6.25 Responding to Good Wishes: Saying Thank You

Your Task. Write a short note thanking a former colleague who sent you good wishes when you recently found a good job after a long hiatus.

6.26 Extending Sympathy: To a Spouse

Your Task. Imagine that a coworker was killed in an automobile accident. Write a letter of sympathy to his or her spouse.

Video Resources

Video Library 2: ***Happy Cows in Harmony With Nature: Organic Valley.*** Organic farmer Paul Deutsche has opened his Wisconsin organic dairy farm to a group of visitors. Paul, with his toddler son Emory, tells how he got started and what motivated him to purchase farmland that became Sweet Ridge Organic Dairy. He answers questions about the term *organic*, and he addresses the problems of meeting high organic standards, including expensive high-quality feed. He is part of a group of Organic Valley family farmers who work in harmony with nature without antibiotics, synthetic hormones, or pesticides. His animals, which you see in the background, are raised humanely and given certified organic feed—never any animal by-products. He's proud that his animals roam freely in certified organic pastures.

Your Task. Assume that you are part of a group of environmentally conscious farmers and activists. You heard that Paul Deutsche, one of Organic Valley's family farmers, occasionally opens his farm for tours. As the leader of your group, you have been given the task of writing a direct request to Organic Valley. You will request permission for your group to visit Paul Deutsche's Sweet Ridge Organic Dairy. Prepare a list of at least six appropriate questions that you would like Mr. Deutsche to discuss when your group visits. Fill in any necessary information and details. Address your direct request to Ms. Ann Simon, Community Service Director, Organic Valley Family of Farms, CROPP Cooperative, One Organic Way, LaFarge, WI 54639. Suggest dates and tell how many people you expect.

Grammar/Mechanics Checkup—6

Commas 1

Review the Punctuation Review section of the Grammar/Mechanics Handbook, Sections 2.01–2.04. Then study each of the following statements and insert necessary commas. In the space provided, write the number of commas that you add; write *0* if no commas are needed. Also record the number of the G/M principle illustrated. When you finish, compare your responses with those shown near the end of the book. For more practice you will find a set of Bonus Grammar/Mechanics exercises with immediate feedback at your premier Web site, **www.cengagebrain.com**. If your answers differ, study carefully the principles shown in parentheses.

2 (2.01) **Example** The hiring manager is looking for candidates who are conscientious, adaptable, and flexible.

______ 1. We do not as a rule hire anyone who has not been interviewed.

______ 2. You may be sure Ms. Ebert that we will notify you immediately.

______ 3. Digital networking involves having your job hunt and qualifications spread virally among friends former colleagues and professional associates.

______ 4. We have scheduled two interviews for December 5 at the Hyatt Regency in Nashville beginning at 1 p.m.

______ 5. As a matter of fact job hunters regularly flub by submitting their résumés to multiple recruiters and hiring managers at the same firm.

______ 6. In the meantime please remember that today's hiring managers regularly search the Internet before hiring anyone.

______ 7. One hiring manager even found digital dirt on a candidate that went back to March 1 2005 in Chicago.

______ 8. Anne Lublin volunteered to move from Albany New York to Atlanta Georgia for a job.

______ 9. Eric Wong Teresa Cabrillo and Elise Rivers are the final three candidates.

______ 10. The benefits package mailed to Ms. Dawn Summers 1339 Kearsley Street Flint MI arrived exactly five days after it was mailed.

______ 11. Many job candidates think needless to say that they will find a job by searching the big job boards.

______ 12. Experienced job counselors feel however that the best way to find a job is through personal networking.

______ 13. Before going to his interview, Jon did three things: researched the hiring company prepared success stories and practiced answering questions.

______ 14. Valuable job leads can develop from projecting yourself online and making sure everyone you know is aware that you are looking for a job.

______ 15. I'm pleased to meet you Mr. Powell.

Editing Challenge—6

As the employee with the best communication skills, you are frequently asked to edit messages. The following letter has problems with spelling, proofreading, comma use, verbs, and other writing techniques you have studied. You may (a) use standard proofreading marks (see Appendix B) to correct the errors here or (b) download the document from **www.meguffey.com** and revise at your computer.

Your instructor may ask you to use the **Track Changes** feature in Word to show your editing comments. Turn on **Track Changes** on the **Review** tab. Click **Show Markup**. Place your cursor at an error, click **New Comment**, and key your edit in the bubble box provided. Study the guidelines in the Grammar/Mechanics Handbook as well as the lists of Confusing Words and Frequently Misspelled Words to sharpen your skills.

January 20, 201x

Mr. Arnold M. Rosen
3201 Rose Avenue
Mar Vista, CA 90066

Dear Mr. Rosan:

Subject: Your February 5 Letter About Our All Natural Products

We have received your letter of February 5, and we are pleased to be able to answer in the affirmative. Yes, our new line of freeze dried back packing foods meet the needs of older adults and young people as well. You asked a number of questions, and here are answers to you're questions about our products.

- Our all natural foods contains no perservatives, sugars or additives. The inclosed list of dinner items tell what foods are cholesterol-, fat-, and salt-free.
- Large orders recieve a five percent discount when they're placed direct with Outfitters, Inc. You can also purchase our products at Malibu Sports Center, 19605 Pacific Coast Highway Malibu CA, 90265.
- Outfitters, Inc., food products are made in our sanitary kitchens which I personally supervise. The foods are flash froze in a patented vacum process that retain freshness, texture and taste.
- Outfitters, Inc. food products are made from choice ingredients that combines good taste and healful quality.
- Our foods stay fresh, and tasty for up to 18 months.

Mr. Rosin I started Outfitters, Inc., five years ago because of the fact that discerning back packers rejected typical camping fare. Its a great pleasure to be able at this point in time to share my custom meals with back packers like you.

By the way I hope you'll enjoy the enclosed sample meal, "Saturday Night on the Trail." This is a four-coarse meal complete with fruit candys and elegant appetizers. Please call me personally at (213) 459-3342 to place an order, or to ask other questions about my backpacking food products.

Sincerely,

April Johnson

April Johnson

Enclosure

Communication Workshop

Using Ethical Tools to Help You Do the Right Thing

In your career you will no doubt face times when you are torn by ethical dilemmas. Should you tell the truth and risk your job? Should you be loyal to your friends even if it means bending the rules? Should you be tactful or totally honest? Is it your duty to help your company make a profit, or should you be socially responsible?

Being ethical, according to the experts, means doing the right thing *given the circumstances*. Each set of circumstances requires analyzing issues, evaluating choices, and acting responsibly. Resolving ethical issues is never easy, but the task can be made less difficult if you know how to identify key issues. The following questions may be helpful.

- **Is the action you are considering legal?** No matter who asks you to do it or how important you feel the result will be, avoid anything that is prohibited by law. Giving a kickback to a buyer for a large order is illegal, even if you suspect that others in your field do it and you know that without the kickback you will lose the sale.
- **How would you see the problem if you were on the opposite side?** Looking at both sides of an issue helps you gain perspective. By weighing both sides of an issue, you can arrive at a more equitable solution.
- **What are the alternative solutions? Consider all dimensions of other options.** Would the alternative be more ethical? Under the circumstances, is the alternative feasible?
- **Can you discuss the problem with someone whose opinion you value?** Suppose you feel ethically bound to report accurate information to a client—even though your boss has ordered you not to do so. Talking about your dilemma with a coworker or with a colleague in your field might give you helpful insights and lead to possible alternatives.
- **How would you feel if your family, friends, employer, or coworkers learned of your action?** If the thought of revealing your action publicly produces cold sweats, your choice is probably not a wise one. Losing the faith of your friends or the confidence of your customers is not worth whatever short-term gains might be realized.

Career Application. One of the biggest accounting firms uses an ethical awareness survey that includes some of the following situations. You may face similar situations with ethical issues on the job or in employment testing.

Your Task. In teams or individually, decide whether each of the following ethical issues is (a) very important, (b) moderately important, or (c) unimportant. Then decide whether you (a) strongly approve of, (b) are undecided about, or (c) strongly disapprove of the action taken.[9] Apply the ethical tools presented here to determine whether the course of action is ethical. What alternatives might you suggest?

- **Recruiting.** You are a recruiter for your company. Although you know company morale is low, the turnover rate is high, and the work environment in many departments is deplorable, you tell job candidates that it is "a great place to work."
- **Training program.** Your company is offering an exciting training program in Hawaii. Although you haven't told anyone, you plan to get another job shortly. You decide to participate in the program anyway because you have never been to Hawaii. One of the program requirements is that participants must have "long-term career potential" with the firm.
- **Thievery.** As a supervisor, you suspect that one of your employees is stealing. You check with a company attorney and find that a lie detector test cannot be legally used. Then you decide to scrutinize the employee's records. Finally, you find an inconsistency in the employee's records. You decide to fire the employee, although this inconsistency would not normally have been discovered.
- **Downsizing.** As part of the management team of a company that makes potato chips, you are faced with the rising prices of potatoes. Rather than increase the cost of your chips, you decide to decrease slightly the size of the bag. Consumers are less likely to notice a smaller bag than a higher price.

Endnotes

[1] Fallows, J. (2005, June 12). Enough keyword searches. Just answer my question. *The New York Times*, p. BU3.

[2] Quinley, K. (2008, May). Apology programs. *Claims*, pp. 14–16. Retrieved from http://www.ebscohost.com/academic/business-source-premier. See also Runnels, M. (2009, Winter). Apologies all around: Advocating federal protection for the full apology in civil cases. *San Diego Law Review*, *46*(1), 137–160. Retrieved from http://search.ebscohost.com

[3] Davidow, M. (2003, February). Organizational responses to customer complaints: What works and what doesn't. *Journal of Service Research*, *5*(3), 225. Retrieved from http://search.ebscohost.com; Blackburn-Brockman, E., & Belanger, K. (1993, June). You-attitude and positive emphasis: Testing received wisdom in business communication. *The Bulletin of the Association for Business Communication*, 1–5; Mascolini, M. (1994, June). Another look at teaching the external negative message. *The Bulletin of the Association for Business Communication*, 46.

[4] Liao, H. (2007, March). Do it right this time: The role of employee service recovery performance in customer-perceived justice and customer loyalty after service failures. *Journal of Applied Psychology*, 92(2), 475. Retrieved October 2, 2009, from http://www.ebscohost.com/academic/business-source-premier; Gilbert, P. (1996, December). Two words that can help a business thrive. *The Wall Street Journal*, p. A12.

[5] Emily Post Institute. (2008). Conveying sympathy Q & A. Retrieved from http://ww31.1800flowers.com

[6] Scenario partially based on Jaroslovsky, R. & Ricardela, A. (2010, August 30–September 5). Salesforce.com channels Facebook. *Bloomberg Businessweek*, pp. 34–35.

[7] Portions based on Gillette, F. (2010, July 19–25). Twitter, twitter, little stars. *Bloomberg Businessweek*, pp. 64–67.

[8] Portions based on Stone, B., & Sheridan, B. (2010, August 30–September 5). The retailer's clever little helper. *Bloomberg Businessweek*, pp. 31–32.

[9] Adapted from Conaway, R. N., & Fernandez, T. L. (2000, March). Ethical preferences among business leaders: Implications for business schools. *Business Communication Quarterly*, 23–38.

Acknowledgments

p. 143 Office Insider based on Caddell, M. H. (2003, November/December). Is letter writing dead? Hardly. *OfficePro*, *63*(8), 23. Retrieved from http://search.ebscohost.com

p. 147 Office Insider cited in National Commission on Writing. (2004, September 14). Writing skills necessary for employment, says big business. [Press release]. Retrieved from http://www.host-collegeboard.com/advocacy/writing

p. 156 Office Insider cited in Ashton, R. (2008, April 11). To whom it may concern. *Utility Week*. Retrieved from http://search.ebscohost.com

p. 158 Office Insider cited in Wisch, N. C. (2005, April). Hey . . . Thank you! *Wearables Business*, p. 39. Retrieved from http://search.ebscohost.com

CHAPTER 7

Negative Messages

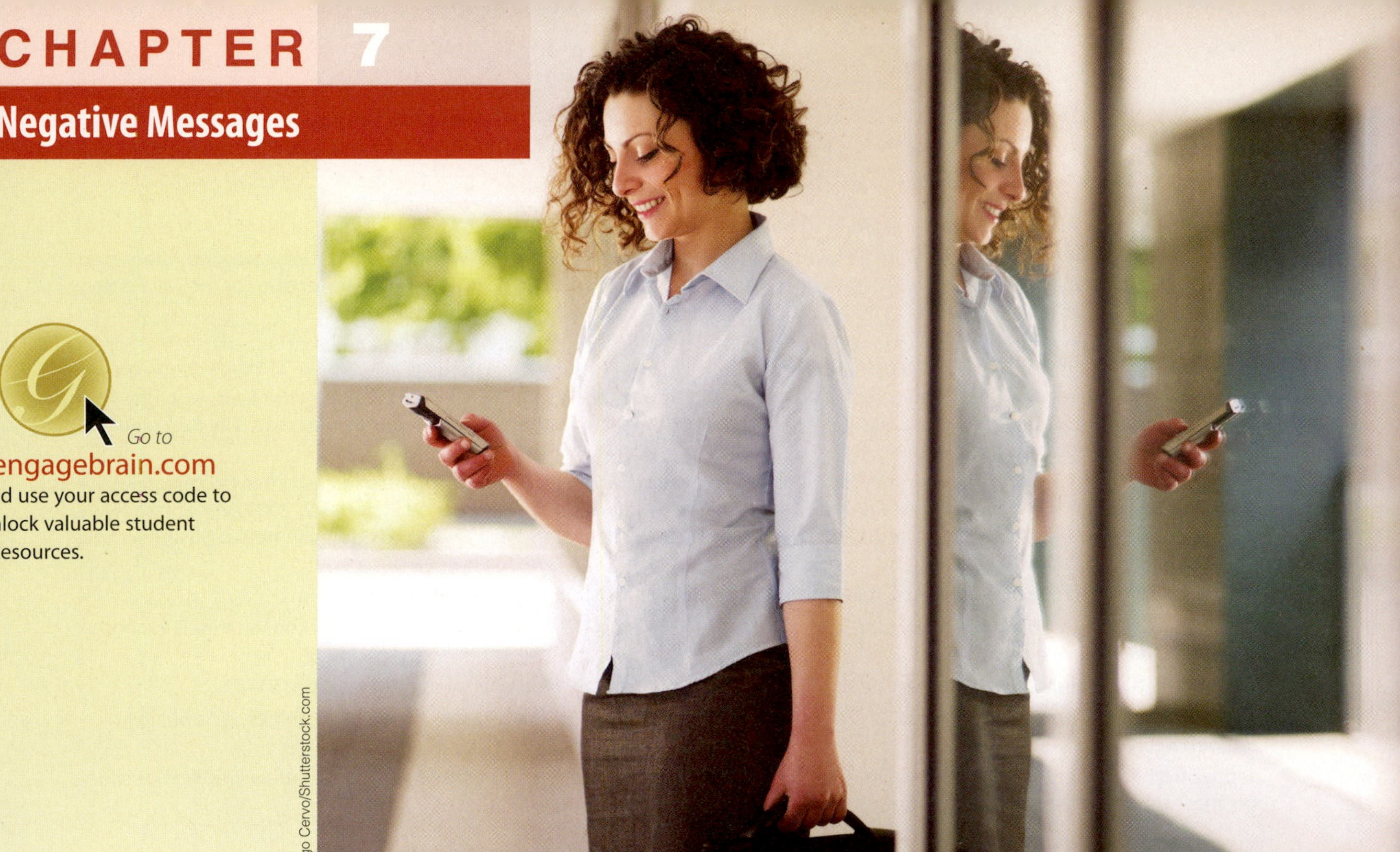

Diego Cervo/Shutterstock.com

Go to **cengagebrain.com** and use your access code to unlock valuable student eResources.

OBJECTIVES

After studying this chapter, you should be able to

- Describe the goals and strategies of business communicators, and decide whether to use the direct or indirect strategy in conveying negative news.
- Analyze the components of effective negative messages, including opening with a buffer, apologizing, conveying empathy, presenting the reasons, cushioning the bad news, and closing pleasantly.
- Outline and apply a plan for refusing typical requests and claims.
- Describe and apply effective strategies for handling bad news with customers.
- Explain and apply effective techniques for breaking bad news within organizations.
- Understand ethical and unethical uses of the indirect strategy.

OFFICE INSIDER

"Delivering difficult messages is part of day-to-day life in all social groups, whether the organization is a family, a nation, or a business."

—John J. Engels, president of Leadership Coaching Inc. in Rochester, New York

Conveying Negative News Effectively

Even the best-run businesses will goof sometimes. Goods arrive late or are not delivered at all, products fail, service disappoints, billing is mishandled, or customers are misunderstood. You may have to write messages ending business relationships, declining proposals, announcing price increases, refusing requests for donations, terminating employees, turning down invitations, or responding to unhappy customers. You might have to apologize for mistakes in orders, the rudeness of employees, overlooked appointments, pricing errors, faulty accounting, defective products, or jumbled instructions. As a company representative, you may even have to respond to complaints voiced to the world on Twitter, Facebook, or consumer comment Web sites.

Every businessperson must occasionally deliver negative news. Because bad news disappoints, irritates, and sometimes angers the receiver, such messages must be written thoughtfully. The bad feelings associated with disappointing news can generally be reduced if the receiver (a) knows the reasons for the rejection,

(b) feels that the news was revealed sensitively, and (c) believes that the matter was treated seriously and fairly.

The sting of bad news can be reduced by giving reasons, communicating sensitively, and treating the receiver fairly.

In this chapter you will learn when to use the direct strategy and when to use the indirect strategy to deliver negative news. You will study the goals of business communicators in working with negative news and learn techniques for achieving those goals.

Establishing Goals in Communicating Negative News

Delivering bad news is not the happiest writing task you may have, but it can be gratifying if you do it effectively. As a business communicator working with bad news, you will have many goals, the most important of which are these:

The goals in communicating negative news are explaining clearly, acting professionally, conveying empathy, being fair, and maintaining friendly relations.

- **Explaining clearly and completely.** Your message should be so clear that the receiver understands and, we hope, accepts the bad news. The receiver should not have to call or write to clarify the message.
- **Projecting a professional image.** You will strive to project a professional and positive image of you and your organization. Even when irate customers use a threatening tone or overstate their claims, you must use polite language, control your emotions, and respond with clear explanations of why a negative message was necessary.
- **Conveying empathy and sensitivity.** Negative news is better accepted if it is delivered sensitively. Use language that respects the receiver and attempts to reduce bad feelings. Accepting blame, when appropriate, and apologizing goes far in smoothing over negative messages. But avoid creating legal liability or responsibility for you or your organization.
- **Being fair.** Show that the situation or decision was fair, impartial, and rational. Receivers are far more likely to accept negative news if they feel they were treated fairly.
- **Maintaining friendly relations.** Make an effort to include statements that show your desire to continue pleasant relations with the receiver. As you learned in Chapter 6 in writing adjustment messages, one of your goals is to regain the confidence of customers.

These goals are ambitious, and we are not always successful in achieving them all. This chapter, however, provides the beginning communicator with strategies and techniques that many writers have found helpful in conveying disappointing news sensitively and safely. With experience, you will be able to vary these strategies and adapt them to your organization's specific communication tasks.

Examining Negative News Strategies

You have at your disposal two basic strategies for delivering negative news: direct and indirect. Which approach is best suited for your particular message? One of the first steps you will take before delivering negative news is analyzing how your receiver will react to this news. In earlier chapters we discussed applying the direct strategy to positive messages. In this chapter we expand on that advice and offer additional considerations to help you decide which strategy to use.

When to Use the Direct Strategy. Many bad-news letters are best organized indirectly, beginning with a buffer and reasons. However, the direct strategy, with the negative news first, may be more effective in situations such as the following:

The direct strategy is appropriate when the bad news is not damaging, when the receiver might overlook the bad news, when directness is preferred, and when firmness is necessary.

- **When the bad news is not damaging.** If the bad news is insignificant (such as a small increase in cost) and doesn't personally affect the receiver, then the direct strategy certainly makes sense.
- **When the receiver may overlook the bad news.** Changes in service, new policy requirements, legal announcements—these critical messages may require boldness to ensure attention.

When a mysterious case of missing hard drives exposed the personal data of 2 million Health Net customers, company executive James Woys sent a letter to notify clients. "We are writing to inform you of an incident involving the personal information of certain former and current Health Net members," the letter began. Woys then offered a three-sentence explanation of the incident before revealing, "We have reason to believe that information that pertains to you is included on the hard disk drives." *Is this a good approach for delivering bad news?*

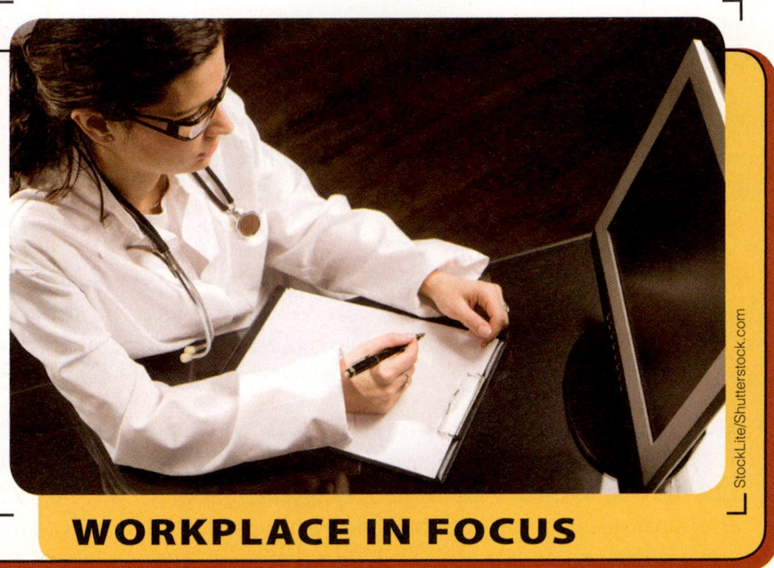

WORKPLACE IN FOCUS

- **When the organization or receiver prefers directness.** Some companies and individuals expect all internal messages and announcements—even bad news—to be straightforward and presented without frills.
- **When firmness is necessary.** Messages that must demonstrate determination and strength should not use delaying techniques. For example, the last in a series of collection letters that seek payment of overdue accounts may require a direct opener.

This direct approach to negative news probably reminds you of the direct strategy you learned to apply to positive news in Chapter 6. Let's now explore when and how to use the indirect strategy in delivering negative news.

The indirect strategy works best when the bad news is personally upsetting, will prompt a hostile reaction, threatens the business relationship, and arrives unexpectedly.

When to Use the Indirect Strategy. Many communicators prefer to use the indirect strategy to present negative news, especially to customers. Not surprisingly, good news can be revealed quickly, but negative news is generally easier to accept when broken gradually. Here are instances in which the indirect strategy works well:

- **When the bad news is personally upsetting.** If the negative news involves the receiver personally, such as a layoff notice, the indirect strategy makes sense. Telling an employee that he or she no longer has a job is probably best done in person and by starting indirectly and giving reasons first. When a company has made a mistake that inconveniences or disadvantages a customer, the indirect strategy makes sense.
- **When the bad news will provoke a hostile reaction.** When your message will irritate or infuriate the recipient, the indirect method may be best. It begins with a buffer and reasons, thus encouraging the reader to finish reading or hearing the message. A blunt announcement may make the receiver stop reading.
- **When the bad news threatens the customer relationship.** If the negative message may damage a customer relationship, the indirect strategy may help salvage the customer bond. Beginning slowly and presenting reasons that explain what happened can be more helpful than directly announcing bad news or failing to adequately explain the reasons.
- **When the bad news is unexpected.** Readers who are totally surprised by bad news tend to have a more negative reaction than those who expected it. If a company suddenly closes an office or a plant and employees had no inkling of the closure, that bad news would be better received if it were revealed cautiously with reasons first.

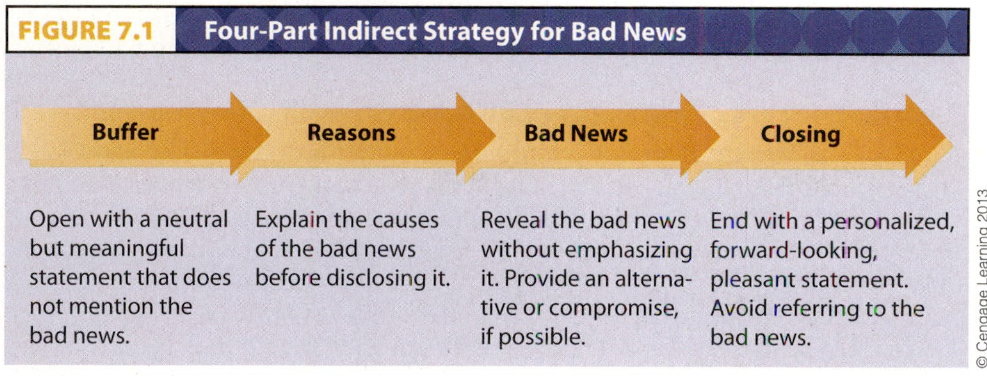

Buffer
Reasons
Bad News
Closing
Open with a neutral but meaningful statement that does not mention the bad news.
Explain the causes of the bad news before disclosing it.
Reveal the bad news without emphasizing it. Provide an alternative or compromise, if possible.
End with a personalized, forward-looking, pleasant statement. Avoid referring to the bad news.

FIGURE 7.1 Four-Part Indirect Strategy for Bad News

Whether to use the direct or indirect strategy depends largely on the situation, the reaction you expect from the audience, and your goals. The direct method saves time and is preferred by some who consider it to be more professional and even more ethical than the indirect method. Others think that revealing bad news slowly and indirectly shows sensitivity to the receiver. By preparing the receiver, you tend to soften the impact. The indirect strategy enables you to keep the reader's attention until you have been able to explain the reasons for the bad news. In fact, the most important part of a negative message is the explanation, which you will learn about shortly. The indirect plan consists of four parts, as shown in Figure 7.1:

- **Buffer.** Introduce the message with a neutral statement that makes the reader continue reading.
- **Reasons.** Explain why the bad news was necessary and that the matter was taken seriously.
- **Bad news.** Provide a clear but understated announcement of the bad news that might include an alternative or a compromise.
- **Closing.** End with a warm, forward-looking statement that might mention good wishes, gifts, or a sales promotion.

Analyzing the Components of Effective Negative Messages

Even though it may be impossible to make the receiver happy when delivering negative news, you can reduce bad feelings and resentment by structuring your message sensitively. As you have just learned, most negative messages contain some or all of these parts: buffer, reasons, bad news, and closing. Figure 7.2

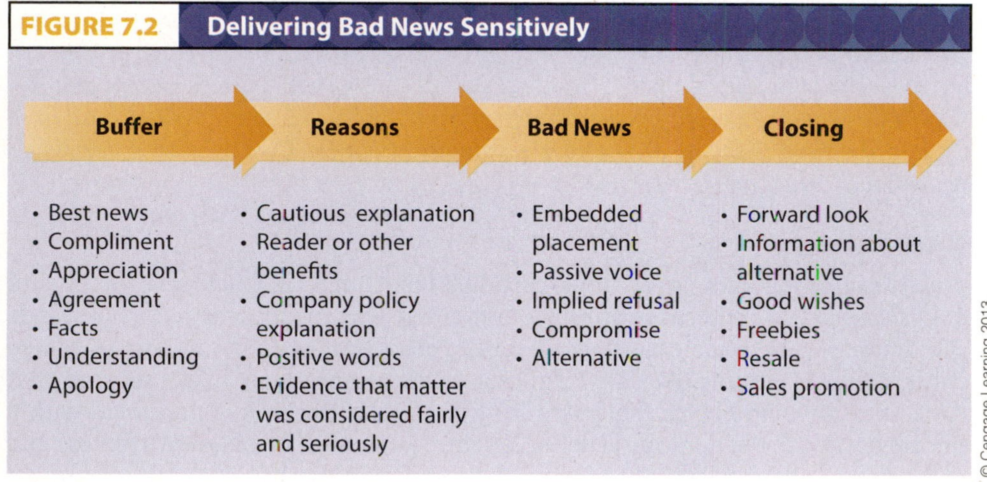

FIGURE 7.2 Delivering Bad News Sensitively

presents these four components of the indirect strategy in greater detail. This section discusses apologies and how to convey empathy in delivering bad news.

Opening Indirect Messages With a Buffer

To reduce negative feelings, use a buffer to open sensitive bad-news messages.

A buffer is a device to reduce shock or pain. To buffer the pain of bad news, begin with a neutral but meaningful statement that makes the reader continue reading. The buffer should be relevant and concise and provide a natural transition to the explanation that follows. The individual situation, of course, will help determine what you should put in the buffer. This section provides some possibilities for opening bad-news messages. Avoid trite buffers such as *Thank you for your letter.*

It should be noted that not all business communication authors agree that buffers actually increase the effectiveness of negative messages. However, in many cultures softening bad news is appreciated. Following are various buffer possibilities.

Best News. Start with the part of the message that represents the best news. For example, a message to workers announced new health plan rules limiting prescriptions to a 34-day supply and increasing co-payments. With home delivery, however, employees could save up to $24 on each prescription. To emphasize the good news, you might write, *You can now achieve significant savings and avoid trips to the drugstore by having your prescription drugs delivered to your home.*

Effective buffers open negative-news messages with compliments, appreciation, agreement, relevant facts, and understanding.

Compliment. Praise the receiver's accomplishments, organization, or efforts, but do so with honesty and sincerity. For instance, in a letter declining an invitation to speak, you could write, *The Thalians have my sincere admiration for their fund-raising projects on behalf of hungry children. I am honored that you asked me to speak Friday, November 5.*

Appreciation. Convey thanks for doing business, for sending something, for conveying confidence in your organization, for expressing feelings, or simply for providing feedback. Suppose you had to draft a letter that refuses employment. You could say, *I appreciated learning about the hospitality management program at Cornell and about your qualifications in our interview last Friday.* Avoid thanking the reader, however, for something you are about to refuse.

Agreement. Make a relevant statement with which both reader and receiver can agree. A letter that rejects a loan application might read, *We both realize how much the export business has been affected by the relative weakness of the dollar in the past two years.*

Facts. Provide objective information that introduces the bad news. For example, in a memo announcing cutbacks in the hours of the employees' cafeteria, you might say, *During the past five years the number of employees eating breakfast in our cafeteria has dropped from 32 percent to 12 percent.*

Understanding. Show that you care about the reader. Notice how in this letter to customers announcing a product defect, the writer expresses concern: *We know that you expect superior performance from all the products you purchase from OfficeCity. That's why we are writing personally about the Omega printer cartridges you recently ordered.*

OFFICE INSIDER

When leaders accept blame or apologize, it is "one of the most powerful and resonant gestures in the human arsenal—almost as powerful as a declaration of love. If love means, 'I care about you, and I'm happy about it,' then an apology means, 'I hurt you, and I'm sorry about it.'"

—Marshall Goldsmith, executive coach

Apologizing

You learned about making apologies in adjustment letters in Chapter 6. We expand that discussion here because apologies are often part of negative-news messages. The truth is that sincere apologies work. Peter Post, great-grandson of famed etiquette expert Emily Post and director of the Emily Post Institute, said that Americans love apologies. They will forgive almost anything if presented with a sincere apology.[1] An apology is defined as an "admission of blameworthiness and regret for an undesirable event."[2] Apologies to customers are especially important if you or your company erred. They cost nothing, and they go a long way in soothing hard feelings. Here are some tips on how to apologize effectively in business messages:

- **Apologize sincerely.** People dislike apologies that sound hollow (*We regret that you were inconvenienced* or *We regret that you are disturbed*). Focusing on your regret does not convey sincerity. Explaining what you will do to prevent recurrence of the problem projects sincerity.
- **Accept responsibility.** One CEO was criticized for the following weak apology: *I want our customers to know how much I personally regret any difficulties you may experience as a result of the unauthorized intrusion into our computer systems.* Communication experts faulted this apology because it did not acknowledge responsibility.[3]
- **Use good judgment.** Don't admit blame if it might prompt a lawsuit.

Consider these poor and improved apologies:

Poor apology: *We regret that you are unhappy with the price of frozen yogurt purchased at one of our self-serve scoop shops.*

Improved apology: *We are genuinely sorry that you were disappointed in the price of frozen yogurt recently purchased at one of our self-serve scoop shops. Your opinion is important to us, and we appreciate your giving us the opportunity to look into the problem you describe.*

Poor apology: *We apologize if anyone was affected.*

Improved apology: *I apologize for the frustration our delay caused you. As soon as I received your message, I began looking into the cause of the delay and realized that our delivery tracking system must be improved.*

Conveying Empathy

Empathy involves understanding and entering into the feelings of someone else.

One of the hardest things to do in apologies is to convey sympathy and empathy. As discussed in Chapter 2, *empathy* is the ability to understand and enter into the feelings of another. When ice storms trapped JetBlue Airways passengers on hot planes for hours, CEO Neeleman wrote a letter of apology that sounded as if it came from his heart. He said, "Dear JetBlue Customers: We are sorry and embarrassed. But most of all, we are deeply sorry." Later in his letter he said, "Words cannot express how truly sorry we are for the anxiety, frustration, and inconvenience that you, your family, friends, and colleagues experienced."[4] Neeleman put himself into the shoes of his customers and tried to experience their pain.

Here are other examples of ways to express empathy in written messages:

- **In writing to an unhappy customer:** *We did not intentionally delay the shipment, and we sincerely regret the disappointment and frustration you must have suffered.*
- **In laying off employees:** *It is with great regret that we must take this step. Rest assured that I will be more than happy to write letters of recommendation for anyone who asks.*
- **In responding to a complaint:** *I am deeply saddened that our service failure disrupted your sale, and we will do everything in our power to . . . .*
- **In showing genuine feelings:** *You have every right to be disappointed. I am truly sorry that . . . .*

Presenting the Reasons

Bad-news messages should explain reasons before stating the negative news.

The most important part of a negative message is the section devoted to reasons. Without sound reasons for denying a request, refusing a claim, or revealing other bad news, a message will fail, no matter how cleverly it is organized or written. For example, if you must deny a customer's request, as part of your planning before

"Dear Valued Customer: We're sorry, but company policy forbids apologies. Sincerely yours. . ."

writing, you analyze the request and decide to refuse it for specific reasons. Where do you place your reasons? In the indirect strategy, explain your reasons before disclosing the bad news. Providing an explanation reduces feelings of ill will and improves the chances that readers will accept the bad news.

Explaining Clearly. If the reasons are not confidential and if they will not create legal liability, you can be specific: *Growers supplied us with a limited number of patio roses, and our demand this year was twice that of last year.* In responding to a billing error, explain what happened: *After you informed us of an error on your January bill, we investigated the matter and admit the mistake was ours. Until our new automated system is fully online, we are still subject to human error. Rest assured that your account has been credited as you will see on your next bill.* In refusing a speaking engagement, tell why the date is impossible: *On January 17 we have a board of directors meeting that I must attend.* However, in an effort to be the "good guy," don't make dangerous or unrealistic promises: *Although we can't contribute now, we expect increased revenues next year and promise a generous gift then.*

Readers accept bad news more readily if they see that someone benefits.

Citing Reader or Other Benefits if Plausible. Readers are more open to bad news if in some way, even indirectly, it may help them. In refusing a customer's request for free hemming of skirts and slacks, Lands' End wrote: "We tested our ability to hem skirts a few months ago. This process proved to be very time-consuming. We have decided not to offer this service because the additional cost would have increased the selling price of our skirts substantially, and we did not want to impose that cost on all our customers."[5] Readers also accept bad news more readily if they recognize that someone or something else benefits, such as other workers or the environment: *Although we would like to consider your application, we prefer to fill managerial positions from within.* Avoid trying to show reader benefits, though, if they appear insincere: *To improve our service to you, we are increasing our brokerage fees.*

Explaining Company Policy. Readers resent blanket policy statements prohibiting something: *Company policy prevents us from making cash refunds* or *Contract bids may be accepted from local companies only* or *Company policy requires us to promote from within.* Instead of hiding behind company policy, gently explain why the policy makes sense: *We prefer to promote from within because it rewards the loyalty of our employees. In addition, we have found that people familiar with our organization make the quickest contribution to our team effort.* By offering explanations, you demonstrate that you care about readers and are treating them as important individuals.

Choosing Positive Words. Because the words you use can affect a reader's response, choose carefully. Remember that the objective of the indirect strategy is holding the reader's attention until you have had a chance to explain the reasons justifying the bad news. To keep the reader in a receptive mood, avoid expressions with punitive, demoralizing, or otherwise negative connotations. Stay away from such words as *cannot, claim, denied, error, failure, fault, impossible, mistaken, misunderstand, never, regret, rejected, unable, unwilling, unfortunately,* and *violate.*

Demonstrating Fairness. In explaining reasons, show the reader that you take the matter seriously, have investigated carefully, and are making an unbiased decision. Receivers are more accepting of disappointing news when they feel that their requests have been heard and that they have been treated fairly. In canceling

© Gregg Segal

WORKPLACE IN FOCUS

The ChicoBag Company knows that it is not what you say but how you say it that matters. While some environmental activists make strident calls to ban plastic bags that "hurt the earth," the California-based bag business takes a humorous approach to the issue. To illustrate the drawbacks of single-use plastic bags, ChicoBag dispatches Bag Monsters to roam the streets in high-visibility locations, such as on the streets at Mardi Gras or in front of the White House. The gimmicky-but-good-natured promotional effort helps the company sell its reusable nylon bags while muting the sometimes-negative tone taken by other eco-minded organizations. *Why is it important to accentuate the positive side of things?*

funding for a program, board members provided this explanation: *As you know, the publication of* Urban Artist *was funded by a renewable annual grant from the National Endowment for the Arts. Recent cutbacks in federally sponsored city arts programs have left us with few funds. Because our grant has been discontinued, we have no alternative but to cease publication of* Urban Artist. *You have my assurance that the board has searched long and hard for some other viable funding, but every avenue of recourse has been closed before us. Accordingly, June's issue will be our last.*

Cushioning the Bad News

Although you can't prevent the disappointment that bad news brings, you can reduce the pain somewhat by breaking the news sensitively. Be especially considerate when the reader will suffer personally from the bad news. A number of thoughtful techniques can cushion the blow.

Techniques for cushioning bad news include positioning it strategically, using the passive voice, focusing on the positive, implying the refusal, and suggesting alternatives or compromises.

Positioning the Bad News Strategically. Instead of spotlighting it, sandwich the bad news between other sentences, perhaps among your reasons. Don't let the refusal begin or end a paragraph; the reader's eye will linger on these high-visibility spots. Another technique that reduces shock is putting a painful idea in a subordinate clause: *Although another candidate was hired, we appreciate your interest in our organization and wish you every success in your job search.* Subordinate clauses often begin with words such as *although, as, because, if,* and *since*.

Using the Passive Voice. Passive-voice verbs enable you to depersonalize an action. Whereas the active voice focuses attention on a person *(We don't give cash refunds)*, the passive voice highlights the action *(Cash refunds are not given because . . .)*. Use the passive voice for the bad news. In some instances you can combine passive-voice verbs and a subordinate clause: *Although franchise scoop shop owners cannot be required to lower their frozen yogurt prices, we are happy to pass along your comments for their consideration.*

Accentuating the Positive. As you learned earlier, messages are far more effective when you describe what you can do instead of what you can't do. Rather than *We will no longer allow credit card purchases,* try a more positive appeal: *We are now selling gasoline at discount cash prices.*

Implying the Refusal. It is sometimes possible to avoid a direct statement of refusal. Often, your reasons and explanations leave no doubt that a request has been denied. Explicit refusals may be unnecessary and at times cruel. In this refusal to contribute to a charity, for example, the writer never actually says *no*: *Because we will soon be moving into new offices in Glendale, all our funds are earmarked for relocation costs. We hope that next year we will be able to support your worthwhile charity.* The danger of an implied refusal, of course, is that it is so subtle that the reader misses it. Be certain that you make the bad news clear, thus preventing the need for further correspondence.

Suggesting a Compromise or an Alternative. A refusal is not so depressing—for the sender or the receiver—if a suitable compromise, substitute, or alternative is available. In denying permission to a group of students to visit a historical private residence, for instance, this writer softens the bad news by proposing an alternative: *Although private tours of the grounds are not given, we do open the house and its gardens for one charitable event in the fall.* You can further reduce the impact of the bad news by refusing to dwell on it. Present it briefly (or imply it), and move on to your closing.

Closing Pleasantly

Closings to bad-news messages might include a forward look, an alternative, good wishes, freebies, resale information, or a sales promotion.

After explaining the bad news sensitively, close the message with a pleasant statement that promotes goodwill. The closing should be personalized and may include a forward look, an alternative, good wishes, freebies, resale information, or a sales promotion. *Resale* refers to mentioning a product or service favorably to reinforce the customer's choice. For example, *you chose our best-selling model.*

Forward Look. Anticipate future relations or business. A letter that refuses a contract proposal might read: *Thanks for your bid. We look forward to working with your talented staff when future projects demand your special expertise.*

"Send him our toughest refusal letter, threaten him with legal action, and don't pull the punches. But put XOXOXO under my signature to show that we still love him as a customer."

Alternative Follow-Up. If an alternative exists, end your letter with follow-through advice. For example, in a letter rejecting a customer's demand for replacement of landscaping plants, you might say: *I will be happy to give you a free inspection and consultation. Please call 301-746-8112 to arrange a date for my visit.* In a message to a prospective home buyer: *Although the lot you saw last week is now sold, we do have two excellent view lots available at a slightly higher price.* In reacting to an Internet misprint: *Please note that our Web site contained an unfortunate misprint offering $850-per-night Bora Bora bungalows at $85. Although we cannot honor that rate, we are offering a special half-price rate of $425 to those who responded.*

Good Wishes. A letter rejecting a job candidate might read: *We appreciate your interest in our company, and we extend to you our best wishes in your search to find the perfect match between your skills and job requirements.*

Freebies. When customers complain—primarily about food products or small consumer items—companies often send coupons, samples, or gifts to restore confidence and to promote future business. In response to a customer's complaint about a frozen dinner, you could write: *Your loyalty and your concern about our frozen entrées are genuinely appreciated. Because we want you to continue enjoying our healthful and convenient dinners, we are enclosing a coupon that you can take to your local market to select your next Green Valley entrée.*

Resale or Sales Promotion. When the bad news is not devastating or personal, references to resale information or promotion may be appropriate: *The computer workstations you ordered are unusually popular because of their stain-, heat-, and scratch-resistant finishes. This is why these machines occasionally ship with slight delays. To help you locate hard-to-find accessories for these workstations, we invite you to visit our Web site where our online catalog provides a huge selection of surge suppressors, multiple outlet strips, security devices, and PC tool kits.*

Avoid endings that sound canned, insincere, inappropriate, or self-serving. Don't invite further correspondence *(If you have any questions, do not hesitate . . .)*, and don't refer to the bad news. To review these suggestions for delivering bad news sensitively, take another look at Figure 7.2.

Refusing Typical Requests and Claims

As you move forward in your career and become a professional or a representative of an organization, you may receive requests for favors or contributions. When you must refuse typical requests, you will first think about how the receiver will react to your refusal and decide whether to use the direct or the indirect strategy. You may also have to say *no* to customer claims, deny credit, and deal with disappointment and even anger. At the same time, your goal is to resolve the situation in a prompt, fair, and tactful manner. If you have any doubt, use the indirect strategy and the following writing plan:

When refusing typical requests and claims, start with a buffer, present valid reasons for the refusal, de-emphasize the bad news, and renew good feelings with a positive closing statement.

WRITING PLAN FOR REFUSING TYPICAL REQUESTS AND CLAIMS

- **Buffer:** Start with a neutral statement on which both reader and writer can agree, such as a compliment, appreciation, a quick review of the facts, or an apology. Try to include a key idea or word that acts as a transition to the reasons.
- **Reasons:** Present valid reasons for the refusal, avoiding words that create a negative tone.
- **Bad news:** Soften the blow by de-emphasizing the bad news, using the passive voice, accentuating the positive, or implying a refusal. Suggest a compromise, alternative, or substitute, if possible. The alternative may be part of the bad-news section or part of the closing.
- **Closing:** Renew good feelings with a positive statement. Avoid referring to the bad news. Include resale or sales promotion material, if appropriate. Look forward to continued business.

Rejecting Requests for Favors, Money, Information, and Action

Requests for favors, money, information, and action may come from charities, friends, or business partners. Many are from people representing commendable causes, and you may wish you could comply. However, resources are usually limited. In a letter from First Franklin Securities, shown in Figure 7.3, the company must refuse a request for a donation to a charity. Following the indirect strategy, the letter begins with a buffer acknowledging the request. It also praises the good works of the charity and uses those words as a transition to the second paragraph. In the second paragraph, the writer explains why the company cannot donate. Notice that the writer reveals the refusal without actually stating it (*Because of sales declines and organizational downsizing, we are forced to take a much harder look at funding requests that we receive this year)*. This gentle refusal makes it unnecessary to be more blunt in stating the denial.

The reasons-before-refusal strategy works well when turning down requests for favors, money, information, or action.

FIGURE 7.3 Refusing Donation Request

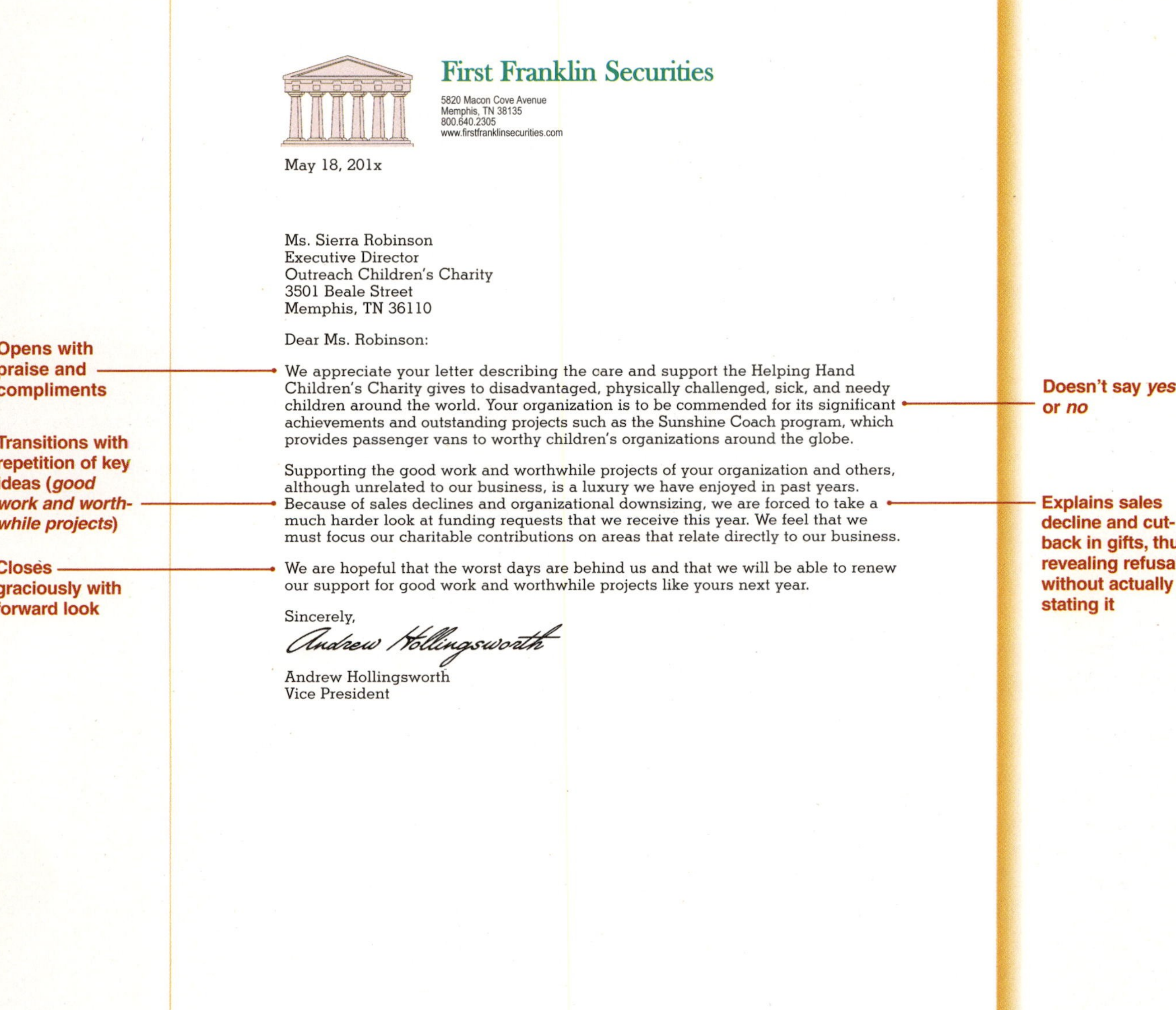

First Franklin Securities
5820 Macon Cove Avenue
Memphis, TN 38135
800.640.2305
www.firstfranklinsecurities.com
Opens with praise and compliments
Transitions with repetition of key ideas (*good work and worthwhile projects*)
Closes graciously with forward look
Doesn't say *yes* or *no*
Explains sales decline and cut-back in gifts, thus revealing refusal without actually stating it

May 18, 201x

Ms. Sierra Robinson
Executive Director
Outreach Children's Charity
3501 Beale Street
Memphis, TN 36110

Dear Ms. Robinson:

We appreciate your letter describing the care and support the Helping Hand Children's Charity gives to disadvantaged, physically challenged, sick, and needy children around the world. Your organization is to be commended for its significant achievements and outstanding projects such as the Sunshine Coach program, which provides passenger vans to worthy children's organizations around the globe.

Supporting the good work and worthwhile projects of your organization and others, although unrelated to our business, is a luxury we have enjoyed in past years. Because of sales declines and organizational downsizing, we are forced to take a much harder look at funding requests that we receive this year. We feel that we must focus our charitable contributions on areas that relate directly to our business.

We are hopeful that the worst days are behind us and that we will be able to renew our support for good work and worthwhile projects like yours next year.

Sincerely,

Andrew Hollingsworth

Andrew Hollingsworth
Vice President

OFFICE INSIDER

"Any declarative sentence starting with 'you' when talking to a customer is best avoided—it comes across as shaking your finger at the customer, and no one wants to feel like we're talking to our mother! Better choices are 'We can' or 'Let's do this together' or 'What I could suggest is.'"

—Kristin Robertson, KR Consulting, Inc.

In some donation refusal letters, the reasons may not be fully explained: *Although we can't provide financial support at this time, we all unanimously agree that the Make-A-Wish Foundation contributes a valuable service to sick children.* The emphasis is on the foundation's good deeds rather than on an explanation for the refusal. In the letter shown in Figure 7.3, the writer felt a connection to the charity. Therefore, he wanted to give a fuller explanation. Businesses that are required to write frequent refusals might prepare a form letter, changing a few variables as needed.

Denying Claims

Customers occasionally want something they are not entitled to or something you can't grant. They may misunderstand warranties or make unreasonable demands. Because these customers are often unhappy with a product or service, they are emotionally involved. Letters that say *no* to emotionally involved receivers will probably be your most challenging communication task. As publisher Malcolm Forbes observed, "To be agreeable while disagreeing—that's an art."[6]

Fortunately, the reasons-before-refusal plan helps you be empathic and artful in breaking bad news. Obviously, in denial letters you will need to adopt the proper tone. Don't blame customers, even if they are at fault. Avoid *you* statements that sound preachy *(You would have known that cash refunds are impossible if you had read your contract)*. Use neutral, objective language to explain why the claim must be refused. Consider offering resale information to rebuild the customer's confidence in your products or organization. In Figure 7.4 the writer denies a customer's claim for the difference between the price the customer paid for speakers and the price he saw advertised locally (which would have resulted in a cash refund of $100). Although the catalog service does match any advertised lower price, the price-matching policy applies *only* to exact models. This claim must be rejected because the advertisement the customer submitted showed a different, older speaker model.

In denying claims, writers use the reasons-before-refusal strategy to set an empathic tone and buffer the bad news.

The letter to Charles Mauppin opens with a key idea of product confidence. The writer agrees with a statement in the customer's letter and repeats the key

FIGURE 7.4 **Denying a Claim**

(((infiniti)))
home theater systems

March 23, 201x

Mr. Charles Mauppin
4290 Emerald Road
Greenwood, SC 29648

Dear Mr. Mauppin:

The Cyborg Alpha home theater speaker system that you purchased last month includes premier concert hall speakers. They are the only ones we present in our catalog because they are the best. You're right, Mr. Mauppin. We do take pride in selling the finest surround sound speakers at rock-bottom prices.

We have such confidence in our products and prices that we offer the price-matching policy you mention in your letter of March 15. That policy guarantees a refund of the price difference if you see one of your purchases offered at a lower price for 30 days after your purchase. To qualify for that refund, customers are asked to send us an advertisement or verifiable proof of the product price and model. As our catalog states, this price-matching policy applies only to exact models with USA warranties.

The Cyborg Alpha speaker set sells for $999.95. You sent us a local advertisement showing a price of $899.95 for Cyborg speakers. This advertisement, however, describes an earlier version, the Cyborg Type I set. The set you received has a wider dynamic range and smoother frequency response than the Cyborg Type I set. Naturally, the improved model you purchased costs a little more than the older Type I model. Your speakers have a new three-chamber bass module that virtually eliminates harmonic distortion. Finally, your speakers are 20 percent more compact than the Type I set.

You bought the finest compact speakers on the market, Mr. Mauppin. If you haven't installed them yet, you may be interested in ceiling mounts, shown in the enclosed catalog on page 48. For the most up-to-date prices and product information, please see our online catalog at our prize-winning Web site at **http://infinityhts.com**. We value your business and invite your continued comparison shopping.

Sincerely,

INFINITY HOME THEATER SYSTEMS

Elijah Mikeska

Elijah Mikeska
Senior Product Manager

Enclosure

245 Commonwealth Avenue, Boston, MA 02116 | phone 617-458-9023 | fax 617-458-3390 | http://infinityhts.com

Combines agreement with resale

Explains price-matching policy and how reader's purchase is different from lower-priced model

Without actually saying *no*, shows why reader's claim cannot be honored

Builds reader's confidence in wisdom of purchase

Continues resale; looks forward to future business

Buffer

Reasons

Implied refusal

Positive closing

idea of product confidence as a transition to the second paragraph. Next comes an explanation of the price-matching policy. Elijah Mikeska does not assume that the customer is trying to pull a fast one. Nor does he suggest that the customer is a dummy who didn't read or understand the price-matching policy. The safest path is a neutral explanation of the policy along with precise distinctions between the customer's speakers and the older ones. The writer also gets a chance to resell the customer's speakers and demonstrate what a quality product they are. By the end of the third paragraph, it is evident to the reader that his claim is unjustified.

Refusing Credit

Goals when refusing credit include maintaining customer goodwill and avoiding actionable language.

When customers apply for credit, they must be notified within 30 days if that application is rejected. The Fair Credit Reporting Act and Equal Credit Opportunity Act state that consumers who are denied loans must receive a notice of "adverse action" from the business declining credit explaining the decision. The business can refer the applicant to the credit-reporting agency, whether Experian, Equifax, or TransUnion, that provided the information upon which the negative decision was based.

If you must deny credit to prospective customers, you have four goals in conveying the refusal:

- Avoiding language that causes hard feelings
- Retaining customers on a cash basis
- Preparing for possible future credit without raising false expectations
- Avoiding disclosures that could cause a lawsuit

"As part of the bank's form reduction policy, you won't have to fill out any additional forms. Your loan application has not been approved."

www.Cartoonstock.com

Because credit applicants are likely to continue to do business with an organization even if they are denied credit, you will want to do everything possible to encourage that patronage. Therefore, keep the refusal respectful, sensitive, and upbeat. A letter to a customer denying her credit application might begin as follows: *We genuinely appreciate your application of January 12 for a Fashion Express credit account.*

To avoid possible litigation, many companies offer no explanation of the reasons for a credit refusal. Instead, they provide the name of the credit-reporting agency and suggest that inquiries be directed to it. In the following example, notice the use of passive voice (*credit cannot be extended)* and a long sentence to de-emphasize the bad news:

> *After we received a report of your current credit record from Experian, it is apparent that credit cannot be extended at this time. To learn more about your record, you may call an Experian credit counselor at (212) 356-0922.*

A cordial closing looks forward to the possibility of a future reapplication:

> *Thanks, Ms. Love, for the confidence you have shown in Fashion Express. We invite you to continue shopping at our stores, and we look forward to your reapplication in the future.*

Some businesses do provide reasons explaining credit denials *(Credit cannot be granted because your firm's current and long-term credit obligations are nearly twice as great as your firm's total assets).* They may also provide alternatives, such as deferred billing or cash discounts. When the letter denies a credit application that accompanies an order, the message may contain resale information. The writer tries to convert the order from credit to cash. For example, if a big order cannot be filled on a credit basis, perhaps part of the order could be filled on a cash basis. Whatever form the bad-news message takes, it is a good idea to have the message reviewed by legal counsel because of the litigation land mines awaiting unwary communicators in this area.

Dealing With Disappointed Customers

All businesses offering products or services must sometimes deal with troublesome situations that cause unhappiness to customers. Whenever possible, these problems should be dealt with immediately and personally. Complaints about products and services now appear on sites such as Complaints.com and iRipoff.com, as well as on Facebook, Twitter, and MySpace. Companies are responding by joining the social media and telling their own stories, putting a positive spin on potentially damaging viral word of mouth.

When a customer problem arises and the company is at fault, many businesspeople call and apologize, explain what happened, and follow up with a goodwill message.

Whether companies deal with unhappy customers in cyberspace or up close and personal, they face the same challenges. Maintaining market share and preserving goodwill require sensitive and skillful communication. Many business professionals strive to control the damage and resolve such problems in the following manner:[7]

- Call the individual involved.
- Describe the problem and apologize.
- Explain why the problem occurred, what your company is doing to resolve it, and how it will ensure that the problem will not happen again.
- Follow up with a message that documents the phone call and promotes goodwill.

Dealing with problems immediately is very important in resolving conflict and retaining goodwill. Written correspondence is generally too slow for problems that demand immediate attention. But written messages are important (a) when personal contact is impossible, (b) to establish a record of the incident, (c) to formally confirm follow-up procedures, and (d) to promote good relations.

A bad-news follow-up letter is shown in Figure 7.5. Consultant Eva Gonzalez Tejo found herself in the embarrassing position of explaining why she had given out the name of her client to a salesperson. The client, Accordia Resources International, had hired her firm, Cartus Consulting Associates, to help find an appropriate service for outsourcing its payroll functions. Without realizing it, Eva had mentioned to a potential vendor (Payroll Services, Inc.) that her client was considering hiring an outside service to handle its payroll. An overeager salesperson from Payroll Services immediately called on Accordia, thus angering the client. The client had hired the consultant to avoid this very kind of intrusion. Accordia did not want to be hounded by vendors selling their payroll services.

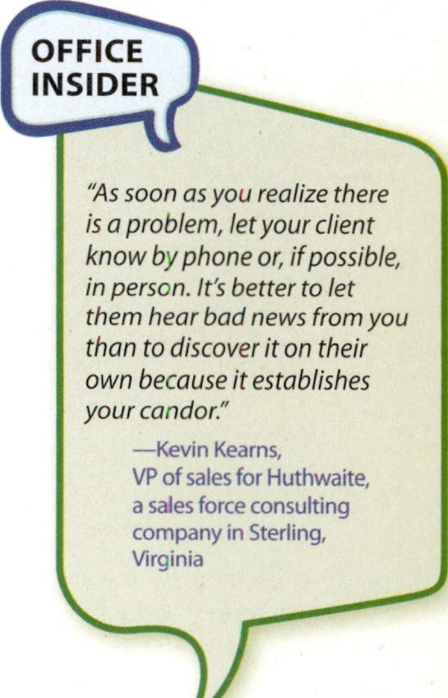

When she learned of the problem, the first thing consultant Eva Gonzalez Tejo did was call her client to explain and apologize. She was careful to control her voice and rate of speaking. A low-pitched, deliberate pace gives the impression that you are thinking clearly, logically, and reasonably—not emotionally and certainly not irrationally. However, she also followed up with the letter shown in Figure 7.5. The letter not only confirms the telephone conversation but also adds the right touch of formality. It sends the nonverbal message that the writer takes the matter seriously and that it is important enough to warrant a letter.

Many consumer problems are handled with letters, either written by consumers as complaints or by companies in response. However, e-mail communication and now the social networking sites on the Internet are emerging as channels for delivering complaints and negative messages.

Breaking Bad News Within Organizations

A tactful tone and a reasons-first approach help preserve friendly relations with customers. These same techniques are useful when delivering bad news within organizations. Interpersonal bad news might involve telling the boss that something went wrong or confronting an employee about poor performance. Organizational bad

Bad news, whether delivered in person or in writing, is usually better received when reasons are given first.

FIGURE 7.5 Bad News Follow-Up Message

CARTUS CONSULTING ASSOCIATES

4350 CamelbackBlvd.
Scottsdale,AZ 85255

Voice:(480)259-0971
Web:www.cartusassociates.com

May 7, 201x

Mr. Carl Shahrazad
Director, Administrative Operations
Accordia Resources International
538 Maricopa Plaza, Suite 1210
Phoenix, AZ 85001

Dear Mr. Shahrazad:

Opens with agreement and apology

You have every right to expect complete confidentiality in your transactions with an independent consultant. As I explained in yesterday's telephone call, I am very distressed that you were called by a salesperson from Payroll Services, Inc. This should not have happened, and I apologize to you again for inadvertently mentioning your company's name in a conversation with a potential vendor, Payroll Services, Inc.

Explains what caused the problem and how it was resolved

Takes responsibility and promises to prevent recurrence

All clients of Cartus Consulting are assured that their dealings with our firm are held in the strictest confidence. Because your company's payroll needs are so individual and because you have so many contract workers, I was forced to explain how your employees differed from those of other companies. Revealing your company name was my error, and I take full responsibility for the lapse. I can assure you that it will not happen again. I have informed Payroll Services that it had no authorization to call you directly and its actions have forced me to reconsider using its services for my future clients.

Closes with forward look

A number of other payroll services offer outstanding programs. I'm sure we can find the perfect partner to enable you to outsource your payroll responsibilities, thus allowing your company to focus its financial and human resources on its core business. I look forward to our next appointment when you may choose from a number of excellent payroll outsourcing firms.

Sincerely,

CARTUS CONSULTING ASSOCIATES

Eva Gonzalez Tejo

Eva Gonzalez Tejo
Partner

Tips for Resolving Problems and Following Up

- Whenever possible, call or see the individual involved.
- Describe the problem and apologize.
- Explain why the problem occurred.
- Take responsibility, if appropriate.
- Explain what you are doing to resolve the problem.
- Explain what you are doing to prevent recurrence.
- Follow up with a message that documents the personal contact.
- Look forward to positive future relations.

news might involve declining profits, lost contracts, harmful lawsuits, public relations controversies, and changes in policy. Whether you use a direct or an indirect strategy in delivering that news depends primarily on the anticipated reaction of the audience. Generally, bad news is better received when reasons are given first. Within organizations, you may find yourself giving bad news in person or in writing.

Delivering Bad News Personally

When you must deliver bad news in person, be sure to gather all the information, prepare, and rehearse.

Whether you are an employee or a supervisor, you may have the unhappy responsibility of delivering bad news. First, decide whether the negative information is newsworthy. For example, trivial, noncriminal mistakes or one-time bad behaviors are best left alone. However, fraudulent travel claims, consistent hostile behavior, or failing projects must be reported.[8] For example, you might have to tell the boss that the team's computer crashed losing all its important files. As a team leader or supervisor, you might be required to confront an underperforming employee. If you know that the news will upset the receiver, the reasons-first strategy is most effective. When the bad news involves one person or a small group nearby, you should generally deliver that news in person. Here are pointers on how to do so tactfully, professionally, and safely:[9]

- **Gather all the information.** Cool down and have all the facts before marching in on the boss or confronting someone. Remember that every story has two sides.
- **Prepare and rehearse.** Outline what you plan to say so that you are confident, coherent, and dispassionate.
- **Explain: past, present, future.** If you are telling the boss about a problem such as the computer crash, explain what caused the crash, the current situation, and how and when you plan to fix it.
- **Consider taking a partner.** If you fear a "shoot the messenger" reaction, especially from your boss, bring a colleague with you. Each person should have a consistent and credible part in the presentation. If possible, take advantage of your organization's internal resources. To lend credibility to your view, call on auditors, inspectors, or human resources experts.
- **Think about timing.** Don't deliver bad news when someone is already stressed or grumpy. Experts also advise against giving bad news on Friday afternoon when people have the weekend to dwell on it.
- **Be patient with the reaction.** Give the receiver time to vent, think, recover, and act wisely.

OFFICE INSIDER

"E-mail and blogging have become such a part of our DNA that people take for granted that it's an OK way to communicate. But actually it's depersonalizing. It chops us off from who we thought we were."

—Ruth Luban, employment counselor and author of *Are You a Corporate Refugee? A Survival Guide for Downsized, Disillusioned and Displaced Workers.*

Refusing Workplace Requests

Internal request refusals focus on explanations and praise, maintaining a positive tone, and offering alternatives.

Occasionally, managers must refuse requests from employees. In Figure 7.6 you see the first draft and revision of a message responding to a request from a key specialist, Donald Gantry. He wants permission to attend a conference. However, he can't attend the conference because the timing is bad; he must be present at budget planning meetings scheduled for the same two weeks. Normally, this matter would be discussed in person. However, Don has been traveling among branch offices, and he just hasn't been in the office recently.

The vice president's first inclination was to send a quickie e-mail, as shown in the Figure 7.6 draft, and "tell it like it is." However, the vice president realized that this message was going to hurt and that it had possible danger areas. Moreover, the message misses a chance to give Don positive feedback. An improved version of the e-mail starts with a buffer that delivers honest praise (*pleased with the exceptional leadership you have provided* and *your genuine professional commitment*). By the way, don't be stingy with compliments; they cost you nothing. To paraphrase the motivational speaker Zig Ziglar, we don't live by bread alone. We need buttering up once in a while.[10] The buffer also includes the date of the meeting, used strategically to connect the reasons that follow.

The middle paragraph provides reasons for the refusal. Notice that they focus on positive elements: Don is the specialist; the company relies on his expertise; and everyone will benefit if he passes up the conference. In this section it becomes obvious that the request will be refused. The writer is not forced to say, *No, you may not attend.* Although the refusal is implied, the reader gets the message.

The closing suggests a qualified alternative (*if our workloads permit, we will try to send you then*). It also ends positively with gratitude for Don's contributions to the organization and with another compliment (*you're a valuable player*). The improved version focuses on explanations and praise rather than on refusals and apologies. The success of this message depends on sincerity and attention to the entire writing process, not just on using a buffer or scattering a few compliments throughout.

Announcing Bad News to Employees

Organizations can sustain employee morale by communicating bad news openly and honestly.

Many of the same techniques used to deliver bad news personally are useful when organizations face a crisis or must deliver bad news to their workers and

FIGURE 7.6 Refusing an Internal Request

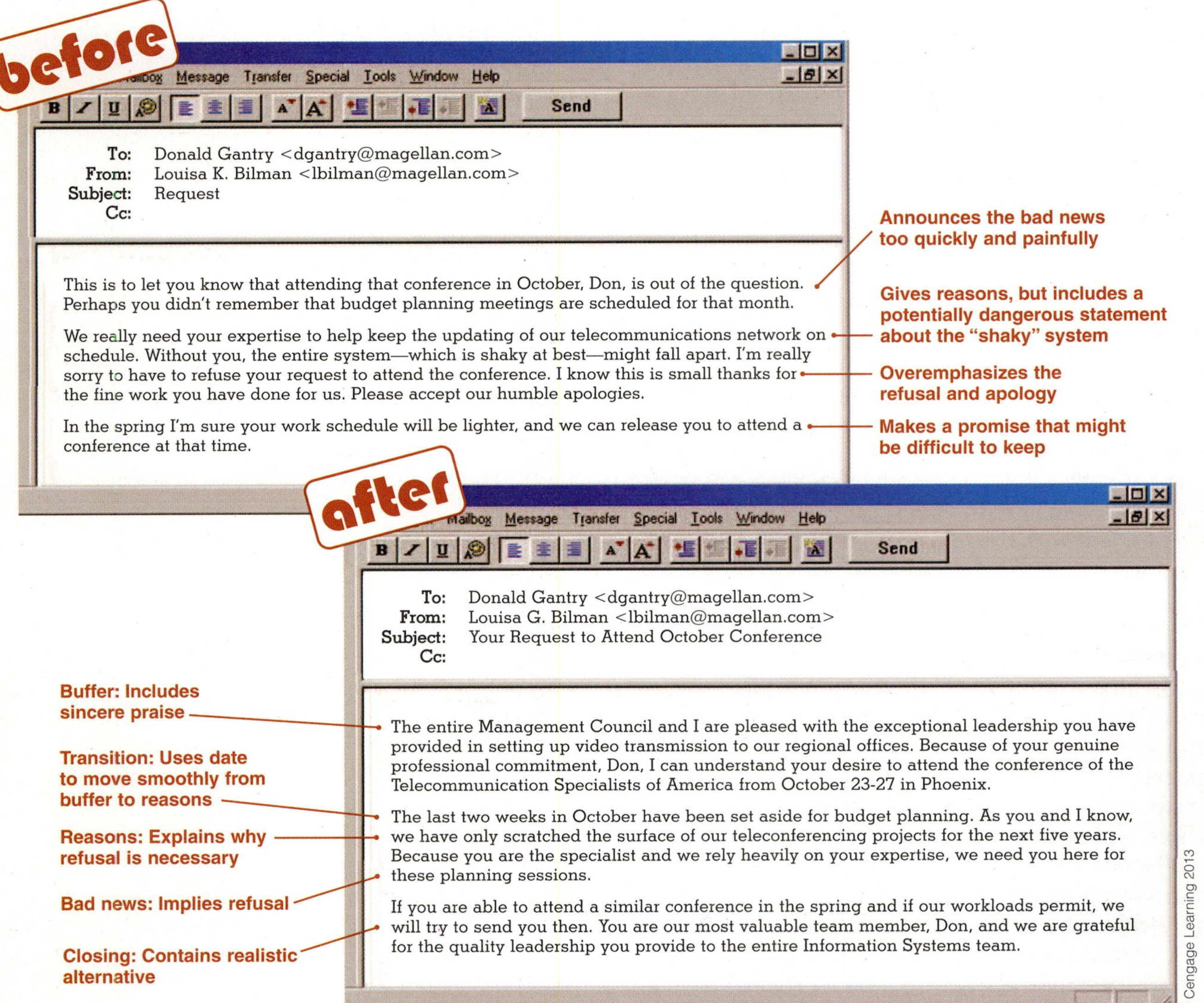

other groups. Smart organizations involved in a crisis prefer to communicate the news openly to employees and stakeholders. A crisis might involve serious performance problems, a major relocation, massive layoffs, a management shakeup, or public controversy. Instead of letting rumors distort the truth, managers explain the organization's side of the story honestly and promptly. Morale can be destroyed when employees learn of major events affecting their jobs through the grapevine or from news accounts—rather than from management.

before
Mailbox Message Transfer Special Tools Window Help
Send
To: Donald Gantry <dgantry@magellan.com>
From: Louisa K. Bilman <lbilman@magellan.com>
Subject: Request
Cc:
This is to let you know that attending that conference in October, Don, is out of the question. Perhaps you didn't remember that budget planning meetings are scheduled for that month.
We really need your expertise to help keep the updating of our telecommunications network on schedule. Without you, the entire system—which is shaky at best—might fall apart. I'm really sorry to have to refuse your request to attend the conference. I know this is small thanks for the fine work you have done for us. Please accept our humble apologies.
In the spring I'm sure your work schedule will be lighter, and we can release you to attend a conference at that time.
Announces the bad news too quickly and painfully
Gives reasons, but includes a potentially dangerous statement about the "shaky" system
Overemphasizes the refusal and apology
Makes a promise that might be difficult to keep
after
Mailbox Message Transfer Special Tools Window Help
Send
To: Donald Gantry <dgantry@magellan.com>
From: Louisa G. Bilman <lbilman@magellan.com>
Subject: Your Request to Attend October Conference
Cc:
The entire Management Council and I are pleased with the exceptional leadership you have provided in setting up video transmission to our regional offices. Because of your genuine professional commitment, Don, I can understand your desire to attend the conference of the Telecommunication Specialists of America from October 23-27 in Phoenix.
The last two weeks in October have been set aside for budget planning. As you and I know, we have only scratched the surface of our teleconferencing projects for the next five years. Because you are the specialist and we rely heavily on your expertise, we need you here for these planning sessions.
If you are able to attend a similar conference in the spring and if our workloads permit, we will try to send you then. You are our most valuable team member, Don, and we are grateful for the quality leadership you provide to the entire Information Systems team.
Buffer: Includes sincere praise
Transition: Uses date to move smoothly from buffer to reasons
Reasons: Explains why refusal is necessary
Bad news: Implies refusal
Closing: Contains realistic alternative

When bad news must be delivered to employees, management may want to deliver the news personally. With large groups, however, this is generally impossible. Instead, organizations deliver bad news through many channels, including traditional interoffice memos. In addition to e-mail distribution, organizations are disseminating important information through the company intranet and other document management platforms. The intranet may feature up-to-date news, blog postings, videos, and webcasts. Still, interoffice memos seem to function most effectively because they are more formal and make a permanent record. The following writing plan outlines the content for such a message:

WRITING PLAN FOR ANNOUNCING NEGATIVE NEWS TO EMPLOYEES

- **Buffer:** Start with a neutral or positive statement that transitions to the reasons for the bad news. Consider opening with the best news, a compliment, appreciation, agreement, or solid facts. Show understanding.
- **Reasons:** Explain the logic behind the bad news. Provide a rational explanation using positive words and displaying empathy. If possible, mention reader benefits.
- **Bad News:** Position the bad news so that it does not stand out. Be positive, but don't sugarcoat the bad news. Use objective language.
- **Closing:** Provide information about an alternative, if one exists. If appropriate, describe what will happen next. Look forward positively.

The draft of the memo shown in Figure 7.7 announces a substantial increase in the cost of employee health care benefits. However, the memo suffers from many problems. It announces jolting news bluntly in the first sentence. Worse, it offers little or no explanation for the steep increase in costs. It also sounds insincere (*We did everything possible . . .*) and arbitrary. In a final miscue, the writer fails to give credit to the company for absorbing previous health cost increases.

In the revision of this bad-news memo, the writer uses the indirect strategy and improves the tone considerably. Notice that the document opens with a relevant, upbeat buffer regarding health care—but says nothing about increasing costs. For a smooth transition, the second paragraph begins with a key idea from the opening (*comprehensive package*). The reasons section discusses rising costs with explanations and figures. The bad news (*you will be paying $119 a month*) is clearly presented but embedded within the paragraph. Throughout, the writer strives to show the fairness of the company's position. The ending, which does not refer to the bad news, emphasizes how much the company is paying and what a wise investment it is.

Notice that the entire memo demonstrates a kinder, gentler approach than that shown in the first draft. Of prime importance in breaking bad news to employees is providing clear, convincing reasons that explain the decision. This memo would most likely be distributed by e-mail, but increasingly such news is also disseminated by company intranet and other digital means.

Keeping the Indirect Strategy Ethical

The indirect strategy is unethical only if the writer intends to deceive the reader.

You may worry that the indirect organizational strategy is unethical or manipulative because the writer deliberately delays the main idea. But consider the alternative. Breaking bad news bluntly can cause pain and hard feelings. By delaying bad news, you soften the blow somewhat, as well as ensure that your reasoning will be read while the receiver is still receptive. One expert communicator recognized the significance of the indirect strategy when she said, "People must believe the reasons why before they will listen to the details of what and when."[11] In using the indirect strategy, your motives are not to deceive the reader or to hide the news. Rather, your goal is to be a compassionate, yet effective communicator.

The key to ethical communication lies in the motives of the sender. Unethical communicators *intend to deceive.* Although the indirect strategy provides a setting in which to announce bad news, it should not be used to avoid or misrepresent the truth. For example, the Internet is rife with bogus "free" trial offers for teeth whiteners and açaí supplements, to name just two of the current scams. Unscrupulous marketers advertise on trusted Web sites of national news organizations and falsely claim endorsements by Oprah Winfrey and Doctor Oz. Unsuspecting consumers end up paying hundreds of dollars, the Better Business Bureau reports.[12] As you will see in Chapter 8, misleading, deceptive, and unethical claims are never acceptable. In fact, many of them are simply illegal.

FIGURE 7.7 Announcing Bad News to Employees

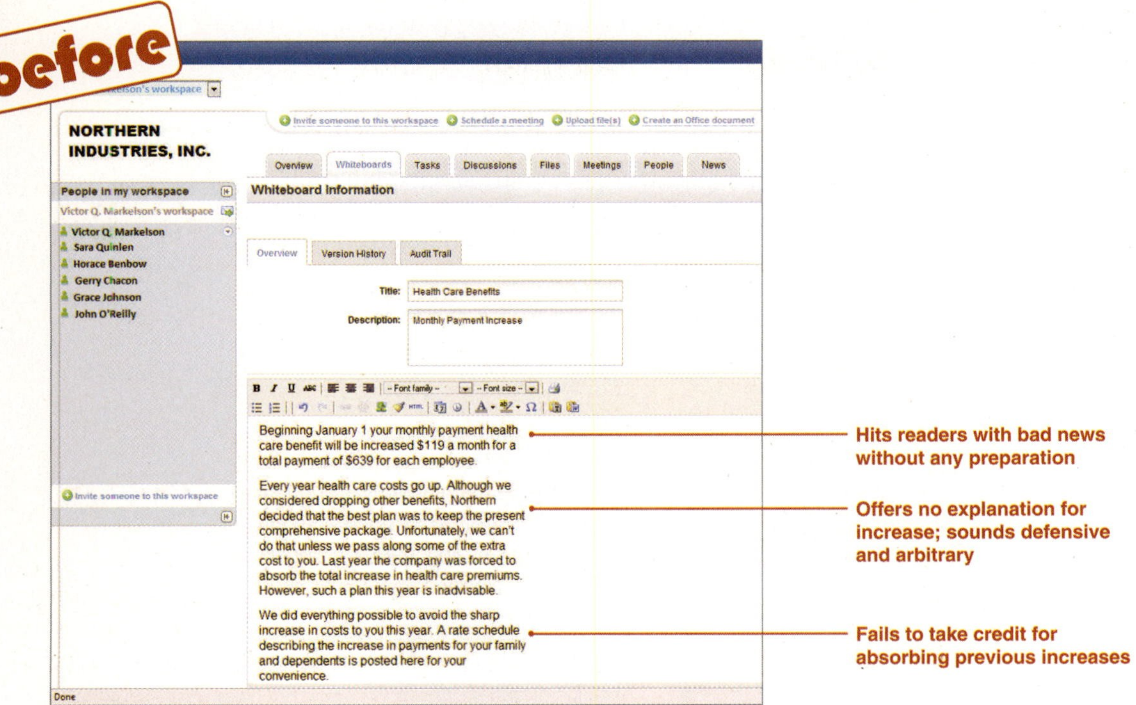

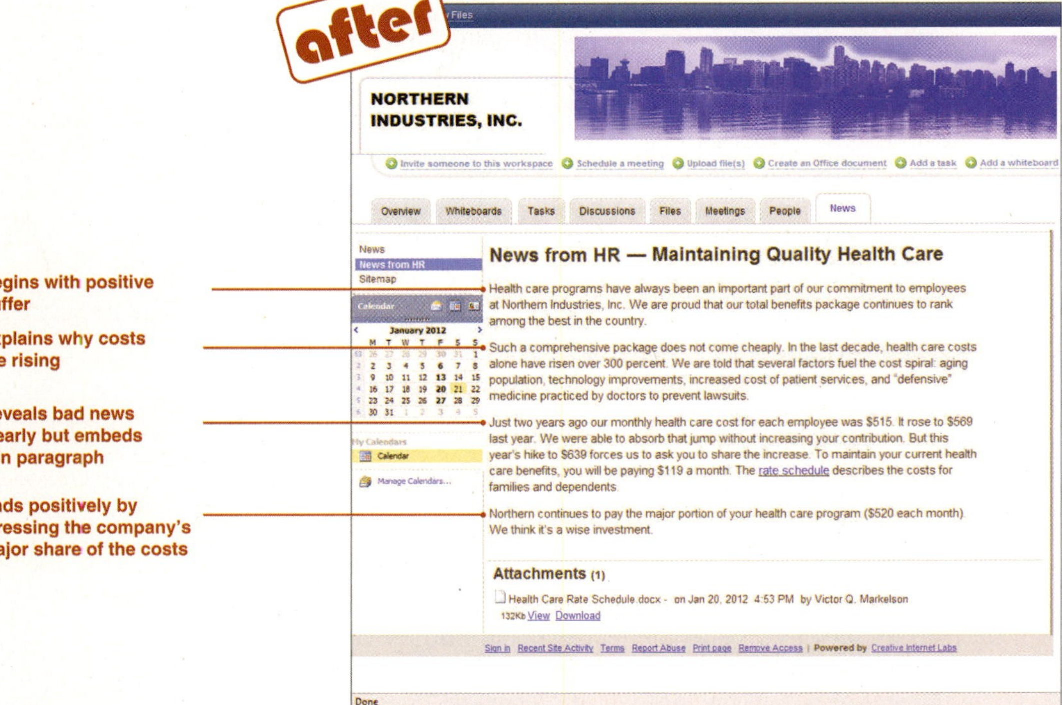

Summing Up and Looking Forward

When faced with delivering bad news, you have a choice. You can announce it immediately, or you can delay it by presenting a buffer and reasons first. Many business communicators prefer the indirect strategy because it tends to preserve goodwill. In some instances, however, the direct strategy is effective in delivering bad news. In this chapter you learned the goals in communicating bad news, and you studied many techniques for delivering bad news sensitively. Then, you learned to apply those techniques in refusing typical requests for favors, money, information, and action. Furthermore, you studied techniques for denying claims, refusing credit, and dealing with disappointed customers. You also gained insight into how companies deliver bad news to audiences inside the organization. Finally, you were taught to recognize unethical applications of the indirect strategy.

Thus far you have studied electronic messages, memos, positive messages, and negative messages. In Chapter 8 you will learn to be persuasive, a powerful skill for any business communicator.

Critical Thinking

1. Communication author Dana Bristol-Smith likens delivering bad news to removing a Band-Aid—you can do it slowly or quickly. She thinks that quickly is better, particularly when companies must give bad news to employees.[13] Do you agree or disagree?
2. Respected industry analyst Gartner Research issued a report naming social networking as one of the top ten "disruptive" (innovative, game-changing) influences shaping information technology today.[14] Should organizations fear Web sites where consumers post negative messages about products and services? What actions can companies take in response to this disruptive influence?
3. Why is the passive voice acceptable, even desirable, in bad-news messages when it's considered poor, impersonal writing in most other situations?
4. Why might it be a bad idea to be blunt and terse toward students and other people on a budget when denying them credit?
5. **Ethical Issue:** Radio Shack infamously fired 400 of its employees by e-mail a few years ago. More recently, the CEO of electric-car manufacturer Tesla, Elon Musk, used his blog to announce layoffs. Why do most business communicators and management experts frown upon such behavior?

Chapter Review

6. What are the business communicator's most important goals in communicating negative news?

7. When is the direct strategy more effective than the indirect strategy in conveying negative news?

8. When is the indirect strategy in communicating bad news preferable?

9. What are some tips for business writers wishing to apologize effectively?

10. What does conveying empathy mean in delivering apologies?

11. Why is the section devoted to reasons the most important part of a negative message, and which five factors ensure the effectiveness of the reasons given?

12. How can the passive voice be used effectively in bad-news messages? Provide an original example.

13. Aside from using a buffer and the indirect strategy, what other techniques can you employ that will cushion the blow of negative news?

14. How can you ensure that you close a bad-news message pleasantly and maintain the reader's goodwill?

15. How would you counter the claim that the indirect organization strategy is unethical or manipulative because the writer deliberately delays the main idea?

Writing Improvement Exercises

Passive-Voice Verbs

Passive-voice verbs may be preferable in breaking bad news because they enable you to emphasize actions rather than personalities. Compare these two refusals:

Example Active voice: I cannot authorize you to take three weeks of vacation in July.

Example Passive voice: Three weeks of vacation in July cannot be authorized.

Your Task. Revise the following refusals so that they use passive-voice instead of active-voice verbs.

16. We do not allow used merchandise to be returned or exchanged.

17. Managers may not advertise any job openings until those positions have first been posted internally.

18. Your car rental insurance does not cover large SUVs.

19. We cannot meet the sales income projected for the fourth quarter.

20. Titan Insurance Company will not process any claim not accompanied by documented proof showing that a physician treated the injuries.

Subordinate Clauses

You can further soften the effect of bad news by placing it in an introductory subordinate clause that begins with *although, since,* or *because.* The emphasis in a sentence is on the independent clause. Instead of saying *We cannot serve you on a credit basis,* try *Because serving you on a credit basis is currently not possible, please consider taking advantage of our cash discounts and sale prices.*

Your Task. Revise the following so that the bad news is de-emphasized in a dependent clause that precedes an independent clause. Use the passive voice and "you" view whenever it is appropriate and safe.

21. Unfortunately, we cannot accept personal checks or unauthorized credit. We encourage you to submit your credit application online before coming to the eBay auction.

22. We appreciate your interest in our organization, but we are unable to extend an employment offer to you at this time.

23. It is impossible for us to ship your complete order at this time. However, we are able to send the two armless task chairs immediately.

24. Air Pacific cannot possibly honor the $51 flight to Fiji that erroneously appeared on Travelocity. We are eager, however, to provide a compromise price to customers who booked at the erroneous price.

Implied Refusals

Bad news can be de-emphasized by implying a refusal instead of stating it directly. Compare these refusals:

Example Direct refusal: We cannot send you a price list, nor can we sell our lawn mowers directly to customers. We sell only through dealers, and your dealer is HomeCo.

Example Implied refusal: Our lawn mowers are sold only through dealers, and your dealer is HomeCo.

Your Task. Revise the following refusals so that the bad news is implied. If possible, use passive-voice verbs and subordinate clauses to further de-emphasize the bad news.

25. Because of the holiday period, all our billboard space was used this month. Therefore, we are sorry to say that we could not give your charitable group free display space. However, next month, after the holidays, we hope to display your message as we promised.

26. We have received your application to enroll your spouse as a dependent in the group insurance plan. But we must reject it because you just missed the deadline. Applications will not be accepted again until January 1, at which time you may enroll your wife.

27. We will not be able to make a pledge in the annual St. John's fund-raising campaign this year. At this time our cash is tied up in building a new production facility in Southport. We look forward to being able to support your campaign in coming years.

Writing Improvement Cases

7.1 Request Refusal: Nuptials Nixed at Napa Inn

The following poorly written letter turns down the request of a bride-to-be seeking to reserve the Napa Valley Inn as a venue for her wedding.

Your Task. Analyze the message. List its weaknesses, and then outline an appropriate writing plan. If your instructor directs, revise the message. A copy of this message is provided at **www.meguffey.com** for revision online.

Current date

Ms. Sonya Capretta
2459 Sierra Avenue
Fresno, CA 93710

Dear Ms. Capretta:

We regret to inform you that the wedding date you request in your letter of February 2 at the Napa Valley Inn is unavailable. Unfortunately, we are fully booked for all of the Saturdays in June, as you probably already suspected.

June is our busiest month, and smart brides make their reservations many months—even years—in advance. That's because the Napa Valley Inn is the ideal romantic getaway for weddings. With unparalleled cuisine and service, along with panoramic Napa Valley and vineyard views, our Inn offers unique, intimate ambiance in a breathtaking location for your special event.

We apologize if we have caused you any inconvenience. However, if you could change your wedding date to the middle of the week, we would try to accommodate your party. We do have a few midweek spots open in June, but even those dates are rapidly filling up. With 45 Mediterranean-style rooms and suites, each with its own sunny private terrace, the Napa Valley Inn is the perfect location for you and your partner to begin your married lives. Afternoon ceremonies typically begin at 11 a.m., while golden sunsets at the Napa Valley Inn offer a romantic prelude of the evening to come. Evening ceremonies usually begin at 6 p.m. I'm available if you want to arrange something.

Sincerely,

1. List at least five weaknesses in this letter.

2. Outline a writing plan for a request refusal:

   Buffer:
   Reasons:

   Bad news:

   Closing:

7.2 Claim Denial: No New Droid for You

Following is a letter to a customer who demanded a brand-new replacement Droid smartphone under her wireless phone protection plan.

Your Task. Analyze the message. List its weaknesses, and then outline an appropriate writing plan. If your instructor directs, revise the message. A copy of this message is provided at **www.meguffey.com** for revision online.

Current date

Ms. Lynda Brownsmith
2402 Prytania Street
New Orleans, LA 70130

Dear Ms. Brownsmith:

This letter is being sent to you to inform you that warranty repairs or replacements are not available for damage caused by operator fault. The dot inside your smartphone indicates in bright red that the device suffered prolonged exposure to liquid. The phone also shows signs of heavy external abuse—quite rightly excluded from coverage under your protection plan.

Your phone retailer, Premier Wireless, at 901 Saint Charles Avenue, forwarded your device to us. Our service technician made an inspection. That's when he discovered that your Droid had not been treated with proper caution and care. He said he had never seen such a gunky phone interior, and that without a doubt the gadget was subjected to blunt force on top of that! You are lucky that the touch screen did not crack or break and that you didn't lose all your data irretrievably since you apparently didn't bother to arrange for a backup. Today's smartphones are sophisticated high-tech devices. They must be handled with utmost respect. You wouldn't believe how many users accidentally drop their phones into the toilet.

Our Peace of Mind Plan gets rave reviews from users. They love the protection their expensive equipment enjoys at a low monthly cost of $5.99. However, the manufacturer's warranty on your Droid covers only this one thing: manufacturing defects. Your warranty has expired by now, but it wouldn't cover neglect and abuse anyway. Your Peace of Mind Plan is in effect but only covers you for theft, loss, and malfunction. It explicitly excludes liquid and physical damage. In any case, there is always a deductible of $89. We can't replace the Droid at no charge. But we could sell you a remanufactured model, at a cost of $49 plus tax. Your other option is to purchase a new device at full retail cost. Furthermore, since you have a two-year contract, you will be eligible for an upgrade as you are nearing month 20.

Let us know what you want to do. We pride ourselves on our unparalleled customer service.

Sincerely,

1. List at least five weaknesses in this letter.

2. Outline a plan for writing a refusal to a request.

   Buffer:

   Reasons:

   Bad news:

   Closing:

7.3 Internal Refusal: Can't Share Software

Sue Wang must refuse the request of some staff engineers. They want to copy for home use the latest version of Adobe Photoshop, an expensive licensed software program that her department just received.

Your Task. Analyze Sue's message. It suffers from many writing faults that you have studied. List its weaknesses, and then outline an appropriate writing plan. If your instructor directs, revise the message.

To: Staff Computer users
From: Sue Wang <swang@csb.com>
Subject: Software Sharing Violates the Law

Unfortunately, I cannot allow copies of our new Adobe Photoshop software to be made for home use. Or for any other use. Some staffers have asked for this privilege. Which is against the law.

This software program has many outstanding features, and I would be happy to demonstrate some of it to anyone who drops by the Document Production Department. Allowing this software to be copied violates company policy as well as the law. Like many licensed products today, it forbids and prohibits copying of all kinds. We have two copies, but we can't even make copies for other computers within our department. And especially not for home use! If you stop and think about it, it makes a lot of sense. Software companies would not be in business for long if it allowed wholesale copying. Eventually, they would not earn enough money to stay in business. Or to develop new software.

This e-mail is to inform you that we cannot allow copies of Adobe Photoshop to be made due to the fact that we agreed to limit its use to one single machine. Thank you for your cooperation.

Sue Wang
Manager | Document Production
E-Mail: swang@csb.com

1. List at least five weaknesses in this e-mail message.

2. Outline a plan for writing a refusal to a request.

   Buffer:

   Reasons:

   Bad news:

   Closing:

7.4 Internal Refusal: No Time for Charity Function

Chester Goings must refuse Sylvia Greene's request to attend a philanthropic event because he doesn't think the heavy workload and the poor financial situation of the company allow it.

Your Task. Analyze Chester's e-mail. It suffers from many writing faults that you have studied. List its weaknesses, and then outline an appropriate writing plan. If your instructor directs, revise the message.

To: Sylvia Greene <sgreene@financialsolutions.com>
From: Chester Goings <cgoings@financialsolutions.com>
Subject: No Go on Baby Charity Thing

Hey, Syl, you're one in a million. But we can't give you time off to work on that charity fashion show/luncheon thingy you want to coordinate. And Financial Solutions can't make a big contribution as we've done in previous years. It's no, no, no, all the way around.

Look, we admire the work you have done for the Newborn Hope Foundation. It has raised millions of dollars to make differences in the lives of babies, particularly premature ones. But we need you here!

With the upcoming release of our Planning Guide 5.0, we need you to interview clients. We need you to make video testimonials, and you are the one to search for stories about customer successes. Plus a zillion other tasks! Our new Web site will launch in just six short weeks, and all that content stuff must be in final form. With the economy in the tank and our bare-bones staff, you certainly must realize that each and every team member must be here and making a difference. If our Planning Guide 5.0 doesn't make a big splash, we'll all have a lot of time off.

Due to the fact that we're the worldwide leader in on-demand financial planning and reporting software, and in view of the fact that we are about to launch our most important new product ever, you must understand our position. When things get better, we might be able to return back to our past practices. But not now!

Chet

1. List at least five weaknesses in this letter.

2. Outline a plan for writing a refusal to a request.

   Buffer:

   Reasons:

   Bad news:

   Closing:

Activities and Cases

7.5 Request Refusal: Helping Abused Children

As a vice president of a real estate brokerage, you serve many clients, and they sometimes ask your company to contribute to their favorite charities. You recently received a letter from Olivia Hernandez asking for a substantial contribution to the National Court Appointed Special Advocate (CASA) Association. On visits to your office, she has told you about its programs to recruit, train, and support volunteers in their work with abused children. She herself is active in your town as a CASA volunteer, helping neglected children find safe, permanent homes. She told you that children with CASA volunteers are more likely to be adopted and are less likely to reenter the child welfare system. You have a soft spot in your heart for children and especially for those who are mistreated. You sincerely want to support CASA and its good work. But times are tough, and you can't be as generous as you have been in the past. Ms. Hernandez wrote a special letter to you asking you to become a Key contributor, with a pledge of $1,000.

Your Task. Write a refusal letter that maintains good relations with your client. Address it to Ms. Olivia Hernandez, 3592 Marine Creek Parkway, Fort Worth, TX 76179.

7.6 Request Refusal: Greening the Office

Hines, an international real estate firm, has developed a green office program designed to enhance the sustainable features and operation of its 230 offices on four continents. Its program, called HinesGO (short for Hines Green Office), helps identify and implement no-cost and low-cost green alternatives for standard indoor office environments. What's outstanding about the HinesGo program is its emphasis on improvements that can be achieved at minimal cost. For example, installation of occupancy light sensors can save enough money to offset the up-front investment.

Scored on a scale of 100, offices are evaluated in seven categories: energy efficiency; people and atmosphere; travel and commuting; reduce, reuse, and recycle; cleaning and pest control; remodeling and construction; and LEED and/or ENERGY STAR. (LEED is an internationally recognized green building certification system.) When a specific strategy has been implemented in the HinesGo program, participants earn Leaf Credits.[15]

Although the HinesGO program was initially intended for Hines offices only, the program generated so much attention that other businesses now want to duplicate its success. As a manager at Hines in charge of communication for HinesGo, you receive numerous invitations to speak to groups interested in creating greener workplace choices. However, you can't always accept. The most recent invitation came from Florida, where a group of realtors wants you to explain the HinesGO program. You were invited to speak October 12, but you are booked. You don't see an opening until sometime in late January.

Your Task. Prepare a letter that refuses the invitation but suggests an alternative and promotes the HinesGO program. Send your letter to Donna Payne, Society of Commercial Realtors of Greater Fort Lauderdale, 1765 NE 26th Street, Fort Lauderdale, FL 33305.

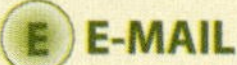

7.7 Request Refusal: Try Applying Online and On Time

Headquartered in San Jose, California, Adobe Systems Incorporated prides itself on its commitment to employees who receive generous benefits and enjoy a supportive corporate culture. This core value may have contributed to the company's ranking among the top 50 of *Fortune* magazine's 100 Best Companies to Work For. The software giant is also known for its community involvement and corporate social responsibility efforts. This is why, like most large companies, Adobe receives many requests for sponsorships of charity events and community projects. True to its innovative spirit, the software company has streamlined the application process by providing an online sponsorship request form at **http://www.adobe.com/aboutadobe/pressroom/sponsorship.html**. Moreover, nonprofit organizations asking for funding can fill out a donation request form—also online.

You work in Corporate Affairs/Community Relations at Adobe and periodically help decide which of the many nonprofits applying for sponsorships and donations will obtain support. However, not all nonprofits know to apply on Adobe's Web site. Just yesterday you received an e-mail from the Pink Dragons of San Diego, a dragon boat racing team of breast cancer survivors. Over the last ten years, the ancient Chinese sport of dragon boat racing has spread around the globe with regular competitions held not only in Asia but also in many Western countries. Dragon boat racing has gained huge popularity in Canada and the United States among breast cancer patients who seek to bond with fellow survivors, engage in healthy competition, and exercise regularly on the water. A dragon boat accommodates a maximum of 20 paddlers in pairs facing toward the bow of the boat. A caller or drummer at the bow faces the paddlers, and a steersperson stands at the helm in the back. Synchronicity and solid technique are more important than brute strength, which is the main reason that even recreational paddlers find great joy in this fast-growing water sport.

The newly formed survivor team in San Diego would like Adobe to sponsor a dragon boat festival taking place in a month, an event potentially drawing at least 20 survivor teams that would compete against each other. You know that your company is already funding several cancer charities and has a policy of sponsoring a wide array of causes. Naturally, no corporate giving program has infinite funds, nor can it green-light every request. Adobe steers clear of religious, political, and "pornographic" events. The company also refuses to support organizations that adopt unlawful discriminatory practices.

The team judging the sponsorship entries wants to ensure that each proposal reaches audiences affiliated with Adobe. Not surprisingly, the company wishes to receive some benefits from its sponsorships. But most of all, applicants must submit their requests at least six weeks before the event.

Your Task. As a junior staff member in Corporate Affairs/Community Relations, write an e-mail to Pink Dragon captain Katrina Rosa (*krosa@pinkdragons.org*) refusing her initial request and explaining the Adobe sponsorship philosophy and submission rules.

7.8 Claim Denial: Sorry—Smokers Must Pay

Recently, the Century Park Hotel embarked on a two-year plan to provide enhanced value and improved product quality to its guests. It always strives to exceed guest expectations. As part of this effort, Century Park has been refurbishing many rooms with updated finishes. The new carpet, paint, upholstery, and draperies, however, absorb the heavy odor of cigarette smoke. In order to protect the hotel's investment, Century Park enforces a strict nonsmoking policy for its nonsmoking rooms.

Century Park makes sure that guests know about its policy regarding smoking in nonsmoking rooms. It posts a notice in each nonsmoking room, and it gives guests a handout from the manager detailing its policy and the consequences for smoking in nonsmoking rooms. The handout clearly says, "Should a guest opt to disregard our nonsmoking policy, we will process a fee of $150 to the guest's account." For those guests who prefer to smoke, a smoking accommodation can be provided.

On May 10 Wilson M. Weber was a guest in the hotel. He stayed in a room clearly marked "Nonsmoking." After he left, the room cleaners reported that the room smelled of smoke. According to hotel policy, a charge of $150 was processed to Mr. Weber's credit card. Mr. Weber has written to demand that the $150 charge be removed. He doesn't deny that he smoked in the room. He just thinks that he should not have to pay.

Your Task. As hotel manager, deny Mr. Weber's claim. You would certainly like to see Mr. Weber return as a Century Park guest, but you cannot budge on your nonsmoking policy. Address your response to Mr. Wilson M. Weber, 634 Wetmore Avenue, Everett, WA 98201.

7.9 Customer Bad News: Bike Is a Lemon

One of your favorite job duties in Corporate Communications at Harley-Davidson is monitoring and addressing customer complaints on the Web and social media networks. You frequently check the various Harley-Davison forums on the Web and the occasional complaint site. Only yesterday you stumbled upon what sounds like a harrowing tale of woe involving a 2011 CVO Softail Springer. The brand-new post is vitriolic and barely literate, and the emotion is raw. Worst of all, after only a day, "Anonymous" already scored over 500 hits and multiple sympathetic comments.

> *Dont buy this piece of junk! I bought this lemon at the worst dealer in Michigan Wareford Harley-Davidson in November 2010. The 2011 CVO Softail Convertible is the hottest machine, but from the start this bike has been underpowered and a gas guzzler. Not much*

help from the Waterford dealer. The dealers general manger told me that my bike and I were no longer welcome. He said to break it in. Some chrome parts were defective, paint was rusty under clear coat, poor gas mileage, under 35, repairs really poor. Harely Davidson company are not standing up to thier responsiblities. $29,600 bike, offered to trade-in for $19,000. that was supposed to be the dealers best offer when I wanted to return the lemon.

Your detective work begins. You call up ABC Harley-Davidson, the only dealer in Waterford, Michigan, and inquire about a customer who had trouble with a 2011 CVO Softail Convertible. Sure enough, you obtain the name and contact information of the unhappy Harley owner. Before calling and writing to Pete Dix, however, you post a response to his scathing review online to limit further damage. You suggest he contact the Harley-Davidson customer Service Department by calling (414) 343-4056 and indicate his name, address, phone number, and the bike's vehicle identification number (VIN) along with the name and location of the dealership.

You find additional negative comments about ABC Harley-Davidson online; therefore, you look up the next closest dealership that could check out the bike, Motor City Harley-Davidson in Farmington Hills, Michigan. You know that all dealerships are independent franchises; hence, the quality of each shop can vary considerably. An inspection by an independent party is the first step. You want to find out if anything is truly wrong with the motorcycle. After all, the bike is still under warranty. Because the customer does not trust his current dealer, choosing a competitor nearby is the best course of action now. Jack Vroman, owner of Motor City Harley-Davidson, is very forthcoming and agrees to inspect the CVO free of charge to the customer. Jack Vroman has already called Pete Dix to offer him a free inspection under the warranty. You have also called Pete and left a voice mail message. Pete Dix's problem does not sound as if the motorcycle would fit the legal definition of a "lemon" under Michigan law, and taking the bike back at full price is out of the question.

You wonder what could have possibly gone wrong with this luxurious motorbike. The new models are a lot more reliable than similar big and heavy machines before them. Starting at $29,599, the 2011 CVO Softail Convertible is the pride of Harley-Davidson's model lineup. Highly customizable, the bike is essentially two motorcycles. In a few simple steps, the owner can remove the fairing, windshield, and other external parts. Instantly, the fully dressed touring bike can be turned into a "naked," yet comfortable cruiser. Unlike BMW and Japanese motorcycles, Harleys are not known for their speed or fuel economy; however, buyers like the "retro" appeal of the legendary brand, the signature engine roar, and the laid-back riding style.

Your Task. Use tact and project empathy when writing a follow-up letter to Pete Dix at 30 Estes Court, Waterford, MI 48327. Your objective is to mollify his frustration by listening to him and helping him get to the bottom of the problems with his bike. Who knows; if you are successful, Pete may even withdraw his negative post. You may want to investigate the lemon laws in your state to better understand the definition of this legal term. You may also want to take a peek at the CVO by visiting Harley-Davidson's official Web site at **http://www.harley-davidson.com**.

7.10 Customer Bad News: The StairClimber or the LifeStep?

You are delighted to receive a large order from Greg Waller at New Bodies Gym. This order includes two Lifecycle Trainers (at $1,295 each), four Pro Abdominal Boards (at $295 each), three Tunturi Muscle Trainers (at $749 each), and three Dual-Action StairClimbers (at $1,545 each).

You could ship immediately except for one problem. The Dual-Action StairClimber is intended for home use, not for gym or club use. Customers like it because they say it is more like scaling a mountain than climbing a flight of stairs. With each step, users exercise their arms to pull or push themselves up. Its special cylinders absorb shock so that no harmful running impact results. However, this model is not what you would recommend for gym use. You feel Mr. Waller should order your premier stair climber, the LifeStep (at $2,395 each) This unit has sturdier construction and is meant for heavy use. Its sophisticated electronics provide a selection of customer-pleasing programs that challenge muscles progressively with a choice of workouts. It also quickly multiplies workout gains with computer-controlled interval training. Electronic monitors inform users of step height, calories burned, elapsed time, upcoming levels, and adherence to fitness goals. For gym use the LifeStep is clearly better than the StairClimber. The bad news is that the LifeStep is considerably more expensive.

You get no response when you try to telephone Mr. Waller to discuss the problem. Should you ship what you can, or hold the entire order until you learn whether he wants the StairClimber or the LifeStep? Or perhaps you should substitute the LifeStep and send only two of them.

Your Task. Decide what to do and write a letter to Greg Waller, New Bodies Gym, 3402 Copeland Drive, Athens, OH 45701.

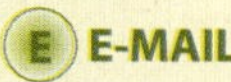

E-MAIL

7.11 Customer Bad News: University Admission Message Erroneously Welcomes All Who Applied

The University of California, San Diego, recently made a big mistake. It inadvertently invited all applicants to the La Jolla campus to an orientation—even those who had been rejected. The message said, "We're thrilled that you've been admitted to UC San Diego, and we're showcasing our beautiful campus on Admit Day." That message was intended to be sent to about 18,000 students who had been accepted. Instead, it went to all 47,000 students who applied. Admissions Director Mae Brown quickly realized the mistake. "The minute the e-mails were sent out, we noted that it was sent to a much larger pool than was admitted. We immediately recognized the error," she said.

What could the university do to correct this massive slip-up? One applicant, who had already received a rejection from UCSD, said she was confused. Her mother said, "It is adding insult to injury for kids who have already been through the wringer." When asked if anyone had been disciplined for the mistake, Brown said that the university was undertaking a complete review of the process.[16]

Your Task. For Admissions Director Mae Brown (*mbrown@ucsd.edu*), write an appropriate bad-news message to the students who received the message in error. Many applicants will be wondering what their real admission status is.

7.12 Customer Bad News: Late Payroll Checks

Trenton Hughes, a printing company sales manager, must tell one of his clients that the payroll checks his company ordered are not going to be ready by the date Hughes had promised. The printing company's job scheduler overlooked the job and didn't get the checks into production in time to meet the deadline. As a result, Hughes' client, a major insurance company, is going to miss its pay run.

Hughes meets with internal department heads. They decide on the following plan to remedy the situation: (a) move the check order to the front of the production line; (b) make up for the late production date by shipping some of the checks—enough to meet their client's immediate payroll needs—by air freight; and (c) deliver the remaining checks by truck.[17]

Your Task. Form groups of three to four students. Discuss the following issues about how to present the bad news to Jessica Dyhala, Hughes' contact person at the insurance company.

a. Should Hughes call Dyhala directly, or delegate the task to his assistant?
b. When should Dyhala be informed of the problem?
c. What is the best procedure for delivering the bad news?
d. What follow-up would you recommend to Hughes?

Be prepared to share your group's responses during a class discussion. Your instructor may ask two students to role-play the presentation of the bad news.

7.13 Credit Refusal: Camcorders for Rudy's Camera Shop

As a Uniworld Electronics sales manager, you are delighted to land a sizable order for your new Canon Vixia camcorder. This hot new camcorder features a sleek, lightweight design, brilliant optical quality, vibrant images, and outstanding image capture in low-light conditions.

The purchase order comes from Rudy's Camera Shop, a retail distributor in Beaumont, Texas. You send the order on to Pamela Kahn, your credit manager, for approval of the credit application attached. To your disappointment, Pam tells you that Rudy's Camera doesn't qualify for credit. Experian, the credit-reporting service, reports that extending credit to Rudy's would be risky for Uniworld. But Experian did offer to discuss your client's report with him.

Because you think you can be more effective in writing than on the telephone, you decide to write to Rudy's Camera with the bad news and offer an alternative. Suggest that Rudy's order a smaller number of the Canon camcorders. If it pays cash, it can receive a 2 percent discount. After Rudy's has sold these fast-moving camcorders, it can place another cash order through your toll-free order number. With your fast delivery system, its inventory will never be depleted. Rudy's can get the camcorders it wants now and can replace its inventory almost overnight. Credit Manager Kahn tells you that your company generally reveals to credit applicants the name of the credit-reporting service it used and encourages them to investigate their credit record.

Your Task. Write a credit refusal to Ron Kasbekar, Rudy's Camera Shop, 3016 East Lucas Drive, Beaumont, TX 77657. Add any information needed.

7. 14 Internal Refusal: Want to Telecommute? Learn to Communicate

Pamela Gershon, a young software developer from Dayton, Ohio, is thrilled at the prospect of working from home where she would be able to take care of her two small children, three dogs, and a cat. Like many forward-looking employers, Northrop Grumman Corporation, a leading aerospace and defense technology company, is encouraging workers to consider telecommuting. The company has created a formal program with specific policies explaining eligibility and requirements. Currently, only positions in technical sales, information technology, Web and graphic design, and software development qualify for telecommuting. In addition, workers must be dependable, self-motivated, and organized. Because telecommuting is a sought-after privilege, employees with proven high performance, seniority, minimal absenteeism, and superb communication skills receive priority consideration. Telecommuters need to follow company policies determining work hours, break times, and work schedules, even off site. Moreover, they must visit the main office located on Wright-Patterson Air Force Base near Dayton at least once every two weeks to report to their supervisors in person.

Northrop Grumman promotes telecommuting because it benefits the company as well as its workers. In addition to flexibility, telecommuters usually experience gains in productivity and efficiency. The employer lowers overhead costs and is able to retain valuable workers who may not be able or willing to commute to remote corporate offices.[18]

Pamela has been a diligent worker, but after only a year and a half at Northrop Grumman, she doesn't have the seniority needed for a successful application. Her performance has been satisfactory but not outstanding. It seems as if she still needs time to prove herself. In addition, her major weakness is average communication skills, something her supervisor has already discussed with Pamela.

Your Task. Draft a memo addressed to Pamela Gershon for Human Resources Director Gabrielle Anicker turning down Pamela's telecommuting application. Be gentle but honest in revealing your reasons for the *no*, but don't close the door on a future application once Pamela meets certain conditions.

7.15 Internal Refusal: We Can't Pay Your Tuition

Yasmin Qajar, a hardworking bank teller, has sent a request asking that the company create a program to reimburse the tuition and book expenses for employees taking college courses. Although some companies have such a program, Middleton Bank has not felt that it could indulge in such an expensive employee perk. Moreover, the CEO is not convinced that companies see any direct benefit from such programs. Employees improve their educational credentials and skills, but what is to keep them from moving that education and those skill sets to other employers? Middleton Bank has over 200 employees. If even a fraction of them started classes, the company could see a huge bill for the cost of tuition and books. Because the bank is facing stiff competition and its profits are sinking, the expense of such a program makes it out of the question. In addition, it would involve administration—applications, monitoring, and record keeping. It is just too much of a hassle. When employees were hard to hire and retain, companies had to offer employment perks. But with a soft economy, such inducements are unnecessary.

Your Task. As director of Human Resources, send an individual response to Yasmin Qajar. The answer is a definite *no*, but you want to soften the blow and retain the loyalty of this conscientious employee.

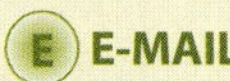

7.16 Employee Bad News: Company Games Are Not Date Nights

As director of Human Resources at Weyerman Paper Company, you received an unusual request. Several employees asked that their spouses or friends be allowed to participate on Weyerman intramural sports teams. Although the teams play only once a week during the season, these employees claim that they can't afford more time away from friends and family. Over 100 employees currently participate on the eight coed volleyball, softball, and tennis teams, which are open to company employees only. The teams were designed to improve employee friendships and to give employees a regular occasion to have fun together.

If nonemployees were to participate, you fear that employee interaction would be limited. Although some team members might have fun if spouses or friends were included, you are not so sure all employees would enjoy it. You are not interested in turning intramural sports into "date night." Furthermore, the company would have to create additional teams if many nonemployees joined, and you don't want the administrative or equipment costs of more teams. Adding teams also would require changes to team rosters and game schedules. This could create a problem for some employees. You do understand the need for social time with friends and families, but guests are welcome as spectators at all intramural games. Also, the company already sponsors a family holiday party and an annual company picnic.

Your Task. Write an e-mail or hard-copy memo to the staff denying the request of several employees to include nonemployees on Weyerman's intramural sports teams.

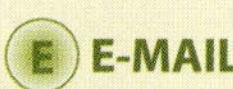

7.17 Employee Bad News: No Facebook on the Company's Dime

Your boss at Contact PR, a hip midsized public relations agency, is concerned that the youngest employee generation may be "oversharing" on Facebook. Two supervisors have complained that they spotted inappropriate photos on Facebook posted by a small group of Millennials on the company payroll. This group of twentysomethings is close-knit. Its members maintain friendships outside the office and in cyberspace. They are smart and plugged in, but they seem to have trouble recognizing boundaries of age and authority. They party every weekend, which is code for a lot of drinking, marijuana use, and even salacious escapades—all of which the young workers generously document with smartphone cameras on the spot and occasionally in real time. Sometimes they share snarky comments about their workplace, such as "Rough day at work" or "Talked to the most idiotic client ever!" On top of that, the young people think nothing of friending their colleagues and supervisors. Their "friends" rank in the hundreds; some in the group have exceeded 1,000 friends on Facebook.

Contact PR has embraced cutting-edge technology because the management believes that information sharing and collaboration tools can lead to networking opportunities and, if used correctly, to increased productivity. The company maintains a permissive stance toward Internet use, but concern is growing that the young people are headed for trouble. The abuses continue despite the company's comprehensive Internet and social media use policy, which was widely disseminated. Probably the biggest risk Contact PR fears is the leaking of confidential information on social networking sites. The managers also complain that the Millennials spend too much time on Facebook during office hours. Your boss is becoming impatient. After several meetings, the management decides to disallow Facebook use during work hours and to caution all employees against dangerous breaches of company policy and social media netiquette.

Your Task. Draft an e-mail to be sent by your boss, Judy L. Shea, Director, Human Resources. Your message should remind all employees about the existing social networking policy and tactfully yet clearly announce the end of Facebook use at the office. The prohibition is effective immediately. Your message should also warn about the pitfalls of oversharing online.

Video Resources

Video Library 2: *Bad News: BuyCostumes.* This video features BuyCostumes, the world's largest online costume and accessories retailer. After watching the video, play the part of a customer-service representative.

BuyCostumes is proud of its extensive stock of costumes, its liberal return policy, and its many satisfied customers. But one day a letter arrived with a request that went beyond the company's ability to deliver. The customer said that he had ordered the Gorilla Blinky Eye with Chest costume. This popular gorilla costume comes with a unique gorilla mask, attractive suit with rubber chest, foot covers, and hands. The customer complained that the gorilla costume did not arrive until two days after his Halloween party. He planned an elaborate party with a gorilla theme, and he was extremely unhappy that he did not have his costume. He asks BuyCostumes to reimburse the $300 that he spent on theme-related decorations, which he says were useless when he failed to receive his costume.

As a customer-service representative, you checked his order and found that it was not received until five days before Halloween, the busiest time of the year for your company. The order was filled the next day, but standard shipping requires three to six business days for delivery. The customer did not order express or premium delivery; his shipping option was marked "Standard."

You showed the letter to the owner, Mr. Getz, who said that this request was ludicrous. However, he wanted to retain the customer's goodwill. Obviously, BuyCostumes was not going to shell out $300 for late delivery of a costume. But Mr. Getz suggested that the company would allow the customer to return the costume (in its original packaging) with a credit for the $134.99 charge. In addition, BuyCostumes would send a coupon for $20 off on the next costume purchase.

Your Task. Mr. Getz asks you to write a letter that retains the goodwill of this customer. Address your bad-news letter to Mr. Christopher King, 3579 Elm Street, Buffalo, NY 14202. Check **http://www.buycostumes.com** for more company information.

Grammar/Mechanics Checkup—7

Commas 2

Review the Grammar/Mechanics Handbook Sections 2.05–2.09. Then study each of the following statements and insert necessary commas. In the space provided, write the number of commas that you add; write *0* if no commas are needed. Also record the number of the G/M principle(s) illustrated. When you finish, compare your responses with those provided at the end of the book. If your answers differ, study carefully the principles shown in parentheses.

1 (2.06a) **Example** When preparing for a job interview, you should conduct considerable research into the target company.

______ 1. If candidates appear overly eager or desperate they may blow the opportunity.

______ 2. Some job seekers are becoming more aggressive and they often end up hurting their chances.

______ 3. You can be best prepared if you look up information about the hiring company and if you know more than just the basics about the company's leadership and core businesses.

______ 4. Deborah Wang who is the founder of an executive search firm says that the most successful candidates offer examples of past accomplishments.

______ 5. Most firms are looking for reliable hardworking candidates who can explain how they will contribute to the organization.

______ 6. During the last 16 months the number of qualified candidates has doubled.

______ 7. The position of marketing manager which has been open for the past six months is difficult to fill.

______ 8. Recruiters look for candidates who are a strong fit for a particular position and who have exactly the skills required.

______ 9. When interviewing a recent candidate the recruiter said that the applicant clearly and effectively explained how he could cut costs and increase sales.

______ 10. The candidates who had the best qualifications were screened by means of telephone interviews before being offered in-person interviews.

Review of Commas 1 and 2

______ 11. To learn about your target company read recent company press releases annual reports media coverage and industry blogs.

______ 12. After he was hired Joseph was told to report for work on Monday May 15 in Atlanta.

______ 13. Regarding the subject of pay which may come up early in an interview it's better to hold off the discussion until you have been extended a job offer.

______ 14. As a matter of fact the salary you request may impact the organization's decision to hire you.

______ 15. Although she wasn't excited about the opportunity Julie scheduled an interview for Tuesday February 3 at 2 p.m.

Editing Challenge—7

As the employee with the best communication skills, you are frequently asked to edit messages. The following letter has problems with spelling, word choice, wordiness, proofreading, comma use, grammar, and other writing techniques you have studied. You may (a) use standard proofreading marks (see Appendix B) to correct the errors here or (b) download the document from **www.meguffey.com** and revise at your computer.

Your instructor may ask you to use the **Track Changes** feature in Word to show your editing comments. Turn on **Track Changes** on the **Review** tab. Click **Show Markup**. Place your cursor at an error, click **New Comment**, and key your edit in the bubble box provided. Study the guidelines in the Grammar/Mechanics Handbook as well as the lists of Confusing Words and Frequently Misspelled Words to sharpen your skills.

CableEx   The Nation's Largest Cable TV Provider

Current date

Mrs. Robert T. Hesser
4430 Poplar Avenue
Memphis, TN 38018

Dear Mr. Hesser:

We at CableEx have been working very hard and diligently to continue to provide you with the highest quality programming and cable features. Because many next generation technology features are available at this point in time we are investing in them to make sure that you have more programming choices and improvments in customer service.

These improvements make it possible for us deliver to you continued innovations such as more high-definition programming, movies on demand, converged services, multiplatform content and faster Internet speeds. Despite the fact that our costs for internet service has increased steady over the passed five years we have absorbed those increases. However this investment in new services when combined with the rising costs of doing business and escalating programming charges has increase our operating budget. As a result we are forced to announce price adjustments in many packages, these adjustments will go into affect January 1.

If you receive the Basic Cable package you wont see a price increase. Depending on where you live that package will remain in the amount of $13 to $18 per month. If you recieve the Digital Economy package you will see a rate decline. Depending on you're package this decline will range from 4 cents to ten dollars per month. Digital Economy provides a basic package of 17 cable channels, it also includes Food Network, History, Disney Channel, Lifetime, AMC and USA.

A complete schedule showing rate adjustments are enclosed. Although the cost of some packages are increasing you are receiving the best in voice, video and data transmission. Its a great entertainment value and we are planning even more innovations for future programming. We appreciate you loyalty and we promise to continue to bring you the best in service and entertainment.

Cordially,

Joshua Luna

Joshua Luna, President

Enclosure

Communication Workshop

Presenting Bad News in Other Cultures

To minimize disappointment, Americans generally prefer to present negative messages indirectly. Other cultures may treat bad news differently, as illustrated in the following:

- In Germany business communicators occasionally use buffers but tend to present bad news directly.
- British writers tend to be straightforward with bad news, seeing no reason to soften its announcement.
- In Latin countries the question is not how to organize negative messages but whether to present them at all. It is considered disrespectful and impolite to report bad news to superiors. Therefore, reluctant employees may fail to report accurately any negative situations to their bosses.
- In Thailand the negativism represented by a refusal is completely alien; the word *no* does not exist. In many cultures negative news is offered with such subtlety or in such a positive light that it may be overlooked or misunderstood by literal-minded Americans.
- In many Asian and some Latin cultures, one must look beyond an individual's actual words to understand what is really being communicated. One must consider the communication style, the culture, and especially the context. Consider the following phrases and their possible meanings:

Phrase	**Possible Meaning**
I agree.	I agree with 15 percent of what you way.
We might be able to . . .	Not a chance!
We will consider . . .	*We* will consider, but the real decision maker will not.
That is a little too much . . .	That is outrageous!
Yes.	Yes, I'm listening. *OR*: Yes, you have a good point. *OR*: Yes, I understand, but I don't necessarily agree.

Career Application. Interview fellow students or work colleagues who are from other cultures. Collect information by asking the following questions:

- How is negative news handled in their cultures?
- How would typical business communicators refuse a request for a business favor (such as a contribution to a charity)?
- How would typical business communicators refuse a customer's claim?
- How would an individual be turned down for a job?

Your Task. Report the findings of your interviews in class discussion or in a memo report. In addition, collect samples of foreign business letters. You might ask foreign students, your campus admissions office, or local export/import companies whether they would be willing to share business letters from other countries. Compare letter styles, formats, tone, and writing strategies. How do these elements differ from those in typical North American business letters?

Endnotes

[1] Brodkin, J. (2007, March 19). Corporate apologies don't mean much. *Networkworld, 24*(11), 8. PDF file retrieved from http://search.ebscohost.com

[2] Schweitzer, M. E. (2006, December). Wise negotiators know when to say "I'm sorry." *Negotiation*, 4. PDF file retrieved from http://search.ebscohost.com

[3] Brodkin, J. (2007, March 19). Rating apologies. *Networkworld, 24*(11), 14. Retrieved from http://search.ebscohost.com

[4] Neeleman, D. (2007). An apology from David Neeleman. Retrieved from http://www.jetblue.com/about/ourcompany/apology/index.html

[5] Letters to Lands' End. (1991, February). 1991 Lands' End catalog. Dodgeville, WI: Lands' End, p. 100.

[6] Forbes, M. (1999). How to write a business letter. In K. Harty (Ed.), *Strategies for business and technical writing*. Boston: Allyn and Bacon, p. 108.

[7] Mowatt, J. (2002, February). Breaking bad news to customers. *Agency Sales*, 30; and Dorn, E. M. (1999, March). Case method instruction in the business writing classroom. *Business Communication Quarterly, 62*(1), 51–52.

[8] Browning, M. (2003, November 24). Work dilemma: Delivering bad news a good way. *Government Computer News*, p. 41; and Mowatt, J. (2002, February). Breaking bad news to customers. *Agency Sales*, p. 30.

[9] Engels, J. (2007, July). Delivering difficult messages. *Journal of Accountancy, 204*(1), 50–52. Retrieved from http://search.ebscohost.com; see also Lewis, B. (1999, September 13). To be an effective leader, you need to perfect the art of delivering bad news. *InfoWorld*, p. 124. Retrieved from http://books.google.com

[10] Ziglar, Z. (2009, July 13). Zig on . . . Overcoming fear. Retrieved from http://www.ziglar.com/newsletter/?tag=goal-setting

[11] O'Neal, S. (2003, November). Quoted in Need to deliver bad news? How & why to tell it like it is. *HR Focus*, p. 3. Retrieved from http://search.ebscohost.com

[12] Council of Better Business Bureaus. (2010, January 5). BBB lists top 10 scams and rip-offs of 2009. Retrieved from http://www.buffalo.bbb.org

[13] Bristol-Smith, D. (2003, November). Quoted in Need to deliver bad news? How & why to tell it like it is. *HR Focus*, p. 3. Retrieved from http://search.ebscohost.com

[14] Gartner identifies top ten disruptive technologies for 2008-2012. (n.d.) Press release. Retrieved from http://www.gartner.com/it/page.jsp?id=68117

[15] Hines unveils HinesGO: A tool to green office space. (2009, February 18). Retrieved from http://www.hines.com/press/releases/2-18-093.aspx

[16] Kucher, K. (2009, March 31). UCSD e-mail erroneously welcomes all who applied. Retrieved from http://www.signonsandiego.com/news/2009/mar/31/bn31letter114447

[17] Mishory, J. (2008, June). Don't shoot the messenger: How to deliver bad news and still keep customers satisfied. *Sales and Marketing Management*, p. 18.

[18] Based on Bonavita, C. V. (2010, August 5). Employers should eye telecommuting's benefits, pitfalls. *The Legal Intelligencer*. Retrieved from http://www.law.com/jsp/lawtechnologynews/PubArticleLTN.jsp?id=1202464268970

Acknowledgments

p. 178 Office Insider cited in Engels, J. (2007, July). Delivering difficult messages. *Journal of Accountancy, 204*(1), 50. Retrieved from http://search.ebscohost.com

p. 182 Office Insider cited in Now go out and lead. (2007, January 8). *Bloomberg Businessweek*. Retrieved from http://www.businessweek.com/magazine/content/07_02/b4016083.htm

p. 191 Office Insider cited in Mishory, J. (2004, June). Don't shoot the messenger: How to deliver bad news and still keep customers satisfied. *Sales & Marketing Management, 156*(6), 18. Retrieved from http://search.ebscohost.com

p. 193 Office Insider cited in Weeks, L. (2008, December 8). Read the blog: You're fired. National Public Radio. Retrieved from http://www.npr.org/templates/story/story.php?storyId=97945811

CHAPTER 8

Persuasive Messages

Go to
cengagebrain.com
and use your access code to unlock valuable student eResources.

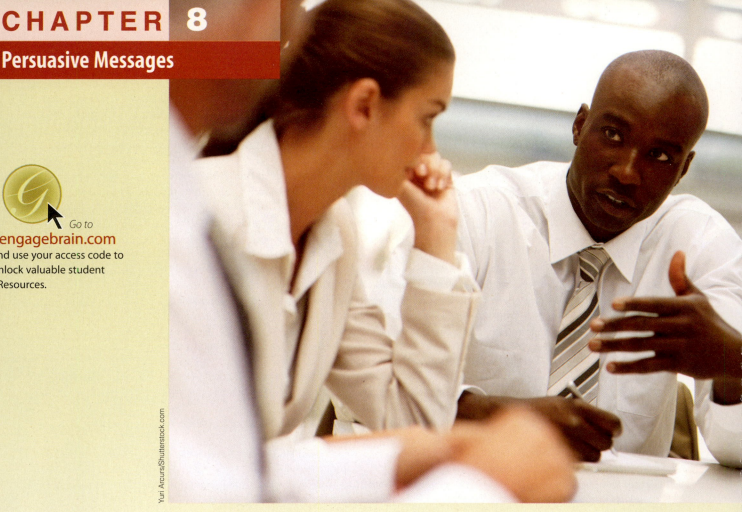

Yuri Arcurs/Shutterstock.com

OBJECTIVES

After studying this chapter, you should be able to

- Outline the opening, body, and closing of persuasive requests.
- Request favors and action convincingly.
- Make reasonable claims and write successful complaints.
- Write effective persuasive messages within organizations.
- Outline sales letters and their AIDA strategy: gaining attention, building interest, developing desire, and motivating action.
- Apply the persuasive strategy to online sales messages.
- Understand how businesses embrace social media to communicate with their stakeholders.

Understanding Persuasive Messages in the Workplace

Much of your success in business and in life will depend on how skilled you are at persuading people to believe, accept, and act on what you are saying. Bill Gates, named one of the world's most influential people, is a business tycoon, philanthropist, author, and founder of Microsoft. He is also on *Forbes'* list of the richest people on earth. To lend urgency to his fight against malaria, he has been known to release mosquitoes into a conference audience. Leveraging his fame, Gates addresses a global audience when condemning poverty or starting a new venture to harness nuclear power. When Bill Gates speaks, the world is listening.

Persuading others skeptical of global warming and fearful of nuclear energy is a tall order. However, Gates uses his celebrity and persuasive skills to mobilize wealthy friends such as Warren Buffett and to urge governments to take action. Leading by example and not one for half measures, Gates has been known to put his money where his mouth is. He founded the Bill & Melinda Gates Foundation, which advocates acting "vigorously but responsibly" in its areas of focus: global development, global health, and education.[1]

Although few of us can claim such a formidable influence in the world today, applying effective persuasive techniques can help you become a winning communicator. Because their ideas generally prevail, persuasive individuals become decision makers—managers, executives, and entrepreneurs. This chapter examines techniques for presenting ideas persuasively, whether in your career or in your personal life.

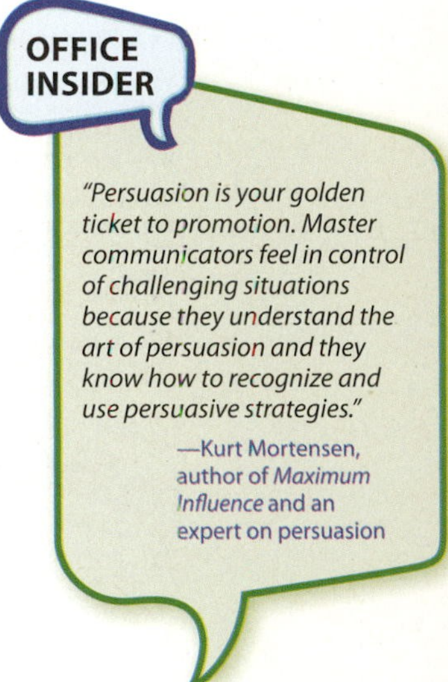

Persuasion is necessary when you anticipate resistance or when you must prepare before you can present your ideas effectively. For example, let's say you bought a new car and the transmission repeatedly required servicing. When you finally got tired of taking it in for repair, you decided to write to the car manufacturer's district office asking that the company install a new transmission in your car. You knew that your request would be resisted. You had to convince the manufacturer that replacement, not repair, was needed. Direct claim letters, such as those you wrote in Chapter 6, are straightforward and direct. Persuasive requests, on the other hand, are generally more effective when they are indirect. Reasons and explanations should precede the main idea. To overcome possible resistance, the writer lays a logical foundation before delivering the request. A writing plan for a persuasive request requires deliberate development.

WRITING PLAN FOR A PERSUASIVE REQUEST

- **Opening:** Capture the reader's attention and interest. Describe a problem, make an unexpected statement, suggest reader benefits, offer praise or compliments, or ask a stimulating question.
- **Body:** Build interest. Explain logically and concisely the purpose of the request. Prove its merit. Use facts, statistics, expert opinion, examples, and specific details. Focus on the reader's direct and indirect benefits. Reduce resistance. Anticipate objections, offer counterarguments, establish credibility, demonstrate competence, and show the value of your proposal.
- **Closing:** Motivate action. Ask for a particular action. Make the action easy to take. Show courtesy, respect, and gratitude.

In this chapter you will learn to apply the preceding writing plan to messages that (a) request favors and action, (b) persuade subordinates and your superiors, and (c) make claims and request adjustments that may meet with opposition.

Requesting Favors and Action

Persuading someone to do something that largely benefits you is not easy. Fortunately, many individuals and companies are willing to grant requests for time, money, information, cooperation, and special privileges. They grant these favors for a variety of reasons. They may just happen to be interested in your project, or they may see goodwill potential for themselves. Often, though, they comply because they see that others will benefit from the request. Professionals sometimes feel obligated to contribute their time or expertise to "give back to the community."

Figure 8.1 shows a persuasive favor request from Michelle Moreno. Her research firm seeks to persuade other companies to complete a questionnaire revealing salary data. To most organizations, salary information is strictly confidential. What can she do to convince strangers to part with such private information?

People are more likely to grant requests if they see direct or indirect benefits to themselves.

FIGURE 8.1 Persuasive Favor Request

Dear Mr. Mansker:

We need your help in collecting salary data for today's workers. Ithaca Research Institute has been collecting business data for 25 years, and we have received awards for accuracy. We know that filling out surveys can be tedious, but the results are very useful.

Companies trust the survey data we compile. We have been in this business long enough to know how important comparative salary data are to most organizations. Filling out our questionnaire will not take very long. If you wish, we could send you some of the results showing not only salaries, but also perks and other benefits.

Please fill out the enclosed questionnaire and call us if you have any questions. Thank you for your cooperation.

Fails to pique interest; provides easy excuse

Does not promote direct and indirect benefits

Does not anticipate objections; fails to motivate action

after

ITHACA RESEARCH INSTITUTE

430 Seneca Street, Ithaca, NY 14850 www.ithacaresearch.com
PH 570.888.2300
FAX 570.888.4359

May 17, 201x

Mr. Trevor M. Mansker
All-Star Financial Advisors
240 Lomb Memorial Drive
Rochester, NY 14623

Dear Mr. Mansker:

Have you ever added a unique job title but had no idea what compensation the position demanded? Has your company ever lost a valued employee to another organization that offered 20 percent more in salary for the same position?

To remain competitive in hiring and to retain qualified workers, companies rely on survey data showing current salaries. Ithaca Research Institute has been collecting business data for a quarter century and has been honored by the American Management Association for its accurate data. We need your help in collecting salary data for today's workers. Information from the enclosed questionnaire will supply companies like yours with such data.

Your information, of course, will be treated confidentially. The questionnaire takes but a few minutes to complete, and it can provide substantial dividends for professional organizations that need comparative salary data.

To show our gratitude for your participation, we will send you comprehensive salary surveys for your industry and your metropolitan area. Not only will you find basic salaries, but you will also learn about bonus and incentive plans, special pay differentials, expense reimbursements, and perquisites such as a company car and credit card.

Comparative salary data are impossible to provide without the support of professionals like you. Please complete the questionnaire and return it in the prepaid envelope before June 1, our spring deadline. Participating in this survey means that you will no longer be in the dark about how much your employees earn compared with others in your industry.

Sincerely yours,

ITHACA RESEARCH INSTITUTE

Michelle Moreno

Michelle Moreno
Director, Survey Research

Enclosure

Poses two short questions related to the reader

Presents reader benefit tied to request explanation; establishes credibility

Anticipates and counters resistance to confidentiality and time/effort objections

Offers free salary data as a direct benefit

Provides deadline and a final benefit to action

Gains attention

Builds interest

Reduces resistance

Appeals to professionalism, an indirect benefit

Motivates action

The hurriedly written first version of the request suffers from many faults. It fails to pique the interest of the reader in the opening. It also provides an easy excuse for Mr. Mansker to refuse (*filling out surveys can be tedious*). In the body, Mr. Mansker doesn't receive any incentive to accept the request. The writing is self-serving and offers few specifics. In addition, the draft does not anticipate objections and fails to suggest counterarguments. Last, the closing does not motivate action by providing a deadline or a final benefit.

In the revised version, Michelle begins her persuasive favor request by posing two short questions that spotlight the need for salary information. To build interest and establish trust, she mentions that Ithaca Research Institute has been collecting business data for a quarter century and has received awards from the American Management Association. Developing credibility is especially important when persuading strangers to do something. Making a reasonable request tied to benefits is also important. Michelle does this by emphasizing the need for current salary information.

To reduce resistance, Michelle promises confidentiality and explains that the questionnaire takes but a few moments to complete. She offers free salary data as a direct benefit. This data may help the receiver learn how its salary scale compares with others in its industry. But Michelle doesn't count on this offer as the only motivator. As an indirect benefit, she appeals to the professionalism of the receiver. She's hoping that the receiver will recognize the value of providing salary data to the entire profession. To motivate action, Michelle closes with a deadline and reminds the reader that her company need not be in the dark about comparative salaries within its industry.

This favor request incorporates many of the techniques that are effective in persuasion: establishing credibility, making a reasonable and precise request, tying facts to benefits, and overcoming resistance.

Composing Persuasive Claims and Complaints

Persuasive claim and complaint messages typically involve damaged products, mistaken billing, inaccurate shipments, warranty problems, limited return policies, insurance snafus, faulty merchandise, and so on. Generally, the direct strategy is best for requesting straightforward adjustments (see Chapter 6). When you believe your request is justified and will be granted, the direct strategy is most efficient. However, if a past request has been refused or ignored or if you anticipate reluctance, then the indirect strategy is appropriate.

Persuasive claim and complaint messages make reasonable requests backed by solid evidence.

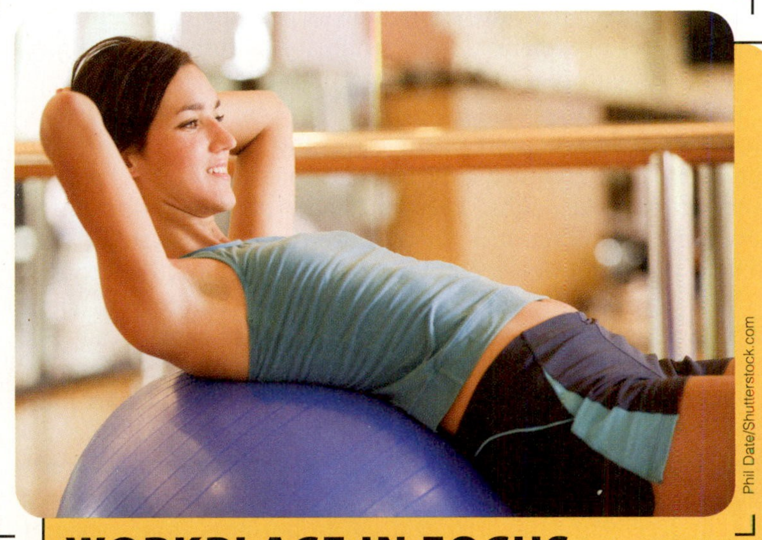
Phil Date/Shutterstock.com

WORKPLACE IN FOCUS

Joining a fitness club is easy, but cancelling membership can be frustrating—especially if the gym closes abruptly. When a Ladies Workout Express near Chicago shut down recently, numerous gym members continued receiving charges. In one situation, a collection agency for the fitness center haggled a member for payment despite the customer's many letters and phone complaints. A spokeswoman at the franchise acknowledged confusion, saying, "It's hard, because a lot of people don't know whom to contact." ***How can individuals file claims that get results?***

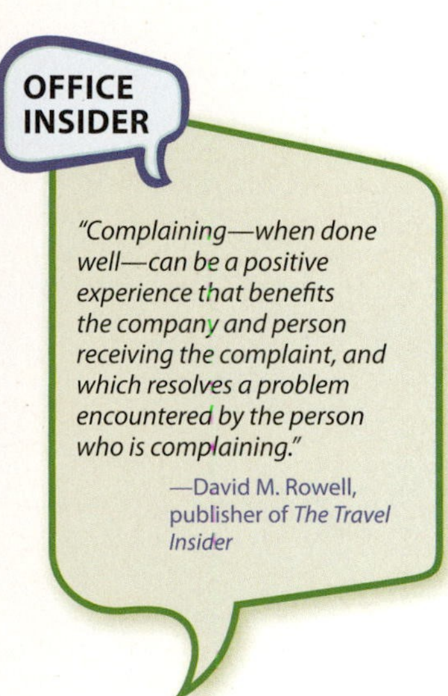

In a sense, a claim is a complaint message that delivers bad news. Someone is complaining about something that went wrong. Some complaint messages just vent anger. However, if the goal is to change something (and why bother to write except to motivate change?), then persuasion is necessary. Effective claim messages make a reasonable and valid request, present a logical case with clear facts, and adopt a moderate tone. Anger and emotion are not effective persuaders.

Logical Development. Strive for logical development in a claim message. You might open with sincere praise, an objective statement of the problem, a point of agreement, or a quick review of what you have done to resolve the problem. Then you can explain precisely what happened or why your claim is legitimate. Don't provide a blow-by-blow chronology of details; just hit the highlights. Be sure to enclose copies of relevant invoices, shipping orders, warranties, and payments. Close with a clear statement of what you want done: a refund, replacement, credit to your account, or other action. Be sure to think through the possibilities and make your request reasonable.

Moderate Tone. The tone of your message is important. Don't suggest that the receiver intentionally deceived you or intentionally created the problem. Rather, appeal to the receiver's sense of responsibility and pride in the company's good name. Calmly express your disappointment in view of your high expectations of the product and of the company. Communicating your feelings without rancor is often your strongest appeal.

If at all possible, address your complaint letter or e-mail to a specific person. If you truly want a problem solved quickly, take the time to call the organization, search its Web site, or send an e-mail. Who should be informed about your issue? Who has the authority to act? Addressing a specific person is more likely to generate action than addressing a generic customer-service department. Whether you approach an individual or a department, the tone of your message should, of course, be moderate.

Martine Romaniack's letter, shown in Figure 8.2, follows the persuasive strategy. She wants to return two voice over Internet protocol (VoIP) telephone systems. Notice her positive opening, her well-documented claims, and her request for specific action.

Writing Persuasive Messages Within Organizations

Internal persuasive messages present honest arguments detailing specific reader or company benefits.

When it comes to persuasion, the power relationships at work determine how we write—whether we choose a direct or indirect strategy, for example. We may consider what type and amount of support we include, depending on whether we wish to persuade subordinates or superiors. The authority of our audience may also help us decide whether to adopt a formal or informal tone.

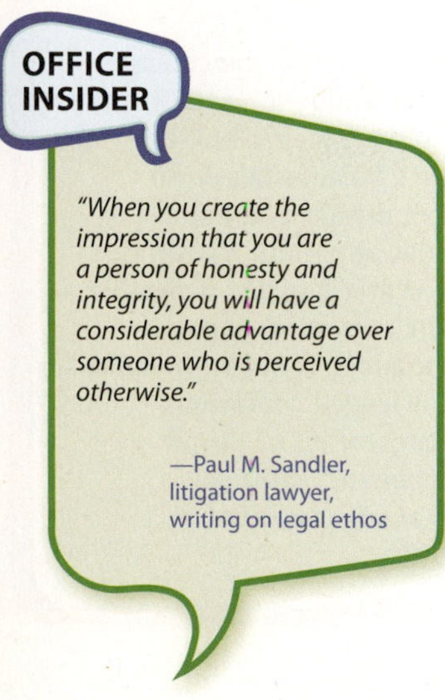

Persuading Subordinates. Instructions or directives moving downward from superiors to subordinates usually require little persuasion. Employees expect to be directed in how to perform their jobs. These messages (such as information about procedures, equipment, or customer service) use the direct strategy, with the purpose immediately stated. However, employees are sometimes asked to volunteer for projects. For example, some organizations encourage employees to join programs to stop smoking, lose weight, or start exercising. Organizations may ask employees to participate in capacities outside their work roles—such as spending their free time volunteering for charity projects. In such cases, the four-part indirect strategy provides a helpful structure.

The goal is not to manipulate employees or to seduce them with trickery. Rather, the goal is to present a strong but honest argument, emphasizing points that are important to the receiver or the organization. In business, honesty is not just the best policy—it's the only policy. People see right through puffery and misrepresentation. For this reason, the indirect strategy is effective only when supported by accurate, honest evidence.

FIGURE 8.2 Claim (Complaint) Letter

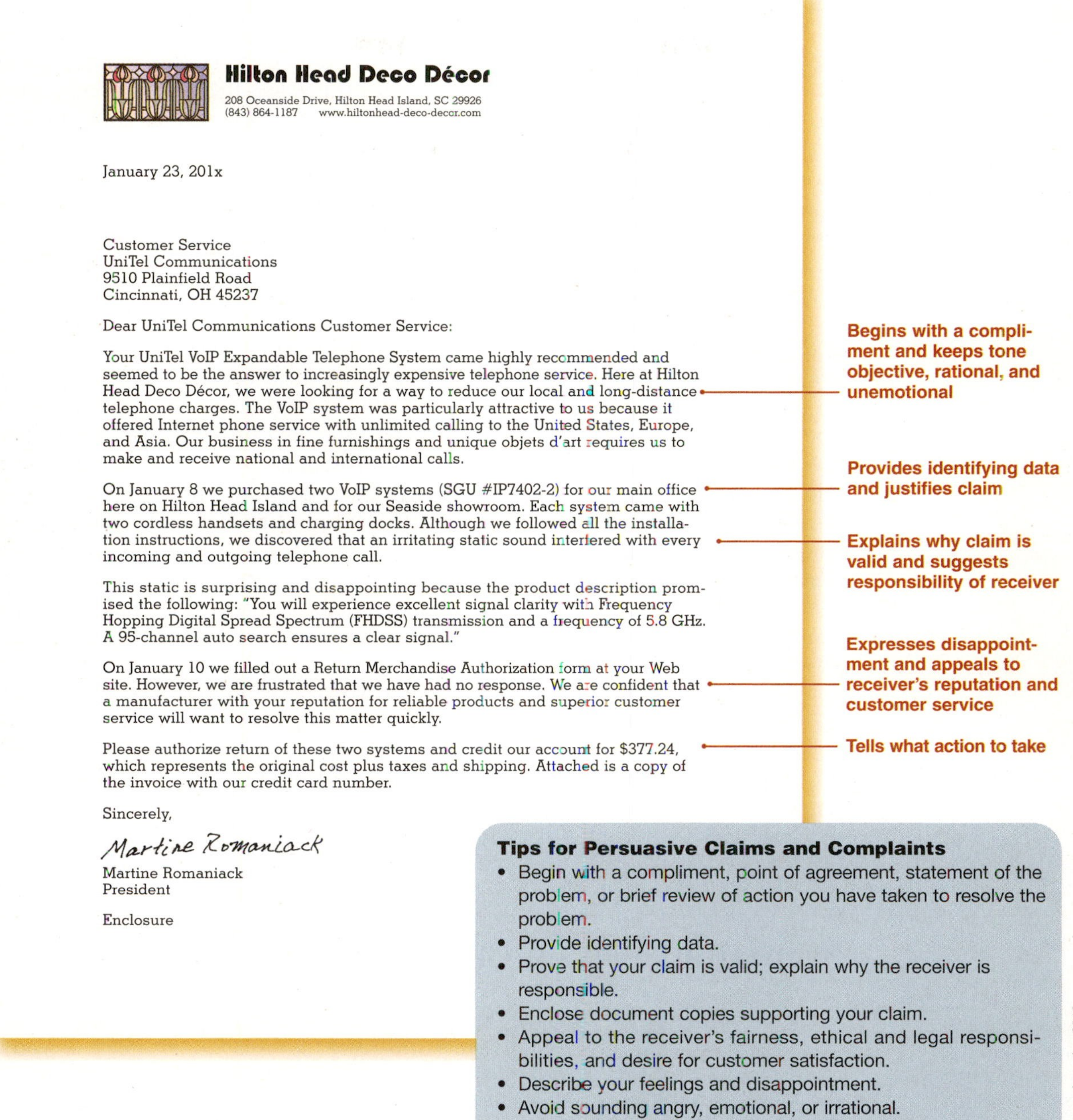

Hilton Head Deco Décor
208 Oceanside Drive, Hilton Head Island, SC 29926
(843) 864-1187 www.hiltonhead-deco-decor.com

January 23, 201x

Customer Service
UniTel Communications
9510 Plainfield Road
Cincinnati, OH 45237

Dear UniTel Communications Customer Service:

Your UniTel VoIP Expandable Telephone System came highly recommended and seemed to be the answer to increasingly expensive telephone service. Here at Hilton Head Deco Décor, we were looking for a way to reduce our local and long-distance telephone charges. The VoIP system was particularly attractive to us because it offered Internet phone service with unlimited calling to the United States, Europe, and Asia. Our business in fine furnishings and unique objets d'art requires us to make and receive national and international calls.

On January 8 we purchased two VoIP systems (SGU #IP7402-2) for our main office here on Hilton Head Island and for our Seaside showroom. Each system came with two cordless handsets and charging docks. Although we followed all the installation instructions, we discovered that an irritating static sound interfered with every incoming and outgoing telephone call.

This static is surprising and disappointing because the product description promised the following: "You will experience excellent signal clarity with Frequency Hopping Digital Spread Spectrum (FHDSS) transmission and a frequency of 5.8 GHz. A 95-channel auto search ensures a clear signal."

On January 10 we filled out a Return Merchandise Authorization form at your Web site. However, we are frustrated that we have had no response. We are confident that a manufacturer with your reputation for reliable products and superior customer service will want to resolve this matter quickly.

Please authorize return of these two systems and credit our account for $377.24, which represents the original cost plus taxes and shipping. Attached is a copy of the invoice with our credit card number.

Sincerely,

Martine Romaniack

Martine Romaniack
President

Enclosure

Begins with a compliment and keeps tone objective, rational, and unemotional
Provides identifying data and justifies claim
Explains why claim is valid and suggests responsibility of receiver
Expresses disappointment and appeals to receiver's reputation and customer service
Tells what action to take

Tips for Persuasive Claims and Complaints

- Begin with a compliment, point of agreement, statement of the problem, or brief review of action you have taken to resolve the problem.
- Provide identifying data.
- Prove that your claim is valid; explain why the receiver is responsible.
- Enclose document copies supporting your claim.
- Appeal to the receiver's fairness, ethical and legal responsibilities, and desire for customer satisfaction.
- Describe your feelings and disappointment.
- Avoid sounding angry, emotional, or irrational.
- Close by telling exactly what you want done.

Persuading the Boss. Another form of persuasion within organizations centers on suggestions made by subordinates. Convincing management to adopt a procedure or invest in a product or new equipment generally requires skillful communication. Managers are just as resistant to change as others are. Providing evidence is critical when subordinates submit recommendations to their bosses. "The key to making a request of a superior," advises communication consultant Patricia Buhler, "is to know your needs and have documentation [facts, figures, evidence]." Another important factor is moderation. "Going in and asking for the world [right] off the cuff is most likely going to elicit a negative response," she added.[2] Equally important is focusing on the receiver's needs. How can you make your suggestion appealing to the receiver?

Obviously, when you set out to persuade someone at work who has more clout than you, do so carefully. Use words such as *suggest* and *recommend*, and craft sentences to begin with these words: *It might be a good idea if* . . . . That lets you offer suggestions without threatening the person's authority.

When Marketing Manager Monique Hartung wanted her boss to authorize the purchase of a multifunction color laser copier, she knew she had to be persuasive. Her memo, shown in Figure 8.3, illustrates an effective approach. First, she researched prices, features, and the maintenance of color laser copiers. These machines often serve as copiers, faxes, scanners, and printers and can cost several thousand dollars. Monique found an outstanding deal offered by a local office supplier. Because she knew that her boss, Samuel Neesen, favored "cold, hard facts," she listed current monthly costs for copying at Copy Quick to increase her chances of gaining approval. Finally, she calculated the amortization of the purchase price and monthly costs of running the new color copier.

Notice that Monique's memo isn't short. A successful persuasive message will typically take more space than a direct message because proving a case requires evidence. In the end, Monique chose to send her memo as an e-mail attachment accompanied by a polite, short e-mail message because she wanted to keep the document format in Microsoft Word intact. She also felt that the message was too long to paste into her e-mail program. Monique's persuasive memo and her e-mail include subject lines that announce the purpose of the message without disclosing the actual request. By delaying the request until she has had a chance to describe the problem and discuss a solution, Monique prevents the reader's premature rejection.

When selling an idea to management, writers often are successful if they make a strong case for saving or earning money.

The strength of this persuasive document, though, is in the clear presentation of comparison figures showing how much money the company can save by purchasing a remanufactured copier. Buying a copier that uses low-cost solid-color ink sticks instead of expensive laser cartridges is another argument in this machine's favor. Although the organization pattern is not obvious, the memo begins with an attention-getter (a frank description of the problem), builds interest (with easy-to-read facts and figures), provides benefits, and reduces resistance. Notice that the conclusion tells what action is to be taken, makes it easy to respond, and repeats the main benefit to motivate action.

Preparing Sales and Marketing Messages

Traditional direct-mail marketing uses snail mail. Electronic marketing uses Internet-based advertising channels such as e-mail, blogs, wikis, and other social media.

Sales messages use persuasion to promote specific products and services. In our coverage in this section, we are most concerned with sales messages delivered as direct mail by the U.S. Postal Service or by e-mail. However, many of the concepts you will learn about sales persuasion apply not only to well-established channels such as direct mail, TV, print, radio, and other traditional media, but also to online marketing and social media. You will learn about nontraditional channels such as Facebook, YouTube, blogs, wikis, and other social media later in this chapter.

The best sales messages, whether delivered by direct mail, e-mail, or other electronic means, have much in common. To reach consumers, smart companies strive to develop a balanced approach to their overall marketing strategy, including both e-marketing and direct mail when appropriate. As one fundraising and technology expert puts it, "Direct mail isn't dead, but single channel communication is."[3] Marketing coach Debra Murphy tells her clients that they must understand who their ideal customers are and "where they hang out." This knowledge then determines which approaches and media will work best for that audience.[4]

Traditional hard-copy sales letters are still the most personal and powerful form of advertising.

When discussing persuasive strategies, we will give most emphasis to traditional direct-mail campaigns featuring letters. Although not as flashy as social media campaigns, direct mail still works as long as it is personalized and thus relevant.[5]

FIGURE 8.3 Persuasive E-Mail and Memo Flowing Upward

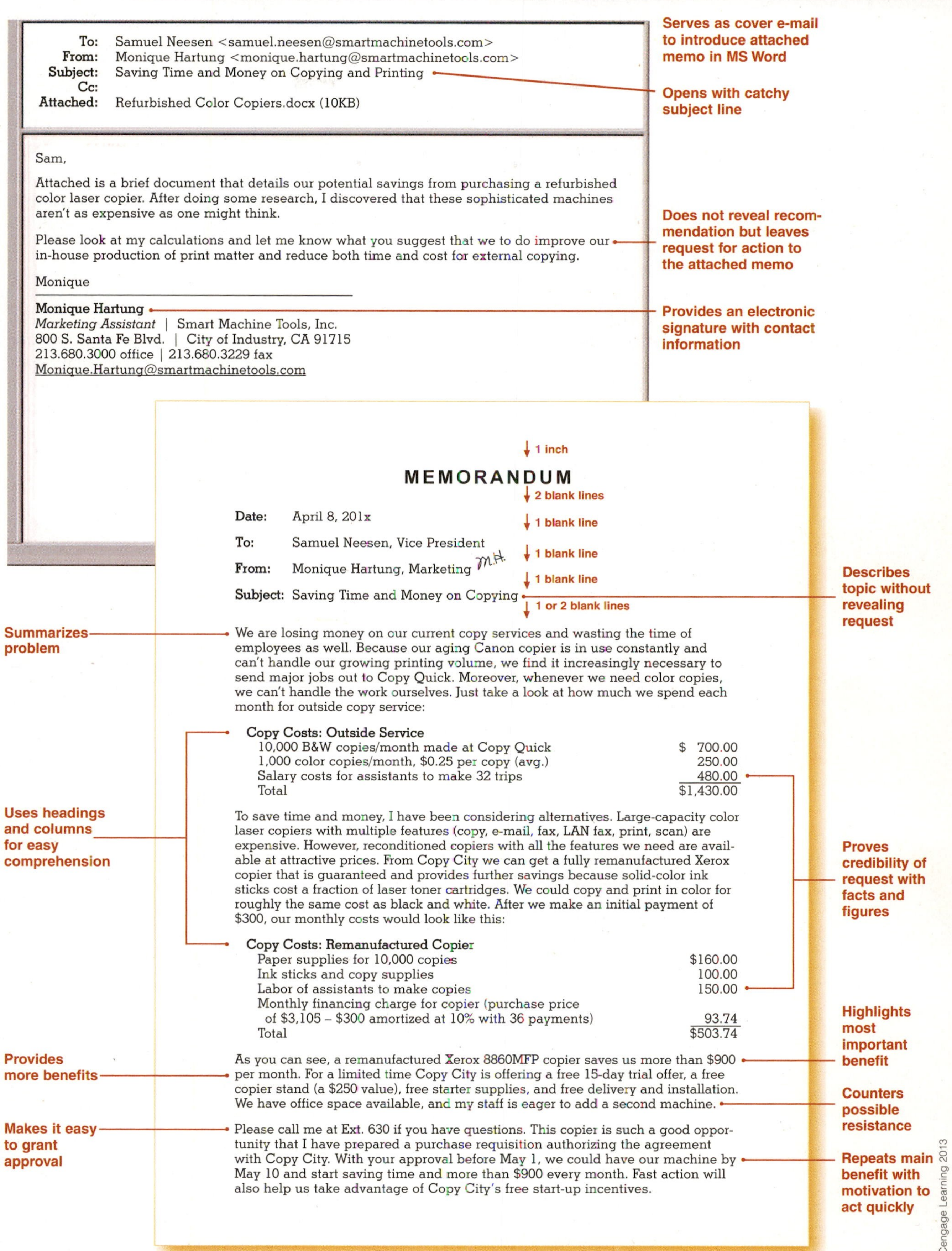

To: Samuel Neesen <samuel.neesen@smartmachinetools.com>
From: Monique Hartung <monique.hartung@smartmachinetools.com>
Subject: Saving Time and Money on Copying and Printing
Cc:
Attached: Refurbished Color Copiers.docx (10KB)

Sam,

Attached is a brief document that details our potential savings from purchasing a refurbished color laser copier. After doing some research, I discovered that these sophisticated machines aren't as expensive as one might think.

Please look at my calculations and let me know what you suggest that we to do improve our in-house production of print matter and reduce both time and cost for external copying.

Monique

Monique Hartung
Marketing Assistant | Smart Machine Tools, Inc.
800 S. Santa Fe Blvd. | City of Industry, CA 91715
213.680.3000 office | 213.680.3229 fax
Monique.Hartung@smartmachinetools.com

MEMORANDUM

Date: April 8, 201x

To: Samuel Neesen, Vice President

From: Monique Hartung, Marketing *M.H.*

Subject: Saving Time and Money on Copying

We are losing money on our current copy services and wasting the time of employees as well. Because our aging Canon copier is in use constantly and can't handle our growing printing volume, we find it increasingly necessary to send major jobs out to Copy Quick. Moreover, whenever we need color copies, we can't handle the work ourselves. Just take a look at how much we spend each month for outside copy service:

Copy Costs: Outside Service	
10,000 B&W copies/month made at Copy Quick	$ 700.00
1,000 color copies/month, $0.25 per copy (avg.)	250.00
Salary costs for assistants to make 32 trips	480.00
Total	$1,430.00

To save time and money, I have been considering alternatives. Large-capacity color laser copiers with multiple features (copy, e-mail, fax, LAN fax, print, scan) are expensive. However, reconditioned copiers with all the features we need are available at attractive prices. From Copy City we can get a fully remanufactured Xerox copier that is guaranteed and provides further savings because solid-color ink sticks cost a fraction of laser toner cartridges. We could copy and print in color for roughly the same cost as black and white. After we make an initial payment of $300, our monthly costs would look like this:

Copy Costs: Remanufactured Copier	
Paper supplies for 10,000 copies	$160.00
Ink sticks and copy supplies	100.00
Labor of assistants to make copies	150.00
Monthly financing charge for copier (purchase price of $3,105 – $300 amortized at 10% with 36 payments)	93.74
Total	$503.74

As you can see, a remanufactured Xerox 8860MFP copier saves us more than $900 per month. For a limited time Copy City is offering a free 15-day trial offer, a free copier stand (a $250 value), free starter supplies, and free delivery and installation. We have office space available, and my staff is eager to add a second machine.

Please call me at Ext. 630 if you have questions. This copier is such a good opportunity that I have prepared a purchase requisition authorizing the agreement with Copy City. With your approval before May 1, we could have our machine by May 10 and start saving time and more than $900 every month. Fast action will also help us take advantage of Copy City's free start-up incentives.

Serves as cover e-mail to introduce attached memo in MS Word
Opens with catchy subject line
Does not reveal recommendation but leaves request for action to the attached memo
Provides an electronic signature with contact information
1 inch
2 blank lines
1 blank line
1 blank line
1 blank line
1 or 2 blank lines
Describes topic without revealing request
Summarizes problem
Uses headings and columns for easy comprehension
Proves credibility of request with facts and figures
Highlights most important benefit
Provides more benefits
Counters possible resistance
Makes it easy to grant approval
Repeats main benefit with motivation to act quickly

OFFICE INSIDER

"Direct mail is perhaps one of the most powerful marketing media in use today. Few other marketing tools can deliver your message with exact precision at such a low cost. The amount of mail in your mailbox every day attests to the effectiveness of this medium (If it didn't work, your mailbox would be empty!)."

—David Frey, president of Marketing Best Practices, Inc., Houston, Texas

Experts know that most recipients do look at their direct mail; in fact, over 70 percent, some say over 80 percent, of such promotional mail pieces are opened.[6] This so-called open rate is much lower for e-mail, hovering at around 19 percent. Direct mail also continues to offer healthy response rates, from 1.4 to 3.4 percent.[7] Hard-copy sales letters are still recognized as "a highly targeted, highly personal and hugely effective way of reaching the target audience."[8] In fact, in its annual survey, the Direct Marketing Association has recently found that spending in direct mail is expected to grow 3.6 percent per year between 2010 and 2014.[9]

Sales letters are generally part of a package that may contain a brochure, price list, illustrations, testimonials, and other persuasive appeals. Professionals who specialize in traditional direct-mail services have made it a science. They analyze a market, develop an effective mailing list, study the product, prepare a sophisticated campaign aimed at a target audience, and motivate the reader to act. You have probably received many direct-mail packages, often derisively called junk mail. Chances are they will keep coming, but they will be a lot more relevant to you and your spending habits.

We are most concerned here with the sales letter: its strategy, organization, and evidence. Because sales letters are usually written by specialists, you may never write one on the job. Why, then, learn how to write a sales letter? In many ways, every letter we create is a form of sales letter. We sell our ideas, our organizations, and ourselves. Learning the techniques of sales writing will help you be more successful in any communication that requires persuasion and promotion. What's more, you will recognize sales strategies that enable you to become a more perceptive consumer of ideas, products, and services.

Your primary goal in writing a sales message is to get someone to devote a few moments of attention to it. You may be promoting a product, a service, an idea, or yourself. In each case the most effective messages will follow the time-honored persuasive strategy in sales, AIDA: attention, interest, desire, and action.

WRITING PLAN FOR A SALES MESSAGE: AIDA

Professional marketers and salespeople follow the AIDA strategy (attention, interest, desire, and action) when persuading consumers. In addition to telemarketing and personal selling, this strategy works very well for written messages as outlined in Figure 8.4.

- **Opening:** Gain ***attention***. Offer something valuable; promise a benefit to the reader; ask a question; or provide a quotation, fact, product feature, testimonial, startling statement, or personalized action setting.
- **Body:** Build ***interest***. Describe central selling points and make rational and emotional appeals. Elicit ***desire*** in the reader and reduce resistance. Use testimonials, money-back guarantees, free samples, performance tests, or other techniques.
- **Closing:** Motivate ***action***. Offer a gift, promise an incentive, limit the offer, set a deadline, or guarantee satisfaction.

Openers for sales messages should be brief, honest, relevant, and provocative.

Attention. One of the most critical elements of a sales message is its opening paragraph. This opener should be short (one to five lines), honest, relevant, and stimulating. Marketing pros have found that eye-catching typographical arrangements or provocative messages, such as the following, can hook a reader's attention:

- **Offer:** A free trip to Hawaii is just the beginning!
- **Benefit:** Now you can raise your sales income by 50 percent or even more with the proven techniques found in . . . .
- **Open-ended suggestive question:** Do you want your family to be safe?

FIGURE 8.4 The AIDA Strategy for Sales Letters

	Strategy	Content	Section
A	Attention	Captures attention, creates awareness, makes a sales proposition, prompts audience to read on	Opening
I	Interest	Describes central selling points, focuses not on features of product/service but on benefits relevant to the reader's needs	Body
D	Desire	Reduces resistance, reassures the reader, elicits the desire for ownership, motivates action	Body
A	Action	Offers an incentive or gift, limits the offer, sets a deadline, makes it easy for the reader to respond, closes the sale	Closing

- **Quotation or proverb:** Necessity is the mother of invention.
- **Compliment:** Life is full of milestones. You have reached one. You deserve . . . .
- **Fact:** The Greenland Eskimos ate more fat than anyone in the world, yet . . . they had virtually no heart disease.
- **Product feature:** Electronic stability control, ABS, and other active and passive safety features explain why the ultra-compact new Smart Fortwo has achieved a four-star crash rating in California.
- **Testimonial:** The most recent J.D. Power survey of "initial quality" shows that BMW ranks at the top of brands with the fewest defects and malfunctions, ahead of Chrysler, Hyundai, Lexus, Porsche, and Toyota.
- **Startling statement:** Let the poor and hungry feed themselves! For just $100 they can.
- **Personalized action setting:** It's 4:30 p.m. and you have got to make a decision. You need everybody's opinion, no matter where they are. Before you pick up your phone and call them one at a time, pick up this card: WebEx web conferencing.

Other openings calculated to capture attention might include a solution to a problem, an anecdote, a personalized statement using the receiver's name, or a relevant current event.

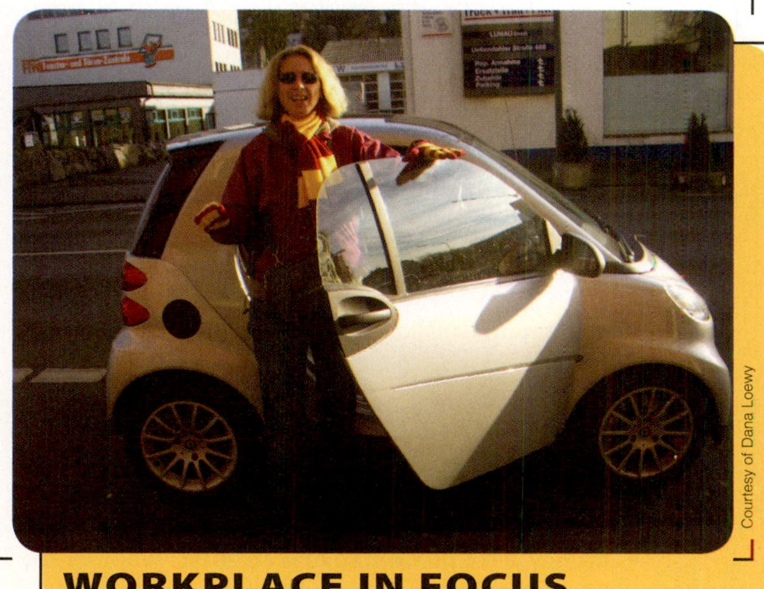

WORKPLACE IN FOCUS

Trying to sell a micro car to Americans is a huge gamble by Daimler AG, manufacturer of the luxurious Mercedes-Benz brand but also maker of the diminutive Smart Fortwo. Prompted by skyrocketing gasoline prices, European and Asian drivers have long embraced small automobiles. But SUV-loving Americans? Although the Smart is well engineered and sells briskly in 36 countries, its promoters will have to work hard to win over Americans. ***What will American car buyers worry about the most when they see an automobile such as the Smart? What strategies might reduce their resistance?***

Build interest by describing the benefits a product or service offers and by making rational or emotional appeals.

Interest. In this phase of your sales message, you should describe clearly the product or service. Think of this part as a promise that the product or service will deliver to satisfy the audience's needs. In simple language emphasize the central selling points that you identified during your prewriting analysis. Those selling points can be developed using rational or emotional appeals.

Rational appeals focus on making or saving money, increasing efficiency, or making good use of resources.

Rational appeals are associated with reason and intellect. They translate selling points into references to making or saving money, increasing efficiency, or making the best use of resources. In general, rational appeals are appropriate when a product is expensive, long-lasting, or important to health, security, and financial success. Emotional appeals relate to status, ego, and sensual feelings. Appealing to the emotions is sometimes effective when a product is inexpensive, short-lived, or nonessential. Many clever sales messages, however, combine emotional and rational strategies for a dual appeal. Consider these examples:

Rational Appeal
You can buy the things you need and want, pay household bills, pay off higher-cost loans and credit cards—as soon as you are approved and your Credit Line account is opened.

Emotional appeals focus on status, ego, and sensual feelings.

Emotional Appeal
Leave the urban bustle behind and escape to sun-soaked Bermuda! To recharge your batteries with an injection of sun and surf, all you need is your bathing suit, a little suntan lotion, and your Credit Line card.

Dual Appeal
New Credit Line cardholders are immediately eligible for a $200 travel certificate and additional discounts at fun-filled resorts. Save up to 40 percent while lying on a beach in picturesque, sun-soaked Bermuda, the year-round resort island.

A physical description of your product is not enough, however. Zig Ziglar, thought by some to be America's greatest salesperson, pointed out that no matter how well you know your product, no one is persuaded by cold, hard facts alone. In the end, he contended, customers don't buy features or functions; they buy product benefits.[10] Your job is to translate those cold facts into warm feelings and reader benefits. Let's say a sales letter promotes a hand cream made with aloe and cocoa butter extracts, along with vitamin A. Those facts become, *Nature's hand helpers—including soothing aloe and cocoa extracts, along with firming vitamin A—form invisible gloves that protect your sensitive skin against the hardships of work, harsh detergents, and constant environmental assaults.*

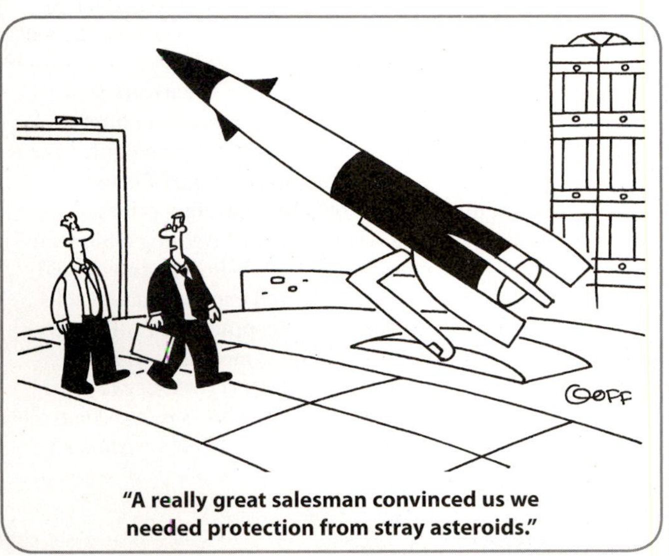

"A really great salesman convinced us we needed protection from stray asteroids."

Desire. Marketing pros use a number of techniques to elicit desire in their audience and to overcome resistance. To make the audience want the product or service and to anticipate objections, focus strongly on reader benefits. Here the promises of the attention and interest sections are covered in great detail.

- **Testimonials:** *Thanks to your online selling workshop, I was able to increase the number of my sales leads from three per month to twelve per week!* —Carlton Strong, Phoenix, Arizona
- **Names of satisfied users (with permission, of course):** Enclosed is a partial list of private pilots who enthusiastically subscribe to our service.
- **Money-back guarantee or warranty:** We offer the longest warranties in the business—all parts and service on-site for five years!

- **Free trial or sample:** We are so confident that you will like our new accounting program that we want you to try it absolutely free.
- **Performance tests, polls, or awards:** Our Audi R8 supercar won World Design Car of the Year and World Performance Car of the Year awards—the first time a single car has received trophies in more than one category.

In addition, you need to anticipate objections and questions the receiver may have. When possible, translate these objections into selling points (*If you are worried about training your staff members on the new software, remember that our offer includes $1,000 worth of on-site one-on-one instruction*). Be sure, of course, that your claims are accurate and do not stretch the truth.

When price is an obstacle, consider these suggestions:

- Delay mentioning price until after you have created a desire for the product.
- Show the price in small units, such as the price per issue of a magazine.
- Demonstrate how the reader saves money—for instance, by subscribing for two or three years.
- Compare your prices with those of a competitor.
- If applicable, offer advantageous financing terms.

Action. All the effort put into a sales message is wasted if the reader fails to act. To make it easy for readers to act, you can provide a reply card, a stamped and preaddressed envelope, a toll-free telephone number, an easy-to-scan Web site, or a promise of a follow-up call. Because readers often need an extra push, consider including additional motivators, such as the following:

Techniques for motivating action include offering a gift or incentive, limiting an offer, and guaranteeing satisfaction.

- **Offer a gift:** You will receive a free iPod nano with the purchase of any new car.
- **Promise an incentive:** With every new, paid subscription, we will plant a tree in one of America's Heritage Forests.
- **Limit the offer:** The first 100 customers receive free travel mugs.
- **Set a deadline:** You must act before June 1 to get these low prices.
- **Guarantee satisfaction:** We will return your full payment if you are not entirely satisfied—no questions asked.

"I find it hard to believe that we've actually won 20 million dollars when they send the letter bulk mail."

Originally printed in *The Wall Street Journal*. Permission granted by United Features Syndicate.

The final paragraph of the sales letter carries the punch line. This is where you tell readers what you want done and give them reasons for doing it. Most sales letters also include postscripts because they make irresistible reading. Even readers who might skim over or bypass paragraphs are drawn to a P.S. Therefore, use a postscript to reveal your strongest motivator, to add a special inducement for a quick response, or to reemphasize a central selling point.

Putting It All Together

Sales letters are a preferred marketing medium because they can be personalized, directed to target audiences, and filled with a more complete message than other advertising media. However, direct mail does not come cheap, although it is one of the least expensive advertising channels. That is why crafting and assembling all the parts of a sales message are so critical.

Because direct mail does not come cheap, messages should present complete information with a personalized tone for specific, well-targeted audiences.

Figure 8.5 shows a sales letter addressed to a target group of small and medium-size business owners. To sell highly customized, efficient information technology services, the letter incorporates all four components of an effective persuasive

FIGURE 8.5 Sales Letter

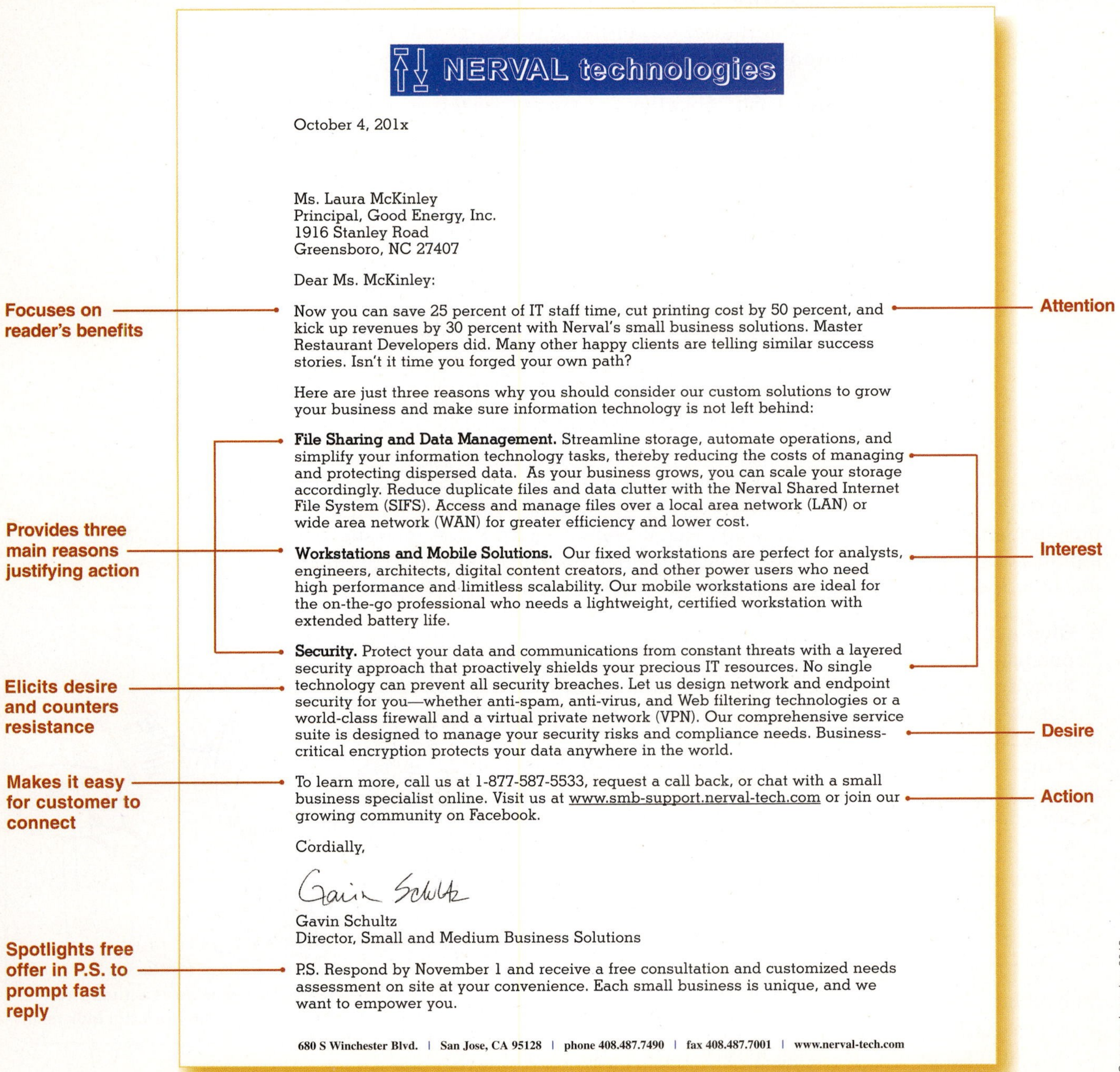
NERVAL technologies

October 4, 201x

Ms. Laura McKinley
Principal, Good Energy, Inc.
1916 Stanley Road
Greensboro, NC 27407

Dear Ms. McKinley:

Now you can save 25 percent of IT staff time, cut printing cost by 50 percent, and kick up revenues by 30 percent with Nerval's small business solutions. Master Restaurant Developers did. Many other happy clients are telling similar success stories. Isn't it time you forged your own path?

Here are just three reasons why you should consider our custom solutions to grow your business and make sure information technology is not left behind:

File Sharing and Data Management. Streamline storage, automate operations, and simplify your information technology tasks, thereby reducing the costs of managing and protecting dispersed data. As your business grows, you can scale your storage accordingly. Reduce duplicate files and data clutter with the Nerval Shared Internet File System (SIFS). Access and manage files over a local area network (LAN) or wide area network (WAN) for greater efficiency and lower cost.

Workstations and Mobile Solutions. Our fixed workstations are perfect for analysts, engineers, architects, digital content creators, and other power users who need high performance and limitless scalability. Our mobile workstations are ideal for the on-the-go professional who needs a lightweight, certified workstation with extended battery life.

Security. Protect your data and communications from constant threats with a layered security approach that proactively shields your precious IT resources. No single technology can prevent all security breaches. Let us design network and endpoint security for you—whether anti-spam, anti-virus, and Web filtering technologies or a world-class firewall and a virtual private network (VPN). Our comprehensive service suite is designed to manage your security risks and compliance needs. Business-critical encryption protects your data anywhere in the world.

To learn more, call us at 1-877-587-5533, request a call back, or chat with a small business specialist online. Visit us at www.smb-support.nerval-tech.com or join our growing community on Facebook.

Cordially,

Gavin Schultz

Gavin Schultz
Director, Small and Medium Business Solutions

P.S. Respond by November 1 and receive a free consultation and customized needs assessment on site at your convenience. Each small business is unique, and we want to empower you.

680 S Winchester Blvd. | San Jose, CA 95128 | phone 408.487.7490 | fax 408.487.7001 | www.nerval-tech.com

Focuses on reader's benefits
Attention
Provides three main reasons justifying action
Interest
Elicits desire and counters resistance
Desire
Makes it easy for customer to connect
Action
Spotlights free offer in P.S. to prompt fast reply

message. Notice that the personalized attention-getter opens with a reader benefit (saving money on IT services) and a testimonial couched in an open-ended suggestive question.The writer develops a rational central selling point (IT services and computing hardware customized to keep step with the changing needs of a growing small to medium-size business) and repeats this selling point in all the components of the letter. Notice, too, how the writer makes it easy for the reader to respond and how the closing pushes for action. This sales letter saves its strongest motivator—a free on-site visit and evaluation—for the high-impact P.S. line.

In developing effective sales messages, some writers may be tempted to cross the line that separates legal from illegal sales tactics. Be sure to check out the Communication Workshop for this chapter to see specific examples of what is legal and what is not.

Writing Successful Online Sales and Marketing Messages

E-mail messages can be used to upsell, cross-sell, cut costs, and attract customers.

To make the best use of limited advertising dollars while reaching an increasingly more targeted segment of potential customers, many businesses are turning to the Internet and to e-mail marketing campaigns in particular. Much like traditional direct mail, e-mail marketing can attract new customers, keep existing ones, encourage future sales, cross-sell, and cut costs. As consumers feel more comfortable and secure with online purchases, they will receive more e-mail sales messages. In fact, growing a healthy 14 percent, online advertising will continue to outpace overall ad spending, predicts Borrell Associates, up to nearly $52 billion. The general ad market is expected to grow only 5 percent to roughly $240 billion. The consultants forecast that the fastest-growing segment of interactive advertising will be local online (think banner ads) as well as any targeted and social media–related advertising.[11]

In the future customers will be more likely to receive ads for products and services they actually use and like, and they can opt out of receiving such marketing e-mails. An eConsultancy study of 1,400 U.S. consumers found that 42 percent prefer to receive ads by e-mail compared to 3 percent who favored social networking sites and only 1 percent who preferred Twitter.[12]

Selling by E-Mail

If you will be writing online sales messages for your organization, try using the following techniques gleaned from the best-performing e-mails. Although much e-marketing dazzles receivers with colorful graphics, we focus on the texts involved in persuasive sales messages.

The first rule of e-marketing is to communicate only with those who have given permission. By sending messages only to "opt-in" folks, you greatly increase your "open rate"—those e-mails that will be opened. E-mail users detest spam. However, receivers are surprisingly receptive to offers tailored specifically for them. Remember that today's customer is somebody—not anybody.

Today's promotional e-mail often comes with eye-catching graphics and a minimum of text. To allow for embedded images, sound, and even video, the e-mail is coded in HTML and can be viewed in an e-mail program or an Internet browser. Software programs make it easy to create e-newsletters for e-mail distribution. Figure 8.6 shows such a promotional message in HTML format by live entertainment company Live Nation. It was sent by e-mail to customers who had bought tickets from Live Nation. They had to create an account and sign up to receive such periodic promotions or e-newsletters. Note that the marketers make it easy for the recipient to unsubscribe.

The principles you have learned to apply to traditional sales messages also work with electronic promotional tools. However, some fundamental differences are obvious when you study Figure 8.6. Online sales messages are much shorter than direct mail, feature colorful graphics, and occasionally even have sound or video clips. They offer a richer experience to readers who can click hyperlinks at will to access content that interests them. When such messages are sent out as ads or periodic e-newsletters, they may not have salutations or closings. Rather, they may resemble Web pages.

Here are a few guidelines that will help you create effective e-mail sales messages:

Send only targeted, not "blanket," mailings. Include something special for a select group.

- **Craft a catchy subject line.** Offer discounts or premiums: *Spring Sale: Buy now and save 20 percent!* Promise solutions to everyday work-related problems. Highlight hot new industry topics. Invite readers to scan a top-ten list of items such as issues, trends, or people.
- **Keep the main information "above the fold."** E-mails should be top heavy. Primary points should appear early in the message so that they capture the reader's attention.

FIGURE 8.6 Live Nation E-Mail Sales Message

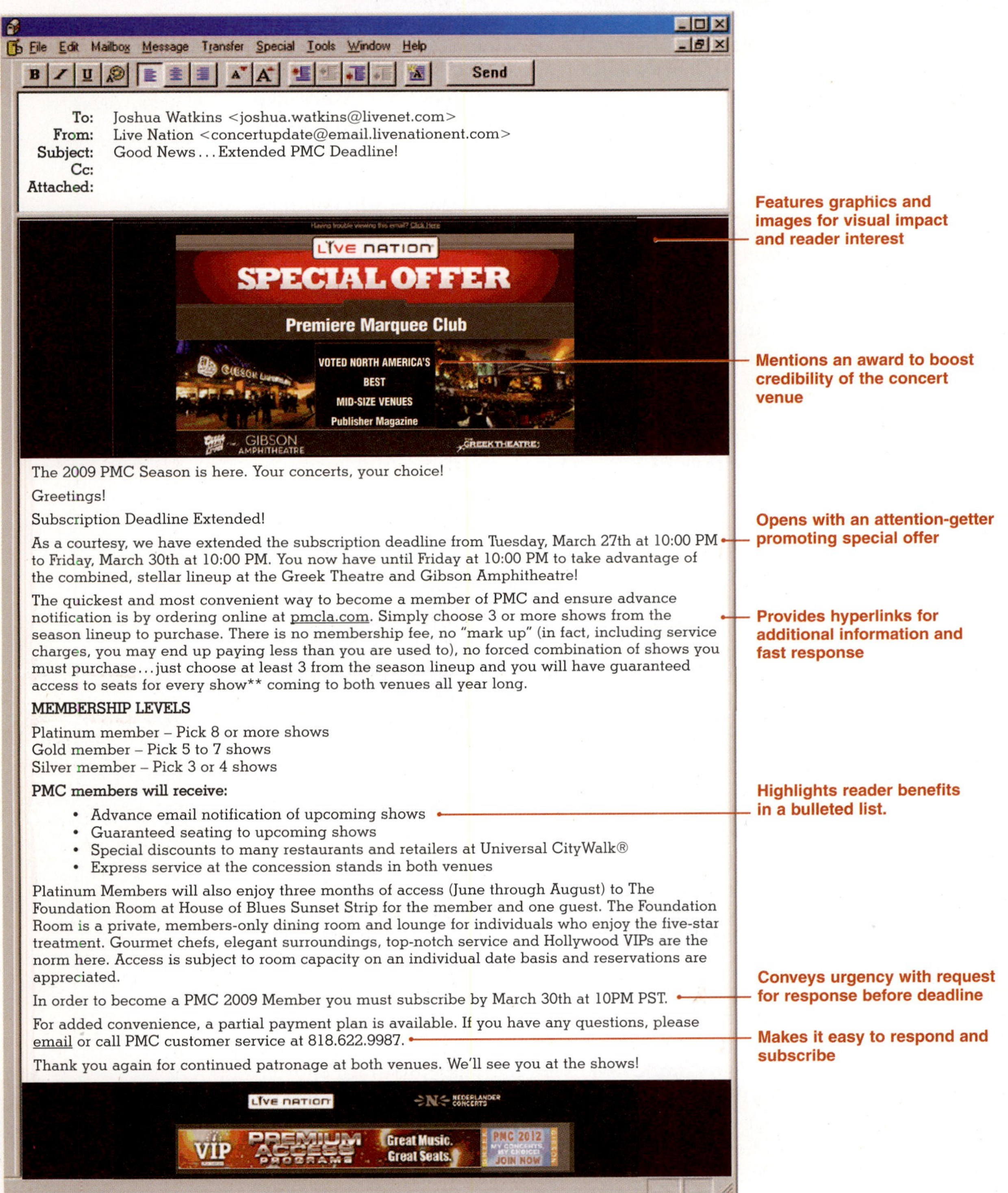
To: Joshua Watkins <joshua.watkins@livenet.com>
From: Live Nation <concertupdate@email.livenationent.com>
Subject: Good News . . . Extended PMC Deadline!
Cc:
Attached:

The 2009 PMC Season is here. Your concerts, your choice!

Greetings!

Subscription Deadline Extended!

As a courtesy, we have extended the subscription deadline from Tuesday, March 27th at 10:00 PM to Friday, March 30th at 10:00 PM. You now have until Friday at 10:00 PM to take advantage of the combined, stellar lineup at the Greek Theatre and Gibson Amphitheatre!

The quickest and most convenient way to become a member of PMC and ensure advance notification is by ordering online at pmcla.com. Simply choose 3 or more shows from the season lineup to purchase. There is no membership fee, no "mark up" (in fact, including service charges, you may end up paying less than you are used to), no forced combination of shows you must purchase . . . just choose at least 3 from the season lineup and you will have guaranteed access to seats for every show** coming to both venues all year long.

MEMBERSHIP LEVELS

Platinum member – Pick 8 or more shows
Gold member – Pick 5 to 7 shows
Silver member – Pick 3 or 4 shows

PMC members will receive:

- Advance email notification of upcoming shows
- Guaranteed seating to upcoming shows
- Special discounts to many restaurants and retailers at Universal CityWalk®
- Express service at the concession stands in both venues

Platinum Members will also enjoy three months of access (June through August) to The Foundation Room at House of Blues Sunset Strip for the member and one guest. The Foundation Room is a private, members-only dining room and lounge for individuals who enjoy the five-star treatment. Gourmet chefs, elegant surroundings, top-notch service and Hollywood VIPs are the norm here. Access is subject to room capacity on an individual date basis and reservations are appreciated.

In order to become a PMC 2009 Member you must subscribe by March 30th at 10PM PST.

For added convenience, a partial payment plan is available. If you have any questions, please email or call PMC customer service at 818.622.9987.

Thank you again for continued patronage at both venues. We'll see you at the shows!

File Edit Mailbox Message Transfer Special Tools Window Help
Send
LIVE NATION
SPECIAL OFFER
Premiere Marquee Club
VOTED NORTH AMERICA'S
BEST
MID-SIZE VENUES
Publisher Magazine
GIBSON AMPHITHEATRE
GREEK THEATRE
LIVE NATION
NEDERLANDER CONCERTS
VIP
PREMIUM ACCESS PROGRAMS
Great Music. Great Seats.
PMC 2012
JOIN NOW
Features graphics and images for visual impact and reader interest
Mentions an award to boost credibility of the concert venue
Opens with an attention-getter promoting special offer
Provides hyperlinks for additional information and fast response
Highlights reader benefits in a bulleted list.
Conveys urgency with request for response before deadline
Makes it easy to respond and subscribe

Courtesy of Live Nation

- **Make the message short, conversational, and focused.** Because on-screen text is taxing to read, be brief. Focus on one or two central selling points only.
- **Convey urgency.** Top-performing e-mails state an offer deadline or demonstrate why the state of the industry demands action on the reader's part. Good messages also tie the product to relevant current events.

- **Sprinkle testimonials throughout the copy.** Consumers' own words are the best sales copy. These comments can serve as callouts or be integrated into the text.
- **Provide a means for opting out.** It's polite and a good business tactic to include a statement that tells receivers how to be removed from the sender's mailing database.

Using Facebook, Blogs, Wikis, and Other Social Media to Connect With Stakeholders

Facebook, blogs, wikis, RSS feeds, and podcasts are some of the social media that companies use to inform and persuade the public, to generate goodwill, and to build a positive brand awareness.

Facebook. Facebook is the Web's dominant social network. Founder and CEO Mark Zuckerberg is confidently predicting a billion Facebook members in the near future. The current number of over 600 million users already represents a huge resource for businesses eager to connect with their customers in unprecedented ways. Nike's three-minute commercial "Write the Future" was first launched on the company's Facebook site. The video went viral, and over one weekend Nike's Facebook fans doubled from 1.6 million to 3.1 million. Soft-drink giant Coca-Cola maintains by far the largest presence on Facebook with more than 12 million fans. The company's vice president of global interactive marketing, Carol Kruse, said that Coca-Cola has made Facebook a central focus of its marketing plans.[13]

A recent study by public relations giant Burson-Marsteller suggests that social media, Facebook foremost among them, offer huge research and brand-building opportunities. Media-savvy businesses face a public that wants to be heard. If they listen to and engage with users, companies can positively affect their customers' beliefs as well as counter potentially negative perceptions.[14] Almost 80 percent of major global companies market their brands and communicate with the public on social media sites.[15] Despite concerns after repeated privacy breaches, to proponents of social media, sites such as Facebook promise advertising that is less obtrusive and more tailored to users' needs than traditional, widely distributed ads.

OFFICE INSIDER
"Facebook is the equivalent to us [of] what TV was for marketers back in the 1960s. It's an integral part of what we do now."
—Davide Grasso, chief marketing officer, Nike Inc.

Blogs. In the right hands, blogs can be powerful marketing tools. Information technology giant Hewlett-Packard invites guest bloggers onto its site as advisors to small businesses, for example. Executives, HP employees, and outside experts discuss a wide range of technology- and company-related topics. Although not overtly pushing a marketing message, ultimately HP wants to generate goodwill; hence, the blogs serve as a public relations tool.[16] Not surprisingly, Burson-Marsteller believes that active and purposeful corporate blogs "provide a useful two-way dialogue for organizations and their stakeholders." The PR firm recommends harnessing the power of multiple social media for their specific benefits because no single social media tool alone is effective.[17] About 33 percent of global companies currently maintain a corporate blog to subtly market their products and develop a brand image.[18]

Wikis. Wikis generally facilitate collaboration inside organizations, but they also do so between companies, thus generating goodwill. A wiki contains digital information available on a Web portal or on a company's protected intranet where visitors can add or edit content. One big advantage of wikis is the ease of information and file sharing. Perhaps the best-known wiki is the online encyclopedia Wikipedia.

In business, wiki users can quickly document and publish a complex process to a group of recipients. Ziba Design of Portland, Oregon, launched what it calls "virtual studios," popular online meeting spots in which the agency and its clients share files, exchange design ideas, and post news.[19] Ziba Design is providing a valuable service to its customers and, in turn, is learning about their needs. You will find out more about wikis as collaboration tools in Chapter 5.

RSS (Really Simple Syndication). RSS (really simple syndication) is yet another tool for keeping customers and business partners up-to-date. Many companies now offer RSS feeds, a format for distributing news or information about recent changes on their Web sites, in wikis, or in blogs. Recipients subscribe to content they want using RSS reader software. Alternatively, they receive news items or articles in their e-mail.[20] The RSS feeds help users to keep up with their favorite Web magazines, Web sites, and blogs. As a promotional tool, this medium can create interest in a company and its products.

Podcasting. Podcasting is emerging as an important Internet marketing tool. Business podcasts are content-rich audio or video files featuring company representatives, business experts, or products and services. They can be distributed by RSS or downloaded from company Web sites and played back on a computer, a smartphone, or an MP3 player.

Facebook, blogs, wikis, RSS, and podcasts are just a few new media tools available to companies for communicating with and persuading the public. Strategic use of these media can enable companies to increase their competitive profiles as well as their awareness of the needs and concerns of their customers.

www.cengagebrain.com

Available with an access code, these eResources will help you prepare for exams:

- **Chapter Review Quizzes**
- **Personal Language Trainer**
- **PowerPoint Slides**
- **Flash Cards**

Summing Up and Looking Forward

The ability to persuade is a powerful and versatile communication tool. In this chapter you learned to apply the indirect strategy in making favor and action requests, creating effective claim and complaint messages, and writing persuasive messages within organizations. This chapter introduced the AIDA strategy, the writing plan for composing sales letters. You also learned techniques for developing successful online sales messages, and how businesses use social media to connect with customers and other stakeholders. In the Communication Workshop at the end of this chapter, you can examine examples of what is legal and what is not in sales letters.

The techniques suggested in this chapter will be useful in many other contexts beyond the writing of business documents. They will come in handy when you apply for a position. Moreover, you will find that organizing your arguments logically is also extremely helpful when expressing ideas orally or any time you must overcome resistance to change.

In coming chapters you will learn how to modify and generalize the techniques of direct and indirect strategies in preparing and writing informal and formal reports and proposals. Nearly all businesspeople today find that they must write an occasional report.

Critical Thinking

1. The word *persuasion* turns some people off. What negative connotations can it have?
2. What motivating impulse may prompt individuals to agree to requests that do not directly benefit themselves or their organizations?
3. Why is it important to know your needs and have documentation when you make requests of superiors?
4. How are direct-mail sales messages and e-mail sales messages similar, and how are they different?
5. **Ethical Issue:** What is puffery, and how can it be justified in marketing messages? Consider the following: Dr. Phil calls himself "America's most trusted relationship counselor." Rush Limbaugh claims to be "America's anchorman." Sony's Cyber-shot camera advertisement says "Make time stand still."

Chapter Review

6. What are the four parts of successful persuasive messages?

7. Why is a written favor request or action request more effective than a face-to-face request?

8. When is persuasion necessary in business messages flowing downward in organizations?

9. When might persuasion be necessary in messages flowing upward?

10. What distinguishes rational, emotional, and dual appeals in persuasion?

11. Name eight or more ways to attract attention in the opening of a sales message.

12. *Recline in your first-class seat and sip a freshly stirred drink while listening to 12 channels of superb audio, or snooze* is an example of what type of persuasive appeal? How does it compare to the following: *Take one of four daily direct flights to Europe on our modern Airbus aircraft, and enjoy the most legroom of any airline. If we are ever late, you will receive coupons for free trips.*

13. Name five techniques for motivating action in the closing of a sales message.

14. Describe the main purposes of using Facebook, business podcasts, blogs, and wikis.

15. What techniques do writers of successful online sales messages use?

Writing Improvement Exercises

Strategies

Your Task. For each of the following situations, check the appropriate writing strategy.

Direct Strategy	Indirect Strategy	
________	________	16. A request from one company to another to verify the previous employment record of a job applicant
________	________	17. An announcement that must convince employees to stop smoking, start exercising, and opt for a healthy diet to lower health care expenses and reduce absenteeism
________	________	18. An e-mail message to employees telling them that the company parking lot will be closed for one week while it is being resurfaced
________	________	19. A letter to a cleaning service demanding a refund for sealing a dirty tiled floor and damaging a fresh paint job
________	________	20. A request for information about a wireless office network
________	________	21. A letter to a grocery store requesting permission to display posters advertising a college fund-raising car wash
________	________	22. A request for a refund of the cost of a computer program that does not perform the functions it was expected to perform
________	________	23. A request for correction of a routine billing error on your company credit card
________	________	24. A letter to the local school board from a nearby convenience store owner expressing disapproval of a proposal allowing Coca-Cola to install vending machines on the school campus
________	________	25. A memo to employees describing the schedule and menu selections of a new mobile catering service

Writing Improvement Cases

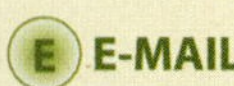

E-MAIL

8.1 Action Request: Protesting Plastic-Wrapped Bananas

Your Task. Analyze the following message and list its weaknesses. If your instructor directs, revise the message. A copy of this e-mail is provided at **www.cengagebrain.com** for revision online.

To: Members of the 7-Eleven Franchise Owners Association of Chicagoland
From: Nicholas Barajas <nicholas.barajas@hotmail.com>
Subject: Can You Believe Plastic-Wrapped Bananas?

Hey, have you heard about this new thing coming at us? As a 7-Eleven franchise owner and member of the 7-Eleven Franchise Owners Association of Chicagoland, I am seriously put off about this move to wrap our bananas in plastic. Sure, it would extend their shelf life to five days. And I know that our customers want yellow—not brown—bananas. But wrapping them in plastic?? I mentioned this at home, and my teenage daughter immediately turned up her nose and said, "A banana wrapped in plastic? Eeeyooo! Do we really need more plastic clogging up the environment?" She's been studying sustainability and said that more plastic packaging is not a sustainable solution to our problem.

I realize that we 7-Eleven franchisees are increasingly dependent on fresh food sales as cigarette sales tank. But plastic-wrapped bananas is going too far, even if the wrapping slows ripening. As members of the 7-Eleven Franchise Owners Association, we have to do something. I think we could insist that our supplier Fresh Del Monte come up with a wrapper that's biodegradable. On the other hand, extending the shelf life of bananas cuts the carbon footprint by cutting down all those deliveries to our stores.

We have a meeting of franchisees coming up on January 20. Let's resist this banana thing!

Nick

1. List at least five weaknesses of this e-mail.

8.2 Persuasive Letter: Seven Cardinal Sins in Food Service

Your Task. Analyze the following poorly written invitation and list its weaknesses. If your instructor directs, revise the letter. A copy of this message is provided at **www.cengagebrain.com** for revision online.

Current date

Ms. Danielle Watkins
The Beverly Hills Hotel
9641 Sunset Boulevard
Beverly Hills, CA 90210

Dear Ms. Watkins:

We know you are a very busy hospitality professional as chef at the Beverly Hills Hotel, but we would like you to make a presentation to the San Francisco chapter of the National Restaurant Association. I was asked to write you since I am program chair.

I heard that you made a good presentation at your local chapter in Los Angeles recently. I think you gave a talk called "Avoiding the Seven Cardinal Sins in Food Service" or something like that. Whatever it was, I'm sure we would like to hear the same or a similar presentation. All restaurant operators are interested in doing what we can to avoid potential problems involving discrimination, safety at work, how we hire people, etc. As you well know, operating a fast-paced restaurant is frustrating—even on a good day. We are all in a gigantic rush from opening the door early in the morning to shutting it again after the last customer has gone. It's a rat race and easy to fall into the trap with food service faults that push a big operation into trouble.

Enclosed please find a list of questions that our members listed. We would like you to talk in the neighborhood of 45 minutes. Our June 10 meeting will be in the Oak Room of the Westin St. Francis Hotel in San Francisco and dinner begins at 7 p.m.

How can we get you to come to San Francisco? We can only offer you an honorarium of $200, but we would pay for any travel expenses. You can expect a large crowd of restaurateurs who are known for hooting and hollering when they hear good stuff! As you can see, we are a rather informal group. Hope you can join us!

Sincerely,

1. List at least five weaknesses of this letter.

8.3 Persuasive Message: Importing T-Shirts From China

Your Task. Analyze the following memo and list its weaknesses. If your instructor directs, revise the message. A copy of this memo is provided at **www.cengagebrain.com** for revision online.

Date: Current
To: Bryanna Mazzetta, Vice President, Marketing
From: Luke Downey, Exhibit Manager
Subject: Possible Change for Saving Money

We always try our best to meet customers and sell Worldclass Trainer equipment at numerous trade shows. But instead of expanding our visits to these trade shows, the company continues to cut back the number that we attend. And we have fewer staff members attending. I know that you have been asking us to find ways to reduce costs, but I don't think we are going about it right.

With increased airfare and hotel costs, my staff has tried to find ways to live within our very tight budget. Yet, we are being asked to find other ways to reduce our costs. I'm currently thinking ahead to the big Las Vegas trade show coming up in September.

One area where we could make a change is in the gift that we give away. In the past we have presented booth visitors with a nine-color T-shirt that is silk-screened and gorgeous. But it comes at a cost of $23 for each and every one of these beauties from a top-name designer. To save money, I suggest that we try a $6 T-shirt made in China, which is reasonably presentable. It's got our name on it, and, after all, folks just use these shirts for workouts. Who cares if it is a fancy silk-screened T-shirt or a functional Chinese one that has "Worldclass Trainer" plastered on the chest? Because we give away 2,000 T-shirts at our largest show, we could save big bucks by dumping the designer shirt. But we have to act quickly. I've enclosed a cheap one for you to see.

Let me know what you think.

1. List at least five weaknesses of this message.

8.4 Favor Request: Facebook Disaster!

Your Task. Analyze the Facebook message requesting a recommendation from a professor, and list its weaknesses. If your instructor directs, revise the message. Decide whether to use Facebook, of which the receiver is a member, or a conventional e-mail to make this request. A copy of this message is provided at **www.cengagebrain.com** for revision online.

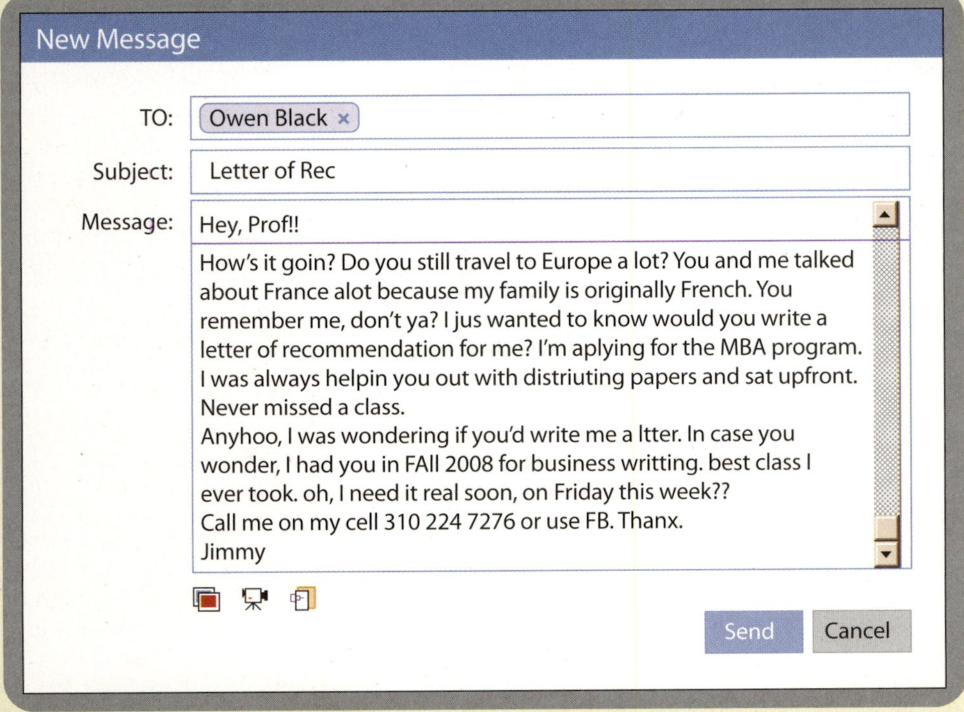
New Message

TO: Owen Black

Subject: Letter of Rec

Message: Hey, Prof!!

How's it goin? Do you still travel to Europe a lot? You and me talked about France alot because my family is originally French. You remember me, don't ya? I jus wanted to know would you write a letter of recommendation for me? I'm aplying for the MBA program. I was always helpin you out with distriuting papers and sat upfront. Never missed a class.
Anyhoo, I was wondering if you'd write me a ltter. In case you wonder, I had you in FAll 2008 for business writting. best class I ever took. oh, I need it real soon, on Friday this week??
Call me on my cell 310 224 7276 or use FB. Thanx.
Jimmy

Send Cancel

1. List at least five weaknesses of this message.

8.5 Sales Letter Analysis

Your Task. Select a one- or two-page sales letter received by you or a friend. (If you are unable to find a sales letter, your instructor may have a collection.) Study the letter and then answer these questions:

a. What techniques were used to capture the reader's attention?

b. Is the opening effective? Explain.

c. What are the central selling points?

d. Does the letter use rational, emotional, or a combination of appeals? Explain.

e. What reader benefits are suggested?

f. How does the letter build interest in the product or service?

g. How is price handled?

h. How does the letter anticipate reader resistance and offer counterarguments?

i. What action is the reader to take? How is the action made easy?

j. What motivators spur the reader to act quickly?

Activities and Cases

E-MAIL

8.6 Persuasive Request: Please Write Me a Letter of Recommendation

As a student, you will need letters of recommendation to find a job, to apply for a scholarship or grant, or to enter graduate school. Naturally, you will consider asking one or several of your college instructors. You talk to a senior you know to find out how to get a busy professor to write you an effective letter. Your friend Paul has the following basic advice for you:

Ask only instructors who have had the opportunity to observe your performance and who may still remember you fondly. Two to five years after you attended a course of 20 to 40 students, your teachers may not recall you at all. Second, contact only professors who can sing your praises. If your grades were lackluster, don't expect a glowing endorsement. Some teachers may flatly refuse to write a recommendation that they cannot make whole-heartedly. Last, make it easy for them to agree to your request and to write a solid letter promptly by following these guidelines:

If possible, make the first request in person. This way, your former instructor will be more likely to remember you. Introduce yourself by name and try to point out something memorable you have done to help your professor recall your performance. Have a copy of the job description, scholarship information, grant requirements, or graduate school application ready. Carry a copy of a recent polished résumé. Alternatively, promise to e-mail these documents and any other information that will help your recommender recall you in a professional setting and understand the nature of the application process. Confirm any agreement by e-mail promptly, and set a firm yet reasonable deadline by which the letter must be received. Don't expect to get a letter if you ask at the last minute. On the other hand, if you give your instructor too much time, he or she may forget. In that case, don't be afraid gently to nudge by e-mail to remind the recommender when the deadline draws closer.

Your Task. Write a persuasive request by e-mail asking your instructor (or supervisor, manager) to write you a letter of recommendation for a job application, grant, scholarship, or graduate school application. Provide all relevant information to make it easy for your reader to write a terrific letter. Explain any potential attachments.

E-MAIL

8.7 Persuasive Favor/Action Request: Inviting an Alumna to Speak

As public relations director for the Business and Accounting Association on your campus, you have been asked to find a keynote speaker for the first meeting of the school year. The owner of a successful local firm, TempHelp4You, is an alumna of your university. You think not only that many students would enjoy learning about how she started her business, but also that some might like to sign up with her temporary help agency. She would need to prepare a 30-minute speech and take questions after the talk. The event will be held from noon until 1:30 p.m. on a date of your choosing in Branford Hall. You can offer her lunch at the event and provide her with a parking permit that she can pick up at the information kiosk at the main entrance to your campus. You need to have her response by a deadline you set.

Your Task. Write a direct approach e-mail to Marion Minter in which you ask her to speak at your club's meeting. Send it to *mminter@temphelp4you.com*.

8.8 Persuasive Favor/Action Request: Asking Beijing to Use Excel

Mario Franchini, regional sales manager for a multinational manufacturer, is always in a hurry and doesn't take the time to write careful messages. As his assistant, you sometimes revise messages for him. Today he asks you to look over his message to Zhu Chen, regional sales manager for the company's prosperous branch in Beijing. On his way out the door, Mario says to you, "Please fix up the following memo. Make it sound better!"

> *Hi there, Zhu! I know you haven't heard from me 4 a while, so don't hit the panic button! I need you to do me a big favor. I'm going to skip the bull and drive right to the point. I need your sales figures to be submitted in Excel spreadsheets. You could hit a home run by zeroing in on the sales for your region and zapping them to us in a better format. We just can't use the ledger account forms you usually send. They may work for your office in Beijing, but they won't fly here in Seattle. I'm counting on you to come through for me by using Excel in submitting your future sales figures. You already have the software available through our home office intranet. Just download it. You will see it's easy as pie to learn. When you send your next quarterly figures at the end of September, I expect to see them in Excel. Chow!*

Your Task. You know that messages to your office from Beijing are usually more formal and often begin with a friendly greeting. You decide to try out your intercultural skills in writing a better favor request. For your boss's signature, revise this message using memo format. After approval, the memo will be faxed.

8.9 Persuasive Favor/Action Request: Borrowing Suits for Interviews

You saw an interesting article describing a Suitable Suits program at Barnard College. Its College of Career Development kept a closet filled with 21 crisp black suits that students could borrow for job interviews. Students made an appointment with the office and agreed to dry clean the suits before returning them. At Barnard the program was paid for with a grant from a prominent financial firm.[21] You think that a Suitable Suits program is worth exploring with your dean.

Your Task. Write a persuasive letter requesting an appointment with your dean to discuss a Suitable Suits program at your school. You don't have all the answers and you are not sure how such a program would operate, but you think the idea is worth discussing. Can you convince the dean to see you?

8.10 Persuasive Claim: Overcharged and Unhappy

As regional manager for an electronics parts manufacturer, you and two other employees attended a conference in Nashville on May 4 and 5. You stayed at the Country Inn because your company recommends that employees use this hotel chain. Generally, your employees have liked their accommodations, and the rates have been within your company's budget. Now, however, you are unhappy with the charges you see on your company's credit statement from Country Inn. When your department's administrative assistant made the reservations, she was assured that you would receive the weekend rates and that a hot breakfast—in the hotel restaurant, the Atrium—would be included in the rate. You hate those cold sweet rolls and instant coffee "continental" breakfasts, especially when you have to leave early and won't get another meal until afternoon. So you and the other two employees went to the restaurant and ordered a hot meal from the menu. When you received the credit statement, though, you see a charge for $114 for three champagne buffet breakfasts in the Atrium on May 5. You hit the ceiling! For one thing, you didn't have a buffet breakfast and certainly no champagne. The three of you got there so early that no buffet had been set up. You ordered pancakes and sausage, and for this you were billed $35 each. You are outraged! What's worse, your company may charge you personally for exceeding the expected rates.

In looking back at this event, you remembered that other guests on your floor were having a "continental" breakfast in a lounge on your floor. Perhaps that's where the hotel expected all guests on the weekend rate to eat. However, your administrative assistant had specifically asked about this matter when she made the reservations, and she was told that you could order breakfast from the menu at the hotel's restaurant.

Your Task. You want to straighten out this matter, and you can't do it by telephone because you suspect that you will need a written record of this entire mess. Write a claim request to Customer Service, Country Inn, Inc., 428 Church Street, Nashville, TN 37219. Should you include a copy of the credit statement showing the charge?

8.11 Persuasive Claim: Botched Print Job

As president of Holiday Travel, you brought a very complex print job to the Jiffy Printers in Brighton, New York. It took almost 15 minutes to explain the particulars of this job to the printer. When you left, you wondered whether all of the instructions would be followed precisely. You even brought in your own special paper, which added to the cost of printing.

When you got the job back (a total of 1,500 sheets of paper) and returned to your office, you discovered a host of problems. One of the pages had 300 copies made on cheap 20-pound paper. This means that the printer must have run out of your special paper and substituted something else for one of the runs. The printer also made copies of your original photos and graphics, so that all the final prints were run from second-generation prints, which reduced the quality of the graphics enormously. What's more, many of the sheets were poorly or improperly cut. In short, the job was unacceptable.

Because you were desperate to complete the job, you allowed the print shop to repeat the job using its paper supply. When you inquired about the cost, the counter person Don was noncommittal. He said you would have to talk to the owner, who worked in the Rochester shop. The repeat print job turned out fairly well, and you paid the full price of $782. But you are unhappy, and Don sensed that Jiffy Printers would not see Holiday Travel again as a customer. He encouraged you to write to the owner and ask for an adjustment.

Your Task. Write a claim letter to Mr. Howard Moscatelli, Jiffy Printers, 3402 South Main Street, Rochester, NY 14634. What is a reasonable claim to make? Do you simply want to register your unhappiness, or do you want a refund? Supply any needed information.

8.12 Persuasive Claim: Honolulu Country Club Gets Scammed on Phony Toner Phoner

Heather W. was new to her job as administrative assistant at the Waialae Country Club in Honolulu. Alone in the office one morning, she answered a phone call from Rick, who said he was the country club's copier contractor. "Hey, look, Babydoll," Rick purred, "the price on the toner you use is about to go way up. I can offer you a great price on this toner if you order right now." Heather knew that the copy machine regularly needed toner, and she thought she should probably go ahead and place the order to save the country club some money. Ten days later two bottles of toner arrived, and Heather was pleased at the perfect timing. The copy machine needed it right away. Three weeks later Maureen, the bookkeeper, called to report a bill from Copy Machine Specialists for $960.43 for two bottles of toner. "What's going on here?" said Maureen. "We don't purchase supplies from this company, and this price is totally off the charts!"[22]

Heather spoke to the manager, Steven Tanaka, who immediately knew what had happened. He blamed himself for not training Heather. "Never, never order anything from a telephone solicitor, no matter how fast-talking or smooth he sounds," warned Steven. He outlined an office policy for future supplies purchases. Only certain people can authorize or finalize a purchase, and purchases require a confirmed price including shipping costs settled in advance. But what to do about this $960.43 bill? The country club had already begun to use the toner, although the current copies were looking faint and streaked.

Your Task. As Steven Tanaka, decide how to respond to this obvious scam. Should you pay the bill? Should you return the unused bottle? Write a persuasive claim to Copy Machine Specialists, 4320 Admiralty Way, Honolulu, HI 96643. Supply any details necessary.

8.13 Persuasive Organizational Messages Flowing Downward: And Now We Want Your Blood!

Companies are increasingly asking employees to take on-site blood tests. Because forcing employees to do so would invade their privacy, companies must persuade them to volunteer. Why should companies bother?

Blood tests are part of health risk assessment. Such assessments are considered the first step toward controlling chronic and expensive health problems such as diabetes, obesity, and tobacco addiction. According to American Healthways, employers using blood tests have seen between a $300 and $1,440 decrease in health care costs per participant, depending on what kind of incentive they offer to participants.

Snap-on, a well-known manufacturer of power and hand tools, began offering blood tests as part of a health assessment program a year ago. Although the first-year sign-up was slow, Snap-on saw a 50 percent increase in sign-ups the following year as employees became familiar with the plan. Employees filled out health risk questionnaires. Then they received the results of their questionnaires so that they could see how their blood work compared with their own assessments. Snap-on assured employees that the company would never see the results. The blood tests, conducted by American Healthways, screened for cholesterol, diabetes, hypertension, body fat, liver function, and nicotine. Employers receive only combined data about their employees.

Even though employees were the benefactors of these blood tests, Snap-on had to offer an incentive to urge them to participate. Employees received a $20 monthly discount on health care premiums for agreeing to the full assessment process, including the blood test.

However, another company found that the penalty approach was more effective in encouraging employee participation. Westell Technologies, which makes broadband communication equipment, charged employees 10 percent higher health care premiums if they refused to take the blood tests. This penalty program resulted in 80 percent participation. Regardless of the method used to encourage participation, any on-site blood testing must be voluntary.[23]

Assume you are part of a group of interns at manufacturer Colman International, which employs 900 people. The director of interns, Christine Davis, is also vice president of Human Resources. One day she calls your group together and says, "Listen up! Colman needs employees to take these blood tests and fill out health risk assessment forms. We know this is a hard sell, but we think it is the right thing to do—not only for employees but also for the company because it will lower our skyrocketing health care costs. So here's what I want you interns to do as a training exercise. Get together and decide what you think is the best way for us to persuade employees to participate. Should we offer incentives or threaten penalties?"

Seeing the blank expressions on your faces, she said, "Oh, you can assume that the company will back whatever decision you make—so long as it's not out of line with what other companies are doing. Once you decide what to do, I want you to prepare a message to employees.

Medical staff from American Healthways will be in the human resources training room to conduct the blood tests on Monday, November 17, through Friday, November 21. Appointments are available between 7:30 a.m. and 5:30 p.m. Employees may sign up for appointments by e-mailing me before November 10 at *cdavis@colman.com* and requesting an appointment time. They will receive a confirmation e-mail stating the date and appointment time."

Your Task. Individually or as a group, prepare two messages. Address one to Christine Davis. Explain what your group decided and justify the rationale for your decisions. Address the second message to Colman employees for the signature of Ms. Davis. Persuade employees to participate in the program. Remember to anticipate objections to your request. How can these objections be overcome? Should you emphasize benefits to the reader or to the company? What direct and indirect benefits can you name? What is the best communication channel for this message? How can you make it easy for receivers to respond?

8.14 Persuasive Organizational Message Flowing Downward: Cutting Overnight Shipping Costs

As office manager of an East Coast software company, write a memo persuading your technicians, engineers, programmers, and other employees to reduce the number of overnight or second-day mail shipments. Your FedEx and other shipping bills have been sky high, and you feel that staff members are overusing these services. You think employees should send messages by e-mail or fax. Sending a zipped file or PDF file as an e-mail attachment costs very little. What's more, a fax costs only about 35 cents a page to most long-distance areas and nothing to local areas. Compare this with $20 or $30 for FedEx service! Whenever possible, staff members should obtain the FedEx account number of the recipient and use it for charging the shipment. If staff members plan ahead and allow enough time, they can use UPS or FedEx ground service, which takes three to five days and is much cheaper. You wonder whether staff members consider whether the recipient is really going to use the message as soon as it arrives. Does it justify an overnight shipment? You would like to reduce overnight delivery services voluntarily by 50 percent over the next two months. Unless a sizable reduction occurs, the CEO threatens severe restrictions in the future.

Your Task. Address your memo to all staff members. What other ways could employees reduce shipping costs?

 **E-MAIL**

8.15 Persuasive Organizational Message Flowing Downward: Supporting Project H.E.L.P.

As employee relations manager of Prudential Financial, one of your tasks is to promote Project H.E.L.P. (Higher Education Learning Program), an on-the-job learning opportunity. Project H.E.L.P. is a combined effort of major corporations and the Newark Unified School District. You must recruit 12 employees who will volunteer as instructors for 50 or more students. The students will spend four hours a week at the Prudential Newark facility earning an average of five units of credit a semester.

This semester the students will be serving in the Claims, Word Processing, Corporate Media Services, Marketing, Communications, Library, and Administrative Support departments. Your task is to convince employees in these departments to volunteer. They will be expected to supervise and instruct the students. In return, employees will receive two hours of release time per week to work with the students. The program has been very successful thus far. School officials, students, and employees alike express satisfaction with the experience and the outcomes.

Your Task. Write a persuasive memo or e-mail with convincing appeals that will bring you 12 volunteers to work with Project H.E.L.P.

 **E-MAIL**

8.16 Persuasive Request Flowing Downward: Please Dump Your Own Trash

In offices across the country, employees are being asked to empty their own desk trash cans instead of having custodial staff empty them. Sure, it sounds like a small thing, but it could make a big difference in custodial fees.

"One of the really labor-intensive parts of custodial work is walking to people's desks and emptying the trash," said Dana Williams, director of facilities for a commission that manages buildings for more than 100 state agencies in Texas. Having employees empty their own waste baskets is expected to save at least $825,000 annually on labor costs in Texas.

In addition to saving money, employees who empty their own trash cans could become more conscious of recycling. At the University of Washington, employees have been emptying their own trash cans for over a decade. The program was started as part of an environmental initiative, but now it is recognized as a money saver. Gene Woodard, the director of building services at the university, admitted that the program was not always enthusiastically welcomed. He said that some employees complained about "stinky trash cans they forgot to empty before a vacation." He noted, however, that such mistakes were made only once.

Dartmouth College recently launched a similar program as part of a sustainability initiative. Psychology professor Catherine Cramer said that she already was recycling nearly all the targeted items. "The only real change will be that I am expected to haul it to some central place myself instead of having custodial staff pick it up. The real goals here, however prettily wrapped in sustainability rhetoric, are rather obvious," she wrote in a university Web site. Professor Cramer questioned the economics of transferring work from the school's lowest-paid workers to higher-paid employees. "While I am certainly not above emptying my own trash," she said, "it's less clear to me that it's a good use of my professional time, especially to make the frequent trips necessitated by a tiny bucket."

In the private sector, companies are also saving money and enhancing recycling by having employees handle their own trash cans. Brewer Science, a semiconductor supplier in Missouri, has had some employees empty their trash cans for many years. Its custodial staff is now a quarter of its original size, and its costs for hauling waste remained the same even as the company doubled in size.

The Business Division at your university has been singled out for a pilot program to determine whether the entire campus will implement a trash-can-emptying program. The primary goal is saving money in the midst of campus-wide budget cuts of 25 percent in every division. The busy dean of the Business Division asks you, his executive assistant, to draft a message for him. He knows that he could simply announce a new trash mandate and demand that faculty members comply. However, he wants to persuade them to buy in to this program so that they comply willingly. He also would like to see his division cited as an example for the entire university.[24]

Your Task. For the signature of Dean Michael Ravera, draft a persuasive e-mail addressed to Business Division faculty members. Ask them to begin emptying their own desk trash cans weekly into the large dumpsters in the basement. Supply additional plausible details to enhance this persuasive message.

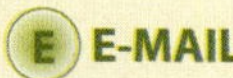

8.17 Persuasive Message Flowing Upward: Dear Boss

In your own work or organization experience, identify a problem for which you have a solution. Should a procedure be altered to improve performance? Would a new or different piece of equipment help you perform your work better? Could some tasks be scheduled more efficiently? Are employees being used most effectively? Could customers be better served by changing something? Do you want to work other hours or perform other tasks? Do you deserve a promotion? Do you have a suggestion to improve profitability?

Your Task. Once you have identified a situation requiring persuasion, write a memo or an e-mail to your boss or organization head. Use actual names and facts. Employ the concepts and techniques in this chapter to help you convince your boss that your idea should prevail. Include concrete examples, anticipate objections, emphasize reader benefits, and end with a specific action to be taken.

8.18 Persuasive Message Flowing Upward: How About a Four-Day Week?

Gas prices are skyrocketing, and many companies and municipalities are switching to a four-day workweek to reduce gas consumption and air pollution. Compressing the workweek into four 10-hour days sounds pretty good to you. You would much prefer having Friday free to schedule medical appointments and take care of family business, in addition to leisurely three-day weekends.

As a manager at Skin Essentials, a mineral-based skin care products and natural cosmetics company, you are convinced that the company's 400 employees could switch to a four-day workweek with many resulting benefits. For one thing, they would save on gasoline and commute time. You know that many cities and companies have already implemented a four-day workweek with considerable success. You took a quick poll of immediate employees and managers and found that 80 percent thought that a four-day workweek was a good idea. One said, "This would be great! Think of what I could save on babysitting and lunches!"

Your Task. With a group of other managers, conduct research on the Web and discuss your findings. What are the advantages of a four-day workweek? What organizations have already tried it? What appeals could be used to persuade management to adopt a four-day workweek? What arguments could be expected, and how would you counter them? Individually or as a group, prepare a one-page persuasive memo addressed to Skin Essentials Management Council. Decide on a goal. Do you want to suggest a pilot study? Meet with management to present your ideas? Start a four-day workweek immediately?

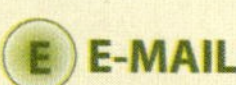

8.19 Persuasive Organizational Message Flowing Upward: An Apple a Day

During the recent economic downturn, Omni Hotels looked for ways to slice expenses. Omni operates 43 luxury hotels and resorts in leading business and leisure destinations across North America. From exceptional golf and spa retreats to dynamic business settings, each Omni showcases the local flavor of the destination while featuring four-diamond services. Omni Hotels ranks in the top three in "Highest in Guest Satisfaction Among Upscale Hotel Chains," according to J. D. Power. One signature amenity it has offered for years is a bowl of free apples in its lobbies. However, the practice of providing apples costs hundreds of thousands of dollars a year. They have to cut costs somewhere, and executives are debating whether to cut out apples as a way to save money with minimum impact on guests.

Omni Hotels prides itself on providing guests with superior service through The Power of One, a service program that provides associates the training and authority to make decisions that exceed the expectations of guests. The entire culture of the hotel provides a positive, supportive environment that rewards associates through the Omni Service Champions program. As an Omni associate, you are disturbed that the hotel is considering giving up its free apples. You hope that executives will find other ways to cut expenses, such as purchasing food in smaller amounts or reducing the hours of its lobby cafes.[25]

Your Task. In the true sense of The Power of One, you decide to express your views to management. Write a persuasive message to Richard Johnson, (*rjohnson@omni.com*), Vice President, Operations, Omni Hotels, 420 Decker Drive, Irving, TX 75062. Should you write a letter or an e-mail? In a separate note to your instructor, explain your rationale for your channel choice and your message strategy.

8.20 Persuasive Organizational Message Flowing Upward: Can We Create Our Own Business Podcasts?

You are working for the small accounting firm, CPA Plus, and your boss, Bradford Trask, wonders whether your company could produce podcasts for its clients without professional help. He doesn't know how podcasting really works, nor what resources or costs would be required. However, he has read about the benefits of providing advice or sending promotional messages to customers who can download them from the company Web site or subscribe to them in a podcast directory.

Conduct some Web research to understand better how podcasting works and what hardware and software are needed. Visit podcast directories such as *Podcast Alley* (**http://www.podcastalley.com**) or Podcast.com (**http://www.podcast.com**) for some ideas, or search iTunes for business and investment podcasts. The Small Business Administration (**http://www.sba.gov**) also offers Web pages devoted to the topic.

Your Task. Consider your accounting firm's needs and its audience. Then write a memo addressed to Bradford Trask that you would send along with a brief e-mail cover message. In your memo argue for or against creating podcasts in house. For professional podcasts listen to *The Wall Street Journal's* The Journal Report or any number of business podcasts on iTunes.

8.21 Persuasive Organizational Message Flowing Upward: Keeping Track of Office Projects

As the supervisor of administrative support at an architectural engineering firm, you serve five project managers. You find it difficult to keep track of what everybody is doing and where they are working. Mike is in New Orleans, Jason just left for Kansas City, Brian is working on a project in St. Louis, and Andrea is completing a job in Houston. With so many people working on projects in various places, it is hard to know where people are and what they are doing. Assigning administrative assistants and tracking their work is difficult. Although digital tools would be ideal, this office has shown no interest in wikis or similar collaborative tools. You decide that you and your managers need a dry erase board in the office to record projects and their statuses. Plain dry erase boards are not expensive at Wal-Mart. But can you persuade the managers to accept this new tool? They are largely independent engineers who are not attuned to following office procedures. Moreover, who will keep the board current?

Your Task. Write a convincing e-mail that persuades managers that your office needs a dry erase board to record weekly projects. Outline the benefits. How can you make it easy for them to buy in to using this new tool? Fill in any details from your imagination, but keep the message fairly simple. Address the first e-mail to *Mike.Kuryia@walters_inc.com.*

8.22 Persuasive Organizational Message Flowing Upward: Training Telecommuters

James Lush arose from bed in his Connecticut home and looked outside to see a heavy snowstorm creating a fairyland of white. But he felt none of the giddiness that usually accompanies a potential snow day. Such days were a gift from heaven when schools closed, businesses shut down, and the world ground to a halt. As an on-and-off telecommuter for many years, he knew that snow days were a thing of the past. These days, work for James Lush and 23.5 million other American employees is no farther than their home offices.[26]

More and more employees are becoming telecommuters. They want to work at home, where they feel they can be more productive and avoid the hassle of driving to work. Some need to telecommute only temporarily, while they take care of family obligations, births, illnesses, or personal problems. Others are highly skilled individuals who can do their work at home as easily as in the office. Businesses definitely see advantages to telecommuting. They don't have to supply office space for workers. What's more, as businesses continue to flatten management structures, bosses no longer have time to micromanage employees. Increasingly, they are leaving workers to their own devices.

But the results have not been totally satisfactory. For one thing, in-house workers resent those who work at home. More important are problems of structure and feedback. Telecommuters don't always have the best work habits, and lack of communication is a major issue. Unless the telecommuter is expert at coordinating projects and leaving instructions, productivity can fizzle. Appreciating the freedom but recognizing that they need guidance, employees are saying, "Push me, but don't leave me out there all alone!"

As the human resources manager at your company, you already have 83 employees who are either full- or part-time telecommuters. With increasing numbers asking to work in remote locations, you decide that workers and their managers must receive training on how to do it effectively. You are considering hiring a consultant to train your prospective telecommuters and their managers. Another possibility is developing an in-house training program.

Your Task. As human resources manager, you must convince Victor Vasquez, vice president, that your company needs a training program for all workers who are currently telecommuting or who plan to do so. Their managers should also receive training. You decide to ask your staff of four to help you gather information. Using the Web, you and your team read several articles on what such training should include. Now you must decide what action you want the vice president to take. Meet with you to discuss a training program? Commit to a budget item for future training? Hire a consultant or agency to come in and conduct training programs? Individually or as a team, write a convincing e-mail to *victor.vasquez@beta.com* that describes the problem, suggests what the training should include, and asks for action by a specific date. Add any reasonable details necessary to build your case.

8.23 Sales Letter: Weighing in at Work

Nearly 68 percent of adults in America are overweight, and 34 percent are obese.[27] In addition to the risks to individuals, obesity costs American companies billions in lost productivity caused by disability, illness, and death.[28] Companies from Wall Street to the Rust Belt are launching or improving programs to help employees lose weight. Union Pacific Railroad is considering giving out pedometers to track workers around the office, as well as dispensing weight loss drugs. Merrill Lynch sponsors Weight Watchers meetings. Caterpillar instituted the Healthy Balance program. It promotes long-term behavioral change and healthier lifestyles for Caterpillar workers. Estimates suggest that employers and employees could save a total of $1,200 a year for each person's medical costs if overweight employees shed their excess pounds.

As a sales representative for Fitness for Life, one of the country's leading fitness operators, you are convinced that your fitness equipment and programs are instrumental in helping people lose weight. With regular exercise at an on-site fitness center, employees lose weight and improve overall health. As employee health improves, absenteeism is reduced and overall productivity increases. What's more, employees love working out before or after work. They make the routine part of their workday, and they often have work buddies who share their fitness regimens.

Although many companies resist spending money to save money, fitness centers need not be large or expensive to be effective. Studies show that moderately sized centers coupled with motivational and training programs yield the greatest success. For just $30,000, Fitness for Life will provide exercise equipment including treadmills, elliptical trainers, exercise bikes, multigyms, and weight machines. Their fitness experts will design a fitness room, set up the equipment, and create appropriate programs. Best of all, the one-time cost is usually offset by cost savings within one year of center installation. For additional fees Fitness for Life can provide fitness consultants for employee fitness assessments. Fitness for Life specialists will also train employees on the proper use of the equipment and clean and manage the facility—for an extra charge, of course.

Your Task. Use the Web to update your obesity statistics. Then prepare a sales letter addressed to Carol Wong, Director, Human Resources, Prophecy Financial Services, 790 Lafayette Boulevard, Bridgeport, CT 06604. Ask for an appointment to meet with her. Send a brochure detailing the products and services that Fitness for Life provides. As an incentive, offer a free fitness assessment for all employees if Prophecy Financial Services installs a fitness facility by December 1.

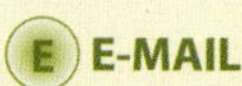

E-MAIL

8.24 E-Mail or Direct Mail Sales Message: Promoting Your Product or Service

Identify a situation in your current job or a previous one in which a sales letter is or was needed. Using suggestions from this chapter, write an appropriate sales message that promotes a product or service. Use actual names, information, and examples. If you have no work experience, imagine a business you would like to start: word processing, pet grooming, car detailing, tutoring, specialty knitting, balloon decorating, delivery service, child care, gardening, lawn care, or something else.

Your Task. Write a sales letter or an online e-mail message selling your product or service to be distributed to your prospective customers. Be sure to tell them how to respond.

You don't need to know HTML to craft a concise and eye-catching online sales message. Try designing it in Microsoft Word and saving it as a Web page (click the Microsoft logo then **Save as** in Word 2007, or go to the **File** menu and select **Save** in Word 2010). Consider adding graphics or photos—either your own or samples borrowed from the Internet. As long as you use them for this assignment and don't publish them online, you are not violating copyright laws.

Video Resources

Video Library 2: *Persuasive Request: Hard Rock Cafe.* This video takes you inside the Hard Rock Cafe where you learn about changes it has undergone in surviving over 30 years in the rough-and-tumble world of hospitality. One problem involves difficulty in maintaining its well-known logo around the world. While watching the video, look for references to the changes taking place and the discussion of brand control.

Your Task. As an assistant in the Hard Rock Corporate Identity Division, you have been asked to draft a persuasive message to be sent to the Edinburgh International Comedy Festival. In doing research, you learned that this festival is one of the three largest comedy festivals in the world, alongside Melbourne Madness Festival and Montreal's Just for Laughs Festival. An annual event, the Edinburgh International Comedy Festival takes over this city in Scotland each autumn with stand-up comedy, cabaret, theater, street performance, film, television, radio, and visual arts programs. Some of the programs raise funds for charity.

The problem is that the festival is staging some of its events at the Hard Rock Cafe, and the festival is using outdated Hard Rock logos at their Web site and in print announcements. Your task is to persuade the Edinburgh International Comedy Festival organizers to stop using the old logos. Explain why it is necessary to use the official Hard Rock logo. Make it easy for them to obtain the official logo. Just search for *Hard Rock Café Logo* and include an appropriate link. Organizers must also sign the logo usage agreement. Organizers may be resistant because they have invested in announcements and Web designs with the old logo. If they don't comply by June 1, Hard Rock attorneys may begin legal actions. However, you need to present this date without making it sound like a threat. Your boss wants this message to develop goodwill, not motivate antagonism. Write a persuasive e-mail message to Edinburgh International Comedy Festival organizer Barry Cook at *bcook@edinburghfestival.com.* Add any reasonable details.

Grammar/Mechanics Checkup—8

Commas 3

Review the Grammar/Mechanics Handbook Sections 2.10–2.15. Then study each of the following statements and insert necessary commas. In the space provided, write the number of commas that you add; write *0* if no commas are needed. Also record the number of the G/M principle(s) illustrated. When you finish, compare your responses with those provided at the end of the book. If your answers differ, study carefully the principles shown in parentheses.

2 (2.12) **Example** Management selected Cynthia Craig, not Michael Crimmins, to be our representative.

______ 1. "Persuasion is not a science" said a wise observer "but an art."

______ 2. The featured speakers are Donna H. Cox PhD and Pam Rankey MBA.

______ 3. The speakers were to focus on persuasion weren't they?

______ 4. Projecting professionalism during your job search helps you stand out in comparison with other candidates and could be the difference between getting the job you want and settling for second best.

______ 5. The more you learn the more you earn.

Review Commas 1, 2, 3

______ 6. As you have probably heard the ability to persuade is a valuable skill that enables you to create instant trust win negotiations and earn what you are worth.

______ 7. Some people think however that persuaders talk too much overpromise and fail to follow through.

______ 8. To fill the open marketing position we hope to hire Geneva Haddock who is known to be an excellent persuader.

______ 9. By the age of 20 the average consumer has been exposed to more than 1 million commercials and is suspicious of tactics people use to sell convince influence or assure.

______ 10. When our Marketing Department launched its campaign we filled 150 orders in the first week; in the second week only 4.

______ 11. In the past five years we have promoted over 20 well-qualified individuals many of whom started in marketing.

______ 12. Carmen Guerro who spoke to our class last week is the author of a book titled *Mastering the Lost Art of Persuasion.*

______ 13. Because nearly all workplace communication involves persuasion not much in the work world gets done without persuading someone to do something.

______ 14. "You can win people over and be more successful" said the author "if you know how to read your audience and how it will respond mentally and emotionally."

______ 15. Whether you are writing a memo corresponding in e-mail delivering a presentation or simply speaking with your boss you must focus on your audience's needs if you want to be a successful persuader.

Editing Challenge—8

As the employee with the best communication skills, you are frequently asked to edit messages. The following persuasive letter has problems with spelling, wordiness, proofreading, comma use, grammar, and other writing techniques you have studied. You may (a) use standard proofreading marks (see Appendix B) to correct the errors here or (b) download the document from **www.cengagebrain.com** and revise at your computer.

Your instructor may ask you to use the **Track Changes** feature in Word to show your editing comments. Turn on **Track Changes** on the **Review** tab. Click **Show Markup**. Place your cursor at an error, click **New Comment**, and key your edit in the bubble box provided. Study the guidelines in the Grammar/Mechanics Handbook as well as the lists of Confusing Words and Frequently Misspelled Words to sharpen your skills.

Current date

Mr. John Kasbekar, General Manager
Crescent Beach & Golf Resort
9891 Gulf Shore Drive
Naples, FL 34108

Dear Mr. Kasbeker:

This letter is to let you know that, even when servers have gave good service some customer's leave no tip. This is a serious problem for we servers in the Lido Beach Club. Many of us have gotten together, and decided to bring the problem, and a possible solution to your attention in this letter.

Restaurants, such as the famous Coach House Restaurant in New York, now add a 15 percent tip to the bill. Other restaurents are printing gratuity guidelines on checks. In fact American Express now provides a calculation feature on it's terminals so that restaurants can chose the tip levels they want printed. In Europe, a service charge of 10 to 15 percent is automatically calculated and added to a check.

Us servers feel that a mandatory tip printed on checks would work good here at the Lido Beach Club. We know that we give good service but some customers forget to tip. By printing a suggested tip on the check we remind them so that they won't forget. A printed mandatory tip also does the math for them which is a advantage for customer's who are not to good with figures.

Printing mandatory tips on checks not only helps customers, but also proves to the staff that you support them in there goal to recieve decent wages for the hard work they do. A few customers might resist but these customers can all ways cross out the printed tip if they wish. If you have any doubts about the plan we could try it for a six-month period, and monitor customers reactions.

We erge you to begin printing a mandatory 15 percent tip on each customers bill. Our American express terminals are all ready equipt to do this. Please let us know your feelings about this proposal because its a serious concern to us.

Sincerely,

Mindy Maldonado

Mindy Maldonado

Communication Workshop

Keeping Sales Letters Legal and Ethical

In promoting products and writing sales letters, be careful about the words you choose and the claims you make. How far can you go in praising and selling your product?

- **Puffery.** In a sales letter, you can write, *Hey, we've got something fantastic! It's the very best product on the market!* Called "puffery," such promotional claims are not taken literally by reasonable consumers.
- **Proving your claims.** If a juice maker touts its product as something close to a magic elixir ("health in a bottle," "antioxidant superpower") that can keep even prostate cancer at bay, it had better have competent and reliable scientific evidence to support the claim. Such a claim goes beyond puffery and requires proof. The Federal Trade Commission (FTC) has accused the makers of Pom Wonderful of hyping the health benefits of the pomegranate juice that sells for five to six times as much as ordinary cranberry juice. The FTC and the Better Business Bureau also considered deceptive a logo used by United Egg Producers ("Animal Care Certified"), which misled consumers by suggesting a higher standard of animal care than was the case. The logo can no longer be used. In a litigious society, marketers who exaggerate are often taken to court.
- **Celebrities.** The unauthorized use of a celebrity's name, likeness, or nickname is not permitted in sales messages. For example, animal rights organization PETA used an image of First Lady Michelle Obama alongside Oprah Winfrey, Tyra Banks, and Carrie Underwood in ads bearing the tagline "Fur-Free and Fabulous!" but failed to secure permission, thus garnering a measured response from the White House that Ms. Obama did not condone the ad. Hip-hop artist 50 Cent settled a lawsuit with Taco Bell under undisclosed terms after suing the chain for allegedly using his persona and trademark to promote new menu items.
- **Misleading statements.** You cannot tell people that they are winners or finalists in a sweepstake unless they actually are. American Family Publishers was found guilty of sending letters tricking people into buying magazine subscription in the belief that they had won $1.1 million. Similarly, it is deceptive to invite unsuspecting consumers to cash a check that will then hook them into entering a legal contract or a subscription. Finally, companies may not misrepresent the nature, characteristics, qualities, or geographic origin of goods or services they are promoting. Most recently, the FTC has warned businesses against making misleading "green" marketing claims and confusing consumers about so-called eco-friendly products.
- **Unwanted merchandise.** If you enclose unsolicited merchandise with a letter, you may not require the receiver to pay for it or return it. Express Publishing, for example, sent a copy of its *Food & Wine Magazine's Cookbook* with a letter inviting recipients to preview the book. "If you don't want to preview the book, simply return the advance notice card within 14 days." Courts, however, have ruled that recipients are allowed to retain, use, or discard any unsolicited merchandise without paying for it or returning it. The FTC is warning the public about companies that advertise free trial periods, chiefly for teeth-whitening products and supplements containing the açaí fruit. The firms later ignore cancellation requests, send unwanted merchandise, and charge customers' credit cards for it.

Career Application. Bring to class at least three sales letters or advertisements that may represent issues described here. What examples of puffery can you identify? Are claims substantiated by reliable evidence? What proof is offered? Do any of your examples include names, images, or nicknames of celebrities? How likely is it that the celebrity authorized this use? Have you ever received unwanted merchandise as part of a sales campaign? What were you expected to do with it?

Endnotes

[1] Walters, H. (2010, February 15). Gates goes nuclear. *BusinessWeek*. Retrieved from http://www.businessweek.com/innovate/next/archives/2010/02/bill_gates_goes_nuclear.html; Bill & Melinda Gates Foundation. (1999–2010). Guiding principles. Retrieved from http://www.gatesfoundation.org/about/Pages/guiding-principles.aspx; Isaacson, W. (1997, January 13). In search of the real Bill Gates. *Time*. Retrieved from http://www.time.com/time/printout/0,8816,1120657,00.html

[2] How to ask for—and get—what you want! (1990, February 1). *Supervision*, p. 11. Retrieved from http://www.allbusiness.com/human-resources/workforce-management/117804-1.html

[3] MacLaughlin, S. (2010, January 11). Direct mail is not dead. Connections [Weblog]. Retrieved from http://forums.blackbaud.com/blogs/connections/archive/2010/01/11/direct-mail-is-not-dead.aspx

[4] Murphy, D. (2010, February 23). Traditional vs. new media channels. Masterful Marketing. Retrieved from http://masterful-marketing.com/marketing-channel-strategy

[5] Direct mail statistics show mailings are still effective. (2011, March 8). The Ballantine Corporation. Retrieved from http://www.ballantine.com/2011/03/08/direct-mail-statistics; Hartong, B. (2011, March). Revitalize your direct mail strategy. *Customer Interaction Solutions*, p. 10. Retrieved from http://proquest.umi.com

[6] DMA releases 2010 response rate trend report. (2010, June 15). Direct Marketing Association. Retrieved from http://www.the-dma.org/cgi/dispannouncements?article=1451; Hartong, B. (2011, March). Revitalize your direct mail strategy. *Customer Interaction Solutions*, p. 10. Retrieved from http://proquest.umi.com

[7] DMA releases 2010 response rate trend report. (2010, June 15). Direct Marketing Association. Retrieved from http://www.the-dma.org/cgi/dispannouncements?article=1451

[8] Direct marketing: Direct mail isn't dead yet. (2010, March 4). B2B Marketing. Retrieved from http://www.b2bmarketing.net/node/12686

[9] Statistical Fact Book. (2011). The Direct Marketing Association. Retrieved from http://www.the-dma.org/cgi/disppressrelease?article=1474

[10] Ziglar, Z. (2004). The features, function and benefits technique. Retrieved from http://www.candogo.com/search/insight?i=3971; Lowenstein, M. (2007, September 24). Make both an emotional and rational appeal to your customers: Inside-out and outside-in commitment and advocacy. CustomerThink.net. Retrieved from http://www.customerthink.com/article/make_emotional_rational_appeal_customers

[11] Borrell Associates. (2010). Borrell Associates' 2011 ad forecast memo. Retrieved from http://www.borrellassociates.com/home

[12] Cited in Rubel, S. (2010, August 9). Hot or not: E-mail marketing vs. social-media marketing. *Advertising Age*. Retrieved from http://adage.com/digital/article?article_id=145285

[13] Stone, B. (2010, September 22). Facebook sells your friends. *BusinessWeek*. Retrieved from http://www.businessweek.com/print/magazine/content/10_40/b4197064860826.htm

[14] The global Fortune 100 social media white paper. (2010). Burson-Marsteller Blog, p. 2. Retrieved from http://www.burson-marsteller.com/Innovation_and_insights/blogs_and_podcasts/BM_Blog/Lists/Posts/Post.aspx?ID=161

[15] Burson-Marsteller Asia-Pacific social media study. (2010, October 28). Retrieved from http://www.burson-marsteller.asia/News/Press%20Releases/2010/Pages/101028_PressRelease.aspx

[16] HP employee business blogs. (2010). Retrieved from http://www.hp.com/phinfo/blogs

[17] The global Fortune 100 social media whitepaper. (2010). Burson-Marsteller Blog. Retrieved from http://www.burson-marsteller.com/Innovation_and_insights/blogs_and_podcasts/BM_Blog/Lists/Posts/Post.aspx?ID=161

[18] Burson-Marsteller Asia-Pacific social media study. (2010, October 28). Retrieved from http://www.burson-marsteller.asia/News/Press%20Releases/2010/Pages/101028_PressRelease.aspx

[19] Based on Asbrand, D. (2007, August 30). Designing a new way to connect. *Microsoft Business & Industry*. Retrieved from http://www.microsoft.com/canada/business/peopleready/business/operations/insight/portals.mspx

[20] Pilgrim, M. (2002, December 18). What is RSS. O'Reilly XML.com. Retrieved from http://www.xml.com/pub/a/2002/12/18/dive-into-xml.html

[21] Suited for employment. (2005, July 15). *The Chronicle of Higher Education*, p. A8.

[22] Based on Fritscher-Porter, K. (2003, June/July). Don't be duped by office supply scam artists. *OfficePro*, pp. 9–10.

[23] Based on Marquez, J. (2006, January 16). On-site blood testing raises privacy issues. *Workplace Management*, p. 10.

[24] Based on Reddy, S. (2010, November 1). Memo to all staff: Dump your trash. *The Wall Street Journal*, p. A4.

[25] Based on Yu, R. (2009, March 13). Hotels take action to pare down food, restaurant expenses. *USA Today*, p. 3D.

[26] Zbar, J. D. (2001, March). Training to telework. *Home Office Computing*, p. 72.

[27] Belluck, P. (2010, January 14). After a longtime rise, obesity rates in U.S. level off, data suggest. *The New York Times*, p. A20(L). Retrieved from http://www.infotrac-college.com/access.html

[28] Know the true cost of obesity: Related lost productivity. (2008, April 1). *Occupational Health Management*. Retrieved from http://www.infotrac-college.com/access.html

Acknowledgments

p. 213 Office Insider cited in Mortensen, K. W. (2006, June 9). The ultra-prosperous study persuasion. EzineArticles. Retrieved from http://ezinearticles.com/?The-Ultra-Prosperous--Study--Persuasion&id=216435

p. 216 Office Insider cited in Rowell, D. M. (2008, January 4). How to create and structure a winning complaint: Being positive and fair gets you more. The Travel Insider. Retrieved from http://thetravelinsider.info/info/howtocomplain2.htm

p. 216 Office Insider based on Sandler, P. M. cited in Power of persuasion. SourceWatch. Retrieved from http://www.sourcewatch.org/index.php?title=Power_of_persuasion

p. 220 Office Insider based on Frey, D. (n. d.). Eight reasons why direct mail is so powerful. Retrieved from http://www.facebook.com/note.php?note_id=10150167591671657&comments

p. 227 Office Insider cited in Stone, B. (2010, September 22). Facebook sells your friends. *Bloomberg Businessweek*. Retrieved from http://www.businessweek.com

UNIT 4

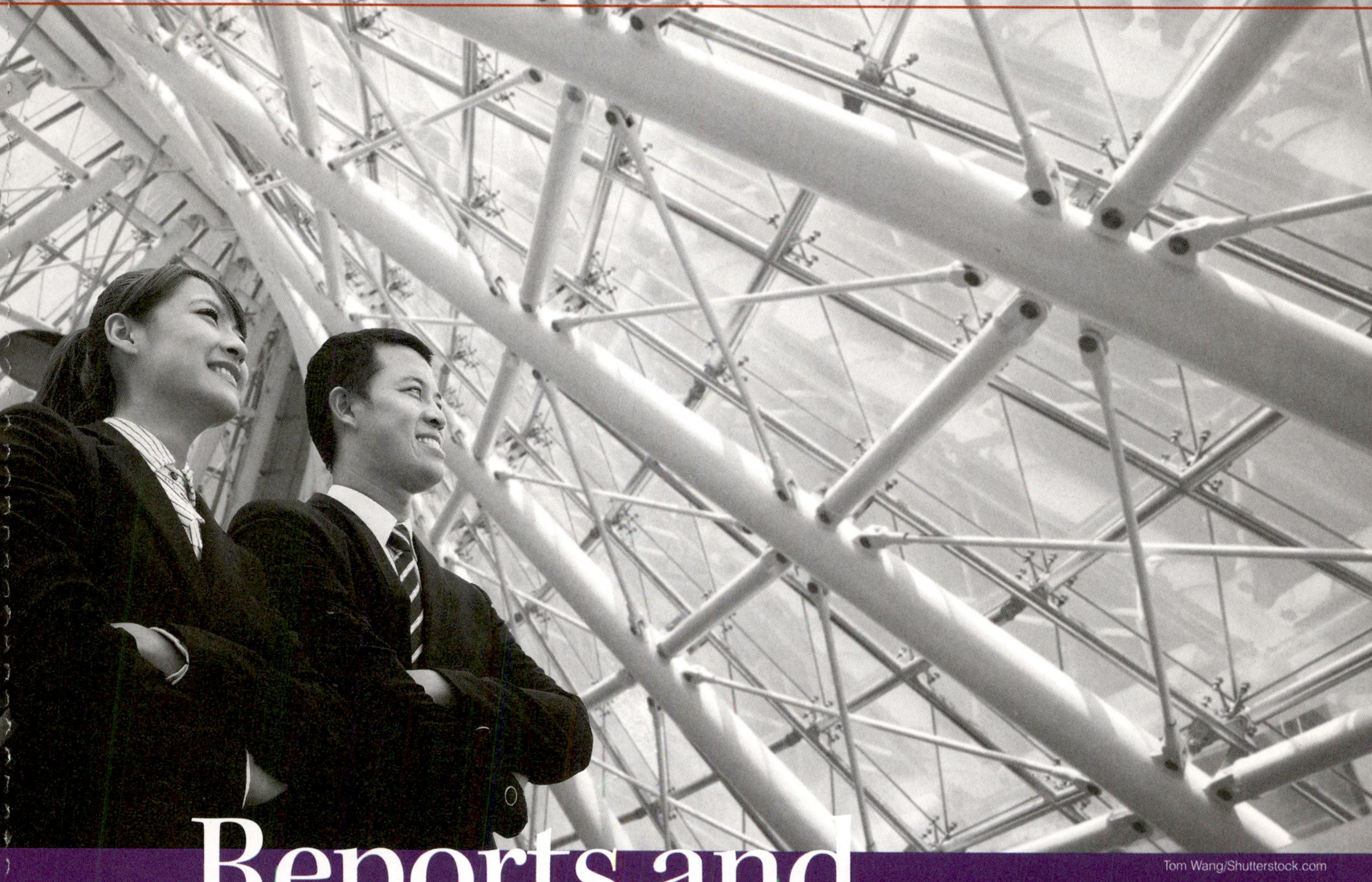

Tom Wang/Shutterstock.com

Reports and Proposals

CHAPTER 9

Informal Reports

Go to
cengagebrain.com
and use your access code to unlock valuable student eResources.

Yuri Arcurs/Shutterstock.com

OBJECTIVES

After studying this chapter, you should be able to

- Understand business report basics, including functions, organizational strategies, and formats.
- Develop informal reports, including determining the problem and purpose, and gathering data.
- Describe six kinds of informal reports.
- Write information and progress reports.
- Create justification/recommendation reports.
- Compose feasibility reports.
- Produce minutes of meetings and summaries of longer publications.
- Adopt an appropriate writing style, be objective, and compose effective headings.

Understanding Reports

Reports are vital to the flow of information in business.

Reports are a fact of life in business today. The larger an organization is, the more important the exchange and flow of information become. Employees report their activities vertically to supervisors. At the same time, the various divisions of a business communicate horizontally with each other through reports. Occasionally, reports are generated for outside organizations or government agencies.

As a business and professional communicator, you will probably have your share of reports to write. With increasing emphasis on performance and profits, businesspeople analyze the pros and cons of problems, studying alternatives and assessing facts, figures, and details. This analysis results in reports.

Informal reports are relatively short (eight or fewer pages) and are usually written in memo or letter format.

Management decisions in many organizations are based on information submitted in the form of reports. Routine reports keep managers informed about completed tasks, projects, and work in progress.

In this chapter we will concentrate on informal reports, the most common type of report in the workplace. These reports tend to be short (usually eight or fewer pages); use letter, memo, or e-mail format; and are personal in tone. You will learn about the functions, strategies, formats, and writing styles of typical business reports. You will also learn to write good reports by examining basic techniques and by analyzing appropriate models.

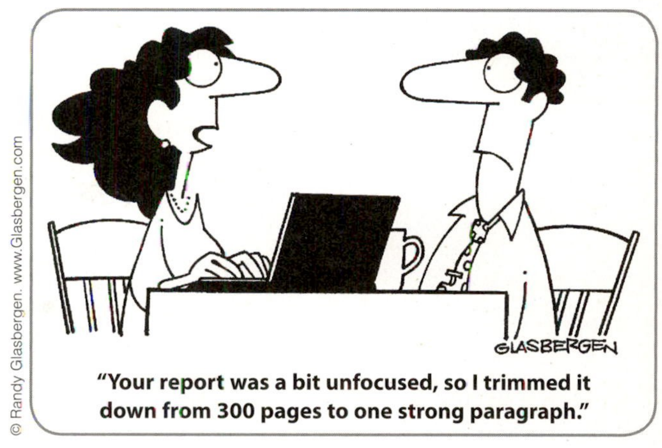

© Randy Glasbergen. www.Glasbergen.com

"Your report was a bit unfocused, so I trimmed it down from 300 pages to one strong paragraph."

Business reports range from informal bulleted lists and half-page trip reports to formal 200-page financial forecasts. Reports may be presented orally in front of a group or electronically on a computer screen. Increasingly, reports are delivered and presented digitally—for instance, as e-mails, PDF (portable document format) files, or electronic slide decks generated with PowerPoint and other presentation software. These files can then be e-mailed, distributed on the company intranet, or posted on the Internet. Hyperlinks tie together content within the document, between associated files, and with Web sources. Such linking adds depth and flexibility to traditional linear texts.

Some reports provide information only; others analyze and make recommendations. Although reports vary in length, content, form, and formality, they all have one or more of the following purposes: *to convey information, answer questions, and solve problems.*

Functions of Reports

In terms of what they do, most reports fit into two broad categories: informational reports and analytical reports.

Informational Reports. Reports that present data without analysis or recommendations are primarily informational. For such reports, writers collect and organize facts, but they do not analyze the facts for readers. A trip report describing an employee's visit to a trade show, for example, presents information. Weekly bulleted status reports distributed by e-mail to a team record the activities of each group member and are shared with supervisors. Other reports that present information without analysis involve routine operations, compliance with regulations, and company policies and procedures.

Informational reports present data without analysis or recommendations.

Analytical reports provide data, analyses, conclusions, and, if requested, recommendations.

Analytical Reports. Reports that provide data or findings, analyses, and conclusions are analytical. Writers may also be asked to supply recommendations. Analytical reports may intend to persuade readers to act or to change their beliefs. Let's say you work for a company that is considering a specific building for a women-only workout center, and you are asked to study the location's suitability. You may have to write a feasibility report—analyzing pros and cons as well as providing a recommendation—that attempts to persuade readers to accept the proposed site.

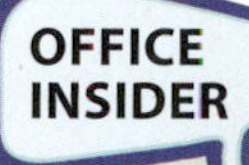

A nonprofit organization polled 120 businesses to find out what type of writing they required of their employees. More than half of the business leaders responded that they "frequently" or "almost always" produce technical reports (59 percent), formal reports (62 percent), and memos and correspondence (70 percent).

—College Board survey of 120 business leaders

Organizational Strategies

Like other business messages, reports may be organized directly or indirectly. The reader's expectations and the content of a report determine its development strategy, as illustrated in Figure 9.1.

Direct Strategy. When the purpose for writing is presented close to the beginning, the organizational strategy is direct. Reports that merely carry information without analysis, such as the letter report shown in Figure 9.2, are usually arranged directly. They open with an introduction, followed by the facts and a summary. In Figure 9.2 the writer explains a legal services plan. The letter report begins with an introduction. Then it presents the facts, which are divided into three subtopics identified by descriptive headings. The letter ends with a summary and a complimentary close. Note that the report was sent as an attachment by e-mail.

Analytical reports may also be organized directly, especially when readers are supportive or are familiar with the topic. Many busy executives prefer this

FIGURE 9.1 Audience Analysis and Report Organization

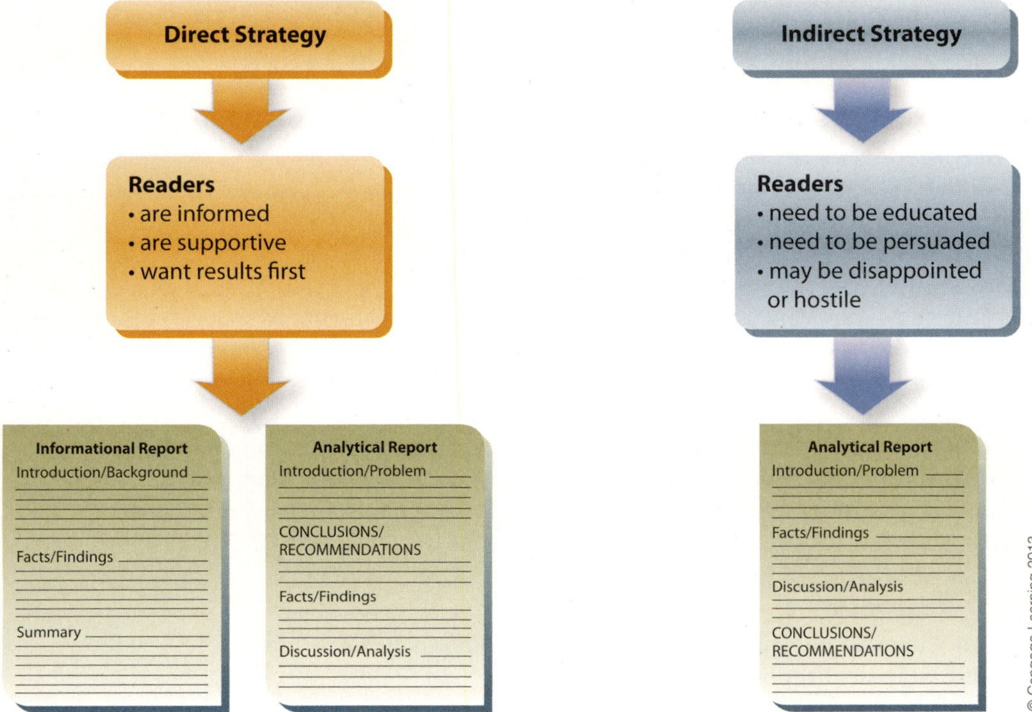

strategy because it gives them the results of the report immediately. They don't have to spend time wading through the facts, findings, discussion, and analyses to get to the two items they are most interested in—the conclusions and recommendations. You should be aware, though, that unless readers are familiar with the topic, they may find the direct strategy confusing. Some readers prefer the indirect strategy because it seems logical and mirrors the way we solve problems.

The indirect strategy is appropriate for analytical reports that seek to persuade or that convey bad news.

Indirect Strategy. When the conclusions and recommendations, if requested, appear at the end of the report, the organizational strategy is indirect. Such reports usually begin with an introduction or description of the problem, followed by facts and interpretation from the writer. They end with conclusions and recommendations. This strategy is helpful when readers are unfamiliar with the problem. It is also useful when readers must be persuaded or when they may be disappointed in or hostile toward the report's findings. The writer is more likely to retain the reader's interest by first explaining, justifying, and analyzing the facts and then making recommendations. This strategy also seems most rational to readers because it follows the normal thought process: problem, alternatives (facts), solution.

Report Formats

How you format a report depends on its length, topic, audience, and purpose.

The format of a report is governed by its length, topic, audience, and purpose. After considering these elements, you will probably choose from among the following four formats.

Letter Format. Use letter format for short (usually eight or fewer pages) informal reports addressed outside an organization. Prepared on a company's letterhead stationery, a letter report contains a date, inside address, salutation, and complimentary close, as shown in Figure 9.2. Although they may carry information

FIGURE 9.2 Informational Report: Letter Format With E-Mail Transmittal

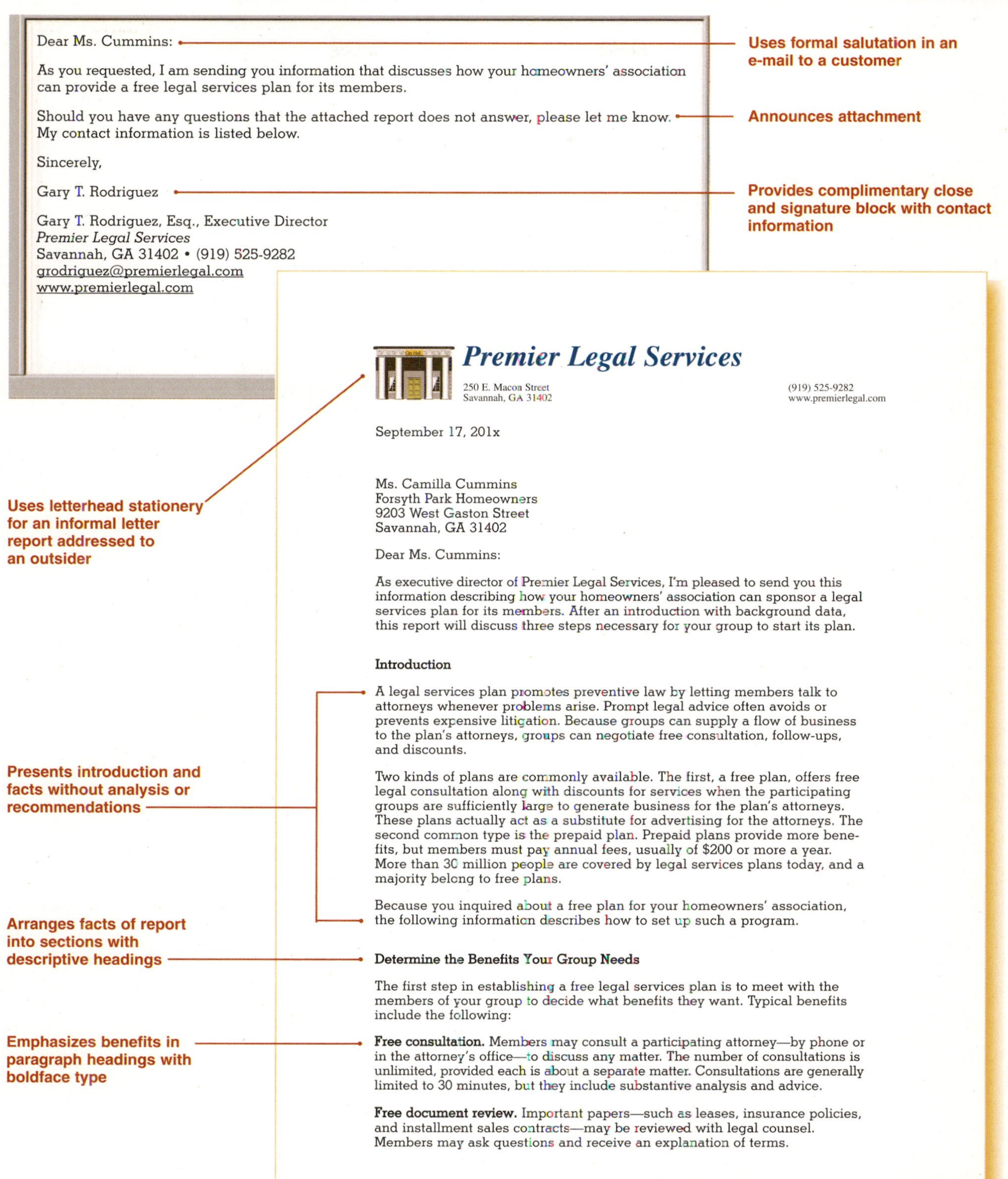

Dear Ms. Cummins:

As you requested, I am sending you information that discusses how your homeowners' association can provide a free legal services plan for its members.

Should you have any questions that the attached report does not answer, please let me know. My contact information is listed below.

Sincerely,

Gary T. Rodriguez

Gary T. Rodriguez, Esq., Executive Director
Premier Legal Services
Savannah, GA 31402 • (919) 525-9282
grodriguez@premierlegal.com
www.premierlegal.com

Premier Legal Services

250 E. Macon Street
Savannah, GA 31402

(919) 525-9282
www.premierlegal.com

September 17, 201x

Ms. Camilla Cummins
Forsyth Park Homeowners
9203 West Gaston Street
Savannah, GA 31402

Dear Ms. Cummins:

As executive director of Premier Legal Services, I'm pleased to send you this information describing how your homeowners' association can sponsor a legal services plan for its members. After an introduction with background data, this report will discuss three steps necessary for your group to start its plan.

Introduction

A legal services plan promotes preventive law by letting members talk to attorneys whenever problems arise. Prompt legal advice often avoids or prevents expensive litigation. Because groups can supply a flow of business to the plan's attorneys, groups can negotiate free consultation, follow-ups, and discounts.

Two kinds of plans are commonly available. The first, a free plan, offers free legal consultation along with discounts for services when the participating groups are sufficiently large to generate business for the plan's attorneys. These plans actually act as a substitute for advertising for the attorneys. The second common type is the prepaid plan. Prepaid plans provide more benefits, but members must pay annual fees, usually of $200 or more a year. More than 30 million people are covered by legal services plans today, and a majority belong to free plans.

Because you inquired about a free plan for your homeowners' association, the following information describes how to set up such a program.

Determine the Benefits Your Group Needs

The first step in establishing a free legal services plan is to meet with the members of your group to decide what benefits they want. Typical benefits include the following:

Free consultation. Members may consult a participating attorney—by phone or in the attorney's office—to discuss any matter. The number of consultations is unlimited, provided each is about a separate matter. Consultations are generally limited to 30 minutes, but they include substantive analysis and advice.

Free document review. Important papers—such as leases, insurance policies, and installment sales contracts—may be reviewed with legal counsel. Members may ask questions and receive an explanation of terms.

Uses formal salutation in an e-mail to a customer
Announces attachment
Provides complimentary close and signature block with contact information
Uses letterhead stationery for an informal letter report addressed to an outsider
Presents introduction and facts without analysis or recommendations
Arranges facts of report into sections with descriptive headings
Emphasizes benefits in paragraph headings with boldface type

similar to that found in correspondence, letter reports usually are longer and show more careful organization than most letters. They also include headings.

Memo and E-Mail Formats. For short informal reports that stay within organizations, the memo format is appropriate. Memo reports begin with essential

FIGURE 9.2 **Informational Report: Letter Format With E-Mail Transmittal (Continued)**

Identifies second and succeeding pages with headings

Ms. Camilla Cummins Page 2 September 17, 201x

Discount on additional services. For more complex matters, participating attorneys will charge members 75 percent of the attorney's normal fee. However, some organizations choose to charge a flat fee for commonly needed services.

Select the Attorneys for Your Plan

Groups with geographically concentrated memberships have an advantage in forming legal plans. These groups can limit the number of participating attorneys and yet provide adequate service. Generally, smaller panels of attorneys are advantageous.

Assemble a list of candidates, inviting them to apply. The best way to compare prices is to have candidates submit their fees. Your group can then compare fee schedules and select the lowest bidder, if price is important. Arrange to interview attorneys in their offices.

After selecting an attorney or a panel, sign a contract. The contract should include the reason for the plan, what the attorney agrees to do, what the group agrees to do, how each side can end the contract, and the signature of both parties. You may also wish to include references to malpractice insurance, assurance that the group will not interfere with the attorney–client relationship, an evaluation form, a grievance procedure, and responsibility for government filings.

Publicize the Plan to Your Members

Members won't use a plan if they don't know about it, and a plan will not be successful if it is unused. Publicity must be vocal and ongoing. Announce it in newsletters, flyers, meetings, and on bulletin boards.

Persistence is the key. All too frequently, leaders of an organization assume that a single announcement is all that's needed. They expect members to see the value of the plan and remember that it is available. Most organization members, though, are not as involved as the leadership. Therefore, it takes more publicity than the leadership usually expects in order to reach and maintain the desired level of awareness.

Summary

A successful free legal services plan involves designing a program, choosing the attorneys, and publicizing the plan. To learn more about these steps or to order a $45 how-to manual, call me at (919) 525-9282.

Sincerely,

Gary T. Rodriguez

Gary T. Rodriguez, Esq.
Executive Director

GTR:pas

Uses parallel side headings for consistency and readability

Includes complimentary close and signature

Tips for Letter Reports

- Use letter format for short informal reports sent to outsiders.
- Organize the facts into divisions with consistent headings.
- Single-space the body.
- Double-space between paragraphs.
- Leave two blank lines above each side heading, if space allows.
- Create side margins of 1 to 1.25 inches.
- Start the date 2 inches from the top or one blank line below the last line of the letterhead.
- Add a second-page heading, if necessary, consisting of the addressee's name, the page number, and the date.

background information, using standard headings: *Date*, *To*, *From*, and *Subject*. Like letter reports, memo reports differ from regular memos in length, use of headings, and deliberate organization. The trip report in Figure 9.3 on next page illustrates the format of an internal memo report. Today, memo reports are rarely distributed in hard copy; rather, they are attached to e-mails or, if short, contained in the body of e-mails.

Manuscript Format. For longer, more formal reports, use the manuscript format. These reports are usually printed on plain paper instead of letterhead stationery or memo forms. They begin with a title followed by systematically displayed headings and subheadings. You will see examples of proposals and formal reports using manuscript formats in Chapter 10.

FIGURE 9.3 **Informational Memo Report: Trip Report With E-Mail Transmittal**

Hi, Dave!

As you requested, I am sending you the attached trip report describing my amazing experiences at the largest IT trade show in the world, the CeBIT.

Thank you for the opportunity. I networked with lots of people and, yes, I had a blast.

Cheers,
Prakash

Prakash Kohli, Developer
Future Engine, Inc.
408.532.3434 Ext. 811
pkohli@future-engine.com
www.future-engine.com

Uses informal form of address

Announces attachment

Uses informal yet professional language

Includes complimentary close and signature block

FUTURE ENGINE, INC.
MEMORANDUM

Date: March 16, 201x
To: David Wong, IT Director
From: Prakash Kohli, Developer PK
Subject: Trip Report from the CeBIT Trade Show in Hannover, Germany

As you know, I attended the huge CeBIT computer show in Hannover on March 4–9. CeBIT runs for six days and attracts almost 500,000 visitors from Germany, Europe, and all over the world to the famed Hannover fairgrounds. It features 27 halls full of technology and people. If you've been to Comdex Las Vegas in the fall, think of a show that is easily five times larger. Let me describe our booth, overall trends, and the contacts I made in Hannover.

Identifies the event

Focuses on three main points

Our Booth at the Fair

Our Future Engine booth spanned two floors. The ground floor had a theater with large screen, demonstration stations, and partners showing their products and services. Upstairs we had tables and chairs for business meetings, press interviews, food, and drinks—along with a cooking area and a dishwasher. Because no one has time to get food elsewhere, we ate in the booth.

Hot Tech Trends

The top story at this year's CeBIT was Green IT. The expo management decided to spotlight a range of topics dealing with Green IT, showcasing many approaches in the Green IT Village in Hall 9. The main focus centered on highly energy-efficient solutions and power-saving technologies and their contribution to climate protection. *Green IT* is the big buzzword now and was even dubbed the "Megatrend of this expo" by the organizer. Only the future will tell whether Green IT will be able to spawn attractive new business areas.

Summarizes key information

Customers and Prospects

CeBIT is a fantastic way to connect with customers and prospects. Sometimes it's a way of meeting people you only knew virtually. In this case, we had three fans of our Internetpakt.com podcast visit us at the booth: Jürgen Schmidt, Karin Richter, and Peter Jahn of MEGAFunk. All three came in our white FE T-Shirts, which could only be rewarded with new black Internetpakt.com T-Shirts. All in all, we made about 600 contacts and have 50 solid leads. The visit was definitely worthwhile and will pay off very soon.

Highlights the value of the trip

In closing, this was probably one of the best conference experiences I've ever had. Customers and partners like FE; they are excited about our technology, and they want more. Some know us because of our software solutions and were surprised to learn that we sell hardware, too (this is a good sign). All want us to grow and gain in influence.

Check out my CeBIT photo gallery on Flickr for some more impressions of our booth at CeBIT with comments. Thank you for giving me the opportunity to network and to experience one of the biggest trade shows in the business. My itemized expenses and receipts are attached.

Shows appreciation and mentions expenses

Tips for Trip Reports

- Use memo format for short informal reports sent within the organization.
- Identify the event (exact date, name, and location) and preview the topics to be discussed.
- Summarize in the body three to five main points that might benefit the reader.
- Itemize your expenses, if requested, on a separate sheet. Mention this in the report.
- Close by expressing appreciation, suggesting action to be taken, or synthesizing the value of the trip or event.

Preprinted Forms. Preprinted forms are often used for repetitive data, such as monthly sales reports, performance appraisals, merchandise inventories, and personnel and financial reports. Standardized headings on these forms save time for the writer. Preprinted forms also make similar information easy to locate and ensure that all necessary information is provided.

Digital Format. Digital media allow writers to produce and distribute reports in electronic form, not in hard copy. With Adobe Acrobat any report can be converted into a PDF document that retains its format and generally cannot be changed. In addition, today's communicators can use programs such as Microsoft's PowerPoint or Apple's Keynote to create electronic presentations in the form of slides. Because the purpose of such presentations is to display concisely the contents of reports, they are often not intended for verbal delivery. Rather, these text-heavy slides are often posted online or e-mailed. When printed out, the stacks of hard-copy slides resemble decks of playing cards, which is why they are called slide decks.

Digital delivery has also changed Microsoft Word documents. This popular program lets users hyperlink multimedia content within the document or with associated text or media files. Thus, such digital documents create a nonlinear reading experience similar to that of browsing Web pages.

Reports in any format can be attached to an e-mail. When using this channel, you will introduce the report and refer clearly to the attachment the body of your e-mail message. Figure 9.2 shows an example of an e-mail transmittal or cover that announces the enclosed letter report and goes to a recipient outside the organization. In Figure 9.3 the writer is sending an internal memo report by e-mail as an attachment within the organization.

Defining the Purpose and Gathering Data

Because business reports are systematic attempts to compile often complex information, answer questions, and solve problems, the best reports are developed methodically. Reports take planning, beginning with defining the project and gathering data. The following guidelines will help you plan your project.

Determining the Problem and Purpose

The first step in writing a report is understanding the problem or assignment clearly. This includes coming up with a statement of purpose. Ask yourself: Am I writing this report to inform, to analyze, to solve a problem, or to persuade? The answer to this question should be a clear, accurate statement identifying your purpose. In informal reports the statement of purpose may be only one sentence; that sentence usually becomes part of the introduction. Notice how the following introductory statement describes the purpose of the report:

This report recommends a plan that provides sales reps with cars to be used in their calls.

Begin the report-writing process by determining your purpose for writing the report.

After writing a statement of purpose, analyze who will read your report. If your report is intended for your immediate supervisors and they are supportive of your project, you need not include extensive details, historical development, definition of terms, or persuasion. Other readers, however, may require background data and persuasive strategies.

The expected audience for your report influences your writing style, research methods, vocabulary, areas of emphasis, and communication strategy. Remember, too, that your audience may consist of more than one set of readers. Reports are often distributed to secondary readers who may need more details than the primary readers.

© REUTERS/Alexander Natruskin /Landov

WORKPLACE IN FOCUS

Though new to the international tourism scene, the Ritz-Carlton, Moscow, has quickly become a hotel hot spot for five-star travelers. Located within walking distance of Red Square and the Kremlin, the 11-story luxury hotel features marble bathrooms, regal amenities, a dedicated concierge staff, and a panoramic view of one of the world's most historic cities. The traditional-styled guest rooms and suites, along with the hotel's ultra-modern rooftop lounge, offer unparalleled comfort with a touch of contemporary ambiance. ***What data sources might an architectural firm use when developing plans for an upscale hotel?***

Gathering Information From Secondary and Primary Sources

One of the most important steps in the process of writing a report is that of gathering information (research). A good report is based on solid, accurate, verifiable facts. This factual information falls into two broad categories: primary and secondary. Primary data result from firsthand experience and observation. Secondary data come from reading what others have experienced or observed and written down. Secondary data are easier and cheaper to gather than primary data, which might involve interviewing large groups or sending out questionnaires. Typical sources of factual information for informal reports include (a) company records; (b) printed material; (c) electronic resources; (d) observation; (e) surveys, questionnaires, and inventories; and (f) interviews.

The facts for reports are often obtained from company records, observation, surveys, interviews, printed material, and electronic resources.

Company Records. Many business reports begin with an analysis of company records and files. From these records you can observe past performance and methods used to solve previous problems. You can collect pertinent facts that will help determine a course of action.

Printed Material. Although we're seeing a steady movement away from print to electronic data, print sources are still the most visible part of most libraries. Much information is available only in print. Print sources include books, newspapers, and periodicals, such as magazines and journals.

Electronic Resources. An extensive source of current and historical information is available electronically by using a computer to connect to the Web, electronic databases, and other online resources. From a personal or office computer you can access storehouses of information provided by the government, newspapers, magazines, nonprofit organizations, and businesses. Business researchers are also using such electronic tools as mailing lists, discussion boards, blogs, Facebook, and Twitter to conduct research. For short, informal reports you will probably find the most usable data in online resources. Chapter 10 gives you more detailed suggestions about online research and electronic research tools.

Observation. In the absence of secondary sources, a logical source of data for many problems lies in personal observation and experience. For example, if you were writing a report on the need for a comprehensive policy on the use of digital media, you might observe how employees are using e-mail and the Web for personal errands or whether they spread potentially damaging company information in their blogs, on Facebook, and in other social media.

Surveys, Questionnaires, and Inventories. If no previously gathered information exists, data from groups of people can be collected most efficiently and economically by using surveys, questionnaires, and inventories. For example, if you were part of a committee investigating the success of an employee carpooling program, you might begin by using a questionnaire.

Interviews provide rich, accurate firsthand information because questions can be explained.

Interviews. Talking with individuals directly concerned with the problem produces excellent firsthand information if published sources are not available. For example, if you are researching whether your company should install wireless technology, you could interview an expert in wireless technology about the pros and cons. Interviews also allow for one-on-one communication, thus giving you an opportunity to explain your questions and ideas in eliciting the most accurate information.

Preparing Informal Reports

OFFICE INSIDER

Two thirds of salaried employees in large American companies have some writing responsibility. "All employees must have writing ability. . . . Manufacturing documentation, operating procedures, reporting problems, lab safety, waste-disposal operations—all have to be crystal clear," said one human resources director.

—College Board survey of 120 business leaders

Informal business reports generally fall into one of six categories. In many instances the boundaries of the categories overlap; distinctions are not always clear-cut. Individual situations, goals, and needs may make one report take on some characteristics of a report in another category. Still, these general categories, presented here in a brief overview, are helpful to beginning writers. Later you will learn how to fully develop each of these reports.

- **Informational reports.** Reports that collect and organize information are informational or investigative. They may record routine activities such as daily, weekly, and monthly reports of sales or profits. They may investigate options, performance, or equipment. Although they provide information, they do not analyze that information. One distinct type of informational report is the trip report. In it business travelers identify the event they attended or the company they visited, objectively summarize three to five main points, and, if requested, itemize their expenses on a separate sheet. Trip reports inform management about new procedures, equipment, trends, and laws or regulations. They may supply information affecting products, operations, and service.
- **Progress reports.** Progress reports monitor the headway of unusual or nonroutine activities. For example, progress reports would keep management informed about a committee's preparations for a trade show 14 months from now. Such reports usually answer three questions: (1) Is the project on schedule? (2) Are corrective measures needed? (3) What activities are next?

Justification/recommendation and feasibility reports attempt to solve problems by presenting data, drawing conclusions, and making recommendations.

- **Justification/recommendation reports.** Justification and recommendation reports are similar to informational reports in that they present information. However, they offer analysis in addition to data. They attempt to solve problems by evaluating options and offering recommendations. These reports are often solicited; that is, the writer has been asked to investigate and report.
- **Feasibility reports.** When a company must decide whether to proceed with a plan of action, it may require a feasibility report. For example, should a company invest thousands of dollars to expand its Web site? A feasibility report would examine the practicality of implementing the proposal.

- **Minutes of meetings.** A record of the proceedings of a meeting is called "the minutes." This record is generally kept by a secretary or recorder. Minutes may be kept for groups that convene regularly, such as clubs, committees, and boards of directors.
- **Summaries.** A summary condenses the primary ideas, conclusions, and recommendations of a longer report or publication. Employees may be asked to write summaries of technical reports. Students may be asked to write summaries of periodical articles or books to sharpen their writing skills. Executive summaries condense long reports such as business plans and proposals.

Minutes of meetings and summaries organize and condense information for quick reading and reference.

Informational Reports

Writers of informational reports provide information without drawing conclusions or making recommendations. Some informational reports are personalized, as illustrated in the letter report shown in Figure 9.2 on pages 251–252. Other informational reports are highly standardized, such as police reports, hospital admittance reports, monthly sales reports, or government regulatory reports. Informational reports generally contain three parts: introduction, body (findings), and conclusion. The body may have many subsections. Consider these suggestions for writing informational reports:

- Explain why you are writing in the introduction.
- Describe what methods and sources were used to gather information and why they are credible.
- Provide any special background information that may be necessary. Preview what is to follow.
- Organize the facts/findings in a logical sequence.
- Consider grouping the facts/findings in one of these patterns: (a) chronological, (b) alphabetical, (c) topical, (d) geographical, (e) journalism style (*who, what, when, where, why*, and *how*), (f) simple to complex, or (g) most to least important. Organizational strategies will be explained in detail in Chapter 10.
- Summarize your findings, synthesize your reactions, suggest action to be taken, or express appreciation in the conclusion.

Organize information chronologically, alphabetically, topically, geographically, journalistically, from simple to complex, or from most to least important.

In the two-page informational report shown in Figure 9.2, Gary Rodriguez responds to an inquiry about prepaid legal services. In the introduction he explains the purpose of the report and previews the organization of the report. In the findings/facts section, he arranges the information topically. He uses the summary to emphasize the three main topics previously discussed.

As the trip report in Figure 9.3 on page 251 demonstrates, internal memo reports in the information-technology industry can be informal if the writer knows that only the boss will read the report. Prakash Kohli organizes his general impressions from the CeBIT trade show by focusing on contacts he established and the main trends that emerged during the annual gathering.

Progress Reports

Continuing projects often require progress reports to describe their status. These reports may be external (telling customers how their projects are advancing) or internal (informing management of the status of activities). Progress reports typically follow this development strategy:

Progress reports tell management whether projects are on schedule.

- Specify in the opening the purpose and nature of the project.
- Provide background information if the audience requires filling in.
- Describe the work completed.
- Explain the work currently in progress, including personnel, activities, methods, and locations.
- Describe current problems and anticipate problems and possible remedies.
- Discuss future activities and provide the expected completion date.

FIGURE 9.4 Progress Report: Memo Format

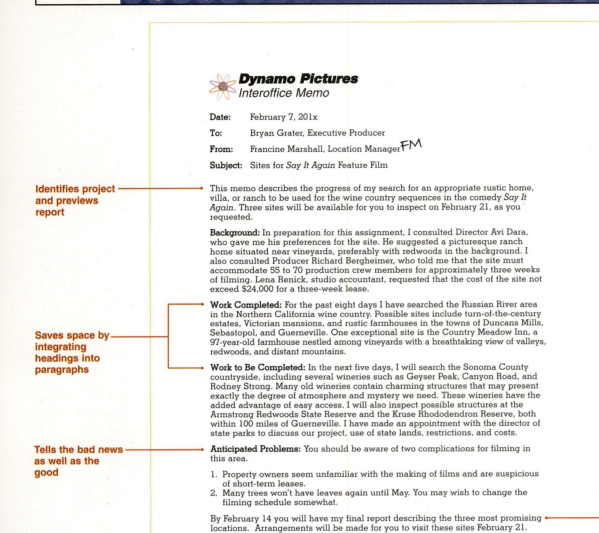

Dynamo Pictures
Interoffice Memo

Date: February 7, 201x

To: Bryan Grater, Executive Producer

From: Francine Marshall, Location Manager FM

Subject: Sites for *Say It Again* Feature Film

Identifies project and previews report

This memo describes the progress of my search for an appropriate rustic home, villa, or ranch to be used for the wine country sequences in the comedy *Say It Again*. Three sites will be available for you to inspect on February 21, as you requested.

Background: In preparation for this assignment, I consulted Director Avi Dara, who gave me his preferences for the site. He suggested a picturesque ranch home situated near vineyards, preferably with redwoods in the background. I also consulted Producer Richard Bergheimer, who told me that the site must accommodate 55 to 70 production crew members for approximately three weeks of filming. Lena Renick, studio accountant, requested that the cost of the site not exceed $24,000 for a three-week lease.

Saves space by integrating headings into paragraphs

Work Completed: For the past eight days I have searched the Russian River area in the Northern California wine country. Possible sites include turn-of-the-century estates, Victorian mansions, and rustic farmhouses in the towns of Duncans Mills, Sebastopol, and Guerneville. One exceptional site is the Country Meadow Inn, a 97-year-old farmhouse nestled among vineyards with a breathtaking view of valleys, redwoods, and distant mountains.

Work to Be Completed: In the next five days, I will search the Sonoma County countryside, including several wineries such as Geyser Peak, Canyon Road, and Rodney Strong. Many old wineries contain charming structures that may present exactly the degree of atmosphere and mystery we need. These wineries have the added advantage of easy access. I will also inspect possible structures at the Armstrong Redwoods State Reserve and the Kruse Rhododendron Reserve, both within 100 miles of Guerneville. I have made an appointment with the director of state parks to discuss our project, use of state lands, restrictions, and costs.

Tells the bad news as well as the good

Anticipated Problems: You should be aware of two complications for filming in this area.

1. Property owners seem unfamiliar with the making of films and are suspicious of short-term leases.
2. Many trees won't have leaves again until May. You may wish to change the filming schedule somewhat.

By February 14 you will have my final report describing the three most promising locations. Arrangements will be made for you to visit these sites February 21.

Concludes by giving completion date and describing what follows

Tips for Writing Progress Reports

- Identify the purpose and nature of the project immediately.
- Supply background information only if the reader must be educated.
- Describe the work completed.
- Discuss the work in progress, including personnel, activities, methods, and locations.
- Identify problems and possible remedies.
- Consider future activities.
- Close by telling the expected date of completion.

As a location manager in the film industry, Francine Marshall frequently writes progress reports, such as the one shown in Figure 9.4. Producers want to be informed of what she is doing, and a phone call does not provide a permanent record. Notice that her progress report identifies the project and provides brief background information. She then explains what has been completed, what is yet to be completed, and what problems she expects.

Justification/Recommendation Reports

Both managers and employees must occasionally write reports that justify or recommend something, such as buying equipment, changing a procedure, hiring an employee, consolidating departments, or investing funds. Large organizations sometimes prescribe how these reports should be organized; they use forms with conventional headings. When you are free to select an organizational plan yourself, however, let your audience and topic determine your choice of the direct or indirect strategy.

Justification/recommendation reports analyze a problem, discuss options, and present a recommendation, solution, or action to be taken.

Direct Strategy. For nonsensitive topics and recommendations that will be agreeable to readers, you can organize directly according to the following sequence:

- In the introduction identify the problem or need briefly.
- Announce the recommendation, solution, or action concisely and with action verbs.
- Explain more fully the benefits of the recommendation or steps necessary to solve the problem.
- Discuss pros, cons, and costs.
- Conclude with a summary specifying the recommendation and necessary action.

Lara Brown, an executive assistant at a large petroleum and mining company in Grand Prairie, Texas, applied the preceding process in writing the recommendation report shown in Figure 9.5. Her boss, the director of Human Resources, asked her to investigate ways to persuade employees to quit smoking. Lara explained that the company had banned smoking many years ago inside the buildings but never tried very hard to get smokers to actually kick their habits. Lara's job was to gather information about the problem and learn how other companies have helped workers stop smoking. The report would go to her boss, but Lara knew he would pass it along to the management council for approval.

If the report were just for her boss, Lara would put her recommendation right up front because she was sure he would support it. But the management council is another story. The managers need to be persuaded because of the costs involved—and because some of them are smokers. Therefore, Lara put the alternative she favored last. To gain credibility, Lara footnoted her sources. She had enough material for a ten-page report, but she kept it to two pages to conform to her company's report policy.

Indirect Strategy. When a reader may oppose a recommendation or when circumstances suggest caution, do not rush to reveal your recommendation. Consider using the following sequence for an indirect approach to your recommendations:

- Refer to the problem in general terms, not to your recommendation, in the subject line.
- Describe the problem or need your recommendation addresses. Use specific examples, supporting statistics, and authoritative quotes to lend credibility to the seriousness of the problem.
- Discuss alternative solutions, beginning with the least likely to succeed.
- Present the most promising alternative (your recommendation) last.
- Show how the advantages of your recommendation outweigh its disadvantages.
- Summarize your recommendation. If appropriate, specify the action it requires.
- Ask for authorization to proceed, if necessary.

Feasibility Reports

Feasibility reports examine the practicality and advisability of following a course of action. They answer this question: Will this plan or proposal work? Feasibility reports typically are internal reports written to advise on matters such as consolidating departments, offering a wellness program to employees, or hiring an outside firm to handle a company's accounting or computing operations. These

Feasibility reports analyze whether a proposal or plan will work.

FIGURE 9.5 Justification/Recommendation Report, Direct Strategy, APA Style

Date: October 11, 201x

To: Gordon McClure, Director, Human Resources

From: Lara Brown, Executive Assistant *LB*

Subject: Smoking Cessation Programs for Employees

At your request, I have examined measures that encourage employees to quit smoking. As company records show, approximately 23 percent of our employees still smoke, despite the antismoking and clean-air policies we adopted in 2012. To collect data for this report, I studied professional and government publications; I also inquired at companies and clinics about stop-smoking programs.

This report presents data describing the significance of the problem, three alternative solutions, and a recommendation based on my investigation.

Significance of Problem: Health Care and Productivity Losses

Employees who smoke are costly to any organization. The following statistics show the effects of smoking for workers and for organizations:

- Absenteeism is 40 to 50 percent greater among smoking employees.
- Accidents are two to three times greater among smokers.
- Bronchitis, lung and heart disease, cancer, and early death are more frequent among smokers (Arhelger, 2012, p. 4).

Although our clean-air policy prohibits smoking in the building, shop, and office, we have done little to encourage employees to stop smoking. Many workers still go outside to smoke at lunch and breaks. Other companies have been far more proactive in their attempts to stop employee smoking. Many companies have found that persuading employees to stop smoking was a decisive factor in reducing their health insurance premiums. Following is a discussion of three common stop-smoking measures tried by other companies, along with a projected cost factor for each (Rindfleisch, 2012, p. 4).

Alternative 1: Literature and Events

The least expensive and easiest stop-smoking measure involves the distribution of literature, such as "The Ten-Step Plan" from Smokefree Enterprises and government pamphlets citing smoking dangers. Some companies have also sponsored events such as the Great American Smoke-Out, a one-day occasion intended to develop group spirit in spurring smokers to quit. "Studies show, however," says one expert, "that literature and company-sponsored events have little permanent effect in helping smokers quit" (Mendel, 2011, p. 108).

Cost: Negligible

Introduces purpose of report, tells method of data collection, and previews organization

Avoids revealing recommendation immediately

Uses headings that combine function and description

Documents data sources for credibility; uses APA style citing author and year in the text

reports may also be written by consultants called in to investigate a problem. The focus in these reports is on the decision: rejecting or proceeding with the proposed option. Because your role is not to persuade the reader to accept the decision, you will want to present the decision immediately. In writing feasibility reports, consider these suggestions:

- Announce your decision immediately.
- Describe the background and problem necessitating the proposal.
- Discuss the benefits of the proposal.
- Describe any problems that may result.
- Calculate the costs associated with the proposal, if appropriate.
- Show the time frame necessary for implementing the proposal.

Claudia Taylor Bernard, human resources manager for a large public accounting firm in Washington, DC, wrote the feasibility report shown

FIGURE 9.5 **(Continued)**

Gordon McClure   October 11, 201x   Page 2

Alternative 2: Stop-Smoking Programs Outside the Workplace

Local clinics provide treatment programs in classes at their centers. Here in Houston we have the Smokers' Treatment Center, ACC Motivation Center, and New-Choice Program for Stopping Smoking. These behavior-modification stop-smoking programs are acknowledged to be more effective than literature distribution or incentive programs. However, studies of companies using off-workplace programs show that many employees fail to attend regularly and do not complete the programs.

Cost: $1,200 per employee, three-month individual program (Your-Choice Program)
$900 per employee, three-month group session

Highlights costs for easy comparison

Alternative 3: Stop-Smoking Programs at the Workplace

Many clinics offer workplace programs with counselors meeting employees in company conference rooms. These programs have the advantage of keeping a firm's employees together so that they develop a group spirit and exert pressure on each other to succeed. The most successful programs are on company premises and also on company time. Employees participating in such programs had a 72 percent greater success record than employees attending the same stop-smoking program at an outside clinic (Honda, 2011, p. 35). A disadvantage of this arrangement, of course, is lost work time—amounting to about two hours a week for three months.

Arranges alternatives so that most effective is last

Cost: $900 per employee, two hours per week of release time for three months

Conclusions and Recommendation

Summarizes findings and ends with specific recommendation

Smokers require discipline, counseling, and professional assistance to kick the nicotine habit, as explained at the American Cancer Society Web site ("Guide to Quitting Smoking," 2012). Workplace stop-smoking programs on company time are more effective than literature, incentives, and off-workplace programs. If our goal is to reduce health care costs and lead our employees to healthful lives, we should invest in a workplace stop-smoking program with release time for smokers. Although the program temporarily reduces productivity, we can expect to recapture that loss in lower health care premiums and healthier employees.

Therefore, I recommend that we begin a stop-smoking treatment program on company premises with two hours per week of release time for participants for three months.

Reveals recommendation only after discussing all alternatives

Lists all references in APA Style

Gordon McClure   October 11, 201x   Page 3

References

Magazine — Arhelger, Z. (2012, November 5). The end of smoking. *The World of Business*, pp. 3–8.

Web site article — Guide to quitting smoking. (2012, October 17). Retrieved from the American Cancer Society Web site: http://www.cancer.org

Journal article, database — Honda, E. M. (2011) Managing anti-smoking campaigns: The case for company programs. *Management Quarterly 32*(2), 29–47. Retrieved from http://search.ebscohost.com/

Book — Mendel, I. A. (2011) *The puff stops here*. Chicago: Science Publications.

Newspaper article — Rindfleisch, T. (2012, December 4). Smoke-free workplaces can help smokers quit, expert says. *Evening Chronicle*, p. 4.

Tips for Memo Reports

- Use memo format for short (eight or fewer pages) informal reports within an organization.
- Create side margins of 1 to 1.25 inches.
- Start the date 2 inches from the top or 1 blank line below the last line of the letterhead.
- Sign your initials on the *From* line.
- Use an informal, conversational style.
- For a receptive audience, put recommendations first.
- For an unreceptive audience, put recommendations last.

FIGURE 9.6 Feasibility Report: Memo Format

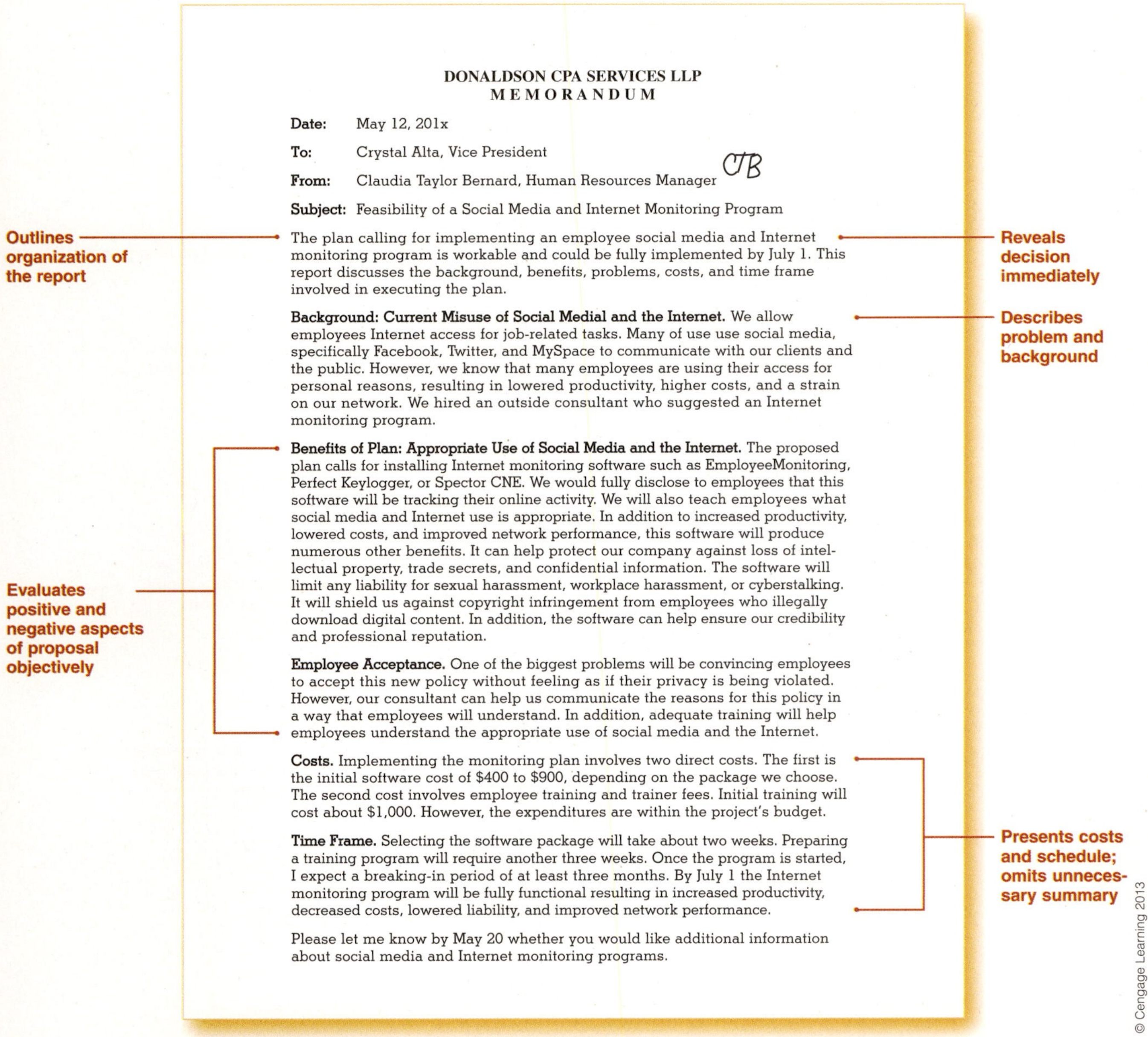

DONALDSON CPA SERVICES LLP
MEMORANDUM

Date: May 12, 201x

To: Crystal Alta, Vice President

From: Claudia Taylor Bernard, Human Resources Manager *CTB*

Subject: Feasibility of a Social Media and Internet Monitoring Program

The plan calling for implementing an employee social media and Internet monitoring program is workable and could be fully implemented by July 1. This report discusses the background, benefits, problems, costs, and time frame involved in executing the plan.

Background: Current Misuse of Social Medial and the Internet. We allow employees Internet access for job-related tasks. Many of use use social media, specifically Facebook, Twitter, and MySpace to communicate with our clients and the public. However, we know that many employees are using their access for personal reasons, resulting in lowered productivity, higher costs, and a strain on our network. We hired an outside consultant who suggested an Internet monitoring program.

Benefits of Plan: Appropriate Use of Social Media and the Internet. The proposed plan calls for installing Internet monitoring software such as EmployeeMonitoring, Perfect Keylogger, or Spector CNE. We would fully disclose to employees that this software will be tracking their online activity. We will also teach employees what social media and Internet use is appropriate. In addition to increased productivity, lowered costs, and improved network performance, this software will produce numerous other benefits. It can help protect our company against loss of intellectual property, trade secrets, and confidential information. The software will limit any liability for sexual harassment, workplace harassment, or cyberstalking. It will shield us against copyright infringement from employees who illegally download digital content. In addition, the software can help ensure our credibility and professional reputation.

Employee Acceptance. One of the biggest problems will be convincing employees to accept this new policy without feeling as if their privacy is being violated. However, our consultant can help us communicate the reasons for this policy in a way that employees will understand. In addition, adequate training will help employees understand the appropriate use of social media and the Internet.

Costs. Implementing the monitoring plan involves two direct costs. The first is the initial software cost of $400 to $900, depending on the package we choose. The second cost involves employee training and trainer fees. Initial training will cost about $1,000. However, the expenditures are within the project's budget.

Time Frame. Selecting the software package will take about two weeks. Preparing a training program will require another three weeks. Once the program is started, I expect a breaking-in period of at least three months. By July 1 the Internet monitoring program will be fully functional resulting in increased productivity, decreased costs, lowered liability, and improved network performance.

Please let me know by May 20 whether you would like additional information about social media and Internet monitoring programs.

Outlines organization of the report
Reveals decision immediately
Describes problem and background
Evaluates positive and negative aspects of proposal objectively
Presents costs and schedule; omits unnecessary summary

in Figure 9.6. Because she discovered that the company was losing time and money as a result of personal social networking and Internet use by employees, she talked with the vice president about the problem. The vice president didn't want Claudia to take time away from her job to investigate what other companies were doing to prevent this type of problem. Instead, she suggested that they hire a consultant to investigate what other companies were doing to prevent or limit personal Internet use. The vice president then wanted to know whether the consultant's plan was feasible. Although Claudia's report is only one page long, it provides all the necessary information: background, benefits, problems, costs, and time frame.

Meeting minutes record summaries of old business, new business, announcements, and reports as well as the precise wording of motions.

Minutes of Meetings

Minutes summarize the proceedings of meetings. Formal, traditional minutes, illustrated in Figure 9.7, are written for large groups and legislative bodies. If you

FIGURE 9.7 Minutes of Meeting

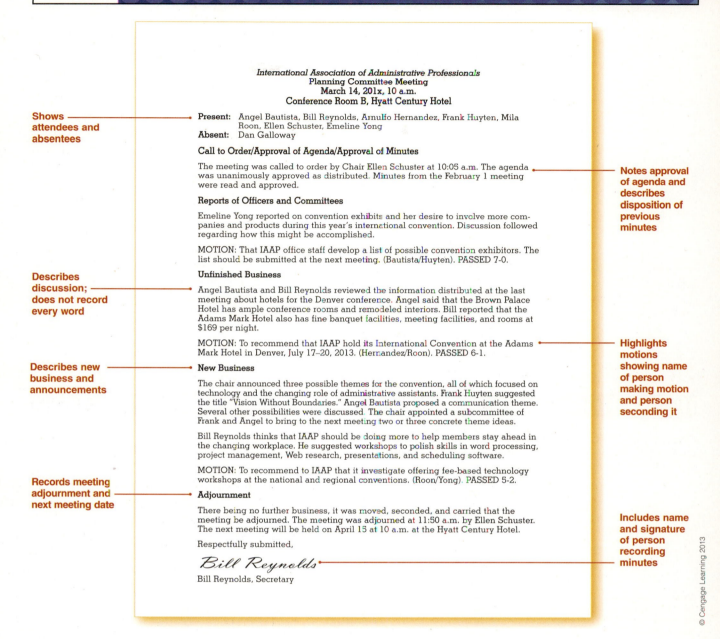

International Association of Administrative Professionals
Planning Committee Meeting
March 14, 201x, 10 a.m.
Conference Room B, Hyatt Century Hotel

Present: Angel Bautista, Bill Reynolds, Arnulfo Hernandez, Frank Huyten, Mila Roon, Ellen Schuster, Emeline Yong
Absent: Dan Galloway

Shows attendees and absentees

Call to Order/Approval of Agenda/Approval of Minutes

The meeting was called to order by Chair Ellen Schuster at 10:05 a.m. The agenda was unanimously approved as distributed. Minutes from the February 1 meeting were read and approved.

Notes approval of agenda and describes disposition of previous minutes

Reports of Officers and Committees

Emeline Yong reported on convention exhibits and her desire to involve more companies and products during this year's international convention. Discussion followed regarding how this might be accomplished.

MOTION: That IAAP office staff develop a list of possible convention exhibitors. The list should be submitted at the next meeting. (Bautista/Huyten). PASSED 7-0.

Unfinished Business

Describes discussion; does not record every word

Angel Bautista and Bill Reynolds reviewed the information distributed at the last meeting about hotels for the Denver conference. Angel said that the Brown Palace Hotel has ample conference rooms and remodeled interiors. Bill reported that the Adams Mark Hotel also has fine banquet facilities, meeting facilities, and rooms at $169 per night.

MOTION: To recommend that IAAP hold its International Convention at the Adams Mark Hotel in Denver, July 17–20, 2013. (Hernandez/Roon). PASSED 6-1.

Highlights motions showing name of person making motion and person seconding it

Describes new business and announcements

New Business

The chair announced three possible themes for the convention, all of which focused on technology and the changing role of administrative assistants. Frank Huyten suggested the title "Vision Without Boundaries." Angel Bautista proposed a communication theme. Several other possibilities were discussed. The chair appointed a subcommittee of Frank and Angel to bring to the next meeting two or three concrete theme ideas.

Bill Reynolds thinks that IAAP should be doing more to help members stay ahead in the changing workplace. He suggested workshops to polish skills in word processing, project management, Web research, presentations, and scheduling software.

MOTION: To recommend to IAAP that it investigate offering fee-based technology workshops at the national and regional conventions. (Roon/Yong). PASSED 5-2.

Records meeting adjournment and next meeting date

Adjournment

There being no further business, it was moved, seconded, and carried that the meeting be adjourned. The meeting was adjourned at 11:50 a.m. by Ellen Schuster. The next meeting will be held on April 15 at 10 a.m. at the Hyatt Century Hotel.

Respectfully submitted,

Bill Reynolds

Bill Reynolds, Secretary

Includes name and signature of person recording minutes

are the secretary or recorder of a meeting, you will want to write minutes that do the following:

- Provide the name of the group, as well as the date, time, and place of the meeting.
- Identify the names of attendees and absentees, if appropriate.
- State whether the previous minutes were approved or revised.
- Record old business, new business, announcements, and reports.
- Include the precise wording of motions; record the vote and action taken.
- Conclude with the name and signature of the person recording the minutes.

"Here are the minutes of our last meeting. Some events have been fictionalized for dramatic purposes."

Notice in Figure 9.7 that the secretary, Bill Reynolds, tries to summarize discussions rather than capture every comment. However, when a motion is made, he records it verbatim. He also shows in parentheses the name of the individual making the motion and the person who seconded it. By using all capital letters for *MOTION* and *PASSED*, he makes these important items stand out for easy reference.

Informal minutes are usually shorter and easier to read than formal minutes. They may be formatted with three categories: summaries of topics discussed, decisions reached, and action items (showing the action item, the person responsible, and the due date).

Although the format of informal minutes and action items varies, spreadsheets or tables work well for readability as Figure 9.8 indicates. The executives of a property management company worried about the cost, effectiveness, and environmental impact of pest control measures for a large number of condominiums and apartment buildings. Osborn Property Management held a meeting, and several attendees assumed research tasks as outlined in Figure 9.8.

Summaries

A summary condenses the primary ideas, conclusions, and recommendations of a longer publication.

A summary compresses the main points from a book, report, article, Web site, meeting, or convention. A summary saves time because it can reduce a report or article 85 to 90 percent. Employees are sometimes asked to write summaries that condense technical reports, periodical articles, or books so that their staffs or superiors may grasp the main ideas quickly. Students may be asked to write summaries of articles, chapters, or books to sharpen their writing skills and to

FIGURE 9.8 Action Item List for Meeting Minutes

Organizations may include a list of action items as part of their minutes so that individuals know what task has been assigned to whom. This list can later be used to track task completion. Osborn Property Management is investigating pest control methods for a large group of apartments and condominiums. The following table was generated in Microsoft Excel to allow easy sorting by due date or other variables.

OSBORN PROPERTY MANAGEMENT
TERMITE ABATEMENT ACTION ITEMS / OPEN ISSUES

Sorted by due date — *Last Update 6/14/12 6:00 p.m. Hassan*

No.	Item	Date	Who	Status	Date completed
1	Review traditional methods of termite abatement, their pros/cons.	6/15/12	Erin to summarize findings	Done Will be distributed at meeting on 6/20	6/4/12
2	Investigate alternative pest control methods and their efficacy in large apartment complexes.	6/15/12	Bob	Done Will report on 6/20	6/14/12
3	Contact at least two independent research chemists about Vikane residue.	6/15/12	Erin	Waiting for callback	
4	Research consumer information and resources.	6/15/12	Hassan		
5	Search for government sources and information.	6/15/12	Chris	CLOSED: none found	6/10/12
6	Call at least five termite control companies for bids; request large-volume discounts, long term.	7/2/12	Chris		

Shows numbered action items with descriptions

Lists names of members responsible for tasks

Indicates dates when tasks were assigned

Identifies dates when tasks were completed

confirm their knowledge of reading assignments. To prepare a helpful summary, include some or all of the following points:

- Present the goal or purpose of the document being summarized. Why was it written?
- Highlight the research methods (if appropriate), findings, conclusions, and recommendations.
- Omit illustrations, examples, and references.
- Organize the readability by including headings and bulleted or enumerated lists.
- Paraphrase from the article. Do not copy passages.
- Include your reactions or an overall evaluation of the document if asked to do so.

In Figure 9.9 executive assistant Alicia Menendez prepared an article summary for her boss, Amir Nasarian. He started a small but growing U.S. sports equipment company. Because he hopes to expand his market to England, he has

FIGURE 9.9 **Article Summary**

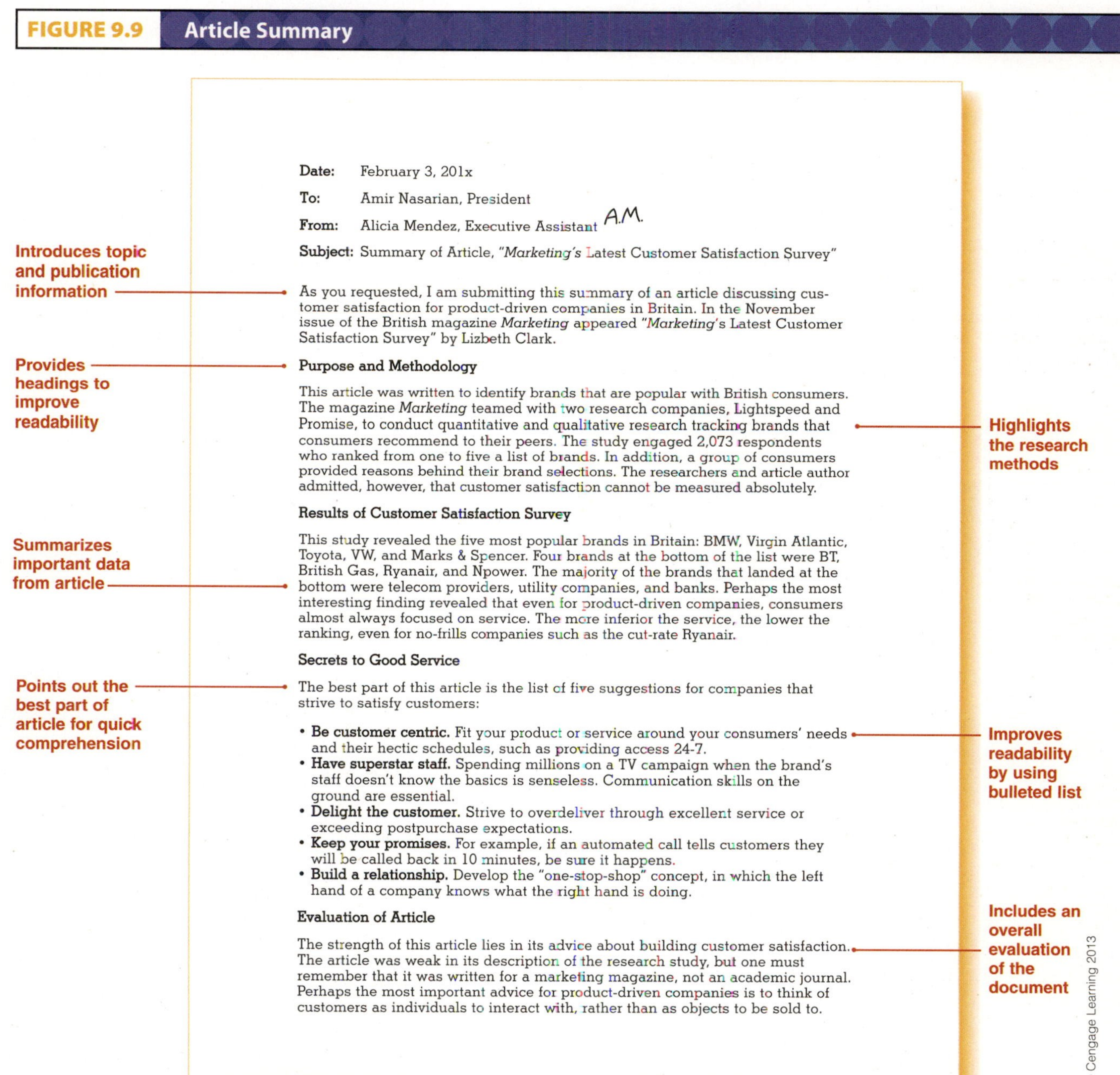

Introduces topic and publication information
Provides headings to improve readability
Summarizes important data from article
Points out the best part of article for quick comprehension
Highlights the research methods
Improves readability by using bulleted list
Includes an overall evaluation of the document

Date: February 3, 201x

To: Amir Nasarian, President

From: Alicia Mendez, Executive Assistant A.M.

Subject: Summary of Article, "*Marketing's* Latest Customer Satisfaction Survey"

As you requested, I am submitting this summary of an article discussing customer satisfaction for product-driven companies in Britain. In the November issue of the British magazine *Marketing* appeared "*Marketing*'s Latest Customer Satisfaction Survey" by Lizbeth Clark.

Purpose and Methodology

This article was written to identify brands that are popular with British consumers. The magazine *Marketing* teamed with two research companies, Lightspeed and Promise, to conduct quantitative and qualitative research tracking brands that consumers recommend to their peers. The study engaged 2,073 respondents who ranked from one to five a list of brands. In addition, a group of consumers provided reasons behind their brand selections. The researchers and article author admitted, however, that customer satisfaction cannot be measured absolutely.

Results of Customer Satisfaction Survey

This study revealed the five most popular brands in Britain: BMW, Virgin Atlantic, Toyota, VW, and Marks & Spencer. Four brands at the bottom of the list were BT, British Gas, Ryanair, and Npower. The majority of the brands that landed at the bottom were telecom providers, utility companies, and banks. Perhaps the most interesting finding revealed that even for product-driven companies, consumers almost always focused on service. The more inferior the service, the lower the ranking, even for no-frills companies such as the cut-rate Ryanair.

Secrets to Good Service

The best part of this article is the list of five suggestions for companies that strive to satisfy customers:

- **Be customer centric.** Fit your product or service around your consumers' needs and their hectic schedules, such as providing access 24-7.
- **Have superstar staff.** Spending millions on a TV campaign when the brand's staff doesn't know the basics is senseless. Communication skills on the ground are essential.
- **Delight the customer.** Strive to overdeliver through excellent service or exceeding postpurchase expectations.
- **Keep your promises.** For example, if an automated call tells customers they will be called back in 10 minutes, be sure it happens.
- **Build a relationship.** Develop the "one-stop-shop" concept, in which the left hand of a company knows what the right hand is doing.

Evaluation of Article

The strength of this article lies in its advice about building customer satisfaction. The article was weak in its description of the research study, but one must remember that it was written for a marketing magazine, not an academic journal. Perhaps the most important advice for product-driven companies is to think of customers as individuals to interact with, rather than as objects to be sold to.

asked her to locate articles involving brands and customer service in England. He is particularly interested in customer satisfaction and how to build brand recognition. Notice in her summary that she selects points that she thinks would be most interesting to Mr. Nasarian. She uses headings to improve readability, and she concludes with her reactions and overall evaluation.

An executive summary presents an overview of a longer report or proposal and focuses on key points.

An *executive summary* summarizes a long report, proposal, or business plan. It concentrates on what management needs to know from a longer report. An example of an executive summary appears in Chapter 10 on page 308 as part of the long report.

Choosing a Report Writing Style and Creating Headings

In previous chapters you have learned that the tone and style we adopt in business documents matter as much as the message we convey. Not surprisingly, reports require an appropriate writing style. They also benefit from objectivity and effective headings.

Adopting an Appropriate Writing Style

An informal writing style includes first-person pronouns, contractions, active-voice verbs, short sentences, and familiar words.

Like other business messages, reports can range from informal to formal, depending on their purpose, audience, and setting. Research reports from consultants to their clients tend to be rather formal. Such reports must project objectivity, authority, and impartiality.

In this chapter we are most concerned with an informal writing style. Your short reports will probably be written for familiar audiences and involve noncontroversial topics. You may use first-person pronouns (*I, we, me, my, us, our*) and contractions (*I'm, it's, let's, can't, didn't*). You will emphasize active-voice verbs and strive for shorter sentences using familiar words. For a comparison of informal and formal writing styles, see Figure 9.10.

Whether you choose a formal or informal writing style, remember to apply the writing techniques you have learned in earlier chapters. The same techniques you have been using to compose effective memos, letters, and e-mails apply to developing outstanding reports. Like all business documents, business reports must be

FIGURE 9.10 Report-Writing Styles

	Informal Writing Style	Formal Writing Style
Use	• Short, routine reports • Reports for familiar audiences • Noncontroversial reports • Most reports to company insiders	• Theses • Research studies • Controversial or complex reports (especially to outsiders)
Effect	• Feeling of warmth • Increased personal involvement • Enhanced closeness	• Impression of objectivity, accuracy • Projection of professionalism, fairness • Distance created between writer and reader
Characteristics	• Use of first-person pronouns (*I, we, me, my, us, our*) • Use of contractions (*can't, don't*) • Emphasis on active-voice verbs (*I conducted the study*) • Shorter sentences; familiar words • Occasional use of humor, metaphors • Occasional use of colorful speech • Acceptance of author's opinions and ideas	• Absence of first-person pronouns; use of third person (*the researcher, the writer*); increasingly, however, the informal style is acceptable • Absence of contractions (*cannot, do not*) • Use of passive-voice verbs (*the study was conducted*) • Complex sentences; long words • Absence of humor and figures of speech • Little use of colorful adjectives and verbs • Elimination of "editorializing" (author's opinions, perceptions)

clear and concise. They should be written using topic sentences, support sentences, and transitional expressions to build coherence. Avoid wordiness, outdated expressions, slang, jargon, and clichés in your reports. Finally, proofread all business reports carefully to make sure that they contain no errors in spelling, grammar, punctuation, names and numbers, or format.

"He says our report is objective. However, quoting Winston Churchill, he writes that the report, by its very length, defends itself against the risk of being read."

Being Objective

Reports are convincing only when the facts are believable and the writer is credible. You can build credibility in a number of ways:

- **Present both sides of an issue.** Even if you favor one possibility, discuss both sides and show through logical reasoning why your position is superior. Remain impartial, letting the facts prove your point.
- **Separate facts from opinions.** Suppose a supervisor wrote, *Our department works harder and gets less credit than any other department in the company.* This opinion is difficult to prove, and it damages the credibility of the writer. A more convincing statement might be, *Our productivity has increased 6 percent over the past year, and I'm proud of the extra effort my employees are making.* After you have made a claim or presented an important statement in a report, ask yourself, *Is this a verifiable fact?* If the answer is *no,* rephrase your statement to make it sound more reasonable.
- **Be sensitive and moderate in your choice of language.** Don't exaggerate. Instead of saying *most people think*. . ., it might be more accurate to say *Some people think*. . . . Better yet, use specific figures such as *Sixty percent of employees agree* . . . . Also avoid using labels and slanted expressions. Calling someone a *loser,* a *control freak,* or an *elitist* demonstrates bias. If readers suspect that a writer is prejudiced, they may discount the entire argument.
- **Cite sources.** Tell your readers where the information came from. For example, *In a telephone interview on October 15, Blake Spence, director of transportation, said . . . OR:* The Wall Street Journal *(August 10, p. 40) reports that* . . . . By referring to respected sources, you lend authority and credibility to your statements. Your words become more believable and your argument, more convincing. In Chapter 10 you will learn how to document your sources properly.

Reports are more believable if the author is impartial, separates facts from opinions, uses moderate language, and cites sources.

Using Effective Report Headings

Good headings are helpful to both the report reader and the writer. For the reader they serve as an outline of the text, highlighting major ideas and categories. They also act as guides for locating facts and pointing the way through the text. Moreover, headings provide resting points for the mind and for the eye, breaking up large chunks of text into manageable and inviting segments. For the writer headings require that the report author organize the data into meaningful blocks. You will learn more about headings in Chapter 10.

You may choose functional or talking heads. Functional heads (such as *Background*, *Findings*, *Staffing*, *Summary*, and *Projected Costs*) describe functions or general topics. They show the outline of a report but provide little insight for readers. Functional heads are useful for routine reports. They are also appropriate for sensitive or controversial topics that might provoke emotional reactions. Figure 9.2 on pages 249 and 250 shows both functional and talking heads.

Functional heads show the outline of a report; talking heads describe the content.

Talking heads (such as *Employees Struggle With Lack of Day-Care Options*) describe content and provide more information to the reader. Many of the examples in this chapter use talking heads, including the informational reports in Figures 9.2 and 9.3. To provide even greater clarity, you can make headings both functional and descriptive, such as *Recommendations: Saving Costs With Off-Site Care*. Whether your headings are talking or functional, keep them brief and clear. To create the most effective headings, follow a few basic guidelines:

- **Use appropriate heading levels.** The position and format of a heading indicate its level of importance and relationship to other points.
- **Strive for parallel construction within levels.** All headings at a given level should be grammatically similar. Use balanced expressions such as *Current Quarterly Budget* and *Next Quarterly Budget* rather than *Current Quarterly Budget* and *Budget Projected in the Next Quarter.*
- **For short reports use first- and second-level headings.** Many business reports contain only one or two levels of headings. For such reports use first-level headings (centered, bolded) and/or second-level headings (flush left, bolded).
- **Capitalize and underline carefully.** Most writers use all capital letters (without underlines) for main titles, such as the report, chapter, and unit titles. For first- and second-level headings, they capitalize only the first letter of main words. For additional emphasis, they use a bold font. Don't enclose headings in quotation marks.
- **Keep headings short but clear.** Try to make your headings brief (no more than eight words) but understandable. Experiment with headings that concisely tell who, what, when, where, and why.
- **Don't use headings as antecedents for pronouns** such as *this, that, these*, and *those*. For example, when the heading reads *Mobile Devices,* don't begin the next sentence with *These are increasingly multifunctional and capable.*
- **Include at least one heading per report page.** Headings increase the readability and attractiveness of report pages. If used correctly, headings help the reader grasp the report structure quickly. Use at least one per page to break up blocks of text.

Breeding beautifully colored koi for collectors is a profitable but hazardous and costly business. Commercial growers need acreage to build breeding and growing ponds, expensive equipment to monitor water quality and prevent diseases, and caring personnel to oversee the intricate breeding program. To secure financial backing, businesses such as bluewater Koi submit proposals that often include summaries, such as that shown in Figure 9.9. *How do business communicators decide what information to include in summaries of long reports?*

© iStockphoto.com/Elena Elisseeva

WORKPLACE IN FOCUS

www.cengagebrain.com

Available with an access code, these eResources will help you prepare for exams:

- **Chapter Review Quizzes**
- **Personal Language Trainer**
- **PowerPoint Slides**
- **Flash Cards**

Summing Up and Looking Forward

This chapter introduced six common types of informal business reports: informational reports, progress reports, justification/recommendation reports, feasibility reports, minutes of meetings, and summaries. Informational reports generally provide data only. Justification/recommendation and feasibility reports are analytical in that they also evaluate the information, draw conclusions, and make recommendations. This chapter also discussed five formats for reports. Letter format is used for reports sent outside an organization; memo or e-mail format is used for internal reports. More formal reports are formatted on plain paper with a manuscript design, while routine reports may be formatted on prepared forms. Increasingly, all types of reports are sent in digital form by e-mail or posted on the company intranet or the Web. The chapter presented several key model documents illustrating the many kinds of reports and their formats. You also learned how to choose the appropriate report writing style and create effective heading.

The examples in this chapter are considered relatively informal. Longer, more formal reports are necessary for major investigations and research. These reports and proposals, along with research methods, are presented in Chapter 10.

Critical Thinking

1. How would you determine whether to use the direct strategy or the indirect strategy for your report?

2. Why would you want to start your research with secondary data rather than gathering primary data right away?

3. How might technology shape business report formats and their delivery in the future?

4. How can report writers ensure that they present their topics objectively and credibly?

5. What are the purposes of headings, and what are the two heading types discussed in this chapter?

Chapter Review

6. Why are reports indispensable documents in business?

7. What is the chief difference between primary and secondary data?

8. Describe the five major formats used for reports. Be prepared to discuss each.

9. Name the six kinds of informal reports. Explain their purpose.

10. From the lists you made in Questions 8 and 9, select a report category and appropriate format for each of the following situations:
    a. Your supervisor wants to know the gist of a recent review in an influential online magazine discussing the Apple iPad.
    b. You wish to propose that the export department hire another marine clerk because the export desk is chronically understaffed and regularly falls behind schedule in loading containers.
    c. Your team was assigned to study how your company, a racing bicycle manufacturer, can comply with the International Cycling Union's regulations before bikes go into production. Your boss wants to know what you have done thus far.
    d. At a meeting of the National Association of Manufacturers, you were asked to record the proceedings and assign lobbying visits to several key representatives in Washington, DC.
    e. You represented your company at the Green Building Conference held by the National Association of Home Builders in Salt Lake City, Utah. Your supervisor asked for a written description of the latest trends.
    f. You are completing annual performance appraisals in your sales department.

g. A recent discovery of bedbugs at the corporate offices of *Time* magazine in New York prompted research into abatement measures that advocated bedbug-sniffing beagles.

11. If you were about to write the following reports, where would you gather information? Be prepared to discuss the specifics of each choice.
    a. Your company would like to know more about and potentially copy the peer-to-peer marketing effort created for Rockstar energy drink. A marketing company recruited 75 student brand evangelists with more than 900 Facebook "friends" to promote the brand to peers.
    b. As HR manager, you must write several letters of reprimand for the inappropriate use of social media and Internet access on the job.
    c. You are proposing a new social media use policy to management.
    d. You were asked to study the need for a child-care facility in your corporate headquarters and recommend for or against it.

12. Why do you need a statement of purpose before you can write your report?

13. List the guidelines for effective headings.

14. What are meeting minutes, and who is their intended audience?

15. How can you ensure that you adopt an appropriate report writing style?

Writing Improvement Exercises

Evaluating Headings and Titles

Your Task. Identify the following report headings and titles as *talking* or *functional*. Discuss the usefulness and effectiveness of each.

16. Background

17. Oil Imports Slow in China

18. Discussion of Findings

19. Rosier Job Outlook: Emerging From the Crisis

20. Recommendation: Return to Stocks Is Paying Off Again

21. Adobe Exceeds Expectations on Creative Suite Sales

22. Best Android Apps for Business: PocketCloud, Ignition, and TouchDown

23. Budget

Activities and Cases

WEB

9.1 Informational Report: Hunting for New Harley Riders

You are a junior sales associate working for Chicago BMW Motorcycle. Because of the economic crisis, sales of motorcycles have taken a huge hit across the board. When money is tight, people tend to cut back on luxurious "toys" such as expensive bikes. BMW relies on a well-heeled clientele, much of it composed of middle-aged men. However, the German motorcycle manufacturer has been trying to capture a share of the market larger than the 2 percent it has occupied for some time in the United States.

Even the ever-popular Harley-Davidson bikes have suffered a decrease in sales of about 30 percent in the last two years. A recent article about the industry in *BusinessWeek* stated that Harley-Davidson is now trying to appeal to women riders. You bring the piece to the attention of your boss, Dale Bell, and he asks you to find out what exactly Harley-Davidson is doing.

Your Task. Visit the Harley-Davidson USA Web site and study how the legendary motorcycle manufacturer is targeting female riders. Write an informational report in memo form addressed to Dale Bell. Which of its motorcycles does your competitor promote as ideal for women and why? How about apparel? What other ways has Harley-Davidson found to attract female riders?

9.2 Informational Report: Showcasing Your Work Experience

Your instructor wants to learn about your employment. Select a position you now hold or one that you have held in the past. If you have not been employed, choose a campus, professional, or community organization to which you belong. You may also select an internship or volunteer activities.

Your Task. Write an informational report describing your employment or involvement. As an introduction describe the company and its products or services, its ownership, and its location. As the main part of the report, describe your position, including its tasks and the skills required to perform these tasks. Summarize by describing the experience you gained. Your memo report should be single-spaced and 1 1/2 to 2 pages long and should be addressed to your instructor.

9.3 Informational Report: Charting Your Career Path

Gather information about a career or position in which you might be interested. Learn about the nature of the job. Discover whether certification, a license, or experience is required. One of the best places to search is the latest *Occupational Outlook Handbook* compiled by the U.S. Bureau of Labor Statistics. Google the latest *Handbook* and either input your desired occupation using the **Search** box or click an **A-Z Index** link.

Your Task. Write an informational report to your instructor that describes your target career area. Discuss the nature of the work, working conditions, necessary qualifications, and the future job outlook for the occupation. Include information about typical salary ranges and career paths. If your instructor wants an extended report, collect information about two companies where you might apply. Investigate each company's history, products and/or services, size, earnings, reputation, and number of employees. Describe the functions of an employee working in the position you have investigated. To do this, interview one or more individuals who are working in that position. Devote several sections of your report to the specific tasks, functions, duties, and opinions of these individuals. You can make this into a recommendation report by drawing conclusions and making recommendations. One conclusion that you could draw relates to success in this career area. Who might be successful in this field?

9.4 Informational Report: Prospecting for Potential Employers

You are considering jobs with a Fortune 500 company, and you want to learn as much as possible about the company.

Your Task. Select a Fortune 500 company and collect information about it on the Web. Use your library's ProQuest subscription to access Hoover's company records for basic facts. Then take a look at the company's Web site; check its background, news releases, and annual report. Learn about its major product, service, or emphasis. Find its Fortune 500 ranking, its current stock price (if listed), and its high and low range for the year. Look up its profit-to-earnings ratio. Track its latest marketing plan, promotion, or product. Identify its home office, major officers, and number of employees. In a memo report to your instructor, summarize your research findings. Explain why this company would be a good or bad employment choice.

9.5 Informational Report: Expanding Operations Overseas

Your boss wants to know more about intercultural and international business etiquette. Today most managers recognize that they need to be polished and professional if they wish to earn the respect of diverse audiences. Assume that your boss will assign various countries to several interns and recent hires. Choose a country that interests you and conduct a Web search. For example, in a Google search, input terms such as *business etiquette*, *business etiquette abroad*, or *intercultural communication*. You could visit Web sites such as the popular, informative etiquette and business guides for specific countries by Kwintessential Ltd. (**http://www.kwintessential.co.uk**).

Your Task. As an intern or a new-hire, write a short memo report about one country that is considerably different from the United States and that offers new business opportunities. Address your report to Jeffrey Brown, CEO. Summarize your research into what U.S. managers need to know about business etiquette in that culture. You should investigate social customs such as greetings, attire, gift giving, formality, business meals, attitudes toward time, communication styles, and so forth, to help your CEO avoid etiquette blunders. The purpose of your report is to promote business, not tourism.

9.6 Progress Report: Heading Toward That Degree

You made an agreement with your parents (or spouse, partner, relative, or friend) that you would submit a progress report describing the progress you have made toward your educational goal (employment, certificate, or degree).

Your Task. Prepare a progress report in letter format. (a) Describe your headway toward your educational goal; (b) summarize the work you have completed thus far; (c) discuss the work currently in progress, including your successes and anticipated obstacles; and (d) outline what you have left to complete.

9.7 Progress Report: Filling in Your Supervisor

As office manager for the Animal Rescue Foundation (**http://www.arf.net**), a nonprofit organization that rescues and finds homes for abandoned and abused animals, you have been asked to come up with ways to increase community awareness of your organization. For the past month, you have been meeting with business and community leaders, conducting Web research, and visiting with representatives from other nonprofit organizations. Your supervisor has just asked you to prepare a written report to outline what you have accomplished so far.

Your Task. In memo format write a progress report to your supervisor. In your memo (a) state whether the project is on schedule; (b) summarize the activities you have completed thus far; (c) discuss thoroughly the work currently in progress; and (d) describe your future activities. Also let your supervisor know any obstacles you have encountered and whether the project is on schedule.

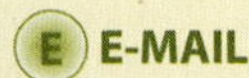

9.8 Progress Report: Checking In

If you are working on a long report for either this chapter or Chapter 10, keep your instructor informed of your progress.

Your Task. Send your instructor a report by e-mail detailing the progress you are making on your long report assignment. Discuss (a) the purpose of the report, (b) the work already completed, (c) the work currently in progress, (d) problems encountered, (e) future activities, and (f) your schedule for completing the report.

9.9 Justification/Recommendation Report: Tackling a Campus Problem

You are the member of a student task force that has been asked to identify problems on campus and suggest solutions.

Your Task. In groups of two to five, investigate a problem on your campus, such as inadequate parking, slow registration, limited dining options, poor class schedules, an inefficient bookstore, meager extracurricular activities, an understaffed library, a weak job placement program, unrealistic degree requirements, or a lack of internship programs. Within your group develop a solution to the problem. If possible, consult the officials involved to ask for their input in arriving at a feasible solution. Do not attack existing programs; instead, strive for constructive discussion and harmonious and feasible improvements. After reviewing the persuasive techniques discussed in Chapter 8, write a justification/recommendation report in memo or letter format. Address your report to the vice president of student affairs or the college president, but submit it to your instructor.

9.10 Justification/Recommendation Report: Developing an Organizational Media Policy

As a manager in a midsized engineering firm, you are aware that members of your department frequently use e-mail, social networking sites, instant messaging, and texting for private messages, shopping, and games. In addition to the strain on computer facilities, you worry about declining productivity, security problems, and liability issues. When you walked by one worker's computer and saw what looked like pornography on the screen, you knew you had to do something. Although workplace privacy is a controversial issue for unions and employee rights groups, employers have legitimate reasons for wanting to know what is happening on their computers or during the time they are paying their employees to work. A high percentage of lawsuits involve the use and abuse of e-mail and increasingly more often other media as well. You think that the executive council should establish some kind of e-mail, Web use, and social media policy. The council is generally receptive to sound suggestions, especially if they are inexpensive. At present, no explicit media use policy exists, and you fear that the executive council is not fully aware of the dangers. You decide to talk with other managers about the problem and write a justification/recommendation report.

Your Task. In teams discuss the need for a comprehensive media use policy. Using the Web and electronic databases, find information about other firms' adoption of such policies. Look for examples of companies struggling with lawsuits over abuse of technology on the job. In your report, should you describe suitable policies? Should you recommend computer monitoring and surveillance software? Should the policy cover instant messaging, social networking sites, blogging, and smartphone use? Each member of the team should present and support his or her ideas regarding what should be included in the policy. Individually or as a team, write a convincing justification/recommendation report in memo or letter format to the executive council based on the conclusions you draw from your research and discussion. Decide whether you should be direct or indirect.

9.11 Justification/Recommendation Report: Trying Peer-to-Peer Marketing on Campus

To create brand awareness among the college crowd, advertisers increasingly go where students hang out—on campus and online. Marketers of products popular with college students have realized that traditional pitches such as TV and magazine ads no longer work with today's twentysomethings. Tethered to their computers and smartphones, college kids prefer to obtain information about products and services on demand on the Internet. To reach them, marketers are attempting to incorporate advertising campaigns into students' lifestyles. They hope to accomplish this objective by enlisting student promoters who spread a specific, targeted brand message to peers, usually virally by Twitter and Facebook.

Clothing manufacturer American Eagle Outfitters, tech firms Apple and Hewlett-Packard, and energy drink maker Red Bull are just a few examples of companies that hire student brand advocates. These peer marketers organize promotional campus events, provide free giveaways, and appeal to fellow students by using social networks. For example, Red Bull alone has millions of fans on Facebook and communicates with students via Twitter. The company also takes advantage of mobile marketing with phone apps and games, some of which it distributes free of charge. The estimated 10,000 student reps on U.S. college campuses today are paid in cash up to $1,500 per semester. They may also receive free products.

Why are marketers so keen on connecting with college kids? First, at 19 million, students may comprise a relatively small demographic, but as a group they have sizable discretionary incomes, often bankrolled by mom and dad. Alloy Media + Marketing estimates that college students spend approximately $76 billion a year.[1] Second, they begin to develop lasting brand loyalty as freshmen. Third, college graduates typically can expect to earn more money in the future than those without college degrees.

Your Task. Your instructor may direct that you write a justification/recommendation report in letter form. Choose a manufacturer of a brand attractive to college students. As a team or individually, brainstorm how your chosen company could unleash the potential of social media and deploy peer marketers to target college students. Consider popular companies such as Coke, Verizon, Taco Bell, Abercrombie & Fitch, or any brand favored by twentysomethings. What could they do to reach out to college kids effectively? Propose specific activities, events, or promotional campaigns. Be sure they are realistic and feasible.

9.12 Feasibility Report: Starting an International Student Organization

To fulfill a student project in your department, you have been asked to submit a letter report to the dean evaluating the feasibility of starting an organization of international students on campus.

Your Task. Find out how many international students are on your campus, what nations they represent, how one goes about starting an organization, and whether a faculty sponsor is needed. Assume that you conducted an informal survey of international students. Of the 39 who filled out the survey, 31 said they would be interested in joining. Write a report in memo or letter format to the dean outlining the advisability of starting an international student organization on your college campus.

9.13 Feasibility Report: Shaping Up at Work

Your company is considering ways to promote employee fitness and morale. Select a fitness program that seems reasonable. Consider a softball league, bowling teams, a basketball league, lunchtime walks, lunchtime fitness speakers and demos, company-sponsored health club memberships, a workout room, a fitness center, nutrition programs, and so on.

Your Task. Assume that your supervisor has tentatively agreed to one of the programs and has asked you to write a memo report investigating its feasibility.

9.14 Minutes: Recording the Proceedings of a Meeting

Attend an open meeting of an organization at your school, in your community, or elsewhere. Assume that you are asked to record the proceedings.

Your Task. Record the meeting proceedings in formal or informal minutes. Review the chapter to be sure you include all the data necessary for minutes. Focus on motions, votes, decisions reached, and action taken.

TEAM

9.15 Minutes and Action Items: Assigning Report-Writing Tasks

When writing a formal report or proposal with a team, take notes at a team meeting about your research, especially one you may schedule with your instructor. Divide research, writing, editing, and formatting responsibilities among the group members.

Your Task. Write minutes recording the meeting. Include a list or table of action items that clearly show how tasks were divided along with names and deadlines. See Figure 9.8 on page 262 for a sample action item list.

WEB

9.16 Article Summary: Putting Business Blogs and Social Media to Work

Your supervisor has just learned about using blogs or social media such as Facebook and Twitter to communicate with the public. He wants to learn more. He asks you to conduct Internet and database research to see what has been written about the business uses of blogs or social media.

Your Task. Using an electronic database or the Web, find an article that discusses the use of blogs or social media in the workplace. In a memo report addressed to your boss, Jin Ree, summarize the primary ideas, conclusions, and recommendations presented in the article. Be sure to identify the author, article name, periodical, and date of publication in your summary. Also include your reaction to and evaluation of the article.

WEB

9.17 Article Summary: Distilling the Facts for Your Boss

Like many executives, your boss is too rushed to read long journal articles. But she is eager to keep up with developments in her field. Assume she has asked you to help her stay abreast of research in her area of expertise. She asks you to submit to her one article summary every month on a topic of interest.

Your Task. In your field of study, select a professional journal, such as the *Journal of Management*. Using an electronic database search or a Web search, look for articles in your target journal. Select an article that is at least five pages long and is interesting to you. Write an article summary in memo format. Include an introduction that might begin with *As you requested, I am submitting this summary of* . . . . Identify the author, article name, journal, and date of publication. Explain what the author intended to do in the study or article. Summarize three or four of the most important findings of the study or article. Include headings, and summarize any recommendations you make. Your boss would also like a concluding statement indicating your evaluation of and reaction to the article. Address your memo to Carole Austin.

9.18 Report Topics

A list of over 90 report topics is available at your book companion site **(www.cengagebrain.com)**. The topics are divided into the following categories: accounting, finance, human resources, marketing, information systems, management, and general business/education/campus issues. You can collect information for many of these reports by using electronic databases and the Web. Your instructor may assign them as individual or team projects. All involve critical thinking in collecting and organizing information into logical reports.

Grammar/Mechanics Checkup—9

Semicolons and Colons

Review Sections 2.16–2.19 in the Grammar/Mechanics Handbook. Then study each of the following statements. Insert any necessary punctuation. Use the delete sign to omit unnecessary punctuation. In the space provided, indicate the number of changes you made and record the number of the G/M principle(s) illustrated. (When you replace one punctuation mark with another, count it as one change.) If you make no changes, write *0*. This exercise concentrates on semicolon and colon use, but you will also be responsible for correct comma use. When you finish, compare your responses with those shown at the end of the book. If your responses differ, study carefully the specific principles shown in parentheses.

2 (2.16a) **Example** Jessica Mayer's task is to ensure that her company has enough cash to meet its obligations; moreover, she is responsible for finding ways to reduce operating expenses.

1. Short-term financing refers to a period of one year or less long-term financing on the other hand refers to a period of more than one year.
2. Jessica Mayer's firm must negotiate short-term financing during the following months October November and December.
3. Jessica was interested in her company's finances however she was also seeking information about improving her personal credit score.
4. Having a long history of making payments on time on all types of credit accounts is important to lenders therefore you should strive to make timely payments.
5. Two of the most highly respected and popular banks for short-term financing are: Bank of America and Chase.
6. People with Fico scores of 700 to 800 are good credit risks people with scores of 400 or less are poor credit risks.
7. Jessica learned that three factors account for about a third of one's credit score (a) length of credit history (b) new credit and (c) type of credit.
8. She attended a credit conference featuring the following speakers Jonathon Cruz certified financial consultant Credit Specialists Margaret Lee founder Credit Solutions and Judith Plutsky legal counsel Liberty Financial.
9. Opening several new credit accounts in a short period of time can lower your credit score but scores are not affected by multiple inquiries from automobile and mortgage lenders over a 30-day period.
10. Your credit score ignores some surprising factors for example your age salary and occupation.
11. Credit Solutions which is a nonprofit counseling and debt management service says that two factors account for two-thirds of your credit score (1) your payment history and (2) the amount owed versus available credit.
12. If you want specific information from Credit Solutions send your request to Margaret Lee 3520 Troy Highway Montgomery AL 36104.
13. Margaret Lee who founded Credit Solutions employs an experienced courteous staff however she also responds to personal requests.
14. Interest rates are at historic lows they may never be this low again.
15. Margaret Lee said "If your goal is to increase your credit score take a look at folks with the highest credit scores. They have four to six credit card accounts no late payment and at least one installment loan with an excellent payment history."

Editing Challenge—9

As the employee with the best communication skills, you are frequently asked to edit messages. The following e-mail has problems with wordiness, spelling, proofreading, commas, semicolons, colons, apostrophes, grammar, and other writing techniques you have studied. You may (a) use standard proofreading marks (see Appendix B) to correct the errors here or (b) download the document from **www.cengagebrain.com** and revise at your computer.

Your instructor may ask you to use the **Track Changes** feature in Word to show your editing comments. Turn on **Track Changes** on the **Review** tab. Click **Show Markup**. Place your cursor at an error, click **New Comment**, and key your edit in the bubble box provided. Study the guidelines in the Grammar/Mechanics Handbook as well as the lists of Confusing Words and Frequently Misspelled Words to sharpen your skills.

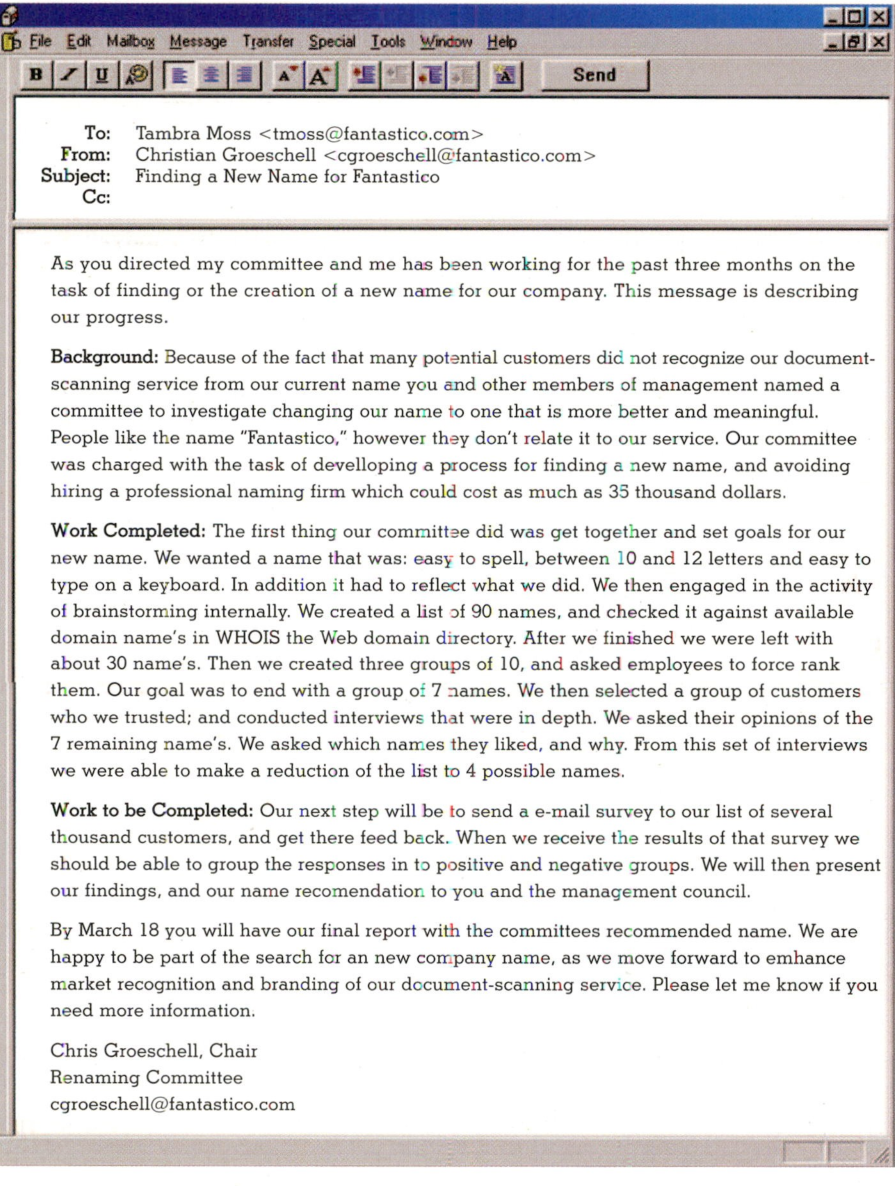

To: Tambra Moss <tmoss@fantastico.com>
From: Christian Groeschell <cgroeschell@fantastico.com>
Subject: Finding a New Name for Fantastico
Cc:

As you directed my committee and me has been working for the past three months on the task of finding or the creation of a new name for our company. This message is describing our progress.

Background: Because of the fact that many potential customers did not recognize our document-scanning service from our current name you and other members of management named a committee to investigate changing our name to one that is more better and meaningful. People like the name "Fantastico," however they don't relate it to our service. Our committee was charged with the task of develloping a process for finding a new name, and avoiding hiring a professional naming firm which could cost as much as 35 thousand dollars.

Work Completed: The first thing our committee did was get together and set goals for our new name. We wanted a name that was: easy to spell, between 10 and 12 letters and easy to type on a keyboard. In addition it had to reflect what we did. We then engaged in the activity of brainstorming internally. We created a list of 90 names, and checked it against available domain name's in WHOIS the Web domain directory. After we finished we were left with about 30 name's. Then we created three groups of 10, and asked employees to force rank them. Our goal was to end with a group of 7 names. We then selected a group of customers who we trusted; and conducted interviews that were in depth. We asked their opinions of the 7 remaining name's. We asked which names they liked, and why. From this set of interviews we were able to make a reduction of the list to 4 possible names.

Work to be Completed: Our next step will be to send a e-mail survey to our list of several thousand customers, and get there feed back. When we receive the results of that survey we should be able to group the responses in to positive and negative groups. We will then present our findings, and our name recomendation to you and the management council.

By March 18 you will have our final report with the committees recommended name. We are happy to be part of the search for an new company name, as we move forward to emhance market recognition and branding of our document-scanning service. Please let me know if you need more information.

Chris Groeschell, Chair
Renaming Committee
cgroeschell@fantastico.com

Communication Workshop

Laying the Groundwork for Team Writing Projects

The chances are that you can look forward to some kind of team writing in your future career. You may collaborate voluntarily (seeking advice and differing perspectives) or involuntarily (through necessity or by assignment). Working with other people can be frustrating, particularly when some team members don't carry their weight or when conflict breaks out. Team projects, though, can be harmonious, productive, and rewarding when members establish ground rules at the outset and adhere to guidelines such as those presented here.

Collaboration tools, such as wikis, allow team members to contribute to and edit a text online. Many businesses today turn to wikis to facilitate teamwork. Your instructor may have access to wiki software or to the wiki function in BlackBoard.

Preparing to Work Together

Before you discuss the project, talk about how your group will function.

- Limit the size of your team, if possible, to two to five members. Larger groups have more difficulties. An odd number is usually preferable to avoid ties in voting.
- Name a team leader (to plan and conduct meetings), a recorder (to keep a record of group decisions), and an evaluator (to determine whether the group is on target and meeting its goals).
- Decide whether your team will be governed by consensus (everyone must agree) or by majority rule.
- Compare team members' schedules, and set up the best meeting times. Plan to meet often. Avoid other responsibilities during meetings. Team meetings can take place face-to-face or virtually.
- Discuss the value of conflict. By bringing conflict into the open and encouraging confrontation, your team can prevent personal resentment and group dysfunction. Conflict can actually create better final documents by promoting new ideas and avoiding groupthink.
- Discuss how you will deal with members who are not pulling their share of the load.

Planning the Document

Once you have established ground rules, you are ready to discuss the project and resulting document. Be sure to keep a record of the decisions your team makes.

- Establish the document's specific purpose and identify the main issues involved.
- Decide on the final form of the document. What parts will it have?
- Discuss the audience(s) for the document and what appeal would help it achieve its purpose.
- Develop a work plan. Assign jobs. Set deadlines.
- Decide how the final document will be written: individuals working separately on assigned portions, one person writing the first draft, the entire group writing the complete document together, or some other method.

Collecting Information

The following suggestions help teams gather accurate information:

- Brainstorm ideas as a group.
- Decide who will be responsible for gathering what information.
- Establish deadlines for collecting information.
- Discuss ways to ensure the accuracy and currency of the information collected.

Organizing, Writing, and Revising

As the project progresses, your team may wish to modify some of its earlier decisions.

- Review the proposed organization of your final document, and adjust it if necessary.
- Write the first draft. If separate team members are writing segments, they should use the same style and format to facilitate combining files.
- Meet to discuss and revise the draft(s).

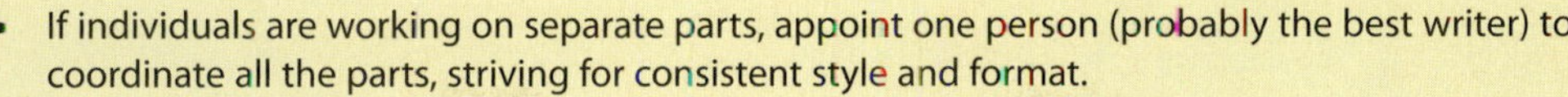

- If individuals are working on separate parts, appoint one person (probably the best writer) to coordinate all the parts, striving for consistent style and format.

Editing and Evaluating

Before submitting the document, complete these steps:

- Give one person responsibility for correcting grammatical and mechanical errors.
- Meet as a group to evaluate the final document. Does it fulfill its purpose and meet the needs of the audience?

Option: Using a Wiki to Collaborate

Hosting companies such as PBWorks (**http://pbworks.com/content/edu+overview**) offer easy-to-use, free wiki accounts to educators to run in their classes without the need of involving the IT department. BlackBoard supports a wiki option as long as a college or university selects it with its subscription. A wiki within Blackboard is a page or multiple pages that students enrolled in the class can edit and change. They may add other content such as images and hyperlinks. A log allows instructors to track changes and the students' contributions. Ask you instructor about these options.

Career Application. Select a report topic from this chapter or Chapter 10. Assume that you must prepare the report as a team project. If you are working on a long report, your instructor may ask you to prepare individual progress reports as you develop your topic.

Your Task

- Form teams of two to five members.
- Prepare to work together by using the suggestions provided here.
- Plan your report by establishing its purpose, analyzing the audience, identifying the main issues, developing a work plan, and assigning tasks.
- Collect information, organize the data, and write the first draft.
- Decide how the document will be revised, edited, and evaluated.

Tip: For revising and editing, consider using the tools in Microsoft Word introduced in Chapter 4 (**Track Changes**) and making comments.

Your instructor may assign grades not only on the final report but also on your team effectiveness and your individual contribution, as determined by fellow team members, and, potentially, by tracking your activities if you are using a wiki.

Endnotes

[1] Scenario is based on Horovitz, B. (2010, December 3). Marketers pull an inside job on college campuses. *USA Today*. Retrieved from http://www.usatoday.com/printedition/money/20101004/collegemarketing04_cv.art.htm

Acknowledgments

p. 247 Office Insider from a report by the College Board: The National Commission on Writing. (2004, September). Writing: A ticket to work . . . or a ticket out. Retrieved from http://www.writingcommission.org/report.html

p. 254 Office Insider from a report by the College Board: The National Commission on Writing. (2004, September). Writing: A ticket to work . . . or a ticket out. Retrieved from http://www.writingcommission.org/report.html

CHAPTER 10

Proposals and Formal Reports

cengagebrain.com
and use your access code to unlock valuable student eResources.

© Ienetstan/Shutterstock.com

OBJECTIVES

After studying this chapter, you should be able to

- Identify and explain the parts of informal and formal proposals.
- Describe the steps in writing a formal report.
- Collect data from secondary sources including print and electronic sources.
- Use Web browsers, search tools, blogs, and other online communication media to locate reliable data.
- Generate primary data from surveys, interviews, observation, and experimentation.
- Understand the need for accurate documentation of data and for developing sound research habits.
- Organize report data, create an outline, and make effective headings.
- Illustrate data using tables, charts, and other graphics.
- Describe and sequence the parts of a formal report.

Preparing Informal Proposals

Proposals are persuasive offers to solve problems, provide services, or sell equipment.

Businesspeople write proposals to solve problems, provide services, or sell equipment. Some proposals are internal, often taking the form of justification and recommendation reports. You learned about these reports in Chapter 9. Most proposals, however, are external and are a critical means of selling equipment and services that generate income for many companies.

Proposals may be divided into two categories: solicited and unsolicited. When government organizations or firms know exactly what they want, they prepare a request for proposal (RFP), specifying their requirements. Government agencies as well as private businesses use RFPs to solicit competitive bids from vendors. Most proposals are solicited, such as that presented by the city of Las Vegas, Nevada. Its 30-page RFP was seeking bids for a parking initiative from public and private funding sources.[1] Enterprising companies looking for work or a special challenge might submit unsolicited proposals—for example, the world-renowned architect who designed the Louvre Museum pyramid in Paris, among other landmarks. I. M. Pei was so intrigued by the mission of the Buck Institute for Age Research that he submitted an unsolicited proposal to design the biomedical research facility in Novato, California.[2]

Both large and small companies are increasingly likely to use RFPs to solicit competitive bids on their projects. This enables them to compare "apples to apples." That is, they can compare prices from different companies on their projects. They also want the legal protection offered by proposals, which are legal contracts.

"I have no objection to creative problem solving as long as it's not too creative and it's not a real problem."

Many companies earn a sizable portion of their income from sales resulting from proposals. That is why creating effective proposals is especially important today. In writing proposals, the most important thing to remember is that proposals are sales presentations. They must be persuasive, not merely mechanical descriptions of what you can do. You may recall from Chapter 8 that effective persuasive sales messages (a) emphasize benefits for the reader, (b) "toot your horn" by detailing your expertise and accomplishments, and (c) make it easy for the reader to understand and respond. Proposals may be informal or formal; they differ primarily in length and format.

Understanding the Components of Informal Proposals

Informal proposals may be presented in short (two- to four-page) letters. Sometimes called *letter proposals*, they contain six principal components: introduction, background, proposal, staffing, budget, and authorization request. The informal letter proposal shown in Figure 10.1 illustrates all six parts of a letter proposal. This proposal is addressed to a Boston dentist who wants to improve patient satisfaction.

Introduction

Informal proposals may contain an introduction, background information, the proposal, staffing requirements, a budget, and an authorization request.

Most proposals begin by briefly explaining the reasons for the proposal and highlighting the writer's qualifications. To make your introduction more persuasive, you need to provide a "hook," such as the following:

- Hint at extraordinary results, with details to be revealed shortly.
- Promise low costs or speedy results.
- Mention a remarkable resource (well-known authority, new computer program, well-trained staff) available exclusively to you.
- Identify a serious problem (worry item) and promise a solution, to be explained later.
- Specify a key issue or benefit that you feel is the heart of the proposal.

Effective proposal openers "hook" readers by focusing on the audience's specific needs and benefits.

Although writers may know what goes into the proposal introduction, many face writer's block before they get started. It doesn't help that most proposals and reports must be completed under pressure by tight deadlines. To get the creative juices flowing, former Raytheon proposal specialist Dr. Mark Grinyer suggests studying the RFP closely to understand what the client really wants. Based on that analysis, he would look for persuasive themes until a proposal outline emerged.[3] Addressing the client's needs may be the ticket to getting off to a good start.

FIGURE 10.1 Informal Proposal

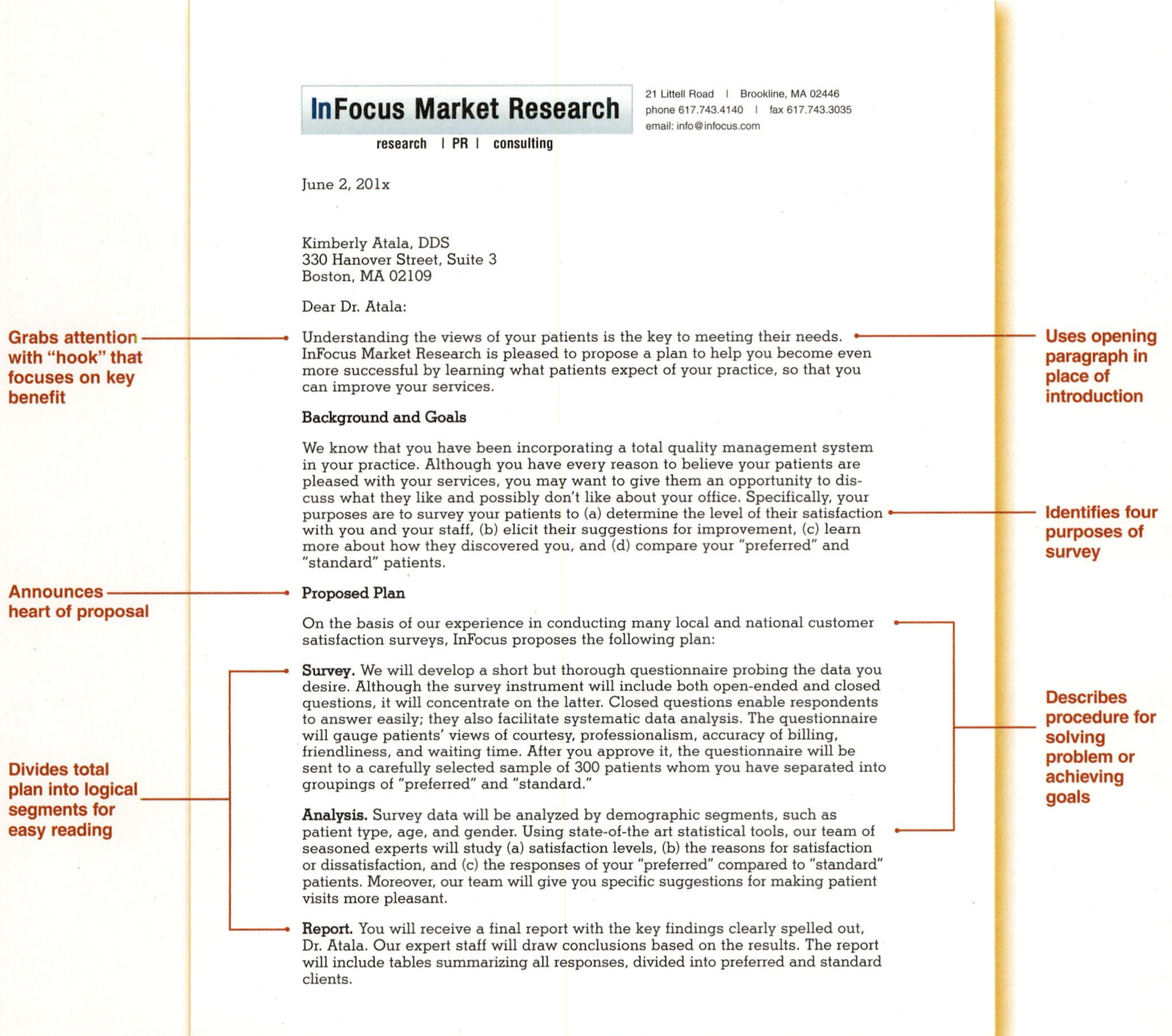

InFocus Market Research
research | PR | consulting

21 Littell Road | Brookline, MA 02446
phone 617.743.4140 | fax 617.743.3035
email: info@infocus.com

June 2, 201x

Kimberly Atala, DDS
330 Hanover Street, Suite 3
Boston, MA 02109

Dear Dr. Atala:

Understanding the views of your patients is the key to meeting their needs. InFocus Market Research is pleased to propose a plan to help you become even more successful by learning what patients expect of your practice, so that you can improve your services.

Background and Goals

We know that you have been incorporating a total quality management system in your practice. Although you have every reason to believe your patients are pleased with your services, you may want to give them an opportunity to discuss what they like and possibly don't like about your office. Specifically, your purposes are to survey your patients to (a) determine the level of their satisfaction with you and your staff, (b) elicit their suggestions for improvement, (c) learn more about how they discovered you, and (d) compare your "preferred" and "standard" patients.

Proposed Plan

On the basis of our experience in conducting many local and national customer satisfaction surveys, InFocus proposes the following plan:

Survey. We will develop a short but thorough questionnaire probing the data you desire. Although the survey instrument will include both open-ended and closed questions, it will concentrate on the latter. Closed questions enable respondents to answer easily; they also facilitate systematic data analysis. The questionnaire will gauge patients' views of courtesy, professionalism, accuracy of billing, friendliness, and waiting time. After you approve it, the questionnaire will be sent to a carefully selected sample of 300 patients whom you have separated into groupings of "preferred" and "standard."

Analysis. Survey data will be analyzed by demographic segments, such as patient type, age, and gender. Using state-of-the art statistical tools, our team of seasoned experts will study (a) satisfaction levels, (b) the reasons for satisfaction or dissatisfaction, and (c) the responses of your "preferred" compared to "standard" patients. Moreover, our team will give you specific suggestions for making patient visits more pleasant.

Report. You will receive a final report with the key findings clearly spelled out, Dr. Atala. Our expert staff will draw conclusions based on the results. The report will include tables summarizing all responses, divided into preferred and standard clients.

Grabs attention with "hook" that focuses on key benefit
Uses opening paragraph in place of introduction
Identifies four purposes of survey
Announces heart of proposal
Describes procedure for solving problem or achieving goals
Divides total plan into logical segments for easy reading

OFFICE INSIDER

"To conquer writer's block, begin with a bulleted list of what the customer is looking for. This list is like a road map; it gets you started and keeps you headed in the right direction."

—Mary Piecewicz, former Hewlett-Packard proposal manager

In the proposal introduction shown in Figure 10.1, Alex Parsons focused on what the customer was looking for. He analyzed the request of the Boston dentist, Dr. Kimberly Atala, and decided that she was most interested in specific recommendations for improving service to her patients. But Alex did not hit on this hook until he had written a first draft and had come back to it later. Indeed, it is often a good idea to put off writing the introduction to a proposal until after you have completed other parts. For longer proposals the introduction also outlines the organization of the material to come.

Background, Problem, and Purpose

The background section identifies the problem and discusses the goals or purposes of the project. In an unsolicited proposal, your goal is to convince the reader that a problem exists. Therefore, you must present the problem in detail, discussing such factors as monetary losses, failure to comply with government regulations,

FIGURE 10.1 **Informal Proposal (Continued)**

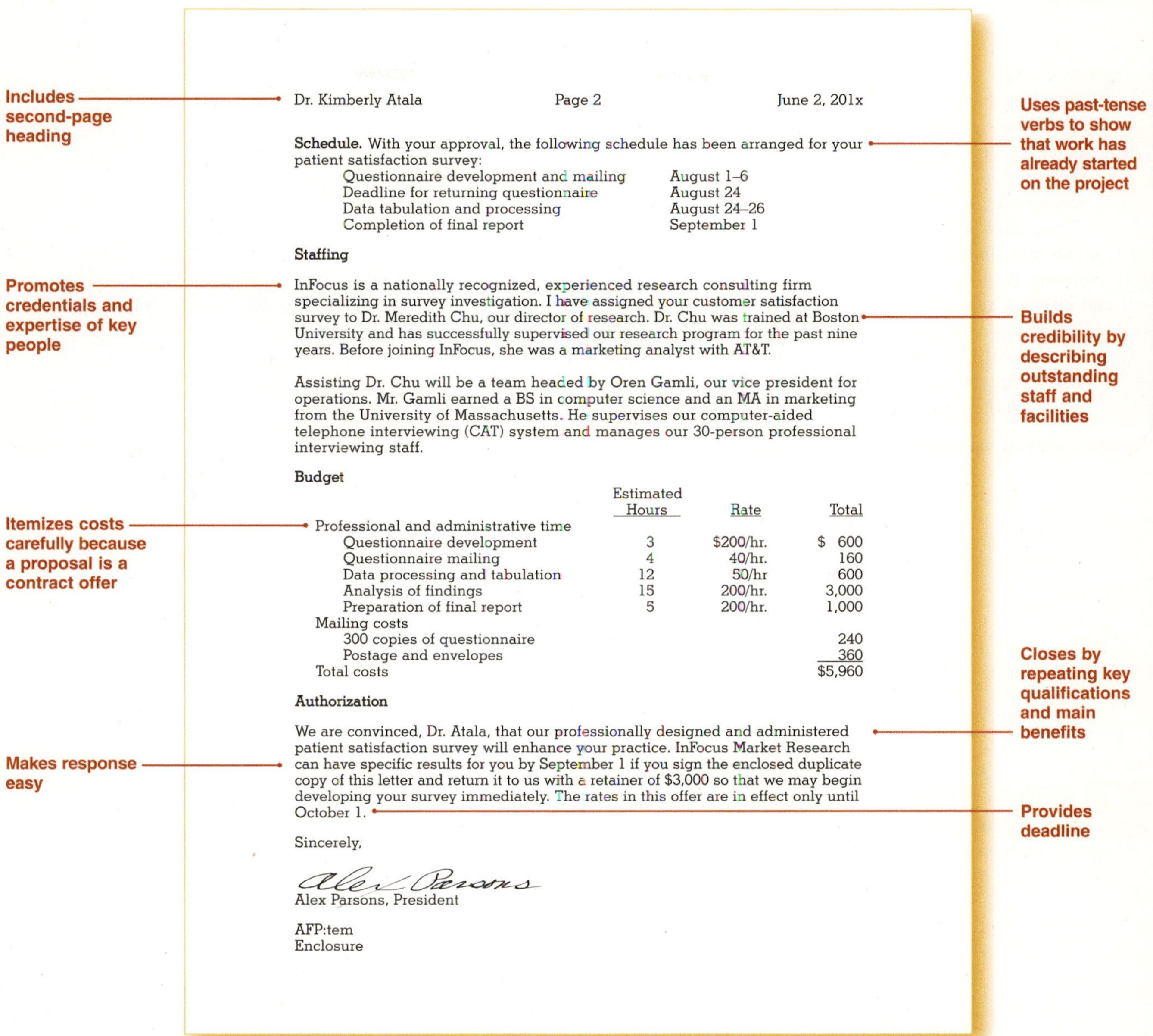

Dr. Kimberly Atala   Page 2   June 2, 201x

Schedule. With your approval, the following schedule has been arranged for your patient satisfaction survey:

Questionnaire development and mailing	August 1–6
Deadline for returning questionnaire	August 24
Data tabulation and processing	August 24–26
Completion of final report	September 1

Staffing

InFocus is a nationally recognized, experienced research consulting firm specializing in survey investigation. I have assigned your customer satisfaction survey to Dr. Meredith Chu, our director of research. Dr. Chu was trained at Boston University and has successfully supervised our research program for the past nine years. Before joining InFocus, she was a marketing analyst with AT&T.

Assisting Dr. Chu will be a team headed by Oren Gamli, our vice president for operations. Mr. Gamli earned a BS in computer science and an MA in marketing from the University of Massachusetts. He supervises our computer-aided telephone interviewing (CAT) system and manages our 30-person professional interviewing staff.

Budget

	Estimated Hours	Rate	Total
Professional and administrative time			
Questionnaire development	3	$200/hr.	$ 600
Questionnaire mailing	4	40/hr.	160
Data processing and tabulation	12	50/hr	600
Analysis of findings	15	200/hr.	3,000
Preparation of final report	5	200/hr.	1,000
Mailing costs			
300 copies of questionnaire			240
Postage and envelopes			360
Total costs			$5,960

Authorization

We are convinced, Dr. Atala, that our professionally designed and administered patient satisfaction survey will enhance your practice. InFocus Market Research can have specific results for you by September 1 if you sign the enclosed duplicate copy of this letter and return it to us with a retainer of $3,000 so that we may begin developing your survey immediately. The rates in this offer are in effect only until October 1.

Sincerely,

Alex Parsons, President

AFP:tem
Enclosure

Includes second-page heading
Promotes credentials and expertise of key people
Itemizes costs carefully because a proposal is a contract offer
Makes response easy
Uses past-tense verbs to show that work has already started on the project
Builds credibility by describing outstanding staff and facilities
Closes by repeating key qualifications and main benefits
Provides deadline

or loss of customers. In a solicited proposal, your aim is to persuade the reader that you understand the problem completely. Therefore, if you are responding to an RFP, this means repeating its language. For example, if the RFP asks for the *design of a maintenance program for wireless communication equipment,* you would use the same language in explaining the purpose of your proposal. This section might include segments titled *Basic Requirements, Most Critical Tasks,* and *Most Important Secondary Problems.*

Proposal, Plan, and Schedule

In the proposal section itself, you should discuss your plan for solving the problem. In some proposals this is tricky because you want to disclose enough of your plan to secure the contract without giving away so much information that your services are not needed. Without specifics, though, your proposal has little chance, so you must decide how much to reveal. Tell what you propose to do and

The proposal section must give enough information to secure the contract but not so much detail that readers may decide they do not need the services.

In a move reminiscent of suburban bomb shelters of the Cold War era, urban planners are preparing "lilypad cities" to house survivors if climate disaster fears ever materialize. Should the planet become inundated by rising sea levels, these zero-emission ships could literally bob around the globe as self-sustaining habitats, complete with energy supplied from solar panels and wind turbines. Designed by award-winning Belgian architect Vincent Callebaut, and inspired by the shape of lilypads, the giant floating metropolises are both stylish and loaded with the comforts of modern living. ***What organizations might submit proposals in the development of lily-pad cities?***

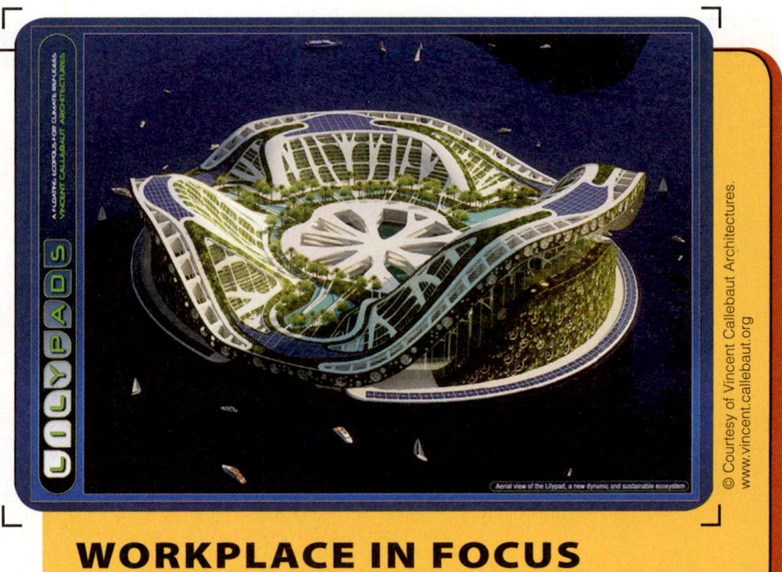

WORKPLACE IN FOCUS

how it will benefit the reader. Remember, too, that a proposal is a sales presentation. Sell your methods, product, and "deliverables" (items that will be left with the client). In this section some writers specify how the project will be managed and how its progress will be audited. Most writers also include a schedule of activities or timetable showing when events will take place.

Staffing

The staffing section promotes the credentials and expertise of the project leaders and support staff.

The staffing section of a proposal describes the credentials and expertise of the project leaders. It may also identify the size and qualifications of the support staff, along with other resources such as computer facilities and special programs for analyzing statistics. The staffing section is a good place to endorse and promote your staff and to demonstrate to the client that your company can do the job. Although some companies use generic rather than actual résumés because they want to be able to replace key individuals during the project, this practice may be unwise. At least two consultants advising proposal writers caution against generic résumés that have not been revised to mirror the RFP's requirements. Only well-tailored résumés will inspire the kind of trust in a team's qualifications that is necessary if a proposal is to be accepted.[4]

Budget

Because a proposal is a legal contract, the budget must be carefully researched.

A central item in most proposals is the budget, a list of proposed project costs. You need to prepare this section carefully because it represents a contract; you cannot raise the price later—even if your costs increase. You can—and should—protect yourself with a deadline for acceptance. In the budget section, some writers itemize hours and costs; others present a total sum only. A proposal to design and build a complex e-commerce Web site might, for example, contain a detailed line-by-line budget. In the proposal shown in Figure 10.1, Alex Parsons felt that he needed to justify the budget for his firm's patient satisfaction survey, so he itemized the costs. However, the budget included for a proposal to conduct a one-day seminar to improve employee communication skills might be a lump sum only. Your analysis of the project will help you decide what kind of budget to prepare.

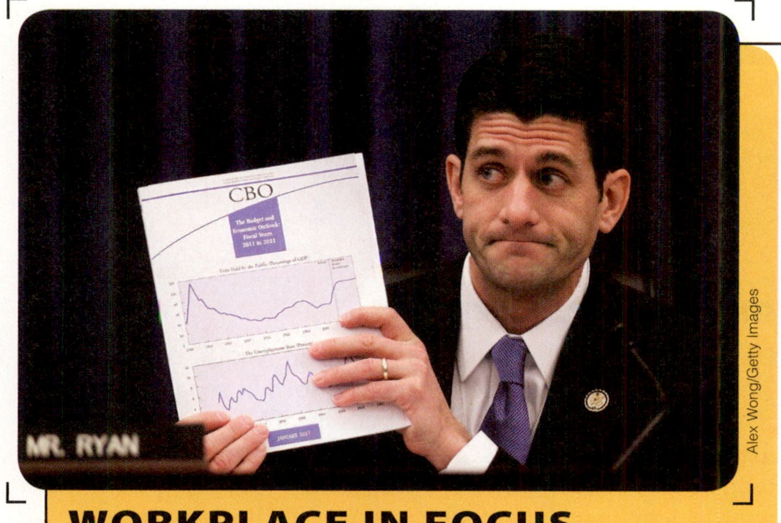

Alex Wong/Getty Images

WORKPLACE IN FOCUS

With the slumping economy and a $15 trillion national debt crisis in the U.S., the Congressional Budget Office (CBO) has transformed from a low-profile legislative research agency to a prominent authority on federal budget decisions. The agency's nonpartisan budget reports and estimates have provided timely fiscal data used for such legislation as the Troubled Asset Relief Program (TARP) and The Patient Protection and Affordable Care Act—commonly known as "Obamacare." ***Why is proper documentation essential for reports published by the CBO?***

Authorization Request

Informal proposals often close with a request for approval or authorization. In addition, the closing should remind the reader of key benefits and motivate action. It might also include a deadline date beyond which the offer is invalid. At defense contractor Raytheon, authorization information can be as simple as naming in the letter of transmittal the company official who would approve the contract resulting from the proposal. However, in most cases, a *model contract* is sent along that responds to the requirements specified by the RFP. This model contract usually results in negotiations before the final project contract is awarded.

"I haven't read your proposal yet, Bob, but I already have some great ideas on how to improve it."

© Randy Glasbergen www.glasbergen.com

Preparing Formal Proposals

Proposals became a staple in the aerospace industry in the 1950s to streamline the bidding for government defense projects. Because proposals are vital to their success, high-tech companies and defense contractors today maintain specialists who do nothing but write proposals. Such proposals typically tell how a problem can be solved, what procedure will be followed, who will do it, how long it will take, and how much it will cost. As you can imagine, writing a formal proposal to bid on a multimillion-dollar contract requires careful preparation, expertise, and countless staff hours.

Formal proposals respond to big projects and may contain 200 or more pages.

Formal proposals differ from informal proposals not in style but in size and format. Formal proposals respond to big projects and may range from 5 to 200 or more pages. To facilitate comprehension and reference, they are organized into many parts. In addition to the six basic parts described for informal proposals, formal proposals may contain some or all of the following additional parts: copy of the RFP, letter or memo of transmittal, abstract and/or executive summary, title page, table of contents, list of figures, list of illustrations, and appendix. In addition, the tone used in formal proposals is often more formal than the tone used in informal proposals.

The primary differences between formal and informal proposals are size and format.

Proposals in the past were always paper-based and delivered by mail or special messenger. Today, however, companies increasingly prefer online proposals.

Receiving companies may transmit the electronic proposal to all levels of management without ever printing a page; this appeals to many environmentally conscious organizations.

Well-written proposals win contracts and business for companies and individuals. In fact, many companies depend entirely on proposals to generate their income, so proposal writing is extremely important.

Writing Formal Business Reports

Formal reports discuss the results of a process of thorough investigation and analysis.

Formal business reports are similar to formal proposals in length, organization, and serious tone. Instead of making an offer, however, formal reports represent the end product of thorough investigation and analysis. They present ordered information to decision makers in business, industry, government, and education. Although formal reports in business are seen infrequently, they serve an important function. They provide management with vital data for decision making. In this section we consider the entire process of writing a formal report: preparing to write, researching secondary data, generating primary data, documenting data, organizing and outlining data, illustrating data, and presenting the final report.

Like proposals and informal reports, formal reports begin with a definition of the project. Probably the most difficult part of this definition is limiting the scope of the report. Every project has limitations. If you are writing a formal report, decide at the outset what constraints influence the range of your project and how you will achieve your purpose. How much time do you have for completing your report? How much space will you be allowed for reporting on your topic? How accessible are the data you need? How thorough should your research be?

If you are writing about low morale among swing-shift employees, for example, how many of your 475 employees should you interview? Should you limit your research to company-related morale factors, or should you consider external factors over which the company has no control? In investigating the relationship between work and student graduation rate, should you focus on particular groups, such as seniors and transfer students, or should you consider all students, including graduate students? The first step in writing a report, then, is determining the precise boundaries of the topic.

The planning of every report begins with a statement of purpose explaining the goal, significance, and limitations of the report.

Once you have defined the project and limited its scope, write a statement of purpose. Preparing a written statement of purpose is a good idea because it defines the focus of the report and provides a standard that keeps the project on target. The statement of purpose should describe the goal, significance, and limitations of the report. In writing useful statements of purpose, choose action verbs telling what you intend to do: *analyze*, *choose*, *investigate*, *compare*, *justify*, *evaluate*, *explain*, *establish*, *determine*, and so on. Notice how the following statement pinpoints the research and report and uses action verbs:

> The purpose of this report is to explore employment possibilities for entry-level clean technology jobs in the Southwest. It will consider typical salaries, skills required, opportunities, and working conditions of insulation workers and solar-energy systems installers. This research is significant because of the increasing number of job openings in the clean tech field. This report won't consider systems and mechanical engineering employment, which requires advanced college degrees and represents a different employment focus.

Researching Secondary Data

One of the most important steps in the process of writing a report is that of gathering information (research). Because a report is only as good as its data, you will want to spend considerable time collecting data before you begin writing.

Data fall into two broad categories, primary and secondary. Primary data result from firsthand experience and observation. Secondary data come from reading what others have experienced or observed and written down. The makers of the energy drink Red Bull, for example, produce primary data when they give away samples, conduct interviews in the streets, and record the reactions of consumers. These same sets of data become secondary after they have been published, and, let's say, a newspaper reporter uses them in an article about the growing popularity of caffeinated energy drinks. Secondary data are easier and cheaper to develop than primary data, which might involve interviewing large groups or sending out questionnaires.

Primary data come from firsthand experience and observation; secondary data, from reading.

You are going to learn first about secondary data because that is where nearly every research project should begin. Often, something has already been written about your topic. Reviewing secondary sources can save time and effort and prevent you from reinventing the wheel. Most secondary material is available either in print or electronically.

Print Resources

Although we're seeing a steady movement away from print data and toward electronic data, print sources are still the most visible parts of most libraries. Much information is available only in print.

Although researchers are increasingly turning to electronic data, some information is available only in print.

If you are an infrequent library user, begin your research by talking with a reference librarian about your project. Librarians won't do your research for you, but they will steer you in the right direction. Moreover, they are very accommodating. Several years ago a *Wall Street Journal* poll revealed that librarians are perceived as among the friendliest, most approachable people in the working world. Many librarians help you understand their computer, cataloging, and retrieval systems by providing advice, brochures, handouts, and workshops.

Books. Although quickly outdated, books provide excellent historical, in-depth data. Books can be located through print catalogs or online catalogs. Most online catalogs today enable you to learn not only whether a book is in the library but also whether it is currently available. Online catalogs can also help you trace and retrieve items from other area libraries if your college doesn't own them.

Periodicals. Magazines, pamphlets, and journals are called *periodicals* because of their recurrent, or periodic, publication. Journals are compilations of scholarly articles. Articles in journals and other periodicals will be extremely useful to you because they are concise, limited in scope, and current and can supplement information in books.

Bibliographic Indexes. Most university libraries now offer online access to the *Readers' Guide to Periodical Literature*. You may still find print copies of this valuable index of general-interest magazine article titles in small libraries. It includes such magazines as *Time, Newsweek, The New Yorker*, and *U.S. News & World Report*. However, business writers today rely almost totally on electronic indexes and databases. Such databases help you locate references, abstracts, and full-text articles from magazines, journals, and newspapers, such as *The New York Times*. Once you locate usable references, you can print a copy of your findings, save them to a USB flash drive, or send them to your e-mail address.

Electronic Databases

As a writer of business reports today, you will probably begin your secondary research with electronic resources. Online databases have become a staple of secondary research. You can conduct detailed searches without ever leaving your office, home, or dorm room.

Commercial databases offer articles, reports, and other information online.

A database is a collection of information stored electronically so that it is accessible by computer and digitally searchable. Databases provide bibliographic information (titles of documents and brief abstracts) and full-text documents. Most researchers prefer full-text documents because they are convenient. Various databases contain a rich array of magazine, newspaper, and journal articles, as well as newsletters, business reports, company profiles, government data, reviews, and directories. The four databases most useful to business writers for general searches are ABI/INFORM Complete (ProQuest), Factiva (Dow Jones), LexisNexis Academic, and Academic Search Premier (EBSCO). Your college library and many businesses subscribe to these expensive resources and perhaps to other, more specialized commercial databases.

The Web

The Web is a collection of hypertext pages that offer information and links on trillions of pages.

Growing at a dizzying pace, the World Wide Web includes an enormous collection of pages created by people around the world. The Web is interactive, mobile, and user-friendly with multimedia content ranging from digital sound files to vivid images and video files. With trillions of pages of information available on the Web, chances are that if you have a question, an answer exists online. To a business researcher, the Web offers a wide range of organizational and commercial information. You can expect to find such items as product and service facts, public relations material, mission statements, staff directories, press releases, current company news, government information, selected article reprints, collaborative scientific project reports, stock research, financial information, and employment information.

The Web is unquestionably one of the greatest sources of information now available to anyone needing simple facts quickly and inexpensively. However, finding relevant, credible information can be frustrating and time-consuming. The constantly changing contents of the Web and its lack of organization irritate budding researchers. Moreover, content isn't always reliable. Anyone posting a Web site is a publisher without any quality control or guarantee. Check out the Communication Workshop at the end of this chapter to learn more about what questions to ask in assessing the quality of a Web document. The problem of gathering information is complicated by the fact that the total number of Web sites recently surpassed about 235 million, growing at a rate of about 4 million new domain addresses each month.[5] Therefore, to succeed in your search for information and answers, you need to understand the search tools available to you. You also need to understand how to evaluate the information you find.

Web browsers are software programs that access Web pages and their links. Increasingly, users access the Web on the go with smartphones and other compact portable devices.

Web Browsers. Searching the Web requires a Web browser, such as Internet Explorer, Safari, or Mozilla Firefox. Browsers are software programs that enable you to view the graphics and text of, as well as access links to, Web pages. Your goal is to locate the top-level Web page (called a *home page* and, in certain cases, a *portal*) of a business organization's site. On this page you will generally find an overview of the site contents or a link to a site map.

Web access has gone mobile in the last few years, as increasingly sophisticated smartphones, netbooks, and tablet devices such as the iPad now offer nearly the same functions as desktop and laptop computers do. Businesspeople can surf Web pages, send text messages, and write e-mail on the go with devices such as the popular iPhone, Android, and BlackBerry, which can fit into their pockets. Similarly, users can listen to podcasts, digital recordings of radio programs, and other audio and video files on demand. Podcasts are distributed for downloading to a computer, a smartphone, or an MP3 audio player such as the iPod and can be enjoyed anywhere you choose.

A search tool or search engine is a service that indexes, organizes, and often rates and reviews Web pages.

Search Tools. The Web is packed with amazing information. Instead of visiting libraries or searching reference books when you need to find something, you can now turn to the Web for all kinds of facts. However, finding what you are looking for on the Web is hopeless without powerful, specialized search tools, such as Google, Bing, Yahoo Search, AOL, and Ask.com. A search tool, also called a search engine, is a service that indexes, organizes, and often rates and reviews Web pages. Some search tools rely on people to maintain a catalog of Web sites or pages. Others use software to identify key information. They all begin a search based on the keywords that you enter. The most-used search engine at this writing is Google.

Internet Search Tips and Techniques. To conduct a thorough search for the information you need, apply these tips and techniques:

You must know how to use search tools to make them most effective.

- **Use two or three search tools.** Begin by conducting a topic search. Use a subject directory such as Yahoo, About.com, or Open Directory Project (**http://www.dmoz.org**). Once you have narrowed your topic, switch to a search engine. At this writing, Google consistently turns up more reliable "hits" than other search tools.
- **Know your search tool.** When connecting to a search site for the first time, always read the description of its service, including its FAQs (frequently asked questions), Help, and How to Search sections. Often there are special features (e.g., news, images, videos, books, scholar, and other categories on Google) that can refine or speed up the search process.
- **Understand case sensitivity.** Generally use lowercase for your searches, unless you are searching for a term that is usually written in upper- and lowercase, such as a person's name.
- **Use nouns as search words and as many as eight words in a query.** The right key words—and more of them—can narrow your search effectively.
- **Combine keywords into phrases.** When searching for a phrase, such as *cost–benefit analysis*, most search tools will retrieve documents having all or some of the terms. This AND/OR strategy is the default of most search tools. To locate occurrences of a specific phrase, enclose it in quotation marks.
- **Omit articles and prepositions.** Known as stop words, articles and prepositions do not add value to a search. Instead of *request for proposal*, use *proposal request*.
- **Use wild cards.** Most search engines support wildcards, such as asterisks. For example, the search term *cent** will retrieve *cents*, whereas *cent*** will retrieve both *center* and *centre*.
- **Proofread your search words.** Make sure you are searching for the right thing by proofreading your search words carefully. For example, searching for *sock market* will come up with substantially different results than searching for *stock market*.
- **Bookmark the best.** To keep track of your favorite Internet sites, save them as bookmarks or favorites.
- **Keep trying.** If a search produces no results, check your spelling. Try synonyms and variations on words. Try to be less specific in your search term. If your search produces too many hits, try to be more specific. Think of words that uniquely identify what you are looking for, and use as many relevant keywords as possible. Use a variety of search tools, and repeat your search a few days later.

Blogs and Social Networks

The Internet continues to grow and expand, offering a great variety of virtual communities and, hence, alternative sources of information. Mentioned most frequently are blogs, the microblogging site Twitter, and social networking sites such as Facebook and LinkedIn.

Blogs and social networking sites can be used to generate primary or secondary data.

One of the newest ways to locate secondary information on the Web is through *blogs.* Individuals' opinions or news items are posted regularly in reverse chronological order, allowing visitors to comment. Blogs are used by business researchers, students, politicians, the media, and many others to share and gather information. Marketing firms and their clients are looking closely at blogs because blogs can produce honest consumer feedback fast and inexpensively. Research published by Technorati confirms that 42 percent of its respondents blog about brands they like or dislike.[6] Employees and executives at companies such as General Motors, Google, Plaxo, IBM, and Hewlett-Packard maintain blogs. They use blogs to communicate internally with employees and externally with the public.

A blog is basically an online diary or journal that allows visitors to leave public comments. At this time, writers have posted 153 million blogs, according to BlogPulse statistics.[7] However, only about half of these blogs are active, meaning that posts were published within three months. A recent Pew Internet study suggested that 32 percent of adult Internet users read a blog once a month and only 17 percent used Twitter or other status-update services.[8] Although blogs and microblogs may have been overrated in their importance, they do represent an amazing new information stream if used wisely. Be sure to evaluate all blog content using the checklist provided in the Communication Workshop at the end of this chapter.

At least as important to business as blogs are popular social networking sites, primarily Facebook. As Technorati reports, 42 percent of all bloggers use social media to follow brands, and 50 percent of those respondents occasionally blog about brands.

Far from being only entertaining leisure sites, social networks such as Facebook and Twitter microblogs are used by businesses, for example, to "listen and engage in customer conversations, address customer complaints and feedback more quickly, and proactively provide information to customers, as well as positively influence customer's opinions."[9] However, these exciting new online tools require sound judgment when researching. The Communication Workshop at the end of this chapter provides reliable evaluation criteria.

Generating Primary Data

Business reports often rely on primary data from firsthand experience.

Although you will begin a business report by probing for secondary data, you will probably need primary data to give a complete picture. Business reports that solve specific current problems typically rely on primary, firsthand data. If, for example, management wants to discover the cause of increased employee turnover in its Seattle office, it must investigate conditions in Seattle by collecting recent information. Providing answers to business problems often means generating primary data through surveys, interviews, observation, or experimentation.

Surveys

Surveys yield efficient and economical primary data for reports.

Surveys collect data from groups of people. Before developing new products, for example, companies often survey consumers to learn their needs. The advantages of surveys are that they gather data economically and efficiently. Snail-mailed, e-mailed, and online surveys reach big groups nearby or at great distances. Moreover, people responding to mailed, e-mailed, and online surveys have time to consider their answers, thus improving the accuracy of the data.

Mailed or e-mailed surveys, of course, have disadvantages. Most of us rank them with junk mail or spam, so response rates may be no higher than 5 percent. Furthermore, those who do respond may not represent an accurate sample of the overall population, thus invalidating generalizations from the group. Let's say, for example, that an insurance company sends out a questionnaire asking about provisions in a new policy. If only older people respond, the questionnaire data cannot be used to generalize what people in other age groups might think. If a survey is only e-mailed, it may miss audiences that do not use the Internet.

A final problem with surveys has to do with truthfulness. Some respondents exaggerate their incomes or distort other facts, thus causing the results to be unreliable. Nevertheless, surveys may be the best way to generate data for business and student reports.

Interviews

Some of the best report information, particularly on topics about which little has been written, comes from individuals. These individuals are usually experts or veterans in their fields. Consider both in-house and outside experts for business reports. Tapping these sources will call for in-person, telephone, or online interviews. To elicit the most useful data, try these techniques:

Interviews with experts produce useful report data, especially when little has been written about a topic.

- **Locate an expert.** Ask managers and individuals who are considered to be most knowledgeable in their areas. Check the membership lists of professional organizations, and consult articles about the topic or related topics. Search business-related blogs to find out who the experts are in your area of interest. Most people enjoy being experts or at least recommending them. You could also post an inquiry to an Internet newsgroup. An easy way to search newsgroups in a topic area is through the **Browse all groups** category indexed by the popular search tool Google.
- **Prepare for the interview.** Learn about the individual you are interviewing, and make sure you can pronounce the interviewee's name correctly. Research the background and terminology of the topic. Let's say you are interviewing a corporate communication expert about producing an in-house newsletter. You ought to be familiar with terms such as *font* and software such as QuarkXPress and Adobe InDesign. In addition, be prepared by making a list of questions that pinpoint your focus on the topic. Ask the interviewee if you may record the talk. Practice using the recording device so that you are familiar with it by the time of the interview.
- **Maintain a professional attitude.** Call before the interview to confirm the arrangements, and then arrive on time. Be prepared to take notes if your recorder fails (and remember to ask permission beforehand if you want to record). Dress professionally, and use your body language to convey respect.
- **Make your questions objective and friendly.** Adopt a courteous and respectful attitude. Don't get into a debating match with the interviewee, and don't interrupt. Remember that you are there to listen, not to talk! Use open-ended questions (*What are your predictions for the future of the telecommunications industry?*), rather than yes-or-no questions (*Do you think we will see more video e-mail in the future?*) to draw experts out.
- **Watch the time.** Tell interviewees in advance how much time you expect to need for the interview. Don't overstay your appointment. If your subject rambles, gently try to draw him or her back to the topic; otherwise, you may run out of time before asking all your questions.
- **End graciously.** Conclude the interview with a general question, such as *Is there anything you would like to add?* Express your appreciation, and ask permission to telephone later if you need to verify points. Send a thank-you note within a day or two after the interview.

Observation and Experimentation

Some kinds of primary data can be obtained only through firsthand observation and investigation. If you determine that the questions you have require observational data, then you need to plan the observations carefully. Most important is deciding what or whom you are observing, and how often those observations are necessary to provide reliable data. For example, if you want to learn more about an organization's customer-service phone service, you probably need to conduct an observation (along with interviews and perhaps even surveys). You will want to answer questions such as, *How long does a typical caller wait before a customer service rep answers the call?* and *Is the service consistent?* Recording observations for 60-minute periods at various times throughout a week will give you a better picture than observing for just an hour on a Friday before a holiday.

Some of the best report data come from firsthand observation and experimentation.

When you observe, plan ahead. Arrive early enough to introduce yourself and set up whatever equipment you think is necessary. Make sure you have received permissions beforehand, particularly if you are recording. In addition, take notes, not only of the events or actions but also of the settings. Changes in environment often have an effect on actions. Famous for his out-of-the box thinking, Howard Schultz, the CEO of Starbucks, is known to hate research, advertising, and customer surveys. Instead of relying on sophisticated marketing research, Schultz visits 25 Starbucks locations a week to learn about his customers.[10]

Experimentation produces data suggesting causes and effects. Informal experimentation might be as simple as a pretest and posttest in a college course. Did students expand their knowledge as a result of the course? More formal experimentation is undertaken by scientists and professional researchers who control variables to test their effects. Assume, for example, that Hershey's wants to test the hypothesis (which is a tentative assumption) that chocolate lifts people out of the doldrums. An experiment testing the hypothesis would separate depressed individuals into two groups: those who ate chocolate (the experimental group) and those who did not (the control group). What effect did chocolate have? Such experiments are not done haphazardly, however. Valid experiments require sophisticated research designs and careful attention to matching the experimental and control groups.

Documenting Information

Report writers document their sources to strengthen an argument, help readers locate data, and protect themselves from charges of plagiarism.

In writing business and other reports, you will often build on the ideas and words of others. In Western culture, whenever you "borrow" the ideas of others, you must give credit to your information sources. This is called *documentation*. Using the ideas of someone else without giving credit is called *plagiarism* and is unethical. Even if you *paraphrase* (put the information in your own words), the ideas must be documented. You will learn more about paraphrasing in this section.

Recognizing the Purposes of Documentation

As a careful writer, you should take pains to document report data properly for the following reasons:

- **To strengthen your argument.** Including good data from reputable sources will convince readers of your credibility and the logic of your reasoning.
- **To instruct the reader.** Citing references enables readers to pursue a topic further and make use of the information themselves.
- **To protect yourself against charges of plagiarism.** Acknowledging your sources keeps you honest. Plagiarism, which is unethical and in some cases illegal, is the act of using others' ideas without proper documentation or paraphrasing poorly.

Plagiarism of words or ideas is a serious charge and can lead to loss of a job. Famous historians, several high-level journalists, and even college professors[11] suffered serious consequences for copying from unnamed sources. Your instructor may use a commercial plagiarism detection service such as Turnitin.com, which can cross-reference much of the information on the Web, looking for documents with similar phrasing. The result, an "originality report," provides the instructor with a clear idea of whether you have been accurate and honest. You can avoid charges of plagiarism as well as add clarity to your work by knowing what to document and by developing good research habits.

Give credit when you use another's ideas, when you cite facts that are not common knowledge, and when you quote or paraphrase another's words.

Learning What to Document

When you write reports, especially in college, you are continually dealing with other people's ideas. You are expected to conduct research, synthesize ideas, and build on the work of others. But you are also expected to give proper credit for borrowed material. To avoid plagiarism, you must give credit whenever you use the following:[12]

- Another person's ideas, opinions, examples, or theory
- Any facts, statistics, graphs, and drawings that are not common knowledge
- Quotations of another person's actual spoken or written words
- Paraphrases of another person's spoken or written words

Information that is common knowledge requires no documentation. For example, the statement The Wall Street Journal *is a popular business newspaper* would require no citation. Statements that are not common knowledge, however, must be documented. For example, *Texas is home to two of the nation's top ten fastest-growing large cities (100,000 or more population): Austin and San Antonio also ranked first and second in jobs*[13] would require a citation because most people don't know this fact. Cite sources for proprietary information such as statistics organized and reported by a newspaper or magazine. You probably know to use citations to document direct quotations, but you must also cite ideas that you summarize in your own words.

OFFICE INSIDER

Many students mistakenly take bad notes during the research process. They write someone else's text verbatim on a card or on their computer and forget quotation marks.

—Boston College Library Guide

Developing Good Research Habits

Report writers who are gathering information should record documentation data immediately after locating the information. This information can then be used in footnotes, endnotes, or in-text citations; and it can be listed in references or a works cited list at the end of the report. Here are some tips for gathering the documentation data you need from some of the most popular types of resources:

- For a book, record the title, author(s), publisher, place of publication, year of publication, and pages cited.
- For newspaper, magazine, and journal articles, record the publication title, article title, author(s), issue/volume number, date, and pages cited.
- For online newspaper and magazine articles, record the author(s), article title, publication title, date the article was written, and the exact URL.
- For an entire Web site, record the name of the company or organization sponsoring the site, and the URL.

Report writers who are gathering information have two methods available for recording the information they find. The time-honored manual method of notetaking works well because information is recorded on separate cards, which can then be arranged in the order needed to develop a thesis or argument. Today, however, writers rely heavily on electronic researching. Instead of recording facts on note cards, savvy researchers manage their data by saving sources to memory sticks and disks, e-mailing documents, bookmarking favorites, and copying and pasting information from the Web into word-processing software for easy storage and retrieval. Beware, though, of cutting-and-pasting your way into plagiarism.

You can learn more about what types of documentation information to record during your research by studying the formal report in Figure 10.17 and by consulting Appendix C.

Practicing the Fine Art of Paraphrasing

In writing reports and using the ideas of others, you will probably rely heavily on *paraphrasing*, which means restating an original passage in your own words and in your own style. To do a good job of paraphrasing, follow these steps:

Paraphrasing involves putting an original passage into your own words.

1. Read the original material carefully to comprehend its full meaning.
2. Write your own version without looking at the original.
3. Avoid repeating the grammatical structure of the original and merely replacing words with synonyms.
4. Reread the original to be sure you covered the main points but did not borrow specific language.

To better understand the difference between plagiarizing and paraphrasing, study the following passages. Notice that the writer of the plagiarized version uses the same grammatical construction as the source and often merely replaces words with synonyms. Even the acceptable version, however, requires a reference to the source author.

Source
While the BlackBerry has become standard armor for executives, a few maverick leaders are taking action to reduce e-mail use. . . . The concern, say academics and management thinkers, is misinterpreted messages, as well as the degree to which e-mail has become a substitute for the nuanced conversations that are critical in the workplace.[14]

The plagiarized version uses the same sentence structure as the original and makes few changes other than replacing some words.

Plagiarized version
Although smartphones are standard among business executives, some pioneering bosses are acting to lower e-mail usage. Business professors and management experts are concerned that messages are misinterpreted and that e-mail substitutes for nuances in conversations that are crucial on the job (Last name, year).

The acceptable paraphrase presents ideas from a different perspective and uses a different sentence structure than the original.

Acceptable paraphrase
E-mail on the go may be the rage in business. However, some executives are rethinking its use, as communication experts warn that e-mail triggers misunderstandings. These specialists believe that e-mail should not replace the more subtle face-to-face interaction needed on the job (Last name, year).

Knowing When and How to Quote

On occasion you will want to use the exact words of a source. Anytime you use the exact words from a source, you must enclose the words in quotation marks. Be careful when doing this that you don't change the wording of the quoted material in any way.

Also beware of overusing quotations. Documents that contain pages of spliced-together quotations suggest that writers have few ideas of their own. Wise writers and speakers use direct quotations for three purposes only:

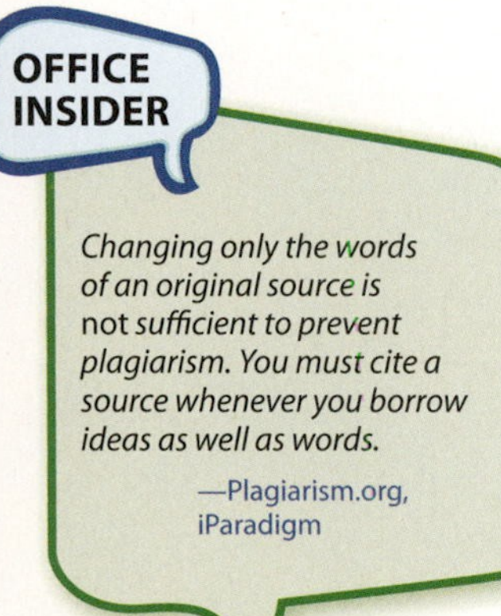

OFFICE INSIDER
Changing only the words of an original source is not sufficient to prevent plagiarism. You must cite a source whenever you borrow ideas as well as words.
—Plagiarism.org, iParadigm

- To provide objective background data and establish the severity of a problem as seen by experts
- To repeat identical phrasing because of its precision, clarity, or aptness
- To duplicate exact wording before criticizing

When you must use a long quotation, try to summarize and introduce it in your own words. Readers want to know the gist of a quotation before they tackle it. For example, to introduce a quotation discussing the shrinking staffs of large companies, you could precede it with your words: *In predicting employment trends, Charles Waller believes the corporation of the future will depend on a small core of full-time employees.* To introduce quotations or paraphrases, use wording such as the following:

According to Waller, ...

Waller argues that . . . .

In his recent study, Waller reported . . . .

Use quotation marks to enclose exact quotations, as shown in the following: *"The current image," says Charles Waller, "of a big glass-and-steel corporate headquarters on landscaped grounds directing a worldwide army of tens of thousands of employees may soon be a thing of the past" (year, page).*

Guidelines for MLA and APA citation formats may be found in Appendix C; guidelines for electronic citations are at **www.cengagebrain.com.**

Using Citation Formats

You can direct readers to your sources with parenthetical notes inserted into the text and with bibliographies, references, or works cited lists. The most common citation formats are those presented by the Modern Language Association (MLA) and the American Psychological Association (APA). Learn more about how to use these formats in Appendix C. For links to the most up-do-date citation formats for electronic references, visit **www.cengagebrain.com**. You will find model citation formats for online magazine, newspaper, and journal articles, as well as for Web references.

Organizing and Outlining Data

Once you have collected the data for a report and recorded that information on notes or printouts, you are ready to organize it into a coherent plan of presentation. First, you should decide on an organizational strategy, and then, following your plan, you will want to outline the report. Poorly organized reports lead to frustration; therefore, it is important to organize your report carefully so that readers will understand, remember, or be persuaded.

Organizational Strategies

The readability and effectiveness of a report are greatly enhanced by skillful organization of the information presented. As you begin the process of organization, ask yourself two important questions: (1) Where should I place the conclusions/recommendations? and (2) How should I organize the findings?

Where to Place the Findings, Conclusions, and Recommendations. As you recall from earlier instruction, the direct strategy requires that we present main ideas first. In formal reports that would mean beginning with your conclusions and recommendations. For example, if you were studying five possible locations for a proposed shopping center, you would begin with the recommendation of the best site. Use this strategy when the reader is supportive and knowledgeable. However, if the reader isn't supportive or needs to be informed, the indirect strategy may be better. This strategy involves presenting the findings (facts and discussion) first, followed by conclusions and recommendations. Since formal reports often seek to educate the reader, this order of presentation is often most effective. Following this sequence, a study of possible locations for a shopping center would begin with data regarding all proposed sites followed by an analysis of the findings and conclusions drawn from that analysis.

In the direct strategy, conclusions and recommendations come first; in the indirect strategy, they are last.

To distinguish among findings, conclusions, and recommendations, consider the example of an audit report. The auditor compiles facts and figures—the findings of the report—to meet the purpose or objective of the audit. Drawing inferences from the findings, the auditor arrives at conclusions. With the audit objectives in mind, the auditor may then propose corrective steps, actions, and recommendations.

How to Organize the Findings. After collecting your facts, you need a coherent plan for presenting them. We describe here three principal organizational patterns: chronological, geographical, and topical. You will find these and other patterns summarized in Figure 10.2. The pattern you choose depends on the material collected and the purpose of your report.

Organize report findings chronologically, geographically, topically, or by one of the other methods shown in Figure 10.2.

- **Chronological order.** Information sequenced along a time line is arranged chronologically. This plan is effective for presenting historical data or for describing a procedure. Agendas, minutes of meetings, progress reports, and procedures are usually organized by time. A report describing an eight-week training program, for example, would most likely be organized by weeks. A plan for step-by-step improvement of customer service would be organized by steps. Often, topics are arranged in a past-to-present or present-to-past sequence.
- **Geographical or spatial arrangement.** Information arranged geographically or spatially is organized by physical location. For instance, a report detailing

FIGURE 10.2 Organizational Patterns for Report Findings

Pattern	Development	Use
Chronology	Arrange information in a time sequence to show history or development of topic.	Useful in showing time relationships, such as five-year profit figures or a series of events leading to a problem
Geography/Space	Organize information by regions or areas.	Appropriate for topics that are easily divided into locations, such as East Coast, West Coast, etc.
Topic/Function	Arrange by topics or functions.	Works well for topics with established categories, such as a report about categories of company expenses
Compare/Contrast	Present problem and show alternative solutions. Use consistent criteria. Show how the solutions are similar and different.	Best used for "before and after" scenarios or for problems with clear alternatives
Journalism Pattern	Arrange information in paragraphs devoted to *who, what, when, where, why,* and *how.* May conclude with recommendations.	Useful with audiences that need to be educated or persuaded
Value/Size	Start with the most valuable, biggest, or most important item. Discuss other items in descending order.	Useful for classifying information in, for example, a realtor's report on home values
Importance	Arrange from most important to least importance or build from least to most important.	Appropriate when persuading the audience to take a specific action or change a belief
Simple/Complex	Begin with simple concept; proceed to more complex idea.	Useful for technical or abstract topics
Best Case/Worst Case	Describe the best and possibly the worst possible outcomes.	Useful when dramatic effect is needed to achieve results; helpful when audience is uninterested or uninformed
Convention	Organize the report using a prescribed plan that all readers understand.	Useful for many operational and recurring reports such as weekly sales reports

company expansion might divide the plan into West Coast, East Coast, and Midwest expansion.

- **Simple/complex arrangement.** Technical or abstract topics lend themselves to a logical order proceeding from a simple concept to more complex ideas. Consider, for example, a report explaining genetic modifications of plants such as soy, organized from simple seed production to complex gene introduction.

Outlines and Headings

Most writers agree that the clearest way to show the organization of a report topic is by recording its divisions in an outline. Although the outline isn't part of the final report, it is a valuable tool of the writer. It reveals at a glance the overall organization of the report. As you learned in Chapter 3, outlining involves dividing a topic into major sections and supporting those with details. Figure 10.3 shows an abbreviated outline of a report about forms of business ownership. Rarely is a real outline so perfectly balanced; some sections are usually longer than others. Remember, though, not to put a single topic under a major component. If you have only one subpoint, integrate it with the main item above it or reorganize. Use details, illustrations, and evidence to support subpoints.

The main points used to outline a report often become the main headings of the written report. In Chapter 9 you studied tips for writing talking and functional headings. Formatting those headings depends on what level they represent. Major headings, as you can see in Figure 10.4, are centered and typed in bold font. Second-level headings start at the left margin, and third-level headings are indented and become part of a paragraph.

FIGURE 10.3 Outline Format

FORMS OF BUSINESS OWNERSHIP

I. **Sole proprietorship (first main topic)**
  A. Advantages of sole proprietorship (first subdivision of Topic I)
    1. Minimal capital requirements (first subdivision of Topic A)
    2. Control by owner (second subdivision of Topic A)
  B. Disadvantages of sole proprietorship (second subdivision of Topic I)
    1. Unlimited liability (first subdivision of Topic B)
    2. Limited management talent (second subdivision of Topic B)

II. **Partnership (second main topic)**
  A. Advantages of partnership (first subdivision of Topic II)
    1. Access to capital (first subdivision of Topic A)
    2. Management talent (second subdivision of Topic A)
    3. Ease of formation (third subdivision of Topic A)
  B. Disadvantages of partnership (second subdivision of Topic II)
    1. Unlimited liability (first subdivision of Topic B)
    2. Personality conflicts (second subdivision of Topic B)

FIGURE 10.4 Levels of Headings in Reports

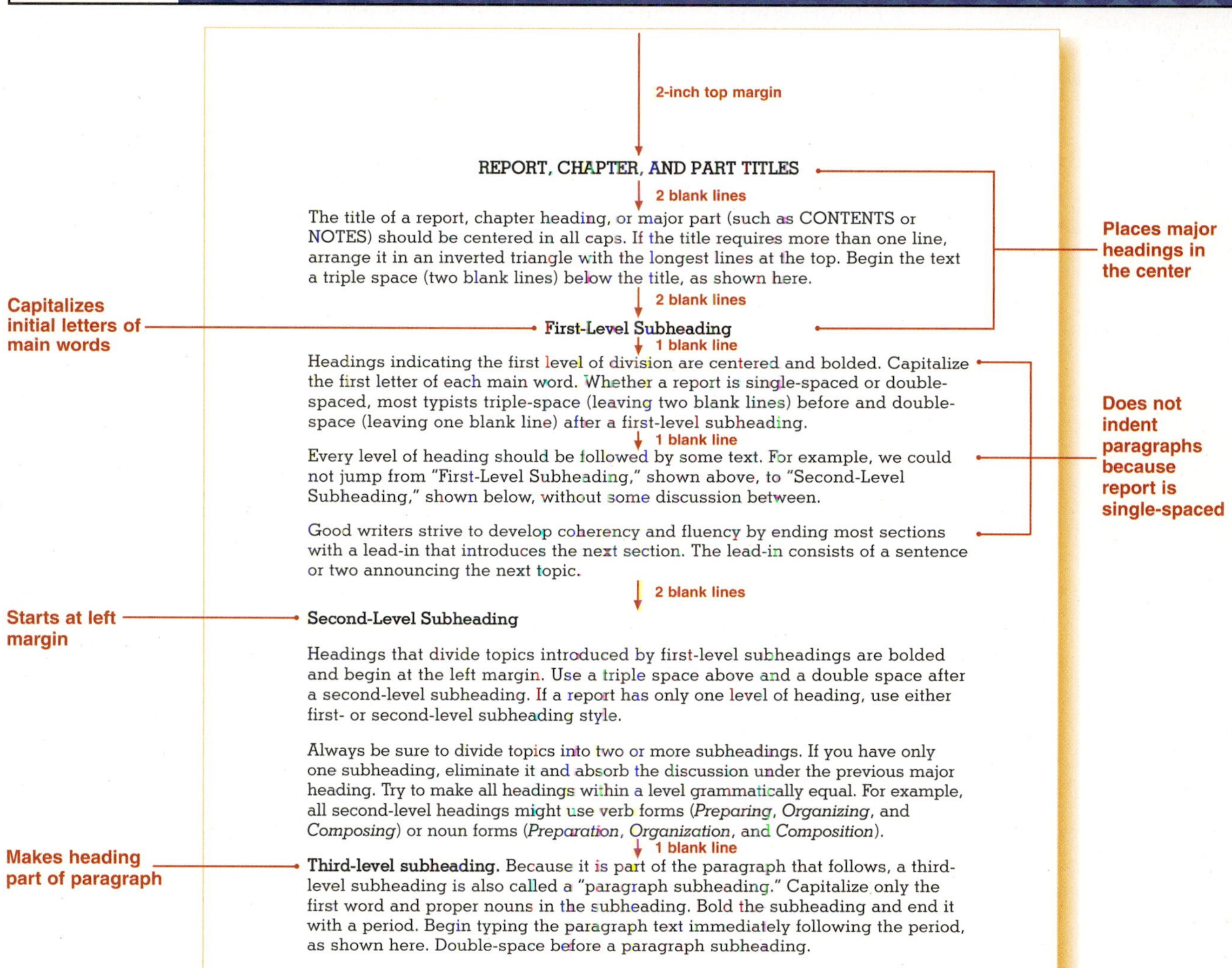

REPORT, CHAPTER, AND PART TITLES

The title of a report, chapter heading, or major part (such as CONTENTS or NOTES) should be centered in all caps. If the title requires more than one line, arrange it in an inverted triangle with the longest lines at the top. Begin the text a triple space (two blank lines) below the title, as shown here.

First-Level Subheading

Headings indicating the first level of division are centered and bolded. Capitalize the first letter of each main word. Whether a report is single-spaced or double-spaced, most typists triple-space (leaving two blank lines) before and double-space (leaving one blank line) after a first-level subheading.

Every level of heading should be followed by some text. For example, we could not jump from "First-Level Subheading," shown above, to "Second-Level Subheading," shown below, without some discussion between.

Good writers strive to develop coherency and fluency by ending most sections with a lead-in that introduces the next section. The lead-in consists of a sentence or two announcing the next topic.

Second-Level Subheading

Headings that divide topics introduced by first-level subheadings are bolded and begin at the left margin. Use a triple space above and a double space after a second-level subheading. If a report has only one level of heading, use either first- or second-level subheading style.

Always be sure to divide topics into two or more subheadings. If you have only one subheading, eliminate it and absorb the discussion under the previous major heading. Try to make all headings within a level grammatically equal. For example, all second-level headings might use verb forms (*Preparing*, *Organizing*, and *Composing*) or noun forms (*Preparation*, *Organization*, and *Composition*).

Third-level subheading. Because it is part of the paragraph that follows, a third-level subheading is also called a "paragraph subheading." Capitalize only the first word and proper nouns in the subheading. Bold the subheading and end it with a period. Begin typing the paragraph text immediately following the period, as shown here. Double-space before a paragraph subheading.

Creating Effective Graphics

Effective graphics clarify numerical data and simplify complex ideas.

After collecting and interpreting information, you need to consider how best to present it. If your report contains complex data and numbers, you may want to consider graphics such as tables and charts. These graphics clarify data, create visual interest, and make numerical data meaningful. By simplifying complex ideas and emphasizing key data, well-constructed graphics make key information more understandable and easier to remember. In contrast, readers tend to be bored and confused by text paragraphs packed with complex data and numbers. However, the same data can be shown in many forms; for example, in a chart, table, or graph. That's why you need to know how to match the appropriate graphic with your objective and how to incorporate it into your report.

Matching Graphics and Objectives

In developing the best graphics, you should first decide what data you want to highlight and which graphics are most appropriate to your objectives. Tables? Bar charts? Pie charts? Line charts? Surface charts? Flowcharts? Organization charts? Pictures? Figure 10.5 summarizes appropriate uses for each type of graphic. The following sections discuss each type in detail.

Tables permit the systematic presentation of large amounts of data, whereas charts enhance visual comparisons.

Tables. Probably the most frequently used graphic in reports is the table. Because a table presents quantitative or verbal information in systematic columns and rows, it can clarify large quantities of data in small spaces. The disadvantage is that tables don't readily display trends. In preparing tables for your readers or

FIGURE 10.5 Matching Graphics to Objectives

Graphic	Objective
Table	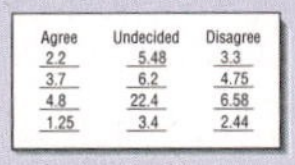 To show exact figures and values
Bar Chart	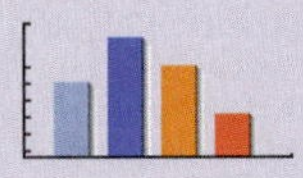 To compare one item with others
Line Chart	 To demonstrate changes in quantitative data over time
Pie Chart	 To visualize a whole unit and the proportions of its components
Flowchart	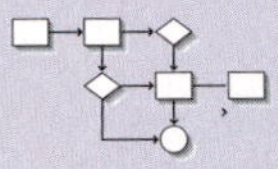 To display a process or procedure
Organization Chart	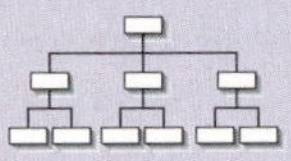 To define a hierarchy of elements
Photograph, Map, Illustration	 To create authenticity, to spotlight a location, and to show an item in use

Jason Stitt/Shutterstock.com

FIGURE 10.6 Table Summarizing Precise Data

Figure 1
MPM Entertainment Company
Income by Division (in millions of dollars)

	Theme Parks	Motion Pictures	DVDs and Blu-ray	Total
2009	$15.8	$39.3	$11.2	$66.3
2010	18.1	17.5	15.3	50.9
2011	23.8	21.1	22.7	67.6
2012	32.2	22.0	24.3	78.5
2013 (projected)	35.1	21.0	26.1	82.2

Source: *Industry Profiles* (New York: DataPro, 2012), 225.

listeners, however, you need to pay attention to clarity and emphasis. Here are tips for designing good tables, one of which is provided in Figure 10.6:

- Place titles and labels at the top of the table.
- Arrange items in a logical order (alphabetical, chronological, geographical, highest to lowest), depending on what you need to emphasize.
- Provide clear headings for the rows and columns.
- Identify the units in which figures are given (percentages, dollars, units per worker hour) in the table title, in the column or row heading, with the first item in a column, or in a note at the bottom.
- Use *N/A* (*not available*) for missing data.
- Make long tables easier to read by shading alternate lines or by leaving a blank line after groups of five.
- Place tables as close as possible to the place where they are mentioned in the text.

Bar Charts. Although they lack the precision of tables, bar charts enable you to make emphatic visual comparisons by using horizontal or vertical bars of varying lengths. Bar charts are useful for comparing related items, illustrating changes in data over time, and showing segments as part of a whole. Figures 10.7 through 10.10 show vertical (also called column charts), horizontal, grouped,

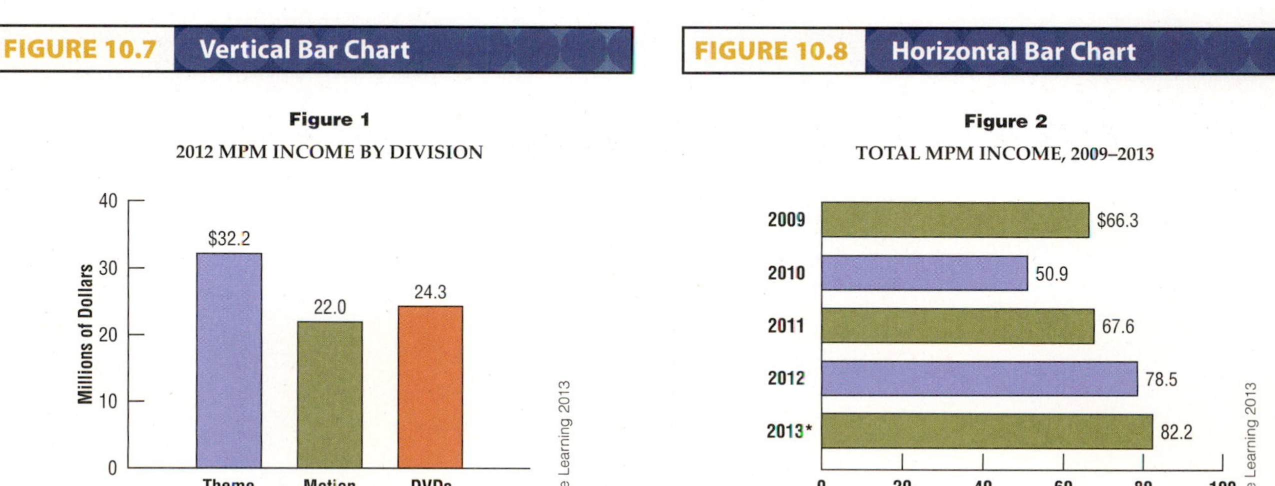

FIGURE 10.9 Grouped Bar Chart

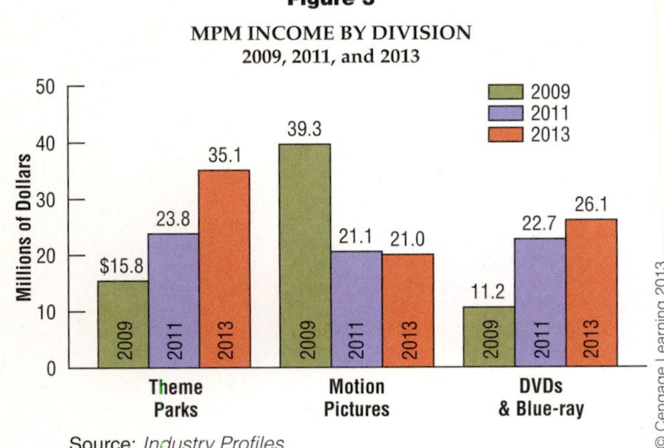

FIGURE 10.10 Segmented 100% Bar Chart

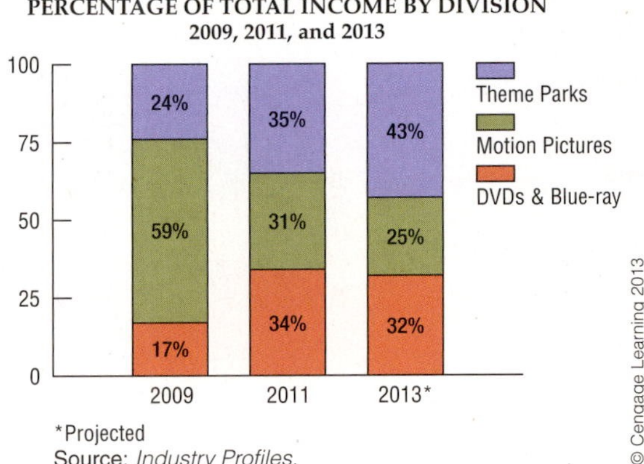

and segmented bar charts that highlight some of the data shown in the MPM Entertainment Company table (Figure 10.6). Note how the varied bar charts present information in differing ways.

Many techniques for constructing tables also hold true for bar charts. Here are a few additional tips:

- Keep the length and width of each bar and segment proportional.
- Include a total figure in the middle of a bar or at its end if the figure helps the reader and does not clutter the chart.
- Start dollar or percentage amounts at zero.
- Place the first bar at some distance (usually half the amount of space between bars) from the *y* axis.
- Avoid showing too much information, thus preventing clutter and confusion.

Line charts illustrate trends and changes in data over time.

Line Charts. The major advantage of line charts is that they show changes over time, thus indicating trends. The vertical axis is typically the dependent variable (such as dollars), and the horizontal axis is the independent one (such as years). Figures 10.11 through 10.13 show line charts that reflect income trends for the three divisions of MPM. Notice that line charts don't provide precise data, such

FIGURE 10.11 Simple Line Chart

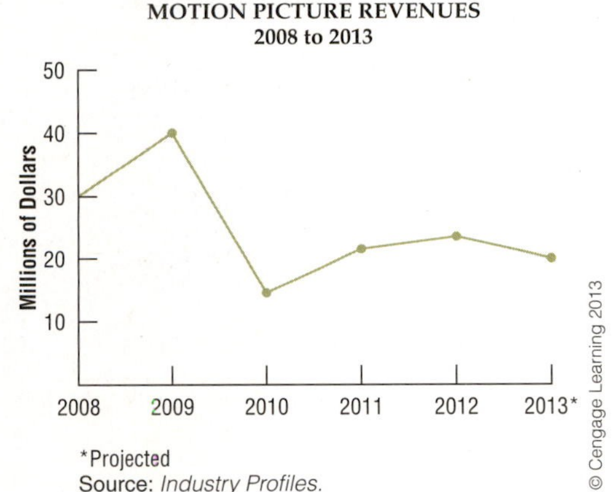

FIGURE 10.12 Multiple Line Chart

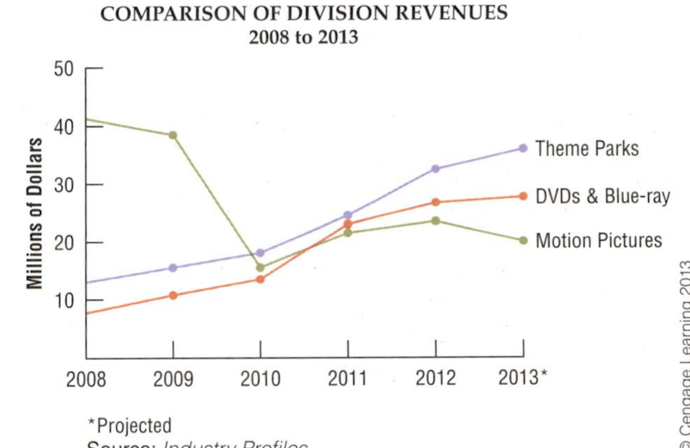

as the 2012 MPM DVD and movies and Blu-ray disc income. Instead, they give an overview or impression of the data. Experienced report writers use tables to list exact data; they use line charts or bar charts to spotlight important points or trends.

Simple line charts (Figure 10.11) show just one variable. Multiple line charts compare items, such as two or more data sets, using the same variable (Figure 10.12). Segmented line charts (Figure 10.13), also called surface charts, illustrate how the components of a whole change over time. To prepare a line chart, remember these tips:

- Begin with a grid divided into squares.
- Arrange the time component (usually years) horizontally across the bottom; arrange values for the other variable vertically.
- Draw small dots at the intersections to indicate each value at a given year.
- Connect the dots and add color if desired.
- To prepare a segmented (surface) chart, plot the first value (say, DVD and Blu-ray disc income) across the bottom; add the next item (say, motion picture income) to the first figures for every increment; for the third item (say, theme park income) add its value to the total of the first two items. The top line indicates the total of the three values.

Pie Charts. Pie charts, or circle graphs, enable readers to see a whole and the proportion of its components, or wedges. Although less flexible than bar or line charts, pie charts are useful for showing percentages, as Figure 10.14 illustrates. They are very effective for lay, or nonexpert, audiences. Notice that a wedge can be "exploded," or popped out, for special emphasis, as seen in Figure 10.14. Microsoft Excel and other spreadsheet programs provide a selection of three-dimensional pie charts. For the most effective pie charts, follow these suggestions:

Pie charts are most useful in showing the proportion of parts to a whole.

- Make the biggest wedge appear first. Computer spreadsheet programs correctly assign the biggest wedge first (beginning at the 12 o'clock position) and arrange the others in order of decreasing size as long as you list the data representing each wedge on the spreadsheet in descending order.
- Include, if possible, the actual percentage or absolute value for each wedge.
- Use four to eight segments for best results; if necessary, group small portions into a wedge called *Other*.

FIGURE 10.13 Segmented Line (Surface) Chart

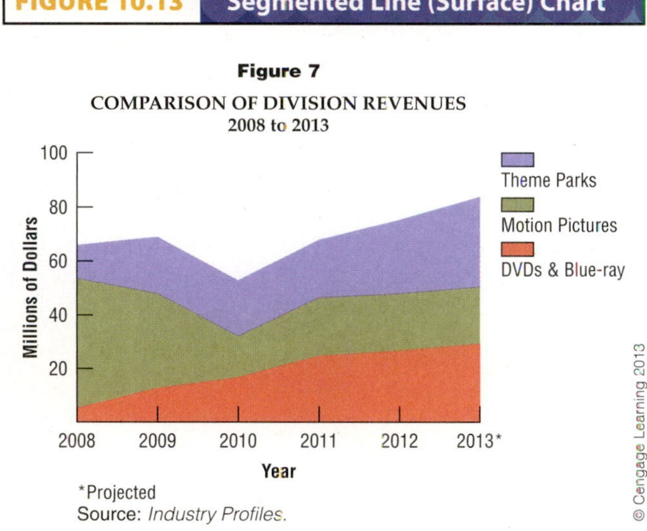

FIGURE 10.14 Pie Chart

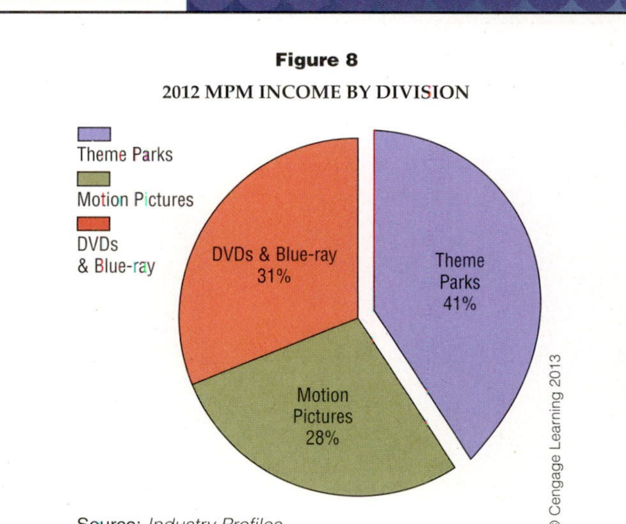

- Draw radii from the center.
- Distinguish wedges with color, shading, or cross-hatching.
- Keep all labels horizontal.

Flowcharts use standard symbols to illustrate a process or procedure.

Flowcharts. Procedures are simplified and clarified by diagramming them in a flowchart, as shown in Figure 10.15. Whether you need to describe the procedure for handling a customer's purchase, highlight steps in solving a problem, or display a problem with a process, flowcharts help the reader visualize the process. Traditional flowcharts use the following symbols:

- Ovals to designate the beginning and end of a process
- Diamonds to indicate decision points
- Rectangles to represent major activities or steps

Software programs such as SmartDraw, EazyDraw, and ConceptDraw can be used to create professional-quality flowcharts.

Organization Charts. Many large organizations are so complex that they need charts to show the chain of command, from the boss down to the line managers and employees. Organization charts like the one in Figure 10.16 provide such information as who reports to whom, how many subordinates work for each manager (the span of control), and what channels of official communication exist. These charts may illustrate a company's structure—for example, by function, customer, or product. They may also be organized by the work being performed in each job or by the hierarchy of decision making.

Photographs, Maps, and Illustrations. Some business reports include photographs, maps, and illustrations to serve specific purposes. Photos, for example, add authenticity and provide a visual record. An environmental engineer may use photos to document hazardous waste sites. Maps enable report writers to depict activities or concentrations geographically, such as dots indicating sales reps in states across the country. Illustrations and diagrams are

FIGURE 10.15 Flowchart

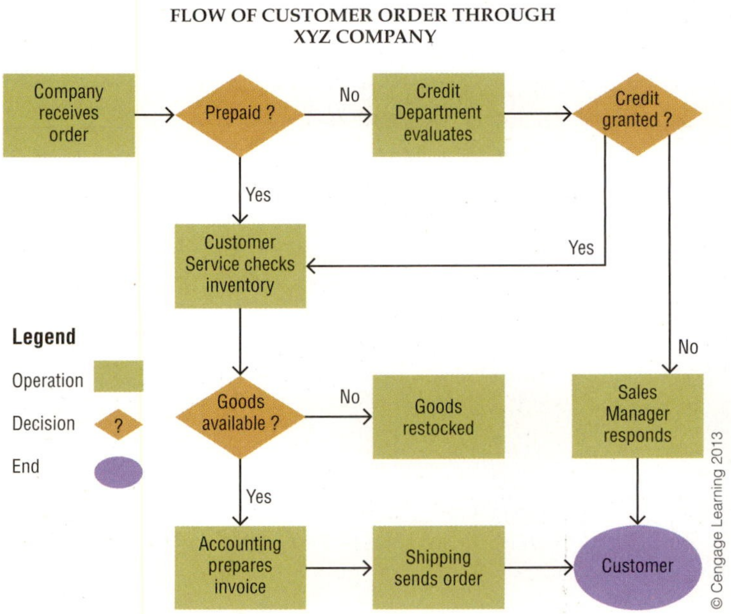

FLOW OF CUSTOMER ORDER THROUGH
XYZ COMPANY

Company receives order
Prepaid ?
No
Credit Department evaluates
Credit granted ?
Yes
Customer Service checks inventory
Yes
No
Goods available ?
No
Goods restocked
Sales Manager responds
Yes
Accounting prepares invoice
Shipping sends order
Customer

Legend
Operation
Decision ?
End

FIGURE 10.16 Organization Chart

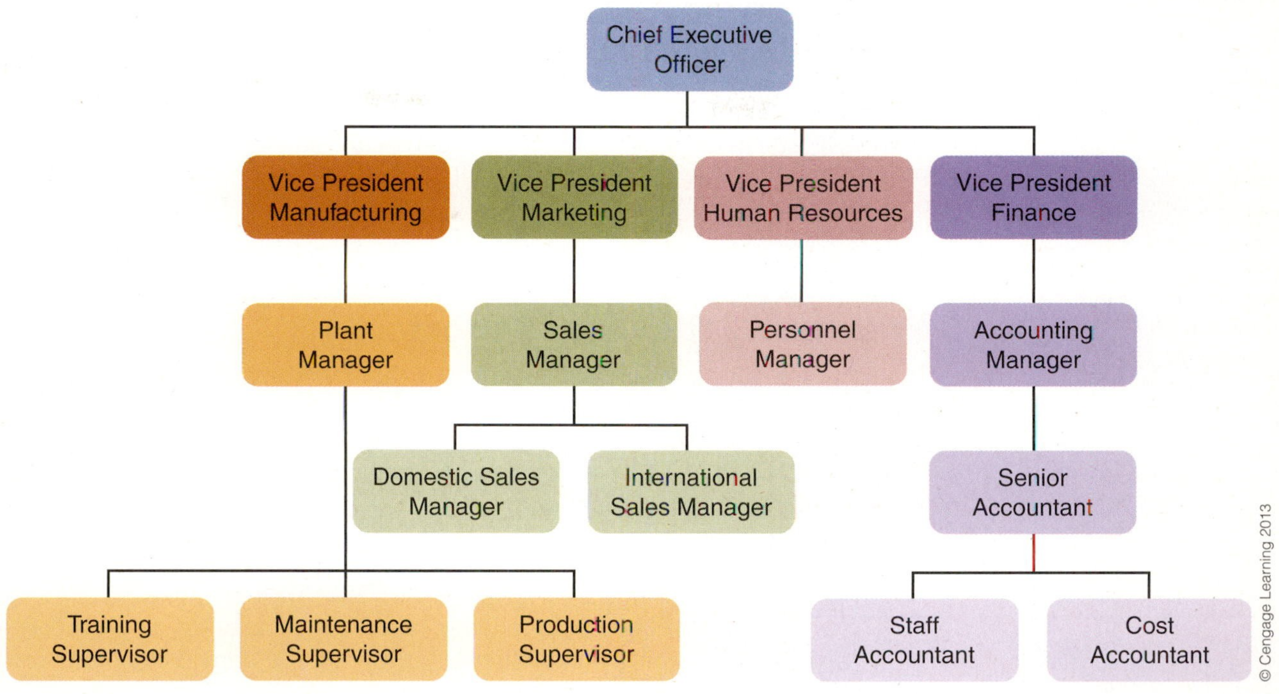

useful in indicating how an object looks or operates. A drawing showing the parts of a printer with labels describing their functions, for example, is more instructive than a photograph or verbal description. With today's computer technology, photographs, maps, and illustrations can be scanned directly into business reports, or accessed through hyperlinks with electronically delivered documents.

Incorporating Graphics in Reports

Used appropriately, graphics make reports more interesting and easier to understand. In putting graphics into your reports, follow these suggestions for best effects:

When creating graphics in reports, consider audience needs, present figures without distortion, introduce your graphs, and use meaningful captions or titles.

- **Evaluate the audience.** Consider the reader, the content, your schedule, and your budget.
- **Use restraint.** Don't overuse color or decorations. Too much color can be distracting and confusing.
- **Be accurate and ethical.** Double-check all graphics for accuracy of figures and calculations. Be certain that your visuals are not misleading—either accidentally or intentionally. Manipulation of a chart scale can make trends look steeper and more dramatic than they really are. Moreover, be sure to cite sources when you use someone else's facts.
- **Introduce a graph meaningfully.** Refer to every graphic in the text, and place the graphic close to the point where it is mentioned. Most important, though, help the reader understand the significance of the graphic. You can do this by telling your audience what to look for or by summarizing the main point of the graphic.
- **Choose an appropriate caption or title style.** Like reports, graphics may use talking titles or generic, functional titles. Talking titles are more persuasive; they tell the reader what to think. Functional titles describe the facts more objectively. These headings were discussed in Chapter 9.

Using Your Computer to Produce Charts

Computer software programs enable you to produce top-quality graphics quickly and cheaply.

Designing effective, accurate bar charts, pie charts, figures, and other graphics is easy with today's software. Spreadsheet programs such as Excel, as well as presentation graphics programs such as PowerPoint, allow even nontechnical people to design high-quality graphics. These graphics can be printed directly on paper for written reports or used for transparency masters and slides for oral presentations. The benefits of preparing visual aids on a computer are near-professional quality, shorter preparation time, and substantial cost savings.

Presenting the Final Report

Long reports are generally organized into three major divisions: (1) front matter, also called prefatory parts or preliminaries, (2) body, and (3) back matter, also known as supplementary parts. Following is a description of the order and content of each part. Refer to the model formal report in Figure 10.17 for illustrations of most of these components.

"Your report just tells me what I already know. Good work. I hate surprises."

Front Matter Components

Front matter items (preceding the body of a report) and back matter items (following the conclusions and recommendations) lengthen formal reports but enhance their professional tone and serve their multiple audiences. Formal reports may be read by many levels of managers, along with technical specialists and financial consultants. Therefore, breaking a long, formal report into small segments makes its information more accessible and easier to understand.

Title Page. A report title page, as illustrated in the Figure 10.17 model report, begins with the name of the report typed in uppercase letters (no underscore and no quotation marks). Next comes *Prepared for* (or *Submitted to*) and the name, title, and organization of the individual receiving the report. Lower on the page is *Prepared by* (or *Submitted by*) and the author's name plus any necessary identification. The last item on the title page is the date of submission. All items after the title appear in a combination of upper- and lowercase letters. The information on the title page should be evenly spaced and balanced on the page for a professional look.

A letter or memo of transmittal presents an overview of the report, suggests how to read it, describes limitations, acknowledges assistance, and expresses appreciation.

Letter or Memo of Transmittal. Generally written on organization letterhead stationery, a letter or memo of transmittal introduces a formal report. You will recall that letters are sent to external audiences; and memos, to internal audiences. A transmittal letter or memo follows the direct strategy and is usually less formal than the report itself. For example, the letter or memo may use contractions and the first-person pronouns *I* and *we*. The transmittal letter or memo typically (a) announces the topic of the report and tells how it was authorized; (b) briefly describes the project; (c) highlights the report's findings, conclusions, and recommendations, if the reader is expected to be supportive; and (d) closes with appreciation for the assignment, instructions for the reader's follow-up actions, acknowledgment of help from others, or offers of assistance in answering questions. If a report is going to various readers, a special transmittal letter or memo should be prepared for each, anticipating how each reader will use the report.

Table of Contents. The table of contents shows the headings in a report and their page numbers. It gives an overview of the report topics and helps readers locate them. You should wait to prepare the table of contents until after you have completed the report. For short reports you should include all headings. For longer reports you might want to list only first- and second-level headings. Leaders (spaced or unspaced dots) help guide the eye from the heading to the page number. Items may be indented in outline form or typed flush with the left margin.

List of Figures. For reports with several figures or tables, you may wish to include a list to help readers locate them. This list may appear on the same page as the table of contents, space permitting. For each figure or table, include a title and page number.

Executive Summary. As you learned in Chapter 9, the purpose of an executive summary is to present an overview of a longer report to people who may not have time to read the entire document. This time-saving device summarizes the purpose, key points, findings, and conclusions. An executive summary is usually no longer than 10 percent of the original document. Therefore, a 20-page report might require a 2-page executive summary. Chapter 9 discussed how to write an article summary and included an example (Figure 9.9 on page 263). An executive summary is featured in Figure 10.17.

Body of Report

The main section of a report is the body. It generally begins with an introduction, includes a discussion of findings, and concludes with a summary and possibly recommendations.

The body of a report includes an introduction, a discussion of findings, and conclusions or recommendations.

Introduction. Formal reports start with an introduction that sets the scene and announces the subject. Because they contain many parts serving different purposes, formal reports are somewhat redundant. The same information may be included in the letter or memo of transmittal, executive summary, and introduction. To avoid sounding repetitious, try to present the information slightly differently in each section.

A good report introduction typically covers the following elements, although not necessarily in this order:

- **Background.** Describe the events leading up to the problem or need.
- **Problem or purpose.** Explain the report topic and specify the problem or need that motivated the report.
- **Significance.** Tell why the topic is important. You may wish to quote experts or cite newspapers, journals, books, Web resources, and other secondary sources to establish the importance of the topic.
- **Scope.** Clarify the boundaries of the report, defining what will be included or excluded.
- **Sources and methods.** Describe your secondary sources (periodicals, books, databases). Also explain how you collected primary data, including survey size, sample design, and statistical programs used.
- **Organization.** Orient readers by giving them a road map that previews the structure of the report.

Discussion of Findings. This is the main section of the report, and it contains numerous headings and subheadings. This section discusses, analyzes, interprets, and evaluates the research findings or solution to the initial problem. This is where you show the evidence that justifies your conclusions. As summarized in Figure 10.2 on page 294, you may organize the findings chronologically, geographically, topically, or by some other method.

Regardless of the organizational pattern, present your findings logically and objectively. In most cases you will want to avoid the use of first-person pronouns *(I, we)*, unless you are certain that your audience prefers informal language. Include tables, charts, and graphs, if necessary, to illustrate your findings. Analytical and scientific reports may include another section titled *Implications of Findings,* in which the writer analyzes the findings and relates them to the problem. Less formal reports contain the author's analysis of the research findings within the *Discussion* section.

Conclusions and Recommendations. The conclusion to a report explains what the findings mean, particularly in terms of solving the original problem. If the report has been largely informational, it ends with a summary of the data presented. If the report analyzes research findings, then it ends with conclusions drawn from the analysis. An analytical report frequently poses research questions. The conclusion to such a report reviews the major findings and answers the research questions. If a report seeks to determine a course of action, it may end with conclusions and recommendations. Recommendations advocating a course of action may be placed in a separate section or incorporated with the conclusions.

Supplementary Parts of Report

Endnotes, a bibliography, and appendixes may appear after the body of the report.

Works Cited, References, or Bibliography. Readers look in the bibliography section to locate the sources of ideas mentioned in a report. Your method of report documentation determines how this section is developed. If you use the Modern Language Association (MLA) referencing format, all citations would be listed alphabetically in the "Works Cited." If you use the American Psychological Association (APA) format, your list would be called "References." Regardless of the format, you must include the author, title, publication, date of publication, page number, and other significant data for all sources used in your report. For electronic references include the URL and the date you accessed the information online. To see electronic and other citations, examine the list of references at the end of Figure 10.17, which follows the MLA documentation style. See Appendix C for more information on documentation formats.

Appendixes. Incidental or supporting materials belong in appendixes at the end of a formal report. These materials are relevant to some readers but not to all. They may also be too bulky to include in the text. Appendixes may include survey forms, copies of other reports, tables of data, large graphics, and related correspondence. If you need more than one appendix, title them *Appendix A, Appendix B,* and so forth. Reference these items in the body of the report.

FIGURE 10.17 Model Formal Report

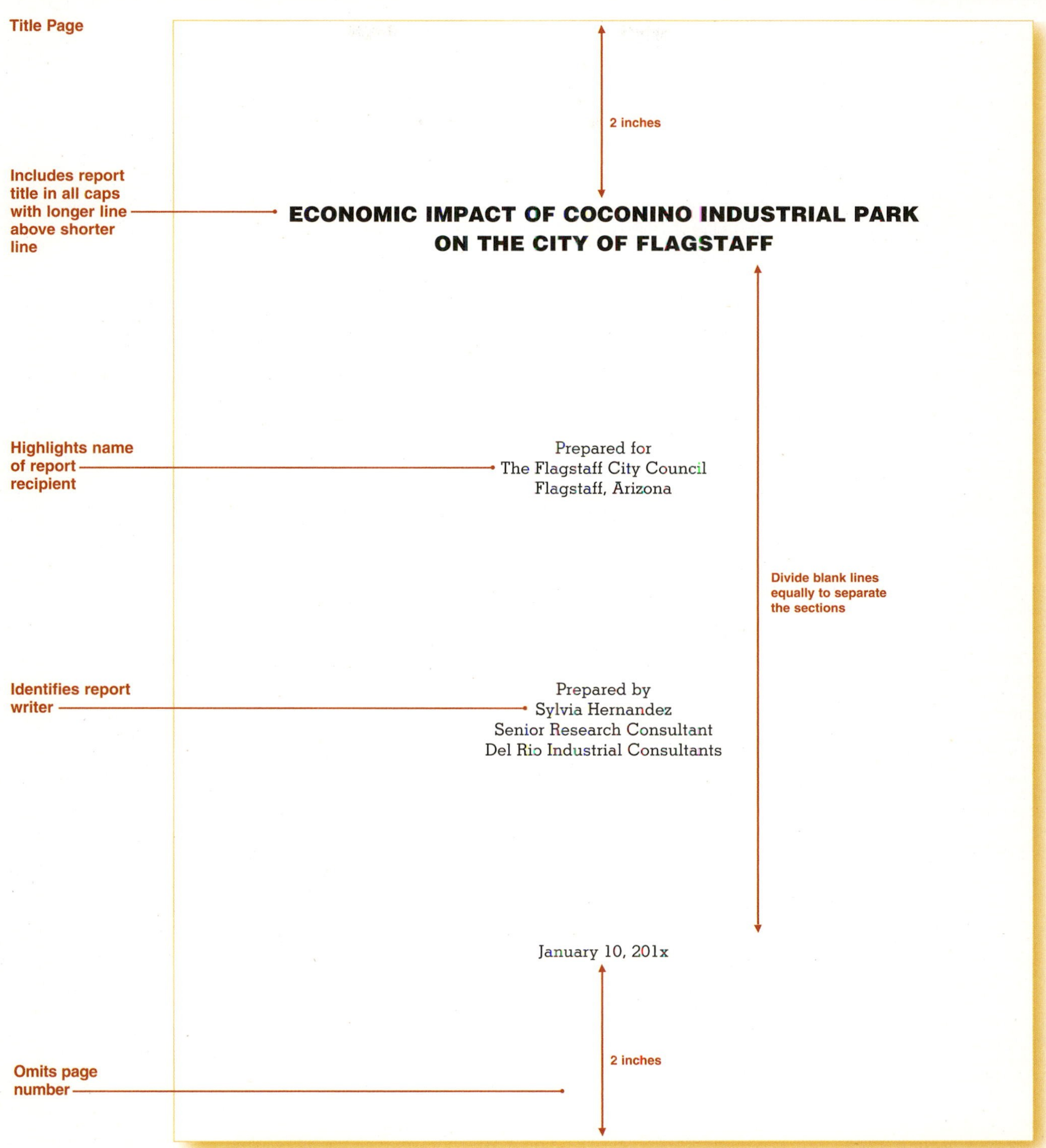

Title Page
2 inches
Includes report title in all caps with longer line above shorter line
ECONOMIC IMPACT OF COCONINO INDUSTRIAL PARK
ON THE CITY OF FLAGSTAFF
Highlights name of report recipient
Prepared for
The Flagstaff City Council
Flagstaff, Arizona
Divide blank lines equally to separate the sections
Identifies report writer
Prepared by
Sylvia Hernandez
Senior Research Consultant
Del Rio Industrial Consultants
January 10, 201x
2 inches
Omits page number

The title page is usually arranged in four evenly balanced areas. If the report is to be bound on the left, move the left margin and center point 0.25 inch to the right. Notice that no page number appears on the title page, although it is counted as page i. In designing the title page, be careful to avoid anything unprofessional—such as too many type fonts, italics, oversized print, and inappropriate graphics. Keep the title page simple and professional. This model report uses MLA documentation style. However, it does not illustrate double-spacing, the recommended format for research papers using MLA style. Instead, this model uses single-spacing, which saves space and is more appropriate for business reports.

FIGURE 10.17 (Continued) Letter of Transmittal

Announces report and identifies authorization

Gives broad overview of report purposes

Uses a bulleted list for clarity and ease of reading

Describes primary and secondary research

Offers to discuss report; expresses appreciation

Uses Roman numerals for prefatory pages

DEL RIO INDUSTRIAL CONSULTANTS

110 West Route 66
Flagstaff, Arizona 86001

www.delrio.com
(928) 774-1101

January 12, 201x

City Council
City of Flagstaff
211 West Aspen Avenue
Flagstaff, AZ 86001

Dear Council Members:

The attached report, requested by the Flagstaff City Council in a letter to Goldman-Lyon & Associates dated October 20, describes the economic impact of Coconino Industrial Park on the city of Flagstaff. We believe you will find the results of this study useful in evaluating future development of industrial parks within the city limits.

This study was designed to examine economic impact in three areas:

- Current and projected tax and other revenues accruing to the city from Coconino Industrial Park
- Current and projected employment generated by the park
- Indirect effects on local employment, income, and economic growth

Primary research consisted of interviews with 15 Coconino Industrial Park tenants and managers, in addition to a 2012 survey of over 5,000 CIP employees. Secondary research sources included the Annual Budget of the City of Flagstaff, county and state tax records, government publications, periodicals, books, and online resources. Results of this research, discussed more fully in this report, indicate that Coconino Industrial Park exerts a significant beneficial influence on the Flagstaff metropolitan economy.

We would be pleased to discuss this report and its conclusions with you at your request. My firm and I thank you for your confidence in selecting our company to prepare this comprehensive report.

Sincerely,

Sylvia Hernandez

Sylvia Hernandez
Senior Research Consultant

SMH:mef
Attachment

ii

A letter or memo of transmittal announces the report topic and explains who authorized it. It briefly describes the project and previews the conclusions, if the reader is supportive. Such messages generally close by expressing appreciation for the assignment, suggesting follow-up actions, acknowledging the help of others, or offering to answer questions. The margins for the transmittal should be the same as for the report, about 1 to 1.25 inches for side margins. The dateline is placed 2 inches from the top, and the margins should be left-justified. A page number is optional.

FIGURE 10.17 (Continued) Table of Contents and List of Figures

Uses leaders to guide eye from heading to page number

Indents secondary headings to show levels of outline

Includes figures (and sometimes tables) in one list for simplified numbering

TABLE OF CONTENTS

LIST OF FIGURES

iii

Because the table of contents and the list of figures for this report are small, they are combined on one page. Notice that the titles of major report parts are in all caps, while other headings are a combination of upper- and lowercase letters. This duplicates the style within the report. Advanced word processing capabilities enable you to generate a contents page automatically, including leaders and accurate page numbering—no matter how many times you revise. Notice that the page numbers are right-justified.

FIGURE 10.17 (Continued) Executive Summary

Opens directly with major research findings

Identifies data sources

Summarizes organization of report

Condenses recommendations

EXECUTIVE SUMMARY

The city of Flagstaff can benefit from the development of industrial parks like the Coconino Industrial Park. Both direct and indirect economic benefits result, as shown by this in-depth study conducted by Del Rio Industrial Consultants. The study was authorized by the Flagstaff City Council when Goldman-Lyon & Associates sought the City Council's approval for the proposed construction of a G-L industrial park. The City Council requested evidence demonstrating that an existing development could actually benefit the city.

Our conclusion that the city of Flagstaff benefits from industrial parks is based on data supplied by a survey of 5,000 Coconino Industrial Park employees, personal interviews with managers and tenants of CIP, city and state documents, and professional literature.

Analysis of the data revealed benefits in three areas:

- **Revenues.** The city of Flagstaff earned nearly $2 million in tax and other revenues from the Coconino Industrial Park in 2012. By 2018 this income is expected to reach $3.4 million (in constant 2012 dollars).
- **Employment.** In 2012 CIP businesses employed a total of 7,035 workers, who earned an average wage of $56,579. By 2018 CIP businesses are expected to employ directly nearly 15,000 employees who will earn salaries totaling over $998 million.
- **Indirect benefits.** Because of the multiplier effect, by 2018 Coconino Industrial Park will directly and indirectly generate a total of 38,362 jobs in the Flagstaff metropolitan area.

On the basis of these findings, it is recommended that development of additional industrial parks be encouraged to stimulate local economic growth.

iv

For readers who want a quick overview of the report, the executive summary presents its most important elements. Executive summaries focus on the information the reader requires for making a decision related to the issues discussed in the report. The summary may include some or all of the following elements: purpose, scope, research methods, findings, conclusions, and recommendations. Its length depends on the report it summarizes. A 100-page report might require a 10-page summary. Shorter reports may contain 1-page summaries, as shown here. Unlike letters of transmittal (which may contain personal pronouns and references to the writer), the executive summary of a long report is formal and impersonal. It uses the same margins as the body of the report. See Chapter 9 for additional discussion of executive summaries.

FIGURE 10.17 (Continued) Page 1

Uses a bulleted list for clarity and ease of reading

Lists three problem questions

Describes authorization for report and background of study

PROBLEM

This study was designed to analyze the direct and indirect economic impact of Coconino Industrial Park on the city of Flagstaff. Specifically, the study seeks answers to these questions:

- What current tax and other revenues result directly from this park? What tax and other revenues may be expected in the future?
- How many and what kind of jobs are directly attributable to the park? What is the employment picture for the future?
- What indirect effects has Coconino Industrial Park had on local employment, incomes, and economic growth?

BACKGROUND

The development firm of Goldman-Lyon & Associates commissioned this study of Coconino Industrial Park at the request of the Flagstaff City Council. Before authorizing the development of a proposed Goldman-Lyon industrial park, the City Council requested a study examining the economic effects of an existing park. Members of the City Council wanted to determine to what extent industrial parks benefit the local community, and they chose Coconino Industrial Park as an example.

For those who are unfamiliar with it, Coconino Industrial Park is a 400-acre industrial park located in the city of Flagstaff about 4 miles from the center of the city. Most of the area lies within a specially designated area known as Redevelopment Project No. 2, which is under the jurisdiction of the Flagstaff Redevelopment Agency. Planning for the park began in 2000; construction started in 2002.

The original goal for Coconino Industrial Park was development for light industrial users. Land in this area was zoned for uses such as warehousing, research and development, and distribution. Like other communities, Flagstaff was eager to attract light industrial users because such businesses tend to "employ a highly educated workforce, are quiet, and do not pollute the environment" (Cohen). The city of Flagstaff recognized the need for light industrial users and widened an adjacent highway to accommodate trucks and facilitate travel by workers and customers coming from Flagstaff.

1

The first page of a formal report generally contains the title printed 2 inches from the top edge. Headings for major parts of a report are centered in all caps. In this model document we show functional heads, such as *PROBLEM, BACKGROUND, FINDINGS,* and *CONCLUSIONS*. However, most business reports would use talking heads or a combination such as *FINDINGS REVEAL REVENUE AND EMPLOYMENT BENEFITS*. First-level headings (such as *Revenues* on page 2) are printed with bold upper- and lowercase letters. Second-level headings (such as *Distribution* on page 3) begin at the side, are bolded, and are written in upper- and lowercase letters. See Figure 10.4 for an illustration of heading formats. This business report is shown with single-spacing, although some research reports might be double-spaced. Always check with your organization to learn its preferred style.

FIGURE 10.17 **(Continued) Page 2**

Provides specifics for data sources

Usess functional heads

Previews organization of report

Places figure close to textual reference

The park now contains 14 building complexes with over 1.25 million square feet of completed building space. The majority of the buildings are used for office, research and development, marketing and distribution, or manufacturing uses. Approximately 50 acres of the original area are yet to be developed.

Data for this report came from a 2012 survey of over 5,000 Coconino Industrial Park employees; interviews with 15 CIP tenants and managers, the Annual Budget of the City of Flagstaff, county and state tax records, current books, articles, journals, and online resources. Projections for future revenues resulted from analysis of past trends and "Estimates of Revenues for Debt Service Coverage, Redevelopment Project Area 2" (Miller 79).

DISCUSSION OF FINDINGS

The results of this research indicate that major direct and indirect benefits have accrued to the city of Flagstaff and surrounding metropolitan areas as a result of the development of Coconino Industrial Park. The research findings presented here fall into three categories: (a) revenues, (b) employment, and (c) indirect effects.

Revenues

Coconino Industrial Park contributes a variety of tax and other revenues to the city of Flagstaff, as summarized in Figure 1. Current revenues are shown, along with projections to the year 2018. At a time when the economy is unstable, revenues from an industrial park such as Coconino can become a reliable income stream for the city of Flagstaff.

Figure 1

REVENUES RECEIVED BY THE CITY OF FLAGSTAFF
FROM COCONINO INDUSTRIAL PARK

Current Revenues and Projections to 2018

	2012	2018
Sales and use taxes	$ 904,140	$1,335,390
Revenues from licenses	426,265	516,396
Franchise taxes	175,518	229,424
State gas tax receipts	83,768	112,134
Licenses and permits	78,331	112,831
Other revenues	94,039	141,987
Total	$1,762,061	$2,448,162

Source: Arizona State Board of Equalization Bulletin. Phoenix: State Printing Office, 2012, 103.

2

Notice that this formal report is single-spaced. Many businesses prefer this space-saving format. However, some organizations prefer double-spacing, especially for preliminary drafts. If you single-space, don't indent paragraphs. If you double-space, do indent the paragraphs. Page numbers may be centered 1 inch from the bottom of the page or placed 1 inch from the upper right corner at the margin. Your word processor can insert page numbers automatically. Strive to leave a minimum of 1 inch for top, bottom, and side margins. References follow the parenthetical citation style (or in-text citation style) of the Modern Language Association (MLA). Notice that the author's name and a page reference are shown in parentheses. The complete bibliographic entry for any in-text citation appears at the end of the report in the works-cited section.

FIGURE 10.17 **(Continued) Page 3**

Continues interpreting figures in table

Includes ample description of electronic reference

Sets stage for next topic to be discussed

Sales and Use Revenues

As shown in Figure 1, the city's largest source of revenues from CIP is the sales and use tax. Revenues from this source totaled $904,140 in 2012, according to figures provided by the Arizona State Board of Equalization (28). Sales and use taxes accounted for more than half of the park's total contribution to the city of $1,762,061.

Other Revenues

Other major sources of city revenues from CIP in 2012 include alcohol licenses, motor vehicle in lieu fees, trailer coach licenses ($426,265), franchise taxes ($175,518), and state gas tax receipts ($83,768). Although not shown in Figure 1, other revenues may be expected from the development of recently acquired property. The U.S. Economic Development Administration has approved a grant worth $975,000 to assist in expanding the current park eastward on an undeveloped parcel purchased last year. Revenues from leasing this property may be sizable.

Projections

Total city revenues from CIP will nearly double by 2018, producing an income of $2.45 million. This estimate is based on an annual growth rate of 0.65 percent, as projected by the Bureau of Labor Statistics and reported at the Web site of Infoplease.com ("Economic Outlook Through 2018").

Employment

One of the most important factors to consider in the overall effect of an industrial park is employment. In Coconino Industrial Park, the distribution, number, and wages of people employed will change considerably in the next six years.

Distribution

A total of 7,035 employees currently work in various industry groups at Coconino Industrial Park. The distribution of employees is shown in Figure 2. The largest number of workers (58 percent) is employed in manufacturing and assembly operations. In the next largest category, the computer and electronics industry employs 24 percent of the workers. Some overlap probably exists because electronics assembly could be included in either group. Employees also work in publishing (9 percent), warehousing and storage (5 percent), and other industries (4 percent).

Although the distribution of employees at Coconino Industrial Park shows a wide range of employment categories, it must be noted that other industrial parks would likely generate an entirely different range of job categories. *The Wall Street Journal* reports that regional industrial parks exert a strong pull on local employees (Pearson).

3

Only the most important research findings are interpreted and discussed for readers. The depth of discussion depends on the intended length of the report, the goal of the writer, and the expectations of the reader. Because the writer wants this report to be formal in tone, she avoids I and we in all discussions.

As you type a report, avoid widows and orphans (ending a page with the first line of a paragraph or carrying a single line of a paragraph to a new page). Strive to start and end pages with at least two lines of a paragraph, even if a slightly larger bottom margin results.

FIGURE 10.17 (Continued) Page 4

Figure 2

EMPLOYMENT DISTRIBUTION OF INDUSTRY GROUPS

Pie chart shows proportion of a whole and includes percentage figures for clarity

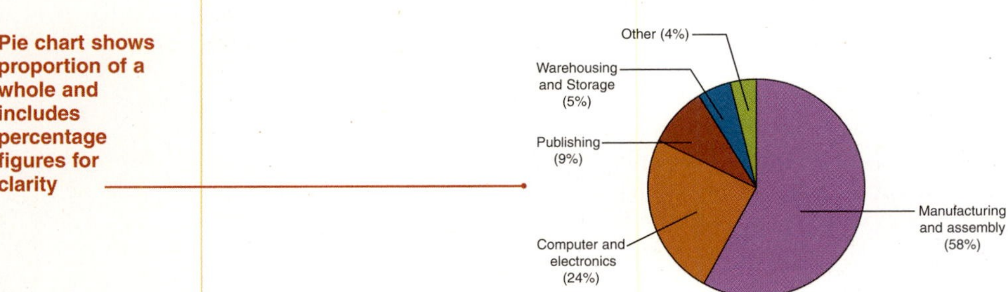

Source: 2012 survey of CIP employees

Wages

Places figure close to textual reference

In 2012 employees at CIP earned a total of $398 million in wages, as shown in Figure 3. The average employee in that year earned $56,579. The highest average wages were paid to employees in white-collar fields, such as computer and electronics ($65,200) and publishing ($61,100). Average wages for workers in blue-collar fields ranged from $53,400 in manufacturing and assembly to $48,500 in warehousing and storage.

Figure 3

AVERAGE ANNUAL WAGES BY INDUSTRIAL GROUPS

Coconino Industrial Park, 2012

Aligns figures on the right and centers headings over columns

Industry Group	Employees	Annual Wages	Total
Manufacturing and assembly	4,073	$53,400	$217,498,200
Computer and electronics	1,657	65,200	108,036,400
Publishing	672	61,100	41,059,200
Warehousing and storage	370	48,500	17,945,000
Other	263	51,300	13,491,900
	7,035		$398,030,700

Source: 2012 Survey of CIP employees

4

If you use figures or tables, be sure to introduce them in the text (for example, as *shown in Figure 3*). Although it isn't always possible, try to place them close to the spot where they are first mentioned. To save space, you can print the title of a figure at its side. Because this report contains few tables and figures, the writer named them all "Figures" and numbered them consecutively.

Clarifies information and tells what it means in relation to original research questions

Projections

By 2018 Coconino Industrial Park is expected to more than double its number of employees, bringing the total to over 15,000 workers. The total payroll in 2018 will also more than double, producing over $998 million (using constant 2012 dollars) in salaries to CIP employees. These projections are based on an 8 percent growth rate (Miller 78), along with anticipated increased employment as the park reaches its capacity.

Future development in the park will influence employment and payrolls. One CIP project manager stated in an interview that much of the remaining 50 acres is planned for medium-rise office buildings, garden offices, and other structures for commercial, professional, and personal services (Novak). Average wages for employees are expected to increase because of an anticipated shift to higher-paying white-collar jobs. Industrial parks often follow a similar pattern of evolution (Badri 41). Like many industrial parks, CIP evolved from a warehousing center into a manufacturing complex.

Summarizes conclusions and recommendations

CONCLUSIONS AND RECOMMENDATIONS

Analysis of tax revenues, employment data, personal interviews, and professional literature leads to the following conclusions and recommendations about the economic impact of Coconino Industrial Park on the city of Flagstaff:

Uses a numbered list for clarity and ease of reading

1. Sales tax and other revenues produced nearly $1.8 million in income to the city of Flagstaff in 2012. By 2018 sales tax and other revenues are expected to produce $2.5 million in city income.

2. CIP currently employs 7,035 employees, the majority of whom are working in manufacturing and assembly. The average employee in 2012 earned $56,579.

3. By 2018 CIP is expected to employ more than 15,000 workers producing a total payroll of over $998 million.

4. Employment trends indicate that by 2018 more CIP employees will be engaged in higher-paying white-collar positions.

On the basis of these findings, we recommend that the City Council of Flagstaff authorize the development of additional industrial parks to stimulate local economic growth.

5

After discussing and interpreting the research findings, the writer articulates what she considers the most important conclusions and recommendations. Longer, more complex reports may have separate sections for conclusions and resulting recommendations. In this report they are combined. Notice that it is unnecessary to start a new page for the conclusions.

FIGURE 10.17 (Continued) Works Cited

Arranges works cited in alphabetical order

WORKS CITED

Brochure – Print

Arizona State Board of Equalization. Bulletin. Phoenix: State Printing Office, 2012. Print.

Magazine – Print

Badri, Masood A. "Infrastructure, Trends, and Economic Effects of Industrial Parks." *Industry Week*. 1 April 2011. Print.

Newspaper – Web

Cohen, Allen P. "Industrial Parks Invade Suburbia." *The New York Times*. The New York Times 10 Dec. 2011. Web. 20 May 2012. <http://www.nytimes.com/2011/12/20/business/19smart.html>.

Government Publication – Web

"Economic Outlook Through 2018." Washington: *Bureau of Labor Statistics*. 24 Nov. 2011. Web. 3 Jan. 2012. <http://www.bls.gov/oco/cg/cgs030.htm#emply2018>.

Book – Print

Miller, Arthur M. *Redevelopment Projects: Future Prospects*. New York: Rincon Press, 2010. Print.

E-mail Interview

Novak, Ivan M. "Re: Redevelopment project plans." E-mail interview with author. E-mail. 30 Nov. 2011.

Newspaper – Web

Pearson, Sandra. "Travel to Work Characteristics for the 50 Largest Metropolitan Areas by Population in the United States." *Online Wall Street Journal*. The Wall Street Journal. 15 Dec. 2011. Web. 8 Jan. 2012. <http://www.wsj.com/article/SB120215930971242053.html>.

Follows Modern Language Association documentation style

6

On this page the writer lists all references cited in the text as well as others that she examined during her research. The writer lists these citations following the MLA referencing style. Notice that all entries are arranged alphabetically. The *MLA Handbook for Writers of Research Papers*, Seventh Edition, 2009, requires italics for titles of books, magazines, newspapers, journals, and Web sites. For electronic sources, the following sequence is suggested: author or editor names; article name in quotation marks; title of Web site, project, or book in italics; any version numbers available; publisher information, including the publisher name and publishing date; page numbers, if available; medium of publication (such as *Web, Print*, or *PDF*); access date; and URL if necessary for retrieval or required by your instructor.

This works-cited page is shown with single-spacing, which is preferable for business reports. However, MLA style recommends double-spacing for research reports, including the works-cited page.

www.cengagebrain.com

Available with an access code, these eResources will help you prepare for exams:

- **Chapter Review Quizzes**
- **Personal Language Trainer**
- **PowerPoint Slides**
- **Flash Cards**

Summing Up and Looking Forward

Proposals are written offers to solve problems, provide services, or sell equipment. Both large and small businesses today write proposals to generate income. Informal proposals may be as short as 2 pages; formal proposals may run 200 pages or more. Regardless of the size, proposals contain standard parts that must be developed persuasively.

Formal business reports present well-organized information systematically. The information may be collected from primary or secondary sources. All ideas borrowed from others must be documented. Good reports contain appropriate headings to help guide readers through the report. In addition, formal reports often contain tables, charts, and graphs to illustrate data.

Written reports are vital to decision makers. But oral reports can be equally important. In Chapter 12 you will learn how to organize and make professional oral presentations. Before discussing oral reports, however, in Chapter 11 you will learn how to become an ethical, polished business professional. In addition to business ethics and etiquette, you will study how to communicate effectively in person, by telephone, in teams, and in meetings.

Critical Thinking

1. Which category of proposal, solicited or unsolicited, is more likely to succeed, and why?
2. How do formal business reports differ from informal business reports?
3. What are primary and secondary data, and why is it best to start your research by gathering secondary data first?
4. Why must researchers document their sources meticulously?
5. How do report writers decide what type of graphic to use in a report?

Chapter Review

6. What purposes do proposals serve?

7. Who uses requests for proposals (RFPs), and why?

8. Why is the budget section of a proposal particularly important?

9. Why are formal reports written in business? Give an original example of a business-related report.

10. If the Web is one of the greatest sources of information, why must researchers exercise caution when using Web sources?

11. Explain how blogs and social media networks can be used by businesses and report writers.

12. Explain what plagiarism is and how you can avoid it.

13. Name the two most common citation formats.

14. Name at least seven organizational patterns for report findings.

15. Briefly compare the advantages and disadvantages of illustrating data with charts (bar and line) versus tables.

Activities and Cases

T TEAM

10.1 Researching Secondary and Primary Data

In teams, discuss how you would collect information for each of the following report topics. Would your research be primary, secondary, or a combination of methods? What resources would be most useful—books, articles, the Web, interviews, surveys?

a. Investigating employee commuting habits for the purpose of creating a carpool program

b. Comparing mine safety in the three largest mining countries: South Africa, the United States, and Australia

c. Finding the best libel lawyer to defend a company under the SPEECH Act of 2010 from defamation claims overseas

d. Establishing the effectiveness of diversity training programs in U.S. businesses

e. Measuring the number of cars passing through an intersection to establish the need for a traffic light

f. Investigating how a recycling program might be introduced in a business organization to ensure effectiveness and compliance

g. Learning the cost and features of a teleconferencing system such as Cisco TelePresence or LifeSize by Logitech to use at your company

h. Learning how wireless customers are responding to the launch of a radically new smartphone

i. Complying with export control laws in the United States prohibiting the unauthorized disclosure of sensitive technology to foreign citizens

10.2 Plagiarism, Paraphrasing, and Citing Sources

One of the biggest problems of student writers is paraphrasing secondary sources correctly to avoid plagiarism.

Your Task. For each of the following, read the original passage. Analyze the paraphrased version. List the weaknesses in relation to what you have learned about plagiarism and the use of references. Then write an improved version.

a. Original Passage

Developing casual online game titles can be much less risky than trying to create a game that runs on a console such as an Xbox. Casual games typically cost less than $200,000 to produce, and production cycles are only six months to a year. There's no shelf space, packaging, or CD production to pay for. Best of all, there's more room for innovation.[15]

Paraphrased Passage: The development of casual online games offers less risk than creating games running on Xbox and other consoles. Usually, casual games are cheaper, costing under $200,000 to create and requiring six to twelve months to produce. Developers save on shelf space, packaging, and CD production too. Moreover, they have more freedom to innovate.

b. Original Passage

The collapse in the cost of computing has made cellular communication economically viable. Worldwide, one in two new phone subscriptions is cellular. The digital revolution in telephony is most advanced in poorer countries because they have been able to skip the outdated technological step of relying on landlines.

Paraphrased Passage: The drop in computing costs now makes cellular communication affordable around the world. In fact, one out of every two new phones is cellular. The digital revolution in cellular telephones is developing faster in poorer countries because they could skip the outdated technological process of using landlines (Henderson 44).

c. Original Passage

Search site Yahoo kept world news prominent on its front page because users feel secure knowing that it is easily accessible, even if they don't often click it. Conspicuous placement also went to entertainment, which draws heavy traffic from people seeking a diversion at work. By contrast, seemingly work-related content such as finance gets ample use in the evening when people pay bills and manage personal portfolios.[16]

Paraphrased Passage: Search giant Yahoo kept news prominent on its portal since its customers feel good knowing it is there, even though they don't read it much. Such noticeable placement was also used for entertainment news that attracts heavy traffic from users searching for a distraction at work. As opposed to that, what may seem work related, such as finance, is much visited at night when people pay their bills and manage their portfolios.

10.3 Gathering and Comparing Data from Secondary Sources

Secondary sources can provide quite different information depending on your mode of inquiry.

Your Task. Pick a business-related subject you want to know more about, and run it through a search engine such as Google. Compare your results with Bing, advertised by Microsoft as a "decision engine," and Dogpile, a metasearch site that combines several search engines. Write a short memo or e-mail to your instructor explaining the differences in the search results. In your message describe what you have learned about the advantages and disadvantages of each search tool.

10.4 Researching Secondary Sources for Reports: Debunking Myths About Young People

Are you tired of hearing that you are spending too much time online? The perception that teens and college students are the biggest consumers of Internet content is intractable—a largely unexamined assumption based on little more than anecdotal evidence. To learn more about young people's true media usage, you could turn to Nielsen Company research.

Your boss, Akiko Kimura, doesn't believe in stereotyping. She encourages her market researchers to be wary of all data. She asked you to explore so-called niche marketing opportunities in targeting teens, a notoriously fickle consumer group. Primarily, Ms. Kimura wants to know how teenagers spend their free time, and, more specifically, how they use media. Understanding teen behavior is invaluable for the success of any promotional or ad campaign.

A casual glance at the latest Nielsen numbers reveals surprising key findings: Teens watch more TV than ever and spend much less time browsing the Internet than adults twenty-five to thirty-four years of age do (11 hours versus the average of 29 hours, 15 minutes for adults). They also spend 35 percent less time watching online videos than adults do. In their preferences for TV shows, top Web sites, and across media, they mirror the tastes of their parents. They also read newspapers, listen to the radio, and like advertising more than most. In short, "teens are actually pretty normal in their usage and more attentive than most give them credit for," said Nic Covey, director of insights for The Nielsen Company.[17]

Your Task. Prepare a brief informational e-mail report summarizing the main Nielsen findings. Address it to *akiko.kimura@premier.com*. Paraphrase correctly and don't just copy from the online report. Ms. Kimura may ask you to analyze more comprehensive data in an analytical report and create a media use profile of U.S. teens. You have already identified additional teenager-related Nielsen studies titled "Special Report: What Do Teens Want?," "Breaking Teen Myths," and "Teens Don't Tweet; Twitter's Growth Not Fueled by Youth."

10.5 Finding Secondary Data for Reports: The Future of Tech

Are you a member of the "thumb generation"? Can you work the keyboard of your smartphone faster than most people can speak? The term *thumb generation* was coined in South Korea and Japan and is applied to people under twenty-five who furiously finger their handheld devices to text at lightning speeds.

More technological innovations are coming that are likely to transform our lives. WiMAX is a new wireless supertechnology that will cover entire cities at cable speeds. Near field communication (NFC) takes the Bluetooth technology a step further to connect cell phones and other devices. Several pending technologies are purported eventually to improve the lives of users and tech support pros alike.[18] Your boss pulled two articles about tech innovations out of his files to show you. However, you know that you can find more current discussions of future trends on MIT's Technology Review Web site at **http://www.technologyreview.com**.

You are one of several marketing interns at MarketNet Global, a worldwide e-commerce specialist. Your busy boss, Jack Holden, wants to be up to speed on cutting-edge tech and communication trends, especially those that could be successfully used in selling and marketing. Individually or as a team, you will research one or several high-tech concepts. On the MIT Technology Review Web site, focus on the tabs **Business**, **Computing**, **Web**, and **Communications**. Chances are you will not find scholarly articles on these subjects because peer-reviewed publications take years to complete. Instead, you must rely on the Web and on electronic databases to find up-to-date information. If you use search engines, you will retrieve many forum and discussion board contributions as well. Examine them critically.

Your Task. In teams or individually, write an e-mail or informational memo to Jack Holden (*jack.holden@basco.com*) complete with a short list of references in MLA or APA documentation style. Explain each new trend. Your instructor may ask you to complete this activity as a report assignment describing to Jack Holden what your sources suggest the new trends may mean for the future of business, specifically e-commerce and online marketing.

10.6 Gathering Data for Reports: Fortune 100 Best Companies to Work For

Even in these tough economic times, some companies continue to spend lavishly on unusual employee perks such as massages and sauna visits, provide generous compensation and benefits, and do not lay off workers as a matter of principle. At the same time, they remain profitable. Chances are that you haven't heard of the newest top three among *Fortune*'s 100 Best Companies to Work For—tech giant SAS, investment advisor Edward Jones, and New York–based Wegmans Food Markets. The perennial favorite, Google, slipped to fourth place. Fourteenth-ranked outdoor powerhouse REI attracts active types who may bring their dogs to work, go on a midday bike ride, and test the products they sell. Sound nice? Just as companies have their distinctive corporate cultures, they also differ in why they are perceived as ideal employers.

Your Task. Visit the *Fortune* magazine Web site at **http://www.fortune.com/bestcompanies** for the most current 100 Best Companies to Work For. Examine the information about the top 20 or 25 highest-ranked companies. Watch the short video clips profiling each business. After studying the information, identify factors that attract and please workers. Take note of features shared across the board, but don't overlook quirky, unusual benefits. Summarize these trends in an informational report addressed to your instructor. Alternatively, prepare an analytical report investigating employee satisfaction gleaned from the secondary data obtained from the *Fortune* site.

TEAM

10.7 Selecting Graphics

In teams identify the best graphic (table, bar chart, line chart, pie chart, flowchart, organization chart, illustration, map) to illustrate the following data:

a. Properties listed for sale in a beach community

b. Month-to-month unemployment figures by the Bureau of Labor Statistics

c. Government unemployment data by industry and sector in percent

d. Figures showing the distribution of the N1H1 virus in humans by state

e. Figures showing the process of delivering electricity to a metropolitan area

f. Areas in the United States likely to have earthquakes

g. Figures showing what proportion of every state tax dollar is spent on education, social services, transportation, debt, and other expenses

h. Academic, administrative, and operational divisions of a college, from the president to department chairs and division managers.

i. Figures comparing the sales of smartphones, netbooks, and laptop computers over the past three years

E-MAIL

WEB

10.8 Evaluating Graphics

Your Task. Select four graphics from newspapers or magazines, in hard copy or online. Look in *The Wall Street Journal, USA Today, BusinessWeek, U.S. News & World Report, Fortune,* or other business news publications. In an e-mail or memo to your instructor, critique each graphic based on what you have learned in this chapter. How effectively could the data have been expressed in words, without the graphics? Is the appropriate graphic form used? How is the graphic introduced in the text? Do you think the graphic is misleading or unethical in any way?

10. 9 Creating a Bar Chart and Writing a Title

Your Task. Prepare a bar chart comparing the tax rates in eight industrial countries: Canada, 33 percent; France, 45 percent; Germany, 41 percent; Japan, 28 percent; Netherlands, 38 percent; Sweden, 49 percent; United Kingdom, 38 percent; United States, 28 percent. These figures represent a percentage of the gross domestic product for each country. The sources of the figures are the rankings of "fiscal freedom" established by the Heritage Foundation. Arrange the entries logically. Write two titles: a talking head and a functional head. What should you emphasize in the chart and title?

10.10 Creating a Line Chart

Your Task. Prepare a line chart showing the sales of Sidekick Athletic Shoes, Inc., for these years: 2013, $6.7 million; 2012, $5.4 million; 2011, $3.2 million; 2010, $2.1 million; 2009, $2.6 million; 2008, $3.6 million. In the chart title, highlight the trend you see in the data.

10.11 Developing an Annotated Bibliography

Select a business topic that interests you. Prepare a bibliography of at least five current magazine or newspaper articles, three books, and five online references that contain relevant information regarding the topic. Your instructor may ask you to divide your bibliography into sections: *Books, Periodicals, Online Resources.* You may also be asked to annotate your bibliography—that is, to compose a brief description of each reference, such as this:

Dumaine, Brian. "Stocks with Upside for a Clean Planet." *Fortune*, Dec. 2010, 85–86.

Dumaine discusses investing in clean energy and recommends several specific solar, wind, and other "green" stocks for investors to buy. He believes that the world will continue to evolve toward a low-carbon, sustainable economy; hence, companies that specialize in energy-efficient technologies should see good long-term growth.

WEB

TEAM

10.12 Set Up a Wiki to Complete a Group Project

Younger workers who grew up with digital technology are spearheading a new trend in business. They are bringing their tech savvy to the table, and, as a result, wikis, blogs, and other new communication channels are being used in the workplace to manage projects and exchange information. When writing a team paper, for example, you could share graphics and other data along with report drafts or the articles you found.

If you would like to try collaborating online, you can set up a free wiki virtually in seconds. Two very popular free sites are Google Sites (**http:www.google.com/sites**) and Wikispaces (**http://wikispaces.com**). At Wikispaces be sure to select **Wikis for Individuals and Groups** or you will be charged for premium membership.

As you register, you can select a variety of features—for example, to make your wiki accessible to anyone or only to invitees whom you choose. Templates and intuitive menus make creating a wiki really simple and easy.

Your Task. Whether you create a wiki to share common interests online with friends or whether you use it to collaborate on a team project, becoming an experienced user of wikis will prepare you for the workplace. Visit either Google Sites or Wikispaces and set up a wiki for yourself and your team. Be sure to invite your instructor as well, so that he or she can observe your online collaboration.

WEB

10.13 Proposals: Comparing Real Proposals

Many new companies with services or products to offer would like to land corporate or government contracts. However, they are intimidated by proposals (the RFP process). You have been asked for help by your friend Mikayla, who has started her own catering business. Her goal is to deliver fresh sandwiches and salads to local offices and shops during lunch hour, either preordered or ready-made. Before writing a proposal, however, she wants to see examples and learn more about the process.

Your Task. Use the Web to find at least two examples of business proposals. Don't waste time on sites that want to sell templates or books. Find actual examples. Then prepare a memo to Mikayla in which you do the following:

a. Identify two sites with sample business proposals.

b. Outline the parts of each proposal.

c. Compare the strengths and weaknesses of each proposal.

d. Draw conclusions. What can Mikayla learn from these examples?

10.14 Unsolicited Proposal: Helping Retailers Nab Shoplifters

The crime of shoplifting seems to be rampant in retail stores. The National Association for Shoplifting Prevention estimates that more than $25 million worth of merchandise is stolen from retailers every day.[19] As a vendor providing security systems, your new employer, SecurityFocus, would like to sell surveillance cameras to retail stores. However, your boss, Dino Prezzi, believes that his unique selling point is that his company offers a comprehensive shoplifting prevention package to his business customers. Not satisfied with merely relying on passive electronic surveillance, SecurityFocus offers advice on theft-resistant store design, effective inventory controls, loss prevention, and proper staffing as well as training. Dino Prezzi wants you to learn about theft-prevention techniques as well as surveillance technology and help him put together a proposal to send to local retailers.

Your Task. Research the cost of and logistics of surveillance technology as well as other measures of theft prevention and deterrence. Present your proposal draft to Dino Prezzi. Because your company's proposal is unsolicited, you will need to be very persuasive to win business.

10.15 Unsolicited Proposal: Requesting Funding for Your Campus Business Club

Let's say you are a member of a campus business club, such as the Society for the Advancement of Management (SAM), the American Marketing Association (AMA), the American Management Association (AMA), the Accounting Society (AS), the Finance Association (FA), or the Association of Information Technology Professionals (AITP). You have managed your finances well, and therefore, you are able to fund your monthly activities. However, membership dues are insufficient to cover any extras. Identify a need such as for a hardware or software purchase, a special one-time event that would benefit a great number of students, or officer training.

Your Task. Request one-time funding to cover what you need by writing an unsolicited letter or memo proposal to your assistant dean, who oversees student business clubs. Identify your need or problem, show the benefit of your request, support your claims with evidence, and provide a budget (if necessary).

10.16 Proposal: Think Like an Entrepreneur

Perhaps you have fantasized about one day owning your own company, or maybe you have already started a business. Proposals are offers to a very specific audience whose business you are soliciting. Think of a product or service that you like or know much about. On the Web or in electronic databases, research the market so that you understand going rates, prices, and costs. Search the Small Business Administration's Web site (**http://www.sba.gov**) for valuable tips on how to launch and manage a business.

Your Task. Choose a product or service you would like to offer to a particular audience, such as a window cleaning business, an online photography business, a new vehicle on the U.S. market, or a new European hair care line. Discuss products and services as well as target audiences with your instructor. Write a letter proposal promoting your chosen product or service.

10.17 Formal Report: Intercultural Communication

U.S. businesses are expanding into foreign markets with manufacturing plants, sales offices, and branch offices abroad. Unfortunately, most Americans have little knowledge of or experience with people from other cultures. To prepare for participation in the global marketplace, you are to collect information for a report focused on an Asian, Latin American, African, or European country where English is not regularly spoken. Before selecting the country, though, consider consulting your campus international student program for volunteers who are willing to be interviewed. Your instructor may make advance arrangements seeking international student volunteers.

Your Task. In teams of two to four, collect information about your target country from electronic databases, the Web, and other sources. If possible, invite an international student representing your target country to be interviewed by your group. As you conduct primary and secondary research, investigate the topics listed in Figure 10.18. Confirm what you learn in your secondary research by talking with your interviewee. When you complete your research, write a report for the CEO of your company (make up a name and company). Assume that your company plans to expand its operations abroad. Your report should advise the company's executives of social customs, family life, attitudes, appropriate business attire, religions, economic institutions, and values in the target country. Remember that your company's interests are business oriented; don't dwell on tourist information. Write your report individually or in teams.

10.18 Formal Report: Coffee Check

The national franchising headquarters for a large coffeehouse chain has received complaints about the service, quality, and cleanliness of one of its cafés in your area. You have been sent to inspect and to report on what you see.

Your Task. Select a nearby coffeehouse. Visit on two or more occasions. Make notes about how many customers were served, how quickly they received their coffee and tea beverages, and how courteously they were treated. Observe the number of employees and supervisors working. Note the cleanliness of observable parts of the café. Inspect the restroom as well as the exterior and surrounding grounds. Sample the beverages and snacks. Your boss is a stickler for details; she has no use for general statements such as *The restroom was not clean.* Be specific. Draw conclusions. Are the complaints justified? If improvements are necessary, make recommendations. Address your report to Phyllis Franz, president.

10.19 Formal Report: The Savvy Buyer

Study a consumer product that you might consider buying. Are you or is your family or your business interested in purchasing a flat-screen TV, home theater system, computer, digital camera, espresso machine, car, SUV, hot tub, or some other product?

Your Task. Use at least five primary and five secondary sources in researching your topic. Your primary research will be in the form of interviews with individuals (owners, users, salespeople, technicians) in a position to comment on attributes of your product. Secondary research will be in the form of print or electronic sources, such as magazine articles, owner manuals, and Web sites. Be sure to use electronic databases and the Web to find appropriate articles. Your report should analyze and discuss at least three comparable models or versions of the target product. Decide what criteria you will use to compare the models, such as price, features, warranty, service, and so forth. The report should include these components: letter of transmittal, table of contents, executive summary, introduction (including background, purpose, scope of the study, and research methods), findings (organized by comparison criteria), summary of findings, conclusions, recommendations, and bibliography. Address the report to your instructor. You may work individually, in pairs, or in teams.

FIGURE 10.18 **Intercultural Interview Topics and Questions**

Social Customs
1. How do people react to strangers? Are they friendly? Hostile? Reserved?
2. How do people greet each other?
3. What are the appropriate manners when you enter a room? Bow? Nod? Shake hands with everyone?
4. How are names used for introductions? Is it appropriate to inquire about one's occupation or family?
5. What are the attitudes toward touching?
6. How does one express appreciation for an invitation to another's home? Bring a gift? Send flowers? Write a thank-you note? Are any gifts taboo?
7. Are there any customs related to how or where one sits?
8. Are any facial expressions or gestures considered rude?
9. How close do people stand when talking?
10. What is the attitude toward punctuality in social situations? In business situations?
11. What are acceptable eye contact patterns?
12. What gestures indicate agreement? Disagreement?

Family Life
1. What is the basic unit of social organization? Basic family? Extended family?
2. Do women work outside of the home? In what occupations?

Housing, Clothing, and Food
1. Are there differences in the kind of housing used by different social groups? Differences in location? Differences in furnishings?
2. What occasions require special clothing?
3. Are some types of clothing considered taboo?
4. What is appropriate business attire for men? For women?
5. How many times a day do people eat?
6. What types of places, food, and drink are appropriate for business entertainment? Where is the seat of honor at a table?

Class Structure
1. Into what classes is society organized?
2. Do racial, religious, or economic factors determine social status?
3. Are there any minority groups? What is their social standing?

Political Patterns
1. Are there any immediate threats to the political survival of the country?
2. How is political power manifested?
3. What channels are used for expressing popular opinion?
4. What information media are important?
5. Is it appropriate to talk politics in social situations?

Religion and Folk Beliefs
1. To which religious groups do people belong? Is one predominant?
2. Do religious beliefs influence daily activities?
3. Which places have sacred value? Which objects? Which events?
4. How do religious holidays affect business activities?

Economic Institutions
1. What are the country's principal products?
2. Are workers organized in unions?
3. How are businesses owned? By family units? By large public corporations? By the government?
4. What is the standard work schedule?
5. Is it appropriate to do business by telephone?
6. How has technology affected business procedures?
7. Is participatory management used?
8. Are there any customs related to exchanging business cards?
9. How is status shown in an organization? Private office? Secretary? Furniture?
10. Are businesspeople expected to socialize before conducting business?

Value Systems
1. Is competitiveness or cooperation more prized?
2. Is thrift or enjoyment of the moment more valued?
3. Is politeness more important than factual honesty?
4. What are the attitudes toward education?
5. Do women own or manage businesses? If so, how are they treated?
6. What are your people's perceptions of Americans? Do Americans offend you? What has been hardest for you to adjust to in America? How could Americans make this adjustment easier for you?

10.20 Formal Report: Avoiding Huge Credit Card Debt for College Students

College students represent a new push for credit card companies. An amazing 84 percent of students carried at least one credit card in the most recent study of undergraduate card use, and half of college students had four or more cards.[20] Credit cards are a contributing factor when students graduate with an average of $20,000 debt. Because they can't buy cars, rent homes, or purchase insurance, graduates with big credit debt see a bleak future for themselves. A local newspaper plans to run a self-help story about college credit cards. The editor asks you, a young part-time reporter, to prepare a memo with information that could be turned into an article. The article would focus on parents of students who are about to leave for college. What can parents do to help students avoid sinking deeply into credit card debt?

Your Task. As a team or individually, use ABI/INFORM, Factiva, or LexisNexis and the Web to locate basic information about student credit card options. In a formal report discuss shared credit cards and other options. Use one or more of the techniques discussed in this chapter to track your sources. Finally, add a memo or letter of transmittal addressed to Janice Arrington, editor.

10.21 Formal Report: Netflix & Company—Movies After DVD and Blu-ray

The competition for consumer film rental dollars is fierce. A 400-employee company, Netflix offers flat rates for DVD and Blu-ray disc rentals by mail. Users can also stream certain movie titles on the Web and view them on their computers and TVs. Netflix has all but won the race against Blockbuster, a company that seemed invincible only a decade ago and traded at around $29 a share. Today, Blockbuster is in trouble; its stock price has slid to the level of penny stocks.

However, Netflix is still competing with Redbox, Amazon, Apple, and the cable companies, all jostling to become the leading provider of online films. After outpacing Blockbuster, Netflix is vying with Apple for leadership in digital streaming services. Experts predict that DVDs and Blu-ray discs will go the way of such dinosaurs as VHS tapes and, eventually, music CDs. Apple's release of the iPad only intensifies the rivalry among the competing streaming services. Netflix CEO Reed Hastings has no plans to stream films to the Apple device.

Your Task. Using ProQuest, Factiva, LexisNexis, or the Web, find information about the movie rental market and video on demand today. Research the latest trends in the use of DVD/Blu-ray discs and Web streaming. In a report, discuss the future of this important entertainment sector. Based on your research, expert opinion, and other resources, reach conclusions about the current state and future prospects of the movie rental business. If possible, in your formal report make recommendations detailing how Netflix could modify its business model to survive the cutthroat competition. Use one or more of the techniques discussed in this chapter to track your sources. If your instructor requires it, write a memo or letter of transmittal to Netflix CEO Reed Hastings.

10.22 More Proposal and Report Topics

A list with over 90 report topics is available at **www.cengagebrain.com**. The topics are divided into the following categories: accounting, finance, human resources, marketing, information systems, management, and general business/education/campus issues. You can collect information for many of these reports by using electronic databases and the Web. Your instructor may assign them as individual or team projects. All involve critical thinking in organizing information, drawing conclusions, and making recommendations. The topics include assignments appropriate for proposals, business plans, and formal reports.

Grammar/Mechanics Checkup—10

Apostrophes

Review Sections 2.20–2.22 in the Grammar/Mechanics Handbook. Then study each of the following statements. Underscore any inappropriate form. Write a correction in the space provided and record the number of the G/M principle(s) illustrated. If a sentence is correct, write C. When you finish, compare your responses with those at the back of the book. If your answers differ, study carefully the principles shown in parentheses.

years' (2.20b) **Example:** In just two years time, Marti earned her MBA degree.

______ 1. Mark Hanleys smartphone was found in the conference room.
______ 2. The severance package includes two weeks salary for each year worked.
______ 3. In only one years time, her school loans totaled $5,000.
______ 4. The board of directors strongly believed that John Petersons tenure as CEO was exceptionally successful.
______ 5. Several employees records were accidentally removed from the files.
______ 6. The last witness testimony was the most convincing to the jury members.
______ 7. Everyone appreciated Robins careful editing of our report.
______ 8. I always get my moneys worth at my favorite restaurant.
______ 9. Three local companies went out of business last month.
______ 10. In one months time, we hope to have our new Web site up and running.
______ 11. I need my boss signature on this expense claim.
______ 12. That legal secretarys credentials and years of experience qualified her for a higher salary.
______ 13. In certain aerospace departments, new applicants must apply for security clearance.
______ 14. Our companys stock price rose dramatically last year.
______ 15. Several businesses opening hours will change in the next three months.

Editing Challenge—10

As the employee with the best communication skills, you are frequently asked to edit messages. The following executive summary has problems with wordiness, spelling, proofreading, apostrophes, pronoun agreement, sentence structure, and other writing techniques you have studied. You may (a) use standard proofreading marks (see Appendix B) to correct the errors here or (b) download the document from **www.cengagebrain.com** and revise at your computer.

Your instructor may ask you to use the **Track Changes** feature in Word to show your editing comments. Turn on **Track Changes** on the **Review** tab. Click **Show Markup**. Place your cursor at an error, click **New Comment**, and key your edit in the bubble box provided. Study the guidelines in the Grammar/Mechanics Handbook as well as the lists of Confusing Words and Frequently Misspelled Words to sharpen your skills.

EXECUTIVE SUMMARY

Problem

Experts agree that the U.S. tuna industry must expand it's markets abroad particularly in regard to Japan. One of the largest consumer's of tuna in the world. Although consumption of tuna is decreasing in the United States they are increasing in Japan. The problem that is occuring for the american tuna industry is developing apropriate marketing strategies to boost its current sale's in Japanese markets. Even tho Japan produces much of it's tuna domesticly, they must still relie on imported tuna to meet its consumers demands.

Summary of Findings

This report analyzes the Japanese market which currently consumes seven hundred thousand tons of tuna per year, and is growing rapidly. In Japan, tuna is primarilly used for sashimi (raw fish) and caned tuna. Tuna is consumed in the food service industry and in home's. Much of this tuna are supplied by imports which at this point in time total about 35% of sales. Our findings indicate that not only will this expand, but that Japans share of imports will continue to grow. The trend is alarming to Japans tuna industry leaders, because this important market, close to a $billion a year, is increasingly subject to the influence of foriegn imports. Declining catches by Japans own Tuna fleet as well as a sharp upward turn in food preference by affluent Japanese consumers, has contributed to this trend. In just two years time, the demand for sashimi alone in Japan has increased in the amount of 15%.

The U.S. tuna industry are in the perfect position to meet this demand. Fishing techniques has been developed that maximize catch rate's, while minimizing danger to the enviroment. Modern packaging procedures assure that tuna reaches Japan in the freshest possible condition. Let it be said that Japanese consumers have rated the qaulity of American tuna high. Which has increased demand.

Recommendations

Based on our analisys, we reccommend the following 5 marketing strategys for the U.S. Tuna industry.

1. Farm greater supplys of tuna to export.
2. Establish new fisheries around the World.
3. We should market our own value added products.
4. Sell fresh tuna direct to the Tokyo Central Wholesale market.
5. Direct sales should be made to Japanese Supermarket chains.

Communication Workshop

Trash or Treasure: Assessing the Quality of Web Documents

Most of us using the Web have a tendency to assume that any information turned up by a search engine has somehow been evaluated as part of a valid selection process. Wrong! The truth is that the Internet is rampant with unreliable sites that reside side by side with reputable ones. Anyone with a computer and an Internet connection can publish anything on the Web.

Unlike the contents of the journals, magazines, and newspapers found in research-oriented libraries, the contents of most Web sites haven't been carefully scrutinized by experienced editors and peer writers. To put it another way, print journals, magazines, and newspapers have traditionally featured reasonably unbiased, trustworthy articles; all too many Web sites, however, have another goal in mind. They are above all else interested in promoting a cause or in selling a product. Much of the contents on the Web is not helpful because it is short-lived. Web sources change constantly and may disappear fast, so that your source cannot be verified. Many do not provide any references or reveal sources that are either obscure or suspect.

To use the Web meaningfully, you must learn to examine carefully what you find there. The following checklist will help you distinguish Web trash from Web treasure.

Checklist for Assessing the Quality of a Web Page

Authority

- Who publishes or sponsors this Web page?
- Is the author or sponsor clearly identified?
- What makes the author or sponsor of the page an authority?
- Is information about the author or creator available?
- If the author is an individual, is he or she affiliated with a reputable organization?
- Is contact information, such as an e-mail address, available?
- To what domain (.com, .org, .edu, .gov, .net, .biz, .tv) does the site containing it belong?
- Is the site based in the United States or abroad (usually indicated by .uk, .ca, ru, or other designation in the URL)?
- Is the site "personal" (often indicated by "~" or "%" in the site's URL)?

Currency

- What is the date of the Web page?
- When was the last time the Web page was updated?
- Is some of the information obviously out-of-date?

Content

- Is the purpose of the page to entertain, inform, convince, or sell?
- How would you classify this page (e.g., news, personal, advocacy, reference)?
- Is the objective or purpose of the Web page clear?
- Who is the intended audience of the page, based on its content, tone, and style?
- Can you judge the overall value of the content as compared with other resources on this topic?
- Does the content seem to be comprehensive (does it cover everything about the topic)?
- Is the site easy to navigate?
- What other sites does the Web page link to? These may give you a clue to the credibility of the target page.
- Does the page contain distracting graphics or fill your screen with unwanted pop-ups?

Accuracy

- Do the facts that are presented seem reliable?
- Do you find spelling, grammar, or usage errors?
- Does the page have broken links or graphics that don't load?
- Do you see any evidence of bias?
- Are footnotes or other documentation necessary? If so, have they been provided?

- If the site contains statistics or other data, are sources, dates, and other pertinent information disclosed?
- Are advertisements clearly distinguished from content?

Career Application. As interns at a news-gathering service, you have been asked to assess the quality of the following Web sites. Which of these could you recommend as sources of valid information?

- Beef Nutrition (**http://www.beefnutrition.org**)
- Edmunds: Where Smart Car Buyers Start (**http://www.edmunds.com**)
- I Hate Windows (**http://ihatewindowsblog.blogspot.com/**)
- EarthSave International (**http://www.earthsave.org**)
- The Vegetarian Resource Group (**http://www.vrg.org/nutshell/nutshell.htm**)
- The White House (**http://www.whitehouse.net**)
- The White House (**http://www.whitehouse.gov**)
- The White House (**http://www.whitehouse.com**)
- The Anaheim White House (**http://www.anaheimwhitehouse.com/**)
- National Anti-Vivisection Society (**http://www.navs.org**)
- Dow Chemical Company (**http://www.dow.com/**)
- Dow: A Chemical Company on the Global Playground (**http://www.dowethics.com/**)
- Smithsonian Institution (**http://www.si.edu**)
- Drudge Report (**http://www.drudgereport.com**)
- American Cancer Society (**http://www.cancer.org**)
- CraigsList (**http://www.craigslist.com**)

Your Task. If you are working with a team, divide the preceding list among team members. If you are working individually, select four of the sites. Answer the questions in the preceding checklist as you evaluate each site. Summarize your evaluation of each site in a memo report to your instructor or in team or class discussion.

Endnotes

[1] City of Las Vegas. (2010, January 4). RFP for public private partnership parking initiative. Onvia DemandStar. Retrieved from http://www.lasvegasnevada.gov/Business/5990.htm?ID

[2] Buck Institute for Research on Aging. (n.d.). Architecture. Retrieved from http://www.buckinstitute.org/architecture

[3] Based on Grinyer, M., Raytheon proposal consultant (personal communication with Mary Ellen Guffey, July 23, 2007).

[4] Greenwood, G., & Greenwood, J. (2008). SBIR proposal writing basics: Resumes must be written well. Greenwood Consulting Group. Retrieved from http://www.g-jgreenwood.com/sbir_proposal_writing_basics91.htm; How to write losing or unsuccessful proposals. (n.d.). Federal Marketplace. Retrieved from http://www.fedmarket.com/contractors/How-to-Write-Losing-or-Unsuccessful-Proposals

[5] Netcraft Ltd., *November 2010 Web Server Survey*. Retrieved from http://news.netcraft.com/archives/2010/01/07/january_2010_web_server_survey.html and Killmer, K. A., & Koppel, N. B. (2002, August). So much information, so little time: Evaluating Web resources with search engines. *THE Journal*. Retrieved from http://www.thejournal.com/articles/16051

[6] Sobel, J. (2010, November 3). State of the blogosphere 2010. Technorati. Retrieved from http://technorati.com/blogging/article/who-bloggers-brands-and-consumers-day/page-3

[7] BlogPulse stats. (2011, January 6). Retrieved from BlogPulse Web site: http://www.blogpulse.com and Beutler, W. (2007, April 10). Yes, but how many blogs are there really? Blog, P. I. Retrieved from http://www.blogpi.net/yes-but-how-many-blogs-are-there-really

[8] Online activities, 2000–2009. (2010, May). Pew Internet. Retrieved from http://www.pewinternet.org/Static-Pages/Trend-Data/Online-Activites-Total.aspx

[9] Petouhoff, N. L. (2010, January 26). How Carphone Warehouse uses Twitter and social media to transform customer service. Forrester. Retrieved from http://www.forrester.com/rb/Research/how_carphone_warehouse_uses_twitter_and_social/q/id/55956/t/2

[10] Berfield, S. (2009, August 17). Howard Schultz versus Howard Schultz. *BusinessWeek*, p. 31.

[11] Arenson, K. W., & Gootman, E. (2008, February 21). Columbia cites plagiarism by a professor. *The New York Times*. Retrieved from http://www.nytimes.com/2008/02/21/education/21prof.html; and Bartlett, T. (2006, September 8). Professor faces firing for plagiarism. *Chronicle of Higher Education*, p. 11. Retrieved from http://search.ebscohost.com

[12] Writing Tutorial Services, Indiana University. (n.d.) Plagiarism: What it is and how to recognize and avoid it. Retrieved from http://www.indiana.edu/~wts/pamphlets/plagiarism.shtml; Learning Center. (2008). iParadigms, LLC. Retrieved from http://www.plagiarism.org

[13] Kotkin, J. (2010, October 10). The fastest-growing cities in the U.S. *Forbes*. Retrieved from http://www.forbes.com/2010/10/11/cities-innovation-texas-great-plains-indianapolis-opinions-columnists-joel-kotkin.html

[14] Brady, D. (2006, December 4). *!#?@ the e-mail. Can we talk? *BusinessWeek*, p. 109.

[15] Reena, J. (2006, October 16). Enough with the shoot-'em-ups. *BusinessWeek*, p. 92; Spake, A. (2003, November 17). Hey kids! We've got sugar and toys. *U.S. News & World Report*, p. 62.

[16] Hibbard, J. (2006, October 9). How Yahoo! gave itself a face-lift. *BusinessWeek*, p. 77.

[17] Teens more "normal" than you think regarding media usage. (2009, June 25). Nielsenwire. Retrieved from http://blog.nielsen.com/nielsenwire/consumer/teens-more-normal-than-you-think-regarding-media-usage

[18] Tynan-Wood, C. (2010, August 17). The (better) future of tech support. Adventures in IT. Retrieved from http://infoworld.com/d/adventures-in-it/the-better-future-tech-support-066?page=0,0; and Edwards, C., & Ihlwan, M. (2006, December 4). Upward mobility. *BusinessWeek*, pp. 68–82.

[19] Waters, S. (n.d.) Shoplifting prevention 101. About.com Guide. Retrieved from http://retail.about.com/od/lossprevention/a/stopshoplifting.htm

[20] How undergraduate students use credit cards. (2009). Sallie Mae. Retrieved from https://www1.salliemae.com/about/news_info/newsreleases/041309.htm

Acknowledgments

p. 280 Office Insider quote from Mary Piecewicz, former HP proposal manager, interview with Mary Ellen Guffey, January 12, 1999.

p. 291 Office Insider cited in Boston College library guide. Retrieved from http://libguides.bc.edu/content.php?pid=613&sid=1356

p. 292 Office Insider based on What is plagiarism? Plagiarism FAQs. (n.d.). Retrieved from http://www.plagiarism.org/learning_center/what_is_plagiarism.html

UNIT 5

Professionalism, Teamwork, Meetings, and Speaking Skills

CHAPTER 11
Professionalism at Work: Business Etiquette, Ethics, Teamwork, and Meetings

CHAPTER 12
Business Presentations

CHAPTER 11

Professionalism at Work: Business Etiquette, Ethics, Teamwork, and Meetings

Go to
cengagebrain.com
and use your access code to unlock valuable student eResources.

StockLite/Shutterstock.com

OBJECTIVES

After studying this chapter, you should be able to

- Show that you understand the importance of professional behavior, business etiquette, and ethics and know what employers want.
- Discuss improving face-to-face workplace communication including using your voice as a communication tool.
- Understand how to foster positive workplace relations through conversation.
- Review techniques for responding professionally to workplace criticism and for offering constructive criticism on the job.
- Explain ways to polish your professional telephone skills and practice proper voice mail etiquette.
- Describe the role of conventional and virtual teams, explain positive and negative team behavior, and identify the characteristics of successful teams.
- Outline procedures for planning, leading, and participating in productive business meetings, including using professional etiquette techniques, resolving conflict, and handling dysfunctional group members.

Embracing Professionalism, Business Etiquette, and Ethical Behavior

Whether we call it *professionalism, business etiquette, ethical conduct, social intelligence*, or *soft skills*, we are referring to a whole range of desirable workplace behaviors.

You probably know that being *professional* is important. When you search for definitions, however, you will find a wide range of meanings. Related terms and synonyms, such as *business etiquette* or *protocol*, *soft skills, social intelligence, polish*, and *civility*, may add to the confusion. However, they all have one thing in common: They describe desirable workplace behavior. Businesses have an interest in employees who get along and deliver positive results that enhance profits and boost the company's image. As a budding business professional, you have a stake in acquiring skills that will make you a strong job applicant and a valuable, successful employee.

In this section you will learn which professional characteristics most business people value in workplace relationships and will expect of you. Next, you will be asked to consider the link between professional and ethical behavior on the job.

Finally, by knowing what recruiters want, you will have the power to shape yourself into the kind of professional they are looking to hire.

Defining Professional Behavior

Smooth relations with coworkers, business partners, and the public are crucial for the bottom line. Conversely, negative behavior comes at a steep price. Business professors Christine Pearson and Christine Porath interviewed 9,000 executives and workers and found that incivility in the workplace is shockingly widespread. Pearson's and Porath's research revealed that almost 50 percent of employees respond to ongoing rude behavior by decreasing their work effort. The study also showed that 12 percent of employees leave their jobs because of bullying and other uncivil acts they have experienced. The average cost of replacing each of these disgruntled employees is $50,000.[1]

Not surprisingly, businesses are responding to increasing incidents of "desk rage" in American workplaces. Many organizations have established protocol procedures or policies to encourage civility. Following are a few synonyms that attempt to define professional behavior to foster positive workplace relations.

OFFICE INSIDER

"Civility on the job creates an atmosphere of respect and appreciation that ultimately translates to better reputation and, hence, to better business."

—Ronald M. Bosrock, founder and director of the Global Institute, a research center

Civility. Management consultant Patricia M. Buhler defines rising incivility at work as "behavior that is considered disrespectful and inconsiderate of others."[2] For an example of a policy encouraging civility, view Wikipedia's guidelines to its editors (**http://en.wikipedia.org/wiki/Wikipedia:Civility**), which offer principles to prevent abuse and hateful responses on the Internet. The largest wiki ever created, the free encyclopedia must ensure that its more than 91,000 active contributors "treat each other with consideration and respect." Wikipedia also clearly defines undesirable behavior: "[I]ncivility consists of personal attacks, rudeness, disrespectful comments, and aggressive behaviours that . . . lead to unproductive stress and conflict."[3] Surely such actions would not be acceptable in most businesses.

Polish. You may hear businesspeople refer to someone as being *polished* or displaying polish when dealing with others. In her book with the telling title *Buff and Polish: A Practical Guide to Enhance Your Professional Image and Communication Style*, corporate trainer Kathryn J. Volin focuses on nonverbal techniques and etiquette guidelines that are linked to career success. For example, she addresses making first impressions, shaking hands, improving one's voice quality, listening, and presentation skills. You will find many of these valuable traits of a polished business professional in this textbook and on the Web (see **www.cengagebrain.com**).

Business and Dining Etiquette. Proper business attire, dining etiquette, and other aspects of your professional presentation can make or break your interview, as you will see in Chapter 14. Even a seemingly harmless act such as sharing a business meal can have a huge impact on your career. In the words of a Fortune 500 executive, "Eating is not an executive skill . . . but it is especially hard to imagine why anyone negotiating a rise to the top would consider it possible to skip mastering the very simple requirements . . . what else did they skip learning?"[4] This means that you will be judged on more than your college-bred expertise. You will need to hone your etiquette skills as a well-rounded future business professional.

Social Intelligence. Occasionally you may encounter the expression *social intelligence*. In the words of one of its modern proponents, it is "the ability to get along well with others and to get them to cooperate with you."[5] Social intelligence points to a deep understanding of culture and life that helps us negotiate interpersonal and social situations. This type of intelligence can be much harder

From meetings and interviews to company parties and golf outings, nearly all workplace-related activities involve etiquette. Take Your Dog to Work Day, the ever-popular morale booster that keeps workers chained to their pets instead of the desk, has a unique set of guidelines to help maximize fun. For employees at the nearly one in five U.S. businesses that allow dogs at work, etiquette gurus say pets must be well behaved, housebroken, and free of fleas to participate in the four-legged festivity. *Why is it important to follow proper business etiquette?*

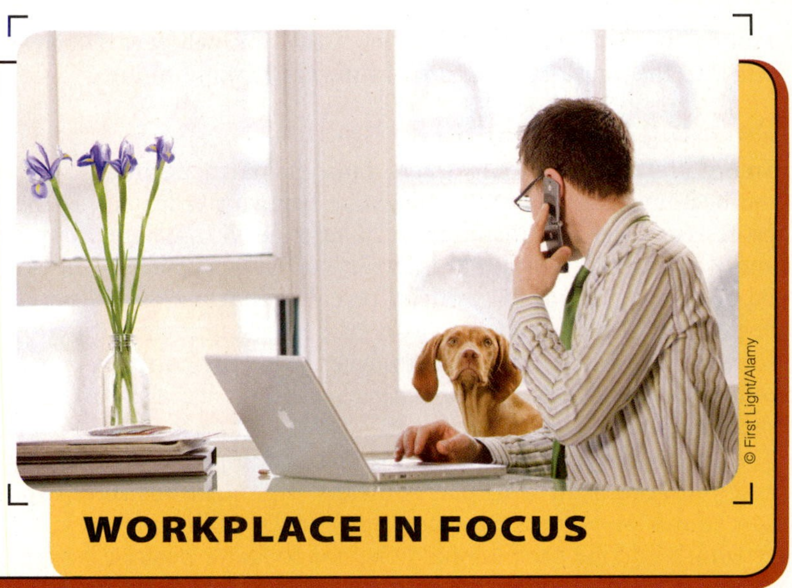
© First Light/Alamy

WORKPLACE IN FOCUS

to acquire than simple etiquette. Social intelligence requires us to interact well, be perceptive, show sensitivity toward others, and grasp a situation quickly and accurately.

OFFICE INSIDER

"Unprofessional conduct around the office will eventually overflow into official duties. Few of us have mastered the rare art of maintaining multiple personalities."

—Douglas Chismar, liberal arts program director at Ringling College of Art and Design

Soft Skills. Perhaps the most common definition of important interpersonal habits is *soft skills*, as opposed to *hard skills*, a term for the technical knowledge in your field. Soft skills are a whole cluster of personal qualities, habits, attitudes (for example, optimism and friendliness), communication skills, and social graces. Employers want managers and employees who are comfortable with diverse coworkers, who can listen actively to customers and colleagues, who can make eye contact, who display good workplace manners, and who possess a host of other interpersonal skills. *Dress for Success* guru John T. Molloy says that 99 out of 100 executives view social skills as prerequisites to success, whether over cocktails, dinner, or in the boardroom.[6] These skills are immensely important not only to be hired but also to be promoted.

Simply put, all these attempts to explain proper behavior at work aim at identifying traits that make someone a good employee and a compatible coworker. You will want to achieve a positive image on the job and to maintain a solid reputation. For the sake of simplicity, in the discussion that follows, the terms *professionalism, business etiquette*, and *soft skills* will be used largely as synonyms.

Relating Professional Behavior to Ethics

Business etiquette is closely related to everyday ethical behavior.

The wide definition of professionalism also encompasses another crucial quality in a businessperson: *ethics* or *integrity*. Perhaps you subscribe to a negative view of business after learning how reckless behavior by major banks contributed to the worst recession since the Great Depression. You may have heard about companies such as Countrywide or Enron. Their demise and fraud charges against their executives have reinforced the cynical perception of business as unethical and greedy. However, for every company that captures the limelight for misconduct, hundreds or even thousands of others operate honestly and serve their customers and the public well. The overwhelming majority of businesses wish to recruit ethical and polished graduates.

The difference between ethics and etiquette is minimal in the workplace. Ethics professor Douglas Chismar—and Harvard professor Stephen L. Carter before him—suggests that no sharp distinction between ethics and etiquette exists. How we approach the seemingly trivial events of work life reflects our character and attitudes when we handle larger issues. Our conduct should be consistently ethical and professional. Professor Chismar believes that "[w]e each have a moral obligation to treat each other with respect and sensitivity every day."[7] He calls on all of us to make a difference in the quality of life, morale, and even productivity at work. When employed appropriately in business, he says, professionalism brings greater good to society and makes for a better workplace.

Figure 11.1 summarizes the many components of professional workplace behavior[8] and identifies six main dimensions that will ease your entry into the world of work. Follow these guidelines to ensure your success on the job and increase the likelihood of promotion.

FIGURE 11.1 The Six Dimensions of Professional Behavior

Professional Dimension	What Professionalism Means on the Job
Courtesy and respect	• Be punctual. • Speak and write clearly and in language others can understand. • Apologize for errors or misunderstandings. • Notify the other person promptly when running late. • Accept constructive criticism. • Provide fair and gentle feedback. • Practice active listening.
Appearance and appeal	• Present yourself pleasantly with good hygiene and grooming. • Choose attractive, yet not distracting business attire. • Understand that appropriate dress and behavior are the first indication of professionalism and create lasting impressions. • Display proper business and dining etiquette.
Tolerance and tact	• Demonstrate self-control. • Stay away from public arguments and disagreements, including in written documents and e-mail. • Eliminate biases and prejudices in all business dealings. • Keep personal opinions of people private. • Avoid snap judgments especially when collaborating with others.
Honesty and ethics	• Avoid even the smallest lies at all cost. • Steer clear of conflicts of interest. • Pay for services and products promptly. • Keep confidential information confidential. • Pass up opportunities to badmouth competitors—emphasize your company's benefits, not your competitors' flaws. • Take positive, appropriate actions; avoid resorting to vengeful behavior when you feel wronged.
Reliability and responsibility	• Be dependable. • Follow through on commitments. • Keep promises and deadlines. • Perform work consistently and deliver effective results. • Make realistic promises about the quantity and quality of work output in a projected time frame.
Diligence and collegiality	• Deliver only work you can be proud of. • Strive for excellence at all times. • Give to customers more than they expect. • Be prepared before meetings and when presenting reports. • Do what needs to be done; do not leave work for others to do. • Show a willingness to share expertise. • Volunteer services to a worthy community or charity group. • Join networking groups and help their members.

Knowing What Recruiters Want

In the workplace we are judged to a great extent on our soft skills and professionalism.

Professional polish is increasingly valuable in our knowledge-based economy and will set you apart in competition with others. Hiring managers expect you to have technical expertise in your field. A good résumé and interview may get you in the door. However, soft skills and professional polish will ensure your long-term success. Advancement and promotions will depend on your grasp of workplace etiquette and the ability to communicate with your boss, coworkers, and customers. You will also earn recognition on the job if you prove yourself as an effective and contributing team member—as a well-rounded professional overall.

Even in technical fields such as accounting and finance, employers are looking for professionalism and soft skills. Based on a survey of international accounting executives, *CA Magazine* concluded that "the future is bright for the next generation of accounting and finance professionals provided they are armed with such soft skills as the ability to communicate, deal with change, and work in a team setting."[9] A survey of chief financial officers revealed that a majority believed that communication skills carry a greater importance today than in the past.[10] Increasingly, finance professionals must be able to interact with the entire organization and explain terms without using financial jargon.

Employers want team players who can work together productively. If you look at current online or newspaper want ads, chances are you will find requirements such as the following examples:

- Proven team skills to help deliver on-time, on-budget results
- Strong verbal and written communication skills as well as excellent presentation skills
- Excellent interpersonal, organizational, and teamwork skills
- Required competencies: interpersonal and team skills plus well-developed communication skills
- Good people skills and superior teamwork abilities

OFFICE INSIDER

"No question, technology is the Great Enabler. But, paradoxically, now the human bit is more, not less, important than ever before."

—Tom Peters, business expert and author of *Re-Imagine!*

In addition, most hiring managers are looking for new-hires who show enthusiasm, are eager to learn, volunteer to tackle even difficult tasks, and exhibit a positive attitude. You will not be hired to warm a seat.

This chapter focuses on developing interpersonal skills, telephone and voice mail etiquette, teamwork proficiency, and meeting management skills. These are some of the soft skills that employers seek in today's increasingly interconnected and competitive environments. You will learn many tips and techniques for becoming a professional communicator, valuable team player, and polished meeting participant.

Succeeding in Face-to-Face Situations

One-dimensional communication technologies cannot replace the richness or effectiveness of face-to-face communication.

Because today's technologies provide many alternate communication channels, you may think that face-to-face communication is no longer essential or even important in business and professional transactions. You have learned that e-mail is still the preferred communication channel because it is faster, cheaper, and easier than telephone, mail, or fax. You also know that businesspeople have embraced instant messaging, texting, and some social media. However, despite their popularity and acceptance, alternate communication technologies can't replace the richness or effectiveness of face-to-face communication.[11] Imagine that you want to tell your boss how you solved a problem. Would you settle for a one-dimensional phone call, a text message, or an e-mail when you could step into her office and explain in person?

Face-to-face conversation has many advantages. It allows you to be persuasive and expressive because you can use your voice and body language to make a point. You are less likely to be misunderstood because you can read feedback and make needed adjustments. In conflict resolution, you can reach a solution more efficiently and cooperate to create greater levels of mutual benefit when communicating face to face.[12] Moreover, people want to see each other to satisfy a deep human need for social interaction. For numerous reasons communicating in person remains the most effective of all communication channels. In this chapter you will explore helpful business and professional interpersonal speaking techniques, starting with viewing your voice as a communication tool.

Using Your Voice as a Communication Tool

It has been said that language provides the words, but your voice is the music that makes words meaningful.[13] You may believe that a beautiful or powerful voice is unattainable. After all, this is the voice you were born with and it can't be changed. Actually, the voice is a flexible instrument. Actors hire coaches to help them eliminate or acquire accents or proper inflection for challenging roles. For example, Nicole Kidman, who speaks with an Australian accent, has taken on other accents, including American Southern and South African, for film roles. Celebrities, business executives, and everyday people consult voice and speech therapists to help them shake bad habits or just help them speak so that they can be understood and not sound less intelligent than they are. Rather than consult a high-paid specialist, you can pick up useful tips for using your voice most effectively by learning how to control such elements as pronunciation, voice quality, pitch, volume, rate, and emphasis.

Like an actor, you can change your voice to make it a more powerful communication tool.

Pronunciation. Proper pronunciation involves saying words correctly and clearly with the accepted sounds and accented syllables. You will have a distinct advantage in your job if, through training and practice, you learn to pronounce words correctly. How can you improve your pronunciation skills? The best ways are to listen carefully to educated people, to look words up in the dictionary, and to practice. Online dictionaries frequently allow you to play back the pronunciation when you have found your desired word.

Proper pronunciation means saying words correctly and clearly with the accepted sounds and accented syllables.

Voice Quality. The quality of your voice sends a nonverbal message to listeners. It identifies your personality and your mood. Some voices sound enthusiastic and friendly, conveying the impression of an upbeat person who is happy to be with the listener. But voices can also sound controlling, patronizing, slow-witted, angry, bored, or childish. This does not mean that the speaker necessarily has that attribute. It may mean that the speaker is merely carrying on a family tradition or pattern learned in childhood. To check your voice quality, record your voice and listen to it critically. Is it projecting a positive quality about you? Do you sound professional?

Pitch. Effective speakers use a relaxed, controlled, well-pitched voice to attract listeners to their message. *Pitch* refers to sound vibration frequency; that is, the highness or lowness of a sound. Voices are most engaging when they rise and fall in conversational tones. Flat, monotone voices are considered boring and ineffectual.

Volume and Rate. The volume of your voice is the loudness or the intensity of sound. Just as you adjust the volume on your MP3 player or television set, you should adjust the volume of your speaking to the occasion and your listeners. *Rate* refers to the pace of your speech. If you speak too slowly, listeners are bored and their attention wanders. If you speak too quickly, listeners may not be able to understand you. Most people normally talk at about 125 words a minute. Monitor the nonverbal signs of your listeners and adjust your volume and rate as needed.

Speaking in a moderately low-pitched voice at about 125 words a minute makes you sound pleasing and professional.

Emphasis. By emphasizing or stressing certain words, you can change the meaning you are expressing. To make your message interesting and natural, use emphasis appropriately.

"Uptalk," in which sentences sound like questions, makes speakers seem weak and tentative.

Some speakers today are prone to *uptalk*. This is a habit of using a rising inflection at the end of a sentence resulting in a singsong pattern that makes statements sound like questions. Once used exclusively by teenagers, uptalk is increasingly found in the workplace with negative results. When statements sound like questions, speakers seem weak and tentative. Their messages lack conviction and authority. On the job, managers afflicted by uptalk may have difficulty convincing staff members to follow directions because their voice inflection implies that other valid options are available. If you want to sound confident and competent, avoid uptalk.

Promoting Positive Workplace Relations Through Conversation

In the workplace, conversations may involve giving and taking instructions, providing feedback, exchanging ideas on products and services, participating in performance appraisals, or engaging in small talk about such things as families and sports. Face-to-face conversation helps people work together harmoniously and feel that they are part of the larger organization. Following are several business etiquette guidelines that promote positive workplace conversations, both in the office and at work-related social functions.

OFFICE INSIDER

"In today's fiercely competitive business arenas, etiquette and protocol intelligence will distinguish you from the crowd. While this unique intelligence alone may not get you anywhere, it will give you an edge that will make the difference between you and another person who is just as smart."

—Dorothea Johnson, author and etiquette expert

Use Correct Names and Titles. Although the world seems increasingly informal, it is still wise to use titles and last names when addressing professional adults (*Ms. O'Malley, Mr. Santiago*). In some organizations senior staff members speak to junior employees on a first-name basis, but the reverse may not be encouraged. Probably the safest plan is to ask your superiors how they want to be addressed. Customers and others outside the organization should always be addressed initially by title and last name. Wait for an invitation to use first names.

When you meet strangers, do you have trouble remembering their names? You can improve your memory considerably if you associate the person with an object, place, color, animal, job, adjective, or some other memory hook. For example, *technology pro Gina, L.A. Matt, silver-haired Mr. Elliott, baseball fan John, programmer Tanya, traveler Ms. Choi.* The person's name will also be more deeply imbedded in your memory if you use it immediately after being introduced, in subsequent conversation, and when you part.

You will be most effective in workplace conversations if you use correct names and titles, choose appropriate topics, avoid negative and judgmental remarks, and give sincere and specific praise.

Choose Appropriate Topics. In some workplace activities, such as social gatherings or interviews, you will be expected to engage in small talk. Be sure to stay away from controversial topics with someone you don't know very well. Avoid politics, religion, or controversial current events that can trigger heated arguments. To initiate appropriate conversations, read newspapers and listen to radio and TV shows discussing current events. Subscribe to e-newsletters and RSS feeds that deliver relevant news to you via e-mail. Visit news portals such as Google News or Yahoo News, or follow CNN and major newspapers online. Make a mental note of items that you can use in conversation, taking care to remember where you saw or heard the news items so that you can report accurately and authoritatively. Try not to be defensive or annoyed if others present information that upsets you.

Avoid Negative Remarks. Workplace conversations are not the place to complain about your colleagues, your friends, the organization, or your job. No one enjoys listening to whiners. What's more, your criticism of others may come back to haunt you. A snipe at your boss or a complaint about a fellow worker may reach him or her, sometimes embellished or distorted with meanings you did not intend. Be circumspect in all negative judgments. Remember, some people love to repeat statements that will stir up trouble or set off internal workplace wars. Don't give them the ammunition!

Listen to Learn. In conversations with managers, colleagues, subordinates, and customers, train yourself to expect to learn something from what you are hearing. Being attentive is not only instructive but also courteous. Beyond displaying good manners, you will probably find that your conversation partner has information that you don't have. Being receptive and listening with an open mind means not interrupting or prejudging. Let's say you want very much to be able to work at home for part of your workweek. You try to explain your ideas to your boss, but he cuts you off shortly after you start. He says, *It is out of the question; we need you here every day.* Suppose instead he had said, *I have strong reservations about your telecommuting, but maybe you will change my mind;* and he settles in to listen to your presentation. Even if your boss decides against your request, you will feel that your ideas were heard and respected.

Give Sincere and Specific Praise. The Greek philosopher Xenophon once said, "The sweetest of all sounds is praise." Probably nothing promotes positive workplace relationships better than sincere and specific praise. Whether the compliments and appreciation are traveling upward to management, downward to workers, or horizontally to colleagues, everyone responds well to recognition. Organizations run more smoothly and morale is higher when people feel appreciated. In your workplace conversations, look for ways to recognize good work and good people. Try to be specific. Instead of *You did a good job in leading that meeting*, say something more specific, such as *Your excellent leadership skills certainly kept that meeting short, focused, and productive.*

OFFICE INSIDER

"I discovered that as much as business people needed training in thinking on their feet, they needed far more training in the fine art of getting along and dealing with people in everyday business and social contacts."

—Andrew Carnegie

Act Professionally in Social Situations. You will likely attend many work-related social functions during your career, including dinners, picnics, holiday parties, and other events. It is important to remember that your actions at these events can help or harm your career. Dress appropriately, and avoid or limit alcohol consumption. Choose appropriate conversation topics, and make sure that your voice and mannerisms communicate that you are glad to be there.

Responding Professionally to Workplace Criticism

Most of us hate giving criticism, but we dislike receiving it even more. However, it is normal to both give and receive criticism on the job. The criticism may be given informally, for example, during a casual conversation with a supervisor or coworker. Or the criticism may be given formally, for example, during a performance evaluation. The important thing is that you are able to accept and respond professionally when receiving criticism.

When being criticized, you may feel that you are being attacked. You can't just sit back and relax. Your heart beats faster, your temperature shoots up, your face reddens, and you respond with the classic fight-or-flight syndrome. You want to instantly retaliate or escape from the attacker. But focusing on your feelings distracts you from hearing the content of what is being said, and it prevents you from responding professionally. Some or all of the following suggestions can help you respond positively to criticism so that you can benefit from it:

When being criticized, you should listen, paraphrase, and clarify what is said; if you agree, apologize or explain what you will do differently.

- **Listen without interrupting.** Even though you might want to protest, make yourself hear the speaker out.
- **Determine the speaker's intent.** Unskilled communicators may throw "verbal bricks" with unintended negative-sounding expressions. If you think the intent is positive, focus on what is being said rather than reacting to poorly chosen words.
- **Acknowledge what you are hearing.** Respond with a pause, a nod, or a neutral statement such as *I understand you have a concern.* This buys you time. Don't disagree, counterattack, or blame, which may escalate the situation and harden the speaker's position.
- **Paraphrase what was said.** In your own words, restate objectively what you are hearing.

- **Ask for more information if necessary.** Clarify what is being said. Stay focused on the main idea rather than interjecting side issues.
- **Agree—if the comments are accurate.** If an apology is in order, give it. Explain what you plan to do differently. If the criticism is on target, the sooner you agree, the more likely you will be to receive respect from the other person.
- **Disagree respectfully and constructively—if you feel the comments are unfair.** After hearing the criticism, you might say, *May I tell you my perspective?* Or you could try to solve the problem by saying, *How can we improve this situation in a way you believe we can both accept?* If the other person continues to criticize, say, *I want to find a way to resolve your concern. When do you want to talk about it next?*
- **Look for a middle position.** Search for a middle position or a compromise. Be genial even if you don't like the person or the situation.
- **Learn from criticism.** Most work-related criticism is given with the best of intentions. You should welcome the opportunity to correct your mistakes and to learn from them. Responding positively and professionally to workplace criticism can help you improve your job performance. As Winston Churchill said, "All men make mistakes, but only wise men learn from their mistakes."[14]

If you feel you are being criticized unfairly, disagree respectfully and constructively; look for a middle position.

Providing Constructive Criticism on the Job

Offering constructive criticism is easier if you plan what you will say, focus on improvement, offer to help, be specific, discuss the behavior and not the person, speak privately face-to-face, and avoid anger.

In the workplace cooperative endeavors demand feedback and evaluation. How are we doing on a project? What went well? What failed? How can we improve our efforts? Today's workplace often involves team projects. As a team member, you will be called on to judge the work of others. In addition to working on teams, you can also expect to become a supervisor or manager one day. As such, you will need to evaluate subordinates. Good employees seek good feedback from their supervisors. They want and need timely, detailed observations about their work to reinforce what they do well and help them overcome weak spots. But making that feedback palatable and constructive is not always easy. Depending on your situation, you may find some or all of the following suggestions helpful when you must deliver constructive criticism:

- **Mentally outline your conversation.** Think carefully about what you want to accomplish and what you will say. Find the right words and deliver them at the right time and in the right setting.
- **Generally, use face-to-face communication.** Most constructive criticism is better delivered in person rather than in e-mail messages or memos. Personal feedback offers an opportunity for the listener to ask questions and give explanations. Occasionally, however, complex situations may require a different strategy. You might prefer to write out your opinions and deliver them by telephone or in writing. A written document enables you to organize your thoughts, include all the details, and be sure of keeping your cool. Remember, though, that written documents create permanent records—for better or worse.
- **Focus on improvement.** Instead of attacking, use language that offers alternative behavior. Use phrases such as *Next time, you could . . . .*"
- **Offer to help.** Criticism is accepted more readily if you volunteer to help eliminate or solve the problem.
- **Be specific.** Instead of a vague assertion such as *Your work is often late*, be more specific: *The specs on the Riverside job were due Thursday at 5 p.m., and you didn't hand them in until Friday.* Explain how the person's performance jeopardized the entire project.
- **Avoid broad generalizations.** Don't use words such as *should, never, always*, and other encompassing expressions as they may cause the listener to shut down and become defensive.
- **Discuss the behavior, not the person.** Instead of *You seem to think you can come to work anytime you want*, focus on the behavior: *Coming to work late means that we have to fill in with someone else until you arrive.*

- **Use the word *we* rather than *you*.** Saying, *We need to meet project deadlines*, is better than saying, *You need to meet project deadlines.* Emphasize organizational expectations rather than personal ones. Avoid sounding accusatory.
- **Encourage two-way communication.** Even if well planned, criticism is still hard to deliver. It may surprise or hurt the feelings of the employee. Consider ending your message with, *It can be hard to hear this type of feedback. If you would like to share your thoughts, I'm listening.*
- **Avoid anger, sarcasm, and a raised voice.** Criticism is rarely constructive when tempers flare. Plan in advance what you will say and deliver it in low, controlled, and sincere tones.
- **Keep it private.** Offer praise in public; offer criticism in private. "Setting an example" through public criticism is never a wise management policy.

Practicing Professional Telephone, Cell Phone, and Voice Mail Etiquette

Despite the heavy reliance on e-mail, the telephone is still an extremely important piece of equipment in offices. With the addition of today's wireless technology, it does not matter whether you are in or out of the office. You can always be reached by phone. As a business communicator, you can be more productive, efficient, and professional by following some simple suggestions. In this chapter we will focus on traditional telephone etiquette as well as cell phone use and voice mail techniques.

Making Telephone Calls Professionally

You can make productive telephone calls by planning an agenda, identifying the purpose, being cheerful and accurate, being professional and courteous, and avoiding rambling.

Before making a telephone call, decide whether the intended call is really necessary. Could you find the information yourself? If you wait a while, would the problem resolve itself? Perhaps your message could be delivered more efficiently by some other means. Some companies have found that telephone calls are often less important than the work they interrupt. Alternatives to telephone calls include texting, instant messaging, e-mail, memos, or calls to voice mail systems. If you must make a telephone call, consider using the following suggestions to make it fully productive:

- **Plan a mini-agenda.** Have you ever been embarrassed when you had to make a second telephone call because you forgot an important item the first time? Before placing a call, jot down notes regarding all the topics you need to discuss. Following an agenda guarantees not only a complete call but also a quick one. You will be less likely to wander from the business at hand while rummaging through your mind trying to remember everything.
- **Use a three-point introduction.** When placing a call, immediately (a) name the person you are calling, (b) identify yourself and your affiliation, and (c) give a brief explanation of your reason for calling. For example: *May I speak to Jeremy Johnson? This is Paula Soltani of Coughlin and Associates, and I'm seeking information about a software program called ZoneAlarm Internet Security.* This kind of introduction enables the receiving individual to respond immediately without asking further questions.
- **Be brisk if you are rushed.** For business calls when your time is limited, avoid questions such as *How are you?* Instead, say, *Lauren, I knew you'd be the only one who could answer these two questions for me.* Another efficient strategy is to set a "contract" with the caller: *Look, Lauren, I have only ten minutes, but I really wanted to get back to you.*
- **Be cheerful and accurate.** Let your voice show the same kind of animation that you radiate when you greet people in person. In your mind try to envision the individual answering the telephone. A smile can certainly affect the tone of your voice; therefore, even though the individual can't see you, smile at that person. Speak with a tone that is enthusiastic, respectful, and attentive. Moreover, be accurate about what you say. *Hang on a second; I will be right*

back rarely is true. It is better to say, *It may take me two or three minutes to get that information. Would you prefer to hold or have me call you back?*

- **Be professional and courteous.** Remember that you are representing yourself and your company when you make phone calls. Use professional vocabulary and courteous language. Say *thank you* and *please* during your conversations. Don't eat, drink, or chew gum while talking on the phone, which can often be heard on the other end. Articulate your words clearly so that the receiver can understand you. Avoid doing other work during the phone call so that you can focus entirely on the conversation.
- **Bring it to a close.** The responsibility for ending a call lies with the caller. This is sometimes difficult to do if the other person rambles on. You may need to use suggestive closing language, such as the following: (a) *I have certainly enjoyed talking with you*, (b) *I have learned what I needed to know, and now I can proceed with my work*, (c) *Thanks for your help*, (d) *I must go now, but may I call you again in the future if I need . . .*? or (e) *Should we talk again in a few weeks*?
- **Avoid telephone tag.** If you call someone who's not in, ask when it would be best for you to call again. State that you will call at a specific time—and do it. If you ask a person to call you, give a time when you can be reached—and then be sure you are in at that time.
- **Leave complete voice mail messages.** Remember that there is no rush when you leave a voice mail message. Always enunciate clearly. Be sure to provide a complete message, including your name, telephone number, and the time and date of your call. Explain your purpose so that the receiver can be ready with the required information when returning your call.

Receiving Telephone Calls Professionally

You can improve your telephone reception skills by identifying yourself, being responsive and helpful, and taking accurate messages.

With a little forethought, you can project a professional image and make your telephone a productive, efficient work tool. Developing good telephone manners also reflects well on you and on your organization. You will be most successful on the job if you practice the following etiquette guidelines:

- **Answer promptly and courteously.** Try to answer the phone on the first or second ring if possible. Smile as you pick up the phone.
- **Identify yourself immediately.** In answering your telephone or someone else's, provide your name, title or affiliation, and a greeting. For example, *Juan Salinas, Digital Imaging Corporation. How may I help you?* Force yourself to speak clearly and slowly. Remember that the caller may be unfamiliar with what you are saying and fail to recognize slurred syllables.
- **Be responsive and helpful.** If you are in a support role, be sympathetic to callers' needs and show that you understand their situations. Instead of *I don't know*, try *That is a good question; let me investigate*. Instead of *We can't do that*, try *That is a tough one; let's see what we can do*. Avoid *No* at the beginning of a sentence. It sounds especially abrasive and displeasing because it suggests total rejection.
- **Be cautious when answering calls for others.** Be courteous and helpful, but don't give out confidential information. It is better to say, *She is away from her desk* or *He is out of the office* than to report a colleague's exact whereabouts. Also be tight-lipped about sharing company information with strangers. Security experts insist that employees answering telephones must become guardians of company information.[15]
- **Take messages carefully.** Few things are as frustrating as receiving a potentially important phone message that is illegible. Repeat the spelling of names and verify telephone numbers. Write messages legibly and record their time and date. Promise to give the messages to intended recipients, but don't guarantee return calls.
- **Leave the line respectfully.** If you must put a call on hold, let the caller know and give an estimate of how long you expect the call to be on hold. Give the caller the option of holding. Say *Would you prefer to hold, or would you like me to call you back?* If the caller is on hold for a long period of time, check back

periodically so that the caller does not think that he or she has been forgotten or that the call has been disconnected.

- **Explain what you are doing when transferring calls.** Give a reason for transferring, and identify the extension to which you are directing the call in case the caller is disconnected.

Using Smartphones for Business

Smartphones are essential workplace communication tools, but they must be used without offending others.

Today's smartphones are very sophisticated mobile devices. They enable you to conduct business from virtually anywhere at any time. The smartphone has become an essential part of communication in the workplace. For a number of years now, the number of U.S. cellular phone users has outpaced the number of landline telephone users, and the number of cell phone, netbook, and tablet computer users keeps growing.[16] More than 80 percent of Americans own a cell phone,[17] and more than a fifth of wireless customers live without landlines.[18]

Today's highly capable smartphones can do much more than making and receiving calls. High-end smartphones function much like laptops or netbooks. They can be used to store contact information, make to-do lists, keep track of appointments and important dates, send and receive e-mail, send and receive text and multimedia messages, search the Web, get news and stock quotes from the Internet, take pictures and videos, synchronize with Outlook and other software applications, and many other functions. Whether businesspeople opt for BlackBerrys, Android phones, or the popular iPhone, thousands of applications ("apps") enable them to stay connected, informed, and entertained on the go.

Because so many people depend on their smartphones and cell phones, it is important to understand proper use and etiquette. How are these mobile devices best used? When is it acceptable to take calls? Where should calls be made? Most of us have experienced thoughtless and rude cell phone behavior. Researchers say that the rampant use of technological devices has worsened workplace incivility. Some employees consider texting and compulsive e-mail checking while working and during meetings disruptive, even insulting. The message the "e-cruising" workers presumably send to their colleagues is that they value the gizmo over human interaction.[19] To avoid offending, smart business communicators practice cell phone etiquette, as outlined in Figure 11.2. In projecting a professional image, they are careful about location, time, and volume in relation to their cell phone calls.

FIGURE 11.2 Practicing Courteous and Responsible Cell Phone Use

Business communicators find cell phones to be enormously convenient and real time-savers. But rude users have generated a backlash against inconsiderate callers. Here are specific suggestions for using cell phones safely and responsibly:

- **Be courteous to those around you.** Don't force those near you to hear your business. Don't step up to a service counter, such as at a restaurant, bank, or post office, while talking on your cell phone. Don't carry on a cell phone conversation while someone is waiting on you. Think first of those in close proximity instead of those on the other end of the phone. Apologize and make amends gracefully for occasional cell phone blunders.
- **Observe wireless-free quiet areas.** Don't allow your cell phone to ring in theaters, restaurants, museums, classrooms, important meetings, and similar places and situations. Use the cell phone's silent/vibrating ring option. A majority of travelers prefer that cell phone conversations *not* be held on most forms of public transportation.
- **Speak in low, conversational tones.** Microphones on cell phones are quite sensitive, thus making it unnecessary to talk loudly. Avoid "cell yell."
- **Take only urgent calls.** Make full use of your cell phone's caller ID feature to screen incoming calls. Let voice mail take those calls that are not pressing.
- **Drive now, talk later.** Pull over if you must make a call. Talking while driving increases the chance of accidents fourfold, about the same as driving while intoxicated. Some companies are implementing cell phone policies that prohibit employees from using cell phones while driving for company business.
- **Choose a professional ringtone.** These days you can download a variety of ringtones, from classical to rap to the *Star Wars* theme. Choose a ringtone that will sound professional.

Location. Use good judgment in placing or accepting cell phone calls. Some places are dangerous or inappropriate for cell phone use. Turn off your cell phone when entering a conference room, interview venue, theater, place of worship, or any other place where it could be distracting or disruptive to others. Taking a call in a crowded room or bar makes it difficult to hear and reflects poorly on you as a professional. Taking a call while driving can be dangerous, leading some states to ban cell phone use while driving. A bad connection also makes a bad impression. Static or dropped signals create frustration and miscommunication. Don't sacrifice professionalism for the sake of a quick phone call. It is smarter to turn off your phone in an area where the signal is weak and when you are likely to have interference. Use voice mail and return the call when conditions are better. Also, be careful about using your cell phone to discuss private or confidential company information.

Time. Often what you are doing is more important than whatever may come over the air waves to you on your phone. For example, when you are having an important discussion with a business partner, customer, or superior, it is rude to allow yourself to be interrupted by an incoming call. It is also poor manners to practice multitasking while on the phone. What's more, it is dangerous. Although you might be able to read and print out e-mail messages, deal with a customer at the counter, and talk on your cell phone simultaneously, doing so is impolite and risky. Lack of attention results in errors. If a phone call is important enough to accept, then it is important enough to stop what you are doing and attend to the conversation.

Volume. Many people raise their voices when using their cell phones because the small devices offer little aural feedback. "Cell yell" results, much to the annoyance of anyone nearby. Raising your voice is unnecessary since most phones have excellent microphones that can pick up even a whisper. If the connection is bad, louder volume will not improve the sound quality. As in face-to-face conversations, a low, modulated voice sounds professional and projects the proper image.

Making the Best Use of Voice Mail

Voice mail eliminates telephone tag, inaccurate message taking, and time zone barriers; it also allows communicators to focus on essentials.

Because telephone calls can be disruptive, most businesspeople are making extensive use of voice mail to intercept and screen incoming calls. Voice mail links a telephone system to a computer that digitizes and stores incoming messages. Some systems also provide functions such as automated attendant menus, allowing callers to reach any associated extension by pushing specific buttons on a touch-tone telephone.

Voice mail is quite efficient for message storage. Because as many as half of all business calls require no discussion or feedback, the messaging capabilities of voice mail can mean huge savings for businesses. Incoming information is delivered without interrupting potential receivers and without all the niceties that most two-way conversations require. Stripped of superfluous chitchat, voice mail messages allow communicators to focus on essentials. Voice mail also eliminates telephone tag, inaccurate message taking, and time zone barriers.

However, voice mail should not be overused. Individuals who screen all incoming calls cause irritation, resentment, and needless telephone tag. Both receivers and callers can use etiquette guidelines to make voice mail work most effectively for them.

"Thank you for calling. Please leave a message. In case I forget to check my messages, please send your message as an audio file to my e-mail, then send me a fax to remind me to check my e-mail, then call back to remind me to check my fax."

On the Receiver's End. Your voice mail should project professionalism and should provide an efficient mechanism for your callers to leave messages for you. Here are some voice mail etiquette tips to follow:

- **Don't overuse voice mail.** Don't use voice mail to avoid taking phone calls. It is better to answer calls yourself than to let voice mail messages build up.

- **Set the number of rings appropriately.** Set your voice mail to ring as few times as possible before picking up. This shows respect for your callers' time.
- **Prepare a professional, concise, friendly greeting.** Make your mechanical greeting sound warm and inviting, both in tone and content. Your greeting should be in your own voice, not a computer-generated voice. Identify yourself and your organization so that callers know they have reached the right number. Thank the caller and briefly explain that you are unavailable. Invite the caller to leave a message or, if appropriate, call back. Here's a typical voice mail greeting: *Hi! This is Larry Lopez of Proteus Software, and I appreciate your call. You have reached my voice mailbox because I'm either working with customers or talking on another line at the moment. Please leave your name, number, and reason for calling so that I can be prepared when I return your call.* Give callers an idea of when you will be available, such as *I'll be back at 2:30* or *I'll be out of my office until Wednesday, May 20*. If you screen your calls as a time management technique, try this message: *I'm not near my phone right now, but I should be able to return calls after 3:30.*
- **Test your message.** Call your number and assess your message. Does it sound inviting? Sincere? Professional? Understandable? Are you pleased with your tone? If not, record your message again until it conveys the professional image you want.
- **Change your message.** Update your message regularly, especially if you travel for your job.
- **Respond to messages promptly.** Check your messages regularly, and try to return all voice mail messages within one business day.
- **Plan for vacations and other extended absences.** If you will not be picking up voice mail messages for an extended period, let callers know how they can reach someone else if needed.

On the Caller's End. When leaving a voice mail message, you should follow these tips:

- **Be prepared to leave a message.** Before calling someone, be prepared for voice mail. Decide what you are going to say and what information you are going to include in your message. If necessary, write your message down before calling.
- **Leave a concise, thorough message.** When leaving a message, always identify yourself using your complete name and affiliation. Mention the date and time you called and a brief explanation of your reason for calling. Always leave a complete phone number, including the area code, even if you think the receiver already has it. Tell the receiver the best time to return your call. Don't ramble.
- **Use a professional and courteous tone.** When leaving a message, make sure that your tone is professional, enthusiastic, and respectful. Smile when leaving a message to add warmth to your voice.
- **Speak slowly and articulate.** You want to make sure that your receiver will be able to understand your message. Speak slowly and pronounce your words carefully, especially when providing your phone number. The receiver should be able to write information down without having to replay your message.
- **Be careful with confidential information.** Don't leave confidential or private information in a voice mail message. Remember that anyone could gain access to this information.
- **Don't make assumptions.** If you don't receive a call back within a day or two after leaving a message, don't get angry or frustrated. Assume that the message wasn't delivered or that it couldn't be understood. Call back and leave another message, or send the person an e-mail.

Becoming a Team Player in Professional Teams

As we discussed in Chapter 1, the workplace and economy are changing. Responding to fierce global competition, businesses are being forced to operate ever more efficiently. One significant recent change is the emphasis on teamwork.

You might find yourself a part of a work team, project team, customer support team, supplier team, design team, planning team, functional team, cross-functional team, or some other group. Such teams are formed to accomplish specific goals, and your career success will depend on your ability to function well in a team-driven professional environment.

Teams can be effective in solving problems and in developing new products. Take, for example, the creation of a unique two-engine digital printing system by a Xerox team. The company did not rely just on the expertise of its 30 engineers and scientists. Rather, Xerox involved more than 1,000 corporate customers who use its commercial printers. Chief Technology Officer Sophie V. Vandebroek named the goal of the collaboration: "Involving experts who know the technology with customers who know the main points."[20] Samsung, the world's largest technology company, used a 40-member task force several years ago to devise strategies and new products that would successfully compete with Apple's admired iPhone. The outcome of this team effort was the Android-based Galaxy smartphone, which so far is outselling the iPhone in the Korean market.[21] Perhaps you can now imagine why forming teams is important.

The Importance of Conventional and Virtual Teams in the Workplace

OFFICE INSIDER
"People exposed to a diversity of information are at higher risk of seeing a new angle, a better way to frame ideas." Companies that harness such social capital "have better growth rates and better patent rates."
—Ronald S. Burt, sociologist, University of Chicago

Businesses are constantly looking for ways to do jobs better at less cost. They are forming teams for the following reasons:

- **Better decisions.** Decisions are generally more accurate and effective because group and team members contribute different expertise and perspectives.
- **Faster responses.** When action is necessary to respond to competition or to solve a problem, small groups and teams can act rapidly.
- **Increased productivity.** Because they are often closer to the action and to the customer, team members can see opportunities for improving productivity.
- **Greater buy-in.** Decisions arrived at jointly are usually better received because members are committed to the solution and are more willing to support it.
- **Less resistance to change.** People who have input into decisions are less hostile, aggressive, and resistant to change.
- **Improved employee morale.** Personal satisfaction and job morale increase when teams are successful.
- **Reduced risks.** Responsibility for a decision is diffused, thus carrying less risk for any individual.

Virtual teams are groups of people who work interdependently with a shared purpose across space, time, and organization boundaries using technology.

To connect with distant team members across borders and time zones, many organizations are creating *virtual teams.* These are groups of people who work interdependently with a shared purpose across space, time, and organization boundaries using technology.[22] The authors of this textbook, for example, work 120 miles apart in their offices in California. Their developmental editor is located in Kentucky, the editor in chief is in Maine, the publisher is in Ohio, and the printer is in Oregon. Important parts of the marketing team are in Singapore and Canada. Although they work in different time zones and rarely see each other, team members use e-mail and teleconferencing to exchange ideas, make decisions, and stay connected.

Virtual teams may be local or global. At Best Buy's corporate headquarters in Richfield, Minnesota, certain employees are allowed to work anywhere and anytime—as long as they successfully complete their assignments on time. They can decide how, when, and where they work.[23] Although few other organizations are engaging in such a radical restructuring of work, many workers today complete their tasks from remote locations, thus creating local virtual teams.

Hyundai Motors exemplifies virtual teaming at the global level. For its vehicles, Hyundai completes engineering in Korea, research in Tokyo and Germany, styling in California, engine calibration and testing in Michigan, and heat testing in the California desert.[24] Members of its virtual teams coordinate their work and complete their tasks across time and geographic zones. Work is increasingly viewed as what you do rather than a place you go.

In some organizations, remote coworkers may be permanent employees from the same office or may be specialists called together for temporary projects. Regardless of the assignment, virtual teams can benefit from shared views and skills.

Professional team members follow team rules, analyze tasks, define problems, share information, listen actively to others, and try to involve quiet members.

Positive and Negative Team Behavior

Team members who are committed to achieving the group's purpose contribute by displaying positive behavior. How can you be a professional team member? The most effective groups have members who are willing to establish rules and abide by those rules. Effective team members are able to analyze tasks and define problems so that they can work toward solutions. They offer information and try out their ideas on the group to stimulate discussion. They show interest in others' ideas by listening actively. Helpful team members also seek to involve silent members. They help to resolve differences, and they encourage a warm, supportive climate by praising and agreeing with others. When they sense that agreement is near, they review significant points and move the group toward its goal by summarizing points of understanding.

Negative team behavior includes insulting, criticizing, lashing out at others, wasting time, and refusing to participate.

Not all groups, however, have members who contribute positively. Negative behavior is shown by those who constantly put down the ideas and suggestions of others. They insult, criticize, and lash out at others. They waste the group's time with unnecessary recounting of personal achievements or irrelevant topics. The team joker distracts the group with excessive joke telling, inappropriate comments, and disruptive antics. Also disturbing are team members who withdraw and refuse to be drawn out. They have nothing to say, either for or against ideas being considered. To be a productive and welcome member of a group, try to exhibit the positive behaviors described in Figure 11.3. Avoid the negative behaviors.

Characteristics of Successful Professional Teams

The use of teams has been called the solution to many ills in the current workplace.[25] Someone even observed that as an acronym TEAM means "Together, Everyone Achieves More."[26] Yet, many teams don't work well together. In fact, some teams can actually increase frustration, lower productivity, and create employee dissatisfaction. Experts who have studied team workings and decisions have discovered that effective teams share some or all of the following characteristics.

FIGURE 11.3 Positive and Negative Group Behavior

Positive Team Behavior	Negative Team Behavior
Setting rules and abiding by them	Blocking the ideas and suggestions of others
Analyzing tasks and defining problems	Insulting and criticizing others
Contributing information and ideas	Wasting the group's time
Showing interest by listening actively	Making inappropriate jokes and comments
Encouraging members to participate	Failing to stay on task
Synthesizing points of agreement	Withdrawing, failing to participate

Small, diverse teams often produce more creative solutions with broader applications than homogeneous teams do.

Small Size, Diverse Makeup. Teams may range from 2 to 25 members, although 4 or 5 is optimum for many projects. Larger groups have trouble interacting constructively, much less agreeing on actions.[27] Jeff Bezos, chairman and CEO of Amazon.com, reportedly said: "If you can't feed a team with two pizzas, the size of the team is too large."[28]

For the most creative decisions, teams generally have male and female members who differ in age, ethnicity, social background, training, and experience. Members should bring complementary skills to a team. Fred Adair, a partner at executive search firm Heidrick & Struggles, had this to say about diverse teams when asked about his study of nearly 700 top business leaders: "Yes, diverse teams are generally better. There is a more balanced consideration of different perspectives, and I'm using the word 'diversity' in the broadest sense—diversity of personality, of opinion, of decision-making style."[29] The key business advantage of diversity is the ability to view a project and its context from multiple perspectives. Many of us tend to think that everyone in the world is like us because we know only our own experience.[30] Teams with members from different ethnicities and cultures can look at projects beyond the limited view of one culture. Many organizations are finding that diverse teams can produce innovative solutions with broader applications than homogeneous teams can.

Agreement on Purpose. An effective team begins with a purpose. Take Dubai, for example. The wealthy business hub had long relied on oil, but its present economy centers on real estate, tourism, and financial services. After the real estate market in the emirate had been clobbered by the global credit crisis, it no longer could borrow capital. The emirate's government established a team of finance experts with a clear purpose: to create a plan to cut spending and increase revenue.[31] Xerox scientists who invented personal computing developed their team purpose after the chairman of Xerox called for an "architecture of information." A team at Sealed Air Corporation developed its purpose when management instructed it to cut waste and reduce downtime.[32] Working from a general purpose to specific goals typically requires a huge investment of time and effort. Meaningful discussions, however, motivate team members to buy in to the project.

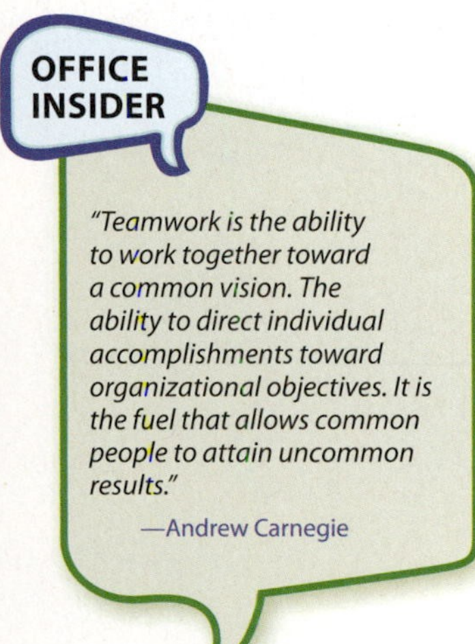

"Teamwork is the ability to work together toward a common vision. The ability to direct individual accomplishments toward organizational objectives. It is the fuel that allows common people to attain uncommon results."
—Andrew Carnegie

Agreement on Procedures. The best teams develop procedures to guide them. They set up intermediate goals with deadlines. They assign roles and tasks, requiring all members to contribute equivalent amounts of real work. They decide how they will reach decisions using one of the strategies discussed earlier. Procedures are continually evaluated to ensure movement toward the attainment of the team's goals.

Ability to Confront Conflict. Poorly functioning teams avoid conflict, preferring sulking, gossiping, or backstabbing. A better plan is to acknowledge conflict and address the root of the problem openly. Although it may feel emotionally risky, direct confrontation saves time and enhances team commitment in the long run. To be constructive, however, confrontation must be task oriented, not person oriented. An open airing of differences, in which all team members have a chance to speak their minds, should center on the strengths and weaknesses of the various positions and ideas—not on personalities. After hearing all sides, team members must negotiate a fair settlement, no matter how long it takes. Good decisions are based on consensus: all members agree.

Effective teams exchange information freely and collaborate rather than compete.

Use of Good Communication Techniques. The best teams exchange information and contribute ideas freely in an informal environment. Team members speak clearly and concisely, avoiding generalities. They encourage feedback. Listeners become actively involved, read body language, and ask clarifying questions before responding. Tactful, constructive disagreement is encouraged. Although a team's task is taken seriously, successful teams are able to inject humor into their interactions.

Ability to Collaborate Rather Than Compete. Effective team members are genuinely interested in achieving team goals instead of receiving individual recognition. They contribute ideas and feedback unselfishly. They monitor team progress, including what is going right, what is going wrong, and what to do about it. They celebrate individual and team accomplishments.

Shared Leadership. Effective teams often have no formal leader. Instead, leadership rotates to those with the appropriate expertise as the team evolves and moves from one phase to another. Many teams operate under a democratic approach. This approach can achieve buy-in to team decisions, boost morale, and create fewer hurt feelings and less resentment. In times of crisis, however, a strong team member may need to step up as a leader.

Acceptance of Ethical Responsibilities. Teams as a whole have ethical responsibilities to their members, to their larger organizations, and to society. Members have a number of specific responsibilities to each other, as shown in Figure 11.4. As a whole, teams have a responsibility to represent the organization's view and respect its privileged information. They should not discuss with outsiders any sensitive issues without permission. In addition, teams have a broader obligation to avoid advocating actions that would endanger members of society at large.

The skills that make you a valuable and ethical team player will serve you well when you run or participate in professional meetings.

FIGURE 11.4 Ethical Responsibilities of Group Members and Leaders

When people form a group or a team to achieve a purpose, they agree to give up some of their individual sovereignty for the good of the group. They become interdependent and assume responsibilities to one another and to the group. Here are important ethical responsibilities for members to follow:

- **Determine to do your best.** When you commit to the group process, you are obligated to offer your skills freely. Don't hold back, perhaps fearing that you will be repeatedly targeted because you have skills to offer. If the group project is worth doing, it is worth the best effort you can offer.
- **Decide to behave with the group's good in mind.** You may find it necessary to set aside your personal goals in favor of the group's goals. Decide to keep an open mind and to listen to evidence and arguments objectively. Strive to evaluate information carefully, even though it may contradict your own views or thwart your personal agendas.
- **Make a commitment to fair play.** Group problem solving is a cooperative, not a competitive, event. Decide that you cannot grind your private ax at the expense of the group project.
- **Expect to give and receive a fair hearing.** When you speak, others should give you a fair hearing. You have a right to expect them to listen carefully, provide you with candid feedback, strive to understand what you say, and treat your ideas seriously. Listeners don't have to agree with you, of course. In turn, you need to extend the same courtesy to others. All speakers have a right to a fair hearing.

- **Be willing to take on a participant/analyst role.** As a group member, it is your responsibility to pay attention, evaluate what is happening, analyze what you learn, and help make decisions.
- **As a leader, be ready to model appropriate team behavior.** A leader's responsibility is to coach team members in skills and teamwork, to acknowledge achievement and effort, to share knowledge, and to periodically remind members of the team's missions and goals.

Conducting Productive Business and Professional Meetings

Because you can expect to attend many workplace meetings, learn to make them efficient, satisfying, and productive.

As businesses turn to team-based and participatory management, workers are attending more meetings than ever. Despite heavy reliance on e-mail, wireless devices, and virtual meetings to stay connected, face-to-face meetings are still the most productive way to exchange information. However, many meetings are a waste of time. Humorist Dave Barry once compared meetings unfavorably to funerals: "The major difference is that most funerals have a definite purpose. Also, nothing is ever really buried in a meeting."[33] One survey showed that a quarter of U.S. workers would rather go to the dentist than attend a boring meeting.[34] Regardless, meetings are here to stay. Our task, then, is to make them efficient, satisfying, and productive.

Meetings consist of three or more individuals who gather to pool information, solicit feedback, clarify policy, seek consensus, and solve problems. For you, however, meetings have another important purpose. They represent opportunities. Because they are a prime tool for developing staff, they are career-critical. The inability to run an effective meeting can sink a career, warned *The Wall Street Journal*.[35] The head of a leadership training firm echoed this warning when he said, "If you can't orchestrate a meeting, you are of little use to the corporation."[36] At meetings, judgments are formed and careers are made. Therefore, instead of treating meetings as thieves of your valuable time, try to see them as golden opportunities to demonstrate your leadership, communication, and problem-solving skills. So that you can make the most of these opportunities, here are techniques for planning and conducting successful meetings. You will also learn how to be a valuable meeting participant.

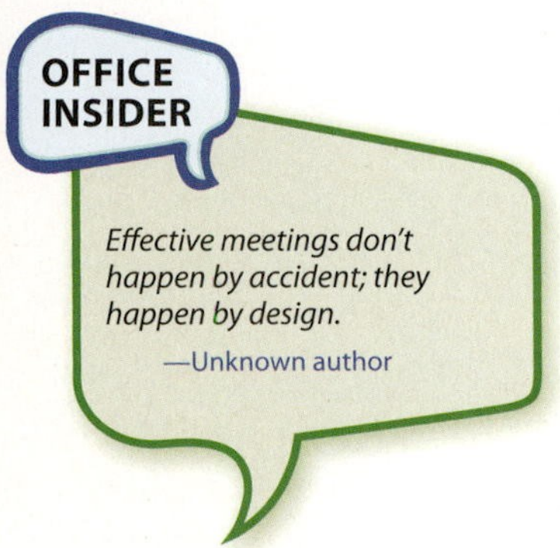

Before the Meeting

Call meetings only when necessary, and invite only key people.

Benjamin Franklin once said, "By failing to prepare, you are preparing to fail."[37] If you are in charge of a meeting, give yourself plenty of preparation time to guarantee the meeting's success. Before the meeting, determine your purpose, decide how and where to meet, organize an agenda, decide who to invite, and prepare the meeting location and materials.

Determining Your Purpose. Before you do anything else, you must decide the purpose of your meeting and whether a meeting is even necessary. No meeting should be called unless the topic is important, can't wait, and requires an exchange of ideas. If the flow of information is strictly one way and no immediate feedback will result, then don't schedule a meeting. For example, if people are merely being advised or informed, send an e-mail, memo, or letter. Leave a telephone or voice mail message, but don't call a costly meeting. Remember, the real expense of a meeting is the lost productivity of all the people attending. To decide whether the purpose of the meeting is valid, it is a good idea to consult the key people who will be attending. Ask them what outcomes they desire and how to achieve them. This consultation also sets a collaborative tone and encourages full participation.

Deciding How and Where to Meet. Once you have determined that a meeting is necessary, you must decide whether to meet face-to-face or virtually. If you decide to meet face-to-face, reserve a meeting room. If you decide to meet virtually, make any necessary advance arrangements for your voice conference, videoconference, or Web conference. These electronic tools were discussed in Chapter 1.

Before a meeting, pass out a meeting agenda showing topics to be discussed and other information.

Organizing an Agenda. Prepare an agenda of topics to be discussed during the meeting. Also include any reports or materials that participants should read in advance. For continuing groups, you might also include a copy of the minutes of the previous meeting. To keep meetings productive, limit the number of agenda items. Remember, the narrower the focus, the greater the chances for success. Consider putting items that the group will complete quickly near the beginning of the agenda to give the participants a sense of accomplishment. Save emotional topics for the end.

FIGURE 11.5 **Typical Meeting Agenda**

AGENDA
Atlantis Global Travel
Staff Meeting
October 13, 201x
1 to 2 p.m.
Conference Room, Fifth Floor

I. Call to order; roll call

II. Approval of agenda

III. Approval of minutes from previous meeting

	Person	Proposed Time
IV. Committee reports		
A. Web site update	Kelly	5 minutes
B. Tour packages	John	10 minutes
V. Old business		
A. Equipment maintenance	Doris	5 minutes
B. Client escrow accounts	Rolla	5 minutes
C. Internal newsletter	Tasha	5 minutes
VI. New business		
A. New accounts	Hung Wei	5 minutes
B Pricing policy for trips	Mark	15 minutes

VII. Announcements

VIII. Chair's summary, adjournment

You should distribute the agenda at least two days in advance of the meeting. A good agenda, as illustrated in Figure 11.5, covers the following information:

- Date and place of meeting
- Start time and end time
- Brief description of each topic, in order of priority, including names of individuals who are responsible for performing some action
- Proposed allotment of time for each topic
- Any premeeting preparation expected of participants

Problem-solving meetings should involve five or fewer people.

Inviting Participants. The number of meeting participants depends on the purpose of the meeting, as shown in Figure 11.6. If the meeting purpose is motivational, such as an awards ceremony for sales reps of Mary Kay Cosmetics, then the number of participants is unlimited. But to make decisions, according to studies at 3M Corporation, the best number is five or fewer participants.[38] Ideally, those attending should be people who will make the decision and people with information necessary to make the decision. Also attending should be people who will be responsible for implementing the decision and representatives of groups who will benefit from the decision. For example, Vermont-based ice cream purveyor Ben & Jerry's offers its employees 40 hours of paid volunteer service time per year to boost community involvement. To match up employee interests, business goals, and community needs, the company brings all parties to the table in meetings.[39]

FIGURE 11.6 Meeting Purpose and Number of Participants

Purpose	Ideal Size
Intensive problem solving	5 or fewer
Problem identification	10 or fewer
Information reviews and presentations	30 or fewer
Motivational	Unlimited

Preparing the Meeting Location and Materials. If you are meeting face-to-face, decide the layout of the room. To maximize collaboration and participation, try to arrange tables and chairs in a circle or a square so that all participants can see one another. Moreover, where you sit at the table or stand in the room signals whether you wish to be in charge or are willing to share leadership.[40] Set up any presentation equipment that the participants will need. Make copies of documents that will be handed out during the meeting. Arrange for refreshments.

During the Meeting

Start meetings on time and open with a brief introduction.

Meetings can be less boring, more efficient, and more productive if leaders and participants recognize how to get the meeting started, move it along, handle conflict, and deal with dysfunctional participants. Whether you are the meeting leader or a participant, it is important to act professionally during the meeting. Figure 11.7 outlines etiquette tips for both meeting leaders and participants. Following are additional guidelines to adhere to during the meeting to guarantee its success.

Getting the Meeting Started. To avoid wasting time and irritating attendees, always start meetings on time—even if some participants are missing. Waiting for latecomers causes resentment and sets a bad precedent. For the same reasons,

FIGURE 11.7 Etiquette Checklist for Meeting Leaders and Participants

Meeting Leader

- ✓ Start and end the meeting on time.
- ✓ Introduce yourself and urge participants to introduce themselves.
- ✓ Make everyone feel welcome and valued.
- ✓ Maintain control of the group members and discussion.
- ✓ Make sure that everyone participates.
- ✓ Stick to the agenda.
- ✓ Encourage everyone to follow the ground rules.
- ✓ Schedule breaks for longer meetings.

Meeting Participants

- ✓ Arrive on time and stay until the meeting ends, unless you have made prior arrangements to arrive late or leave early.
- ✓ Leave the meeting only for breaks and emergencies.
- ✓ Come to the meeting prepared.
- ✓ Silence cell phones and other electronic devices.
- ✓ Follow the ground rules.
- ✓ If you are on the agenda as a presenter, don't go over your allotted time.
- ✓ Don't exhibit nonverbal behavior that suggests you are bored, frustrated, angry, or negative in any way.
- ✓ Don't interrupt others or cut anyone off.
- ✓ Make sure your comments, especially negative comments, are about ideas, not people.
- ✓ Listen carefully to what other meeting participants are saying.
- ✓ Participate fully.
- ✓ Don't go off on tangents; be sure that you stick to the topic being discussed.
- ✓ Don't engage in side conversations.
- ✓ Clean up after yourself when leaving the meeting.
- ✓ Complete in a timely manner any follow-up work that you are assigned.

WORKPLACE IN FOCUS

While most people know to turn off cell phones at company meetings, some employees show little hesitation in sending text messages during group presentations. Whether one is tapping away sneakily under the table or ripping off full e-mails in plain view, texting during meetings is an inappropriate practice that distracts others and sends a message that the gathering is unimportant. The behavior has reached epidemic proportions, especially among young college graduates. ***What can team leaders do to prevent unwanted texting at meetings?***

don't give a quick recap to anyone who arrives late. At the appointed time, open the meeting by having all participants introduce themselves, if necessary. Then continue with a three- to five-minute introduction that includes the following:

- Goal and length of the meeting
- Background of topics or problems
- Possible solutions and constraints
- Tentative agenda
- Ground rules to be followed

A typical set of ground rules might include arriving on time, communicating openly, being supportive, listening carefully, participating fully, confronting conflict frankly, silencing cell phones and other digital devices, and following the agenda. Participants should also determine how the group will make decisions. More formal groups follow parliamentary procedures based on Robert's Rules of Order. After establishing basic ground rules, the leader should ask whether participants agree thus far. The next step is to assign one attendee to take minutes and one to act as a recorder. The recorder stands at a flipchart or whiteboard and lists the main ideas being discussed and agreements reached.

"In many ways, leading a meeting is like juggling. A good leader keeps the balls in the air, stays focused, makes it a little entertaining, and ends with a big finish. Taking responsibility for this role is half the battle in leading good meetings. Remember, everyone wants somebody to lead."

—Suzanne Bates, consultant and author of *Speak Like a CEO*

Moving the Meeting Along. After the preliminaries, the leader should say as little as possible. Like a talk show host, an effective leader makes "sure that each panel member gets some air time while no one member steals the show."[41] Remember that the purpose of a meeting is to exchange views, not to hear one person, even the leader, do all the talking. If the group has one member who monopolizes, the leader might say, *Thanks, Gary, for that perspective, but please hold your next point while we hear how Rachel would respond to that.* This technique also encourages quieter participants to speak up.

To avoid allowing digressions to sidetrack the group, try generating a "parking lot" list. This is a list of important but divergent issues that should be discussed at a later time. Another way to handle digressions is to say, *Look, folks, we are veering off track here. Let's get back to the central issue of . . . .* It is important to adhere to the agenda and the time

"Wow! This meeting lasted longer than I thought. It appears the year is now 2053."

schedule. Equally important, when the group seems to have reached a consensus, is to summarize the group's position and check to see whether everyone agrees.

When a conflict develops between two members, allow each to make a complete case before the group.

Dealing With Conflict. Conflict is a normal part of every workplace. Although conflict may cause you to feel awkward and uneasy, it is not always negative. In fact, conflict in the workplace can even be desirable. When managed properly, conflict can improve decision making, clarify values, increase group cohesiveness, stimulate creativity, decrease tensions, and reduce dissatisfaction. Unresolved conflict, however, can destroy productivity and seriously reduce morale.

In meetings, conflict typically develops when people feel unheard or misunderstood. If two people clash, the best approach is to encourage each to make a complete case while group members give their full attention. Let each one question the other. Then, the leader should summarize what was said, and the group should offer comments. The group may modify a recommendation or suggest alternatives before reaching consensus on a direction to follow.

To control dysfunctional behavior, team leaders should establish rules and seat problem people strategically.

Handling Difficult Group Members. When individuals are exhibiting dysfunctional behavior (such as blocking discussion, monopolizing the conversation, attacking other speakers, joking excessively, not paying attention, or withdrawing), they should be handled with care and tact. The following specific techniques can help a meeting leader control some group members and draw others out.[42]

"I'm going to train you to 'Confront Difficult People'. . . okay, raise your hands if you're a difficult person."

- **Lay down the rules in an opening statement.** Give a specific overall summary of topics, time allotment, and expected behavior. Warn that speakers who digress will be interrupted.
- **Seat potentially dysfunctional members strategically.** Experts suggest seating a difficult group member immediately next to the leader. It is easier to control a person in this position. Make sure the person with dysfunctional behavior is not seated at a power point, such as at the end of table or across from the leader.
- **Avoid direct eye contact.** In North America direct eye contact is a nonverbal signal that encourages talking. Therefore, when asking a question of the group, look only at those whom you wish to answer.
- **Assign dysfunctional members specific tasks.** Ask a potentially disruptive person, for example, to be the group recorder.
- **Ask members to speak in a specific order.** Ordering comments creates an artificial, rigid climate and should be done only when absolutely necessary. But such a regimen ensures that everyone gets a chance to participate.
- **Interrupt monopolizers.** If a difficult member dominates a discussion, wait for a pause and then break in. Summarize briefly the previous comments, or ask someone else for an opinion.
- **Encourage nontalkers.** Give only positive feedback to the comments of reticent members. Ask them direct questions about which you know they have information or opinions.
- **Give praise and encouragement** to those who seem to need it, including the distracters, the monopolizers, the blockers, and the withdrawn.

Ending the Meeting and Following Up

How do you know when to stop a meeting? Many factors determine when a meeting should be adjourned, including (a) when the original objectives have been accomplished, (b) when the group has reached an impasse, or (c) when the agreed-upon ending time arrives. To show respect for participants, the leader should be sure the meeting stops at the promised time. It may be necessary to table (postpone for another meeting) some unfinished agenda items. Concluding a meeting effectively helps participants recognize what the team accomplished so that they feel that the meeting was worthwhile. Effective leaders perform a number of activities in ending a meeting and following up.

Concluding the Meeting. When the agreed-upon stopping time arrives or when the objectives have been met, discussion should stop. The leader should summarize what the group decided and who is going to do what. Deadlines for action items should also be established. It may be necessary to ask people to volunteer to take responsibility for completing action items agreed to in the meeting. No one should leave the meeting without a full understanding of what was accomplished. One effective technique that encourages full participation is "once around the table." Everyone summarizes briefly his or her interpretation of what the group decided and what happens next. Of course, this closure technique works best with smaller groups.

End the meeting with a summary of accomplishments and a review of action items; follow up by distributing meeting minutes and reminding participants of their assigned tasks.

An effective leader concludes by asking the group to set a time for the next meeting. The leader should also assure the group that a report will follow and thank participants for attending. Participants should vacate the meeting room once the meeting is over, especially if another group is waiting to enter. The room should be returned to a neat and orderly condition.

Distributing Minutes. If minutes were taken during the meeting, they should be keyed in an appropriate format. You will find guidelines for preparing meeting minutes in Chapter 9. Minutes should be distributed within a couple of days after the meeting. Send the minutes to all meeting participants and to anyone else who needs to know what was accomplished and discussed during the meeting.

Completing Assigned Tasks. It is the leader's responsibility to see that what was decided at the meeting is accomplished. The leader may need to call people to remind them of their assignments and also to volunteer to help them, if necessary. Meeting participants should complete any assigned tasks by the agreed-upon deadline.

www.cengagebrain.com

Available with an access code, these eResources will help you prepare for exams:

- **Chapter Review Quizzes**
- **Personal Language Trainer**
- **PowerPoint Slides**
- **Flash Cards**

Summing Up and Looking Forward

In this chapter you studied how to practice professional behavior in individual face-to-face settings, on the phone, as well as in teams and meetings. You learned how to use your voice as a communication tool, how to promote positive workplace relations through conversation, and how to give and take constructive criticism on the job. You were given tips on professional telephone, cell phone, and voice mail etiquette, including making and receiving productive telephone calls. You learned about a variety of tools enabling you to participate constructively in professional teams. Finally, the chapter presented techniques for planning and participating in productive business and professional meetings, both face-to-face and virtual.

The next chapter covers an additional facet of oral communication, that of making business presentations. Learning to speak before groups is important to your career success because you will probably be expected to do so occasionally. You will learn helpful techniques and get practice applying them so that you can control stage fright in making polished presentations.

Critical Thinking

1. Many people have a negative image of business and believe in the cliché that "nice guys finish last." Relate what you read about professionalism in this chapter to this conventional perception.
2. How does professionalism relate to ethics?
3. Describe the advantages of face-to-face communication as opposed to interactions facilitated by technology such as telephones, e-mail, instant messaging, texting, the Web, social networking sites, and so on. When is face-to-face communication more effective?
4. How does conflict develop in teams and at meetings, and how can you address it?
5. Most workers groan and grumble when they must attend meetings. How can you ensure that the meetings you run are productive?

Chapter Review

6. What do the various definitions of *professionalism* have in common, and why should you work hard to develop professional traits?

7. Explain briefly what each of the five synonyms used to describe professional behavior in this chapter means.

8. What do hiring managers in our knowledge-based economy look for in job candidates?

9. What is uptalk, and why is it unprofessional? What other poor voice habits can you identify?

10. How can you enhance your face-to-face conversations in the workplace and improve your image as a professional?

11. List at least eight strategies that will help you to provide constructive criticism on the job.

12. How can you ensure that your telephone calls on the job are productive? Name at least six suggestions.

13. Compare and contrast positive team behavior and negative team behavior.

14. Name the components of an effective meeting agenda.

15. List the ethical responsibilities of group members and leaders.

Activities and Cases

(T) TEAM (W) WEB

11.1 Research Definitions and Compile an Annotated Works-Cited List

The ability to scan articles quickly, summarize them efficiently, and list sources in the correct MLA or APA format will be very useful to you. In your classes and as you continue learning throughout your life, you will need to be a quick study who demonstrates attention to detail. Moreover, frequently you will need to grasp a new subject area or field in a relatively short amount of time. Naturally, research typically starts with definitions of key terms. You have seen that many definitions for *professionalism* exist. Recently, an opportunity to practice your research skills has arisen when your boss was invited to make a presentation to a group of human relations officers. He asked you and a small group of fellow interns to help him find articles about professionalism, soft skills, and other interpersonal qualities.

Your Task. Review Activity 10.11 in Chapter 10, and as a team divide your research in such a way that each intern is responsible for one or two search terms, depending on the size of your group. Look for articles with definitions of *professionalism, business etiquette, civility, business ethics, social skills, soft skills,* and *social intelligence.* Find at least three useful articles for each search term. If you get bogged down in your research, consult with a business librarian on campus or report to your instructor. After compiling your findings, as a team present your annotated works-cited list in an informational memo report to your boss, Ted Rollins.

11.2 Professionalism and Ethics in Action

Working adults may encounter ethical dilemmas and workplace challenges that test their professionalism and engage their moral compass.

Your Task. Individually or as a team, describe one or more challenges that you or someone you know encountered in the workplace for each of the six dimensions of professional behavior listed in Figure 11.1. You may also draw on your experience during an internship, in college, or among friends and family. Where appropriate, suggest remedies or preventive measures that demonstrate professionalism. To jog your memory, draw on the specific examples listed in the column titled "What Professionalism Means on the Job" in the table shown in Figure 11.1.

Example 1:
Courtesy and respect: You or someone you know was late to work repeatedly.
Result: Reprimand or dismissal from the job. Remedy: When exceptional circumstances will cause you to be late, promptly notify the boss that you are running late. Factor in rush hour traffic and other delays, and leave your house with plenty of time to spare.

Example 2:
Appearance and appeal: Someone you encountered on the job exhibited poor hygiene.
Result: Loss of credibility on the part of the culprit and possibly the company, discomfort, and unpleasantness around the office. Remedy: Talk to the supervisor, who may opt for a discreet one-on-one conversation with the offender. You may choose to ignore the problem if the guilty party is a person with more power than you.

The six dimensions of professional behavior are the following:

a. Courtesy and respect
b. Appearance and appeal
c. Tolerance and tact
d. Honesty and ethics
e. Reliability and responsibility
f. Diligence and collegiality

11.3 Soft Skills: Checking Job Ads

What soft skills do employers request when they list job openings in your field?

Your Task. Check job listings in your field at an online job board. Visit a job board such as Monster, College Recruiter, CareerBuilder.com, or Yahoo Careers. Follow the instructions to search job categories and locations. Study many job listings in your field. Then prepare a list of the most frequently requested soft skills in your area of interest. Next to each item on the list, indicate how well you think you would qualify for the skill or trait mentioned. Your instructor may ask you to submit your findings and/or report to the class. If you are not satisfied with the job selection at any job site, choose another job board.

11.4 Voice Quality

Recording your voice gives you a chance to learn how your voice sounds to others and provides an opportunity for you to improve its effectiveness. Don't be surprised if you fail to recognize your own voice.

Your Task. Record yourself reading a newspaper or magazine article.

a. If you think your voice sounds a bit high, practice speaking slightly lower.
b. If your voice is low or expressionless, practice speaking slightly louder and with more inflection.
c. Ask a colleague, teacher, or friend to provide feedback on your pronunciation, pitch, volume, rate, and professional tone.

11.5 Researching Business Etiquette

In today's competitive labor market, many job seekers realize they need to brush up on their business etiquette in order to find and keep a position. Yet if you are like most workers, you may not always know appropriate conduct in every given social situation. For example, many Americans fear formal dinners and other workplace-related events because they are unsure about proper dining etiquette. Formal table settings intimidate a lot of people. They may fear making fools of themselves because they don't know where to put their napkins and which tableware to use and in what order. To lessen such anxieties, you will research an important element of business etiquette.

Your Task. Research an aspect of business etiquette about which you are particularly concerned. If dining etiquette and table manners scare you, resolve to find out how to use dishware and tableware like a pro and how to act in formal dining situations. Individually or as a team, you may want to present your findings to the class; for example, you could show diagrams of table settings or provide an in-class demonstration using plates and silverware. Similarly, teams could investigate topics such as proper greetings and introductions, professional attire, dealing with difficult coworker or bosses, tattoos and piercings, social media manners, and many more. For a list of potential etiquette topics to research, visit the Web site of the Emily Post Institute run by several descendants of the famous etiquette maven.

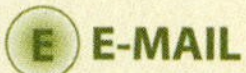

11.6 Surviving a Social Business Function

The idea of attending a social business function provokes anxiety in many businesspeople. What should you talk about? What should you wear? How can you make sure you maintain your professionalism?

Your Task. In groups of two to four, discuss appropriate behavior in four social situations. Decide appropriate attire, suitable topics of conversation, and other etiquette guidelines that you should follow. Present your decisions regarding the following social functions to your instructor in a memo or e-mail:

a. Company picnic
b. Holiday party
c. Formal dinner
d. Business luncheon

11.7 Providing Constructive Criticism in the Workplace

No one likes to give it or receive it, but sometimes criticism is unavoidable: Constructive criticism in the workplace is necessary when team members need feedback and managers must assess team effectiveness.

Your Task. To remedy each of the following unprofessional actions, supply the appropriate solution following the guidelines provided in this chapter.

a. Supervisor Ed is tempted to deliver his negative feedback of a team member by e-mail.

b. Linda provided feedback to a dysfunctional team by spontaneously approaching team members in the hallway. Face-to-face with the argumentative team, she was at a loss for words and felt that she did not convey her points fully.

c. Manager Paul has a hot temper. He exploded when Jack, one of his subordinates, came late to a staff meeting. Paul told Jack that he hated his tardiness and that Jack was always late.

d. Hot-headed manager Paul loudly confronted Anita in her cubicle within earshot of staff. Anita had requested time off as an important deadline was looming, and the project was already late.

e. Regional manager Edna delivered a stern lecture to an underperforming sales rep who was clearly stunned and hurt.

11.8 Delivering and Responding to Criticism

Develop your skills in handling criticism by joining with a partner to role-play critical messages you might deliver and receive on the job.

Your Task. Designate one person as A and the other B. A describes the kinds of critical messages she or he is likely to receive on the job and identifies who might deliver them. In Scenario 1, B takes the role of the critic and delivers the criticism in an unskilled manner. A responds using techniques described in this chapter. In Scenario 2, B again is the critic but delivers the criticism using techniques described in this chapter. A responds again. Then A and B reverse roles and repeat Scenarios 1 and 2.

 TEAM  E-MAIL

11.9 Discussing Workplace Criticism

In the workplace, criticism is often delivered thoughtlessly.

Your Task. In teams of two or three, describe a time when you were criticized by an untrained superior or colleague. What made the criticism painful? What goal do you think the critic had in mind? How did you feel? How did you respond? Consider techniques discussed in this chapter; how could the critic have improved his or her delivery? How does the delivery technique affect the way a receiver responds to criticism? Your instructor may ask you to submit a memo or e-mail analyzing an experience in which you received criticism.

11.10 Making It a Team Effort at Timberland

He introduces himself as a New Hampshire bootmaker, but Timberland CEO Jeffrey B. Swartz is much more. Although he heads a highly successful global company that produces boots and sportswear, he is strongly committed to corporate social responsibility (CSR) and employee involvement. A third-generation CEO, Swartz has run Timberland for 30 years and made CSR part of every corporate and executive decision. With the zeal of a missionary, the enthusiastic, fast-talking Swartz travels extensively, preaching the power of volunteerism among the 300 Timberland stores and factories.[43]

Your Task. Let's say that you work for Timberland, and Swartz asks you to organize an extensive volunteer program using Timberland employees. The program involves much planning and cooperation to be successful. You are flattered that he respects you and thinks that you are capable of completing the task. But you think that a team could do a better job than an individual. What arguments would you use to convince him that a team could work better than a single person?

 TEAM  E-MAIL

11.11 Meetings: Managing Difficult or Reticent Team Members and Other Challenges

As you have learned, facilitating a productive meeting requires skills that may be critical to your career success.

Your Task. Individually or as a team describe how you would deal with the following examples of unproductive or dysfunctional behavior and other challenges in a team meeting that you are running. Either report your recommendations verbally, or, if your instructor directs, summarize your suggestions in an e-mail or memo.

a. Jimmy, a well-known office clown, is telling off-color jokes while others are discussing the business at hand.

b. Anna is quiet, although she is taking notes and seems to be following the discussion attentively.

c. Peter likes to make long-winded statements and often digresses to unrelated subjects.

d. Carla keeps interrupting other speakers and dominates the discussion.

e. Ron and Mark are hostile toward each other and clash over an agenda item.

f. Elena arrives 15 minutes late and noisily unpacks her briefcase.

g. Kristen, Shelley, and Paul are reading e-mails and texting under the table.

h. The meeting time is up, but the group has not met the objective of the meeting.

11.12 Analyzing a Meeting

You have learned a number of techniques in this chapter for planning and participating in meetings. Here's your chance to put your knowledge to work.

Your Task. Attend a structured meeting of a college, social, business, community, or other organization. Compare the manner in which the meeting is conducted with the suggestions presented in this chapter. Why did the meeting succeed or fail? Prepare a memo for your instructor, or be ready to discuss your findings in class.

11.13 Planning a Meeting

Assume that at the next meeting of your Associated Students Organization (ASO), you will discuss preparations for a job fair in the spring. The group will hear reports from committees working on speakers, business recruiters, publicity, reservations of campus space, setup of booths, and any other matters you can think of.

Your Task. As president of your ASO, prepare an agenda for the meeting. Compose your introductory remarks to open the meeting. Your instructor may ask you to submit these two documents or use them in staging an actual meeting in class.

11.14 Leading a Meeting

Your boss is unhappy at the way some employees lead meetings. Because he knows that you have studied this topic, he asks you to send him a memo or e-mail listing specific points that he can use in an in-house training session in which he plans to present ideas on how to conduct business meetings.

Your Task. Using an electronic database, locate articles providing tips on leading meetings. Three particularly good articles are listed here. Prepare a memo to your boss, Mark Shields, outlining eight or more points on how to lead a meeting. Include at least five tips that are not found in this chapter.

Brown, C. (2010, November 10). Make meetings productive. *Nursing Standard, 25*(10), pp. 64–65. Retrieved from http://content.ebscohost.com
Powell, R. S. (2010, March 5). The art of meeting. *Chronicle of Higher Education, 56*(25), pp. 49–51. Retrieved from http://content.ebscohost.com
Spittle, B. (2010). Let your staff run your staff meetings. *Review of Optometry*, pp. 31–33. Retrieved from http://content.ebscohost.com

11.15 Improving Telephone Skills by Role-Playing

Acting out the roles of telephone caller and receiver is an effective technique for improving skills. To give you such practice, your instructor will divide the class into pairs.

Your Task. For each scenario take a moment to read and rehearse your role silently. Then play the role with your partner. If time permits, repeat the scenarios, changing roles.

Partner 1

A. You are the personnel manager of Wireless World, Inc. Call Susan Campbell, office manager at Digitron Corporation. Inquire about a job applicant, Lisa Chung, who listed Ms. Campbell as a reference.

B. Call Ms. Campbell again the following day to inquire about the same job applicant, Lisa Chung. Ms. Campbell answers today, but she talks on and on, describing the applicant in great detail. Tactfully close the conversation.

C. You are now the receptionist for Cyrus Artemis, of Artemis Imports. Answer a call for Mr. Artemis, who is working in another office, at Ext. 2219, where he will accept calls.

D. You are now Cyrus Artemis, owner of Artemis Imports. Call your attorney, Maria Solomon-Williams, about a legal problem. Leave a brief, incomplete message.

E. Call Ms. Solomon-Williams again. Leave a message that will prevent telephone tag.

Partner 2

A. You are the receptionist for Digitron Corporation. The caller asks for Susan Campbell, who is home sick today. You don't know when she will be able to return. Answer the call appropriately.

B. You are now Ms. Campbell, office manager. Describe Lisa Chung, an imaginary employee. Think of someone with whom you have worked. Include many details, such as her ability to work with others, her appearance, her skills at computing, her schooling, her ambition, and so forth.

C. You are now an administrative assistant for attorney Maria Solomon-Williams. Call Cyrus Artemis to verify a meeting date Ms. Solomon-Williams has with Mr. Artemis. Use your own name in identifying yourself.

D. You are now the receptionist for attorney Maria Solomon-Williams. Ms. Solomon-Williams is skiing in Aspen and will return in two days, but she does not want her clients to know where she is. Take a message.

E. Take a message again.

 TEAM  WEB 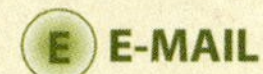 E-MAIL

11.16 Voice Mail: Recording a Concise, Friendly Greeting

To present a professional image, smart businesspeople carefully prepare their outgoing voice mail greetings and announcements. After all, they represent their companies and want to be perceived as polished and efficient. Before recording a greeting, most workers plan and perhaps even jot down what they will say. To be concise, the greeting should not run longer than 25 seconds.

Your Task. Use the guidelines in this chapter to plan your greeting. Invent a job title and the name of your company. Indicate when and how callers can reach you. Individually or as a team, record a professional voice mail greeting using a smartphone or another digital recording device. If the instructor directs, share your recording by sending it via e-mail to a designated address for evaluation. Alternatively, team members may be asked to exchange their recorded greetings for a peer critique. If you own an iPhone or an iPod Touch with a microphone, download a free app such as **Voice Memos** that allows voice recordings. Android phone owners can likewise download a free app such as **Voice Recorder**. These mobile applications are easy to use, and when the recording is completed, you have the option of sharing it by e-mail, by Bluetooth, on Facebook, and so forth.

11.17 Leaving a Professional Voice Mail Message

Voice mail messages can be very effective communication tools as long as they are professional and make responding to them easy.

Your Task. If your instructor allows, call his or her office number after hours or within a specified time frame. Plan what you will say; if needed, jot down a few notes. Leave a professional voice mail message as described in this chapter. Start by introducing yourself by name, then give your telephone number, and finally, leave a brief message about something you discussed in class, read in the chapter, or want the instructor to know about you. Speak slowly, loudly enough, and clearly, so that your instructor won't need to replay your message.

Grammar/Mechanics Checkup—11

Other Punctuation

Although this checkup concentrates on Sections 2.23–2.29 in the Grammar/Mechanics Handbook, you may also refer to other punctuation principles. Insert any necessary punctuation and change any incorrect punctuation. In the space provided, indicate the number of changes you make and record the number of the G/M principle(s) illustrated. Count each mark separately; for example, a set of parentheses counts as 2. If you make no changes, write *0*. Use the underscore to show italics. When you finish, compare your responses with those provided at the end of the book. If your responses differ, study carefully the specific principles shown in parentheses.

2 (2.27) **Example** (De-emphasize) Current sales projections (see page 11 in the attached report) indicate a profitable year ahead.

______ 1. (Emphasize) Three outstanding employees Santiago Wilson, Rae Thomas, and Charles Stoop will receive bonuses.

______ 2. Will you please Jonathon complete your assignment by six o'clock?

______ 3. To determine whether to spell e-mail with or without the hyphen be sure to consult our company style sheet.

______ 4. Cargill, Koch Industries, and Bechtel these are the most profitable private companies in America.

______ 5. (De-emphasize) Today's employers regularly conduct three kinds of background checks drug, credit, and criminal before hiring employees.

______ 6. Was it Warren Buffet who said "The rearview mirror is always clearer than the windshield

______ 7. Did you see the article titled Wireless Riches From Serving the Poor that appeared in The New York Times

______ 8. (Emphasize) Three cities considered the best places in the world to live Vienna, Zurich, and Geneva are all in Europe.

______ 9. Did you send invitations to Dr Lisa Uhl, Ms Ginger Ortiz, and Mr Orrin T Tapia

______ 10. Our instructor recommended the chapter titled The Almost Perfect Meeting that appeared in Emily Post's book called The Etiquette Advantage in Business.

______ 11. Incredible Did you see the price of gold today

______ 12. Susan wondered what keywords would attract the most clicks in her Google ad?

______ 13. The owner of Smash Party Entertainment found that the best keyword for her online ad business was party.

______ 14. Is the reception scheduled to begin at 6 pm

______ 15. The term autoregressive is defined as using past data to predict future data.

Editing Challenge—11

As the employee with the best communication skills, you are frequently asked to edit messages. The following meeting minutes have problems with grammar, punctuation, wordiness, spelling, proofreading, apostrophes, sentence structure, and other writing techniques you have studied. You may either (a) use standard proofreading marks (see Appendix B) to correct the errors here or (b) download the document from **www.cengagebrain.com** and revise at your computer. Study the guidelines in the Grammar/Mechanics Handbook to sharpen your skills.

Mountain View Parks and Recreation Board
Board Room, City Hall, 10 Main Street, Mountin View, Colorado
October 29, 201x

Present: Scott Almquist, Sue Hjortsberg, Bob Taft, Shirley Bailey, Michelle Esteban, Terri Rogers, David Kazanis
Absent: Kathie Muratore

The meeting was called to order at 7:03 pm in the evening by Vice Chair Michelle Esteban. Minutes from the September 28th meeting was read and approved.

Old Business

Manager Scott Almquist reported that a ten thousand dollar gift from the Partners of Parks & Recreation, Inc., had been recieved. The gift according to the donors request will be used for renovation of the Community Center. Bids were coming in considerable higher then anticipated, however, Mr. Almquist is confident that the project will move foreward on schedule.

Sue Hjortsberg reported on her research into municipal park festivitys. She reccomended that Board members read an article titled Guide to Park Celebrations which appeared in the July issue of Park Management.

New Business

Discussion was held in a matter related to a donation request from Plains Real Estate Co., Inc. This donation involves three lots on Rancho Street, see pages 2-4 of your board packet. Because these lots is near Buffalo park Bob Taft stated that he couldn't hardly see any value in adding another "small tot" park to that area.

MOTION: To deny request from Plans Real Estate Co, Inc., to donate 3 lots on Rancho Street for Park purposes. (Taft/Bailey). Passed unanimously.

Discussion was held about proposed bonuses in view of the fact that the budget has been cut. Should the planned bonuses for three outstanding gardeners: Hector Valdez, Heather York, and Juan Rio, be postponed. The matter was tabled untill the next meeting.

Board members discussed the facility fee schedule for community use. David Kazanis suggested that fees should not be charged for Senior or Youth programs held in Mountain View facilitys but he thought that fees for adult sport's and fitness programs would need to be increase to cover added expenses.

MOTION: To increase fees for adult sport's and fitness programs held in Mountain View Park and Recreation District facilities. (Kazanis/Rogers). Failed 2-5.

Adjournment
The meeting was adjorned at 8:35 pm. The next meeting of the Mountain View Parks and Recreation Board will be held November 28th at the City Hall Board Room.

Respectfully submitted,

Communication Workshop

Dr. Guffey's Guide to Business Etiquette and Workplace Manners

Etiquette, civility, and goodwill efforts may seem out of place in today's fast-paced, high-tech offices. However, etiquette and courtesy are more important than ever if diverse employees want to work cooperatively and maximize productivity and workflow. Many organizations recognize that good manners are good for business. Some colleges and universities offer management programs that include a short course in manners. Companies are also conducting manners seminars for trainees and veteran managers. Why is politeness regaining legitimacy as a leadership tool? Primarily because courtesy works.

Good manners convey a positive image of an organization. We like to do business with people who show respect and treat others civilly. People also like to work in an environment that is pleasant. Considering how much time is spent at work, wouldn't an agreeable environment be preferable to one in which people are rude and uncivil?

You can brush up your workplace etiquette skills online at *Dr. Guffey's Guide to Business Etiquette and Workplace Manners* (**www.cengagebrain.com**). Of interest to both workplace newcomers and veterans, this guide covers the following topics:

Professional Image
Introductions and Greetings
Networking Manners
General Workplace Manners
Coping With Cubicles
Interacting With Superiors
Managers' Manners
Business Meetings
Business Gifts
Business Cards
Dealing With Angry Customers
Telephone Manners
Cell Phone Etiquette
E-Mail Etiquette
Gender-Neutral Etiquette
Business Dining
Avoiding Social Blunders When Abroad

To gauge your current level of knowledge of business etiquette, take the preview quiz at **www.cengagebrain.com**. Then, study all 17 business etiquette topics. These easy-to-read topics are arranged in bulleted lists of dos and don'ts. After you complete this etiquette module, your instructor may test your comprehension by giving a series of posttests.

Career Application. As manager at OfficeTemps, a company specializing in employment placement and human resources information, you received a request from a reporter. She is preparing an article for a national news organization about how workplace etiquette is changing in today's high-tech environment. The reporter asks for any other information you can share with her regarding her topic, "Information Age Etiquette."

Her letter lists the following questions:

- Are etiquette and workplace manners still important in today's fast-paced Information Age work environment? Why or why not?
- Do workers need help in developing good business manners? Why or why not?
- Are the rules of office conduct changing? If so, how?
- What advice can you give about gender-neutral etiquette?
- What special manners do people working in shared workspaces need to observe?

Your Task. In teams or individually, prepare an information response letter addressed to Ms. Lindsey Ann Evans, National Press Association, 443 Riverside Drive, New York, NY 10024. Use the data you learned in this workshop. Conduct additional Web research if you wish. Remember that you will be quoted in her newspaper article, so make it interesting!

Endnotes

[1] Pearson, C., & Porath, C. (2009). *The cost of bad behavior: How incivility is damaging your business and what to do about it.* New York, NY: Portfolio/Penguin.

[2] Buhler, P. M. (2003, April 1). Managing in the new millennium; workplace civility: Has it fallen by the wayside? *Supervision*. Retrieved from http://www.allbusiness.com/human-resources/workforce-management/513719-1.html

[3] Wikipedia: Civility. (2011, January 6). Wikipedia. Retrieved from http://en.wikipedia.org/wiki/Wikipedia:Civility

[4] Johnson, D. (1988–2006). Dine like a diplomat. Seminar Script. The Protocol School of Washington, Columbia, South Carolina.

[5] Albrecht, K. (2005). *Social intelligence: The new science of success*. San Francisco: Pfeiffer, p. 3.

[6] Cited in Johnson, D. (1995-2005). Outclass the competition—Business etiquette. The Protocol School of Washington, Columbia, South Carolina.

[7] Chismar, D. (2001). Vice and virtue in everyday (business) life. *Journal of Business Ethics*, *29*, 169–176. doi: 10.1023/A:1006467631038

[8] Hughes, T. (2008). Being a professional. Wordconstructions.com. Retrieved from http://www.wordconstructions.com/articles/business/professional.html; Grove, C., & Hallowell, W. (2002). The seven balancing acts of professional behavior in the United States: A cultural values perspective. Grovewell.com. Retrieved from http://www.grovewell.com/pub-usa-professional.html

[9] Brent, P. (2006, November). Soft skills speak volumes. *CA Magazine*, *139*, p. 112. Retrieved from http://web.ebscohost.com

[10] Laff, M. (2006, December). Wanted: CFOs with communications skills. *ASTD*, *60*(12), 20. Retrieved from http://store.astd.org

[11] Martin, C. (2007, March 6). The importance of face-to-face communication at work. CIO.com. Retrieved from http://www.cio.com/article/29898/The_Importance_of_Face_to_Face_Communication_at_Work; Duke, S. (2001, Winter). E-mail: Essential in media relations, but no replacement for face-to-face communication. *Public Relations Quarterly*, p. 19.

[12] Brenner, R. (2007, October 17). Virtual conflict. *Point Lookout*, Chaco Canyon Consulting. Retrieved from http://www.chacocanyon.com/pointlookout/071017.shtml; Drolet, A. L., & Morris, M. W. (2000, January). Rapport in conflict resolution: Accounting for how face-to-face contact fosters mutual cooperation in mixed-motive conflicts. *Journal of Experimental Social Psychology*, p. 26.

[13] Miculka, J. (1999). *Speaking for success*. Cincinnati: South-Western, p. 19.

[14] Motivational and Inspirational Corner. (2005, June 27). Retrieved from http://www.motivational-inspirational-corner.com/getquote.html?startrow=11&categoryid=207

[15] Burge, J. (2002, June). Telephone safety protocol for today. *The National Public Accountant*. FindArticles.com. Retrieved from http://findarticles.com/p/articles/mi_m4325/is_2002_June/ai_n25049376

[16] Smith, A. (2010, July 7). Mobile access 2010. Pew Internet. Retrieved from http://www.pewinternet.com/Reports/2010/Mobile-Access-2010.aspx; Lanman, S. (2005, July 9). Mobile-phone users become a majority. *San Francisco Chronicle*, p. C1.

[17] Smith, A. (2010, July 7). Mobile access 2010. Pew Internet. Retrieved from http://www.pewinternet.com/Reports/2010/Mobile-Access-2010.aspx; Sidener, J. (2008, January 27). Cell phones taking on many roles, transforming market, generation. SignOnSanDiego.com. Retrieved from http://www.signonsandiego.com/news/metro/20080127-9999-1n27phone.html

[18] Study: More cellular-only homes as Americans expand mobile media usage. (2009, December 21). Nielsen Wire. Retrieved from http://blog.nielsen.com/nielsenwire/online_mobile/study-more-cellular-only-homes-as-americans-expand-mobile-media-usage; Hockenberry, J., Adaora, U., & Colgan, J. (2008, May 20). For many Americans, cell phones are supplanting the landline. The Take Away. Retrieved from http://www.thetakeaway.org/2008/may/20/for-many-americans-cell-phones-are-supplanting-the-landline

[19] Pearson, C. (2010, May 16). Sending a message that you don't care. *The New York Times*. Retrieved from http://www.nytimes.com

[20] Xerox' new design team: Customers. (2007, May 7). *Bloomberg Businessweek*. Retrieved from http://www.businessweek.com/magazine/content/07_19/b4033087.htm

[21] Glionna, J. M., & Choi, J. (2011, January 22). Apple grows on Samsung's soil. *Los Angeles Times*, p. B3.

[22] Brown, M. K., Huettner, B., & James-Tanny, C. (2007). *Managing virtual teams: Getting the most of wikis, blogs, and other collaborative tools*. Plano, TX: Wordware Publishing; Lipnack, J. & Stamps, J. (2000). *Virtual teams: People working across boundaries with technology* (2nd ed.). New York: Wiley, p. 18.

[23] Kiger, P. J. (2006, September 25). Flexibility to the fullest: Throwing out the rules of work—Part 1 of 2. *Workforce Management*, *85*(18), p. 1. See also Holland, K. (2006, December). When work time isn't face time. *The New York Times*, p. BU 3.

[24] Cutler, G. (2007, January–February). Mike leads his first virtual team. *Research-Technology Management*, *50*(1), 66. Retrieved from http://web.ebscohost.com

[25] Rey, J. (2010, June). Team building. *Inc.*, *32*(5), 68–71; Romando, R. (2006, November 9). Advantages of corporate team building. Ezine Articles. Retrieved from http://ezinearticles.com/?Advantages-of-Corporate-Team-Building&id=352961; Amason, A. C., Hochwarter, W. A., Thompson, K. R., & Harrison, A. W. (1995, Autumn). Conflict: An important dimension in successful management teams. *Organizational Dynamics*, *24*(2), 1. Retrieved from http://web.ebscohost.com; Romando, R. (2006, November 9). Advantages of corporate team building. Ezine Articles. Retrieved from http://ezinearticles.com/?Advantages-of-Corporate-Team-Building&id=352961

[26] Ruffin, B. (2006, January). T.E.A.M. work: Technologists, educators, and media specialists collaborating. *Library Media Connection*, 24(4), p. 49. Retrieved from http://web.ebscohost.com

[27] Pratt, E. L. (2010). Virtual teams in very small classes. In: R. Ubell (Ed.), *Virtual teamwork: Mastering the art and practice of online learning and corporate collaboration.* Hoboken, NJ: Wiley, pp. 93–94; Katzenbach, J. R., & Smith, K. (1994). *The wisdom of teams*. New York: HarperBusiness, p. 45.

[28] Pratt, E. L. (2010). Virtual teams in very small classes. In: R. Ubell (Ed.), *Virtual teamwork: Mastering the art and practice of online learning and corporate collaboration*. Hoboken, NJ: Wiley, p. 93.

[29] Holstein, W. J. (2008, May 30). Getting the most from management teams. *BusinessWeek*. Retrieved from http://www.businessweek.com/managing/content/may2008/ca20080530_775110.htm?chan=search

[30] Weiten, W. (2010). *Psychology: Themes and variations* (8th ed.). Belmont, CA: Wadsworth/Cengage, pp. 74–75; Gale, S. F. (2006, July). Common ground. *PM Network*, p. 48. Retrieved from http://web.ebscohost.com

[31] Sharif, A., & Chmaytelli, M. (2010, April 11). Dubai forms a team to prepare medium-term finance plan. *Bloomberg Businessweek*. Retrieved from http://www.bloomberg.co.jp/apps/news?pid=90970900&sid=a5mvKBZqcMv8

[32] Katzenbach, J. R., & Smith, K. (1994). *The wisdom of teams*. New York: HarperBusiness, p. 50.

[33] Quoted in Rothwell, J. D. (2010). *In mixed company: Communicating in small groups and teams* (7th ed.). Stamford, CT: Cengage, p. 261.

[34] Dull meeting? I'd rather see the dentist. (2004, October 19). *Personnel Today*, p. 1. Retrieved from http://web.ebscohost.com

[35] Maher, K. (2004, January 13). The jungle: Focus on recruitment, pay and getting ahead. *The Wall Street Journal*, p. B6.

[36] Schechtman, M. quoted in Lancaster, H. (1998, May 26). Learning some ways to make meetings less awful. *The Wall Street Journal*, p. B1; Wuorio, J. (2010). Eight way to show speaking skills in a meeting. Microsoft Business. Retrieved from http://www.microsoft.com/business/en-us/resources/management/leadership-training/8-ways-to-show-speaking-skills-in-a-meeting.aspx#waystoshowspeakingskillsinameeting

[37] ThinkExist.com. Retrieved from http://en.thinkexist.com/quotation/by_failing_to_prepare-you_are_preparing_to_fail/199949.html

[38] Bruening, J. C. (1996, July). There's good news about meetings. *Managing Office Technology*, pp. 24–25. Retrieved from http://proquest.umi.com

[39] Lapowsky, I. (2010, June 9). How to start a volunteer program. Inc. Retrieved from http://www.inc.com/guides/2010/06/volunteer-program.html

[40] Imperato, G. (2007, December 19). You have to start meeting like this! FastCompany.com. Retrieved from http://www.fastcompany.com/magazine/23/begeman.html

[41] Schabacker, K. (1991, June). A short, snappy guide to meaningful meetings. *Working Women*, p. 73.

[42] Hamilton, C., & Parker, C. (2001). *Communicating for success* (6th ed.). Belmont, CA: Wadsworth, pp. 311–312.

[43] 2007–2008 Corporate social responsibility report. Timberland.com. Retrieved from http://community.timberland.com/Reporting-Downloads; Marquis, C. (2003, July). Doing well and doing good. *The New York Times*, p. BU 2.

Acknowledgments

p. 331 Office Insider cited in Bosrock, R. M. (2005, October 5). Business forum: Good manners bring good results. *Star Tribune.com*. Retrieved from http://www.startribune.com/business/11050361.html?elr=KArksUUUoDEy3LGDiO7aiU

p. 332 Office Insider cited in Chismar, D. (2001). Vice and virtue in everyday (business) life. *Journal of Business Ethics*, 29, 169–176. doi: 10.1023/A:1006467631038

p. 334 Office Insider from Tom Peters quoted in Begley, K. A. (2004). Face to face communication: Making human connections in a technology-driven world. NETg. Retrieved from http://www.axzopress.com/downloads/pdf/1560526998pv.pdf

p. 336 Office Insider cited in Johnson, D. (1988–2006). Dine like a diplomat. Seminar Script. The Protocol School of Washington. Columbia, South Carolina.

p. 337 Office Insider based on Andrew Carnegie quoted in Johnson, D. (1988–2006). Dine like a diplomat. Seminar Script. The Protocol School of Washington. Columbia, South Carolina.

p. 344 Office Insider cited in Edmondson, G. (2006, October 16). The secret of BMW's success. *Bloomberg Businessweek*. Retrieved from http://www.businessweek.com/magazine/content/06_42/b4005078.htm

p. 346 Office Insider based on Andrew Carnegie quoted in HeartQuotes: Quotes of the Heart. Retrieved from http://www.heartquotes.net/teamwork-quotes.html

p. 348 Office Insider quoted in Gantz, N. R. (2009). *101 Global leadership lessons for nurses*. Indianapolis, IN: Sigma Theta Tau International, p. 278.

p. 351 Office Insider cited in Bates, S. (2011). "Running a meeting: Ten rookie mistakes and how to avoid them. *Management Consulting News*. Retrieved from http://www.managementconsultingnews.com/articles/bates_meeting.php

CHAPTER 12

Business Presentations

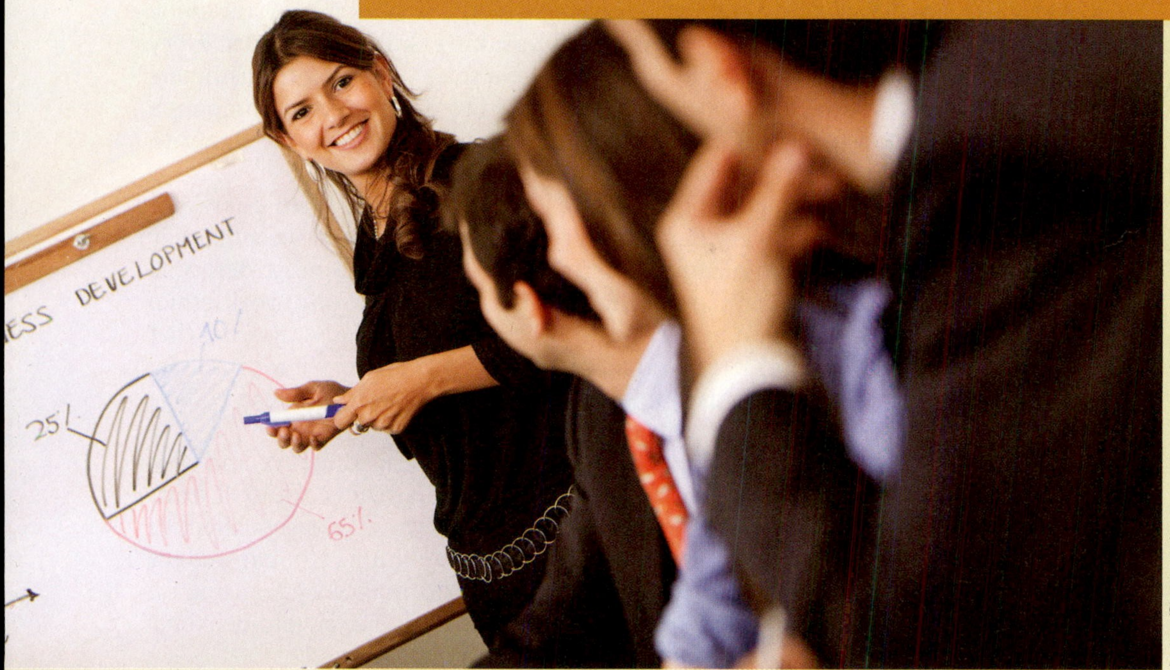

Andresr/Shutterstock.com

Go to **cengagebrain.com** and use your access code to unlock valuable student eResources.

OBJECTIVES

After studying this chapter, you should be able to

- Discuss two important first steps in preparing effective oral presentations.
- Explain the major elements of a presentation: the introduction, body, and conclusion.
- Identify techniques for gaining audience rapport, including using effective imagery, providing verbal signposts, and sending appropriate nonverbal messages.
- Discuss types of visual aids, including multimedia slides, handouts, overhead transparencies, and speaker's notes.
- Explain how to design an impressive multimedia presentation, including adapting template and color schemes; organizing, composing, and editing your slideshow; rehearsing your talk; and keeping audiences engaged.
- Specify delivery techniques for use before, during, and after a presentation.

Preparing Effective Oral Presentations

Perhaps you have admired the speaking skills of such well-known orators as motivational expert Anthony Robbins, self-help guru Zig Ziglar, and the late Apple CEO Steve Jobs. Few of us will ever talk to an audience of millions—whether face-to-face or aided by technology. We won't be introducing a spectacular new product or motivating millions. At some point, however, all businesspeople have to inform others or sell an idea. Such information and persuasion are often conveyed in person and involve audiences of various sizes. If you are like most people, you have some apprehension when speaking in public. That's normal. Good speakers are made, not born. The good news is that you can conquer the fear of public speaking and hone your skills with instruction and practice.

Speaking Skills and Your Career

Effective speaking skills and career success go hand in hand.

Many future businesspeople fail to take advantage of opportunities in college to develop speaking skills. However, such skills often play an important role in

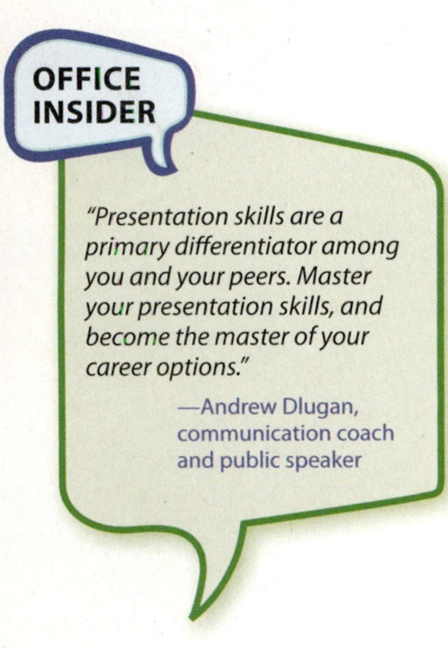

a successful career. In fact, the No. 1 predictor of success and upward mobility, according to an AT&T and Stanford University study, is how much you enjoy public speaking and how effective you are at it.[1] Speaking skills are useful at every career stage. You might, for example, have to make a sales pitch before customers or speak to a professional gathering. You might need to describe your company's expansion plans to your banker, or you might need to persuade management to support your proposed marketing strategy.

As you have seen in Chapter 11, technical skills aren't enough to guarantee success. Speaking skills rank very high on recruiters' wish lists. In a recent survey of employers, spoken communication took the top spot as the most desirable "soft skill" sought in job candidates. It even ranks above a strong work ethic, teamwork, analytical skills, and initiative.[2] Another employer study reported that 70 percent of executives considered oral communication skills very important for high school graduates entering the job market; 82 percent for two-year college graduates, and a whopping 95 percent for four-year college graduates.[3]

This chapter prepares you to use speaking skills in making effective and professional oral presentations, whether alone or as part of a team. You will learn what to do before, during, and after your presentation; and how to design effective visual aids and multimedia presentations. For any presentation, you can reduce your fears and lay the foundation for a professional performance by focusing on five areas: preparation, organization, audience rapport, visual aids, and delivery.

Knowing Your Purpose

Preparing for an oral presentation means identifying your purpose and understanding the audience.

The most important part of your preparation is deciding what you want to accomplish. Do you want to sell a health care program to a prospective client? Do you want to persuade management to increase the marketing budget? Do you want to inform customer service reps of three important ways to prevent miscommunication? Whether your goal is to persuade or to inform, you must have a clear idea of where you are going. At the end of your presentation, what do you want your listeners to remember or do?

Nicholas Gilmore, a loan officer at First Fidelity Trust, faced such questions as he planned a talk for a class in small business management. (You can see the outline for his talk in Figure 12.3 on page 370.) Nicholas's former business professor had asked him to return to campus and give the class advice about borrowing money from banks in order to start new businesses. Because Nicholas knew so much about this topic, he found it difficult to extract a specific purpose statement for his presentation. After much thought he narrowed his purpose to this: *To inform potential entrepreneurs about three important factors that loan officers consider before granting start-up loans to launch small businesses*. His entire presentation focused on ensuring that the class members understood and remembered three principal ideas.

Knowing Your Audience

Audience analysis issues include size, age, gender, experience, attitude, and expectations.

A second key element in preparation is analyzing your audience, anticipating its reactions, and adjusting to its needs if necessary. Audiences may fall into four categories, as summarized in Figure 12.1. By anticipating your audience, you have a better idea of how to organize your presentation. A friendly audience, for example, will respond to humor and personal experiences. A neutral audience requires an even, controlled delivery style. You would want to fill the talk with facts, statistics, and expert opinions. An uninterested audience that is forced to attend requires a brief presentation. Such an audience might respond best to humor, cartoons, colorful visuals, and startling statistics. A hostile audience demands a calm, controlled delivery style with objective data and expert opinion. Whatever type of audience you will have, remember to plan your presentation so that it focuses on audience benefits. The members of your audience will want to know what's in it for them.

FIGURE 12.1 Succeeding With Four Audience Types

Audience Members	Organizational Pattern	Delivery Style	Supporting Material
Friendly			
They like you and your topic.	Use any pattern. Try something new. Involve the audience.	Be warm, pleasant, and open. Use lots of eye contact and smiles.	Include humor, personal examples, and experiences.
Neutral			
They are calm, rational; their minds are made up, but they think they are objective.	Present both sides of the issue. Use pro/con or problem/solution patterns. Save time for audience questions.	Be controlled. Do nothing showy. Use confident, small gestures.	Use facts, statistics, expert opinion, and comparison and contrast. Avoid humor, personal stories, and flashy visuals.
Uninterested			
They have short attention spans; they may be there against their will.	Be brief—no more than three points. Avoid topical and pro/con patterns that seem lengthy to the audience.	Be dynamic and entertaining. Move around. Use large gestures.	Use humor, cartoons, colorful visuals, powerful quotations, and startling statistics.
	Avoid darkening the room, standing motionless, passing out handouts, using boring visuals, or expecting the audience to participate.		
Hostile			
They want to take charge or to ridicule the speaker; they may be defensive, emotional.	Organize using a non-controversial pattern, such as a topical, chronological, or geographical strategy.	Be calm and controlled. Speak evenly and slowly.	Include objective data and expert opinion. Avoid anecdotes and humor.
	Avoid a question-and-answer period, if possible; otherwise, use a moderator or accept only written questions.		

Other elements, such as age, gender, education, experience, and the size of the audience will affect your style and message. Analyze the following questions to determine your organizational pattern, delivery style, and supporting material.

- How will this topic appeal to this audience?
- How can I relate this information to my listeners' needs?
- How can I earn respect so that they accept my message?
- What would be most effective in making my point? Facts? Statistics? Personal experiences? Expert opinion? Humor? Cartoons? Graphic illustrations? Demonstrations? Case histories? Analogies?
- What measures must I take to ensure that this audience remembers my main points?

If you have agreed to speak to an audience with which you are unfamiliar, ask for the names of a half dozen people who will be in the audience. Contact them and learn about their backgrounds and expectations for the presentation. This information can help you answer questions about what they want to hear and how deeply you should explore the subject. You will want to thank these people when you start your speech. Doing this kind of homework will impress the audience.

Organizing the Content for a Powerful Impact

Once you have determined your purpose and analyzed the audience, you are ready to collect information and organize it logically. Good organization and conscious repetition are the two most powerful keys to audience comprehension and retention. In fact, many speech experts recommend the following deliberately repetitious, but effective, plan:

Good organization and intentional repetition help your audience understand and retain what you say.

Step 1: Tell them what you are going to tell them.
Step 2: Tell them.
Step 3: Tell them what you have just told them.

"Always start your presentation with a joke, but be careful not to offend anyone! Don't mention religion, politics, race, age, money, technology, men, women, children, plants, animals, food...."

In other words, repeat your main points in the introduction, body, and conclusion of your presentation. Although it is redundant, this strategy works well because most people retain information best when they hear it repeatedly. Let's examine how to construct the three parts of an effective presentation: introduction, body, and conclusion.

Capturing Attention in the Introduction

How many times have you heard a speaker begin with, *It's a pleasure to be here.* Or, *I'm honored to be asked to speak.* Boring openings such as these get speakers off to a dull start. Avoid such banalities by striving to accomplish three goals in the introduction to your presentation:

- Capture listeners' attention and get them involved.
- Identify yourself and establish your credibility.
- Preview your main points.

If you are able to appeal to listeners and involve them in your presentation right from the start, you are more likely to hold their attention until the finish. Consider some of the same techniques that you used to open sales letters: a question, a startling fact, a joke, a story, or a quotation. Some speakers achieve involvement by opening with a question or command that requires audience members to raise their hands or stand up. Ten techniques to gain and keep audience attention are presented in Figure 12.2.

Attention-grabbing openers include questions, startling facts, jokes, anecdotes, and quotations.

To establish your credibility, you need to describe your position, knowledge, or experience—whatever qualifies you to speak. Try also to connect with your audience. Listeners respond particularly well to speakers who reveal something of themselves and identify with them. A consultant addressing office workers might reminisce about how she started as a temporary worker; a CEO might tell a funny story in which the joke is on himself. Use humor if you can pull it off (not everyone can); self-effacing humor may work best for you.

However, a joke at one's own expense can also backfire and defeat its purpose, which is to allow the audience to identify with the speaker who thus demonstrates that he or she is not pompous or arrogant. Netflix CEO Reed Hastings set off a storm of criticism after making an ill-conceived joke in an interview with *The Hollywood Reporter.* Hastings had said that Americans are too self-absorbed to notice the price disparity between Netflix's cheaper new Canadian subscription service and rates in the United States. A red-blooded American himself, Hastings thought he could score points by invoking yet ridiculing the stereotype of the uninformed American. Nevertheless, instead of appearing likeable and funny by poking fun at his compatriots and himself, the speaker alienated his audience.[4]

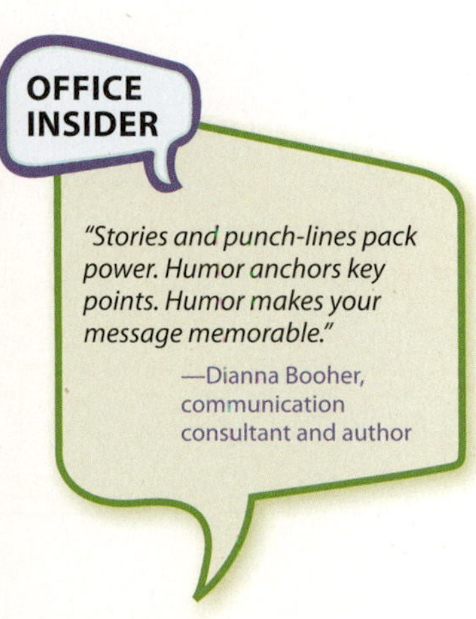

OFFICE INSIDER
"Stories and punch-lines pack power. Humor anchors key points. Humor makes your message memorable."
—Dianna Booher, communication consultant and author

After capturing attention and establishing yourself, you will want to preview the main points of your topic, perhaps with a visual aid. You may wish to put off actually writing your introduction, however, until after you have organized the rest of the presentation and crystallized your principal ideas.

Take a look at Nicholas Gilmore's introduction, shown in Figure 12.3, to see how he integrated all the elements necessary for a good opening.

Organizing the Body

The best oral presentations focus on a few key ideas.

The biggest problem with most oral presentations is a failure to focus on a few principal ideas. This is why the body of your short presentation (20 or fewer minutes) should include a limited number of main points, say, two to four. Develop each main point with adequate, but not excessive, explanation and details. Too many details can obscure the main message, so keep your presentation simple and logical. Remember, listeners have no pages to leaf back through should they become confused.

FIGURE 12.2 Gaining and Keeping Audience Attention

Dmitriy Shironosov/Shutterstock.com

Experienced speakers know how to capture the attention of an audience and how to maintain that attention during a presentation. You can spruce up your presentations by trying these ten proven techniques.

- **A promise.** Begin with a realistic promise that keeps the audience expectant (for example, *By the end of this presentation, you will know how you can increase your sales by 50 percent!*).
- **Drama.** Open by telling an emotionally moving story or by describing a serious problem that involves the audience. Throughout your talk include other dramatic elements, such as a long pause after a key statement. Change your vocal tone or pitch. Professionals use high-intensity emotions such as anger, joy, sadness, and excitement.
- **Eye contact.** As you begin, command attention by surveying the entire audience to take in all listeners. Give yourself two to five seconds to linger on individuals to avoid fleeting, unconvincing eye contact. Don't just sweep the room and the crowd.
- **Movement.** Leave the lectern area whenever possible. Walk around the conference table or down the aisles of your audience. Try to move toward your audience, especially at the beginning and end of your talk.
- **Questions.** Keep listeners active and involved with rhetorical questions. Ask for a show of hands to get each listener thinking. The response will also give you a quick gauge of audience attention.
- **Demonstrations.** Include a member of the audience in a demonstration (for example, *I'm going to show you exactly how to implement our four-step customer courtesy process, but I need a volunteer from the audience to help me*).
- **Samples/props.** If you are promoting a product, consider using items to toss out to the audience or to award as prizes to volunteer participants. You can also pass around product samples or promotional literature. Be careful, though, to maintain control.
- **Visuals.** Give your audience something to look at besides yourself. Use a variety of visual aids in a single session. Also consider writing the concerns expressed by your audience on a flipchart or on the board as you go along.
- **Dress.** Enhance your credibility with your audience by dressing professionally for your presentation. Professional attire will help you look more competent and qualified, which will make your audience more likely to listen to you and take you seriously.
- **Self-interest.** Review your entire presentation to ensure that it meets the critical *What's-in-it-for-me* audience test. Remember that people are most interested in things that benefit them.

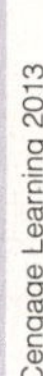

When Nicholas Gilmore began planning his presentation, he realized immediately that he could talk for hours on his topic. He also knew that listeners are not good at separating major and minor points. Therefore, instead of submerging his listeners in a sea of information, he sorted out a few main ideas. In the banking industry, loan officers generally ask the following three questions of each applicant for a small business loan: (a) Are you ready to "hit the ground running" in starting your business? (b) Have you done your homework? and (c) Have you made realistic projections of potential sales, cash flow, and equity investment? These questions would become his main points, but Nicholas wanted to streamline them further so that his audience would be sure to remember them. He summarized the questions in three words: *experience, preparation*, and *projection*. As you can see in Figure 12.3, Nicholas prepared a sentence outline showing these three main ideas. Each is supported by examples and explanations.

How to organize and sequence main ideas may not be immediately obvious when you begin working on a presentation. The following patterns, which review and amplify those discussed in Chapter 10, provide many possible strategies and examples to help you organize a presentation:

Organize your report by time, geography, function, importance, or some other method that is logical to the receiver.

- **Chronology.** Example: A presentation describing the history of a problem, organized from the first sign of trouble to the present.
- **Geography/space.** Example: A presentation about the changing diversity of the workforce, organized by regions in the country (East Coast, West Coast, and so forth).

FIGURE 12.3 Oral Presentation Outline

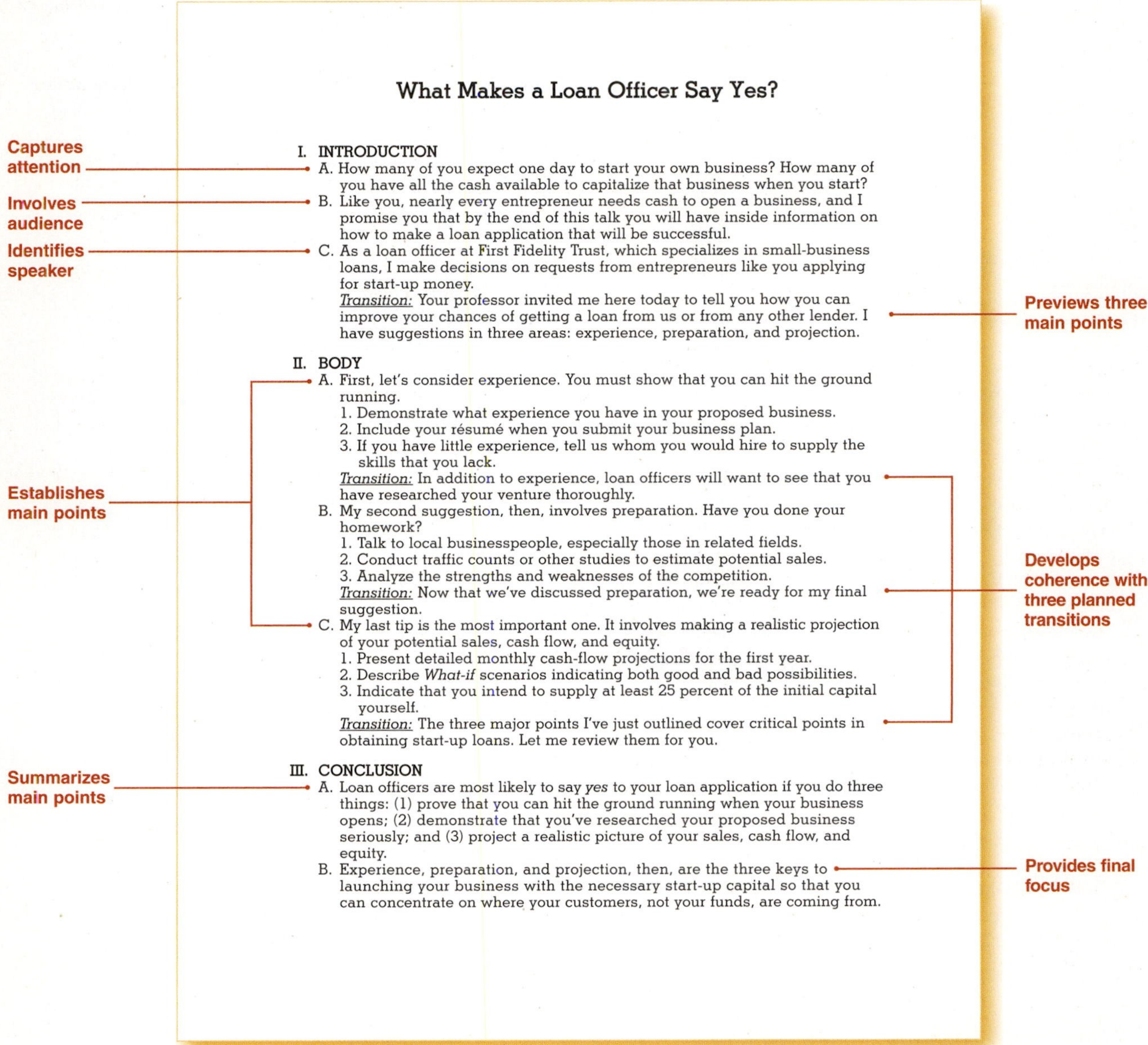
What Makes a Loan Officer Say Yes?

I. INTRODUCTION
A. How many of you expect one day to start your own business? How many of you have all the cash available to capitalize that business when you start?
B. Like you, nearly every entrepreneur needs cash to open a business, and I promise you that by the end of this talk you will have inside information on how to make a loan application that will be successful.
C. As a loan officer at First Fidelity Trust, which specializes in small-business loans, I make decisions on requests from entrepreneurs like you applying for start-up money.
Transition: Your professor invited me here today to tell you how you can improve your chances of getting a loan from us or from any other lender. I have suggestions in three areas: experience, preparation, and projection.

II. BODY
A. First, let's consider experience. You must show that you can hit the ground running.
1. Demonstrate what experience you have in your proposed business.
2. Include your résumé when you submit your business plan.
3. If you have little experience, tell us whom you would hire to supply the skills that you lack.
Transition: In addition to experience, loan officers will want to see that you have researched your venture thoroughly.
B. My second suggestion, then, involves preparation. Have you done your homework?
1. Talk to local businesspeople, especially those in related fields.
2. Conduct traffic counts or other studies to estimate potential sales.
3. Analyze the strengths and weaknesses of the competition.
Transition: Now that we've discussed preparation, we're ready for my final suggestion.
C. My last tip is the most important one. It involves making a realistic projection of your potential sales, cash flow, and equity.
1. Present detailed monthly cash-flow projections for the first year.
2. Describe *What-if* scenarios indicating both good and bad possibilities.
3. Indicate that you intend to supply at least 25 percent of the initial capital yourself.
Transition: The three major points I've just outlined cover critical points in obtaining start-up loans. Let me review them for you.

III. CONCLUSION
A. Loan officers are most likely to say *yes* to your loan application if you do three things: (1) prove that you can hit the ground running when your business opens; (2) demonstrate that you've researched your proposed business seriously; and (3) project a realistic picture of your sales, cash flow, and equity.
B. Experience, preparation, and projection, then, are the three keys to launching your business with the necessary start-up capital so that you can concentrate on where your customers, not your funds, are coming from.

- **Topic/function/conventional grouping.** Example: A presentation discussing mishandled airline baggage, organized by names of airlines.
- **Comparison/contrast (pro/con).** Example: A presentation comparing organic farming methods with those of modern industrial farming.
- **Journalistic pattern (the six Ws).** Example: A presentation describing how identity thieves can steal your money and ruin your good name. Organized by *who, what, when, where, why,* and *how*.
- **Value/size.** Example: A presentation describing fluctuations in housing costs, organized by prices of homes.
- **Importance.** Example: A presentation describing five reasons a company should move its headquarters to a specific city, organized from the most important reason to the least important.
- **Problem/solution.** Example: A company faces a problem such as declining sales. A presentation offers a solution such as reducing staff.

- **Simple/complex.** Example: A presentation explaining genetic modification of plants such as corn, organized from simple seed production to complex gene introduction.
- **Best case/worst case.** Example: A presentation analyzing whether two companies should merge, organized by the best-case results (improved market share, profitability, employee morale) as opposed to the worst-case results (devalued stock, lost market share, employee malaise).

In the presentation shown in Figure 12.3, Nicholas arranged the main points by importance, placing the most important point last, where it had maximum effect. When organizing any presentation, prepare a little more material than you think you will actually need. Savvy speakers always have something useful in reserve such as an extra handout, transparency, or idea—just in case they finish early. At the same time, most speakers go about 25 percent over the allotted time as opposed to their practice runs at home in front of the mirror. If your speaking time is limited, as it usually is in your classes, aim for less than the limit when rehearsing, so that you don't take time away from the next presenters.

Summarizing in the Conclusion

Nervous speakers often rush to wrap up their presentations because they can't wait to flee the stage. However, listeners will remember the conclusion more than any other part of a speech. That's why you should spend some time to make it most effective. Strive to achieve three goals:

An effective conclusion summarizes the main points and allows the speaker to exit gracefully.

- Summarize the main themes of the presentation.
- Leave the audience with a specific and memorable take-away.
- Include a statement that allows you to exit the podium gracefully.

Some speakers end limply with comments such as *I guess that's about all I have to say* or *That's it*. Such lame statements show little enthusiasm and are not the culmination of the talk that listeners expect. Skilled speakers alert the audience that they are finishing. They use phrases such as, *In conclusion, As I end this presentation,* or, *It's time for me to sum up*. Then they proceed immediately to the conclusion. Audiences become justly irritated with a speaker who announces the conclusion but then talks on for ten more minutes.

A straightforward summary should review major points and focus on what you want the listeners to do, think, or remember. You might say, *In bringing my presentation to a close, I will restate my major purpose . . . ,* or, *In summary, my major purpose has been to . . . . In support of my purpose, I have presented three major points. They are (1) . . . , (2) . . . , and (3) . . . .* Notice how Nicholas Gilmore, in the conclusion shown in Figure 12.3, summarized his three main points and provided a final focus to listeners.

If you are promoting a recommendation, you might end as follows: *In conclusion, I recommend that we retain Matrixx Marketing to conduct a telemarketing campaign beginning September 1 at a cost of X dollars. To complete this recommendation, I suggest that we (a) finance this campaign from our operations budget, (b) develop a persuasive message describing our new product, and (c) name Riley Robinson to oversee the project*. Avoid using phrases such as *I think, I believe,* or *I feel,* which state the obvious and will weaken your presentation.

A conclusion is like a punch line and must be memorable. Think of it as the high point of your presentation, a valuable kernel of information to take away. The valuable kernel of information, or take-away, should tie in with the opening and present a forward-looking idea. Avoid merely rehashing, in the same words, what you said before. Instead, ensure that the audience will take away very specific information or benefits and a positive impression of you and your company. The take-away is the value of the presentation to the audience and the benefit audience members believe to have received. The tension that you built in the early parts of the talk now culminates in the close.

In your conclusion you might want to use an anecdote, an inspiring quotation, or a statement that ties in the opener and offers a new insight. Whatever you choose, be sure to include a closing thought that indicates you are finished. For example, *This concludes my presentation. After investigating many marketing firms, we are convinced that Matrixx is the best for our purposes. Your authorization of my recommendations will mark the beginning of a very successful campaign for our new product. Thank you.*

Building Audience Rapport Like a Pro

Use analogies, metaphors, similes, personal anecdotes, personalized statistics, and worst- and best-case scenarios instead of dry facts.

Good speakers are adept at building audience rapport. They form a bond with the audience; they entertain as well as inform. How do they do it? Based on observations of successful and unsuccessful speakers, we learn that the good ones use a number of verbal and nonverbal techniques to connect with the audience. Their helpful techniques include providing effective imagery, supplying verbal cues, and using body language strategically.

Effective Imagery

You will lose your audience quickly if you fill your talk with abstractions, generalities, and dry facts. To enliven your presentation and enhance comprehension, try using some of the following techniques. However, beware of exaggeration or distortion. Keep your imagery realistic and credible:

- **Analogies.** A comparison of similar traits between dissimilar things can be effective in explaining and drawing connections. For example, *Product development is similar to the process of conceiving, carrying, and delivering a baby*. Or, *Downsizing or restructuring is similar to an overweight person undergoing a regimen of dieting, habit changing, and exercise.*
- **Metaphors.** A comparison between otherwise dissimilar things without using the words *like* or *as* results in a metaphor. For example, *Our competitor's CEO is a snake when it comes to negotiating,* or *My desk is a garbage dump*.
- **Similes.** A comparison that includes the words *like* or *as* is a simile. For example, *Our critics used our background report like a drunk uses a lamppost—for support rather than for illumination.* Or: *She's as happy as someone who just won the lottery.*
- **Personal anecdotes.** Nothing connects you faster or better with your audience than a good personal story. In a talk about e-mail techniques, you could reveal your own blunders that became painful learning experiences. In a talk to potential investors, the founder of a new ethnic magazine might tell a story about growing up without positive ethnic role models.
- **Personalized statistics.** Although often misused, statistics stay with people—particularly when they relate directly to the audience. A speaker discussing job searching might say, *Look around the room. Only one in four graduates will find a job immediately after graduation*. If possible, simplify and personalize facts. For example, *The sales of Coca-Cola beverages around the world totaled nearly 24 billion cases last year. That means that every man, woman, and child on this planet consumed 3.5 cases of soda and other Coca-Cola products.*
- **Worst- and best-case scenarios.** Hearing the worst that could happen can be effective in driving home a point. For example, *If we do nothing about our computer backup system now, it's just a matter of time before the entire system crashes and we lose all of our customer contact information. Can you imagine starting from scratch in building all of your customer files again? However, if we fix the system now, we can expand our customer files and actually increase sales at the same time.*

Verbal Signposts

Speakers must remember that listeners, unlike readers of a report, cannot control the rate of presentation or flip back through pages to review main points. As a result, listeners get lost easily. Knowledgeable speakers help the audience recognize the organization and main points in an oral message with verbal signposts. They keep listeners on track by including helpful previews, summaries, and transitions, such as these:

Knowledgeable speakers provide verbal signposts to indicate when they are previewing, summarizing, or switching directions.

- **Previewing**
  The next segment of my talk presents three reasons for . . . .
  Let's now consider two causes of . . . .
- **Summarizing**
  Let me review with you the major problems I have just discussed.
  You see, then, that the most significant factors are . . . .
- **Switching directions**
  Thus far we have talked solely about . . . ; now let's move to . . . .
  I have argued that . . . and . . . , but an alternate view holds that . . . .

You can further improve any oral presentation by including appropriate transitional expressions such as *first, second, next, then, therefore, moreover, on the other hand, on the contrary*, and *in conclusion*. These transitional expressions build coherence, lend emphasis, and tell listeners where you are headed. Notice in Nicholas Gilmore's outline in Figure 12.3, on page 370, the specific transitional elements designed to help listeners recognize each new principal point.

Nonverbal Messages

Although what you say is most important, the nonverbal messages you send can also have a powerful effect on how well your audience receives your message. How you look, how you move, and how you speak can make or break your presentation. The following suggestions focus on nonverbal tips to ensure that your verbal message resonates with your audience.

A speaker's appearance, movement, and speech affect the success of your presentation.

- **Look terrific!** Like it or not, you will be judged by your appearance. For everything but small in-house presentations, be sure you dress professionally. The rule of thumb is that you should dress at least as well as the best-dressed person in the audience. However, even if you know that your audience will be dressed casually, showing up in professional attire will help you build credibility. You will feel better about yourself too!
- **Animate your body.** Be enthusiastic and let your body show it. Stand with good posture to show confidence. Emphasize ideas to enhance points about size, number, and direction. Use a variety of gestures, but don't consciously plan them in advance.
- **Speak extemporaneously.** Do not read from notes or a manuscript, but speak freely. Use your presentation slides to guide your talk. You will come across as more competent and enthusiastic if you are not glued to your notes or manuscript. Use note cards or a paper outline only if presenting without an electronic slideshow.
- **Punctuate your words.** You can keep your audience interested by varying your tone, volume, pitch, and pace. Use pauses before and after important points. Allow the audience to take in your ideas.
- **Use appropriate eye contact.** Maintaining eye contact with your audience shows that you are confident and prepared. In addition, looking at audience members, rather than looking at your notes or your computer screen, helps them feel more involved.
- **Get out from behind the podium.** Avoid being planted behind the podium. Movement makes you look natural and comfortable and helps you connect more with your audience. You might pick a few places in the room to walk to.

Even if you must stay close to your visual aids, make a point of leaving them occasionally so that the audience can see your whole body.

- **Vary your facial expression.** Begin with a smile, but change your expressions to correspond with the thoughts you are voicing. You can shake your head to show disagreement, roll your eyes to show disdain, look heavenward for guidance, or wrinkle your brow to show concern or dismay. To see how speakers convey meaning without words, mute the sound on your TV or streaming video clips online and watch the facial expressions of a talk show personality, newscaster, or politician.

Whenever possible, beginning presenters should have an experienced speaker watch them and give them tips as they rehearse. Your instructor is an important coach who can provide you with invaluable feedback. In the absence of helpers, record your talk and watch for your nonverbal behavior on camera.

Planning Visual Aids and Multimedia Presentations

Before you make a business presentation, consider this wise proverb: "Tell me, I forget. Show me, I remember. Involve me, I understand." Your goals as a speaker are to make listeners understand, remember, and act on your ideas. To get them interested and involved, include effective visual aids. Some experts say that we acquire as much as 85 percent of all our knowledge visually: "Professionals everywhere need to know about the incredible inefficiency of text-based information and the incredible effects of images," says developmental biologist John Medina.[5] Therefore, audiences are far more likely to grasp and retain an oral presentation that incorporates visual aids than one lacking visual enhancement.

Visual aids clarify points, improve comprehension, and aid retention.

Good visual aids serve many purposes. They emphasize and clarify main points, thus improving comprehension and retention. They increase audience interest, and they make the presenter appear more professional, better prepared, and more persuasive. Well-designed visual aids illustrate and emphasize your message more effectively than words alone; therefore, they may help shorten a meeting or achieve your goal faster. Visual aids are particularly helpful for inexperienced speakers because the audience concentrates on the aid rather than on the speaker. However, experienced speakers work hard at not allowing their slideshows to eclipse them. Good visuals also serve to jog the memory of a speaker, thus improving self-confidence, poise, and delivery.

Types of Visual Aids

Today, speakers have many forms of visual media at their fingertips if they wish to enhance a presentation. Figure 12.4 describes the pros and cons of several visual aids and can guide you in selecting the best one for any speaking occasion. Three of the most popular visuals are multimedia slides, overhead transparencies, and handouts.

Multimedia Slides. With today's excellent software programs—such as Microsoft PowerPoint, Apple Keynote, Lotus Freelance Graphics, Corel Presentations, and Adobe Presenter or Adobe Ovation—you can create dynamic, colorful presentations with your computer. The output from these programs is generally shown on a computer monitor, a TV monitor, an LCD (liquid crystal display) panel, or a screen. With a little expertise and advanced equipment, you can create a multimedia presentation that includes stereo sound, videos, and hyperlinks, as described shortly in the discussion of multimedia presentations. Multimedia slides can also be uploaded to a Web site or broadcast live over the Internet.

FIGURE 12.4 Pros and Cons of Visual Aid Options

Medium	Pros	Cons
Multimedia slides	Create professional appearance with many color, art, graphic, and font options. Easy to use and transport via removable storage media, Web download, or e-mail attachment. Inexpensive to update.	Present potential incompatibility issues. Require projection equipment and practice for smooth delivery. Tempt user to include razzle-dazzle features that may fail to add value.
Transparencies	Give professional appearance with little practice. Easy to (a) prepare, (b) update and maintain, (c) locate reliable equipment, and (d) limit information shown at one time.	Appear to some as an outdated presentation method. Hold speaker captive to the machine. Provide poor reproduction of photos and some graphics.
Handouts	Encourage audience participation. Easy to maintain and update. Enhance recall because audience keeps reference material.	Increase risk of unauthorized duplication of speaker's material. Can be difficult to transport. May cause speaker to lose audience's attention.
Flipcharts or whiteboards	Provide inexpensive option available at most sites. Easy to (a) create, (b) modify or customize on the spot, (c) record comments from the audience, and (d) combine with more high-tech visuals in the same presentation.	Require graphics talent. Difficult for larger audiences to see. Prepared flipcharts are cumbersome to transport and easily worn with use.
Video	Gives an accurate representation of the content and a strong indication of forethought and preparation.	Creates potential for compatibility issues related to computer video formats. Expensive to create and update.
Props	Offer a realistic reinforcement of message content. Increase audience participation with close observation.	Lead to extra work and expense in transporting and replacing worn objects. Limited use with larger audiences.

Overhead Transparencies. Some speakers still rely on the overhead projector for many reasons. Most meeting rooms are equipped with projectors and screens. Moreover, acetate transparencies for the overhead are cheap, easily prepared on a computer or copier, and simple to use. Because rooms need not be darkened, a speaker using transparencies can maintain eye contact with the audience. Many experienced speakers create overhead slides in addition to their electronic slides to have a backup plan in the case of malfunctioning presentation technology. More important, though, overhead transparencies are ideal if the speaker needs to draw on the images or data using a marker. A word of caution, however, when using transparencies: stand to the side of the projector so that you don't obstruct the audience's view.

Handouts. You can enhance and complement your presentations by distributing pictures, outlines, brochures, articles, charts, summaries, or other supplements. Speakers who use multimedia presentation software often prepare a set of their slides along with notes to hand out to viewers. Timing the distribution of any handout, though, is tricky. If given out during a presentation, your handouts tend to distract the audience, causing you to lose control. Therefore, you should discuss handouts during the presentation but delay distributing them until after you finish.

To maintain control, distribute handouts after you finish speaking.

Speaker's Notes. You have a variety of options for printing hard-copy versions of your presentation. You can, for example, make speaker's notes, which are a wonderful aid for practicing your talk. Beneath the miniature image of each slide is space for you to key in your supporting comments for the abbreviated material in your slides. You can also include up to nine miniature versions of your slides per printed page. These miniatures are handy if you want to preview your talk to a sponsoring organization or if you want to supply the audience with a summary of your presentation. However, resist the temptation to read from your notes during the slide presentation. It might turn off your audience and make you appear insecure and incompetent.

Designing an Impressive Multimedia Presentation

Microsoft PowerPoint has become the business standard for presenting, defending, and selling ideas.

Few corporate types or entrepreneurs would do without snazzy colorful images to make their points. Electronic slideshows, PowerPoint in particular, have become a staple of business presentations. However, overuse or misuse may be the downside of the ever-present multimedia slideshow. Over the more than two decades of the software program's existence, millions of poorly created and badly delivered PowerPoint presentations have tarnished PowerPoint's reputation as an effective communication tool. Tools are helpful only when used properly.

Imagine those who sit through the more than 30 million PowerPoint presentations that Microsoft estimates are made each day.[6] No doubt, many of them would say this "disease" has reached epidemic proportions. PowerPoint, say its detractors, dictates the way information is structured and presented. They say that the program is turning the nation's businesspeople into a "mindless gaggle of bullet-pointed morons."[7] If you typed *death by PowerPoint* in your favorite search engine, you would score millions of hits. However, text-laden, amateurish slides that distract and bore audiences are the fault of their creator and not the software program itself.

In the last few years, several communication consultants have tried to show business how it can move "beyond bullet points." The experts recommend creating slideshows that tell a story and send a powerful message with much less text and more images.[8] Presentation guru Garr Reynolds urges readers to unleash their creativity: "Do not rely on Microsoft or Apple or anyone else to dictate your choices. Most of all, do not let mere habit—and the habits of others—dictate your decisions on how you prepare and design and deliver your presentations."[9] When you are ready to explore highly visual, less text-laden design choices, consider the advice of the authorities on presentation skills, Cliff Atkinson, Guy Kawasaki, Garr Reynolds, and Tad Simons.

Critics say that PowerPoint is too rigid and produces "bullet-pointed morons."

In the sections that follow, you will learn to create an impressive multimedia presentation using the most widely used presentation software program, PowerPoint. With any software program, of course, gaining expertise requires your investment of time and effort. You could take a course, or you could teach yourself through

an online tutorial such as those found at **http://office.microsoft.com**. Another way to master PowerPoint is to read a book such as Faithe Wempen's *PowerPoint 2010 Bible.* If operated by a proficient slide preparer and a skillful presenter, PowerPoint can add a distinct visual impact to any presentation.

Preparing a Visually Appealing PowerPoint Presentation

Some presenters prefer to create their slides first and then develop the narrative around their slides. Others prepare their content first and then create the visual component. The risk associated with the first approach is that you may be tempted to spend too much time making your slides look good and not enough time preparing your content. Remember that great-looking slides never compensate for thin content. In the following discussion, you will learn how to adjust the content and design of your slides to the situation or purpose and your audience. You will also receive detailed how-to instructions for creating a PowerPoint slideshow.

Analyzing the Situation and Purpose. Making the best content and design choices for your slides depends greatly on your analysis of the presentation situation and the purpose of your slideshow. Will your slides be used during a live presentation? Will they be part of a self-running presentation such as in a store kiosk? Will they be saved on a server so that Internet users can watch the presentation at their convenience? Will they be sent as a PowerPoint show or a PDF document—also sometimes called a deck—to a client instead of a hard-copy report? Are you converting PowerPoint slideshows for viewing on smartphones or tablets?

If you are e-mailing the presentation or posting it online as a self-contained file, the slides will typically feature more text than if they were delivered orally. If, on the other hand, you are creating slides for a live presentation, your analysis will prompt you to choose powerful, telling images over boring text-laden slides.

"My presentation lacks power and it has no point. I assumed the software would take care of that!"

Anticipating Your Audience. Think about how you can design your presentation to get the most positive response from your audience. Audiences respond, for example, to the colors you use. Primary ideas are generally best conveyed with bold colors such as blue, green, and purple. Because the messages that colors convey can vary from culture to culture, presenters must choose colors carefully. In the United States, blue is the color of credibility, tranquility, conservatism, and trust. Therefore, it is the background color of choice for many business presentations. Green relates to interaction, growth, money, and stability. It can work well as a background or an accent color. Purple can also work as a background or accent color. It conveys spirituality, royalty, dreams, and humor.[10] As for slide text, adjust the color in such a way that it provides high contrast and is readable as a result. White or yellow, for example, usually works well on dark backgrounds.

Just as you anticipate audience members' reactions to color, you can usually anticipate their reaction to special effects. Using animation and sound effects—flying objects, swirling text, clashing cymbals, and the like—only because they are available is not a good idea. Special effects distract your audience, drawing attention away from your main points. You should add animation features only if doing so helps convey your message or adds interest to the content. When your audience members leave, they should be commenting on the ideas you conveyed—not the cool swivels and sound effects.

Adapting Text and Color Selections. Adapt the amount of text on your slide to how your audience will use the slides. As a general guideline, most graphic

Follow the 6-x-6 rule and select background and text colors based on the lightness of the room.

designers encourage the 6-x-6 rule: "Six bullets per screen, max; six words per bullet, max."[11] **You may find, however, that breaking this rule is sometimes necessary, particularly when your users will be viewing the presentation on their own with no speaker assistance.** For most purposes, though, strive to break free from bulleted lists whenever possible and minimize the use of text.

Adapt the colors based on where you will give the presentation. Use light text on a dark background for presentations in darkened rooms. Use dark text on a light background for presentations in lighted rooms. Avoid using a dark font on a dark background, such as red text on a dark blue background. In the same way, avoid using a light font on a light background, such as white text on a pale blue background. Dark on dark or light on light results in low contrast, making the slides difficult to read.

Organizing Your Slides. When you prepare your slides, translate the major headings in your presentation outline into titles for slides. Then build bullet points using short phrases. In Chapter 4 you learned to improve readability by using graphic highlighting techniques, including bullets, numbers, and headings. In preparing a PowerPoint presentation, you will use those same techniques.

The slides you create to accompany your spoken ideas can be organized with visual elements that will help your audience understand and remember what you want to communicate. Let's say, for example, that you have three points in your presentation. You can create a blueprint slide that captures the three points in a visually appealing way, and then you can use that slide several times throughout your presentation. Near the beginning, the blueprint slide provides an overview of your points. Later, it will provide transitions as you move from point to point. For transitions, you can direct your audience's attention by highlighting the next point you will be talking about. Finally, the blueprint slide can be used near the end to provide a review of your key points.

Working With Templates. All presentation programs require you to (a) select or create a template that will serve as the background for your presentation and (b) make each individual slide by selecting a layout that best conveys your message. Novice and even advanced users choose existing templates because they are designed by professionals who know how to combine harmonious colors, borders, bullet styles, and fonts for pleasing visual effects. If you prefer, you can alter existing templates so they better suit your needs. Adding a corporate logo, adjusting the color scheme to better match the colors used on your organization's Web site, or selecting a different font are just some of the ways you can customize existing templates. One big advantage of templates is that they get you started quickly.

Overused templates and clip art produce "visual clichés" that bore audiences.

Be careful, though, of what one expert has labeled "visual clichés."[12] Overused templates and even clip art that ship with PowerPoint can weary viewers who have seen them repeatedly in presentations. Instead of using a standard template, search for *PowerPoint template* in your favorite search engine. You will see hundreds of template options available as free downloads. Unless your employer requires that presentations all have the same look, your audience will most likely appreciate fresh templates that complement the purpose of your presentation and provide visual variety.

Composing Your Slideshow. During the composition stage, many users fall into the trap of excessive formatting and programming. They fritter away precious time fine-tuning their slides. They don't spend enough time on what they are going to say and how they will say it. To avoid this trap, set a limit for how much time you will spend making your slides visually appealing. Your time limit will be based on how many "bells and whistles" (a) your audience expects and (b) your content requires to make it understandable. Remember that not every point nor every thought requires a visual. In fact, it's smart to switch off the slides occasionally and direct the focus to yourself. Darkening the screen while you discuss a point, tell a story, give an example, or involve the audience will add variety to your presentation.

Create a slide only if the slide accomplishes at least one of the following purposes:

- Generates interest in what you are saying and helps the audience follow your ideas
- Highlights points you want your audience to remember
- Introduces or reviews your key points
- Provides a transition from one major point to the next
- Illustrates and simplifies complex ideas

In a later section of this chapter, you will find very specific steps to follow as you create your presentation.

Designing for Optimal Effect. Try to avoid long, boring bulleted lists in a presentation. You can alter layouts by repositioning, resizing, or changing the fonts for the placeholders in which your titles, bulleted lists, organization charts, video clips, photographs, or other elements appear. Figure 12.5 illustrates two of the many layout and design options for creating your slides. The figure shows that you can make your slides visually more appealing and memorable even with relatively small changes.

Notice that the bulleted items on the first slide in Figure 12.5 are not parallel. The slide looks as if the author had been brainstorming or freewriting a first draft. The second and sixth bullet points express the same thought, that shopping online is convenient and easy for customers. Some bullet points are too long. The bullets on the improved slide are very short, well within the 6-x-6 rule, although they are complete sentences. The photograph in the revised slide adds interest and illustrates the point. You may use stock photos that you can download from the Web for personal or school use without penalty. Alternatively, consider taking your own pictures if you own a digital camera or a camera-equipped smartphone.

Figure 12.6 shows how to add variety and pizzazz to your slides. Notice that the same information that appeared as bullet points in Figure 12.5 now appears as exciting spokes radiating from the central idea: Why You Should Sell Online. This spoke diagram is just one of numerous **SmartArt graphics** in the **Illustrations**

FIGURE 12.5 **Revising and Enhancing Slides for Greater Impact**

Before Revision

Reasons for Selling Online

- Your online business can grow globally.
- Customer convenience.
- Conduct business 24/7.
- No need for renting a retail store or hiring employees.
- Reduce inquiries by providing policies and a privacy statement.
- Customers can buy quickly and easily.

After Revision

Why You Should Sell Online

- Grow business globally.
- Offer convenience to customers.
- Conduct business 24/7.
- Save on rent and staff.
- Create policies to reduce inquiries.

The slide on the left contains bullet points that are not parallel and that overlap in meaning. The second and sixth bullet points say the same thing. Moreover, some bullet points are too long. After revision, the slide on the right has a more convincing title illustrating the "you" view. The bullet points are shorter, and each begins with a verb for parallelism and an emphasis on action. The photo adds interest.

FIGURE 12.6 Converting a Bulleted Slide Into a Diagram

Revised With a SmartArt Graphic

SmartArt Graphics Options

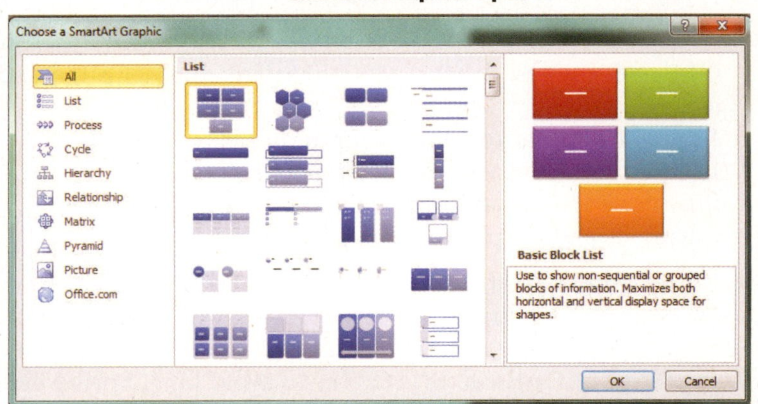

The same content that appears in the Figure 12.5 slides takes on a totally different look when arranged as spokes radiating from a central idea. Add a 3-D effect and a muted background image to the middle shape, for example, and you depart from the usual boring template look. When presenting this slide, you can animate each item and control when it is revealed, further enlivening your presentation. PowerPoint 2010 provides SmartArt graphics with many choices of diagrams and shapes for arranging information.

tab in PowerPoint. You can also animate each item in the diagram. Occasionally, try to convert pure text and bullet points to graphics, charts, and other images to add punch to your slideshow. You will keep your audiences interested and help them retain the information you are presenting.

Use animation to introduce elements of a presentation as they unfold in your spoken remarks.

Your audience will grasp numeric information more easily in charts or graphs than in a listing of numbers. Moreover, in most programs, you can animate your graphs and charts. Say, for instance, you have four columns in your bar chart. You can control the entry of each column by determining in what order and how each column appears on the screen. The goal is to use animation strategically to introduce elements of the presentation as they unfold in your spoken remarks. Figure 12.7 shows how a chart can illustrate a concept discussed in the presentation about selling online.

Revising, Proofreading, and Evaluating Your Slideshow. Use PowerPoint's **Slide Sorter** view to rearrange, insert, and delete slides during the revision process. This is the time to focus on making your presentation as clear and concise as possible. If you are listing items, be sure that all items use parallel grammatical form. Figure 12.8 shows how to revise a slide to improve it for conciseness, parallelism, and other features. Study the design tips described in the first slide and determine which suggestions their author did not follow. Then compare it with the revised slide.

Notice that both slides in Figure 12.8 feature a calm blue background, the color of choice for many business presentations. However, the background swirls on the first slide are distracting. In addition, the uppercase white font contributes to the busy look, making the image hard to read. Inserting a transparent overlay and choosing a dark font to mute the distracting waves create a cleaner-looking slide.

As you are revising, check carefully to find spelling, grammar, punctuation, and other errors. Use the PowerPoint spell-checker, but don't rely on it without careful proofing, preferably from a printed copy of the slideshow. Nothing is as embarrassing as projecting errors on a huge screen in front of your audience. Also, check for consistency in how you capitalize and punctuate points throughout the presentation.

Finally, critically evaluate your slideshow. Consider whether you have done all you can to use the tools PowerPoint provides to communicate your message in a visually appealing way. In addition, test your slides on the equipment and in the room you will be using during your presentation. Do the colors you selected

FIGURE 12.7 Using a Bar Chart (Column Chart) to Illustrate a Concept

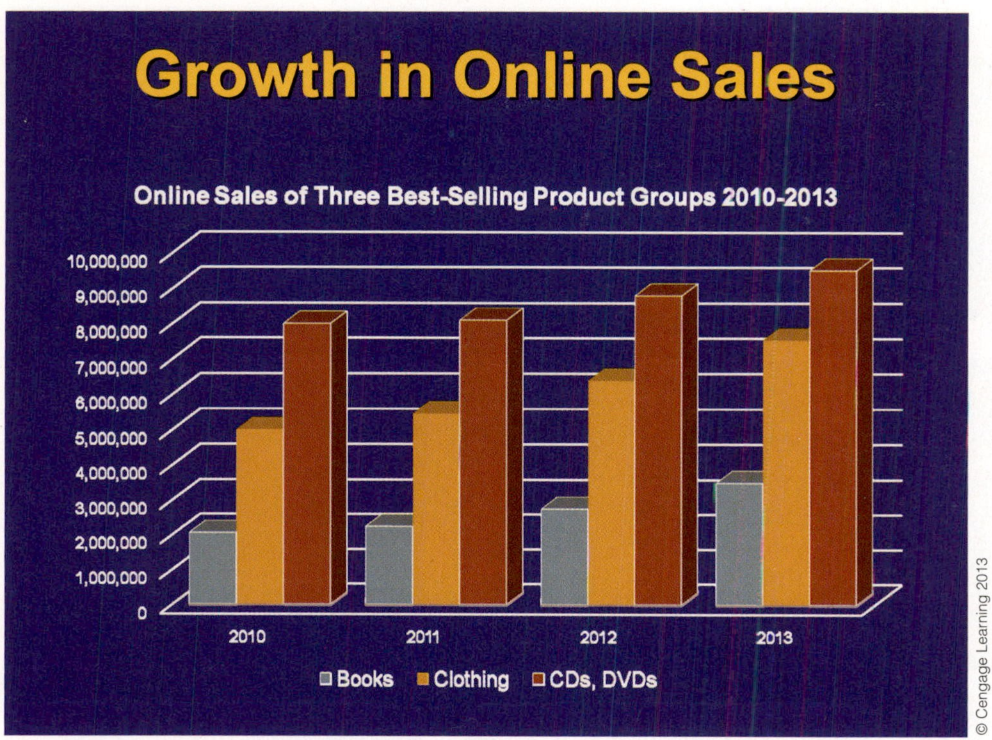

This slide was created using PowerPoint's **Insert, Chart** function. The information presented here is more exciting and easier to comprehend than if it had been presented in a bulleted list.

work in this new setting? Are the font styles and sizes readable from the back of the room? Figure 12.9 shows examples of slides that incorporate what you have learned in this discussion.

The dark, purple-colored background and the green and blue hues in the slideshow shown in Figure 12.9 are standard choices for many business presentations. With an unobtrusive dark background, white fonts are a good option for maximum contrast and, hence, readability. The creator of the presentation varied the

FIGURE 12.8 Designing More Effective Slides

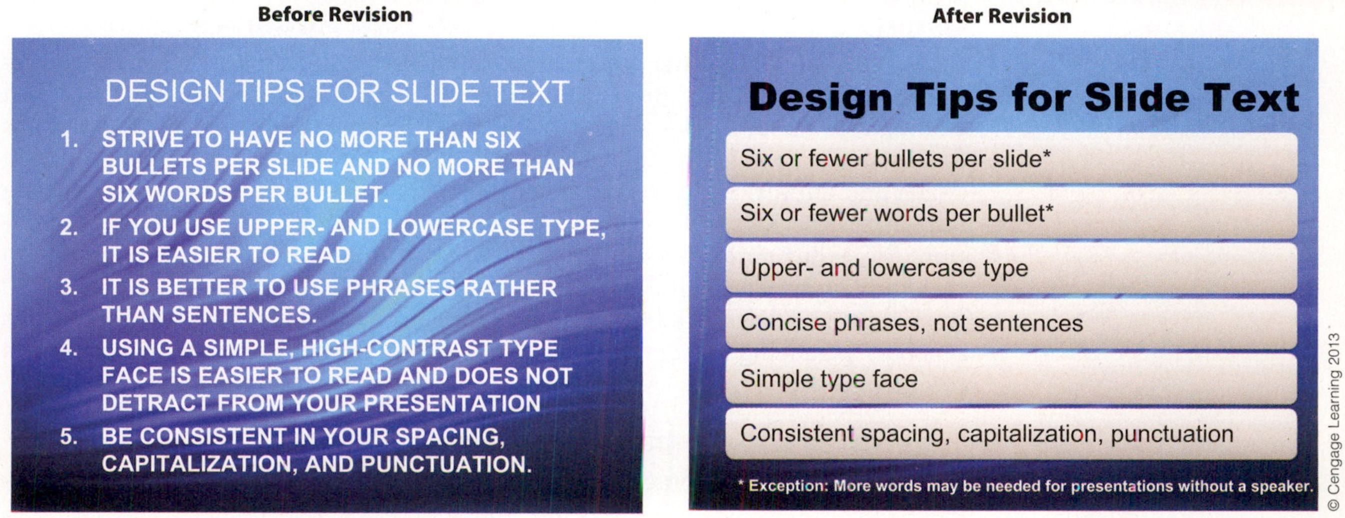

Before Revision

DESIGN TIPS FOR SLIDE TEXT

1. STRIVE TO HAVE NO MORE THAN SIX BULLETS PER SLIDE AND NO MORE THAN SIX WORDS PER BULLET.
2. IF YOU USE UPPER- AND LOWERCASE TYPE, IT IS EASIER TO READ
3. IT IS BETTER TO USE PHRASES RATHER THAN SENTENCES.
4. USING A SIMPLE, HIGH-CONTRAST TYPE FACE IS EASIER TO READ AND DOES NOT DETRACT FROM YOUR PRESENTATION
5. BE CONSISTENT IN YOUR SPACING, CAPITALIZATION, AND PUNCTUATION.

After Revision

Design Tips for Slide Text

- Six or fewer bullets per slide*
- Six or fewer words per bullet*
- Upper- and lowercase type
- Concise phrases, not sentences
- Simple type face
- Consistent spacing, capitalization, punctuation

* Exception: More words may be needed for presentations without a speaker.

The slide on the left is difficult to read and understand because it violates many slide-making rules. How many violations can you detect? The slide on the right illustrates an improved version of the same information. Which slide do you think viewers would rather read?

FIGURE 12.9 PowerPoint Slides That Illustrate Multimedia Presentations

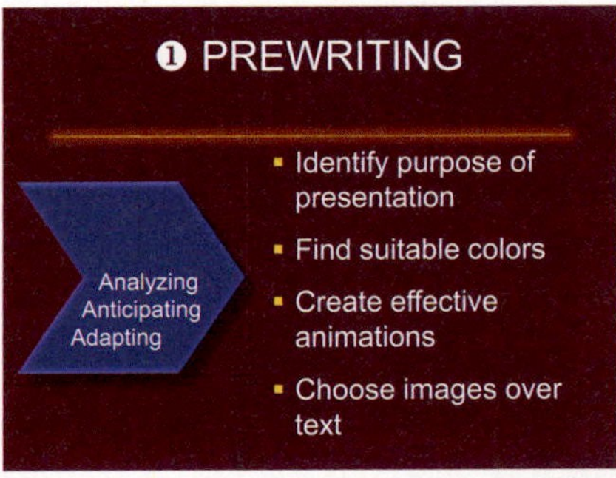

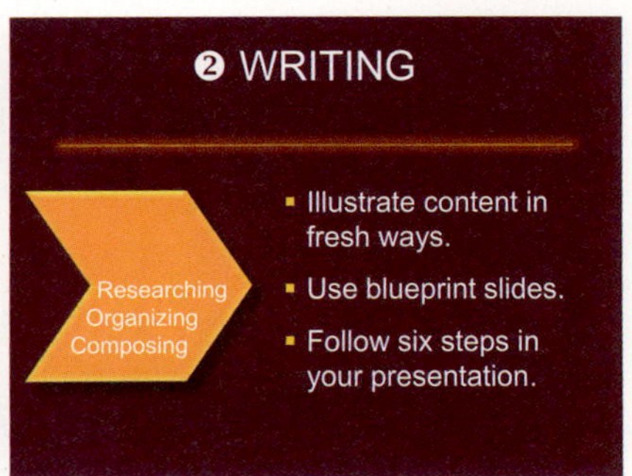

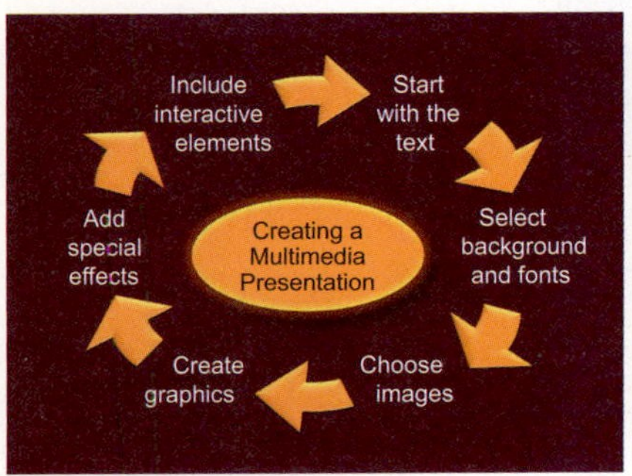

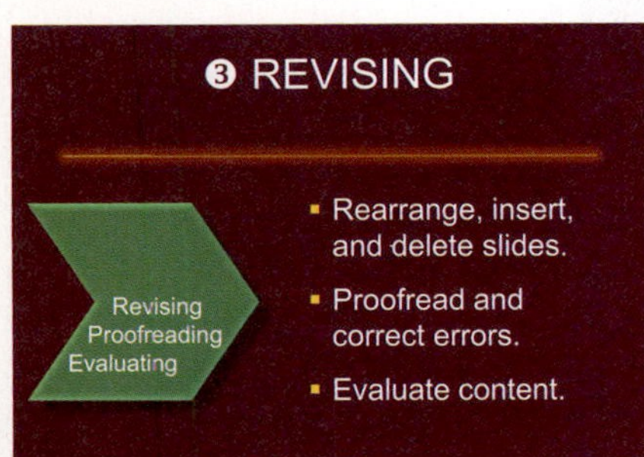

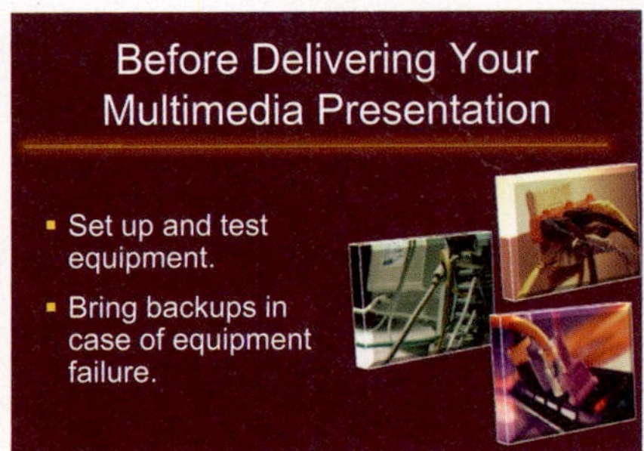

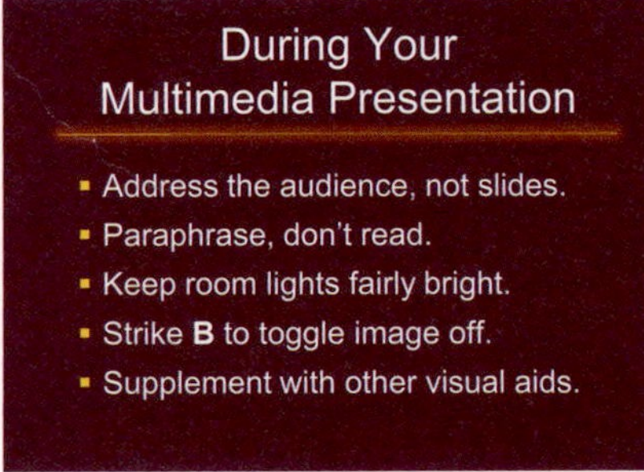

slide design to break the monotony of bulleted or numbered lists. Images and animated diagrams add interest and zing to the slides.

Using PowerPoint Effectively With Your Audience

A fabulous slideshow can be ruined if you are unfamiliar with the equipment.

Technology glitches or the presenter's unfamiliarity with the equipment have sabotaged many promising presentations. Fabulous slides are of value only if you can manage the technology expertly. The late Apple CEO Steve Jobs was famous for his ability to wow his audiences during his keynote addresses. Communication coach and author Carmine Gallo credits extensive preparation for Jobs' amazing impact. "Steve Jobs spends hours of grueling practice before a keynote presentation. Superstar performers in all fields leave nothing to chance. If you want to thrill any audience, steal a page from the Jobs playbook and start practicing!"[13] At a recent Macworld rehearsal, for example, Jobs spent more than four hours on stage practicing and reviewing every technical and performance aspect of his product launch.

Practicing and Preparing

Solid preparation and practice are crucial. One expert advises presenters to complete their slideshows a week before the actual talk and rehearse several times each day before the presentation.[14] Allow plenty of time before your presentation to set up and test your equipment.[15] Confirm that the places you plan to stand are not in the line of the projected image. Audience members don't appreciate having part of the slide displayed on your body. Make sure that all video or Web links are working and that you know how to operate all features the first time you try. No matter how much time you put into preshow setup and testing, you still have no guarantee that all will go smoothly. Therefore, you should always bring backups of your presentation. Overhead transparencies and handouts of your presentation provide good substitutes. Transferring your presentation to a CD or a USB flash drive that could run from any available notebook might prove useful as well.

Keeping Your Audience Engaged

In addition to using the technology to enhance and enrich your message, here are additional tips for performing like a professional and keeping the audience engaged:

To keep your audience interested, maintain eye contact, don't read from your slides, use a radio remote and a laser pointer, and turn off an image after discussing it.

- Know your material. This will free you to look at your audience and gaze at the screen, not your practice notes. Maintain genuine eye contact to connect with individuals in the room.
- As you show new elements on a slide, allow the audience time to absorb the information. Then paraphrase and elaborate on what the listeners have seen. Don't insult your audience's intelligence by reading verbatim from a slide.
- Leave the lights as bright as you can. Make sure the audience can see your face and eyes.
- Use a radio remote control (not infrared) so you can move freely rather than remain tethered to your computer. Radio remotes allow you to be up to 50 feet away from your laptop.
- Maintain a connection with the audience by using a laser pointer to highlight slide items to discuss. Be aware, however, that a dancing laser point in a shaky hand may make you appear nervous. Steady your hand.
- Don't leave a slide on the screen when you have finished discussing it. While you are running your presentation in **Slide Show** mode, strike *B* on the keyboard to turn on or off the screen image by blackening it. Pushing *W* will turn the screen white.

Before PowerPoint.

Some presenters allow their PowerPoint slides to steal their thunder. One expert urges speakers to "use their PowerPresence in preference to their PowerPoint."[16] Although multimedia presentations supply terrific sizzle, they cannot replace the steak. In developing a presentation, don't expect your slides to carry the show. You can avoid being upstaged by not relying totally on your slides. Help the audience visualize your points by using other techniques. For example, drawing a diagram on a white board or flipchart can be more engaging than showing slide after slide of static drawings. Demonstrating or displaying real objects or props is a welcome relief from slides. Remember that slides should be used only to help your audience understand the message and to add interest. You are still the main attraction!

Eight Steps to Making a Powerful Multimedia Presentation

We have now discussed many suggestions for making effective PowerPoint presentations, but you may still be wondering how to put it all together. Here is a step-by-step process for creating a powerful multimedia presentation:

1. **Start with the text.** The text is the foundation of your presentation. Express your ideas using words that are clear, concise, and understandable. Once the entire content of your presentation is in place, you are ready to begin adding color and all the other elements that will make your slides visually appealing.

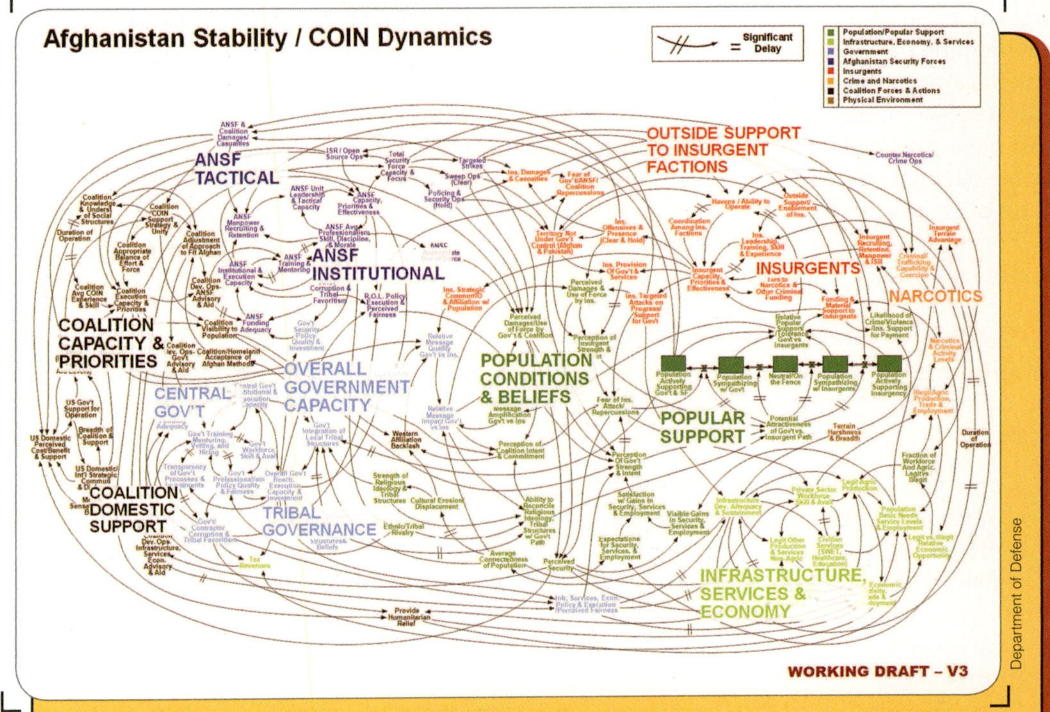

Department of Defense

WORKPLACE IN FOCUS

"When we understand that slide, we'll have won the war." General Stanley McChrystal, former U.S. commander in Afghanistan, echoes the military's ambivalence about fuzzy PowerPoint slides in briefings. Other critics in the military, General McMaster among them, suggest that PowerPoint reduces complex issues to simplistic bullet points. Decisions may be made hastily in the absence of well-developed written orders and without much time to think. Too much information on slides and an emphasis on style over substance may create dangerous confusion in the armed forces. Junior officers, called "PowerPoint Rangers," occupy most of their time with creating slideshows. General McMaster cautioned that PowerPoint "can create the illusion of understanding and the illusion of control." ***Why are confusing slideshows bad news in the armed forces? How could the use of PowerPoint be improved?***

For a powerful presentation, first write the text, and then work on templates, font styles, and colors.

2. **Select background and fonts.** Select a template that will provide consistent font styles and sizes and a background for your slides. You can create your own template or use one included with PowerPoint. You can also download free templates or pay for templates from many online sites. You can't go wrong selecting a basic template design with an easy-to-read font, such as Times New Roman or Arial. As a general rule, use no more than two font styles in your presentation. The point size should be between 24 and 36. Title fonts should be larger than text font. The more you use PowerPoint and find out what works and doesn't work, the more you can experiment with bolder, more innovative background and font options that effectively convey your message.
3. **Choose images that help communicate your message.** Images, such as clip art, photographs, and maps, should complement the text. Never use an image that is not immediately relevant. Microsoft Office Online can be accessed in PowerPoint and contains thousands of clip art images and photographs, most of which are in the public domain and require no copyright permissions. Before using images from other sources, determine whether permission from the copyright holder is required. Bear in mind that some people consider clip art amateurish, so photographs are usually preferable. In addition, clip art is available to any user, so it tends to become stale fast. Consider the drastic, yet eloquent photograph shown in Figure 12.10. A striking image can tell a

FIGURE 12.10 Harnessing the Appeal of Powerful Images

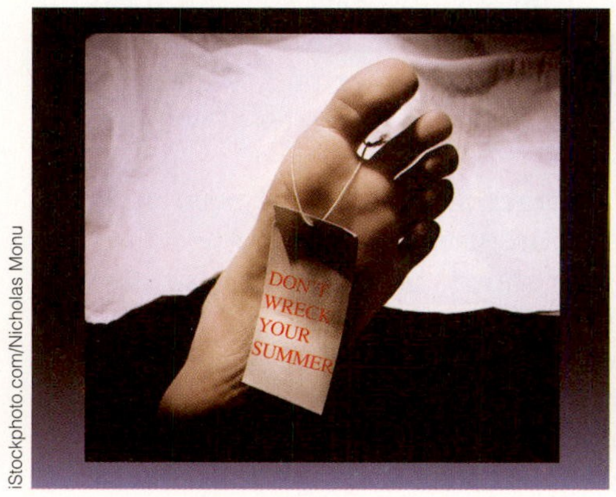

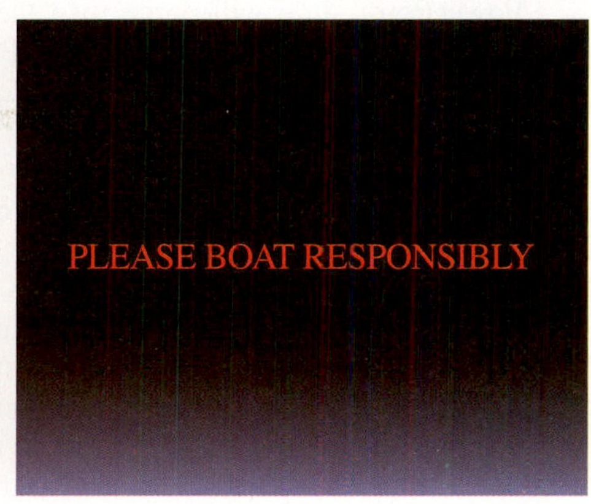

iStockphoto.com/Nicholas Monu

The image of a toe-tagged body used in the left slide is shocking to most viewers. The purpose of the two slides is to create a strong emotional appeal for boating safety. The message of these two sparse slides is more eloquent than bulleted text ever could be.

OFFICE INSIDER

"Keep it simple. Limit the number of illustrations and reduce the number of words. One concept on a slide is sufficient. Remember: Less is better!"

—Joyce Kupsh, PowerPoint expert and coauthor of *Presentation Design and Delivery*

persuasive story, as the United States Coast Guard's photograph does in the service of boating safety. Inserted in a slide such as the one in Figure 12.10, this picture is indeed worth a thousand words.

Learn to simplify complex information in visually appealing graphics.

4. **Create graphics.** PowerPoint includes a variety of tools to help you simplify complex information or to transform a boring bulleted list into a visually appealing graphic. You can use PowerPoint's **Illustrations** tools in the **Insert** tab. The **SmartArt** graphic options in particular will help you create organization charts (*Hierarchy*), cycles and radials (*Cycle*), timelines (*Process*), as well as pyramids, matrixes, Venn diagrams, and more. With the **Chart** function in the **Illustrations** group, you can select 11 types of chart including line, pie, and bar charts. All of these tools require practice before you can create effective visuals. Remember that graphics should be easy to understand without overloading your audience with unnecessary details or too much text. In fact, it's a good idea to put such details in handouts rather than cluttering your slides with them.
5. **Add special effects.** To keep your audience focused on what you are discussing, use PowerPoint's **Animations** tab to control when objects or text appear on the screen. Animate points in a bulleted list to appear one at a time, for example, or the boxes (or circles) in a radial diagram to appear as you are discussing each box. Keep in mind that the first thing your audience sees on every slide should describe the slide's content. With motion paths and other animation options, you can move objects to different positions on the slide; or to minimize clutter, you can dim or remove them once they have served their purpose.

   In addition, as you move from slide to slide in a presentation, you can select transition effects, such as *Fade* or *Dissolve*. The animation and transition options range from subtle to flashy—choose them with care so that the visual delivery of your presentation doesn't distract from the content of your message. An option at this step is to purchase a PowerPoint add-in product, such as Adobe Ovation or Presenter, that can add professional-looking special effects to your presentation with very little effort.
6. **Create hyperlinks to approximate the Web browsing experience.** Make your presentation more interactive and intriguing by connecting your PowerPoint presentation, via hyperlinks, to other sources that provide content that will enhance your presentation. You can hyperlink to (a) other slides within the presentation or in other PowerPoint files; (b) other programs that will open a second window that displays items such as spreadsheets, documents, and videos; and (c) if you have an Internet connection, Web sites.

When you finish discussing the hyperlinked source or watching the video that opened in a second window, close that window. Your hyperlinked PowerPoint slide will come into view again. In this way, you can break up the monotony of typical linear PowerPoint presentations. Instead, your hyperlinked show approximates the viewing experience of a Web user who enters a site through a main page or portal and then navigates at will to reach second- and third-level pages.

7. **Engage your audience by asking for interaction.** When you need audience response and feedback, interactive tools are useful. Audience response systems may be familiar to you from game shows, but they are also used for surveys and opinion polls, group decision making, voting, quizzes and tests, and many other applications. To interact with your audience, present polling questions. Audience members submit their individual or team responses using handheld devices ("clickers") read by a PowerPoint add-in program. The audience immediately sees a chart that displays the response results. If you would like to know more about audience response systems, visit the Web sites of commercial providers—for example, Audience Response Systems or Turning Technologies.

Internet options for slide presentations range from posting slides online to conducting a live Web conference with slides, narration, and speaker control.

8. **Move your presentation to the Internet.** You have a range of alternatives, from simple to complex, for moving your multimedia presentation to the Internet or your company's intranet. The simplest option is posting your slides online for others to access. Even if you are giving a face-to-face presentation, attendees appreciate these *electronic handouts* because they don't have to lug them home. The most complex option for moving your multimedia presentation to the Internet involves a Web conference or broadcast.

   Web presentations with slides, narration, and speaker control have emerged as a way for anyone who has access to the Internet to attend your presentation without leaving the office. For example, you could initiate a meeting via a conference call, narrate using a telephone, and have participants see your slides from the browsers on their computers. If you prefer, you could skip the narration and provide a prerecorded presentation. Web-based presentations have many applications, including providing access to updated training or sales data whenever needed.[17]

   Some businesses convert their PowerPoint presentations to common video formats. Alternatively, they save their slides as PDF documents or send PowerPoint shows (file extension *.ppsx), which open directly in **Slide Show** mode, ready to run. Simple slideshows are highly suitable for e-mailing; larger files can't be e-mailed. They need to be posted online in some form for streaming or downloading.

Polishing Your Delivery and Following Up

Once you have organized your presentation and prepared visuals, you are ready to practice delivering it. You will feel more confident and appear more professional if you know more about various delivery methods and techniques to use before, during, and after your presentation.

Choosing a Delivery Method

Presentations delivered using the "notes" method are more convincing than presentations that are memorized or read.

Inexperienced speakers often believe that they must memorize an entire presentation to be effective. Unless you are an experienced performer, however, you will sound wooden and unnatural. What's more, forgetting your place can be disastrous! That's why we don't recommend memorizing an entire oral presentation. However, memorizing significant parts—the introduction, the conclusion, and perhaps a meaningful quotation—can be dramatic and impressive.

If memorizing your business presentation won't work, is reading from a manuscript the best plan? Definitely not! Reading to an audience is boring and ineffective. Because reading suggests that you don't know your topic well, the audience loses confidence in your expertise. Reading also prevents you from maintaining eye contact. You can't see audience reactions; consequently, you can't benefit from feedback.

Neither memorizing nor reading creates very convincing business presentations. The best plan, by far, is to present *extemporaneously,* especially when you are displaying an electronic slideshow such as PowerPoint. Extemporaneous delivery means speaking freely, generally without notes, after preparation and rehearsing. It means that in your talk you comment on the electronic slideshow you have prepared and rehearsed several times. Remember, PowerPoint and other presentation software have replaced traditional outlines and notes. Reading notes or a manuscript in addition to PowerPoint slides will damage your credibility.

Extemporaneous delivery results in more convincing presentations than those that are memorized or read.

If you give a talk without PowerPoint, however, you may use note cards or an outline containing key sentences and major ideas. At the same time, beware of reading from a script. By preparing and then practicing with your notes, you can talk to your audience in a conversational manner. Your notes should be neither entire paragraphs nor single words. Instead, they should contain a complete sentence or two to introduce each major idea. Below the topic sentence(s), outline subpoints and illustrations. Note cards will keep you on track and prompt your memory, but only if you have rehearsed the presentation thoroughly.

"Fear of public speaking is quite common. If dressing up as Speaker Man makes you feel more confident, then so be it."

Combating Stage Fright

Nearly everyone experiences some stage fright when speaking before a group. "If you hear someone say he or she isn't nervous before a speech, you are talking either to a liar or a very boring speaker," says corporate speech consultant Dianna Booher.[18] Being afraid is quite natural and results from actual physiological changes occurring in your body. Faced with a frightening situation, your body responds with the fight-or-flight response, discussed more fully in Figure 12.11. You can learn to control and reduce stage fright, as well as to incorporate techniques for effective speaking, by using the following strategies and techniques before, during, and after your presentation.

Stage fright is both natural and controllable.

Before Your Presentation

Speaking in front of a group will become less daunting if you prepare adequately and practice sufficiently. Interacting with the audience and limiting surprises such as malfunctioning equipment will also add to your peace of mind. Review the following tips for a smooth start:

Thorough preparation, extensive rehearsal, and stress-reduction techniques can lessen stage fright.

- **Prepare thoroughly.** One of the most effective strategies for reducing stage fright is knowing your subject thoroughly. Research your topic diligently and prepare a careful sentence outline. Those who try to "wing it" usually suffer the worst butterflies—and make the worst presentations.
- **Rehearse repeatedly.** When you rehearse, practice your entire presentation, not just the first half. In PowerPoint you may print out speaker's notes, an outline, or a handout featuring miniature slides, which are excellent for practice. If you don't use an electronic slideshow, place your outline sentences on separate note cards. You may also wish to include transitional sentences to help you move to the next topic as you practice. Rehearse alone or before friends and family.

FIGURE 12.11 **Conquer Stage Fright With These Techniques**

Ever get nervous before giving a speech? Everyone does! And it's not all in your head, either. When you face something threatening or challenging, your body reacts in what psychologists call the *fight-or-flight response*. This physical reflex provides your body with increased energy to deal with threatening situations. It also creates those sensations—dry mouth, sweaty hands, increased heartbeat, and stomach butterflies—that we associate with stage fright. The fight-or-flight response arouses your body for action—in this case, making a presentation.

Because everyone feels some form of apprehension before speaking, it is impossible to eliminate the physiological symptoms altogether. However, you can reduce their effects with the following techniques:

- **Breathe deeply.** Use deep breathing to ease your fight-or-flight symptoms. Inhale to a count of ten, hold this breath to a count of ten, and exhale to a count of ten. Concentrate on your counting and your breathing; both activities reduce your stress.
- **Convert your fear.** Don't view your sweaty palms and dry mouth as evidence of fear. Interpret them as symptoms of exuberance, excitement, and enthusiasm to share your ideas.
- **Know your topic and come prepared.** Feel confident about your topic. Select a topic that you know well and that is relevant to your audience. Test your equipment and arrive with time to spare.
- **Use positive self-talk.** Remind yourself that you know your topic and are prepared. Tell yourself that the audience is on your side—because it is! Moreover, most speakers appear to be more confident than they feel. Make this apparent confidence work for you.
- **Take a sip of water.** Drink some water to alleviate your dry mouth and constricted voice box, especially if you are talking for more than 15 minutes.
- **Shift the spotlight to your visuals.** At least some of the time the audience will be focusing on your slides, transparencies, handouts, or whatever you have prepared—and not totally on you.
- **Ignore any stumbles.** Don't apologize or confess your nervousness. If you keep going, the audience will forget any mistakes quickly.
- **Don't admit you are nervous.** Never tell your audience that you are nervous. They will probably never notice!
- **Feel proud when you finish.** You will be surprised at how good you feel when you finish. Take pride in what you have accomplished, and your audience will reward you with applause and congratulations. Your body, of course, will call off the fight-or-flight response and return to normal!

Also try an audio or video recording of your rehearsals so that you can evaluate your effectiveness.

- **Time yourself.** Most audiences tend to get restless during longer talks. Therefore, try to complete your presentation in no more than 20 minutes. If you have a time limit, don't go over it. Set a simple kitchen timer during your rehearsal to keep track of time. Better yet, PowerPoint offers a function **Rehearse Timings** in the **Slide Show** tab that can measure the length of your talk as you practice.
- **Dress professionally.** Dressing professionally for a presentation will make you look more credible to your audience. You will also feel more confident. If you are not used to professional attire, practice wearing it or you may appear uncomfortable in formal wear.
- **Request a lectern.** Every beginning speaker needs the security of a high desk or lectern from which to deliver a presentation. It serves as a note holder and a convenient place to rest wandering hands and arms. Don't, however, lean on it. Eventually you will want to interact with the audience without any physical barriers.
- **Check the room.** If you are using a computer, a projector, or sound equipment, be certain they are operational. Before you start, check electrical outlets and the position of the viewing screen. Ensure that the seating arrangement is appropriate to your needs.
- **Greet members of the audience.** Try to make contact with a few members of the audience when you enter the room, while you are waiting to be introduced, or when you walk to the podium. Your body language should convey friendliness, confidence, and enjoyment.
- **Practice stress reduction.** If you feel tension and fear while you are waiting your turn to speak, use stress-reduction techniques, such as deep breathing. Additional techniques to help you conquer stage fright are presented in Figure 12.11.

During Your Presentation

To stay in control during your talk, to build credibility, and to engage your audience, follow these time-tested guidelines for effective speaking:

Eye contact, a moderate tone of voice, and natural movements enhance a presentation.

- **Begin with a pause.** When you first approach the audience, take a moment to make yourself comfortable. Establish your control of the situation.
- **Present your first sentence from memory.** By memorizing your opening, you can immediately establish rapport with the audience through eye contact. You will also sound confident and knowledgeable.
- **Maintain eye contact.** If the size of the audience overwhelms you, pick out two individuals on the right and two on the left. Talk directly to these people. Don't ignore listeners in the back of the room. If you are presenting to a smaller audience, try to make genuine, not fleeting eye contact with everyone in the room at least once during your presentation.
- **Control your voice and vocabulary.** This means speaking in moderated tones but loudly enough to be heard. Eliminate verbal static, such as *ah, er, like, you know,* and *um*. Silence is preferable to meaningless fillers when you are thinking of your next idea.
- **Skip the apologies.** Don't begin with a weak opening, such as *I will not take much time. I know you are busy.* Or: *I know you have heard this before, but we need to review it anyway.* Or: *I had trouble with my computer and the slides, so bear with me.* Unless the issue is blatant, such as not being able to load the presentation or make the projector work, apologies are counterproductive. Focus on your presentation. Dynamic speakers never say they are sorry.
- **Put the brakes on.** Many novice speakers talk too rapidly, displaying their nervousness and making it very difficult for audience members to understand their ideas. Slow down and listen to what you are saying.
- **Incorporate pauses when appropriate.** Silence can be effective especially when you are transitioning from one point to another. Pauses are also effective in giving the audience time to absorb an important point.

"This is where you all went wrong, causing my plan to fail."

- **Move naturally.** If you have a lectern, don't remain glued to it. Move about casually and naturally. Avoid fidgeting with your clothing, hair, or items in your pockets. Do not roll up your sleeves or put your hands in your pockets. Learn to use your body to express a point.
- **Use visual aids effectively.** You should discuss and interpret each visual aid for the audience. Move aside as you describe it so that it can be seen fully. Use a pointer if necessary, but steady your hand if it is shaking.
- **Avoid digressions.** Stick to your outline and notes. Don't suddenly include clever little anecdotes or digressions that occur to you on the spot. If it is not part of your rehearsed material, leave it out so that you can finish on time. Remember, too, that your audience may not be as enthralled with your topic as you are.
- **Summarize your main points and arrive at the high point of your talk.** Conclude your presentation by reiterating your main points or by emphasizing what you want the audience to think or do. Once you have announced your conclusion, proceed to it directly.
- **Show enthusiasm.** If you are not excited about your topic, how can you expect your audience to be? Show passion for your topic through your tone, facial expressions, and gestures. Adding variety to your voice also helps to keep your audience alert and interested.

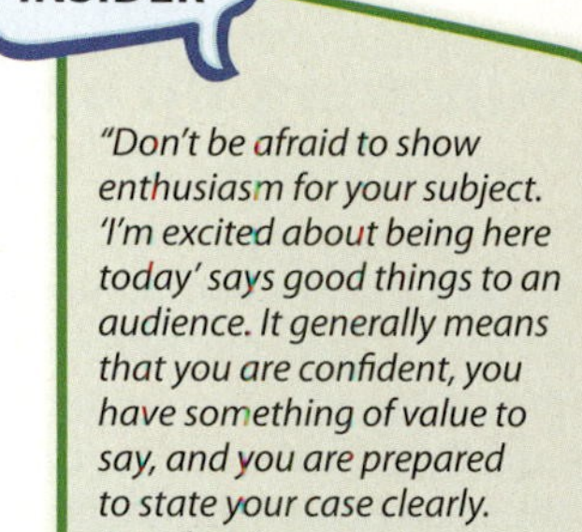

"Don't be afraid to show enthusiasm for your subject. 'I'm excited about being here today' says good things to an audience. It generally means that you are confident, you have something of value to say, and you are prepared to state your case clearly. Boredom is contagious."

—Dianna Booher, communication consultant and author

After Your Presentation

The time to answer questions, distribute handouts, and reiterate main points is after a presentation.

As you are concluding you presentation, handle questions and answers competently and provide handouts, if appropriate. Try the following techniques:

- **Distribute handouts.** If you prepared handouts with data the audience will not need during the presentation, pass them out when you finish.
- **Encourage questions.** If the situation permits a question-and-answer period, announce it at the beginning of your presentation. Then, when you finish, ask for questions. Set a time limit for questions and answers. If you don't know the answer to a question, don't make one up or panic. Instead, offer to find the answer within a day or two. If you make such a promise to your audience, be sure to follow through.
- **Repeat questions.** Although the speaker may hear the question, audience members often do not. Begin each answer by repeating the question. This also gives you thinking time. Then, direct your answer to the entire audience.
- **Reinforce your main points.** You can use your answers to restate your primary ideas (*I'm glad you brought that up because it gives me a chance to elaborate on . . .*). In answering questions, avoid becoming defensive or debating the questioner.
- **Keep control.** Don't allow one individual to take over. Keep the entire audience involved.
- **Avoid *Yes, but* answers.** The word *but* immediately cancels any preceding message. Try replacing it with *and*. For example, *Yes, X has been tried. And Y works even better because . . . .*
- **End with a summary and appreciation.** To signal the end of the session before you take the last question, say something like *We have time for just one more question*. As you answer the last question, try to work it into a summary of your main points. Then, express appreciation to the audience for the opportunity to talk with them.

www.cengagebrain.com

Available with an access code, these eResources will help you prepare for exams:

- **Chapter Review Quizzes**
- **Personal Language Trainer**
- **PowerPoint Slides**
- **Flash Cards**

Summing Up and Looking Forward

This chapter presented techniques for making effective oral presentations. Good presentations begin with analyses of your audience and your purpose. Organizing the content involves preparing an effective introduction, body, and closing. The introduction should capture the listener's attention, identify the speaker, establish credibility, and preview the main points. The body should discuss two to four main points, with appropriate explanations, details, and verbal signposts to guide listeners. The conclusion should review the main points, provide a final focus, and allow the speaker to leave the podium gracefully. You can improve audience rapport by using effective imagery including analogies, metaphors, similes, personal anecdotes, statistics, and worst- and best-case scenarios. In illustrating a presentation, use simple, easily understood visual aids to emphasize and clarify main points. If you choose PowerPoint, you can enhance the presentation by using templates, layout designs, bullet points, and multimedia elements. Don't allow your PowerPoint slides, however, to "steal your thunder."

Before delivering your presentation, rehearse repeatedly. Check your equipment before the talk. During the presentation consider beginning with a pause and presenting your first sentence from memory. Dress professionally, make eye contact, control your voice, show enthusiasm for your topic, speak and move naturally, and avoid digressions. After your talk distribute handouts and answer questions. End gracefully and express appreciation.

The final two chapters of this book focus on your ultimate goal—getting a job or advancing in your career. In Chapter 13 you will learn how to write a persuasive résumé and other employment documents. In Chapter 14 you will discover how to ace an employment interview.

Critical Thinking

1. Why should even practiced speakers plan their presentations when addressing a business audience instead of just "winging it"?
2. "Communicate—don't decorate." This principle is one of 20 rules that graphic designer and educator Timothy Samara discusses in his book *Design Elements: A Graphic Style Manual*. How could you apply this principle to the design of your PowerPoint presentations?
3. What are detractors saying about PowerPoint, and why are they condemning it? Can you present a counterargument?
4. Communication expert Dianna Booher believes that "Humor anchors key points" and "makes your message memorable."[19] Discuss the role of humor in business presentations.
5. Communication expert Dianna Booher claims that enthusiasm is infectious and "boredom is contagious."[20] What does this mean for you as a presenter? How can you avoid being a boring speaker?

Chapter Review

6. How do speaking skills affect promotions and career success?

7. Why is redundancy—usually condemned in business communication—a smart strategy in organizing the main points in the introduction, body, and conclusion of your presentation?

8. How can you learn more about an unfamiliar audience before creating your presentation?

9. Can speaking skills be improved, or do we have to be "born" communicators?

10. Why are analyzing an audience and anticipating its reaction particularly important before business presentations, and how would you adapt to the four categories of listeners?

11. In preparing an oral presentation, you can reduce fears and lay a foundation for a professional performance by focusing on what five areas?

12. Why should speakers deliver the first sentence from memory?

13. List suggestions that would ensure that your nonverbal messages reinforce your verbal messages effectively.

14. Name specific advantages and disadvantages of multimedia presentation software.

15. How can speakers overcome stage fright? Name six helpful techniques.

Activities and Cases

12.1 Critiquing a Speech

Your Task. Search online for a speech that was delivered by a significant businessperson or a well-known political figure. Consider watching Steve Jobs' excellent 15-minute "Stay Hungry, Stay Foolish" commencement speech at Stanford University on YouTube. Transcripts of that well-known speech by the CEO of Apple, Inc., are also available online. Write a memo report or give a short presentation to your class critiquing the speech in terms of the following:

a. Effectiveness of the introduction, body, and conclusion
b. Evidence of effective overall organization
c. Use of verbal signposts to create coherence
d. Emphasis of two to four main points
e. Effectiveness of supporting facts (use of examples, statistics, quotations, and so forth)
f. Focus on audience benefits
g. Enthusiasm for the topic

12.2 Knowing Your Audience

Your Task. Select a recent issue of *Fortune, The Wall Street Journal, Fast Company, Bloomberg BusinessWeek, The Economist*, or another business periodical approved by your instructor. Based on your analysis of your classmates, select an article that will appeal to them and that you can relate to their needs. Submit to your instructor a one-page summary that includes the following: (a) the author, article title, source, issue date, and page reference; (b) a one-paragraph article summary; (c) a description of why you believe the article will appeal to your classmates; and (d) a summary of how you can relate the article to their needs.

12.3 Hiring a Business Tycoon Who Is an Accomplished Public Speaker

Have you ever wondered why famous business types, politicians, athletes, and other celebrities can command high speaking fees? How much are they really making per appearance, and what are factors that may justify their sometimes exorbitant fees? You may also wonder how a motivational speaker or corporate trainer might benefit you and your class or your campus community. Searching for and selecting an expert is easy online with several commercial speaker bureaus vying for clients. All services provide detailed speaker bios, areas of expertise, and fees. One agency even features video previews of its clients.

The three preeminent agencies for booking talent are All American Talent & Celebrity Network, BigSpeak, and Brooks International Speakers & Entertainment Bureau. All American represents, for example, the likes of economist Nouriel Roubini, Donald Trump, Jack Welch, Richard Branson, and Suze Orman. BigSpeak standouts are Deepak Chopra, Dr. Susan Love, and distance swimmer Diana Nyad. Brooks International features financier and philanthropist Mike Milken and TV commentator and personal finance expert Terry Savage, among others. Imagine that you have a budget of up to $100,000 to hire a well-known public speaker.

Your Task. In teams or individually, select a business-related category of speaker by visiting one of the speaker bureaus online. For example, choose several prominent personal finance gurus (Orman, Savage, and others) or successful entrepreneurs and venture capitalists (Branson, Trump, Jack Welch, and so forth). Other categories could include motivational speakers, philanthropists, or famous economists. Study their bios for clues to their expertise and accomplishments. Comparing at least three, come up with a set of qualities that apparently make these individual sought-after speakers. Consider how those qualities could enlighten you and your peers. To enrich your experience and enhance your knowledge, watch videos of your chosen speakers on YouTube, if available. Check talent agencies, personal Web sites, and Facebook for further information. Write a memo report about your speaker group, or present your findings orally, with or without PowerPoint. If your instructor directs, recommend your favorite speaker and give reasons for your decision.

WEB

TEAM

12.4 Twitter: Follow Your Favorite Entrepreneur or Tycoon

Your Task. Go to **http://twitter.com** and sign up for a Twitter account if you don't have one yet, so that you can follow businesspeople and examine the topics they like to tweet about. In the **Search** window on top of the page, enter the name of the businessperson whose tweets you wish to follow. Donald Trump, Jack Welch, Richard Branson, Suze Orman, Guy Kawasaki, and other well-known businesspeople are avid Twitter users. Over the course of a few days, read the tweets of your favorite expert. After a while, you should be able to discern certain trends and areas of interest. Note whether and how your subject responds to queries from followers. What are his or her favorite topics? Report your findings to the class, verbally with notes or using PowerPoint. If you find particularly intriguing tweets and links, share them with the class.

WEB

12.5 Exploring the New World of Web Conferencing

Your boss at the Home Realty Company is interested in learning more about Web conferencing but doesn't have time to do the research herself. She asks you to find out the following:

a. In terms of revenue, how big is the Web conferencing industry?
b. Who are the leading providers of Web conferencing tools?
c. What are the typical costs associated with holding a Web conference?
d. What kind of equipment does Web conferencing usually require?
e. How are other realtors using Web conferencing?

Your Task. Using electronic databases and the Internet, locate articles and Web sites that will provide the information your boss has outlined. Be prepared to role-play an informal presentation to your boss in which you begin with an introduction, answer the four questions in the body, and present a conclusion.

TEAM

12.6 Overcoming Stage Fright

What scares you the most about making a presentation before class? Being tongue-tied? Fearing all eyes on you? Messing up? Forgetting your ideas and looking silly?

Your Task. Discuss the previous questions as a class. Then, in groups of three or four, talk about ways to overcome these fears. Your instructor may ask you to write a memo (individual or collective) summarizing your suggestions, or you may break out of your small groups and report your best ideas to the entire class.

12.7 Investigating Oral Communication in Your Field

Your Task. Interview one or two individuals in your professional field. How is oral communication important in this profession? Does the need for oral skills change as one advances? What suggestions can these people make to newcomers to the field for developing proficient oral communication skills? Discuss your findings with your class.

12.8 Outlining an Oral Presentation

One of the hardest parts of preparing an oral presentation is developing the outline.

Your Task. Select an oral presentation topic from the list in Activity 12.15, or suggest an original topic. Prepare an outline for your presentation using the following format:

Title	
Purpose	
	I. INTRODUCTION
State your name	A.
Gain attention and involve the audience	B.
Establish credibility	C.
Preview main points	D.
Transition	
	II. BODY
Main point	A.
Illustrate, clarify, contrast	1.
	2.
	3.
Transition	
Main point	B.
Illustrate, clarify, contrast	1.
	2.
	3.
Transition	
Main point	C.
Illustrate, clarify, contrast	1.
	2.
	3.
Transition	
	III. CONCLUSION
Summarize main points	A.
Provide final focus or take-away	B.
Encourage questions	C.

WEB

12.9 YouTube: Critiquing a Satirical Clip Lampooning PowerPoint

Your Task. Watch Don McMillan's now famous YouTube hit "Life After Death by PowerPoint" from 2008 or the expanded version "Life After Death by PowerPoint 2010." Which specific PowerPoint ills is McMillan satirizing? Write a brief summary of the short clips for discussion in class. With your peers, discuss whether the bad habits the YouTube videos parody correspond with design principles introduced in this chapter.

WEB

E-MAIL

12.10 Evaluating and Outlining Podcasts of Apple Keynotes

To learn from the presentation skills of one of the best corporate speakers today, visit iTunes and watch one or more of the Apple keynotes posted there. They mostly cover Steve Jobs' famous product launches, including that of the iPad, and other important announcements.

Your Task. Download iTunes if you don't yet have a copy of the software and search for *apple keynotes.* If your instructor directs, watch one of the keynotes and outline it. You may also be asked to critique Steve Jobs' presentation techniques based on the guidelines you have studied in this chapter. Jot down your observations either as notes for a classroom discussion or to serve as a basis for an informative memo or e-mail.

12.11 Creating an Oral Presentation: Outline Your Job Duties

What if you had to create a presentation for your classmates and instructor, or perhaps a potential recruiter, that describes the multiple tasks you fulfill at work? Could you do it in a five-minute PowerPoint presentation?

Your instructors, for example, may wear many hats. Most academics (a) teach; (b) conduct research to publish; and (c) provide service to the department, college, university, and community. Can you see how those aspects of their profession lend themselves to an outline of primary slides (teaching, publishing, service) and second-level slides (instructing undergraduate and graduate classes, presenting workshops, and giving lectures under the *teaching* label)?

Your Task. Now it's your turn to introduce the duties of a current position or a past job, volunteer activity, or internship in a brief, simple, yet well-designed PowerPoint presentation. Your goal is to inform your audience of your job duties in a three- to five-minute talk. Use animation features and graphics where appropriate. Your instructor may show you a completed example of this project.

12.12 Creating an Oral Presentation: Pitch to Guy Kawasaki

Venture capitalist and angel investor Guy Kawasaki believes that persuasive PowerPoint presentations should be no more than 10 slides long, last 20 minutes at most, and contain 30-point fonts or bigger (the 10/20/30 rule). Kawasaki is convinced that presentations deviating from this rule will fall short of their purpose, which is typically to reach some type of agreement.

Could you interest an investor such as Guy Kawasaki in your business idea? The venture capitalist believes that if you must use more than 10 slides to explain your business, you probably don't have one. Furthermore, Kawasaki claims that the 10 topics a venture capitalist cares about are the following:

1. Problem
2. Your solution
3. Business model
4. Underlying magic/technology
5. Marketing and sales
6. Competition
7. Team
8. Projections and milestones
9. Status and time line
10. Summary and call to action

Your Task. Dust off that start-up fantasy you may have, and get to work. Prepare a slideshow that would satisfy Kawasaki's 10/20/30 rule: In 10 slides and a presentation of no more than 20 minutes, address the 10 topics that venture capitalists care about. Make sure that the fonts on your slides are at least 30 points in size.

12.13 Delivering an Impromptu Elevator Speech

"Can you pass the elevator test?" asks presentation whiz Garr Reynolds in a new twist on the familiar scenario.[21] He suggests this technique as an aid in sharpening your core message. In this exercise you need to pitch your idea in a few brief moments instead of the 20 minutes you had been granted with your vice president of product marketing. You arrive at her door for your appointment as she is leaving, coat and briefcase in hand. Something has come up. This meeting is a huge opportunity for you if you want to get the OK from the executive team. Could you sell your idea during the elevator ride and the walk to the parking lot? Reynolds asks. Although this scenario may never happen, you will possibly be asked to shorten a presentation, say, from an hour to 30 minutes or from 20 minutes to 5 minutes. Could you make your message tighter and clearer on the fly?

Your Task. Take a business idea you may have, a familiar business topic you care about, or a promotion or raise you wish to request in a time of tight budgets. Create a spontaneous two- to five-minute speech making a good case for your core message. Even though you won't have much time to think about the details of your speech, you should be sufficiently familiar with the topic to boil it down and yet be persuasive.

12.14 Researching Fortune List Information

Your Task. Using an electronic database, perform a search to learn how *Fortune* magazine determines which companies make its annual lists. Research the following lists. Then organize and present a five- to ten-minute informative talk to your class.

a. Fortune 500
b. Global 500
c. 100 Best Companies to Work For
d. America's Most Admired Companies

12.15 Choosing a Topic for an Oral Presentation

Your Task. Select a report topic from the following suggestions or from the expanded list of Report Topics at **www.cengagebrain.com.** Prepare a five- to ten-minute oral presentation. Consider yourself an expert who has been called in to explain some aspect of the topic before a group of interested people. Because your time is limited, prepare a concise yet forceful presentation with effective visual aids.

a. How can businesses benefit from Twitter? Cite specific examples in your chosen field.
b. Which is financially more beneficial to a business, leasing or buying company cars?
c. Tablet computers are eroding the market share previously held by laptops and netbooks. Which brands are businesses embracing and why? Which features are a must-have?
d. What kind of marketing works with students on college campuses? Word of mouth? Internet advertising? Free samples? How do students prefer to get information about goods and services?
e. How can consumers protect themselves from becoming victims of identity theft?

f. How could the lunch line in a school cafeteria be redesigned to encourage healthier menu choices?
g. Should students be required to pay for college athletic budgets in their fees?
h. How could an intercultural training program be initiated in your school?
i. Companies usually do not admit shortcomings. However, some admit previous failures and use them to strategic advantage. For example, Domino's Pizza ran a commercial with its customers saying its pizza tasted like ketchup and cardboard. Find three or more examples of companies admitting weaknesses and draw conclusions from their strategies. Would you recommend this as a sound marketing ploy?
j. How can students and other citizens contribute to conserving gasoline and other fossil fuel in order to save money and help slow global climate change?
k. What is the career outlook in a field of your choice? Consider job growth, compensation, and benefits. What kind of academic or other experience is typically required in your field?
l. How could students in the United States be motivated to learn languages and study abroad in greater numbers?
m. What is telecommuting, and for what kinds of workers is it an appropriate work alternative?
n. What criteria should parents use in deciding whether their young child should attend a public, private, or parochial school, or be home-schooled?
o. What is the economic outlook for a given product, such as hybrid cars, laptop computers, digital cameras, fitness equipment, or a product of your choice?
p. What are the Webby Awards, and what criteria do the judges use to evaluate Web sites?
q. What franchise would offer the best investment opportunity for an entrepreneur in your area?
r. How should a job candidate dress for an interview?
s. What should a guide to proper cell phone use include?
t. Are internships worth the effort?
u. Why should a company have a written e-mail and social media policy?
v. Where should your organization hold its next convention?
w. What is the outlook for real estate (commercial or residential) investment in your area?
x. What do the personal assistants for celebrities do, and how does one become a personal assistant? (Investigate the Association of Celebrity Personal Assistants.)
y. What kinds of gifts are appropriate for businesses to give clients and customers during the holiday season?
z. What scams are on the Federal Trade Commission's List of Top 10 Consumer Scams, and how can consumers avoid falling for them?

WEB

12.16 Creepy Crawlies—Unwanted Souvenirs

North America is rapidly becoming infested with bedbugs, blood-sucking pests that seem to be experiencing a comeback. Hotels in particular, but many private homes and business offices as well, have fallen victim to the pesky insects. For example, *Time* magazine headquarters and former President Clinton's Manhattan offices have suffered infestations.

Recently, the nation's two largest pest extermination companies, Orkin LLC and Terminix, "crowned" America's most infested cities. Not surprisingly, they are densely populated urban areas that attract many tourists: New York City, Chicago, Los Angeles, and Washington, DC. Strangely enough, the most infested state is Ohio. Canada, too, has a bedbug problem, most prominently in Vancouver, BC.[22]

You work for a midsized local boutique hotel that is not part of a national chain. You have just read an alarming article about bedbugs conquering the United States. As far as you know, your hotel has not yet been affected, but after what you've read, it may be only a question of time. Your boss suggests that you prepare a briefing for hotel staff to alert the employees to the problem. You decide to check the Orkin and Terminix Web sites. In addition to an article search, you may want to visit the Web sites of the National Pesticide Information Center, the U.S. Centers for Disease Control and Prevention, and the U.S. Environmental Protection Agency.

Consider these and similar questions: How serious is the situation? Who or what is affected? How do the pests spread? How does an infestation manifest itself? What has caused the reappearance of bedbugs after decades of dormancy? Can your employer do anything to prevent an infestation? Once infested, what can a hotel do to eradicate the pests?

Your Task. Create an informative PowerPoint presentation that briefs the hotel staff and addresses the issues raised here.

12.17 Self-Contained Multimedia Activity: Creating a PowerPoint Presentation (No additional research required)

You are a consultant who has been hired to improve the effectiveness of corporate trainers. These trainers frequently make presentations to employees on topics such as conflict management, teamwork, time management, problem solving, performance appraisals, and employment interviewing. Your goal is to teach these trainers how to make better presentations.

Your Task. Create six visually appealing slides. Base the slides on the following content, which will be spoken during the presentation titled "Effective Employee Training." The comments shown here are only a portion of a longer presentation.

Trainers have two options when they make presentations. The first option is to use one-way communication in which the trainer basically dumps the information on the employees and leaves. The second option is to use a two-way audience involvement approach. The two-way approach can accomplish many purposes, such as helping the trainer connect with the employees, helping the trainer reinforce key points, increasing the employees' retention rates, and changing the pace and adding variety. The two-way approach also encourages employees to get to know each other better. Because today's employees demand more than just a "talking head," trainers must engage their audiences by involving them in a two-way dialogue.

When you include interactivity in your training sessions, choose approaches that suit your delivery style. Also, think about which options your employees would be likely to respond to most positively. Let's consider some interactivity approaches now. Realize, though, that these ideas are presented to help you get your creative juices flowing. After I present the list, we will think about situations in which these options might be effective. We will also brainstorm to come up with creative ideas we can add to this list.

- Ask employees to guess at statistics before revealing them.
- Ask an employee to share examples or experiences.
- Ask a volunteer to help you demonstrate something.
- Ask the audience to complete a questionnaire or worksheet.
- Ask the audience to brainstorm or list something as fast as possible.
- Ask a variety of question types to achieve different purposes.
- Invite the audience to work through a process or examine an object.
- Survey the audience.
- Pause to let the audience members read something to themselves.
- Divide the audience into small groups to discuss an issue.

12.18 Improving the Design and Content of PowerPoint Slides

Your Task. Identify ways to improve the design and content of the three slides presented in Figure 12.12. Classify your comments under the following categories: (a) color choices, (b) font choice including style and point size, (c) 6-x-6 rule, (d) listings in parallel grammatical form, (e) consistent capitalization and punctuation, and (f) graphics and images. Identify what needs to be improved and exactly how you would improve it. For example, if you identify category (d) as an area needing improvement, your answer would include a revision of the listing. When you finish, your instructor may show you a revised set of slides.

FIGURE 12.12 **PowerPoint Slides Needing Revision**

Webcasting Basics

- Inexpensive way to hold conferences and meetings
- Presenter broadcasts via one of many Webcast platforms available today.
- Participants access meeting from anywhere via Internet connection and free software.
- Capabilities include live Q&A sessions and live polls of audience members.
- Those who missed the event can access stored presentations when convenient

Voice Quality During Webcast

- The Three Ps are critical
  - Pacing
  - Pausing
  - Passion

Webcasting Pointers

- To engage audience early on, tell personal stories.
- Standing while webcasting adds energy to your voice.
- Remember, smiles are audible.
- Change slides frequently.
- Prepare a brief summary conclusion to follow Q&A session.

Video Resources

Video Library 1: ***Building Workplace Skills***
Effective On-the-Job Oral Presentations
Watch this video to see how businesspeople apply a writing process in developing a persuasive oral presentation.

Grammar/Mechanics Checkup—12

Capitalization

Review Sections 3.01–3.16 in the Grammar/Mechanics Handbook. Then study each of the following statements. Draw three underlines below any letter that should be capitalized. Draw a slash (/) through any capital letter that you wish to change to lowercase. Indicate in the space provided the number of changes you made in each sentence, and record the number of the G/M principle(s) illustrated. If you made no changes, write *0*. When you finish, compare your responses with those provided at the back of the book. If your responses differ, study carefully the principles in parentheses.

5 (3.01) **Example** The consumer product safety act was revised specifically to ensure the safety of Children's toys.

1. Employees of bank of america had to evacuate their Headquarters in suite 200 after the scottsdale fire department units arrived.
2. Americans are reluctant to travel to europe because of the weak dollar; however, more british and french citizens are traveling to the United States, according to Maurice Dubois, Vice President at Hilton hotels.
3. Once the Management Team and the Union members finally agreed, mayor Faria signed the Agreement.
4. The boston marathon is an annual sporting event hosted by the city of boston on patriot's day.
5. Luis was disappointed when he learned that the university of new mexico eliminated italian from its curriculum; now he must take history, geography, and political science classes to learn about italy.
6. The most popular sites on the internet are those operated by google, facebook, and youtube.
7. According to a Federal Government report issued in january, any regulation of State and County banking must receive local approval.
8. The position of director of research must be filled before summer.
9. The Vice President of MegaTech Industries reported to the President that the securities and exchange commission was beginning an investigation of their Company.
10. My Uncle, who lives near surfrider beach in malibu, says that the Moon and Stars are especially brilliant on cool, clear nights.
11. Our marketing director met with Adrienne Hall, Manager of our advertising media department, to plan an Adwords campaign for google.
12. During the Fall our Faculty Advisor explored new exchange and semester-abroad opportunities in asia, australia, and china.
13. Last february my Father and I headed south to visit the summer waves water park located on jekyll island in georgia.
14. On page 6 of my report, you will find a list of all instructors in our business division with Master's degrees.
15. Please consult figure 5.1 in chapter 5 of the book *analysis of population growth* for the latest U.S. census bureau figures regarding non-english-speaking residents.

Editing Challenge—12

As the employee with the best communication skills, you are frequently asked to edit messages. The following outline of a presentation, written by your office manager, has problems with capitalization, grammar, punctuation, spelling, proofreading, number expression, and other writing techniques you have studied. He may need to submit this to management, and he asks you to clean it up. You may (a) use standard proofreading marks (see Appendix B) to correct the errors here or (b) download the document from **www.cengagebrain.com** and revise at your computer.

Your instructor may ask you to use the **Track Changes** feature in Word to show your editing comments. Turn on **Track Changes** on the **Review** tab. Click **Show Markup**. Place your cursor at an error, click **New Comment**, and key your edit in the bubble box provided. Study the guidelines in the Grammar/Mechanics Handbook as well as the lists of Confusing Words and Frequently Misspelled Words to sharpen your skills.

Developing an Office Recycling Plan

I. Introduction

Paper makes up about 40 percent of the solid waste stream in our City. By recycling our office paper we can help the Environment and save trees. Every ton of paper made from recycled fiber saves about 17 trees. It also saves about 25 gallons of Water, and reduces air pollution by an estimated 60 pounds. Here in our office we use a lot of white Paper. When Paper is recycled it goes into such products as tissue, paperboard, stationary, magazines, new office paper and other paper products. In interviewing 3 experts including Dr Walter Yang at the university of west virginia I learned how we can develop our own office recycling plan that could be implemented within 60 days.

II. Body

Companies can easily integrate Paper recycling into their normal business operations. One of the first steps is placing Recycling Bins next to employees desks. In addition the most successful programs conduct Seminars to educate employee. They also hire an Office Recycling Coordinator to facilitate the program. Some examples include the following:

- Bank of america initiated a program that grew from recycling 1,400 tons per year of computer and white paper to nearly fifteen thousand tons within 20 years. This Program saved nearly 500 thousand dollars in trash hauling fees.
- Hewlett Packard was able to divert 91 million pounds of Solid Waste, including 43 million pounds of Paper. H-P vice president william morris said that it saved more than 367,000 trees!

Our Vice President agrees with me that setting up a Office Recycling Program doesn't happen over night. It usually involves finding motivated employees, and educating the Office Staff. It may also require a Capitol investment in recycling bins.

A successful paper recycling plan will work best if we keep it very, very simple. First however we will need top Managements support. We must also provide sufficient instructions on what to put in, and what to keep out. We will need surveys, interviews and inspections to see how the Plan is working. Because the recycling bins and trash cans must be clean and items sorted properly we will need monitors checking to be sure every one is following instrutions.

III. Conclusion

Paper recycling is relatively easy to do, we just need to make a committment. We could start with 5 of our 15 offices to work out the best procedures. If you all agree I will meet with the CEO within 1 week. If Management supports the idea our goal should be to start a Program within 2 months. Our Companies disposal costs can decrease dramatically and we can help the Environment as well. Let's do it!

Communication Workshop

Techniques for Taking Part in Effective and Professional Team Presentations

You may have to join a team that will prepare and deliver an oral presentation. This can happen in the classroom and on the job. If you have been part of any team before, you also know that such projects can be very frustrating—particularly when some team members don't carry their weight or when members cannot resolve conflict. On the other hand, team projects can be harmonious and productive when members establish ground rules and follow these steps:

- **Prepare to work together.** First, you should (a) compare schedules of team members in order to set up the best meetings times, (b) plan to meet often, and (c) discuss how you will deal with team members who are not contributing to the project.
- **Plan the presentation.** Your team will need to agree on (a) the specific purpose of the presentation, (b) your audience, (c) the length of the presentation, (d) the types of visuals to include, and (e) the basic structure and content of the presentation.
- **Make assignments.** Once you decide what your presentation will cover, give each team member a written assignment that details his or her responsibilities for researching content, producing visuals, developing handouts, building transitions between segments, and showing up for team meetings and rehearsals.
- **Collect information.** To gather or generate information, teams can brainstorm together, conduct interviews, or search the Web for information. The team should decide on deadlines for collecting information and should discuss how to ensure the accuracy and currency of the information collected. Team members should exchange periodic progress reports on how their research is coming along.
- **Organize and develop the presentation.** Once your team has gathered all research, start working on the presentation. Determine the organization of the presentation, compose a draft in writing, and prepare PowerPoint slides and other visual aids. The team should meet often to discuss the presentation and to decide which team member will be responsible for delivering what parts of the presentation. Be sure each member builds a transition to the next presenter's topic and launches it smoothly. Strive for logical connections between segments.
- **Edit, rehearse, and evaluate.** Before you deliver the presentation, rehearse several times as a team. Make sure that transitions from speaker to speaker are smooth. For example, you might say, *Now that I have discussed how to prepare for the meeting, Ashley is going to discuss how to get the meeting started*. Decide who will be responsible for advancing slides during the presentation. Practice fielding questions if you plan to have a question-and-answer session. Decide how you are going to dress to look professional and competent. Run a spell-check and proofread your PowerPoint slides to ensure that the design, format, and vocabulary are consistent.
- **Deliver the presentation.** Show up on time for your presentation and wear appropriate attire. Deliver your part of the presentation with professionalism and enthusiasm. Remember that your audience is judging the team on its performance, not the individuals. Do what you can to make your team shine!

Career Application. Your boss named you to a team that is to produce an organizational five-year plan for your company. You know this assignment will end with an oral presentation to management and stockholders. Your first reaction is dismay. You have been on teams before in the classroom, and you know how frustrating they can be. However, you want to give your best, and you resolve to contribute positively to this team effort.

Your Task. In small groups or with the entire class, discuss effective collaboration. How can one contribute positively to a team? How should teams deal with members who aren't contributing or who have negative attitudes? What should team members do to ensure that the final presentation is professional and well coordinated?

Endnotes

[1] Hooey, B. (2005). Speaking for success! *Speaking success.* Retrieved from Toastmasters International Web site http://members.shaw.ca/toasted/speaking_succes.htm

[2] Korn, M. (2010, December 3). Wanted: Good speaking skills. *The Wall Street Journal.* Retrieved from Hire Education blog at http://blogs.wsj.com/hire-education/2010/12/03/wanted-good-speaking-skills

[3] Barrington, L., Casner-Lotto, J., & Wright, M. (2008, May). Are they really ready to work? The Conference Board. Retrieved from http://www.conference-board.org/pdf_free/BED-06-Workforce.pdf

[4] Vlessing, E. (2010, September 23). What Netflix CEO hopes U.S. won't notice. *The Hollywood Reporter.* Retrieved from http://www.hollywoodreporter.com/news/what-netflix-ceo-hopes-us-28218

[5] Dr. John J. Medina quoted in Reynolds, G. (2010). *Presentation Zen design.* Berkeley, CA: New Riders, p. 97.

[6] Pope, J. (2007, August 5). Business school requires PowerPoint. *Oakland Tribune*, p. 1. Retrieved from http://proquest.umi.com

[7] Journalist Tad Simons arguing against Ian Parker's *The New Yorker* article: Simons, T. (2001, July). When was the last time PowerPoint made you sing? *Presentations,* p. 6. Retrieved from http://www.presentations.com; Parker, I. (2001, May 28). Absolute PowerPoint: Can a software package edit our thoughts? *The New Yorker.* Retrieved from http://www.newyorker.com/archive/2001/05/28/010528fa_fact_parker; see also Tufte, E. R. (2006). *The cognitive style of PowerPoint: Pitching out corrupts within.* Cheshire, CT: Graphics Press.

[8] Atkinson, C. (2008). *Beyond bullet points* (2nd ed.). Redmond, WA: Microsoft Press.

[9] Reynolds, G. (2008). *Presentation Zen.* Berkeley, CA: New Riders, p. 220. See also Reynolds, G. (2010). *Presentation Zen design.* Berkeley, CA: New Riders.

[10] Booher, D. (2003). *Speak with confidence: Powerful presentations that inform, inspire, and persuade.* New York: McGraw-Hill Professional, p. 126. See also http://www.indezine.com/ideas/prescolors.html

[11] Bates, S. (2005). *Speak like a CEO: Secrets for commanding attention and getting results.* New York: McGraw-Hill Professional, p. 113.

[12] Sommerville, J. (n. d.). The seven deadly sins of PowerPoint Presentations. About.com: Entrepreneurs. Retrieved from http://entrepreneurs.about.com/cs/marketing/a/7sinsofppt.htm

[13] Gallo, C. (2010). *The presentation secrets of Steve Jobs: How to be insanely great in front of any audience.* New York: McGraw-Hill, p. 194; Burrows, P., Grover, R., & Green, H. (2006, February 6). Steve Jobs' magic kingdom. *BusinessWeek,* p. 62. Retrieved from http://www.businessweek.com

[14] Kupsh, J. (2011, January 21). Presentation delivery guidelines to remember. *Training.* Retrieved from http://www.trainingmag.com/article/presentation-delivery-guidelines-remember

[15] PowerPoint pre-show checklist. (n.d.). TLC Creative Services. Retrieved from http://www.tlccreative.com/images/tutorials/PreShowChecklist.pdf

[16] Ellwood, J. (2004, August 4). Less PowerPoint, more powerful points, *The Times* (London), p. 6.

[17] Boeri, R. J. (2002, March). Fear of flying? Or the mail? Try the Web conferencing cure. *Emedia Magazine*, p. 49.

[18] Booher, D. (2003). *Speak with confidence.* New York: McGraw-Hill, p. 14.

[19] Ibid., p. 106.

[20] Ibid., p. 9.

[21] Reynolds, G. (2008). *Presentation Zen.* Berkeley, CA: New Riders, pp. 64ff.

[22] Based on Brennan, M. (2010, December 22). America's most bed bug-infested cities. *Forbes.* Retrieved from http://www.forbes.com/2010/12/22/worst-cities-bed-bugs-real-estate-personal-finance.html

Acknowledgments

p. 366 Office Insider cited in Dlugan, A. (2008, April 10). 10 ways your presentation skills generate career promotions. Six Minutes. Retrieved from http://sixminutes.dlugan.com/2008/04/10/career-promotions-presentation-skills

p. 368 Office Insider cited in Booher, D. (2003). On speaking. Quotes by Dianna Booher. Booher Consultants. Retrieved from http://www.booher.com/quotes.html#speaking

p. 377 Office Insider cited in Paradi, D. (2004). PowerPoint sucks! No it doesn't!! Think Outside The Slide. Retrieved from http://www.thinkoutsidetheslide.com/articles/powerpointnotsucks.htm

p. 385 Office Insider cited in Kupsh, J. (2010, November 4). 15 guidelines to effective presentations. *Training.* Retrieved from http://www.trainingmag.com/article/15-guidelines-effective-presentations

p. 389 Office Insider cited in Booher, D. (2003). On speaking. Quotes by Dianna Booher. Booher Consultants. Retrieved from http://www.booher.com/quotes.html#speaking

p. 384 Photo Essay (Is PowerPoint the Enemy?) based on Bumiller, E. (2010, April 26). We have met the enemy and he is PowerPoint. *The New York Times.* Retrieved from http://www.nytimes.com; Hammes, T. X. (2009, July). Essay: Dumb-dumb bullets. *Armed Forces Journal.* Retrieved from http://armedforcesjournal.com/2009/07/4061641; Burke, C. (2009, July 24). The TX Hammes PowerPoint challenge (essay contest). *Small Wars Journal.* Retrieved from http://smallwarsjournal.com/blog/2009/07/draft-draft-draftpowerpoint-1

UNIT 6

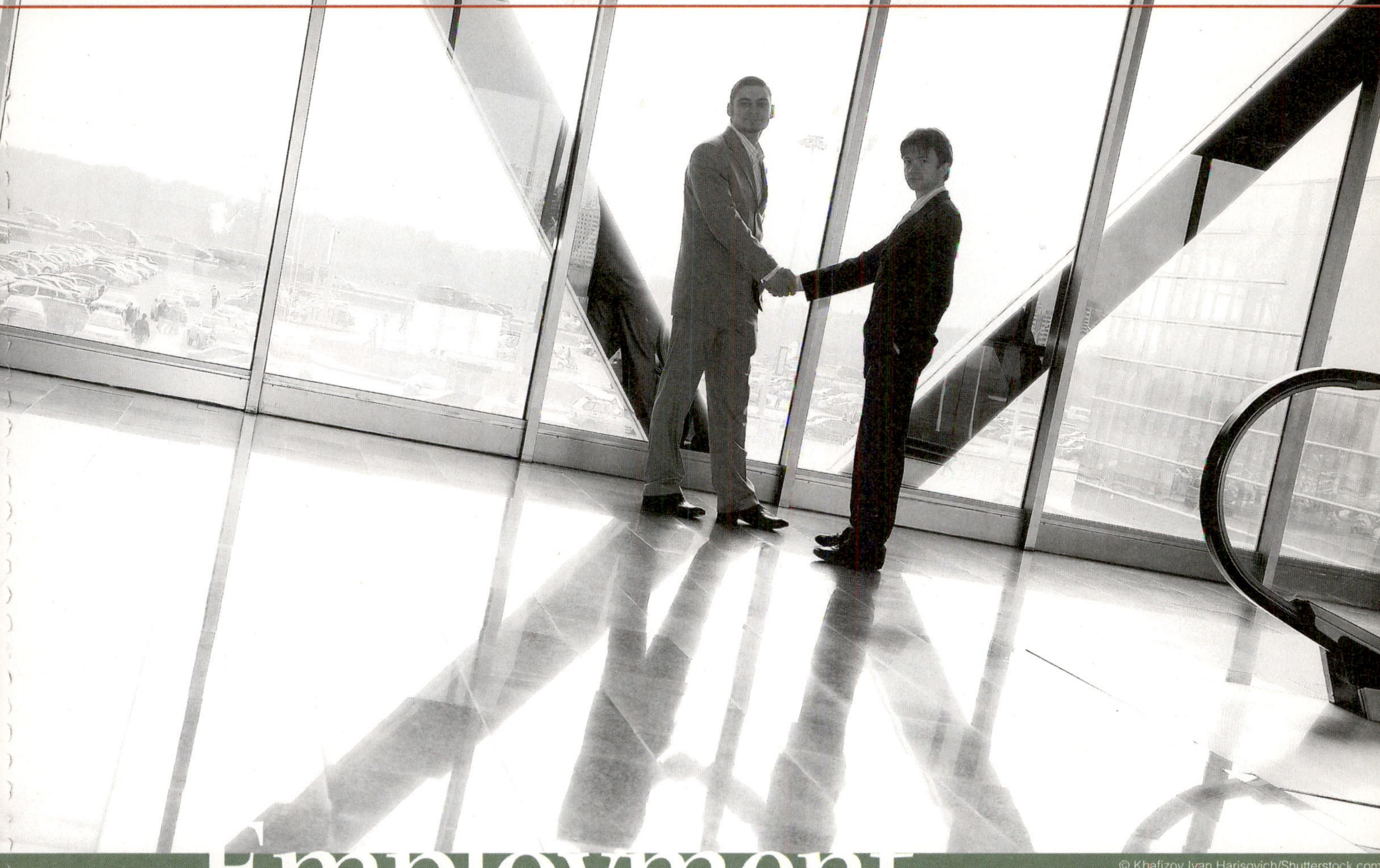

Employment Communication

CHAPTER 13

The Job Search, Résumés, and Cover Letters

Dmitriy Shironosov/Shutterstock.com

Go to **cengagebrain.com** and use your access code to unlock valuable student eResources.

OBJECTIVES

After studying this chapter, you should be able to

- Prepare for a successful job search by identifying your interests, evaluating your assets, recognizing employment trends, and choosing a career path.
- Apply both electronic and traditional job-search techniques.
- Appreciate the need to customize your résumé, and know whether to choose a chronological or a functional résumé format.
- Organize your qualifications and information into effective résumé categories.
- Describe techniques that optimize a résumé for today's technologies, including preparing a scannable résumé and an e-portfolio.
- Write a customized cover letter to accompany your résumé.

Preparing for a Successful Job Search

Today's graduates face a tough job market and a recessionary economy. Competition for employment is keener than ever in recent history. In addition, the Web has changed the way we look for jobs. Workplace experts point out that the Web has made job searching easier but also more challenging.[1] Because hundreds and perhaps thousands of candidates may be applying for an advertised position, you must work hard to be noticed and to outshine the competition. You must also look beyond the Web.

The better prepared you are, the more confident you will feel during your search. This chapter provides expert current advice in preparing for a job search, scouring the job market, writing a customized résumé, and developing a persuasive cover letter. What you learn here can lead to a successful job search and maybe even your dream job.

Finding a satisfying career requires learning about yourself, the job market, and the employment process.

You may think that the first step in finding a job is writing a résumé. Wrong! The job-search process actually begins long before you are ready to prepare your résumé. Regardless of the kind of employment you seek, you must invest time and effort getting ready. You can't hope to find the position of your dreams without (a) knowing yourself, (b) knowing the job market, and (c) knowing the employment process.

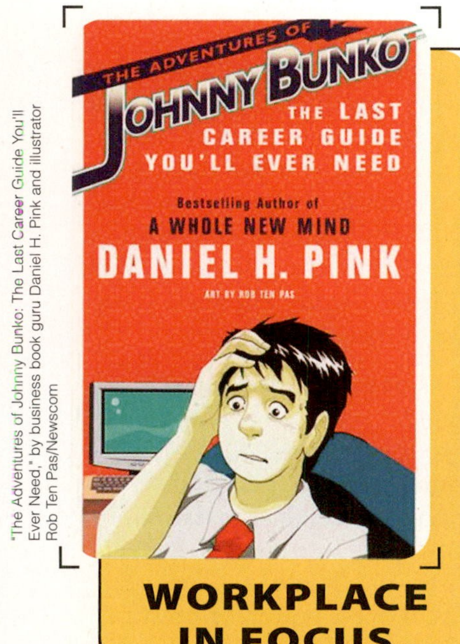

"The Adventures of Johnny Bunko: The Last Career Guide You'll Ever Need," by business book guru Daniel H. Pink and illustrator Rob Ten Pas/Newscom

WORKPLACE IN FOCUS

Given the box-office success of comic book heroes such as Batman and Spider Man, it is not surprising that the hottest career hero of the new generation is also a fictional character—Johnny Bunko. In the Japanese magna book *The Adventures of Johnny Bunko: The Last Career Guide You'll Ever Need*, anime character Johnny Bunko is a disillusioned office worker who longs to escape his dead-end job and find true occupational happiness. Aided by the spellbinding avatar Diana and a pair of magic chopsticks, Bunko embarks on an action-packed career journey that gives readers valuable insights into their own career paths. *Why should job seekers consult career guides when preparing for employment?*

Begin the job-search process by identifying your interests and goals and evaluating your qualifications. This self-evaluation will help you choose a suitable career path and job objective. At the same time, you should be studying the job market and becoming aware of substantial changes in the workplace and hiring techniques. You will want to understand how to use the latest Web tools along with traditional resources in your job search. Both the Web and traditional approaches are necessary to help you effectively search the open and hidden job markets. Once you know what jobs are available in your field, you will need to design a résumé and cover letter that you can customize for small businesses as well as for larger organizations. Following these steps, summarized in Figure 13.1 and described in this chapter, gives you a master plan for securing a job you really want.

FIGURE 13.1 The Employment Search

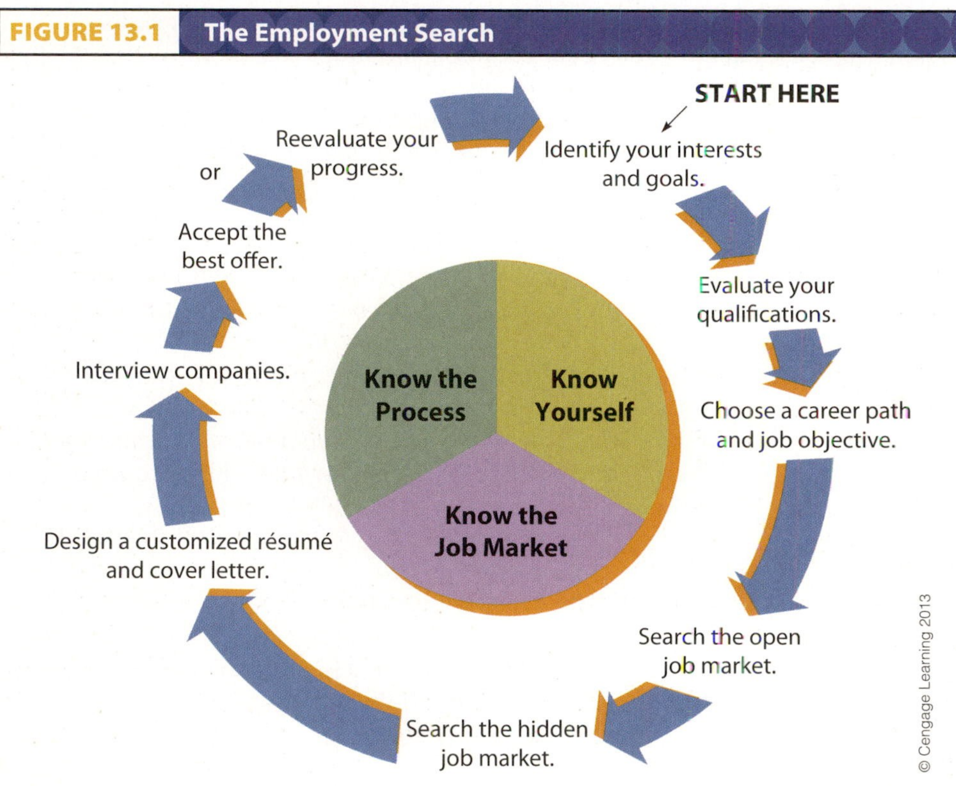

Identifying Your Interests and Goals

Analyzing your likes and dislikes helps you make wise employment decisions.

Buddha is believed to have said, "Your work is to discover your work and then with all your heart to give yourself to it." Following this ancient wisdom, you should begin the employment process with introspection. This means looking inside yourself to analyze what you like and dislike so that you can make good employment choices. Career counselors charge large sums for helping individuals learn about themselves. You can do the same kind of self-examination—without spending a dime. For guidance in choosing a career that eventually proves to be satisfying, answer the following questions. If you have already chosen a career path, think carefully about how your answers relate to that choice.

Answering specific questions can help you choose a career.

- What are you passionate about? Can you turn this passion into a career?
- Do you enjoy working with people, data, or things?
- Would you like to work for someone else or be your own boss?
- How important are salary, benefits, technology support, and job stability?
- How important are working environment, colleagues, and job stimulation?
- Would you rather work for a large or small company?
- Must you work in a specific city, geographical area, or climate?
- Are you looking for security, travel opportunities, money, power, or prestige?
- How would you describe the perfect job, boss, and coworkers?

To aid you with appraising your abilities, many college career centers offer skills assessment and personality type testing. Be sure to explore resources available on campus, including one-on-one sessions with career counselors, job-search and etiquette workshops, local employer job postings, internships, and more.

Evaluating Your Qualifications

Decide what qualifications you possess and how you can prove them.

In addition to your interests, assess your qualifications. Employers today want to know what assets you have to offer them. Your responses to the following questions will target your thinking as well as prepare a foundation for your résumé. Remember, though, that employers seek more than empty assurances; they will want proof of your qualifications.

- *What technology skills can you offer?* Employers are often interested in specific computer software programs, Web experience, and social media skills.
- *What other skills have you acquired in school, on the job, or through activities?* How can you demonstrate these skills?
- *Do you work well with people? Do you enjoy teamwork?* What proof can you offer? Consider extracurricular activities, clubs, class projects, and jobs.
- *Are you a leader, self-starter, or manager?* What evidence can you offer? What leadership roles have you held?
- *Do you speak, write, or understand another language?* In today's global economy, being able to communicate in more than one language is an asset.
- *Do you learn quickly? Are you creative?* How can you demonstrate these characteristics?
- *Do you communicate well in speech and in writing?* How can you verify these talents?
- *What are the unique qualifications you can offer that will make you stand out among other candidates?* Think about what you offer that will make you memorable during your job search.

Recognizing Employment Trends in Today's Workplace

People feel less job security after downsizing, outsourcing, and offshoring of jobs.

As you learned in Chapter 1, the workplace is changing. One of the most significant changes involves the concept of the job. Following the downsizing of corporations and the outsourcing and offshoring of jobs in recent years, companies are employing fewer people in permanent positions.

Other forms of employment are replacing traditional jobs. In many companies teams complete special projects and then disband. Work may also be outsourced to a group that is not even part of the organization. Because new technologies can spring up overnight making today's skills obsolete, employers are less willing to hire people into jobs with narrow descriptions. Instead, they are hiring contingency employees who work temporarily and then leave. What's more, big companies are no longer the main employers. People work for smaller companies, or they are starting their own businesses. According to the Small Business Administration, small companies employ over half of all private sector employees, and that number is expected to grow over the next decade.[2]

"We found someone overseas who can drink coffee and talk about sports all day for a fraction of what we're paying you."

What do these changes mean for you? For one thing, you should probably forget about a lifelong career with a single company. Don't count on regular pay raises, promotions, and a comfortable retirement income. You should also become keenly aware that a career that relies on yesterday's skills is headed for trouble. You are going to need updated, marketable skills that serve you well as you move from job to job. Technology skills will become increasingly important over the next decade as more than 2 million jobs are expected to be created by 2018, according to the Bureau of Labor Statistics.[3] This means that upgrading your skills and retraining yourself constantly are the best career strategies for the twenty-first century. People who learn quickly and adapt to change will always be in demand even in a climate of surging change.

Jobs are becoming more flexible and less permanent.

Choosing a Career Path

The job picture in the United States is extraordinarily dynamic and flexible. On average, workers between ages eighteen and thirty-eight in the United States will have ten different employers; the median job tenure of wage earners and salaried workers with the current employer is 4.4 years.[4] Although you may be frequently changing jobs in the future (especially before you reach forty), you still need to train for a specific career now. In choosing an area, you will make the best decisions when you can match your interests and qualifications with the requirements and rewards in specific careers. Where can you find the best career data? Here are some suggestions:

Career information can be obtained at campus career centers and libraries, from the Web, in classified ads, and from professional organizations.

- **Visit your campus career center.** Most campus career centers have literature, inventories, career-related software programs, and employment or internship databases that allow you to explore such fields as accounting, finance, office technology, information systems, hotel management, and so forth. Some have well-trained job counselors who can tailor their resources to your needs. They may also offer career exploration workshops, job skills seminars, career days with visiting companies, assistance with résumé preparation, and mock interviews.
- **Search the Web.** Many job-search sites on the Web offer career-planning information and resources. You will learn about some of the best career sites in the next section.
- **Use your library.** Print and online resources in your library are especially helpful. Consult *O*NET Occupational Information Network, Dictionary of Occupational Titles, Occupational Outlook Handbook,* and *Jobs Rated Almanac* for information about job requirements, qualifications, salaries, and employment trends.
- **Take a summer job, internship, or part-time position in your field.** Nothing is better than trying out a career by actually working in it or in a related area. Many companies offer internships and temporary or part-time jobs to begin

Summer jobs, part-time employment, and internships are good opportunities to learn about various careers and to establish a professional network.

training college students and to develop relationships with them. Experts commonly believe that at least 60 percent of these relationships blossom into permanent positions. Recent polls suggest that as many as 90 percent of employers offer full-time job positions to their interns.[5]

- **Interview someone in your chosen field.** People are usually flattered when asked to describe their careers. Inquire about needed skills, required courses, financial and other rewards, benefits, working conditions, future trends, and entry requirements.
- **Volunteer with a nonprofit organization.** Many colleges and universities encourage service learning. In volunteering their services, students gain valuable experience, and nonprofits appreciate the expertise and fresh ideas that students bring.
- **Monitor the classified ads.** Early in your college career, begin monitoring want ads and Web sites of companies in your career area. Check job availability, qualifications sought, duties, and salary range. Don't wait until you are about to graduate to see how the job market looks.
- **Join professional organizations in your field.** Frequently, professional organizations offer student membership status and reduced rates. You will receive inside information on issues, career news, and possibly jobs. Student business clubs and organization such as Phi Beta Lambda can also provide leadership development trainings, career tips, and networking opportunities.

Conducting a Successful Job Search

Employment Web sites list many jobs, but finding a job electronically requires more work than simply clicking a mouse.

Searching for a job today is vastly different than it used to be as a result of the Web. Until fairly recently a job seeker browsed the local classified ads, found a likely-sounding job listing, prepared an elegant résumé on bond paper, and sent it out by U.S. mail. All that has changed because of the Web. The challenge today is knowing how to use the Web to your advantage, while realizing that traditional job-search techniques can still be effective. Like other smart job seekers, you can combine both online and traditional job-search tactics to land the job of your dreams.

Searching for a Job Online

OFFICE INSIDER
"The recruiting game has become an arms race of sorts. Recruiters, job boards, and Web sites like ResumeBomber .com have built technological systems to store and ship unprecedented numbers of [résumés]. . . . Companies have developed equally sophisticated programs to sort, select, and scrap all of those resumes."
—Kyle Stock, business journalist, The Wall Street Journal

Searching for a job electronically has become a common, but not always fruitful, approach. With all the publicity given to Web-based job boards and career sites, you might think that online job searching has totally replaced traditional methods. Not so! Although Web sites such as CareerBuilder.com and Monster.com list millions of jobs, actually landing a job is much harder than just clicking a mouse. In addition, these job boards now face competition from social networking sites such as LinkedIn, Facebook, and Twitter.[6]

Both recruiters and job seekers complain about online job boards. Corporate recruiters say that the big job boards bring a flood of candidates, many of whom are not suited for the listed jobs. Workplace experts estimate that the average Fortune 500 company is inundated with 2,000 résumés a day.[7] Job candidates grumble that listings are frequently outdated and fail to produce leads. Some career advisors call these sites black holes,[8] into which résumés vanish without a trace. Applicants worry about the privacy of information posted at big boards. Most important, a recent study has shown that the percentage of external hires resulting from job boards is astonishingly low—3.14 percent at Monster.com, 3.95 percent at CareerBuilder.com, and 1.35 percent at HotJobs.com, before Yahoo sold HotJobs to Monster.[9] Workplace expert Liz Ryan advises job seekers not to count on finding a job by devoting all their energy to searching online job boards.[10]

FIGURE 13.2 Searching the Big Boards

Monster.com is one of several popular Web sites that allow you to search for jobs but also provides excellent tips for conducting job searches, writing résumés, organizing cover letters, preparing for job interviews, and planning careers.

Using the Big Job Boards. Despite these gloomy prospects, many job seekers use job boards to gather job-search information, such as résumé, interviewing, and salary tips. Job boards also serve as a jumping-off point in most searches. They can inform you about the kinds of jobs that are available and the skill sets required. With tens of thousands of job boards and employment Web sites deluging the Internet, it is hard to know where to start. We have listed a few of the best-known online job sites here:

Many job seekers start searching by visiting the big online job boards.

- **CareerBuilder** claims to be the nation's largest employment network. Users can search for millions of jobs by job category, keywords, geographic location, industry, or type of job (full-time, part-time, internship, and so on).
- **Monster**, shown in Figure 12.3, offers access to information on millions of jobs worldwide. With the acquisition of Yahoo HotJobs, this volume will grow even larger. Monster.com uses a search technology called 6Sense to match applicants with the best job opportunities. Because of this cutting-edge search system, many consider Monster.com to be the Web's premier job site.
- **CollegeGrad** describes itself as the "number one entry-level job site" for students and graduates. In addition to searching for entry-level jobs, users can also search for undergraduate and graduate degree programs to help them become more marketable.
- **CareerJournal,** which is part of *The Wall Street Journal*, focuses on listing high-level executive and finance positions.

Forbes media reporter Elaine Wong sums up the relative strengths of LinkedIn and job boards as follows: "LinkedIn offers a targeted, easy to home in approach, but Monster and CareerBuilder still offer scale and reach."[11]

Beyond the Big Online Job Boards. Disillusioned job seekers may turn their backs on job boards but not on online job-searching tactics. Savvy candidates know how to use their computers to search for jobs at Web sites such as the following:

Job prospects may be more promising at the Web sites of corporations, professional organizations, employers' organizations, niche fields, and, most recently, professional networking sites.

- **Company Web sites.** Probably the best way to find a job online is at a company's own Web site. Many companies now post job openings only on their own Web sites to avoid being inundated by the volume of applicants that respond to postings on online job boards. Job seekers also find that they are more likely to obtain an interview if they post their résumés on company sites. In addition to finding a more direct route to decision makers, job hunters find that they can keep their job searches more private than at big board sites.
- **Professional organization Web sites.** Online job listings have proved to be the single-most popular feature of many professional organizations such as the International Association of Administrative Professionals, the American Institute of Certified Public Accountants, the National Association of Sales Professionals, the National Association of Legal Assistants, and the Association of Information Technology Professionals. Although you pay a fee, the benefits of joining a professional association in your career field are enormous. Remember that it is never too early to start networking. If you join a professional organization while you are still in college, you will jump-start your professional connections.
- **JobCentral National Labor Exchange.** JobCentral is a public service Web site provided by the DirectEmployers Association, a nonprofit consortium of Fortune 500 and other leading U.S. corporations. Many companies now use JobCentral as a gateway to job listing at their own Web sites, advertising millions of jobs. Best of all, this service is free, bypassing the big commercial job boards. You can enter a job description or job title, and a list of openings pops up. When you click one, you are taken straight to the company's Web site, where you can apply.
- **Local employment Web sites.** Although many of the big job boards allow you to search for jobs geographically, frequently job seekers have more luck using local employment Web sites such as Craigslist, Cumulus Jobs, and JobStar.
- **Niche Web sites.** If you want a job in a specialized field, look for a niche Web site, such as Dice for technology jobs, Advance for Health Care Careers for medical occupations, and Accountemps for accounting positions. Niche Web sites also exist for job seekers with special backgrounds or needs, such as the disabled (GettingHired), and older workers (Workforce50). New Grad Life, an aggregate job-search site, offers free resources for recent college graduates such as a list of 100 top niche job sites. However, don't rely on any single search strategy. A recent poll suggests that less than 20 percent of job seekers find a position with the help of such specialized job market sites.[12] Your prospects are brighter with social media such as LinkedIn and Twitter.
- **Social media sites.** Perhaps you use Facebook or Google+ to communicate with friends and family. However, users are increasingly tapping into social media sites to prospect for jobs; and recruiters also use these sites to find potential employees. LinkedIn is currently the top site for job seekers, with over 42 million users, both job seekers and recruiters. Other popular sites include Facebook, Plaxo, TheLadders, BlueSteps, and Jobster.[13] Twitter has created a job-search engine called TwitJobSearch, and many companies now post recruitment videos on YouTube. Smart job seekers use these tools to network and to search for available positions. Of course, the most successful job seekers understand that they must maintain a professional online appearance at all times.

"Your resume is excellent, but your Facebook page lacks the imagination we want in a new employee."

Safe Online Job Hunting. You need to be aware of the dangers associated with using online job boards and other employment sites. Your current boss might see your résumé posted online, or a fraudster could use the information in your résumé to steal your identity. The following tips can help you conduct a safe, effective Web job search:

You can ensure a safe online search by choosing reputable sites, protecting your personal information and that of your references, keeping careful records, and renewing your posts regularly.

- **Use reputable sites.** Stick to the well-known, reputable job boards. Never use a site that makes you pay to post your résumé.
- **Be selective.** Limit the number of sites on which you post your résumé. Employers dislike "résumé spammers."
- **Use a dedicated e-mail address.** Set up a separate e-mail account with a professional-sounding e-mail address for your job search.
- **Limit personal information.** Never include your social security or other identification numbers on your résumé. Consider omitting your home address and home phone number to protect your privacy.
- **Post privately.** If given an option, choose to post your résumé privately. Doing so means that you can control who has access to your e-mail address and other contact information.
- **Count the days.** Renew your résumé posting every 14 days. If you keep it up longer, it will look as if employers have no interest in you. If you haven't received a response in 45 days, pull your résumé from the site and post it somewhere else.
- **Keep careful records.** Keep a record of every site on which you post your résumé. At the end of your job search, remove all posted résumés.
- **Protect your references.** If you post your résumé online, don't include your references. It is unethical for job seekers to post their references' personal contact information online without their knowledge.
- **Don't respond to a "blind" job posting.** Respond only to job postings that include a company name and contact information. It is unfortunate that many scammers use online job boards to post fake job ads as a way to gather your personal information.

Despite these dangers, job seekers use online sites to search millions of openings. The harsh reality, however, is that landing a job still depends largely on personal contacts. One employment expert believes that overreliance on technology may have made job seekers lazy: "At the end of the day, the job hunt is largely about people and it is about networking—looking at who you know and where they work."[14] Job-search consultant Debra Feldman concurs: "More important than what you know is who knows what you know. Make sure you are on the radar of people who have access to the kind of job leads you want."[15]

Many jobs are listed on the Web, but most hiring is still done through personal contact.

Searching for a Job Using Traditional Techniques

Finding the perfect job requires an early start and a determined effort. A research study of college graduates revealed that those with proactive personalities were the most successful in securing interviews and jobs. Katharine Brooks, career services director in Austin, Texas, recommends: "Look for opportunities to learn, take a risk, try things out, see what you like, and always be open to the next opportunity."[16]

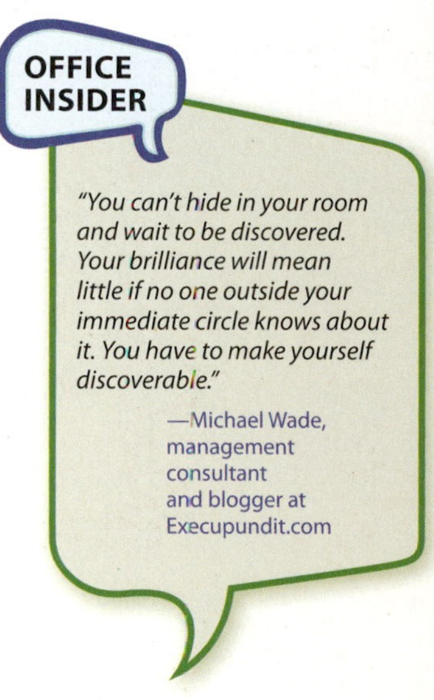

OFFICE INSIDER
"You can't hide in your room and wait to be discovered. Your brilliance will mean little if no one outside your immediate circle knows about it. You have to make yourself discoverable."
—Michael Wade, management consultant and blogger at Execupundit.com

Whether you use traditional or online job-search techniques, you should be prepared to launch an aggressive campaign—and you can't start too early. Some universities now require first- and second-year students to take an employment seminar called Reality 101. Students learn early on that a college degree alone does not guarantee a job. They are cautioned that grade point averages make a difference to employers.[17] They are also advised of the importance of experience, such as internships. Traditional job-search techniques, such as those described here, continue to be critical in landing jobs.

The most successful job seekers are those who launch aggressive campaigns employing a wide array of techniques such as these.

- **Check classified ads in local and national newspapers.** You can find classified job ads in print or online versions of newspapers. Be aware, though, that classified ads are only one small source of jobs.
- **Check announcements in publications of professional organizations.** If you don't have a student membership, ask your instructors to share current copies of professional journals, newsletters, and so on. Your college library is another good source.
- **Contact companies in which you are interested, even if you know of no current opening.** Write an unsolicited letter and include your résumé. Follow up with a telephone call. Check the company's Web site for employment opportunities and procedures. To learn immediately of job openings, use Twitter to follow companies where you would like to work.
- **Sign up for campus interviews with visiting company representatives.** Campus recruiters may open your eyes to exciting jobs and locations. They may also help you prepare by offering mock interviews.
- **Attend career fairs.** Job fairs are invaluable in your quest to learn about specific companies and your future career options. Recruiters say that the more you know about the company and its representatives, the more comfortable you will be in an interview.[18]
- **Ask for advice from your instructors.** Your teachers often have contacts and ideas for conducting and expanding your job search.
- **Develop your own network of contacts.** Networking still accounts for most of the jobs found by candidates. Therefore, plan to spend a considerable portion of your job-search time developing a personal network. The Communication Workshop at the end of this chapter gives you step-by-step instructions for traditional networking as well as some ideas for online networking.

Creating a Customized Résumé

A customized résumé means that you will prepare a special résumé for each position you want.

After using both traditional and online resources to learn about the employment market and to develop job leads, you will focus on writing a customized résumé. This means you will prepare a special résumé for every position you want. The competition is so stiff today that you cannot get by with a generic, all-purpose résumé. Although you can start with a basic résumé, you should customize it to fit each company and position if you want your résumé to stand out from the crowd. Include many keywords that describe the skills, traits, tasks, and job titles associated with your targeted job. You will learn more about keywords shortly.

The Internet has made it so easy to apply that recruiters are swamped with applications. As a job seeker, you have about five seconds to catch the recruiter's eye—if your résumé is even read by a person. Many companies use computer scanning technologies to weed out unqualified candidates. Your goal is to make your résumé fit the targeted position and be noticed. Such a résumé does more than merely list your qualifications. It packages your assets into a convincing advertisement that sells you for a specific job.

In the scramble to get noticed, some job seekers—particularly in creative professions—occasionally resort to unusual job-hunting tactics, for example, sending a recruiter a shoe "to get a foot in the door" or a bowling pin to suggest "I'll bowl you over."[19] The survey of hiring managers revealed that more than half of marketing and a quarter of advertising executives view such unconventional approaches as unprofessional. Whereas in advertising gimmicky applications may be acceptable to almost half of the executives polled, in most business disciplines they would be a huge gamble. Perhaps you should think twice before drawing attention to yourself the way one applicant did by putting up posters of himself in the garage where the executives parked.

The goal of a résumé is winning an interview. Even if you are not in the job market at this moment, preparing a résumé now has advantages. Having a current résumé makes you look well organized and professional should an unexpected employment opportunity arise. Moreover, preparing a résumé early can help you recognize weak areas and give you time to bolster them. Even after you have accepted a position, it is a good idea to keep your résumé up-to-date. You never know when an opportunity might come along!

Winning an interview is the goal of a customized résumé.

Choosing a Résumé Style

Résumés usually fall into two categories: chronological and functional. In this section we present basic information as well as insider tips on how to choose an appropriate résumé style, how to determine its length, and how to arrange its parts. You will also learn about adding a summary of qualifications, which busy recruiters increasingly want to see. Models of the résumés in the following discussion are shown in our comprehensive Résumé Gallery beginning on page 421.

See our comprehensive Résumé Gallery beginning on page 421.

Chronological. The most popular résumé format is the chronological résumé, shown in Figures 13.6 through 13.9 in our Résumé Gallery. It lists work history job by job, starting with the most recent position. Recruiters favor the chronological format because it quickly reveals a candidate's education and experience. Recruiters are familiar with the chronological résumé, and one research study showed that 75 percent of employers prefer to see a candidate's résumé in this format.[20] The chronological style works well for candidates who have experience in their field of employment and for those who show steady career growth, but it is less appropriate for people who have changed jobs frequently or who have gaps in their employment records. For college students and others who lack extensive experience, the functional résumé format may be preferable.

Chronological résumés focus on job history with the most recent positions listed first.

Functional. The functional résumé, shown in Figure 13.10 on page 425, focuses on a candidate's skills rather than on past employment. Like a chronological résumé, the functional résumé begins with the candidate's name, contact information, job objective, and education. Instead of listing jobs, though, the functional résumé groups skills and accomplishments in special categories, such as *Supervisory and Management Skills* or *Retailing and Marketing Experience.* This résumé style highlights accomplishments and can de-emphasize a negative employment history. People who have changed jobs frequently, who have gaps in their employment records, or who are entering an entirely different field may prefer the functional résumé. Recent graduates with little or no related employment experience often find the functional résumé useful. Older job seekers who want to downplay a long job history and job hunters who are afraid of appearing overqualified may also prefer the functional format. Be aware, though, that online job boards may insist on chronological format. In addition, some recruiters are suspicious of functional résumés, thinking the candidate is hiding something.

Because functional résumés focus on skills, they may be more advisable for graduates with little experience.

Deciding on Length

Experts simply do not agree on how long a résumé should be. Conventional wisdom has always held that recruiters prefer one-page résumés. A survey of 150 senior executives, however, revealed that 52 percent of executives polled believe a single page is the ideal length for a staff-level résumé, but 44 percent said they prefer two pages. Nearly one third of those surveyed (31 percent) also said that three pages is ideal for executive positions.[21] Recruiters who are serious about candidates often prefer the kind of details that a two-page résumé can provide. On the other hand, many recruiters are said to be extremely busy and prefer concise résumés.

Recruiters may say they prefer one-page résumés, but many choose to interview those with longer résumés.

Perhaps the best advice is to make your résumé as long as needed to sell your skills to recruiters and hiring managers. Individuals with more experience will naturally have longer résumés. Those with fewer than ten years of experience, those making a major career change, and those who have had only one or two employers will likely have one-page résumés. Those with ten years or more of related experience may have two-page résumés. Finally, some senior-level managers and executives with lengthy histories of major accomplishments might have résumés that are three pages or longer.[22]

Organizing Your Information Into Effective Résumé Categories

The parts of résumés should be arranged with the most important qualifications first.

Although résumés have standard parts, their arrangement and content should be strategically planned. A customized résumé emphasizes skills and achievements aimed at a particular job or company. It shows a candidate's most important qualifications first, and it de-emphasizes any weaknesses. In arranging your information and qualifications, try to create as few headings as possible; more than six generally makes the résumé look cluttered. No two résumés are ever exactly alike, but most writers consider including all or some of these categories: main heading, career objective, summary of qualifications, education, experience, capabilities and skills, awards and activities, personal information, and references.

Main Heading

Your résumé, whether it is chronological or functional, should start with a main heading that is as uncluttered and simple as possible. The first line of the main heading should always be your name; add your middle initial for an even more professional look. Format your name so that it stands out on the page. Below your name, list your contact information, including your complete address, area code and phone number, and e-mail address. Be sure to include a telephone number where you can receive messages. The outgoing message at this number should be in your voice, it should mention your full name, and it should be concise and professional. If you include your cell phone number and are expecting an important call from a recruiter, pick up only when you are in a quiet environment and can concentrate.

"That's my resume, my autobiography, and six of my last projects."

For your e-mail address, be sure it sounds professional instead of something like *toosexy4you@hotmail.com* or *sixpackguy@yahoo.com*. Also be sure that you are using a personal e-mail address. Putting your work e-mail address on your résumé announces to prospective employers that you are using your current employer's resources to look for another job. If you have a Web site where an e-portfolio or samples of your work can be viewed, include the address in the main heading.

Career Objective

Career objectives are most appropriate for specific, targeted positions, but they may limit a broader job search.

Opinion is divided about the effect of including a career objective on a résumé. Recruiters think such statements indicate that a candidate has made a commitment to a career and is sure about what he or she wants to do. Career objectives, of course, make the recruiter's life easier by quickly classifying the résumé. Such declarations, however, can also disqualify a candidate if the stated objective does not match a company's job description.[23] A well-written objective—customized for the job opening—can add value to either a chronological or a functional résumé.

A person applying for an auditor position might include the following objective: *Seeking an auditor position in an internal corporate accounting department where my accounting skills, computer experience, knowledge of GAAP, and attention to detail will help the company run efficiently and ensure that its records are kept accurately.*

Your objective should also focus on the employer's needs. Therefore, it should be written from the employer's perspective, not your own. Focus on how you can contribute to the organization, not on what the organization can do for you. A typical self-serving objective is *To obtain a meaningful and rewarding position that enables me to learn more about the graphic design field and allows for advancement*. Instead, show how you will add value to the organization with an objective such as *Position with advertising firm designing Web sites, publications, logos, and promotional displays for clients, where creativity, software knowledge, and proven communication skills can be used to build client base and expand operations.* As Rick Saia, a certified professional résumé writer, advises, these days, "the company is really not as interested in what they can do for you as in what you can do for them.[24]

Also be careful that your career objective does not downplay your talents. For example, some consultants warn against using the words *entry-level* in your objective, as these words emphasize lack of experience or show poor self-confidence. Finally, your objective should be concise. Try to limit your objective to no more than three lines. Avoid using complete sentences and the pronoun *I*.

If you choose to omit the career objective, be sure to discuss your objectives and goals in your cover letter. Savvy job seekers are also incorporating their objectives into a summary of qualifications, which is discussed next.

Summary of Qualifications

"The biggest change in résumés over the last decade has been a switch from an objective to a summary at the top," says career expert Wendy Enelow.[25] Recruiters are busy, and smart job seekers add a summary of qualifications to their résumés to save the time of recruiters and hiring managers. Once a job is advertised, a hiring manager may get hundreds or even thousands of résumés in response. A summary at the top of your résumé makes it easier to read and ensures that your most impressive qualifications are not overlooked by a recruiter, who skims résumés quickly. Job applicants must often capture a recruiter's attention in less than ten seconds.[26] A well-written summary, therefore, motivates the recruiter to read further.

A summary of qualifications section lists your most impressive accomplishments and qualifications in one concise bulleted list.

OFFICE INSIDER

"I know many days I have reviewed hundreds of resumes and most in less than 20 seconds. . . . [T]he average is probably around 5 to 7 seconds. So for the record when you hear or read about, 'reading a resume in 20 seconds,' that isn't completely true. It is more than likely, 'reviewed the resume in 20 seconds.'"

—Brad Remillard, executive recruiter and hiring expert

A summary of qualifications (also called *career profile, job summary*, or *professional highlights*) should include three to eight bulleted statements that prove you are the ideal candidate for the position. When formulating these statements, consider your experience in the field, your education, your unique skills, awards you have won, certifications, and any other accomplishments that you want to highlight. Include numbers wherever possible. Target the most important qualifications an employer will be looking for in the person hired for this position. Examples of summaries of qualifications appear in Figures 13.6, 13.7, 13.9, and 13.11 in the résumé models found in our Résumé Gallery.

Education

The next component in a chronological résumé is your education—if it is more noteworthy than your work experience. In this section you should include the name and location of schools, dates of attendance, major fields of study, and degrees received. By the way, once you have attended college, you should not list high school information on your résumé.

The education section shows degrees and GPA but does not list all courses a job applicant has taken.

Your grade point average and/or class ranking may be important to prospective employers. The National Association of Colleges and Employers found that 66 percent of employers screen candidates by GPA, and 58 percent of those surveyed said they would be much less likely to hire applicants with college GPAs of less than 3.0.[27] One way to enhance your GPA is to calculate it in your major courses only (for example, *3.6/4.0 in major*). It is not unethical to showcase your GPA in your major—as long as you clearly indicate what you are doing. Although some hiring managers may think that applicants are hiding something if they omit a poor record of grades, consultant Terese Corey Blanck suggests leaving out a poor GPA. Instead, she advises that students try to excel in internships, show extracurricular leadership, and target smaller, lesser-known companies to offset low grades.[28] Remember, however, that many employers will assume your GPA is lower than 3.0 if you omit it.[29]

Under *Education* you might be tempted to list all the courses you took, but such a list makes for very dull reading and uses valuable space. Refer to courses only if you can relate them to the position sought. When relevant, include certificates earned, seminars attended, workshops completed, scholarships awarded, and honors earned. If your education is incomplete, include such statements as *BS degree expected 6/14* or *80 units completed in 120-unit program.* Title this section *Education, Academic Preparation,* or *Professional Training.* If you are preparing a functional résumé, you will probably put the education section below your skills summaries, as Kevin Touhy has done in Figure 13.10.

Work Experience or Employment History

The work experience section of a résumé should list specifics and quantify achievements.

If your work experience is significant and relevant to the position sought, this information should appear before your education section. List your most recent employment first and work backward, including only those jobs that you think will help you win the targeted position. A job application form may demand a full employment history, but your résumé may be selective. Be aware, though, that time gaps in your employment history will probably be questioned in the interview. For each position show the following:

- Employer's name, city, and state
- Dates of employment (month and year)
- Most important job title
- Significant duties, activities, accomplishments, and promotions

Describe your employment achievements concisely but concretely to make what résumé consultants call "a strong value proposition."[30] Avoid generalities such as *Worked with customers*. Be more specific, with statements such as *Served 40 or more retail customers a day; Successfully resolved problems about custom stationery orders;* or *Acted as intermediary among customers, printers, and suppliers.* If possible, quantify your accomplishments, such as *Conducted study of equipment needs of 100 small businesses in Houston; Personally generated orders for sales of $90,000 annually;* or *Keyed all the production models for a 250-page employee procedures manual.* One professional recruiter said, "I spend a half hour every day screening 50 résumés or more, and if I don't spot some [quantifiable] results in the first 10 seconds, the résumé is history."[31]

Your employment achievements and job duties will be easier to read if you place them in a bulleted list. When writing these bullet points, don't try to list every single thing you have done on the job; instead, customize your information so that it relates to the target job. Make sure your list of job duties shows what you have to contribute and how you are qualified for the position you are applying for. Do not make your bullet points complete sentences, and avoid using personal pronouns (*I, me, my*). If you have performed a lot of the same duties for multiple employers, you don't have to repeat them.

In addition to technical skills, employers seek individuals with communication, management, and interpersonal capabilities. This means you will want to select work experiences and achievements that illustrate your initiative, dependability, responsibility, resourcefulness, flexibility, and leadership. Employers also want people who can work together in teams. Therefore, include statements such as *Collaborated with interdepartmental task force in developing ten-page handbook for temporary workers* and *Headed student government team that conducted most successful voter registration in campus history.*

Statements describing your work experience can be made forceful and persuasive if you use action verbs, such as those listed in Figure 13.3 and illustrated in Figure 13.4. Starting each of your bullet points with an action verb will help ensure that your bulleted lists are parallel.

FIGURE 13.3 Action Verbs for Powerful Résumés

The underlined words are especially good for pointing out accomplishments.

Communication Skills

arbitrated
arranged
authored
clarified
collaborated
convinced
corresponded
defined
developed
directed
drafted
edited
enlisted
explained
formulated
influenced
integrated
interpreted
mediated
moderated
negotiated
participated
persuaded
promoted
publicized
reconciled
recruited
resolved
spoke
specified
suggested
summarized
translated
wrote

Teamwork, Supervision Skills

adapted
advised
assessed
assisted
clarified
coached
collaborated (with)
communicated
coordinated
counseled
demonstrated
demystified
developed
enabled
encouraged
evaluated
expedited
explained
facilitated
guided
informed
instructed
motivated
persuaded
set goals
stimulated
teamed (with)
trained

Management, Leadership Skills

administered
analyzed
assigned
attained
authorized
chaired
consolidated
contracted
coordinated
delegated
developed
directed
evaluated
executed
handled
headed
implemented
improved
increased
led
modeled
organized
oversaw
planned
prioritized
produced
recommended
reorganized
reviewed
scheduled
strengthened
supervised
trained

Research Skills

analyzed
clarified
collected
critiqued
diagnosed
evaluated
examined
experimented
extracted
formulated
gathered
identified
informed
inspected
interpreted
interviewed
invented
investigated
located
measured
observed
organized
researched
reviewed
searched
solved
studied
summarized
surveyed
systematized

Clerical, Detail Skills

activated
approved
arranged
catalogued
classified
collected
compiled
edited
executed
generated
implemented
inspected
logged
maintained
monitored
operated
organized
prepared
processed
proofread
purchased
recorded
retrieved
screened
specified
streamlined
systematized
tabulated
updated
validated

Creative Skills

acted
conceptualized
created
customized
designed
developed
directed
established
fashioned
founded
illustrated
initiated
instituted
integrated
introduced
invented
originated
performed
planned
revitalized
shaped

Technical Skills

assembled
built
calculated
computed
configured
designed
devised
engineered
fabricated
installed
maintained
operated
overhauled
performed troubleshooting
programmed
remodeled
repaired
retrieved
solved
upgraded

Financial Skills

administered
allocated
analyzed
appraised
audited
balanced
budgeted
calculated
computed
developed
forecast
managed
marketed
planned
projected
researched

More Accomplishment Verbs

achieved
expanded
improved
pioneered
reduced (losses)
resolved (problems)
restored
revamped
spearheaded

FIGURE 13.4 Use Action Verbs in Statements That Quantify Achievements
Identified weaknesses in internships and **researched** five alternate programs
Reduced delivery delays by an average of three days per order
Streamlined filing system, thus reducing 400-item backlog to zero
Organized holiday awards program for 1,200 attendees and 140 workers
Designed three pages in HTML for company Web site
Represented 2,500 students on committee involving university policies and procedures
Calculated shipping charges for overseas deliveries and **recommended** most economical rates
Managed 24-station computer network linking data in three departments
Distributed and **explained** voter registration forms to over 500 prospective voters
Praised by top management for enthusiastic teamwork and achievement
Secured national recognition from National Arbor Foundation for tree project

Capabilities and Skills

Emphasize the skills and aptitudes that prove you are qualified for a specific position.

Recruiters want to know specifically what you can do for their companies. Therefore, list your special skills, such as *Proficient in preparing federal, state, and local payroll tax returns as well as franchise and personal property tax returns.* Include your ability to use the Internet, social media, software programs, office equipment, and communication technology tools. If you speak a foreign language or use sign language, include it on your résumé. Describe proficiencies you have acquired through training and experience, such as *Certified in computer graphics and Web design through an intensive 350-hour classroom program.* Use expressions such as *competent in, skilled in, proficient with, experienced in,* and *ability to;* for example, *Competent in writing, editing, and proofreading reports, tables, letters, memos, manuscripts, and business forms.*

You will also want to highlight exceptional aptitudes, such as working well under stress, learning computer programs quickly, and interacting with customers. If possible, provide details and evidence that back up your assertions; for example, *Mastered PhotoShop in 25 hours with little instruction.* Include examples of your writing, speaking, management, organizational, and interpersonal skills—particularly those talents that are relevant to your targeted job. For recent graduates, this section can be used to give recruiters evidence of your potential. Instead of *Capabilities,* the section might be called *Skills and Abilities.*

Those job hunters preparing a functional résumé will place more focus on skills than on any other section. A well-written functional résumé groups skills into categories such as *Accounting/Finance Skills, Management/Leadership Skills, Communication/Teamwork Skills*, and *Computer/Technology Skills*. Each skills category includes a bulleted list of achievements and experience that demonstrate the skill, including specific numbers whenever possible. These skills categories should be placed in the beginning of the résumé, where they will be highlighted, followed by education and work experience. The action verbs shown in Figures 13.3 and 13.4 can also be used when constructing a functional résumé.

Awards, Honors, and Activities

Awards, honors, and activities are appropriate for the résumé.

If you have three or more awards or honors, highlight them by listing them under a separate heading. If not, put them in the education or work experience section, whichever is appropriate. Include awards, scholarships (financial and other), fellowships, dean's list, honors, recognitions, commendations, and certificates. Be sure to identify items clearly. Your reader may be unfamiliar, for example, with

Greek organizations, honors, and awards; tell what they mean. Instead of saying *Recipient of Star Award,* give more details: *Recipient of Star Award given by Pepperdine University to outstanding graduates who combine academic excellence and extracurricular activities.*

It is also appropriate to include school, community, volunteer, and professional activities. Employers are interested in evidence that you are a well-rounded person. This section provides an opportunity to demonstrate leadership and interpersonal skills. Strive to use action statements. For example, instead of saying *Treasurer of business club,* explain more fully: *Collected dues, kept financial records, and paid bills while serving as treasurer of 35-member business management club.*

Personal Data

Omit personal data not related to job qualifications.

Today's résumés omit personal data, such as birth date, marital status, height, weight, national origin, health, disabilities, and religious affiliation. Such information does not relate to genuine occupational qualifications, and recruiters are legally barred from asking for such information. Some job seekers do, however, include hobbies or interests (such as skiing or photography) that might grab the recruiter's attention or serve as conversation starters. For example, let's say you learn that your hiring manager enjoys distance running. If you have run a marathon, you may want to mention it. Many executives practice tennis or golf, two sports highly suitable for networking. You could also indicate your willingness to travel or to relocate since many companies will be interested.

References

References are unnecessary for the résumé, but they should be available for the interview.

Listing references directly on a résumé takes up valuable space. Moreover, references are not normally instrumental in securing an interview—few companies check them before the interview. Instead, recruiters prefer that you bring to the interview a list of individuals willing to discuss your qualifications. Therefore, you should prepare a separate list, such as that in Figure 13.5, when you begin your job search. Ask three to five individuals—instructors, your current employer or previous employers, colleagues or subordinates, and other professional

FIGURE 13.5 Sample Reference List

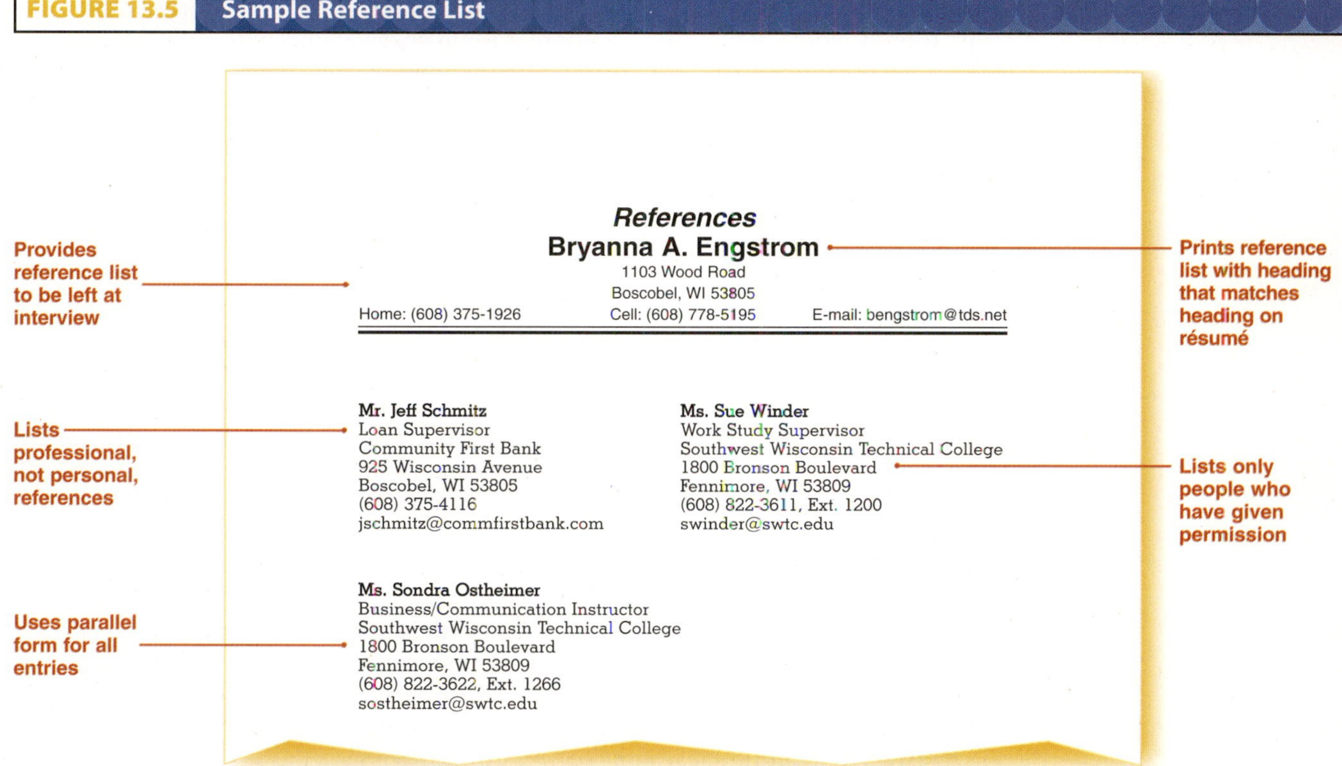
Provides reference list to be left at interview
Lists professional, not personal, references
Uses parallel form for all entries
Prints reference list with heading that matches heading on résumé
Lists only people who have given permission
© Cengage Learning 2013

References

Bryanna A. Engstrom

1103 Wood Road
Boscobel, WI 53805
Home: (608) 375-1926 Cell: (608) 778-5195 E-mail: bengstrom@tds.net

Mr. Jeff Schmitz
Loan Supervisor
Community First Bank
925 Wisconsin Avenue
Boscobel, WI 53805
(608) 375-4116
jschmitz@commfirstbank.com

Ms. Sue Winder
Work Study Supervisor
Southwest Wisconsin Technical College
1800 Bronson Boulevard
Fennimore, WI 53809
(608) 822-3611, Ext. 1200
swinder@swtc.edu

Ms. Sondra Ostheimer
Business/Communication Instructor
Southwest Wisconsin Technical College
1800 Bronson Boulevard
Fennimore, WI 53809
(608) 822-3622, Ext. 1266
sostheimer@swtc.edu

"I don't have any references, but 4 out of 5 phone psychics say I'm destined for greatness."

contacts—whether they would be willing to answer inquiries regarding your qualifications for employment. Be sure, however, to provide them with an opportunity to refuse. No reference is better than a negative one. Better yet, to avoid rejection and embarrassment, ask only those people who will give you a glowing endorsement.

Do not include personal or character references, such as friends, family, or neighbors, because recruiters rarely consult them. Companies are more interested in the opinions of objective individuals who know how you perform professionally and academically. One final note: most recruiters see little reason for including the statement *References furnished upon request.* It is unnecessary and takes up precious space.

In Figures 13.6 through 13.10 beginning on page 421, you will find our Résumé Gallery, which contains models of chronological and functional résumés. Use these models to help you organize the content and format of your own persuasive résumé.

Optimizing Your Résumé for Today's Technologies

Because résumés are increasingly becoming part of searchable databases, you may need three versions.

Thus far we have aimed our résumé advice at human readers. However, the first reader of your résumé may well be a computer. Hiring organizations today use a variety of methods to process incoming résumés. Some organizations still welcome traditional print-based résumés that may include attractive formatting. Larger organizations, however, must deal with thousands of incoming résumés. Increasingly, they are placing those résumés directly into searchable databases.

To improve your chances, you will need various versions of your résumé. For starters, we recommend that you create a traditional print-based résumé in Microsoft Word. To preserve your formatting, you may opt to convert this Word document to a PDF file. Then, when pursuing a job with a large, popular company, be sure to make your résumé scannable so that a computer can read it. Finally, some job hunters prepare a plain-text version with minimal formatting for cutting and pasting into company application forms online. If you are very creative, you may even craft an e-portfolio or a video résumé to showcase your qualifications. Most job applicants, however, will focus on a print-based résumé first.

Designing a Print-Based Résumé

Print-based résumés (also called *presentation résumés*) are attractively formatted to maximize readability. You can create a professional-looking résumé by using your word processing program to highlight your qualifications. The Résumé Gallery in this chapter provides ideas for simple layouts that are easily duplicated. You can also examine résumé templates for design and format ideas. Their inflexibility, however, may lead to frustration as you try to force your skills and experience into a predetermined template sequence. What's more, recruiters who read hundreds of résumés can usually spot a template-based résumé. Instead, create your own original résumé that fits your unique qualifications.

Your print-based résumé should be in an outline format with headings and bullet points to present information in an orderly, uncluttered, easy-to-read format. An attractive print-based résumé is necessary (a) when you are competing for a job that does not require electronic submission, (b) to present in addition to an electronic submission, and (c) to bring with you to job interviews. Even if a résumé is submitted electronically, nearly every job candidate will want to have an attractive traditional résumé handy for human readers.

Résumé Gallery

FIGURE 13.6 **Chronological Résumé: Current College Student With Limited Experience**

To highlight her skills and capabilities, Bryanna Engstrom placed them in the summary of qualifications at the top of her résumé. She used the tables feature of her word processing program to create neat, invisible columns and to fit more information on one page, the length favored by most recruiters.

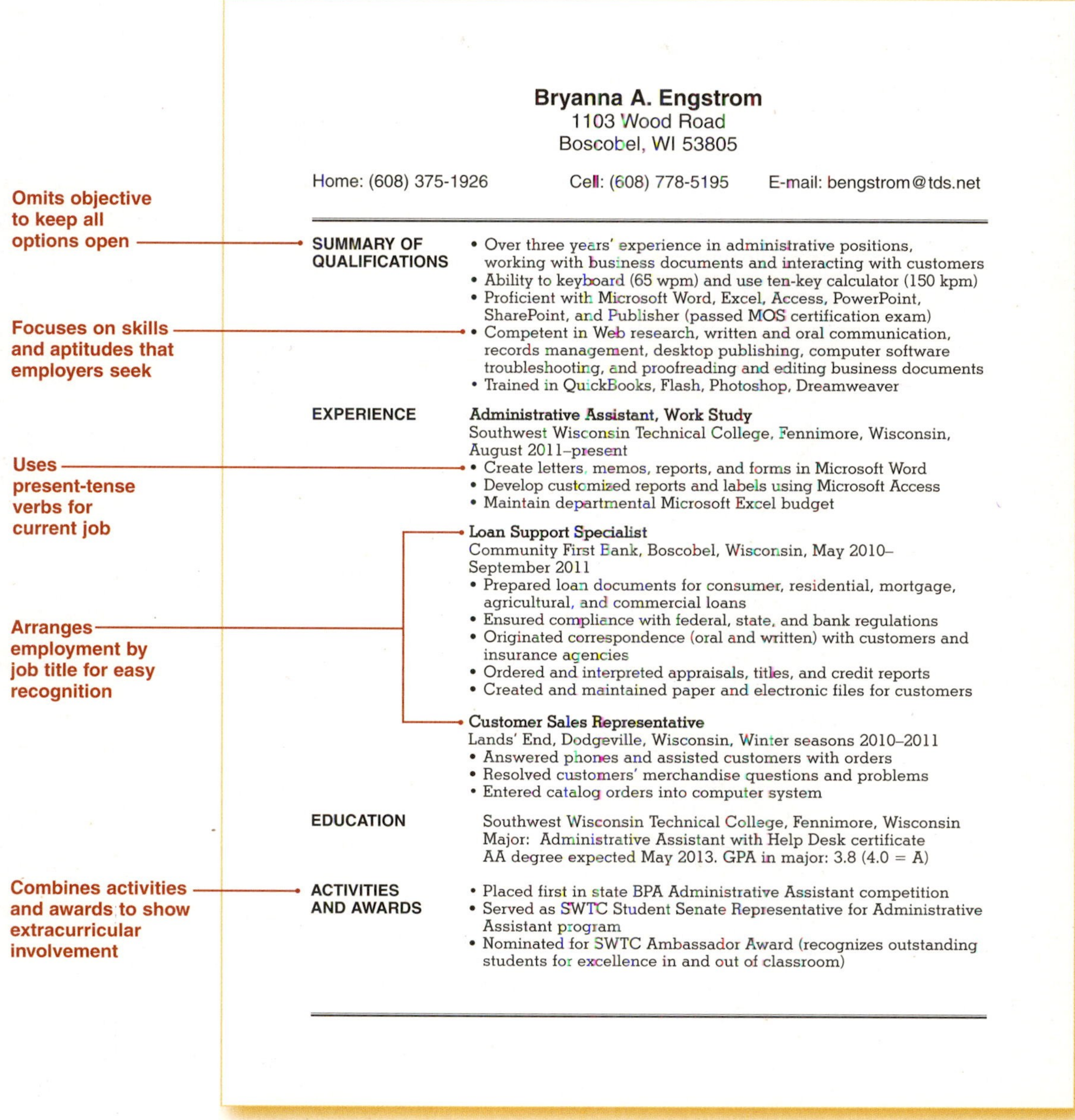

Bryanna A. Engstrom
1103 Wood Road
Boscobel, WI 53805

Home: (608) 375-1926 Cell: (608) 778-5195 E-mail: bengstrom@tds.net

SUMMARY OF QUALIFICATIONS

- Over three years' experience in administrative positions, working with business documents and interacting with customers
- Ability to keyboard (65 wpm) and use ten-key calculator (150 kpm)
- Proficient with Microsoft Word, Excel, Access, PowerPoint, SharePoint, and Publisher (passed MOS certification exam)
- Competent in Web research, written and oral communication, records management, desktop publishing, computer software troubleshooting, and proofreading and editing business documents
- Trained in QuickBooks, Flash, Photoshop, Dreamweaver

EXPERIENCE

Administrative Assistant, Work Study
Southwest Wisconsin Technical College, Fennimore, Wisconsin, August 2011–present
- Create letters, memos, reports, and forms in Microsoft Word
- Develop customized reports and labels using Microsoft Access
- Maintain departmental Microsoft Excel budget

Loan Support Specialist
Community First Bank, Boscobel, Wisconsin, May 2010–September 2011
- Prepared loan documents for consumer, residential, mortgage, agricultural, and commercial loans
- Ensured compliance with federal, state, and bank regulations
- Originated correspondence (oral and written) with customers and insurance agencies
- Ordered and interpreted appraisals, titles, and credit reports
- Created and maintained paper and electronic files for customers

Customer Sales Representative
Lands' End, Dodgeville, Wisconsin, Winter seasons 2010–2011
- Answered phones and assisted customers with orders
- Resolved customers' merchandise questions and problems
- Entered catalog orders into computer system

EDUCATION

Southwest Wisconsin Technical College, Fennimore, Wisconsin
Major: Administrative Assistant with Help Desk certificate
AA degree expected May 2013. GPA in major: 3.8 (4.0 = A)

ACTIVITIES AND AWARDS

- Placed first in state BPA Administrative Assistant competition
- Served as SWTC Student Senate Representative for Administrative Assistant program
- Nominated for SWTC Ambassador Award (recognizes outstanding students for excellence in and out of classroom)

Omits objective to keep all options open
Focuses on skills and aptitudes that employers seek
Uses present-tense verbs for current job
Arranges employment by job title for easy recognition
Combines activities and awards to show extracurricular involvement

Preparing a Scannable Résumé

A scannable résumé is one that is printed on plain white paper and read by a computer. According to Pat Kendall, former president of the National Resume Writers' Association, more than 80 percent of résumés are scanned by companies using automated applicant-tracking software.[32] These systems scan an incoming résumé with optical character recognition (OCR) looking for keywords or keyword phrases. The most sophisticated programs enable recruiters and hiring managers to rank résumés based on the number of "hits" and generate reports. Information from your résumé is stored, usually for from six months to a year.

Applicant-tracking software scans incoming résumés searching for keywords.

FIGURE 13.7 Chronological Résumé: Recent College Graduate With Related Experience

Jessica Fuentes used a chronological résumé to highlight her work experience, most of which was related directly to the position she seeks. Although she is a recent graduate, she has accumulated experience in two part-time jobs and one full-time job. She included a summary of qualifications to highlight her skills, experience, and interpersonal traits aimed at a specific position. Notice that Jessica designed her résumé in two columns with five major categories listed in the left column. In the right column she included bulleted items for each of the five categories. Conciseness and parallelism are important in writing an effective résumé. In the *Experience* category, she started each item with an active verb, which improved readability and parallel form.

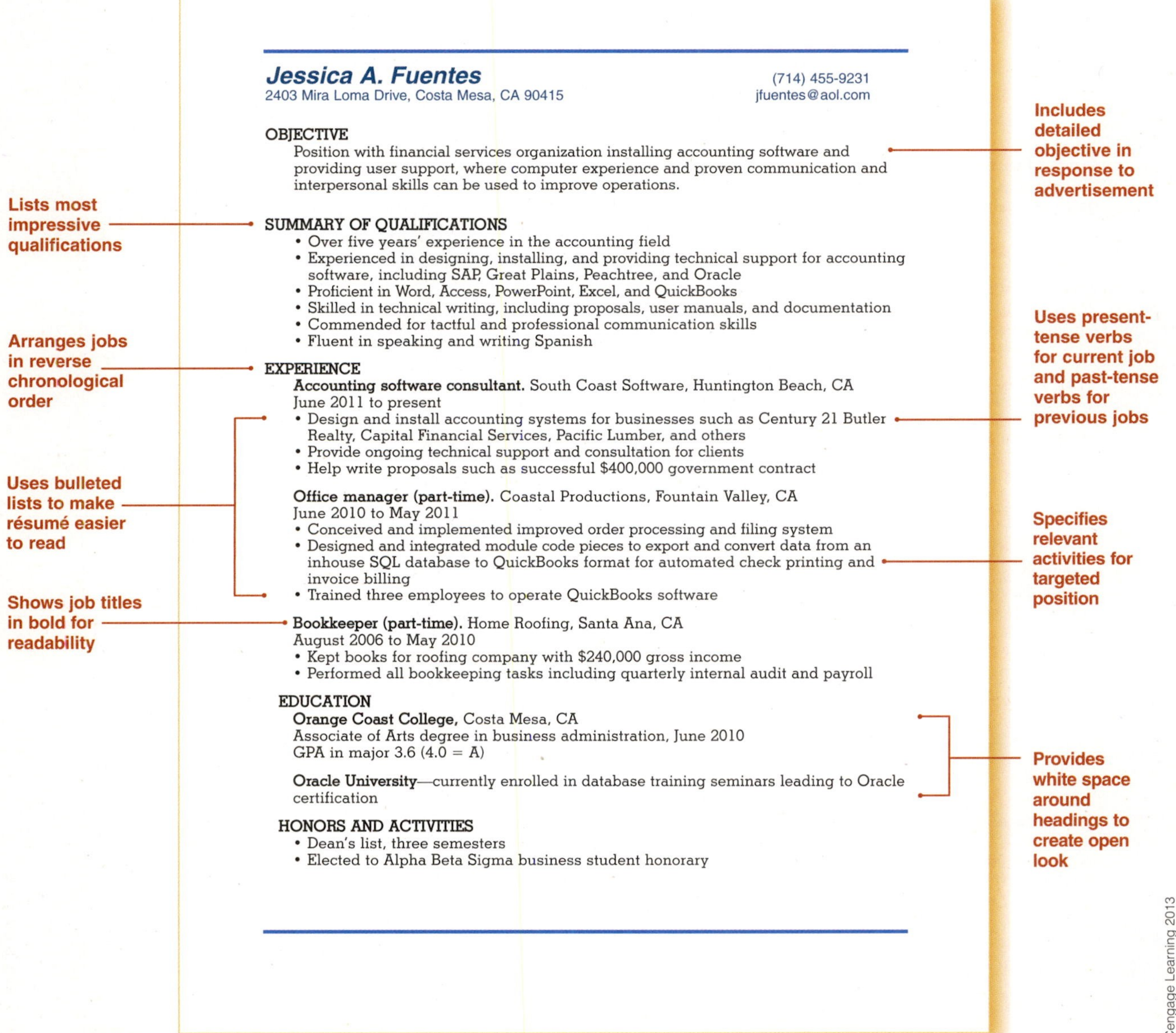
Jessica A. Fuentes
2403 Mira Loma Drive, Costa Mesa, CA 90415
(714) 455-9231
jfuentes@aol.com

OBJECTIVE
Position with financial services organization installing accounting software and providing user support, where computer experience and proven communication and interpersonal skills can be used to improve operations.

SUMMARY OF QUALIFICATIONS
- Over five years' experience in the accounting field
- Experienced in designing, installing, and providing technical support for accounting software, including SAP, Great Plains, Peachtree, and Oracle
- Proficient in Word, Access, PowerPoint, Excel, and QuickBooks
- Skilled in technical writing, including proposals, user manuals, and documentation
- Commended for tactful and professional communication skills
- Fluent in speaking and writing Spanish

EXPERIENCE
Accounting software consultant. South Coast Software, Huntington Beach, CA
June 2011 to present
- Design and install accounting systems for businesses such as Century 21 Butler Realty, Capital Financial Services, Pacific Lumber, and others
- Provide ongoing technical support and consultation for clients
- Help write proposals such as successful $400,000 government contract

Office manager (part-time). Coastal Productions, Fountain Valley, CA
June 2010 to May 2011
- Conceived and implemented improved order processing and filing system
- Designed and integrated module code pieces to export and convert data from an inhouse SQL database to QuickBooks format for automated check printing and invoice billing
- Trained three employees to operate QuickBooks software

Bookkeeper (part-time). Home Roofing, Santa Ana, CA
August 2006 to May 2010
- Kept books for roofing company with $240,000 gross income
- Performed all bookkeeping tasks including quarterly internal audit and payroll

EDUCATION
Orange Coast College, Costa Mesa, CA
Associate of Arts degree in business administration, June 2010
GPA in major 3.6 (4.0 = A)

Oracle University—currently enrolled in database training seminars leading to Oracle certification

HONORS AND ACTIVITIES
- Dean's list, three semesters
- Elected to Alpha Beta Sigma business student honorary

Includes detailed objective in response to advertisement
Lists most impressive qualifications
Uses present-tense verbs for current job and past-tense verbs for previous jobs
Arranges jobs in reverse chronological order
Uses bulleted lists to make résumé easier to read
Specifies relevant activities for targeted position
Shows job titles in bold for readability
Provides white space around headings to create open look

Before sending your résumé, find out whether the recipient uses scanning software. If you can't tell from the job announcement, call the company to ask whether it scans résumés electronically. If you have even the slightest suspicion that your résumé might be read electronically, you will be smart to prepare a plain, scannable version as shown in Figure 13.11. Although current scanning software can read a résumé in any format, many companies still use older versions that have difficulty with complex fonts and formatting. Therefore, it pays to follow these tips for maximizing scannability and "hits."

FIGURE 13.8 Chronological Résumé: Current University Student With Limited Relevant Experience

Hung-Wei Chun used MS Word to design a traditional chronological print-based résumé that he plans to give to recruiters at the campus job fair or during an interview. Although Hung-Wei has work experience not related to his future employment, his résumé looks impressive because he has transferable skills. His internship is related to his future career, and his language skills and study abroad experience will help him score points in competition with applicants. Hung-Wei's volunteer experience is also attractive because it shows him as a well-rounded, compassionate individual. Because his experience in his future field is limited, he omitted a summary of qualifications.

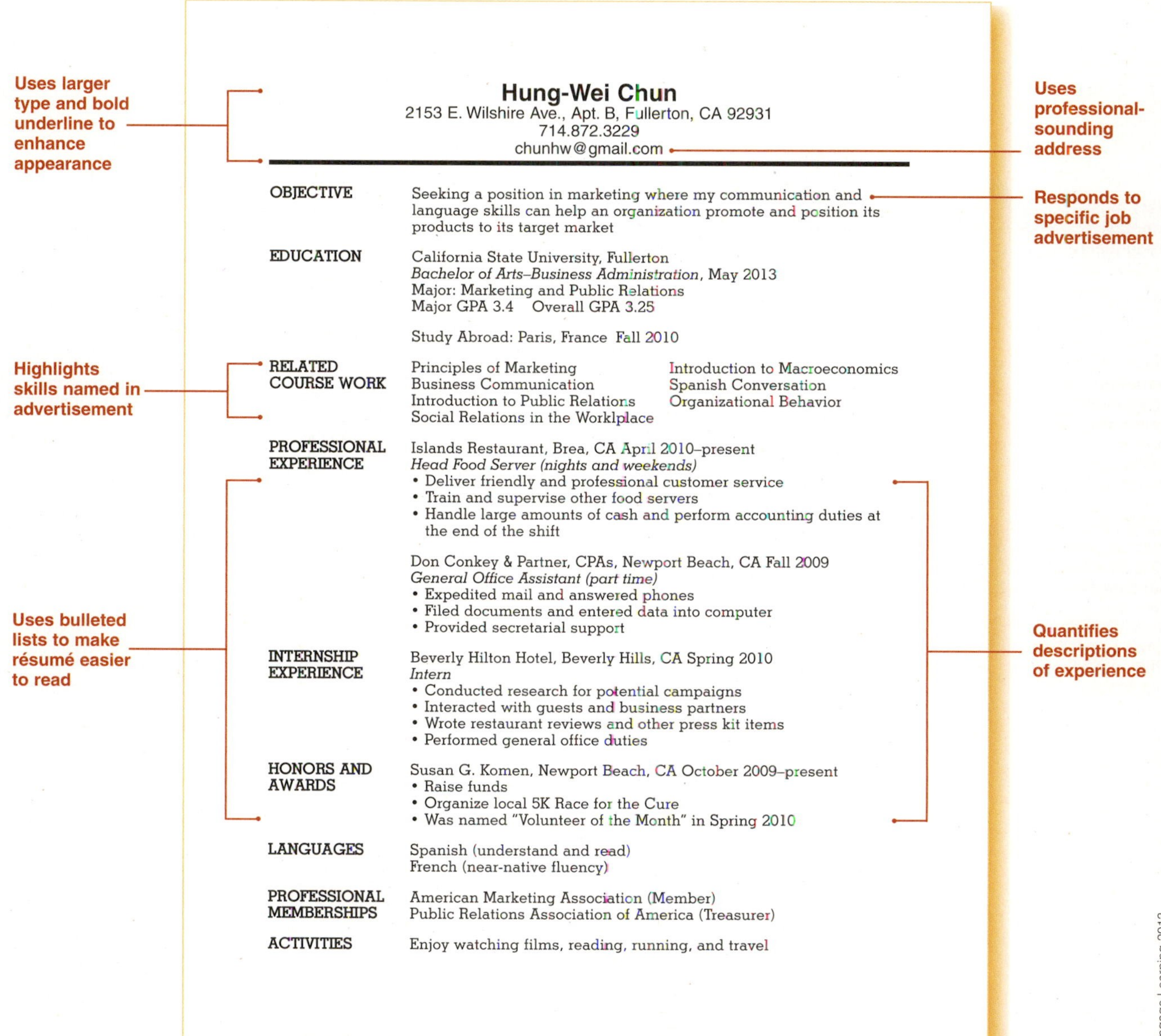

Uses larger type and bold underline to enhance appearance
Uses professional-sounding address
Responds to specific job advertisement
Highlights skills named in advertisement
Uses bulleted lists to make résumé easier to read
Quantifies descriptions of experience

Hung-Wei Chun
2153 E. Wilshire Ave., Apt. B, Fullerton, CA 92931
714.872.3229
chunhw@gmail.com

OBJECTIVE
Seeking a position in marketing where my communication and language skills can help an organization promote and position its products to its target market

EDUCATION
California State University, Fullerton
Bachelor of Arts–Business Administration, May 2013
Major: Marketing and Public Relations
Major GPA 3.4 Overall GPA 3.25

Study Abroad: Paris, France Fall 2010

RELATED COURSE WORK
Principles of Marketing
Business Communication
Introduction to Public Relations
Social Relations in the Worklplace
Introduction to Macroeconomics
Spanish Conversation
Organizational Behavior

PROFESSIONAL EXPERIENCE
Islands Restaurant, Brea, CA April 2010–present
Head Food Server (nights and weekends)
• Deliver friendly and professional customer service
• Train and supervise other food servers
• Handle large amounts of cash and perform accounting duties at the end of the shift

Don Conkey & Partner, CPAs, Newport Beach, CA Fall 2009
General Office Assistant (part time)
• Expedited mail and answered phones
• Filed documents and entered data into computer
• Provided secretarial support

INTERNSHIP EXPERIENCE
Beverly Hilton Hotel, Beverly Hills, CA Spring 2010
Intern
• Conducted research for potential campaigns
• Interacted with guests and business partners
• Wrote restaurant reviews and other press kit items
• Performed general office duties

HONORS AND AWARDS
Susan G. Komen, Newport Beach, CA October 2009–present
• Raise funds
• Organize local 5K Race for the Cure
• Was named "Volunteer of the Month" in Spring 2010

LANGUAGES
Spanish (understand and read)
French (near-native fluency)

PROFESSIONAL MEMBERSHIPS
American Marketing Association (Member)
Public Relations Association of America (Treasurer)

ACTIVITIES
Enjoy watching films, reading, running, and travel

Tips for Maximizing Scannability. A scannable résumé must sacrifice many of the graphic enhancements you might have used to make your traditional print résumé attractive. To maximize scannability, follow these steps:

Scannable résumés use plain formatting, large fonts, quality printing, and white space.

- **Use 10- to 14-point type.** Use a well-known font such as Times New Roman or Arial. The font size in the body of your résumé should be 10-, 11-, or 12-point, and headings should be no larger than 14-point.
- **Avoid fancy formatting.** Do not use underlining, italics, borders, shading, or other graphics to highlight text. These features don't scan well. Most

FIGURE 13.9 Chronological Résumé: University Graduate With Substantial Experience

Because Rachel Chowdhry has many years of experience and seeks executive-level employment, she highlighted her experience by placing it before her education. Her summary of qualifications highlighted her most impressive experience and skills. This chronological two-page résumé shows the steady progression of her career to executive positions, a movement that impresses and reassures recruiters.

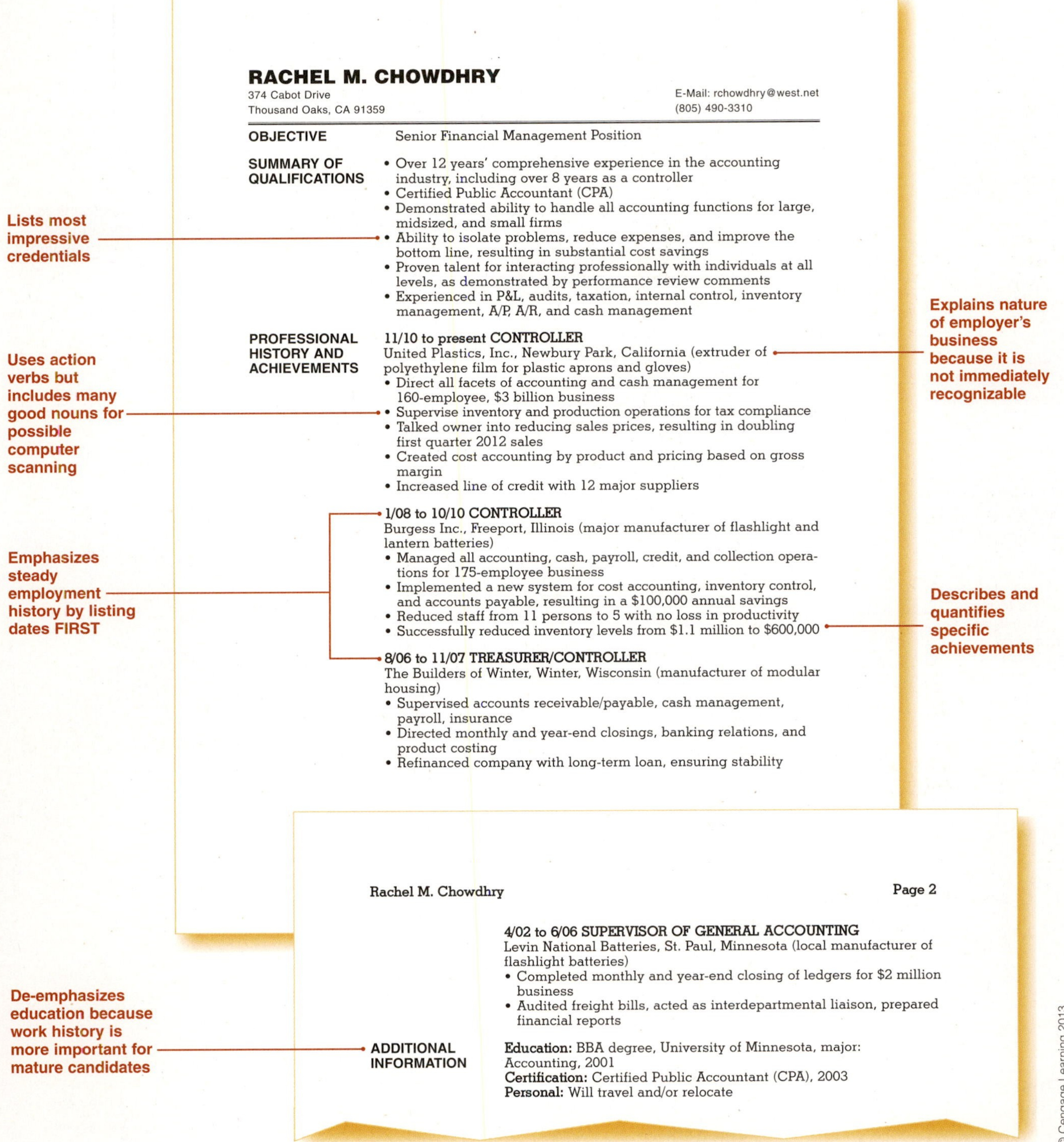

RACHEL M. CHOWDHRY

374 Cabot Drive
Thousand Oaks, CA 91359

E-Mail: rchowdhry@west.net
(805) 490-3310

OBJECTIVE Senior Financial Management Position

SUMMARY OF QUALIFICATIONS

- Over 12 years' comprehensive experience in the accounting industry, including over 8 years as a controller
- Certified Public Accountant (CPA)
- Demonstrated ability to handle all accounting functions for large, midsized, and small firms
- Ability to isolate problems, reduce expenses, and improve the bottom line, resulting in substantial cost savings
- Proven talent for interacting professionally with individuals at all levels, as demonstrated by performance review comments
- Experienced in P&L, audits, taxation, internal control, inventory management, A/P, A/R, and cash management

PROFESSIONAL HISTORY AND ACHIEVEMENTS

11/10 to present CONTROLLER
United Plastics, Inc., Newbury Park, California (extruder of polyethylene film for plastic aprons and gloves)

- Direct all facets of accounting and cash management for 160-employee, $3 billion business
- Supervise inventory and production operations for tax compliance
- Talked owner into reducing sales prices, resulting in doubling first quarter 2012 sales
- Created cost accounting by product and pricing based on gross margin
- Increased line of credit with 12 major suppliers

1/08 to 10/10 CONTROLLER
Burgess Inc., Freeport, Illinois (major manufacturer of flashlight and lantern batteries)

- Managed all accounting, cash, payroll, credit, and collection operations for 175-employee business
- Implemented a new system for cost accounting, inventory control, and accounts payable, resulting in a $100,000 annual savings
- Reduced staff from 11 persons to 5 with no loss in productivity
- Successfully reduced inventory levels from $1.1 million to $600,000

8/06 to 11/07 TREASURER/CONTROLLER
The Builders of Winter, Winter, Wisconsin (manufacturer of modular housing)

- Supervised accounts receivable/payable, cash management, payroll, insurance
- Directed monthly and year-end closings, banking relations, and product costing
- Refinanced company with long-term loan, ensuring stability

Rachel M. Chowdhry **Page 2**

4/02 to 6/06 SUPERVISOR OF GENERAL ACCOUNTING
Levin National Batteries, St. Paul, Minnesota (local manufacturer of flashlight batteries)

- Completed monthly and year-end closing of ledgers for $2 million business
- Audited freight bills, acted as interdepartmental liaison, prepared financial reports

ADDITIONAL INFORMATION

Education: BBA degree, University of Minnesota, major: Accounting, 2001
Certification: Certified Public Accountant (CPA), 2003
Personal: Will travel and/or relocate

Lists most impressive credentials
Uses action verbs but includes many good nouns for possible computer scanning
Emphasizes steady employment history by listing dates FIRST
De-emphasizes education because work history is more important for mature candidates
Explains nature of employer's business because it is not immediately recognizable
Describes and quantifies specific achievements

applicant-tracking programs, however, can accurately read bold print, solid bullets, and asterisks.

- **Place your name on the first line.** Reports generated by applicant-tracking software usually assume that the first line of a résumé contains the applicant's name.

FIGURE 13.10 **Functional Résumé: Recent College Graduate With Unrelated Part-Time Experience**

Recent graduate Kevin Touhy chose this functional format to de-emphasize his meager work experience and emphasize his potential in sales and marketing. This version of his résumé is more generic than one targeted for a specific position. Nevertheless, it emphasizes his strong points with specific achievements and includes an employment section to satisfy recruiters. The functional format presents ability-focused topics. It illustrates what the job seeker can do for the employer instead of narrating a history of previous jobs. Although recruiters prefer chronological résumés, the functional format is a good choice for new graduates, career changers, and those with employment gaps.

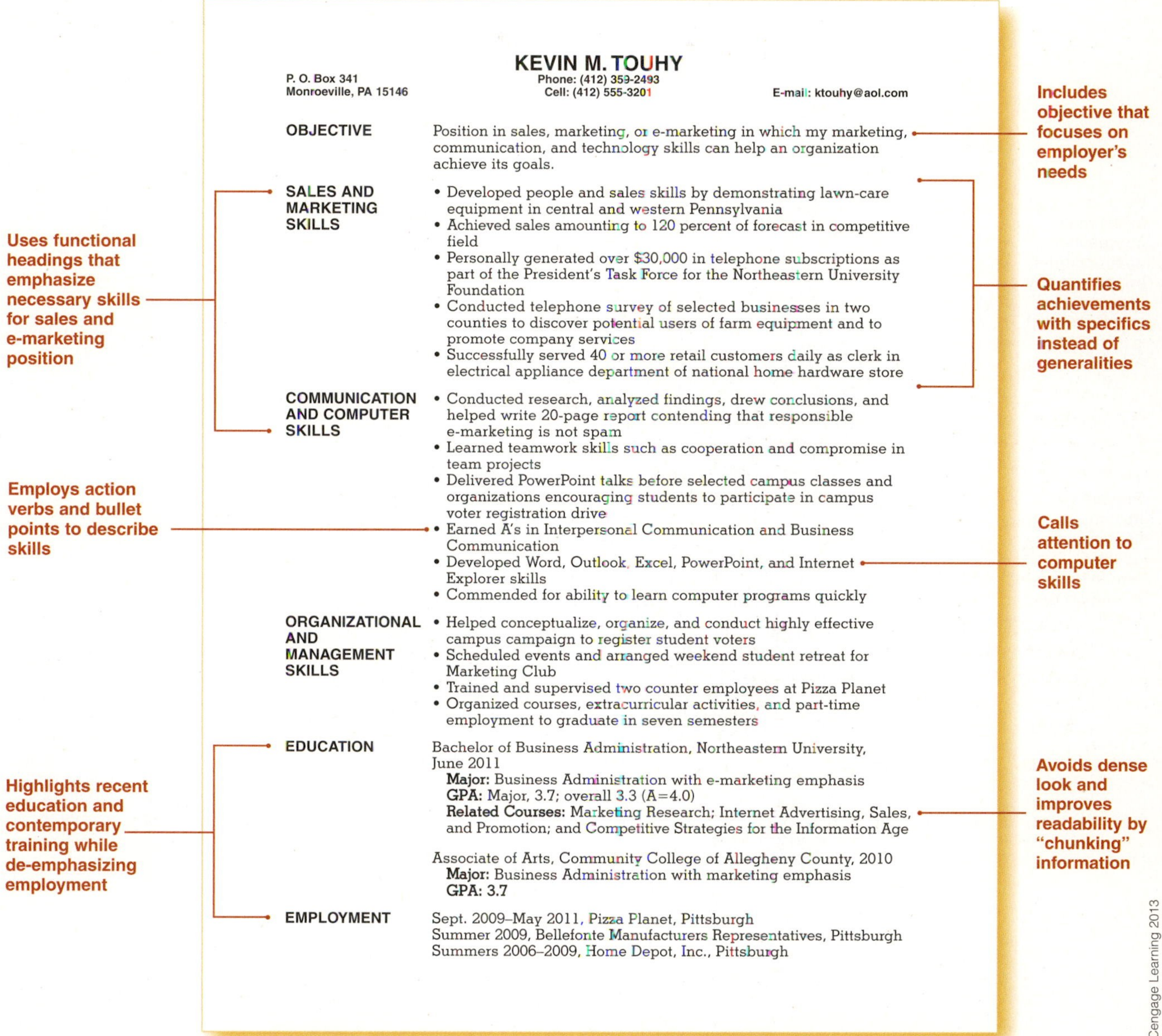

KEVIN M. TOUHY

P. O. Box 341
Monroeville, PA 15146

Phone: (412) 359-2493
Cell: (412) 555-3201

E-mail: ktouhy@aol.com

OBJECTIVE

Position in sales, marketing, or e-marketing in which my marketing, communication, and technology skills can help an organization achieve its goals.

SALES AND MARKETING SKILLS

- Developed people and sales skills by demonstrating lawn-care equipment in central and western Pennsylvania
- Achieved sales amounting to 120 percent of forecast in competitive field
- Personally generated over $30,000 in telephone subscriptions as part of the President's Task Force for the Northeastern University Foundation
- Conducted telephone survey of selected businesses in two counties to discover potential users of farm equipment and to promote company services
- Successfully served 40 or more retail customers daily as clerk in electrical appliance department of national home hardware store

COMMUNICATION AND COMPUTER SKILLS

- Conducted research, analyzed findings, drew conclusions, and helped write 20-page report contending that responsible e-marketing is not spam
- Learned teamwork skills such as cooperation and compromise in team projects
- Delivered PowerPoint talks before selected campus classes and organizations encouraging students to participate in campus voter registration drive
- Earned A's in Interpersonal Communication and Business Communication
- Developed Word, Outlook, Excel, PowerPoint, and Internet Explorer skills
- Commended for ability to learn computer programs quickly

ORGANIZATIONAL AND MANAGEMENT SKILLS

- Helped conceptualize, organize, and conduct highly effective campus campaign to register student voters
- Scheduled events and arranged weekend student retreat for Marketing Club
- Trained and supervised two counter employees at Pizza Planet
- Organized courses, extracurricular activities, and part-time employment to graduate in seven semesters

EDUCATION

Bachelor of Business Administration, Northeastern University, June 2011
Major: Business Administration with e-marketing emphasis
GPA: Major, 3.7; overall 3.3 (A=4.0)
Related Courses: Marketing Research; Internet Advertising, Sales, and Promotion; and Competitive Strategies for the Information Age

Associate of Arts, Community College of Allegheny County, 2010
Major: Business Administration with marketing emphasis
GPA: 3.7

EMPLOYMENT

Sept. 2009–May 2011, Pizza Planet, Pittsburgh
Summer 2009, Bellefonte Manufacturers Representatives, Pittsburgh
Summers 2006–2009, Home Depot, Inc., Pittsburgh

Includes objective that focuses on employer's needs
Uses functional headings that emphasize necessary skills for sales and e-marketing position
Quantifies achievements with specifics instead of generalities
Employs action verbs and bullet points to describe skills
Calls attention to computer skills
Highlights recent education and contemporary training while de-emphasizing employment
Avoids dense look and improves readability by "chunking" information

- **List each phone number on its own line.** Your landline and cell phone numbers should appear on separate lines to improve recognition.
- **Avoid double columns.** When listing job duties, skills, computer programs, and so forth, don't tabulate items into two- or three-column lists. Scanners read across and may convert tables into nonsensical output.
- **Take care when printing and mailing.** When printing your scannable résumé for mailing, use smooth white paper and black ink and print it on a quality printer. Mail your résumé in a large envelope to avoid folding it. If your résumé is longer than one page, don't staple it.

FIGURE 13.11 **Scannable Résumé**

Letitia P. Lopez prepared this "plain Jane" résumé free of graphics and fancy formatting so that it would scan well if read by a computer. With the résumé, she included many job titles, skills, traits, and other descriptive keywords that scanners are programmed to recognize. To improve accurate scanning, she avoided bullets, italics, underlining, and columns. If she had more information to include, she could have gone to a second page because a résumé to be scanned need not be restricted to one page.

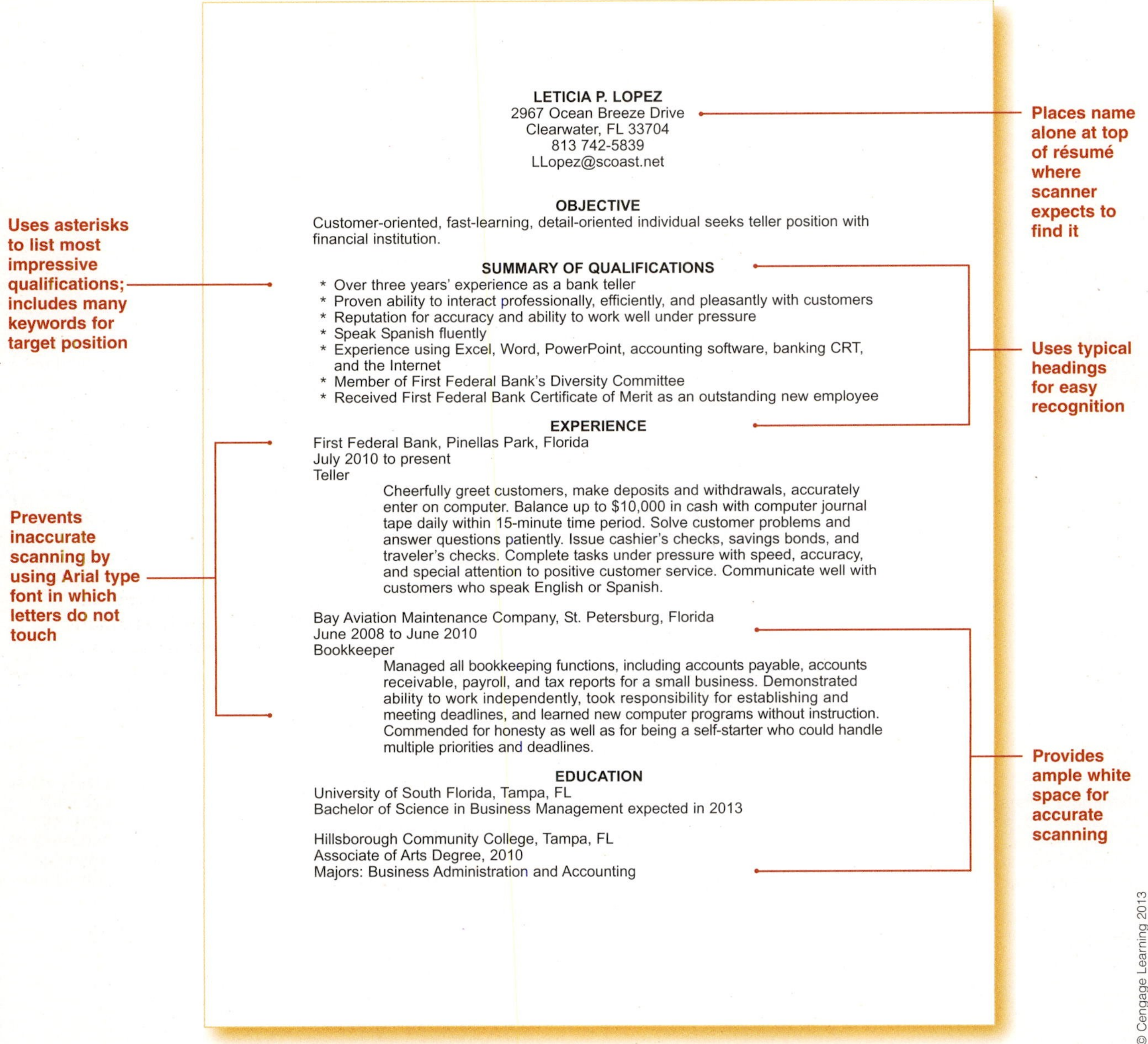

LETICIA P. LOPEZ
2967 Ocean Breeze Drive
Clearwater, FL 33704
813 742-5839
LLopez@scoast.net

OBJECTIVE
Customer-oriented, fast-learning, detail-oriented individual seeks teller position with financial institution.

SUMMARY OF QUALIFICATIONS
* Over three years' experience as a bank teller
* Proven ability to interact professionally, efficiently, and pleasantly with customers
* Reputation for accuracy and ability to work well under pressure
* Speak Spanish fluently
* Experience using Excel, Word, PowerPoint, accounting software, banking CRT, and the Internet
* Member of First Federal Bank's Diversity Committee
* Received First Federal Bank Certificate of Merit as an outstanding new employee

EXPERIENCE
First Federal Bank, Pinellas Park, Florida
July 2010 to present
Teller
Cheerfully greet customers, make deposits and withdrawals, accurately enter on computer. Balance up to $10,000 in cash with computer journal tape daily within 15-minute time period. Solve customer problems and answer questions patiently. Issue cashier's checks, savings bonds, and traveler's checks. Complete tasks under pressure with speed, accuracy, and special attention to positive customer service. Communicate well with customers who speak English or Spanish.

Bay Aviation Maintenance Company, St. Petersburg, Florida
June 2008 to June 2010
Bookkeeper
Managed all bookkeeping functions, including accounts payable, accounts receivable, payroll, and tax reports for a small business. Demonstrated ability to work independently, took responsibility for establishing and meeting deadlines, and learned new computer programs without instruction. Commended for honesty as well as for being a self-starter who could handle multiple priorities and deadlines.

EDUCATION
University of South Florida, Tampa, FL
Bachelor of Science in Business Management expected in 2013

Hillsborough Community College, Tampa, FL
Associate of Arts Degree, 2010
Majors: Business Administration and Accounting

Places name alone at top of résumé where scanner expects to find it
Uses asterisks to list most impressive qualifications; includes many keywords for target position
Uses typical headings for easy recognition
Prevents inaccurate scanning by using Arial type font in which letters do not touch
Provides ample white space for accurate scanning

Scanners produce "hits" when they recognize targeted keywords such as nouns describing skills, traits, tasks, and job titles.

Tips for Maximizing "Hits." In addition to paying attention to the physical appearance of your résumé, you must also be concerned with keywords or keyword phrases that produce "hits," or recognition by the scanner. The following tips will help you to maximize hits:

- **Focus on specific keywords or keyword phrases.** Study carefully any advertisements and job descriptions for the position you want. Describe your experience, education, and qualifications in terms associated with the job advertisement or job description for this position. Select keywords or phrases that describe specific skills, traits, expertise, tasks, and job titles.

- **Use accurate names.** Spell out complete names of schools, degrees, and dates. Include specific names of companies, products, and services, as appropriate.
- **Be careful of abbreviations and acronyms.** Spell out unfamiliar abbreviations and acronyms, but maximize easily recognized abbreviations and acronyms—especially those within your field, such as CAD, JPG, or JIT.
- **Describe interpersonal traits and attitudes.** Hiring managers look for keywords and phrases that describe interpersonal traits and attitudes that are related to the specific position; for example, *time management skills, dependability, high energy, leadership, sense of responsibility*, and *team player*.

Showcasing Your Qualifications in an E-Portfolio or a Video Résumé

As the workplace becomes increasingly digital, you have new ways to display your qualifications to prospective employers—in digitized e-portfolios and video résumés. Resourceful job candidates in certain fields—writers, models, artists, and graphic artists—have been creating print portfolios to illustrate their qualifications and achievements for some time. Now business and professional job candidates are using electronic portfolios to show off their talents.

An e-portfolio offers links to examples of a job candidate's performance, talents, and accomplishments in digital form.

"I want my résumé to be the one you remember. It's also available as a music video, interpretive dance, and a haiku."

Understanding the E-Portfolio. An e-portfolio is a collection of digital files that can be navigated with the help of menus and hyperlinks much like a personal Web site. An e-portfolio provides viewers with a snapshot of a candidate's performance, talents, and accomplishments. A digital portfolio may include a copy of your résumé, reference letters, commendations for special achievements, awards, certificates, work samples, a complete list of your courses, thank-you letters, and anything else that touts your accomplishments. An e-portfolio might include links to electronic copies of your artwork, film projects, videos, blueprints, documents, photographs, multimedia files, and blog entries that might otherwise be difficult to share with potential employers.

E-portfolios are generally accessed at Web sites, where they are available around-the-clock to employers. Some colleges and universities not only make Web site space available for student e-portfolios, but also provide instruction and resources for scanning photos, digitizing images, and preparing graphics. E-portfolios may also be burned onto CDs and DVDs to be mailed to prospective employers. Whichever medium you choose, respect the intellectual property of your employers before sharing professional work samples online. Don't post them without permission.[33]

Job candidates generally offer e-portfolios at Web sites, but they may also burn them onto CDs or DVDs.

E-portfolios have many advantages. On Web sites they can be viewed at employers' convenience. Let's say you are talking on the phone with an employer in another city who wants to see a copy of your résumé. You can simply refer the employer to the Web address where your résumé resides. E-portfolios can also be seen by many individuals in an organization without circulating a paper copy. But the real reason for preparing an e-portfolio is that it shows off your talents and qualifications more thoroughly than a print résumé does.

Understanding the Video Résumé. Tech-savvy applicants even use videos to profile their skills. A professional-grade video résumé may open doors and secure an interview when other techniques have failed.[34] However, some recruiters are skeptical about digital or video portfolios because they fear that such applications take more time to view than paper-based résumés do. One time-strapped recruiter clearly favors traditional applications: "If I have a stack of resumes and a good highlighter, I can do that much faster."[35] Nontraditional applications may end up at the bottom of the pile or be ignored.

Moreover, humiliation looms if the applicant produces an amateurish result with low-quality video, poor sound, and inappropriate lighting. Finally, video résumés are most appropriate for positions requiring creativity, salesmanship, and presentation skills in the visual and performing arts, advertising, and public relations fields. Video résumés are much less suitable for more traditional positions—for example, in banking or accounting.[36]

A truly weighty reason to exercise caution when creating and sharing video résumés is the risk of discrimination lawsuits. Employment decisions must be based on objective criteria related to the position, not on subjective factors such as appearance. Corporate lawyers advise their clients to refuse to view online video résumés or traditional résumés with pictures. New Jersey attorney Steven Harz warns: "Video resumes lend themselves to making decisions based on race, gender, national origin and other protected classifications plus other subjective issues. Subjective decisions are difficult to defend in court."[37]

Not long ago, fewer than a quarter of senior executives in the United States accepted video résumés, but multimedia resources are growing. Within a few years, video résumé sites, such as BriteTab.com, OptimalResume.com, InterviewStudio.com, and Resumebook.tv, were launched.[38] They propose to make creating e-video résumés an easy task with customizable templates. Experts agree that the new medium will need to mature before smart use guidelines can emerge. You can learn more about video résumés by searching the Web.

Ensuring Integrity and Polishing Your Résumé

Because your résumé is probably the most important message you will ever write, you will revise it many times. With so much information in concentrated form and with so much riding on its outcome, your résumé demands careful polishing, proofreading, and critiquing.

As you revise, be certain to verify all the facts, particularly those involving your previous employment and education. Don't be caught in a mistake, or worse, a distortion of previous jobs and dates of employment. These items likely will be checked, and the consequences of puffing up a résumé with deception or flat-out lies are simply not worth the risk.

Being Honest and Ethical

Lying on a résumé is illegal and fudging the facts is unethical. Either can destroy a career.

A résumé is expected to showcase a candidate's strengths and minimize weaknesses. For this reason, recruiters expect a certain degree of self-promotion. Some résumé writers, however, step over the line that separates honest self-marketing from deceptive half-truths and flat-out lies. Distorting facts on a résumé is unethical; lying is illegal. Most important, either practice can destroy a career.

Given the competitive job market, it might be tempting to puff up your résumé. What's more, you would not be alone in telling fibs or outright whoppers. A survey of 8,700 workers found that only 8 percent admitted to lying on their résumés; however, the same study found that of the 3,100 hiring managers surveyed, 49 percent caught a job applicant lying on some part of his or her résumé. And 57 percent of employers will automatically dismiss applicants who lie on any part of their résumés. According to Rosemary Haefner, vice president of Human Resources for CareerBuilder.com, "Even the slightest embellishment can come back to haunt you and ruin your credibility. If you're concerned about gaps in employment, your academic background or skill sets, invention is not the answer."[39] Although recruiters can't check all information, most will verify previous employment and education before hiring candidates. Over half will require official transcripts.

After hiring, the checking process may continue. If hiring officials find a discrepancy in GPA or prior experience and the error is an honest mistake, they meet with the new-hire to hear an explanation. If the discrepancy wasn't a mistake,

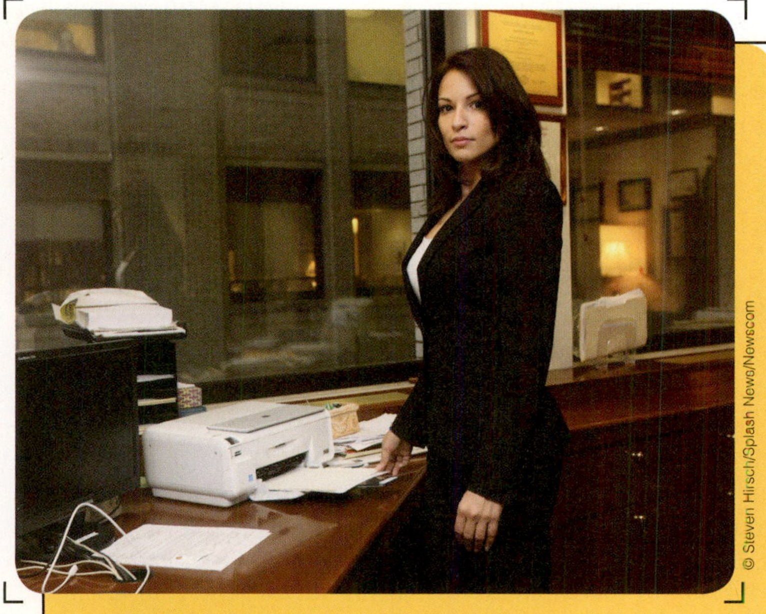

© Steven Hirsch/Splash News/Newscom

WORKPLACE IN FOCUS

Whether legally risky or merely unprofessional, sending personal photos to recruiters is a mistake, employment experts say. Hiring based on looks has triggered discrimination lawsuits for Southwest Airlines and Hooters Restaurants, and fashion brand American Apparel is under fire for requiring full-body photos for all job applicants. In one high-profile case about looks and professionalism, Citibank fired an employee for accentuating sex appeal at work. *Is it possible to keep appearance out of the employment process in the age of Facebook?*

they will likely fire the person immediately. No job seeker wants to be in the unhappy position of explaining résumé errors or defending misrepresentation. Avoiding the following common problems can keep you off the hot seat:

- **Inflated education, grades, or honors.** Some job candidates claim degrees from colleges or universities when in fact they merely attended classes. Others increase their grade point averages or claim fictitious honors. Any such dishonest reporting is grounds for dismissal when discovered.
- **Enhanced job titles.** Wishing to elevate their status, some applicants misrepresent their titles. For example, one technician called himself a programmer when he had actually programmed only one project for his boss. A mail clerk who assumed added responsibilities conferred upon herself the title of supervisor. Even when the description seems accurate, it is unethical to list any title not officially granted.
- **Puffed-up accomplishments.** Some job seekers inflate their employment experience or achievements. One clerk, eager to make her photocopying duties sound more important, said that she assisted the *vice president in communicating and distributing employee directives.* An Ivy League graduate who spent the better part of six months watching rented movies on his DVD player described the activity as *Independent Film Study.* The latter statement may have helped win an interview, but it lost him the job. In addition to avoiding puffery, guard against taking sole credit for achievements that required many people. When recruiters suspect dubious claims on résumés, they nail applicants with specific—and often embarrassing—questions during their interviews.
- **Altered employment dates.** Some candidates extend the dates of employment to hide unimpressive jobs or to cover up periods of unemployment and illness. Let's say that several years ago Cindy was unemployed for 14 months between working for Company A and being hired by Company B. To make her employment history look better, she adds seven months to her tenure with Company A and seven months to Company B. Now her

"I typed up my résumé on the computer. The spell-checker accidentally changed 'Mid-State Junior College' to 'Harvard.'"

© Randy Glasbergen www.glasbergen.com

employment history has no gaps, but her résumé is dishonest and represents a potential booby trap for her.

- **Hidden keywords.** One of the latest sneaky tricks involves inserting invisible keywords in electronic résumés. To fool scanning programs into ranking their résumés higher, some job hunters use white type on a white background or they use Web coding to pack their résumés with target keywords. However, newer recruiter search tools detect such mischief, and those résumés are tossed.[40]

If your honest qualifications aren't good enough to get you the job you want, start working now to improve them. No job seeker should want to be hired based on lies.

Polishing Your Résumé

Studying models for ideas can help you improve your résumé format.

While you continue revising, look for other ways to improve your résumé. For example, consider consolidating headings. By condensing your information into as few headings as possible, you will produce a clean, professional-looking document. Study other résumés for valuable formatting ideas. Ask yourself what graphic highlighting techniques you can use to improve readability: capitalization, underlining, indenting, and bulleting. Experiment with headings and styles to achieve a pleasing, easy-to-read message. Moreover, look for ways to eliminate wordiness. For example, instead of *Supervised two employees who worked at the counter*, try *Supervised two counter employees*. Review Chapter 4 for more tips on writing concisely.

"It sounds basic, but make sure that your résumé is free of typos and other errors. When applying by e-mail, there is more of a tendency to rush and make careless mistakes. For many employers, this shows a lack of attention to detail and is an easy way to eliminate someone from consideration."

—Wendy S. Enelow, executive director of Career Masters Institute

In addition to making your résumé concise, make sure that you haven't included any of the following information, which does not belong on a résumé:

- Any basis for discrimination (age, marital status, gender, national origin, religion, race, number of children, disability)
- A photograph
- Reasons for leaving previous jobs
- The word *résumé*
- Social security number
- Salary history or requirements
- High school information
- References
- Full addresses of schools or employers (include city and state only)

Above all, make sure your print-based résumé look professional. Avoid anything humorous or "cute," such as a help-wanted poster with your name or picture inside. Eliminate the personal pronoun *I* to ensure an objective style. Use high-quality paper in a professional color, such as white, off-white, or light gray. Print your résumé using a first-rate printer. Be prepared with a résumé for people to read as well as versions for computer scanning, sending by e-mail, and posting to Web sites.

Proofreading Your Résumé

In addition to being well written, a résumé must be carefully formatted and meticulously proofread.

After revising, you must proofread, proofread, and proofread again for spelling, grammar, mechanics, content, and format. Then have a knowledgeable friend or relative proofread it yet again. This is one document that must be perfect. Because the job market is so competitive, one typo, misspelled word, or grammatical error could eliminate you from consideration.

By now you may be thinking that you'd like to hire someone to write your résumé. Don't! First, you know yourself better than anyone else could know you. Second, you will end up with a generic or a one-time résumé. A generic résumé in today's tight job market will lose out to a customized résumé nine times out of ten. Equally useless is a one-time résumé aimed at a single job. What if you don't get that job? Because you will need to revise your résumé many times as you seek a variety of jobs, be prepared to write (and rewrite) it yourself.

Submitting Your Résumé

If you are responding to a job advertisement, be sure to read the job listing carefully to make sure you know how the employer wants you to submit your résumé. Not following the prospective employer's instructions can eliminate you from consideration before your résumé is even reviewed. Employers will probably ask you to submit your résumé as a Word, plain-text, or PDF document. You may also be asked to submit it in the company database or by fax.

Send your résumé in the format the employer requests.

- **Word document.** Recruiters may still ask candidates to send their résumés and cover letters by postal mail. They may also allow applicants to attach their résumés as Microsoft Word documents to e-mails, despite the fear of viruses.
- **Plain-text document.** Some employers expect applicants to submit résumés and cover letters as plain-text documents. This format is widely used for posting to an online job board and sometimes for sending by e-mail. Plain-text résumés may be embedded within or attached to e-mails. Convert your files to plain text in Microsoft Word with the **Save As** option. Select *Plain Text* as the file type. Because you will lose nearly all formatting after converting your file to plain text, you will have to examine the resulting document carefully in your word processor and check it again once you paste the plain-text résumé into your e-mail.
- **PDF document.** For safety reasons, many hiring managers prefer PDF (portable document format) files. A PDF résumé will look exactly like the original and cannot be altered without Adobe Acrobat or other conversion software. Most computers have Adobe Acrobat Reader installed for easy reading of PDF files. Converting your Microsoft Word and other Office documents to a PDF file, however, requires an add-in for older word processing software or Adobe Acrobat. The 2010 Office versions allow you to select **Save as** and **Print** to a PDF.
- **Company database.** Some organizations prefer that you complete an online form with your résumé information. This enables them to plug your data into their formats for rapid searching. You might be able to cut and paste your information into the online form.
- **Fax.** Although still a popular way of sending résumés, faxing presents problems such as blurry text and lost information. If you must fax your résumé, use at least 12-point font to improve readability. Thinner fonts—such as Times New Roman, Palatino, New Century Schoolbook, Arial, and Bookman—are clearer than thicker ones. Avoid underlines, which may look broken or choppy when faxed. Follow up with your polished, printed résumé.

Whether you are mailing your résumé the traditional way, submitting it by e-mail, or transmitting it by fax, don't send it on its own. Regardless of the submission format, in most cases a résumé should be accompanied by a cover letter, which will be discussed next.

Creating a Customized, Persuasive Cover Letter

Job candidates often labor over their résumés but treat the cover letter as an afterthought. Some send out résumés without including a cover letter at all. These critical mistakes could destroy a job search. Even if an advertisement does not request one, be sure to distinguish your application with a persuasive cover letter (also called a *letter of application*). Some hiring managers won't even look at a résumé if it is not accompanied by a cover letter. A cover letter has three purposes: (a) introducing the résumé, (b) highlighting your strengths in terms of benefits to the reader, and (c) helping you gain an interview. In many ways your cover letter is a sales letter; it sells your talent and tries to beat the competition. It will, accordingly, include many of the techniques you learned for persuasive messages in Chapter 8, especially if your letter is unsolicited.

Cover letters introduce résumés, relate writer strengths to reader benefits, and seek an interview.

Recruiting professionals disagree about how long to make a cover letter. Many prefer short letters with no more than three paragraphs. Others desire longer letters that supply more information, thus giving them a better opportunity to evaluate a candidate's qualifications and writing ability. These recruiters argue that hiring and training new employees is expensive and time consuming; therefore, they welcome extra data to guide them in making the best choice the first time. Follow your judgment in writing a brief or a longer cover letter. If you think, for example, that you need space to explain in more detail what you can do for a prospective employer, do so.

Regardless of its length, a cover letter should have three primary parts: (a) an opening that captures attention, introduces the message, and identifies the position; (b) a body that sells the candidate and focuses on the employer's needs; and (c) a closing that requests an interview and motivates action. When putting your cover letter together, remember that the biggest mistake job seekers make when writing cover letters is making them sound too generic. You should, therefore, write a personalized, customized cover letter for every position you apply for.

Gaining Attention in the Opening

The opening in a cover letter gains attention by addressing the receiver by name.

Your cover letter will be more appealing, and more likely to be read, if it begins by addressing the reader by name. Rather than sending your letter to the *Hiring Manager* or *Human Resources Department*, try to identify the name of the appropriate individual. Kelly Renz, vice president for a recruiting outsourcing firm, says that resourceful job seekers "take control of their application's destiny." She suggests looking on the company's Web site, doing an Internet search for a name, or calling the human resources department and asking the receptionist the name of the person in charge of hiring.

In addition, Ms. Renz suggests using professional networking sites such as LinkedIn to find someone working in the same department as the posted job. This person may know the name of the hiring manager.[41] If you still cannot find the name of any person to address, you might replace the salutation of your letter with a descriptive subject line such as *Application for Marketing Specialist Position.*

How you open your cover letter depends largely on whether the application is solicited or unsolicited. If an employment position has been announced and applicants are being solicited, you can use a direct approach. If you don't know whether a position is open and you are prospecting for a job, use an indirect approach. Whether direct or indirect, the opening should attract the attention of the reader. Strive for openings that are more imaginative than *Please consider this letter an application for the position of . . .* or *I would like to apply for . . . .*

Openers for solicited jobs refer to the source of the information, the job title, and qualifications for the position.

Openings for Solicited Jobs. When applying for a job that has been announced, consider some of the following techniques to open your cover letter:

- **Refer to the name of an employee in the company.** Remember that employers always hope to hire known quantities rather than complete strangers:

  Mitchell Sims, a member of your Customer Service Department, told me that IntriPlex is seeking an experienced customer-service representative. The enclosed summary of my qualifications demonstrates my preparation for this position.

  At the suggestion of Ms. Jennifer Larson of your Human Resources Department, I submit my qualifications for the position of staffing coordinator.

- **Refer to the source of your information precisely.** If you are answering an advertisement, include the exact position advertised and the name and date of the publication. If you are responding to a position listed on an online job board, include the Web site name and the date the position was posted:

Your advertisement in Section C-3 of the June 1 Daily News *for an accounting administrator greatly appeals to me. With my accounting training and computer experience, I am confident I could serve Quad Graphics well.*

From your company's Web site, I learned about your need for a sales representative for the Ohio, Indiana, and Illinois regions. I am very interested in this position and am confident that my education and experience are appropriate for the opening.

Susan Butler, placement director at Sierra University, told me that Data-Tech has an opening for a technical writer with knowledge of Web design and graphics.

My talent for interacting with people, coupled with more than five years of customer-service experience, makes me an ideal candidate for the director of customer relations position you advertised on the CareerJournal.com Web site on August 3.

- **Refer to the job title and describe how your qualifications fit the requirements.** Hiring managers are looking for a match between an applicant's credentials and the job needs:

Will an honors graduate with a degree in recreation and two years of part-time experience organizing social activities for a convalescent hospital qualify for your position of activity director?

Because of my specialized training in finance and accounting at Boise State University, I am confident that I have the qualifications you described in your advertisement for a staff accountant trainee.

Openings for unsolicited jobs show an interest in and knowledge of the company, as well as spotlight reader benefits.

Openings for Unsolicited Jobs. If you are unsure whether a position actually exists, you might use a more persuasive opening. Because your goal is to convince this person to read on, try one of the following techniques:

- **Demonstrate interest in and knowledge of the reader's business.** Show the hiring officer that you have done your research and that this organization is more than a mere name to you:

Because Signa HealthNet, Inc., is organizing a new information management team for its recently established group insurance division, could you use the services of a well-trained information systems graduate who seeks to become a professional systems analyst?

- **Show how your special talents and background will benefit the company.** Human resource managers need to be convinced that you can do something for them:

Could your rapidly expanding publications division use the services of an editorial assistant who offers exceptional language skills, has an honors degree from the University of Maine, and has two years of experience producing a campus literary publication?

Do recruiters really read cover letters? Although some hiring managers ignore them, others read them carefully. Given the stiff competition for jobs today, making an effort to write a cover letter and to customize it for the position makes sense. Crafting a letter specifically for a job opening enables the job seeker to stand out from all those who skip this important step.

In applying for an advertised job, Tonya Powell wrote the solicited cover letter shown in Figure 13.12. Notice that her opening identifies the position advertised on the company's Web site, so that the reader knows exactly what advertisement

FIGURE 13.12 Solicited Cover Letter

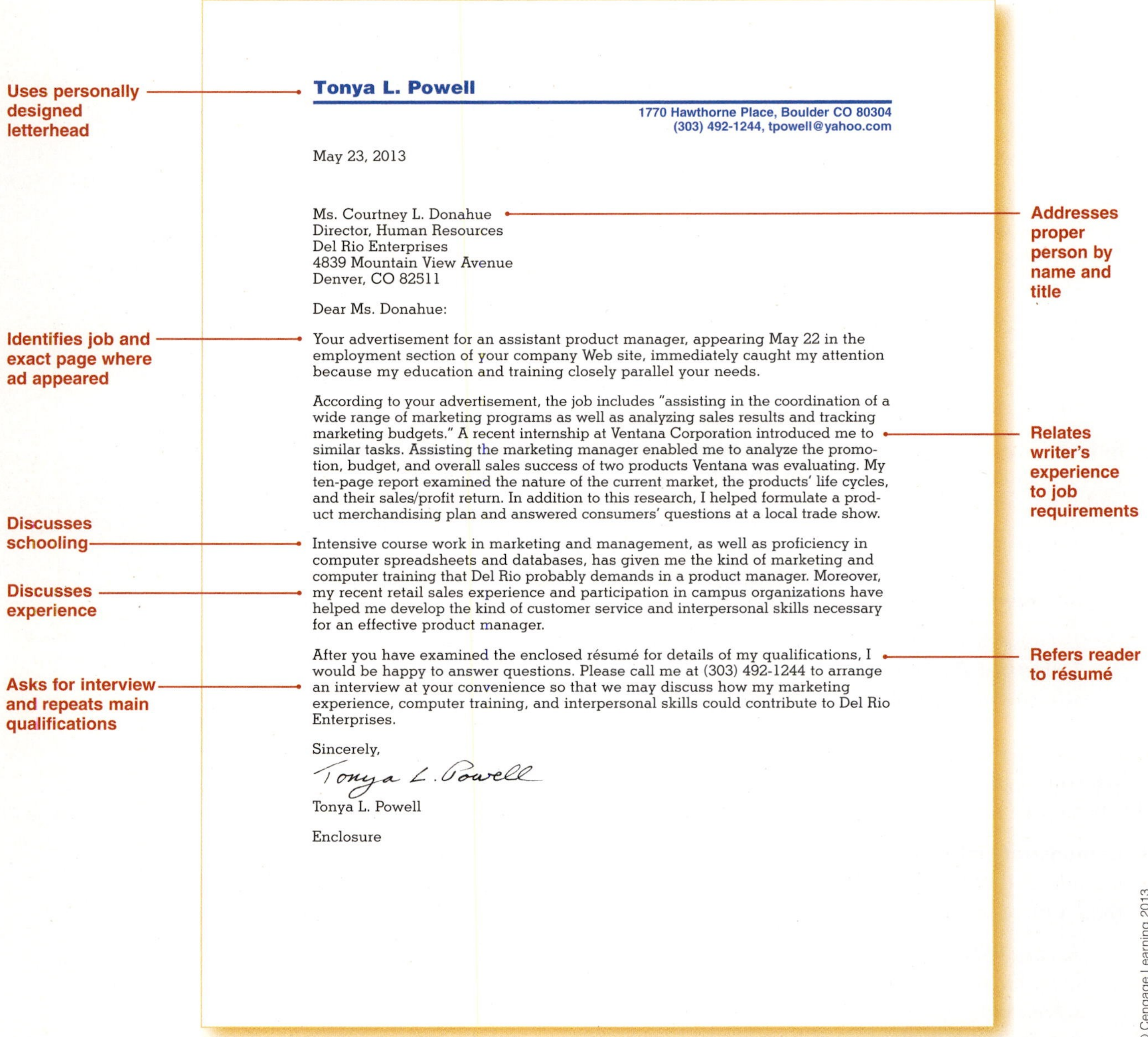

Uses personally designed letterhead
Addresses proper person by name and title
Identifies job and exact page where ad appeared
Relates writer's experience to job requirements
Discusses schooling
Discusses experience
Refers reader to résumé
Asks for interview and repeats main qualifications
© Cengage Learning 2013

Tonya L. Powell

1770 Hawthorne Place, Boulder CO 80304
(303) 492-1244, tpowell@yahoo.com

May 23, 2013

Ms. Courtney L. Donahue
Director, Human Resources
Del Rio Enterprises
4839 Mountain View Avenue
Denver, CO 82511

Dear Ms. Donahue:

Your advertisement for an assistant product manager, appearing May 22 in the employment section of your company Web site, immediately caught my attention because my education and training closely parallel your needs.

According to your advertisement, the job includes "assisting in the coordination of a wide range of marketing programs as well as analyzing sales results and tracking marketing budgets." A recent internship at Ventana Corporation introduced me to similar tasks. Assisting the marketing manager enabled me to analyze the promotion, budget, and overall sales success of two products Ventana was evaluating. My ten-page report examined the nature of the current market, the products' life cycles, and their sales/profit return. In addition to this research, I helped formulate a product merchandising plan and answered consumers' questions at a local trade show.

Intensive course work in marketing and management, as well as proficiency in computer spreadsheets and databases, has given me the kind of marketing and computer training that Del Rio probably demands in a product manager. Moreover, my recent retail sales experience and participation in campus organizations have helped me develop the kind of customer service and interpersonal skills necessary for an effective product manager.

After you have examined the enclosed résumé for details of my qualifications, I would be happy to answer questions. Please call me at (303) 492-1244 to arrange an interview at your convenience so that we may discuss how my marketing experience, computer training, and interpersonal skills could contribute to Del Rio Enterprises.

Sincerely,

Tonya L. Powell

Tonya L. Powell

Enclosure

Tonya means. Using word processing, Tonya designed her own letterhead that uses her name and looks like professionally printed letterhead paper. Notice that Tonya chose a blue color accent for her letter. When used sparingly and strategically, color can help job hunters stand out. Personal branding expert William Arruda believes, "Color is a valuable tool in your personal branding toolbox that will help express your brand attributes and create emotional connections with hiring managers and recruiters." Arruda does not promote gaudy-looking application documents but suggests the consistent use of just one color—one that is best suited to reinforce an applicant's brand message.[42]

More challenging are unsolicited cover letters, such as Donald Vinton's shown in Figure 13.13. Because he hopes to discover or create a job, his opening must grab the reader's attention immediately. To do that, he capitalizes on company information appearing in an online article. Donald purposely kept his cover letter short and to the point because he anticipated that a busy executive would be

FIGURE 13.13 Unsolicited Cover Letter

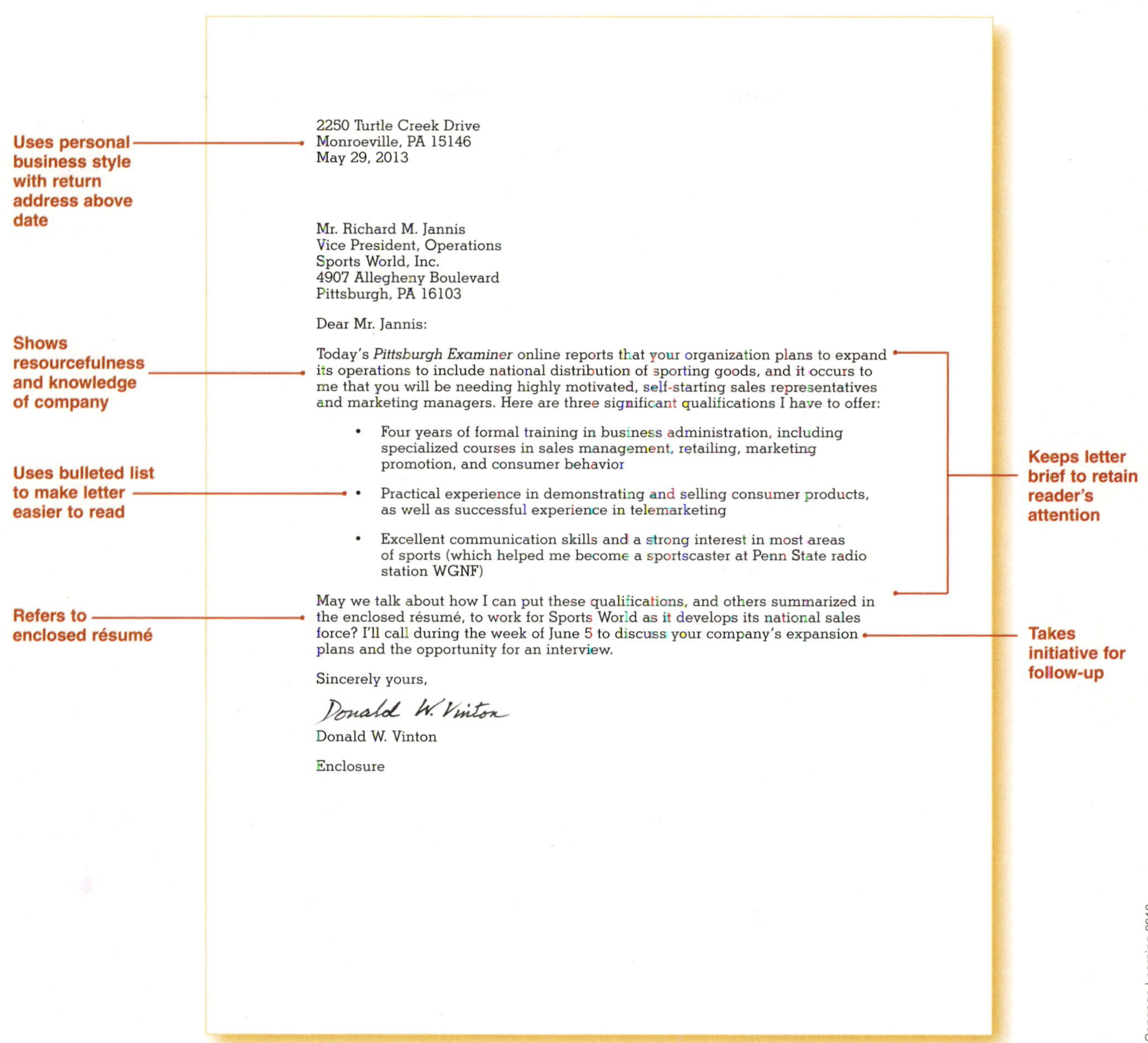

Uses personal business style with return address above date
Shows resourcefulness and knowledge of company
Uses bulleted list to make letter easier to read
Refers to enclosed résumé
Keeps letter brief to retain reader's attention
Takes initiative for follow-up

2250 Turtle Creek Drive
Monroeville, PA 15146
May 29, 2013

Mr. Richard M. Jannis
Vice President, Operations
Sports World, Inc.
4907 Allegheny Boulevard
Pittsburgh, PA 16103

Dear Mr. Jannis:

Today's *Pittsburgh Examiner* online reports that your organization plans to expand its operations to include national distribution of sporting goods, and it occurs to me that you will be needing highly motivated, self-starting sales representatives and marketing managers. Here are three significant qualifications I have to offer:

- Four years of formal training in business administration, including specialized courses in sales management, retailing, marketing promotion, and consumer behavior
- Practical experience in demonstrating and selling consumer products, as well as successful experience in telemarketing
- Excellent communication skills and a strong interest in most areas of sports (which helped me become a sportscaster at Penn State radio station WGNF)

May we talk about how I can put these qualifications, and others summarized in the enclosed résumé, to work for Sports World as it develops its national sales force? I'll call during the week of June 5 to discuss your company's expansion plans and the opportunity for an interview.

Sincerely yours,

Donald W. Vinton

Donald W. Vinton

Enclosure

unwilling to read a long, detailed letter. Donald's unsolicited letter "prospects" for a job. Some job candidates believe that such letters may be even more productive than efforts to secure advertised jobs, since prospecting candidates face less competition and show initiative. Notice that Donald's letter uses a personal business letter format with his return address above the date.

Highlighting Your Strengths in the Body

Once you have captured the attention of the reader and identified your purpose in the letter opening, you should use the body of the letter to promote your qualifications for this position. If you are responding to an advertisement, you will want to explain how your preparation and experience fill the stated requirements. If you are prospecting for a job, you may not know the exact requirements. Your employment research and knowledge of your field, however, should give you a reasonably good idea of what is expected for this position.

The body of the cover letter promotes the candidate's qualifications for the targeted job.

It is also important to stress reader benefits. In other words, you should describe your strong points in relation to the needs of the employer. Hiring officers want you to tell them what you can do for their organizations. This is more important than telling what courses you took in college or what duties you performed in your previous jobs. Instead of *I have completed courses in business communication, report writing, and technical writing,* try this:

Courses in business communication, report writing, and technical writing have helped me develop the research and writing skills required of your technical writers.

Employers seek employees who are team players, take responsibility, show initiative, and learn easily.

Choose your strongest qualifications and show how they fit the targeted job. Remember that students with little experience are better off spotlighting their education and its practical applications, as these candidates did:

Because you seek an architect's apprentice with proven ability, I submit a drawing of mine that won second place in the Sinclair College drafting contest last year.

Composing e-mails, business letters, memos, and reports in my business communication and office technology courses helped me build the writing, language, proofreading, and computer skills mentioned in your ad for an administrative assistant.

In the body of your letter, you may choose to discuss relevant personal traits. Employers are looking for candidates who, among other things, are team players, take responsibility, show initiative, and learn easily. Do not just list several personal traits, though; instead, include documentation that proves you possess these traits. Notice how the following paragraph uses action verbs to paint a picture of a promising candidate:

In addition to honing technical and academic skills at Mid-State University, I have gained interpersonal, leadership, and organizational skills. As vice president of the business students' organization, Gamma Alpha, I helped organize and supervise two successful fund-raising events. These activities involved conceptualizing the tasks, motivating others to help, scheduling work sessions, and coordinating the efforts of 35 diverse students in reaching our goal. I enjoyed my success with these activities and look forward to applying such experience in your management trainee program.

Finally, in this section or the next, you should refer the reader to your résumé. Do so directly or as part of another statement, as shown here:

As you will notice from my enclosed résumé, I will graduate in June with a bachelor's degree in business administration. Please refer to the attached résumé for additional information regarding my education, experience, and references.

Motivating Action in the Closing

The closing of a cover letter confidently requests an interview and makes it easy to respond.

After presenting your case, you should conclude by asking confidently for an interview. Don't ask for the job. To do so would be presumptuous and naïve. In requesting an interview, you might suggest reader benefits or review your strongest points. Sound sincere and appreciative. Remember to make it easy for the reader to agree by supplying your telephone number and the best times to call you. In addition, keep in mind that some hiring officers prefer that you take the initiative to call them. Avoid expressions such as *I hope*, which will weaken your closing. Here are possible endings:

This brief description of my qualifications and the additional information on my résumé demonstrate my genuine desire to put my skills in accounting to work for McLellan and Associates. Please call me at (405) 488-2291 before 10 a.m. or after 3 p.m. to arrange an interview.

To add to your staff an industrious, well-trained administrative assistant with proven word processing and communication skills, call me at (350) 492-1433 to arrange an interview. I look forward to meeting with you to further discuss my qualifications.

Please allow me to discuss my qualifications for the financial analyst position more fully in an interview. You can reach me at (213) 458-4030. Next week, after you have examined the enclosed résumé, I will call you to discuss the possibility of arranging an interview.

Sending Your Cover Letter

More than 90 percent of résumés at Fortune 500 companies arrive by e-mail or are submitted through the corporate Web site.[43] Many applicants using technology make the mistake of not including cover letters with their résumés submitted by e-mail or by fax. A résumé that arrives without a cover letter makes the receiver wonder what it is and why it was sent. Recruiters want you to introduce yourself, and they also are eager to see some evidence that you can write. Some candidates either skip the cover letter or think they can get by with one-line cover letters such as this: *Please see attached résumé, and thanks for your consideration.*

Serious job candidates send a professional cover letter even if the résumé is submitted online, by e-mail, or by fax.

If you are serious about landing the job, take the time to prepare a professional cover letter. If you are sending your résumé by e-mail, you may use the same cover letter you would send by postal mail but shorten it a bit. As illustrated in Figure 13.14, an inside address is unnecessary for an e-mail recipient. Also, move your return address from the top of the letter to just below your name. Include your e-mail address and phone number. Remove tabs, bullets, underlining, and italics that might be problematic in e-mail messages. If you are submitting your résumé by fax, send the same cover letter you would send by postal mail. If you are submitting your résumé as a PDF file, do the same for your cover letter.

FIGURE 13.14 **E-Mail Cover Letter**

File Edit Mailbox Message Transfer Special Tools Window Help

Send

To: Courtney L. Donahue <courtney.donahue@delrio.com>
From: Tonya L. Powell <tpowell@yahoo.com>
Subject: Application for Assistant Product Manager Position Advertised 5-22-13
Cc:

Provides complete subject line identifying purpose

Addresses proper person by name

Dear Ms. Donahue:

Transfers traditional cover letter to e-mail

Your advertisement for an assistant product manager, appearing May 22 in the employment section of your company Web site, immediately caught my attention because my education and training closely parallel your needs. The advertisement says the job involves coordinating marketing programs, analyzing sales results, and tracking marketing budgets.

I would like to discuss my qualifications with you and answer any questions you have about my résumé, which is embedded below. The best way to reach me is to call my cell at (713) 343-2910. I look forward to putting my skills to work for Del Rio Enterprises.

Calls attention to résumé embedded in same message

Sincerely,

Tonya L. Powell
1770 Hawthorne Place
Boulder, CO 80304
E-mail; tpowell@yahoo.com
Cell: (713) 343-2910

Uses signature block for all contact information

Plain-text résumé embedded below. Attractive print résumé available on request.

Reminds receiver that attractive print résumé is available

Look for ways to reduce the overuse of *I*.

Final Tips for Successful Cover Letters

As you revise your cover letter, notice how many sentences begin with *I*. Although it is impossible to talk about yourself without using *I*, you can reduce "I" domination with this writing technique. Make activities and outcomes, and not yourself, the subjects of sentences. For example, rather than *I took classes in business communication and computer applications,* say *Classes in business communication and computer applications prepared me to . . . .* Instead of *I enjoyed helping customers,* say *Helping customers was a real pleasure.*

Because the beginning of a sentence is a prominent position, avoid starting sentences with *I* whenever possible. Use the "you" view (*You are looking for a hardworking team player . . .*), or try opening with phrases that de-emphasize you, the writer—for example, *All through college, I worked full time at . . .* Above all, strive for a comfortable style. In your effort to avoid sounding self-centered, don't write unnaturally.

Like the résumé, your cover letter must look professional and suggest quality. This means using a traditional letter style, such as block or modified block. Also, be sure to print it on the same quality paper as your résumé. As with your résumé, proofread it several times yourself; then have a friend read it for content and mechanics. Don't rely on spell-check to find all the errors. Just like your résumé, your cover letter must be perfect.

OFFICE INSIDER

"Unless you are applying for a position as a snake charmer, the following opening line from an actual cover letter will definitely nix your chances of winning an interview: 'I have seven years of expertise as an international press editor, *proven* journalism skills, *and* excellent writhing skills.'"

—Patrick Beausoleil, Bouma Construction Company

www.cengagebrain.com

Available with an access code, these eResources will help you prepare for exams:

- **Chapter Review Quizzes**
- **Personal Language Trainer**
- **PowerPoint Slides**
- **Flash Cards**

Summing Up and Looking Forward

In today's competitive job market, an employment search begins with identifying your interests, evaluating your qualifications, and choosing a career path. Finding the perfect job will mean a concentrated effort devoted to searching online job listings, checking classified advertisements, and networking. In applying for jobs, you will want to submit a customized, persuasive résumé that advertises your skills and experience. Whether you choose a chronological or a functional résumé style, you should tailor your assets to fit the position sought. If you think your résumé might be scanned, emphasize keywords and keep the format simple. A persuasive cover letter should introduce your résumé and describe how your skills and experiences match those required.

Now, if your résumé and cover letter have been successful, you will proceed to the employment interview, one of life's most nerve-wracking experiences. The last chapter in this book provides helpful suggestions for successful interviewing and follow-up communication.

Critical Thinking

1. In regard to hiring, conventional wisdom holds that it's all about whom you know. How can job candidates find an insider to refer them for a job opening?
2. Discuss the advantages and disadvantages of using video résumés and other creative but unconventional job-application strategies.
3. Why is searching for a job both exhilarating and intimidating? How can you overcome feelings of intimidation?
4. Is it easier to search for a job by visiting online job boards or by networking? Which method do you think is more successful?
5. **Ethical Issue:** Job candidate Karen is an older job seeker who is worried that her age will hurt her during her job search. While preparing her résumé, she has decided to omit the year she graduated from college and to leave off several positions she held earlier in her career so that she will appear younger to recruiters. Is what she is doing unethical?

Chapter Review

6. What employment trends are occurring in the workplace today?

7. What can you do to determine a career path?

8. What are some tips you should follow to ensure a safe and effective online job search?

9. Even with the popularity of online job-search sites, traditional job-search techniques are still important. What are some traditional sources for finding jobs?

10. What is a customized résumé, and why should you have one?

11. Compare and contrast chronological and functional résumés. Name the advantages and disadvantages of each.

12. Should résumé writers provide career objectives?

13. Why should you create several different versions of your résumé? What formats or styles do you know?

14. What are the three main purposes of a cover letter?

15. What is an e-portfolio? How can having one benefit you?

Activities and Cases

13.1 Revising Heather's Résumé

One effective way to improve your writing skills is to critique and edit the résumé of someone else.

Your Task. Analyze the following poorly organized résumé. List its weaknesses. Your instructor may ask you to revise sections of this résumé before showing you an improved version.

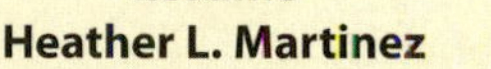

Résumé
Heather L. Martinez
503 West Austin Avenue, Apt. D • New Braunfels, TX
Phone (830) 652-3252 • E-Mail: Hotchilibabe08@gmail.com

OBJECTIVE
I would love to find a first job in the "real world" with a big accounting company that will help me get ahead in the accounting field

SKILLS
Word processing, Internet browsers (Explorer and Google), PowerPoint, Excel, type 30 wpm, databases, spreadsheets; great composure in stressful situations; 3 years as leader and supervisor and 4 years in customer service

EDUCATON
Alamo Community College, St. Philip Campus. New Braunfels, Texas. AA degree Fall 2010

Now I am pursuing a BA in Accounting at TSU-San Marcos, majoring in Accounting; my minor is Marketing. Expected degree date is June 2012; I recieved a Certificate of Completion in Entry Level Accounting in June 2010

I went to Scranton High School, Scranton, PA. I graduated in June 2007.

Highlights:

- Named Line Manger of the Month at Home Depot, 09/2007 and 08/2006
- Obtained a Certificate in Entry Level Accounting, June 2008
- Chair of Accounting Society, Spring and fall 2010
- Dean's Honor List, Fall 2011
- Financial advisor training completed through Primerica (May 2011)
- Webmaster for M.E.Ch.A., Spring 2012

Part-Time Employment
Financial Consultant, 2011 to present

I worked only part-time (January 2011-present) for Primerica Financial Services, San Marcos, TX to assist clients in obtaining a mortgage or consolidating a current mortgage loan and also to advise clients in assessing their need for life insurance.

Home Depot, Kyle, TX. As line manager, from September 2007-March 2011, I supervised 50 cashiers and front-end associates. I helped to write schedules, disciplinary action notices, and performance appraisals. I also kept track of change drawer and money exchanges; occasionally was manager on duty for entire store.

Penn Foster Career School-Scranton, PA where I taught flower design, I supervised 15 florists, made floral arrangements, sent them to customers, and restocked flowers.

List at least six weaknesses in this résumé.

13.2 Revising Heather's Cover Letter

The following cover letter accompanies Heather Martinez's résumé (Activity 13.1).

Your Task. Analyze each section of the following cover letter written by Heather and list its weaknesses. Your instructor may ask you to revise this letter before showing you an improved version.

To Whom It May Concern:

I saw your internship position yesterday and would like to apply right away. It would be so exciting to work for your esteemed firm! An internship would really give me much needed real-world experience and help my career.

I have all the qualifications you require in your ad and more. I am a junior at Texas State University-San Marcos and an Accounting major (with a minor in Finance). Accounting and Finance are my passion and I want to become a CPA and a financial advisor. I have taken Intermediate I and II and now work as a financial advisor with Primerica Financial Services in San Marcos. I should also tell you that I was at Home Depot for four years. I learned a lot, but my heart is in accounting and finance.

I am a team player, a born leader, motivated, reliable, and I show excellent composure in stressful situation, for example, when customers complain. I put myself through school and always carry at least 15 units while working part time.

You will probably agree that I am a good candidate for your internship position, which should start July 1. I feel that my motivation, passion, and strong people skills will serve your company well.

Best regards,

List at least six weaknesses in the cover letter.

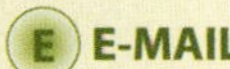 

13.3 Identifying Your Employment Interests and Goals

Your Task. In an e-mail or a memo addressed to your instructor, answer the questions in the section "Identifying Your Interests and Goals" at the beginning of the chapter. Draw a conclusion from your answers. What kinds of career, company, position, and location seem to fit your self-analysis?

13.4 Evaluating Your Qualifications

Your Task. Prepare worksheets that inventory your qualifications in four areas: employment, education, capabilities and skills, and honors and activities. Use active verbs when appropriate.

- **a. Employment.** Begin with your most recent job or internship. For each position list the following information: employer; job title; dates of employment; and three to five duties, activities, or accomplishments. Emphasize activities related to your job goal. Strive to quantify your achievements.
- **b. Education.** List degrees, certificates, and training accomplishments. Include courses, seminars, and skills that are relevant to your job goal. Calculate your grade point average in your major.
- **c. Capabilities and skills.** List all capabilities and skills that recommend you for the job you seek. Use words such as *skilled, competent, trained, experienced*, and *ability to*. Also list five or more qualities or interpersonal skills necessary for success in your chosen field. Write action statements demonstrating that you possess some of these qualities. Empty assurances aren't good enough; try to show evidence (*Developed teamwork skills by working with a committee of eight to produce a . . .*).
- **d. Awards, honors, and activities.** Explain any awards so that the reader will understand them. List campus, community, and professional activities that suggest you are a well-rounded individual or possess traits relevant to your target job.

13.5 Choosing a Career Path

Many job applicants know amazingly little about the work done in various occupations and the training requirements.

Your Task. Use the online *Occupational Outlook Handbook* at **http://www.bls.gov/OCO**, prepared by the Bureau of Labor Statistics, to learn more about an occupation of your choice. Find the description of a position for which you could apply in two to five years. Learn about what workers do on the job, working conditions, training and education needed, earnings, and expected job prospects. Print the pages from the *Occupational Outlook Handbook* that describe employment in the area in which you are interested. If your instructor directs, attach these copies to the cover letter you will write in Activity 13.10. For further information, explore options at your campus career placement office; find out if you have access to personality and aptitude testing to help you flesh out a likely career path.

13.6 Locating Salary Information

What salary can you expect in your chosen career?

Your Task. Visit CareerOneStop at **http://www.careeronestop.org** or Salary.com and select an occupation based on the kind of employment you are seeking now or will be seeking after you graduate. Use your current geographic area or the location where you would like to work after graduation. What wages can you expect in this occupation? Click to learn more about this occupation. Take notes on three or four interesting bits of information you uncovered about this career. Bring a printout of the wage information to class, and be prepared to discuss what you learned.

13.7 Searching the Job Market

Where are the jobs? Even though you may not be in the market at the moment, become familiar with the kinds of available positions because job awareness should become an important part of your education. Also, as a future business professional, you will need to stay current on global and domestic news because external events affect business profoundly. To be successful, you need to be a well-informed and well-rounded individual.

Your Task. Download or print a job advertisement or announcement from a (a) company Web site, (b) job board on the Web, (c) professional association listing or (d) classified section of a newspaper. Alternatively, check whether your college maintains listings of local job opportunities, especially if your campus has a career center. Select an advertisement or announcement describing the kind of employment you are seeking now or plan to seek when you graduate. Save this advertisement or announcement to attach to the résumé you will write in Activity 13.9.

13.8 Posting a Résumé on the Web

Learn about the procedure for posting résumés at job boards on the Web. Estimates put the number of specialty or niche job boards at about 100,000 worldwide.[44] Therefore, you are facing a sheer inexhaustible supply of employment information.

Your Task. Choose the three best Web sites for your career and explain why you picked those job sites. Describe the procedure involved and the advantages for each site.

13.9 Writing Your Résumé

Your Task. Using the data you developed in Activity 13.4, write your résumé. Aim it at a full-time job, part-time position, or internship. Attach a job listing for a specific position (from Activity 13.7). Also prepare a list of references. Revise your résumé until it is perfect.

13.10 Preparing Your Cover Letter

Your Task. Using the job listing you found for Activity 13.7, write a cover letter introducing your résumé. Again, revise until it is perfect.

13.11 Using Social Media in the Job Search

One of the fastest-growing trends in employment is using social media sites during the job search.

Your Task. Locate one social media site and set up an account. Explore the site to discover how job seekers can use it to search for a job and how employers can use it to find job candidates. Be prepared to share your findings in class.

13.12 Tweeting to Find a Job

Twitter résumés are a new twist on job hunting. While most job seekers struggle to contain their credentials on one page, others are tweeting their credentials in 140 characters or fewer! Here is an example from The Ladders.com:

> *RT #Susan Moline seeks a LEAD/SR QA ENG JOB http://bit.ly/1ThaW @TalentEvolution - http://bit.ly/QB5DC @TweetMyJobs.com #résumé #QA-Jobs-CA*

Are you scratching your head? Let's translate: (a) RT stands for retweet, allowing your Twitter followers to repeat this message to their followers. (b) The hashtag (#) always means *subject;* prefacing your name, it makes you easy to find. (c) The uppercase abbreviations indicate the job title, here *Lead Quality Assurance Engineer.* (d) The first link is a "tiny URL," a short, memorable Web address or alias provided free by TinyURL.com and other URL-shrinking services. The first short link reveals the job seeker's Talent Evolution profile page; the second directs viewers to a job seeker profile created on TweetMyJOBS.com. (e) The hashtags indicate the search terms used as seen here: name, quality assurance jobs in California, and the broad term *résumé.* You may want to visit the career site The Ladders.com at **http://www.theladders.com** and view the many articles for job seekers under **Career Advice**. When doing research from within Twitter, use the @ symbol with a specific Twitter user name or the # symbol for a subject search.

Your Task. As a team or individually, search the Web for *Tweet Résumé.* Pick one of the sites offering to tweet your résumé out for you, for example, TweetMyJOBS.com (**http://tweetmyjobs.com**) or Tweet My Résumé. Describe to your peers the job-search process via Twitter presented on that Web site. Some services are free, whereas others come with charges. If you select a commercial service, critically evaluate its sales pitch and its claims. Is it worthwhile to spend money on this service? Do clients find jobs? How does the service try to demonstrate that? As a group or individually, share the results with the class.

 WEB  TEAM

13.13 E-Portfolios: Job Hunting in the Twenty-First Century

In high-tech fields, digital portfolios have been steadily gaining in popularity and now seem to be going mainstream as universities are providing space for student job seekers to profile their qualifications in e-portfolios online. Although digital portfolios are unlikely to become widely used very soon, you would do well to learn about them by viewing many samples—good and bad.

Your Task. Conduct a Google search using the search term *student e-portfolios* or *student digital portfolios*. You will see long lists of hits, some of which will be actual digital document samples on the Web or instructions for creating an e-portfolio. Your instructor may assign you individually or as a team to visit specific digital portfolio sites and summarize your findings in a memo or a brief oral presentation. You could focus on the composition of the site, page layout, links provided, colors used, types of documents included, and so forth. A fine site to start from that offers many useful links is maintained by the Center for Excellence in Teaching (CET) at the University of Southern California. Visit **http://www.usc.edu** and type *student e-portfolios* to search the USC Web pages. Click the link to the CET site.

Alternatively, teams or the whole class could study sites that provide how-to instructions and then combine the advice of the best among them to create practical tips for making a digital portfolio. This option would lend itself to team writing; consider using a wiki or a document-sharing tool such as Google Docs.

Grammar/Mechanics Checkup—13

Number Style

Review Sections 4.01–4.13 in the Grammar/Mechanics Handbook. Then study each of the following pairs. Assume that these expressions appear in the context of letters, reports, or memos. In the answer spaces provided, write the preferred number style and the number of the G/M principle illustrated. When you finish, compare your responses with those at the end of the book. If your responses differ, study carefully the principles in parentheses.

three (4.01a) **Example:** He had (three, 3) cell phones.

________ 1. At least (20, twenty) candidates applied for the opening.

________ 2. The interview was on (Fourth, 4th) Street.

________ 3. Angelica saw (12, twelve) possible jobs listed on the Web.

________ 4. One job started on (June 1, June 1st).

________ 5. She filled her gas tank for ($40, forty dollars).

________ 6. She hoped to have a job by the (15th, fifteenth) of June.

________ 7. Her interview started at (3 p.m., 3:00 p.m.).

________ 8. The assistant edited (4 three-page, four 3-page) memos.

________ 9. She founded her company over (40, forty) years ago.

________ 10. About (3 million; 3,000,000) people visited Monster.com.

________ 11. (16, Sixteen) candidates applied for one open position.

________ 12. I need (50, fifty) cents for the machine.

________ 13. She graduated at the age of (21, twenty-one).

________ 14. The interest rate on her loan was (7, seven) percent.

________ 15. Only (4, four) of the 35 e-mail messages were undelivered.

Editing Challenge—13

As the employee with the best communication skills, you are frequently asked to edit messages. The following résumé has problems with number usage, capitalization, spelling, proofreading, and other writing techniques you have studied. You may (a) use standard proofreading marks (see Appendix B) to correct the errors here or (b) download the document from **www.cengagebrain.com** and revise at your computer.

Your instructor may ask you to use the **Track Changes** feature in Word to show your editing comments. Turn on **Track Changes** on the **Review** tab. Click **Show Markup**. Place your cursor at an error, click **New Comment**, and key your edit in the bubble box provided. Study the guidelines in the Grammar/Mechanics Handbook as well as the lists of Confusing Words and Frequently Misspelled Words to sharpen your skills.

Tracy M Williams
1436 East 9th Avenue
Monroe, Mich. 48162

Summary of qualifications

- Over three years experience in working in customer relations
- Partnered with Assistant Manager to create mass mailing by merging three thousand customers names and addresses in ad campaign
- Hold AA Degree in Administrative Assisting
- Proficient with MS Word, excel, powerpoint, and the internet

Experience

Administrative Assistant, Monroe Mold and Machine Company, Munroe, Michigan
June 2012 to present

- Answer phones, respond to e-mail and gather information for mold designers
- Key board and format proposals for various machine Platforms and Configurations
- Help company with correspondence to fulfill it's guarantee that a prototype mold can be produced in less than 1 week
- Worked with Assistant Manger to create large customer mailings
- Use the internet to Research prospective customers; enter data in Excel

Shift Supervisor, Monroe Coffee Shop, Monroe, Michigan
May 2011 to May 2012

- Trained 3 new employees, opened and closed shop handled total sales
- Managed shop in the owners absence
- Builded satisfied customer relationships

Server, Hostess, Expeditor, Busser, Roadside Girll, Toledo, Ohio
April 2009 to April 2011

- Created customer base and close relationships with patrons of resterant
- Helped Owner expand menu from twenty to thirty-five items
- Develop procedures that reduce average customer wait time from sixteen to eight minutes

Awards and Achievements

- Deans List, Spring, 2012, Fall, 2011
- Awarded 2nd prize in advertise essay contest, 2011

Education

- AA degree, Munroe Community College, 2012
- Major: Office Administation and Technology
- GPA in major: 3.8 (4.0 = A)

Communication Workshop

Network Your Way to a Job in the Hidden Market

According to Cornell University Career Services, the "hidden" job market accounts for up to 80 percent of all positions available.[45] Companies do not always announce openings publicly because interviewing all the applicants, many of whom aren't qualified, is time consuming. What's more, even when a job is advertised, companies dislike hiring "strangers." The key to finding a good job, then, is converting yourself from a "stranger" into a known quantity through networking. This can take time. As Walter Kraft, vice president for communications for Eastern Michigan University, reminds us, "Finding a job is a full-time job. It is far more than making a phone call and sending out a resume." Here are traditional and online resources for tapping into the hidden job market.[46]

Traditional Networking

- **Develop a list.** Make a list of anyone who would be willing to talk with you about finding a job. List your friends, relatives, former employers, former coworkers, members of professional organizations, members of your religious community, people in social and athletic clubs, present and former teachers, neighbors, and friends of your parents, even if you haven't talked with them in years. Also consider asking your campus career center for alumni contacts who will talk with students.
- **Make contacts.** Call the people on your list, or even better, try to meet with them in person. To set up a meeting, say, *Hi, Aunt Martha! I'm looking for a job and I wonder if you could help me out. When could I come over to talk about it?* During your visit be friendly, well organized, polite, and interested in what your contact has to say. Provide a copy of your résumé, and try to keep the conversation centered on your job-search area. Your goal is to get two or more referrals. In pinpointing your request, ask, *Do you know of anyone who might have an opening for a person with my skills?* If the person does not, ask, *Do you know of anyone else who might know of someone who would?*
- **Follow up on your referrals.** Call the people whose names are on your referral list. You might say something like, *Hello. I'm Eric Rivera, a friend of Meredith Medcalf. She suggested that I call and ask you for help. I'm looking for a position as a marketing trainee, and she thought you might be willing to spare a few minutes and steer me in the right direction.* Don't ask for a job. During your referral interview, ask how the individual got started in this line of work, what he or she likes best (or least) about the work, what career paths exist in the field, and what problems a newcomer must overcome. Most important, ask how a person with your background and skills might get started in the field. Send an informal thank-you note to anyone who helps you in your job search, and stay in touch with the most promising contacts. Ask whether you may call every three weeks or so during your job search.

Online Networking

As with traditional networking, the goal of online networking is to make connections with people who are advanced in their fields. Ask for their advice about finding a job.

- **Join a career networking group.** Build your own professional network by joining one or more of the following: LinkedIn, Twitter, Facebook, Ryze Business Networking (**http://ryze.com**), Zero Degrees Network (**http://zerodegreenetwork.com**), and Ziggs (**http://ziggs.com**). You can also sign up for a universal address book at Plaxo (**http://www.plaxo.com**) to help you keep your network contacts organized. Typically, joining a network requires creating a password, filling in your profile, and adding your business contacts. Once you connect with an individual, the content of your discussions and the follow-up is similar to that of traditional networking.
- **Participate in a discussion group or mailing lists.** Two especially good discussion group resources for beginners are Yahoo Groups (**http://groups.yahoo.com**) and Google Groups (**http://groups.google.com**). You may choose from groups in a variety of fields including business and computer technology.
- **Locate a relevant blog.** Blogs are another opportunity for networking and sharing information. A quick Web search reveals hundreds of career-related blogs and blogs in your field of

study. Many companies, such as Microsoft, also maintain employment-related blogs. A good list of career blogs can be found at Quintessential Careers (**http://www.quintcareers.com/career_blog**). You can also search a worldwide blog directory at **http://www.blogcatalog.com**. Once you locate a relevant blog, you can read recent postings, search archives, and reply to postings.

- **Start tweeting.** Set up a Twitter account at **http://twitter.com** so that you can start marketing yourself, following employers, and getting updates from recruiters. According to Miriam Salpeter from Keppie Careers, "With over 3 million users, Twitter offers an unparalleled opportunity to create an extended network.[47] Experts offer this advice to Twitter users seeking employment: include appropriate keywords in your profile; use the "More Info URL" to send potential employers to your LinkedIn profile or online résumé; and follow those who are interesting or share your interests.[48]

Career Application. Begin developing your network. Conduct at least one referral interview or join one online networking group. Record the results you experienced and the information you learned from the networking option you chose. Report to the class your reactions and findings.

Endnotes

[1] Ryan, L. (2007). Online job searching. *BusinessWeek*. Video interview retrieved from http://feedroom.businessweek.com; Wolgemuth, L. (2008, February 25). Using the Web to search for a job. *U.S. News & World Report*. Retrieved from http://www.usnews.com/articles/business/careers/2008/02/25/using-the-web-to-search-for-a-job.html

[2] U.S. Small Business Administration Office of Advocacy. (2009, September). FAQs: Frequently asked questions. Retrieved from http://web.sba.gov/faqs

[3] Middleton, D. (2009, December 28). Landing a job of the future takes a two-track mind. *The Wall Street Journal, CareerJournal*. Retrieved from http://online.wsj.com

[4] Bureau of Labor Statistics. (2010, September 14). Economic news release: Employee tenure in 2010. Retrieved from http://www.bls.gov/news.release/tenure.nr0.htm; Kimmit, R. M. (2007, January 23). Why job churn is good. *The Washington Post*, p. A17. Retrieved from http://www.washingtonpost.com/wp-dyn/content/article/2007/01/22/AR2007012201089.html

[5] Employers report internships lead to full-time hires. (n.d.). The Career Exposure Network. Retrieved from http://careerexposure.com/resources/resources_internship.jsp; Kahney, M. (2009, March 16). Top 20 undergraduate internship programs for college students. EduChoices.org. Retrieved from http://educhoices.org/articles/Top_20_Undergraduate_Internship_Programs_for_College_Students.html

[6] Wong, E. (2011, January 18). Why LinkedIn is every recruiter's hot search tool. *Forbes*. Retrieved from http://blogs.forbes.com/elainewong/2011/01/18/why-linkedin-is-every-recruiters-hot-search-tool; Levy, R. (2010). How to use social media in your job search. About.com. Retrieved from http://jobsearch.about.com/od/networking/a/socialmedia.htm; 20 Twitter tips for new grads and entrepreneurs. (2009, June 29). EduChoices.org. Retrieved from http://educhoices.org/articles/20_Twitter_Tips_for_New_Grads_and_Entrepreneurs.html; Kharif, O. (2007, January 3). Online job sites battle for share. *BusinessWeek*. Retrieved from http://www.businessweek.com/technology/content/jan2007/tc20070103_369308.htm

[7] Korkki, P. (2007, July 1). So easy to apply, so hard to be noticed. *The New York Times*. Retrieved from http://proquest.umi.com

[8] Marquardt, K. (2008, February 21). 5 tips on finding a new job. *U.S. News & World Report*. Retrieved from http://www.usnews.com/articles/business/careers/2008/02/21/5-tips-on-finding-a-new-job.html; Wolgemuth, L. (2008, February 25). Using the Web to search for a job. *U.S. News & World Report*. Retrieved from http://www.usnews.com/articles/business/careers/2008/02/25/using-the-web-to-search-for-a-job.html

[9] Crispin, G., & Mehler, M. (2009, February). CareerXroads 8th annual sources of hire study. CareerXroads.com. Retrieved from http://www.careerxroads.com/news/SourcesOfHire09.pdf

[10] Ryan, L. (2007). Online job searching. *BusinessWeek*. Video interview retrieved from http://feedroom.businessweek.com/index.jsp?fr_story=5e1ec1bacf73ae689d381f30e80dfea30cd52108

[11] Wong, E. (2011, January 18). Why LinkedIn is every recruiter's hot search tool. *Forbes*. Retrieved from http://blogs.forbes.com/elainewong/2011/01/18/why-linkedin-is-every-recruiters-hot-search-tool

[12] Dickey-Chasins, J. (2010, October 5). Results of the Job Board Future survey are here! Job Board Doctor Blog. Retrieved from http://www.jobboarddoctor.com/2010/10/05/results-of-the-job-board-future-survey-are-here

[13] Boyle, M. (2009, June 25). Recruiting: Enough to make a monster tremble. *BusinessWeek*. Retrieved from http://www.businessweek.com/magazine/content/09_27/b4138043180664.htm; and Shawbel, D. (2009, February 24). Top ten social sites for finding a job. Mashable: The Social Media Guide. Retrieved from http://mashable.com/?s=Top+ten+social+sites+for+finding+a+job

[14] Cheesman, J. quoted by Wolgemuth, L. (2008, February 25). Using the Web to search for a job. *U.S. News & World Report*. Retrieved from http://www.usnews.com/articles/business/careers/2008/02/25/using-the-web-to-search-for-a-job.html

[15] Feldman, D. quoted by Marquardt, K. (2008, February 21). 5 tips on finding a new job. *U.S. News & World Report*. Retrieved from http://www.usnews.com/articles/business/careers/2008/02/21/5-tips-on-finding-a-new-job.html

[16] Korkki, P. (2010, May 22). Graduates' first job: Marketing themselves. *The New York Times*. Retrieved from http://www.nytimes.com/2010/05/23/jobs/23search.html?_r=2&pagewan

[17] Koeppel, D. (2006, December 31). Those low grades in college may haunt your job search. *The New York Times*, p. 1. Retrieved from http://web.ebscohost.com

[18] Black, D. quoted by Brandon, E. (2007, January 31). Tips for getting that first job. *U.S. News & World Report*. Retrieved from http://www.usnews.com/usnews/biztech/articles/070131/31firstjob.htm

[19] The Creative Group. (2008, February 21). Substance over style: Survey shows off-the-wall job-hunting tactics can be risky. Press Release. Retrieved from http://www.creativegroup.com/portal/site/tcg-us/template.PAGE/menuitem.926b08198c67974b735e0c5c02f3dfa0

[20] Jones, C. (2007). What do recruiters want anyway? Yahoo HotJobs Exclusive. Retrieved from http://hotjobs.yahoo.com/jobseeker/tools/article_print.html?id=What_Do_Recruiters_Want_Anyway__20021114-1412.xml

[21] Résumés inching up. (2009, March 20). Accountemps. Retrieved from http://accountemps.rhi.mediaroom.com/index.php?s=189&item=210

[22] Isaacs, K. (2007). How to decide on résumé length. Resume Power. Retrieved from http://www.resumepower.com/resume-length.html; Fisher, A. (2007, March 29). Does a resume have to be one page long? CNNMoney.com. Retrieved from http://money.cnn.com/2007/03/28/news/economy/resume.fortune/index.htm

[23] Hansen, K. (2010, January 10). Should you use a career objective on your résumé? JobsDB.com. Retrieved from http://sg.jobsdb.com/SG/EN/Resources/JobSeekerArticle/28.htm?ID=374

[24] Coombes, A. (2010, February 7). First aid for your résumé. *The Wall Street Journal*. Retrieved from http://online.wsj.com/article/SB126550131743542087.html

[25] Korkki, P. (2007, July 1). So easy to apply, so hard to be noticed. *The New York Times*. Retrieved from http://www.nytimes.com/2007/07/01/business/yourmoney/01career.html?_r=1

[26] Remillard, B. (2010, January 8). How recruiters read resumes in 10 seconds or less. IMPACT Hiring Solutions Career Blog. Retrieved from http://www.impacthiringsolutions.com/careerblog/2010/01/18/how-recruiters-read-resumes-in-10-seconds-or-less

[27] Koeppel, D. (2006, December 31). Those low grades in college may haunt your job search. *The New York Times*, p. 1. Retrieved from http://www.nytimes.com/2006/12/31/jobs/31gpa.html

[28] Ibid.

[29] Mulligan, B. (2007, November 30). Build the résumé employers want. JobWeb. Retrieved from http://www.jobweb.com/Resume/help.aspx?id=858&terms=Build+the+resume+employers+want

[30] Locke, A. (2008, June 18). Is your resume telling the wrong story? The Ladders.com. Retrieved from http://www.theladders.com

[31] Washington, T. (2009) Effective resumes bring results to life. *Career Journal Europe/The Wall Street Journal*. Retrieved from http://careerjournaleurope.com/jobhunting/resumes/20000913-washington.html

[32] Hansen, K. (2010). Tapping the power of keywords to enhance your résumé's effectiveness. QuintCareers.com. Retrieved from http://www.quintcareers.com/resume_keywords.html

[33] Condon, J. (2009, April 2). An online toolbox starts with a polished résumé. *The New York Times*, p. B5.

[34] The video resume technique. (2007). CollegeGrad.com. Retrieved from http://www.collegegrad.com/jobsearch/guerrilla-insider-techniques/the-video-resume-technique

[35] Donna Farrugia quoted in Dizik, A. (2010, May 20). Wooing job recruiters with video résumés. *The Wall Street Journal*, p. D4.

[36] Vaas, L. (2010, June 22). Are video resumes ready for their closeup? The Ladders.com. Retrieved from http://www.theladders.com/career-advice/are-video-resumes-ready-for-closeup?fromSearch=true&start=&contentSearchKeyword=video%20resume

[37] Benedict, A. (2008, August 27). Online video résumés. The Ladders.com. Retrieved from http://www.theladders.com/career-advice/online-video-resumes

[38] Dizik, A. (2010, May 20). Wooing job recruiters with video résumés. *The Wall Street Journal*, p. D4.

[39] Zupek, R. (2008). Honesty is the best policy in résumés and interviews. CareerBuilder.com. Retrieved from http://www.careerbuilder.com

[40] Needleman, S. E. (2007, March 6). Why sneaky tactics may not help résumé. *The Wall Street Journal*, p. B8.

[41] Korkki, P. (2009, July 18). Where, oh where, has my application gone? *The New York Times*. Retrieved from http://www.nytimes.com

[42] Arruda, W. (2011, January 5). Use color to get your next job. The Ladders.com. Retrieved from http://www.theladders.com/career-advice/use-color-to-get-next-job

[43] Korkki, P. (2007, July 1). So easy to apply, so hard to be noticed. *The New York Times*. Retrieved from http://www.nytimes.com

[44] Frauenheim, E. (2009, June 22). Logging off of job boards. Special report 2: Talent acquisition. *Workforce Management*, p. 26.

[45] Gabbard, D. (2009, June 12). Unlocking the hidden job market. Examiner.com Retrieved from http://www.examiner.com

[46] Borney, N. (2010, February 16). 10 ways to crack Michigan's hidden job market. AnnArbor.com. Retrieved from http://www.annarbor.com/business-review/ann-arbor-human-resources-experts-offer-tips-how-to-get-hired-in-2010

[47] Salpeter, M. (2010). Leverage Twitter for your job search. Twitip.com. Retrieved from http://www.twitip.com/leverage-twitter-for-your-job-search

[48] 20 Twitter tips for new grads and entrepreneurs. (2009, June 29). EduChoices.org. Retrieved from http://educhoices.org/articles/20_Twitter_Tips_for_New_Grads_and_Entrepreneurs.html

Acknowledgments

p. 408 Office Insider cited in Stock, K. (2010, July 27). How to keep your online resume exclusive and effective. *FINS, The Wall Street Journal*. Retrieved from http://www.fins.com/Finance/Articles/SB127956336878218653/How-to-Keep-Your-Online-Resume-Exclusive-and-Effective

p. 411 Office Insider based on Wade, M. quoted in Win at work. (2009, May). *U.S. News & World Report*. Retrieved from http://web.ebscohost.com

p. 415 Office Insider cited in Remillard, B. (2010, January 18). How recruiters read resumes in 10 seconds or less. IMPACT Hiring Solutions. Retrieved from http://www.impacthiringsolutions.com/careerblog/2010/01/18/how-recruiters-read-resumes-in-10-seconds-or-less

p. 428 Office Insider based on Cheesman, J. quoted in Wolgemuth, L. (2008, February 25). Using the Web to search for a job. *U.S. News & World Report*. Retrieved from http://www.usnews.com/articles/business/careers/2008/02/25/using-the-web-to-search-for-a-job.html

p. 430 Office Insider based on Enelow, W. S. quoted in Korkki, P. (2007, July 1). So easy to apply, so hard to be noticed. *The New York Times*. Retrieved from http://proquest.umi.com

p. 438 Office Insider based on Patrick Beausoleil, Bouma Construction Company. (2008, March 3). E-mail message to Mary Ellen Guffey.

p. 443 Activity 13.12 based on Harkins, R. (2010, March/April). Tweet your way to a new job. *OfficePRO*, p. 30.

CHAPTER 14

Interviewing and Following Up

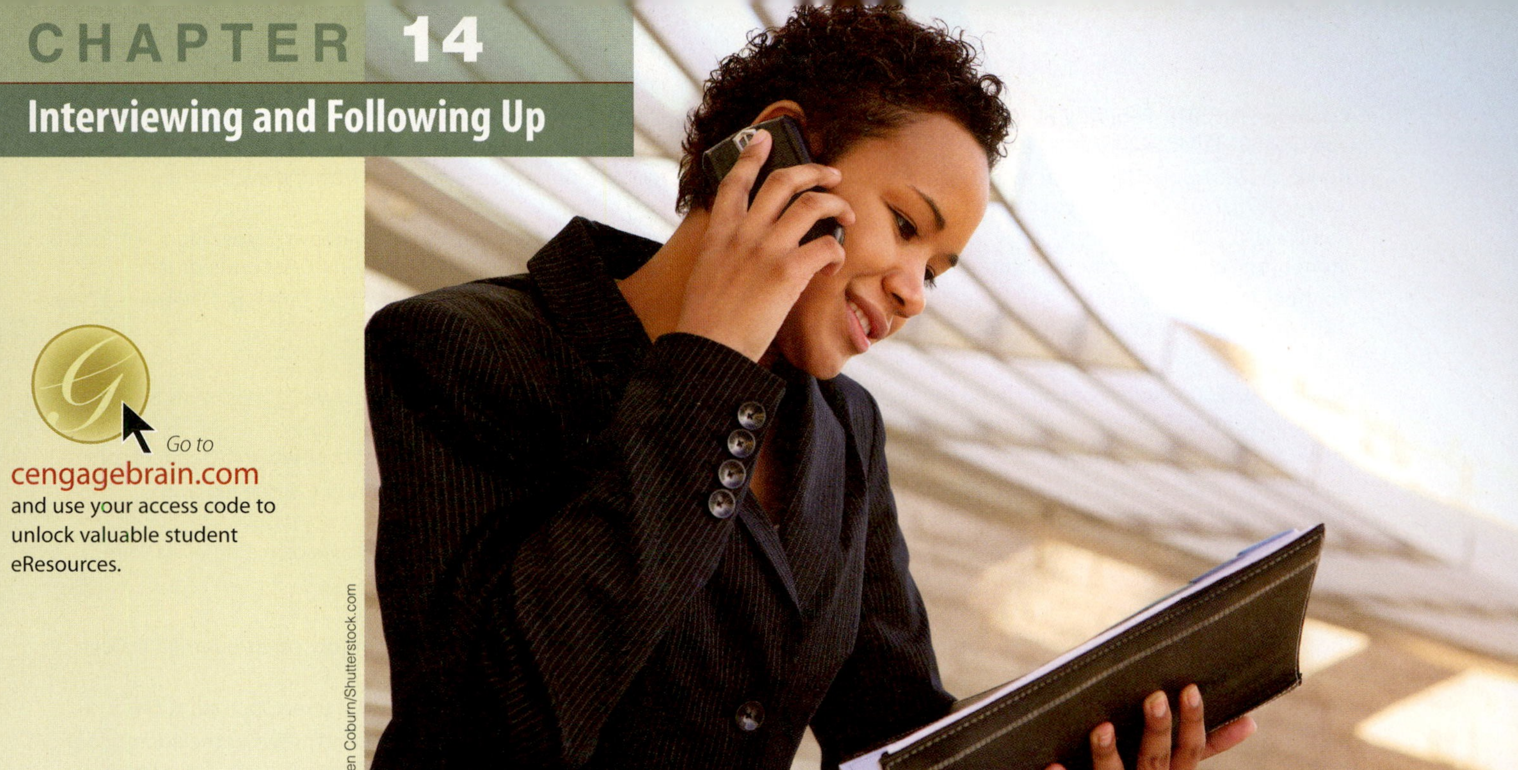

Go to **cengagebrain.com** and use your access code to unlock valuable student eResources.

Stephen Coburn/Shutterstock.com

OBJECTIVES

After studying this chapter, you should be able to

- Explain the purposes and types of job interviews, including screening, one-on-one, panel, group, sequential, stress, and online interviews.
- Describe what to do before an interview, including researching the company, rehearsing success stories, practicing responses to potential interview questions, and cleaning up digital dirt.
- Explain how to prepare for employment interviews, including researching the target company.
- Recognize how to fight interview fears and control nonverbal messages.
- Answer common interview questions and close an interview positively.
- Outline the activities that take place after an interview, including thanking the interviewer and contacting references.
- Write follow-up letters and e-mails and other employment messages.

The Purposes and Types of Job Interviews

Knowing the job interview process reduces your anxiety and boosts confidence.

Whether you are completing your education and searching for your first serious position or whether you are in the workforce and striving to change jobs—a job interview can be life changing. Because employment is a major part of everyone's life, the job interview takes on enormous importance.

Most people consider job interviews extremely stressful. However, the more you learn about the process and the more prepared you are, the less stress you will feel. Moreover, a job interview is a two-way street. It is not just about being judged by the employer. You, the applicant, will be using the job interview to evaluate the employer. Do you really want to work for this organization?

This chapter will increase your interviewing effectiveness and confidence by explaining the purposes and kinds of interviews and how to prepare for them. You will learn how to project a professional image throughout the interview process, gather information about an employer, and reduce nervousness. You will receive advice on how to send positive nonverbal messages that will help you stay in control during your interview. You will pick up tips for responding to recruiters' favorite questions and learn how to cope with illegal questions and salary matters. Moreover, you will receive pointers on significant questions you can ask during an interview. Finally, you will learn what you should do as a successful follow-up to an interview.

Yes, job interviews can be intimidating and stressful. However, you can expect to ace an interview when you know what's coming and when you prepare thoroughly. Remember, preparation often determines who gets the job. First, though, you need to know the purposes of employment interviews and what types of interviews you might encounter in your job search.

Purposes of Employment Interviews

An interview has several purposes for you as a job candidate. It is an opportunity to (a) convince the employer of your potential, (b) learn more about the job and the company, and (c) expand on the information in your résumé. This is the time for you to gather information about whether you would fit into the company culture. You should also be thinking about whether this job suits your career goals.

From the employer's perspective, the interview is an opportunity to (a) assess your abilities in relation to the requirements for the position; (b) discuss your training, experience, knowledge, and abilities in more detail; (c) see what drives and motivates you; and (d) decide whether you would fit into the organization.

Types of Employment Interviews

Job applicants generally face two kinds of interviews: screening interviews and hiring/placement interviews. You must succeed in the first to proceed to the second. Once you make it to the hiring/placement interview, you will find a variety of interview styles, including one-on-one, panel, group, sequential, stress, and online interviews. You will be better prepared if you know what to expect in each type of interview.

Screening interviews are intended to eliminate those who fail to meet minimum requirements.

Screening Interviews. Screening interviews do just that—they screen candidates to eliminate those who fail to meet minimum requirements. Companies use screening interviews to save time and money by weeding out lesser-qualified candidates before scheduling face-to-face interviews. Although some screening interviews are conducted during job fairs or on college campuses, many screening interviews take place on the telephone, and some take place online.[1]

Some companies computerize their screening interviews. For example, Lowe's Home Improvement has applicants access a Web site where they answer a series of ethics-related questions. Retail giant Walmart screens cashiers, stockers, and customer-service representatives with a multiple-choice questionnaire that applicants answer by pushing buttons on a phone keypad.[2] Even more cutting-edge, some employers, such as Hewlett-Packard, Microsoft, Sodexo, and Verizon are using Second Life, an online virtual community, to hold virtual job fairs and to screen job applicants.[3]

During a screening interview, the interviewer will probably ask you to provide details about the education and experience listed on your résumé; therefore, you must be prepared to promote your qualifications. Remember that the person conducting the screening interview is trying to determine whether you should move on to the next step in the interview process.

A screening interview may be as short as five minutes. Even though it may be short, don't treat it casually. If you don't perform well during the screening interview, it may be your last interview with that organization. You can use the tips that follow in this chapter to succeed during the screening process.

In hiring/placement interviews, recruiters try to learn how the candidate would fit into their organization.

Hiring/Placement Interviews. The most promising candidates selected from screening interviews are invited to hiring/placement interviews. Hiring managers want to learn whether candidates are motivated, qualified, and a good fit for

"You seem intelligent, capable, level-headed and mature. That's a shame because I was really hoping you'd fit in here."

the position. Their goal is to learn how the candidate would fit into their organization. Conducted in depth, hiring/placement interviews may take many forms.

One-on-One Interviews. In one-on-one interviews, which are the most common type, you can expect to sit down with a company representative and talk about the job and your qualifications. If the representative is the hiring manager, questions will be specific and job related. If the representative is from human resources, the questions will probably be more general.

Panel Interviews. Panel interviews are typically conducted by people who will be your supervisors and colleagues. Usually seated around a table, interviewers take turns asking questions. Panel interviews are advantageous because they save the company time and money, and they show you how the staff works together. For these interviews, you can prepare basic biographical information about each panel member. When answering questions, maintain eye contact with the questioner as well as with the others.[4] Try to take notes during the interview so that you can remember each person's questions and what was important to that individual.

Hiring interview types include one-on-one, panel, group, sequential, stress, and online.

Group Interviews. Group interviews occur when a company interviews several candidates for the same position at the same time. Some employers use this technique to measure leadership skills and communication styles. During a group interview, stay focused on the interviewer, and treat the other candidates with respect. Even if you are nervous, try to remain calm, take your time when responding, and express yourself clearly. The key during a group interview is to make yourself stand out from the other candidates in a positive way.[5]

Sequential Interviews. In a sequential interview, you meet individually with two or more interviewers one-on-one over the course of several hours or days. For example, you may meet with human resources representatives, your hiring manager, and potential future supervisors and colleagues in your division or department. You must listen carefully and respond positively to all interviewers. Promote your qualifications to each one; don't assume that any interviewer knows what was said in a previous interview. Keep your responses fresh, even when repeating yourself many times over. Subsequent interviews also tend to be more in-depth than first interviews, which means that you need to be even more prepared and know even more about the company. According to Chantal Verbeek-Vingerhoed, head of enterprise talent for ING, during subsequent interviews, "They dig deeper into your technical skills, and make connections about how you'd add value and solve issues in the department. If you know the exact job requirements and expectations, you can really shine."[6]

Mastering stress interviews requires you to remain calm, keep a sense of humor, and avoid becoming defensive.

Stress Interviews. Stress interviews are meant to test your reactions during nerve-racking situations and are common for jobs in which you will face significant stress. You may be forced to wait a long time before being greeted by the interviewer, you may be given a test with an impossible time limit, or one or more of the interviewers may treat you rudely.

Another stress interview technique is to have interviewers ask questions at a rapid rate. If asked rapid-fire questions from many directions, take the time to slow things down. For example, you might say, *I would be happy to answer your question, Ms. X, but first I must finish responding to Mr. Z.* If greeted with silence (another stress technique), you might say, *Would you like me to begin the interview? Let me tell you about myself.* Or ask a question such as *Can you give me more information about the position?* One career expert says, "The key to surviving stress interviews is to remain calm, keep a sense of humor, and avoid getting angry or defensive."[7]

Online Interviews. Many companies today use technology to interview job candidates from a distance. Although conference call interviews have a long tradition, today's savvy companies such as Zappos.com use webcams and videoconferencing software to conduct interviews. If an applicant doesn't have a webcam, Zappos sends one with a return label.[8]

Using the free Skype service and a webcam saves job applicants and companies time and money, especially when applicants are not in the same geographic location as the company. Even though your interview may be online, conducted with videoconferencing software and a webcam, don't take it any less seriously than a face-to-face interview.

No matter what interview structure you encounter, you will feel more comfortable and be better prepared if you know what to do before, during, and after the interview.

Before the Interview

Once you have sent out at least one résumé or filled out at least one job application, you must consider yourself an active job seeker. Being active in the job market means that you should be prepared to be contacted by potential employers. As discussed earlier, employers often use screening interviews to narrow the list of candidates. If you do well in the screening interview, you will be invited to an in-person or online meeting.

After submitting your résumé, you may be contacted by potential employers for a screening interview.

Ensuring Professional Phone Techniques

Even with the popularity of e-mail, most employers contact job applicants by phone to set up interviews. Employers can judge how well applicants communicate by hearing their voices and expressions over the phone. Therefore, once you are actively looking for a job, anytime the phone rings, it could be a potential employer. Don't make the mistake of letting an unprofessional voice mail message or a lazy roommate ruin your chances. To make the best impression, try these tips:

- Invest in a good answering machine or voice mail service. Make sure that your outgoing message is concise and professional, with no distracting background sounds. It should be in your own voice and include your full name for clarity. You can find more tips for creating professional outgoing messages in Chapter 11.
- Tell those who might answer your phone at home about your job search. Explain to them the importance of acting professionally and taking complete messages. Family members or roommates can affect the first impression an employer has of you.
- If you have children, prevent them from answering the phone during your job search. Children of all ages are not known for taking good messages!
- If you have put your cell phone number on your résumé, don't answer unless you are in a good location to carry on a conversation with an employer. It is hard to pay close attention when you are driving down the highway or eating in a noisy restaurant!
- Use voice mail to screen calls. By screening incoming calls, you can be totally in control when you return a prospective employer's call. Organize your materials and ready yourself psychologically for the conversation.

Making the First Conversation Impressive

Whether you answer the phone directly or return an employer's call, make sure you are prepared for the conversation. Remember that this is the first time the employer has heard your voice. How you conduct yourself on the phone will

Sounding flustered, unprepared, or unprofessional when an employer calls may ruin a job seeker's chances with that company.

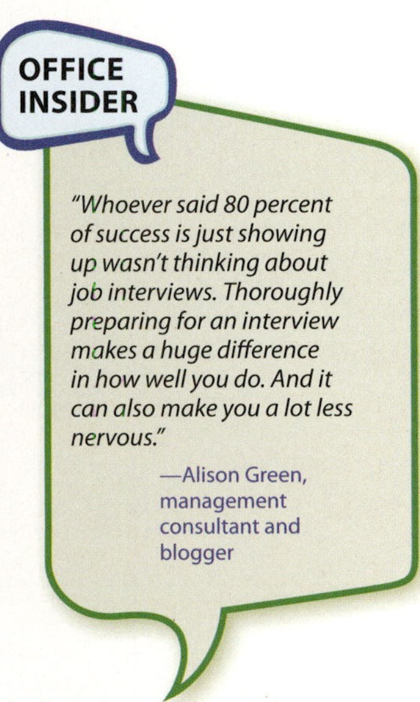

create a lasting impression. To make that first impression a positive one, follow these tips:

- Keep a list near the telephone of positions for which you have applied.
- Treat any call from an employer just like an interview. Use a professional tone and businesslike language. Be polite and enthusiastic, and sell your qualifications.
- If caught off guard by the call, ask whether you can call back in a few minutes. Take that time to organize your materials and yourself.
- Have a copy of your résumé available so that you can answer any questions that come up. Also have your list of references, a calendar, and a notepad handy.
- Be prepared for a screening interview. As discussed earlier, this might occur during the first phone call.
- Take good notes during the phone conversation. Obtain accurate directions, and verify the spelling of your interviewer's name. If you will be interviewed by more than one person, get all of their names.
- Before you hang up, reconfirm the date and time of your interview. You could say something like *I look forward to meeting with you next Wednesday at 2 p.m.*

Researching the Target Company

Before your interview, take time to research the target company and learn about its goals, customers, competitors, reputation, and so forth.

Once you have scheduled an in-person or online interview, you need to start preparing for it. One of the most important steps in effective interviewing is gathering detailed information about a prospective employer. Never enter an interview cold. Recruiters are impressed by candidates who have done their homework. Search the potential employer's Web site, news sources, trade journals, and industry directories. Unearth information about the job, the company, and the industry. Don't forget to Google the interviewer.[9] Learn all you can about the company's history, mission and goals, size, geographic locations, number of employees, customers, competitors, culture, management structure, reputation in the community, financial condition, strengths and weaknesses, and future plans, as well as the names of its leaders. Also, learn what you can about the industry in which the company operates. Visit the library and explore your campus career center to find additional information about the target company and its field, service, or product.

Analyze the company's advertising, including sales and marketing brochures. One candidate, a marketing major, spent a great deal of time poring over brochures from an aerospace contractor. During his initial interview, he shocked and impressed the recruiter with his knowledge of the company's guidance systems. The candidate had, in fact, relieved the interviewer of his least-favorite task—explaining the company's complicated technology.

Talking with company employees is always a good idea, if you can manage it. They are probably the best source of inside information. Try to speak to someone who is currently employed—but not working in the immediate area where you wish to be hired. Be sure to seek out someone who is discreet.

Blogs can provide authentic information about a company's culture, current happenings, and future plans.

Blogs are also good sources for company research. One marketing specialist calls them "job posting gold mines."[10] Many employees maintain both formal and informal blogs, where they share anecdotes and information about their employers. You can use these blogs to learn about a company's culture, its current happenings, and its future plans. Many job seekers find that they can get a more realistic picture of a company's day-to-day culture by reading blogs than they would by reading news articles or company Web site information. Blogs written by employees and ex-employees can be particularly informative.[11] If you can bring up a suitable post on the company blog in your cover letter or mention it in the interview, you may have a leg up over the competition.

Finally, you may also want to connect with the company through social media. "Like" the company on Facebook and comment shrewdly on the organization's status updates and other posts. You may hear about vacancies before they are advertised. If you follow the company and its key people on Twitter, you may draw some positive attention to yourself, perhaps even hear about up-to-the-minute job openings. If you know the interviewers' names, look up their profiles on LinkedIn, but don't try to connect with them before actually meeting them. You may find more in-depth information about these individuals on LinkedIn than on Facebook.[12]

In learning about a company, you may uncover information that convinces you that this is not the company for you. It is always better to learn about negatives early in the process. More likely, though, the information you collect will help you tailor your interview responses to the organization's needs. You know how flattered you feel when an employer knows about you and your background. That feeling works both ways. Employers are pleased when job candidates take an interest in them. Be ready to put in plenty of effort in investigating a target employer because this effort really pays off at interview time.

Preparing and Practicing

After you have learned about the target organization, study the job description or job listing. The most successful job candidates never go into interviews unprepared. They rehearse success stories and practice answers to typical questions. They clean up digital dirt and plan their responses to any problem areas on their résumés. As part of their preparation before the interview, they decide what to wear, and they gather the items they plan to take with them.

Rehearse Success Stories. To feel confident and be able to sell your qualifications, prepare and practice success stories. These stories are specific examples of your educational and work-related experience that demonstrate your qualifications and achievements. Look over the job description and your résumé to determine what skills, training, personal characteristics, and experience you want to emphasize during the interview. Then prepare a success story for each one. Incorporate numbers, such as dollars saved or percentage of sales increase, whenever possible. Your success stories should be detailed but brief. Think of them as 30-second sound bites.

Practice success stories that emphasize your most strategic skills, areas of knowledge, strongest personality traits, and key accomplishments.

Practice telling your success stories until they fluently roll off your tongue and sound natural. Then in the interview be certain to find places to insert them. Tell stories about (a) dealing with a crisis, (b) handling a tough interpersonal situation, (c) successfully juggling many priorities, (d) changing course to deal with changed circumstances, (e) learning from a mistake, (f) working on a team, and (g) going above and beyond expectations.[13]

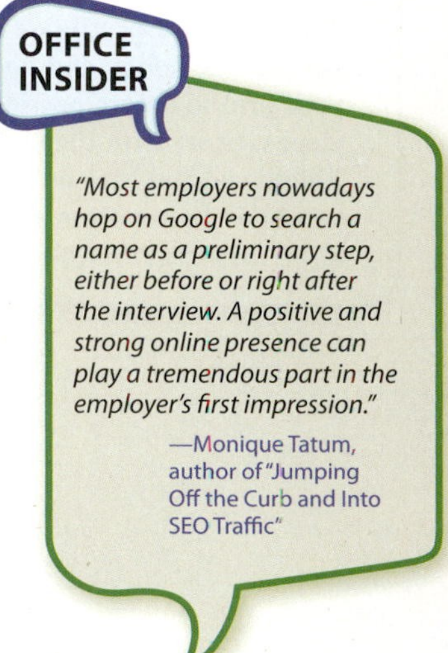

OFFICE INSIDER
"Most employers nowadays hop on Google to search a name as a preliminary step, either before or right after the interview. A positive and strong online presence can play a tremendous part in the employer's first impression."
—Monique Tatum, author of "Jumping Off the Curb and Into SEO Traffic"

Practice Answers to Possible Questions. Imagine the kinds of questions you may be asked and work out sample answers. Although you can't anticipate precise questions, you can expect to be asked about your education, skills, experience, salary expectations, and availability. Recite answers to typical interview questions in front of a mirror, with a friend, while driving in your car, or in spare moments. Keep practicing until you have the best responses down pat. Consider recording a practice session to see and hear how you answer questions. Do you look and sound enthusiastic?

Clean Up Any Digital Dirt. A study showed that 45 percent of employers screen candidates using Google and social networking sites such as Facebook, LinkedIn, MySpace, and Twitter.[14] Even more important, 70 percent of recruiters have found something online that caused them not to hire a candidate.[15] The top reasons cited for not considering an applicant after an online search were that the candidate (a) posted provocative or inappropriate photographs or information; (b) posted content about drinking or doing drugs; (c) talked negatively about current or previous employers, colleagues, or clients; (d) exhibited poor communication skills; (e) made discriminatory comments; (f) lied about qualifications; or (g) revealed a current or previous employer's confidential information.[16]

Make sure everything posted about you online is professional and positive.

For example, the president of a small consulting company in Chicago was about to hire a summer intern when he discovered the student's Facebook page.

Mikael Damkier /Shutterstock.com

WORKPLACE IN FOCUS

How can you protect your career prospects online? Imagine that your search using Google, 123people.com, Snitch.name, or PeekYou.com unearthed negative information about you. What to do? Look for contact information on the Web site and ask the owner to remove any offensive information about you. In serious cases, you may need legal advice. Understand that digital dirt can persist on other Web sites even after it is removed on the one you found. To prevent future problems, consider using nicknames or pseudonyms when starting a new profile on a social network. Know the privacy policy and understand who can view your profile before posting any text, images, or videos. Start with the strictest privacy settings. Finally, accept "friend" requests only from people you know, never from strangers. ***What else can you do to impress curious recruiters in cyberspace?***

The candidate described his interests as "smokin' blunts [cigars hollowed out and stuffed with marijuana], shooting people and obsessive sex."[17] The executive quickly lost interest in this candidate. Even if the student was merely posturing, it showed poor judgment. Teasing photographs and provocative comments about drinking, drug use, and sexual exploits make students look immature and unprofessional. You should, therefore, follow these steps to clean up your online presence:

- **Remove questionable content.** Remove any incriminating, provocative, or distasteful photos, content, and links that could make you look unprofessional to potential employers.
- **Stay positive.** Don't complain about things in your professional or personal life online. Even negative reviews you have written on sites such as Amazon.com can turn employers off.
- **Be selective about who is on your list of friends.** You don't want to miss out on an opportunity because you seem to associate with negative, immature, or unprofessional people. Your best bet is to make your personal social networking pages private.
- **Avoid joining groups or fan pages that may be viewed negatively.** Remember that online searches can turn up your online activities, including group memberships, blog postings, and so on. If you think any activity you are involved in might show poor judgment, remove yourself immediately.
- **Don't discuss your job search if you are still employed.** Employees can find themselves in trouble with their current employers by writing status updates or sending tweets about their job search.
- **Set up a professional social networking page or create your own personal Web site.** Use Facebook, LinkedIn, or other social networking sites to create a professional page. Many employers actually find information during their online searches that convinces them to hire candidates. Make sure your professional page demonstrates creativity, strong communication skills, and well-roundedness.[18]

Expect to Explain Problem Areas on Your Résumé. Interviewers are certain to question you about problem areas on your résumé. If you have little or no experience, you might emphasize your recent training and up-to-date skills. If you have gaps in your résumé, be prepared to answer questions about them positively and truthfully. If you were fired from a job, accept some responsibility for what happened and explain what you gained from the experience. Don't criticize a previous employer, and don't hide the real reasons. If you received low grades for one term, explain why and point to your improved grades in subsequent terms.

Decide How to Dress. What you wear to a job interview still matters. Even if some employees in the organization dress casually, you should look qualified, competent, and successful. One young applicant complained to his girlfriend about having to wear a suit for an interview when everyone at the company dressed casually. She replied, "You don't get to wear the uniform, though, until you make the team!" If uncertain, call the company and ask about the dress code. Research the culture at your target company. When in doubt, don a suit. Avoid loud colors; strive for a coordinated, natural appearance. Favorite "power" colors for interviews are gray and dark blue. Cover tattoos and conceal body piercings; these can be a turnoff for many interviewers. Don't overdo jewelry, and make sure that what you do wear is clean, pressed, odor-free, and lint-free. Shoes should be polished and scuff-free. Forget about flip-flops. To summarize, ensure that what you wear projects professionalism and shows your respect for the interview situation.

Gather Items to Bring. Decide what you should bring with you to the interview, and get everything ready the night before. You should plan to bring copies of your résumé, and your reference list, a notebook and pen, money for parking and tolls, and samples of your work, if appropriate. Place everything in a businesslike briefcase to add that final professional touch to your look.

Traveling to and Arriving at Your Interview

The big day has arrived! Ideally, you are fully prepared for your interview. Now you need to make sure that everything goes smoothly. That means making sure the trip to the potential employer's office goes well and that you arrive on time.

Allow ample time to arrive unflustered, and be congenial to everyone who greets you.

On the morning of your interview, give yourself plenty of time to groom and dress. Then make sure you can arrive at the employer's office without being rushed. If something unexpected happens that will to cause you to be late, such as an accident or bridge closure, call the interviewer right away to explain what is happening. Most interviewers will be understanding, and your call will show that you are responsible. On the way to the interview, don't smoke, don't eat anything messy or smelly, and don't load up on perfume or cologne. Arrive at the interview five or ten minutes early, but not earlier. If you are very early, wait in the car or in a café nearby. If possible, check your appearance before going in.

When you enter the office, be courteous and congenial to everyone. Remember that you are being judged not only by the interviewer but also by the receptionist and anyone else who sees you before and after the interview. They will notice how you sit, what you read, and how you look. Introduce yourself to the receptionist, and wait to be invited to sit. You may be asked to fill out a job application while you are waiting. You will find tips for doing this effectively later in this chapter.

Greet the interviewer confidently, and don't be afraid to initiate a handshake. Doing so exhibits professionalism and confidence. Extend your hand, look the interviewer directly in the eye, smile pleasantly, and say, *I'm pleased to meet you, Mr. Thomas. I am Constance Ferraro.* In this culture a firm, not crushing, handshake sends a nonverbal message of poise and assurance. Once introductions have taken place, wait for the interviewer to offer you a chair. Make small talk with upbeat comments, such as *This is a beautiful headquarters or I'm very impressed with the facilities you have here.* Don't immediately begin rummaging in your briefcase for your résumé. Being at ease and unrushed suggest that you are self-confident.

Fighting Fear

Expect to be nervous before and during the interview. It is natural! Other than public speaking, employment interviews are the most dreaded events in people's lives. One of the best ways to overcome fear is to know what happens in a typical interview. You can further reduce your fears by following these suggestions:

Fight fear by practicing, preparing thoroughly, dressing professionally, breathing deeply, and knowing that you are in charge for part of the interview.

- **Practice interviewing.** Try to get as much interviewing practice as you can—especially with real companies. The more times you experience the interview situation, the less nervous you will be. If offered, campus mock interviews also provide excellent practice, and the interviewers will offer tips for improvement.
- **Prepare thoroughly.** Research the company. Know how you will answer the most frequently asked questions. Be ready with success stories. Rehearse your

closing statement. One of the best ways to reduce anxiety is to know that you have done all you can to be ready for the interview.

- **Understand the process.** Find out ahead of time how the interview will be structured. Will you be meeting with an individual, or will you be interviewed by a panel? Is this the first of a series of interviews? Don't be afraid to ask about these details before the interview so that an unfamiliar situation won't catch you off guard.
- **Dress professionally.** If you know you look sharp, you will feel more confident.
- **Breathe deeply.** Take deep breaths, particularly if you feel anxious while waiting for the interviewer. Deep breathing makes you concentrate on something other than the interview and also provides much-needed oxygen.
- **Know that you are not alone.** Everyone feels some anxiety during a job interview. Interviewers expect some nervousness, and a skilled interviewer will try to put you at ease.
- **Remember that an interview is a two-way street.** The interviewer isn't the only one who is gleaning information. You have come to learn about the job and the company. In fact, during some parts of the interview, you will be in charge. This should give you courage.

During the Interview

Throughout the interview you will be answering questions and asking your own questions. Your demeanor, body language, and other nonverbal cues will also be on display. The interviewer will be trying to learn more about you, and you should be learning more about the job and the organization. Although you may be asked some unique questions, many interviewers ask standard, time-proven questions, which means that you can prepare your answers ahead of time.

Sending Positive Nonverbal Messages and Acting Professionally

Send positive nonverbal messages by arriving on time, being courteous, dressing professionally, greeting the interviewer confidently, controlling your body movements, making eye contact, listening attentively, and smiling.

You have already sent nonverbal messages to your interviewer by arriving on time, being courteous, dressing professionally, and greeting the receptionist confidently. You will continue to send nonverbal messages throughout the interview. Remember that what comes out of your mouth and what is written on your résumé are not the only messages an interviewer receives from you. Nonverbal messages also create powerful impressions on people. Here are suggestions that will help you send the right nonverbal messages during face-to-face and online interviews:

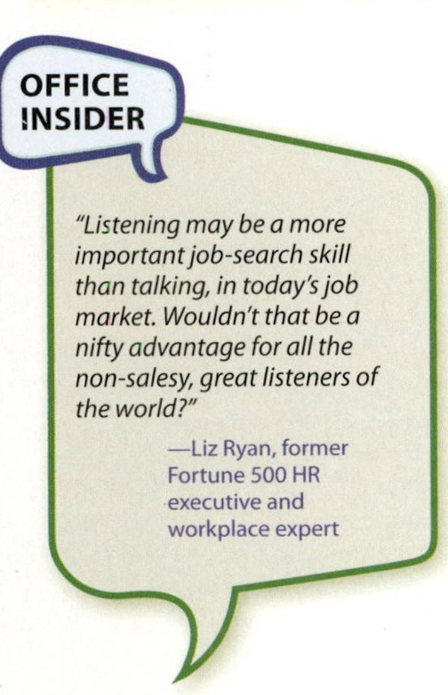

OFFICE INSIDER
"Listening may be a more important job-search skill than talking, in today's job market. Wouldn't that be a nifty advantage for all the non-salesy, great listeners of the world?"
—Liz Ryan, former Fortune 500 HR executive and workplace expert

- **Control your body movements.** Keep your hands, arms, and elbows to yourself. Don't lean on a desk. Keep your feet on the floor. Don't cross your arms in front of you. Keep your hands out of your pockets.
- **Exhibit good posture.** Sit erect, leaning forward slightly. Don't slouch in your chair; at the same time, don't look too stiff and uncomfortable. Good posture demonstrates confidence and interest.
- **Practice appropriate eye contact.** A direct eye gaze, at least in North America, suggests interest and trustworthiness. If you are being interviewed by a panel, remember to maintain eye contact with all interviewers.
- **Use gestures effectively.** Nod to show agreement and interest. Gestures should be used as needed, but don't overdo it.
- **Smile enough to convey a positive attitude.** Have a friend give you honest feedback on whether you generally smile too much or not enough.
- **Listen attentively.** Show the interviewer you are interested and attentive by listening carefully to the questions being asked. This will also help you answer questions appropriately.

- **Turn off your cell phone or other electronic devices.** Avoid the embarrassment of allowing your iPhone or BlackBerry to ring, or even as much as buzz, during an interview. Turn off your electronic devices completely; don't just switch them to vibrate.
- **Don't chew gum.** Chewing gum during an interview is distracting and unprofessional.
- **Sound enthusiastic and interested—but sincere.** The tone of your voice has an enormous effect on the words you say. Avoid sounding bored, frustrated, or sarcastic during an interview. Employers want employees who are enthusiastic and interested.
- **Avoid empty words.** Filling your answers with verbal pauses such as *um*, *uh*, *like*, and *basically* communicates that you are not prepared. Also avoid annoying distractions such as clearing your throat repeatedly or sighing deeply.
- **Be confident, but not cocky.** Most recruiters want candidates who are self-assured but not too casual or even arrogant. Let your body language, posture, dress, and vocal tone prove your confidence. Speak at a normal volume and enunciate words clearly without mumbling.[19]

"I'm in the middle of a job interview. What are you doing?"

Naturally, hiring managers make subjective decisions based on intuition, but they need to ferret out pleasant people who fit in. To that end, some recruiters apply "the airport test" to candidates: "Would I want to be stuck in the airport for 12 hours with this person if my flight were delayed?"[20]

Answering Typical Interview Questions

Remember that the way you answer questions can be almost as important as what you say. Use the interviewer's name and title from time to time when you answer. *Ms. Lyon, I would be pleased to tell you about . . . .* People like to hear their own names. Be sure you are pronouncing the name correctly, and don't overuse this technique. Avoid answering questions with a simple *yes* or *no*; elaborate on your answers to better promote yourself and your assets. Keep your answers positive; don't criticize anything or anyone.

How you answer questions can be as important as the answers themselves.

During the interview it may be necessary to occasionally refocus and clarify vague questions. Some interviewers are inexperienced and ill at ease in the role. You may even have to ask your own question to understand what was asked, *By _____, do you mean _____?* Consider closing out some of your responses with *Does that answer your question?* or *Would you like me to elaborate on any particular experience?*

Always aim your answers at the key characteristics interviewers seek: expertise, competence, motivation, interpersonal skills, decision-making skills, enthusiasm for the company and the job, and a pleasing personality. Remember to stay focused on your strengths. Don't reveal weaknesses, even if you think they make you look human. You won't be hired for your weaknesses, only for your strengths.

Be sure to use good English and enunciate clearly. Avoid slurred words such as *gonna* and *din't*, as well as slangy expressions such as *yeah, like*, and *ya know*. As you practice answering expected interview questions, it is always a good idea to make a recording. Is your speech filled with verbal static?

Stay focused on the skills and traits that employers seek; don't reveal weaknesses.

You can't expect to be perfect in an employment interview. No one is. But you can avert sure disaster by avoiding certain topics and behaviors such as those described in Figure 14.1.

Employment interviews are all about questions, and many of the questions interviewers ask are not new. You can anticipate a large percentage of questions that will be asked before you ever walk into an interview room. Although you can't anticipate every question, you can prepare for various types.

FIGURE 14.1 Twelve Interview Actions to Avoid

1. **Don't be late or too early.** Arrive five to ten minutes before your scheduled interview.
2. **Don't be rude or annoying.** Treat everyone you come into contact with warmly and respectfully. Avoid limp handshakes, poor eye contact or staring, and verbal ticks such as *like, you know*, and *umm.*
3. **Don't ask for the job.** Asking for the job is naïve, undignified, and unprofessional. Wait to see how the interview develops.
4. **Don't criticize anyone or anything.** Don't criticize your previous employer, supervisors, colleagues, or job. The tendency is for interviewers to wonder if you would speak about their companies similarly.
5. **Don't be a threat to the interviewer.** Avoid suggesting directly or indirectly that your goal is to become head honcho, a path that might include the interviewer's job.
6. **Don't act unprofessionally.** Don't discuss controversial subjects, and don't use profanity. Don't answer your cell phone or fiddle with it. Silence all electronic devices so that they don't even buzz, or turn them off completely. Don't bring food or coffee.
7. **Don't emphasize salary or benefits.** Don't address salary, vacation, or benefits early in an interview. Let the interviewer set the pace; win him or her over first.
8. **Don't focus on your imperfections.** Never dwell on your liabilities or talk negatively about yourself.
9. **Don't interrupt.** Interrupting is not only impolite but also prevents you from hearing a complete question or remark. Don't talk too much or too little. Answer interview questions to the best of your ability, but avoid rambling as much as terseness.
10. **Don't bring someone along.** Don't bring a friend or relative with you to the interview. If someone must drive you, ask that person to drop you off and come back later.
11. **Don't appear impatient or bored.** Your entire focus should be on the interview. Don't glance at your watch, which can imply that you are late for another appointment. Be alert and show interest in the company and the position.
12. **Don't act desperate.** A sure way to turn off an interviewer is to act too desperate. Don't focus on why you *need* the job; focus on how you will add value to the organization.

You can anticipate a large percentage of the questions you will be asked in an interview.

This section presents questions that may be asked during employment interviews. Some questions are meant to help the interviewer become acquainted with you. Others are aimed at measuring your interest, experience, and accomplishments. Still others will probe your future plans and challenge your reactions. Some will inquire about your salary expectations. Your interviewer may use situational or behavioral questions and may even occasionally ask an illegal question. To get you thinking about how to respond, we have provided an answer for, or a discussion of, one or more of the questions in each of the following groups. As you read the remaining questions in each group, think about how you could respond most effectively. For additional questions, contact your campus career center, or consult one of the career Web sites listed in Chapter 13.

"Yes, I think I have good people skills. What kind of idiot question is that?"

Questions to Get Acquainted. After opening introductions, recruiters generally try to start the interview with personal questions designed to put you at ease. They are also striving to gain an overview to see whether you will fit into the organization's culture. When answering these questions, keep the employer's needs in mind and try to incorporate your success stories.

Prepare for get-acquainted questions by practicing a short formula response.

1. Tell me about yourself.

Experts agree that you must keep this answer short (one to two minutes tops) but on target. Use this chance to promote yourself. Stick to educational, professional, or business-related strengths; avoid personal or humorous references. Be ready with at least three success stories illustrating characteristics important to this job. Demonstrate responsibility you have been given; describe how you contributed as a team player. Try practicing this formula: *I have completed a ______ degree with a major in ____. Recently I worked for ______ as a _______. Before that I worked for _______ as a _____. My strengths are ________ (interpersonal) and _________ (technical).* Try rehearsing your response in 30-second segments devoted to your education, work experience, qualifications, and skills.

OFFICE INSIDER

"Occasionally you bump into a talented and competent candidate . . . who's so lacking in the EQ components of humility and realness that you can't take a chance. This young man had a lot of the right stuff, but when he started telling us that he had never made a mistake in his life and didn't expect to, we knew we'd heard enough."

—Jack and Suzy Welch, management consultants and authors

2. What are your greatest strengths?

Stress your strengths that are related to the position, such as *I am well organized, thorough, and attentive to detail.* Tell success stories and give examples that illustrate these qualities: *My supervisor says that my research is exceptionally thorough. For example, I recently worked on a research project in which I . . . .*

3. Do you prefer to work by yourself or with others? Why?

This question can be tricky. Provide a middle-of-the-road answer that not only suggests your interpersonal qualities but also reflects an ability to make independent decisions and work without supervision.

4. What was your major in college, and why did you choose it?
5. What are some things you do in your spare time?

Questions to Gauge Your Interest. Interviewers want to understand your motivation for applying for a position. Although they will realize that you are probably interviewing for other positions, they still want to know why you are interested in this particular position with this organization. These types of questions help them determine your level of interest.

Recruiters want to know how interested you are in their organization and in the open position.

1. Why do you want to work for [name of company]?

Questions like this illustrate why you must research an organization thoroughly before the interview. The answer to this question must prove that you understand the company and its culture. This is the perfect place to bring up the company research you did before the interview. Show what you know about the company, and discuss why you want to become a part of this organization. Describe your desire to work for this organization not only from your perspective but also from its point of view. What do you have to offer that will benefit the organization?

2. Why are you interested in this position?
3. What do you know about our company?
4. Why do you want to work in the ______________ industry?
5. What interests you about our products (or services)?

Questions About Experience and Accomplishments. After questions about your background and education and questions that measure your interest, the interview generally becomes more specific with questions about your experience and accomplishments. Remember to show confidence when you answer these questions. If you are not confident in your abilities, why should an employer be?

1. Why should we hire you when we have applicants with more experience or better credentials?

In answering this question, remember that employers often hire people who present themselves well instead

"Besides 'a great smile' do you have any other qualifications we could consider?"

Questions about your experience and accomplishments enable you to work in your success stories.

of others with better credentials. Emphasize your personal strengths that could be an advantage with this employer. Are you a hard worker? How can you demonstrate it? Have you had recent training? Some people have had more years of experience but actually have less knowledge because they have done the same thing over and over. Stress your experience using the latest methods and equipment. Be sure to mention your computer training and use of the Web. Tell success stories. Emphasize that you are open to new ideas and learn quickly. Above all, show that you are confident in your abilities.

2. Describe the most rewarding experience of your career so far.
3. How have your education and professional experiences prepared you for this position?
4. What were your major accomplishments in each of your past jobs?
5. What was a typical workday like?
6. What job functions did you enjoy most? Least? Why?
7. Tell me about your computer skills.
8. Who was the toughest boss you ever worked for and why?
9. What were your major achievements in college?
10. Why did you leave your last position? *OR:* Why are you leaving your current position?

Questions About the Future. Questions that look into the future tend to stump some candidates, especially those who have not prepared adequately. Employers ask these questions to see whether you are goal oriented and to determine whether your goals are realistic.

1. Where do you expect to be five (or ten) years from now?

When asked about the future, show ambition and interest in succeeding with this company.

Formulate a realistic plan with respect to your present age and situation. The important thing is to be prepared for this question. It is a sure kiss of death to respond that you would like to have the interviewer's job! Instead, show an interest in the current job and in making a contribution to the organization. Talk about the levels of responsibility you would like to achieve. One employment counselor suggests showing ambition but not committing to a specific job title. Suggest that you hope to have learned enough to have progressed to a position in which you will continue to grow. Keep your answer focused on educational and professional goals, not personal goals.

2. If you got this position, what would you do to be sure you fit in?
3. This is a large (or small) organization. Do you think you would like that environment?
4. Do you plan to continue your education?
5. What do you predict for the future of the ______________ industry?
6. How do you think you can contribute to this company?
7. What would you most like to accomplish if you get this position?
8. How do you keep current with what is happening in your profession?

Challenging Questions. The following questions may make you uncomfortable, but the important thing to remember is to answer truthfully without dwelling on your weaknesses. As quickly as possible, convert any negative response into a discussion of your strengths.

1. What is your greatest weakness?

Strive to convert a discussion of your weaknesses to topics that show your strengths.

It is amazing how many candidates knock themselves out of the competition by answering this question poorly. Actually, you have many choices. You can present a strength as a weakness (*Some people complain that I'm a workaholic or too attentive to details*). You can mention a corrected weakness (*Because I needed to learn about designing Web sites, I took a course.*) You could cite an unrelated skill (*I really need to brush up on my Spanish*). You can cite a learning objective (*One of my long-term goals is to learn more about international management. Does your company have any plans to expand overseas?*). Another possibility is to reaffirm your qualifications (*I have no weaknesses that affect my ability to do this job*). Be careful that your answer doesn't sound too cliché (*I tend to be a perfectionist*) and instead shows careful analysis of your abilities.

2. What type of people do you have no patience for?

   Avoid letting yourself fall into the trap of sounding overly critical. One possible response is, *I have always gotten along well with others. But I confess that I can be irritated by complainers who don't accept responsibility.*

Answer challenging questions truthfully, but try to turn the discussion into one that emphasizes your strengths.

3. If you could live your life over, what would you change and why?
4. How would your former (or current) supervisor describe you as an employee?
5. What do you want the most from your job?
6. What is your grade point average, and does it accurately reflect your abilities?
7. Have you ever used drugs?
8. Who in your life has influenced you the most and why?
9. What are you reading right now?
10. Describe your ideal work environment.
11. Is the customer always right?
12. How do you define success?

Situational Questions. Questions related to situations help employers test your thought processes and logical thinking. When using situational questions, interviewers describe a hypothetical situation and ask how you would handle it. Situational questions differ based on the type of position for which you are interviewing. Knowledge of the position and the company culture will help you respond favorably to these questions. Even if the situation sounds negative, keep your response positive. Here are just a few examples:

Employers find that situational and behavioral interview questions give them useful information about job candidates.

1. You receive a call from an irate customer who complains about the service she received last night at your restaurant. She is demanding her money back. How would you handle the situation?
2. If you were aware that a coworker was falsifying data, what would you do?
3. Your supervisor has just told you that she is dissatisfied with your work, but you think it is acceptable. How would you resolve the conflict?
4. Your supervisor has told you to do something a certain way, and you think that way is wrong and that you know a far better way to complete the task. What would you do?
5. Assume that you are hired for this position. You soon learn that one of the staff is extremely resentful because she applied for your position and was turned down. As a result, she is being unhelpful and obstructive. How would you handle the situation?
6. A colleague has told you in confidence that she suspects another colleague of stealing. What would your actions be?
7. You have noticed that communication between upper management and first-level employees is eroding. How would you solve this problem?

"We look for people who can quickly adapt to changes in the workplace."

www.cartoonstock.com

Behavioral Questions. Instead of traditional interview questions, you may be asked to tell stories. The interviewer may say, *Describe a time when . . .* or *Tell me about a time*

The STAR technique (Situation, Task, Action, Results) helps you respond logically to behavioral questions.

when . . . . To respond effectively, learn to use the storytelling, or STAR, technique. Ask yourself, what the **S**ituation or **T**ask was, what **A**ction you took, and what the **R**esults were.[21] Practice using this method to recall specific examples of your skills and accomplishments. To be fully prepared, develop a coherent and articulate STAR narrative for every bullet point on your résumé. When answering behavioral questions, describe only educational and work-related situations or tasks, and try to keep them as current as possible. Here are a few examples of behavioral questions:

1. Tell me about a time when you solved a difficult problem.

   Tell a concise story explaining the situation or task, what you did, and the result. For example, *When I was at Ace Products, we continually had a problem of excessive back orders. After analyzing the situation, I discovered that orders went through many unnecessary steps. I suggested that we eliminate much paperwork. As a result, we reduced back orders by 30 percent.* Go on to emphasize what you learned and how you can apply that learning to this job. Practice your success stories in advance so that you will be ready.

2. Describe a situation in which you were able to use persuasion to convince someone to see things your way.

   The recruiter is interested in your leadership and teamwork skills. You might respond, *I have learned to appreciate the fact that the way you present an idea is just as important as the idea itself. When trying to influence people, I put myself in their shoes and find some way to frame my idea from their perspective. I remember when I . . . .*

3. Describe a time when you had to analyze information and make a recommendation.
4. Describe a time that you worked successfully as part of a team.
5. Tell me about a time that you dealt with confidential information.
6. Give me an example of a time when you were under stress to meet a deadline.
7. Tell me about a time when you had to go above and beyond the call of duty to get a job done.
8. Tell me about a time you were able to deal with another person successfully even though that individual did not like you personally (or vice versa).
9. Give me an example of when you showed initiative and took the lead.
10. Tell me about a recent situation in which you had to deal with an upset customer or coworker.

Candidates who are asked illegal questions must decide whether to answer, deflect the question tactfully, or confront the interviewer.

Illegal and Inappropriate Questions. Federal laws prohibit employment discrimination based on gender, age, religion, color, race, national origin, and disability. In addition, federal civil service statutes and many state and city laws prohibit employment discrimination based on factors such as sexual orientation.[22] Therefore, it is inappropriate for interviewers to ask any question related to these areas. These questions become illegal, though, only when a court of law determines that the employer is asking them with the intent to discriminate.[23] Most illegal interview questions are asked innocently by inexperienced interviewers. Some are only trying to be friendly when they inquire about your personal life or family. Regardless of the intent, how should you react?

If you find the question harmless and if you want the job, go ahead and answer it. If you think that answering it would damage your chance to be hired, try to deflect the question tactfully with a response such as *Could you tell me how my marital status relates to the responsibilities of this position?* or, *I prefer to keep my personal and professional lives separate*. If you are uncomfortable answering a question, try to determine the reason behind it; you might answer, *I don't let my personal life interfere with my ability to do my job*, or, *Are you concerned with my availability to work overtime?* Another option, of course, is to respond to any inappropriate or illegal question by confronting the interviewer and threatening a lawsuit or refusing to answer. However, you could not expect to be hired under these circumstances. In any case, you might wish to reconsider working for an organization that sanctions such procedures.

Here are some inappropriate and illegal questions that you may or may not want to answer:[24]

You may respond to an inappropriate or illegal question by asking tactfully how it relates to the responsibilities of the position.

1. What is your marital status? Are you married? Do you live with anyone? Do you have a boyfriend (or girlfriend)? (However, employers can ask your marital status after hiring for tax and insurance forms.)
2. Do you have any disabilities? Have you had any recent illnesses? (But it is legal to ask if the person can perform specific job duties, such as, *Can you carry a 50-pound sack up a 10-foot ladder five times daily?*)
3. I notice you have an accent. Where are you from? What is the origin of your last name? What is your native language? (However, it is legal to ask what languages you speak fluently if language ability is related to the job.)
4. Have you ever filed a workers' compensation claim or been injured on the job?
5. Have you ever had a drinking problem or been addicted to drugs? (But it is legal to ask if a person uses illegal drugs.)
6. Have you ever been arrested? (But it is legal to ask, *Have you ever been convicted of ___________?* when the crime is related to the job.)
7. How old are you? What is your date of birth? When did you graduate from high school? (But it is legal to ask, *Are you 16 years [or 18 years or 21 years] old or older?* depending on the age requirements for the position.)
8. Of what country are you a citizen? Are you a U.S. citizen? Where were you born? (But it is legal to ask, *Are you authorized to work in the United States?*)
9. What is your maiden name? (But it is legal to ask *What is your full name?* or, *Have you worked under another name?*)
10. Do you have any religious beliefs that would prevent you from working weekends or holidays? (An employer can, however, ask you if you are available to work weekends and holidays or otherwise within the company's required schedule.)
11. Do you have children? Do you plan to have children? Do you have adequate child-care arrangements? (However, employers can ask for dependent information for tax and insurance purposes after you are hired. Also, they can ask if the candidate would be able to travel or work overtime on occasion.)
12. How much do you weigh? How tall are you? (However, employers can ask you about your height and weight if minimum standards are necessary to safely perform a job.)[25]

Interview questions become illegal only if a court of law determines that the intent was to discriminate.

Asking Your Own Questions

At some point in the interview, usually near the end, you will be asked whether you have any questions. The worst thing you can do is say *No,* which suggests that you are not interested in the position. Instead, ask questions that will help you gain information and will impress the interviewer with your thoughtfulness and interest in the position. Remember that this interview is a two-way street. You must be happy with the prospect of working for this organization. You want a position that matches your skills and personality. Use this opportunity to learn whether this job is right for you. Be aware that you don't have to wait for the interviewer to ask you for questions. You can ask your own questions throughout the interview to learn more about the company and position. Here are some questions you might ask:

Your questions should impress the interviewer but also provide valuable information about the job.

1. What will my duties be (if not already discussed)?
2. Tell me what it is like working here in terms of the people, management practices, workloads, expected performance, and rewards.

Most job hunters know that answering the cell phone during an employment interview would cost them the job. However, in a CareerBuilder survey, 71 percent of hiring managers cited yakking on the phone during a job interview as job candidates' most common blunder—closely followed at 69 percent each by inappropriate attire and appearing uninterested. Seeming arrogant is a close third at 66 percent. Other pet peeves the recruiters cited were maligning a former employer (63 percent), chewing gum (59 percent), not providing specific answers (35 percent), and not asking good questions (32 percent.) The most spectacular offenses? Hugging the recruiter at the end of the interview, emptying the candy jar, and wearing a hat that says "Take this job and shove it." ***How can job candidates demonstrate their interest in the interviewer's company, avoid seeming arrogant, provide specific answers, and ask good questions?***

WORKPLACE IN FOCUS

3. What training programs are available from this organization? What specific training will be given for this position?
4. Who would be my immediate supervisor?
5. What is the organizational structure, and where does this position fit in?
6. Is travel required in this position?
7. How is job performance evaluated?
8. Assuming my work is excellent, where do you see me in five years?
9. How long do employees generally stay with this organization?
10. What are the major challenges for a person in this position?
11. What do you see in the future of this organization?
12. What do you like best about working for this organization?
13. May I have a tour of the facilities?
14. When do you expect to make a decision?

Do not ask about salary or benefits, especially during the first interview. It is best to let the interviewer bring those topics up first.

Ending Positively

At the end of the interview, summarize your strongest qualifications, thank the interviewer, and ask for the interviewer's card.

After you have asked your questions, the interviewer will signal the end of the interview, usually by standing up or by expressing appreciation that you came. If not addressed earlier, you should at this time find out what action will follow. Demonstrate your interest in the position by asking when it will be filled or what the next step will be. Too many candidates leave the interview without knowing their status or when they will hear from the recruiter. Don't be afraid to say that you want the job!

Before you leave, summarize your strongest qualifications, show your enthusiasm for obtaining this position, and thank the interviewer for a constructive interview and for considering you for the position. Ask the interviewer for a business card, which will provide the information you need to write a thank-you letter, which is discussed later. Shake the interviewer's hand with confidence, and acknowledge anyone else you see on the way out. Be sure to thank the receptionist. Departing gracefully and enthusiastically will leave a lasting impression on those responsible for making the final hiring decision.

After the Interview

After leaving the interview, immediately make notes of what was said in case you are called back for a second interview. Write down key points that were discussed, the names of people you spoke with, and other details of the interview. Ask yourself what went really well and what you could improve. Note your strengths and weaknesses during the interview so that you can work to improve in future interviews. Next, write down your follow-up plans. To whom should you send thank-you messages? Will you contact the employer by phone? By e-mail? If so, when? Then be sure to follow up on those plans, beginning with writing a thank-you e-mail or letter and contacting your references.

Thanking Your Interviewer

After a job interview, you should always send a thank-you note, also called a follow-up message. This courtesy sets you apart from other applicants, most of whom will not bother. Your message also reminds the interviewer of your visit and shows your good manners and genuine enthusiasm for the job.

A follow-up thank-you message shows your good manners and your enthusiasm for the job.

Follow-up messages are most effective if sent immediately after the interview. Experts believe that a thoughtful follow-up note carries as much weight as the cover letter does. Almost nine out of ten senior executives admit that in their evaluation of a job candidate they are swayed by a written thank-you.[26] In your thank-you message, refer to the date of the interview, the exact job title for which you were interviewed, and specific topics discussed. "An effective thank-you letter should hit every one of the employer's hot buttons," author and career consultant Wendy Enelow says.[27]

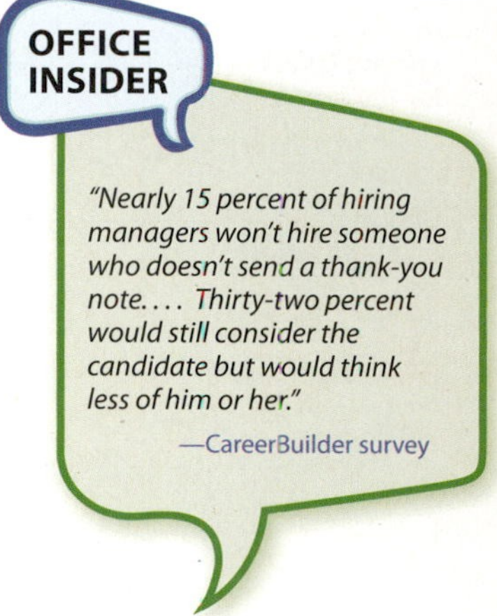

Note, however, that some employers are more digitally inclined and prefer e-mail; they frown upon a traditional thank-you note through the mail.[28] In any case, avoid worn-out phrases, such as *Thank you for taking the time to interview me*. Be careful, too, about overusing *I*, especially to begin sentences. Most important, show that you really want the job and that you are qualified for it. Notice how the letter in Figure 14.2 conveys enthusiasm and confidence.

If you have been interviewed by more than one person, send a separate thank-you message to each interviewer. It is also a good idea to send a thank-you message to the receptionist and to the person who set up the interview. Your preparation and knowledge of the company culture will help you determine whether a traditional thank-you letter sent by mail or an e-mail is more appropriate. Make sure that you write your e-mail using professional language, standard capitalization, and proper punctuation. One job candidate makes a follow-up e-mail her standard practice. She summarizes what was discussed during the face-to-face interview and adds information that she had not thought to mention during the interview.[29]

Contacting Your References

Once you have thanked your interviewer, it is time to alert your references that they may be contacted by the employer. You might also have to request a letter of recommendation to be sent to the employer by a certain date. As discussed in Chapter 13, you should have already asked permission to use these individuals as references, and you should have supplied them with a copy of your résumé, and information about the types of positions you are seeking

To provide the best possible recommendation, your references need information. What position have you applied for with what company? What should they stress to the prospective employer? Let's say you are applying for a specific job that requires a letter of recommendation. Professor Angus has already agreed to be a reference for you. To get the best

© Ted Goff www.tedgoff.com

"Why do all your references scream and slam down the phone when I mention your name?"

FIGURE 14.2 Interview Follow-Up Message

Eugene H. Vincente

1308 Big Ridge Rd., Apt. 3, Biloxi, MS 39530
(228) 627-4362, evincente@gmail.com

May 28, 201x

Mr. André G. Mercier
3D Signs
5505 Industrial Parkway, Ste. 200
New Orleans, LA 70129

Dear Mr. Mercier:

Talking with you Thursday, May 27, about the graphic designer position was both informative and interesting.

Thanks for describing the position in such detail and for introducing me to Ms. Sasaki, the designer. Her current project designing an annual report in four colors sounds fascinating as well as quite challenging.

Now that I've learned in greater detail the specific tasks of your graphic designers, I'm more than ever convinced that my computer and creative skills can make a genuine contribution to your graphic productions. My training in design and layout using Photoshop and InDesign ensures that I could be immediately productive on your staff.

You will find me an enthusiastic and hardworking member of any team effort. As you requested, I'm enclosing additional samples of my work. I'm eager to join the graphics staff at your New Orleans headquarters, and I look forward to hearing from you soon.

Sincerely,

Eugene H. Vincente

Eugene H. Vincente

Enclosures

Uses customized letterhead but could have merely typed street and city address above dateline

Mentions the interview date and specific job title

Personalizes the message by referring to topics discussed in the interview

Highlights specific skills for the job

Shows good manners, appreciation, and perseverance—traits that recruiters value

Reminds reader of interpersonal skills as well as enthusiasm and eagerness for the job

letter of recommendation from Professor Angus, help her out. Write an e-mail or letter telling her about the position, its requirements, and the recommendation deadline. Include copies of your résumé, college transcript, and, if applicable, the job posting or ad with detailed information about the opening. You might remind her of a positive experience with you that she could use in the recommendation. Remember that recommenders need evidence to support generalizations. Give them appropriate ammunition, as the student has done in the following request:

In a reference request letter, tell immediately why you are writing. Identify the target position and company.

Dear Professor Angus:

Recently I interviewed for the position of administrative assistant in the Human Resources Department of Host International. Because you kindly agreed to help me, I am now asking you to write a letter of recommendation to Host.

Specify the job requirements so that the recommender knows what to stress.

The position calls for good organizational, interpersonal, and writing skills, as well as computer experience. To help you review my skills and training, I enclose my résumé. As you may recall, I earned an A in your business communication class last fall; and you commended my long report for its clarity and organization.

Please send your letter to Mr. James Jenkins at Host International before July 1 in the enclosed stamped, addressed envelope. I'm grateful for your support and promise to let you know the results of my job search.

Provide a stamped, addressed envelope.

Sincerely,

Following Up

If you don't hear from the interviewer within five days, or at the specified time, consider following up. The standard advice to job candidates is to call to follow up a few days after the interview. However, some experts suggest that cold calling a hiring manager is fraught with risk. You may be putting a busy recruiter on the spot and force him or her to search for your application. In addition, don't assume you are the only candidate; multiply your phone call by the 200 applicants whom some hiring managers interview.[30] Therefore, you don't want to be a pest. An e-mail to find out how the decision process is going may be your best bet because such a message is much less intrusive.

However, if you believe it is safe to follow up by phone or if the recruiter suggested it, practice saying something like, *I'm wondering what else I can do to convince you that I'm the right person for this job, or, I'm calling to find out the status of your search for the ____________ position.* When following up, it is important to sound professional and courteous. Sounding desperate, angry, or frustrated that you have not been contacted can ruin your chances. The following follow-up e-mail message would impress the interviewer:

Dear Ms. Kahn:

A follow-up message inquires courteously but does not sound angry or desperate.

I enjoyed my interview with you last Thursday for the receptionist position. You should know that I'm very interested in this opportunity with Coastal Enterprises. Because you mentioned that you might have an answer this week, I'm eager to know how your decision process is coming along. I look forward to hearing from you.

Sincerely,

Depending on the response you get to your first follow-up request, you may have to follow up additional times.[31] Keep in mind, though, that some employers won't tell you about their hiring decision unless you are the one hired. Don't harass the interviewer, and don't force a decision. If you don't hear back from an employer within several weeks after following up, it is best to assume that you didn't get the job and to continue with your job search.

Other Employment Documents and Follow-Up Messages

Although the résumé and cover letter are your major tasks, other important documents and messages are often required during the employment process. You may need to complete an employment application form and write follow-up letters. You might also have to write a letter of resignation when leaving a job. Because each of these tasks reveals something about you and your communication skills, you will want to put your best foot forward. These documents often subtly influence company officials to offer a job.

Application Form

Some organizations require job candidates to fill out job application forms instead of, or in addition to, submitting résumés. This practice permits them to gather and store standardized data about each applicant. Whether the application is on paper

When applying for jobs, keep with you a card summarizing your important data.

or online, follow the directions carefully and provide accurate information. The following suggestions can help you be prepared:

- Carry a card summarizing vital statistics not included on your résumé. If you are asked to fill out an application form in an employer's office, you will need a handy reference to the following data: graduation dates; beginning and ending dates of all employment; salary history; full names, titles, and present work addresses of former supervisors; full addresses and phone numbers of current and previous employers; and full names, occupational titles, occupational addresses, and telephone numbers of persons who have agreed to serve as references.
- Look over all the questions before starting.
- Fill out the form neatly, using blue or black ink. Many career counselors recommend printing your responses; cursive handwriting can be difficult to read.
- Answer all questions honestly. Write *Not applicable* or *N/A* if appropriate. Don't leave any sections blank.
- Use accurate spelling, grammar, capitalization, and punctuation.
- If asked for the position desired, give a specific job title or type of position. Don't say, *Anything* or *Open.* These answers make you look unfocused; moreover, they make it difficult for employers to know what you are qualified for or interested in.
- Be prepared for a salary question. Unless you know what comparable employees are earning in the company, the best strategy is to suggest a salary range or to write *Negotiable* or *Open.* See the Communication Workshop at the end of this chapter for tips on dealing with money matters while interviewing.
- Be prepared to explain the reasons for leaving previous positions. Use positive or neutral phrases such as *Relocation, Seasonal, To accept a position with more responsibility, Temporary position, To continue education,* or *Career change*. Avoid words or phrases such as *Fired*, *Quit*, *Didn't get along with supervisor*, or *Pregnant*.
- Look over the application before submitting to make sure it is complete and that you have followed all instructions. Sign and date the application.

Application or Résumé Follow-Up Message

If your résumé or application generates no response within a reasonable time, you may decide to send a short follow-up e-mail or letter such as the following. Doing so (a) jogs the memory of the personnel officer, (b) demonstrates your serious interest, and (c) allows you to emphasize your qualifications or to add new information.

Dear Ms. Gutierrez:

Open by reminding the reader of your interest.

Please know I am still interested in becoming an administrative support specialist with Quad, Inc.

Review your strengths or add new qualifications.

Since submitting an application [or résumé] in May, I have completed my degree and have been employed as a summer replacement for office workers in several downtown offices. This experience has honed my word processing and communication skills. It has also introduced me to a wide range of office procedures.

Close positively; avoid accusations that make the reader defensive.

Please keep my application in your active file and let me know when my formal training, technical skills, and practical experience can go to work for you.

Sincerely,

Rejection Follow-Up Message

If you didn't get the job and you think it was perfect for you, don't give up. Employment specialists encourage applicants to respond to a rejection. The candidate who was offered the position may decline, or other positions may open up. In a rejection follow-up e-mail or letter, it is OK to admit you are disappointed.

Be sure to add, however, that you are still interested and will contact the company again in a month in case a job opens up. Then follow through for a couple of months—but don't overdo it. You should be professional and persistent, not annoying. Here is an example of an effective rejection follow-up message:

Dear Mr. O'Leary:

Although disappointed that someone else was selected for your accounting position, I appreciate your promptness and courtesy in notifying me.

Subordinate your disappointment to your appreciation at being notified promptly and courteously.

Because I am confident that you would benefit from my technical and interpersonal skills in your fast-paced environment, please consider keeping my résumé in your active file. My desire to become a productive member of your Transamerica staff remains strong.

Emphasize your continuing interest.

Our interview on ______ was very enjoyable, and I especially appreciate the time you and Ms. Goldstein spent describing your company's expansion into international markets. To enhance my qualifications, I have enrolled in a course in international accounting at CSU.

Refer to specifics of your interview.

Should you have an opening for which I am qualified, you may reach me at (818) 719-3901. In the meantime, I will call you in a month to discuss employment possibilities.

Take the initiative; tell when you will call for an update.

Sincerely,

Job Acceptance and Rejection Message

When all your hard work pays off, you will be offered the position you want. Although you will likely accept the position over the phone, it is a good idea to follow up with an acceptance e-mail or letter to confirm the details and to formalize the acceptance. Your acceptance message might look like this:

Dear Ms. Doyle:

It was a pleasure talking with you earlier today. As I mentioned, I am delighted to accept the position of web designer with Innovative Creations, Inc., in your Seattle office. I look forward to becoming part of the IC team and starting work on a variety of exciting and innovative projects.

Confirm your acceptance of the position with enthusiasm.

As we agreed, my starting salary will be $46,000, with a full benefits package including health and life insurance, retirement plan, and two weeks of vacation per year.

Review salary and benefits details.

I look forward to starting my position with Innovative Creations on September 15, 2011. Before that date I will send you the completed tax and insurance forms you need. Thanks again for everything, Ms. Doyle.

Include the specific starting date.

Sincerely,

If you must turn down a job offer, show your professionalism by writing a sincere letter. This letter should thank the employer for the job offer and explain briefly that you are turning it down. Taking the time to extend this courtesy could help you in the future if this employer has a position you really want. Here's an example of a job rejection letter:

Dear Mr. Rosen:

Thank you very much for offering me the position of sales representative with Bendall Pharmaceuticals. It was a difficult decision to make, but I have accepted a position with another company.

Thank the employer for the job offer and decline the offer without giving specifics.

I appreciate your taking the time to interview me, and I wish Bendall much success in the future.

Express gratitude and best wishes for the future.

Sincerely,

Resignation Letter

After you have been in a position for a period of time, you may find it necessary to leave. Perhaps you have been offered a better position, or maybe you have decided to return to school full-time. Whatever the reason, you should leave your position gracefully and tactfully. Although you will likely discuss your resignation in person with your supervisor, it is a good idea to document your resignation by writing a formal letter. Some resignation letters are brief, while others contain great detail. Remember that many resignation letters are placed in personnel files; therefore, you should format and write yours using the professional business letter-writing techniques you learned earlier. Here is an example of a basic letter of resignation:

Dear Ms. Byrne:

Confirm the exact date of resignation. Remind the employer of your contributions.

This letter serves as formal notice of my resignation from Allied Corporation, effective Friday, August 15. I have enjoyed serving as your office assistant for the past two years, and I am grateful for everything I have learned during my employment with Allied.

Offer assistance to prepare for your resignation.

Please let me know what I can do over the next two weeks to help you prepare for my departure. I would be happy to help with finding and training my replacement.

Offer thanks and end with a forward-looking statement.

Thanks again for providing such a positive employment experience. I will long remember my time here.

Sincerely,

Although the employee who wrote the preceding resignation letter gave the standard two-week notice, you may find that a longer notice is necessary. The higher your position and the greater your responsibility, the longer the notice you give your employer should be. You should, however, always give some notice as a courtesy.

Writing job acceptance, job rejection, and resignation letters requires effort. That effort, however, is worth it because you are building bridges that may carry you to even better jobs in the future.

www.cengagebrain.com

Available with an access code, these eResources will help you prepare for exams:

- **Chapter Review Quizzes**
- **Personal Language Trainer**
- **PowerPoint Slides**
- **Flash Cards**

Summing Up and Looking Forward

Whether you face a screening interview or a hiring/placement interview, you must be well prepared. You can increase your chances of success and reduce your anxiety considerably by knowing how interviews are typically conducted and by researching the target company thoroughly. Practice answering typical questions, including situational, behavioral, and challenging ones. Consider audio or video recording a mock interview so that you can check your body language and improve your answering techniques.

At the end of the interview, thank the interviewer, review your main strengths for the position, and ask what the next step is. Follow up with a thank-you letter and a follow-up call or message, if appropriate. Prepare other employment-related documents as needed, including application forms, application and résumé follow-up messages, rejection follow-up letters, job acceptance and rejection letters, and resignation letters.

You have now completed 14 chapters of rigorous instruction aimed at developing your skills so that you can be a successful business communicator in today's rapidly changing world of information. Remember that this is but a starting point. Your skills as a business communicator will continue to grow on the job as you apply the principles you have learned and expand your expertise.

Critical Thinking

1. Why do you think so many employers search for information about job applicants online using Google, Facebook, Twitter, and other online tools? Do you think these kinds of searches are ethical or appropriate? Isn't this similar to snooping?
2. What can you do to appear professional when a potential employer contacts you by phone for a screening interview or to schedule a job interview?
3. If you are asked an illegal interview question, why is it important to first assess the intentions of the interviewer?
4. Why is it a smart strategy to thank an interviewer, to follow up, and even to send a rejection follow-up message? Are any risks associated with this strategy?
5. Should you try to inflate your previous salary in a job interview to receive a higher offer if, for example, you believe you were worth more than what you were paid or if you were about to get a raise?

Chapter Review

6. Name the two main types of employment interviews, and explain how they differ.

7. What are stress interviews, and what purpose do they serve? How can you shine in a stress interview?

8. What are success stories, and how can you use them?

9. What is digital dirt, and what should you do to clean it up during the employment process?

10. Name at least five techniques that allow you to prepare for and practice before an important interview.

11. What are situational and behavioral interview questions, and how can you craft responses that will make a favorable impression on the interviewer?

12. What should you do if asked a salary question early in an interview?

13. What kinds of questions should you ask during an interview?

14. How can you show courtesy after the interview and restate your interest in the job?

15. If you receive a job offer, why is it important to write an acceptance message, and what should it include?

Activities and Cases

W WEB

14.1 Researching an Organization

An important part of your preparation for an interview is learning about the target company.

Your Task. Select an organization where you would like to be employed. Assume you have been selected for an interview. Using resources described in this chapter, locate information about the organization's leaders and their business philosophies. Discover information about the organization's accomplishments, setbacks, finances, products, customers, competition, and advertising. Prepare a summary report documenting your findings.

W WEB

14.2 Learning What Jobs Are Really About Through Blogs, Facebook, and Twitter

Blogs and social media sites such as Facebook and Twitter are becoming important tools in the employment search process. By accessing blogs, company Facebook pages, and Twitter feeds, job seekers can locate much insider information about a company's culture and day-to-day activities.

Your Task. Using the Web, locate a blog that is maintained by an employee of a company where you would like to work. Monitor the blog for at least a week. Also access the company's Facebook page and monitor Twitter feeds for at least a week. Prepare a short report summarizing what you learned about the company through reading the blog postings, status updates, and tweets. Include a statement of whether this information would be valuable during your job search.

WEB

14.3 Taking a Look at Corporate Web Videos

Would you like to know what it is like to work for the company that interests you? Check out Web videos posted by companies on their career pages, job boards, and even YouTube. Currently about 7,000 corporate videos await you on Jobing.com, a job board that lists openings in specific geographic regions.

Your Task. Search company recruiting Web sites, YouTube, or Jobing.com for videos featuring two or three companies in your chosen industry. Compare how the employers introduce themselves, which aspects they emphasize about their organizations, how they present their employees, what they offer potential applicants, and so forth. Write a short report addressed to your instructor comparing and contrasting the corporate Web videos you examined.

14.4 Building Interview Skills With Worksheets

Successful interviews require diligent preparation and repeated practice. To be well prepared, you need to know what skills are required for your targeted position. In addition to computer and communication skills, employers generally want to know whether a candidate works well with a team, accepts responsibility, solves problems, is efficient, meets deadlines, shows leadership, saves time and money, and is a hard worker.

Your Task. Consider a position for which you are eligible now or one for which you will be eligible when you complete your education. Identify the skills and traits necessary for this position. If you prepared a résumé in Chapter 13, be sure that it addresses these targeted areas. Now prepare interview worksheets listing at least ten technical and other skills or traits you think a recruiter will want to discuss in an interview for your targeted position.

14.5 Preparing Success Stories

You can best showcase your talents if you are ready with your own success stories that illustrate how you have developed the skills or traits required for your targeted position.

Your Task. Using the worksheets you prepared in Activity 14.4, prepare success stories that highlight the required skills or traits. Select three to five stories to develop into answers to potential interview questions. For example, here is a typical question: *How does your background relate to the position we have open?* A possible response: *As you know, I have just completed an intensive training program in ______________. In addition, I have over three years of part-time work experience in a variety of business settings. In one position I was selected to manage a small business in the absence of the owner. I developed responsibility and customer-service skills in filling orders efficiently, resolving shipping problems, and monitoring key accounts. I also inventoried and organized products worth over $200,000. When the owner returned from a vacation to Florida, I was commended for increasing sales and was given a bonus in recognition of my efforts.* People relate to and remember stories. Try to shape your answers into memorable stories.

WEB

14.6 Digging for Digital Dirt: Keeping a Low Profile Online

Before embarking on your job hunt, you may want to know what employers might find if they searched your personal life in cyberspace, specifically on Facebook, MySpace, Twitter, and so forth. Running your name through Google and other search engines, particularly enclosed in quotation marks to lower the number of hits, is usually the first step. Assembling a digital portrait of an applicant is easier than ever thanks to new spy-worthy Web sites such as Snitch.name (**http://snitch.name**) that collect information from a number of search engines, Web sites, and social networks. Self-titled "The Social White Pages," Snitch.name not only looks for people's profiles in social networks, but also compiles publicly available data found on services such as 123people.com, PeekYou.com, and so forth.

Your Task. Use Google, Snitch.name, Bing, or Dogpile to search the Web for your full name, enclosed in quotation marks. In Google, don't forget to run an *Image* search at **http://www.google.com/images** to find any photos of questionable taste. If the instructor requests, share your insights with the class—not the salacious details, but general observations—or write a short memo summarizing the results.

WEB

14.7 Exploring Appropriate Interview Attire

As you prepare for your interview by learning about the company and the industry, don't forget a key component of interview success: creating a favorable first impression by wearing appropriate business attire. Job seekers often have nebulous ideas about proper interview wear. Some wardrobe mishaps include choosing a conservative "power suit" but accessorizing it with beat-up casual shoes or a shabby bag. Grooming glitches include dandruff on dark suit fabric, dirty fingernails, or mothball odor. Women sometimes wrongly assume that any black clothing items are acceptable, even if they are too tight, revealing, sheer, or made of low-end fabrics. Most image consultants agree that workplace wardrobe falls into three main categories: business formal, business casual, and casual. Only business formal is considered proper interview apparel.

Your Task. To prepare for your big day, search the Web for descriptions and images of *business formal*. You may research *business casual* and *casual* styles, but for an interview, always dress on the side of caution—conservatively. Compare prices and look for suit sales to buy one or two attractive interview outfits. Share your findings (notes, images, and price range for suits, solid shoes, and accessories) with the class and your instructor.

14.8 Polishing Answers to Interview Questions

Practice makes perfect in interviewing. The more often you rehearse responses to typical interview questions, the closer you are to getting the job.

Your Task. Select three questions from each of these question categories discussed in this chapter: questions to get acquainted, questions to gauge your interest, questions about your experience and accomplishments, questions about the future, and challenging questions. Write your answers to each set of questions. Try to incorporate skills and traits required for the targeted position, and include success stories where appropriate. Polish these answers and your delivery technique by practicing in front of a mirror or by making an audio or video recording. Your instructor may choose this assignment as a group activity in class.

14.9 Learning to Answer Situational Interview Questions

Situational interview questions can vary widely from position to position. You should know enough about a position to understand some of the typical situations you would encounter on a regular basis.

Your Task. Use your favorite search tool to locate typical job descriptions of a position in which you are interested. Based on these descriptions, develop a list of six to eight typical situations someone in this position would face; then write situational interview questions for each of these scenarios. In pairs, role-play interviewer and interviewee, alternating with your listed questions.

14.10 Developing Skills With Behavioral Interview Questions

Behavioral interview questions are increasingly popular, and you will need a little practice before you can answer them easily.

Your Task. Use your favorite search tool to locate lists of behavioral questions on the Web. Select five skills areas such as communication, teamwork, and decision making. For each skill area, find three behavioral questions that you think would be effective in an interview. In pairs, role-play interviewer and interviewee, alternating with your listed questions. You goal is to answer effectively in one or two minutes. Remember to use the STAR method when answering.

14.11 Creating an Interview "Cheat Sheet"

Even the best-rehearsed applicants sometimes forget to ask the questions they prepared, or they fail to stress their major accomplishments in job interviews. Sometimes applicants are so rattled they even forget the interviewer's name. To help you keep your wits during an interview, make a "cheat sheet" that summarizes key facts, answers, and questions. Review it before the interview and again as the interview is ending to be sure you have covered everything that is critical.

Your Task. Prepare a cheat sheet with the following information:

Day and time of interview:
Meeting with: [Name of interviewer(s), title, company, city, state, zip, telephone, cell, fax, e-mail]
Major accomplishments: (four to six)
Management or work style: (four to six)
Things you need to know about me: (three to four items)
Reason I left my last job:
Answers to difficult questions: (four to five answers)
Questions to ask interviewer:
Things I can do for you:

14.12 Handling Inappropriate and Illegal Interview Questions

Although some questions are considered inappropriate and potentially illegal by the government, many interviewers will ask them anyway—whether intentionally or unknowingly. Being prepared is important.

Your Task. How would you respond in the following scenario? Assume you are being interviewed at one of the top companies on your list of potential employers. The interviewing committee consists of a human resources manager and the supervising manager of the department where you would work. At various times during the interview, the supervising manager asks questions that make you feel uncomfortable. For example, he asks whether you are married. You know this question is inappropriate, but you see no harm in answering it. Then, however, he asks how old you are. Because you started college early and graduated in three and a half years, you are worried that you may not be considered mature enough for this position. However, you have most of the other qualifications required, and you are convinced you could succeed on the job. How should you answer this question?

14.13 Knowing What to Ask

When it is your turn to ask questions during the interview process, be ready.

Your Task. Decide on three to five questions that you would like to ask during an interview. Write these questions out and practice asking them so that you sound confident and sincere.

TEAM

14.14 Role-Playing in a Mock Interview

One of the best ways to understand interview dynamics and to develop confidence is to role-play the parts of interviewer and candidate in a mock interview.

Your Task. Choose a partner for this activity. Each partner makes a list of two interview questions for each of the eight interview question categories presented in this chapter. In team sessions you and your partner will role-play an actual interview. One acts as interviewer; the other is the candidate. Prior to the interview, the candidate tells the interviewer the job he or she is applying for and the name of the company. For the interview, the interviewer and candidate should dress appropriately and sit in chairs facing each other. The interviewer greets the candidate and makes the candidate comfortable. The candidate gives the interviewer a copy of his or her résumé. The interviewer asks three (or more depending on your instructor's time schedule) questions from the candidate's list. The interviewer may also ask follow-up questions, if appropriate. When finished, the interviewer ends the meeting graciously. After one interview, partners reverse roles and repeat.

14.15 Recording an Interview

Seeing how you look and hearing how you sound during an interview can help you improve your body language and presentation style. Your instructor may act as an interviewer, or an outside businessperson may be asked to conduct mock interviews in your classroom.

Your Task. Engage a student or campus specialist to prepare a video or audio recording of your interview. Review your performance and critique it looking for ways to improve. Your instructor may ask class members to offer comments and suggestions on individual interviews. Alternatively, visit your campus career center, if available, and sign up for a mock interview. Ask if your session could be recorded for subsequent viewing.

WEB

14.16 YouTube: Critiquing Interview Skills

The adage *Practice makes perfect* is especially true for interviewing. The more you confront your fears in mock or real interviews, the calmer and more confident you will be when your dream job is on the line. Short of undergoing your own interview, you can also learn from observation. The Web offers countless video clips showing examples of excellent, and poor, interviewing techniques.

Your Task. Visit YouTube, Monster.com, or Best-Interview-Strategies.com for interview videos. Select a clip that you find particularly entertaining or informative. Watch it multiple times and jot down your observations. Then summarize the scenario in a paragraph or two. Provide examples of interview strategies that worked and those that didn't, applying the information you learned in this chapter. If required, share your insights about the video with the class.

WEB

14.17 Mastering Interviews Over Meals

Although they are less likely for entry-level candidates, nevertheless, interviews over business meals are a popular means to size up the social skills of a job seeker, especially in second and subsequent interviews. Candidates coveting jobs with a lot of face-to-face contact with the public may be subjected to the ultimate test: table manners. Interviews are nerve-racking and intimidating enough, but imagine having to juggle silverware, wrangle potentially messy food, and keep your clothing stain-free—all this while listening carefully to what is being said around the table and giving thoughtful, confident answers.

Your Task. Research tips can help you avoid the most common pitfalls associated with interviews over meals. Use your favorite search engine and try queries such as *interview dining tips*, *interviewing over meals*, and so forth. Consider the credibility of your sources. Are they authorities on the subject? Compile your list of tips, and jot down your sources. Share the list with your peers. If you instructor directs, discuss the categories of advice provided. Then, as a class assemble a universal list of the most common interview tips.

14.18 Saying Thanks for the Interview

You have just completed an exciting employment interview, and you want the interviewer to remember you.

Your Task. Write a follow-up thank-you letter to Ronald T. Ranson, Human Resources Development, Electronic Data Sources, 1328 Peachtree Plaza, Atlanta, GA 30314 (or a company of your choice). Make up any details needed.

14.19 Requesting a Reference

Your favorite professor has agreed to be one of your references. You have just arrived home from a job interview that went well, and you must ask your professor to write a letter of recommendation.

Your Task. Write to the professor requesting that he or she send a letter of recommendation to the company where you interviewed. Explain that the interviewer asked that the letter be sent directly to him. Provide information about the job and about yourself so that the professor can target its content.

14.20 Following Up After Submitting Your Résumé

A month has passed since you sent your résumé and cover letter in response to a job advertisement. You are still interested in the position and would like to find out whether you still have a chance.

Your Task. Write a follow-up e-mail or letter to an employer of your choice that does not offend the reader or damage your chances of employment.

14.21 Refusing to Take No for an Answer

After an excellent interview with Electronic Data Sources (or a company of your choice), you are disappointed to learn that someone else was hired. However, you really want to work for EDS.

Your Task. Write a follow-up message to Ronald T. Ranson, Human Resources Development, Electronic Data Sources, 1328 Peachtree Plaza, Atlanta, GA 30314 (or a company of your choice). Indicate that you are disappointed but still interested.

14.22 Saying *Yes* to a Job Offer

Your dream has come true: you have just been offered an excellent position. Although you accepted the position on the phone, you want to send a formal acceptance letter.

Your Task. Write a job acceptance letter to an employer of your choice. Include the specific job title, your starting date, and details about your compensation package. Make up any necessary details.

14.23 Searching for Advice

You can find wonderful, free, and sometimes entertaining job-search strategies and career tips, as well as interview advice, on the Web.

Your Task. Use the Web to locate articles or links to sites with job-search, résumé, and interview information. Make a list of at least five good job-search pointers—ones that were not covered in this chapter. Send an e-mail to your instructor describing your findings, or post your findings to a class discussion board to share with your classmates.

14.24 Evaluating Your Course

Your boss has paid your tuition for this course. As you complete the course, he (or she) asks you for a letter about your experience in the course.

Your Task. Write a letter to a boss in a real or imaginary organization explaining how this course made you more valuable to the organization.

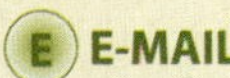

14.25 Grounding Helicopter Parents

Overprotective couples hovering over their Millennial offspring have been dubbed helicopter parents by some human resources specialists. These take-charge parents now seem to extend their involvement into managing their adult children's job searches. Recruiters and career counselors are reporting that parents accompany their kids to job fairs and job interviews. Some don't think twice about attempting to arrange interview appointments for their kids. Others go as far as calling hiring managers to ask why their twenty-four-year-old didn't get the job. Experts explain that the Millennials grew up on an electronic leash. When in trouble, they could rely on a cell phone, IM or text messages, or e-mail to contact their parents for help and advice. Millennials view their parents as trusted advisors. Second, the skyrocketing costs of a college education have prompted parents to become more hands-on to protect their investment.

Most hiring managers are troubled by this trend. After all, they want to employ mature, independent individuals. Whereas most recruiters frown on parental involvement and would not hire a recent graduate who brings mom or dad to a job interview, some employers are beginning to reach out to parents. Merrill Lynch, Office Depot, and others may hold a parents' day, send a letter of introduction to parents of recent hires, or instruct parents on the corporate Web site on how to strike a balance between support and meddling.[32]

Your Task. Ponder this information about helicopter parents in light of what you learned in this chapter. Consider the following questions: How do you feel about parents who hover around their kids and intervene in their job searches? Can you name benefits of parental involvement? What are the advantages of the opposite—the hands-off approach? Do hands-on parents improve or hurt their children's job prospects? What specific problems do helicopter parents pose for hiring managers and their companies? How involved are your parents in your education? Are they supportive? Intrusive? After jotting down answers to these and similar questions, discuss parental involvement with your peers in class. Your instructor may ask you to summarize your thoughts in a memo or e-mail.

Video Resources

Video Library 1: ***Building Workplace Skills***
Sharpening Your Interview Skills
In the video titled ***Sharpening Your Interview Skills,*** you see the job interview of Betsy Chin. Based on what you learned in this chapter and your own experience, critique her performance. What did she do well, and what could she improve?

Grammar/Mechanics Checkup—14

Total Review

This exercise reviews all of the guidelines in the Grammar/Mechanics Handbook as well as the lists of Confusing Words and Frequently Misspelled Words. Use proofreading marks to correct capitalization, number expression, grammar, and spelling in the following sentences. When you finish, compare your responses with those at the end of the book.

Example: Just between you and ~~I~~ me, we expect to raise over ~~two thousand dollars~~ $2,000 during the four-week campaign that ends June 1.

1. In the evening each of the female nurses are escorted to there cars.
2. It must have been him who received the highest score although its hard to understand how he did it.
3. Our Office Manager asked Rachel and I to fill in for him for 4 hours on Saturday morning.
4. Working out at the Gym and jogging twenty miles a week is how she stays fit.
5. 3 types of costs must be considered for proper inventory controll, holding costs, ordering costs and stockout costs.
6. If I was him I would fill out the questionaire immediately so that I would qualify for the drawing.
7. Higher engine revolutions per mile mean better acceleration, however lower revolutions mean the best fuel economy.
8. Our teams day to day operations include: setting goals, improving customer service, manufacturing quality products and hitting sales targets.
9. If I had saw the shippers bill I would have payed it immediately.
10. When convenent will you please send me 3 copys of the companys color logo?
11. Do you think it was him who left the package on the boss desk.
12. About 1/2 of Pizza Huts six thousand outlets will make deliverys, the others concentrates on walk in customers.
13. Every thing accept labor is covered in this five year warranty.
14. Our Director of Human Resources felt nevertheless that the applicant should be given a interview.
15. When Keisha completes her degree she plans to apply for employment in: Seattle, Dallas and Atlanta.

Editing Challenge—14

As the employee with the best communication skills, you are frequently asked to edit messages. The following interview follow-up letter, written by your friend Tracy, has problems with punctuation, wordiness, proofreading, capitalization, sentence structure, and other writing techniques you have studied. You may (a) use standard proofreading marks (see Appendix B) to correct the errors here or (b) download the document from **www.cengagebrain.com** and revise at your computer.

Your instructor may ask you to use the **Track Changes** feature in Word to show your editing comments. Turn on **Track Changes** on the **Review** tab. Click **Show Markup**. Place your cursor at an error, click **New Comment**, and key your edit in the bubble box provided. Study the guidelines in the Grammar/Mechanics Handbook as well as the lists of Confusing Words and Frequently Misspelled Words to sharpen your skills.

3249 West Olive Avenue
Glendale, AZ 85302
June 17, 201x

Mr. Michael Searle
Vice President
Mariposa Agency
3021 East Van Buren Street
Phoenix, AZ 85022

Dear Mr. Searle:

It was extremely enjoyable to talk with you on tuesday about the Assistant Account Manager position at the Mariposa Agency. The position as you presented it seems to be a excelent match for my training and skills. The creative approach to Account Management that you described, confirmed my desire to work in a imaginative firm such as the Maraposa Agency.

In addition to an enthusiastic attitude I would bring to the position strong communication skills, and the ability to encourage others to work cooperatively within the department. My Graphic Arts training and experience will help me work with staff artists, and provide me with a understanding of the visual aspects of you work.

I certainly understand your departments need for strong support in the administrative area. My attention to detail and my organizational skills will help to free you to deal with more pressing issues in the management area. Despite the fact that it was on my résumé I neglected to emphasize during our interview that I had worked for 2 summers as a temporary office worker. This experience helped me to develop administrative support and clerical skills as well as to understand the every day demands of a busy office.

Thanks for taking the time to interview me, and explain the goals of your agency along with the dutys of this position. As I mentioned during the interview I am very interested in working for the Maraposa agency, and look forward to hearing from you about this position. In the event that you might possibly need additional information from me or facts about me, all you need to do is shoot me an e-mail at tteslenko@hotmail.com.

Sincerely,

Tracy A. Teslenko

Tracy A. Teslenko

Communication Workshop

Let's Talk Money: Negotiating a Salary

When to talk about salary causes many job applicants concern. The important thing to remember is that almost all salaries are negotiable. Research conducted by the Society for Human Resource Management and CareerJournal.com shows that approximately 90 percent of human resources professionals say salaries are negotiable, and 78 percent of employees report negotiating salary.[33] If you have proved your worth throughout the interview process, employers will want to negotiate with you. To discuss compensation effectively, though, you must be prepared for salary questions, and you should know what you are worth. You also need to know basic negotiation strategies. As negotiation expert Chester L. Karrass said, "In business, you don't get what you deserve, you get what you negotiate."[34] The following negotiating rules, recommended by various career experts, can guide you to a better beginning salary.[35]

Rule No. 1: Avoid discussing salary for as long as possible in the interview process.

The longer you delay salary discussion, the more time you will have to convince the employer that you are worth what you are asking for. Ideally, you should try to avoid discussing salary until you know for sure that the interviewing company is making a job offer. The best time for you to negotiate your salary is between the time you are offered the position and the time you accept it. Wait for the employer to bring salary up first. If salary comes up and you are not sure whether the job is being offered to you, it is time for you to be blunt. Here are some things you could say:

Are you making me a job offer?

What is your salary range for positions with similar requirements?

I'm very interested in the position, and my salary would be negotiable.

Tell me what you have in mind for the salary range.

Rule No. 2: Know in advance the probable salary range for similar jobs in similar organizations.

Many job-search Web sites provide salary information. But it is probably better for you to call around in your area to learn what similar jobs are paying. The important thing here is to think in terms of a wide range. Let's say you are hoping to start at between $45,000 and $50,000. To an interviewer, you might say, *I was looking for a salary in the high forties to the low fifties*. This technique is called bracketing. In addition, stating your salary range in an annual dollar amount sounds more professional than asking for an hourly wage. Be sure to consider such things as geographic location, employer size, industry standards, the strength of the economy, and other factors to make sure that the range you come up with is realistic.

Rule No. 3: When negotiating, focus on what you are worth, not on what you need.

Throughout the interview and negotiation process, focus continually on your strengths. Make sure that the employer knows everything of value that you will bring to the organization. You have to prove that you are worth what you are asking for. Employers pay salaries based on what you will accomplish on the job and contribute to the organization. When discussing your salary, focus on how the company will benefit from these contributions. Don't bring personal issues into the negotiation process. No employer will be willing to pay you more because you have bills to pay, mouths to feed, or debt to settle.

Rule No. 4: Never say *no* to a job before it is offered.

Why would anyone refuse a job offer before it is made? It happens all the time. Let's say you were hoping for a salary of, say, $45,000. The interviewer tells you that the salary scheduled for this job is $40,000. You respond, *Oh, that is out of the question!* Before you were offered the job, you have, in effect, refused it. Instead, wait for the job offer; then start negotiating your salary.

Rule No. 5: Ask for a higher salary first, and consider benefits.

Within reason, always try to ask for a higher salary first. This will leave room for this amount to decrease during negotiations until it is closer to your original expectations. Remember to consider the entire compensation package when negotiating. You may be willing to accept a lower salary if benefits such as insurance, flexible hours, time off, and retirement are attractive.

Rule No. 6: Be ready to bargain if offered a low starting salary.

Many salaries are negotiable. Companies are often willing to pay more for someone who interviews well and fits their culture. If the company seems right to you and you are pleased with the sound of the open position but you have been offered a low salary, say, *That is somewhat lower than I had hoped, but this position does sound exciting. If I were to consider this, what sorts of things could I do to quickly become more valuable to this organization?* Also discuss such factors as bonuses based on performance or a shorter review period. You could say something like, *Thanks for the offer. The position is very much what I wanted in many ways, and I am delighted at your interest. If I start at this salary, may I be reviewed within six months with the goal of raising the salary to ____?*

Another possibility is to ask for more time to think about the low offer. Tell the interviewer that this is an important decision, and you need some time to consider the offer. The next day you can call and say, *I am flattered by your offer, but I cannot accept because the salary is lower than I would like. Perhaps you could reconsider your offer or keep me in mind for future openings.*

Rule No. 7: Be honest.

Be honest throughout the entire negotiation process. Don't inflate the salaries of your previous positions to try to get more money. Don't tell an employer that you have received other job offers unless it is true. These lies can be grounds for being fired later on.

Rule No. 8: Get the final offer in writing.

Once you have agreed on a salary and compensation package, get the offer in writing. You should also follow up with a position acceptance letter, as discussed earlier in the chapter.

Career Application. You have just passed the screening interview and have been asked to come in for a personal interview with the human resources representative and the hiring manager of a company where you are very eager to work. Although you are delighted with the company, you have promised yourself that you will not accept any position that pays less than $45,000 to start.

Your Task. In teams of two, role-play the position of interviewer and interviewee. The interviewer sets the scene by discussing preliminaries and offers a salary of $42,500. The interviewee responds to preliminary questions and to the salary offer of $42,500. Then, reverse roles so that the interviewee becomes the interviewer, and repeat the scenario.

Endnotes

[1] Bergey, B. (2009, December 10). Online job interviews becoming more popular. WKOW.com. Retrieved from http://www.wkowtv.com/Global/story.asp?S=11655389; Kennedy, J. L. (2008). *Job interviews for dummies*. Hoboken, NJ: Wiley Publishing, p. 20.

[2] Wilmott, N. (n.d.). Interviewing styles: Tips for interview approaches. About.com: Human Resources. Retrieved from http://humanresources.about.com/cs/selectionstaffing/a/interviews.htm

[3] Mease, B. (2010, June 4). Employers using Second Life to scout out job candidates. Ezine Articles. Retrieved from http://ezinearticles.com/?Employers-Using-Second-Life-to-Scout-Out-Job-Candidates&id=4422448; Athavaley, A. (2007, June 20). A job interview you don't have to show up for. *The Wall Street Journal*. Retrieved from http://online.wsj.com/article/SB118229876637841321.html#articleTabs%3Darticle

[4] Ziebarth, B. (2009, December 10). Tips to ace your panel job interview. Associated Content, Inc. Retrieved from http://www.associatedcontent.com/article/2470148/tips_to_ace_your_panel_job_interview.html?cat=31

[5] Cristante, D. (2009, June 15). How to succeed in a group interview. CareerFAQs. Retrieved from http://www.careerfaqs.com.au/job-interview-tips/1116/How-to-succeed-in-a-group-interview

[6] Weiss, T. (2009, May 12). Going on the second interview. *Forbes*. Retrieved from http://www.forbes.com/2009/05/12/second-interview-advice-leadership-careers-basics.html

[7] Hansen, R. (2010). Situational interviews and stress interviews: What to make of them and how to succeed in them. Quintessential Careers. Retrieved from http://www.quintcareers.com/situational_stress_interviews.html

[8] Bergey, B. (2009, December 10). Online job interviews becoming more popular. WKOWTV. Retrieved from http://www.wkowtv.com/Global/story.asp?S=11655389

[9] Rossheim, J. (2011, February 24). Do your homework before the big interview. Monster.com. Retrieved from http://career-advice.monster.com/job-interview/interview-preparation/do-your-homework-before-interview/article.aspx

[10] Gold, T. (2010, November 28). How social media can get you a job. Marketing Trenches. Retrieved from http://www.marketingtrenches.com/marketing-careers/how-social-media-can-get-you-a-job

[11] Doyle, A. (n.d.) Job research: Find what you need to know about a job or a company. About.com. Retrieved from http://jobsearch.about.com/od/companyresearch/a/jobresearch.htm

[12] Bowles, L. (2010, December 20). How to research a company for a job search. eHow.com. Retrieved from http://www.ehow.com/how_7669153_research-company-job-search.html; Gold, T. (2010, November 28). How social media can get you a job. Marketing Trenches. Retrieved from http://www.marketingtrenches.com/marketing-careers/how-social-media-can-get-you-a-job

[13] Ryan, L. (2007, May 6). Job seekers: Prepare your stories. Ezine Articles. Retrieved from http://practicaljobsearchadvice.blogspot.com/2007/05/job-seekers-prepare-your-stories.html

[14] Haefner, R. (2009, June 10). More employers screening candidates via social networking sites. CareerBuilder. Retrieved from http://www.careerbuilder.com/Article/CB-1337-Getting-Hired-More-Employers-Screening-Candidates-via-Social-Networking-Sites

[15] Lynch, B. (2010, January 28). Online reputation in a connected world. [Presentation]. Data Privacy Day. Retrieved from http://www.microsoft.com

[16] Haefner, R. (2009, June 10). More employers screening candidates via social networking sites. CareerBuilder. Retrieved from http://www.careerbuilder.com/Article/CB-1337-Getting-Hired-More-Employers-Screening-Candidates-via-Social-Networking-Sites

[17] Finder, A. (2006, June 11). For some, online persona undermines a résumé. *The New York Times*. Retrieved from http://www.nytimes.com/2006/06/11/us/11recruit.html?_r=1&scp=1&sq=For%20some,%20online%20persona%20undermines&st=cse&oref=slogin

[18] Haefner, R. (2009, June 10). More employers screening candidates via social networking sites. CareerBuilder. Retrieved from http://www.careerbuilder.com/Article/CB-1337-Getting-Hired-More-Employers-Screening-Candidates-via-Social-Networking-Sites

[19] Korkki, P. (2009, September 13). Subtle cues can tell an interviewer "pick me." *The New York Times*. Retrieved from http://www.nytimes.com

[20] Susan L. Hodas cited in Korkki, P. (2009, September 13). Subtle cues can tell an interviewer "pick me." *The New York Times*. Retrieved from http://www.nytimes.com

[21] Tyrell-Smith, T. (2011, January 25). Tell a story that will get you hired. *Money/U.S. News & World Report*. Retrieved from http://money.usnews.com/money/blogs/outside-voices-careers/2011/01/25/tell-a-story-that-will-get-you-hired

[22] The U.S. Equal Employment Opportunity Commission. (2009, November 21). Federal laws prohibiting job discrimination: Questions and Answers. Retrieved from http://www.eeoc.gov/facts/qanda.html

[23] Doyle, A. (n.d.). Illegal interview questions. About.com. Retrieved from http://jobsearchtech.about.com/od/interview/l/aa022403.htm

[24] Ibid.; 30 interview questions you can't ask and 30 sneaky, legal alternatives to get the same info. (2007, November 15). *HR World*. Retrieved from http://www.hrworld.com/features/30-interview-questions-111507

[25] Ibid.

[26] Lublin, J. S. (2008, February 5). Notes to interviewers should go beyond a simple thank you. *The Wall Street Journal,* p. B1. Retrieved from http://proquest.umi.com

[27] Ibid.

[28] Korkki, P. (2009, September 13). Subtle cues can tell an interviewer "pick me." *The New York Times*. Retrieved from http://www.nytimes.com

[29] Olson, L. (2010, September 16). Why you should never skip the interview thank-you note. *Money/U.S.News & World Report*. Retrieved from http://money.usnews.com/money/blogs/outside-voices-careers/2010/09/16/why-you-should-always-send-an-interview-thankyou-note; Needleman, S. E. (2006, February 7). Be prepared when opportunity calls. *The Wall Street Journal*, p. B4.

[30] Green, A. (2010, December 27). How to follow up after applying for a job. *Money/U.S.News & World Report*. Retrieved from http://money.usnews.com/money/blogs/outside-voices-careers/2010/12/27/how-to-follow-up-after-applying-for-a-job

[31] Korkki, P. (2009, August 23). No response after an interview? What to do. *The New York Times*. Retrieved from http://www.nytimes.com.

[32] Based in part on Weiss, T. (2006, November 9). Are parents killing their kids' careers? *Forbes*. Retrieved from http://www.forbes.com/2006/11/08/leadership-careers-jobs-lead-careers-cx_tw_1109kids.html

[33] Glover, B. (2009, May 12). The importance of negotiating salary. *Bloomberg Businessweek*. Retrieved from http://www.businessweek.com/bschools/blogs/mba_admissions/archives/2009/05/the_importance.html; Green, A. (2010, December 20). What to consider before accepting a job offer. *Money/U.S.News & World Report*. Retrieved from http://money.usnews.com/money/blogs/outside-voices-careers/2010/12/20/what-to-consider-before-you-accept-a-job-offer; Patterson, V. (2004, March 30). Earning the salary you want in today's tough economy. *The Wall Street Journal*. Retrieved from http://proquest.umi.com

[34] About Karrass: The Karrass Story. (n.d.). Retrieved from http://www.karrass.com/kar_eng/about.htm

[35] Boardman, J. (n.d.). Know what you're worth BEFORE your salary negotiation. CBsalary.com. Retrieved from http://www.cbsalary.com; Dawson, R. (2006). *Secrets of power salary negotiating*. Franklin Lakes, NJ: Career Press, pp. 117–125; Hansen, R. S. (n.d.). Job offer too low? Use these key salary negotiation techniques to write a counter proposal letter. Quintessential Careers. Retrieved from http://www.quintcareers.com/salary_counter_proposal.html; Hansen, R. S. (n.d.). Salary negotiation do's and don'ts. Quintessential Careers. Retrieved from http://www.quintcareers.com/salary-dos-donts.html; Susan Ireland, S. (n.d.). Salary negotiation skills. Retrieved from http://susanireland.com/salarywork.html; Powell, J. (n.d.). Salary negotiation: The art of the deal. Resume-Resource. Retrieved from http://www.resume-resource.com/article16.html

Acknowledgments

p. 454 Office Insider cited in Green, A. (2011, February 7). How to prepare for a job interview. *Money. U.S. News & World Report*. Retrieved from http://money.usnews.com/money/blogs/outside-voices-careers/2011/02/07/how-to-prepare-for-a-job-interview

p. 455 Office Insider quoted in Zupek, R. (2009, October 12). "Digital dirt" can haunt your job search. CNN.com. Retrieved from http://edition.cnn.com/2009/LIVING/worklife/10/24/cb.digital.trail.job.search/index.html

p. 458 Office Insider cited in Ryan, L. (2009, June 23). Winning over an interviewer. *Bloomberg Businessweek*. Retrieved from http://www.businessweek.com/managing/content/jun2009/ca20090623_323874.htm

p. 461 Office Insider from Welch, J., & Welch, S. (2008, July 7). Hiring is hard work. *BusinessWeek*, p. 80.

p. 467 Office Insider cited in Bachel, B. (2007, February/March). Fantastic follow-ups: Touching base after a good interview can give you an edge. *Career World*, p. 20. Retrieved from http://web.ebscohost.com

p. 456 Workplace in Focus based on Sarno, D. (2009, August 16). It's getting hard to hide in cyberspace. *Los Angeles Times*, p. B4.

p. 466 Workplace in Focus based on Jones, S. M. (2011, January 15). On a job interview? Don't answer cellphone. *Los Angeles Times*, p. B3.

Business communicators produce numerous documents that have standardized formats. Becoming familiar with these formats is important because business documents actually carry two kinds of messages. Verbal messages are conveyed by the words chosen to express the writer's ideas. Nonverbal messages are conveyed largely by the appearance of a document and its adherence to recognized formats. To ensure that your documents carry favorable nonverbal messages about you and your organization, you will want to give special attention to the appearance and formatting of your e-mails, letters, envelopes, and fax cover sheets.

E-Mails

E-mails are sent by computers through networks. After reading e-mails, receivers may print, store, or delete them. E-mail is an appropriate channel for *short* messages. E-mails should not replace business letters or memos that are lengthy, require permanent records, or transmit confidential or sensitive information. Chapter 5 presented guidelines for preparing e-mails. This section provides additional information on formats and usage. The following suggestions, illustrated in Figure A.1 and also in Figure 5.1 on page 110, may guide you in setting up the parts of any e-mail. Always check, however, with your organization so that you can follow its practices.

To Line. Include the receiver's e-mail address after *To*. If the receiver's address is recorded in your address book, you just have to click it. Be sure to enter all addresses very carefully since one mistyped letter prevents delivery.

From Line. Most mail programs automatically include your name and e-mail address after *From.*

Cc and Bcc. Insert the e-mail address of anyone who is to receive a copy of the message. *Cc* stands for carbon copy or courtesy copy. Don't be tempted, though, to send needless copies just because it is easy. *Bcc* stands for blind carbon copy. Some writers use *bcc* to send a copy of the message without the addressee's knowledge. Writers also use the *bcc* line for mailing lists. When a message is sent to a number of people and their e-mail addresses should not be revealed, the *bcc* line works well to conceal the names and addresses of all receivers.

Subject. Identify the subject of the e-mail with a brief but descriptive summary of the topic. Be sure to include enough information to be clear and compelling. Capitalize the initial letters of main words. Main words are all words except (a) the articles *a, an,* and *the*; (b) prepositions containing two or three letters (such as *at, to, on, by, for*); (c) the word *to* in an infinitive (*to work, to write*); and (d) the word *as*—unless any of these words are the first or last word in the subject line.

Salutation. Include a brief greeting, if you like. Some writers use a salutation such as *Dear Erica* followed by a comma or a colon. Others are more informal with *Hi, Erica; Hello, Erica; Good morning*; or *Greetings*. See Chapter 5 for additional discussion of e-mail greetings.

FIGURE A.1 E-Mail

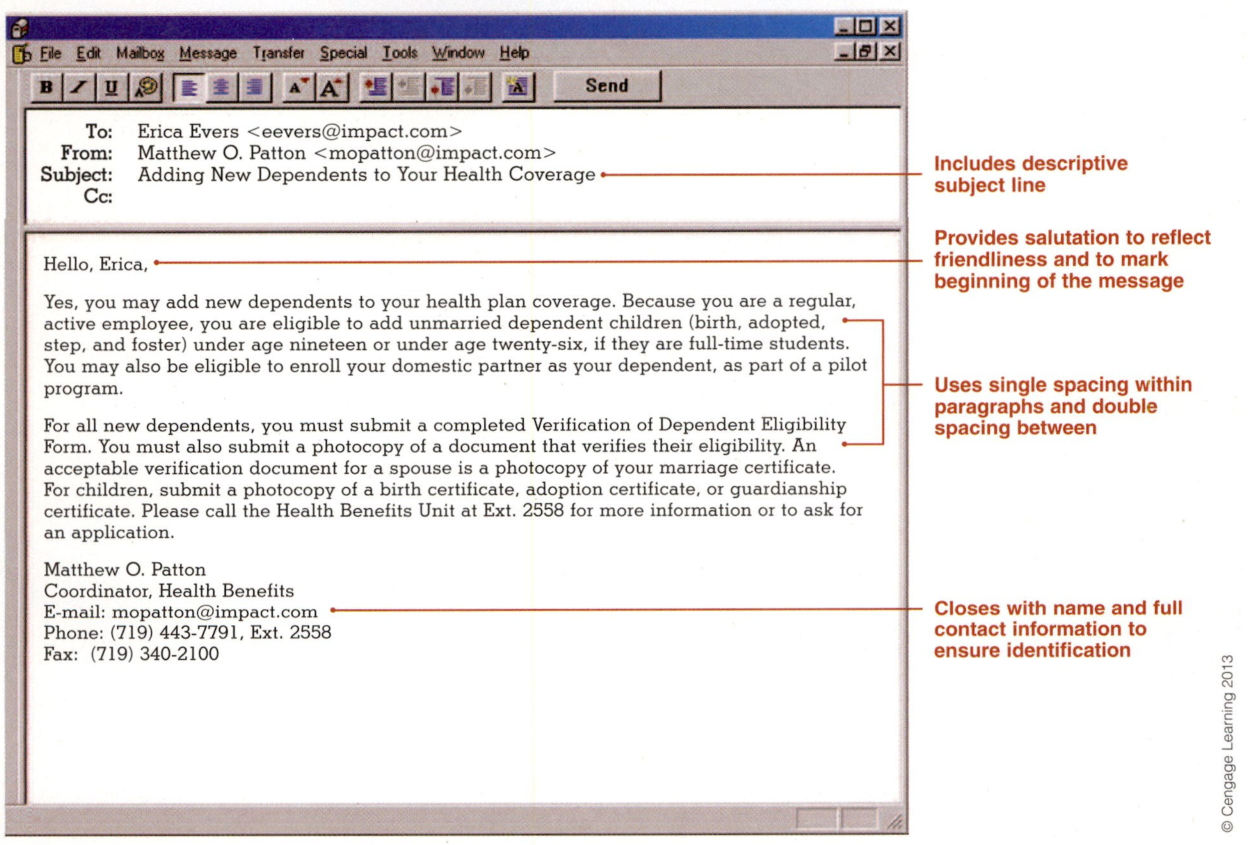
File Edit Mailbox Message Transfer Special Tools Window Help
Send
Includes descriptive subject line
Provides salutation to reflect friendliness and to mark beginning of the message
Uses single spacing within paragraphs and double spacing between
Closes with name and full contact information to ensure identification
© Cengage Learning 2013

To: Erica Evers <eevers@impact.com>
From: Matthew O. Patton <mopatton@impact.com>
Subject: Adding New Dependents to Your Health Coverage
Cc:

Hello, Erica,

Yes, you may add new dependents to your health plan coverage. Because you are a regular, active employee, you are eligible to add unmarried dependent children (birth, adopted, step, and foster) under age nineteen or under age twenty-six, if they are full-time students. You may also be eligible to enroll your domestic partner as your dependent, as part of a pilot program.

For all new dependents, you must submit a completed Verification of Dependent Eligibility Form. You must also submit a photocopy of a document that verifies their eligibility. An acceptable verification document for a spouse is a photocopy of your marriage certificate. For children, submit a photocopy of a birth certificate, adoption certificate, or guardianship certificate. Please call the Health Benefits Unit at Ext. 2558 for more information or to ask for an application.

Matthew O. Patton
Coordinator, Health Benefits
E-mail: mopatton@impact.com
Phone: (719) 443-7791, Ext. 2558
Fax: (719) 340-2100

Message. Cover just one topic in your message, and try to keep your total message under three screens in length. Single-space and be sure to use both upper- and lowercase letters. Double-space between paragraphs.

Closing. Conclude an e-mail, if you like, with *Cheers, Best wishes,* or *Warm regards,* followed by your name and complete contact information. Some people omit their e-mail address because they think it is provided automatically. However, programs and routers do not always transmit the address. Therefore, always include it along with other identifying information in the closing.

Attachment. Use the attachment window or button to select the path and file name of any file you wish to send with your e-mail. You can also attach a Web page to your message.

Business Letters

Business communicators write business letters primarily to correspond with people outside the organization. Letters may go to customers, vendors, other businesses, and the government, as discussed in Chapters 6, 7, and 8. The following information will help you format your letters following conventional guidelines.

Conventional Letter Placement, Margins, and Line Spacing

To set up business letters using conventional guidelines, follow these steps:

- For a clean look, choose a sans serif font such as Arial, Calibri, Tahoma, or Verdana. For a more traditional look, choose a serif font such as Times New Roman. Use a 10-point, 11-point, or 12-point size.

- Use a 2-inch top margin for the first page of a letter printed on letterhead stationery. This will place the date on line 12. Use a 1-inch top margin for second and succeeding pages.
- Justify only the left margin. Set the line spacing to single.
- Choose side margins according to the length of your letter. Set 1.5-inch margins for short letters (under 200 words), and 1-inch margins for longer letters (200 or more words).
- Leave from 2 to 10 blank lines following the date to balance the message on the page. You can make this adjustment after keying your message.

Formatting Letters With Microsoft Word 2007 and 2010

If you are working with Microsoft Word 2007 or 2010, the default margins are set at 1 inch with 11-point Calibri font set. The default setting for line spacing is 1.15, and the paragraph default is 10 points of blank space following each paragraph or each tap of the **Enter** key. Many letter writers find this extra space excessive, especially after parts of the letter that are normally single-spaced. The model documents in this book show conventional single-spacing with one blank line between paragraphs.

To format your documents with conventional spacing and yet retain a clean look, we recommend that you change the Microsoft defaults to the following: Arial font set for 11 points, line spacing at 1.0, and spacing before and after paragraphs at 0.

Spacing and Punctuation

For some time typists left two spaces after end punctuation (periods, question marks, and so forth). This practice was necessary, it was thought, because typewriters did not have proportional spacing and sentences were easier to read if two spaces separated them. Professional typesetters, however, never followed this practice because they used proportional spacing, and readability was not a problem. Influenced by the look of typeset publications, many writers now leave only one space after end punctuation. As a practical matter, however, it is not wrong to use two spaces.

Business Letter Parts

Professional-looking business letters are arranged in a conventional sequence with standard parts. Following is a discussion of how to use these letter parts properly. Figure A.2 illustrates the parts of a block style letter. See Chapter 6 for additional discussion of letters and their parts.

Letterhead. Most business organizations use 8½ × 11-inch paper printed with a letterhead displaying their official name, street address, Web address, e-mail address, and telephone and fax numbers. The letterhead may also include a logo and an advertising message.

Dateline. On letterhead paper you should place the date one blank line below the last line of the letterhead or 2 inches from the top edge of the paper (line 12 or 13). On plain paper place the date immediately below your return address. Because the date goes on line 12 or 13, start the return address an appropriate number of lines above it. The most common dateline format is as follows: *June 9, 2013*. Don't use *th* (or *rd, nd,* or *st*) when the date is written this way. For European or military correspondence, use the following dateline format: *9 June 2013*. Notice that no commas are used.

Addressee and Delivery Notations. Delivery notations such as *FAX TRANSMISSION, FEDEX, MESSENGER DELIVERY, CONFIDENTIAL,* or *CERTIFIED MAIL* are typed in all capital letters two blank lines above the inside address.

FIGURE A.2 Block and Modified Block Letter Styles

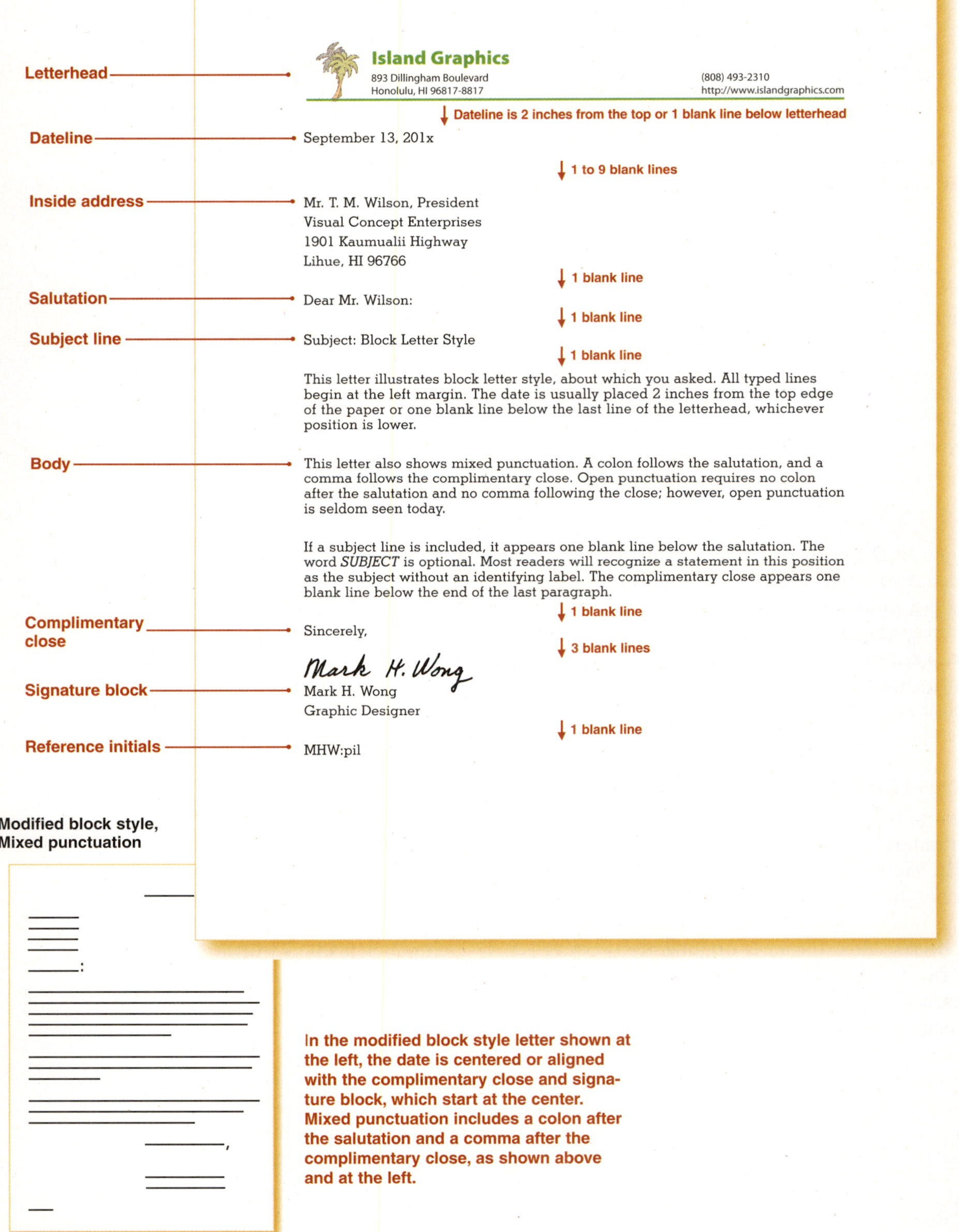

Island Graphics
893 Dillingham Boulevard
Honolulu, HI 96817-8817
(808) 493-2310
http://www.islandgraphics.com

September 13, 201x

Mr. T. M. Wilson, President
Visual Concept Enterprises
1901 Kaumualii Highway
Lihue, HI 96766

Dear Mr. Wilson:

Subject: Block Letter Style

This letter illustrates block letter style, about which you asked. All typed lines begin at the left margin. The date is usually placed 2 inches from the top edge of the paper or one blank line below the last line of the letterhead, whichever position is lower.

This letter also shows mixed punctuation. A colon follows the salutation, and a comma follows the complimentary close. Open punctuation requires no colon after the salutation and no comma following the close; however, open punctuation is seldom seen today.

If a subject line is included, it appears one blank line below the salutation. The word *SUBJECT* is optional. Most readers will recognize a statement in this position as the subject without an identifying label. The complimentary close appears one blank line below the end of the last paragraph.

Sincerely,

Mark H. Wong

Mark H. Wong
Graphic Designer

MHW:pil

Inside Address. Type the inside address—that is, the address of the organization or person receiving the letter—single-spaced, starting at the left margin. The number of lines between the dateline and the inside address depends on the size of the letter body, the type size (point or pitch size), and the length of the typing lines. Generally, one to nine blank lines are appropriate.

Be careful to duplicate the exact wording and spelling of the recipient's name and address on your documents. Usually, you can copy this information from the letterhead of the correspondence you are answering. If, for example, you are responding to *Jackson & Perkins Company*, do not address your letter to *Jackson and Perkins Corp.*

Always be sure to include a courtesy title such as *Mr., Ms., Mrs., Dr.,* or *Professor* before a person's name in the inside address—for both the letter and the envelope. Although many women in business today favor *Ms.*, you should use whatever title the addressee prefers.

In general, avoid abbreviations such as *Ave.* or *Co.* unless they appear in the printed letterhead of the document being answered.

Attention Line. An attention line allows you to send your message officially to an organization but to direct it to a specific individual, officer, or department. However, if you know an individual's complete name, it is always better to use it as the first line of the inside address and avoid an attention line. Two common formats for attention lines follow:

The MultiMedia Company
931 Calkins Avenue
Rochester, NY 14301

ATTENTION MARKETING DIRECTOR

The MultiMedia Company
Attention: Marketing Director
931 Calkins Avenue
Rochester, NY 14301

Attention lines may be typed in all caps or with upper- and lowercase letters. The colon following *Attention* is optional. Notice that an attention line may be placed one blank line below the address block or printed as the second line of the inside address. Use the latter format so that you may copy the address block to the envelope and the attention line will not interfere with the last-line placement of the zip code. Mail can be sorted more easily if the zip code appears in the last line of a typed address. Whenever possible, use a person's name as the first line of an address instead of putting that name in an attention line.

Salutation. For most letter styles, place the letter greeting, or salutation, one blank line below the last line of the inside address or the attention line (if used). If the letter is addressed to an individual, use that person's courtesy title and last name (*Dear Mr. Lanham*). Even if you are on a first-name basis (*Dear Leslie*), be sure to add a colon (not a comma or a semicolon) after the salutation. Do not use an individual's full name in the salutation (not *Dear Mr. Leslie Lanham*) unless you are unsure of gender (*Dear Leslie Lanham*).

For letters with attention lines or those addressed to organizations, the selection of an appropriate salutation has become more difficult. Formerly, writers used *Gentlemen* generically for all organizations. With increasing numbers of women in business management today, however, *Gentlemen* is problematic. Because no universally acceptable salutation has emerged as yet, you could use *Ladies and Gentlemen* or *Gentlemen and Ladies.*

Subject and Reference Lines. Although experts suggest placing the subject line one blank line below the salutation, many businesses actually place it above the salutation. Use whatever style your organization prefers. Reference lines often show policy or file numbers; they generally appear one blank line above the salutation. Use initial capital letters for the main words or all capital letters.

Body. Most business letters and memorandums are single-spaced, with double-spacing between paragraphs. Very short messages may be double-spaced with indented paragraphs.

Complimentary Close. Typed one blank line below the last line of the letter, the complimentary close may be formal (*Very truly yours*) or informal (*Sincerely* or *Cordially*).

Signature Block. In most letter styles, the writer's typed name and optional identification appear three or four blank lines below the complimentary close. The combination of name, title, and organization information should be arranged to achieve a balanced look. The name and title may appear on the same line or on separate lines, depending on the length of each. Use commas to separate categories within the same line, but not to conclude a line.

Sincerely yours,	*Cordially yours,*
Jeremy M. Wood	Casandra Baker-Murillo
Jeremy M. Wood, Manager *Technical Sales and Services*	*Casandra Baker-Murillo* *Executive Vice President*

Some organizations include their names in the signature block. In such cases the organization name appears in all caps one blank line below the complimentary close, as shown here:

Cordially,

LIPTON COMPUTER SERVICES

Shelina A. Simpson

Shelina A. Simpson
Executive Assistant

Reference Initials. If used, the initials of the typist and writer are typed one blank line below the writer's name and title. Generally, the writer's initials are capitalized and the typist's are lowercased, but this format varies.

Enclosure Notation. When an enclosure or attachment accompanies a document, a notation to that effect appears one blank line below the reference initials. This notation reminds the typist to insert the enclosure in the envelope, and it reminds the recipient to look for the enclosure or attachment. The notation may be spelled out (*Enclosure, Attachment*), or it may be abbreviated (*Enc., Att.*). It may indicate the number of enclosures or attachments, and it may also identify a specific enclosure (*Enclosure: Form 1099*).

Copy Notation. If you make copies of correspondence for other individuals, you may use *cc* to indicate courtesy copy, *pc* to indicate photocopy, or merely *c* for any kind of copy. A colon following the initial(s) is optional.

Second-Page Heading. When a letter extends beyond one page, use plain paper of the same quality and color as the first page. Identify the second and succeeding pages with a heading consisting of the name of the addressee, the page number, and the date. Use the following format or the one shown in Figure A.3:

Ms. Sara Hendricks	2	*May 3, 2013*

Both headings appear six blank lines (1 inch) from the top edge of the paper followed by two blank lines to separate them from the continuing text. Avoid using a second page if you have only one line or the complimentary close and signature block to fill that page.

FIGURE A.3 Second-Page Heading

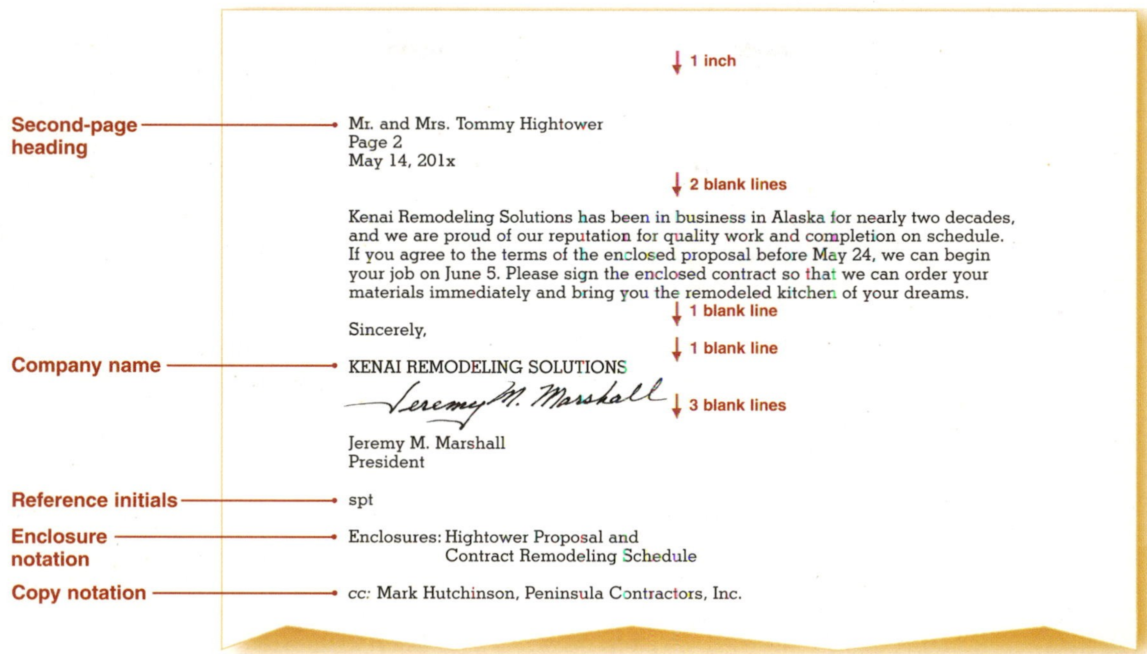

Plain-Paper Return Address. If you prepare a personal or business letter on plain paper, place your address immediately above the date. Do not include your name; you will type (and sign) your name at the end of your letter. If your return address contains two lines, begin typing so that the date appears 2 inches from the top. Avoid abbreviations except for a two-letter state abbreviation. Shown here is a return address in block style beginning at the left margin.

580 East Leffels Street
Springfield, OH 45501
December 14, 201x

Ms. Ellen Siemens
Escrow Department
TransOhio First Federal
1220 Wooster Boulevard
Columbus, OH 43218-2900

Dear Ms. Siemens:

For letters in the modified block style, start the return address at the center to align with the complimentary close.

Letter and Punctuation Styles

Most business letters today are prepared in either block or modified block style, and they generally use mixed punctuation.

Block Style. In the block style, shown in Figure A.2, all lines begin at the left margin. This style is a favorite because it is easy to format.

Modified Block Style. The modified block style differs from block style in that the date and closing lines appear in the center, as shown at the bottom of Figure A.2. The date may be (a) centered, (b) begun at the center of the page (to align with the closing lines), or (c) backspaced from the right margin. The signature block—including the complimentary close, writer's name and title, or organization identification—begins at the center. The first line of each paragraph may begin at the left margin or may be indented five or ten spaces. All other lines begin at the left margin.

Mixed Punctuation Style. Most businesses today use mixed punctuation, shown in Figure A.2. It requires a colon after the salutation and a comma after the complimentary close. Even when the salutation is a first name, a colon is appropriate.

Envelopes

An envelope should be of the same quality and color of stationery as the letter it carries. Because the envelope introduces your message and makes the first impression, you need to be especially careful in addressing it. Moreover, how you fold the letter is important.

Return Address. The return address is usually printed in the upper left corner of an envelope, as shown in Figure A.4. In large companies some form of identification (the writer's initials, name, or location) may be typed above the company name and address. This identification helps return the letter to the sender in case of nondelivery.

On an envelope without a printed return address, single-space the return address in the upper left corner. Beginning on line 3 on the fourth space (½ inch) from the left edge, type the writer's name, title, company, and mailing address. On a word processor, select the appropriate envelope size and make adjustments to approximate this return address location.

FIGURE A.4 Envelope Formats

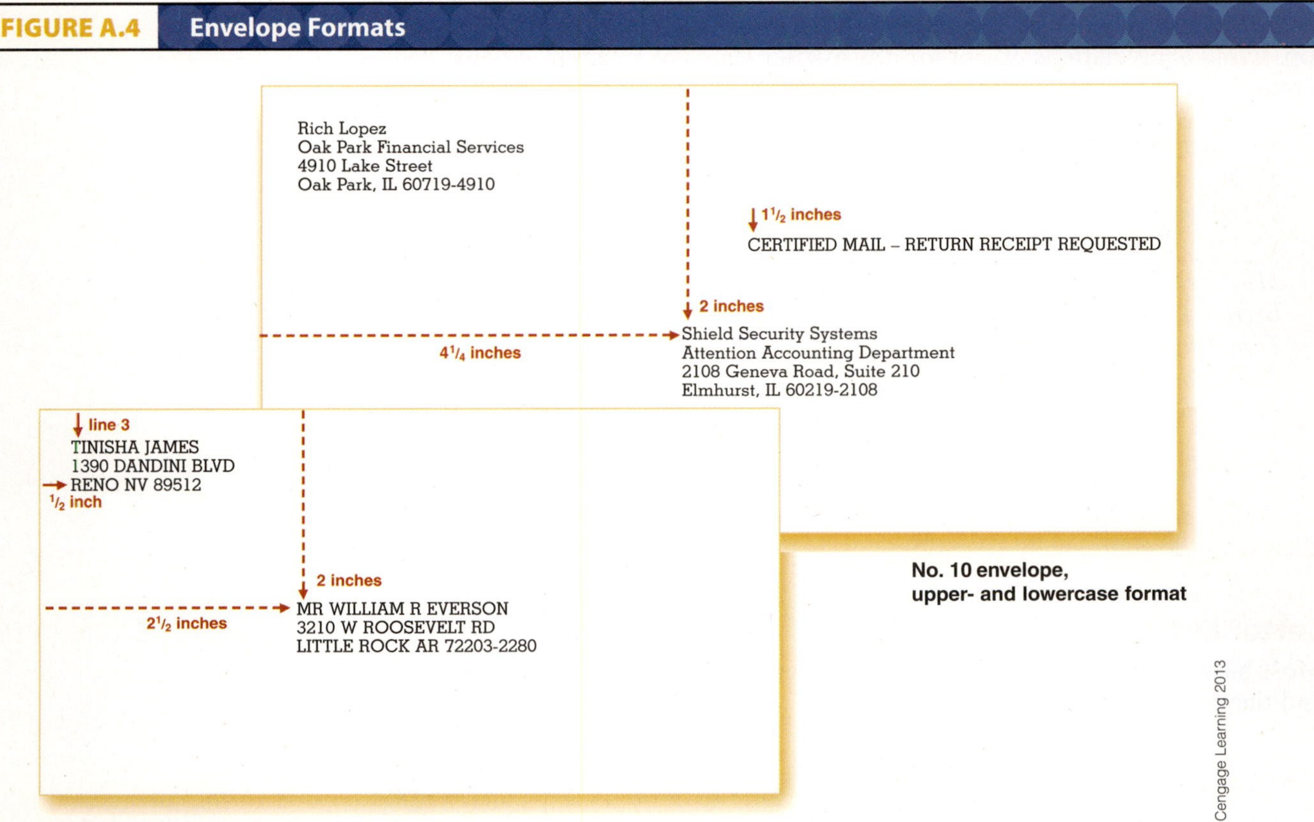

Mailing Address. On legal-sized No. 10 envelopes (4⅛ × 9½ inches), begin the address on line 13 about 4¼ inches from the left edge, as shown in Figure A.4. For small envelopes (3⅝ × 6½ inches), begin typing on line 12 about 2½ inches from the left edge. On a word processor, select the correct envelope size and check to be sure your address falls in the desired location.

In the past the U.S. Postal Service recommended that addresses be typed in all caps without any punctuation. This Postal Service style, shown in the small envelope in Figure A.4, was originally developed to facilitate scanning by optical character readers. Today's OCRs, however, are so sophisticated that they scan upper- and lowercase letters easily. Many companies today do not follow the Postal Service format because they prefer to use the same format for the envelope as for the inside address. If the same format is used, writers can take advantage of word processing programs to copy the inside address to the envelope, thus saving keystrokes and reducing errors. Having the same format on both the inside address and the envelope also looks more professional and consistent. For those reasons you may choose to use the familiar upper- and lowercase combination format. But you will want to check with your organization to learn its preference.

In addressing your envelopes for delivery in this country or in Canada, use the two-letter state and province abbreviations shown in Figure A.5. Notice that these abbreviations are in capital letters without periods.

Folding. The way a letter is folded and inserted into an envelope sends additional nonverbal messages about a writer's professionalism and carefulness. Most businesspeople follow the procedures shown here, which produce the least number of creases to distract readers.

For large No. 10 envelopes, begin with the letter face up. Fold slightly less than one third of the sheet toward the top, as shown in the following diagram. Then fold down the top third to within ⅓ inch of the bottom fold. Insert the letter into the envelope with the last fold toward the bottom of the envelope.

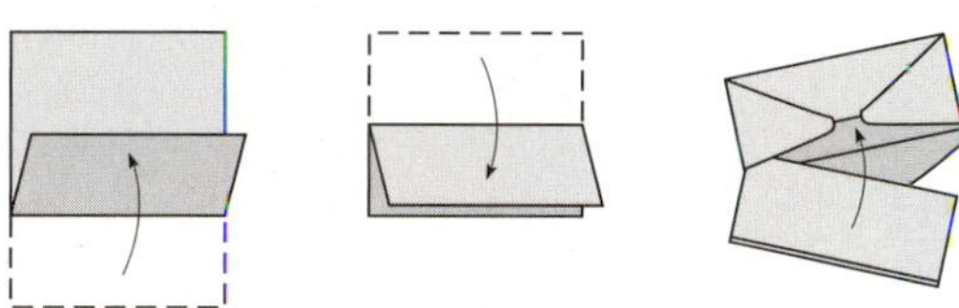

For small No. 6¾ envelopes, begin by folding the bottom up to within ⅓ inch of the top edge. Then fold the right third over to the left. Fold the left third to within ⅓ inch of the last fold. Insert the last fold into the envelope first.

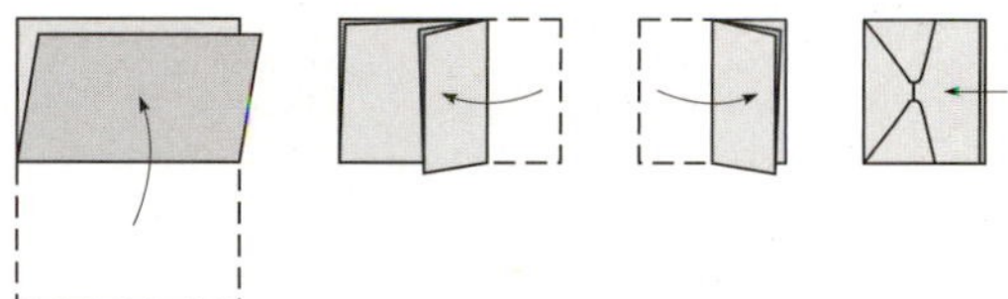

Fax Cover Sheet

Documents transmitted by fax are usually introduced by a cover sheet, such as that shown in Figure A.6. As with memos, the format varies considerably. Important items to include are (a) the name and fax number of the receiver, (b) the name and fax number of the sender, (c) the number of pages being sent, and (d) the name and telephone number of the person to notify in case of unsatisfactory transmission.

FIGURE A.5 Abbreviations of States, Territories, and Provinces

State or Territory	Two-Letter Abbreviation	State or Territory	Two-Letter Abbreviation
Alabama	AL	North Dakota	ND
Alaska	AK	Ohio	OH
Arizona	AZ	Oklahoma	OK
Arkansas	AR	Oregon	OR
California	CA	Pennsylvania	PA
Canal Zone	CZ	Puerto Rico	PR
Colorado	CO	Rhode Island	RI
Connecticut	CT	South Carolina	SC
Delaware	DE	South Dakota	SD
District of Columbia	DC	Tennessee	TN
Florida	FL	Texas	TX
Georgia	GA	Utah	UT
Guam	GU	Vermont	VT
Hawaii	HI	Virgin Islands	VI
Idaho	ID	Virginia	VA
Illinois	IL	Washington	WA
Indiana	IN	West Virginia	WV
Iowa	IA	Wisconsin	WI
Kansas	KS	Wyoming	WY
Kentucky	KY		
Louisiana	LA		
Maine	ME	**Canadian Province**	
Maryland	MD	Alberta	AB
Massachusetts	MA	British Columbia	BC
Michigan	MI	Labrador	LB
Minnesota	MN	Manitoba	MB
Mississippi	MS	New Brunswick	NB
Missouri	MO	Newfoundland	NF
Montana	MT	Northwest Territories	NT
Nebraska	NE	Nova Scotia	NS
Nevada	NV	Ontario	ON
New Hampshire	NH	Prince Edward Island	PE
New Jersey	NJ	Quebec	PQ
New Mexico	NM	Saskatchewan	SK
New York	NY	Yukon Territory	YT
North Carolina	NC		

When the document being transmitted requires little explanation, you may prefer to attach an adhesive note (such as a Post-it fax transmittal form) instead of a full cover sheet. These notes carry essentially the same information as shown in our printed fax cover sheet. They are perfectly acceptable in most business organizations and can save considerable paper and transmission costs.

FIGURE A.6 Fax Cover Sheet

FAX TRANSMISSION

DATE: ______________________

TO: ______________________ FAX NUMBER: ______________________

____

____

FROM: ______________________ FAX NUMBER: ______________________

____

____

NUMBER OF PAGES TRANSMITTED INCLUDING THIS COVER SHEET: ______________________

MESSAGE:

If any part of this fax transmission is missing or not clearly received, please call:

NAME: ______________________

PHONE: ______________________

CORRECTION SYMBOLS AND PROOFREADING MARKS

APPENDIX B

In marking your papers, your instructor may use the following symbols or abbreviations to indicate writing weaknesses. Studying these symbols and suggestions will help you understand your instructor's remarks. Knowing this information can also help you evaluate and improve your own memos, e-mails, letters, reports, and other writing. These symbols are keyed to your Grammar/Mechanics Handbook and to the text.

Adj	Hyphenate two or more adjectives that are joined to create a compound modifier before a noun. See G/M 1.17e.
Adv	Use adverbs, not adjectives, to describe or limit the action. See G/M 1.17d.
Apos	Use apostrophes to show possession. See G/M 2.20–2.22.
Assgn	Follow the assignment instructions.
Awk	Recast to avoid awkward expression.
Bias	Use inclusive, bias-free language. See Chapter 2, page 46.
Cap	Use capitalization appropriately. See G/M 3.01–3.16.
CmConj	Use a comma before the coordinating conjunction in a compound sentence. See G/M 2.05.
CmDate	Use commas appropriately in dates, addresses, geographical names, degrees, and long numbers. See G/M 2.04.
CmIn	Use commas to set off internal sentence interrupters. See G/M 2.06c.
CmIntr	Use commas to separate introductory clauses and certain phrases from independent clauses. See G/M 2.06.
CmSer	Use commas to separate three or more items (words, phrases, or short clauses) in a series. See G/M 2.01.
Coh	Improve coherence between ideas. Repeat key ideas, use pronouns, or use transitional expressions. See Chapter 3, page 70.
Cl	Improve the clarity of ideas or expression so that the point is better understood.
CS	Avoid comma-splice sentences, Do not use a comma to splice (join) two independent clauses. See Chapter 3, page 65.
CmUn	Avoid unnecessary commas. See G/M 2.15.
:	Use a colon after a complete thought that introduces a list of items. Use a colon in business letter salutations and to introduce long quotations. See G/M 2.17–2.19.
Direct	Use the direct strategy by emphasizing the main idea. See Chapter 3, page 61.
Dash	Use a dash to set off parenthetical elements, to emphasize sentence interruptions, or to separate an introductory list from a summarizing statement. See G/M 2.26.
DM	Avoid dangling modifiers by placing modifiers close to the words they describe or limit. See Chapter 3, page 69.
Filler	Avoid fillers such as *there are* or long lead-ins such as *this is to inform you that*. See Chapter 4, page 84.
Format	Choose an appropriate format for this document.

Frag	Avoid fragments by expressing ideas in complete sentences. A fragment is a broken-off part of a sentence. See Chapter 3, page 65.
GH	Use graphic highlighting (bullets, lists, indentions, or headings) to enhance readability. See Chapter 4, pages 89–91.
MM	Avoid misplaced modifiers by placing modifiers close to the words they describe or limit. See Chapter 3, page 69.
Num	Use number or word form appropriately. See G/M 4.01–4.13.
Ob	Avoid stating the obvious.
Org	Improve organization by grouping similar ideas.
Par	Express ideas in parallel form. See Chapter 3, page 68.
Paren	Use parentheses to set off nonessential sentence elements such as explanations, directions, questions, or references. See G/M 2.27.
Period	Use one period to end a statement, command, indirect question, or polite request. See G/M 2.23.
Pos	Express an idea positively rather than negatively. See Chapter 2, page 45.
PosPro	Use possessive-case pronouns to show ownership. See G/M 1.07 and 1.08d.
Pro	Use nominative-case pronouns as subjects of verbs and as subject complements. Use objective-case pronouns as objects of prepositions and verbs. See G/M 1.07 and 1.08.
ProAgr	Make pronouns agree in number and gender with the words to which they refer (their antecedents). See G/M 1.09.
ProVag	Be sure that pronouns such as *it, which, this*, and *that* refer to clear antecedents.
?	Use a question mark after a direct question and after statements with questions appended. See G/M 2.24.
Quo	Use quotation marks to enclose the exact words of a speaker or writer; to distinguish words used in a special sense; or to enclose titles of articles, chapters, or other short works. See G/M 2.28.
Redun	Avoid expressions that repeat meaning or include unnecessary words. See Chapter 4, page 84.
RunOn	Avoid run-on (fused) sentences. A sentence with two independent clauses must be joined by a coordinating conjunctions (*and, or, nor, but*) or by a semicolon (;). See Chapter 3, page 65.
Sp	Check misspelled words.
Self	Use *self*-ending pronouns only when they refer to previously mentioned nouns or pronouns. See G/M 1.08h.
;	Use a semicolon to join closely related independent clauses. A semicolon is also an option to join separate items in a series when one or more of the items contain internal commas. See G/M 2.16.
Shift	Avoid a confusing shift in verb tense, mood, or voice. See G/M 1.15c.
Trans	Use an appropriate transition. See Chapter 3, page 70, and Chapter 12, page 373.
Tone	Use a conversational, positive, and courteous tone that promotes goodwill. See Chapter 2, page 44.
You	Focus on developing the "you" view. See Chapter 2, page 43.
VbAgr	Make verbs agree with subjects. See G/M 1.10.
VbMood	Use the subjunctive mood to express hypothetical (untrue) ideas. See G/M 1.12.

VbTnse	Use present-tense, past-tense, and part-participle forms correctly. See G/M 1.13.
VbVce	Use active- and passive-voice verbs appropriately. See G/M 1.11.
WC	Focus on precise word choice. See Chapter 4, pages 87.
Wordy	Avoid wordiness including flabby expressions, long lead-ins, unnecessary *there is/are* fillers, redundancies, and trite business phrases. See Chapter 4, pages 83.

Proofreading Marks

Proofreading Mark	Draft Copy	Final Copy
Align horizontally	TO: Rick Munoz	TO: Rick Munoz
Align vertically	166.32 132.45	166.32 132.45
Capitalize	Coca-cola sending a pdf file	Coca-Cola sending a PDF file
Close up space	meeting at 3 p. m.	meeting at 3 p.m.
Center	Recommendations	Recommendations
Delete	in my final judgement	in my judgment
Insert apostrophe	our companys product	our company's product
Insert comma	you will of course	you will, of course,
Insert hyphen	tax free income	tax-free income
Insert period	Ms Holly Hines	Ms. Holly Hines
Insert quotation mark	shareholders receive a bonus.	shareholders receive a "bonus."
Insert space	wordprocessing program	word processing program
Lowercase (remove capitals)	the Vice President HUMAN RESOURCES	the vice president Human Resources
Move to left	I. Labor costs	I. Labor costs
Move to right	A. Findings of study	A. Findings of study
Spell out	aimed at 2 depts	aimed at two departments
Start new paragraph	Keep the screen height of your computer at eye level.	Keep the screen height of your computer at eye level.
Stet (don't delete)	officials talked openly	officials talked openly
Transpose	accounts recievable	accounts receivable
Use boldface	Conclusions bf	**Conclusions**
Use italics	The Perfect Résumé ital	*The Perfect Résumé*

For many reasons business writers are careful to properly document report data. Citing sources strengthens a writer's argument, as you learned in Chapter 10. Acknowledging sources also shields writers from charges of plagiarism. Moreover, good references help readers pursue further research.

Before we discuss specific documentation formats, you must understand the difference between *source* notes and *content* notes. Source notes identify quotations, paraphrased passages, and author references. They lead readers to the sources of cited information, and they must follow a consistent format. Content notes, on the other hand, enable writers to add comments, explain information not directly related to the text, or refer readers to other sections of a report. Because content notes are generally infrequent, most writers identify them in the text with a raised asterisk (*). At the bottom of the page, the asterisk is repeated with the content note following. If two content notes appear on one page, a double asterisk identifies the second reference.

Your real concern will be with source notes. These identify quotations or paraphrased ideas in the text, and they direct readers to a complete list of references (a bibliography) at the end of your report. Researchers have struggled for years to develop the perfect documentation system, one that is efficient for the writer and crystal clear to the reader. As a result, many systems exist, each with its advantages. The important thing for you is to adopt one system and use it consistently.

Students frequently ask, "But what documentation system is most used in business?" Actually, no one method dominates. Many businesses have developed their own hybrid systems. These companies generally supply guidelines illustrating their in-house style to employees. Before starting any research project on the job, you will want to inquire about your organization's preferred documentation style. You can also look in the files for examples of previous reports.

References are usually cited in two places: (a) a brief citation appears in the text, and (b) a complete citation appears in a bibliography at the end of the report. The two most common formats for citations and bibliographies in academic work are those of the Modern Language Association (MLA) and the American Psychological Association (APA). Each has its own style for textual references and bibliography lists. The citations in this textbook are based on the APA style, which is increasingly the standard in business communication.

Modern Language Association Format

Writers in the humanities and liberal arts frequently use the MLA format, which is illustrated in Figure C.1. In parentheses close to the textual reference appears the author's name and page cited. If no author is known, a shortened version of the source title is used. At the end of the report, the writer lists alphabetically all references in a bibliography called "Works Cited." The MLA no longer requires the use of URLs in Web citations because Web addresses change and most readers can find Web addresses by using a Web browser and searching for the publication title. In another recent change, MLA style now requires identification of the publication medium, such as *Print* or *Web.* For more information consult *MLA Handbook for Writers of Research Papers*, 7e (New York: The Modern Language Association of America, 2009) or Jill Rossiter's *The MLA Pocket Handbook* (DW Publishing, 2008).

FIGURE C.1 Portions of MLA Text Page and Works Cited

Peanut butter was first delivered to the world by a St. Louis physician in 1890. As discussed at the Peanut Advisory Board's Web site, peanut butter was originally promoted as a protein substitute for elderly patients ("History"). However, it was the 1905 Universal Exposition in St. Louis that truly launched peanut butter. Since then, annual peanut butter consumption has zoomed to 3.3 pounds a person in the United States (Barrons).

America's farmers produce 1.6 million tons of peanuts annually, about half of which is used for oil, nuts, and candy. Lisa Gibbons, executive secretary of the Peanut Advisory Board, says that "peanuts in some form are in the top four candies: Snickers, Reese's Peanut Butter Cups, Peanut M&Ms, and Butterfingers" (Meadows 32).

Works Cited

Barrons, Elizabeth Ruth. "A Comparison of Domestic and International Consumption of Legumes." *Journal of Economic Agriculture* 23 (2010): 45–49. Print.

"History of Peanut Butter." *Peanut Advisory Board.* Alabama Peanut Producers Association. n.d. Web. 19 Jan. 2011.

Meadows, Mark Allen. "Peanut Crop Is Anything but Peanuts at Home and Overseas." *Business Monthly* May 2011: 31–34. Print.

MLA In-Text Format. In-text citations generally appear close to the point where the reference is mentioned or at the end of the sentence inside the closing period. Follow these guidelines:

- Include the last name of the author(s) and the page number. Do not use a comma, as (Smith 310).
- If the author's name is mentioned in the text, cite only the page number in parentheses. Do not include either the word *page* or the abbreviations *p.* or *pp.*
- If no author is known, refer to the document title or a shortened version of it, as ("Facts at Fingertips" 102).

MLA Bibliographic Format. In the "Works Cited" bibliography, list all references cited in a report. Some writers include all works consulted. A portion of an MLA bibliography is shown in Figure C.1. A more complete list of model references appears in Figure C.2. Following are selected guidelines summarizing important points regarding MLA bibliographic format:

- Use italics for the titles of books, magazines, newspapers, journals, and Web sites. Capitalize all main words.
- Enclose the titles of magazine, newspaper, and journal articles in quotation marks. Include volume and issue numbers for journals only.
- Use the following sequence for electronic sources: author; article name in quotation marks; title of Web site, project, or book in italics; name of institution, organization, or publisher affiliated with the site; page numbers if available; URL (only if necessary for retrieval); publication medium (such as *Web, Print,* or *PDF*); and access date.

FIGURE C.2 MLA Sample Works Cited

Works Cited

American Airlines. *2011 Annual Report.* Fort Worth, TX: AMR Corporation. Print.	Annual report, print
Atamian, Richard A., and Ellen Ferranto. *Driving Market Forces.* New York: HarperCollins, 2010. Print.	Book, two authors, print
Austin, Anthony. "Re: Job Networking." Message to the author. 16 Jan. 2012. E-mail.	E-mail interview
Balcazar, Saul. "The Future of Investing," *Fortune* 1 Mar. 2010: 62–67. *ABI/Inform*. Web. 15 Mar. 2010.	Magazine article, Web database
Berss, Marcia. "Protein Man," *Forbes* 24 Oct. 2011: 65–66. Print.	Magazine article, print
Cantrell, Mark R., and Hilary Watson. "Violence in Today's Workplace." *Office Review* 10 Jan. 2010: 24–27. PDF. 23 May 2011.	Magazine article, PDF
"Globalization Often Means That the Fast Track Leads Overseas." *The Washington Post* 16 June 2011: A1, A4. Print.	Newspaper article, no author, print
Grover, Hal. "When Taking a Tip From a Job Network, Proceed With Caution." *The Wall Street Journal* 7 Feb. 2011: B1. Print.	Newspaper article, one author, print
Gutzman, Debra. "Corporate Ghostwriting," *Financial Times* 14 Apr. 2011: n.pag. *FT.com.* Web. 20 Apr. 2011.	Newspaper article, Web, no page
Lynch, Diane. "Wired Women: Gender in High-Tech Workplace." *abcnews.go.com Technology*. n.d. Web. 24 Apr. 2011.	Web document without print version
Tedeschi, Bob. "Searching for a Job? Try Looking at Your Hand-Held First." *The New York Times*. 19 May 2011. Web. 9 June 2011. <http://www.nytimes.com/2011/05/19/technology/personaltech/19smart.html>	Web newspaper article with URL
U.S. Dept. of Labor. *Child Care as a Workforce Issue*. Washington, DC: Government Printing Office, 2010. Print.	Government publication
Vitalari, Nicholas P., James C. Patton, and Andrew Milner. "Key Trends in Systems Development in Europe and North America." *Journal of Global Information Management* 3.2 (2010): 5–20. Print. [*3.2* signifies volume 3, issue 2]	Journal article with volume and issue numbers, print
Walker, Robyn C., and Jolanta Aritz. "Cognitive Organization and Identity Maintenance in Multicultural Teams." *Journal of Business Communication* 47.1 (2010): 20–41. Business Source Complete database. Web. 15 Mar. 2011.	Journal, electronic database
"Writing With Inferential Statistics." *The OWL at Purdue*. Purdue University Online Writing Lab, n.d. Web. 20 Feb. 2011.	Web document, no author, no date
Yellin, Mike. "Re: Managing Managers and Cell Phones." *Yahoo Groups*. E-commerce. 9 Sept. 2011. Web. 15 Sept. 2011.	Listserv, discussion group, blog posting

Note 1: MLA style recommends listing URLs for Web sites only if necessary for location. However, many instructors require that all Web citations in student research papers be identified by URL. If adding a URL, place it within angle brackets (< >) as the last item in the citation.

Note 2: To prevent confusion, you might add the words *Accessed* or *Retrieved* preceding the date you accessed the online source.

Note 3: Although MLA style prescribes double-spacing for the works cited, we show single spacing to conserve space and to represent preferred business usage.

American Psychological Association Format

Popular in the social and physical sciences, the American Psychological Association (APA) documentation style uses parenthetic citations. That is, each author reference is shown in parentheses when cited in the text, as shown in Figure C.3. At the end of the report, all references are listed alphabetically in a bibliography called "References." Because online materials can change, APA now recommends providing a digital object identifier (DOI) when available rather than the URL. In

FIGURE C.3 Portions of APA Text Page and References

Peanut butter was first delivered to the world by a St. Louis physician in 1890. As discussed at the Peanut Advisory Board's Web site, peanut butter was originally promoted as a protein substitute for elderly patients (History, n.d.). However, it was the 1905 Universal Exposition in St. Louis that truly launched peanut butter. Since then, annual peanut butter consumption has zoomed to 3.3 pounds a person in the United States (Barrons, 2010, p. 46).

America's farmers produce 1.6 million tons of peanuts annually, about half of which is used for oil, nuts, and candy. Lisa Gibbons, executive secretary of the Peanut Advisory Board, says that "peanuts in some form are in the top four candies: Snickers, Reese's Peanut Butter Cups, Peanut M&Ms, and Butterfingers" (Meadows, 2011, p. 32).

References

Barrons, E. R. (2010, November). A comparison of domestic and international consumption of legumes. *Journal of Economic Agriculture*, *23*(3), 45–49.

History of peanut butter. (n.d.). Peanut Advisory Board. Alabama Peanut Producers Association. Retrieved from http://www.alpeanuts.com/consumer_interest/articles.phtml?articleID=102

Meadows, M. A. (2011, May). Peanut crop is anything but peanuts at home and overseas. *Business Monthly*, 31–34.

another departure from previous advice, APA style no longer requires the date of retrieval. For more information about APA formats, see the *Publication Manual of the American Psychological Association*, 6e (Washington, DC: American Psychological Association, 2009) or Jill Rossiter's *The APA Pocket Handbook* (DW Publishing, 2007).

APA In-Text Format. Within the text, document each specific textual source with a short description in parentheses. Following are selected guidelines summarizing important elements of APA style:

- For a direct quotation, include the last name of the author(s), date of publication, and page number, as (Jones, 2010, p. 36). Use *n.d.* if no date is available.
- If no author is known, refer to the first few words of the reference list entry and the year, as (Computer Privacy, 2011).
- Include page numbers only for direct quotations.

APA Reference Format. List all citations alphabetically in a section called "References." A portion of an APA reference page is shown in Figure C.3. A more complete list of model references appears in Figure C.4. APA style requires specific capitalization and sequencing guidelines, some of which are summarized here:

- Include an author's name with the last name first followed by initials, such as *Smith, M. A.* First and middle names are not used.
- Show the date of publication in parentheses immediately after the author's name, as *Smith, M. A. (2011, March 2).*
- Italicize the titles of books. Use "sentence-style" capitalization. This means capitalize only the first word of a title, proper nouns, and the first word after an internal colon.

FIGURE C.4 APA Sample References

References

American Airlines. (2011). *2011 Annual Report.* Fort Worth, TX: AMR Corporation. — Annual report

Atamian, R. A., & Ferranto, E. (2010). *Driving market forces.* New York: HarperCollins. — Book, two authors

Audio conferencing. (2010). In *Encyclopaedia Britannica*. Retrieved October 19, 2011, from Encyclopaedia Britannica Online: http://www.britannica.com/eb/article-61669 — Encyclopedia, online

Balcazar, S. (2010, March 1). The future of investing. [Electronic version]. *Fortune*, 62–67. — Magazine article, online, without DOI, print version available

Beardsley, E. (2011, April 6). Building gone wild in China. [Electronic version]. *Asia Today*, 102, pp. 42–44. doi: 10.1090/14733300410001676403 — Magazine article, with DOI

Berss, M. (2008, October 24). Protein man. *Forbes*, 65–66. — Magazine article, print

Clay, R. (2008, June). Science vs. ideology: Psychologists fight back about the misuse of research. *Monitor on Psychology*, 39(6). Retrieved from http://www.apa.org.monitor/ — Magazine article, online

Globalization often means that the fast track leads overseas. (2011, June 16). *The Washington Post*, pp. A1, A4. — Newspaper article, no author, print

Guzman, D. (2011, April 20). Corporate ghostwriting. *Financial Times*. Retrieved from http://www.ft.com — Newspaper article, online

U.S. Department of Health and Human Services, National Institutes of Health, National Heart, Lung, and Blood Institute. (2003). *Managing asthma: A guide for schools* (NIH Publication No. 02-2650). Retrieved from http://www.nhlbi.nih.gov/health/prof/lung/asthma/asth_sch.pdf — Government report

Varma, P., Sivakumaran, B., and Marshall, R. (2010, March). Impulse buying and variety seeking: A trait-correlates perspective. *Journal of Business Research, 63*(3), 276–283. [*63*(3) signifies volume 63, series or issue 3] — Journal article from database (see Note 1 below)

Vitalari, N. P., Patton, J. C., & Milner, A. (2010, May). Key trends in systems development in Europe and North America. *Journal of Global Information Management, 3*(2), 5–20. — Journal article without DOI

Walker, R. D., & Aritz, J. (2010, January). Cognitive organization and identity maintenance in multicultural teams. [Electronic version]. *Journal of Business Communication, 47*(1): 20–41. doi: 10.1177/0021943609340669 — Journal article with DOI

Writing with inferential statistics. (n.d.). *The OWL at Purdue*. Retrieved from http://owl.english.purdue.edu/owl/resource/672/06/ — Web document, no author, no date

Yerkes, J. (2010, February 24). Re: Emerging business models [Online forum comment]. Retrieved from http://www1.wipo.int:8080/roller/trackback/ipisforum/Weblog/theme_nine_emerging_business_models — Web posting to newsgroup, online forum, or discussion group

Note 1: Database identification is unnecessary if the article is easily located through its primary publication.

Note 2: Do not include retrieval dates unless the source material may change over time (e.g., wikis).

Note 3: Although APA style prescribes double spacing for the References page, we show single spacing to conserve space and to represent preferred business usage.

- Do not italicize or underscore the titles of magazine and journal articles. Use sentence-style capitalization for article titles.
- Italicize the names of magazines, newspapers, and journals. Capitalize the initial letters of all main words.
- Include the document object identifier (DOI) when available for online periodicals. If no DOI is available, include the URL but no date of retrieval.
- For an online periodical that also appears in a printed version, include *Electronic version* in brackets after the article's title. Do not include a URL.
- For articles easily obtained from an online database (such as that in a school library), provide print information. The database need not be identified. You may include an accession number in parentheses at the end, but APA style does not require it.

Introduction

Because many students need a quick review of basic grammar and mechanics, we provide a number of resources in condensed form. The Grammar/Mechanics Handbook, which offers you a rapid systematic review, consists of four parts:

- **Grammar/Mechanics Diagnostic Test.** This 65-point pretest helps you assess your strengths and weaknesses in eight areas of grammar and mechanics. Your instructor may later give you a posttest to assess your improvement.
- **Grammar/Mechanics Profile.** The G/M Profile enables you to pinpoint specific areas in which you need remedial instruction or review.
- **Grammar/Mechanics Review.** Provided here is a concise review of basic principles of grammar, punctuation, capitalization, and number style. The review also provides reinforcement and quiz exercises that help you interact with the principles of grammar and test your comprehension. The guidelines not only provide a study guide for review but will also serve as a reference manual throughout the writing course. The grammar review can be used for classroom-centered instruction or for self-guided learning.
- **Confusing Words and Frequently Misspelled Words.** A list of selected confusing words, along with a list of 160 frequently misspelled words, completes the Grammar/Mechanics Handbook.

More Help to Improve Your Grammar Skills

Some of you want all the help you can get in improving your language skills. For additional assistance with grammar and language fundamentals, *Essentials of Business Communication,* 9e, offers you unparalleled interactive and print resources at **www.meguffey.com**.

- **Your Personal Language Trainer.** In this self-paced learning tool, Dr. Guffey acts as your personal trainer in helping you pump up your language muscles. *Your Personal Language Trainer* provides the rules plus hundreds of sentence applications so that you can try out your knowledge and build your skills with immediate feedback and explanations.
- **Sentence Competency Skill Builders** offer interactive exercises similar to the grammar/mechanics checkups in this book. These drills focus on common writing weaknesses so that you can learn to avoid them.
- **Speak Right!** reviews frequently mispronounced words. You'll hear correct pronunciations from Dr. Guffey so that you will never be embarrassed by mispronouncing these terms.
- **Spell Right!** presents frequently misspelled words along with exercises to help you improve your skills.
- **Advanced Grammar/Mechanics Checkups** take you to the next level in language confidence. These self-teaching exercises provide challenging sentences that test your combined grammar, punctuation, spelling, and usage skills.

A more comprehensive treatment of grammar, punctuation, and usage can be found in Clark and Clark's *A Handbook for Office Workers* or Guffey's *Business English.* The first step in your systematic review of grammar and mechanics involves completing a diagnostic pretest found on the next page.

Grammar/Mechanics Diagnostic Pretest

Name____________________

This diagnostic pretest is intended to reveal your strengths and weaknesses in using the following:

plural nouns	adjectives	punctuation
possessive nouns	adverbs	capitalization style
pronouns	prepositions	number style
verbs	conjunctions	

The pretest is organized into sections corresponding to the preceding categories. In Sections A through H, each sentence is either correct or has one error related to the category under which it is listed. If a sentence is correct, write *C*. If it has an error, underline the error and write the correct form in the space provided. When you finish, check your answers with your instructor and fill out the Grammar/Mechanics Profile at the end of the test.

A. Plural Nouns

companies____________

Example: Large companys hire numerous CPAs and accountants.

1. All job candidates are asked whether they can work on Saturday's.
2. Two freshmans discussed the pros and cons of using laptops and cell phones in their classes.
3. Both of Jeff's sister-in-laws worked as secretaries at different facilities.
4. Neither the Sanchezes nor the Harris's knew about the changes in beneficiaries.
5. Since the early 2000s, most judicial systems and attornies have invested in packages that detect computer viruses.

B. Possessive Nouns

6. We sincerely hope that the jurys judgment reflects the stories of all the witnesses.
7. In a little over two months time, the analysts finished their reports.
8. Ms. Porters staff is responsible for all accounts receivable for customers purchasing electronics parts.
9. At the next stockholders meeting, we will discuss benefits for employees and dividends for shareholders.
10. For the past 90 days, employees in the sales department have complained about Mr. Navetta smoking.

C. Pronouns

me____________

Example: Whom did you ask to replace Francisco and I?

11. The chief and myself were quite willing to send copies to whoever requested them.
12. Much of the project assigned to Samantha and I had to be reassigned to Matt and them.
13. Although it's CPU was noisy, the computer worked for Jeremy and me.
14. Just between you and me, only you and I know that she will be transferred.
15. My friend and I applied at GE because of their excellent benefits.

D. Verb Agreement

Example: The list of payments <u>have</u> to be approved by the boss. has

16. This cell phone and its calling plan costs much less than I expected.
17. A description of the property, together with several other legal documents, were submitted by my attorney.
18. There are a wide range of proposals for reducing e-mail overload.
19. Neither the manager nor the employees in the office think the solution is fair.
20. Because of the holiday, our committee were unable to meet.

E. Verb Mood, Voice, and Tense

21. If I was in charge, I would certainly change things.
22. To make a copy, first open the disk drive door and then you insert the disk.
23. If I could chose any city, I would select Hong Kong.
24. Those contracts have laid on his desk for more than two weeks.
25. The auditors have went over these accounts carefully, and they have found no discrepancies.

F. Adjectives and Adverbs

26. Until we have a more clearer picture of what is legal, we will proceed cautiously.
27. Britney thought she had done good in her job interview.
28. A recently appointed official was in charge of monitoring peer to peer file-sharing systems.
29. Robert only has two days before he must submit his end-of-the-year report.
30. The architects submitted there drawings in a last-minute attempt to beat the deadline.

G. Prepositions and Conjunctions

31. Can you tell me where the meeting is scheduled at?
32. It seems like we have been taking this pretest forever.
33. Our investigation shows that cell phones may be cheaper then landlines.
34. My courses this semester are totally different than last semester's.
35. Do you know where this shipment is going to?

H. Commas

For each of the following sentences, insert any necessary commas. Count the number of commas that you added. Write that number in the space provided. All punctuation must be correct to receive credit for the sentence. If a sentence requires no punctuation, write *C*

Example: Because of developments in theory and computer applications, management is becoming more of a science. 1

36. For example management determines how orders assignments and responsibilities are delegated to employees.
37. Your order Ms. Lee will be sent from Memphis Tennessee on July 1.
38. When you need service on any of your equipment we will be happy to help you Mr. Lopez.
39. Michelle Wong who is the project manager at TeleCom suggested that I call you.
40. You have purchased from us often and your payments in the past have always been prompt.

I. Commas and Semicolons 1

Add commas and semicolons to the following sentences. In the space provided, write the number of punctuation marks that you added.

41. The salesperson turned in his report however he did not indicate the time period it covered.
42. Interest payments on bonds are tax deductible dividend payments are not.
43. We are opening a branch office in Scottsdale and hope to be able to serve all your needs from that office by the middle of January.
44. As suggested by the committee we must first secure adequate funding then we may consider expansion.
45. When you begin to research a report consider many sources of information namely think about using the Internet, books, periodicals, government publications, and databases.

J. Commas and Semicolons 2

46. After our chief had the printer repaired it jammed again within the first week although we treated it carefully.
47. Our experienced courteous staff has been trained to anticipate your every need.
48. In view of the new law that went into effect on April 1 our current liability insurance must be increased therefore we need to adjust our budget.
49. As stipulated in our contract your agency will develop a social media program and supervise our media budget.
50. As you know Ms. Okui we aim for long-term business relationships not quick profits.

K. Other Punctuation

Each of the following sentences may require colons, question marks, quotation marks, periods, parentheses, and underscores, as well as commas and semicolons. Add the appropriate punctuation to each sentence. Then in the space provided, write the total number of marks that you added or changed.

2 **Example:** Fully recharging your digital camera's battery(see page 6 of the instruction manual)takes only 90 minutes.

51. The following members of the department volunteered to help on Saturday Kim Carlos Dan and Sylvia.
52. Mr Phillips, Miss Reed, and Mrs. Garcia usually arrived at the office by 8 30 a m.
53. We recommend that you use hearing protectors see the warning on page 8 when using this electric drill.
54. Did the president really say "All employees may take Friday off
55. We are trying to locate an edition of BusinessWeek that carried an article titled Who Is Reading Your E-Mail

L. Capitalization

For each of the following sentences, underline any letter that should be capitalized. In the space provided, write the number of words you marked.

4 **Example:** vice president rivera devised a procedure for expediting purchase orders from area 4 warehouses.

56. although english was his native language, he also spoke spanish and could read french.
57. on a trip to the east coast, uncle henry visited the empire state building.
58. karen enrolled in classes in history, german, and sociology.
59. the business manager and the vice president each received a new dell computer.
60. james lee, the president of kendrick, inc., will speak to our conference in the spring.

M. Number Style

Decide whether the numbers in the following sentences should be written as words or as figures. Each sentence either is correct or has one error. If it is correct, write *C*. If it has an error, underline it and write the correct form in the space provided.

Example: The bank had 5 branches in three suburbs. five

61. More than 3,000,000 people have visited the White House in the past five years. ________
62. Of the 28 viewer comments we received regarding our online commercial, only three were negative. ________
63. We set aside forty dollars for petty cash, but by December 1 our fund was depleted. ________
64. The meeting is scheduled for May fifth at 3 p.m. ________
65. In the past five years, nearly fifteen percent of the population changed residences at least once. ________

Grammar/Mechanics Profile

In the spaces at the right, place a check mark to indicate the number of correct answers you had in each category of the Grammar/Mechanics Diagnostic Pretest.

		Number Correct				
		5	4	3	2	1
1-5	Plural Nouns	____	____	____	____	____
6-10	Possessive Nouns	____	____	____	____	____
11-15	Pronouns	____	____	____	____	____
16-20	Verb Agreement	____	____	____	____	____
21-25	Verb Mood, Voice, and Tense	____	____	____	____	____
26-30	Adjectives and Adverbs	____	____	____	____	____
31-35	Prepositions and Conjunctions	____	____	____	____	____
36-40	Commas	____	____	____	____	____
41-45	Commas and Semicolons 1	____	____	____	____	____
46-50	Commas and Semicolons 2	____	____	____	____	____
51-55	Other Punctuation	____	____	____	____	____
56-60	Capitalization	____	____	____	____	____
61-65	Number Style	____	____	____	____	____

Note: 5 = have excellent skills; 4 = need light review; 3 = need careful review; 2 = need to study rules; 1 = need serious study and follow-up reinforcement.

Grammar/Mechanics Review

Parts of Speech (1.01)

1.1 Functions. English has eight parts of speech. Knowing the functions of the parts of speech helps writers better understand how words are used and how sentences are formed.

a. **Nouns:** name persons, places, things, qualities, concepts, and activities (for example, *Kevin, Phoenix, computer, joy, work, banking*)

b. **Pronouns:** substitute for nouns (for example, *he, she, it, they*).

c. **Verbs:** show the action of a subject or join the subject to words that describe it (for example, *walk, heard, is, was jumping*).

d. **Adjectives:** describe or limit nouns and pronouns and often answer the questions *what kind? how many?* and *which one?* (for example, *red* car, *ten* items, *good* manager).

e. **Adverbs:** describe or limit verbs, adjectives, or other adverbs and frequently answer the questions *when? how? where?* or *to what extent?* (for example, *tomorrow, rapidly, here, very*).

f. **Prepositions:** join nouns or pronouns to other words in sentences (for example, desk *in* the office, ticket *for* me, letter *to* you).

g. **Conjunctions:** connect words or groups of words (for example, you *and* I, Mark *or* Jill).

h. **Interjections:** express strong feelings (for example, *Wow! Oh!*).

Nouns (1.02–1.06)

Nouns name persons, places, things, qualities, concepts, and activities. Nouns may be classified into a number of categories.

1.02 Concrete and Abstract. Concrete nouns name specific objects that can be seen, heard, felt, tasted, or smelled. Examples of concrete nouns are *telephone, dollar, IBM,* and *tangerine.* Abstract nouns name generalized ideas such as qualities or concepts that are not easily pictured. *Emotion, power*, and *tension* are typical examples of abstract nouns.

Business writing is most effective when concrete words predominate. It is clearer to write *We need 16-pound copy paper* than to write *We need office supplies.* Chapter 4 provides practice in developing skill in the use of concrete words.

1.03 Proper and Common. Proper nouns name specific persons, places, or things and are always capitalized *(General Electric, Baltimore, Jennifer*). All other nouns are common nouns and begin with lowercase letters *(company, city, student*). Rules for capitalization are presented in Sections 3.01–3.16.

1.04 Singular and Plural. Singular nouns name one item; plural nouns name more than one. From a practical view, writers seldom have difficulty with singular nouns. They may need help, however, with the formation and spelling of plural nouns.

1.05 Guidelines for Forming Noun Plurals

a. Add *s* to most nouns *(chair, chairs; mortgage, mortgages; Monday, Mondays*).

b. Add *es* to nouns ending in *s, x, z, ch,* or *sh (bench, benches; boss, bosses; box, boxes; Lopez, Lopezes*).

c. Change the spelling in irregular noun plurals *(man, men; foot, feet; mouse, mice; child, children*).

d. Add *s* to nouns that end in *y* when *y* is preceded by a vowel *(attorney, attorneys; valley, valleys; journey, journeys)*.

e. Drop the *y* and add *ies* to nouns ending in *y* when *y* is preceded by a consonant *(company, companies; city, cities; secretary, secretaries)*.

f. Add *s* to the principal word in most compound expressions *(editors in chief, fathers-in-law, bills of lading, runners-up)*.

g. Add *s* to most numerals, letters of the alphabet, words referred to as words, degrees, and abbreviations (*5s, 2000s, Bs, ands, CPAs, qts.*).

h. Add *'s* only to clarify letters of the alphabet that might be misread, such as *A's, I's, M's,* and *U's* and *i's, p's,* and *q's.* An expression like *c.o.d.s* requires no apostrophe because it would not easily be misread.

1.06 Collective Nouns. Nouns such as *staff, faculty, committee, group,* and *herd* refer to a collection of people, animals, or objects. Collective nouns may be considered singular or plural depending on their action. See Section 1.10i for a discussion of collective nouns and their agreement with verbs.

Review Exercise A—Nouns

In the space provided for each item, write *a* or *b* to complete the following statements accurately. When you finish, compare your responses with those provided. Answers are provided for odd-numbered items. Your instructor has the remaining answers. For each item on which you need review, consult the numbered principle shown in parentheses.

1. Two of the contest (a) *runner-ups,* (b) *runners-up* protested the judges' choice. ________
2. Several (a) *attorneys,* (b) *attornies* worked on the case together. ________
3. Please write to the (a) *Davis's,* (b) *Davises* about the missing contract. ________
4. The industrial complex has space for nine additional (a) *companys,* (b) *companies.* ________
5. That accounting firm employs two (a) *secretaries,* (b) *secretarys* for five CPAs. ________
6. Four of the wooden (a) *benches,* (b) *benchs* must be repaired. ________
7. The home was constructed with numerous (a) *chimneys,* (b) *chimnies.* ________
8. Tours of the production facility are made only on (a) *Tuesdays,* (b) *Tuesday's.* ________
9. We asked the (a) *Lopez's,* (b) *Lopezes* to contribute to the fund-raising drive. ________
10. Both my (a) *sister-in-laws,* (b) *sisters-in-law* agreed to the settlement. ________
11. The stock market is experiencing abnormal (a) *ups and downs,* (b) *up's and down's.* ________
12. Three (a) *mouses,* (b) *mice* were seen near the trash cans. ________
13. This office is unusually quiet on (a) *Sundays,* (b) *Sunday's.* ________
14. Several news (a) *dispatchs,* (b) *dispatches* were released during the strike. ________
15. Two major (a) *countries,* (b) *countrys* will participate in arms negotiations. ________
16. Some young children have difficulty writing their (a) *bs* and *ds,* (b) *b's* and *d's.* ________
17. The (a) *board of directors,* (b) *boards of directors* of all the major companies participated in the surveys. ________
18. In their letter the (a) *Metzes,* (b) *Metzs* said they intended to purchase the property. ________
19. In shipping we are careful to include all (a) *bill of sales,* (b) *bills of sale.* ________
20. Over the holidays many (a) *turkies,* (b) *turkeys* were consumed. ________

---

1. b (1.05f) 3. b (1.05b) 5. a (1.05e) 7. a (1.05d) 9. b (1.05b) 11. a (1.05g) 13. a (1.05a) 15. a (1.05e) 17. b (1.05f) 19. b (1.05f) (Only odd-numbered answers are provided. Consult your instructor for the others.)

Pronouns (1.07–1.09)

Pronouns substitute for nouns. They are classified by case.

1.07 Case. Pronouns function in three cases, as shown in the following chart.

Nominative Case *(Used for subjects of verbs and subject complements)*	**Objective Case** *(Used for objects of prepositions and objects of verbs)*	**Possessive Case** *(Used to show possession)*
I	me	my, mine
we	us	our, ours
you	you	your, yours
he	him	his
She	her	her, hers
it	it	its
they	them	their, theirs
who, whoever	whom, whomever	whose

1.08 Guidelines for Selecting Pronoun Case

a. Pronouns that serve as subjects of verbs must be in the nominative case:

> *He* and *I* (not *Him* and *me*) decided to apply for the jobs.

b. Pronouns that follow linking verbs (such as *am, is, are, was, were, be, being, been*) and rename the words to which they refer must be in the nominative case.

> It must have been *she* (not *her*) who placed the order. (The nominative-case pronoun *she* follows the linking verb *been* and renames *it.*)
>
> If it was *he* (not *him*) who called, I have his number. (The nominative-case pronoun *he* follows the linking verb *was* and renames *it.*)

c. Pronouns that serve as objects of verbs or objects of prepositions must be in the objective case:

> Mr. Andrews asked *them* to complete the proposal. (The pronoun *them* is the object of the verb *asked.*)
>
> All computer printouts are sent to *him.* (The pronoun *him* is the object of the preposition *to.*)
>
> Just between you and *me,* profits are falling. (The pronoun *me* is one of the objects of the preposition *between.*)

d. Pronouns that show ownership must be in the possessive case. Possessive pronouns (such as *hers, yours, ours, theirs,* and *its*) require no apostrophes:

> I bought a cheap cell phone, but *yours* (not *your's*) is expensive.
>
> All parts of the machine, including *its* (not *it's*) motor, were examined.
>
> The house and *its* (not *it's*) contents will be auctioned.
>
> Don't confuse possessive pronouns and contractions. Contractions are shortened forms of subject–verb phrases (such as *it's* for *it is, there's* for *there is,* and *they're* for *they are*).

e. When a pronoun appears in combination with a noun or another pronoun, ignore the extra noun or pronoun and its conjunction. In this way pronoun case becomes more obvious:

> The manager promoted Jeff and *me* (not I). (Ignore *Jeff and.*)

f. In statements of comparison, mentally finish the comparative by adding the implied missing words:

 Next year I hope to earn as much as *she.* (The verb *earns* is implied here: . . . *as much as she earns.*)

g. Pronouns must be in the same case as the words they replace or rename. When pronouns are used with appositives, ignore the appositive:

 A new contract was signed by *us* (not *we*) employees. (Temporarily ignore the appositive *employees* in selecting the pronoun.)

 We (not us) citizens have formed our own organization. (Temporarily ignore the appositive *citizens* in selecting the pronoun.)

h. Pronouns ending in *self* should be used only when they refer to previously mentioned nouns or pronouns:

 The CEO *himself* answered the telephone.

 Robert and *I* (not *myself*) are in charge of the campaign.

i. Use objective-case pronouns as objects of the prepositions *between, but, like* and *except:*

 Everyone but John and *him* (not *he*) qualified for the bonus.

 Employees like Miss Gillis and *her* (not *she*) are hard to replace.

j. Use *who* or *whoever* for nominative-case constructions and *whom* or *whomever* for objective-case constructions. In making the correct choice, it's sometimes helpful to substitute *he* for *who* or *whoever* and *him* for *whom* or *whomever:*

 For *whom* was this book ordered? *(This book was ordered for him/whom?)*

 Who did you say would drop by? *(Who/He … would drop by?)*

 Deliver the package to *whoever* opens the door. (In this sentence the clause *whoever opens the door* functions as the object of the preposition *to.* Within the clause itself, *whoever* is the subject of the verb *opens.* Again, substitution of *he* might be helpful: *He/Whoever opens the door.*)

1.09 Guidelines for Making Pronouns Agree With Their Antecedents. Pronouns must agree with the words to which they refer (their antecedents) in gender and in number.

a. Use masculine pronouns to refer to masculine antecedents, feminine pronouns to refer to feminine antecedents, and neuter pronouns to refer to antecedents without gender:

 The man opened *his* office door. (Masculine gender applies.)

 A woman sat at *her* desk. (Feminine gender applies.)

 This computer and *its* programs fit our needs. (Neuter gender applies.)

b. Use singular pronouns to refer to singular antecedents:

 Common-gender pronouns (such as *him* or *his*) traditionally have been used when the gender of the antecedent is unknown. Sensitive writers today, however, prefer to recast such constructions to avoid gender-biased pronouns. Study these examples for bias-free pronouns. See Chapter 2 for additional discussion of bias-free language.

Each student must submit *a* report on Monday.

All students must submit *their* reports on Monday.

Each student must submit *his or her* report on Monday. (This alternative is least acceptable since it is wordy and calls attention to itself.)

c. Use singular pronouns to refer to singular indefinite subjects and plural pronouns for plural indefinite subjects. Words such as *anyone, something,* and *anybody* are considered indefinite because they refer to no specific person or object. Some indefinite pronouns are always singular; others are always plural.

Always Singular			Always Plural
anybody	either	nobody	both
anyone	everyone	no one	few
anything	everything	somebody	many
each	neither	someone	several

Somebody in the group of touring women left *her* (not *their*) purse in the museum.

Either of the companies has the right to exercise *its* (not *their*) option to sell stock.

d. Use singular pronouns to refer to collective nouns and organization names:

The engineering staff is moving *its* (not *their*) facilities on Friday. (The singular pronoun *its* agrees with the collective noun *staff* because the members of *staff* function as a single unit.)

Jones, Cohen, & Chavez, Inc., *has* (not *have*) canceled *its* (not *their*) contract with us. (The singular pronoun *its* agrees with *Jones, Cohen, & Chavez, Inc.,* because the members of the organization are operating as a single unit.)

e. Use a plural pronoun to refer to two antecedents joined by *and,* whether the antecedents are singular or plural:

Our company president and our vice president will be submitting *their* expenses shortly.

f. Ignore intervening phrases—introduced by expressions such as *together with, as well as,* and *in addition to*—that separate a pronoun from its antecedent:

One of our managers, along with several salespeople, is planning *his* retirement. (If you wish to emphasize both subjects equally, join them with *and:* One of our managers *and* several salespeople are planning *their* retirements.)

g. When antecedents are joined by *or* or *nor,* make the pronoun agree with the antecedent closest to it.

Neither Jackie nor Kim wanted *her* (not *their*) desk moved.

Review Exercise B—Pronouns

In the space provided for each item, write *a, b,* or *c* to complete the statement accurately. When you finish, compare your responses with those provided. For each item on which you need review, consult the numbered principle shown in parentheses.

______ 1. Send e-mail copies of the policy to the manager or (a) *me,* (b) *myself.*

______ 2. James promised that he would call; was it (a) *him,* (b) *he* who left the message?

______ 3. Much preparation for the seminar was made by Mrs. Washington and (a) *I,* (b) *me* before the brochures were sent out.

______ 4. The Employee Benefits Committee can be justly proud of (a) *its,* (b) *their* achievements.

5. A number of inquiries were addressed to Jeff and (a) *I,* (b) *me,* (c) *myself.*
6. (a) *Who,* (b) *Whom* did you say the letter was addressed to?
7. When you visit Franking Savings Bank, inquire about (a) *its,* (b) *their* certificates.
8. All e-mail messages for Taylor and (a) *I,* (b) *me,* (c) *myself* will become part of the lawsuit.
9. Apparently one of the female applicants forgot to sign (a) *her,* (b) *their* application.
10. Both the printer and (a) *it's,* (b) *its* cover are missing.
11. I've never known any man who could work as fast as (a) *him,* (b) *he.*
12. Just between you and (a) *I,* (b) *me,* the stock price will fall by afternoon.
13. Give the supplies to (a) *whoever,* (b) *whomever* ordered them.
14. (a) *Us,* (b) *We* employees have been given an unusual voice in choosing benefits.
15. When he finally found a job, Dante, along with many other recent graduates, described (a) *his,* (b) *their* experience in an employment blog.
16. Either James or Robert must submit (a) *his,* (b) *their* report next week.
17. Any woman who becomes a charter member of this organization will be able to have (a) *her,* (b) *their* name inscribed on a commemorative plaque.
18. We are certain that (a) *our's,* (b) *ours* is the smallest camera phone available.
19. Everyone has completed the reports except Debbie and (a) *he,* (b) *him.*
20. Lack of work disturbs Mr. Thomas as much as (a) *I,* (b) *me.*

---

1. a (1.08h) 3. b (1.08c) 5. b (1.08c, 1.08e) 7. a (1.09d) 9. a (1.09b) 11. b (1.08f) 13. a (1.08j) 15. a (1.09f) 17. a (1.09b) 19. b (1.08i)

Cumulative Editing Quiz 1

Use proofreading marks (see Appendix B) to correct errors in the following sentences. All errors must be corrected to receive credit for the sentence. Check with your instructor for the answers.

Example: Max and ~~her~~ *she* started ~~there~~ *their* own company in early 2000's.

1. Neither the citys nor the countys would take responsibility for there budget overruns.
2. Can we keep this matter just between you and I?
3. Only a few attornies still have private secretarys.
4. Our staff committee gave their recommendation to the president and I as soon as they finished deliberating.
5. Theres really no excuse for we citizens to have no voice in the matter.
6. The manager and myself will deliver supplies to whomever ordered them.
7. Many basketball and football star's earn huge salarys.
8. Are you sure that this apartment is their's?
9. Each student must submit their report on Monday.
10. Both the network administrator and myself are concerned about the increase in personal Web use and it's tendency to slow productivity.

Verbs (1.10-1.15)

Verbs show the action of a subject or join the subject to words that describe it.

1.10 Guidelines for Agreement With Subjects. One of the most troublesome areas in English is subject–verb agreement. Consider the following guidelines for making verbs agree with subjects.

a. A singular subject requires a singular verb:

The stock market *opens* at 10 a.m. (The singular verb *opens* agrees with the singular subject *market.*)

He *doesn't* (not *don't*) work on Saturday.

b. A plural subject requires a plural verb:

On the packing slip several items *seem* (not *seems*) to be missing.

c. A verb agrees with its subject regardless of prepositional phrases that may intervene:

This list of management objectives *is* extensive. (The singular verb *is* agrees with the singular subject *list.*)

Every one of the letters *shows* (not *show*) proper form.

d. A verb agrees with its subject regardless of intervening phrases introduced by *as well as, in addition to, such as, including, together with,* and similar expressions:

An important memo, together with several contracts, *is* missing. (The singular verb *is* agrees with the singular subject *memo.*)

The president as well as several other top-level executives *approves* of our proposal. (The singular verb *approves* agrees with the subject *president.*)

e. A verb agrees with its subject regardless of the location of the subject:

Here *is* one of the contracts about which you asked. (The verb *is* agrees with its subject *one,* even though it precedes *one.* The adverb *here* cannot function as a subject.)

There *are* many problems yet to be resolved. (The verb *are* agrees with the subject *problems.* The word *there* does not function as a subject.)

In the next office *are* several printers. (In this inverted sentence, the verb *are* must agree with the subject *printers.*)

f. Subjects joined by *and* require a plural verb:

Analyzing the reader and organizing a strategy *are* the first steps in message writing. (The plural verb *are* agrees with the two subjects, *analyzing* and *organizing.*)

The tone and the wording of the message *were* persuasive. (The plural verb *were* agrees with the two subjects, *tone* and *wording.*)

g. Subjects joined by *or* or *nor* may require singular or plural verbs. Make the verb agree with the closer subject:

Neither the memo nor the report *is* ready. (The singular verb *is* agrees with *report,* the closer of the two subjects.)

h. The following indefinite pronouns are singular and require singular verbs: *anyone, anybody, anything, each, either, every, everyone, everybody, everything, many a, neither, nobody, nothing, someone, somebody,* and *something:*

Either of the alternatives that you present *is* acceptable. (The verb *is* agrees with the singular subject *either.*)

i. Collective nouns may take singular or plural verbs, depending on whether the members of the group are operating as a unit or individually:

Our management team *is* united in its goal.

The faculty *are* sharply divided on the tuition issue. (Although acceptable, this sentence sounds better recast: The faculty *members* are sharply divided on the tuition issue.)

j. Organization names and titles of publications, although they may appear to be plural, are singular and require singular verbs.

Clark, Anderson, and Horne, Inc., *has* (not *have*) hired a marketing consultant.

Thousands of Investment Tips is (not *are*) again on the best-seller list.

1.11 Voice. Voice is that property of verbs that shows whether the subject of the verb acts or is acted upon. Active-voice verbs direct action from the subject toward the object of the verb. Passive-voice verbs direct action toward the subject.

Active voice: Our employees *send* many e-mail messages.
Passive voice: Many e-mail messages *are sent* by our employees.

Business writers generally prefer active-voice verbs because they are specific and forceful. However, passive-voice constructions can help a writer be tactful. Chapter 3 presents strategies for effective use of active- and passive-voice verbs.

1.12 Mood. Three verb moods express the attitude or thought of the speaker or writer toward a subject: (a) the indicative mood expresses a fact; (b) the imperative mood expresses a command; and (c) the subjunctive mood expresses a doubt, a conjecture, or a suggestion.

Indicative: I *am looking* for a job.
Imperative: *Begin* your job search with the want ads.
Subjunctive: I wish I *were* working.

Only the subjunctive mood creates problems for most speakers and writers. The most common use of subjunctive mood occurs in clauses including *if* or *wish.* In such clauses substitute the subjunctive verb *were* for the indicative verb *was:*

If he *were* (not *was*) in my position, he would understand.

Mr. Simon acts as if he *were* (not *was*) the boss.

We wish we *were* (not *was*) able to ship your order.

The subjunctive mood can maintain goodwill while conveying negative information. The sentence *We wish we were able to ship your order* sounds more pleasing to a customer than *We cannot ship your order*. However, for all practical purposes, both sentences convey the same negative message.

1.13 Tense. Verbs show the time of an action by their tense. Speakers and writers can use six tenses to show the time of sentence action; for example:

Present tense: I *work;* he *works.*
Past tense: I *worked;* she *worked.*
Future tense: I *will work;* he *will work.*
Present perfect tense: I *have worked;* he *has worked.*
Past perfect tense: I *had worked;* she *had worked.*
Future perfect tense: I *will have worked;* he *will have worked.*

1.14 Guidelines for Verb Tense

a. Use present tense for statements that, although introduced by past-tense verbs, continue to be true:

What did you say his name *is*? (Use the present tense *is* if his name has not changed.)

b. Avoid unnecessary shifts in verb tenses:

The manager *saw* (not *sees*) a great deal of work yet to be completed and *remained* to do it herself.

Although unnecessary shifts in verb tense are to be avoided, not all the verbs within one sentence have to be in the same tense; for example:

She *said* (past tense) that she *likes* (present tense) to work late.

1.15 Irregular Verbs. Irregular verbs cause difficulty for some writers and speakers. Unlike regular verbs, irregular verbs do not form the past tense and past participle by adding *-ed* to the present form. Here is a partial list of selected troublesome irregular verbs. Consult a dictionary if you are in doubt about a verb form.

Troublesome Irregular Verbs

Present	**Past**	**Past Participle** *(always use helping verbs)*
begin	began	begun
break	broke	broken
choose	chose	chosen
come	came	come
drink	drank	drunk
go	went	gone
lay (to place)	laid	laid
lie (to rest)	lay	lain
ring	rang	rung
see	saw	seen
write	wrote	written

a. Use only past-tense verbs to express past tense. Notice that no helping verbs are used to indicate simple past tense:

The auditors *went* (not *have went*) over our books carefully.

He *came* (not *come*) to see us yesterday.

b. Use past-participle forms for actions completed before the present time. Notice that past-participle forms require helping verbs:

Steve *had gone* (not *had went*) before we called. (The past-participle *gone* is used with the helping verb *had.*)

c. Avoid inconsistent shifts in subject, voice, and mood. Pay particular attention to this problem area because undesirable shifts are often characteristic of student writing.

Inconsistent: When Mrs. Taswell read the report, the error was found. (The first clause is in the active voice; the second, passive.)

Improved: When Mrs. Taswell read the report, she found the error. (Both clauses are in the active voice.)

Inconsistent: The clerk should first conduct an inventory. Then supplies should be requisitioned. (The first sentence is in the active voice; the second, passive.)

Improved: The clerk should first conduct an inventory. Then he or she should requisition supplies. (Both sentences are in the active voice.)

Inconsistent:	All workers must wear security badges, and you must also sign a daily time card. (This sentence contains an inconsistent shift in subject from *all workers* in the first clause to *you* in the second clause.)
Improved:	All workers must wear security badges, and they must also sign a daily time card.
Inconsistent:	Begin the transaction by opening an account; then you enter the customer's name. (This sentence contains an inconsistent shift from the imperative mood in the first clause to the indicative mood in the second clause.)
Improved:	Begin the transaction by opening an account; then enter the customer's name. (Both clauses are now in the imperative mood.)

Review Exercise C—Verbs

In the space provided for each item, write *a* or *b* to complete the statement accurately. When you finish, compare your responses with those provided. For each item on which you need review, consult the numbered principle shown in parentheses.

1. Our directory of customer names and addresses (a) *was* (b) *were* out-of-date. ________
2. There (a) *is,* (b) *are* a customer-service engineer and two salespeople waiting to see you. ________
3. Improved communication technologies and increased global competition (a) *is,* (b) *are* changing the world of business. ________
4. Crews, Meliotes, and Bove, Inc., (a) *has,* (b) *have* opened an office in Boston. ________
5. Yesterday Mrs. Phillips (a) *choose,* (b) *chose* a new office on the second floor. ________
6. The man who called said that his name (a) *is,* (b) *was* Hernandez. ________
7. Our management team and our attorney (a) *is,* (b) *are* researching the privacy issue. ________
8. Either of the flight times (a) *appears,* (b) *appear* to fit my proposed itinerary. ________
9. If you had (a) *saw,* (b) *seen* the rough draft, you would better appreciate the final copy. ________
10. Across from our office (a) *is,* (b) *are* the parking structure and the information office. ________
11. Although we have (a) *began,* (b) *begun* to replace outmoded equipment, the pace is slow. ________
12. Specific training as well as ample experience (a) *is,* (b) *are* important for that position. ________
13. Changing attitudes and increased job opportunities (a) *is,* (b) *are* resulting in increased numbers of working women. ________
14. Neither the organizing nor the staffing of the program (a) *has been,* (b) *have been* completed. ________
15. If I (a) *was,* (b) *were* you, I would ask for a raise. ________
16. If you had (a) *wrote,* (b) *written* last week, we could have sent a brochure. ________
17. The hydraulic equipment that you ordered (a) *is,* (b) *are* packed and will be shipped Friday. ________
18. One of the reasons that sales have declined in recent years (a) *is,* (b) *are* lack of effective online advertising. ________
19. Either of the proposed laws (a) *is,* (b) *are* going to affect our business negatively. ________
20. Merger statutes (a) *requires,* (b) *require* that a failing company accept bids from several companies before merging with one. ________

---

1. a (1.10c) 3. b (1.10f) 5. b (1.15a) 7. b (1.10f) 9. b (1.15b) 11. b (1.15b) 13. b (1.10f) 15. b (1.12) 17. a (1.10a) 19. a (1.10h)

Review Exercise D—Verbs

In the following sentence pairs, choose the one that illustrates consistency in use of subject, voice, and mood. Write *a* or *b* in the space provided. When you finish, compare your responses with those provided. For each item on which you need review, consult the numbered principle shown in parentheses.

______ 1. (a) You need more than a knowledge of technology; one also must be able to interact well with people.
(b) You need more than a knowledge of technology; you also must be able to interact well with people.

______ 2. (a) Tim and Jon were eager to continue, but Bob wanted to quit.
(b) Tim and Jon were eager to continue, but Bob wants to quit.

______ 3. (a) The salesperson should consult the price list; then you can give an accurate quote to a customer.
(b) The salesperson should consult the price list; then he or she can give an accurate quote to a customer.

______ 4. (a) Read all the instructions first; then you install the printer program.
(b) Read all the instructions first, and then install the printer program.

______ 5. (a) She was an enthusiastic manager who always had a smile for everyone.
(b) She was an enthusiastic manager who always has a smile for everyone.

---

1. b (1.15c) 3. b (1.15c) 5. a (1.14b)

Cumulative Editing Quiz 2

Use proofreading mark (see Appendix B) to correct errors in the following sentences. All errors must be corrected to receive credit for the sentence. Check with your instructor for the answers.

1. The production cost and the markup of each item is important in calculating the sale price.
2. Sheila acts as if she was the manager, but we know she is not.
3. The committee are reconsidering their decision in view of recent health care legislation.
4. My all-in-one computer and it's lightweight keyboard is attractive but difficult to use.
5. Waiting in the outer office is a job applicant and a sales representative who you told to stop by.
6. Each applicant could have submitted his application online if he had went to our Web site.
7. One of the reasons she applied are that she seen the salarys posted at our Web site.
8. Either of the options that you may chose are acceptable to Jake and myself.
9. Although there anger and frustration is understandable, both editor in chiefs decided to apologize and reprint the article.
10. The Lopez'es, about who the article was written, accepted the apology graciously.

Adjectives and Adverbs (1.16–1.17)

Adjectives describe or limit nouns and pronouns. They often answer the questions *what kind? how many?* or *which one?* Adverbs describe or limit verbs, adjectives, or other adverbs. They often answer the questions *when? how? where?* or *to what extent?*

1.16 Forms. Most adjectives and adverbs have three forms, or degrees: positive, comparative, and superlative.

	Positive	Comparative	Superlative
Adjective:	clear	clearer	clearest
Adverb:	clearly	more clearly	most clearly

Some adjectives and adverbs have irregular forms.

	Positive	Comparative	Superlative
Adjective:	good	better	best
	bad	worse	worst
Adverb:	well	better	best

Adjectives and adverbs composed of two or more syllables are usually compared by the use of *more* and *most;* for example:

The Payroll Department is *more efficient* than the Shipping Department.

Payroll is the *most efficient* department in our organization.

1.17 Guidelines for Use

a. Use the comparative degree of the adjective or adverb to compare two persons or things; use the superlative degree to compare three or more:

Of the two plans, which is *better* (not *best*)?

Of all the plans, we like this one *best* (not *better*).

b. Do not create a double comparative or superlative by using *-er* with *more* or *-est* with *most:*

His explanation couldn't have been *clearer* (not *more clearer*).

c. A linking verb (*is, are, look, seem, feel, sound, appear,* and so forth) may introduce a word that describes the verb's subject. In this case be certain to use an adjective, not an adverb:

The characters on the monitor look *bright* (not *brightly*). (Use the adjective *bright* because it follows the linking verb *look* and modifies the noun *characters.*)

The company's letter made the customer feel *bad* (not *badly*). (The adjective *bad* follows the linking verb *feel* and describes the noun *customer.*)

d. Use adverbs, not adjectives, to describe or limit the action of verbs:

The business is running *smoothly* (not *smooth*). (Use the adverb *smoothly* to describe the action of the verb *is running. Smoothly* tells how the business is running.)

Don't take his remark *personally* (not *personal*). (The adverb *personally* describes the action of the verb *take.*)

Serena said she did *well* (not *good*) on the test. (Use the adverb *well* to tell how she did.)

e. Two or more adjectives that are joined to create a compound modifier before a noun should be hyphenated:

The *four-year-old* child was tired.

Our agency is planning a *coast-to-coast* campaign.

Hyphenate a compound modifier following a noun only if your dictionary shows the hyphen(s):

Our speaker is very *well-known.* (Include the hyphen because most dictionaries do.)

The tired child was four years old. (Omit the hyphens because the expression follows the word it describes, *child,* and because dictionaries do not indicate hyphens.)

f. Keep adjectives and adverbs close to the words they modify:

She asked for *a cup of hot coffee* (not *a hot cup of coffee*).

Patty *had only two days* of vacation left (not *only had two days*).

Students may sit in the *first five rows* (not *in five first rows*).

He *has saved almost* enough money for the trip (not *has almost saved*).

g. Don't confuse *there* with the possessive pronoun *their* or the contraction *they're:*

Put the documents *there.* (The adverb *there* means "at that place or at that point.")

There are two reasons for the change. (The pronoun *there* is used as function word to introduce a sentence or a clause.)

We already have *their* specifications. (The possessive pronoun *their* shows ownership.)

They're coming to inspect today. (The contraction *they're* is a shortened form of *they are.*)

Review Exercise E—Adjectives and Adverbs

In the space provided for each item, write *a, b,* or *c* to complete the statement accurately. If two sentences are shown, select *a* or *b* to indicate the one expressed more effectively. When you finish, compare your responses with those provided. For each item on which you need review, consult the numbered principle shown in parentheses.

1. After the interview, Tim looked (a) *calm,* (b) *calmly.*
2. If you had been more (a) *careful,* (b) *carefuler,* the box might not have broken.
3. Because we appointed a new manager, the advertising campaign is running (a) *smooth,* (b) *smoothly.*
4. To avoid a (a) *face to face,* (b) *face-to-face* confrontation, she sent an e-mail.
5. Darren completed the employment test (a) *satisfactorily,* (b) *satisfactory.*
6. I felt (a) *bad,* (b) *badly* that he was not promoted.
7. Which is the (a) *more,* (b) *most* dependable of the two cars?
8. Can you determine exactly what (a) *there,* (b) *their,* (c) *they're* company wants us to do?
9. Of all the copiers we tested, this one is the (a) *easier,* (b) *easiest* to operate.
10. (a) Mr. Aldron almost was ready to accept the offer.

    (b) Mr. Aldron was almost ready to accept the offer.
11. (a) We only thought that it would take two hours for the test.

    (b) We thought that it would take only two hours for the test.
12. (a) Please bring me a glass of cold water.

    (b) Please bring me a cold glass of water.
13. (a) The committee decided to retain the last ten tickets.

    (b) The committee decided to retain the ten last tickets.
14. New owners will receive a (a) *60-day,* (b) *60 day* trial period.
15. The time passed (a) *quicker,* (b) *more quickly* than we expected.
16. We offer a (a) *money back,* (b) *money-back* guarantee.
17. Today the financial news is (a) *worse,* (b) *worst* than yesterday.

18. Please don't take his comments (a) *personal,* (b) *personally.*
19. You must check the document (a) *page by page,* (b) *page-by-page.*
20. (a) We try to file only necessary paperwork.
    (b) We only try to file necessary paperwork.

---

1. a (1.17c) 3. b (1.17d) 5. a (1.17d) 7. a (1.17a) 9. b (1.17a) 11. b (1.17f) 13. a (1.17f) 15. b (1.17d) 17. a (1.17a) 19. a (1.17e)

Prepositions (1.18)

Prepositions are connecting words that join nouns or pronouns to other words in a sentence. The words *about, at, from, in,* and *to* are examples of prepositions.

1.18 Guidelines for Use

a. Include necessary prepositions:

What type *of* software do you need (not *what type software*)?

I graduated *from* high school two years ago (not *I graduated high school*).

b. Omit unnecessary prepositions:

Where is the meeting? (Not *Where is the meeting at?*)
Both printers work well. (Not *Both of the printers.*)
Where are you going? (Not *Where are you going to?*)

c. Avoid the overuse of prepositional phrases.

Weak: We have received your application for credit at our branch in the Fresno area.
Improved: We have received your Fresno credit application.

d. Repeat the preposition before the second of two related elements:

Applicants use the résumé effectively by summarizing their most important experiences and *by* relating their education to the jobs sought.

e. Include the second preposition when two prepositions modify a single object:

George's appreciation *of* and aptitude *for* computers led to a promising career.

Conjunctions (1.19)

Conjunctions connect words, phrases, and clauses. They act as signals, indicating when a thought is being added, contrasted, or altered. Coordinate conjunctions (such as *and, or, but*) and other words that act as connectors (such as *however, therefore, when, as*) tell the reader or listener in what direction a thought is heading. They are like road signs signaling what's ahead.

1.19 Guidelines for Use

a. Use coordinating conjunctions to connect only sentence elements that are parallel or balanced.

Weak: His report was correct and written in a concise manner.
Improved: His report was correct and concise.

Weak: Management has the capacity to increase fraud, or reduction can be achieved through the policies it adopts.
Improved: Management has the capacity to increase or reduce fraud through the policies it adopts.

b. Do not use the word *like* as a conjunction:

It seems *as if* (not *like*) this day will never end.

c. Avoid using *when* or *where* inappropriately. A common writing fault occurs in sentences with clauses introduced by *is when* and *is where.* Written English ordinarily requires a noun (or a group of words functioning as a noun) following the linking verb *is.* Instead of acting as conjunctions in these constructions, the words *where* and *when* function as adverbs, creating faulty grammatical equations (adverbs cannot complete equations set up by linking verbs). To avoid the problem, revise the sentence, eliminating *is when* or *is where.*

Weak: A bullish market is when prices are rising in the stock market.
Improved: A bullish market is created when prices are rising in the stock market.

Weak: A flowchart is when you make a diagram showing the step-by-step progression of a procedure.
Improved: A flowchart is a diagram showing the step-by-step progression of a procedure.

Weak: A podcast is where a prerecorded audio program posted to a Web site.
Improved: A podcast is a prerecorded audio program posted to a Web site.

A similar faulty construction occurs in the expression *I hate when.* English requires nouns, noun clauses, or pronouns to act as objects of verbs, not adverbs.

Weak: I hate when we're asked to work overtime.
Improved: I hate it when we're asked to work overtime.
Improved: I hate being asked to work overtime.

d. Don't confuse the adverb *then* with the conjunction *than. Then* means "at that time"; *than* indicates the second element in a comparison:

We would rather remodel *than* (not *then*) move.

First, the equipment is turned on; *then* (not *than*) the program is loaded.

Review Exercise F—Prepositions and Conjunctions

In the space provided for each item, write *a* or *b* to indicate the sentence that is expressed more effectively. When you finish, compare your responses with those provided. For each item on which you need review, consult the numbered principle shown in parentheses.

1. (a) The chief forgot to tell everyone where today's meeting is.
   (b) The chief forgot to tell everyone where today's meeting is at.
2. (a) She was not aware of nor interested in the company insurance plan.
   (b) She was not aware nor interested in the company insurance plan.
3. (a) Mr. Samuels graduated college last June.
   (b) Mr. Samuels graduated from college last June.
4. (a) "Flextime" is when employees arrive and depart at varying times.
   (b) "Flextime" is a method of scheduling worktime in which employees arrive and depart at varying times.
5. (a) Both employees enjoyed setting their own hours.
   (b) Both of the employees enjoyed setting their own hours.
6. (a) I hate when my cell loses its charge.
   (b) I hate it when my cell loses its charge.
7. (a) What style of typeface should we use?
   (b) What style typeface should we use?
8. (a) Business letters should be concise, correct, and written clearly.
   (b) Business letters should be concise, correct, and clear.
9. (a) Mediation in a labor dispute occurs when a neutral person helps union and management reach an agreement.

(b) Mediation in a labor dispute is where a neutral person helps union and management reach an agreement.

10. (a) It looks as if the plant will open in early January. ____________

(b) It looks like the plant will open in early January.

11. (a) We expect to finish up the work soon. ____________

(b) We expect to finish the work soon.

12. (a) At the beginning of the program in the fall of the year at the central office, we experienced staffing difficulties. ____________

(b) When the program began last fall, the central office experienced staffing difficulties.

13. (a) Your client may respond by e-mail or a telephone call may be made. ____________

(b) Your client may respond by e-mail or by telephone.

14. (a) A résumé is when you make a written presentation of your education and experience for a prospective employer. ____________

(b) A résumé is a written presentation of your education and experience for a prospective employer.

15. (a) Stacy exhibited both an awareness of and talent for developing innovations. ____________

(b) Stacy exhibited both an awareness and talent for developing innovations.

16. (a) This course is harder then I expected. ____________

(b) This course is harder than I expected.

17. (a) An ombudsman is an individual hired by management to investigate and resolve employee complaints. ____________

(b) An ombudsman is when management hires an individual to investigate and resolve employee complaints.

18. (a) I'm uncertain where to take this document to. ____________

(b) I'm uncertain where to take this document.

19. (a) By including accurate data and by writing clearly, you will produce effective messages. ____________

(b) By including accurate data and writing clearly, you will produce effective messages.

20. (a) We need computer operators who can load software, monitor networks, and files must be duplicated. ____________

(b) We need computer operators who can load software, monitor networks, and duplicate files.

---

1. a (1.18b) 3. b (1.18a) 5. a (1.18b) 7. a (1.18a) 9. a (1.19c) 11. b (1.18b) 13. b (1.19a) 15. a (1.18e) 17. a (1.19c) 19. a (1.18d)

Cumulative Editing Quiz 3

Use proofreading marks (see Appendix B) to correct errors in the following sentences. All errors must be corrected to receive credit for the sentence. Check with your instructor for the answers.

1. Her new computer is definitely more faster then her previous computer.
2. Max said that he felt badly that he missed his appointment with you and myself.
3. Neither the managers nor the union are happy at how slow the talks are progressing.
4. Just between you and I, we have learned not to take the boss's criticism personal.

5. After completing a case by case search, the consultant promised to send his report to Carlos and I.
6. If you was me, which of the two job offers do you think is best?
7. Did your team members tell you where there meeting is at?
8. Jason felt that he had done good on the three hour certification exam.
9. It seems like our step by step instructions could have been more clearer.
10. I hate when I'm expected to finish up by myself.

Punctuation Review

Commas 1 (2.01–2.04)

2.01 Series. Commas are used to separate three or more equal elements (words, phrases, or short clauses) in a series. To ensure separation of the last two elements, careful writers always use a comma before the conjunction in a series:

> Business letters usually contain a dateline, address, salutation, body, and closing. (This series contains words.)
>
> The job of an ombudsman is to examine employee complaints, resolve disagreements between management and employees, and ensure fair treatment. (This series contains phrases.)
>
> Trainees complete basic keyboarding tasks, technicians revise complex documents, and editors proofread completed projects. (This series contains short clauses.)

2.02 Direct Address. Commas are used to set off the names of individuals being addressed:

> Your inquiry, *Mrs. Johnson,* has been referred to me.
>
> We genuinely hope that we may serve you, *Mr. Lee.*

2.03 Parenthetical Expressions. Skilled writers use parenthetical words, phrases, and clauses to guide the reader from one thought to the next. When these expressions interrupt the flow of a sentence and are unnecessary for its grammatical completeness, they should be set off with commas. Examples of commonly used parenthetical expressions follow:

all things considered	however	needless to say
as a matter of fact	in addition	nevertheless
as a result	incidentally	no doubt
as a rule	in fact	of course
at the same time	in my opinion	on the contrary
consequently	in the first place	on the other hand
for example	in the meantime	therefore
furthermore	moreover	under the circumstances

> *As a matter of fact,* I wrote to you just yesterday. (Phrase used at the beginning of a sentence.)
>
> We will, *in the meantime,* send you a replacement order. (Phrase used in the middle of a sentence.)
>
> Your satisfaction is our first concern, *needless to say.* (Phrase used at the end of a sentence.)

Do not use commas if the expression is necessary for the completeness of the sentence:

> Kimberly had *no doubt* that she would finish the report. (Omit commas because the expression is necessary for the completeness of the sentence.)

2.04 Dates, Addresses, and Geographical Items. When dates, addresses, and geographical items contain more than one element, the second and succeeding elements are normally set off by commas.

a. Dates:

> The conference was held February 2 at our home office. (No comma is needed for one element.)
>
> The conference was held February 2, 2012, at our home office. (Two commas set off the second element.)
>
> The conference was held Tuesday, February 2, 2012, at our home office. (Commas set off the second and third elements.)
>
> In February 2012 the conference was held. (This alternate style omitting commas is acceptable if only the month and year are written.)

b. Addresses:

> The letter addressed to Mr. Jim W. Ellman, 600 Via Novella, Agoura, CA 91306, should be sent today. (Commas are used between all elements except the state and zip code, which in this special instance act as a single unit.)

c. Geographical items:

> She moved from Toledo, Ohio, to Champaign, Illinois. (Commas set off the state unless it appears at the end of the sentence, in which case only one comma is used.)

In separating cities from states and days from years, many writers remember the initial comma but forget the final one, as in the examples that follow:

> The package from Austin, Texas{,} was lost.
>
> We opened June 1, 2007{,} and have grown steadily since.

Review Exercise G—Commas 1

Insert necessary commas in the following sentences. In the space provided, write the number of commas that you add. Write *C* if no commas are needed. When you finish, compare your responses with those provided. For each item on which you need review, consult the numbered principle shown in parentheses.

1. As a rule, we do not provide complimentary tickets. ____________
2. You may be certain Mr. Martinez that your policy will be issued immediately. ____________
3. I have no doubt that your calculations are correct. ____________
4. The safety hazard on the contrary can be greatly reduced if workers wear rubber gloves. ____________
5. Every accredited TV newscaster radio broadcaster and blogger had access to the media room. ____________
6. Deltech's main offices are located in Boulder Colorado and Seattle Washington. ____________
7. The employees who are eligible for promotions are Terry Evelyn Vicki Rosanna and Steve. ____________
8. During the warranty period of course you are protected from any parts or service charges. ____________

9. Many of our customers include architects engineers attorneys and others who are interested in database management programs.
10. I wonder Mrs. Stevens if you would send my letter of recommendation as soon as possible.
11. The new book explains how to choose appropriate legal protection for ideas trade secrets copyrights patents and restrictive covenants.
12. The factory is scheduled to be moved to 2250 North Main Street Ann Arbor Michigan 48107 within two years.
13. You may however prefer to correspond directly with the manufacturer in Hong Kong.
14. Are there any alternatives in addition to those that we have already considered?
15. The rally has been scheduled for Monday January 12 in the football stadium.
16. A check for the full amount will be sent directly to your home Mr. Jefferson.
17. Goodstone Tire & Rubber for example recalled 400,000 steelbelted radial tires because some tires failed their rigorous tests.
18. Kevin agreed to unlock the office open the mail and check all the equipment in my absence.
19. In the meantime thank you for whatever assistance you are able to furnish.
20. Research facilities were moved from Austin Texas to Santa Cruz California.

1. rule, (2.03) 3. C (2.03) 5. newscaster, radio broadcaster, (2.01) 7. Terry, Evelyn, Vicki, Rosanna, (2.01) 9. architects, engineers, attorneys, (2.01) 11. ideas, trade secrets, copyrights, patents, (2.01) 13. may, however, (2.03) 15. Monday, January 12, (2.04a) 17. Rubber, for example, (2.03) 19. meantime, (2.03)

Commas 2 (2.05–2.09)

2.05 Independent Clauses. An independent clause is a group of words that has a subject and a verb and that could stand as a complete sentence. When two such clauses are joined by *and, or, nor,* or *but,* use a comma before the conjunction:

> We can ship your merchandise July 12, but we must have your payment first.
>
> Net income before taxes is calculated, and this total is then combined with income from operations.

Notice that each independent clause in the preceding two examples could stand alone as a complete sentence. Do not use a comma unless each group of words is a complete thought (that is, has its own subject and verb).

> Our CPA calculates net income before taxes *and* then combines that figure with income from operations. (No comma is needed because no subject follows *and.*)

2.06 Dependent Clauses. Dependent clauses do not make sense by themselves; for their meaning they depend on independent clauses.

a. **Introductory clauses.** When a dependent clause precedes an independent clause, it is followed by a comma. Such clauses are often introduced by *when, if,* and *as:*

> *When your request came,* we responded immediately.
>
> *As I mentioned earlier,* Mrs. James is the manager.

b. **Terminal clauses.** If a dependent clause falls at the end of a sentence, use a comma only if the dependent clause is an afterthought:

We have rescheduled the meeting for October 23, *if this date meets with your approval.* (Comma used because dependent clause is an afterthought.)

We responded immediately *when we received your request.* (No comma is needed.)

c. **Essential versus nonessential clauses.** If a dependent clause provides information that is unneeded for the grammatical completeness of a sentence, use commas to set it off. In determining whether such a clause is essential or nonessential, ask yourself whether the reader needs the information contained in the clause to identify the word it explains:

Our district sales manager, *who just returned from a trip to the Southwest District,* prepared this report. (This construction assumes that there is only one district sales manager. Because the sales manager is clearly identified, the dependent clause is not essential and requires commas.)

The salesperson *who just returned from a trip to the Southwest District* prepared this report. (The dependent clause in this sentence is necessary to identify which salesperson prepared the report. Therefore, use no commas.)

The position of assistant sales manager, *which we discussed with you last week,* is still open. (Careful writers use *which* to introduce nonessential clauses. Commas are also necessary.)

The position *that we discussed with you last week* is still open. (Careful writers use *that* to introduce essential clauses. No commas are used.)

2.07 Phrases. A phrase is a group of related words that lacks both a subject and a verb. A phrase that precedes a main clause is followed by a comma if the phrase contains a verb form or has five or more words:

Beginning November 1, Worldwide Savings will offer two new combination checking/savings plans. (A comma follows this introductory phrase because the phrase contains the verb form *beginning.*)

To promote our plan, we will conduct an extensive social media advertising campaign. (A comma follows this introductory phrase because the phrase contains the verb form *to promote.*)

In a period of only one year, we were able to improve our market share by 30 percent. (A comma follows the introductory phrase—actually two prepositional phrases—because its total length exceeds five words.)

In 2012 our organization installed a multiuser system that could transfer programs easily. (No comma needed after the short introductory phrase.)

2.08 Two or More Adjectives. Use a comma to separate two or more adjectives that equally describe a noun. A good way to test the need for a comma is this: Mentally insert the word *and* between the adjectives. If the resulting phrase sounds natural, a comma is used to show the omission of *and:*

We're looking for a *versatile, error-free* operating system. (Use a comma to separate *versatile* and *error-free* because they independently describe *operating system. And* has been omitted.)

Our *experienced, courteous* staff is ready to serve you. (Use a comma to separate *experienced* and *courteous* because they independently describe *staff. And* has been omitted.)

It was difficult to refuse the *sincere young* telephone caller. (No commas are needed between *sincere* and *young* because *and* has not been omitted.)

2.09 Appositives. Words that rename or explain preceding nouns or pronouns are called *appositives.* An appositive that provides information not essential to the identification of the word it describes should be set off by commas:

> James Wilson, *the project director for Sperling's,* worked with our architect. (The appositive, *the project director for Sperling's,* adds nonessential information. Commas set it off.)

Review Exercise H—Commas 2

Insert only necessary commas in the following sentences. In the space provided, indicate the number of commas that you add for each sentence. If a sentence requires no commas, write *C.* When you finish, compare your responses with those provided. For each item on which you need review, consult the numbered principle shown in parentheses.

1. A corporation must register in the state in which it does business and it must operate within the laws of that state.
2. The manager made a point-by-point explanation of the distribution dilemma and then presented his plan to solve the problem.
3. If you will study the cost analysis you will see that our company offers the best system at the lowest price.
4. Molly Epperson who amassed the greatest number of sales points won a bonus trip to Hawaii.
5. The salesperson who amasses the greatest number of sales points will win a bonus trip to Hawaii.
6. To promote goodwill and to generate international trade we are opening offices in South Asia and in Europe.
7. On the basis of these findings I recommend that we retain Jane Rada as our counsel.
8. Scott Cook is a dedicated hardworking employee for our company.
9. The bright young student who worked for us last summer will be able to return this summer.
10. When you return the completed form we will be able to process your application.
11. We will be able to process your application when you return the completed form.
12. The employees who have been with us over ten years automatically receive additional insurance benefits.
13. Knowing that you wanted this merchandise immediately I took the liberty of sending it by FedEx.
14. The central processing unit requires no scheduled maintenance and has a self-test function for reliable performance.
15. A tax credit for energy-saving homes will expire at the end of the year but Congress might extend it if pressure groups prevail.
16. Stacy Wilson our newly promoted office manager has made a number of worthwhile suggestions.
17. For the benefit of employees recently hired we are offering a two-hour seminar regarding employee benefit programs.
18. Please bring your suggestions and those of Mr. Mason when you attend our meeting next month.
19. The meeting has been rescheduled for September 30 if this date meets with your approval.
20. Some of the problems that you outline in your recent memo could be rectified through more stringent purchasing procedures.

1. business, (2.05) 3. analysis, (2.06a) 5. C (2.06c) 7. findings, (2.07) 9. C (2.08) 11. C (2.06b) 13. immediately, (2.07) 15. year, (2.05) 17. hired, (2.07) 19. September 30, (2.06b)

Commas 3 (2.10–2.15)

2.10 Degrees and Abbreviations. Degrees following individuals' names are set off by commas. Abbreviations such as *Jr.* and *Sr.* are also set off by commas unless the individual referred to prefers to omit the commas:

Anne G. Turner, *MBA*, joined the firm.

Michael Migliano, *Jr.*, and Michael Migliano, *Sr.*, work as a team.

Anthony A. Gensler *Jr.* wrote the report. (The individual referred to prefers to omit commas.)

The abbreviations *Inc.* and *Ltd.* are set off by commas only if a company's legal name has a comma just before this kind of abbreviation. To determine a company's practice, consult its stationery or a directory listing:

Firestone and Blythe, *Inc.*, is based in Canada. (Notice that two commas are used.)

Computers *Inc.* is extending its franchise system. (The company's legal name does not include a comma before *Inc.*)

2.11 Omitted Words. A comma is used to show the omission of words that are understood:

On Monday we received 15 applications; on Friday, only 3. (Comma shows the omission of *we received.*)

2.12 Contrasting Statements. Commas are used to set off contrasting or opposing expressions. These expressions are often introduced by such words as *not, never, but,* and *yet:*

The president suggested cutbacks, *not* layoffs, to ease the crisis.

Our budget for the year is reduced, *yet* adequate.

The greater the effort, the greater the reward.

If increased emphasis is desired, use dashes instead of commas, as in *Only the sum of $100—not $1,000—was paid on this account.*

2.13 Clarity. Commas are used to separate words repeated for emphasis. Commas are also used to separate words that may be misread if not separated:

The building is a long, long way from completion.

Whatever is, is right.

No matter what, you know we support you.

2.14 Quotations and Appended Questions

a. A comma is used to separate a short quotation from the rest of a sentence. If the quotation is divided into two parts, two commas are used:

The manager asked, "Shouldn't the managers control the specialists?"

"Perhaps the specialists," replied Tim, "have unique information."

b. A comma is used to separate a question appended (added) to a statement:

You will confirm the shipment, won't you?

2.15 Comma Overuse. Do not use commas needlessly. For example, commas should not be inserted merely because you might drop your voice if you were speaking the sentence:

> One of the reasons for expanding our East Coast operations is{,} that we anticipate increased sales in that area. (Do not insert a needless comma before a clause.)
>
> I am looking for an article entitled{,} "State-of-the-Art Communications." (Do not insert a needless comma after the word *entitled.*)
>
> Customers may purchase many food and nonfood items in convenience stores *such as*{,} 7-Eleven and Stop-N-Go. (Do not insert a needless comma after *such as.*)
>
> We have{,} at this time{,} an adequate supply of parts. (Do not insert needless commas around prepositional phrases.)

Review Exercise I—Commas 3

Insert only necessary commas in the following sentences. Remove unnecessary commas with the delete sign ( ). In the space provided, indicate the number of commas inserted or deleted in each sentence. If a sentence requires no changes, write *C.* When you finish, compare your responses with those provided. For each item on which you need review, consult the numbered principle shown in parentheses.

1. We expected Anna Cortez not Tyler Rosen to conduct the audit.
2. Brian said "We simply must have a bigger budget to start this project."
3. "We simply must have" said Brian "a bigger budget to start this project."
4. In August customers opened at least 50 new accounts; in September only about 20.
5. You returned the merchandise last month didn't you?
6. In short employees will now be expected to contribute more to their own retirement funds.
7. The better our advertising and recruiting the stronger our personnel pool will be.
8. Mrs. Delgado investigated selling her stocks not her real estate to raise the necessary cash.
9. "On the contrary" said Mr. Stevens "we will continue our present marketing strategies."
10. Our company will expand into surprising new areas such as, women's apparel and fast foods.
11. What we need is more not fewer suggestions for improvement.
12. Randall Clark Esq. and Jonathon Georges MBA joined the firm.
13. "America is now entering" said President Saunders "the Age of Information."
14. One of the reasons that we are inquiring about the publisher of the software is, that we are concerned about whether that publisher will be in the market five years from now.
15. The talk by D. A. Spindler PhD was particularly difficult to follow because of his technical and abstract vocabulary.
16. The month before a similar disruption occurred in distribution.
17. We are very fortunate to have, at our disposal, the services of excellent professionals.
18. No matter what you can count on us for support.
19. Mrs. Sandoval was named legislative counsel; Mr. Freeman executive advisor.

20. The data you are seeking can be found in an article entitled, "The 100 Fastest Growing Games in Computers."

---

1. Cortez, Rosen, (2.12) 3. have," said Brian, (2.14a) 5. month, (2.14b) 7. recruiting, (2.12) 9. contrary," Stevens, (2.14a) 11. more, not fewer, (2.12) 13. entering," Saunders, (2.14a) 15. Spindler, PhD, (2.10) 17. have at our disposal (2.15) 19. Freeman, (2.11)

Cumulative Editing Quiz 4

Use proofreading marks (see Appendix B) to correct errors and omissions in the following sentences. All errors must be corrected to receive credit for the sentence. Check with your instructor for the answers.

1. E-mails must be written clear and concise, to ensure that receivers comprehend the message quick.
2. Our next sales campaign of course must target key decision makers.
3. In the meantime our online sales messages must include more then facts testimonials and guarantees.
4. The Small Business Administration which provide disaster loans are establishing additional offices in Miami New Orleans and Biloxi.
5. Because we rely on e-mail we have reduced our use of faxes, and voice messages.
6. In business time is money.
7. "The first product to use a bar code" said Alice Beasley "was Wrigley's gum."
8. In 1908, the Model T went into production in Henry Ford's plant in Detroit Michigan.
9. As Professor Perez predicted the resourceful well trained graduate was hired quick.
10. The company's liability insurance in view of the laws that went into effect January 1 need to be increased.

Semicolons (2.16)

2.16 Independent Clauses, Series, Introductory Expressions

a. **Independent clauses with conjunctive adverbs.** Use a semicolon before a conjunctive adverb that separates two independent clauses. Some of the most common conjunctive adverbs are *therefore, consequently, however,* and *moreover:*

> Business messages should sound conversational; *therefore,* writers often use familiar words and contractions.
>
> The bank closes its doors at 5 p.m.; *however,* the ATM is open 24 hours a day.

Notice that the word following a semicolon is *not* capitalized (unless, of course, that word is a proper noun).

b. **Independent clauses without conjunctive adverbs.** Use a semicolon to separate closely related independent clauses when no conjunctive adverb is used:

> Bond interest payments are tax deductible; dividend payments are not.
>
> Ambient lighting fills the room; task lighting illuminates each workstation.

Use a semicolon in *compound* sentences, not in *complex* sentences:

> After one week the paper feeder jammed; we tried different kinds of paper. (Use a semicolon in a compound sentence.)

After one week the paper feeder jammed, although we tried different kinds of paper. (Use a comma in a complex sentence. Do not use a semicolon after *jammed.*)

The semicolon is very effective for joining two closely related thoughts. Don't use it, however, unless the ideas are truly related.

c. **Independent clauses with other commas.** Normally, a comma precedes *and, or,* and *but* when those conjunctions join independent clauses. However, if either clause contains commas, the writer may elect to change the comma preceding the conjunction to a semicolon to ensure correct reading:

Our primary concern is financing; and we have discovered, as you warned us, that money sources are quite scarce.

d. **Series with internal commas.** Use semicolons to separate items in a series when one or more of the items contains internal commas:

Delegates from Miami, Florida; Freeport, Mississippi; and Chatsworth, California, attended the conference.

The speakers were Kevin Lang, manager, Riko Enterprises; Henry Holtz, vice president, Trendex, Inc.; and Margaret Woo, personnel director, West Coast Productions.

e. **Introductory expressions.** Use a semicolon when an introductory expression such as *namely, for instance, that is,* or *for example* introduces a list following an independent clause:

Switching to computerized billing are several local companies; namely, Ryson Electronics, Miller Vending Services, and Black Home Heating.

The author of a report should consider many sources; for example, books, periodicals, databases, and newspapers.

Colons (2.17–2.19)

2.17 Listed Items

a. **With colon.** Use a colon after a complete thought that introduces a formal list of items. A formal list is often preceded by such words and phrases as *these, thus, the following,* and *as follows.* A colon is also used when words and phrases like these are implied but not stated:

Additional costs in selling a house involve *the following:* title examination fee, title insurance costs, and closing fee. (Use a colon when a complete thought introduces a formal list.)

Collective bargaining focuses on several key issues: cost-of-living adjustments, fringe benefits, job security, and work hours. (The introduction of the list is implied in the preceding clause.)

b. **Without colon.** Do not use a colon when the list immediately follows a *to be* verb or a preposition:

The employees who should receive the preliminary plan are James Sears, Monica Spears, and Rose Lopez. (No colon is used after the verb *are.*)

We expect to consider equipment for Accounting, Legal Services, and Payroll. (No colon is used after the preposition *for.*)

2.18 Quotations. Use a colon to introduce long one-sentence quotations and quotations of two or more sentences:

Our consultant said: "This system can support up to 32 users. It can be used for decision support, computer-aided design, and software development operations at the same time."

2.19 Salutations. Use a colon after the salutation of a business letter:

Gentlemen: Dear Mrs. Seaman: Dear Jamie:

Review Exercise J—Semicolons, Colons

In the following sentences, add semicolons, colons, and necessary commas. For each sentence indicate the number of punctuation marks that you add. If a sentence requires no punctuation, write *C*. When you finish, compare your responses with those provided. For each item on which you need review, consult the numbered principle shown in parentheses.

1. Technological advances make full-motion video viewable on small screens consequently mobile phone makers and carriers are rolling out new services and phones. __________
2. Our branch in Sherman Oaks specializes in industrial real estate our branch in Canoga Park concentrates on residential real estate. __________
3. The sedan version of the automobile is available in these colors Olympic red metallic silver and Aztec gold. __________
4. If I can assist the new manager please call me however I will be gone from June 10 through June 15. __________
5. The individuals who should receive copies of this announcement are Jeff Doogan Alicia Green and Kim Wong. __________
6. We would hope of course to send personal letters to all prospective buyers however we have not yet decided just how to do this. __________
7. Many of our potential customers are in Southern California therefore our promotional effort will be strongest in that area. __________
8. Since the first of the year we have received inquiries from one attorney two accountants and one information systems analyst. __________
9. Three dates have been reserved for initial interviews January 15 February 1 and February 12. __________
10. Several staff members are near the top of their salary ranges and we must reclassify their jobs. __________
11. Several staff members are near the top of their salary ranges we must reclassify their jobs. __________
12. Several staff members are near the top of their salary ranges therefore we must reclassify their jobs. __________
13. If you apply for an Advantage Express card today we will waive the annual fee moreover you will earn 10,000 bonus miles and reward points for every $1 you spend on purchases. __________
14. Monthly reports from the following departments are missing Legal Department Human Resources Department and Engineering Department. __________
15. Monthly reports are missing from the Legal Department Human Resources Department and Engineering Department. __________
16. Since you became director of that division sales have tripled therefore I am recommending you for a bonus. __________
17. The convention committee is considering Portland Oregon New Orleans Louisiana and Phoenix Arizona. __________
18. Several large companies allow employees access to their personnel files namely General Electric Eastman Enterprises and Infodata. __________

19. Sherry first asked about salary next she inquired about benefits.

20. Sherry first asked about the salary and she next inquired about benefits.

1. screens; consequently, (2.16a) 3. colors: Olympic red, metallic silver, (2.01, 2.17a) 5. Doogan, Alicia Green, (2.01, 2.17b) 7. California; therefore, (2.16a) 9. interviews: January 15, February 1, (2.01, 2.17a) 11. ranges; (2.16b) 13. today, fee; moreover, (2.06a, 2.16a) 15. Department, Human Resources Department, (2.01, 2.17b) 17. Portland, Oregon; New Orleans, Louisiana; Phoenix, (2.16d) 19. salary; (2.16b)

Apostrophes (2.20–2.22)

2.20 Basic Rule. The apostrophe is used to show ownership, origin, authorship, or measurement.

Ownership:	We are looking for *Brian's keys.*
Origin:	At the *president's suggestion,* we doubled the order.
Authorship:	The *accountant's annual report* was questioned.
Measurement:	In *two years' time* we expect to reach our goal.

a. **Ownership words not ending in *s*.** To place the apostrophe correctly, you must first determine whether the ownership word ends in an *s* sound. If it does not, add an apostrophe and an *s* to the ownership word. The following examples show ownership words that do not end in an *s* sound:

the employee's file	(the file of a single employee)
a member's address	(the address of a single member)
a year's time	(the time of a single year)
a month's notice	(notice of a single month)
the company's building	(the building of a single company)

b. **Ownership words ending in *s*.** If the ownership word does end in an *s* sound, usually add only an apostrophe:

several employees' files	(files of several employees)
ten members' addresses	(addresses of ten members)
five years' time	(time of five years)
several months' notice	(notice of several months)
many companies' buildings	(buildings of many companies)

A few singular nouns that end in *s* are pronounced with an extra syllable when they become possessive. To these words, add *'s.*

my boss's desk the waitress's table the actress's costume

Use no apostrophe if a noun is merely plural, not possessive:

All the sales representatives, as well as the assistants and managers, had their names and telephone numbers listed in the directory.

2.21 Names Ending in *s* or an *s* sound. The possessive form of names ending in *s* or an *s* sound follows the same guidelines as for common nouns. If an extra syllable can be pronounced without difficulty, add *'s* . If the extra syllable is hard to pronounce, end with an apostrophe only.

Add apostrophe and *s*	**Add apostrophe only**
Russ's computer	New Orleans' cuisine
Bill Gates's business	Los Angeles' freeways
Mrs. Jones's home	the Morrises' family
Mr. Lopez's desk	the Lopezes' pool

Individual preferences in pronunciation may cause variation in a few cases. For example, some people may prefer not to pronounce an extra *s* in examples such as *Bill Gates' business.* However, the possessive form of plural names is consistent: *the Joneses' home, the Burgesses' children, the Bushes' car.* Notice that the article *the* is a clue in determining whether a name is singular or plural.

2.22 Gerunds. Use *'s* to make a noun possessive when it precedes a gerund, a verb form used as a noun:

> Mr. Smith's smoking prompted a new office policy. (Mr. *Smith* is possessive because it modifies the gerund *smoking.*)
>
> It was Betsy's careful proofreading that revealed the discrepancy.

Review Exercise K—Apostrophes

Insert necessary apostrophes and corrections in the following sentences. In the space provided for each sentence, write the corrected word. If none were corrected, write *C.* When you finish, compare your responses with those provided. For each item on which you need review, consult the numbered principle shown in parentheses.

1. In five years time, Lisa hopes to repay all of her student loans. ____________
2. If you go to the third floor, you will find Mr. Londons office. ____________
3. All the employees personnel folders must be updated. ____________
4. In a little over a years time, that firm was able to double its sales. ____________
5. The Harrises daughter lived in Florida for two years. ____________
6. A patent protects an inventors invention for 17 years. ____________
7. Both companies headquarters will be moved within the next six months. ____________
8. That position requires at least two years experience. ____________
9. Some of their assets could be liquidated; therefore, a few of the creditors received funds. ____________
10. All secretaries workstations were equipped with Internet access. ____________
11. The package of electronics parts arrived safely despite two weeks delay. ____________
12. Many nurses believe that nurses notes are not admissable evidence. ____________
13. According to Mr. Cortez latest proposal, all employees would receive an additional holiday. ____________
14. Many of our members names and addresses must be checked. ____________
15. His supervisor frequently had to correct Jacks financial reports. ____________
16. We believe that this firms service is much better than that firms. ____________
17. Mr. Jackson estimated that he spent a years profits in reorganizing his staff. ____________
18. After paying six months rent, we were given a receipt. ____________
19. The contract is not valid without Mrs. Harris signature. ____________
20. It was Mr. Smiths signing of the contract that made us happy. ____________

---

1. years' (2.20b) 3. employees' (2.20b) 5. Harrises' (2.21) 7. companies' (2.20b) 9. C (2.20b) 11. weeks' (2.20b) 13. Cortez's (2.21) 15. Jack's (2.21) 17. year's (2.20a) 19. Harris's (2.21)

Cumulative Editing Quiz 5

Use proofreading marks (see Appendix B) to correct errors and omissions in the following sentences. All errors must be corrected to receive credit for the sentence. Check with your instructor for the answers.

1. Mark Zuckerberg worked for years to build Facebook however it was years' before the company made a profit.
2. E-businesses has always been risky, online companys seem to disappear as quick as they appear.
3. According to a leading data source three of the top European entertainment companys are the following Double Fusion, Jerusalem, Israel, Echovoc, Geneva, Switzerland, and IceMobile, Amsterdam, The Netherlands.
4. By the way Tess e-mail was forwarded to Mr. Lopezes incoming box in error and she was quite embarrassed.
5. The SECs findings and ruling in the securitys fraud case is expected to be released in one hours time.
6. Only one HMOs doctors complained that they were restricted in the time they could spend listening to patients comments.
7. Any one of the auditors are authorized to conduct an independent action however only the CEO can change the councils directives.
8. Charles and Les mountain bicycles were stole from there garage last night.
9. Five of the worst computer passwords are the following your first name, your last name, the Enter key, *Password,* and the name of a sports' team.
10. On January 15 2012 we opened an innovative full equipped fitness center.

Other Punctuation (2.23–2.29)

2.23 Periods

a. **Ends of sentences.** Use a period at the end of a statement, command, indirect question, or polite request. Although a polite request may have the same structure as a question, it ends with a period:

Corporate legal departments demand precise skills from their workforce. (End a statement with a period.)

Get the latest data by reading current periodicals. (End a command with a period.)

Mr. Rand wondered whether we had sent any follow-up literature. (End an indirect question with a period.)

Would you please reexamine my account and determine the current balance. (A polite request suggests an action rather than a verbal response.)

b. **Abbreviations and initials.** Use periods after initials and after many abbreviations.

R. M. Johnson	c.o.d.	Ms.
p.m.	a.m.	Mr.
Inc.	i.e.	Mrs.

The latest trend is to omit periods in degrees and professional designations: BA, PhD, MD, RN, DDS.

Use just one period when an abbreviation falls at the end of a sentence:

Guests began arriving at 5:30 p.m.

2.24 Question Marks. Direct questions are followed by question marks:

Did you send your proposal to Datatronix, Inc.?

Statements with questions added are punctuated with question marks.

We have completed the proposal, haven't we?

2.25 Exclamation Points. Use an exclamation point after a word, phrase, or clause expressing strong emotion. In business writing, however, exclamation points should be used sparingly:

Incredible! Every terminal is down.

2.26 Dashes. The dash (constructed at a keyboard by striking the hyphen key twice in succession) is a legitimate and effective mark of punctuation when used according to accepted conventions. As a connecting punctuation mark, however, the dash loses effectiveness when overused.

a. **Parenthetical elements.** Within a sentence a parenthetical element is usually set off by commas. If, however, the parenthetical element itself contains internal commas, use dashes (or parentheses) to set it off:

Three top salespeople—Tom Judkins, Tim Templeton, and Mary Yashimoto—received bonuses.

b. **Sentence interruptions.** Use a dash to show an interruption or abrupt change of thought:

News of the dramatic merger—no one believed it at first—shook the financial world.

Ship the materials Monday—no, we must have them sooner.

Sentences with abrupt changes of thought or with appended afterthoughts can usually be improved through rewriting.

c. **Summarizing statements.** Use a dash (not a colon) to separate an introductory list from a summarizing statement:

Sorting, merging, and computing—these are tasks that our data processing programs must perform.

2.27 Parentheses. One means of setting off nonessential sentence elements involves the use of parentheses. Nonessential sentence elements may be punctuated in one of three ways: (a) with commas, to make the lightest possible break in the normal flow of a sentence; (b) with dashes, to emphasize the enclosed material; and (c) with parentheses, to de-emphasize the enclosed material. Parentheses are frequently used to punctuate sentences with interpolated directions, explanations, questions, and references:

The cost analysis (which appears on page 8 of the report) indicates that the copy machine should be leased.

Units are lightweight (approximately 13 oz.) and come with a leather case and operating instructions.

The latest laser printer (have you heard about it?) will be demonstrated for us next week.

A parenthetical sentence that is not embedded within another sentence should be capitalized and punctuated with end punctuation:

The Model 20 has stronger construction. (You may order a Model 20 brochure by circling 304 on the reader service card.)

2.28 Quotation Marks

a. **Direct quotations.** Use double quotation marks to enclose the exact words of a speaker or writer:

"Keep in mind," Mrs. Frank said, "that you'll have to justify the cost of networking our office."

The boss said that automation was inevitable. (No quotation marks are needed because the exact words are not quoted.)

b. **Quotations within quotations.** Use single quotation marks (apostrophes on the keyboard) to enclose quoted passages within quoted passages:

In her speech, Mrs. Deckman remarked, "I believe it was the poet Robert Frost who said, 'All the fun's in how you say a thing.'"

c. **Short expressions.** Slang, words used in a special sense, and words following *stamped* or *marked* are often enclosed within quotation marks:

Jeffrey described the damaged shipment as "gross." (Quotation marks enclose slang.)

Students often have trouble spelling the word "separate." (Quotation marks enclose words used in a special sense.)

Jobs were divided into two categories: most stressful and least stressful. The jobs in the "most stressful" list involved high risk or responsibility. (Quotation marks enclose words used in a special sense.)

The envelope marked "Confidential" was put aside. (Quotation marks enclose words following *marked.*)

In the four preceding sentences, the words enclosed within quotation marks can be set in italics, if italics are available.

d. **Definitions.** Double quotation marks are used to enclose definitions. The word or expression being defined should be underscored or set in italics:

The term *penetration pricing* is defined as "the practice of introducing a product to the market at a low price."

e. **Titles.** Use double quotation marks to enclose titles of literary and artistic works, such as magazine and newspaper articles, chapters of books, movies, television shows, poems, lectures, and songs. Names of major publications—such as books, magazines, pamphlets, and newspapers—are set in italics (underscored).

Particularly helpful was the chapter in Smith's *Effective Writing Techniques* entitled "Right Brain, Write On!"

In the *Los Angeles Times* appeared John's article, "E-Mail Blunders"; however, we could not locate it online.

f. **Additional considerations.** In this country periods and commas are always placed inside closing quotation marks. Semicolons and colons, on the other hand, are always placed outside quotation marks:

Mrs. James said, "I could not find the article entitled 'Cell Phone Etiquette.'"

The president asked for "absolute security": All written messages were to be destroyed.

Question marks and exclamation points may go inside or outside closing quotation marks, as determined by the form of the quotation:

Sales Manager Martin said, "Who placed the order?" (The quotation is a question.)

When did the sales manager say, "Who placed the order?" (Both the incorporating sentence and the quotation are questions.)

Did the sales manager say, "Ryan placed the order"? (The incorporating sentence asks a question; the quotation does not.)

"In the future," shouted Bob, "ask me first!" (The quotation is an exclamation.)

2.29 Brackets. Within quotations, brackets are used by the quoting writer to enclose his or her own inserted remarks. Such remarks may be corrective, illustrative, or explanatory:

> Mrs. Cardillo said, "OSHA [Occupational Safety and Health Administration] has been one of the most widely criticized agencies of the federal government."

Review Exercise L—Other Punctuation

Insert necessary punctuation in the following sentences. In the space provided for each item, indicate the number of punctuation marks that you added. Count sets of parentheses, dashes, and quotation marks as two marks. Emphasis or de-emphasis will be indicated for some parenthetical elements. When you finish, compare your responses with those provided. For each item on which you need review, consult the numbered principle shown in parentheses.

1. Will you please send me your latest catalog ____________
2. (Emphasize) Three of my friends Carmen Lopez, Stan Meyers, and Ivan Sergo were promoted. ____________
3. Mr Lee, Miss Evans, and Mrs Rivera have not responded. ____________
4. We have scheduled your interview for 4 45 p m ____________
5. (De-emphasize) The appliance comes in limited colors black, ivory, and beige , but we accept special orders. ____________
6. The expression de facto means exercising power as if legally constituted. ____________
7. Was it the president who said "This, too, will pass ____________
8. Should this package be marked Fragile ____________
9. Did you see the Newsweek article titled How Far Can Wireless Go ____________
10. Amazing All sales reps made their targets ____________

---

1. catalog. (2.23a) 3. Mr. Mrs. (2.23) 5. colors (black, ivory, and beige) (2.26a) 7. said, pass"? (2.28f) 9. *Newsweek* "How Go?" (2.28e)

Cumulative Editing Quiz 6

Use proofreading marks (see Appendix B) to correct errors and omissions in the following sentences. All errors must be corrected to receive credit for the sentence. Check with your instructor for the answers.

1. We wondered whether Ellen Hildago PhD would be the speaker at the Cairo Illinois event?
2. Our operating revenue for 2012 see Appendix A exceeded all the consultants expectations.
3. Four features, camera, text messaging, Web access, and voice mail—are what Americans want most on there cell phones.
4. Louis Camilleri CEO of Philip Morris said "We're being socially responsible in a rather controversial industry.
5. Kym Andersons chapter titled Subsidies and Trade Barriers appears in the book How to Spend $50 Billion to Make the World a Better Place.
6. Wasnt it Zack Woo not Ellen Trask who requested a 14 day leave.
7. Was it Oprah Winfrey who said that the best jobs are those we'd do even if we didn't get paid.
8. The word mashup is a technology term that is defined as a Web site that uses content from more then one source to create a completely new service.

9. Miss. Rhonda Evers is the person who the employees council elected as there representative.
10. Would you please send a current catalog to Globex, Inc?

Style and Usage

Capitalization (3.01–3.16)

Capitalization is used to distinguish important words. However, writers are not free to capitalize all words they consider important. Rules or guidelines governing capitalization style have been established through custom and use. Mastering these guidelines will make your writing more readable and more comprehensible.

3.01 Proper Nouns. Capitalize proper nouns, including the *specific* names of persons, places, schools, streets, parks, buildings, holidays, months, agreements, Web sites, software programs, historical periods, and so forth. Do not capitalize common nouns that make only *general* references.

Proper nouns	Common nouns
Barbara Walters	the first female news anchor
Mexico, Canada	U.S. trading partners
El Camino College	a community college
Sam Houston Park	a park in the city
Phoenix Room, Statler Inn	a meeting room in the hotel
Memorial Day, New Year's Day	two holidays
Google, Facebook, Wikipedia	popular Web sites
George Washington Bridge	a bridge
Consumer Product Safety Act	a law to protect consumers
Orlando Chamber of Commerce	a chamber of commerce
Will Rogers World Airport	a municipal airport
January, February, March	months of the year

3.02 Proper Adjectives. Capitalize most adjectives that are derived from proper nouns:

Greek symbol	British thermal unit
Roman numeral	Freudian slip
Xerox copy	Hispanic markets

Do not capitalize the few adjectives that, although originally derived from proper nouns, have become common adjectives through usage. Consult your dictionary when in doubt:

manila folder	diesel engine
venetian blinds	china dishes

3.03 Geographic Locations. Capitalize the names of *specific* places such as continents, countries, states, mountains, valleys, lakes, rivers, oceans, and geographic regions:

New York City	Great Salt Lake
Allegheny Mountains	Pacific Ocean
San Fernando Valley	Delaware Bay
the East Coast	the Pacific Northwest

3.04 Organization Names. Capitalize the principal words in the names of all business, civic, educational, governmental, labor, military, philanthropic, political, professional, religious, and social organizations:

Genentech	Board of Directors, Midwest Bank
*The Wall Street Journal**	San Antonio Museum of Art
New York Stock Exchange	Securities and Exchange Commission
United Way	National Association of Letter Carriers
Commission to Restore the Statue of Liberty	Association of Information Systems Professionals

3.05 Academic Courses and Degrees. Capitalize particular academic degrees and course titles. Do not capitalize general academic degrees and subject areas:

Professor Bernadette Ordian, *PhD,* will teach *Accounting* 221 next fall.

Mrs. Snyder, who holds *bachelor's* and *master's degrees,* teaches *marketing* classes.

Jim enrolled in classes in *history, business English,* and *management.*

3.06 Personal and Business Titles

a. Capitalize personal and business titles when they precede names:

Vice President Ames	Uncle Edward
Board Chairman Frazier	Councilman Herbert
Governor G. W. Thurmond	Sales Manager Klein
Professor McLean	Dr. Samuel Washington

b. Capitalize titles in addresses, salutations, and closing lines:

Mr. Juan deSanto	Very truly yours,
Director of Purchasing	
Space Systems, Inc.	Clara J. Smith
Boxborough, MA 01719	Supervisor, Marketing

c. Generally, do not capitalize titles of high government rank or religious office when they stand alone or follow a person's name in running text.

The president conferred with the joint chiefs of staff and many senators.

Meeting with the chief justice of the Supreme Court were the senator from Ohio and the mayor of Cleveland.

Only the cardinal from Chicago had an audience with the pope.

d. Do not capitalize most common titles following names:

The speech was delivered by Robert Lynch, *president,* Academic Publishing. Lois Herndon, *chief executive officer,* signed the order.

e. Do not capitalize common titles appearing alone:

Please speak to the *supervisor* or to the *office manager.*

Neither the *president* nor the *vice president* could attend.

**Note*: Capitalize *the* only when it is part of the official name of an organization, as printed on the organization's stationery.

However, when the title of an official appears in that organization's minutes, bylaws, or other official document, it may be capitalized.

f. Do not capitalize titles when they are followed by appositives naming specific individuals:

We must consult our *director of research,* Ronald E. West, before responding.

g. Do not capitalize family titles used with possessive pronouns:

my mother	your father
our aunt	his cousin

h. Capitalize titles of close relatives used without pronouns:

Both *Mother* and *Father* must sign the contract.

3.07 Numbered and Lettered Items. Capitalize nouns followed by numbers or letters (except in page, paragraph, line, and verse references):

Flight 34, Gate 12	Plan No. 2
Volume I, Part 3	Warehouse 33-A
Invoice No. 55489	Figure 8.3
Model A5673	Serial No. C22865404-2
State Highway 10	page 6, line 5

3.08 Points of the Compass. Capitalize *north, south, east, west,* and their derivatives when they represent *specific* geographical regions. Do not capitalize the points of the compass when they are used in directions or in general references.

Specific regions	**General references**
from the South	heading north on the highway
living in the Midwest	west of the city
Easterners, Southerners	western Nevada, southern Indiana
going to the Middle East	the northern part of the United States
from the East Coast	the east side of the street

3.09 Departments, Divisions, and Committees. Capitalize the names of departments, divisions, or committees within your own organization. Outside your organization capitalize only *specific* department, division, or committee names:

The inquiry was addressed to the *Legal Department* in our *Consumer Products Division.*

John was appointed to the *Employee Benefits Committee.*

Send your résumé to their *human resources division.*

A *planning committee* will be named shortly.

3.10 Governmental Terms. Do not capitalize the words *federal, government, nation,* or *state* unless they are part of a specific title:

Unless *federal* support can be secured, the *state* project will be abandoned.

The *Federal Deposit Insurance Corporation* protects depositors from bank failure.

3.11 Product Names. Capitalize product names only when they refer to trademarked items. Except in advertising, common names following manufacturers' names are not capitalized:

Magic Marker	Dell computer
Kleenex tissues	Swingline stapler
Q-tip swab	ChapStick lip balm
Levi 501 jeans	Excel spreadsheet
DuPont Teflon	Canon camera

3.12 Literary Titles. Capitalize the principal words in the titles of books, magazines, newspapers, articles, movies, plays, songs, poems, and reports. Do *not* capitalize articles (*a, an, the*), short conjunctions (*and, but, or, nor*), and prepositions of fewer than four letters (*in, to, by, for*) unless they begin or end the title:

Jackson's *What Job Is for You?* (Capitalize book titles.)

Gant's "Software for the Executive Suite" (Capitalize principal words in article titles.)

"Performance Standards to Go By" (Capitalize article titles.)

"The Improvement of Fuel Economy With Alternative Fuels" (Capitalize report titles.)

3.13 Beginning Words. In addition to capitalizing the first word of a complete sentence, capitalize the first word in a quoted sentence, independent phrase, item in an enumerated list, and formal rule or principle following a colon:

The business manager said, "*All* purchases must have requisitions." (Capitalize first word in a quoted sentence.)

Yes, if you agree. (Capitalize an independent phrase.)

Some of the duties of the position are as follows:

1. *Editing* and formatting Word files
2. *Arranging* video and teleconferences
3. *Verifying* records, reports, and applications (Capitalize items in a vertical enumerated list.)

One rule has been established through the company: *No* smoking is allowed in open offices. (Capitalize a rule following a colon.)

3.14 Celestial Bodies. Capitalize the names of celestial bodies such as *Mars, Saturn,* and *Neptune.* Do not capitalize the terms *earth, sun,* or *moon* unless they appear in a context with other celestial bodies:

Where on *earth* did you find that manual typewriter?

Venus and *Mars* are the closest planets to *Earth.*

3.15 Ethnic References. Capitalize terms that refer to a particular culture, language, or race:

Asian	Hebrew
Caucasian	Indian
Latino	Japanese
Persian	Judeo-Christian

3.16 Seasons. Do not capitalize seasons:

In the *fall* it appeared that *winter* and *spring* sales would increase.

Review Exercise M—Capitalization

In the following sentences, correct any errors that you find in capitalization. Underscore any lowercase letter that should be changed to a capital letter. Draw a slash (/) through a capital letter that you wish to change to a lowercase letter. In the space provided, indicate the total number of changes you have made in each sentence. If you make no changes, write *0*. When you finish, compare your responses with those provided.

5 **Example** Bill McAdams, currently Assistant Manager in our Personnel department, will be promoted to Manager of the Employee Services division.

1. The social security act, passed in 1935, established the present system of social security.
2. Our company will soon be moving its operations to the west coast.
3. Marilyn Hunter, mba, received her bachelor's degree from Ohio university in athens.
4. The President of Datatronics, Inc., delivered a speech entitled "Taking off into the future."
5. Please ask your Aunt and your Uncle if they will come to the Attorney's office at 5 p.m.
6. Your reservations are for flight 32 on american airlines leaving from gate 14 at 2:35 p.m.
7. Once we establish an organizing committee, arrangements can be made to rent holmby hall.
8. Bob was enrolled in history, spanish, business communications, and physical education courses.
9. Either the President or the Vice President of the company will make the decision about purchasing xerox copiers.
10. Rules for hiring and firing Employees are given on page 7, line 24, of the Contract.
11. Some individuals feel that american companies do not have the sense of loyalty to their employees that japanese companies do.
12. Where on Earth can we find better workers than Robots?
13. The secretary of state said, "we must protect our domestic economy from foreign competition."
14. After crossing the sunshine skyway bridge, we drove to Southern Florida for our vacation.
15. All marketing representatives of our company will meet in the empire room of the red lion motor inn.
16. Richard Elkins, phd, has been named director of research for spaceage strategies, inc.
17. The special keyboard for the Dell Computer must contain greek symbols for Engineering equations.
18. After she received a master's degree in electrical engineering, Joanne Dudley was hired to work in our product development department.
19. In the Fall our organization will move its corporate headquarters to the franklin building in downtown los angeles.
20. Dean Amador has one cardinal rule: always be punctual.

---

1. Social Security Act (3.01) 3. MBA University Athens (3.01, 3.05) 5. aunt uncle attorney's (3.06e, 3.06g) 7. Holmby Hall (3.01) 9. president vice president Xerox (3.06e, 3.11) 11. American Japanese (3.02) 13. We foreign (3.10, 3.13) 15. Empire Room Red Lion Motor Inn (3.01) 17. computer Greek engineering (3.01, 3.02, 3.11) 19. fall Franklin Building Los Angeles (3.01, 3.03, 3.16)

Cumulative Editing Quiz 7

Use proofreading marks (see Appendix B) to correct errors and omissions in the following sentences. All errors must be corrected to receive credit for the sentence. Check with your instructor for the answers.

1. I wonder whether president Jackson invited our Marketing Vice President to join the upcoming three hour training session?
2. Our Sales Manager said that you attending the two day seminar is fine however we must find a replacement.
3. The boston marathon is an annual Sporting Event hosted by the City of Boston, Massachusetts on patriot's day the third monday of April.
4. Steve Chen one of the founders of YouTube hurried to gate 44 to catch flight 246 to north carolina.
5. Jake noticed that the english spoken by asians in hong kong sounded more british than american.
6. Memorial day is a Federal holiday therefore banks will be closed.
7. Because the package was marked fragile the mail carrier handled it careful.
8. Money traders watched the relation of the american dollar to the chinese yuan, the european euro and the japanese yen.
9. My Aunt and me travel South each Winter to vacation in Southern Georgia with our friends the Gonzalez's.
10. Mary Minnick former Executive Vice President of the Coca-cola company now serves as president of the companys marketing, strategy, and innovation department.

Number Style (4.01–4.13)

Usage and custom determine whether numbers are expressed in the form of figures (for example, *5, 9*) or in the form of words (for example, *five, nine*). Numbers expressed as figures are shorter and more easily understood, yet numbers expressed as words are necessary in certain instances. The following guidelines are observed in expressing numbers in written sentences. Numbers that appear on business forms—such as invoices, monthly statements, and purchase orders—are always expressed as figures.

4.01 General Rules

a. The numbers *one* through *ten* are generally written as words. Numbers above *ten* are written as figures:

   The bank had a total of *nine* branch offices in *three* suburbs.

   All *58* employees received benefits in the *three* categories shown.

   A shipment of *45,000* lightbulbs was sent from *two* warehouses.

b. Numbers that begin sentences are written as words. If a number beginning a sentence involves more than two words, however, the sentence should be revised so that the number does not fall at the beginning.

   Fifteen different options were available in the annuity programs.

   A total of 156 companies participated in the promotion (not *One hundred fifty-six companies participated in the promotion*).

4.02 Money. Sums of money $1 or greater are expressed as figures. If a sum is a whole dollar amount, omit the decimal and zeros (whether or not the amount appears in a sentence with additional fractional dollar amounts):

> We budgeted *$300* for a digital camera, but the actual cost was *$370.96.*
>
> On the invoice were items for *$6.10, $8, $33.95,* and *$75.*

Sums less than $1 are written as figures that are followed by the word *cents:*

> By shopping carefully, we can save *15 cents* per unit.

4.03 Dates. In dates, numbers that appear after the name of the month are written as cardinal figures (*1, 2, 3,* etc.). Those that stand alone or appear before the name of a month are written as ordinal figures *(1st, 2nd, 3rd,* etc.):

> The Personnel Practices Committee will meet *May 7.*
>
> On the *5th* day of February and again on the *25th,* we placed orders.

In domestic business documents, dates generally take the following form: *January 4, 2012.* An alternative form, used primarily in military and foreign correspondence, begins with the day of the month and omits the comma: *4 January 2012.*

4.04 Clock Time. Figures are used when clock time is expressed with *a.m.* or *p.m.* Omit the colon and zeros in referring to whole hours. When exact clock time is expressed with the contraction *o'clock,* either figures or words may be used:

> Mail deliveries are made at *11 a.m.* and *3:30 p.m.*
>
> At *four* (or *4*) *o'clock* employees begin to leave.

4.05 Addresses and Telephone Numbers

a. Except for the number *one,* house numbers are expressed in figures:

540 Elm Street	17802 Washington Avenue
One Colorado Boulevard	2 Highland Street

b. Street names containing numbers *ten* or lower are written entirely as words. For street names involving numbers greater than *ten,* figures are used:

330 Third Street	3440 Seventh Avenue
6945 East 32nd Avenue	4903 West 23rd Street

c. Telephone numbers are expressed with figures. When used, the area code is placed in parentheses preceding the telephone number:

> Please call us at *(818) 347-0551* to place an order.
>
> Mr. Sims asked you to call *(619) 554-8923,* Ext. 245, after 10 a.m.

4.06 Related Numbers. Numbers are related when they refer to similar items in a category within the same reference. All related numbers should be expressed as the largest number is expressed. Thus if the largest number is greater than *ten,* all the numbers should be expressed in figures:

> Only *5* of the original *25* applicants completed the processing. (Related numbers require figures.)
>
> The *two* plans affected *34* employees working in *three* sites. (Unrelated numbers use figures and words.)
>
> Exxon Oil operated *86* rigs, of which *6* were rented. (Related numbers require figures.)

The company hired *three* accountants, *one* customer-service representative, and *nine* sales representatives. (Related numbers under ten use words.)

4.07 Consecutive Numbers. When two numbers appear consecutively and both modify a following noun, generally express the first number in words and the second in figures. If, however, the first number cannot be expressed in one or two words, place it in figures also (*120 70-cent* stamps). Do not use commas to separate the figures.

Historians divided the era into *four 25-year* periods. (Use word form for the first number and figure form for the second.)

We ordered *ten 30-page* color brochures. (Use word form for the first number and figure form for the second.)

Did the manager request *150 100-watt* bulbs? (Use figure form for the first number since it would require more than two words.)

4.08 Periods of Time. Seconds, minutes, days, weeks, months, and years are treated as any other general number. Numbers above ten are written in figure form. Numbers below ten are written in word form unless they represent a business concept such as a discount rate, interest rate, or warranty period.

This business was incorporated over *50* years ago. (Use figures for a number above ten.)

It took *three* hours to write this short report. (Use words for a number under ten.)

The warranty period is limited to *2* years. (Use figures for a business term.)

4.09 Ages. Ages are generally expressed in word form unless the age appears immediately after a name or is expressed in exact years and months:

At the age of *twenty-one,* Elizabeth inherited the business.

Wanda Tharp, *37,* was named acting president.

At the age of *4 years and 7 months,* the child was adopted.

4.10 Round Numbers. Round numbers are approximations. They may be expressed in word or figure form, although figure form is shorter and easier to comprehend:

About *600* (or *six hundred*) stock options were sold.

It is estimated that *1,000* (or *one thousand*) people will attend.

For ease of reading, round numbers in the millions or billions should be expressed with a combination of figures and words:

At least *1.5 million* readers subscribe to the ten top magazines.

Deposits in money market accounts totaled more than *$115 billion.*

4.11 Weights and Measurements. Weights and measurements are expressed with figures:

The new deposit slip measures *2* by *6 inches.*

Her new suitcase weighed only *2 pounds 4 ounces.*

Toledo is *60 miles* from Detroit.

4.12 Fractions. Simple fractions are expressed as words. Complex fractions may be written either as figures or as a combination of figures and words:

Over *two thirds* of the stockholders have already voted.

This microcomputer will execute the command in *1 millionth* of a second. (A combination of words and numbers is easier to comprehend.)

She purchased a *one-fifth* share in the business.*

4.13 Percentages and Decimals. Percentages are expressed with figures that are followed by the word *percent.* The percent sign (%) is used only on business forms or in statistical presentations:

We had hoped for a *7 percent* interest rate, but we received a loan at *8 percent.*

Over *50 percent* of the residents supported the plan.

Decimals are expressed with figures. If a decimal expression does not contain a whole number (an integer) and does not begin with a zero, a zero should be placed before the decimal point:

The actuarial charts show that *1.74* out of *1,000* people will die in any given year.

Inspector Norris found the setting to be *.005* inch off. (Decimal begins with a zero and does not require a zero before the decimal point.)

Considerable savings will accrue if the unit production cost is reduced *0.1* percent. (A zero is placed before a decimal that neither contains a whole number nor begins with a zero.)

Quick Chart—Expression of Numbers

Use Words	**Use Figures**
Numbers *ten* and under	Numbers *11* and over
Numbers at beginning of sentence	Money
Ages	Dates
Fractions	Addresses and telephone numbers
	Weights and measurements
	Percentages and decimals

Review Exercise N—Number Style

Write the preferred number style on the lines provided. Assume that these numbers appear in business correspondence. When you finish, compare your responses with those provided. For each item on which you need review, consult the numbered principle shown in parentheses.

1. (a) 2 alternatives (b) two alternatives
2. (a) Seventh Avenue (b) 7th Avenue
3. (a) sixty sales reps (b) 60 sales reps
4. (a) November ninth (b) November 9
5. (a) forty dollars (b) $40
6. (a) on the 23rd of May (b) on the twenty-third of May
7. (a) at 2:00 p.m. (b) at 2 p.m.
8. (a) 4 two-hundred-page books (b) four 200-page books
9. (a) at least 15 years ago (b) at least fifteen years ago
10. (a) 1,000,000 viewers (b) 1 million viewers
11. (a) twelve cents (b) 12 cents
12. (a) a sixty-day warranty (b) a 60-day warranty

**Notes*: Fractions used as adjectives require hyphens.

13. (a) ten percent interest rate	(b) 10 percent interest rate
14. (a) 4/5 of the voters	(b) four fifths of the voters
15. (a) the rug measures four by six feet	(b) the rug measures 4 by 6 feet
16. (a) about five hundred people attended	(b) about 500 people attended
17. (a) at eight o'clock	(b) at 8 o'clock
18. (a) located at 1 Wilshire Boulevard	(b) located at One Wilshire Boulevard
19. (a) three computers for twelve people	(b) three computers for 12 people
20. (a) 4 out of every 100 licenses	(b) four out of every 100 licenses

1. b (4.01a) 3. b (4.01a) 5. b (4.02) 7. b (4.04) 9. a (4.08) 11. b (4.02) 13. b (4.13) 15. b (4.11) 17. a or b (4.04) 19. b (4.06)

Cumulative Editing Quiz 8

Use proofreading marks (see Appendix B) to correct errors and omissions in the following sentences. All errors must be corrected to receive credit for the sentence. Check with your instructor for the answers.

1. My partner and myself will meet at our attorneys office at three p.m. on June ninth to sign our papers of incorporation.
2. Emily prepared 2 forty page business proposals to submit to the Senior Account Manager.
3. Of the 235 e-mail messages sent yesterday only seven bounced back.
4. Your short term loan for twenty-five thousand dollars covers a period of sixty days.
5. Each new employee must pick up their permanent parking permit for lot 3-A before the end of the 14 day probationary period.
6. 259 identity theft complaints were filed with the Federal trade commission on November second alone.
7. Robertas 11 page report was more easier to read then Davids because her's was better organized and had good headings.
8. Every morning on the way to the office Tatiana picked up 2 lattes that cost a total of six dollars.
9. Taking 7 years to construct the forty thousand square foot home of Bill Gates reportedly cost more then fifty million dollars.
10. Many companys can increase profits nearly ninety percent by retaining only 5% more of there current customers.

Confusing Words

accede:	to agree or consent
exceed:	over a limit
accept:	to receive
except:	to exclude; (prep) but
adverse:	opposing; antagonistic
averse:	unwilling; reluctant
advice:	suggestion, opinion
advise:	to counsel or recommend
affect:	to influence
effect:	(n) outcome, result; (v) to bring about, to create
all ready:	prepared
already:	by this time
all right:	satisfactory
alright:	unacceptable variant spelling
altar:	structure for worship
alter:	to change
appraise:	to estimate
apprise:	to inform
ascent:	(n) rising or going up
assent:	(v) to agree or consent

assure: to promise
ensure: to make certain
insure: to protect from loss
capital: (n) city that is seat of government; wealth of an individual; (adj) chief
capitol: building that houses state or national lawmakers
cereal: breakfast food
serial: arranged in sequence
cite: to quote; to summon
site: location
sight: a view; to see
coarse: rough texture
course: a route; part of a meal; a unit of learning
complement: that which completes
compliment: (n) praise, flattery; (v) to praise or flatter
conscience: regard for fairness
conscious: aware
council: governing body
counsel: (n) advice, attorney; (v) to give advice
credible: believable
creditable: good enough for praise or esteem; reliable
desert: arid land; to abandon
dessert: sweet food
device: invention or mechanism
devise: to design or arrange
disburse: to pay out
disperse: to scatter widely
elicit: to draw out
illicit: unlawful
envelop: (v) to wrap, surround, or conceal
envelope: (n) a container for a written message
every day: each single day
everyday: ordinary
farther: a greater distance
further: additional
formally: in a formal manner
formerly: in the past
grate: (v) to reduce to small particles; to cause irritation; (n) a frame of crossed bars blocking a passage
great: (adj) large in size; numerous; eminent or distinguished
hole: an opening
whole: complete
imply: to suggest indirectly
infer: to reach a conclusion
lean: (v) to rest against; (adj) not fat
lien: (n) a legal right or claim to property
liable: legally responsible
libel: damaging written statement
loose: not fastened
lose: to misplace
miner: person working in a mine
minor: a lesser item; person under age
patience: calm perseverance
patients: people receiving medical treatment
personal: private, individual
personnel: employees
plaintiff: (n) one who initiates a lawsuit
plaintive: (adj) expressive of suffering or woe
populace: (n) the masses; population of a place
populous: (adj) densely populated
precede: to go before
proceed: to continue
precedence: priority
precedents: events used as an example
principal: (n) capital sum; school official; (adj) chief
principle: rule of action
stationary: immovable
stationery: writing material
than: conjunction showing comparison
then: adverb meaning "at that time"
their: possessive form of *they*

there: at that place or point

they're: contraction of *they are*

to: a preposition; the sign of the infinitive

too: an adverb meaning "also" or "to an excessive extent"

two: a number

waiver: abandonment of a claim

waver: to shake or fluctuate

160 Frequently Misspelled Words

absence
accommodate
achieve
acknowledgment
across
adequate
advisable
analyze
annually
appointment
argument
automatically
bankruptcy
becoming
beneficial
budget
business
calendar
canceled
catalog
changeable
column
committee
congratulate
conscience
conscious
consecutive
consensus
consistent
control
convenient
correspondence
courteous
criticize
decision
deductible
defendant
definitely
dependent
describe
desirable
destroy
development
disappoint
dissatisfied
division
efficient
embarrass
emphasis
emphasize
employee
envelope
equipped
especially
evidently
exaggerate
excellent
exempt
existence
extraordinary
familiar
fascinate
feasible
February
fiscal
foreign
forty
fourth
friend
genuine
government
grammar
grateful
guarantee
harass
height
hoping
immediate
incidentally
incredible
independent
indispensable
interrupt
irrelevant
itinerary
judgment
knowledge
legitimate
library
license
maintenance
manageable
manufacturer
mileage
miscellaneous
mortgage
necessary
nevertheless
ninety
ninth
noticeable
occasionally
occurred
offered
omission
omitted
opportunity
opposite
ordinarily
paid
pamphlet
permanent
permitted
pleasant
practical
prevalent
privilege
probably
procedure
profited
prominent
qualify
quantity
questionnaire
receipt
receive
recognize
recommendation
referred
regarding
remittance
representative
restaurant
schedule
secretary
separate
similar
sincerely
software
succeed
sufficient
supervisor
surprise
tenant
therefore
thorough
though
through
truly
undoubtedly
unnecessarily
usable
usage
using
usually
valuable
volume
weekday
writing
yield

KEY TO GRAMMAR/MECHANICS CHECKUPS

Chapter 1

1. boundaries (1.05e) **2.** C (1.05g) **3.** companies (1.05e) **4.** Sundays (1.05a) **5.** attorneys (1.05d) **6.** Sanchezes (1.05b) **7.** 2000s (1.05g) **8.** editors in chief (1.05f) **9.** CPAs (1.05g) **10.** counties (1.05e) **11.** runners up (1.05f) **12.** C (1.05d) **13.** liabilities (1.05e) **14.** C (1.05h) **15.** brothers-in-law (1.05.f)

Chapter 2

1. he (1.08b) **2.** his (1.09b) **3.** me (1.08c) **4.** Who (1.08j) **5.** yours (1.08d) **6.** me (1.08c) **7.** I (1.08a) **8.** ours (1.08d) **9.** whoever (1.08j) **10.** me (1.08i) **11.** he (1.08f) **12.** we (1.08g) **13.** her (1.09b) **14.** she (1.08f) **15.** his or her (1.09b)

Chapter 3

1. *are* for *is* (1.10e) **2.** *has* for *have* (1.10c) **3.** *offers* for *offer* (1.10d) **4.** *is* for *are* (1.10g) **5.** C (1.10f) **6.** *is* for *are* (1.10i) **7.** C (1.10h) **8.** *chosen* for *chose* (1.15) **9.** *lain* for *laid* (1.15) **10.** *were* for *was* (1.12) **11.** *is* for *are* (1.10c) **12.** b (1.15c) **13.** b (1.15c) **14.** a (1.15c) **15.** b (1.15c)

Chapter 4

1. state-of-the-art (1.17e) **2.** quickly (1.17d) **3.** their (1.17g) **4.** collected only (1.17f) **5.** 18-week (1.17e) **6.** site-by-site (1.17e) **7.** their (1.17g) **8.** spur-of-the-moment (1.17e) **9.** badly (1.17d) **10.** well-thought-out (1.17e) **11.** bad (1.17d) **12.** more (1.16) **13.** run faster (1.17d) **14.** case-by-case (1.17e) **15.** smoothly (1.17d)

Chapter 5

1. a (1.18a) **2.** b (1.19c) **3.** b (1.19d) **4.** b (1.19c) **5.** a. (1.19a) **6.** a (1.18b) **7.** b (1.19d) **8.** b (1.18c) **9.** b (1.19c) **10.** b (1.18b) **11.** a (1.19a) **12.** b (1.19b) **13.** a (1.18d) **14.** b (1.18b) **15.** b (1.18a)

Chapter 6

1. 2 (2.03) not, as a rule, **2.** 2 (2.02) may be sure, Ms. Ebert, **3.** 2 (2.01) among friends, former colleagues, **4.** 0 **5.** 1 (2.03) As a matter of fact, **6.** 1 (2.03) In the meantime, **7.** 2 (2.04a) March 1, 2005, **8.** 4 (2.04c) Albany, New York, to Atlanta, Georgia, **9.** 2 (2.01) Eric Wong, Teresa Cabrillo, **10.** 4 (2.04b) Summers, 1339 Kearsley Street, Flint, MI, **11.** 2 (2.03) think, needless to say, **12.** 2 (2.03) feel, however, **13.** 2 (2.01) hiring company, prepared success stories, **14.** 0 **15.** 1 (2.02) you, Mr. Powell.

Chapter 7

1. 1 (2.06a) desperate, they **2.** 1 (2.05) more aggressive, and **3.** 0 (2.05) **4.** 2 (2.09) Deborah Wang, search firm, **5.** 1 (2.08) reliable, hardworking **6.** 1 (2.07) 16 months, **7.** 2 (2.06c) manager, six months, **8.** 0 (2.05) **9.** 1 (2.06a) candidate, **10.** 0 (2.06c) **11.** 4 (2.07, 2.01) company, press releases, annual reports, media coverage, **12.** 3 (2.06a, 2.04a) hired, Monday, May 15, **13.** 2 (2.07, 2.06c) pay, interview, **14.** 1 (2.03) As a matter of fact, **15.** 3 (2.06a, 2.04a) opportunity, Tuesday, February 3,

Chapter 8

1. 2 (2.14a) science, observer, **2**. 3 (2.10) Cox, PhD, Pam Rankey, MBA **3.** 1 (2.14b) persuasion, **4.** 0 (2.15) **5.** 1 (2.12) learn, **6.** 3 (2.06a, 2.01) heard, trust, negotiations, **7**. 4 (2.03, 2.01) think, however, much, overpromise, **8**. 2 (2.07, 2.06c) position, Haddock, **9**. 4 (2.07, 2.01) 20, sell, convince, influence, **10**. 2 (2.06a, 2.11) campaign, first week; second week, only 4 **11**. 2 (2.07, 2.09) years, individuals, **12**. 2 (2.06c, 2.15) Guerro, week, **13**. 1 (2.06a) persuasion, **14**. 2 (2.14a) successful, author, **15**. 4 (2.01, 2.06) memo, e-mail, presentation, boss,

Chapter 9

1. 3 (2.03, 2.16b) less; financing, hand, **2.** 3 (2.01, 2.17a) months: October, November, **3.** 2 (2.16a) finances; however, **4**. 2 (2.16a) lenders; therefore, **5**. 1 (2.17b) are [delete colon] **6**. 1 (2.16b) credit risks; **7**. 3 (2.17a, 2.01) credit score: credit history, (b) new credit, **8.** 9 (2.16d, 2.17) speakers: Cruz, consultant, Credit Specialists; Margaret Lee, founder, Credit Solutions; and Judith Plutsky, legal counsel, Liberty Financial **9.** 1 (2.05) score, **10.** 4 (2.16e, 2.01) factors; for example, your age, salary, **11**. 3 (2.06c, 2.17) Credit Solutions, service, score: **12.** 4 (2.06a, 2.04b) Credit Solutions, Margaret Lee, 3520 Troy Highway, Montgomery, AL 36104 **13**. 5 (2.06c, 2.08, 2.16a) Lee, Solutions, experienced, courteous staff; however, **14**. 1 (2.16c) historic lows; **15.** 4 (2.18, 2.06a, 2.01) said: score, card accounts, no late payments,

Chapter 10

1. (2.20a) Hanley's **2.** (2.20b) weeks' **3.** (2.20b) year's **4.** (2.21) Peterson's **5.** (2.20b) employees' **6.** (2.20b) witness's **7.** (2.22) Robin's **8.** (2.20a) money's **9.** C **10.** (2.20a) month's **11.** (2.20b) boss's **12.** (2.20a) secretary's **13.** C **14.** (2.20a) company's **15.** (2.20b) businesses'

Chapter 11

1. 2 (2.26a) employees–Santiago Wilson, Rae Thomas, and Charles Stoop– **2.** 3 (2.02, 2.23a) please, Jonathon, six o'clock. [delete question mark] **3.** 3 (2.28c, 2.06a) "e-mail" without the hyphen, **4.** 1 (2.26c) Bechtel– **5.** 2 (2.26a) checks (drug, credit, and criminal)

6. 3 (2.28f) said, windshield"? **7.** 4. (2.28e, 2.28f) "Wireless Poor" The New York Times? (italics possible) **8.** 2 (2.26a) live–Vienna, Zurich, and Geneva– **9.** 5 (2.23a, 2.23b, 2.24) Dr. Lisa Uhl, Ms. Ginger Ortiz, and Mr. Orrin T. Tapia? **10.** 3 (2.28e) "The Almost Perfect Meeting" The Etiquette Advantage in Business (italics possible) **11.** 2 (2.25, 2.24) Incredible! today! **12.** 1 (2.23) Google ad. [delete question mark] **13.** 2 (2.28c, 2.28f) "party." **14.** 3 (2.23b, 2.24) 6 p.m.? **15.** 3 (2.28d) autoregressive "using past data to predict future data."

Chapter 12

1. 7 (3.01, 3.07) Bank America headquarters Suite Scottsdale Fire Department **2.** 6 (3.01, 3.02, 3.06d) Europe British French vice president Hotels **3.** 5 (3.01, 3.06a) management team union Mayor agreement **4.** 5 (3.01, 3.05) Boston Marathon Boston Patriot's Day **5.** 5 (3.01, 3.05) University New Mexico Italian Italy **6.** 5 (3.01). Internet Google Facebook YouTube **7.** 5 (3.01, 3.10) federal government January state county **8.** 0 (3.06e, 3.16) **9.** 7 (3.01, 3.04, 3.06e) vice president president Securities Exchange Commission company **10.** 6 (3.01, 3.06g, 3.14) uncle Surfrider Beach Malibu moon stars **11.** 5 (3.06d, 3.06e, 3.09, 3.01) manager Advertising Media Department Google **12.** 6 (3.316, 3.06a, 3.01) fall faculty advisor Asia Australia China **13.** 9 (3.01, 3.06g, 3.03) February father Summer Waves Water Park Jekyll Island Georgia **14.** 3 (3.07, 3.09, 3.05) Business Division master's **15.** 8 (3.07, 3.12, 3.04, 3.02) Figure Chapter Analysis Population Growth Census Bureau non-English

Chapter 13

1. 20 (4.01a) **2.** Fourth (4.05b) **3.** 12 (4.01a) **4.** June 1 (4.03) **5.** $40 (4.02) **6.** 15th (4.03) **7.** 3 p.m. (4.04) **8.** four 3-page (4.07) **9.** 40 (4.01, 4.08) **10.** 3 million (4.10) **11.** Sixteen (4.01b) **12.** 50 (4.02) **13.** twenty-one (4.09) **14.** 7 (4.13) **15.** 4 (4.06)

Chapter 14

1. nurses is escorted to her car **2.** must have been he score, although it's **3.** office manager asked Rachel and me four hours **4.** gym and jogging 20 miles a week are **5.** Three types control: holding costs, ordering costs, **6.** If I were he, questionnaire **7.** acceleration; however, lower revolutions mean better **8.** team's day-to-day operations include [delete colon] products, **9.** had seen the shipper's bill, paid **10.** convenient, three copies company's color logo. [no question mark] **11.** it was he boss's desk? **12.** one half of Pizza Hut's 6,000 deliveries; concentrate on walk-in **13.** Everything except 5-year **14.** director felt, nevertheless, an interview **15.** degree, in [delete colon] Dallas,

INDEX

Italic page numbers indicate illustrative information in figures.

A

B

C

D

E

F

G

Q

R

S

T